THE EUROPEAN UNION AND SPORT:
LEGAL AND POLICY DOCUMENTS

*This publication was realised with the cooperation of the*

INTERNATIONAL OLYMPIC COMMITTEE
FIFPRO

*and supported by*

ERNST & YOUNG / HOLLAND VAN GIJZEN
DE KEERSMAEKER VROMANS
INFOSTRADA SPORTS


*Partners of the ASSER International Sports Law Centre*

LARRAURI &
LÓPEZ ANTE

C/M/S/ **Derks Star Busmann**
ATTORNEYS AT LAW CIVIL LAW NOTARIES TAX ADVISERS

T.M.C. ASSER INSTITUUT
ASSER International Sports Law Centre

# The European Union and Sport: Legal and Policy Documents

Edited by

Robert C.R. Siekmann

and

Janwillem Soek

THE NETWORKS OF THE ASSER INTERNATIONAL SPORTS LAW CENTRE

T·M·C·Asser Press

Published by T·M·C·Asser press
P.O.Box 16163, 2500 BD The Hague, The Netherlands
<www.asserpress.nl>


T·M·C·Asser press' English language books are distributed exclusively by:

Cambridge University Press, The Edinburgh Building, Shaftesbury Road,
Cambridge CB2 2RU, UK,
or
for customers in the USA, Canada and Mexico:
Cambridge University Press, 40 West 20th Street, New York, NY 10011-4211, USA
<www.cambridge.org>

Cover photograph: Courtesy of The Press Association, London.
*Jensen of Denmark scoring for 'The Three' v. 'The Six' in the EEC Enlargement Celebration Match of January 3, 1973 at Wembley Stadium in London.*

| | | |
|---|---|---|
| The Three (New) 2 | | HT: 0-0 |
| (Henning Jensen 49, Colin Stein 70) | | Att: 36,500 |
| The Six 0 | | Ref: Norman Burtenshaw (Eng) |

**The Three**: Pat Jennings (NIR/UK) – Peter Edwin Storey (ENG/UK), Bobby Moore (ENG/UK), Norman Hunter (ENG/UK), - Colin Bell (ENG/UK) (John Steen Olsen, DEN, 74), Johnny giles (IRL), Bobby Charlton (ENG/UK) – Peter Lorimer (SCO/UK), Colin Stein (SCO/UK), Henibng Jensen (DEN), (Alan Ball ENG/UK, 60). Manager: Alf Ramsey (ENG).
**The Six**: Christian Piot (BEL) (Dino Zoff, ITA, 46) – Marius Trésor (FRA) (Wim Suurbier, NED, 46), Franz Beckenbauer (FRG) (Ruud Krol, NED, 46), Horst Blankenburg (FRG), Berti Vogts (FRG) – Willem van Hanegem (NED) (Herbert Wimmer, FRG, 46), Günther Netzer (FRG), Johan Neeskens (NED) – Jürgen Grabowski (FRG), Gerd Müller (FRG), Georges Bereta (FRA). Manager: Helmut Schön (FRG).
© Infostrada Sports 2002
http://www.sportsdeskonline.com

ISBN 90-6704-194-7
© 2005, T.M.C. Asser press, The Hague, The Netherlands


**T.M.C. Asser Instituut - Institute for Private and Public International Law, International Commercial Arbitration and European Law**

Institute Address: R.J. Schimmelpennincklaan 20-22, The Hague, The Netherlands; Mailing Address: P.O. Box 30461, 2500 GL The Hague, The Netherlands; Tel.: +3170 342 0300; Fax: +3170 3420 359; Internet: www.asser.nl.
Over thirty years, the T.M.C. Asser Institute has developed into a leading scientific research institute in the field of international law. It covers private international law, public international law, including international humanitarian law, the law of the European Union, the law of international commercial arbitration and increasingly, also, international economic law, the law of international commerce and international sports law. Conducting scientific research, either fundamental or applied, in the aforementioned domains, is the main activity of the Institute. In addition, the Institute organizes congresses and postgraduate courses, undertakes contract-research and operates its own publishing house.
Because of its inter-university background, the Institute often cooperates with Dutch law faculties as well as with various national and foreign institutions. The Institute organizes *Asser College Europe*, a project in cooperation with East and Central European countries whereby research and educational projects are organized and implemented.

# FOREWORD

The present publication entitled *The European Union and Sport – Legal and Policy Documents* is the first volume in the Asser series of collections of documents on international sports law containing material on the intergovernmental (inter-state) part of international sports law. In the previous volumes, NGO material, i.e. statutes and constitutions, doping rules and regulations and arbitral and disciplinary rules of the international Olympic sports organisations were published.

The texts in this book cover the period since the Walrave judgment, when the Court of Justice established that sport is subject to Community law to the extent that it constitutes an economic activity, up to the present time. The book provides a detailed insight in what could be called the *acquis communautaire sportive* for the present and future Member States. This *acquis* was developed over the years in numerous decisions and policy documents of the Council, the Commission, the European Parliament and the Court of Justice in particular.

A reference book such as this is an extremely valuable tool for both legal practice and research purposes in the field of sport and the law, in this case: sport and European law and policy.

Brussels, August 2004          Viviane REDING
                               *EU Commissioner for Education and Culture*

# SUMMARY OF CONTENTS

# INTRODUCTION

In 1998, the publication entitled *Basic Documents of International Sports Organisations* was realised within the framework of the T.M.C. Asser Institute's research project on international sports law.[1] This collection of documents deals with the non-governmental, 'autonomous' part of international sports law[2], and includes documents of an institutional character, i.e., the Statutes and Constitutions of universal sports organisations. Two main categories of universal sports organisations are represented in *Basic Documents*: (1) international ('umbrella') organisations which are not limited to any single sport, including the Olympic Charter and the Statutes of the Court of Arbitration for Sport (CAS); and (2) what are known as international sports federations which are organised per sport, insofar as they concern Olympic sports. In 1999, *Doping Rules of International Sports Organisations* was published as a comprehensive follow-up publication to *Basic Documents*, which concerns the general organisational network of international sports. *Doping Rules* concentrates on one of the main areas of international sports law, namely the international regulation of doping.[3] Finally, in 2001, *Arbitral and Disciplinary Rules of International Sports Organisations* was the third volume in the Asser series of documents on international sports law. It concerns the general aspects of 'the administration of justice', i.e., the law on disputes and disciplinary action, in the international sporting world. The present publication entitled *The European Union and Sport: Legal and Policy Documents* is the first volume in the Asser series of collections of documents on international sports law containing material on the intergovernmental (interstate) part of international sports law.

There is no specific reference to sport in the EC Treaty. However, sport has always been one of the Community's concerns. The inclusion of a Declaration on Sport in the 1997 Amsterdam Treaty gave a strong political signal as regards the new importance which the Heads of State and Government attach to sport and its values by. Moreover, sport is indirectly affected by many Community policies, such as those to do with health (doping), audiovisual policy, education, training and youth, etc. In the (draft) Treaty establishing a Constitution for Europe which was approved by the Heads of State or Government at the Intergovernmental Conference in Brussels on 18 June 2004, sport is included in Article 282 (Part III, Title III, Chapter V, Section 4 on Education, youth, sport and vocational train-

---

[1] Robert C.R. Siekmann and Janwillem Soek (eds), *Basic Documents of International Sports Organisations*, T.M.C. Asser Instituut/Kluwer Law International, The Hague/Boston/London 1998.

[2] Robert C.R. Siekmann, Janwillem Soek, and Andrea Bellani (eds), *Doping Rules of International Sports Organisations,* T.M.C. Asser Instituut/T.M.C. Asser Press, The Hague 1999.

[3] Robert C.R. Siekmann and Janwillem Soek (eds), *Arbitral and Disciplinary rules of International Sports Organisations,* T.M.C.Asser Instituut/T.M.C. Asser Press, The Hague 2001.

ing). It is stated that the Union shall contribute to the promotion of European sporting issues, while taking account of its specific nature, its structures based on voluntary activity and its social and educational function (paragraph 1, final sentence), and that the Union shall be aimed at developing the European dimension of sport, by promoting fairness and openness in sporting competitions and cooperation between bodies responsible for sports, and by protecting the physical and moral integrity of sportsmen and sportswomen, especially young sportsmen and sportswomen (paragraph 2 sub g).

Sport, as an economic activity in the sense of Article 2 of the EC Treaty, must comply with Community law, in particular the provisions relating to the free movement of workers. A Court of Justice judgment in 1974 (Walrave) established that sport is subject to Community law to the extent that it constitutes an economic activity. Since then, various cases (Dona, Bosman, Deliege, Lehtonen) have confirmed this approach. It is a significant fact that the one judgment which has aroused more media interest than any other in the history of Community case law was sports-related (Bosman).[4]

The legal and policy texts in the present book are arranged in thematical, alphabetical order and are chronologically sub-ordered per theme. They cover the period since the Walrave judgment up to and including 2003. The book in fact gives a detailed insight in what could be called the '*EU Sport Acquis*' for the present and future (candidate) Member States. This *acquis* was developed over the years in numerous decisions and policy documents by the Council, Commission, European Parliament and by the Court of Justice in particular. It is subdivided into three parts covering all themes which the EC/EU has dealt with so far. The first part headed 'General' contains general policy documents, such as, for example, the European Model of Sport and the Helsinki Report on Sport. Specific subjects (part two) concern Boycott, Broadcasting (in particular the Television without Frontiers Directive), Community Aid and Sport Funding (for example, the Eurathlon Programme), Competition (central selling of the TV rights of the UEFA Champions League, German Bundesliga, English Premier League, etc., Formula One, World Cup ticketing arrangements, players' agents), Customs, Diplomas (Heylens), Discrimination (Walrave, Dona, Kolpak, and documents concerning women in sport), Doping (Community Support Plan and Pilot Project for Campaigns to Combat Doping in Sport), Education/Youth (European Year of Education through Sport 2004 and documents concerning child protection in sport and trafficking in young footballers), the freedoms of establishment, services (Deliège) and movement of workers (Bosman, Lehtonen), Olympic Games, State Aid, Tax, Tobacco Advertising, Trade Mark (Arsenal/Reed), Vandalism and Violence (football hooliganism). The third part contains Miscellanea (Fishing, Horses, Hunting, etc.).

---

[4] Cf., in this context in particular: Richard Parrish, *Sports law and policy in the European Union*, European Policy Research Unit Series, Manchester University Press, Manchester and New York, 2003, p. 271.

This Volume contains a *selection* of the documents which are most relevant from a legal and policy perspective. The full texts of documents which are marked with an asterisk (*) are not incorporated in the book itself, but are freely accessible on the website of the ASSER International Sports Law Centre, at <www.sportslaw.nl> – documentation.

Apart from the invaluable support of the Directorate-General for Education and Culture and the Directorate-General for Competition, the realisation of this project would not have been possible without the assistance of Ms Victorine Verkruissen at the Documentation and Information Department of the T.M.C. Asser Institute. Additionally, trainees of the ASSER International Sports Law Centre contributed to the work by collecting and arranging the material for this publication. We thank them all very much, in particular Ms Geraldine Gonzales (France) and Ms Patricia Stroh (Germany).

Finally, we thank in particular the International Olympic Committee for their generous financial support to the project which led to the publication of the book.


The Hague, August 2004          Robert SIEKMANN and Janwillem SOEK
                                *ASSER International Sports Law Centre*

Part 1

General

**\* 1.1.   REPORT DRAWN UP ON BEHALF OF THE COMMITTEE ON YOUTH, CULTURE, EDUCATION, INFORMATION AND SPORT ON SPORT AND THE COMMUNITY, 2 APRIL 1984[1]**

Rapporteur: Mr A. Bord

——

**1.2.   RESOLUTION OF THE EUROPEAN PARLIAMENT ON SPORT IN THE COMMUNITY, 13 APRIL 1984[2]**

*The European Parliament,*

- having regard to the Treaty establishing the European Economic Community,
- having regard to the work of the Council of Europe for the promotion of sport,
- having regard to the following motions for resolutions:
  - motion for a resolution tabled by Mr Hahn and others on the launching of European schools sports competitions (Doc. 1-977/80),
  - motion for a resolution tabled by Mr Brok and others on the holding of games in the European Community (Doc. 1-12/82),
  - motion for a resolution tabled by Mr Verges and others on the participation of football teams from the Third World (Doc. 1-514/82),
  - motion for a resolution tabled by Mr Junot and others on the establishment of a sporting competition to be known as the 'Community Games' (Doc. 1-746/82),
  - motion for a resolution tabled by Mr Gontikas on the establishment of Community athletic games (Doc. 1-823/82),
  - motion for a resolution tabled by Mr Calvez and Mr Damseaux on the organization of a European athletics meeting in Strasbourg (Doc. 1-1046/82),
  - motion for a resolution tabled by Mr Fernandez on the training of personnel engaged in physical activities and sport (Doc. 1-571/83),
  - motion for a resolution tabled by Mr Fernandez on physical education and sports instruction (Doc. 1-572/83),
  - motion for a resolution tabled by Mr Fernandez on professional sport (Doc. 1-573/83),
  - motion for a resolution tabled by Mr Purvis and Mr Simmonds on discipline during and after football matches (Doc. 1-1085/83),
  - motion for a resolution tabled by Mr Romualdi and others on a common emblem for athletes of the 10 Community countries taking part in the next Olympic Games (Doc. 1-1170/83),
  - motion for a resolution tabled by Mr Lecanuet and others on the participation of European athletes in the forthcoming Olympic Games in Los Angeles (Doc. 1-1324/83),

---

\* The full texts of documents which are marked with an asterisk (\*) are not incorporated in the book itself, but are freely accessible on the website of the ASSER International Sports Law Centre, at <www.sportslaw.nl> – documentation.

[1] A1-53/84.

[2] OJ C 127, 14-5-1984, p. 142.

–   having regard to the report of the Committee on Youth, Culture, Education, Information and Sport (Doc. 1-53/84),

A.  whereas in the twentieth century sport has become a social phenomenon totally integrated within the cultural, economic and political framework of the 10 Member States of the European Community, and the latter cannot therefore ignore its development;

B.  whereas the development of sport is necessarily linked to that of leisure, tourism and mass communication;

C.  whereas sport is an eminently suitable means of promoting contacts between individuals and facilitating mutual understanding between nations;

D.  stressing that international events in particular at European level, such as the European Football Cup, have greatly contributed to arousing interest in sport as a means of communication and contact between the European nations;

E.  whereas the ever-higher demands that are made on top-class sportsmen and the commercialization of sport leads to situations that are at variance with the objectives of sport, i.e. health, balanced personality, recreation and mutual understanding;

F.  having regard to the serious financial problems facing clubs and associations with the formation of ever larger groupings, particularly in the field of sport, and the growing demands of an increasingly exacting public,

1.  Supports the efforts made by the representatives of clubs and federations and by all associations that seek to promote the development of their particular disciplines and sport in general, while limiting the unfavourable effects of uncontrolled expansion;

2.  Supports all efforts to coordinate the sports policies of the European nations;

3.  Welcomes the declaration by the European Ministers of Sport on practical measures to reduce violence among the public at sporting events, in particular football matches, and calls for greater cooperation between the governments, which are responsible for maintaining public order, the federations and the sports clubs to ensure that the necessary measures are taken to prevent all violence and all practices that run counter to the true sporting spirit;

4.  Draws attention to the possibility of cooperating with the Council of Europe in this field;

5.  Calls on the Commission to assemble the studies drawn up in the various Member States in consultation with the competent bodies on the phenomenon of supporter violence in order to gain insight into what underlies it and thus allow it to be combated in a more direct fashion;

6.  Requests the international sports federations to harmonize their rules in order to facilitate mobility and contacts among sportsmen;

7.  Urges these federations to consider the possibility of introducing rules better suited to ensuring the fair representation of Third World countries at international events;

8.  Requests the Commission of the European Communities to take energetic steps against rules that limit the freedom of movement and establishment of Member State citizens engaged in certain sports and thus run counter to the Treaty of Rome;

9.  Requests the Commission to urge that the qualifications required of sports teachers and sports instructors should be harmonized;

10. Requests the Commission to study the various means employed to finance sports clubs and associations in the Community Member States and to propose, in collabo-

ration with these organizations and the Member State governments, solutions designed to increase the financial resources of clubs, allowing them clearly to meet all their obligations;

11. Requests the Commission to contact the federations, the Member State sports authorities and the Youth Forum with a view to launching 'Community Games' at junior, intermediate, school and university level;

12. Requests that, following the decision to designate 1985 a year of youth, sport be associated with events for young people, thus demonstrating the importance attached by our institutions to young people's sporting activities;

13. Requests the Commission to work out pilot projects for the organization of contacts between young people engaged in sport and also to make an inventory of existing plans in the Member States, as for example Rotterdam municipality's plan to organize an international youth sports festival in 1985, and to provide financial support for these plans;

14. Requests that a special budget heading be introduced for this purpose;

15. Also requests the Commission to consider the possibility of establishing a Community programme for the provision of sports facilities under which a financial contribution is given by the Community to all facilities intended for European sports events;

16. Requests the Commission to hold consultations with all those concerned, that is to say the sports authorities, advertising agencies and television authorities, with a view to adopting a European charter on the allocation to sports clubs and federations of the proceeds from the broadcasting of European sporting events;

17. Welcomes the adoption by the Council of Regulation (EEC) No 3/84 introducing arrangements for movement within the Community of goods sent from one Member State for temporary use in one or more other Member States[3] but protests vigorously at the exclusion from these new arrangements of items of sports equipment accompanying sports teams, although they were expressly included in the Commission's proposal[4];

18. Requests that, when the Lomé Convention is renewed, a special section be devoted to sports events, with the objective of promoting contacts between young people engaged in sport, providing assistance for the provision of facilities and training competent personnel;

19. Calls on the Member States to refuse to organize any sporting event in conjunction with South Africa as the apartheid regime is contrary to the spirit of mutual comprehension between peoples which sport must seek to develop;

20. Instructs its President to forward this resolution to the Council and Commission, the Member State Governments and the main international sporting federations.

———

[3] OJ L 2, 4-1-1984, p. 1.
[4] OJ C 227, 8-9-1981, p. 3.

## 1.3.    RESOLUTION OF THE EUROPEAN PARLIAMENT ON A PEOPLE'S EUROPE, 13 NOVEMBER 1985[5]

*The European Parliament,*

A.    having regard to the conclusions of the June 1984 Fontainebleau European Council and the setting up during that Council of an *ad hoc,* committee on a people's Europe (the Adonnino Committee),

B.    having regard to the interim report submitted by the *ad hoc* Committee to the December 1984 Dublin European Council and approved by the latter,

C.    having regard to the first report by the *ad hoc* Committee, submitted to the March 1985 Brussels European Council and approved by the latter[6]

D.    having regard to the final report submitted by the *ad hoc* Committee to the June 1985 Milan European Council and approved by the latter[7]

E.    having regard to the French memorandum of 26 June 1985 on progress in the construction of Europe, especially the suggestions concerning youth and culture in the section entitled 'A people's Europe',

F.    having regard to the conclusions of the June 1985 Milan European Council, especially as regards 'A people's Europe'[8],

G.    having regard to the initial report by the committee of prominent European personalities (the Colombo committee) to the Council of Europe of 12 June 1985 on prospects for European cooperation over the next decade,

H.    having regard to its past resolutions on various aspects of a people's Europe[9],

I.    having regard to its resolutions of 14 June 1985
   –    on strengthening the citizens' right to petition the European Parliament[10],
   –    on the European Passport[11],
   –    on the report from the *ad hoc* Committee on a People's, Europe to the European Council meeting of 29 June 1985 in Milan[12],
   –    on the removal of obstacles to traffic at the Community's internal borders[13],

J.    having regard to the motions for resolutions
   –    by Mr Gaibisso and others on the formation of European sports teams (Doc. 2-893/84),
   –    by Mr Romualdi and others on a badge for athletes of the 10 Community countries and a European year of sport (Doc. 2-1034/84),
   –    by Mr Turner on grants for students in higher and further education (Doc. 2-1511/84),
   –    by Mrs Lizin on the introduction of a system of free travel on all public transport (road, rail and sea) for the young unemployed and students under 25 throughout the Community (Doc. B2-26/85),

---

[5]   OJ C 345, 31-12-1985, p. 27.
[6]   SN/848/6/85.
[7]   SN/2536/3/85.
[8]   EP Bulletin of 8-7-1985, p. 7.
[9]   See selection shown in Annex I to Doc. A2-133/85.
[10]  OJ C 175, 15-7-1985, p. 273.
[11]  Idem, pp. 275 and 276.
[12]  Idem, p. 276.
[13]  Idem, pp. 277 and 278.

-   by Mr Vandemeulebroucke and Mr Kuijpers on the propagation of the European idea among young people through education (Doc. B2-69/85),
-   by Mr Welsh en the fostering of exchange visits by schoolchildren in the Member States (Doc. B2-92/85),
-   by Mr Parodi and others on the introduction of the European Community as a subject taught in schools (Doc. B2-601/85),
-   by Mr Münch and others on common European symbols (Doc. B2-47/85),

K.  having regard to the communication from the Commission to the Council on implementing the conclusions of the Fontainebleau European Council concerning a people's Europe[14],

L.  having regard to the Commission white paper on completing the internal market submitted to the Milan European Council[15],

M.  having regard to the Commission's programma of work from 1985, especially the passages concerning a people's Europe[16],

N.  having regard to the proposals of the *ad hoc* Committee on Institutional Affairs[17],

O.  having regard to the proposal from the Commission for a Council Directive on a general system for the recognition of higher education diplomas[18],

P.  having regard to the report of the Committee on Youth, Culture, Education, Information and Sport and the opinions of the Committee on Transport and the Committee on the Environment, Public Health and Consumer Protection (Doc. A2-133/85),

Q.  whereas the Council has been instructed to draw up an initial report on action taken, for submission to the December 1985,European Council in Brussels,

R.  whereas the June 1984 direct elections to the European Parliament again demonstrated an inadequate awareness of Europe among the people of the Community, due to the irrelevance of many Community policies to the problems of working people in Europe,

S.  fearing that, unless the European dimension is rapidly impressed on the public and unless unemployment in the Member States is tackled in a rigorous manner, the public is likely to lose all interest in Community affairs,

T.  having regard to the danger that might jeopardize the development of the Community and European integration as such,

U.  aware of the urgent need for concrete and visible steps to bring early improvements in the various aspects of the everyday life of the general public,

V.  convinced that the public in the Community will give credit to a successful Community scheme for rapid and unbureaucratic action, and positive proposals to tackle unemployment in the Member States,

**General**

1.  Pays tribute to the work of the *ad hoc* Committee on a People's Europe (the Adonnino Committee) and supports in principle its many and well-founded proposals for short and medium-term action;

2.  Welcomes the fact that the European Council has in principle approved the proposals of the Adonnino Committee;

---

[14]  COM(84) 446 final.
[15]  COM(85) 310 – Doc. C2-63/85.
[16]  Chapter VI 6.2.1.
[17]  SN/1187/88(Spaak II).
[18]  COM(85) 355 final – Doc. C2-71/85.

3. Criticizes the Council, therefore, for not moving quickly to implement these proposals;

4. Considers it necessary for the Commission, pending the implementation of these proposals, to adhere very closely to the texts submitted by the *ad hoc* Committee, so that the Council is not released from the obligation deriving from the positive attitude of the European Council;

5. Believes that the more far-reaching proposals of the Commission and the European Parliament should be tackled in a second phase;

6. Considers it appropriate for the majority of the proposals to be implemented by all Member States;

7. Considers it necessary that where measures and projects are co-financed from the Community budget, the public should always be informed of this Community contribution by an appropriate means (e.g. signs and announcements in the press);

8. Calls upon the Council rapidly to adopt all Commission proposals before it which concern a people's Europe, in order to demonstrate the advantages of a united Europe to the public as a whole;

9. Calls upon the Member States of the Community to impress up on the competent national departments the need to reach the decisions for a people's Europe they are called upon to take in their spheres in an unbureaucratic and Community-oriented spirit, especially in difficult individual cases;

10. Believes that to achieve declared aims in a number of sectors, more extensive cooperation needed across Community frontiers;

11. Stresses the important role of non-governmental organizations in constructing a people's Europe, and advocates financial support for these organizations;

12. Draws attention in this context to the activities in Europe of private organizations such as the European Cultural Foundation, which seeks to promote the European idea under its statutes, and calls for their activities to achieve a people's Europe to be coordinated, in cooperation with the European institutions;

13. Takes the view that the public in the Community must be encouraged to object to obstacles to the attainment of a people's Europe;

14. Proposes therefore that points for receiving such information and complaints be set up in the Member States so that action on them ma be taken, in order to bring about a people's Europe.

[...]

**Youth, education, exchanges and sport**

29. Calls for greater emphasis on the European Community in school curricula and examination syllabuses, in curricula and examination syllabuses for trainee teachers, and in school textbooks and teaching materials;

30. Emphasizes the important role for young people in the development of the Europe of the future and therefore considers it essential to interest young people in European events and encourage them to take an active part;

31. Welcomes the fact that the *ad hoc* Committee is advocating intensified exchange programmes for young people, as they will be the bearers of the European ideal in the future, and advocates a substantial increase in the existing Community youth exchange programma, particularly encouraging cultural and human relations across frontiers;

(a)   supports therefore the committee's proposals for pupil exchanges between schools in the partner countries;

(b)   calls, in the long-term, for the progressive opening up of the European Youth Exchange programma now in preparation to young people from Central and Eastern Europe, as Europe cannot be confined to its Western part and an exchange of young people between the nations of East and West would be a contribution to a genuine peace policy, as young people who know each other cannot be driven into war by any government;

(c)   calls therefore for the required funds to be made available for the youth exchange scheme;

(d)   advocates further the expansion of the programmes for the exchange of young workers in the Community, and calls upon the Commission to draw up proposals for improved harmonization of vocational training systems between the Member States, so that exchanges of young trainees may take place without loss of quality in such training;

32.   Regards education as an area offering great scope for developing a people's Europe, by:

—   cooperation between European universities,

—   extra-mural education,

—   training and adult education schemes,

—   fostering exchanges for schoolchildren and students,

—   regulations on grants and tuition fees which preclude discrimination against students from other Member States;

33.   Regards increased foreign language teaching in the Community as both a means of international understanding and a way to help the public to make genuine use of freedom of movement; and therefore requests that in each Member State at least two foreign languages are included in the basic curriculum;

34.   Supports the suggestions of the *ad hoc* Committee for Community sports events, the formation of Community teams, the exchange of sportsmen, athletes and trainers, and encouragement of sport for the handicapped;

35.   Regards sport as an important sphere of international communication and therefore advocates measures to:

—   encourage exchanges of sportsmen and athletes, and

—   introduce common symbols and joint sports events, also involving schools;

[...]

———

**\* 1.4.   REPORT DRAWN UP ON BEHALF OF THE COMMITTEE ON YOUTH, CULTURE, EDUCATION, INFORMATION AND SPORT ON SPORT IN THE EUROPEAN COMMUNITY AND A PEOPLE'S EUROPE, 1 DECEMBER 1988[19]**

Rapporteur: Mrs. J. Larive

———

---

[19]  Doc. A2-282/88.

### 1.5.    RESOLUTION OF THE EUROPEAN PARLIAMENT ON SPORT IN THE EUROPEAN COMMUNITY AND A PEOPLE'S EUROPE, 17 FEBRUARY 1989[20]

*The European Parliament,*

–    having regard to its resolutions:
  –    of 13 April 1984 on sport in the Community[21],
  –    of 21 January 1988 on vandalism and violence in sport[22],
  –    of 16 September 1988 on Europe's contribution to Olympic Year 1992[23],
–    having regard to the motions for resolutions:
  –    on the European Games of the future (Doc. B2-230/85),
  –    on the institutionalization and establishment of sports meetings and events by and for the Europe of the Twelve (Doc. B2-1099/86),
  –    on the organizations of competitions, contests and championships for young people in the European Community (Doc. B2-1110/86),
  –    on sport in schools (Doc. B2-1622/86 and Doc. B2-98/87),
  –    on the drawing up of a common team sports programme (Doc. B2-498187),
  –    on the need for Community representation in sport (Doc. B2-636/87),
  –    on the organization of European Community games (Doc. B2-1803187),
  –    on an exchange programme for young amateur sportsmen and women (Doc. B2247/88),
–    having regard to the activities of the Council of Europe in promoting cooperation in sport,
–    having regard to the adoption by the European Council in Milan in June 1985 of the report of the Adonnino Committee on a People's Europe which paved the way for action by the European Community and the Commission in particular, in the area of sport,
–    having regard to the first informal Sports Council held in Athens on 16 and 17 July 1988,
–    having regard to the report of the Committee on Youth, Culture, Education, Information and Sport on sport in the Community (Doc. A2-282/88),

A.    whereas in this century sport has become a social phenomenon that is an integral part of the culture, social, economic and political life of the citizens of the 12 Member States of the Community and whereas the European Community should therefore play a role in sports policy,
B.    whereas since ancient times sport has been an important forum for communication among peoples and sport is an excellent way of enabling European citizens and peoples to get to know and appreciate each other's worth and to develop a sense of belonging to the Community,
C.    whereas active participation in sport should be encouraged as far as possible, partly for reasons of public health, and specific attention should be paid to certain groups such as the disabled, old people and minorities,

---

[20]  OJ C 69, 20-3-1989, p. 234.
[21]  OJ C 127, 14-5-1984, p. 142.
[22]  OJ C 49, 22-2-1988, p. 168.
[23]  OJ C 262, 10-10-1988, p. 208.

D.    whereas more women should be actively encouraged to take up sport as a vital part of the Community policy on equal opportunities,

E.    whereas children should be encouraged to take part in sport and to develop a sporting mentality from an early age and whereas proper teaching of sport in schools is of the utmost importance,

F.    whereas the passive enjoyment of sport is also a form of relaxation on which the media exercise considerable influence,

G.    whereas there is also a negative side to sport and the efforts of the Member States within the Community to combat the problems now facing sport need to be better integrated and coordinated with the activities of the Council of Europe,

H.    whereas, as a result of technological developments, an increasing number of TV stations will be broadcasting for longer and longer periods per day, thus creating an ever-growing demand for sports coverage,

I.    whereas completion of the internal market by 1992 means that there is a greater need for the European Community to have a coherent and coordinated sports policy, in close cooperation with the Council of Europe,

1.    Calls on the Commission of the European Communities, in close cooperation with the Council of Europe, to develop a coherent sports policy[24], to submit a communication to the European Parliament by June 1989 and subsequently to draw up an action programme for the period up to 1992;

2.    Considers that this policy should tackle sport on three fronts:
      (a)   international approach to the social aspects of sport,
      (b)   the implications of Europe 1992 for sport,
      (c)   promotion of the Community dimension in sport;

*Social aspects of sport*

3.    Urges the Commission to ensure that the following social aspects of sport are covered by the action programme:
      (a)   stepping-up and coordination of measures to combat violence and drug taking in sport[25], as stressed by the Sports Council of July 1988 and repeatedly called for by the European Parliament[26],
      (b)   encouragement of active participation in sport, particularly by certain less active groups in the population such as old people, the disabled and minorities,
      (c)   encouraging women to take part in sport as a vital part of the policy of equal opportunities,
      (d)   exchanges of sportsmen, athletes and coaches through Community programmes particularly by expanding the YES programme and with special reference to peripheral areas,
      (e)   organization of sporting activities for sports clubs, schools and students in conjunction with the twinning of schools and towns[27],
      (f)   encouragement of sport in schools and training and refresher courses for sports teachers and coaches[28],
      (g)   recognition of the role of sport in the rehabilitation of society's rejects;

---

[24]  Adonnino report adopted by the European Council in Milan (June 1985).
[25]  Adonnino report adopted by the European Council in Milan (June 1985).
[26]  EP resolution of 21-1-1988.
[27]  Adonnino report adopted by the European Council in Milan (June 1985).
[28]  Adonnino report adopted by the European Council in Milan (June 1985).

## Europe 1992 and sport

4.    Considers that Europe 1992 will affect the sporting world in a number of ways, such, as the free movement of professional sportsmen and coaches – to be regulated after the sports bodies responsible have been consulted – European tender procedures and safety standards for sports facilities, mutual recognition of qualifications and diplomas, fiscal harmonization, harmonization of national legislation and drug abuse, etc., and calls on the Commission to draw up specific proposals in these areas;

5.    Believes that, along with adoption of the directive on a general system for the recognition of higher education, diplomas awarded on completion of professional education and training of at least three years' duration, it is of pressing importance to make progress in coordinating the syllabuses and recognizing the qualifications of physical education teachers, for example through Community exchange programmes similar to Erasmus;

6.    Supports the request made by the national Olympic Committee to e Commission that a joint conference of all those involved be held in 1989 to examine the implications of the free internal market for sport;

7.    Considers that the Commission should strongly oppose regulations in certain sectors of sport, if they contravene the Treaty of Rome, and abolish or reform them where necessary, with a view to securing freedom of movement and freedom of establishment, while taking into account the position of the sports bodies responsible;

8.    Calls on the Commission to include in Regulation No 3/84 introducing arrangements for movement within the Community of goods sent from one Member State for temporary use in one or more other Member States[29] sports goods which are part of the equipment of sporting teams in order to promote freedom of movement for teams;

## The Community dimension in sport

9.    Is fully aware that a number of recent studies based on opinion pons conducted by the European Commission have clearly shown that the vast majority of Community citizens welcome the initiatives so far taken by the Community in the area of sport and would like to see this policy continued and developed;

10.   Would like to see the Community dimension in sport and sport as a means of communication between European citizens consolidated by the following action taken in conjunction with the sports governing bodies:

      (a)    organization by the Community of more European sporting events[30],
      (b)    creation of Community teams for some sports[31],
      (c)    inviting sporting teams to wear the Community emblem in addition to their national colours at major sporting events[32],
      (d)    creation of Community trophies[33],
      (e)    organization of Community Games[34],

---

[29]   OJ L 2, 4-1-1984, p. 1.
[30]   Adonnino report adopted by the European Council in Milan (June 1985).
[31]   Adonnino report adopted by the European Council in Milan (June 1985).
[32]   Adonnino report adopted by the European Council in Milan (June 1985).
[33]   Adonnino report adopted by the European Council in Milan (June 1985).
[34]   Adonnino report adopted by the European Council in Milan (June 1985).

11. Considers that in doing so the Commission should be guided by the following principles:
    (a) the need to achieve a broad balance between the different sports and countries selected,
    (b) the involvement of both professional sportsmen and amateurs,
    (c) selective and modest funding for a limited period;

12. Supports the Commission's policy of providing sponsorship and Community patronage for a number of existing major sports events but hopes that the policy of organizing Community competitions will be continued on the basis of a clear and properly funded programme;

13. Considers that limited support for national, regional or even local sports events could greatly help to bring the Community closer to its citizens and considers that the Commission should develop a strategy in this area in consultation with the national information offices;

14. Calls on the Commission to keep up its efforts to create European sports teams, however difficult this may be;

15. Urges that at the Olympic Games in Barcelona and Albertville in 1992 all teams from the Member States will wear a Community emblem and that other Community activities will be arranged;

16. Hopes that the current talks with university sports associations in the Member States will result in their athletes wearing a Community emblem at the next 'Universiades' in 1989;

17. Calls on the Commission to draw up proposals for the award of Community prizes to deserving and above all sporting athletes and teams and to institute a special prize for the best supporters club;

18. Regrets the fact that the European Community Games have been postponed and asks the Commission to involve the national Olympic Committees and national sports federations more closely in preparing its revised plans for European Community Games;

19. Calls on the Commission to give its backing to the proposals for a 'European Stars' sports TV programme in which each Member State will be represented by a sports team of well known personalities and which is to be broadcast by Eurovision;

### Sport and the European institutions

20. Would like to see the special budget item (Article 673) for sport for the handicapped, created on the initiative of the European Parliament in 1987, maintained and if possible increased since the present allocation must be regarded as an absolute minimum;

21. Considers also that the separate item created in the 1988 budget (Article 675) to promote public awareness of the Community's activities through sport meets a real need;

22. Would like to see the Commission establishing clear objectives, criteria and decision-making procedures for awarding grants to international, national, regional and local sporting events and making an annual assessment of the sporting events it has supported;

23. Recommends, on the basis of the requested communication and action programme for the period up to 1992, that a general budget line for sport be created;

24. Urges the Ministers responsible for sport to meet in 1989 to discuss an action programme up to 1992 on the basis of the Commission communication;

25. Instructs its President to forward this resolution to the Council and Commission, the International Olympic Committee and the Council of Europe.

---

**\* 1.6. COMMISSION COMMUNICATION TO THE COUNCIL AND THE EUROPEAN PARLIAMENT ON THE EUROPEAN COMMUNITY AND SPORT, 31 JULY 1991**[35]

---

**\* 1.7. ANSWER ON BEHALF OF THE COMMISSION TO WRITTEN QUESTION NO 2801/92 BY MR MARC GALLE (S), 7 JULY 1993**[36] \*

Subject: Community representation at sport events

---

**\* 1.8. ANSWER ON BEHALF OF THE COMMISSION TO WRITTEN QUESTION E-245/93 BY FREDDY BLAK (PSE), 28 FEBRUARY 1994**[37] \*

Subject: Relative importance of sport and olive oil

---

**\* 1.9. REPORT OF THE COMMITTEE ON CULTURE, YOUTH, EDUCATION AND THE MEDIA ON THE EUROPEAN COMMUNITY AND SPORT, 27 AND 29 APRIL 1994**[38]

Rapporteur: Mrs J. Larive

---

**1.10. RESOLUTION OF THE EUROPEAN PARLIAMENT ON THE EUROPEAN COMMUNITY AND SPORT, 6 MAY 1994**[39]

*The European Parliament,*

–   having regard to the motions for resolutions by:
    (a) Mrs Ewing on the protection of popular sporting traditions in Europe (B3-1909/90),
    (b) Mrs Banotti on the need to reappraise the EC's sports policy (B3-0862/91),
    (c) Mr Gutiérrez Díaz on professional boxing (B3-1512/91),
    (d) Mrs Muscardini on a common logo for athletes from the 12 Community Member States taking part in the next Olympic Games (B3-1725/91),
    (e) Mr Bofill Abeilhe on legislation to outlaw symbols which incite violence in sport (B3-0456/92),
    (f) Mrs Muscardini on the safety of sports installations (B3-0714/92),

---

[35] SEC(91) 1438/F.
[36] Question of 16-11-1992; OJ C 292, 28-10-1993, p. 14.
[37] Question of 23-2-1993; OJ C 310, 7-11-1994, p. 2.
[38] A3-0326/94.
[39] OJ C 205, 25-7-1994, p. 486.

- having regard to its resolutions of 13 April 1984 on sport in the Community [40], 11 July 1985 on hooliganism and violence in sport[41] 14 October 1987 on women in sport [42], 22 January 1988 on hooliganism and violence in sport [43], 16 September 1988 on the European Community's contribution to the Olympic Year 1992 [44], and 17 February 1989 on sport in the European Community and a People's Europe[45],
- having regard to the work of the Council of Europe concerning sport,
- having regard to the Adonnino report on a People's Europe, which was adopted by the Milan Council in 1985, and more particularly to the passage in this report concerning the contribution of sport to enhancing European citizenship,
- having regard to the decisions which have resulted from the informal Councils of Ministers responsible for sport since 1988,
- having regard to the Commission communication to the Council and the European Parliament of 31 July 1991 on 'The European Community and Sport' (SEC(91) 1438),
- having regard to the consultations and decisions resulting from the meetings of the European Sports Forum in 1991, 1992 and 1993,
- having regard to the hearing on 'The European Community and Sport' held by the Committee on Culture, Youth, Education and the Media on Thursday 25 November 1993,
- having regard to Rule 45 of the Rules of Procedure,
- having delegated the power of decision to the Committee on Culture, Youth, Education and the Media, pursuant to Rule 52 of the Rules of Procedure,
- having regard to the report of the Committee on Culture, Youth, Education and the Media and the opinion of the Committee on Legal Affairs and Citizens' Rights (A3-0326/94),

A. whereas sport is a focus of interest for many tens of millions of citizens of the European Union in their daily lives, and whereas it should therefore receive political attention and be taken into account in policy at European level as well as at other levels,

B. whereas both active participation in sport and passive spectating make a substantial contribution to the social and cultural identity of European citizens and peoples,

C. whereas the Maastricht Treaty confers new powers on the European Union in the cultural and social sphere and thus strengthens the legal basis for a European policy on sport,

D. whereas any action by the authorities with regard to sport – including action at European level – must be assessed in the light of the principle of subsidiarity and must therefore supplement private initiative and national, regional and local policy and must be determined in close consultation with the parties concerned,

E. whereas the establishment of the Single Market has important consequences both for sports associations and for individual sportsmen and women, because active participation in sport and passive spectating result in substantial amounts of economic activity,

---

[40] OJ C 127, 14-5-1984, p. 142.
[41] OJ C 229, 9-9-1985, p. 99.
[42] OJ C 305, 16-1-1987, p. 62.
[43] OJ C 49, 22-2-1988, p. 168.
[44] OJ C 262, 10-1-1988, p. 208.
[45] OJ C 69, 20-3-1989, p. 234.

F.       whereas sport is endangered by a number of undesirable phenomena – among which hooliganism, racism and drug abuse are not the least significant – which can be effectively combated only by means of a transfrontier policy approach,

G.       whereas action by the authorities in the sports sector should be primarily designed to promote active participation in sport and amateur sport,

H.       whereas, bearing in mind the above observations, a more active policy is needed at European Union level and must replace the hesitant and fragmentary action so far taken by the Commission, which has moreover focused too exclusively on external communication,

1.       Takes the view that sport and activities associated with it should be governed by general European and national legislation and subject to the jurisdiction of the general European and national courts;

2.       Recognizes the important function of sponsoring and patronage in sport but considers that abuses and unacceptable influence must be combated;

3.       Takes the view that EU subsidies for top-class sport should make way for a genuine EU policy on sport, which should be elaborated as a supplement to and in conjunction with
         –       the sector itself and should be concerned with the application of EU legislation to sport,
                 promoting active sport,
         –       combating dangers which threaten sport,
         –       expanding instruments for an EU sport policy, and therefore:

### as regards the consequences of the Single Market

4.       Calls on the Commission to pursue an information policy which achieves genuine results, so as to ensure that EU legislation relevant to sport meets with prompt and effective acceptance;

5.       Urges that it be made clear to the sporting world that the legislation of and the administration of justice by the European Union take precedence over internal sports Regulations and disciplinary procedures;

6.       Calls for obstacles to participation in sport by EU citizens based on nationality, such as 'foreigners rules', to be phased out more rapidly;

7.       Demands the elimination of discrimination on grounds of nationality, which is also practised in amateur sport;

8.       Calls for the right to join and leave sports clubs freely to be guaranteed without making it dependent on additional conditions which conflict with general law (the transfer system);

9.       Urges the Commission to investigate immediately whether both the rules and practices of FIFA, UEFA, and the national football associations and clubs are compatible with EU legislation, to take the appropriate decisions following this investigation and to act accordingly;

10.      Calls for the necessary legislation for recognition of diplomas and certificates to be adopted without delay so that trainers, coaches, therapists, etc., may practise their profession in the EU without discrimination on grounds of nationality;

11.      Calls for the derogation for sport in the Directive on protection against child labour not to result in children being exploited or put under excessive pressure to perform;

12.      Calls on the Commission to carry out careful monitoring to ensure that free competition between top-class sports clubs is not distorted by excessive public financing;

13. Hopes that the Commission, the Member States, the two sides of industry and sports associations will draw up a social charter for sportsmen and women;

### as regards the promotion of active participation in sport

14. Calls for progress to be made, in connection with the European Year of the Elderly, in the adoption of a specific programme to promote active participation in sport by the elderly;
15. Calls for the emancipatory aspects of sport to be exploited in combating disadvantage by including sport in the relevant EU programmes;
16. Calls, further, for the appropriations for sport for the disabled to be maintained but allocated to projects which genuinely give disabled people the opportunity to participate in sport;
17. Calls upon the two sides of industry to provide scope for sport at the workplace and for the EU institutions to set an example in this respect;
18. Stresses the contribution of school sport to public health, calls on the Member States to include sufficient time for physical recreation in school syllabuses and recommends that the Commission study the participation of young people in sport at school;
19. Hopes that the Commission will support the promotion of women's sport and an increase in the proportion of women in key posts in sport and more actively pursue the recommendations of the its abovementioned resolution of 14 October 1987;

### as regards combating violence in and on the periphery of sport

20. Calls on the Commission at long last to tackle seriously the issue of European safety standards for sports stadiums, in accordance with its abovementioned resolution of 22 January 1988;
21. Calls on the Commission, the Member States, European citizens, education systems, sports associations and the media persistently to promote the cause of ethics and fair play in sport and supports the measures taken by the Council of Europe in this respect;
22. Encourages sports associations and Member States to continue without any relaxation their policies to prevent and combat violence among supporters and recommends a comparative study of the impact of this policy on violence in and around sports grounds;
23. Calls on the Commission, Member States, sports associations, sportsmen and women and the media to work actively to eliminate expressions of racism and xenophobia in and in connection with sport;
24. Calls upon officers of sports associations and Member States' policy-makers to ensure strict compliance with safety regulations concerning the equipment and design of sports venues;

### as regards instruments for an active EU policy on sport

25. Welcomes the setting up of the European Sports Forum, would like to be involved in it on a permanent basis, would like its activities to be stepped up, and calls on the Council to recognize the role of the European Sports Forum;
26. Urges that sport be used as a means of reducing obstacles to access so as to strengthen, *inter alia*, the Youth for Europe programme and improve the outreach and accessibility of Community programmes;

27. Calls for EU sports subsidies to be reallocated to small-scale, transfrontier amateur sport which enables citizens to share the European experience and for subsidies to be awarded in consultation with the sporting world, in a more transparent and de-centralized manner, and on the basis of objective criteria;

28. Calls on the Commission to draw up a specific programme to promote regional and traditional sports;

29. Calls, in view of the value of sport to society and the economic and employment opportunities it presents, for measures concerning sport to be incorporated in the EU's policy instruments, with appropriations within the Structural Funds being ear-marked for sports facilities and training, including vocational training, etc.;

30. Calls on the Commission to promote sports management and international research into sport, *inter alia* by means of exchanges, international seminars and training courses;

31. Calls on the Council and Commission to recognize the opportunities presented by sport in external policy (development policy, association agreements and central and eastern Europe);

32. Proposes that, when the Treaty is revised, sport should be included as an area of policy of the European Union and that, until then, the sports unit should remain re-sponsible for coordination and liaison within the Commission (DG X);

33. Instructs its President to forward this resolution to the Commission, the Council, the governments of the Member States and the Council of Europe.

---

**\* 1.11. ANSWER ON BEHALF OF THE COMMISSION TO WRITTEN QUESTION E-542/96 BY IRINI LAMBRAKI (PSE), 15 APRIL 1996[46] \***

Subject: Application of Community law to the statutes of international and national sport federations

---

**\* 1.12. ANSWER ON BEHALF OF THE COMMISSION TO WRITTEN QUESTION E-1269/96 BY ANTONI GUTIÉRREZ DÍAZ (GUE/NGL), 5 JULY 1996[47]**

Subject: Professional boxing

---

**\* 1.13. REPORT OF THE COMMITTEE ON CULTURE, YOUTH, EDUCATION AND THE MEDIA ON THE ROLE OF THE EUROPEAN UNION IN THE FIELD OF SPORT, 28 MAY 1997[48]**

Rapporteur: Mrs Doris Pack

---

[46] Question of 11-3-1996; OJ C 217, 26-7-1996, p. 66.
[47] Question of 24-5-1996; OJ C 305, 15-10-1996, p. 76.
[48] A4-0197/97.

## 1.14. RESOLUTION OF THE EUROPEAN PARLIAMENT ON THE ROLE OF THE EUROPEAN UNION IN THE FIELD OF SPORT, 13 JUNE 1997[49]

*The European Parliament,*

–    having regard to the motion for a resolution by Mr Willockx and Mr De Coene on setting up a European youth sport fund (B4-0467/96),
–    having regard to its previous resolutions on the relationship between the European Community and sport and in particular its resolution of 6 May 1994 on the European Community and sport (205, 25-7-1994, p. 486),
–    having regard to its resolution of 13 March 1996 embodying (i) its opinion on the convening of the Intergovernmental Conference, and (ii) an evaluation of the work of the Reflection Group and a definition of the political priorities of the European Parliament with a view to the Intergovernmental Conference (OJ C 96, 1-4-1996, p. 77.) and in particular to paragraph 4.18 thereof,
–    having regard to its resolution of 19 September 1996 on the role of public service, television in a multi-media society (OJ C 320, 28-10-1996, p. 180.),
–    having regard to its decision of 10 June 1997 on the joint text approved by the Conciliation Committee for a European Parliament and Council Directive amending Council Directive 89/552/EEC on the coordination of certain provisions laid down by law, regulation or administrative action in Member States concerning the pursuit of television broadcasting activities (Minutes of that Sitting, Part II, Item 1.),
–    having regard to the judgment of the Court of Justice of 15 December 1995 in Case C-415/93 ('the Bosman case') (Reports of Cases 1995, pp. I-4921.), and in particular grounds 105 to 110 thereof,
–    having regard to the debates at the Sixth European Sports Forum organized by the Commission on 16 and 17 December 1996 in Brussels,
–    having regard to the resolution of the European sports movement of 17 December 1996 on the inclusion of sport in the EU Treaty and to the draft article annexed thereto,
–    having regard to the public hearings organized by the Committee on Culture, Youth, Education and the Media on 20 March 1996 on the implications of the Bosman ruling and on 19 March 1997 on Sport, Youth and the Media: should the EU play too?,
–    having regard to Rule 148 of its Rules of Procedure,
–    having regard to the report of the Committee on Culture, Youth, Education and the Media and the opinion of the Committee on Budgets (A4-0197/97),

A.    whereas more than 100 million European citizens participate in sporting activities; whereas such activities are organized by some tens of thousands of sports groups which are themselves members of a plethora of associations and federations; whereas the sports movement is one of the most significant movements involving European Union citizens; and whereas sport, therefore, besides being an economic phenomenon, constitutes a basic cultural and social phenomenon,

B.    whereas access to sport and the practice of sport, like access to culture, promote personal development and a well-balanced personality,

---

[49]    OJ C 200, 30-6-1997, p. 252.

C.    whereas more people enjoy sport than participate in sporting activities, and whereas all citizens are entitled to information about major sporting events, as confirmed by the European Parliament and Council Directive on television without frontiers,

D.    whereas sport is also an important sector of the economy which generates an estimated 1.5% of the European Union's GDP and whereas it therefore represents a not inconsiderable source of employment in the services sector,

E.    whereas education for sport and sports training for young people, in particular, are of fundamental importance for health especially for combating smoking and alcohol and drug abuse and for preventing cancer and cardio-vascular problems – for physical and mental well-being and for social integration; whereas that aspect of social integration is crucial for the most vulnerable social groups,

F.    whereas there is a tendency for the time devoted to sport and education for sport in schools to be reduced to the bare minimum, and whereas it is essential for that trend to be reversed; whereas sports clubs act as an addition to, a link with and frequently a substitute for school, and whereas it is crucial to establish more structured relationships between sports clubs and schools,

G.    whereas, in general terms, and for certain socio-cultural reasons, women do not have adequate access to sporting activities, and whereas specific schemes to promote women's sport especially among young women – are required,

H.    emphasizing that, while -sport can foster positive values such as determination, courage, tolerance, loyalty, friendship and team spirit, it may, in certain cases, and without being the root cause, act as a catalyst for negative values such as intolerance, chauvinism, racism and violence as well as cheating – both of oneself and one's opponents – by resorting to drugs; whereas the positive values must be encouraged and the negative values combated with the utmost vigour,

I.    whereas, although the European Union has taken an interest in professional sport as an economic activity, it has, to date, only taken account in a very marginal fashion of the cultural, educational and social dimension of sport, and whereas such neglect stems basically from the fact that there is no explicit reference to sport in the Treaty,

J.    whereas the specific nature of sport and the autonomy of the sports movement and of the organizations which give it a structure must be acknowledged where the sporting activity concerned is not primarily a form of economic activity; whereas the economic activity generated by professional sport may not, however, be exempt from the provisions of Community law,

K.    whereas it is vital for the current Intergovernmental Conference to include a reference to sport in Article 128 of the Treaty, without prejudice to the inclusion in the Treaty of an article devoted to sport or the annexing thereto of a protocol on that subject,

L.    whereas, as they are worded at present, and while they could usefully be interpreted in that sense, Articles 126 and 127 of the Treaty concerning education, vocational training and youth must already be deemed to apply to sport,

M.    whereas, in its ruling in Case C-415/93 ('the Bosman case'), the Court of Justice of the European Communities prohibited the practice of requiring the payment of a transfer fee if professional sportsmen change clubs at the end of their contracts; whereas, in its grounds for the judgment, the Court admitted that 'it must be accepted that the prospect of receiving transfer, development or training fees is indeed likely to encourage football clubs to seek new talent and train young players, (Ground 108) but took the view that 'the same aims can be achieved at least as efficiently by other means which do not impede freedom of movement for workers' (Ground 110),

N. whereas, therefore, as the Court of Justice itself suggested, efficient solidarity and redistribution mechanisms must be guaranteed and developed to ensure that young players are trained and the continued existence of amateur clubs is not jeopardized, and whereas this must be done in such a way that, in practice, players from disadvantaged backgrounds are not excluded,

O. whereas, in sports where fees are paid, some redistribution of television broadcasting rights may help to provide funds for such mechanisms, and whereas any system for negotiating such rights must facilitate their implementation,

P. whereas, moreover, solutions must be found which comply with Community law and which, in practice, do not dissuade big, medium-sized and small professional and amateur clubs from making significant efforts to train young players and thereby fulfil their educational and social role,

Q. whereas the line separating professional from amateur sport must be discussed since, in practice, it frequently varies from one Member State to another and from one sport to another; whereas, logically, a sportsman who receives in return for his services payment which is more than simple travel expenses but less than the lowest wages paid for ordinary work should not be regarded as a professional sportsman,

R. whereas the maintenance of a balance between clubs, or, in the words of the Court of Justice, the preservation of a certain degree of equality and uncertainty as to results, is essential if fair and attractive competitions are to be organized; whereas such a balance and the very nature of European competitions may be adversely affected by distortions of competition connected with existing disparities as regards subsidies and obligations to which the clubs are subject, with particular regard to their obligation to balance their books and to their social security and tax burdens,

S. whereas the financial situation referred to above may also be altered if clubs are taken over by undertakings which have only a commercial relationship with sport and which naturally rate commercial considerations higher than sporting objectives,

T. recalling that Article B3-305 in the Community budget was created by Parliament with a view to encouraging some specific initiatives, in particular the Eurathlon programme and sport for the disabled,

U. whereas the Community budget for 1997 has an article (B3-305) (OJ L 44, 14-2-1997) devoted to a pilot programme entitled 'Sport in Europe' with an appropriation of ECU 3 million in commitment appropriations; whereas that article is included in the chapter entitled 'Information and Communication', which is indicative of the fact that, to date, sport has not been considered by the Community on own merits but as a means of implementing other policies; whereas that article basically finances the Eurathlon programme and provides ECU 1 million for sport for the disabled; whereas, despite its merits, this vulnerable budget article, against which the Commission usually makes no more than a token entry in its preliminary draft budget, cannot cover, either in terms of its structure or its endowment, the measures expected in this field of a European Union which claims to put 'Citizens First',

V. emphasizing that, in the Remarks against this budget article, the budgetary authority asks the Commission not only to submit to it a report on the impact of this measure but also to accompany it by a study on the formulation of a full-scale Community action programme in the field of sport, geared to its social and educational dimension and integrational function,

W.    recalling that some of the appropriations from Article B3-305 must be used to assist
      the training of young people in all branches of sport,

X.    taking the view, on the basis of the foregoing considerations, that it is a matter of
      urgency for the Commission to set up a task force with a remit to review all the as-
      pects of sport which are of interest to the European Union and its policies – whether
      cultural, social or educational, pertaining to health or economic – and to draw up,
      after consulting the various participants in the sports movement, a Green Paper with
      a view to the elaboration of a proper full-scale action plan in the field of sport,

Y.    whereas, pending the implementation of an action plan of that nature, account must
      be taken of sport forthwith through a variety of Community programmes which, to
      date, have largely or entirely ignored it, in particular the programmes covered by
      the regional and social policies, those concerning education, training and youth ex-
      changes – Socrates, Leonardo and Youth for Europe – the action programme con-
      cerning equal opportunities for men and women, action in the field of health,
      measures to combat racism, and the research policy (links between sport and health,
      campaign against doping, etc.),

1.    Takes the view that, in the Treaty on which it is based and through its actions, the
      European Union must acknowledge the basic cultural, economic and social phe-
      nomenon that sport rep resents;

2.    Calls on the current Intergovernmental Conference, to that end, to include at all
      events an explicit reference to sport in Article 128 of the Treaty;

3.    Emphasizes that the European Union must recognize the specific nature of sport and
      the autonomy of the sports movement it being understood that the economic activity
      generated by professional sport cannot be exempt from the provisions of Commu-
      nity law;

4.    Urges each member State to use the opportunity provided for by the new Article 3a
      of the 'Television without frontiers' Directive by taking steps to ensure that TV
      broadcasters under its jurisdiction do not broadcast on an exclusive basis events, in
      this instance sporting events, which are regarded by that Member State as being of
      major importance to the general public in such a way as to deprive a substantial pro-
      portion of the public in that Member State of the opportunity of watching those
      events on free television and to draw up a list of designated events, national or oth-
      erwise, in due course, in accordance with a transparent procedure, which involves
      the sports associations concerned;

5.    Urges the Commission to set up forthwith a Task Force on Sport and to draw up,
      after consulting the entire sports movement, a Green Paper with a view to the elabo-
      ration of a comprehensive action plan of the European Union in the field of sport;

6.    Calls in particular on the Commission, as part of the work of that Task Force:

      (a)   to take account of sport across the entire spectrum of its activities, especially
            in the regional, social, education, youth training and health fields, and, as a
            result, to reshape its pilot programme in the field of sport,

      (b)   since it has failed to refer to sport in its White Paper on Education and Train-
            ing, to rectify that omission, on the basis of Article 126 of the Treaty, in the
            activities to be carried out on the basis of that White Paper, to encourage the
            Member States to reverse the trend to reduce the time devoted to sport in
            schools and to encourage the establishment of closer links between schools
            and sports clubs,

(c)    to contribute, by means of appropriate activities in the field of sport, to social integration and to the campaign against racism,

(d)    to implement an awareness, promotion and profile-raising campaign geared to women's amateur and professional sport,

(e)    to give active support, with the associations involved, to the introduction of efficient redistribution and solidarity mechanisms so that the training of young players and the continued existence of amateur clubs may be financed by means compatible with Community law,

(f)    to examine whether the various schemes for state aid to professional clubs applied in the Member States and the current disparities relating to social security and tax burdens have an effect on the fairness of European competitions and whether the transparency of the financial situation of the various professional clubs in the Community should be guaranteed,

(g)    to make the necessary proposals to regulate the permitted transfer from one club to another within one and the same competition, without infringing the freedom of players to change clubs, in order to counter distortion of competition,

(h)    to conclude an agreement with national and international sports federations concerning the observance of relevant Community legislation and in particular, with reference to major sporting events (championships, Olympic Games, etc.), Council Directive 85/337/EEC (and subsequent amendments) on the assessment of the effects of certain public and private projects on the environment (OJ L 175, 5-7-1985, p. 40.);

7.    Calls for the convening of a Council of Ministers for Sport;

8.    Instructs its appropriate committee to establish structured and permanent relations with the European sports movement;

9.    Calls for the organization of a European Year of Sport;

10.   Instructs its President to forward this resolution to the Commission. the Council, the Committee of the Regions, the governments and parliaments of the Member States, the European Olympic Committee and the European non-governmental sports organizations which are members of ENGSO.

———

**\* 1.15.   ANSWER ON BEHALF OF THE COMMISSION TO WRITTEN QUESTION E-2109/97 BY JOHANNA BOOGERD-QUAAK (ELDR), 15 SEPTEMBER 1997**[50]

Subject: Promoting the euro in connection with European sport policy

———

**1.16.   TREATY OF AMSTERDAM, AMENDING THE TREATY ON EUROPEAN UNION, THE TREATIES ESTABLISHING THE EUROPEAN COMMUNITIES AND CERTAIN RELATED ACTS, ANNEX, 2 OCTOBER 1997**

[...]

---

[50]   Question of 23-6-1997; OJ C 082, 17-3-1998, p. 30.

**29. Declaration on sport**
The Conference emphasises the social significance of sport, in particular its role in forging identity and bringing people together. The Conference therefore calls on the bodies of the European Union to listen to sports associations when important questions affecting sport are at issue. In this connection, special consideration should be given to the particular characteristics of amateur sport.

[...]

---

**\* 1.17.  ANSWER ON BEHALF OF THE COMMISSION TO WRITTEN QUESTION NO. 3426/97 BY MARJO MATIKAINEN-KALLSTRÖM (PPE), 27 NOVEMBER 1997**[51]

Subject: Creation of a Task Force on Sport

---

**1.18.  PRESIDENCY CONCLUSIONS OF THE CARDIFF EUROPEAN COUNCIL, 15 AND 16 JUNE 1998**

**IV. BRINGING THE UNION CLOSER TO PEOPLE**

[...]

31.  The European Council invites the Council and the Member States to consider ideas to promote more contacts between young people, e.g. through the Internet, and the scope for tackling social exclusion among young people, including through sport.

[...]

---

**\* 1.19.  COMMISSION STAFF WORKING PAPER, THE DEVELOPMENT AND PROSPECTS FOR COMMUNITY ACTION IN THE FIELD OF SPORT, 29 SEPTEMBER 1998**

---

**1.20.  COMMISSION, CONSULTATION DOCUMENT OF DG X, THE EUROPEAN MODEL OF SPORT**

Table of contents
Introduction
Chapter one – The European model of sport
1    The European Model of Sport
   1.1   Organisation of sport in Europe
      1.1.1  Pyramid Structure
         1.1.1.1   The Clubs

---

[51]  Question of 31-10-1997; OJ C 134, 30-4-1998, p. 162.

## INTRODUCTION

In its September 1998 working paper the Commission identified sport as performing five functions: an educational, a public health, a social, a cultural and a recreational function. In economic terms sport is a rapidly growing area accounting for 3% of world trade and is one of the sectors most likely to generate new employment. In recent years, sport in Europe has developed rapidly. The increasing economic and commercial slant of sport has created a real change, for example in the field of TV-rights for sports events. Since 1974[52] the European Union has been dealing with sport and observing these changes from an economic point of view.

Provisions in the EC Treaty, secondary legislation, Community policies and decisions have an increasing impact on sporting practices and activities. These developments have caused a number of problems for sport in Europe. The Directorate-General for Competition (DG IV) of the European Commission, for example, has received 55 complaints relating to sport, on matters such as the role of sports organisations, television rights or commercial sponsoring. Most of these actions were brought after the ruling of the ECJ in the Bosman case.[53] This increase in the number of actions also reveals that there is a gap between the real world of sport and its regulatory framework.

In September 1998 the Commission issued a working paper in which it identified its policy on sport. It recognises that sport is not only an economic activity but also part of European identity.

This social function of sport was also identified by the Intergovernmental Conference set up to revise the Maastricht Treaty, and a Declaration on sport was annexed to the Treaty of Amsterdam.

The Commission is aware that these developments raise questions regarding the future organisation of sport in Europe. It is ready and willing to help sport organisations to find solutions on the basis of their own initiatives. In order to assist the sports associations and following the Declaration of Amsterdam, the Commission wishes to consult the sports world to reflect on the future development of sport in Europe. In order to prepare the ground, the Commission is conducting a survey which will enable all parties involved to identify the problems caused by the changing situation and give them an opportunity to express their views and make suggestions on the future development of sport in Europe.

The Commission will use the findings for two purposes:

–    to prepare for the European Conference on Sport (*Assises européennes du sport*) to be held in May 1999
–    to identify more clearly the real features of European sport and to preserve them.

This paper describes the organisation of sport in Europe, its features and the recent developments. It highlights the problems which have arisen, and the attached questionnaire will

---

[52]  Ruling of the ECJ C-36/74 *Walrave* v *UCI* [1974] ECR I-1405.
[53]  Case C-415/93.

enable the Commission to receive the comments of those concerned. All the interested parties are asked to send their answers to the European Commission (Directorate-General X, Sport Unit, Rue de la Loi 102, 1049 Brussels) by 25 February 1999.

## CHAPTER ONE – THE EUROPEAN MODEL OF SPORT

## 1 THE EUROPEAN MODEL OF SPORT

From the end of World War II until the mid 80s two different models of sport existed in Europe, namely the East and the West European model. The former was more or less ideologically oriented; sport was a part of propaganda. In western countries European sport developed a mixed model, in which actions performed by governmental and non-governmental organisations existed side by side. It is also important to underline that sport has grown in parallel with television, basically in an environment of exclusively public television. Western European sport is thus the result of private and public activity. In the northern countries, the state does not regulate, whereas in the southern countries, the states play a regulatory role in sport.

### 1.1 Organisation of sport in Europe

In the Member States sport is traditionally organised in a system of national federations. Only the top federations (usually one per country) are linked together in European and international federations. Basically the structure resembles a pyramid with a hierarchy.

### *1.1.1 Pyramid Structure*

1.1.1.1 The Clubs

The *clubs* form the foundation of this pyramid. They offer everyone the possibility of engaging in sport locally, thereby promoting the idea of 'sport for all'. They also foster the development of new generations of sportsmen/women. At this level unpaid participation is particularly important and beneficial to the development of European sport. In Portugal, for example, there are about 70.000 unpaid coaches and 40.000 unpaid board and committee members.[54]

One feature of European Sport that is closely linked to this level is amateur sport. As stressed by Marcelino Oreja, Member of the European Commission responsible for sport, addressing the 7th European Sports Forum in 1997, amateur sport reflects that genuine, disinterested love of taking part in a sport. In this field, sport has a strong social function by bringing people together. In Austria, for example, about 39% of the population are members of a sport club or a federation.[55]

1.1.1.2 The Regional Federations

Regional federations form the next level; the clubs are usually members of these organisations. Their area of interest is limited to a region in which they are responsible for organising regional championships or coordinating sport on a regional level. In some countries, Germany for example, there are regional-level umbrella organisations, which comprise all the clubs in one region.

---

[54] Final Draft on Sport in the Member States, 1991.
[55] Sports Information Bulletin, 'Sport for All'; Clearing House, 1997, 19.

1.1.1.3 The National Federations
National federations, one for each discipline, represent the next level. Usually all the regional federations are members of the respective national federation. These federations regulate all general matters within their discipline and at the same time represent their branch in the European or International federations. They also organise national championships and act as regulatory bodies. As there is only one national federation for each discipline, they have a monopolistic position. In each country there is, for example, only one football federation. Only this federation can organise recognised championships. In some countries the role of the federation is regulated by national legislation.

1.1.1.4 The European Federations
The top of the pyramid is formed by the European Federations, which are organised along the same lines as the national federations. Every European federation allows only one national federation from each country to be a member. By means of rules, usually involving sanctions for those taking part in championships which have not been recognised or authorised by the international federation, these organisations try to maintain their position.

*1.1.2 A System of Promotion and Relegation*
The pyramid structure implies interdependence between the levels, not only on the organisational side but also on the competitive side, because competitions are organised on all levels. Thus, a football club playing at a regional level can qualify for championships on a national or even international level (e.g. the UEFA Cup) by winning promotion. On the other hand a club will be relegated if it fails to qualify. Relegation and promotion are standard features of every national championship. Because of the arrival of new competitors the championships are more interesting than closed competitions.
This system of promotion and relegation can also be found on a European level. In all disciplines the national federations (i.e. the top of the pyramid) are members of both European and international federations which in their turn organise European and international championships. Qualification for most of these tournaments, however, is usually decided at a national level.
This system of promotion and relegation is one of the key features of the European model of sport. The US has developed the model of closed championships and multiple sport federations. The same teams, once in this championship, keep on playing in this league. In Europe, there is a new tendency to try and combine both systems. In a recent proposal by UEFA, clubs would qualify not only by a system of promotion and relegation, but also by fulfilling economic and technical criteria.

**1.2 The features of sport in Europe**
*1.2.1 Grassroots approach*
One of the features of sport in Europe is that sport is based on a grassroots approach. The development of sport originates from the level of clubs. They organise sport on a local level. Sport traditionally has not been linked to a state or a business.
This is illustrated by the fact that sport in Europe is run mainly by non-professionals and unpaid volunteers. They are responsible for the operation of sport in Europe. For them sport is a pastime and a way of contributing to society. In this way sport in Europe differs from sport in the US where it is linked to business. In the US sport is based on a more professional approach and is operated mainly by professionals.

*1.2.2 Commitment to national identity*
As is recognised by the Amsterdam Declaration, sport in Europe has important social relevance. The Declaration states explicitly that sport has a role in forging identity and bringing people together.
Sport represents and strengthens national or regional identity by giving people a sense of belonging to a group. It unites players and spectators giving the latter the possibility of identifying with their nation. Sport contributes to social stability and is an emblem for culture and identity.
Although sport in Europe has been confronted with globalisation, it can be seen as one of the last national passions. The commitment to national identity or even regional identity, therefore, is one of the features of sport in Europe.

*1.2.3 International competitions*
National teams are seen as representing a nation. The tradition in Europe has been for the different countries to compete against each other and to hold international competitions.
In Europe sport is one of the last national passions; a psychological need exists to confront to one another. Sport is a way of doing this without bloodshed. International competitions are an opportunity for European countries to demonstrate their culture and tradition, thus safeguarding the cultural diversity, which is one of the characteristics of Europe.
In this respect Europe differs from the US where there is no need for inter-State competitions. In the US for example, California does not have to compete against Texas.

*1.2.4 Negative aspects*
The social function of forging identity can have negative aspects as well, such as the rise of ultra-nationalism or racism and intolerance.
In the past dictatorships exploited the popularity of sport in Europe to promote their own ideology. The Nazi regime, for example, used the Olympic Games in Berlin as a means of promoting its ideology. Victories of national teams are often used as a tool for propaganda. The Mussolini regime presented Italy's success in the 1934 and 1938 football world cups as proof of the superiority of fascism over democracy. Also in the former East-bloc countries sport was ideologically oriented and used as propaganda.
The violence of hooligans is a problem facing sport in Europe. Hooliganism does not always have a link with politics. Some spectators who are victims of social or economic exclusion use sports events to express their frustration. These negative consequences of sport are unknown in the US.

**1.3 The importance of sport in Europe**
Traditionally the Member States of the European Union have hosted a significantly large percentage of world sports events: for example, 54% of Summer Olympics between 1896-1996 and 50% of football world cups between 1930 and 1998. This remarkable concentration of world sport events within the EU has been partly a result of history. Europe saw the start of the industrial revolution. The ensuing development towards economic and social progress enhanced the development of sport in Europe.
Traditionally sport has its origins on the European continent; the Olympic movement, for example, came about as the result of a European initiative. Moreover, most of the important international sport organisations are based in Europe. Europe can therefore be considered the powerhouse of world sport. The latest developments are evidence that sport in

Europe is very dynamic. The most important changes in sport in Europe will be presented in the next chapter.

There is a European model of sport with its own characteristics. This model has been exported to almost all other continents and countries, with the exception of North America. Sport in Europe has a unique structure. For the future development of sport in Europe these special features should be taken into account.

## 2 CHANGES

### 2.1 Moves towards globalisation

Before the 50s sport at European level was a matter for national teams and representatives. Only teams and individuals representing their country went to compete abroad. One of the earliest examples is the World Cup, which dates from the first half of the 20th century.

After World War II the European countries agreed that in their own interest it was necessary to prevent future conflicts and peace needed to be safeguarded by common action. This move towards cooperation lent support to the first European community in 1952 and was behind the creation of pan-European television with the establishment of Eurovision and the European Broadcasting Union.

In parallel to these first steps towards European integration at political level came the emergence of European competitions for sport. UEFA was founded in 1954 and the European club competitions emerged. In 1955 the French newspaper L'Equipe came up with the idea of staging a European Cup.

Although the World Cup dates from the 1930s, only recently has sport become really global. An important factor has been television exposure of the most popular sporting events such as the Olympic Games and the World Cup.

### 2.2 Major changes in the 80s

The IOC decided to abolish the distinction between amateur and professional sport, thus opening the Olympic games to everyone. It also allowed the games to be commercially sponsored, which led to a general commercialisation of sport. Sponsorship has now become one of the major sources of funding for sport.

In the mid-80s in most Western European countries, the state television monopoly was broken. As in the US, fierce competition ensued to win the broadcasting rights for major events. The sale of television rights and sponsorship account for 65-85% of the funding of sports events and have become the primary source of financing professional sport in Europe. What should also be taken into account is the rapid and far-reaching technological change affecting television.

The East bloc disappeared and with it the restrictions for those engaging in sport. This resulted in an increase in the number of eastern Europeans practising sport professionally.

The European Court of Justice recognised in the Bosman case that there is no reason why professional sports people should not enjoy the benefits of the single market and in particular the free movement of workers. This has resulted in national competitions being open to players throughout Europe and has revitalised major European Leagues.[56]

### 2.3 Recent developments in the 90s

In order to contend with the creation of European super-leagues, many important clubs

---

[56] Consequences of the Bosman Judgment, memorandum from Commissioners Van Miert, Flynn and Oreja, SEC (96) 212 of 2-2-1996.

had to think about new ways of financing. Since November 1997 English football clubs (Manchester United, Tottenham Hotspur and many others) have been listed on the stock exchange. This allows them to acquire the financial means necessary to maintain their leading position in European sport. On the other hand, some investment companies gained influence by acquiring majority shareholdings in several football clubs, for instance the English National Investment Company (ENIC) already controls 4 clubs, namely Glasgow Rangers, Slavia Prague, Vicenza (Italy) and AEK Athens

The proposal for a closed league outside UEFA is new and has attracted the interest of many of Europe's top clubs. Within this league there is no system of promotion and relegation. It is a new form of competition, which has no link with the existing pyramidal structure.

The top clubs are interested in this Super League mainly because they are dissatisfied with UEFA's distribution of Champions League revenues. They see the initiative as a possibility of more money going direct to the participants and less to the administration of the competition. If things develop as in the US, where the system of closed competitions has existed for many years, the top clubs could increase their profits enormously. The new approach will see the big teams playing one another regularly, something the US has known for a long time with its major sports

UEFA has been forced to react by proposing a new initiative which seeks to combine the traditional system of promotion and relegation and the closed championship system.

What UEFA is offering clubs is a bigger share of the revenues generated by the sale of broadcasting rights.

## 3 PROBLEMS

### 3.1 The role of sports federations

Up to the 1980s sports federations were mainly regulatory bodies. As TV rights grew in importance, they began to negotiate these rights, thus acting like any other commercial company. The question that arises then is whether the federations can be regulatory bodies and private business entities at the same time. The top members of these federations as well as the grassroots members feel that their interests are no longer adequately represented.

What is more, in some countries leagues have been created that are independent of the national federation. In England and Spain this is true for football, in Spain, Italy and France for basketball.

#### 3.1.1 Problems with top members

The most successful members of federations want a bigger share of the money earned by the federations, threatening otherwise to leave the federations and set up their own championships. Most national federations have rules which refuse their members the right to take part in championships that are not organised or authorised by themselves and penalising them if they do. If the leading European clubs were to participate in closed competitions, would they be excluded from the national championships? This would mean the end of one key feature of the European model, namely the commitment to national identity. Should this national orientation be retained and if so, what is the best way to safeguard it?

#### 3.1.2 Problems with the grassroots members

The grassroots members for their part complain that the federations no longer fulfil their 'public' task, namely the promotion of sport. They also claim that the solidarity system providing them with money earned by the federation does not work properly. The question then is whether federations, which operate as private companies and at the same time have the role of promoting sport, can succeed in striking the right balance between these two tasks or whether a public organisation should be responsible for the promotion of sport. It is not clear what will happen to the federations if they lose both their top members and their grassroots members.

### 3.2 Competition law

In general the monopolistic role of the federations is not called into question, as their institutional structure is recognised to be the most efficient way of organising sport. The rules of most national and international federations stipulate that their members may only participate in sport events organised or at least authorised by the federations themselves. Problems may arise when one variant of the game thinks its interests would be better represented by a new federation. Should federations be allowed to compete freely for this market? In the case of boxing such competition is already reality: there are several international federations, such as WBF, WBO, WBA, WBC and IBF.

The question that arises then is whether the federations will have to change their internal rules and structure (only one federation per country and discipline) in order to comply with the EC Treaty provisions on competition and the single market and with judgments of the ECJ. If they do so, what will be the impact on the European system (Pyramid model)? In a recent decision, the Court of Arbitration for Sport[57] maintains that sportsgoverning bodies resemble governmental bodies as far as their structure and their role as regulatory bodies are concerned. It states that similar principles govern their actions, for example when changing the legislation or administrative rules.

### 3.3 Multiple ownership

As mentioned before, some investment companies control different football clubs listed on the stock exchange. This might be detrimental to sport, for genuine sporting competition might be distorted. In response to a parliamentary question the Commission stressed that rules laid down by sports organisations to prevent clubs with the same owner taking part in the same competitions, whether national or international, would not be covered by the competition rules laid down in the EC treaty. These rules, however, have to be limited to their purpose, namely to ensure the uncertainty as to the results of competitions, and must remain in proportion to the sporting objective pursued.[58] In a recent case brought by AEK Athens and Slavia Prague against UEFA, the Court of Arbitration for Sport ruled that it was unlawful for UEFA to pass new rules prohibiting participation in the same competition by clubs jointly owned without giving the football clubs concerned a reasonable time to prepare for this change. The Court found that these new rules were put into force in haste, thus surprising the clubs and depriving them of the chance to take measures. The Court, however, did not refer to the lawfulness of these rules.[59]

### 3.4 Finance

The Bosman case has had huge financial repercussions for sport in Europe. Before the Bosman ruling transfer fees provided the game with much of its financial resources.

---

[57] Court of Arbitration for Sport, 17-7-1998, CAS 98/200.

[58] Answer given by Mr Van Miert on behalf of the Commission to a written question, OJ C 310, 9-10-1998.

[59] Court of Arbitration for Sport, 17-7-1998, CAS 98/200.

When transfer fees were abolished, footballers' salaries soared and clubs had to make huge investments. The financing of sport in Europe since then has changed dramatically. It now depends increasingly on revenues derived from sponsorship and other commercial communications.

The revenues from sports events depend on the attractiveness of a sport for the general public. The problem is that not every sport is as suited to television as football. There is a risk that only the commercially attractive sports will survive and other smaller sports become endangered. The income received from the sale of broadcasting rights is transforming the sports world and widening the gulf between amateurs and professionals and between the top and bottom of sport in Europe.[60]

The characteristics of sport (uncertainty of results, equality of competitors) recognised by Advocate-General Lenz in the Bosman case make the sport market different from any other commercial market. The Advocate-General suggested that there should be a distribution of income in order to maintain a competitive balance. It is necessary to examine if and how sports income needs to be distributed among the clubs and associations. This can have consequences for the financing of sport in Europe. UEFA has established a solidarity system for the distribution of Champions League revenues. According to UEFA this system serves to maintain a competitive and financial balance among the clubs and to promote football in general.[61] The large football clubs accuse UEFA of not being transparent in financing and distribution. The smaller clubs complain that more money should go to the lower levels of the pyramid. It is debatable whether the UEFA system is operating properly and whether there is a need for such a system.

In most Member States lotteries finance sport. Most money is derived from betting on football results. Football feels that it is entitled to more of the money than other sports.

There is a problem of how the money should be spent. The existing sports federations in Europe receive money from the state and also receive revenues from the sale of television rights. But can this still be justified? How should state aids be awarded to sport?

In closed competitions the money stays within the organisation, which is self-sufficient and does not therefore feel any need to help other sports. Any move towards such competitions could be detrimental to sport in Europe.

## 4 QUESTIONS

### 4.1 Role of the national federations

1. Can we keep the model of only one federation for each Member State?
2. Is it satisfactory to have one federation doing everything from management of teams – thus acting as a multinational – to organisation of leagues and promotion of sport? Are they able to combine these tasks adequately?
3. Do you think the national federations are capable of fulfilling their new commercial role i.e. the selling of television rights, making of contracts, alongside the other roles of promoting sport and organising competitions?
4. Public non-profit organisations organise large-scale 'sport for all' events. Does this mean that national federations cannot organise such competitions?
5. Does this threaten the position of the federations?
6. What will happen to federations if they lose the grassroots members and the top members? What will be the role of the federations?

---

[60] Competition Policy Newsletter No 2 1998.
[61] UEFA solidarity system, 16.

7.      Should federations do no more than set the rules, promote sport and organise competitions for national teams?

## 4.2 Emergence of closed competitions

1.      When closed competitions emerge, the top clubs will leave national competitions. Will national leagues still be attractive in future or will they become too small? Could national leagues be devalued because of closed competitions?
2.      Will the emergence of closed competitions jeopardise inter-country competitions?
3.      Will closed leagues threaten the link between sport and nationality?
4.      If private leagues go ahead (closed competitions) what ties should they have with existing federations?
5.      If Europe starts to move towards this model, should conditions be imposed on these leagues?
6.      Participation in closed leagues will be by invitation, thus breaking with the principle of qualification. Is it necessary to have a system of qualification and promotion and relegation? Do you think it is important to have a link with the national pyramid structure?
7.      Is there any advantage for Europe in moving towards the US model for sport?
8.      Closed competitions cause practical problems. Do you foresee any problem for having players available for national competitions? Are there problems in setting the calendar? Is there a need for coordination and in what way could this be achieved?

## 4.3 Solidarity

1.      Is it necessary to have solidarity between the top and the grass roots of sport?
2.      Do you think that because of closed leagues the solidarity between top-class professional sport and the grass roots will be broken?
3.      Is there a need for a solidarity system? Which sports should receive contributions and how can the distribution be justified?
4.      Are there positive or negative effects when the solidarity is broken? Must public funds be provided to replace the present income generated by federations?
5.      Do you think the UEFA solidarity system operates properly to produce equality between the different clubs and sports?

## 4.4 Promotion of sport

1.      How should this objective be achieved?
2.      Should there be a separation of public money for promotion of sport and private money generated by commercial activities?
3.      Should there be a public budget for promotion of sport? Is there a need for a division between amateur and professional sport?
4.      Do you think the national federations are capable of promoting sport?
5.      Do you think that with a system of closed competitions sport can be adequately promoted?

## 4.5 European model of sport

1.      Can we keep the European model of sport as it exists today?
2.      Should we keep the status quo or does the system need adjusting?

## CHAPTER TWO – SPORT AND TELEVISION

## 5 DEVELOPMENT OF SPORT AND TELEVISION IN EUROPE

Since the 1950s television and sport have been developing in parallel: both were organised at a national level, with one public TV-channel and one federation per country. At a European level, they are members of European federations or organisations, such as the UEFA for European football or the EBU (Eurovision) for the western TV stations. The equivalent to the European movement on political level is the emergence of European competitions for sport. UEFA was founded in 1954 and the European club competitions emerged. In 1955 the French newspaper L'Equipe came up with the idea of staging a European Cup.

The scene in the US was different: private TV stations and professional sporting federations were interested in higher profits. The TV-networks compete with each other for the most interesting and spectacular sports events. Advertisers, in their turn, are out to attract big audiences, which they usually find at sports events. This close interdependence of sport, television and advertisers in the US has led to a completely different approach towards sport as compared with Europe.

In the mid 1980s private television arrived in most west European countries, thus braking the public television monopoly. Since then competition between TV networks has pushed up prices for the broadcasting rights of major sports events, such as the World Championship.

Another reason for the keener competition was the progress in audiovisual technology. The development from analog to digital television led to the appearance of many new broadcasters in Europe. This new audiovisual framework, particularly the arrival of pay-per-view television, led to intensified competition for broadcasting major sports events, which has always been an appropriate way of attracting new viewers or new subscribers to pay-per-view networks.

To meet the needs of televised sport, some sports federations changed the rules or introduced new ones. This suggests that there is already close interdependence as far as the commercial side of sport is concerned. The FIBA, the International Basketball Federation, for example, introduced the time-out for TV-sports, and the International Tennis Federation the tie-break, which stops tennis matches from going on indefinitely.

The International Volleyball World Union has recently changed the rules to allow a point to be scored in each *exchange*, rather than, as was the case up to now, only by the serving team.

## 6 BROADCASTING RIGHTS

TV-rights have become the major source of income for most sports disciplines. In football, for example, they bring in more than gate money, so most clubs are more interested in selling TV-rights to the highest bidder than in selling all tickets.

For TV-networks, on the other hand, broadcasting major sports events, especially football matches, has always been a way of obtaining the best viewing figures. This, together with fierce competition in the audiovisual sector, led to the explosion of prices for broadcasting rights.

### 6.1 Ownership of broadcasting rights

A fundamental element concerns the ownership of broadcasting rights to sports events.
This question has been dealt with under national law. Cases before several national courts concerning broadcasting rights to national football matches give some indications. In a re-

cent case in Germany the Bundesgerichtshof took the view that broadcasting rights generally belong to the clubs, which are considered to be the natural owners of these rights. The question whether federations may also have a claim to ownership in different circumstances has not been answered.[62]

After this decision, the Bundestag inserted a clause in the German cartel law, stating that the German Football Federation can sell the broadcasting rights of the future closed leagues.[63] The German Football Federation and representatives of the clubs agreed that the clubs themselves could sell the broadcasting rights of their home matches in the UEFA-Cup, the Cup Winners Cup and the UI Cup.

## 6.2 Collective selling

Sport is, according to the ECJ 'subject to Community law only in so far as it constitutes an economic activity within the meaning of Article 2 of the Treaty'.[64] Nonetheless, sport differs from other economic activities: usually a market player is trying to compete with others to get a bigger share of the market, and a loss of one market player, for example due to his financial instability, will be a gain for the others. In sport, however, the competing clubs need their competitors in order to make the championship interesting and exciting. Therefore a competitive balance between competitors has to be maintained. A championship comprising one major club that attracts all the financial resources and therefore dominates the tournament will not be as interesting as a championship with equal and economically solid competitors. This difference compared with the competitive relationship between undertakings in other markets was already identified by the Advocate-General in the Bosman case.[65]

As the selling of TV-rights constitutes the major source of income, smaller or lesser-known clubs could find themselves in financial difficulties, whereas top European clubs will be able to ask for more money than today. In order to prevent the gap between big and small clubs widening, the Advocate-General Lenz acknowledges the need to adopt rules that guarantee a certain equality among clubs. The question arises whether the collective selling of broadcasting rights could be a means of preserving this balance.

Collective selling of broadcasting rights may constitute an arrangement restrictive of competition contrary to Article 85(1) of the EC Treaty, if it affects trade between Member States. In this case the Commission will have to examine whether such arrangements satisfy the criteria for exemption.

## 6.3 Exclusivity

Broadcasters depending financially on advertising revenue try to attract as many viewers as possible in order to generate revenue. Sports, particularly football, attract large audiences and are therefore a prime target for broadcasters. Exclusive broadcasting rights allow the broadcasters to offer programmes not available on other channels, thus, building up audience, substantially increasing revenue and differentiating themselves from other broadcasters. For the organisers, on the other hand, exclusive broadcasting rights ensure maximum short-term profitability of an event.

The Commission does not believe that exclusive broadcasting rights are anticompetitive

---

[62] Decision of the German Bundesgerichtshof, 11-12-1997 in *Deutscher Fussball-Bund, UFA Film and ISPR v Bundeskartellamt.*

[63] Franfurter Allgemeine Zeitung, 8-5-1998.

[64] Case C-36/74 *Walrave* v *UCI* [1974] ECR I-1405.

[65] Case C-415/93; paragraph 227 of the opinion of the Advocate General.

*per se*, the duration and the scope of exclusivity might, however, infringe the treaty provisions on competition. The anti-competitive nature of exclusive broadcasting rights depends on the individual circumstances of a case. In the *CODITEL II* decision,[66] the ECJ found that exclusive licences of performing rights did not *per se* infringe Article 85(1). The Court concluded by stating that the exercise of these rights may infringe Article 85(1) where there is a specific situation 'in the economic or legal sphere the object or effect of which is to prevent or restrict the distribution [...] or to distort competition on the [...] market [...]'. The Court pointed out that the specific characteristics of this market had to be taken into account.

Certain parallels could be drawn with exclusive broadcasting rights to sports events, the special features, however, of the relationship between sport and television have to be considered.

## 6.4 Acquisition of football clubs

In recent years, large media groups have been buying an increasing number of football clubs. The French group Canal+, for example, controls Paris Saint Germain and Servette Genève. The question arises whether this monopolistic position – owning the broadcasting rights and exploiting them by one's own networks – is compatible with EU competition policy. In connection with the proposed acquisition of Manchester United by Rupert Murdoch's BskyB, Mr Van Miert, Commissioner responsible for competition, stated in reply to a parliamentary question that this acquisition was not caught by the turnover threshold tests set by Community legislation, and therefore national law was applicable.[67]

The Commission stressed, however, that it will keep a close watch on all instances of interpenetration between sport and the audiovisual industry and that it will ensure that such acquisitions comply with Community rules, where appropriate.[68]

## 7 RIGHT TO INFORMATION

While the television monopoly existed, viewers who wanted to could usually watch popular sports events without problems. Today, however, a viewer might have to buy a decoder, take out a cable subscription or make additional payments (pay per view).

Some sports are considered to be of national or heritage importance, therefore, free broad access by the means of free access television should be guaranteed. This essential right to information led to the amendment of the 'Television without frontiers'[69] Directive, and the insertion of the new Article 3a. It stipulates that Member States may take measures to ensure that broadcasters under their jurisdiction do not broadcast major events on an exclusive basis, thus depriving a substantial proportion of the public in this Member State of the possibility of watching these events. The Member State concerned must draw up a list of designated events, whether national or international, which it considers important for society. Member States must also ensure that broadcasters under their jurisdiction do not exercise exclusive rights in such a way that a substantial proportion of the public in an-

---

[66] Case C-262/81.

[67] Answer given by Mr Van Miert on behalf of the Commission to a parlementary question, OJ to be published.

[68] Answer of the Commission in response to a parlementary question, OJ to be published.

[69] Directive 97/36/EC of the European Parliament and of the Council of 30-6-1997 amending Council, Directive 89/552/EEC on the coordination of certain provisions laid down by law, regulation or administrative action in the Member States concerning the pursuit of television broadcasting activities. (OJ L 202/60 of 30-7-1997).

other Member State is deprived of the possibility of watching the events designated by another Member State.

## 8 THE FUTURE ROLE OF PUBLIC TV IN EUROPE

The Court of First Instance declared in its judgment in *Telecinco v European Commission*[70] that the European Commission failed to fulfil its obligations under the EC Treaty by not adopting a decision following two complaints about state aids for Spanish public television. The Commission wants public television channels to introduce separate accounting to differentiate between programmes that serve the public basic supply as defined by law and all other programmes, such as sports or entertainment, which will have to be financed by advertisements and sponsorship. State aids will only be allowed for the public tasks; for all other tasks public funding would be subject to the provisions of the Treaty. This could imply that public broadcasters would have to look for other ways of financing in order to purchase the broadcasting rights of sport events.

It then has to be seen whether this development is detrimental to sport as such, in that the general public might be obliged to pay more (whether decoders or pay per view) in order to watch sport events. On the other hand, some TV-networks with smaller financial resources may have to consider broadcasting less popular sports, thus promoting 'minority' sports, which have received less public attention up to now. A good example of this is snooker, which has grown from a minority sport to a leading television sport in the UK.

## 9 QUESTIONS

### 9.1 Collective selling and duration of exclusivity

1. Is collective selling an appropriate means of preserving financial equality in European sport?
2. In the event of collective selling, how should the revenues be allocated at European level?
3. Where commercial leagues exist, how should they work with the grassroots sport?
4. Should collective selling be allowed only as a guarantee for equal competition (as is the case in the US, where the commercial leagues state that they need the collective selling of broadcasting rights in order to work properly) or should it be attached to a solidarity fund as suggested by Advocate-General Lenz?
5. What in your view are the criteria for determining the length of exclusivity?
6. If federations keep their monopolistic role, is it necessary to organise the sale of broadcasting rights by a call for tenders?

### 9.2 Interpenetration between sport and the audiovisual industry

1. Do you think that the purchase of sports clubs by audiovisual groups could have a negative influence on the development of sport?
2. Could such interpenetration interfere with the normal development of sports competitions in Europe?
3. How could the ethics of sport be protected in these cases?

### 9.3 The right to information

1. Do you think that sport is threatened by pay-per-view television?
2. How must a balance be struck between the interest of sports organisations to gener-

---

[70] Case T-95/96.

ate revenues by selling broadcasting rights and the need for public exposure of sport on public television?

## 9.4 The role of public TV

1. What should be the role of public TV in promoting sport?
2. Should public TV broadcast 'minority' sports as part of its public supply task?
3. Is it therefore right that public television using public funds should compete with private television in order to purchase broadcasting rights for sports events?

## CHAPTER THREE – SPORT AND SOCIAL POLICY

Sport has significant social functions, identified by the Commission in its working paper on sport.[71] The role of sport in our society in the fields of education, environment, health and employment will be outlined in the following paragraphs.

## 10 SPORT AND EDUCATION

Sport can perform an educational function, in that it is a means of giving a true view of some values in life, such as competitiveness. In today's world, children have to realise that life is not always easy and that one has to fight for one's ideas and aims in order to achieve them. On the other hand, the competitive features of sport should not be exaggerated; respect for other people is important. This is the point of the concept of 'fair play'. Sport is extraordinary in that it combines these two features, and that is why the influence of sport in the education of adolescents is particularly important. Another value that can be derived from practising sports is the ability to resist the temptation to give up at the first hurdle but to overcome it. Sport is a means of identifying our limits, abilities, strengths and weaknesses. The refusal to give up and the determination to win can be transferred to real life.

Both amateur and professional sport are a major entertainment industry, but sports people also have to spend much time training. So sport shields those who practise it from many of the dangers of modern society, such as alcohol, tobacco or drugs in general.

## 11 SPORT AS A MEANS OF SOCIAL INTEGRATION, COMBATING RACISM AND PROMOTING TOLERANCE

While sport promotes a number of positive ideals, it also has negative aspects in relation both to individuals (injuries, doping) and collectively (intolerance, violence). Some European initiatives have been launched to combat racism, discrimination and violence.

These initiatives, described in the document 'Sport Society',[72] can be distinguished by their target groups (such as immigrants, national minorities, women, homosexuals, disabled and socially less privileged people) and countries. It is interesting to note the importance attached to sport as a means of promoting greater involvement of immigrants, for example, in the life of society. These initiatives are designed to help build a society that is more open and tolerant.

Another social aspect of sport is its important integration function. For example disabled people often are better integrated in a community through their participation in a team or championship.

---

[71] The Development and Prospects for Community Action in the Field of Sport, Brussels, 29-9-1998.

[72] SportSociety, study carried out by Clearing House in the framework of the Eurathlon programme.

## 12 SPORT AND ENVIRONMENT

Problems linked to the environment usually attract wide attention on account of their impact on our everyday life.

The Olympic movement, which unites sports organisations, athletes and individuals under the guidance of the Olympic Charter, has a very important role in the fields of sport and the environment. It has two main objectives – to ensure that the Olympic Games take place in a spirit of respect for the environment and to lead a global awareness programme promoting respect for the environment.

But to what extent can sport be a danger to environment? Some sports, football for example, need extensive facilities and specific infrastructure. Others (such as skiing) take place entirely in the natural environment. Sport and its facilities have a multifaceted impact on nature: the conservation of biological diversity, the protection of the ecosystem, pollution, handling of resources and waste, health, safety and safeguarding the cultural heritage.

## 13 SPORT AND PUBLIC HEALTH

The Latin tag *Mens sana in corpore sano* – a healthy mind in a healthy body – is more apposite than ever today. In the information society, where people spends so much of their working and leisure time at the computer, physical activity is more and more important as a means of keeping fit.

The link between practising sport and the beneficial effects on health is no longer questioned. Many studies had been carried out showing that practising sport leads to an improved physical condition. Another finding of these studies was that inactivity, being a risk factor for many illnesses, is a major health problem for western societies.

Two questions then arise: What form of physical exercise offers most benefits to most people and what is the best policy to encourage the practise of this sport.

Another important aspect is sports injuries. It has been recognised that a preventive approach is needed in order to limit injuries. The Council of Europe has launched research under the WHO's 'health for all' action plan in order to improve understanding of this problem and elaborate a preventive strategy. The main risk factors can be divided into two categories – internal risks, i.e. those linked to the person practising sport, and external risks, i.e. those not linked to the person but to other circumstances. Preventive measures come in various forms, including warm-up exercises, strict enforcement by referees and heavier punishments.

Although there is an inherent risk of injury in all physical activity, the other beneficial effects of sport make up for it.

## 14 SPORT AND DOPING

In the world of both amateur and professional sports, the importance of revenues is increasing, and many top athletes therefore go to their physical limits in an effort to outdo each other. The increasing use of illicit substances to enhance performance in this competitive climate has become a major problem in the world of sport. An important aspect of this problem is that it is very hard to detect these substances in the human body. Although the problem is seen as a recent one (Tour de France 1998), it should not be forgotten that it has been with us for years.

The Olympic Games have always been confronted with this problem. The first champions hardly hid their magic potions. It was the death of an athlete in Rome 1960 that alerted sport authorities to the dangers of doping. But the problem really blew up in 1998: routine check detected banned pharmaceutical substances at the Festina team. To make matters worse, huge sums of money are involved – 1 billion dollars.

The situation in the Member States is quite different. In some Member States, for example in Spain or Great Britain, the government has introduced anti-doping legislation in accordance with rules issued by the IOC or the national federations. In other Member States, Germany or Italy for example, regulation is in the hands of the national federations. French legislation provides for criminal penalties for use of medicinal substances. As usual, differences between the legislation of the Member States can constitute a potential barrier to the free movement of services. In sport, an athlete may be allowed to take medicinal substances in one Member State whereas the same substance is on the prohibited list in another Member State.

The Community does not have powers to develop a policy to combat doping. The Commission, however, is aware of the importance of this problem and is willing to act under different policies and in the context of cooperation in the fields of justice and home affairs.

Some Community Directives on health issues are also important for sport, as they prohibit the use of medicinal products for purposes other than those for which authorisation was given (the diagnosis or treatment of recognised pathological states) and the use of these substances in non-authorised forms and doses.[73] Furthermore Community legislation bans the sale of such substances without prescription[74] and advertising of such products.[75] This recent activity of the European Union has been emphasised by a Resolution of the Council of 3 December 1990 on Community action to combat the use of drugs, including the abuse of medicinal products, particularly in sport.[76] It is underlined that cooperation between the Member States of the Community and the Council of Europe takes place in a spirit of complementarity.

Sports people are covered by the provisions of the Directive on the introduction of measures to encourage improvements in the safety and health of workers at work,[77] Article 6 of which provides that the employer shall take measures for the safety and health protection of workers, and in particular in order to avoid risks. The use of medicinal substances, which often have severe side effects, can constitute a risk that has to be avoided by the employer.

## 15 SPORT AND EMPLOYMENT

Sport has developed into a major source of employment, already identified as such by the Commission in its White Paper on growth, competitiveness and employment. The Commission suggests that 'Member States should address existing barriers to maximising the job creation potential of [...] areas of new employment growth and activity by a range of measures aimed at anticipating and accelerating [...] new jobs growth.' Measures could include those which 'promote the development of new employment opportunities through the use of public-private partnerships at all levels, and notably in potential growth areas such as [...] sport [...]'.[78]

---

[73] Directive 65/65/EEC, as last amended by Directive 89/341/EEC.

[74] Directive 75/319/EEC, as last amended by Directive 89/341/EEC.

[75] Directive 84/450/EEC.

[76] Resolution of the Council and of the representatives of the Governments of the Member States, meeting within the Council of 3-12-1990 on Community action to combat the use of drugs, including the abuse of medicinal products, particularly in sport, OJ C 329.

[77] Directive 89/391/EEC.

[78] White Paper on growth, competitiveness, and employment The challenges and ways forward into the 21st century, COM(93) 700 final, Brussels, 5-12-1993.

Originally sport was mainly organised by unpaid amateurs. But now, many people want to practise sport on a professional basis to earn their living. This trend towards the development of professional sport, coupled with the fact that most people have greater leisure time and prefer to practise sport, has led to the creation and growth of employment in the fields of sport.

But there is a downside too. The risk of injuries and the risk of lacking adequate education are problems that particularly concern adolescent sport people. Most of them start at an early age in order to turn professional and tend to neglect their education. By the age of 30 their career is usually at an end, for two reasons: first, most of the professionals have pushed their body to its limits for the last years, and second, a new generation of professionals is taking over. Therefore, these problems concern the problem of protecting minors as well. Children are often pushed to turn professional by their parents or trainers for different reasons, but only sometimes they really succeed in professional sport and earn a living from it.

In 1994 the Council adopted a directive on the protection of young people at work.[79] It applies to any person under 18 years of age having an employment contract. The directive requires the Member States to adopt measures to prohibit work by children.

Yet, Member States may make legislative or regulatory provision for the prohibition not to apply in certain areas, such as cultural activities.

## 16    QUESTIONS
### 16.1  Education
1.    Do you think that the European network of Universities and sport schools should be strengthened?
2.    Is there a problem in the mutual recognition of qualifications?
3.    Do you think that the sport is well integrated in the education system?

### 16.2  Social integration
1.    What form of European action can most effectively combat racism and intolerance?
2.    How could Community action best contribute to the integration of less privileged groups?
3.    How can sport contribute to combating inequality between men and women?
4.    What does positive discrimination mean in the context of sport competitions?
5.    How could Community action best contribute to the integration of disabled people?

### 16.3  Environment
1.    In what field should the Community act? Better information, subsidies for pilot projects or support for research on the impact of sports facilities?

### 16.4  Public health
1.    What is the role played by 'sports for all' in the improvement of public health?
2.    Do you have the means of determining whether the negative impacts of sport on health (injuries etc.) are offset by the positive effects?
3.    Are the federations capable of promoting the 'sports for all' idea?

### 16.5  Doping
1.    Does the absence of a common list of medicinal substances constitute a barrier for the practise of sport?

---

[79]  Council Directive 94/33/EC of 22-6-1994, OJ L 216.

2. Do you think that excessively restrictive legislation could endanger the attribution/allocation of sports events in Europe?
3. Do you think it is desirable to strengthen the approximation of national legislation?
4. Which is in your view the degree of responsibility of the different persons involved in doping, such as athletes, doctors or executives?
5. In some US major leagues, athletes are allowed to take medicinal substances. Do you think that this could be a model for Europe?
6. On which field should possible Community action focus? Education, research, awareness campaign, cooperation in the fields of justice and home affairs or information in the package leaflet of medications?

## 16.6 Employment
1. Should there be greater training facilities for those who want to become professional sports people?
2. Should there be a management/labour dialogue in the fields of sport?
3. Should there be framework (contractual or regulatory) for working hours and pay, and what are your suggestions for the establishment of this framework?
4. Should there be training schemes adapted to the career structure of sport?

----

## 1.21. PRESIDENCY CONCLUSIONS OF THE VIENNA EUROPEAN COUNCIL, 11 AND 12 DECEMBER 1998

[...]

## XII. SPORT
95. Recalling the Declaration on Sport attached to the Treaty of Amsterdam and recognising the social role of sport, the European Council invites the Commission to submit a report to the Helsinki European Council with a view to safeguarding current sports structures and maintaining the social function of sport within the Community framework.
96. The European Council underlines its concern at the extent and seriousness of doping in sports, which undermines the sporting ethic and endangers public health. It emphasises the need for mobilisation at European Union level and invites the Member States to examine jointly with the Commission and international sports bodies possible measures to intensify the fight against this danger, in particular through better coordination of existing national measures.

[...]

----

## * 1.22. ANSWER ON BEHALF OF THE COMMISSION TO WRITTEN QUESTION E-2876/98 BY MARJO MATIKAINEN-KALLSTRÖM (PPE), 14 DECEMBER 1998[80]

Subject: Green Paper on sport

----

---

[80] Question of 28-9-1998; OJ C 289, 11-10-1999, p. 9.

* 1.23.   CONCLUSIONS OF THE FIRST EUROPEAN UNION CONFERENCE
          ON SPORT, OLYMPIA (GREECE), 20-23 MAY 1999

          ———

1.24.     CONCLUSIONS OF THE COUNCIL PRESIDENCY ON THE
          OCCASION OF THE INFORMAL MEETING OF THE SPORTS
          MINISTERS OF THE EUROPEAN UNION, PADERBORN 31 MAY TO
          2 JUNE 1999 ['PADERBORN CONCLUSIONS']

**First Subject**
**The Fight against Doping**
The Sport Ministers of the Member States of the European Union hold the view that
–    the co-ordination of the doping legislation and of the other anti-doping measures is
     vital to efficiently combat doping;
–    the use of doping substances in organised as well as in non-organised sports endan-
     ger public health. Governments feel the responsibility to combat this negative phe-
     nomenon in all its forms;
–    a uniform list of prohibited substances and methods is to be created which is appli-
     cable to all sports and countries. The impact on mass sports are to be taken into
     account;
–    effective doping prevention cannot do without deterring sanctions and that there-
     fore a system of internationally applicable and equivalent sanctions is needed, such
     as a two-year minimum ban for first-time offenders;
–    the fight against doping can only be effective if it is launched jointly in cooperation
     between the sport organisations and the governments;
–    the EU Commission be requested to continue, with the help of the Council of Eu-
     rope, the co-ordination of anti-doping work at national level in the Working Group
     which has been set up by the EU Commission;
–    an international independent and transparent Anti-Doping Agency is needed to
     implement an efficient fight against doping. On the basis of the draft submitted by
     the German EU Council Presidency, which is contained in Annex 1 and which
     builds on the considerations by the EU and Council of Europe Working Groups,
     they have agreed on a proposal;
–    the EU Commission should be requested to look into whether it is possible to in-
     volve the EU in the Anti-Doping Agency and for the EU Commission to co-finance
     the Agency;
–    it is necessary that the existing Community instruments of police, judicial and cus-
     toms co-operation include the fight against the trade in doping products in their
     scope of action;
–    co-operation between the Member States of the European Union, within the frame-
     work of the existing and future research work, for instance on EPO, should be es-
     tablished to improve prevention and co-operation measures.

**Second Subject:**
**Employment and Sport**
As part of the high-priority fight against unemployment – especially youth unemployment
– in the European Union, the Sport Ministers of the Member States of the European
Union support the employment and training measures and initiatives in the field of sport.
In the context of the development of the ever-diverse leisure-time and sport activities,

sport is an important potential for employment in connection with sport animation, social integration tasks , management, training and information.

In light of the great diversity of employment requirements in connection with sport, the Sport Ministers of the European Union suggest that all employment opportunities be identified and supported in the Member States of the European Union.

The Ministers underline the importance of removing the obstacles which are an encumbrance to the creation of new jobs in the field of sport, in particular with regard to the differing training levels and the recognition of degrees and diplomas.

The Sport Ministers of the EU agree to pursue firmly the issue of sport and employment, in particular in light of the presentation of the results of a study for the European Council in Helsinki as announced by the EU Commission.

**Third Subject:**
**improving the portrayal of sport for the disabled in the media**
The promotion and development of sport for the disabled with all its aspects are important parts of the European Sport Ministers' policy.

The Sport Ministers of the European Union call on
–    the media of the Member States to give adequate weight to the events of disabled sportsmen and women in their coverage. In this respect, targeted measures to inform journalists may be useful;
–    the broadcasting stations of the EU countries to extend their television coverage of the Paralympics Sydney 2000;
–    the EU Commission to support the television broadcasting stations in their efforts to cover the Paralympics Sydney 2000.

**Fourth Subject:**
**Implementation and perspectives of the Joint Declaration on Sport**
The Sport Ministers of the EU Member States call on the European Commission and the European Council to increasingly support the particular concerns of sport, based on the Joint Declaration on Sport and the conclusions of the Vienna Summit.

The Sport Ministers welcome the initiative taken by the European Commission of organising the first EU Conference on Sport in Olympia to answer in particular the invitation to dialogue with the sport organisations, as laid down in the Joint Declaration on Sport. The conclusions of this conference mean a step forward to safeguard the particular characteristics of sport.

So as to safeguard the ethics and the social significance of sport, the particular concerns of sport should be supported especially in the following areas:
–    the application of competition law and internal market rules
–    the European Union measures relating to sport and television
–    Community actions of the European Union in the field of sport
–    the assistance programmes of the European Union, in order to achieve greater transparency as regards the taking into account of sports
–    in light of the interest that the European Union attaches to the campaign of the Member States and of the sport organisations relating to the protection of minor athletes, the training of young persons, the social significance and the solidarity functions of sport.

The Sport Ministers invite the European Commission to set up a working group composed of representatives of the Member States of the European Union and of the Commission, which is to work out how the concerns of sport can be taken into account in the EU Treaty. In so doing, the Working Group will consult the sport organisations.

---

## * 1.25.  OPINION OF THE COMMITTEE OF THE REGIONS ON THE EUROPEAN MODEL OF SPORT, 16 SEPTEMBER 1999[81]

---

## 1.26.  REPORT FROM THE COMMISSION TO THE EUROPEAN COUNCIL WITH A VIEW TO SAFEGUARDING CURRENT SPORTS STRUCTURES AND MAINTAINING THE SOCIAL FUNCTION OF SPORT WITHIN THE COMMUNITY FRAMEWORK, 1 DECEMBER 1999 [THE HELSINKI REPORT ON SPORT][82]

**Table of contents**

## 1. INTRODUCTION

*'Recalling the Declaration on Sport attached to the Treaty of Amsterdam and recognising the social role of sport'*, the European Council, meeting in Vienna on 11 and 12 December 1998, invited *'the Commission to submit a report to the Helsinki European Council with a view to safeguarding current sports structures and maintaining the social function of sport within the Community framework'*. This report by the Commission is the response to the European Council's invitation.

Following this invitation and in accordance with the Amsterdam Declaration, numerous consultations were held (Olympic movement, sporting federations, sports industries, media, governments and Community institutions), especially at the 'European Union Conference on Sport' organised in Olympia from 20 to 23 May 1999. Sport is one of the areas of activity that most concerns and brings together the citizens of the European Union, irrespective of age and social origin. More than half of them regularly do sport, either in one of the 700 000 clubs that exist in the Union or outside these clubs. Almost two million teachers, instructors and voluntary workers spend their working or leisure time organising sporting activities.

---

[81]  OJ C 374 , 23-12-1999, pp. 56-66.
[82]  COM(1999) 644.

This social function of sport, which is in the general interest, has for some years been affected by the emergence of new phenomena which sometimes call into question the ethics of sport and the principles on which it is organised, be they violence in the stadiums, the increase in doping practices or the search for quick profits to the detriment of a more balanced development of sport.

This report gives pointers for reconciling the economic dimension of sport with its popular, educational, social and cultural dimensions.

## 2. THE DEVELOPMENT OF SPORT IN EUROPE RISKS WEAKENING ITS EDUCATIONAL AND SOCIAL FUNCTION

There are many common features in the ways in which sport is practised and organised in the Union, in spite of certain differences between the Member States, and it is therefore possible to talk of a European approach to sport based on common concepts and principles.

For several years, the European approach to sport has been affected by several phenomena:

- the *rise in the popularity of sport* in terms of the number of people doing and watching sport. A total of 37 billion television viewers watched the matches of the most recent football World Cup, which is nearly 600 million television viewers per match,

- the *internationalisation of sport*, with the increase in the number of international competitions. In 1999, 77 world championships and 102 European championships were organised in Europe,

- the *unprecedented development of the economic dimension of sport*, with, for example, the spectacular increase in television rights: the value of the television rights negotiated by the IOC has risen from USD 441 million in 1992 (Barcelona Olympic Games) to an expected USD 1.318 billion for the 2000 Olympic Games in Sydney.

These phenomena provide certain advantages for sport and society. Accordingly, the number of jobs created directly or indirectly by the sport industry has risen by 60% in the past ten years to each nearly 2 million. It has to be recognised, however, that these phenomena may also cause tension.

One of the first signs of these developments is the overloading of sporting calendars, which, linked to the need to produce results under the pressure of sponsors, may be considered to be one of the causes of the expansion of doping.

A second consequence is the increase in the number of lucrative sporting events, which may end up promoting the commercial approach, to the detriment of sporting principles and the social function of sport.

A third symptom is the temptation for certain sporting operators and certain large clubs to leave the federations in order to derive the maximum benefit from the economic potential of sport for themselves alone. This tendency may jeopardise the principle of financial solidarity between professional and amateur sport and the system of promotion and relegation common to most federations.

Another consequence that has been observed is the hazardous future facing young people who are being led into top-level competitive sport at an increasingly early age, often with no other vocational training, with the resulting risks for their physical and mental health and their subsequent switch to other employment.

## 3. THE COMMUNITY, ITS MEMBER STATES AND THE SPORTING MOVE-MENT NEED TO REAFFIRM AND STRENGTHEN THE EDUCATIONAL AND SOCIAL FUNCTION OF SPORT

The Declaration on sport annexed to the Amsterdam Treaty 'emphasises the social signifi-cance of sport, in particular its role in forging identity and bringing people together'. Physical and sporting activities need to find their place in the education system of each Member State.

The values that they represent (equal opportunities, fair play, solidarity, etc.) must also be passed on by sports associations. Sport affects all social classes and age groups and is an essential tool for social integration and education.

### 3.1. Enhancing the educational role of sport

The Commission's White Paper on Education and Training[83] stresses that *'knowledge is defined as an acquired corpus of fundamental and technical knowledge and social skills' that concern 'relational skills, such as the ability to cooperate and work as part of a team, creativeness and the quest for quality'*, all of which are values conveyed by sport. With this in mind, Community action, within the context of its educational and training programmes, could focus on the following objectives:

–    *improving* the position of sport and physical education at school through the Com-munity programmes;

–    *promoting* the subsequent switch to other employment and future integration onto the labour market of sportsmen and women;

–    *promoting* convergence between the training systems for sports workers in each Member State.

Moreover, the Council of Europe rightly stressed that sport is also *'an ideal platform for social democracy*[84]'. It is therefore important for the existing Community programmes to make use of sport in combating exclusion, inequalities, racism and xenophobia.

Furthermore, the violence that sometimes develops at sporting events is unacceptable. As part of the European Union's objective to provide its citizens with a high level of protec-tion in an area of freedom, safety and justice, the responsible authorities will have to step up their cooperation in order to prevent this type of violence.

### 3.2. Joining forces to combat doping

The Vienna European Council also wished to underline *'its concern at the extent and seri-ousness of doping in sports'*. It mentioned the need for mobilisation at European Union level and invited the Member States and the Commission 'to *examine possible measures to intensify the fight against this danger'*, together with the sports bodies.

The measures implemented by the Commission,[85] in close cooperation with the Member States, have focused on three fronts:

–    *Referring* this matter to the European Group on Ethics. The opinion issued by this Group suggests a number of avenues that could be explored by the State authorities and sporting organisations;

---

[83] 'Teaching and learning – towards the knowledge-based society', Commission White Paper on Education and Training, OPOCE, Luxembourg, 1995.

[84] 'Social cohesion and sport' Clearing House – Sport Division of the Council of Europe – Committee for the Development of Sport, Strasbourg, March 1999.

[85] Community support plan in the combat against doping in sport, COM(1999) 643 of 1-12-1999.

- *Cooperating* with the Olympic movement to create a world anti-doping agency and to make sure that it works independently and transparently;
- *Mobilising* Community instruments to supplement and strengthen the work already carried out by the Member States in the areas of research, public health, education and youth, but also cooperation, as provided for by the third pillar. Further work needs to be done to improve legislative coordination.

However, this work will come to nothing unless the public authorities and the sporting organisations tackle the root causes of the rise in doping. The development of the fight against doping also depends on the general development of sport.

## 4. CLARIFYING THE LEGAL ENVIRONMENT OF SPORT

As underlined by the conclusions of the European Union Conference on Sport organised by the Commission in Olympia in May 1999, *'sport must be able to assimilate the new commercial framework in which it must develop, without at the same time losing its identity and autonomy, which underpin the functions it performs in the social, cultural, health and educational areas.*

While the Treaty contains no specific provisions on sport, the Community must nevertheless ensure that the initiatives taken by the national State authorities or sporting organisations comply with Community law, including competition law, and respect in particular the principles of the internal market (freedom of movement for workers, freedom of establishment and freedom to provide services, etc.).

In this respect, accompanying, coordination or interpretation measures at Community level might prove to be useful, for example in the area of the fight against doping'. They would be designed to strengthen the legal certainty of sporting activities and their social function at Community level. However, as Community powers currently stand, there can be no question of large-scale intervention or support programmes or even of the implementation of a Community sports policy.

### 4.1. The increase in the number of conflicts

The economic developments observed in the area of sport and the responses of the various State authorities and sporting organisations to the problems that they raise do not go far enough to guarantee that the current structures of sport and its social function can be safeguarded. The increase in the number of court proceedings is the sign of growing tension.

- Certain clubs contest the collective sale of television rights. Several complaints have been submitted to national courts, and the judgments delivered at national level have come to differing conclusions. The question of the collective sale of such rights is also raised in certain cases pending before the Commission.
- The Bosman judgment, delivered by the Court of Justice in December 1995 on the basis of the principle of freedom of movement for workers, has had major repercussions on the organisation of sport in Europe. It has done much to eliminate certain abuses and to promote the mobility of sportsmen and women. However, the sporting federations – which, incidentally, have not set up a new alternative system to the one condemned by the Court – consider that it has widened the economic gap between clubs and between players and has caused problems for the training of young people in clubs. Certain clubs which have established training centres for professional sportsmen and women have seen their best people leave, without them receiving any compensation for the investment they have made in training.
- There are differences in fiscal legislation, and hence in the taxation of professional

sportsmen and women or of sporting clubs, within the European Union. This situation is a source of inequality between countries and clubs and contributes to the phenomenon of ever higher offers.

–    Several Member States of the European Union have recently announced measures to limit or manage the effects of the commercialisation of sport. While these measures obviously help to preserve the principles and social function of sport, they may increase the disparities between Member States of the European Union and cause problems in the area of Community law.

–    Certain complaints also concern the monopoly of federations on the organisation of sporting competitions, the ownership of several clubs by one person (multiple ownership), the rules on the geographical organisation of sport, the statutes of professional clubs and certain commercial operations carried out by the federations.

On the other hand, other measures have been taken at Community level, in keeping with the principle of subsidiarity, which are strengthening the legal framework while preserving the 'common interest' dimension of sport. One example is the decision taken at the time of the 1997 revision of the 'Television without frontiers' Directive. Under the terms of the revised text, the Member States may take measures, in keeping with Community law, to ensure that the general public has access to major sporting events.

### 4.2. The need for convergent endeavours

If it is advisable, as wished by the European Council, but also the European Parliament[86] and the Committee of the Regions[87], to preserve the social function of sport, and therefore the current structures of the organisation of sport in Europe, there is a need for a new approach to questions of sport both at European Union level and in the Member States, in compliance with the Treaty, especially with the principle of subsidiarity, and the autonomy of sporting organisations.

This new approach involves preserving the traditional values of sport, while at the same time assimilating a changing economic and legal environment. It is designed to view sport globally and coherently. This overall vision assumes greater consultation between the various protagonists (sporting movement, Member States and European Community) at each level. It should lead to the clarification, at each level, of the legal framework for sports operators.

The European Union would have an essential part to play in implementing this new approach, given the increasing internationalisation of sport and the direct impact of Community policies on European sport.

### 4.2.1. The Community level

In terms of the economic activity that it generates, the sporting sector is subject to the rules of the EC Treaty, like the other sectors of the economy. The application of the Treaty's competition rules to the sporting sector must take account of the specific characteristics of sport, especially the interdependence between sporting activity and the economic activity that it generates, the principle of equal opportunities and the uncertainty of the results.

With a view to an improved definition of the legal environment, it is possible to give ex-

---

[86] Resolution of the European Parliament on the role of the European Union in the field of sport, OJ C 200, 30-6-1997.

[87] Opinion of the Committee of the Regions on 'The European model of sport', CdR 37/99, 16-9-1999.

amples, without prejudice to the conclusions that the Commission could draw from the in-depth analysis of each case, of practices of sports organisations.

### 4.2.1.1. Practices which do not come under the competition rules

The regulations of sporting organisations drawing up rules without which a sport could not exist, or which are necessary for its organisation or for the organisation of competitions, might not be subject to the competition rules. The rules inherent to sport are, first and foremost, the 'rules of the game'. The aim of these rules is not to distort competition.

### 4.2.1.2. Practices that are, in principle, prohibited by the competition rules

These are restrictive practices in the economic activities generated by sport. They may concern, in particular, restrictions on parallel imports of sports products and the sale of entrance tickets to stadiums that discriminate between users who are resident in a particular Member State and those who live outside that Member State.

Sponsoring agreements that close a market by removing other suppliers for no objective reason are prohibited. The systems of international transfers based on arbitrarily calculated payments which bear no relation to training costs seem to have been prohibited, irrespective of the nationality of the player concerned.

Lastly, it is likely that there would be a ban on the practice of a sporting organisation using its regulatory power to exclude from the market, for no objective reason, any economic operator which, even though it complies with the justified quality or safety standards, has not been able to obtain a document from this organisation certifying to the quality or safety of its products.

### 4.2.1.3. Practices likely to be exempted from the competition rules

–   *The Bosman* judgment mentioned above recognised as legitimate the objectives designed to maintain a balance between clubs, while preserving a degree of equality of opportunity and the uncertainty of the result, and to encourage the recruitment and training of young players. Consequently, it is likely that agreements between professional clubs or decisions by their associations that are really designed to achieve these two objectives would be exempted. The same would be true of a system of transfers or standard contracts based on objectively calculated payments that are related to the costs of training, or of an exclusive right, limited in duration and scope, to broadcast sporting events. It goes without saying that the other provisions of the Treaty must also be complied with in this area, especially those that guarantee freedom of movement for professional sportsmen and women.

–   It is likely that short-term sponsoring agreements based on an invitation to tender and with clear and non-discriminatory selection criteria would be authorised.

–   Any exemptions granted in the case of the joint sale of broadcasting rights must take account of the benefits for consumers and of the proportional nature of the restriction on competition in relation to the legitimate objective pursued. In this context, there is also a need to examine the extent to which a link can be established between the joint sale of rights and financial solidarity between professional and amateur sport, the objectives of the training of young sportsmen and women and those of promoting sporting activities among the population. However, with regard to the sale of exclusive rights to broadcast sporting events, it is likely that any exclusivity which, by its duration and/or scope, resulted in the closing of the market, would be prohibited.

### 4.2.2. The national level

The national State authorities also need to clarify the legal rules in order to safeguard the current structures and the social function of sport.

One way of safeguarding the national federal structures could be to provide for them to be recognised by law in each Member State of the Union. Other ways of achieving this objective would be the partnership agreements between the State and the sporting federations and to grant the representative sporting federations a specific status which could be based on that of the professional associations. There is also a need to examine, in legal terms, the legal status of clubs, their purchase or the participation of commercial or financial groups in their equity.

### 4.2.3. The level of sporting organisations

In order to clarify the legal environment of sport, it is also necessary for the federations to make an effort to define their missions and statutes more precisely. The pyramid structure of the organisation of sport in Europe gives sporting federations a practical 'monopoly'. The existence of several federations in one discipline would risk causing major conflicts. Indeed, the organisation of national championships and the selection of national athletes and national teams for international competitions often require the existence of one umbrella organisation bringing together all the sports associations and competitors of one discipline.

The federations should also perform tasks such as the promotion of amateur and professional sport and carry out a role of integration into society (young people, the disabled, etc.). Their statutes should explicitly state these missions. These responsibilities should be translated effectively into practice by financial mechanisms of internal solidarity and the structural and solidarity-based relationship between competitive sport and amateur sport. Operations with an economic dimension should be founded on the principles of transparency and balanced access to the market, effective and proven redistribution and clarification of contracts, while prominence is given to the 'specific nature of sport'.

It must be stressed that the basic freedoms guaranteed by the Treaty do not generally conflict with the regulatory measures of sports associations, provided that these measures are objectively justified, non-discriminatory, necessary and proportional.

There is also a need to find solutions, in partnership with the sporting federations, in order to develop alternatives to the transfer systems condemned by the Bosman judgment.

### 5. CONCLUSION

If the Commission is asked whether it can guarantee that the current development of sport will not jeopardise the current structures and social function of sport, its unequivocal answer is that it cannot. However the Commission has no direct competence for sport under the Treaty.

In order to safeguard the current sports structures and maintain the social function of sport, there is a need for a new approach to questions of sport. The first step towards such a new approach is for the various protagonists involved to respect a common foundation of sporting principles:

–   The European Union recognises the eminent role played by sport in European society and attaches the greatest importance to the maintenance of its functions of promoting social integration and education and making a contribution to public health and to the general interest function performed by the federations;

–   The integrity and autonomy of sport must be preserved. The purchase of sporting clubs by commercial bodies (communication groups etc.) must, if permitted, be governed by clear rules, out of a concern for the preservation of sporting structures and ethics;

– The system of promotion and relegation is one of the characteristics of European sport. This system gives small or medium-sized clubs a better chance and rewards sporting merit;

– Doping and sport are diametrically opposed. There can be no let-up in the fight against doping;

– The 'trade' in young sportsmen and women must be combated. Each young sportsman or woman trained by a club for top-level competition must receive vocational training in addition to sports training.

On the basis of these principles, there is a need for a new partnership between the European institutions, the Member States and the sports organisations, all moving in the same direction, in order to encourage the promotion of sport in European society, while respecting sporting values, the autonomy of sporting organisations and the Treaty, especially the principle of subsidiarity.

Insufficient coordination between the protagonists of sport (federations, Member States and the European Community), all of them working in isolation, would risk thwarting the efforts to achieve these shared principles. However, the convergent efforts of the European Community, the Member States and the sporting federations could make an effective contribution to the promotion in Europe of sport that is true to its social role, while ensuring that its organisational aspects assimilate the new economic order.

---

## * 1.27.   ANSWER ON BEHALF OF THE COMMISSION TO WRITTEN QUESTION E-2187/99 BY CHRISTOS FOLIAS (PPE-DE) AND IOANNIS MARINOS (PPE-DE), 20 DECEMBER 1999[88]

Subject: Treaty of Amsterdam and sport

---

## * 1.28.   ANSWER ON BEHALF OF THE COMMISSION TO WRITTEN QUESTION P-2424/99 BY ROBERTA ANGELILLI (UEN), 7 JANUARY 2000[89]

Subject: Recognition of sport in the Treaty

---

## * 1.29.   ANSWER ON BEHALF OF THE COMMISSION TO WRITTEN QUESTION E-2256/99 BY ROBERT EVANS (PSE), 10 JANUARY 2000[90]

Subject: 'Horse wrestling'

---

[88]   Question of 29-11-1999; OJ C 170 E, 20-6-2000, p. 149-150.
[89]   Question of 13-12-1999; OJ C 219 E, 1-8-2000, p. 159-160.
[90]   Question of 13-12-1999; OJ C 203 E, 18-7-2000, p. 158.

**\* 1.30.   ANSWER ON BEHALF OF THE COMMISSION TO WRITTEN QUESTION P-102/00 BY PIETRO-PAOLO MENNEA (ELDR), 18 FEBRUARY 2000**[91]

Subject: Request for specific recognition of amateur sport

———

**\* 1.31.   ANSWER ON BEHALF OF THE COMMISSION TO WRITTEN QUESTION P-1445/00 BY ARIENE MCCARTHY (PSE), 24 MAY 2000**[92]

Subject: Sport and the EU Treaties

———

**1.32.   PRESIDENCY CONCLUSIONS OF THE SANTA MARIA DA FEIRA EUROPEAN COUNCIL, 20 JUNE 2000**

[...]

**IV. EUROPE AND THE CITIZEN**

[...]

D. Sport

50.    The European Council requests the Commission and the Council to take account of the specific characteristics of sport in Europe and its social function in managing common policies.

[...]

———

**\* 1.33.   OPINION OF THE COMMITTEE ON LEGAL AFFAIRS AND THE INTERNAL MARKET FOR THE COMMITTEE ON CULTURE, YOUTH, EDUCATION, THE MEDIA AND SPORT ON THE REPORT FROM THE COMMISSION TO THE EUROPEAN COUNCIL WITH A VIEW TO SAFEGUARDING CURRENT SPORTS STRUCTURES AND MAINTAINING THE SOCIAL FUNCTION OF SPORT WITHIN THE COMMUNITY FRAMEWORK – THE HELSINKI REPORT ON SPORT, 22 JUNE 2000**[93]

Draftsman: Klaus-Heiner Lehne

———

---

[91]   Question of 18-1-2000; OJ C 225 E, 8-8-2000, p. 219.
[92]   Question of 3-5-2000; OJ C 026 E, 26-1-2001, p. 166.
[93]   A5-0208/2000.

**\* 1.34.  REPORT OF THE COMMITTEE ON CULTURE, YOUTH, EDUCATION, THE MEDIA AND SPORT ON THE COMMISSION REPORT TO THE EUROPEAN COUNCIL WITH A VIEW TO SAFEGUARDING CURRENT SPORTS STRUCTURES AND MAINTAINING THE SOCIAL FUNCTION OF SPORT WITHIN THE COMMUNITY FRAMEWORK – THE HELSINKI REPORT ON SPORT, 18 JULY 2000[94]**

Rapporteur: Pietro-Paolo Mennea

———

**1.35.  RESOLUTION OF THE EUROPEAN PARLIAMENT ON THE COMMISSION REPORT TO THE EUROPEAN COUNCIL WITH A VIEW TO SAFEGUARDING CURRENT SPORTS STRUCTURES AND MAINTAINING THE SOCIAL FUNCTION OF SPORT WITHIN THE COMMUNITY FRAMEWORK – THE HELSINKI REPORT ON SPORT, 7 SEPTEMBER 2000[95]**

*The European Parliament,*

–   having regard to the Commission report (COM(1999) 644 – C5-0088/2000),
–   having regard to the European Union Conference on Sport, held in Olympia from 20 to 23 May 1999, which underlined the importance of sport for bringing the citizens of the European Union closer together,
–   having regard to Declaration No 29 on sport, annexed to the Amsterdam Treaty,
–   having regard to the Commission White Paper on Education and Training (COM(1995) 590),
–   having regard to the opinion of the Committee of the Regions on the European Model of Sport[96],
–   having regard to its resolution of 17 December 1998 on urgent measures to be taken against doping in sport[97],
–   having regard to the conclusions of the Vienna European Council meeting held on 11-12 December 1998,
–   having regard to its resolutions of 22 May 1996 on the broadcasting of sports events[98] and 13 June 1997 on the role of the European Union in the field of sport[99],
–   having regard to Point 50 of the Conclusions of the European Council of Santa Maria da Feira of 19-20 June 2000, calling for account to be taken of the special characteristics of sport in Europe and its social function,
–   having regard to the Bosman judgment of the EC Court of Justice[100],
–   having regard to the Deliège (C-191/1997) and Lehtonen (C-176/1996) judgments of the EC Court of Justice,

---

[94]  COM(1999) 644.
[95]  Minutes of 7-9-2000, Provisional Edition.
[96]  OJ C 374, 23-12-1999, p. 56.
[97]  OJ C 98, 9-4-1999, p. 291.
[98]  OJ C 166, 10-6-1996, p. 109.
[99]  OJ C 200, 30-6-1997, p. 252.
[100]  ECR 1995, I-4921.

–       having regard to its resolution of 18 November 1999 on preparation for reform of
        the treaties and the next intergovernmental conference[101],
–       having regard to the Communication from the Commission on the Community sup-
        port plan to combat doping in sport (COM(1999) 643,
–       having regard to the recommendations of the Helsinki Spirit 2000 Conference of
        the European Women and Sport Network (EWS),
–       having regard to the Commission's unsatisfactory reply to the Parliamentary ques-
        tion of 13 January 2000 on the request for specific recognition of amateur sport (P-
        0102/2000),
–       having regard to Rule 47(1) of its Rules of Procedure,
–       having regard to the report by the Committee on Culture, Youth, Education, the
        Media and Sport and the opinion of the Committee on Legal Affairs and the Inter-
        nal Market (A5-0208/2000),

A.      whereas sport is an ideal platform for social inclusion and cohesion and as such
        should be an integral part of existing Community programmes, which should make
        use of it to combat social exclusion, violence, inequalities, racism and xenophobia,
B.      whereas there is widespread concern regarding the reprehensible outbreaks of
        forms of violence, racism and xenophobia at sporting events,
C.      whereas Member States and sporting organisations, in organising sporting events,
        have a duty to provide their citizens with protection in an area of freedom and jus-
        tice,
D.      having regard to the increase in doping and the alarming infiltration of this sector
        by organised crime, with serious consequences as a result of the ongoing legislative
        vacuum; having regard to the increasing abuse of pharmaceutical products which is
        seriously damaging the health of sportspersons; having regard to the need for Euro-
        pean sporting authorities to draw up a common set of rules to be applied to the is-
        sue of doping,
E.      having regard to the economic imbalances in professional sport between clubs and
        athletes, not to mention the problems in training young athletes, which have arisen
        in the wake of the Bosman judgment,
F.      whereas professional sport and the marketing of professional sport have become a
        business; whereas, therefore, competition law and the four freedoms must apply to
        the commercial aspects of sport; whereas, further, in applying the Treaty rules to
        sport, the special characteristics of the sector must be taken into account, as already
        indicated by the European Court of Justice,
G.      having regard to the position adopted by the Commission, and Parliament's afore-
        mentioned resolution of 22 May 1996, concerning the granting of exclusive broad-
        casting rights to non-encrypted channels, with a view to enabling the majority of
        the population to participate in sporting events of general interest,
H.      having regard to the enormous expansion of sport in economic terms, which has led
        to an increase in the value of television rights, sponsorships, merchandising and all
        other ancillary activities, and to the multiplication of international competitions,
        with a consequent increase in jobs in the sector,
I.      whereas the pursuit of sports-related economic activities by both organisations and
        individuals is subject to the rules of the EC Treaty and Community law,
J.      whereas sport can be of enormous benefit to all social groups, both educationally

---

[101] Texts Adopted, Item 4.

and in terms of social integration, and this should be reflected in national and Community policies,

K.   whereas the practice of sport has very positive implications for the development of European health policy,

L.   whereas the work and status of sportspersons should be properly appreciated and safeguarded and taken into consideration by Member States and by national and international sporting federations,

M.   having regard to the importance of establishing, in each Member State, a sporting federation to supervise the growth of sport amongst the disabled and the less advantaged sections of the population and to encourage them to become involved in it; whereas greater attention should be paid to sporting programmes and events geared to the needs of such groups,

1.   Welcomes the Commission's statements regarding the significant educational and social functions of sport; emphasises the integrative nature of sport and its importance not only as regards physical development but also in intellectual terms through the inculcation of important social values, such as team spirit, fair competition, cooperation, tolerance and solidarity;

2.   Underlines the need for the Community to take account of the autonomy and competence of recognised sports bodies both at national and international level with regard to the governance and organisation of the sports concerned;

3.   Calls on the Commission to involve the existing work of the European Network of Sport Sciences in Higher Education (ENSSHE) and the subjects of vocational training and qualifications for sportspersons in the EU's Socrates and Leonardo Programmes, together with the reintegration of sportspersons in the labour market when their sporting activity comes to an end;

4.   Welcomes the Commission's willingness in the Helsinki Report to come forward with accompanying, coordination or interpretation measures at Community level to strengthen the legal certainty of sport and its specific social and educational functions;

5.   Underlines the importance of sports education at school; calls on the Member States to attach due importance to the teaching of physical education in the curricula of all schools and to encourage young people to take part in amateur sports;

6.   Takes it for granted that the Commission acknowledges the principles laid down in the Bosman judgment as firmly established ones, and therefore calls on the Commission to support structures of self-government within sport that promote solidarity and the training and development of players, as much in smaller local clubs as in great internationally recognised ones; reminds the Commission that such structures and aims are fully compatible with the opinion of the EC Court of Justice in the Bosman case; and calls on the Commission to refrain from taking measures or putting forward proposals which might call into question the principle established in the Bosman judgement;

7.   Calls on the sports federations to revitalise their internal democracy and take account of the different needs and management methods of professional and amateur sport, by setting up the appropriate representative structures;

8.   Calls on the Intergovernmental Conference to include an explicit reference to sport in Article 151 of the Treaty, so that in its action the EU can recognise the cultural, economic and social phenomenon that sport represents;

9.      Reiterates the call it issued to the Commission in paragraph 6(f) of its aforemen-
        tioned resolution of 13 June 1997 to investigate the national rules governing public
        subsidies for professional clubs and to seek to bring about transparency with regard
        to the financial situation of such clubs;

10.     Calls particularly on the Commission to take account of the positive aspect of sport
        with regard to health in the development of a Community health policy;

11.     Draws attention to the conclusions of its aforementioned resolution of 13 June
        1997 concerning the organisation of a European Year of Sport;

12.     Calls on the Commission to give favourable consideration, but in a manner strictly
        consistent with the Treaty, to those practices which promote the grass-roots devel-
        opment of sport and which provide for equality of opportunity and thus contribute
        to the healthy and diverse development of European sport;

13.     Expresses its respect for those persons who perform voluntary work in sports clubs
        set up to offer sport as a leisure activity, in particular work with young people and
        minority groups in sports and society; reiterates the need for special coordination to
        be given to the particular characteristics of amateur sport;

14.     Takes the view that such activities merit greater support and calls on the Commis-
        sion to consider how this support can be provided more effectively and on a
        broader basis at European level;

15.     Warns about the major differences which may emerge between elite sport and
        smaller sports clubs and between professional and amateur sport; points out that, in
        both these cases, the one cannot do without the other, so that efforts must be made
        to ensure that mutual support continues to be provided;

16.     Calls for the establishment of sporting associations to be encouraged, wherever this
        is intended to support amateur sport and show solidarity with the less-advantaged
        sections of society;

17.     Acknowledges the European Communities' framework for sport, but asks the
        Commission, in accordance with the spirit of declaration 29 in the Amsterdam
        Treaty annex, to take due account of the national and regional character of sports
        structures and the historic tradition of sport in Europe;

18.     Calls on the Commission to collect and disseminate widely best practice developed
        by local and regional authorities as community leaders and key players in local re-
        generation partnerships, as well as providers and enablers of services to all people
        in the community;

19.     Calls for the Member States and sporting federations to protect sportsmen and
        women under the age of eighteen and to envisage strict arrangements for their care
        and education which might even include a ban on any commercial transactions in-
        volving them and to conduct a study into the 'trade' in young sportsmen and
        women, focusing in particular on the effect on young athletes under the age of
        eighteen who enter into professional sport;

20.     Urges the International Gymnastic Federation not to encourage extreme thinness,
        by penalising gymnasts and other sportspersons;

21.     Calls on sporting bodies to establish principles whereby all young athletes who are
        being trained to participate in high-level sporting competitions also receive an edu-
        cation and vocational training to complement their sports training; calls on the
        Commission to incorporate these aspects in the Socrates and Leonardo
        Programmes;

22.     Reminds sporting bodies and the Member States of the European Union's objective
        to provide its citizens with protection in the areas of freedom and safety and asks

the responsible authorities to step up their cooperation in order to prevent violence at sporting events;

23. Calls on the Member States to transpose the Council recommendation of 22 April 1996 relating to the prevention and control of disturbances in connection with football matches into their national legislations as soon as possible and to adopt the tightest possible sanctions against those responsible, in accordance with the handbook for international police cooperation approved by the Council resolution of 21 June 1999[102];

24. Calls on the Member States to adopt practical measures in their legislation to encourage private investment in sport;

25. Urges those Member States that have not yet done so to establish a sporting federation for disabled people, both the physically disabled and those with learning difficulties, recognised and assisted by official sporting bodies;

calls on the Member States to give particular attention to the development, funding and promotion of sport for disabled people and to safeguard their special needs as a part of sports culture and to provide exchanges between disabled and non-disabled sportspersons;

and calls on the Member States and the Commission to encourage sport and physical activities for people with disabilities through the Community programmes;

26. Calls on sports organisations to share out responsibilities in sport between women and men, strengthen women's role in the decision-making process, and develop gender equality plans for their members;

27. Calls for television rights to be granted in compliance with the antitrust law and to companies which take responsibility for the risks involved in preparing the sporting event;

calls also for transparency in the granting of television rights;

28. Draws attention to the need to comply with Community law, in view of the enormous economic importance of the manufacture of sports articles and clothing, and – particularly in the area of development cooperation – the need to prevent imports into the Community of products whose manufacture does not comply with ILO and environmental standards;

29. Calls on the Commission, bearing in mind the conclusions of the Portuguese Presidency and the European Council of Santa Maria da Feira, to submit a Communication on the integration of sport into the various Community policies and ways of acknowledging the work of the sports organisations, the extent of sports education in the curricula of the individual Member States, and sexual harassment and abuse in sport;

30. Insists that consumers must be allowed a fair share of the resulting benefit, and in particular that European citizens should not be deprived of the opportunity to view important sporting events live through public service broadcasting, or through other channels that are free at the point of delivery; therefore calls on the Commission to give favourable consideration to practices which bring this about and, pursuant to Article 81(3) of the EC Treaty, to clear the way for some exemptions from competition rules;

31. Reiterates the call it issued to all the Member States in paragraph 4 of its aforementioned resolution of 13 June 1997 to make use of the right provided for in Article 3a of the television directive in order to ensure that a substantial proportion of the

---

[102] OJ C 196, 13-7-1999, p. 1.

public is not deprived of the possibility of following events of major social importance because the latter are broadcast on an exclusive basis;

32.　Requests the Member States to promote ways of ensuring that part of the revenue from sponsorship and advertising goes towards supporting amateur sport;

33.　Calls on the Member States to upgrade schools specialising in sports medicine and to set up vocational training courses for specialists in the various sectors of sports medicine;

34.　Instructs its President to forward this resolution to the Council and Commission.

———

**\* 1.36.　REPLY ON BEHALF OF THE COUNCIL TO WRITTEN QUESTION P-1528/00 BY JOSÉ RIBEIRO E CASTRO (UEN), 18 AND19 SEPTEMBER 2000**[103]

Subject: The 'Bosman case' – revision of the EC Treaty and addition of a protocol on professional football or sport in general

———

**\* 1.37.　ANSWER ON BEHALF OF THE COMMISSION TO WRITTEN QUESTION E-2501/00 BY JOSÉ RIBEIRO E CASTRO (UEN), 25 SEPTEMBER 2000**[104]

Subject: Recognition of the specific characteristics of sport in the Treaties

———

**\* 1.38.　ANSWER ON BEHALF OF THE COMMISSION TO WRITTEN QUESTION E-2609/00 BY JOSÉ RIBEIRO E CASTRO (UEN), 26 SEPTEMBER 2000**[105]

Subject: UEFA – EURO 2000: punishment of professional Portuguese footballers in violation of fundamental legal guarantees

———

**\* 1.39.　REPLY ON BEHALF OF THE COUNCIL TO WRITTEN QUESTION P-2475/00 BY JOSÉ RIBEIRO E CASTRO (UEN), 16 NOVEMBER 2000**[106]

Subject: Recognition of the specific nature of sport in the Treaties.

———

**1.40.　PRESIDENCY CONCLUSIONS OF THE NICE EUROPEAN COUNCIL MEETING, 7-9 DECEMBER 2000**

[...]

---

[103]　Question of 10-5-2000; OJ C 72 E, 6-3-2001, p. 70
[104]　Question of 2-8-2000; OJ C 89 E, 20-3-2001, p. 203-204.
[105]　Question of 1-8-2000; OJ C 103 E, 3-4-2001, p. 196.
[106]　Question of 11-7-2000; OJ C 113 E, 18-4-2001, p. 104.

## VI. CITIZEN'S EUROPE

[...]

### H. Europe of culture

[...]

### Sport

54. The European Council notes the declaration adopted by the Council (see Annex) on the specific characteristics of sport. The European Council also welcomes the Council conclusions concerning the World Anti-Doping Agency and agrees to intensify European cooperation in this area. It also noted the UN Millennium Declaration on the promotion of peace and mutual comprehension by means of sport and the Olympic Truce.

[...]

## ANNEX IV
## DECLARATION ON THE SPECIFIC CHARACTERISTICS OF SPORT AND ITS SOCIAL FUNCTION IN EUROPE, OF WHICH ACCOUNT SHOULD BE TAKEN IN IMPLEMENTING COMMON POLICIES

1. The European Council has noted the report on sport submitted to it by the European Commission in Helsinki in December 1999 with a view to safeguarding current sports structures and maintaining the social function of sport within the European Union. Sporting organisations and the Member States have a primary responsibility in the conduct of sporting affairs. Even though not having any direct powers in this area, the Community must, in its action under the various Treaty provisions, take account of the social, educational and cultural functions inherent in sport and making it special, in order that the code of ethics and the solidarity essential to the preservation of its social role may be respected and nurtured.

2. The European Council hopes in particular that the cohesion and ties of solidarity binding the practice of sports at every level, fair competition and both the moral and material interests and the physical integrity of those involved in the practice of sport, especially minors, may be preserved.

### Amateur sport and sport for all

3. Sport is a human activity resting on fundamental social, educational and cultural values. It is a factor making for integration, involvement in social life, tolerance, acceptance of differences and playing by the rules.

4. Sporting activity should be accessible to every man and woman, with due regard for individual aspirations and abilities, throughout the whole gamut of organised or individual competitive or recreational sports.

5. For the physically or mentally disabled, the practice of physical and sporting activities provides a particularly favourable opening for the development of individual talent, rehabilitation, social integration and solidarity and, as such, should be encouraged. In this connection, the European Council welcomes the valuable and exemplary contribution made by the Paralympic Games in Sydney.

6.    The Member States encourage voluntary services in sport, by means of measures providing appropriate protection for and acknowledging the economic and social role of volunteers, with the support, where necessary, of the Community in the framework of its powers in this area.

**Role of sports federations**

7.    The European Council stresses its support for the independence of sports organisations and their right to organise themselves through appropriate associative structures. It recognises that, with due regard for national and Community legislation and on the basis of a democratic and transparent method of operation, it is the task of sporting organisations to organise and promote their particular sports, particularly as regards the specifically sporting rules applicable and the make-up of national teams, in the way which they think best reflects their objectives.

8.    It notes that sports federations have a central role in ensuring the essential solidarity between the various levels of sporting practice, from recreational to top-level sport, which co-exist there; they provide the possibility of access to sports for the public at large, human and financial support for amateur sports, promotion of equal access to every level of sporting activity for men and women alike, youth training, health protection and measures to combat doping, acts of violence and racist or xenophobic occurrences.

9.    These social functions entail special responsibilities for federations and provide the basis for the recognition of their competence in organising competitions.

10.   While taking account of developments in the world of sport, federations must continue to be the key feature of a form of organisation providing a guarantee of sporting cohesion and participatory democracy.

**Preservation of sports training policies**

11.   Training policies for young sportsmen and -women are the life blood of sport, national teams and top-level involvement in sport and must be encouraged. Sports federations, where appropriate in tandem with the public authorities, are justified in taking the action needed to preserve the training capacity of clubs affiliated to them and to ensure the quality of such training, with due regard for national and Community legislation and practices.

**Protection of young sportsmen and -women**

12.   The European Council underlines the benefits of sport for young people and urges the need for special heed to be paid, in particular by sporting organisations, to the education and vocational training of top young sportsmen and -women, in order that their vocational integration is not jeopardised because of their sporting careers, to their psychological balance and family ties and to their health, in particular the prevention of doping. It appreciates the contribution of associations and organisations which minister to these requirements in their training work and thus make a valuable contribution socially.

13.   The European Council expresses concern about commercial transactions targeting minors in sport, including those from third countries, inasmuch as they do not comply with existing labour legislation or endanger the health and welfare of young sportsmen and -women. It calls on sporting organisations and the Member States to investigate and monitor such practices and, where necessary, to consider appropriate measures.

**Economic context of sport and solidarity**

14.  In the view of the European Council, single ownership or financial control of more than one sports club entering the same competition in the same sport may jeopardise fair competition. Where necessary, sports federations are encouraged to introduce arrangements for overseeing the management of clubs.

15.  The sale of television broadcasting rights is one of the greatest sources of income today for certain sports. The European Council thinks that moves to encourage the mutualisation of part of the revenue from such sales, at the appropriate levels, are beneficial to the principle of solidarity between all levels and areas of sport.

**Transfers**

16.  The European Council is keenly supportive of dialogue on the transfer system between the sports movement, in particular the football authorities, organisations representing professional sportsmen and -women, the Community and the Member States, with due regard for the specific requirements of sport, subject to compliance with Community law.

17.  The Community institutions and the Member States are requested to continue examining their policies, in compliance with the Treaty and in accordance with their respective powers, in the light of these general principles.

———

**1.41.   STATEMENT BY THE SPORTS MINISTERS OF THE EUROPEAN UNION MEMBER STATES PERTAINING TO SPORT SAFETY, THE FIGHT AGAINST DOPING AND THE SPECIFIC FUNCTION OF SPORT WITHIN THE CONTEXT OF COMMUNITY INTEGRATION, 12 NOVEMBER 2001**

Recalling the conclusions of the European Council in Nice on the specific characteristics of sport and its social function in Europe,

Supported by the 1999 Helsinki report on sport, presented by the Commission to the European Council 'with a view to safeguarding current sports structures and maintaining the social function of sport within the Community framework',

With reference to the European Community initiatives announced in the Community support plan to combat doping in sport (1999),

The Sports Ministers of the 15 EU Member States, assembled in Brussels on 12 November 2001, underline

**I. With regard to safety and tolerance in sports**

In a world in which international tensions have escalated considerably, sport can often help to reconcile people from different countries and cultures. Sport and the Olympic ideal must play a greater role, and bring a message of tolerance and mutual respect.

Taking account of the priority which has to be given to the safety of all those involved in sports events, the Ministers are of the opinion that everything possible must be done that all sports events and in particular the next Olympic Winter Games in Salt Lake City and the World Cup Football 2002 to take place in conditions of optimum safety and honesty, and with the highest possible number of participants.

The Ministers strongly urge to take all necessary measures be taken to combat racism and xenophobia in sports.

## II. With regard to the fight against doping

The use of doping agents does not conform to the call for tolerance and mutual respect. Consequently, the Ministers call on the EU Member States and the Community institutions to do everything within their competences to put a stop to this abuse. Doping no longer seems to be a marginal phenomenon in the world of sports, but it is an increasingly heavy burden on the credibility of sport. It is unacceptable that sportsmen and sportswomen and their entourage should attempt to engage in the deceitful manipulation of sporting challenges and to endanger their own health.

In view of the increased mobility of sportsmen and sportswomen and the growing number of international competitions, all sports federations and public authorities concerned are encouraged within the framework of their competences, to work closely together with WADA to implement the international standards for doping control and to use it as the basis for mutual cooperation, including to accept the result of testing from countries within the European Union.

In addition, the sports federations and public authorities, as appropriate, are encouraged to work towards a greater efficiency in the application of sportive sanctions including the examination of the issue of mutual recognition of sportive sanctions.

## III. With regard to the future role and the specific characteristics of sports

Finally, the Ministers recall the Nice Declaration and encourage an open debate on the social, educational and cultural values in Sport in order to guarantee the specific characteristics of Sport in Europe at all levels.

———

## * 1.42.  ANSWER ON BEHALF OF THE COMMISSION TO WRITTEN QUESTION E-2937/01 BY JUAN NARANJO ESCOBAR (PPE-DE), 19 DECEMBER 2001[107]

Subject: Common policies – implementation integrating sport

———

## * 1.43.  ANSWER ON BEHALF OF THE COMMISSION TO WRITTEN QUESTION E-512/02 BY THERESA ZABELL (PPE-DE), 12 APRIL 2002[108]

Subject: Sport

———

## * 1.44.  COMMISSION'S CALL FOR PROPOSALS – DG EAC NO 33/02 – PREPARATORY MEASURES FOR A COMMUNITY POLICY IN THE FIELD OF SPORT, 11 JULY 2002

———

[107] Question of 24-10-2001; OJ C 134 E, 6-6-2002, p. 155.
[108] Question of 28-2-2002; OJ C 172 E, 18-7-2002, p. 206.

**\* 1.45. ANSWER ON BEHALF OF THE COMMISSION TO WRITTEN QUESTION E-1470/02 BY THERESA ZABELL (PPE-DE), 15 JULY 2002**[109]

Subject: Actions connected with sport

———

**\* 1.46. ANSWER ON BEHALF OF THE COMMISSION TO WRITTEN QUESTION P-1900/02 BY PIETRO-PAOLO MENNEA (PPE-DE), 17 JULY 2002**[110]

Subject: 2002 World Cup

———

**\* 1.47. ANSWER ON BEHALF OF THE COMMISSION TO WRITTEN QUESTION E-2897/02 BY MARGRIETUS VAN DEN BERG (PSE), 27 NOVEMBER 2002**[111]

Subject: Agreement of international rules concerning top-class sport

———

**1.48. 2003/2004 IGC PROVISIONAL CONSOLIDATED VERSION OF THE DRAFT TREATY ESTABLISHING A CONSTITUTION FOR EUROPE, BRUSSELS, 25 JUNE 2004**[112]

[...]
**PART III: THE POLICIES AND FUNCTIONING OF THE UNION**
[...]
**TITLE III – INTERNAL POLICIES AND ACTION**
[...]
Chapter V – Areas where the union may take coordinating, complementary or supporting action
[...]
Section 4 – Education, youth, sport and vocational training,
Article III-182 (ex Article 149 TEC)
1.    [...]
      The Union shall contribute to the promotion of European sporting issues, while taking account of its specific nature, its structures based on voluntary activity and its social and educational function.
2.    Union action shall be aimed at:
      [...]
      (g)    developing the European dimension in sport, by promoting fairness and openness in sporting competitions and cooperation between bodies responsible for sports, and by protecting the physical and moral integrity of

---

[109] Question of 27-5-2002; OJ C 301 E, 5-12-2002, p. 154.
[110] Question of 20-6-2002; OJ C 301 E, 5-12-2002, p. 243.
[111] Question of 14-10-2002; OJ C 92 E, 17-4-2003, p. 217-218.
[112] CIG 86/04.

sportsmen and sportswomen, especially young sportsmen and sportswomen.

3.      The Union and the Member States shall foster cooperation with third countries and
        the competent international organisations in the field of education and sport, in
        particular the Council of Europe.

4.      In order to contribute to the achievement of the objectives referred to in this Ar-
        ticle,

        (a)    European laws or framework laws shall establish incentive actions, exclud-
               ing any harmonisation of the laws and regulations of the Member States.
               They shall be adopted after consultation of the Committee of the Regions
               and the Economic and Social Committee;

        (b)    the Council, on a proposal from the Commission, shall adopt recommenda-
               tions.

———

Part 2

# Specific Subjects

# 2.1. BOYCOTT*

**\* 2.1.1. COMMON POSITION BY THE COUNCIL ON THE BASIS OF ARTICLE J.2 OF THE TREATY ON EUROPEAN UNION ON NIGERIA, 4 DECEMBER 1995[1]**

---

**\* 2.1.2. DECISION OF THE COUNCIL ON THE IMPLEMENTATION OF COMMON POSITION 95/544/CFSP ON NIGERIA, 28 NOVEMBER 1997[2]**

---

**\* 2.1.3. REPLY ON BEHALF OF THE COUNCIL TO WRITTEN QUESTION E-40/98 BY ULF HOLM (V), 27 APRIL 1998[3]**

Subject: Nigeria's participation in international sports events

---

**\* 2.1.4. ANSWER ON BEHALF OF THE COMMISSION TO WRITTEN QUESTION P-1180/98 BY EDITH MÜLLER (V), 20 MAY 1998[4]**

Subject: The international football matches between Germany and Nigeria on 22 April 1998 and between the Netherlands and Nigeria on 5 June 1998

---

**\* 2.1.5. ANSWER ON BEHALF OF THE COMMISSION TO WRITTEN QUESTION E-1428/98 BY JOHN IVERSEN (PSE), 6 JULY 1998[5]**

Subject: Football international between Germany and Nigeria

---

**\* 2.1.6. EUROPEAN COUNCIL – GENERAL AFFAIRS, 26 APRIL 1999[6]**

---

**\* 2.1.7. EUROPEAN COUNCIL – GENERAL AFFAIRS, 31 MAY 1999[7]**

---

---

\* The full texts of documents which are marked with an asterisk (\*) are not incorporated in the book itself, but are freely accessible on the website of the ASSER International Sports Law Centre, at <www.sportslaw.nl> – documentation.

[1] OJ L 309 , 21-12-1995, p. 1 (no longer in force).
[2] OJ L 338 , 9-12-1997, p. 7.
[3] Question of 28-1-1998; OJ C 223, 17-7-1998, p. 91.
[4] Question of 6-4-1998; OJ C 354, 19-11-1998, p. 76.
[5] Question of 11-5-1998; OJ C 323, 21-10-1998, p. 130.
[6] Bulletin EU 4-1999.
[7] Press 171-G Nr: 8657/99.

**\* 2.1.8.   PRESIDENCY CONCLUSIONS OF THE COLOGNE EUROPEAN COUNCIL, 3 AND 4 JUNE 1999**

———

**\* 2.1.9.   REPLY ON BEHALF OF THE COUNCIL TO WRITTEN QUESTION E-1580/99 BY ERIK MEIJER (GUE/NGL), 22 OCTOBER 1999[8]**

Subject: Exclusion of sportsmen and women of Yugoslav from sporting events

———

---

[8]  Question of 8-9-1999; OJ C 27 E, 29-1-2000, p. 139.

## 2.2.    BROADCASTING*

### 2.2.1.    RESOLUTION OF THE EUROPEAN PARLIAMENT ON THE BROADCASTING OF SPORTS EVENTS, 22 MAY 1996[9]

*The European Parliament,*

A.    whereas the costs of the right to broadcast sports events are reaching levels that only make it possible for the most capital-rich broadcasters to bid for them successfully,

B.    whereas Article 9 of the Council of Europe Convention on Transfrontier Television binds parties to the Convention to avoid the right of the public to information being undermined due to the exercise by a broadcaster of exclusive rights for the transmission or retransmission of an event of high public interest and which has the effect of depriving a large part of the public in one or more other Parties of the opportunity to follow that event on television, where the definition of an event of high public interest includes sports events which are of general interest in one or more Member States,

C.    whereas the general position of DG IV at the Commission is that exclusive broadcasting rights for television coverage of sports events should only be for limited duration (e.g. one football season), although such rights may be renewed; and that if such rights are for longer periods, then specific grounds for exemption are required (for example, an exemption was available for a longer term of three years to facilitate BSkyB entry to develop direct-to-home satellite broadcasting),

D.    whereas however in the current competition situation long-term contracts constitute the best guarantee for free-to-air channels to broadcast major sports events in a manner accessible to the population as a whole,

E.    whereas the organizer of a sports event normally owns the television rights and so makes the decision to guarantee exclusivity to one broadcaster; whereas televised sports organizations need to exploit this market for greater revenue due to the ever increasing costs of sports infrastructure and the salaries of professional sportsmen and women,

F.    whereas exclusive broadcasting rights are a necessary part of the normal functioning of the highly competitive broadcasting market and are seen as a central driving force in the generation of revenue for both sports organizations and television broadcasters;
whereas this exclusivity has led to an increase in both the amount of sport broadcast and the number of different sports televised, particularly with the rise of televised minority sports,

G.    whereas rising costs increase the probability that exclusive rights to transmit major sports events, such as the Olympics or the World Football Championship, may be attributed to commercial broadcasters that operate subscription channels or that do not have universal reach in the country where they are licensed,

H.    whereas, should this happen, the broadcasting of major sports events could only be-

---

* The full texts of documents which are marked with an asterisk (*) are not incorporated in the book itself, but are freely accessible on the website of the ASSER International Sports Law Centre, at <www.sportslaw.nl> – documentation.

    [9] OJ C 166, 10-6-1996, p. 109.

come accessible to those citizens of the Union who have access to channels only available on subscription or in certain parts of their country and not in others,

I.    whereas public service channels in most EU Member States have a specific obligation to ensure that the broadcasting of major sports events reaches free-to-air all the population,

J.    whereas general-interest private non-encrypted channels also have the purpose of safeguarding the broadcasting of such sp orts events,

K.    whereas the European Broadcasting Union, through the contract signed with the International Olympic Committee, has succeeded in guaranteeing free-to- air broadcasting, accessible to the whole population, until 2008, also enabling future applicant cities to prepare their bids on sounder and more practical bases and enhancing the financial stability of all members of the Olympic movement for the coming years,

L.    whereas an extremely high bid had been made for exclusive rights to the retransmission in Europe of Summer and Winter Olympic Games in the years 2000 to 2008 by an operator of pay-TV channels,

*The European Parliament,*

1.    Considers it essential for all spectators to have a right of access to major sports events, just as they have a right to information;

2.    Welcomes the decision of the International Olympic Committee which reflects its concern that the democratic, widespread and charge-free broadcasting of sports events should prevail over purely commercial considerations;

3.    Considers that increased revenue from broadcasting rights has greatly contributed to promoting sports in general and to improving facilities available to athletes at all levels of performance;

4.    Welcomes the amendment of 6 February 1996 to the UK Broadcasting Bill which guarantees that the broadcasting of sports events of general interest is not the exclusive preserve of pay-TV but is part of the service offered by channels with general coverage in the country;

5.    Considers that exclusive broadcasting rights for certain sports events which are of general interest in one or more Member States must be granted to channels which broadcast in non-encrypted form so that these events remain accessible to the population a s a whole;

6.    Emphasises that the news media have a right to free news gathering and the public a right to adequate and rapid information, and that holders of 'exclusive broadcasting rights' should not therefore prevent other TV broadcasters from showing excerpts from or summaries of events in which there is a great public interest by demanding payment beyond that required to cover costs or by making stipulations as to the time of the broadcast; therefore calls upon the Commission to draw up proposals for legislation, and to devise a competition policy, which limit the exclusive nature of broadcasting rights for sporting contests and other public events as set out above;

7.    Considers it advisable for radio and television coverage of such events not to be the exclusive prerogative of State concerns but to be open to private stations that provide guarantees of pluralism, economic reliability, technical efficiency and transmission coverage in keeping with the requirements laid down in this resolution and in line with the principles underlying a public service;

8.    Considers it the duty of the European Union to identify appropriate monitoring and intervention mechanisms to prevent the emergence, with respect to the negotiations on radio an d television rights, of a speculative market in sports events of general

interest that conflicts with the rules of pluralism, free movement, competition and equal opportunities enshrined in the Treaty on European Union;

9. Considers that, to promote competition and maximise public access to sport, different transmission rights to the same event should not be sold to a single broadcaster in one package but unbundled and put on the market separately (e.g. live television coverage of an event separate from television highlights and radio transmission rights);

10. Requests that where the broadcasting rights for national sports events have been acquired at national level, these events should actually be broadcast throughout the territory of the country in question;

11. Requests that where the broadcasting rights for a sports event are granted to an encrypted channel, this channel should be obliged to make available, in return for a reasonable fee, extracts of this event to other channels which express an interest;

12. Instructs its President to forward this resolution to the Commission and the governments and parliaments of the Member States.

———

## 2.2.2. DIRECTIVE 97/36/EC OF THE EUROPEAN PARLIAMENT AND OF THE COUNCIL AMENDING COUNCIL DIRECTIVE 89/552/EEC ON THE COORDINATION OF CERTAIN PROVISIONS LAID DOWN BY LAW, REGULATION OR ADMINISTRATIVE ACTION IN MEMBER STATES CONCERNING THE PURSUIT OF TELEVISION BROADCASTING ACTIVITIES, 30 JUNE 1997 ('TELEVISION WITHOUT FRONTIERS')[10]

*The European Parliament and the Council of the European Union,*

– Having regard to the Treaty establishing the European Community, and in particular Articles 57(2) and 66 thereof,
– Having regard to the proposal from the Commission[11],
– Having regard to the opinion of the Economic and Social Committee[12],
– Acting in accordance with the procedure laid down in Article 189b of the Treaty[13] in the light of the joint text approved by the Conciliation Committee on 16 April 1997,

(1) Whereas Council Directive 89/552/EEC[14] constitutes the legal framework for television broadcasting in the internal market;

(2) Whereas Article 26 of Directive 89/552/EEC states that the Commission shall, not later than the end of the fifth year after the date of adoption of the Directive, submit to the European Parliament, the Council and the Economic and Social Committee a report on the application of the Directive and, if necessary, make further proposals to adapt it to developments in the field of television broadcasting;

---

[10] OJ L 202, 30-7-1997, p. 60-70.
[11] OJ C 185, 19-7-1995, p. 4 and OJ C 221, 30-7-1996, p. 10.
[12] OJ C 301, 13-11-1995, p. 35.
[13] Opinion of the European Parliament of 14-2-1996 (OJ C 65, 4-3-1996, p. 113). Council Common Position of 18-7-1996 (OJ C 264, 11-9-1996, p. 52) and Decision of the European Parliament of 12-11-1996 (OJ C 362, 2-12-1996, p. 56). Decision of the European Parliament of 10-6-1997 and Decision of the Council of 19-6-1997.
[14] OJ L 298, 17-10-1989, p. 23. Directive as amended by the 1994 Act of Accession.

(3)    Whereas the application of Directive 89/552/EEC and the report on its application have revealed the need to clarify certain definitions or obligations on Member States under this Directive;

(4)    Whereas the Commission, in its communication of 19 July 1994 entitled 'Europe's way to the information society: an action plan', underlined the importance of a regulatory framework applying to the content of audiovisual services which would help to safeguard the free movement of such services in the Community and be responsive to the opportunities for growth in this sector opened up by new technologies, while at the same time taking into account the specific nature, in particular the cultural and sociological impact, of audiovisual programmes, whatever their mode of transmission;

(5)    Whereas the Council welcomed this action plan at its meeting of 28 September 1994 and stressed the need to improve the competitiveness of the European audiovisual industry;

(6)    Whereas the Commission has submitted a Green Paper on the Protection of Minors and Human Dignity in audiovisual and information services and has undertaken to submit a Green Paper focusing on developing the cultural aspects of these new services;

(7)    Whereas any legislative framework concerning new audiovisual services must be compatible with the primary objective of this Directive which is to create the legal framework for the free movement of services;

(8)    Whereas it is essential that the Member States should take action with regard to services comparable to television broadcasting in order to prevent any breach of the fundamental principles which must govern information and the emergence of wide disparities as regards free movement and competition;

(9)    Whereas the Heads of State and Government meeting at the European Council in Essen on 9 and 10 December 1994 called on the Commission to present a proposal for a revision of Directive 89/552/EEC before their next meeting;

(10)   Whereas the application of Directive 89/552/EEC has revealed the need to clarify the concept of jurisdiction as applied specifically to the audiovisual sector; whereas, in view of the case law of the Court of Justice of the European Communities, the establishment criterion should be made the principal criterion determining the jurisdiction of a particular Member State;

(11)   Whereas the concept of establishment, according to the criteria laid down by the Court of Justice in its judgment of 25 July 1991 in the Factortame case[15], involves the actual pursuit of an economic activity through a fixed establishment for an indefinite period;

(12)   Whereas the establishment of a television broadcasting organization may be determined by a series of practical criteria such as the location of the head office of the provider of services, the place where decisions on programming policy are usually taken, the place where the programma to be broadcast to the public is finally mixed and processed, and the place where a significant proportion of the workforce required for the pursuit of the television broadcasting activity is located;

(13)   Whereas the fixing of a series of practical criteria is designed to determine by an exhaustive procedure that one Member State and one only has jurisdiction over a broadcaster in connection with the provision of the services which this Directive addresses; nevertheless, taking into account the case law of the Court of Justice and so as to avoid cases where there is a vacuum of jurisdiction it is appropriate to refer to

[15] Case C-221/89, Queen v. Secretary of State for Transport, ex parte Factortame Ltd. and Others, (1991) ECR 1-3905, paragraph 20.

the criterion of establishment within the meaning of Articles 52 and following of the Treaty establishing the European Community as the final criterion determining the jurisdiction of a Member State;

(14) Whereas the Court of Justice has constantly held[16] that a Member State retains the right to take measures against a television broadcasting organization that is established in another Member State but directs all or most of its activity to the territory of the first Member State if the choice of establishment was made with a view to evading the legislation that would have applied to the organization had it been established on the territory of the first Member State;

(15) Whereas Article F(2) of the Treaty on European Union stipulates that the Union shall respect fundamental rights as guaranteed by the European Convention for the Protection of Human Rights and Fundamental Freedoms as general principles of Community law; whereas any measure aimed at restricting the reception and/or suspending the retransmission of television broadcasts taken under Article 2a of Directive 89/552/EEC as amended by this Directive must be compatible with such principles;

(16) Whereas it is necessary to ensure the effective application of the provisions of Directive 89/552/EEC as amended by this Directive throughout the Community in order to preserve free and fair competition between firms in the same industry;

(17) Whereas directly affected third parties, including nationals of other Member States, must be able to assert their rights, according to national law, before competent judicial or other authorities of the Member State with jurisdiction over the television broadcasting organization that may be failing to comply with the national provisions arising out of the application of Directive 89/552/EEC as amended by this Directive;

(18) Whereas it is essential that Member States should be able to take measures to protect the right to information and to ensure wide access by the public to television coverage of national or non-national events of major importance for society, such as the Olympic games, the football World Cup and European football championship; whereas to this end Member States retain the right to take measures compatible with Community law aimed at regulating the exercise by broadcasters under their jurisdiction of exclusive broadcasting rights to such events;

(19) Whereas it is necessary to make arrangements within a Community framework, in order to avoid potential legal uncertainty and market distortions and to reconcile free circulation of television services with the need to prevent the possibility of circumvention of national measures protecting a legitimate general interest;

(20) Whereas, in particular, it is appropriate to lay down in this Directive provisions concerning the exercise by broadcasters of exclusive broadcasting rights that they may have purchased to events considered to be of major importance for society in a Member State other than that having jurisdiction over the broadcasters, and whereas, in order to avoid speculative rights purchases with a view to circumvention of national measures, it is necessary to apply these provisions to contracts entered into after the publication of this Directive and concerning events which take place after the date of implementation, and whereas, when contracts that predate the publication of this Directive are renewed, they are considered to be new contracts;

(21) Whereas events of major importance for society should, for the purposes of this Directive, meet certain criteria, that is to say be outstanding events which are of inter-

---

[16] See, in particular, the judgments in Case 33/74, Van Binsbergen v. Bestuur van de Bedrijfsvereniging, (1974) ECR 1299 and in Case C-23/93, TV 10 SA v. Commissariaat voor de Media, (1994) ECR 1-4795.

est to the general public in the European Union or in a given Member State or in an important component part of a given Member State and are organized in advance by an event organizer who is legally entitled to sell the rights pertaining to that event;

(22) Whereas, for the purposes of this Directive, 'free television' means broadcasting on a channel, either public or commercial, of programmes which are accessible to the public without payment in addition to the modes of funding of broadcasting that are widely prevailing in each Member State (such as licence fee and/or the basic tier subscription fee to a cable network);

(23) Whereas Member States are free to take whatever measures they deem appropriate with regard to broadcasts which come from third countries and which do not satisfy the conditions laid down in Article 2 of Directive 891552/EEC as amended by this Directive, provided they comply with Community law and the international obligations of the Community;

(24) Whereas in order to eliminate the obstacles arising from differences in national legislation on the promotion of European works, Directive 89/552/EEC as amended by this Directive contains provisions aimed at harmonizing such legislation; whereas those provisions which, in general, seek to liberalize trade must contain clauses harmonizing the conditions of competition;

(25) Whereas, moreover, Article 128(4) of the Treaty establishing the European Community requires the Community to take cultural aspects into account in its action under other provisions of the Treaty;

(26) Whereas the Green Paper on 'strategy options to strengthen the European programma industry in the context of the audiovisual policy of the European Union', adopted by the Commission on 7 April 1994, puts forward inter alia measures to promote European works in order to further the development of the sector; whereas the Media II programma, which seeks to promote training, development and distribution in the audiovisual sector, is also designed to enable the production of European works to be developed; whereas the Commission has proposed that production of European works should also be promoted by a Community mechanism such as a Guarantee Fund;

(27) Whereas broadcasting organizations, programma makers, producers, authors and other experts should be encouraged to develop more detailed concepts and strategies aimed at developing European audiovisual fiction films that are addressed to an international audience;

(28) Whereas, in addition to the considerations cited above, it is necessary to create conditions for improving the competitiveness of the programme industry; whereas the communications on the application of Articles 4 and 5 of Directive 89/552/EEC, adopted by the Commission on 3 March 1994 and 15 July 1996 pursuant to Article 4(3) of that Directive, draw the conclusion that measures to promote European works can contribute to such an improvement but that they need to take account of developments in the field of television broadcasting;

(29) Whereas channels broadcasting entirely in a language other than those of the Member States should not be covered by the provisions of Articles 4 and 5; whereas, nevertheless, where such a language or languages represent a substantial part but not all of the channel's transmission time, the provisions of Articles 4 and 5 should not apply to that part of transmission time;

(30) Whereas the proportions of European works must be achieved taking economic realities into account; whereas, therefore, a progressive system for achieving this objective is required;

(31) Whereas, with a view to promoting the production of European works, it is essential that the Community, taking into account the audiovisual capacity of each Member

State and the need to protect lesser used languages of the European Union, should promote independent producers; whereas Member States, in defining the notion of 'independent producer', should take appropriate account of criteria such as the ownership of the production company, the amount of programmes supplied to the same broadcaster and the ownership of secondary rights;

(32) Whereas the question of specific time scales for each type of television showing of cinematographic works is primarily a matter to be settled by means of agreements between the interested parties or professionals concerned;

(33) Whereas advertising for medicinal products for human use is subject to the provisions of Directive 92/28/EEC[17];

(34) Whereas daily transmission time allotted to announcements made by the broadcaster in connection with its own programmes and ancillary products directly derived from these, or to public service announcements and charity appeals broadcast free of charge, is not to be included in the maximum amounts of daily or hourly transmission time that may be allotted to advertising and teleshopping;

(35) Whereas, in order to avoid distortions of competition, this derogation is limited to announcements concerning products that fulfil the dual condition of being both ancillary to and directly derived from the programmes concerned; whereas the term ancillary refers to products intended specifically to allow the viewing public to benefit fully from or to interact with these programmes;

(36) Whereas in view of the development of teleshopping, an economically important activity for operators as a whole and a genuine outlet for goods and services within the Community, it is essential to modify the rules on transmission time and to ensure a high level of consumer protection by putting in place appropriate standards regulating the form and content of such broadcasts;

(37) Whereas it is important for the competent national authorities, in monitoring the implementation of the relevant provisions, to be able to distinguish, as regards channels not exclusively devoted to teleshopping, between transmission time devoted to teleshopping spots, advertising spots and other forms of advertising on the one hand and, on the other, transmission time devoted to teleshopping windows; whereas it is therefore necessary and sufficient that each window be clearly identified by optical and acoustic means at least at the beginning and the end of the window;

(38) Whereas Directive 89/552/EEC as amended by this Directive applies to channels exclusively devoted to teleshopping or self-promotion without conventional programma elements such as news, sports, films, documentaries and drama, solely for the purposes of these Directives and without prejudice to the inclusion of such channels in the scope of other Community instruments;

(39) Whereas it is necessary to make clear that self-promotional activities are a particular form of advertising in which the broadcaster promotes its own products, services, programmes or channels; whereas, in particular, trailers consisting of extracts from programmes should be treated as programmes; whereas selfpromotion is a new and relatively unknown phenomenon and provisions concerning it may therefore be particularly subject to review in future examinations of this Directive;

(40) Whereas it is necessary to clarify the rules for the protection of the physical, mental and moral development of minors; whereas the establishment of a clear distinction between programmes that are subject to an absolute ban and those that may be authorized subject to the use of appropriate technical means should satisfy concern about the public interest expressed by Member States and the Community;

---

[17] OJ L 113, 30-4-1992, p. 13.

(41) Whereas none of the provisions of this Directive that concern the protection of minors and public order requires that the measures in question must necessarily be implemented through the prior control of television broadcasts;

(42) Whereas an investigation by the Commission, in liaison with the competent Member State authorities, of the possible advantages and drawbacks of further measures to facilitate the control exercised by parents or guardians over the programmes that minors may watch shall consider, inter alia, the desirability of:
- the requirement for new television sets to be equipped with a technical device enabling parents or guardians to filter out certain programmes,
- the setting up of appropriate rating systems,
- encouraging family viewing policies and other educational and awareness measures,
- taking into account experience gained in this field in Europe and elsewhere as well as the views of interested parties such as broadcasters, producers, educationalists, media specialists and relevant associations, with a view to presenting, if necessary before the deadline laid down in Article 26, appropriate proposals for legislative or other measures;

(43) Whereas it is appropriate to amend Directive 89/552/EEC to allow natural or legal persons whose activities include the manufacture or the sale of medicinal products and medical treatment available only on prescription to sponsor television programmes, provided that such sponsorship does not circumvent the prohibition of television advertising for medicinal products and medical treatment available only on prescription;

(44) Whereas the approach in Directive 89/552/EEC and this Directive has been adopted to achieve the essential harmonization necessary and sufficient to ensure the free movement of television broadcasts in the Community; whereas Member States remain free to apply to broadcasters under their jurisdiction more detailed or stricter rules in the fields coordinated by this Directive, including, inter alia, rules concerning the achievement of language policy goals, protection of the public interest in terms of television's role as a provider of information, education, culture and entertainment, the need to safeguard pluralism in the information industry and the media, and the protection of competition with a view to avoiding the abuse of dominant positions and/or the establishment or strengthening of dominant positions by mergers, agreements, acquisitions or similar initiatives;
whereas such rules must be compatible with Community law;

(45) Whereas the objective of supporting audiovisual production in Europe can be pursued within the Member States in the framework of the organization of their broadcasting services, inter alia, through the definition of a public interest mission for certain broadcasting organizations, including the obligation to contribute substantially to investment in European production;

(46) Whereas Article 8 of the Treaty on European Union states that one of the objectives the Union shall set itself is to maintain in full the 'acquis communautaire',

Have adopted this directive:

Article 1
Directive 89/552/EEC is hereby amended as follows:
1.    in Article 1:
      (a)    the following new point (b) shall be inserted:
             '(b)   'broadcaster' means the natural or legal person who has editorial responsibility for the composition of schedules of television programmes

within the meaning of (a) and who transmits them or has them transmitted by third parties; '

(b)    the former point (b) shall become point (c) and shall read as follows: '(c) 'television advertising' means any form of announcement broadcast whether in return for payment or for similar consideration or broadcast for selfpromotional purposes by a public or private undertaking in connection with a trade, business, craft or profession in order to promote the supply of goods or services, including immovable property, rights and obligations, in return for payment; '

(c)    the former points (c) and (d) shall become points (d) and (e);

(d)    the following point shall be added:
       '(f) 'teleshopping' means direct offers broadcast to the public with a view to the supply of goods or services, including immovable property, rights and obligations, in return for payment.';

2.    Article 2 shall be replaced by the following:
'Article 2

1.    Each Member State shall ensure that all television broadcasts transmitted by broadcasters under its jurisdiction comply with the rules of the system of law applicable to broadcasts intended for the public in that Member State.

2.    For the purposes of this Directive the broadcasters under the jurisdiction of a Member State are:
      –    those established in that Member State in accordance with paragraph 3;
      –    those to whom paragraph 4 applies.

3.    For the purposes of this Directive, a broadcaster shall be deemed to be established in a Member State in the following cases:
      (a)    the broadcaster has its head office in that Member State and the editorial decisions about programma schedules are taken in that Member State;
      (b)    if a broadcaster has its head office in one Member State but editorial decisions on programma schedules are taken in another Member State, it shall be deemed to be established in the Member State where a significant part of the workforce involved in the pursuit of the television broadcasting activity operates; if a significant part of the workforce involved in the pursuit of the television broadcasting activity operates in each of those Member States, the broadcaster shall be deemed to be established in the Member State where it has its head office; if a significant part of the workforce involved in the pursuit of the television broadcasting activity operates in neither of those Member States, the broadcaster shall be deemed to be established in the Member State where it first began broadcasting in accordance with the system of law of that Member State, provided that it maintains a stable and effective link with the economy of that Member State;
      (c)    if a broadcaster has its head office in a Member State but decisions on programme schedules are taken in a third country, or vice-versa, it shall be deemed to be established in the Member State concerned, provided that a significant part of the workforce involved in the pursuit of the broadcasting activity operates in that Member State.

4.    Broadcasters to whom the provisions of paragraph 3 are not applicable shall be deemed to be under the jurisdiction of a Member State in the following cases:
      (a)    they use a frequency granted by that Member State;

(b)      although they do not use a frequency granted by a Member State they do use a satellite capacity appertaining to that Member State;

(c)      although they use neither a frequency granted by a Member State nor a satellite capacity appertaining to a Member State they do use a satellite up-link situated in that Member State.

5.      If the question as to which Member State has jurisdiction cannot be determined in accordance with paragraphs 3 and 4, the competent Member State shall be that in which the broadcaster is established within the meaning of Articles 52 and following of the Treaty establishing the European Community.

6.      This Directive shall not apply to broadcasts intended exclusively for reception in third countries, and which are not received directly or indirectly by the public in one or more Member States.';

3.      the following Article shall be inserted:

'Article 2a

1.      Member States shall ensure freedom of reception and shall not restrict retransmissions on their territory of television broadcasts from other Member States for reasons which fall within the fields coordinated by this Directive. 2. Member States may, provisionally, derogate from paragraph 1 if the following conditions are fulfilled:

(a)      a television broadcast coming from another Member State manifestly, seriously and gravely infringes Article 22 (1) or (2) and/or Article 22a;

(b)      during the previous 12 months, the broadcaster has infringed the provision(s) referred to in (a) on at least two prior occasions;

(c)      the Member State concerned has notified the broadcaster and the Commission in writing of the alleged infringements and of the measures it intends to take should any such infringement occur again;

(d)      consultations with the transmitting Member State and the Commission have not produced an amicable settlement within 15 days of the notification provided for in (c), and the alleged infringement persists.

The Commission shall, within two months following notification of the measures taken by the Member State, take a decision on whether the measures are compatible with Community law. If it decides that they are not, the Member State will be required to put an end to the measures in question as a matter of urgency. 3. Paragraph 2 shall be without prejudice to the application of any procedure, remedy or sanction to the infringements in question in the Member State which has jurisdiction over the broadcaster concerned.'

4.      Article 3 shall be replaced by the following:

'Article 3

1.      Member States shall remain free to require television broadcasters under their jurisdiction to comply with more detailed or stricter rules in the areas covered by this Directive.

2.      Member States shall, by appropriate means, ensure, within the framework of their legislation, that television broadcasters under their jurisdiction effectively comply with the provisions of this Directive.

3.      The measures shall include the appropriate procedures for third parties directly affected, including nationals of other Member States, to apply to the competent judicial or other authorities to seek effective compliance according to national provisions.

Article 3a

1.      Each Member State may take measures in accordance with Community law to ensure that broadcasters under its jurisdiction do not broadcast on an exclu-

sive basis events which are regarded by that Member State as being of major importance for society in such a way as to deprive a substantial proportion of the public in that Member State of the possibility of following such events via live coverage or deferred coverage on free television. If it does so, the Member State concerned shall draw up a list of designated events, national or non-national, which it considers to be of major importance for society. It shall do so in a clear and transparent manner in due and effective time. In so doing the Member State concerned shall also determine whether these events should be available via whole or partial live coverage, or where necessary or appropriate for objective reasons in the public interest, whole or partial deferred coverage.

2. Member States shall immediately notify to the Commission any measures taken or to be taken pursuant to paragraph 1. Within a period of three months from the notification, the Commission shall verify that such measures are compatible with Community law and communicate them to the other Member States. It shall seek the opinion of the Committee established pursuant to Article 23a. It shall forthwith publish the measures taken in the Official Journal of the European Communities and at least once a year the consolidated list of the measures taken by Member States.

3. Member States shall ensure, by appropriate means, within the framework of their legislation that broadcasters under their jurisdiction do not exercise the exclusive rights purchased by those broadcasters following the date of publication of this Directive in such a way that a substantial proportion of the public in another Member State is deprived of the possibility of following events which are designated by that other Member State in accordance with the preceding paragraphs via whole or partial live coverage or, where necessary or appropriate for objective reasons in the public interest, whole or partial deferred coverage on free television as determined by that other Member State in accordance with paragraph 1.';

5. in Article 4(1), the words 'and teletext services' shall be replaced by the words 'teletext services and teleshopping';

6. in Article 5, the words 'and teletext services' shall be replaced by the words 'teletext services and teleshopping';

7. Article 6 shall be amended as follows:

(a) paragraph 1 (a) shall be replaced by the following:
'(a) works originating from Member States;'

(b) in paragraph 1, the following subparagraph shall be added:
'Application of the provisions of (b) and (c) shall be conditional on works originating from Member States not being the subject of discriminatory measures in the third countries concerned.';

(c) paragraph 3 shall be replaced by the following:
'3. The works referred to in paragraph 1 (c) are works made exclusively or in coproduction with producers established in one or more Member States by producers established in one or more European third countries with which the Community has concluded agreements relating to the audiovisual sector, if those works are mainly made with authors and workers residing in one or more European States.';

(d) paragraph 4 shall become paragraph 5 and the following paragraph shall be inserted:
'4. Works that are not European works within the meaning of paragraph 1 but that are Produced within the framework of bilateral

co-production treaties concluded between Member States and third countries shall be deemed to be European works provided that the Community co-producers supply a majority share of the total cost of the production and that the production is not controlled by one or more producers established outside the territory of the Member States.';

(e)  in the new paragraph 5, the words 'paragraph 1' shall be replaced by the words 'paragraphs 1 and 4';

8.   Article 7 shall be replaced by the following:
'Article 7
Member States shall ensure that broadcasters under theirjurisdiction do not broadcast cinematographic works outside periods agreed with the rights holders.';

9.   Article 8 shall be deleted;

10.  Article 9 shall be replaced by the following:
'Article 9
This Chapter shall not apply to television broadcasts that are intended for local audiences and do not form part of a national network.';

11.  the title of Chapter IV shall be replaced by the following:
'Television advertising, sponsorship and teleshopping'.

12.  Article 10 shall be replaced by the following:
'Article 10
1.   Television advertising and teleshopping shall be readily recognizable as such and kept quite separate from other parts of the programma service by optical and/or acoustic means.
2.   Isolated advertising and teleshopping spots shall remain the exception.
3.   Advertising and teleshopping shall not use subliminal techniques.
4.   Surreptitious advertising and teleshopping shall be prohibited.';

13.  Article 11 shall be replaced by the following:
'Article 11
1.   Advertising and teleshopping spots shall be inserted between programmes. Provided the conditions set out in paragraphs 2 to 5 are fulfilled, advertising and teleshopping spots may also be inserted during programmes in such a way that the integrity and value of the programme, taking into account natural breaks in and the duration and nature of the programma, and the rights of the rights holders are not prejudiced.
2.   In programmes consisting of autonomous parts, or in sports programmes and similarly structured events and performances containing intervals, advertising and teleshopping spots shall only be inserted between the parts or in the intervals.
3.   The transmission of audiovisual works such as feature films and films made for television (excluding series, serials, light entertainment programmes and documentaries), provided their scheduled duration is more than 45 minutes, may be interrupted once lor each period of 45 minutes. A further interruption shall be allowed if their scheduled duration is at least 20 minutes longer than two or more complete periods of 45 minutes.
4.   Where programmes, other than those covered by paragraph 2, are interrupted by advertising or teleshopping spots, a period of at least 20 minutes should elapse between each successive advertising break within the programma.
5.   Advertising and teleshopping shall not be inserted in any broadcast of a religious service. News and current affairs programmes, documentaries, religious programmes and children's programmes, when their scheduled duration is

less than 30 minutes, shall not be interrupted by advertising or by teleshopping. If their scheduled duration is 30 minutes or longer, the provisions of the previous paragraphs shall apply.';

14. in Article 12, the introductory words shall be replaced by the following: 'Television advertising and teleshopping shall not:';

15. Article 13 shall be replaced by the following: 'Article 13 All forms of television advertising and teleshopping tor cigarettes and other tobacco products shall be prohibited.';

16. in Article 14, the present text shall become paragraph 1 and the following paragraph shall be added:
    '2.    Teleshopping for medicinal products which are subject to a marketing authorization within the meaning of Council Directive 65/65/EEC of 26 January 1965 on the approximation of provisions laid down by law, regulation or administrative action relating to medicinal products[18], as well as teleshopping for medical treatment, shall be prohibited;

17. in Article 15, the introductory words shall be replaced by the following: 'Television advertising and teleshopping for alcoholic beverages shall comply with the following criteria:';

18. in Article 16, the present text shall become paragraph 1 and the following paragraph shall be added:
    '2.    Teleshopping shall comply with the requirements referred to in paragraph 1 and, in addition, shall not exhort n-linors to contract for the sale or rental of goods and services.';

19. Article 17 shall be amended as follows:
    (a)   paragraph 2 shall be replaced by the following:
          '2.    Television programmes may not be sponsored by undertakings whose principal activity is the manufacture or sale of cigarettes and other tobacco products.';
    (b)   paragraph 3 shall become paragraph 4 and the following paragraph shall be inserted:
          '3.    Sponsorship of television programmes by undertakings whose activities include the manufacture or sale of medicinal products and medical treatment may promote the name or the image of the undertaking but may not promote specific medicinal products or medical treatments available only on prescription in the Member State within whose jurisdiction the broadcaster falls.';

20. Article 18 shall be replaced by the following:
    'Article 18
    1.    The proportion of transmission time devoted to teleshopping spots, advertising spots and other forms of advertising, with the exception of teleshopping windows within the meaning of Article 18a, shall not exceed 20% of the daily trans'ssion time. The transmission time for advertising spots shall not exceed 15% of the daily transmission time.
    2.    The proportion of advertising spots and teleshopping spots within a given clock hour shall not exceed 20%.
    3.    For the purposes of this Article, advertising does not include:
          –     announcements made by the broadcaster in connection with its own

---

[18] OJ 22, 9-2-1965, p. 369. Directive as last amended by Directive 93/39/EEC (OJ L 214, 24-8-1993, p. 22).

      programmes and ancillary products directly derived from those pro-
      grammes;

      –   public service announcements and charity appeals broadcast free of
          charge.';

21.   the following Article shall be inserted:

'Article 18a

1.   Windows devoted to teleshopping broadcast by a channel not exclusively de-
     voted to teleshopping shall be of a minimum uninterrupted duration of 15 min-
     utes.

2.   The maximum number of windows per day shall be eight. Their overall dura-
     tion shall not exceed three hours per day. They must be clearly identified as
     teleshopping windows by optical and acoustic means.';

22.   Article 19 shall be replaced by the following:

'Article 19

Chapters 1, 11, IV, V, VI, VIa and VII shall apply mutatis mutandis to channels exclusively devoted to teleshopping. Advertising on such channels shall be allowed
within the daily limits established by Article 18(1). Article 18(2) shall not apply.';

23.   the following Article shall be inserted:

'Article 19a

Chapters I, II, IV, V, VI, VIa and VII shall apply mutatis mutandis to channels exclusively devoted to self-promotion. Other forms of advertising on such channels
shall be allowed within the limits established by Article 18 (1) and (2). This provision in particular shall be subject to review in accordance with Article 26.';

24.   Article 20 shall be replaced by the following:

'Article 20

Without prejudice to Article 3, Member States may, with due regard for Community
law, lay down conditions other than those laid down in Article 11(2) to (5) and Articles 18 and 18a in respect of broadcasts intended solely for the national territory
which cannot be received, directly or indirectly by the public, in one or more other
Member States.';

25.   Article 21 shall be deleted.

26.   the title of Chapter V shall be replaced by the following:

'Protection of minors and public order';

27.   Article 22 shall be replaced by the following:

'Article 22

1.   Member States shall take appropriate measures to ensure that television broad-
     casts by broadcasters under their jurisdiction do not include any programmes
     which might seriously impair the physical, mental or moral development of
     'nors, in particular programmes that involve pornography or gratuitous vio-
     lence.

2.   The measures provided for in paragraph 1 shall also extend to other pro-
     grammes which are likely to impair the physical, mental or moral development
     of minors, except where it is ensured, by selecting the time of the broadcast or
     by any technical measure, that minors in the area of transmission will not nor-
     mally hear or see such broadcasts.

3.   Furthermore, when such programmes are broadcast in unencoded form Member
     States shall ensure that they are preceded by an acoustic warning or are identi-
     fied by the presence of a visual symbol throughout their duration.';

28.   the following Article shall be inserted:

'Article 22a

Member States shall ensure that broadcasts do not contain any incitement to hatred
on grounds of race, sex, religion or nationality.';

29. the following Article shall be inserted:
    'Article 22b
    1. The Commission shall attach particular importance to application of this Chapter in the report provided for in Article 26.
    2. The Commission shall within one year from the date of publication of this Directive, in liaison with the competent Member State authorities, carry out an investigation of the possible advantages and drawbacks of further measures with a view to facilitating the control exercised by parents or guardians over the programmes that minors may watch. This study shall consider, inter alia, the desirability of:
       – the requirement for new television sets to be equipped with a technical device enabling parents or guardians to filter out certain programmes;
       – the setting up of appropriate rating systems,
       – encouraging family viewing policies and other educational and awareness measures,
       – taking into account experience gained in this field in Europe and elsewhere as well as the views of interested parties such as broadcasters, producers, educationalists, media specialists and relevant associations. 1;
       30. Article 23 (1) shall be replaced by the following:
       '1. Without prejudice to other Provisions adopted by the Member States under civil, administrative or criminal law, any natural or legal person, regardless of nationality, whose legitimate interests, in particular reputation and good name, have been damaged by an assertion of incorrect facts in a television Programme must have a right of reply or equivalent remedies. Member States shall ensure that the actual exercise of the right of reply or equivalent remedies is not hindered by the imposition of unreasonable terins or conditions. The reply shall be transmitted within a reasonable time subsequent to the request being substantiated and at a time and in a manner appropriate to the broadcast to which the request refers.';

31. after Article 23, the following new Chapter VIa shall be inserted:
    'CHAPTER VIa
    Contact committee
    Article 23a
    1. A contact committee shall be set up under the aegis of the Commission. It shall be composed of representatives of the competent authorities of the Member States.
       It shall be chaired by a representative of the Commission and meet either on his initiative or at the request of the delegation of a Member State.
    2. The tasks of this committee shall be:
       (a) to facilitate effective implementation of this Directive through regular consultation on any practical problems arising from its application, and particularly from the application of Article 2, as well as on any other matters on which exchanges of views are deemed useful;
       (b) to deliver own-initiative opinions or opinions requested by the Commission on the application by the Member States of the provisions of this Directive;
       (c) to be the forum for an exchange of views on what matters should be dealt with in the reports which Member States must submit pursuant to Article 4 (3), on the methodology of these, on the terras of reference for the independent study referred to in Article 25a, on the evaluation of

tenders for this and on the study itself; (d) to discuss the outcome of regular consultations which the Commission holds with representatives of broadcasting organizations, producers, consumers, manufacturers, service providers and trade unions and the creative community; (e) to facilitate the exchange of information between the Member States and the Commission on the situation and the development of regulatory activities regarding television broadcasting services, taking account of the Community's audiovisual policy, as well as relevant developments in the technical field; (f) to examine any development arising in the sector on which an exchange of views appears useful.';

32.   the following Article shall be inserted:
'Article 25a
A further review as provided for in Article 4(4) shall take place before 30 June 2002. It shall take account of an independent study on the impact of the measures in question at both Community and national level.';

33.   Article 26 shall be replaced by the following:
'Article 26
Not later than 31 December 2000, and every two years thereafter, the Commission shall submit to the European Parliament, the Council and the Economic and Social Committee a report on the application of this Directive as amended and, if necessary, make further proposals to adapt it to developments in the field of television broadcasting, in particular in the light of recent technological developments.'

Article 2
1.   Member States shall bring into force the laws, regulations and administrative provisions necessary to comply with this Directive not later than 31 December 1998. They shall immediately inform the Commission thereof.
When Member States adopt these measures, they shall contain a reference to this Directive or be accompanied by such reference on the occasion of their official States. publication. The methods of making such reference shall be laid down by Member States.,
2.   Member States shall communicate to the Commission the text of the main provisions of national law which they adopt in the field covered by this Directive.

Article 3
This Directive shall enter into force on the date of its publication in the Official Journal of the European Communities.

Article 4
This Directive is addressed to the Member States.

Done at Luxembourg, 30 June 1997. For the Parliament
The President
J.M. Gil-Robles
For the Council
The President
A. Nuis

### 2.2.3. RESOLUTION OF THE COMMITTEE OF THE REGIONS ON THE BROADCASTING RIGHTS OF MAJOR SPORT EVENTS, 17 SEPTEMBER 1997[19]

*The committee of the regions,*

– having regard to its decision on 11 June 1997 under the fourth paragraph of Article 198c of the Treaty establishing the European Community, to draw up a resolution on the subject and to instruct Subcommission 7 – Youth and Sport – to draw up the resolution;

– having regard to the draft resolution (CdR 183/97 rev.) adopted by Subcommission 7 on 11 July 1997 (rapporteurs: Mrs Bolger, Mr Bellotti);

– having regard to the Council Directive 89/552/EEC on the coordination of certain provisions laid down by law, regulation and administrative action in Member States concerning the pursuit of television broadcasting activities (Television Without Frontiers);[20]

– having regard to Directive 97/36/EEC of the European Parliament and of the Council amending Council Directive 89/552/EEC on the coordination of certain provisions laid down by law, regulation or administrative action in Member States concerning the pursuit of television broadcasting activities;[21]

– having regard to the Commission Communication on the initiative of Commissioner Oreja on exclusive rights for television broadcasting of major sports events;[22]

– having regard to Resolution EP No B4-0326/96 regarding retransmission of major sporting events, adopted on 22 May 1996;

– having regard to the EP Report and Resolution on Public Service Broadcasting adopted on 19 September 1996 (paragraphs 21 and 22 of EP document No A4-0243/96);

– having regard to the EP Report on the role of the EU in the field of sport, adopted on 13 June 1997, No A4-0197/97;

– having regard to the issues arising from the debates of the Sixth European Sports Forum organized by the Commission on 16 and 17 December 1996 in Brussels;

– whereas the citizens of Europe have an inalienable right to access to culture and to affirm and express their national or regional cultural identity;

– whereas the issue of public access to broadcasts of major sporting events has wide cultural, economic and commercial implications;

– whereas the Council Directive 89/552/EEC (Television Without Frontiers), which is based on Articles 57(2) and 66 of the Treaty, aims to produce an instrument that can provide the legal framework conducive to ensuring the free movement of broadcast services within the Union until the end of the century and beyond;

– whereas television is a major source of information for the European citizen, the exercise of exclusive rights for television broadcasts in encrypted form may prove to be detrimental to the right of access of the public to information in one or several countries covered by the broadcaster that holds the exclusive rights;

– whereas it is vital for the pursuit of the public interest and to development of the broadcasting industry in the Union to balance the right of the citizen to public ac-

---

[19]  OJ C 379 , 15-12-1997, p. 67.
[20]  OJ L 298, 17-10-1989, p. 23.
[21]  OJ L 202, 30-7-1997, p. 60.
[22]  SEC(97) 174/9.

cess to events of national importance with the right of 'pay per view' broadcasters to vie for market share;
– whereas the sense of community and citizenship experienced on national or regional days of sporting celebration and add much to the notion of diversity, a notion which the Union is at present striving to promote;
– whereas sport and culture promote personal development, help to bridge regional and national divides and contribute to breaking down social barriers;
– whereas 'events of major importance' for society should meet certain criteria, that is to say be outstanding events which are of interest to the general public in the European Union or in a given Member State or in an important component part of a given Member State and are organized in advance by an event organizer who is legally entitled to sell the rights pertaining to that event;
– whereas the quantity and quality of sports coverage broadcast on television has grown significantly in recent years since the entry of subscription channels distributed via cable or satellite;
– whereas national sporting events have taken on a lucrative commercial value, 'pay-per-view' broadcasters who have secured exclusive rights to many major sporting events, are strategically positioned to earn enormous profits;
– whereas issues relating to sport are not specifically catered for in the Treaty, it must be acknowledged that the economic activity revolving around professional sport must not be exempt from the provisions of Community Law;
– whereas the regional, cultural, economic and social aspects of this issue demand that the Committee of the Regions make a declaration on this issue,
– adopted the following resolution at its 19th plenary session on 17 and 18 September 1997 (meeting of 17 September) unanimously.

The Committee of the Regions
1.  Calls on the Member States to protect the European citizen's inalienable right to access to culture and to affirm and express their regional and national cultural identity through sport.
2.  In Article 10 of the European Convention on Human Rights (ECHR) the public's access to freedom of information is protocoled and seeing sporting events is important to our citizens.
3.  Recommends that any measures put in place to protect public access to major sporting events are consistent with Community law and are proportionate and non-discriminatory. Voluntary agreements between those concerned should be the preferred solution.
4.  Urges Member States to draw up a list of special sporting events that are to be broadcast live on 'free to air' television. This list of events should be drawn up effectively and well in advance in a clear and transparent fashion, as provided for in the Community rules.
    Experts – including regional, national or international representatives of sports associations, 'free to air' and 'pay per view' television broadcasters and government representatives with responsibility for sporting and cultural affairs in the Member States – should be consulted beforehand. It should also be ensured that appropriate sanctions are applied for violations of national rules.
5.  Proposes that Member States provide for a periodic review of the list of events of major importance to society, thus allowing for additions or withdrawals of events from the list over time.
6.  Calls on the Member States to take account of distinctive regional interest when deciding on the events deemed to be of major importance to society and in so doing,

the Member States will promote the principles of diversity and inclusiveness. This approach is wholly consistent with the principle of subsidiarity since Member States retain competence to decide what events are of importance to their populations.

7. Calls on the Member States to keep restrictive practices to a minimum when deciding upon measures to protect free access to events of major importance.

8. Calls on the Member States to ensure that, where primary or exclusive rights to a sporting event have been agreed, liberal secondary distribution rights are provided for on a transnational basis.

9. Calls on Member States to consider the possibility of enacting national legislation requiring subscription broadcasters to make a contribution to national sports development along with other broadcasting services.

10. Calls on Member States to consider the adoption of legal and technical provisions permitting subscription broadcasters or public franchise holders to broadcast sports events in unencrypted form, even if not with exclusive rights, in limited areas of a region or country if this is in keeping with the prevailing interest of local or regional residents.

11. Urges the Commission to monitor on an annual basis the distribution agreements entered into by broadcasters, sporting bodies and Member States, so as to prevent the emergence of cartels and to ensure that Community competition law is not contravened.

12. Urges the Commission to publish guidelines on the application of Article 3a paragraph 2 of the 'Television Without Frontiers' Directive, in particular on the criteria it will take into account when verifying that the measures notified by the Member States are compatible with Community law; such guidelines should provide predictability for Member States, sports events organizers and broadcasters.

13. Compliments the Commission's stringent efforts to create a balanced regulatory framework, which protects the citizens right to information while concurrently liberalizing distribution rights, in the European broadcasting sector.

Brussels, 17 September 1997.
The Chairman of the Committee of the Regions
Pasqual Maragall i Mira

———

**\* 2.2.4. INFORMATION FROM THE COMMISSION – PUBLICATION PURSUANT TO ARTICLE 3(A)(2) OF COUNCIL DIRECTIVE 89/552/ EC[23] ON THE COORDINATION OF CERTAIN PROVISIONS LAID DOWN BY LAW, REGULATION OR ADMINISTRATIVE ACTION IN MEMBER STATES CONCERNING THE PURSUIT OF TELEVISION BROADCASTING ACTIVITIES, AS AMENDED BY DIRECTIVE 97/36/ EC OF THE EUROPEAN PARLIAMENT AND OF THE COUNCIL, 19 JANUARY 1999[24, 25]**

———

[23] OJ L 298, 17-10-1989, p. 23.
[24] OJ L 202, 30-7-1997, p. 60.
[25] OJ C 14, 19-1-1999, p. 6.

* 2.2.5.    INFORMATION FROM THE COMMISSION – PUBLICATION IN
            ACCORDANCE WITH ARTICLE 3(A)(2) OF COUNCIL DIRECTIVE
            89/552/EEC ON THE COORDINATION OF CERTAIN PROVISIONS
            LAID DOWN BY LAW, REGULATION OR ADMINISTRATIVE
            ACTION IN MEMBER STATES CONCERNING THE PURSUIT OF
            TELEVISION BROADCASTING ACTIVITIES, AS AMENDED BY
            DIRECTIVE 97/36/EC OF THE EUROPEAN PARLIAMENT AND OF
            THE COUNCIL, 30 SEPTEMBER 1999[26]

* 2.2.6.    INFORMATION FROM THE COMMISSION – PUBLICATION
            PURSUANT TO ARTICLE 3(A)(2) OF COUNCIL DIRECTIVE 89/552/
            EEC[27] ON THE COORDINATION OF CERTAIN PROVISIONS LAID
            DOWN BY LAW, REGULATION OR ADMINISTRATIVE ACTION IN
            MEMBER STATES CONCERNING THE PURSUIT OF TELEVISION
            BROADCASTING ACTIVITIES, AS AMENDED BY DIRECTIVE 97/36/
            EC OF THE EUROPEAN PARLIAMENT AND OF THE COUNCIL,
            29 SEPTEMBER 2000[28] .[29]

* 2.2.7.    INFORMATION FROM THE COMMISSION – PUBLICATION
            PURSUANT TO ARTICLE 3A(2) OF COUNCIL DIRECTIVE 89/552/
            EEC (OJ L 298, 17-10-1989, P. 23) ON THE COORDINATION OF
            CERTAIN PROVISIONS LAID DOWN BY LAW, REGULATION OR
            ADMINISTRATIVE ACTION IN MEMBER STATES CONCERNING
            THE PURSUIT OF TELEVISION BROADCASTING ACTIVITIES, AS
            AMENDED BY DIRECTIVE 97/36/EC OF THE EUROPEAN
            PARLIAMENT AND OF THE COUNCIL (OJ L 202, 30-7-1997, P. 60) –
            UNITED KINGDOM, 18 NOVEMBER 2000[30]

* 2.2.8.    INFORMATION FROM THE COMMISSION – PUBLICATION IN
            ACCORDANCE WITH ARTICLE 3(A)(2) OF COUNCIL DIRECTIVE
            89/552/EEC ON THE COORDINATION OF CERTAIN PROVISIONS
            LAID DOWN BY LAW, REGULATION OR ADMINISTRATIVE
            ACTION IN MEMBER STATES CONCERNING THE PURSUIT OF
            TELEVISION BROADCASTING ACTIVITIES, AS AMENDED BY
            DIRECTIVE 97/36/EC OF THE EUROPEAN PARLIAMENT AND OF
            THE COUNCIL, 19 JANUARY 2002[31]

---

[26] OJ C 277 , 30-9-1999 p. 3.
[27] OJ L 298, 17-10-1989, p. 23.
[28] OJ L 202, 30-7-1977, p. 60.
[29] OJ C 277, 29-9-2000, p. 4.
[30] OJ C 328, 18-11-2000, p. 2-7.
[31] OJ C 16 , 19-1-2002, p. 8-10.

**\* 2.2.9. INFORMATION FROM THE COMMISSION – PUBLICATION OF CONSOLIDATED MEASURES IN ACCORDANCE WITH ARTICLE 3A(2) OF COUNCIL DIRECTIVE 89/552/EEC ON THE COORDINATION OF CERTAIN PROVISIONS LAID DOWN BY LAW, REGULATION OR ADMINISTRATIVE ACTION IN MEMBER STATES CONCERNING THE PURSUIT OF TELEVISION BROADCASTING ACTIVITIES, AS AMENDED BY DIRECTIVE 97/36/EC OF THE EUROPEAN PARLIAMENT AND OF THE COUNCIL, 9 AUGUST 2002**[32]

———

**\* 2.2.10. ANSWER ON BEHALF OF THE COMMISSION TO WRITTEN QUESTION E-3912/02 BY DIRK STERCKX (ELDR), 7 FEBRUARY 2003**[33]

Subject: UEFA exclusive contracts and the right to information and press freedom

———

**\* 2.2.11. ANSWER ON BEHALF OF THE COMMISSION TO WRITTEN QUESTION E-246/03 BY RAINA ECHERER (VERTS/ALE) AND MONICA FRASSONI (VERTS/ALE), 14 MARCH 2003**[34]

Subject: Media: mini-ads during the transmission of sporting events in Italy

———

[32] OJ C 189, 9-8-2002, p. 2-20, OJ L 298, 17-10-1989, p. 23.
[33] Question 14-1-2003; OJ C 155 E, 3-7-2003, p. 204.
[34] Question of 4-2-2003; OJ C 161 E, 10-7-2003, p. 201.

## 2.3. COMMUNITY AID AND SPORT FUNDING*

**\* 2.3.1. ANSWER ON BEHALF OF THE COMMISSION TO WRITTEN QUESTION NO 218/90 BY MR JOHN TOMLINSON (S), 17 APRIL 1990**[35]

Subject: Community aid to sport

----

**\* 2.3.2. ANSWER ON BEHALF OF THE COMMISSION TO WRITTEN QUESTION E-1922/94 BY JESSICA LARIVE (ELDR), 20 OCTOBER 1994**[36]

Subject: Spending of European money on sport in the European Union

----

**\* 2.3.3. EURATHLON – COMMISSION PROGRAMME IN FAVOUR OF SPORT, 25 OCTOBER 1994**[37]

----

**2.3.4. EURATHLON II EUROPEAN COMMISSION PROGRAMMA FOR SPORT, 7 OCTOBER 1995**[38]

----

**\* 2.3.5. ANSWER ON BEHALF OF THE COMMISSION TO WRITTEN QUESTION E-2365/94 BY GIOVANNI BURTONE (PPE), 11 JANUARY 1995**[39]

Subject: Support for the World Student Games in Sicily

----

**\* 2.3.6. ANSWER ON BEHALF OF THE COMMISSION TO WRITTEN QUESTION E-2171/95 BY MARIANNE THYSSEN (PPE), 6 OCTOBER 1995**[40]

Subject: Sports policy

----

\* The full texts of documents which are marked with an asterisk (\*) are not incorporated in the book itself, but are freely accessible on the website of the ASSER International Sports Law Centre, at <www.sportslaw.nl> – documentation.

[35] Question of 14-1-1990; 90/C 233/36, OJ C 233/19, 17-9-1990.
[36] Question of 12-9-1994; 95/C 30/84, OJ C 30/34, 6-2-1995.
[37] OJ C 297, 25-10-1994, p. 7.
[38] OJ C 262, 7-10-1995, p. 32.
[39] Question of 15-11-1994; OJ C 81, 3-4-1995, p. 27.
[40] Question of 28-7-1995; OJ C 79, 18-3-1996, p. 6.

**\* 2.3.7.   ANSWER ON BEHALF OF THE COMMISSION TO WRITTEN QUESTION E-2718/95 BY LUIGI MORETTI (ELDR), 23 NOVEMBER 1995[41]**

Subject: European Commission programme to promote sport

———

**\* 2.3.8.   ANSWER ON BEHALF OF THE COMMISSION TO WRITTEN QUESTION E-3029/95 BY WOLFGANG NUSSBAUMER (NI), 22 JANUARY 1996[42]**

Subject: Infrastructure for sports facilities

———

**\* 2.3.9.   ANSWER ON BEHALF OF THE COMMISSION TO WRITTEN QUESTION E-259/96 BY LUIGI MORETTI (ELDR), 19 MARCH 1996[43]**

Subject: Commission programme to promote sport

———

**\* 2.3.10.  ANSWER ON BEHALF OF THE COMMISSION TO WRITTEN QUESTION E-546/96 BY CHRISTINE CRAWLEY (PSE), 28 MARCH 1996[44]**

Subject: Bullfighting

———

**\* 2.3.11.  ANSWER ON BEHALF OF THE COMMISSION TO WRITTEN QUESTION E-1714/96 BY GLENYS KINNOCK (PSE), 22 JULY 1996[45]**

Subject: Evaluation of projects approved under the Eurathlon programme

———

**\* 2.3.12.  EURATHLON 1997 – EUROPEAN COMMISSION PROGRAMMA FOR SPORT, 31 JULY 1996[46]**

———

**\* 2.3.13.  ANSWER ON BEHALF OF THE COMMISSION TO WRITTEN QUESTION E-1774/96 BY ERICH SCHREINER (NI), 16 SEPTEMBER 1996[47]**

Subject: Sponsorship for the Vienna marathon

———

---

[41] Question of 6-10-1995; OJ C 66, 4-3-1996, p. 25.
[42] Question of 13-11-1995; OJ C 112, 17-4-1996, p. 16-17.
[43] Question of 9-2-1996; OJ C 173, 17-6-1996, p. 40.
[44] Question of 11-3-1996; OJ C 185, 25-6-1996, p. 70.
[45] Question of 25-6-1996; OJ C 322, 28-10-1996, p. 100.
[46] OJ C 222, 31-7-1996, p. 13.
[47] Question of 3-7-1996; OJ C 385, 19-12-1996, p. 35.

**\* 2.3.14.  ANSWER ON BEHALF OF THE COMMISSION TO WRITTEN QUESTION E-646/97 BY ELISABETH SCHROEDTER (V), 8 APRIL 1997**[48]

Subject: Investment grant from the Government of the Land of Brandenburg for a motor racing track

———

**\* 2.3.15.  EURATHLON 1998 – EUROPEAN COMMISSION PROGRAMMA FOR SPORT, 19 JULY 1997**[49]

———

**\* 2.3.16.  EURATHLON 98 – PRACTICAL GUIDE**

———

**\* 2.3.17.  ANSWER ON BEHALF OF THE COMMISSION TO WRITTEN QUESTION E-3163/97 BY CONCEPCIÓ FERRER (PPE), 6 NOVEMBER 1997**[50]

Subject: Eurathlon programme

———

**\* 2.3.18.  ANSWER ON BEHALF OF THE COMMISSION TO WRITTEN QUESTION E-4121/97 BY GERHARD HAGER (NI), 2 MARCH 1998**[51]

Subject: Declaration on sport

———

**\* 2.3.19.  ANSWER ON BEHALF OF THE COMMISSION TO WRITTEN QUESTION P-3383/98 BY FREDDY BLAK (PSE), 9 DECEMBER 1998**[52]

Subject: Aid programmes

———

**\* 2.3.20.  ANSWER ON BEHALF OF THE COMMISSION TO WRITTEN QUESTION E-3922/98 BY HILDE HAWLICEK (PSE) AND HERBERT BÖSCH (PSE), 23 FEBRUARY 1999**[53]

Subject: Support for sporting activities for the disabled

———

**\* 2.3.21.  ANSWER ON BEHALF OF THE COMMISSION TO WRITTEN QUESTION E-390/99 BY GERHARD SCHMID (PSE), 7 APRIL 1999**[54]

Subject: Use of Objective 5b funds to finance the construction of golf courses in Bavaria

———

[48]  Question of 6-3-1997; OJ C 319, 18-10-1997, p. 146.
[49]  OJ C 222, 19-7-1997, p. 7.
[50]  Question of 13-10-1997; OJ C 117, 16-4-1998, p, 158.
[51]  Question of 16-1-1998; OJ C 196, 22-6-1998 p. 82.
[52]  Question of 9-11-1998; OJ C 142, 21-5-1999, p. 126.
[53]  Question of 4-1-1999; OJ C 289, 11-10-1999, p. 105.
[54]  Question of 1-3-1999; OJ C 341, 29-11-1999, p. 105.

**\* 2.3.22. ANSWER ON BEHALF OF THE COMMISSION TO WRITTEN QUESTION E-1606/00 BY ALEXANDROS ALAVANOS (GUE/NGL), 27 JULY 2000**[55]

Subject: Sport event for kidney sufferers

———

**\* 2.3.23. ANSWER ON BEHALF OF THE COMMISSION TO WRITTEN QUESTION E-2920/00 BY CHARLES TANNOCK (PPE-DE), 9 NOVEMBER 2000**[56]

Subject: Sporting and leisure activities in Andalusia

———

**\* 2.3.24. ANSWER ON BEHALF OF THE COMMISSION TO WRITTEN QUESTION E-489/01 BY DANIEL HANNAN (PPE-DE), 11 APRIL 2001**[57]

Subject: Sport funding

———

**\* 2.3.25. ANSWER ON BEHALF OF THE COMMISSION TO WRITTEN QUESTION E-2867/01 BY JONAS SJÖSTEDT (GUE/NGL), 30 NOVEMBER 2001**[58]

Subject: Commission projects to strengthen sport

———

**\* 2.3.26. ANSWER ON BEHALF OF THE COMMISSION TO WRITTEN QUESTION E-3291/01 BY CHRISTOPHER HEATON-HARRIS (PPE-DE), 21 DECEMBER 2001**[59]

Subject: Funding for sport

———

**\* 2.3.27. ANSWER ON BEHALF OF THE COMMISSION TO WRITTEN QUESTION E-41/02 BY DANA SCALLON (PPE-DE), 11 FEBRUARY 2002**[60]

Subject: Funds for retired people engaged in educational, social, cultural and sport activities

———

---

[55] Question of 29-5-2000; OJ C 072 E, 6-3-2001, p. 86.
[56] Question of 19-9-2000; OJ C 151 E, 22-05-2001, p. 25.
[57] Question of 22-2-2001; OJ C 235 E, 21-8-2001, p. 215.
[58] Question of 17-10-2001; OJ C 115 E, 16-5-2002, p. 180.
[59] Question of 27-11-2001; OJ C 134 E, 6-6-2002, p. 216.
[60] Question of 23-1-2002; OJ C 147 E, 20-6-2002, p. 234.

**\* 2.3.28.  ANSWER ON BEHALF OF THE COMMISSION TO WRITTEN QUESTION E-1219/02 BY DANIELA RASCHHOFER (NI), 28 JUNE 2002**[61]

Subject: Subsidies for sports clubs

——

**\* 2.3.29.  ANSWER ON BEHALF OF THE COMMISSION TO WRITTEN QUESTION E-860/03 BY ROBERTA ANGELILLI (UEN), 2O MARCH 2003**[62]

Subject: Use of funds under the Sport for the disabled programme by the City of Frosinone[63]

——

**\* 2.3.30.  EUROPEAN COURT OF JUSTICE, JUDGMENT OF THE COURT OF FIRST INSTANCE (FOURTH CHAMBER), STADTSPORTVERBAND NEUSS EV V COMMISSION OF THE EUROPEAN COMMUNITIES, CASE T-137/01, 17 SEPTEMBER 2003**[64]

——

[61] Question of 29-4-2002; OJ C 301 E , 5-12-2002, p. 109.
[62] Question of 20-3-2003; OJ C 11, 15-1-2004, p. 148.
[63] Roberta Angelilli tabled similar questions concerning the municipalities of Siena, Prato, Pistoia, Pisa, Pesaro, Perugia, Massa, Macerata, Livorno, Florence, Carrara, Ancona, Fiumicino and Terni; written questions E-0885/03, E-1192/03, E-1193/03, E-1194/03, E-1195/03, E-1196/03, E-1197/03, E-1198/03, E-1199/03, E-1202/03, E-1201/03, E -1200/03. [*Eds.*]
[64] ECR 2003, not yet published.

# 2.4.    COMPETITION*

## 2.4.1.    COMMISSION DECISION RELATING TO A PROCEEDING UNDER ARTICLE 85 OF THE EEC TREATY (IV/29.395 – WINDSURFING INTERNATIONAL), 11 JULY 1983[65]

*The Commission of the European Communities,*

–    Having regard to the Treaty establishing the European Economic Community,
–    Having regard to Council Regulation No 17 of 6 February 1962[66], first Regulation implementing Articles 85 and 86 of the Treaty, as last amended by the Act of Accession of Greece, and in particular Articles 3(1), 4 and 15(2) thereof,
–    Having regard to the complaints lodged with the Commission pursuant to Article 3(1) of Regulation No 17 by the undertakings IMA AG, Arbon Tabur Marine SA, Paris, Dufour SA, Paris, and Tabur Marine (Great Britain) Ltd, Slough; SC France, Marseille, Surfer's Paradise GmbH, Rosenheim, Cowabanga Sportartikel, Munich, European Surfing Company BV, Amersfoort, Alpina Plast AG, Eichberg, Kunststofftechnik Peter Degler GmbH and SC-Products Surfgeraet – und Zubehoer-Handels Ges. mbH, both of Grassau; Seal Marine Ltd, Liskeard, and Surf Sales Ltd, St Leonards-on-Sea; Point Sportgeraete GmbH, Point AG and Exa Point Marine Vertrieb GmbH, all of Munich, Sodim Paris, Brakeborough Ltd, Headley Down (Nr. Bordon), Daher France, Marseille, and Skipper International, Hennebont; Crit. SA, Saint-Ouen, and Open Surf, Saint-Rémy-les-Chevreuses and Helmut Kertscher and Co., Hamburg,
–    Having regard to the Commission Decision of 7 June 1982 to initiate proceedings in this case,
–    Having given the undertakings concerned the opportunity to make known their views on the objections raised by the Commission, pursuant to Article 19(1) of Regulation No 17 a nd Regulation No 99/63/EEC of 25 July 1963 concerning the hearing as laid down in Article 19(1) and (2) of Council Regulation No 17(2), and having regard to the written comments of the undertakings Windsurfing International Inc., Ostermann, Akutec, Klepper and Windsurfing Central and having regard to the oral hearing of the undertakings Windsurfing International Inc. and Windsurfing Central on 20 September 1982,
–    Having regard to the opinion delivered by the Advisory Committee on Restrictive Practices and Dominant Positions on 23 March 1983;
Whereas:

### A. THE FACTS
The facts may be summarized as follows:

### I. THE PRODUCT
Sailboards were developed with the idea of enabling surfboards, which have been known

---

*    The full texts of documents which are marked with an asterisk (*) are not incorporated in the book itself, but are freely accessible on the website of the ASSER International Sports Law Centre, at <www.sportslaw.nl> – documentation.
    [65]    OJ L 229, 20-8-1983, p. 1-21.
    [66]    OJ 13, 21-2-1962, p. 204-262.

for a long time, to be used as wind-propelled watercraft in waters not having the necessary amount of surf. Sailboards consist of a board-shaped foam-filled plastic hull with a daggerboard inserted through its centre and a sail rig which is attached to the hull and can be angled and rotated in all directions. The sail rig consists essentially of a mast, a mast pivot, a sail and a pair of curved booms, and is referred to below as a 'rig'.

As a result of the further development of this new product, there are nowadays differences between boards in respect of the material used for the foam filling and for the outer surface, the type of construction (one-piece or in parts that can be assembled) and the types of application, which are dependent on the shape (all-round boards, regatta boards, fun boards or boards for heavy surf). Sail sizes also vary according to the type of use (regatta sails, normal sails and storm sails). In April 1980 an industrial standard DIN-7873 was introduced in Germany which lays down the safety requirements for sailboards within the meaning of the Appliance Safety Law (BGBI, Part I, 1968, No 42).

Individual parts of the rigs as well as complete rigs and hulls can frequently be combined with one another irrespective of their origin. All the individual components of the product are marketed separately as replacement parts. The manufacturing costs and prices for hulls are on average between 50 and 100% more than those for rigs. It also happens that amateur enthusiasts who have access to the necessary specifications and building instructions through specialist magazines, construct do-it-yourself boards for their own use.

## II. UNDERTAKINGS CONCERNED

1.    Windsurfing International Inc. ('WSI'), Torrance, California, USA, is a company founded as a family firm by Hoyle Schweitzer, a key figure in the development of the sailboard. The company has worldwide operations.

Its turnover in 1980 was [...][67], which was achieved partly from sales of sailboards and partly through income from licensing contracts for their manufacture. Until recently, WSI did not manufacture any sailboards in Europe. Its direct activities here were confined to administering and exploiting its industrial property rights, responsibility for which was largely placed in the hands of Axel Hansmann, a Munich patent lawyer.

The 'Windsurfer' sailboard model developed by WSI was first distributed in Europe by the firm Koninklijke Textielfabrieken Nijverdal Ten Cate. NV through its subsidiary Ten Cate Sports BV ('Ten Cate'). By an agreement dated 1 January 1973, WSI granted to Ten Cate the exclusive right to manufacture and market the 'Windsurfer' for Europe in accordance with technical know-how to be furnished by WSI on a continuing basis. Furthermore, by this agreement, the word marks 'Windsurfer' and 'Windsurfing' as well as a design mark showing the abstract shape of a sail (a so-called 'logo'), all registered in Germany and France, were assigned to Ten Cate. Ten Cate was obliged to use them and also to apply for registration of them in other European countries. On termination of the agreement, all registered trade marks are to be reassigned to WSI.

In addition, Ten Cate was initially – at least de facto – the exclusive licensee with respect to any industrial property rights that might be obtained for the transferred technical know-how or parts of it in various European countries and was entitled, in agreement with WSI, to grant sublicenses. Accordingly, Ten Cate, as sublicensor, concluded with Ostermann in 1976 (see point 2 below) and with Shark in 1977 (see point 3 below) sublicence contracts for the exploitation of German patent No

---

[67] Pursuant to Article 21(2) of Regulation No 17, turnover figures are not published in the Official Journal.

19 14 602.4-22 which had been applied for at that time and of other European patent applications. By amendments to these agreements dated 6 July 1978, WSI itself took over the position of licensor. All further licensing agreements were concluded directly by WSI. A special agreement concluded between WSI and Ten Cate on 9 August 1979 specifically laid down that WSI alone had the right to conclude further licensing agreements.

Since 21 April 1982, a new contractual relationship has existed between Ten Cate and WSI; under this agreement, the two firms are first to form a joint undertaking 'Windsurfing International Europe BV', with WSI acquiring all the shares held by Ten Cate by the end of 1984. WSI intends to build up its own production and marketing of sailboards in Europe through this firm. Ten Cate is to receive a non-exclusive licence in respect of WSI's industrial property rights and will no longer be permitted to use the trade marks mentioned. The contractual relationship between WSI and Ten Cate is not the subject of this Decision.

2.  Windglider Fred Ostermann GmbH ('Ostermann'), Altforweiler, Germany, is engaged solely in the manufacture and marketing of sailboards and of the relevant ancillary equipment. It has been doing so since 1976, on the basis of the licensing agreement concluded initially with Ten Cate and subsequently assigned to WSI. Ostermann's turnover in sailboards was as follows:

1978 DM[...],
1979 DM[...],
1980 DM[...].

Apart from the hulls, some of which are manufactured by the firm itself, Ostermann purchases elsewhere all the other elements of sailboards, complete or for assembly. Ostermann's models include one marketed under are name of 'Windglider'. By a decision of the competent sport associations, this sailboard has been provisionally chosen as the Olympic regatta class board. Windsurfing is to be included in the 1984 Olympic Games.

At the beginning of 1982, Ostermann was taken over by the French group Bic Marine SA. This group includes the firm Dufour, which is currently reckoned to be the largest manufacturer of sailboards in the world.

3.  Shark Wasserportgeraete GmbH ('Shark'), Bassum, Germany, is a wholly-owned subsidiary of Kolbus Kunststoffwerke GmbH. Initially, from 30 March 1977, it was a sublicensee of Ten Cate. Since 6 July 1978, there has been a direct licensing agreement with WSI. Shark's total turnover in sailboards was as follows:

1978 DM[...],
1979 DM[...],
1980 DM[...].

Shark procures all its hulls, masts, mast heels and curved booms from the parent company Kolbus, which also supplies Ten Cate and other licensees. Like most of its competitors, Shark purchases its sails from a manufacturer in Hong Kong. Shark has so far manufactured mainly boards that can be assembled, known as 'Systemboards'. Its output is still relatively limited.

4.  Akutec Angewandte Kunststofftechnik GmbH ('Akutec'), Munich, Germany is a plastics-processing firm. It manufactures and distributes sailboards on the basis of a licensing agreement concluded with WSI on 1 July 1978. Its sales of sailboards were as follows:

1978 DM[...],
1979 DM[...],
1980 DM[...].

Until 1980, Akutec procured all its parts from subcontractors. Recently, the firm has also begun manufacturing hulls and booms itself. Aktuec's models all bear the name 'HiFly'.

5.   S.A.N. Warenvertriebsgesellschaft mbH ('S.A.N.'), Neckarsulm, Germany, is a wholly-owned subsidiary of Binder Kunststofftechnik GmbH. S.A.N. has been a licensee of WSI since 1 January 1979. Its sales of sailboards were as follows:
1978 DM[...],
1979 DM[...],
1980 DM[...].
S.A.N. does not have any manufacturing facilities of its own. All its components are purchased or are made by other manufacturers to S.A.N.'s specifications.

6.   Klepper Beteiligungs GmbH and Co, Bootsbau KG ('Klepper'), Rosenheim, Germany, belongs to Klepper Beteiligungs-GmbH and Co., which, in addition to boat and yacht building, is engaged in the manufacture of gymnastic and sports equipment and clothing. Klepper obtained a licence from WSI with effect from 1 January 1979, though it had already begun building and distributing sailboards earlier. Its sales of sailboards were as follows:
1978 DM[...],
1979 DM[...],
1980 DM[...].
Klepper manufactures mast heels, booms and sails itself, but it purchases the masts and has the hulls manufactured to order. Klepper's models bear the letter 'S'.

7.   Marker Surf GmbH ('Marker'), Garmisch-Partenkirchen, Germany, is a wholly-owned subsidiary of Marker GmbH, whose main activity is the manufacture of ski bindings. The licensing agreement between WSI and Marker was concluded on 21 August 1980. Marker had not yet begun selling sailboards in 1980. Since 1981, Marker has been assembling sailboards from parts which it has purchased or which have been manufactured to order according to its specifications, and marketing them under the name 'Mark 1'.

8.   Windsurfing Central GmbH ('WSC'), Rodgau, Germany, is a trading firm which specializes in the distribution of sailboards and accessories. It is an independent firm which acts as Ten Cate's sole importer in Germany. It supplies some 400 retail outlets in Germany. Its sales of sailboards amounted to around DM[...] in 1980. WSC now also distributes windsurfing equipment manufactured by other firms.
Licensing contracts which WSI has concluded with other firms since the end of 1981/beginning of 1982 are not the subject to this Decision.

## III. THE MARKET IN SAILBOARDS

The relatively new European sailboard market is a very buoyant market. In recent years it has been marked by considerable growth rates (though these have differed widely from one Member State to another) and by rapidly changing market positions of the numerous suppliers. WSI's German patent concerning a 'rig for a sailboard' (details under IV.1) and even more extensive patent protection for sailboards in the United Kingdom (referred to as UK patent below) have significantly influenced competition. In the absence of more precise statistical data, the figures given below are no more than estimates, although they do adequately reflect the proportions involved.

1.   Around one-third of total European output of sailboards is sold in Germany; up to the beginning of 1980, about 70 000 had been sold. In 1980, at least a further 80 000 sailboards were sold on the German market.
In 1979 and 1980, the combined market share of all the licensees in Germany was around 70%. According to Ten Cate's estimates, the numbers of sailboards sold and the relevant percentages were approximately as follows:

| | 1979 | | 1980 | |
|---|---|---|---|---|
| Firm | Numbers sold | % | Numbers sold | % |
| Ostermann | ca. 12.000 | 30 | ca. 20.000 | 25 |
| Ten Cate (WSC) | ca. 6.000 | 20 | ca. 12.000 | 15 |
| S.A.N. | ca. 4.500 | 11 | ca. 12.000 | 15 |
| Akutec | ca. 3.500 | 9 | ca. 5.600 | 7 |
| Klepper | ca. 2.500 | 7 | ca. 3.200 | 4 |
| Shark | — | — | ca. 3.200 | 4 |
| Total licensees | 28.500 | 77 | 56.000 | 70 |
| Market volume | 35.000 | 100 | 80.000 | 100 |

The relative market positions of the various licensees have since changed considerably However, their total market share of 70% in Germany has been maintained and has probably risen even further owing to more rigorous application of patent protection against non-licensed suppliers, some of whom confine themselves to offering boards without rigs or supply the German market from manufacturing and marketing establishments outside Germany but near the frontier.

2.  The total numbers of sailboards sold in other Member States in 1980 were approximately as follows:

France          ca. 85.000
Netherlands     ca. 40.000
Italy           ca. 10.000
United Kingdom  5.000
Belgium         3.000

The above figures show that, apart from Germany, the most important sales areas in the Community are the Netherlands and France. The licensees have estimated their market share in the European Community (excluding Germany) in 1980 at some 35%. Out of a total of 40 manufacturers, the major competitors of the licensees in the Member States in which no patent protection exists are Mistral, Dufour (Bic Marine), Skipper International and Sainval (all France) and Sordelli (Italy).

The licensees have estimated their share of the Dutch market in 1980 at some 40% and that of the French market at some 15 to 20%. According to other information, their share of the French market was somewhat lower, as follows:

In 1979 and 1980, the licensees' exports to other Member States accounted for between 45 and 50% of their total sales (with variations according to the firm in question).

| | Sailboards | % |
|---|---|---|
| Ten Cate | 6.000 | ca. 7 |
| S.A.N. | 2.400 | ca. 3 |
| Ostermann | 1.500 | ca. 1,8 |
| Akutec | 500 | ca. 0,5 |
| Klepper | 170 | ca. 0,2 |
| Total licensees | — | ca. 12,5 |

## IV. THE AGREEMENTS BETWEEN WSI AND THE GERMAN LICENSEES

### 1. Subject of the licensing agreements

The subject of the licensing agreements is the German patent No 19 14 602.4-22 and the United Kingdom patent No 1.258.317 (together with supplementary patent No 1.551.426).

(a)  Invoking the priority arising from the application field in the United States on 27 March 1968, Hoyle Schweitzer and the co-inventor James Drake applied for a patent for the Federal Republic of Germany on 21 March 1969. The original patent claims referred to a 'wind-propelled vehicle'(application filed on 21 March 1969) or a 'sailboard with a sail-bearing mast'(amended application filed on 18 July 1973). Having expressed reservations as to the claims formulated in these patent applications on state-of-the-art grounds, the German Patent Office, in a notice dated 21 August 1973, held out the prospect of a patent being granted for the combination of a sailboard with a mast that could be moved in all directions and a main boom in the form of an oval-shaped two-part split boom. As a result, WSI submitted, on 7 and 9 January 1974, amended claims which again referred to a 'sailboard' and stated that the aim of the invention was to design a sailboard in such a way that it did not exhibit the manoeuvring defects common to existing designs based on the hitherto current state-of-the-art. However, the Patent Office did not agree to the claims, but proposed instead, in a notice dated 24 January 1974, a principal claim which referred to a 'rig for a sailboard'. It accordingly also altered the content of the patent description to the effect that the aim of the invention was to 'design the rig for the sailboard in such a way that the user can also sail relatively close to the wind with the sailboard while still being able to remove the sail or rig easily so as to enable the board to withstand strong gusts without being overturned or upset'. The manner in which this was to be achieved was characterized by the fact 'that the foot of the mast is fixed to the sailboard by means of a joint allowing it to be angled and rotated freely in all directions, and that, as spars for holding and trimming the sail or rig, two opposed outward curving main booms in the nature of a split gaff are used to whose ends the sail is attached and between which it is passed loosely, with the underleech of the sail running from the ends diagonally down to the mast and the two main booms being fixed to the mast above the tack of the sail'.

WSI agreed with this amended wording. It was accordingly laid open to public inspection on 27 June 1974 in patent class B63H (ship propulsion and steering equipment), subclass 9/00 (wind-propelled elements; specifications). By a decision of 31 March 1978, the German Patent Office granted the patent in a form not substantially different from the specification laid open to public inspection. The aim of the invention was now defined as follows: 'To design a rig for a sailboard in such a way that it is possible for the user to turn and set the sail easily, even under difficult sailing conditions, in the various positions necessary for the desired manoeuvre and without the mast becoming separated from the board – this despite the fact that the foot of the mast can be angled and rotated freely in all directions in relation to the board'. The patent description stated it to be significant amongst other things, that the proposed arrangement made the rig manoeuvrable in a way that, in contrast to existing manual sail arrangements, allowed tacking very close to the wind and stable handling even in strong gusts or in disturbed coastal waters. During the course of this proceeding, the Commission has examined the certificates of acceptance of the German Patent Office.

A large number of parties appealed against the decision of acceptance on state-of-the-art grounds, and the Bundespatentgericht gave a ruling by decision of 28 November 1979. In the decision, the appeals were in substance dismissed and the principal claim of the patent was replaced, in line with the applicant's alternative claim II of 13 November 1979, by the following wording: 'Rig for a sailboard, with a sail held taut between a mast and a curved spar, with the instayed rig, which is fixed to the sailboard by means of a joint that can be angled and rotated freely in all directions, being held by the user by the spar and thus being trimmed relative to the sailboard and wind, and with the sail being secured to the spar only at its ends, the underleech of the sail running from the ends diagonally down to the mast and the spar being attached to the mast above the tack of the sail, characterized by the fact that the sail [...] is held by its foreleech [...] to the mast [...] and that, as a spar for holding and trimming the sail or rig, a split boom consisting of two opposed outward curving main booms [...] is provided, between which the sail [...] is passed loosely.'In its decision, the Federal Patent Court stated that the essential feature of the invention was the two opposed outward-curving booms.

The German patent was the subject of numerous actions for infringement brought by WSI against various firms. In its judgment of 10 December 1983[68] (file No X ZR 70/80) in the case brought against a manufacturer of sails which were particularly suited for use in sailboard rigs, the Bundesgerichtshof referred, in stating the facts of the case, to the mast that can be angled and rotated freely in all directions, the sail and the outward-curving booms as elements in combination. WSI also endeavoured, through a further suit filed against an importer of boards before the Landgericht Muenchen I, to get the Court to prohibit the distribution of boards in Germany on the grounds that this represented at least an indirect patent infringement since the board formed part of the patent-protected combination. Invoking the abovementioned judgment of the Bundesgerichtshof, the Landgericht Muenchen I, in its judgment of 2 March 1982, dismissed this complaint partly on the grounds that the patent in no way involved a 'rig with a sailboard' but only a 'rig for a sailboard'. WSI's appeal against this judgment was rejected by a judgment of the Oberlandesgericht Muenchen of 13 January 1983 (file No 6 U 2244/82).

(b)     In the United Kingdom, the patent protection for WSI arises from a main patent No 1.258.317 – filed on 28 February 1969, invoking the United States priority already mentioned and published on 30 December 1971 – and from a supplementary patent No 1.551.426 – filed on 8 November 1976 with additions in 1977 and published in full on 30 August 1979.

## 2. Contents of the agreements

With differences of drafting from case to case, the agreements have hitherto provided essentially for the following:

(a)     The licensed product was specified as being a complete sailboard consisting of the rig and a precisely-defined type of board manufactured by the licensee; the specifi-

---

[68] Reported in 'Gewerblicher Rechtsschutz und Urheberrecht', 1982, p. 165.
Claim No 1 in patent No 1.258.317 reads as follows : 'A wind-propelled vehicle comprising body means, an unstayed spar connected to said body means through a joint which will provide universal-type movement of the spar in the absence of support thereof by a user of the vehicle, a sail attached along one edge thereof to the spar, and a pair of arcuate booms, first ends of the booms being connected together and laterally connected on said spar, second ends of the booms being connected together and having means thereon connected to the sail such that said sail is held taut between the booms'. The further claims 2 to 7 clarify individual elements of claim 1, in particular that the vehicle may be a watercraft which is also equipped with a leeboard.
Patent No 1.551.426 extends the patent claim chiefly to vehicles of the type just mentioned in which the two booms are not curved opposite each other but – by means of the necessary joints – form a right angel, a triangle or other shapes. Substructure specifications are included only where provision is made for an opening for inserting an adjustable leeboard (claim No 16).
In an action for infringement brought by WSI before the High Court in London, the patents were revoked by the Court following a counterclaim by the defendant on the grounds of lack of novelty and absence of an inventive step (Windsurfing International Inc. v. Tabur Marine (Great Britain) Ltd – Judgment of 7 April 1982 – Whitford, J.). An appeal has been lodged against this judgment.
In view of the uncertainty surrounding the United Kingdom patent, the Commission has not included the United Kingdom market in this proceeding.

cations of the board were set out in an annex as an integral part of the agreement. WSI granted each licensee a non-exclusive licence for the manufacture, use and distribution of the complete product so defined under the abovementioned German patent. The licence under the United Kingdom partent was limited to the right to distribute the product.

The agreement with Shark, which did not expressly cover the United Kingdom patent, contained no precise definition of a given board model in the above sense and also referred only to a 'rig for a sailboard' as the subject of the licence. However, Shark was prohibited from manufacturing, supplying and distributing rigs otherwise than 'in connection with sailboards consisting of several parts'.

It was also stipulated in the agreements that any change by the licensee in the board type defined as part of the licensed product or any combination by the licensee of the rig covered by the patent with other board types required WSI's authorization. WSI stated that it proposed not to withhold its authorization unreasonably, provided that the intended change did not detract from the quality of the licensed product. A further condition was that any new board should not be prejudicial to the 'rights of Ten Cate' (as stated in the agreement with Akutec) or the 'rights of other licensees' (as stated in the agreements with S.A.N., Klepper and Marker). Ostermann was absolutely prohibited from manufacturing polyethylene boards.

(b)     As in the case of the agreement with Shark, the agreements with S.A.N., Klepper and Marker also specifically stipulated that the licensee could manufacture items or parts thereof only for use in the complete licensed product defined in the agreement and could supply them only in connection with that product.

(c)     The royalty agreed was a specific percentage of the net selling price of the licensed product specified in each agreement, i.e. of the complete sailboard. In some cases (Akutec, S.A.N. and Klepper), it was also stipulated that a royalty of the same amount was payable on net income from rentals of the relevant sailboard.

(d)     As to the territorial limits of the licence, the agreements contained differing provisions.

The agreement with Ostermann provided for a right to manufacture and market throughout Europe. Shark's right to manufacture was limited to the territory of the Federal Republic of Germany.

Akutec's manufacturing licence was expressly restricted to the place where the manufacturing plant of the licensee was situated at the time the agreement was concluded. The same applied – following amending agreements of December 1980 – to the agreements with S.A.N., Klepper and Marker. Any change in the place of manufacture entitled WSI to terminate the agreement immediately.

The agreements with S.A.N., Klepper and Marker had originally granted a right of manufacture for the whole of the Federal Republic of Germany, while at the same time permitting these licensees to manufacture individual components of the licensed product outside the licensed territory so long as they were brought back into the licensed territory and assembled there. However, it was stipulated that the direct marketing outside the licensed territory of individual components manufactured outside it, and any transfer of the entire production establishment outside the licensed territory, would be regarded as entitling WSI to terminate the agreement immediately.

(e)     The licensees were obliged to affix to the hull of each of the sailboards in their range a notice indicating that it was licensed by WSI or by Hoyle Schweitzer (the agreements with Ostermann and Shark originally stipulated that the notice must indicate that the board was licensed by Ten Cate).

(f)     The licensees undertook not to use the word marks 'Windsurfer' and 'Windsurfing' – hitherto used by Ten Cate in Europe – or the 'logo' design mark and to acknowledge them as valid trade marks.

(g)     The agreements with Ostermann and Shark contained the requirement that licensees should not challenge the licensed patents.

Since the end of 1981/beginning of 1982, WSI has concluded new agreements with all the licensees mentioned above. In these agreements, the said obligations have been removed or modified. These new agreements are not the subject of this Decision, but the Commission reserves the right to examine them subsequently in the light of Articles 85 and 86 of the EEC Treaty.

### 3. The agreements in practice

The following further facts emerge from the documents which the Commission has available as a result of its investigations:

(a)     WSI's key criterion for granting licenses and approval for licensees' new boards was that the various types of board should be sufficiently 'distant' from each other. Accordingly, it was continually pointed out in the numerous exchanges of correspondence to which the Commission has had access that 'only products and not firms were licensed' by WSI. In this context 'products' meant the boards of sailboards. WSI also arranged for licensees to submit their new models, before they were finally approved by itself, to other licensees for their opinion, without, however, granting the latter a formal right of approval. Thus, certain types of board were in fact rejected because, in WSI's opinion, they were too similar to existing boards produced by other licensees. By contrast, quality or safety requirements played no part in the approval of the various boards. Nor did WSI exercise any sort of control over licensees' day-to-day production in this regard.

(b)     In addition to the numerous actions for patent infringement brought by WSI as already mentioned, WSI arranged for its German patent lawyer to send a number of letters to German manufacturers and also to dealers warning them that actions for patent infringement would be brought if, for example, they marketed non-licensed boards or supplied rigs separately. Furthermore, WSI repeatedly sent circulars to licensees warning against the danger of outsiders penetrating the market if these were supplied with rigs. Some licensees expressly agreed with this. As recently as October 1981, WSI warned several licensees, including Akutec, that their licensing agreements would be terminated if they were to supply rigs separately except where needed as replacement parts.

Independent manufacturers or importers of boards who inquired of various licensees about the supply of rigs only were therefore turned down by most licensees. Where they answered such inquiries at all, licensees referred sometimes to the structure of their range, which contained no separate rigs, sometimes to their own requirements, which accounted for their entire capacity, and sometimes to the danger of patent infringement which they claimed existed. At WSI's instigation, the licensees also agreed at a joint meeting in Munich on 9 October 1980 that, in advertisements and exhibitions, they would in future show only complete sailboards.

### V. SALES POLICY OF A NUMBER OF GERMAN LICENSEES AND OF SOLE IMPORTERS IN VARIOUS MEMBER STATES

#### 1. Distribution of Ostermann products ('Windglider')

For the purposes of this procedure, the Commission investigated sales of these products in the Netherlands, Belgium and Germany.

(a)    Distribution outside Germany
       (aa)  In the Netherlands, Ostermann's sole importer is Thijs, Middelburg. It was
             not possible to establish whether there was a written agreement. However,
             the Commission has in its possession a draft import agreement for 1980
             originating from Thijs in which Thijs undertakes' to sell only in Holland the
             goods procured from Windglider. Supplies to other countries are subject to
             prior approval by Ostermann. Thijs undertakes to conclude with its custom-
             ers only agreements which prohibit those customers from selling boards di-
             rectly or indirectly abroad'.
             This provision, if no others, was put into effect by the parties. Thus Thijs re-
             fused to supply a Dutch retailer who had turned to Thijs to meet a large order
             from Germany. From various exchanges of telex between Ostermann and
             Thijs, it is evident that, in other instances too, Ostermann together with Thijs
             was on the alert to ensure that sailboards supplied in the Netherlands re-
             mained there and, in the event of deliveries outside the Netherlands, cau-
             tioned the relevant dealers. Surveillance relied partly on a 'board card
             system' introduced in 1981: as stipulated in the instructions sent by
             Ostermann 'to all general importers', a carbon copy of the 'control card'was
             to be kept by Ostermann, one copy was to go to the importer and one copy,
             with the name and address of the final consumer, was to be kept by the re-
             tailer. Thijs was required to pass on the necessary instructions to the Dutch
             retailers.
       (bb)  In Belgium Ostermann orally granted d'leteren, Braine-le-Château, exclusive
             distribution rights. Here, too, there was an understanding between the parties
             that supplies outside the allotted territory should not be permitted. This can
             be seen for example, from the communication from d'leteren to Ostermann
             dated 9 April 1981 reporting that d'leteren and Thijs had assured each other
             that within their respective territories they would enforce export bans even at
             retail level.
(b)    Domestic sales
       In Germany Ostermann sells its products direct to retailers called 'specialist deal-
       ers', although the term 'specialist dealer' is not defined. Until 1982, Ostermann
       had concluded 'partnership agreements' with these dealers which required the re-
       tailer to supply goods covered by the agreements only to final consumers. Goods
       could not be supplied to domestic and foreign retailers, even to other 'partners' of
       Ostermann.

## 2. Distribution of Akutec products ('HiFly')

For the purpose of this procedure, the Commission investigated sales of these products in
the Netherlands, Belgium, Italy and Germany.
(a)    Distribution outside Germany
       Akutec has appointed sole importers (known as 'agents') for the Netherlands
       (Horwa BV, Oosterhout; since 1981, the firm Taselaar BV, Zwijndrecht), for Bel-
       gium (Ertisport NV, Destelbergen) and for Italy (RaFly, Spinea / Venice).
       A standard agreement concluded with these firms contained a clause prohibiting
       the 'agent' from effecting re-imports into the country of the manufacturer or carry-
       ing out sales outside his allotted territory on pain of a penalty.
(b)    Domestic sales
       Akutec products are distributed in Germany through a network of several indepen-
       dent 'stock depots'. These depots supply the goods only to dealers included in a
       'customer list' kept jointly with Akutec. Until 1982, dealers wishing to be admitted

to the list had to undertake not to pass on to other retailers goods supplied by Akutec, unless Akutec had first expressly agreed to such a delivery. Dealers then received a 'dealer's pass' entitling them to obtain goods from the Akutec depot. Any infringement of the ban on horizontal supplies would result in expulsion from the group of authorized dealers. In 1980, Akutec had also introduced a numbering control system which, according to a circular sent to dealers by Akutec, was designed to trace and eliminate horizontal supplies and re-imports.

### 3. Distribution of Klepper products

Klepper distributes sailboards outside Germany through sole importers on the basis of agreements, each of which contained, until 1982, a supplementary clause prohibiting importers from exporting the goods. This clause was worded as follows: 'Re-imports into Germany and imports into countries other than[...] (the territory covered by the agreement) shall require our express approval'.

Such agreements existed with Telstar in Harderwijk, Netherlands and Citabel Sports in Luxembourg until 1982. The very same agreements existed from 1979 to 1981 with Intersurf in Sterzing, Italy and Media Loisirs in Strasbourg, France.

### 4. Distribution of Shark products ('Systemboard')

Between January 1978 and December 1980, a distribution agreement existed between Shark and the Dutch importer Renka Sport BV, Almelo, which included the following clause: 'Renka undertakes not to supply or offer for sale Shark products outside Holland. Exception from this shall require prior approval by Shark'.

### 5. Distribution of Ten Cate products by WSC ('Windsurfer')

WSC has organized distribution in Germany on the basis of what are called 'partnership agreements' with retailers. The aim of these agreements, as stated in paragraph 1 of each of them, has hitherto been to maintain an 'orderly distribution system'. Paragraph 3 required the dealer 'not in any circumstances to sell the products supplied by WSC to dealers, but only to final consumers'.

All the abovementioned distribution restrictions were – as far as they still existed – abandoned by the parties concerned during the course of the Commission's investigations.

## B. LEGAL ASSESSMENT

## I. APPLICABILITY OF ARTICLE 85(1) OF THE EEC TREATY

Article 85(1) of the EEC Treaty prohibits as incompatible with the common market all agreements between undertakings, decisions by associations of undertakings and concerted practices which may affect trade between Member States and which have as their object or effect the prevention, restriction or distortion of competition within the common market.

All the parties concerned are undertakings within the meaning of the above provision.

### 1. The agreements between WSI and the German licensees

(a)     The restriction of the right to exploit the licensed invention to certain types of board laid down in the agreements, on which alone patented rigs could be mounted, and the obligation on the licensees to submit for the licensor's prior approval any new board types on which they intended to use the rigs constituted a restriction of the licensees entrepreneurial freedom of action, prohibited under Article 85(1) of the EEC Treaty.

(aa)  The scope of the patent protection – even if that protection covered the hull in Germany as well – could not by itself in any way justify these restrictions, since they constituted restrictions on use within the same technical field of application – namely the construction of sailboards for use on water.

(bb)  Further, WSI's assertion of the right to exercise control over boards with a view to ensuring their quality and safety did not arise, at any rate on the basis of the facts investigated here, from the specific subject matter of the licensed patent rights, so that this restriction on the licensees is not excluded from the scope of Article 85(1) of the EEC Treaty. Such a right could be recognized as forming part of the specific subject matter of the patent right only if the licensor's quality and safety requirements were limited to a product in fact covered by the patent protection or to a protected part thereof, if they were also intended to ensure no more than that the technical instructions as described in the patent and used by the licensee may be carried into effect and if they were agreed upon in advance and on the basis of objectively verifiable criteria.

There is no need at this point to go into the actual extent of the protection afforded by the licensed patents, in particular German Patent No 19 14 602.4-22, since the requirement of prior approval contained in the agreements in respect of possible quality and safety requirements was in any case worded so vaguely that, instead of meeting the abovementioned criteria, it left licensees' model policy largely in the licensor's hands. During the course of the Commission's enquiries, WSI did submit a list of a number of technical criteria which, according to WSI's statements, were applied in exercising control over boards. Quite apart from the question of whether this list would satisfy the abovementioned principles, it should be noted that it was not contained in the agreements examined here and was thus not binding between the contracting parties. While a licensee would also in theory have been able to contest before a court WSI's refusal to sanction a board as being 'unreasonable', this was scarcely ever contemplated in practice in order to avoid straining relations with the licensor. Moreover, such action would have considerably delayed the licensee's introduction of a new models onto the market and would thus have restricted his entrepreneurial freedom. Where WSI – again independently of the extent of the patent protection – refers to the need to monitor quality and safety owing to the product liability requirements to which it is subject as a licensor in the USA, this has no bearing on the circumstances investigated here in view of the different legal situations in the Community Member States. Furthermore, it should be pointed out that WSI did not continually monitor its licensees' production.

(cc)  If, therefore, the requirement of prior approval imposed by WSI in respect of quality and safety requirements does not escape the scope of Article 85(1) of the EEC Treaty because they are too vague, this applies all the more to the right which WSI claims in the same connection, through prior control over new models, to prevent slavish imitation of boards already on the market.

Protection against slavish imitation does not form part of the specific subject matter of any industrial property right, but is a protection developed by the courts of many countries against passing off of products by competitors. Even if one starts from the principle that Article 85(1) of the EEC Treaty is intended to protect only forms of fair competition, it must be borne in mind that actually defining the limits of slavish imitation in individual cases is a difficult exercise and is to a significant extent at the discretion of the court in question. If the licensor himself, through an appropriate clause in the agreement, sets himself up as the sole arbiter in place of the court for any cases of doubt that might arise, there is a danger that he will use this discretion solely in his own favour and thus restrict his licensees in their competitive freedom to an extent that goes beyond the limits of unfair competition.

In particular, this allows a licensor to limit competition from the licensees against himself and competition amongst the licensees by using 'selective' approval to ensure that his licensees products are isolated one from another. That this possibility was in the present instance also deliberately exploited by WSI in agreement with the licensees is indicated by the 'consultations' held with individual licensees in connection with the authorization of new board types (see A.IV. 3 above). Safety requirements or quality aspects were barely touched on, whereas the possible competitive disadvantages consequent on the approval of new boards were discussed in detail.

There was thus no legal justification for regarding the abovementioned restriction on licensees as outside the scope of Article 85(1) of the EEC Treaty.

(b)    The requirement that licensees – apart from meeting replacement part needs – should supply individual components (i.e. in particular rigs) covered by the licensed German patent No 19 14 602.4-22 only in conjunction with the board types approved by the licensor, that is to say only as complete sailboards, also constituted a restriction of competition prohibited under Article 85(1) of the EEC Treaty. It restricted the licensees in their freedom to decide whether they wanted to act on the market as manufacturers and distributors only of boards of their own production or also as suppliers of rigs separately to third parties. Furthermore, manufacturers and distributors of other sailboards were prevented from supplying such boards to licensees or completing their own range by rigs of the licensees.

(aa)   Though this requirement was expressly stipulated only in the agreements with Shark, S.A.N., Klepper and Marker, it was also indirectly provided for in the other agreements, since under those agreements the licensee was granted distribution rights only in respect of the relevant licensed product laid down by the licensor according to the board type approved by it and defined as a complete sailboard. Where WSI contests this interpretation of the agreements, it bases itself on isolated sections without taking into account the text of the agreements as a whole. Furthermore, WSI's own behaviour and that of its representatives clearly show that WSI itself interpreted the agreements in the manner described above and also indicated this to the licensees. Thus, there were numerous occasions on which pressure was brought to bear on the licensees – including those, such as Akutec, in whose contracts the abovementioned prohibition was not specifically contained – to the effect that they should not, beyond providing spare parts, supply rigs separately (see A.IV.3 above).

Despite enquiries from third parties, the licensees have therefore largely refrained from supplying rigs separately. WSI seeks to explain this by claiming that these were autonomous decisions of each independent licensee, deriving from their own interest to reserve rigs, in accordance with their own capacity, only for boards of their own manufacture for the purpose of their own sales of complete sailboards. It must be pointed out that, in view of the existing specific or at least indirect contractual obligations on licensees, these decisions could not have been entirely autonomous. Moreover, these decisions were prompted by the numerous additional 'exhortations' addressed to all licensees, which carried the underlying threat that their licensing agreements might at any time be terminated. Furthermore, as regards the licensees' economic self-interest, WSI's statement is refuted by the fact that the production of rigs on the one hand and of boards on the other is technically completely unrelated and that many licensees do not manufacture rigs at all for themselves but buy them from various specialized subcontractors. Accordingly, the separate supply of rigs might be of substantial economic interest to them, so that to prevent such supplies constituted an appreciable restriction of competition.

(bb)  The abovementioned restriction was also not covered by the specific subject matter of the German patent and is therefore still caught by Article 85(1) of the EEC Treaty, since the patent protection extends in Germany only to the rig.

The patent in question is a combination patent. In order to be covered by the scope of the patent, therefore, the board would have to be part of the protected combination. The combination elements mentioned in the patent claims – the patent claims are the primary basis for determining the scope of the protection (see Article 84 of the European Patent Convention) – concern only elements of a rig which, as a result of their particular arrangement and interaction, produce a given new effect. Where reference is also made in the patent claims to the board, this is clearly only for the purpose of describing the general technical framework within which this effect is produced.

Even when account is taken of the patent description and the corresponding drawings, the result is no different. Parts of a combination to which the invention idea does not directly relate do not belong to a protected combination, even though their use may be stipulated or absolutely indispensable. The aim referred to in the patent description and the proposed solution (see A.IV.A above) relate simply to a new rigging system for floating boards. The idea protected by the patent in question is limited to this. This is also shown by the details of the state-of-the-art given in the patent description; according to these at the time of the patent grant several hand-sailing devices were already known for use, among other things, on surfboards. Patent protection can only be considered, however, where an idea goes beyond the known state-of-the-art. Even if one were to go beyond the currently applicable interpretation rule in Article 14 of the German Patents Law (see also Article 69 of the European Patent Convention) and extend the scope of the patent protection to elements in which only the general idea underlying the patented invention, in line with principles of interpretation used by the German courts hitherto, is reflected, the result would be no different since the idea is restricted to a new rigging system to which the board as such does not belong.

This interpretation is confirmed by the outcome of the proceedings for grant before the German Patent Office. The fact that the Patent Office has limited the patent claim to the rig is clearly reflected in the alteration of the original principal claim to a 'rig for a sailboard' and in the new wording of the patent aim and its solution in the patent description. This was also made sufficiently clear to the patent applicant by the German Patent Office. This interpretation is further confirmed in the judgments already pronounced by German courts on this issue, and particularly in the abovementioned judgment of the Bundesgerichtshof of 10 December 1981, where, in the presentation of the facts of the case, the board is not mentioned as an element of the protected combination. In view of this clear state of affairs, it is not necessary to await the final outcome of the action for patent infringement brought against an importer of boards by WSI and referred to by it as a 'test case' (see A.IV. 3b above), quite apart from the fact that even a judgment favourable to WSI would in no way determine the scope of the patent erga omnes.

It follows from the above that it may also be left open whether Article 85(1) would in fact cease to apply if the German patent were to include the board.

(cc) Nor, finally, could the requirement that the licensees were to supply rigs only in conjunction with approved board types be derived from the specific subject matter of a patent right on 'indirect patent infringement' grounds. This is an action which a patentee can bring against third parties in order to prevent them 'from offering or supplying to a person, other than a party entitled to exploit the patented invention, with means relating to an essential element of that invention, for putting it into effect therein when the third party knows, or it is obvious in the circumstances, that these means are suitable and intended for putting that invention into effect' (see section 10(1) of the German Patents Law as at 16 December 1980, BGBl 1981, Part I, p. 1).

In view of the scope of the patent claim in Germany, it is doubtful whether boards are 'means' within the meaning of the above provision. At any rate, no right would ensue to prevent licensees from marketing rigs otherwise than in conjunction with such 'means', since the licensees are all ' persons entitled to exploit the patented invention'within the meaning of this provision. For the same reason, such a right of prohibition could not be invoked against non-licensed manufacturers of boards for sailboards, at any rate where they restrict themselves to manufacturing such boards alone and supply these boards only to licensees for the purpose of combining them with patent protected rigs or purchase from them rigs for the purpose of combining them with their boards.

(c) The abovementioned restriction of competition was repeated in the method of calculating royalties, as laid down in the agreements, on the basis of the net selling price of the complete sailboard supplied by the licensee. This obligation too – where it concerned sailboards manufactured under German patent No 19 14 602.4-22 – fell in the circumstances of the present case, under Article 85(1) of the EEC Treaty.

If the calculation of royalties, when payable on the basis of individual sales, is not linked to the products covered by the licensed invention there is a danger of the licensee's production, as compared with that of competitors, having to bear costs for which the licensee is not compensated through the advantages conferred by exploitation of the patent. As already explained above, the German patent does not include the board. Of course it may for practical reasons be necessary in many cases not to take the individual items covered by the licensed patent as the basis for calculating the royalties, but to refer instead to a product at a more advanced stage of the manufacturing process, into which the patented item is incorporated and in conjunction with which it is marketed. The reasons for this may be, for example, that the number of items manufactured or consumed or their value are difficult to establish separately in a complex production process, or that there is for the patented item on its own no separate demand which the licensee would be prevented from satisfying through such a method of calculation. Under such circumstances, this kind of calculation may be regarded as neutral under the competition rules; but this is not necessarily the case simply because a mode of calculation is ' usual commercial practice', as WSI states.

However, such circumstances as outlined above did not exist in the present case: The production of the rigs and their individual parts on the one hand and the boards on the other is not technically related: The licensees obtain their supplies to a large extent from subcontractors of various kinds, who charge for each element separately. Even though it is only through the combination of board and rig that a final product ready for use is arrived at, the combination is so easy for everyone to carry out that there is brisk demand for each part, whether from manufacturers of other board types, from wholesalers or retailers or from final consumers. Owing to the growing popularity of windsurfing it is very likely that such demand will expand even more since an increasing number of experienced sportsmen is going to want to acquire different types of boards for various events that may all, nevertheless, be equipped with the same rig.

Whereas there were no objective technical reasons to support this method of calculating royalties, it prevented the licencees from acting in the separate markets for boards and rigs.

First, the method of royalty payments as described above meant that WSI claimed royalties for each of the principal parts of a sailboard, in other words the board and the rig, supplied by a licensee. That meant that the licensees were obliged to pay royalties even where they only sold the board alone, which is not covered by the German patent.

Furthermore, where one of the principal parts, namely a board or a rig, was sold separately, the royalties had to be calculated on the basis of the fictitious price of a complete sailboard. In particular, in the case of a sale of a rig alone, the burden of such royalties, taking into consideration the lower price of a rig in comparison with a board, would constitute an enormous increase in the costs. Although identical or similar costs might have occurred if WSI had managed to impose a proportionally higher level of royalties based on the sale price of a rig alone, as long as the sole basis for calculating royalties was the complete sailboard, the licensees were incited to apportion the costs of the royalties between the board and the rig. Consequently, the sale of rigs alone was not economically viable, for the proceeds that one could obtain by such a sale would have had to cover royalties calculated on the basis of the sale price of a much dearer product. Added to this was the difficulty in practice for the licensees of determining which of the different models of their range of sailboards should have been the basis for a fictitious calculation according to the cost of a complete sailboard. In the circumstances, the aforementioned method of calculating royalties tended to prevent the licensees from selling rigs alone and this independently from the express contractual prohibition aiming at the same objective. The outcome was that, on the one hand, other producers of boards were prevented from completing their products with the patented rigs and, on the other, the licensees were persuaded to sell boards and rigs as a combination only, even though there is a demand for the two parts separately.

(d)     Article 85(1) of the EEC Treaty also applies to the restriction whereby the manufacturing licence for German patent No 19 14 602.4-22 which relates to the complete sailboard, was limited to a specific manufacturing plant in the Federal Republic of Germany, given the fact that any change in the place of manufacture on the part of the licensee (with the exception of Ostermann and Shark) entitled WSI to terminate the agreement immediately.

Because of the constant threat that the licensor might terminate the agreement, each licensee was in practice obliged not to manufacture boards and rigs anywhere else other than in the stipulated place of manufacture. He thereby relinquished the opportunity open to any third party of taking up the manufacture of sailboards in areas of the common market in which the licensor did not enjoy patent protection and of distributing them there without having to bear the costs of the royalty payable for exploitation of the patent. Such was the unmistakeable purpose and result-ant effect of the version of the agreements between WSI and S.A.N, Klepper and Market which applied until the end of 1980. Although this was then replaced by a less clear wording which was already contained in the other licensing agreements, this in no way meant that a de facto restriction did not or did no longer exist. It remained a condition that any change in the place of manufacture on the part of the licensee could lead WSI to terminate the agreement, irrespective of whether the production were transferred wholly or only partly outside the licensed terri-tory.

Consequently, in the case under discussion, WSI obtained royalties for all the sailboards sold by the licensees throughout the common market, since they could not in fact be manufactured outside the licensed territory. It is true that the manu-facture of a patented product is exclusively reserved for the patentee, so that the obligation to pay royalties for manufacture within the area in which a patent is valid is covered by its specific subject matter. However, it is not part of the spe-cific subject matter of the patent right if the patentee so formulates the conditions of the licence as to make it impossible, at least in practice, for the licensee to en-gage in royalty-free manufacture in areas not covered by the patent and thus indi-rectly to secure for the patentee a 'reward' for his invention even in places where he does not enjoy any patent protection at all.

Therefore, this restriction was neither covered by the Commission Notice on Patent Licensing Agreements (Official Journal of the European Communities No 139 of 24 December 1962, p. 2922/82) where the Commission stated that, on the basis of the facts known to it at that time, the prohibition laid down in Article 85(1) of the EEC Treaty did not apply inter alia to a territorial restriction of the licensee which would limit the license to a specific factory (loc. cit. point 4 (b)). In any event, this statement covers only territories where patent protection was effec-tively granted. The further question relating to whether the prohibition on the lic-ensees to transfer their production plant within the territory where a valid patent exists, also falls under Article 85(1) of the EEC Treaty can be left open for the purposes of this proceeding[69].

(e)     The obligation that the licensees affix to boards manufactured and marketed in Germany a notice stating that they were 'licensed by Hoyle Schweitzer' or were 'licensed by WSI' was also an infringment of Article 85(1) of the EEC Treaty. This is because such a notice gave the impression that each licensee's board was manufactured on the basis of certain industrial property rights or at least in accor-dance with certain technical know-how made available by the licensor. However, the opposite was the case. The licensees were thus restricted in representing them-selves as technically independent, at least as far as the board was concerned, and in consolidating the reputation of their firms through the respective board types developed by themselves independently.

(f)     The fact that the agreements require the German licensees to recognize as valid trade marks the word marks 'Windsurfer' and 'Windsurfing' and the 'logo' design

---

[69] See Fourth Report on Competition Policy (1974), points 22 et seq.; Fifth Report on Competi-tion Policy (1975), point 11, where the Commission, the establishment of the internal market having basically been accomplished, has already moved away from the view that territorial restrictions in patent licensing agreements are in principle harmless for the purpose of Article 85(1) of the EEC Treaty. See also the Commission's announcement given in the Official Journal of the European Communities No C 58, 3-3-1979, p. 11, of its intention to withdraw the abovementioned Notice.

mark that Ten Cate has hitherto used in Europe for its sailboards also infringed Article 85(1) of the EEC Treaty.

In the present case, WSI and Ten Cate have themselves intimated that considerable doubts exist as to whether these trade marks are sufficiently distinctive in character and whether in particular the terms 'Windsurfer' and and 'Windsurfing' have not in current language become a common name for the sport and item of sporting equipment in question. Such circumstances would, however, militate against their registration or maintenance as valid trade marks under the laws of all the Member States[70].

In relinquishing by contract the possibility of bringing these circumstances into play, the licensee renounced the opportunity of using names or symbols that might indicate generally, and without reference to a specific undertaking, a particular sport in a striking way to a broad public. Such a possibility might have represented an important element in their competitive behaviour, particularly in advertising. Conversely, WSI could gain an unjustified competitive advantage if it succeeded in monopolizing the use of any such name or symbol for itself. The obligation of the licensees not to challenge the trade marks was advantageous in this context. Whether a no-challenge clause concerning a trade mark also falls under Article 85(1) of the EEC Treaty when it is part of an agreement concerning the licensing of this very trade mark can be left undecided for the purposes of this proceeding. In any event, the conclusion of a licensing agreement concerning patents only must not be used in order to induce the patent licensee to acknowledge the validity of trade marks belonging to the licensor or third parties and thus to deny him the opportunity of clarifying whether use of the relevant marks is open to all competitors.

(g)     The obligation imposed on Ostermann and Shark not to challenge the licensed patent also constituted an infringement of Article 85(1) of the EEC Treaty. This no-challenge clause denied the licensees in the present case the opportunity, open to any third party, of removing an obstacle – which was essential bearing in mind the importance of the patents on the economical level as well – to their economic activity by means of proceedings attacking the patent's validity. Such a restriction is also of importance where a patent is granted by a patent office only after examination of the invention for novelty and inventive step, for despite such an examination, as regards the question of patentability, the opposition of firms interested in the refusal of the patent or any possible actions for invalidity must still be permitted.

(h)     The abovementioned clauses were, individually and taken as a whole, likely to affect trade between Member States. The effect of the restrictions as described in B.I.1 (a) to (c) was to render trade in boards and rigs between Germany and the other Member States at least substantially more difficult. The limitation of the licence to certain board-types restricted the possible demand of the licensees for boards of other manufacturers from other Member States. These manufacturers

---

[70] See also Articles 2(1) and 14 (2) of the proposal for a first Council Directive to approximate the laws of the Member States relating to trade marks, OJ No C 351, 31-12-1980, p. 1, and Article 6(1) of the proposal for a Council Regulation on Community trade marks, OJ No C 35 1, 31-12-1980, p. 5.
Even if it is only through information made available to him by the licensor that a licensee is put in a position to challenge the patent, the interest of the public in a basically free competition system and therefore in the removal of a monopoly perhaps wrongly granted to the licensee must still prevail over the special relationship which exists between the partners to a licensing agreement.

were impeded from adding rigs to their boards so as to form a complete sailboard unit by the ban on the separate sale of the former, which was safeguarded and enforced by the mode of calculating the royalties, and were thus obstructed in their marketing efforts in the Federal Republic of Germany. The same was true for importers of boards from other Member States. The fixing of the place of manufacture (see B.I.1 (d) above) forced the licensees concerned to serve the markets of other Member States only from the Federal Republic of Germany; otherwise they might have served these markets from other places where production would not have borne the burden of royalties. The obligation to affix a licence notice on the board (see B.I.1 (e) above) and the obligation to acknowledge the licensor's trade mark (see B.I.1 (f) above) impeded the licensees' scope for developing their businesses throughout the Community. The no-challenge clause imposed on Ostermann and Shark (see B.I.1 (g) above) reinforced the licensor's patent right not only vis-à-vis the relevant licensees, but also vis-à-vis all competitors throughout the Community.

Bearing in mind that the licensees together with Ten Cate (WSC) hold a strong position in the German market, and the exceptional economic importance of the patent in question, these restrictions on trade were appreciable.

**2. Restrictions of competition in distribution**

(a)   Exclusive dealing agreements, particularly when concluded between firms from different Member States, may be caught by Article 85(1) of the EEC Treaty because of the obligation imposed on the supplier to supply the relevant goods within a specified territory only to the sole importer and because of the territorial restrictions imposed on the sole importer regarding sales of the relevant goods. The exclusive dealing agreements concluded between various parties in the case under consideration are as such, however, not the subject of these proceedings, in so far as they are covered by exemptions under Article 1(1) and (2) of Commission Regulation No 67/67/EEC (3).

(aa)   However, the following agreements also contained a ban preventing the sole importer not only from pursuing any active sales policy outside his allotted territory (see Article 2(1) (b) of Regulation No 67/67/EEC, but also from furnishing any supplies whatsoever:

1.   the agreements between Akutec on the one hand and Horwa (until 1981), then Taselaar (Netherlands), Ertisport (Belgium) and RaFly (Italy) on the other;

2.   the agreements between Ostermann on the one hand and Thijs (Netherlands) and d'Ieteren (Belgium) on the other, between Klepper on the one hand and Telstar (Netherlands), Intersurf (Italy), Media Loisirs (France) and Citabel Sports (Luxembourg) on the other; and between Shark on the one hand and Renka Sport (Netherlands) on the other.

In the agreements included under (1), these restrictions appear from the actual wording of the standard agreement. In the agreements included under (2), it is merely stipulated that the supplier's approval must be obtained for supplies outside the agreed territory; however, this sort of approval requirement interferes with the sole importer's potential sales strategy. It thus constitutes a restriction of competition within the meaning of Article 85(1) of the EEC Treaty. The absolute ban on supplies from the allotted territory of the possibility of refusing to approve such supplies makes it possible to isolate the individual sales territories completely from one another. These agreements were thus designed to affect trade between Member States in a way which was no longer covered by Regulation No 67/67/EEC.

(bb)    Akutec, Ostermann, Klepper and Shark together occupy a substantial position on the German market (accounting for approximately 40% of that market). Their individual positions are also significant. While the market shares of the individual firms differ considerably, none of these market shares is so small as to mean that the isolation of the German market achieved though the reimport bans has not been appreciable.

The products of Akutec, Ostermann, Klepper and Shark are well established in other Member States; this applies particularly to the important French and Dutch markets (see A.III.2 above). Even though their market shares are not equally large everywhere and they could not be determined with certainty because of the relative newness of the market in windsurfing equipment and its resulting fluctuations, exports to Community countries do at all events represent an important business factor for all undertakings concerned. Accordingly, the fact that the agreements were intended to prevent the sole importers altogether from supplying other Community sales territories directly must also be seen as an appreciable restriction of competition.

(b)    In standardized supply agreements, Akutec (using the 'dealer's pass') and WSC and Ostermann (using the ' partnership agreements') had obliged retailers in Germany to sell their products only to final consumers.

(aa)    These obligations prevented the retailers from selling to other retailers and constituted, at least in so far as this prohibition concerned sales to retailers in other Member States, an infringement of Article 85(1) of the EEC Treaty.

(bb)    In the present case, these agreements also affected trade between Member States and were appreciable: the sailboards manufactured by Akutec and Ostermann, and those of Ten Cate distributed in Germany by WSC are marketed in many Member States of the Community. Their products are well represented on the French and Dutch markets in particular (see A.III.2 above). Dealers in these areas might in principle have been interested in obtaining these products from dealers on the German market, on which in the period under investigation Ten Cate (WSC) and Ostermann had a substantial market share (15% and 25% respectively) and Akutec a significant share (7%). Account must also be taken of the fact that, because these three firms as a whole had adopted the same approach, almost half of the supply available on the German market was withheld from potential trade between Member States.

## II. APPLICABILITY OF ARTICLE 85(3) OF THE EEC TREATY

Under Article 85(3), the provisions of Article 85(1) may be declared inapplicable in the case of any agreement between undertakings which contributes to improving the production or distribution of goods or to promoting technical or economic progress, while allowing consumers a fair share of the resulting benefit, and which does not:

(a)    impose on the undertakings concerned restrictions which are not indispensable to the attainment of these objectives;

(b)    afford such undertakings the possibility of eliminating competition in respect of a substantial part of the products in question.

None of the agreements and concerted practices examined here have been notified to the Commission, so that in principle, under Article 4(1) of Regulation No 17, application of Article 85(3) of the EEC Treaty cannot, for formal reasons, be considered.

1.    The patent licensing agreements also do not fall under Article 4 (2) (2) (b) of Regulation No 17. This applies to the obligation not to supply rigs manufactured under the German patent except with previously approved board types, since this obligation restricts licensees not only in relation to the exercise of the licensed right, but furthermore impedes their liberty to decide whether and to what extent they will act as a competitor on the market for boards, which are not covered by the German patent. Although markets for rigs and boards are related in that rigs only form a final product ready for use when combined with boards or other types of base, both markets are nevertheless distinguishable as regards demand. In the same way the contractual obligations relating to the calculation of royalties on the basis of the selling price of a complete sailboard as well as the obligation to affix a notice about the licence on the board went beyond the limits of those restrictions not needing notification under Article 4 (2) (2) (b).

This Article is also inapplicable to the obligation to acknowledge as valid the trade marks of the WSI / Ten Cate as these rights are not licensed to the licensees. Nor is this Article applicable to the obligation imposed on Ostermann and Shark not to challenge the licensed rights, since this obligation is not aimed at restricting the licensees in their exercise of the licensed patent rights but at denying to them the opportunity of attacking the very existence of the licensed rights.

Furthermore, there is no basis to believe that the conditions of Article 85(3) of the EEC Treaty would have been met:

–    The restrictions of the licences to certain board types and the need to obtain approval for new boards had purely restrictive direct effects on the production and distribution of goods. Quality and safety requirements in respect of the licensed product which go beyond the specific subject matter of the patent right may certainly lead, in particular cases, to an improvement in the production of goods and benefit the consumer. In principle, therefore, it cannot be denied that the licensor may also have an interest in the observance of such standards. Even where he does not encounter the consumer in the licensed territory as the manufacturer and seller of the licensed product, the consumer may form particular ideas about the identity of the patentee and the 'value' of his patented invention – whether because it has become known through public discussion, or because the patentee himself draws attention to himself through the notice referring to the inventor, or because the consumer encounters him as a supplier on markets outside the licensed territory. However, the formulation of such standards also entails special dangers for the entrepreneurial independence of the licensees and competitive freedom on the relevant market as a whole. They must therefore be limited to what is objectively necessary, they must be notified to the licensee in advance and in a clear and detailed fashion and must apply to all licensees and also to the licensor without distinction. In view of the vagueness of the relevant clause in the agreements, these conditions have not been met in the case under consideration. This is further reinforced by the fact that the control exercised over boards was at the same time designed to ensure that there was a competitive 'distance' between all involved.

–    The obligation to sell rigs only as part of complete sailboards merely constitutes a restriction of distribution of goods.

–    The requirement that royalties be paid on the basis of the selling price of complete sailboards and the requirement that the sailboards carry a notice indicating that they were 'licensed by Hoyle Schweitzer' served merely to consolidate and reinforce the abovementioned restrictions of competition.

–    The imposition on the licensees of the place of manufacture, the obligation on them to acknowledge certain trade marks as legally valid and the obligation imposed on Ostermann and Shark not to challenge the licensed patents did not result in any improvements or benefits within the meaning of Article 85(3) of the EEC Treaty.

2.    The distribution agreements concluded by Akutec, WSC and Ostermann with retailers in Germany were also not caught by Article 4 (2) (1) of Regulation No 17. The ban on supplies to other dealers contained in the agreements also applied, without restriction, to any supplies to dealers in other Member States and thus constituted a ban on exports, so that these agreements also related to imports and exports within the meaning of this provision.

     Moreover, there are no circumstances underlying these restrictions which might have justified exemption under Article 85(3) of the EEC Treaty. It is true that the retailers covered by the agreements were referred to as 'specialist dealers' and that the firms involved have also claimed that it was necessary, owing to the special nature of the sailboard product, to exercise control over the eligibility of dealers. However, none of the firms involved have mentioned any objective criteria on the basis of which the dealers were in fact selected. In any case, even if a permissible selective distribution system had existed, the complete ban on any supplies to other dealers, including therefore those in the distribution system itself, would have imposed too great a restriction.

## III. APPLICATION OF ARTICLE 15(2) (a) OF REGULATION No 17

Under Article 15(2) (a) of Regulation No 17, the Commission may by decision impose on undertakings fines of from 1 000 to 1 000 000 units of account, or a sum in excess thereof but not exceeding 10% of the turnover in the preceding business year of each of the undertakings participating in the infringement where, either intentionally or negligently, they infringe Article 85(1) of the EEC Treaty. In fixing the amount of the fine, regard must be had both to the gravity and to the duration of the infringement.

### 1. Culpability
(a)   Patent licensing agreements

     While WSI and the licensees may have originally assumed that the ban on the separate supply of rigs, the calculation of the royalty on the basis of the selling price of the complete sailboard and the affixing of the licence notice to the board were covered by the scope of the German patent in the form of the original application, they could not in good faith maintain that view once the German Patent Office, at the beginning of 1974, had decided on the final version of the document laid open for public inspection on 27 June 1974. The adoption of this version and its wording clearly resulted in the patent protection being restricted to the rig. Where, in legal actions brought against third parties, WSI continues to put forward the view that the scope of the patent protection extends in Germany also to the board and that the abovementioned restrictions had therefore been covered by the specific subject matter of the patent right, the maintenance of this legal standpoint – at any rate as regards the applicability of the competition rules in the EEC Treaty – does not exclude the reproach of negligent infringement. This would be true even if it were established that third-party suppliers of boards for windsurfing might under certain circumstances be committing an 'indirect patent infringement' on the German market, since licensees at any rate, being persons entitled to exploit the invention, can supply rigs to anyone and purchase boards from anyone. The culpability of the licensees as regards the abovementioned restrictions must be deemed to be slight, however, as they had to submit to the relevant conditions imposed by WSI in order to obtain a licence. Similarly, in the implementation of the licensing agreements, it was primarily WSI that insisted on the observance of the relevant restrictions and in particular sought to prevent the separate supply of rigs, so that the main burden of responsibility, as far as the application of Article 15(2) is concerned, lies with WSI alone. Therefore it has been thought fit not to fine the licensees.

In assessing the culpability of WSI, the Commission has given consideration to the fact that no decision has ever before taken on restrictions of competition of the kind under consideration here.

The culpability of WSI, Ostermann and Shark regarding the agreement concluded between them not to challenge the licensed patent must be judged quite independently of their own assessment of the patent situation. Even in the abovementioned Commission Notice on Patent Licensing Agreements of 24 December 1962, such no-challenge clauses were not included in the list of clauses unobjectionable under the terms of Article 85(1) of the EEC Treaty. Since 1972, the Commission has in its decisions consistently pointed out the incompatibility of such clauses with this provision[71]. Ignorance of this legal position by the parties concerned is at the very least grossly negligent. However, the culpability of the licensees Ostermann and Shark must also be deemed to be slight, since they too had to submit to this condition imposed by WSI; therefore, once again, a fine is to be imposed only on WSI.

Against that WSI claims that it had to accept this clause of the agreements since it had originally been agreed by Ten Cate with the firms concerned and these firms had refused any change when the licensing agreement was transferred to WSI. However, this explanation cannot be accepted, since the no-challenge clause is an agreement to the disadvantage of the licensees alone. It has also not been confirmed by the licensees.

(b)    Restrictions of competition in distribution

It has been a principle established in Commission decisions since as early as 1964[72], and confirmed frequently by the Court of Justice of the European Communities[73], that export or reimport bans imposed on sole distributors and bans imposed on other types of dealers preventing them from supplying other dealers constitute infringements of the Community competition rules in that they tend to isolate national markets, in so far as such restrictions go beyond the limits set in Regulation No 67/67/EEC and are not limited to the obligation to observe the conditions of a selective distribution system.

The firms involved in these restrictions of competition − namely Ostermann, Akutec, Klepper, Shark and WSC − have intentionally infringed one of the basic prohibitions laid down in the Community competition rules: for in all the abovementioned instances, the aim was the complete isolation of the respective national markets. The fact that they might not have realized in detail the scope of

[71] Decision of 9-6-1972, Davidson Rubber : OJ No L 143, 23-6-1972, p. 31, and in particular p. 32; Decision of 18-7-1975, Kabelmetal / Luchaire: OJ No L 222, 22-8-1975, p. 34, and in particular p. 35; Decision of 2-12-1975, AOIP / Beyrard: OJ No L 6, 13-1-1976, p. 8, and in particular p. 12.

[72] See Decision of 23-9-1964, Grundig / Consten: OJ No 161, 20-10-1964, p. 2545 ; see also, for example, Decision of 1-12-1976, Miller International: OJ No L 357, 29-12-1976, p. 40 ; Decision of 23-12-1977, BMW Belgium NV: OJ No L 46, 17-2-1978, p. 33; Decision of 14-12-1979, Pioner Hi-Fi Equipment: OJ No L 60, 5-3-1980, pp. 21 et seq.; Decision of 25-11-1980, Johnson and Johnson: OJ No L 377 31-12-1980, p. 16.

[73] Judgment of 13-7-1966, Grundig / Consten (1966) ECR 429; see also judgment of 1-2-1978, Miller International (1978) ECR 131; judgment of 12-7-1979, BMW Belgium NV (1979) ECR 2435.

these rules is irrelevant, since they were in any case aware of and sought to achieve the restrictive effects of their agreements[74].

## 2. Gravity and duration of the infringement

(a)    Patent licensing agreements

The ban on the separate sale of rigs and the associated restrictions concerning the calculation of royalties and the affixing of the licence notice had a considerable influence on the supply of sailboards on the German market. Other Community suppliers wishing to market boards in Germany combined with the rigs manufactured under licence were thus in principle shut out, though in practice the attempt to exclude them was not always entirely successful. The effect of these restrictions must have been appreciable as from the time when the patent was published on 27 June 1974 and even more so when the patent was finally granted by the German Patent Office (decision of 31 March 1978), because suppliers, from the latter time at the latest, were dependent on the supply of rigs from the licensees if they wished to avoid what was then a clear risk of patent infringement proceedings. The full effect of the restrictions was finally felt after the termination of the litigation on the granting of the licensed patent brought before the Bundespatentgericht (decision of 28 November 1979) in which the validity of the patent for the rig was in substance confirmed. It must therefore be assumed that these restrictions of competition significantly affected the marketing campaigns for sailboards in 1978 and 1979 and had a major effect on such campaigns in 1980 and 1981.

With regard to the no-challenge clause imposed by WSI on Ostermann and Shark, particular account must be taken of the fact that the sail system protected by the patent is considered at present to be the only usable one on the market and that the patent is accordingly also of outstanding importance economically.

(b)    Restrictions of competition in distribution

It is difficult to assess in detail the extent of the movements of goods which might have taken place if they had not been prevented by the distribution restrictions agreed by Ostermann, Akutec, Klepper and Shark with sole importers in other Member States and by Ostermann, Akutec and WSC with retailers in Germany. They were in force for between two and three years. In view of their purpose, which runs directly counter to the Community's objective of integration, and their not inconsiderable duration, the abovementioned restrictions must be regarded as serious. However, account must be taken of the fact that the firms involved have been able to show that the distribution restrictions were in many cases not observed; measures to counter this were taken only by Ostermann and then only to a limited extent. In fixing the amount of the fine, apart from the turnover, the number of restrictive distribution agreements concluded by each undertaking must also be considered.

## IV. APPLICABILITY OF ARTICLE 3 OF REGULATION No 17

Where the Commission finds that there is infringement of Articles 85 or 86 of the EEC Treaty, it may, under Article 3 of Regulation No 17, require the undertakings concerned to bring such infringement to an end.

After the suppression of the said agreements, at least in the version under consideration here, the need to require the termination of the infringements contained in these agree-

---

[74]  See judgment of 1-2-1978, Miller International (1978) ECR p. 131, and in particular ground of judgment No 18.

ments no longer exists. But there remains a continuing interest in confirming the existence of infringements in the past. This follows in the first place from Article 15(2) of Regulation No 17, since fines are being imposed with regard to a number of these agreements. However, this is also true for those restrictive agreements for which a fine is not imposed since it is necessary vis-à-vis the interested public to clarify the Commission's assessment of these agreements taken as a whole. The complainants have a particular interest therein.

HAS ADOPTED THIS DECISION:

Article 1

1.   The following provisions in the patent licensing agreements which existed until 1981/82 between WSI and the licensees Ostermann, Shark, Akutec, S.A.N., Klepper and Marker constituted an infringement of Article 85(1) of the EEC Treaty:

    1.   the obligation on the licensees to exploit the licensed patents only for the manufacture of sailboards using boards which had been given WSI's prior approval;

    2.   the obligation on the licensees not to supply rigs manufactured under German patent No 19 14 602.4-22 separately and without the boards approved by WSI;

    3.   the obligation on the licensees to pay royalties for rigs manufactured under German patent No 19 14 602.4-22 only on the basis of the net selling price of a complete sailboard;

    4.   the obligation on the licensees to affix to the boards in their range a notice stating that such boards are 'licensed by Hoyle Schweitzer' or 'licensed by WSI';

    5.   the obligation on the licensees to acknowledge the word marks 'Windsurfer' and 'Windsurfing'as well as a design mark showing the abstract shape of a sail (so-called 'logo') as valid trade marks.

2.   The provision in the agreements between WSI and Akutec, S.A.N., Klepper and Marker for termination of the licensing agreements should the licensees start production in a territory not covered by a patent also constituted an infringement of Article 85(1) of the EEC Treaty.

3.   Furthermore, the obligation on the licensees, stipulated in the agreements with Ostermann and Shark, not to challenge the licensed patents constituted an infringement of Article 85(1) of the EEC Treaty.

Article 2

1.   The prohibition contained in the distribution agreements as listed below under (a) to (d) preventing each sole distributor from selling outside his allotted territory, or the latters' obligation to ask the manufacturer for approval of any such sales, constituted infringements of Article 85(1) of the EEC Treaty:

    (a)   agreements between Akutec on the one hand and the undertakings Horwa, Taselaar, Ertisport and RaFly on the other;

    (b)   agreements between Ostermann on the one hand and the undertakings Thijs and d'Ieteren on the other;

    (c)   agreements between Klepper on the one hand and the undertakings Telstar, Intersurf, Media Loisirs and Citabel Sports on the other;

    (d)   the agreement between Shark on the one hand and Renka Sport on the other.

2.   The prohibition on retailers according to the agreements as listed below under (a) to (c) to supply contract products to other dealers in other Member States also constituted an infringement of Article 85(1) of the EEC Treaty:

(a)   the 'dealer passes' distributed by Akutec to retailers;
(b)   the 'partnership agreements' concluded between Ostermann and retailers;
(c)   the 'partnership agreements' concluded between WSC and retailers.

Article 3
The following fines are hereby imposed:
1.   on the undertaking WSI a total fine of 50 000 (fifty thousand) ECU or DM 113 793
     in respect of the ban on the separate supply of rigs (Article 1(1) (2)), the obligation
     to pay royalties on the basis of the net selling price of a complete sailboard (Article
     1(1) (3)), the obligation to affix the licence notice on the board (Article 1(1) (4)),
     the factual ban on production in territories not covered by a patent (Article 1 (2))
     and the stipulation of a no-challenge clause (Article 1 (3));
2.   in respect of the export bans imposed on sole distributors in other Member States
     and the bans imposed on dealers in Germany from supplying other dealers:
     1.   a fine of 15 000 (fifteen thousand) ECU or DM 34 138 on the undertaking
          Ostermann;
     2.   a fine of 10 000 (ten thousand) ECU or DM 22 759 on the undertaking
          Akutec;
     3.   a fine of 10 000 (ten thousand) ECU or DM 22 759 on the undertaking
          Klepper;
     4.   a fine of 5 000 (five thousand) ECU or DM 11 379 on the undertaking
          Shark;
     5.   a fine of 5 000 (five thousand) ECU or DM 11 379 on the undertaking WSC.
     The abovementioned amounts shall be paid within three months of notification of
     this Decision to account No 260/00/64910 of the Commission of the European
     Communities with Sal. Oppenheimer, Cologne.

Article 4
This Decision is addressed to:
1.   Windsurfing International Inc.
     (a)   1955 West 190th Street, Torrance,
           California 90509,
           USA;
     (b)   for the attention of
           Herrn Patentanwalt Axel Hansmann
           c / o Licht, Schmidt, Hansmann and Hermann,
           Albert-Rosshaupter-Str. 65,
           D-8000 Muenchen 70
2.   Windglider Fred Ostermann GmbH,
     Comotorstr. 12,
     D-6636 Ueberherrn-Altforweiler;
3.   Shark Wassersportgeraete GmbH,
     Auf den Hoehen,
     D-2830 Bassum;
4.   Akutec Angewandte Kunststofftechnik GmbH,
     Staeblistr. 6,
     D-8000 Muenchen 71;
5.   S.A.N. Warenvertriebsgesellschaft mbH,
     Roetelstr. 30,
     D-7107 Neckarsulm;

6.  Klepper BeteiligungsGmbH and Co. Bootsbau KG,
    Klepperstr. 18,
    D-8200 Rosenheim;
7.  Marker Surf GmbH,
    Hauptstr. 51 – 53,
    D-8100 Garmisch-Partenkirchen;
8.  Windsurfing Central GmbH,
    Hainburgstr. 47,
    D-6054 Rodgau.

This Decision is enforceable in accordance with Article 192 of the EEC Treaty.
Done at Brussels, 11 July 1983.
For the Commission
Frans Andriessen
Member of the Commission

———

### 2.4.2. COMMISSION DECISION RELATING TO A PROCEEDING PURSUANT TO ARTICLE 85 OF THE EEC TREATY (IV/32.524 – SCREENSPORT/EBU MEMBERS), 19 FEBRUARY 1991[75]

*The Commission of the European Communities,*

–   Having regard to the Treaty establishing the European Economic Community,
–   Having regard to Council Regulation No 17 of 6 February 1962, first Regulation implementing Articles 85 and 86 of the EEC Treaty[76], as last amended by the Act of Accession of Spain and Portugal, and in particular Article 3(1) thereof,
–   Having regard to the application for a finding of an infringement submitted on 17 December 1987 pursuant to Article 3 of Regulation No 17, by W. H. Smith & Son Ltd and Screen Sport (formerly Screensport Ltd) (hereinafter 'Screensport'),
–   Having regard to the notification and application for negative clearance submitted to the Commission by the Eurosport consortium, Sky Television plc (hereinafter 'Sky'), Satellite Sport Sales Ltd, Satellite Sports Services Ltd and News International plc (hereinafter 'NI') on 17 January 1989,
–   Having regard to the Commission Decision of 5 December 1988 to initiate proceedings in this case,
–   Having given the undertakings and association of undertakings concerned the opportunity to make known their views on the objections raised by the Commission, pursuant to Article 19(1) and (2) of Regulation No 17 and Commission Regulation No 99/63/EEC of 25 July 1963 on the hearings provided for in Article 19(1) and (2) of council Regulation No 17[77],
–   After consulting the Advisory Committee on Restrictive Practices and Dominant Positions,
Whereas:

---

[75] OJ L 63 , 9-3-1991 p. 32-44.
[76] OJ No 13, 21-2-1962, p. 204.
[77] OJ No 127, 20-8-1963, p. 2268.

## I. THE FACTS
### Complaint and notification

(1)     On 17 December 1987 Screensport registered a complaint at the Commission concerning the following:
   (i)     certain activities of the European Broadcasting Union (hereinafter 'EBU') and/or its members, in particular, the refusal to grant Screensport sublicences to sports events to which the EBU and/or its members have acquired exclusive rights, with the effect that commercial cable and satellite companies such as Screensport are prevented from competing with the EBU and/or its members, in the field of sports programmes;
   and
   (ii)    the joint venture between the EBU and/or certain of its members with NI establishing a television sports channel 'Eurosport'.
(2)     This Decision, while mentioning the EBU's activities, does not deal with the first aspect of this complaint, which is the subject of separate proceedings initiated by the Commission (Case IV/32.150). A statement of objections was sent by the Commission to the Eurosport Consortium and NI in connection with point (ii) above on 20 December 1988.
(3)     On 17 January 1989 the Commission received a notification and application for negative clearance concerning a series of agreements relating to the Eurosport sports channel television service, including:
   (i)     the Eurosport Consortium Agreement, signed on 5 May 1988 between 16 members of the EBU (hereinafter 'Members'). Following withdrawals from and additions to the consortium the current membership is 17, namely ORF (Austria), BRT (Belgium), RTBF (Belgium), DR (Denmark), YLE (Finland), ERT (Greece), RUV (Iceland), RTE (Ireland), RAI (Italy), NRK (Norway), SVT (Sweden), SSR (Switzerland), BBC (United Kingdom), JRT (Yugoslavia), CYBC (Cyprus), TRT (Turkey) and IBA (Israel);
   (ii)    a Shareholders Agreement signed on 23 December 1988 between Sky Television plc and the Eurosport Consortium, providing inter alia for exclusive ownership of Satellite Sport Sales Ltd by Sky (see recitals (21) and (32));
   (iii)   a Services Agreement, signed on 23 December 1988 between Satellite Sport Services Ltd (hereinafter 'the service company') jointly owned by the Eurosport Consortium, and Sky;
   (iv)    a Facilities Agreement, signed on 23 December 1988 between Sky and the service company;
   (v)     a Guarantee, signed on 23 December, given by NI, parent company of Sky, to the Eurosport Consortium.
   A supplementary statement of objections was sent by the Commission to the Eurosport Consortium and Sky on 10 April 1989.

### The complainant
(4)     Screensport is a company registered in England providing a commercial transnational satellite television sports channel service which has been in operation since March 1984. Until March 1989 it delivered its programmes by low power satellite to cable systems in various parts of Europe. Since then, in addition, the service has also been available directly to consumers by means of domestic satellite dishes following the launch of the Astra satellite in February 1989. The service, which is multilingual, is currently available in 12 European countries, including seven EEC Member States, provided either by Screensport alone or in conjunction

with partners in certain countries (such as France, Germany and the Netherlands). 75% of the shareholding in Screensport is owned by W. H. Smith Ltd. The remaining shares are held by ESPN Inc., the major satellite cable channel in the USA which is jointly owned by ABC and Capital Cities. In the year up to June 1989 Screensport's turnover was £ 3,3 million, resulting in a loss for the company in the same period.

(5)  The Screensport channel consists exclusively of sports programmes, transmitted in four languages – English, French, German and Dutch.

**Eurosport**

(6)  Eurosport, like Screensport, is a transnational satellite television channel service dedicated to sport, which came into operation on 5 February 1989 on the Astra satellite. Television viewers within the footprint of the satellite receive the service either by cable television operators or directly by domestic satellite dishes. It is currently received in 22 European countries, including eight EEC Member States, and it broadcasts for 17 hours a day in English, German and Dutch.

(7)  The Eurosport Consortium is the product of an agreement concluded between a group of EBU members. The Consortium is contractually linked to Sky, and/or undertakings within the Sky group of companies, and NI, parent of Sky.

**The Eurosport Consortium**

(8)  The Eurosport Consortium is a consortium of members of the EBU, an association of broadcasting organizations established in 1950. Membership of the EBU is open to broadcasting organizations or groups of such organizations from a member country of the International Telecommunication Union (ITU) situated in the European Broadcasting Area as defined by the Radio Regulations annexed to the International Telecommunication Convention, which provide in that country, with the authorization of the competent authorities, a broadcasting service of national character and national importance, and which furthermore prove that they fulfil all the conditions set out below:

(a)  they are under an obligation to cover the entire national population and in fact cover at least a substantial part thereof, while using their best endeavours to achieve full coverage in due course;

(b)  they are under an obligation to, and actually do, provide varied and balanced programming for all sections of the population, including a fair share of programmes catering for special-minority interests of various sections of the public, irrespective of the ratio of programme cost to audience;

(c)  they actually produce and/or commission under their own editorial control a substantial proportion of the programmes broadcast.

The EBU currently has 39 active members in 32 countries situated within the European Broadcasting Area, most of them public service broadcasters. Membership is also open to consortia, including the Eurosport Consortium.

(9)  All active EBU members are eligible to participate in an institutionalized exchange system for TV programmes, including sports programmes, via a European network, known as 'Eurovision', in which all but two members currently participate. The system is also open to consortia, consisting exclusively of active members from different countries providing together a transnational television programme service. Eurovision is based on reciprocity: whenever a broadcasting organization covers an event – including sports events – which takes place on its own national territory and is of potential interest to other Eurovision members, it offers the signal (basic video and international sound feed) free of charge to all the other Eurovision members,

on the understanding that in return it will receive corresponding offers from all the other members regarding events taking place in their respective countries. The originating broadcasting organization also provides the necessary infrastructure to enable visiting broadcasters to function properly (commentary positions, etc.).

(10)  Reciprocal arrangements of a similar kind exist with Intervision, the eastern European counterpart of Eurovision. Reciprocity has also been agreed among the six broadcasting unions which have jointly acquired world rights in the FIFA World Cup both in the past and for the future.

(11)  While facing growing competition from the new commercial broadcasters (see below), at present EBU and its members are still able to provide exclusive programming with respect to many major sports events. They achieve this mainly by jointly acquiring the rights to sports events and exchanging the signal. This is part of the Eurovision system referred to above. At present the major proportion of the exchanges made under Eurovision consist of sports programmes (the balance being made up almost entirely of news items).

(12)  While acquiring the rights to such sports events, however, most EBU members in fact transmit only a small proportion of the events in question. Indeed, on average, members transmit only about 15% of all sports events that are potentially available through the Eurovision system. EBU members attribute this to their 'public mission' obligations, which prevent them from concentrating unduly on only one type of programme. Thus, in order to provide more extensive coverage of these events, as sought by international sports federations, together with the need to reinforce its own negotiating position for the acquisition of rights to sports events in the face of the new and growing competition from commercial broadcasters for such rights, the EBU began in 1986 to examine the feasibility of an association establishing a satellite television channel dedicated to sport. A working group was set up to this effect, which reported to the interested member organizations of EBU. On the basis of this report it was decided to proceed with the establishment of such a channel. However, having already experienced a commercial failure in the establishment of a previous joint satellite channel (Europa TV), it was decided that a future joint sports channel should not be carried by EBU members alone but in conjunction with an undertaking experienced in the field of commercial satellite television and one which would be willing to bear the financial risk of such a project. Sky was selected from amongst four applicants, as was first announced to the press on 2 December 1987. Prior to its selection, Sky had been planning its own sports channel, as one of a number of specialist channels it intended to launch (see below).

(13)  The Eurosport consortium was established expressly to provide the Eurosport service on the part of the EBU members. The Agreement to this effect was formally signed on 5 May 1988, originally by 16 Members. Certain Members have subsequently withdrawn from the Agreement, while the Consortium has also attracted new membership, all members of the EBU in principle being eligible to participate. New Members are admitted with the consent of two-thirds of existing Members. There are currently 17 Members (see recital (3)).

(14)  The Agreement provides that the Consortium, an association without legal personality, is established for a period of 10 years ending on the 10th anniversary of the start of the Eurosport service. The service itself comprises principally programmes based on material made available to the Consortium by EBU members, including the Members of the Consortium. The Members of the Consortium accept, however, that the Consortium is to be free to operate its own programme policy. In particular, it is entitled to include any programme in the service at such time and in such manner as it thinks fit. No Member, therefore, can withhold from the Consortium

any programme or any right in any programme with a view to preventing or delaying its inclusion in the service. With regard to each sports programme produced or acquired by a Member, that Member must, at the request of the Consortium:

(a)    make the programme and such rights the Member has in relation to it freely available to the Consortium without restriction for the purpose of the service;

(b)    use its best endeavours to secure, in consultation with the Consortium or its representatives, such additional rights as are necessary to permit the programme to be included in the service;

(c)    use its best endeavours, in consultation with the Consortium, to extend the coverage of an event as long as the production facilities are on site;

(d)    make its commentary available to the Consortium as a guide;

and

(e)    provide commentary positions at the event for the Consortium or its representatives in accordance with Eurovision reciprocity rules.

In this context it should be noted that under the Eurovision rules the EBU member originating a programme (the host broadcaster) is entitled to prevent Eurosport from broadcasting the same programme into its territory in its own language. However this limitation does not apply in the case of those sports events which belong to the common sports heritage of all European nations (Winter Olympic Games, Summer Olympic Games, Football World Cup, European Football Championships).

(15)    Members are entitled to contributions from the Consortium for costs incurred in connection with the programmes made available and included in the service. These contributions take into account the type of sports programme made available by each Member and the number of hours of programme material made available by them included in the service. In addition Members suffering a disproportionate impact of loss of audience due to the existence of the service are compensated from part of the profits arising from the activities of the Consortium

(16)    Members wishing to withdraw from the Consortium may do so up to the fourth anniversary of the date on which that Member joined, by giving at least one year's written notice of that fact while undertaking thereafter to use all reasonable endeavours during such notice to make available at the Consortium's request such sports programme material of the same type as it has previously at any time during the period offered to make available through the Eurovision programme exchanges.

(17)    The Consortium is required to inform the EBU Administrative Council regularly of its activities.

**Sky**

(18)    Sky Television plc (formerly Satellite Television plc), a company registered in England, is a subsidiary of NI. The ultimate parent company is the News Corporation Ltd, a company incorporated in South Australia. In 1988 the consolidated turnover of the group as a whole was £ 2 500 million. The turnover of NI is more than £450 million. Sky itself remains a loss-making undertaking at present.

(19)    The principal activity of Sky is the transmission of an English language satellite broadcasting service in Europe. In the past this has centred on Sky Channel, a general entertainment satellite channel, including sports programmes, which is received by over 15 million households in 18 countries in Europe, including nine EEC Member States.

In June 1988 it was announced that the channel would be relaunched as part of a four-channel direct braodcasting network called Sky Television. The four channels

– including Eurosport and (a revamped) Sky Channel (now known as Sky One in the United Kingdom) – began transmission on the Astra satellite in February 1989. Sky Channel has also continued to acquire rights to broadcast certain sports events.

(20) The involvement of Sky in a proposed European sports channel was made public by an announcement made to the press on 2 December 1987 that NI was involved in a joint venture with a group of EBU Members to launch a satellite sports channel to be known as Eurosport. In fact, representatives from NI had participated in previous meetings of the EBU Sports Working Party held to discuss and organize the setting up of the channel. Certain elements of each party's involvement in the venture were made known at the time of the press announcement and in the following months, in particular the lease of transponders on the Astra satellite for the Sky channels, including Eurosport. Final details, however, were completed only on the signing of a series of agreements on 23 December 1988. These are as follows:

(21) The Shareholders Agreement (signed by Sky and the Eurosport Consortium) which provides inter alia that Sky and the Eurosport Consortium share equally in the ownership and management of the service company. As regards management, in particular, Sky and the Eurosport Consortium are each entitled to appoint three directors to the company; the Eurosport Consortium nominates the Head of Programming, while Sky nominated the Managing Director. The Agreement also provides that the sales company is wholly owned by Sky. Sky agrees, however, to appoint one director of this company on the nomination of the Eurosport Consortium, this director being provided with all data relating to the sales company available to all other members of the Board of Directors (including management accounts) and information on the trading position of the sales company, which he/she is then entitled to disclose to the Eurosport Consortium. In addition, the Agreement provides that:

(a) the Eurosport Consortium is required to execute the Services Agreement while Sky and the Eurosport Consortium use their respective powers to procure the execution of that Agreement by the service company;

(b) the Eurosport Consortium is required to execute the Sales Agreement and Sky shall procure the execution of that Agreement by the sales company;

(c) Sky is required to execute and procure the execution by the sales company of the Finances Agreement;

and

(d) Sky is required to execute the Facilities Agreement and Sky and the Consortium use their respective powers to procure the execution of that agreement by the service company.

(22) Furthermore, the Shareholders Agreement also details the sports programming material which the Eurosport Consortium undertakes to make available for broadcasting on Eurosport. This is:

(a) all sports programming produced or acquired by Members (other than such programming described in subparagraph (b) below);

(b) all sports programming acquired by Members which is programming offered to the EBU Eurovision programme exchanges ('Eurovision') by members of the EBU who are not Members of Eurosport provided that programming forms part of Eurovision and;

(i) it is not contrary to the national law of the place of incorporation or establishment of the relevant Member for such programming to be so made available;

(ii) that any additional rights necessary have been acquired at the request of the service company by or through the Members concerned;

(iii)   the said programming shall be made available on a non-exclusive basis;

and

(iv)   in the case of such programming, it shall be made available subject to such conditions, reservations or other qualifications as may be imposed in accordance with the regulations governing Eurovision from time to time.

(23)   However, the Members undertake to Sky that, whenever granting a sublicence permitting the inclusion of such programming as is described in subparagraph (a) of recital (22) in a 'Reserved Service' (as defined below), which is provided primarily for reception within the service area of the transponder which for the time being is used for the transmission of Eurosport, they shall reserve priority for Eurosport for 48 hours after the end of an event or of the daily competition where an event lasts more than one day. It is understood that if a Member gives the service company notice that it wishes to sublicense programming specified in the notice to a Reserved Service without such reservation of priority, then, unless within 48 hours of receipt of such notice the service company gives that Member notice that it has selected such programming for inclusion in Eurosport within the 48-hour priority period described above, the Member may sublicense such programming without reservation of priority. For the purposes of this clause.

'Reserved Service' means:

(i)   a transnational television service, that is to say a television broadcasting service intended for reception in more than one country which is not aimed primarily at audiences in a single country;

or

(ii)   a third party national satellite television service, that is to say a television broadcasting service provided by means of a satellite (whether in the fixed-satellite or broadcasting-satellite service) aimed primarily at audiences in a single country, in which no Member has any bona fide economic interest except as a provider of programme material;

other than

(i)   any service provided by a Eurovision member (as that term is from time to time defined by the EBU);

(ii)   any service to which any Member is required in sublicensing such programming to do so without such reservation of priority by reason of any applicable law, regulation or decision of a court or other competent authority or by reason of any contract existing at the date of the Agreement which has been disclosed to Sky prior to the date thereof.

The application of the abovementioned clause may have been modified following a change to the EBU sublicensing rules. On 2 July 1990 the EBU adopted a new scheme for sublicences to non-members. This is dealt with in case IV/32.150 EBU/ Eurovision. Under the scheme, sublicences are made available to all interested third parties subject to an embargo for a limited number of hours and further restrictions on the timing and volume of the transmissions.

(24)   A list of sports events to which the EBU, on behalf of its Members, has already acquired 'standard' or 'world' rights, as defined therein, was also attached to the Agreement. The Eurosport Consortium warranted to Sky that such rights were subsisting at the time of signature.

(25)   The Agreement is intended to continue for a period of 10 years. Early termination is permitted in certain circumstances. Provision is also made for extension of the Agreement.

(26)   The Services Agreement, concluded between the Eurosport Consortium and the
       service company (owned jointly by the Eurosport Consortium and Sky), provides
       that the latter supplies certain facilities and services to the Consortium, including:
       (i)    those relating to the establishment of the Eurosport-channel, including nego-
              tiation (on the Consortium's behalf) for the transponder and uplink facility
              together with technical support and liaison with suppliers, regulatory au-
              thorities, etc. necessary to establish the channel;
       (ii)   those relating to the operation of the Eurosport channel, including prepara-
              tion and selection of programme material for inclusion on the channel;
       (iii)  accounting and administrative services and personnel and other services nec-
              essary for the operation and distribution of the services.
(27)   Copyright in the programmes included in the service and in all material included in
       them belongs to and remains the property of the Eurosport Consortium Members
       (whether as owners or licensees).
(28)   The Sales Agreement is concluded between the Eurosport Consortium and Satellite
       Sport Sales Ltd (hereinafter 'the sales company') which is wholly owned by Sky,
       but which includes one director nominated by the Eurosport Consortium.
       Under the Agreement the Eurosport Consortium:
       (i)    grants to the sales company the exclusive right to contract for the transmis-
              sion of advertizements on Eurosport;
       (ii)   authorizes the sales company to impose charges for the reception and (where
              appropriate) the retransmission of the satellite service. The contracts made
              with cable operators to this effect are required to be in a form previously ap-
              proved in writing by the service company;
       (iii)  grants to the sales company the right to enter into agreements with persons
              or organizations for programme association ('on-air sponsorship of
              programmes') included in the service. The agreements are in accordance in-
              ter alia with any guidelines laid down by the service company and with any
              existing sponsorship obligations of the Eurosport Consortium or any of its
              Members and which have been notified to the sales company.
       In return, the Eurosport Consortium inter alia agrees to include in the satellite ser-
       vice the advertisements delivered by the sales company, and to provide the service
       itself on a daily basis as agreed. In addition, the Eurosport Consortium undertakes
       to make the satellite service available for distribution so as to enable the sales com-
       pany to comply with its own obligations under the Agreement concerning the avail-
       ability of the satellite service to the public generally within the coverage area.
(29)   The Facilities Agreement between Sky and the service company provides that Sky
       agrees to provide or procure for the service company, at cost, such experienced
       personnel, facilities, recommendations, information, know-how and advice as rea-
       sonably requested by the latter so as to enable it to carry out its obligations under
       the Services Agreement.
(30)   The Finances Agreement between Sky and the sales company provides that Sky
       agrees to provide the sales company such facilities (including know-how, executive
       and technical personnel and premises), services and funds (by way of interest-free
       loans) as the sales company shall require in order to carry out its obligations and
       activities under the Sales Agreement. In return, the sales company is required to
       pay Sky for the facilities and services provided.
(31)   NI, parent of Sky Television plc, irrevocably guarantees to the Eurosport Consor-
       tium, in consideration of the Eurosport Consortium entering into the Shareholders
       Agreement with its subsidiary, the due and punctual performance and observance
       by Sky and the sales company of their respective obligations under their Agree-

ments, and in the case of their default, to perform and observe these obligations itself.

### The nature of Eurosport

(32)  While accepting the need for Eurosport to be commercially viable, the Eurosport Consortium has constantly stressed that it represents an extension of its Members' activities and, as such, constitutes a public service channel. (At present about 50% of the Eurosport programme schedule is made up of EBU programme material, 34% of which is produced by Members of the Consortium, 16% by other members of the EBU.) Emphasis is placed on the fact that the service is broadcast by the Eurosport Consortium and that they are responsible for its programme schedule. The services provided by Sky through the sales and service companies take the form of a subcontracting relationship. On this basis Eurosport enjoys the rights of an EBU member as far as the Eurovision system is concerned. Cable operators and sports organizers and/or their agents, in particular, are encouraged to accept the public service character of Eurosport. As such, it is inevitable that the service is considered by these bodies to be closely associated with the EBU and its members, including those which are not themselves Members of the Eurosport Consortium.

(33)  By contrast, the viewing public has tended to associate Eurosport more closely with Sky. On its inauguration the channel was heavily advertised, in the United Kingdom at least, as one of the four 'Sky' satellite channels launched by Sky Television on the Astra satellite. On the continent the channel has also been closely linked to Sky Channel by the fact that the two services have shared the same cable channel, with Eurosport replacing Sky Channel after 6 p.m. on certain cable networks receiving the service from another satellite.

### The market

(34)  Until recently television viewers have been dependent upon their national public broadcasting organizations for access to televised sport, television itself being transmitted via national terrestrial networks, and licences to operate generally were confined to public organizations charged with 'public service' obligations relating to programme quality, diversity, education, etc.

(35)  Sport has generally been considered to fall within the scope of this public mission, at least coverage of certain major international events, such as the Olympic Games, Football World Cup and European Football Championships, together with national events of particular interest to the domestic public. Some organizations have chosen to highlight sport or at least certain events more than others. However, in each case, extensive coverage has been constrained by the obligation to televise other types of programmes.

(36)  At the same time, however, the monopolies conferred upon national broadcasting services enabled them to secure exclusive and, frequently, long-term broadcasting rights to sports events – particularly where such rights were negotiated through the EBU. Furthermore, the Eurovision system guaranteed members free access to the signal for programmes broadcast in other members' territories, as well as other privileges. Prices for these rights were kept relatively low as sports organizers were more concerned to secure television coverage in order to attract sponsorship and widest promotion of their events through television audiences.

(37)  In recent years, technical innovation has resulted in the introduction of cable and satellite television services – that is the transmission of a television signal via a satellite to cable operators which have contracted to receive the service(s) in question, and then distribute it/them to the viewers in a given area. This, together with the

deregulation of television broadcasting which has taken place in some Member States, has led to the establishment of a number of commercial broadcasters. They operate on a local, national or transnational basis, providing either a diversified range of programmes, including sport, or a more specialist service, such as sports, films, arts or children's programmes, etc.

(38)   The latest technical development has been direct-to-home broadcasting, whereby satellite signals may be picked up directly from small domestic satellite dishes erected for this purpose. Both Eurosport and Screensport operate on this basis, providing a transnational service across most of Europe. However, access to viewers via cable operators remains vital for both services at present, particularly in heavily cabled countries, pending growth of the domestic satellite market.

(39)   All commercial broadcasters are financed principally by advertizing revenue although some, in addition, charge a subscription fee. They therefore compete with one another for such revenue, which is based upon the audience ratings for their services. High ratings, in turn, depend upon the attractiveness of the programme content and its scheduling by the broadcasters concerned.

(40)   Public broadcasters have not been immune from the impact of commercial television, even if they are not to the same degree financially dependent upon advertising revenue. On the contrary, all strive to attain the highest possible audience ratings for their services, even while other conditions of operating have also to be fulfilled.

(41)   Sport is one area which has been particularly attractive to a number of the new commercial operators, whether as part of general entertainment channels or specialist sports channels. Audience ratings can be very high for certain events, and are also popular with commercial sponsors. National commercial channels are able to select events of particular interest to the domestic audience, while transnational services are attracted by the fact that sports programmes, above all others, transcend linguistic boundaries, making them especially suitable for transnational broadcasting and advertizing. As a result, public broadcasters have increasingly faced competition in the acquisition of broadcasting rights to certain sports events. At the same time, organizers of such events, or their agents, have become more and more aware of the value of their events to broadcasters, and prices have accordingly increased. In addition, there has been an increasing tendency to 'unbundle' the rights themselves, that is, to distinguish between, for example, terrestrial, cable and/or satellite rights, whether events can be shown 'live' or on a deferred basis only, and/or whether extensive coverage is permitted or limited highlights only, and to sell these various rights separately.

(42)   At present a number of national commercial broadcasters offering general entertainment services include a certain amount of sports programmes for national viewers in various Member States. Prominent amongst these are SAT 1 and RTL Plus in Germany, as well as Canal Plus, La Cinq and M6 in France. Some of these channels have outbid the EBU for specific sports events. In addition, UFA, a member of the Bertelsmann group, has purchased the exclusive world rights for Wimbledon other than the United Kingdom, previously shown on Eurovision.

(43)   A commercial satellite channel dedicated to sport began operations in the United Kingdom during May 1990 (British Satellite Broadcasting). On 10 November 1990 this company agreed to merge with Sky, creating a new company, British Sky Broadcasting. It is currently proposed that this company will operate a sports channel (Sky Sports) directed at the United Kingdom, while the Eurosport channel will be directed at audiences in continental Europe. Plans for a national commercial satellite sports channel also exist in France (Sport-2-3).

(44)  Transnational satellite sports channels are currently limited to Screensport and Eurosport. Since both are transmitted on the Astra satellite their footprint covers the same geographical area, which includes most of the Member States of the European Community.

(45)  Nevertheless, many sports organizers and/or their agents have sought to maintain their relationships with public broadcasters, a number of which have well-established reputations for the quality of the sports events which they transmit, and can guarantee national coverage of their events. In addition, the Eurovision system – which enables sports organizers or their agents to negotiate the sales rights for a number of countries, or indeed over the Eurovision area as a whole, through a single body, the EBU, and guarantees coverage to all EBU members wishing to participate in a particular event – greatly simplifies the dealing/selling process (notwithstanding its negative impact on competitors outside the system). In any event, the EBU currently still holds the exclusive rights to a number of major international events, the contracts to which have not yet expired.

(46)  Moreover, while increased competition from private broadcasters has led to certain major events traditionally broadcast by EBU members (including the Wimbledon Open Tennis Championship) moving into the hands of private broadcasters, in practice the EBU is continuing to acquire rights to other major events. For example, the EBU has secured the rights to both the Summer and Winter Olympic Games taking place in 1992. It also has purchased the rights to the Football World Cup Championships until 1998, together with rights for the European Champion Cup and the final stages of the European Cupwinners' Cup competition.

(47)  The creation of Eurosport, it is claimed by Screensport, has exacerbated its previous problems in acquiring access to major sports events, and in particular European events – national and international – which it would like to show on its own transnational channel. Eurosport has direct access to programmes produced by EBU members (both Members and even non-members of the Eurosport Consortium) whereas Screensport does not, since it is not connected to the Eurovision network. This, it is claimed, discriminates against Screensport and prevents it from broadcasting more European-based sports events which it would like. Of particular concern to Screensport in this respect is that Eurosport has access to 'live' events, either simultaneously with one or more Member of the Eurosport Consortium, or even on its own (the Consortium Member may choose instead to show selected highlights at a later stage). Indeed the Eurosport Consortium has itself admitted that some programme coordination takes place between itself and Eurosport.

(48)  As a result of the above, Screensport claims that cable networks cannot but favour Eurosport by comparison to its own service – including networks in countries where Consortium Members do not exist. This problem has been accentuated by Sky's policy of replacing the Sky Channel service each evening with Eurosport on established networks, and seeking to replace this service entirely by Eurosport once current contracts have expired.

(49)  By contrast, Sky claims that the creation of Eurosport is pro- rather than anti-competitive, since consumers benefit from the introduction of a new, dedicated sports channel enabling them to have much more extensive coverage of sports events shown on national television, either live or possibly at a more convenient time, and possibly in combination with the national channel itself (e. g. early rounds of a competition shown on Eurosport, with the finals on the national channel). In addition, the viewer may be able to see, possibly for the first time, certain new events previously shown only to other national audiences.

## II. LEGAL ASSESSMENT

### Article 85(1)

(50)  The parties concerned in this case are undertakings within the meaning of Article 85(1).

(51)  The basic agreement establishing the transnational satellite television sports channel service Eurosport is the Shareholders Agreement signed by Sky and the Eurosport Consortium on 23 December 1989 and which inter alia creates the service company. However, full details of the operation of the channel and of the rights and obligations of the parties thereto can only be found by reference to a complex series of agreements signed (i) between, currently, 17 members of the EBU which have signed the Eurosport Consortium Agreement, and (ii) between the Eurosport Consortium and Sky and/or undertakings within the Sky Group, together with the guarantee provided by NI, parent of Sky. These are agreements within the meaning of Article 85(1).

(52)  Collectively, these agreements have the object and/or effect of restricting and distorting competition:

    (i)    between the partners to the joint venture, to the extent that they are actual and/or potential competitors on the market for broadcasting sports events;

and

    (ii)    with regard to third parties seeking to broadcast sports events, in particular, transnational dedicated sports channels.

### Re (i)

(53)  Prior to launching the package of four satellite channels including Eurosport in the United Kingdom and other Community countries, Sky (then Satellite Television plc) already operated a transnational satellite and cable television service known as Sky Channel, available to viewers in the UK and four other Community countries (Belgium, Germany, Ireland and the Netherlands).

(54)  While being a general entertainment channel, the service included a number of sports events, and Sky was actively involved in seeking to acquire rights to such events for inclusion on the channel. Moreover, having decided to enter into direct satellite broadcasting, it was generally known that Sky was contemplating one channel dedicated to sports. Thus, when considering Sky as a potential partner in their own venture, the interested EBU members, later the Eurosport Consortium, were not only aware of Sky's qualities as an experienced broadcaster in transnational commercial satellite television, including sports events, but also of the threat that Sky might become a direct competitor as a transnational commercial satellite channel dedicated to sport. Sky, for its part, must have known that, in establishing such a channel on its own, it would encounter the same problems as, for example, Screensport, in acquiring sports programming material in competition with the EBU, or in the form of sublicences from the EBU itself.

(55)  For its part, a consortium of EBU members, such as the Eurosport Consortium, can be regarded as a potential competitor to Sky, as it was clear that members of the EBU were contemplating the establishment of a transnational satellite sports channel. This is so even though it was decided to carry out this venture in collaboration with another undertaking. In this respect, it should be recalled that three undertakings, in addition to Sky, applied to enter into such collaboration. None of these applicants, however, were actual or potential sports channels, as far as was known at the time.

(56)  It follows, therefore, that any incentive for Sky to offer substantive competition to

Eurosport was eliminated and that any potential competition between the two parents in the form of rival transnational satellite television channels dedicated to sport ceased as a consequence of their agreement to establish Eurosport together.

**Re (ii)**

(57)   It is pointed out by Sky that Eurosport is but one of many television channels whose programmes include sports programmes, and that more are planned for the near future, including a number of channels dedicated entirely to sport. As such, it is claimed by both Sky and the Eurosport Consortium that the existence of their own channel cannot have any restrictive effect on the market but, on the contrary, is entirely pro-competitive in nature and a stimulus for other potential channels.

(58)   In this respect it is appropriate to examine the market for televised sports programmes in more detail. First, there are the established public broadcasters which are required to televise the most important major events, or at least extracts thereof, as well as events of great interest to the domestic audience, including sports of otherwise minority appeal. These broadcasters have an established national audience who expect the above-described events to be included on national television.

(59)   The new commercial national television channels have recognised that certain sports events attract high ratings amongst domestic audiences – and hence advertising revenue – and have therefore sought to exploit this market by purchasing rights to specific sports events by which they aim to attract national audiences away from public broadcasters to their own services. Transnational commercial channels providing a general entertainment service may also seek to use sport to the same effect, the particular attraction of sport to these channels being that it transcends linguistic boundaries. These channels, however, may elect not to select the same sports events as national commercial channels but may instead choose those which have a wider international appeal.

(60)   Transnational channels dedicated wholly to sport cannot adopt such a selective policy. On the contrary, their mandate must be to carry a wide variety of sport including, as far as possible, the most extensive coverage of the greatest number of events of interest to their potential audience (including minority groups), taking into account that their financial viability rests on attracting advertising (and/or possibly subscription) revenue from high audience ratings. At present, only two transnational commercial television channels of this type are in operation, namely Screensport and Eurosport. Since both transmit from the Astra satellite they are direct competitors for the same geographic audience. They therefore compete for the same type of programme material, the same sponsors and also the same advertisers. In addition, they are also both seeking to succeed in a new domain, namely the direct satellite market. While awaiting the development of this market, however, both are dependent upon reaching the widest possible audience through cable network operators.

(61)   When comparing the position of Eurosport with that of Screensport and other potential transnational commercial satellite television sports channels, the terms of the joint venture clearly confer a privileged position on the former over the latter. First, with regard to programme material, Eurosport is granted unrestricted access to all programmes produced or acquired by Members of the Eurosport Consortium, including programmes which they acquire through the Eurovision system from other EBU members which are not Members of the Consortium. No other service has priority access to these programmes, not even through sublicences granted by the EBU and/or its members (see recital (63)). A list of events to which the EBU

and/or its members had already acquired exclusive 'standard' or 'world' rights (as defined therein) was included in the joint venture Agreements, including certain major international events. Eurosport is entitled to select from this list − and of course any rights subsequently acquired − the events it wishes to include in its service. It may also freely choose the extent of coverage it requires, and, what is of utmost importance, whether to offer the programmes live or on a deferred basis. It may do so independently of the Consortium Members themselves or it may choose to coordinate with them the scheduling of the event in question.

(62)  It should be recalled in this context that EBU members reserve exclusivity for themselves for all rights to live sports programmes produced or acquired by their members. By virtue of the Agreements at issue in this Decision, the Eurosport channel is included in this system.

(63)  In contrast to Eurosport, therefore, third parties may only acquire limited access to Eurovision material through sublicences granted by the EBU or individual members, the priority for live broadcasting being given to participants in the Eurovision system. Sublicences are in principle available only for deferred transmissions subject to an embargo and various other restrictions regarding the timing and volume of transmissions. Eurosport, however, has direct access to all EBU programmes without any restrictions imposed upon it. This effectively deprives third parties (in particular transnational television channels and nationally-orientated direct satellite broadcasting or satellite-to-cable channels) of an equal opportunity to compete with Eurosport for such programmes, in particular to show any 'live' coverage.

(64)  In addition, Eurosport has access free of charge to the signal transmitting the abovementioned programmes from the host nation, in the same way as all other members of the EBU, as part of the Eurovision system of reciprocity. No similar concession is available to other commercial sports channels which would always be required to pay for this signal, or provide it themselves.

(65)  Secondly, as to the market for the acquisition of rights to sports events, an important objective of Eurosport as far as the interested EBU members are concerned is to increase the benefits of the collective negotiating position of EBU members with regard to numerous international events. It enables them to make package deals including events which, though being of little interest to many national public broadcasters, constitute useful programme material for a dedicated sports channel. In the view of the Commission, the joint purchasing policy operated by the EBU through the Eurovision scheme already confers upon EBU members a certain degree of market power. This is so despite the fact that private broadcasters have been able to outbid the EBU for certain events. Even if the EBU's current market power appears to be rather diminished compared to its former position, it still continues to be a powerful body in a privileged situation on the market for the acquisition of programme rights, and is likely to remain so during the next years. For members of such a body to reinforce not only their own position but also that of a potential competitor (Sky) by long-term agreements favouring a joint transnational commercial satellite channel wholly dedicated to sports events can only reduce the opportunities for third parties, in particular independent transnational sports channel services, to compete on an equal footing with Eurosport for the acquisition of satellite cable rights from the EBU.

(66)  Thirdly, the close link between the Eurosport channel and the EBU, through the Eurosport Consortium, and hence to Eurovision programme material, is a factor favouring Eurosport over other potential transnational sports channels as far as cable operators are concerned when determining which sports channel service(s) they may wish to include on their networks. Pending further development of the

domestic satellite dish market, the role of cable operators may well be crucial to the continuing financial viability of transnational satellite sports channels, in securing sufficiently high audiences for them to attract enough advertising revenue to continue operation. In this respect, cable operators have been attracted by the claimed 'public service' character of Eurosport. In addition, a number accepted the daily switch from Sky Channel to Eurosport in their contractual relationships with Sky, thereby enabling Eurosport very quickly to have access to a very large audience.

**Effect on trade between Member States**

(67) Given the transnational character of Eurosport, which is available either directly by satellite or via cable distribution throughout most of Western Europe, and includes sports programmes on events taking place in many parts of the world, the rights to which have been acquired by a group of broadcasting organizations from many countries in Western Europe, the restrictions on competition stated above affect trade within the common market as a whole. This is all the more so as the relevant advertizing markets present strong transnational elements, given the interest of important advertizers engaged in the import and export business, to reach potential clients in other Member States. As such, therefore, this falls within the scope of Article 85(1). The case is confined, however, to effects felt within the Community itself.

**Article 90(2)**

(68) It is claimed by the Eurosport Consortium that its Members need the satellite channel created together with Sky in order to fulfil their public mission, the purpose of the Eurosport channel being to transmit throughout Europe more of the programmes produced or acquired by the Members of the Consortium. Due to the subcontracting relationship on the basis of which the services to the Eurosport Consortium are provided, the channel is said to be a public broadcasters' channel whatever may be the commercial incentives for its creation. (Reference is made to the Members' wish to recover the costs of those sports programmes which they have to produce but which they are otherwise not able to broadcast in view of the general programme constraints imposed on them.) For this reason the Eurosport Consortium argues that the exception provided for by Article 90 (2), under which undertakings entrusted with the operation of services of general economic interest must not be hindered by the competition rules from performing the particular tasks assigned to them, applies.

(69) While it may be possible that the public mission obligations imposed by Member States on their national broadcasting organizations renders them undertakings entrusted with services of general economic interest to this extent, it is highly doubtful that, given the national character of these obligations, they could be interpreted as extending to transnational activities of a collective nature such as Eurosport. In any event, there is nothing in the possible application of Article 85(1) to their joint venture Agreements with the Sky group which would prevent them from fulfilling these missions, not to mention the readily admitted commercial character of the venture which Sky has entered into for purely economic reasons, providing for management expertise and financial assistance, in the expectation of some day making a profit.

**Article 85(3)**

Improvement in the production or distribution of goods or to promoting technical or economic progress

(70)   It is claimed by Sky that Eurosport improves production and distribution in the market in a number of respects: it is one of the first thematic television channels broadcasting across national boundaries promoting sport in general and less well-known sports in particular, thereby promoting a new audience, for the benefit of other channels to follow. Technical and/or economic progress is said to be encouraged through the increased use of satellite technology, the promotion of sport and increased investment in sport and opportunities for sponsors, advertisers Eurosport, etc. For its part, the Eurosport Consortium emphasizes the fact that Eurosport enables its members to optimize the exploitation of their transmission rights thereby recouping their investment. Screensport however rejects this argument by claiming that the same benefit could be achieved by licensing surplus rights to a multiplicity of parties, including Screensport, while Eurosport, it says, tends to narrow distribution because EBU members prefer to continue channelling surplus rights through a sole outlet rather than being obliged by increasing commercial pressure to license them more widely or to desist in the first place from acquiring rights which they cannot exploit.

(71)   In reply to this argument the Commission acknowledges the achievement of Eurosport in setting up a second transnational commercial satellite television channel dedicated to sports. However, this is not an 'improvement' within the meaning of Article 85(3) if, in practice, its effect is a disproportionate distortion of competition in the market in question. Nor is technical or economic progress 'promoted' in such circumstances. The Commission takes the view that it is of vital importance in new, developing industries, requiring considerable investment in technology and development, that priority must be given to ensuring that competition at all levels should remain as open as possible so as to confer upon all potential market entrants an equal opportunity to compete.

**Benefit to consumers**

(72)   As claimed by the parties, it is arguable that, in the short term at least, consumers benefit from the introduction of a new, dedicated sports channel enabling them to have much more extensive coverage of sports events shown on national television, either live or possibly at a more convenient time, and possibly in combination with the national channel itself (e.g. early rounds of a competition shown on Eurosport, with the finals on the national channel). In addition, the viewer may be able to see, possibly for the first time, certain new events previously shown only to other national audiences.

(73)   However, this reasoning fails to consider the possibilities offered by an autonomous development of a dedicated sport channel by the Sky group. It has already been publicly announced that the Sky group would go on anyway with extensive broadcasting of sports events. This being so, the consumer may be better served by being able to make an informed choice between at least two channels offering an equally wide variety of European sports programmes, including the major international events, which may differ in style, presentation, quality and content. In those circumstances, it is the consumer who decides ultimately which/how many channels of this kind should eventually succeed.

**Indispensability**

(74)   Contrary to the arguments of the parties, the Commission is not convinced that a transnational sports channel such as Eurosport could only come into existence on the basis of such a joint venture between a group of members of the EBU, with the backing of the organization itself, and the most likely main competitor capable of

creating an alternative venture. In the view of the Commission, the creation of a joint venture on the basis of the present Agreements is excessive, and the implied restrictions of competition cannot be regarded as indispensable to the establishment of a dedicated sports channel with a transnational dimension capable of rivalling other sports channels to the benefit of the consumers.

(75) Indeed, the Commission cannot accept that all the restrictions contained in the Agreements themselves are indispensable to the operation of the venture. In particular, the channel has a privileged position compared to other channels broadcasting sports events, especially transnational sports channels.

**Conclusion**

(76) In these circumstances, from the viewpoint of competition law, the disadvantages linked to the scheme notified by the parents of Eurosport outweigh possible improvements and benefits on the market in question. For these reasons the Commission rejects the application for an exemption under Article 85(3),

**HAS ADOPTED THIS DECISION:**

Article 1
The joint venture Agreements and all related contractual provisions between, on the one hand, the Members of the Eurosport Consortium, and, on the other hand, Sky Television plc, Satellite Sports Sales Ltd, Satellite Sports Services and News International plc which were notified to the Commission on 17 January 1989, constitute an infringement of Article 85(1) of the EEC Treaty in so far as they have as their effect the granting of direct access to the Eurovision system.

Article 2
An exemption under Article 85(3) of the EEC Treaty for the Agreements and implementing and related rules as mentioned in Article 1 is hereby refused.

Article 3
This Decision is addressed to the following undertakings:
(a)     The Members of the Eurosport Consortium,
        c/o Union Européenne de Radiodiffusion,
        Case postale 67,
        CH-1218 Grand-Saconnex (Geneva);
(b)     Sky Television plc,
        Sky Television Centre,
        6 Centaurs Business Park,
        Grant Way,
        Isleworth,
        UK-Middlesex TW7 5QK;
(c)     Satellite Sport Sales Ltd,
        PO Box 495,
        Virginia Street,
        UK-London E1 9XY;
(d)     Satellite Sports Services Ltd,
        PO Box 495,
        Virginia Street,
        UK-London E1 9XY;

(e)    News International plc,
       PO Box 481,
       Virginia Street,
       UK-London E1 9BD.

Done at Brussels, 19 February 1991.
For the Commission
Leon Brittan
Vice-President

———

### 2.4.3.    EUROPEAN COURT OF JUSTICE, ORDER OF THE COURT OF FIRST INSTANCE (FIRST CHAMBER), EUROSPORT CONSORTIUM V COMMISSION OF THE EUROPEAN COMMUNITIES, CASE T-35/91, 28 NOVEMBER 1991[78]

*Procedure – Intervention – Interested persons – Dispute relating to the validity of a decision applying the rules on competition – Complainant undertaking – Undertaking to which the decision was addressed failed to bring an independent action – Procedural rights*
*(Statute of the Court of Justice of the EEC, Art. 37)*

*The right to intervene in a dispute between one of the addressees of a Commission decision applying the rules on competition and the Commission is granted by Article 37 of the Statute of the Court to any person establishing an interest in the result of such a case. The undertaking whose complaint caused the proceeding to be initiated which was concluded by the decision at issue has such an interest. So does an undertaking which, like the applicant, was the addressee of the decision and, as a result, enjoyed an independent right of action under the second paragraph of Article 173 of the Treaty. That interest is not negated by the fact that it did not bring such an action, but means that its rights as intervener must be confined to supporting the form of order sought by the applicant.*

In Case T-35/91,
Eurosport Consortium, represented by Michel Waelbroeck and Denis Waelbroeck, of the Brussels Bar, with an address for service in Luxembourg at the Chambers of Ernest Arendt, 4 Avenue Marie-Thérèse, applicant, v Commission of the European Communities, represented by Julian Currall and Berend Jan Drijber, members of its Legal Service, acting as Agents, with an address for service in Luxembourg at the office of R. Hayder, a national official temporarily attached to the Commission's Legal Service, Wagner Centre, Kirchberg, defendant,

Application for a declaration that Commission Decision 91/130/EEC of 19 February 1991 relating to a proceeding pursuant to Article 85 of the EEC Treaty (IV/32.524 – Screensport/EBU Members) (Official Journal 1991 L 63, p. 32) is void,

*The Court of First Instance of the European Communities*
(First Chamber)
composed of: D.A.O. Edward, President of the Chamber, R. García-Valdecasas, K.

---

[78]  ECR 1991, p. II-1359.

Lenaerts, H. Kirschner and R. Schintgen, Judges, Registrar: B. Pastor, Administrator, makes the following

Order

1. By an application lodged at the Registry of the Court of First Instance on 21 August 1991, The European Sports Network (formerly Screensport Limited), whose registered office is at London, represented by Jonathan Scott and Stephen Kinsella, Solicitors, of Messrs Herbert Smith, Brussels, with an address for service in Luxembourg at the Chambers of Georges Baden, 8 Boulevard Royal, applied for leave to intervene in Case T-35/91 in support of the defendant.

2. The application for leave to intervene was submitted in accordance with Article 115 of the Rules of Procedure of the Court of First Instance, pursuant to the second paragraph of Article 37 and the first paragraph of Article 46 of the EEC Statute of the Court of Justice.

3. The applicati on was served on the parties. The defendant stated that it had no comments to make on the application. The applicant declared that it had no objection against the intervention.

4. In accordance with the third subparagraph of Article 116(1) of the Rules of Procedure, the President of the First Chamber referred the decision to the Chamber.

5. It appears from the decision in issue in this case that on 17 December 1987 The European Sports Network submitted a complaint to the Commission under Article 3 of Council Regulation No 17 of 6 February 1962, First Regulation implementing Articles 85 and 86 of the Treaty (Official Journal, English Special Edition 1959-1962, p. 87), on the basis of which the Commission initiated a proceeding pursuant to Article 85 of the EEC Treaty and adopted the contested decision. The European Sports Network therefore has an interest in seeing that decision upheld.

6. The European Sports Network's application for leave to intervene must therefore be granted.

7. By an application lodged at the Registry of the Court of First Instance on 19 September 1991, Sky Television plc, whose registered office is at London, represented by Mario Siragusa, of the Rome Bar, and Michael Bowsher, of the Bar of England and Wales, with an address for service in Luxembourg at the Chambers of Messrs Elvinger, Hoss & Prussen, 15 Côte d' Eich, applied to intervene in the same case in support of the applicant.

8. The application to intervene was submitted in accordance with Article 115 of the Rules of Procedure of the Court of First Instance, pursuant to the second paragraph of Article 37 and the first paragraph of Article 46 of the EEC Statute of the Court of Justice.

9. In accordance with the third subparagraph of Article 116(1) of the Rules of Procedure, the President of the First Chamber referred the decision to the Chamber.

10. In support of its application, Sky Television claims, first, that it has an interest in seeing the contested decision annulled because it was one of the parties directly involved in the administrative procedure and the contested decision was addressed to it.

11. Secondly, Sky Television claims that it has an interest in seeing the contested decision annulled because its legal position stands to be affected by that decision and by the outcome of the action brought before the Court of First Instance by the Eurosport consortium. That situation arises as a result of an action for damages brought against Sky Television, among others, by The European Sports Network, the complainant in the administrative proceedings, and Sportskanal GmbH. That action was commenced by writ issued in the High Court of Justice, Chancery Divi-

sion, London, on 14 May 1991, by which time Sky Television asserts that it had withdrawn from the operation of the Eurosport channel. The writ was served on it on 4 July 1991.

12. Sky Television states that in the High Court action the two plaintiffs mentioned claim damages for, inter alia, breach of Article 85 and/or Article 86 of the EEC Treaty in and about the creation and operation of the Eurosport channel. In the statement of claim served on Sky Television on 30 July 1991, the two plaintiffs specifically rely upon the Commission's finding in the contested decision of an infringement of Article 85 in support of their claim for damages. In Sky Television's opinion, the contested decision will form an important element of any decision in the High Court action, and its legal position will therefore be directly affected by the final decision of the Court of First Instance.

13. Finally, Sky Television claims that its interest in the outcome of the present action is continuing, notwithstanding the fact that it did not exercise its right to appeal against the contested decision as provided for in Article 173 of the Treaty. At no time, it stresses, did it waive, either expressly or by implication, its right to intervene in the present action.

14. The application for leave to intervene by Sky Television was served on the parties. The defendant stated that it had no observations to make on the application. The applicant declared that it had no objection against the intervention.

15. Article 37 of the EEC Statute of the Court of Justice provides that the right to intervene is to be open to any person establishing an interest in the result of a case such as the present. Sky Television's interest, as an addressee of the contested decision, is confirmed by the fact that it enjoyed an independent right of action under the second paragraph of Article 173 of the EEC Treaty (order of the Court of Justice of 28 January 1987 in Case 150/86 Usinor and Sacilor v Commission, not published). That interest is not negated by the fact that Sky Television did not bring such an action. However, since it did not do so, Sky Television's rights as intervener must be confined to supporting the form of order sought by the applicant.

16. Its application for leave to intervene must therefore be granted.

17. Under Article 116(2) of the Rules of Procedure of the Court of First Instance, if the Court allows the intervention, the intervener is to receive a copy of every document served on the parties.

On those grounds,
*The Court of First Instance*
(First Chamber)
hereby orders as follows:

1. The European Sports Network is granted leave to intervene in Case T-35/91 in support of the defendant;
2. Sky Television is granted leave to intervene in Case T-35/91 in support of the applicant;
3. The Registrar shall serve on the interveners a copy of every document served on the parties;
4. A period shall be prescribed within which the interveners must state in writing their pleas in law in support of the forms of order sought by them;
5. Costs are reserved.

Luxembourg, 28 November 1991.

**2.4.4. COMMISSION DECISION RELATING TO A PROCEEDING PURSUANT TO ARTICLE 85 OF THE EEC TREATY (IV/32.290 – NEWITT/DUNLOP SLAZENGER INTERNATIONAL AND OTHERS), 18 MARCH 1992**[79]

*The Commission of the European Communities,*

– Having regard to the Treaty establishing the European Economic Community,
– Having regard to Council Regulation No 17 of 6 February 1962, First Regulation implementing Articles 85 and 86 of the Treaty[80], as last amended by the Act of Accession of Spain and Portugal, and in particular Articles 3, 15 and 16 thereof,
  Having regard to the application submitted on 18 March 1987 by Newitt & Co. Ltd (United Kingdom) requesting the Commission to find, pursuant to Article 3 of Regulation No 17, that Dunlop Slazenger International Ltd (United Kingdom) and some of its exclusive distributors had infringed Article 85 of the Treaty,
– Having regard to the decision taken by the Commission, on 7 May 1990, to initiate proceedings in this case,
– Having given the undertakings concerned the opportunity of being heard on the matters to which the Commission has taken objection, in accordance with Article 19(1) of Regulation No 17 and Commission Regulation No 99/63/EEC of 25 July 1963 on the hearings provided for in Article 19(1) and (2) of Council Regulation No 17[81],
– Having consulted the Advisory Committee on Restrictive Practices and Dominant Positions,

Whereas:

## A. THE FACTS

### I. The parties

1. DSI and the BTR group
(1)    Dunlop Slazenger International Ltd (DSI) is a company incorporated under British law and controlled by the BTR plc group, whose activities cover many different sectors. DSI is concerned with the group's activities relating to the manufacture and distribution of sports goods and is engaged in such activities worldwide. Its turnover was £ 114 million in 1988 (ECU 172 million). The turnover of the BTR group as a whole was £ 5 473 million (ECU 8 242 million).
2. Newitt
(2)    Newitt & Co. Ltd (Newitt) is also a company incorporated under British law and is a wholesaler and retailer of sports goods. Its turnover in 1988 was £ 3,7 million (ECU 5,8 million). Up to 1986, Newitt was one of the main parallel exporters, if not the main parallel exporter, of DSI products.
3. All Weather Sports
(3)    All Weather Sports BV (AWS) was, at the time of the facts described, DSI's exclusive distributor for the Dunlop brand in the Benelux countries. Its turnover in 1988 was Hfl 30 million (ECU 13 million). In 1989, AWS was purchased by its manage-

---

[79] OJ L 131, 16-5-1992, pp. 32-49, including full formatted annexes at pp. 46-49.
[80] OJ No 13, 21-2-1962, p. 204.
[81] OJ No 127, 20-8-1963, p. 2268.

ment from the group Buehrmann-Tetterode Nederland BV, which controlled it, and took the name All Weather Sports Benelux BV.

4. Pinguin Sports

(4)    Pinguin Sports BV (Pinguin) was, at the time of the facts described, DSI's exclusive distributor for the Slazenger brand in the Netherlands. In 1987, its turnover in Slazenger products amounted to some Hfl 2,4 million (ECU 1 million).

## II. Newitt's Complaint

(5)    On 18 March 1987, Newitt complained to the Commission that DSI had, by means of various measures, notably prices, impeded exports of tennis-balls and squash-balls to other Member States in order to protect its exclusive distribution network in such other Member States.

Newitt claimed that DSI, which had a dominant position in the market for tennis and squash-balls and was acting in order to ensure compliance with its distribution agreements, was infringement both Article 85 and Article 86 of the Treaty.

## III. The main products and their markets

1. Tennis balls

(6)    The tennis-balls market is oligopolistic. Five manufacturers accounted for some 90% of the Community market in 1989 (see Annex 1.1) [82]: DSI (some 39%: 28% accounted for by Dunlop and 11% by Slazenger), Dunlop France (19%)[83], Penn (some 16%), Tretorn (some 11%) and Wilson (some 6%). Since sales by Tretorn and Dunlop France are virtually confined to Europe, the main producers at world level (1986) are Wilson (some 30%), Penn (some 24%) and DSI (some 21%). Wilson and Penn share most of the US market, while DSI leads the European market by a considerable margin.

(7)    Although there are some technological barriers to entry, the oligopolistic nature of the tennis-balls market appears to be due more to barriers of an economic nature and to the importance of the brand image of the products. This latter type of obstacle, which is difficult to overcome in introducing a new name into the market, is kept at a high level by means of systematic and expensive sponsoring of major tournaments by the manufacturers and by means of the widespread use of the system of 'official' recognition of tennis balls by federations, such recognition being conferred on the basis of financial contributions from manufacturers and/or their official distributors.

2. Squash-balls

(8)    The structure of the squash-balls market is characterized by the dominance, and virtual monopoly in certain countries, of DSI, its share of the Community market being 60 to 70% (1986). Its share is 80% in the United Kingdom, 85% in Ireland and 90% in Spain (see Annex 1.2). Its only real competitor as regards squash-balls is Elastomer Technology Pty (Australia), which manufactures Merco balls and holds approximately 11% of the Community market.

---

[82] These figures apply only to what are known as 'first-grade tennis-balls', i.e. top quality balls used in matches and competitions, though these are also the ones most commonly used in general.

[83] Controlled by the Japanese Sumitomo group.

3. Other products

(9)    DSI manufactures and/or distributes a very large variety of sports equipment, in-
       cluding clothes and shoes. Most of these products are less homogeneous and the
       number of manufacturers much greater, and competition is consequently stronger.
       In the case of some articles, such as tennis-rackets and golfing equipment, how-
       ever, concentration is greater, and DSI is among the leading manufacturers in the
       case of all such goods.

## IV. DSI's Distribution system

1. Distribution network

(10)   DSI has no appointed distributor in the United Kingdom. It does business direct
       with retailers or, in certain segments of the market, sells through a limited number
       of wholesalers. In the other Member States, DSI has a network of exclusive dis-
       tributors, albeit different ones for the Dunlop and Slazenger brands, or operates
       through other group companies.

2. Distribution agreements

(11)   Though they sometimes differ formally, DSI's distribution agreements are broadly
       similar in the types of obligation they impose. Thus, as regards territorial represen-
       tation, all the agreements are exclusive distribution agreements, and the differences
       between 'exclusive distributor', 'principal distributor' and 'representative' are es-
       sentially terminological. All the distributors concerned are allocated a territory in
       which they hold the exclusive distribution rights for the Dunlop or Slazenger
       brands and outside which they may not engage in active selling. Under the written
       terms of the agreements, however, there is no prohibition on passive selling or any
       absolute territorial protection. For the rest, the other terms of the agreements are
       along the usual lines of standard exclusive distribution agreements.

3. Pricing policy

(12)   DSI has two price-lists for all its products, one for the UK market (trade price-list)
       and one for the export market (export price-list), the latter generally offering lower
       prices.
       Annex 2 provides an overview of the extent of the differences between the two
       lists, for the most representative tennis- and squash-balls, in the period 1982 to
       1989.
       This shows that export prices, with one or two exceptions, are consistently lower
       than UK domestic prices for both tennis- and squash-balls. The extent of the price
       differences varies, however, from year to year and is much greater for squash balls
       (between 15 and 30%) than for tennis balls (from 3 to 15%).
       A similar analysis of a sample of other DSI products (tennis- and squash-rackets,
       ping-pong bats, balls and tables, sports bags) shows that UK domestic prices for
       these products are also usually, despite fairly large variations and excluding 1985,
       appreciably higher than export prices. The disparities, of the order of 15 to 30%,
       can in some cases reach nearly 50%.
       DSI's exclusive distributors in the Community are charged the export prices less
       (according to information provided by DSI in reply to a request for information) a
       standard 20% discount. It has emerged in fact that the discount is generally much
       larger: 25 to 45%[84].

---

[84]  See recital 34 below and Annex 2.

## V. Barriers erected by DSI against the export of its products

Summary

(13)    Since 1977 at least, DSI has pursued a commercial policy which in general prohibits all exports. Since 1985 at least, DSI has erected a series of specific barriers to the export of certain of its products – principally but not exclusively tennis-balls and tennis-rackets – to other Member States, notably the Benelux countries, in collaboration with its exclusive distributors in those countries, for the purpose of protecting its distribution network from all parallel imports.

(14)    The barriers consisted of:
–    a ban on exporting without DSI's agreement,
–    specific refusals to fill orders,
–    pricing measures against UK dealers to prevent them from exporting at competitive rates,
–    buying back low-price parallel exports to prevent them from undermining the prices of DSI's official distribution network,
–    marking of products to identify their origin and final destination,
–    using tennis federation labels to promote DSI's official distribution network only.

(15)    The measures taken were applied mainly (but not solely) to Newitt. They were not, however, necessarily aimed at Newitt, since the identity of the exporter was not always known at the outset. Furthermore, the measures should be viewed in the context of DSI's general policy of prohibiting all exports to countries where it has an exclusive distributor.

1. Export ban

(16)    It is evident that, for many years, Dunlop has sold its products to UK wholesalers only on condition that they were not exported. A letter dated 14 December 1977 from Dunlop Sports Company (whose assets were taken over by DSI) to Newitt contains the following statements:
'May I emphasize that this offer is made on the understanding that the goods offered by you will be through your normal retail premises and not for export in bulk to overseas without our prior permission or to other outlets within the UK for resale by companies with whom Dunlop Sports Company do not have a trading account.'
In practice, however, such exports were tolerated – at least as regards the complainant – over a long period, with Dunlop confining itself, according to Newitt, to issuing a number of formal protests, though without taking any specific action. As from 1985/86, DSI changed its attitude: pressure was brought to bear on Newitt, and concrete action was taken.

(17)    On 5 August 1985, though it accepted an order from Newitt, DSI added in the letter confirming the order:
'I would confirm our export policy as quite simply not allowing shipments to any world market where we have local legal distributor agreements where to supply via a third party would be both a breach of contract and poor commercial practice. In essence all European markets are covered by such agreements.'

(18)    At a meeting on 12 May 1986, DSI informed Newitt of the complaints made by AWS, its exclusive distributor for Dunlop products in the Benelux countries[85], concerning parallel imports of Dunlop products and announced its intention of putting an end to such practices. By letter dated 16 June 1986 to Newitt, DSI specified the measures taken to prevent all parallel exports:

---

[85]    See recital 3 above.

1. all direct exporting of Dunlop and Slazenger products was prohibited, except products specifically agreed by DSI;
2. in the event that Newitt received any export enquiries, these should be passed on to DSI for individual consideration. In certain circumstances, orders could be dealt with directly by DSI, with a commission for Newitt. A subsequent letter[86] stated, however, that this type of operation could normally involve only third countries, such as 'the African markets';
3. the export account opened for Newitt on DSI's books was closed. All sales to Newitt were to take place through the UK sales account and would be handled by the UK sales office (and would thus be invoiced on the basis of UK domestic prices).

The letter also suggested that a further meeting be held to discuss other ways in which DSI 'could achieve greater control of unwelcome cross-frontier trading within Europe, particularly those from the UK in Holland, France and Germany'.

2. Refusal to supply
(19) In October 1986, DSI refused to supply two large orders by Newitt for tennis-balls (57 000 dozen worth a total value of some £ 270 000) intended for dispatch to France, reiterating its policy on exports and the 'considerable difficulties' which it had experienced with 'substantial quantities' of balls sold by Newitt in France and re-exported to the Netherlands and Belgium.
(20) Faced with the obstacles erected by DSI to the export of its products, Newitt sought alternative sources of supply. A source for tennis-balls was found in the United States. DSI attempted to identify the source of such supplies[87].
At the same time, DSI put pressure on Newitt by deciding, in June 1987, to place an embargo on deliveries to it. However, although it acknowledges that such a measure was taken because DSI had reached the view that Newitt was no longer respecting 'the position' of its distributors in Europe – BTR, the DSI holding company, denies that there was ever any question of making the ban permanent and total[88].
(21) Up to the end of 1987, Newitt managed to obtain supplies of tennis-balls from DSI's US subsidiary. From January 1988, however, that company stopped supplies to Newitt 'due to adjusted policy'[89].

3. Pricing measures
3.1. Changes in price-lists and discounts granted to UK wholesalers
(22) DSI's abovementioned letter dated 16 June 1986 prohibiting Newitt from exporting again without its approval also announced a change in the prices charged and discounts granted to Newitt for squash-balls, namely a switch from the export price-list (substantially cheaper[90], to which Newitt had had access since 1978) with a 20% discount to the domestic price-list with a 15% discount. These changes meant that Newitt's purchasing prices jumped sharply, by some 27% for coloured squash-balls and by some 54% for black squash-balls.
(23) Similar price and discount changes affected tennis-balls in 1986 to 1987. Having previously been charged export prices minus a discount of 20% in principle in 1985

---

[86] Letter dated 15-10-1986 to Newitt.
[87] See recital 33 below.
[88] Letter dated 3-9-1987 from BTR to Newitt's solicitors.
[89] Telex sent on 1 February 1989 by Dunlop USA to Newitt.
[90] See recital 12 above.

and 16,5% in 1986, Newitt was charged UK domestic prices minus a discount of 15%, subsequently negotiated to 20%, and then reduced to 17,5% in 1988. The impact of these measures compared to the prices charged to a number of DSI's exclusive distributors is illustrated in Annex 3. The prices charged Newitt, which were between 0 and 10% higher than those charged such distributors, gradually rose to become 25 to 40% higher (Annex 3.3).

(24)  In the letter dated 3 September 1987 already referred to above, while proposing to Newitt the resumption of normal business relations following the embargo imposed on some or all of its orders, BTR specified that Newitt would be entitled to export prices only for 'specific' export orders to 'named' customers, with discounts that would take account of the 'responsibilities' borne in the relevant territory by DIS's distributors there.

3.2. Measures to support exclusive distributors

(25)  In certain cases, DSI backed up the pricing measures described above by taking specific measures to support some of its exclusive distributors (ad hoc price reductions, compensation for inadequate profit margins, etc.) in order to keep the ratio of prices charged the exclusive distribution network to prices charged UK exporters sufficiently low to prevent the latter from exporting again[91].

4. Buying-back of parallel exports

(26)  In 1985 and 1986, parallel imports of Dunlop Max 200 G rackets were put on sale at low prices by two Dutch chains of shops. Following complaints by AWS, DSI undertook to contribute financially to the total buying-back of these rackets by AWS (250 rackets) by compensating its exclusive distributor for the difference between the buy-back price paid by the latter to the shops in question and the price AWS would normally have paid for the rackets from DSI. The operation was followed by a widespread advertising and promotion campaign supported financially by DSI which was aimed at publicizing the buy-back and thus re-establishing the retail trade's confidence in DSI's distribution network. The first buy-back was apparently followed by a second, at the end of 1986, of 200 new Max 200 G models sold by Kwantum.

5. Marking of products

5.1. Identification codes

(27)  It is also apparent that DSI started to place identification codes on some of its products, such as tennis-rackets, to enable it to identify the origins of parallel imports and take appropriate measures to 'eliminate' them[92].

5.2. Marks

(28)  For the same purpose, DSI placed special marks on its tennis-ball tins. It was this process which, according to the complainant, allowed DSI to identify the final destination of the tennis-balls which it had sold it.

6. Use of tennis federation labels for exclusive distributors only

(29)  The technical approval of tennis-balls takes place at International Tennis Federation level. Any ball meeting the technical standards laid down by the ITF may be

---

[91]  See recitals 34 and 35 below.

[92]  See in particular the telex sent on 10 March 1986 by DSI to AWS.

approved, subject to payment of a fixed amount to cover the costs of tests and analyses. Approved balls are designated as 'first-grade tennis-balls' and thus recognized as suitable for use in all tournaments and matches.

However, most of the national tennis federations apply what might be termed a second level of approval or selection, based on purely financial criteria. In return for payment of a fixed amount or, in some cases, on the basis of negotiations or even bidding procedures, one or more brands of tennis-ball may be labelled as 'official balls' of individual national federations, or as 'official balls' of major tournaments organized by them (such as Wimbledon and Roland Garros). The label may be placed on the tins or even printed on the balls. The label 'official balls' may in many cases include the description of the balls as being 'selected' or 'recommended' by the federations.

In addition to the promotional advantage which use of this label represents, these 'official' balls will generally be the only ones that can be used in competitions organized by the federations.

In response to the parallel imports flooding the Dutch market, DSI decided in 1986 to print the label 'KNLTB official' on its 'Fort' balls (KNLTB being the initials of the Dutch tennis federation)[93], and to place a sticker bearing the same message on its new tins, adding the following legend 'the only approved and recommended tennis-ball' (meaning approved and recommended by the KNLTB), it being understood that such balls and tins were to be supplied only to DSI's exclusive distribution network in the Netherlands. Similar markings were added in Belgium.

## VI. The role played by certain DSI exclusive distributors in determining its policy

(30)   An investigation carried out on 3 November 1988 on the premises of AWS, DSI's exclusive distributor for Dunlop products in the Benelux countries, revealed the active part placed by AWS in support of DSI's export policy to those countries. An investigation carried out on 4 November 1988 at Pinguin, DSI's exclusive distributor for Slazenger in the Netherlands, revealed that Pinguin had at the very least played a passive role in that policy.

### 1. AWS

(31)   On the basis of the documents obtained during the abovementioned investigation, the role played by AWS consisted essentially in informing DSI of the flow of parallel imports into the Benelux countries, in helping to identify their origin, in encouraging DSI to take steps to end such imports and participating in the implementation of such measures. The products involved in the concerted practices between DSI and AWS appear to have been chiefly, but not exclusively, tennis-balls and tennis-rackets. To these must be added, at least, golfing equipment and squash-balls. The respective roles played by AWS and DSI were described in detail in the Statement of Objections[94] (recitals 42 to 76), and this Decision provides only a summary of them.

---

[93]   KNLTB: Koninklijke Nederlandse Lawn Tennis Bond.

[94]   Letters sent on 29-5-1990 by the Commission to DSI, BTR, AWS and Pinguin. However, it should be noted that the Commission's interpretation, in the Statement of Objections, of a number of documents obtained during the investigation at AWS has been challenged by AWS. The Commission's interpretation is not maintained here in respect of the following: Statement of Objections point 37 in fine (not 'various', but 'one' document), point 53 in fine ('eigen kenmerken'), point 64 first paragraph in fine ('inkoop' and 'verkoopprijzen'), point 72 in fine ('artificial exchange rates') and point 74.

1.1. Exchange of information and pressure on DSI

(32)    Numerous documents obtained on the premises of AWS show that there was close
        collaboration between AWS and DSI to identify the origin of parallel imports into
        the Netherlands and Belgium so as to eliminate them.

        From 1985 to the end of 1987 at least, AWS regularly informed DSI of the immi-
        nent arrival or sale at low prices on the Dutch market of parallel imports of Dunlop
        products, from whatever country. Such information was generally transmitted in
        the form of a complaint, with AWS accusing DSI of not being able to control its
        distribution channels and pointing out on occasion that such control was one of the
        conditions for their collaboration. AWS frequently accompanied its complaints
        with threats: threats that it would stop doing business with DSI and threats that it
        would not place planned orders or would return unsold stocks. Where it was aware
        of them, AWS informed DSI of the country of origin of parallel imports or the
        identity of the parallel importer or any other information likely to help in such
        identification.

        The documents show, moreover, that DSI took action (generally very rapidly) on
        the complaints from its distributor and sought actively to identify the origin of the
        parallel imports complained about and the channels through which the goods had
        been imported, taking specific measures in this respect (codification, marking,
        etc.). Once the sources had been identified, DSI attempted by various means to
        eliminate such imports. At all stages of this process, DSI in turn requested AWS's
        collaboration.

1.2. Stopping of supplies to Newitt

(33)    While DSI's export ban was intended to provide general protection for the whole
        of its exclusive distribution network[95], the documents and the complainant's alle-
        gations (not denied by DSI) show that AWS played a particular role in stopping
        supplies to Newitt. Thus, in announcing in May 1986 that it intended to put an end
        to parallel imports, DSI referred to AWS's complaints[96]. It also made reference to
        the question of balls sold by Newitt in France and re-exported to the Netherlands
        and Belgium in refusing, in October 1986, to supply orders placed by Newitt for
        dispatch to France[97]. It was also in response to complaints by AWS concerning the
        arrival on the Dutch market of Dunlop balls originating in the United States that
        DSI sought to identify the source or sources in question and got its American sub-
        sidiary to stop supplying Newitt[98].

1.3. Pricing measures

(34)    The documents obtained during the investigation carried out at AWS show that the
        pricing measures taken by DSI against British traders[99] were also in response to
        complaints made by AWS. The prices for Dunlop products imported through paral-
        lel channels into the Netherlands were much lower than those charged by AWS.
        AWS wanted a ratio to be set (for the most widely sold tennis-balls and tennis-
        rackets in any case) between UK domestic prices and the prices it was charged,
        with such a ratio enabling it to sell in the Netherlands at a price equal to the net

---

[95]   See recitals 16 to 18 above.
[96]   See recital 18 above.
[97]   See recital 19 above.
[98]   See in particular the telefax sent on 16-11-1987 by AWS to DSI and the telefax sent on 17-
11-1987 by DSI to AWS. See also recital 21 above.
[99]   See recitals 22 et seq. above.

purchasing prices of the UK parallel exporters, with the aim of removing any incentive for the latter to export. Taking account of the net trading margin which it wanted to reserve for itself and transport costs, AWS took the view that the net prices which it should be allowed should be equal to 65 to 66% of the net domestic prices charged to British traders:

Net purchasing price for UK traders = 100% = AWS's selling price in the Netherlands, − 32,5% = AWS's net trading margin, − (±) 2,5% = transport costs ± 65% = AWS's net purchasing prices.

However, DSI did not accept AWS's proposals as they stood, since it found them too rigid, and requested further discussion and examination of the figures. It informed AWS, however, that the net prices charged to Newitt for tennis-balls had already risen from £ 7,50 per dozen in 1985 to £ 8,50 in order 'to make exporting impossible' (meeting held on 15 and 16 May 1986). After fairly lengthy negotiations (AWS again demanded the introduction of a fixed ratio), DSI decided to increase UK domestic prices in general, to increase in addition the 'lowest UK net trade prices' charged to Newitt and two other UK traders and, conversely, to reduce (temporarily) the net prices charged to AWS. AWS thus was charged 'the lowest prices for Dunlop Fort balls' and this solution was intended 'in theory to make parallel imports impossible'[100].

In general, it is evident from Annex 3.3 that the index of prices charged to Newitt as compared with those charged to AWS rose from + 109% in 1984 to + 112% in 1985, + 121% in 1986, + 125% in 1987, + 134% in 1988, falling again to + 123% in 1989.

(35)   The documents show that similar measures involving the setting of 'ad hoc' prices[101], intended to eliminate parallel imports by removing any commercial advantage while at the same time maintaining AWS's profit margin at the desired level, were also taken, in collaboration between DSI and AWS, in respect of other products (tennis-rackets and golf equipment at least). So as to make this dissuasive price difference permanent, these prices were supposed to move in parallel with those charged to UK wholesalers.

(36)   It should lastly be mentioned that DSI closed all export accounts for UK traders[102]. AWS stated that this measure was also the result of its 'very tough position'[103].

1.4. Buy-back of products exported through parallel channels

(37)   The documents also show that it was on a proposal by AWS[104] that DSI decided in May 1986 to contribute financially to the buy-back of parallel imports of Dunlop Max 200 G rackets from two chains of shops (see recital 26 above).

1.5. Marking of products
1.5.1. Identification codes

(38)   DSI's practice of marking some of its tennis-rackets with identification codes (see recital 27 above) does not appear to be directly due to pressure exercised by AWS, since it seems to predate such pressure. However, the documents show clearly that

---

[100]   AWS internal memorandum dated 4 March 1987.
[101]   Sometimes referred to as 'special net prices' by AWS.
[102]   For the significance of this measure, see recital 18 above.
[103]   Meeting of the NSF (Dutch sports federation) on 20-10-1986.
[104]   See in particular the record of the meeting of Dunlop racket sports goods distributors on 6 and 7-5-1987, record of the meeting between DSI and AWS on 15 and 16 May 1986 and AWS's internal memorandum of 7-11-1986.

when consignments of rackets imported through parallel channels appeared on the Dutch or Belgian markets, AWS noted the codes and passed them on to DSI for the purposes of identifying the exporter (see recital 32 above).

### 1.5.2. Marking
(39)   The documents obtained do not show whether AWS played an active role as regards the marking of tennis-ball tins (see recital 28 above), but the context within which this operation took place leaves little if any doubt that it represented one of DSI's responses to the complaints made by AWS, if not by other of its exclusive distributors (see recital 32 above), with a view to identifying parallel exporters.

### 1.6. Reserved use of tennis federation labels
(40)   Although the implementation of this measure (see recital 29 above) was due to DSI, the documents obtained show that it represented once agin one of the responses made to AWS's complaints. The documents show that, regardless of the promotional effects anticipated for AWS, the measure was also intended to facilitate the identification of parallel imports. The cost of stamping the initials was borne by DSI, the major advertising campaigns accompanied the operation.

### 1.7. Miscellaneous
(41)   The documents also show that the requests for protection did not necessarily emanate exclusively from AWS, but also from DSI. In May 1986, DSI asked AWS not to supply squash-balls for export to the United Kingdom 'because of its low prices'[105].

### 2. Pinguin
(42)   By letter dated 12 August 1987, DSI informed AWS and Pinguin, as well as its other distributors, that the Commission had received a complaint from Newitt 'concerning action we took against the resale of our products, by Newitt, outside the UK'. It asked AWS and Pinguin, if contacted by the Commission, not to make any response without first contacting DSI, so as to ensure that responses were provide 'in a coordinated way'. In the margin of the letter, Pinguin replied:
'Don't supply Newitt unless you can make an arrangement with him. If making arrangements is impossible because Newitt does not keep them, them don't do business with him. Pirate traders like Newitt and others have harmed our mutual business for hundreds of thousands of pounds in the past'.

## VII. The conduct of the undertakings concerned following the complaint by Newitt and the Statement of Objections by the Commission
### 1. DSI
(43)   After having been informed of the complaint by Newitt in June 1987 (letter dated 23 June 1987) and despite a clear warning from the Commission (letter dated 20 October 1987)[106], DSI did not alter its conduct, which it justified to the Commis-

---

[105] Meeting on 15 and 16-5-1986.

[106] The warning was expressed in the following terms: 'You will not be unaware of the importance the Commission attaches to compliance with the Treaty's competition rules and more particularly those concerning the free movement of goods within the Community. The Commission has always taken the view that any barrier to exports must be considered a particularly serious infringement of those rules. If, therefore, as the complainant maintains − and the documents supporting his complaint seem at first sight to confirm the validity of this claim − you have exerted pressure on him

sion on the grounds of its obligation to support its exclusive distributors in view of the specific responsibilities they bore (letter dated 9 November 1987). On 12 August 1987, it sent a letter to its exclusive distributors warning them of the investigation initiated by the Commission and asking them not to make any response to the Commission without first contacting DSI[107] and at the end of 1987/beginning of 1988, it got its American subsidiary to stop supplying Newitt[108].

(44)   It was only after having received the Commission's Statement of Objections (29 May 1990) that DSI, in its written (16 July 1990) and oral (hearing of 5 October 1990) replies, acknowledged that most of the measures which it had taken against Newitt and other UK exporters constituted infringements of Article 85 of the Treaty and gave undertakings in this respect regarding future action.

2. AWS and Pinguin

(45)   In its written (31 July 1990) and oral (hearing of 5 October 1990) replies, AWS, while acknowledging most of the facts outlined by the Commission, denied that they could – with a few exceptions – have constituted infringements of Article 85 of the Treaty. Pinguin did not reply to the Statement of Objections.

**VIII. Development of Newitt's exports**

(46)   DSI products accounted for a large proportion of Newitt's exports to the Community. From 1985 to 1988, these fell by 40%, while its turnover rose by 42% during the same period: its exports of DSI products to the Community accounted for only 7,6% of its turnover in 1988 compared with 18,3% in 1985. With more particular regard to tennis-balls, having, according to its own estimates, exported 44 000 dozen DSI tennis-balls to the Community, Newitt exported only 9 000 in 1987 and none in 1988.

**B. LEGAL ASSESSMENT**

**I. Article 85(1)**

(47)   The barriers erected by DSI to the export of its products are not unilateral acts by DSI, but must be regarded as an integral, although frequently unwritten, part of its distribution or sales agreements, or are the result of concerted action by DSI and some of its distributors. The barriers had the direct object and the effect of restricting competition and affecting trade between Member States.

**A. AGREEMENTS, CONCERTED PRACTICES AND RESTRICTIONS OF COMPETITION**

1. Ban on exports (recitals 16, 17 and 18)

(48)   The various letters from DSI to Newitt and more particularly the letter dated 5 August 1985, which confirms DSI's export policy of 'quite simply not allowing ship-

---

of any kind whatsoever with a view to restricting his freedom to export within the common market, I call upon you to cease doing so immediately.'

    [107] 'It is just possible that the Commission may contact you as one of our European distributors. If so, please do not make any response without first contacting myself. This is most important. We obviously wish to assist the Commission with their investigations, but to do so in a coordinated way' (letter dated 12 August from the Managing Director).

    [108] See recital 21 above.

ment to any world market where we have local legal distributor agreements', indicate clearly that:

- DSI's exclusive distribution system contains an unwritten clause whereby DSI undertakes to provide its exclusive distributors with absolute territorial protection,
- the sales agreements between DSI and its retailers and distributors also contain an unwritten condition of sale which prohibits them from exporting to the territories of other distributors.
- Such unwritten clauses, by their very nature, have the object of restricting competition and of impeding trade between Member States, in breach of Article 85(1). By eliminating all scope for economic operators to engage in parallel exports, they result in a sharing of the market for Dunlop-Slazenger products between DSI's various exclusive distributors and create the prerequisites for a differentiated pricing policy.

(49) DSI's letter of 5 August 1985 and a letter dated 15 October 1986 stipulate further that the general export ban covers the whole of Europe. As has been seen, DSI has, in all the Member States, either exclusive distributors or subsidiaries or branches which perform that function[109].

(50) BTR's letter dated 3 September 1987 – sent in response to the Commission's communication of Newitt's complaint – does little if anything to alter this general export ban: the possibility of exporting which it re-establishes is purely formal in that the new conditions which it introduces remove any real incentive for economic operators to export, since the prices they would be charged would be determined according to the 'responsibilities' of DSI's exclusive distributor in the country of destination, in other words, on the basis of the profit margin fixed for that distributor[110]. There is also the fact that the obligation on the exporter to reveal the identity of the final customer – an obligation which the decisions and case law of the Commission and the Court of Justice have always opposed – is liable to jeopardize the goodwill on which his business is based.

2. Refusal to supply (recitals 19, 20, 21, 33 and 42)

(51) The refusal to fill two large orders from Newitt for tennis-balls for France in October 1986, followed by the embargo, albeit temporary, on (some) supplies to the company in June 1987, and the subsequent stopping of supplies by the American subsidiary in 1988 were all measures designed to put an end to Newitt's exports, which had continued despite DSI's ban.

As has been seen (recitals 32 and 33), these refusals to supply were the result both of concerted practices by DSI and AWS and of the export ban governing DSI's sales agreements with UK traders.

Article 85 (1) prohibits such agreements and such concerted practices, which had the direct object and effect of restricting competition and of affecting trade between Member States and which prevented Dutch consumers from benefiting from lower prices than those charged by DSI's exclusive distributor.

(52) A document obtained at the premises of Pinguin shows that it too urged DSI to stop supplying Newitt unless an 'arrangement' was possible. The wording of the text is

---

[109] See recital 10 above.

[110] This was actually implemented by DSI in collaboration with AWS in the Netherlands: see recitals 34 and 35 above. See also recital 56 below on the reasons adduced by DSI to justify these protection measures.

such that it must be concluded that the 'arrangement' would in one way or another restrict Newitt's freedom to export and that here too there was a concerted practice in breach of Article 85(1).

(53)     In its written and oral replies to the Statement of Objections, DSI, while denying that it imposed a permanent export ban, acknowledges that 'on occasion' it took such measures in respect of countries where it had exclusive distributors. It acknowledges that it thus refused to supply Newitt's orders for France and that, following AWS's request, it took action to get its American subsidiary to stop supplies to Newitt. It regrets having taken such measures, which it now regards as 'incorrect', but takes the view that 'the matter should have been dealt with entirely through the mechanism of price and discount adjustment', which is not any more acceptable for the Commission (see recital 56 below).

3. Pricing measures (recitals 22 to 25, 34, 35 and 36)

(54)     The fact that DSI no longer allowed Newitt to benefit from its export prices and that it reduced the discounts usually granted to Newitt constituted measures aimed at preventing Newitt from remaining competitive in relation to DSI's exclusive distributors on the export markets[111]. These measures, which together had the effect of increasing Newitt's purchase prices by between 15 and over 50% in the case of certain articles, effectively prevented it from continuing to export certain DSI products, such as tennis- and squash-balls, to other Community countries and compelled it to seek alternative sources of supply in third countries. As outlined in recital 34, these measures, which infringe Article 85(1), were the result of close collaboration between DSI und AWS, and the level of the new prices charged to Newitt was specifically calculated to remove any incentive for that company to continue to export to the Benelux countries and to enable AWS to retain artificially its profit margins on the DSI products concerned.

(55)     Certain documents show that, when it was impossible to raise the prices charged to British exporters – either for commercial reasons, or because the parallel imports had already taken place – DSI, in certain cases, subsidized the products of AWS byx covering part of the losses or loss of profit resulting from the 'special' prices which AWS was obliged to charge in order to combat such parallel imports. These ad hoc measures must be considered to be measures having an equivalent effect to the higher prices charged to British exporters.

(56)     In its written and oral replies to the Statement of Objections, DSI defends the abovementioned pricing measures by referring to the specific costs borne by exclusive distributors and not borne by the parallel exporters. It thus argues that the measures taken in 1986 to 1987 against Newitt were intended merely to put an end to an unfair and commercially unjustified advantage whose origin was to be sought in a certain degree of management laxity prior to the takeover of DSI by BTR.

---

[111] Indeed, the very existence of two price-lists, one for all export countries, the other for the United Kingdom only, is questionable in terms of its economic justification or, in any event, in terms of the frequently large disparities between the two sets of prices, which are usually to the disadvantage of the UK. The fact that domestic prices are for the most part considerably higher (15 to 50%) (see recital 12 above) removes, in many cases, any incentive for UK firms to export. DSI has announced that it intends to do away with this double price list within the Community. The Commission reserves the right – if this intention is not put into effect – to return to this question and examine its compatibility with Article 85(1) (possible existence of indirect export barriers) and, for products where DSI proves to hold a dominant position, with Article 86 (possible discriminatory pricing practices).

The Commission cannot accept this argument, for several reasons.

Firstly, it is not apparent (see Annex 3.1) that the prices charged to Newitt before the 1986 to 1988 measures gave it any unfair advantage, given the volumes involved, over DSI's other major wholesalers, selling mainly, or indeed virtually exclusively, on the UK market. During this entire period, the net prices charged to Newitt were, moreover, already significantly higher (some 9 to 12%) than those charged to AWS (see Annex 3.3). On the contrary, the 1986 to 1988 measures affecting mainly Newitt, whose purchase prices exceeded those charged to smaller firms (Annex 3.1) and were at dissuasive levels compared with DSI's exclusive distributors (Annex 3.2 and 3.3), were in point of fact discriminatory in character.

The 'specific' costs referred to by DSI and cited during the hearing[112] do not, moreover, in any way properly derive from the function of exclusive distributor. Such costs are normal costs borne by any distribution firm, and their scale is primarily linked to the volume of turnover. The only particular costs of any scale which DSI's exclusive distributors have to bear, compared with independent firms, relate to advertising and promotional expenditure for the brand (some 6% of its turnover according to AWS). However, it should firstly be noted that such expenditure is partly financed by DSI, which indeed makes a considerable contribution towards it. In addition, such expenditure is certainly not without benefit to the exclusive distributor in so far as his name — and his title of 'exclusive' or 'official' distributor — are broadly associated with the brand in the advertising and promotional measures. If there are specific costs, they are thus counterbalanced by specific benefits.

At any rate, the view must be taken that any specific costs borne by exclusive distributors are largely offset by the granting of exclusivity, which constitutes a key commercial advantage. They do not justify the additional application to exclusive distributors of special prices intended to protect them from parallel imports.

Lastly, it should be pointed out that the documents obtained from AWS show that it was not the economic considerations claimed by DSI in its written and oral replies to the Statement of Objections which guided it in the measures it took against parallel exporters. The setting of the relative prices for UK firms and exclusive distributors was never based on their respective commercial importance or even on the amount of the 'specific' costs referred to by DSI. Such relative prices were set precisely, in collusion with AWS, at the level which would remove any incentive for British firms to continue exporting. This was the only criterion, inended to prevent parallel imports, which was taken into consideration[113].

(57) AWS for its part maintains that it was DSI which decided to increase the prices charged to United Kingdom traders and that it sought only to reduce its purchasing prices, which could only stimulate competition.

It has been abundantly evident that AWS's requests were not intended to obtain purchasing prices at an economically justified level, but the setting of an artificial ratio between them and the prices charged to British firms in order, on the contrary, to prevent all competition.

---

[112] Administrative and sales staff, advertising and promotion, storage costs, distribution costs, travel and entertainment expenses, postage, telex, fax, bad debts.

[113] DSI acknowledges this, moreover, indirectly in its written reply to the Statement of Objections – and shows that it persists in this view – when, expressing regret at the export bans imposed on Newitt and the interruptions in supply, it adds that 'this matter should have been dealt with entirely through the mechanism of price and discount adjustment' (see recital 53 above).

4. Buying-back of parallel imports (recitals 26 and 37)

(58)   As indicated in recitals 26 and 37, the repurchasing by AWS of parallel imports of low-price tennis-rackets on sale in Dutch chain stores and the reimbursement by DSI of the difference between the buy-back price paid by AWS and the price it normally paid DSI were also carried out at AWS's request and involved close collaboration between the two companies. These concerted practices were designed to protect AWS from competition and to enable it to maintain a high level of prices. They prevented consumers from benefiting from the cheaper prices charged by the parallel exporters and clearly infringe Article 85(1). THe same applies to the advertising and promotion campaigns organized by AWS, with the support of DSI, which were intended to heighten the dissuasive effect of the buy-back operations.

5. Product marking (recitals 27 and 28, 38 and 39)

(59)   DSI marked its products with codes or marks in order to make it easier to identify parallel exporters, with a view to terminating their activities. DSI acknowledged this operation, and the documents obtained from AWS also show that AWS actively participated in efforts to identify such exporters. Such concerted practices, once again aimed at protecting the DSI distribution network from parallel imports, also infringe Article 85(1).

6. Use of the tennis federation label for the benefit of exclusive distributors only (recitals 29 and 40)

(60)   The printing of the initials of the Dutch tennis federation ('KNLTB official') only on tennis-balls sold to AWS and the use of stickers bearing the same message together with the legend 'the only approved and recommended tennis-ball' on the corresponding tins were intended to achieve two objectives. They were intended, on the one hand, to facilitate (by allowing immediate identification) the tracing of balls imported through parallel channels and, on the other, whatever DSI and AWS say, to give the DSI exclusive distribution network an edge over competitors by inducing consumers erroneously to believe that only the balls distributed by that network met the technical standards supposedly imposed by the federation[114] and, incidentally, that the higher prices charged were justified. These measures must be regarded as constituting concerted practices that infringe Article 85(1), since DSI implemented them and bore the financial costs of them in response to urgent requests from AWS to identify and halt parallel imports into the Benelux countries.

The exclusivity agreement between the KNLTB and AWS (which AWS refers to in its written reply to the Statement of Objections) does not alter the facts of the situation. Regardless of the question of the compatibility of the exclusivity agreement with Article 85

– a question on which the Commission has not expressed an opinion in this case, since it had no knowledge of the existence of the agreement – it has always been considered that the concerted use, within the framework of an exclusive distribution agreement, of an intellectual property right with the sole aim of impeding parallel imports constitutes an infringement of Article 85(1)[115].

---

[114] The consumer certainly cannot imagine that the selection of the 'official' balls is carried out solely on a financial basis and not on the basis of their technical properties (see recital 29), particularly when the 'official' sticker is followed by the legend 'the only approved and recommended tennis-ball', – referring to approval and recommendation by the KNLTB. It is significant in this respect that AWS urged DSI to take back its old stocks of balls not marked with this label.

[115] See in particular Joined Cases 56 and 58/64 Consten and Grundig v. Commission [1966] ECR 299. See also Article 3 (d) of Regulation (EEC) No 1983/83 (OJ No L 173, 30-6-1983, p. 1).

## B. EFFECT ON TRADE BETWEEN MEMBER STATES

(61)    The ban on exports contained in the DSI distribution agreements and conditions of sale had the direct object of impeding trade between Member States. The ban was a general one, in that it concerned all DSI products and all the Community countries. In view, moreover, of DSI's importance in the markets for sports equipment, especially the market for tennis, squash and golf equipment[116], the effect on trade between Member States was particularly appreciable.

(62)    The concerted practices by DSI and AWS aimed at eliminating parallel imports into the Benelux countries also had the object of impeding trade between Member States. In many cases, they enabled such imports to be halted or cancelled their effects on prices, preventing consumers in those countries from enjoying lower prices than those charged by AWS. The concerted practices led to the virtual elimination of all exports by Newitt of Dunlop products to other Member States[117] and probably also to that of parallel exports by other UK traders.

## II. Regulation (EEC) No 1983/83

(63)    Article 1 of Regulation (EEC) No 1983/83 provides that exclusive distribution agreements are in general exempt from the prohibition laid down in Article 85(1) if they fulfil the conditions set out in the Regulation. The exclusive distribution agreements concluded by DSI do not, however, qualify for such block exemption as they impose on the parties obligations which are liable to restrict competition other than the restrictions authorized in Article 2 of the Regulation and because they are accompanied by an unwritten clause giving absolute territorial protection to DSI distributors. Furthermore, the implementation of the agreements also involves concerted practices. Both the provisions of the agreements and the concerted practices are caught by Article 3 (d) of the Regulation.

## III. Article 85(3)

(64)    The DSI distribution agreements in the United Kingdom and in the other Member States were not notified to the Commission and do not therefore qualify for an individual exemption. In any event, even if they had been notified, they would not have qualified for such exemption in view of the export bans aimed at total territorial protection which they contain and which are not indispensable to the effectiveness of DSI's distribution system.

## IV. Article 3 of Regulation No 17

(65)    Pursuant to Article 3(1) of Regulation No 17, the Commission may, if it finds that there has been an infringement of Article 85, require by decision that the undertakings concerned bring such infringement to an end.

(66)    DSI is required, if it has not already done so, to terminate the export bans governing its sales agreements in the United Kingdom and the absolute territorial protection included in the exclusive distribution agreements it has in other Member States. It is also required to terminate the various measures (notably as regards prices) applied to Newitt and other UK traders with a view to preventing them from exporting, thus protecting its exclusive distributors.

---

[116] See recitals 6 to 9 above.
[117] See recital 46 above.

## V. Article 15(2) of Regulation No 17

(67) Pursuant to Article 15(2) (a) of Regulation No 17, the Commission may, by decision, impose fines of from ECU 1 000 to 1 000 000 or a sum in excess thereof, but not exceeding 10% of the turnover in the previous business year, on undertakings which, either intentionally or negligently, infringe Article 85. In setting the amount of the fine, regard must be had both to the gravity and to the duration of the infringement.

(68) DSI could not have been unaware that the export ban (which applied to all its products and all the Member States) governing its distribution agreements and conditions of sale infringed Article 85(1) and that the Court of Justice and the Commission have always regarded such bans, which undermine one of the fundamental objectives of the EEC Treaty, as particularly serious infringements. DSI and AWS could not have been unaware that the same applied to the various concerted practices employed in order to prevent parallel imports into the Benelux countries. Consequently, a fine should be imposed on DSI and AWS.

(69) Neither the communication of Newitt's complaint to DSI in June 1987 nor the formal warning given by the Commission in October 1987 against these restrictions on exports induced DSI to change its behaviour[118]. The only response which the communication of Newitt's complaint to DSI appears to have evoked was that DSI sent a letter to its distributors on 12 August 1987 requesting them to coordinate their replies to any questions the Commission might ask.

In its written and oral replies to the Statement of Objections, by contrast, DSI acknowledge that a number (but not all) of the measures it had taken constituted infringements of the competition rules, said that it regretted this and announced that it would take a series of corrective measures, namely instructions to its staff and exclusive distributors, new distribution agreements and new conditions of sale [119]. However, at the same time, it made clear its intention of continuing to protect its exclusive distributors through a system of differentiated prices or discounts [120].

(70) Account must be taken of the fact that the infringements committed by DSI date back to at least 1977 (see the letter dated 14 December 1977 stressing that Dunlop products supplied to Newitt may not be exported) [121] and that they stopped in 1990, except in the case of the measures relating to prices. Account must also be taken of the fact that the infringements committed by AWS date back to at least 1985(see the telexes dated 1 February and 29 April 1985 showing that AWS was noting the identification codes on Dunlop rackets and the telex dated 27 February 1986 in which it states that it agreed to DSI's pricing policy in 1985 only on the express condition that DSI had 'its distribution under control') and that the infringements stopped in April 1989, the date on which AWS ceased to be DSI's exclusive distributor.

(71) In setting the amount of the fine, the Commission has also taken account of the fact that, although the export ban governing DSI's distribution agreements was general and covered all products, the concerted practices engaged in with AWS were apparently (on the basis of the information available to the Commission) limited to only some of the products (tennis-balls, squash-balls, tennis-rackets and golfing

---

[118] See recital 43 above.

[119] In this context, BTR communicated to the Commission by letter dated 12 December 1990 a 'competition law compliance manual' and, by letter dated 22 January 1991, a new standard distribution agreement.

[120] See in particular 53 above.

[121] However, the Commission acknowledges that this export ban was not always applied.

equipment). The Commission has also taken DSI's importance on the relevant markets into consideration.

As regards AWS, the Commission has taken account of the financial problems which it has encouraged and which have culminated in a takeover,

## HAS ADOPTED THIS DECISION:

Article 1

Dunlop Slazenger International Ltd has infringed Article 85(1) of the EEC Treaty by applying in its business relations with its customers a general ban on exporting its products, designed to protect its exclusive distribution network, and by implementing, in respect of some of its products (tennis-balls, squash-balls, tennis-rackets and golfing equipment), various measures – refusal to supply, dissuasive pricing measures, marking and follow-up of exported products, buy-back of exported products and the discriminatory use of official labels – in order to ensure enforcement of the export ban.

All Weather Sports International BV has infringed Article 85(1) by urging and participating in the implementation of such measures in the Netherlands in respect of Dunlop products.

Pinguin Sports BV has infringed Article 85(1) by urging the implementation of similar measures in the Netherlands in respect of Slazenger products.

Article 2

A fine of ECU 5 000 000 is hereby imposed on Dunlop Slazenger International Ltd and a fine of ECU 150 000 on All Weather Sports Benelux BV (which has taken over the assets of All Weather Sports BV) in respect of the infringements referred to in Article 1.

The fine shall be paid, in ecus, to the Commission of the European Communities, account No 310-0933000-43, Banque Bruxelles Lambert, Agence Européenne, Rond Point Schuman 5, 1040 Brussels, within a period of three months of the notification of this Decision. After the expiry of that period, interest shall automatically be payable at the rate charged by the European Monetary Cooperation Fund on its ecu operations on the first working day of the month in which this Decision is adopted, plus three and a half percentage points.

Article 3

Dunlop Slazenger International Ltd shall, in so far as it has not already done soe, terminate the infringements referred to in Article 1 of this Decision. It shall refrain from adopting any measure having equivalent effect.

Article 4

This Decision is addressed to:
Dunlop Slazenger International Ltd,
Challenge Court,
Barnett Wood Lane,
Leatherhead,
UK – Surrey KT22 2LW,
BTR plc,
Vincent Square,
UK – London SW1P 2PL,
All Weather Sports Benelux BV,
Postbus 295,
Wattstraat 20,

NL-2700 AG-Zoetemeer,
Pinguin Sports BV,
Postbus 30,
Industrieweg 50,
NL-2380 AA Zoeterwoude/Rijndijk.

This Decision shall be enforceable pursuant to Article 192 of the EEC Treaty. Done at Brussels, 18 March 1992. For the Commission
Leon BRITTAN
Vice-President

**ANNEX 1.1** – NB: for full formatted annexes see OJ L 131, 16-5-1992, pp. 32-49, at pp. 46-49.
First-grade tennis-balls – Market shares and dimensions in the Community – 1989
Member States Market Dimension (1000 dozen) Dunlop Slazenger Total DSI Penn Wilson Tretorn Dunlop France Others Belgium/
Luxembourg 160 5 12 17 14 5 44 3 17 Denmark 45 5 25 30 15 5 33 – 17 Ireland 20 35 8 43 37 8 10 – 2 France 1 800 5 10 15 16 3 5 48 13 Germany 1 700 57 7 64 12 4 12 – 8 (Pirelli: 7) Greece 10 40 5 45 20 15 15 – 5 Netherlands 210 38 21 59 12 3 20 2 4 Italy 540 28 5 33 10 6 20 4 27 (Pirelli: 25) Portugal 12 30 10 40 32 8 – 10 10 Spain 180 18 3 21 31 19 2 20 7 United Kingdom 290 11 39 50 20 25 5 – – Total EEC 4 967 28 11 39 16 6 11 19 9

**ANNEX 1.2** – NB: for full formatted annexes see OJ L 131, 16-5-1992, pp. 32-49, at pp. 46-49.
Squash-balls – Market shares in the Community[122] – 1989
Member States Dunlop Slazenger Total DSI Belgium/Luxembourg 33 17 50 Denmark – – – Ireland 85 – 85 France – 10 10 Germany 43 3 46 Netherlands 50 5 55 Italy 53 15 68 Portugal – – – Spain 80 10 90 United Kingdom 70 10 80 Greece – – – Total EEC 56 7 63

**ANNEX 2** – NB: for full formatted annexes see OJ L 131, 16-5-1992, pp. 32-49, at pp. 46-49.
DSI – United Kingdom domestic price-list and export price-list – Differentials for tennis-balls and squash-balls – United Kingdom domestic list price = 100
Dunlop Slazenger Date Tennis-balls[123] Squash-balls[124] Date Tennis-balls[125] Squash-balls[126] United Kingdom price (a) Export price (b) United Kingdom price Export price United Kingdom price Export price United Kingdom price Export price £ Index £ Index £ Index £ Index £ Index £ Index £ Index £ Index 1982 1982 1. 9 ? 7,87 5,07 1. 10 ? 8,30 ? 4,50 – 1983 1983 1. 3 / 1. 4 8,55 100 8,26 (7,87) (*) 96,6 6,05 100 5,58 92,2 31. 1 8,15 100 101,8 5,20 100 86,5 1. 10 8,67 (7,87) 101,4 5,58 92,2 3. 10 8,98 9,15 101,9 6,66 100 5,20 78,1 1984 1984 1. 10 / 1. 11 9,40 100 9,10 (7,87) 96,8 6,66 100 5,58 83,8 2. 4 8,98 101,9 6,66 100 78,1 1. 10 9,40 97,3 6,66 100 78,1 1985 1985 25. 2 / 4. 3 9,40 100 9,10 96,8 8,08 100 5,58 69,1 4. 3 9,40 ? ? 6,66 100 ? ? 1. 9 / 1. 10 10,45 100 10,20 97,6 8,08 100 5,58 69,1 1. 10 10,45 ? ? 6,66 100 ? ? 2. 12 11,20 100 91,1 1986 1986 2. 4 11,90 100 85,7 8,08 69,1 1. 3 / 2. 4 11,20 10,75 96,0 6,66 100 5,58 83,8 1. 9 / 29. 9 11,90 100 11,00

---

[122] DSI estimates and commercial audits.
[123] Dunlop Fort 601.331 (1-9-1982-1-10-1983) – 601.332 and 601.330 (1-10-1984-2-12-1985) – 601.336 (2-4-1986-1-9-1988) – Dunlop T.P. 601.362 (since 1-9-1989).
[124] Black Yellow Dot 750 890 (1- 9-1982-1-10-1984) – XX Black Yellow Dot 750 440 (since 4-3-1985).
[125] Slazenger Yellow 340 430 (1-10-1982-1-9-1986) – 340 454 (since 1-9-1986).
[126] Navy Blue Yellow Dot 419 043 (1-10-1982-4-3-1985) – 419 047 (1-10-1985-2-4-1986) – 419 173 (since 1-9-1986).

92,4 8,08 100 5,75 71,2 1. 9 / 29. 9 11,90 11,00 92,4 6,66 100 5,75 86,3 1987 1987 13. 4
11,90 100 92,4 8,75 65,7 13. 4 11,90 92,4 6,66 86,3 1. 7 6,20 70,9 1. 7 6,20 93,1 1. 9 / 28.
9 12,40 100 11,75 94,8 8,75 70,9 1. 9 / 28. 9 12,40 11,75 94,8 6,66 6,20 93,1 1988 1988 1.
4 12,40 100 94,8 9,09 68,2 1. 4 12,40 94,8 6,66 93,1 1. 7 6,65 73,2 1. 9 / 3. 10 13,02 13,15
101,0 6,66 6,90 1. 9 / 3. 10 13,02 100 13,15 101,0 6,65 73,2 1989 1989 3. 4 13,02 100
101,0 3. 4 13,02 101,0 1. 7 9,54 7,10 74,4 1. 7 6,66 6,90 103,6 1. 9 / 2. 10 13,02 100 13,15
101,0 9,54 74,4 1. 9 / 2. 10 13,02 13,14 100,9 6,66 103,6
(a) Carriage paid.
(b) fob.
(*) Figures supplied by Newitt.

**ANNEX 3.1** – NB: for full formatted annexes see OJ L 131, 16-5-1992, pp. 32-49, at pp. 46-49.
DSI first-grade tennis-balls – Volumes/Prices/Discounts
Date United Kingdom List price (A) Export List price (B) AWS (Benelux) (export price
only) Newitt (United Kingdom and export price) . . . (*) (United Kingdom price only) . . .
(United Kingdom price only) . . . (United Kingdom price only) ' 000 dozen Price Discount on B ' 000 dozen Price Discount ' 000 dozen Price Discount on A ' 000 dozen Price
Discount on A ' 000 dozen Price Discount on A on B on A 1984 8,55 8,67 1/11 9,40 9,10
1985 9,40 9,10 1/9 10,45 10,20 2/12 11,20 10,20 1986 11,20 10,20 2/4 11,90 10,20 1/9
11,90 11,00 1987 11,90 11,00 1/9 12,40 11,75 1988 12,40 11,75 1/9 13,02 13,15 1989
13,02 13,15
1. Year-end figures.
2. Price = weighted average price.
3. AWS 1989 sales: January-April only (distribution agreements terminated).
Source: DSI.
(*) In the published version of the Decision, some information has hereinafter been omitted, pursuant to the provisions of Article 21 of Regulation No 17 concerning non-disclosure of business secrets.

**ANNEX 3.2** – NB: for full formatted annexes see OJ L 131, 16-5-1992, pp. 32-49, at pp. 46-49.
DSI 'first-grade' tennis-balls – Volumes/Prices/Discounts
Date Export list price Benelux three distributors Italy two distributors Spain two distributors Newitt ' 000 dozen Price Discount ' 000 dozen Price Discount ' 000 dozen Price Discount ' 000 dozen Price Discount 1984 8,67 1/11 9,10 1985 9,10 1/9 10,20 1986 10,20 1/9
11,00 1987 11,00 1/9 11,75 1988 11,75 1/9 13,15 1989 13,15
1. Sales in Spain in 1984 were affected by late purchases in 1983 (total 1983 = [. . .]
dozen).
Source: DSI.

**ANNEX 3.3** – NB: for full formatted annexes see OJ L 131, 16-5-1992, pp. 32-49, at pp. 46-49.
Ratio of prices charged to Newitt and to certain DSI exclusive distributors – Index
Year Newitt price AWS price Newitt price Italian distributor price Newitt price Spanish
distributor price 1984 109 100 94 100 101 100 1985 112 100 104 100 109 100 1986 121
100 113 100 116 100 1987 123 100 115 100 117 100 1988 134 100 123 100 124 100 1989
123 100 120 100 140 100

## 2.4.5. COMMISSION DECISION RELATING TO A PROCEEDING UNDER ARTICLE 85 OF THE EEC TREATY (IV/33.384 AND IV/33.378 – DISTRIBUTION OF PACKAGE TOURS DURING THE 1990 WORLD CUP), 27 OCTOBER 1992[127]

*The Commission of the European Communities,*

– Having regard to the Treaty establishing the European Economic Community,
– Having regard to Council Regulation No 17 of 6 February 1962, first Regulation implementing Articles 85 and 86 of the Treaty[128], as last amended by the Act of Accession of Spain and Portugal, and in particular Article 3 thereof,
– Having regard to the application made by Pauwels Travel BVBA on 28 November 1989, in accordance with Article 3 of Regulation No 17, for a finding that Article 85 had been infringed,
– Having regard to the Commission's decision of 22 January 1991 to initiate a proceeding in this case,
– Having given the undertakings concerned the opportunity to make known their views on the objections raised by the Commission, pursuant to Article 19(1) of Regulation No 17 and Commission Regulation No 99/63/EEC of 25 July 1963 on the hearings provided for in Article 19(1) and (2) of Council Regulation No 17 (2),
– After consulting the Advisory Committee on Restrictive Practices and Dominant positions,

Whereas:

## I. THE FACTS

### A. Subject of the Decision

(1) On 28 November 1989, the Commission received a complaint from the travel agency Pauwels Travel BVBA ('Pauwels Travel') against:
  – FIFA Local Organizing Committee Italia '90,
  – 90 Tour Italia SpA,
  – NV CIT Belgique.

(2) The complaint, based on the provisions of Article 3 of Regulation No 17, related to the ticket distribution system applied during the FIFA World Cup held in Italy in 1990.

(3) Pauwels Travel wanted to put together and sell in Belgium World Cup package tours comprising transport, accommodation and entrance tickets to the stadia in which the various matches were to be played. However, it found that the ticket distribution system that had been decided on did not allow travel agencies to acquire stadium entrance tickets for the purpose of putting together package tours.

(4) The attempts made by Pauwels Travel to sell such package tours by procuring entrance tickets through parallel channels resulted in an action to cease and desist being brought before the Belgian national courts by the travel agency authorized by the World Cup organizers to sell package tours in Belgium.

(5) This Decision does not relate to the whole of the ticket distribution system, but only to the contracts through which the World Cup organizers conferred on the company 90 Tour Italia world exclusive rights for the supply of stadium entrance tickets for the purpose of putting together package tours.

---

[127] OJ L 326 , 12-11-1992, p. 31-42.
[128] ECR 1405 [1974].

(6)     The market on which the effects of the contracts must be assessed is thus that for the sale of package tours to the World Cup held in Italy.

In accordance with the case law of the Court of Justice, in particular in Case 23/67, Brasserie de Haecht v. Wilkin (1), however, the whole of the distribution system must be examined and the contracts must be assessed in the context within which they operated.

## B. General organization of the World Cup

(7)     On 5 August 1983, the International Federation of Association Football (Fédération internationale de football association – FIFA) drew up the specifications and conditions for the federation organizing the 1990 World Cup.

The specifications and conditions, signed by the General Secretary of FIFA, state that the World Cup is a FIFA competition and that FIFA is to appoint one of the national associations affiliated to FIFA as the organizer (executive agent) of the World Cup.

(8)     Under Article 1.1 of the specifications and conditions, the national association appointed may carry out its task directly itself or it may request FIFA to appoint a local organizing committee comprising representatives of the national association concerned and of FIFA.

(9)     The specifications and conditions also stipulate that the national association appointed and its local organizing committee are placed under the control of the FIFA World Cup organizing committee, which has the last word in all matters.

(10)    On 19 May 1984, FIFA appointed the Federazione italiana gioco calcio (FIGC) as organizer of the 1990 World Cup.

(11)    In accordance with the FIFA specifications and conditions for the organization of the World Cup, FIFA and the FIGC agreed to set up a local organizing committee on 3 December 1984.

(12)    The document establishing the local organizing committee provides that the committee is to comprise a maximum of 15 members, including five from FIFA and 10 from Italy, and that its head office will be in Zurich under the auspices of FIFA, with a branch office in Rome.

(13)    In fact, the number of members was limited to 11, i.e. two from FIFA and 9 from the FIGC.

(14)    The setting up of the local organizing committee was ratified by the FIFA executive committee at a meeting held in Zurich on 28 April 1985, and on 11 June 1985 FIFA drew up the regulations governing the organization and operation of the local organizing committee for the 1990 World Cup.

(15)    The function of the local organizing committee is specified in Article 3 of the regulation as being to perform all activities relating, directly or indirectly, to the technical and logistical organization of the World Cup in Italy in 1990, in compliance with the operating limits laid down in the specifications and conditions drawn up by FIFA and the 1990 FIFA World Cup regulations.

(16)    Amongst such activities, the local organizing committee is in particular required to propose to FIFA the plan for distributing and setting entrance tickets and to deal subsequently with the implementation of the plan.

(17)    Lastly, a number of aspects of relations between FIFA and the local organizing committee were covered in a document entitled 'Agreement between FIFA and the local organizing committee Italia 90', signed by the administrative director of the local organizing committee and the General Secretary of FIFA.

With regard to the sale of tickets, the document stipulates that the directives governing the sale of tickets and their prices must be approved by FIFA (a requirement which FIFA considered essential).

## C. The parties concerned

(18)  FIFA is a federation of national football associations from 158 countries and is based in Zurich. Its object is to promote football and, for this purpose, to organize the World Cup every four years.

FIFA's revenue derives from the dues paid by its members and from a percentage of revenue from international matches and world championships.

(19)  The Federazione italiana gioco calcio (FIGC) represents the various Italian football associations.

It is based in Rome and has a Chairman and a General Secretary.

(20)  The Compagnia italiana turismo SpA (CIT) is a subsidiary of the Ente ferrovie dello Stato.

It is one of the main travel agencies in Italy.

CIT Italia also has subsidiaries in other European countries, including Belgium, France and the United Kingdom.

(21)  Italia Tour SpA (Italia Tour) is a subsidiary of Alitalia – Linee Aeree Italiana SpA, which also carries out travel agency activities within and outside Italy.

(22)  90 Tour Italia SpA (90 Tour Italia) is a company created jointly by CIT and Italia Tour for the purpose of marketing package tours to the 1990 World Cup. Its existence is closely bound up with the organization of the 1990 World Cup.

## D. The financing of the World Cup

(23)  The expenditure involved in establishing the infrastructure required for the World Cup was borne by the organizing federation or the organizing country. This applied to the work involved in converting grounds, improving roads, hotels, etc.

(24)  The organizing federation received the following revenue:
   (a)  some 15% of net competition profits, calculated as follows:
      –  proceeds from television rights plus the sale of tickets,
      –  minus the expenses entailed in organizing the World Cup;
   (b)  the commercial exploitation in Italy of the 1990 World Cup emblem, created by the organizing federation;
   (c)  a proportion of match revenue to cover the reimbursement of State, provincial and municipal taxes and the hire of grounds;
   (d)  a percentage of ticket revenue, to be determined with FIFA as a contribution towards the organization expenses proper.

(25)  Contracts relating to advertising and the commercial exploitation of emblems and television contracts were concluded directly by FIFA.

(26)  Estimated total World Cup revenue was Sfr 220 million, made up as follows:
   –  Sfr 75 million from the sale of tickets,
   –  Sfr 55 million from the sale of advertising rights,
   –  Sfr 90 million from the sale of television rights.

## E. The general ticket distribution system

(27)  The general ticket distribution system covered a total of some 2 700 000 tickets broken down as follows:
   –  12% distributed in Italy by the national football associations,
   –  4% distributed in Italy by the official World Cup sponsors,
   –  34% distributed in Italy by the Banca Nazionale del Lavoro ('BNL'),
   –  15% distributed outside Italy by the national sport associations,
   –  5% distributed outside Italy by the main European football association,
   –  5% distributed outside Italy by BNL or its representatives,
   –  25% distributed outside Italy by 90 Tour Italia as part of package tours.

**F. The conditions governing distribution of tickets not included in package tours**
(28)   The distribution of tickets by the football associations was subject to restrictions set
       out in a FIFA circular sent on 23 October 1989 to all the national FIFA associa-
       tions, the main provisions of which were as follows:
       –    ticket sales were intended only for the associations themselves,
       –    sale to travel agencies or other bodies was prohibited. If the national associa-
            tion intended to organize a trip through the intermediary of a travel agency
            normally used by it, it was asked to contact 90 Tour Italia in order to ensure
            that such arrangements were coordinated, and
       –    sales were to take place only in the country itself.
(29)   The distribution of tickets by BNL and its agents was also subject to certain restric-
       tions. BNL could not sell tickets to travel agencies, nor could BNL agents resell
       their tickets to travel agencies.
       In addition, each spectator could acquire no more than a maximum of four series,
       so as to prevent any parallel procurement by travel agencies.
       BNL agents could sell such tickets only in their own countries and had to inform
       BNL of the identity of those acquiring tickets.
       These requirements were also set out in a letter which BNL sent on 16 March 1989
       to the Crédit communal de Belgique as its agent for the sale of tickets in Belgium.

**G. The distribution of tickets as part of package tours**
(30)   On 26 June 1987, a contract was concluded between the local organizing commit-
       tee, on the one hand, and CIT and Italia Tour, on the other, the main provisions of
       which are as follows:
       –    the local organizing committee entrusted CIT and Italia Tour with the task
            of providing, through the intermediary of 90 Tour Italia, a joint company to
            be created, all the tourist, hotel and transport services requested by the local
            organizing committee in connection with the 1990 World Cup in order to
            meet its requirements and the requirements of FIFA, referees, official del-
            egations and teams, journalists and any persons specified by the local orga-
            nizing committee,
       –    the local organizing committee also conferred on 90 Tour Italia exclusive
            world rights for the organization of:
       –    the various 1990 World Cup package tours and any services connected with
            the World Cup during the period 1987 to 1990, and
       –    an appropriate network for distributing such services both in Italy and in the
            rest of the world,
       –    the local organizing committee granted 90 Tour Italia exclusive world rights
            for the issue of stadium entrance tickets to be included in package tours and
            assured it of a number of tickets at least equal to 30% of the capacity of the
            stadia,
       –    in return for the concession of the abovementioned rights, 90 Tour Italia was
            to pay to the local organizing committee a percentage of the turnover
            achieved under the contract throughout its period of validity, such percent-
            age being equal to 0,5% of the gross turnover, or Lit 700 million, whichever
            sum was the higher,
       –    in carrying out its tasks, 90 Tour Italia was authorized to present itself as the
            exclusive authorized agent of the local organizing committee in the area of
            tourism and to use the title 'tour operator for the local organizing committee
            Italia '90',

- CIT and Italia Tour were jointly responsible together with 90 Tour to the local organizing committee,
- the contract was valid until 31 December 1990.

(31) A second contract was concluded on 11 February 1988 between the local organizing committee and 90 Tour Italia, with the counter-signature of the chairman of CIT SpA and Italia Tour SpA.

This contract reiterates that CIT and Italia Tour have declared themselves willing to provide the local organizing committee with all the tourist services which the local organizing committee requires in connection with the World Cup and to put together package tours including entrance tickets to the various World Cup matches, package tours which would be marketed on an exclusive basis throughout the world.

The contract then goes on to repeat the provisions of the contract concluded on 26 June 1987 between the local organizing committee on the one hand and CIT and Italia Tour on the other, notably as regards:

- the supply of tourist, hotel and transport services by 90 Tour Italia to the local organizing committee,
- the world exclusive rights granted to 90 Tour Italia by the local organizing committee for the issuing of tickets as part of package tours,
- the world exclusive rights granted to 90 Tour Italia to acquire, exclusively for the package tours sector, all or some of any tickets still available when the local organizing committee has fulfilled its other engagements. This agreement was valid until 31 December 1990.

(32) For the purpose of marketing its package tours, 90 Tour Italia concluded contracts with travel agencies in the various countries.

As far as the Member States were concerned, 90 Tour Italia concluded a contract with one agency in Ireland and one in Belgium/Luxembourg. In the other Community countries, contracts were concluded with a number of agencies.

(33) In all cases, the agencies approved by 90 Tour Italia undertook to resell the package tours at retail level only on their own territories. The agencies could if they wished resell the package tours at the wholesale level, but only to:

- agencies selling at the retail level which were established on their respective territories and which undertook to resell the package tours at the retail level,

or

- agencies selling at the wholesale level which were established on their respective territories and which undertook to resell the package tours to agencies selling at the retail level which were themselves established within the relevant territory.

(34) The authorized agencies were not in any circumstances allowed to resell the entrance tickets separately from the package tours.

(35) The relevant contracts related to a total of some 540 000 tickets to be included in the package tours.

The prices of the package tours differed considerably depending on aspects such as the number of days, the type of accommodation, the type of transport, distance and the meals included.

The prices of the package deals sold in Belgium by the agency authorized by 90 Tour Italia, for example, ranged from ECU 143 to ECU 840.

## H. The question of safety

(36) The organization of the World Cup raises problems relating to safety that have to be taken into account. Such problems were outlined during the course of the pro-

ceeding by the deputy procurator of the Republic (sostituto procuratore della Repubblica Italiana), responsible for coordinating the organization of safety arrangements during the World Cup, and by the representatives of the local organizing committee and may be summarized as follows.

(37)  The main problem for the organizers was to ensure that opposing groups of supporters were kept separate from one another and did not clash in or around the grounds. It was therefore necessary to ensure that spectators were grouped together by nationality within the grounds.

(38)  For this purpose, the organizers carried out work within the grounds that would in particular allow all spectators to be seated.

(39)  In addition, a central computerized system managed by BNL was set up with the aim of identifying the nationality of all the spectators and allowing seats to be allocated on the basis of nationality. The tickets distributed by BNL and its agents were sold only on presentation of an identity document, and the relevant information was entered in the central BNL computer.

(40)  The procedure was the same for package tours; each person purchasing a package tour had to provide evidence of his identity, which was entered in the BNL computer via a computerized sub-system managed by 90 Tour Italia. Each person travelling on a package tour thus received a ticket corresponding to his nationality.

(41)  The organizational arrangements still left open the possibility that individual supporters could purchase tickets not intended for them, notably on the black market. However, according to the organizers, such practices were not widespread and posed little risk in terms of safety. The main problem was the formation of 'groups' of supporters close to or among opposing supporters.

(42)  According to the organizers, it had therefore to be ensured that independent travel agencies not controlled by the local organizing committee could not acquire tickets. Such travel agencies would have been able to resell such tickets, either separately or as part of package tours, to supporters of a different nationality than that for which they were intended, thus jeopardizing spectator safety.

## II. LEGAL ASSESSMENT

### A. The concept of undertaking

(43)  In accordance with the case law of the Court of Justice, any entity carrying on activities of an economic nature, regardless of its legal form, constitutes an undertaking within the meaning of Article 85 of the EEC Treaty (see in particular Cases 36/74 of 12 December 1974, Walrave v. Union Cycliste Internationale[129] and C-41/90 of 23 April 1991, Hoefner v. Elser/Macrotron[130]).
An activity of an economic nature means any activity, whether or not profit-making, that involves economic trade (see Case 41/83 of 20 March 1985, Italy v. Commission (British Telecommunications)[131]).

(44)  Regarding the commercial nature of the World Cup
The World Cup is indisputably a major sporting event.
However, it also involves activities of an economic nature, notably as regards:
–      the sale of 2 700 000 entrance tickets for matches, more than 20% of which are included in package tours comprising hotel accommodation, transport and sightseeing,

---

[129]  OJ L 173, 30-6-1983, p. 1.
[130]  ECR I-1979 [1991].
[131]  ECR 873 [1985].

- the conclusion of contracts for advertising on panels within the grounds,
- the commercial exploitation of the FIFA emblems, the World Cup, the FIFA fair-play trophy and the World Cup mascot,
- the commercial exploitation by the local organizer of a specific emblem for the 1990 World Cup, and
- the conclusion of television broadcasting contracts.

(45) The economic value of the World Cup is, moreover, acknowledged in Article 3.4 of the specifications and conditions laid down by FIFA for the organizing federation.

(46) The economic value of the World Cup was also acknowledged by FIFA representatives at the hearing (see page 126 of the hearing record).

(47) FIFA

FIFA is a federation of sports associations and accordingly carries out sports activites.

However, FIFA also carries out activities of an economic nature, notably as regards:
- the conclusion of advertising contracts,
- the commercial exploitation of the World Cup emblems, and
- the conclusion of contracts relating to television broadcasting rights.

(48) In the case of the 1990 World Cup, the sale of advertising and television broadcasting rights by FIFA accounted for some 65% of total World Cup revenue, estimated at Sfr 220 million.

(49) It must therefore be concluded that FIFA is an entity carrying on activities of an economic nature and constitutes an undertaking within the meaning of Article 85 of the EEC Treaty.

(50) The Federazione Italiana Gioco Calcio (FIGC) is the national Italian football association, appointed by FIFA to organize the 1990 World Cup.

(51) The FIGC was accordingly responsible for the entire organization of the event in accordance with the provisions of the 1990 World Cup regulations and had in particular the task of ensuring that grounds were in order, press facilities provided, parking spaces laid out, etc.

(52) For the purpose of financing such expenditure, the FIGC had a share in the net profits of the competition and was able to exploit commercially in Italy the 1990 World Cup emblem, which it had itself created.

(53) The FIGC thus also carries on activities of an economic nature and is consequently an undertaking within the meaning of Article 85 of the EEC Treaty.

(54) Local organizing committee

The local organizing committee is a body set up jointly by FIFA and the FIGC for the purpose of carrying on all activities relating directly or indirectly to the technical and logistical organization of the World Cup.

The local organizing committee's tasks included the establishment and implementation of the ticket distribution arrangements.

(55) The local organizing committee's revenue derived partly from television rights, advertising rights, the sale of tickets and the commercial exploitation in Italy of the World Cup emblem.

(56) The exclusive rights granted to 90 Tour Italia resulted in remuneration for the local organizing committee, in accordance with the provisions of Article 5 of the contract of 26 June 1987.

(57) It must therefore be concluded that the local organizing committee was a body carrying on activities of an economic nature and consequently constituted an undertaking within the meaning of Article 85.

(58)    The Compagnia Italiana Tourismo SpA (CIT) is an Italian company engaged in travel agency activities. It is therefore an undertaking within the meaning of Article 85.

(59)    Italia Tour SpA is a company carrying on an activity similar to that of CIT and is thus also an undertaking within the meaning of Article 85.

(60)    90 Tour Italia SpA is a company established under Italian law by CIT and Italia Tour for the purpose of putting together and marketing package tours to the 1990 World Cup. It is therefore an undertaking within the meaning of Article 85 of the EEC Treaty.

**B. The contracts**

(61)    The conditions under which 90 Tour Italia was active in marketing the package tours derive from two contracts:
    −    a contract concluded on 26 June 1987 between the local organizing committee on the one hand and CIT SpA and Italia Tour on the other, and
    −    a contract concluded on 11 February 1988 between the local organizing committee and 90 Tour Italia reiterating the main provisions of the abovementioned contract.

(62)    These two contracts were for an identical term of validity, ending on 31 December 1990. The contract concluded on 11 February 1988 does not contain any provision cancelling or replacing the contract concluded on 26 June 1987.

(63)    It should also be noted that the contract concluded on 11 February 1988 between the local organizing committee and 90 Tour Italia was countersigned by CIT and Italia Tour which, under Article 8 of the contract, declared themselves jointly responsible with 90 Tour Italia vis-à-vis the local organizing committee.

(64)    Consequently, contrary to the statements made by the representatives of CIT during the proceeding, it cannot be argued that any anti-competitive effect of the contract between the local organizing committee and 90 Tour Italia cannot be blamed on CIT and Italia Tour. The two abovementioned contracts must therefore be taken into account in this proceeding.

**C. On the responsibility of FIFA and FIGC**

(65)    The two contracts which are the subject of this proceeding were concluded between the local organizing committee on the one hand and 90 Tour Italia, CIT and Italia Tour on the other. The contracts were not signed by FIFA or the FIGC.

(66)    However, it should be borne in mind that the local organizing committee, although having a separate legal personality, did not have any real autonomy as regards its conduct. Such lack of autonomy is due in particular to the following aspects.

(67)    The local organizing committee was set up jointly by the FIGC and FIFA specifically for the purpose of carrying on all activities relating directly or indirectly to the technical and logistical organization of the 1990 World Cup in Italy, in compliance with the operating constraints laid down in the specifications and conditions established by FIFA and the 1990 World Cup regulations (Article 3 of the local organizing committee regulations of 14 August 1985).

(68)    The existence of the local organizing committee was consequently closely linked to the organization of the 1990 World Cup and was to end once the 1990 World Cup was over.

(69)    The local organizing committee comprised 9 representatives of the FIGC and the President and General Secretary of FIFA. These 11 members, meeting in plenary session, had full powers of decision over the committees' activities.

(70)    The lcoal organizing committee's restricted executive committee, which included

FIFA's General Secretary, could be drawn only from the local organizing committee's own members.

(71) As a result of the presence of their representatives within the local organizing committee's decision-making body, the FIGC and FIFA directly and effectively controlled the whole of the committee's activities on a joint basis, notably as regards ticket distribution.

In this area, the local organizing committee was subject to the instructions of FIFA and the FIGC.

(72) In addition, in accordance with the provisions stipulated in the specifications and conditions, FIFA had the last word in all decisions of principle in all matters, including the ticket distribution system, which was a key element in the organization of the World Cup.

(73) The ticket distribution system had in any case to be approved by FIFA. Thus, the contracts concluded on 26 June 1987 between the local organizing committee and CIT/Italia Tour and on 11 February 1988 between the local organizing committee and 90 Tour Italia regarding the distribution of tickets to be included in package tours included a suspensory clause to the effect that the policy on ticket sales had to be approved by FIFA.

(74) All in all, it must be concluded that the local organizing committee was not in a position to determine in a really autonomous manner its behaviour on the market and that the conclusion of the above-mentioned contracts of 26 June 1987 and 11 February 1988 is attributable jointly to the local organizing committee, the FIGC and FIFA.

## D. The concept of agreement

(75) The two contracts of 26 June 1987 and 11 February 1988 constitute agreements between undertakings within the meaning of Article 85 of the EEC Treaty.

## E. On the nature of the contracts in question

(76) During the proceeding, some of the parties stated that the purpose of the contracts was to entrust to 90 Tour Italia the function of carrying out a task which the local organizing committee was not in a position to perform.

It might be concluded from this that 90 Tour Italia acted solely as an agent and that the contracts in question were not caught by the provisions of Article 85 of the Treaty.

(77) Such an analysis cannot be accepted for the following reasons:
- – 90 Tour Italia was able to acquire entrance tickets to the grounds from the local organizing committee, but subsequently it provided different services, namely package tours, of which the tickets were only one element; the package tours were marketed at the prices and on the conditions set by 90 Tour Italia,
- – 90 Tour Italia had to undertake to acquire, and did actually acquire, a considerable number of tickets for matches whose appeal to spectators was heavily dependent on the qualification of their team and hence unpredictable, and
- – 90 Tour Italia thus accepted a high commercial risk, as the representatives of CIT pointed out at the hearing (see pages 60 and 70 of the hearing record).

(78) Accordingly, the functions of 90 Tour Italia went well beyond those of a mere agent, and the contracts are therefore caught by Article 85 of the Treaty.

## F. Effect on competition

(79) The purpose of this Decision is solely to establish the effect on competition produced by the two abovementioned contracts concluded between the local organizing committee, 90 Tour Italia, CIT and Italia Tour.

However, in assessing the object and effects of the contracts in the light of Article 85(1) of the Treaty, it is necessary to take into account the context within which they operated, notably entire ticket distribution system as described above.

(80) Under the two contracts of 26 June 1987 and 11 February 1988, the local organizing committee:
- conferred on 90 Tour Italia world exclusive rights in organizing the various package tours to the World Cup and in establishing an appropriate network for the distribution of such package tours in Italy and in the rest of the world,
- allowed 90 Tour Italia to present itself as the exclusive agent of the local organizing committee and to use the description 'Tour Operator for Italia 90', and
- within this framework, also granted 90 Tour Italia world exclusive rights to issue ground entrance tickets for inclusion in package tours and made available to it a number of tickets at least equal to 30% of the capacity of the grounds.

(81) These exclusive rights were not granted by the local organizing committee free of charge, but entailed remuneration by 90 Tour Italia in accordance with the provisions of Article 5 of the contract of 26 June 1987.

(82) 90 Tour Italia subsequently authorized agencies in the various countries to sell its package tours.

(83) The result of these exclusive rights was that 90 Tour Italia was the only tour operator able to acquire ground entrance tickets from the local organizing committee for the purpose of putting together and selling package tours that included such tickets.

(84) Other tour operators, and travel agencies as well, were not able to acquire ground entrance tickets from the local organizing committee or from other sources of supply such as the sports associations or BNL because of the restrictions imposed on the sale of such tickets, and in particular the ban on resale to travel agencies.

(85) Consequently, the only package tours including ground entrance tickets available on the market were those put together by 90 Tour Italia. Other tour operators were able to offer only package tours that did not inlude ground entrance tickets.

(86) Obviously, for anyone wishing to go to Italy for the World Cup, it was crucial to have a package tour that did include ground entrance tickets.
Consequently, tour operators that were not able to offer such package tours were at a considerable competitive disadvantage vis-à-vis 90 Tour Italia.

(87) The world exclusive rights granted to 90 Tour Italia thus had the effect of restricting competition between tour operators in the Community.

(88) Furthermore, travel agencies wishing to sell package tours that included match entrance tickets were able to obtain such package tours from only one tour operator.
If world exclusive rights had not been granted to 90 Tour Italia, travel agencies would have been able to choose between a number of tour operators and possibly obtain more favourable terms, thus enabling them to gain a competitive edge over other travel agencies.

(89) Consequently, the world exclusive rights enjoyed by 90 Tour Italia also had the effect of restricting competition between travel agencies within the Community.

(90) During the proceeding, the parties argued that tour operators could sell package tours without ground entrance tickets and ask their customers to obtain the tickets from BNL or from the football associations.

(91) This cannot regarded as a valid option. In such a situation, a customer buying a package tour without tickets would have to go to a BNL branch or agent to obtain tickets corresponding to the dates of the package tour. Given the time and effort this would entail, potential customers would obviously give preference to the travel agencies authorized by 90 Tour Italia to sell package tours with tickets.

(92) A second possibility suggested by the parties during the proceeding was that poten-

tial customers could book a package tour without tickets at a travel agency and ask the travel agency to purchase the ground entrance tickets for them.

(93) This approach similarly cannot be regarded as a satisfactory alternative solution.

Such a procedure would have meant that, for each package tour sold, a travel agency not authorized by 90 Tour Italia would have to go to the BNL branch or agent with the customer's identity papers in order to obtain the ground entrance tickets.

This procedure would have meant extra work and hence extra costs for the non-authorized travel agency and would still have left some doubt in the mind of the customer as to the real chances of obtaining the entrance tickets.

This sort of procedure thus placed agencies that did not have tickets at a competitive disadvantage vis-à-vis the agencies authorized by 90 Tour Italia, which were the only ones that were able to state in their advertising that they were able to guarantee entrance tickets.

(94) Account must also be taken of the fact that, by fax dated 26 January 1990, BNL instructed all its sales outlets outside Italy to stop selling entrance tickets as from 31 January 1990.

(95) As a result, as from 1 February 1990, tour operators other than 90 Tour Italia were unable to sell package tours for which their customers were supposed to purchase the tickets from BNL branches or agents.

(96) All in all, by granting exclusive rights to 90 Tour Italia to supply entrance tickets to be included in package tours, alternative sources for the procurement of tickets not being available, the agreements concluded between, on the one hand, the local organizing committee in its capacity as a body belonging jointly to FIFA and the FIGC and, on the other, 90 Tour Italia, CIT and Italia Tour had the effect of restricting competition in the Community within the meaning of Article 85(1) of the Treaty between our operators and between travel agencies on the market for the sale of package tours to the 1990 World Cup. The conditions of Article 85(1) are thus met.

## G. Commission Regulation (EEC) No 1983/83 (1)

(97) During the proceeding, the parties argued that the agreements could have been exempted under Regulation (EEC) No 1983/83 on the application of Article 85(3) of the Treaty to categories of exclusive distribution agreements.

(98) Regulation (EEC) No 1983/83 was adopted by the Commission pursuant to Council Regulation (EEC) No 19/65/EEC of 2 March 1965 on the application of Article 85(3) of the Treaty to certain categories of agreements and concerted practices[132].

(99) Article 1(1) of Regulation (EEC) No 19/65/EEC explicitly limits the Commission's power to adopt an exemption regulation to agreements relating to goods only.

This restriction is also evident in the wording of the Article, which covers transactions in which one party purchases a good for resale.

(100) Such purchasing and reselling transactions cannot be applied to services.

(101) It must therefore be concluded that services are excluded from the scope of Council Regulation (EEC) No 19/65/EEC.

(102) Regulation (EEC) No 1983/83 is thus bound to have the same scope of application, defined as 'agreements to which only two undertakings are party and whereby one party agrees with the other to supply certain goods for resale within the whole or a defined area of the common market only to that other'.

---

[132] OJ 36, 6-3-1965, p. 533/65.

(103) In point 11 of its Notice concerning Regulation (EEC) No 1983/83[133], the Commission stipulated that 'exclusive agreements for the supply of services rather than the resale of goods are not covered by the Regulation'.

(104) The agreements to which this proceeding relates concern the supply on an exclusive basis of entrance tickets to grounds for the purpose of putting together package tours comprising transport, accommodation and meals.

(105) It is thus obvious that the agreements relate to the supply of services and do not fall within the scope of application of Regulation (EEC) No 1983/83.

(106) Even if the package tours in question had been deemed to be goods within the meaning of Article 1 of Regulation (EEC) No 1983/83, the conditions for exemption set out in Article 3 of the Regulation were not met.

Thus, contrary to the provisions of Article 3 (c), users could obtain the package tours with match entrance tickets in the contract territory only from the exclusive distributor or its representatives and had no alternative source of supply outside the contract territory, the contract territory being the entire world.

(107) With regard to the exclusive rights enjoyed by 90 Tour Italia, the representatives of the local organizing committee stated during the proceeding that such exclusive rights were de facto exclusive rights resulting from the lack of any other tour operator interested in concluding a contract with the local organizing committee.

(108) This argument cannot be accepted for the following three reasons:
- if the parties did not wish to conclude an exclusive contract, there is no reason why they should have incorporated such a clause in the contract,
- the first contract between the local organizing committee and CIT/Italia Tours, signed on 26 June 1987, already provided for such exclusivity. As from that date, the local organizing committee was thus not in a position to conclude a contract with any other interested tour operator,
- if exclusivity had not been desired by the parties, there is no reason why the parties should have provided by contract for the financial consideration in respect of such exclusivity.

## H. The question of safety

(109) During the proceeding, the parties claimed that any restrictions of competition were justified by safety requirements.

The separation of spectators within the grounds by nationality and the need for safety arrangements around the grounds, it was claimed, meant that only one tour operator could be authorized to put together the package tours comprising entrance tickets for sale at world level.

(110) From the legal point of view, the parties argued that such restrictions of competition had to be examined in the light of Article 36 of the Treaty, whose provisions took precedence over the competition rules laid down in Article 85. The parties referred in this respect to the judgment of the Court of Justice in Case 40/70 Sirena v. Eda[134].

(111) With regard to the application of Article 36 of the EEC Treaty, the court of Justice held, in its judgment in Case 40/70 referred to by the parties, that 'Article 36, although it appears in the chapter of the Treaty dealing with quantitative restrictions on trade between Member States, is based on a principle equally applicable to the question of competition, in the sense that even if the rights recognized by the legislation of a Member State on the subject of industrial and commercial property are

---

[133] OJ C 101, 13-4-1984, p. 2.
[134] ECR 69 [1971].

not affected, so far as their existence is concerned, by Articles 85 and 86 of the Treaty, their exercise may still fall under the prohibitions imposed by those provisions'.

(112) It must be deduced from this judgment that, as in the case of the rules governing the free movement of goods, the competition rules may set limits to the exercise of industrial property rights. The argument put forward by the parties takes the opposite line in that it claims that Article 36 sets limits to the application of the competition rules.

(113) At all events, even if this principle were accepted, it would be necessary to ensure that, in accordance with the provisions of Article 36, the practices in question did not constitute disguised restrictions of competition and that they were indispensable to the attainment of their objective.

(114) In his evidence on the problems of safety, the deputy procurator of the Republic, who was responsible for the coordination of safety arrangements during the World Cup, did not mention the need to establish world exclusivity for the distribution of package tours inclusive of entrance tickets to the grounds.

(115) During the hearing, a representative of the local organizing committee stated, with regard to the package tours, that all the tour operators willing to create a computerized subsystem and ensure its coordination with that of BNL could have been selected. The local organizing committee's representative stated in particular that 'two, fifteen or twenty' tour operators could have been selected (see page 89 of the hearing record).

(116) It must therefore be concluded from the statements of the local organizing committee's representative himself that the world exclusive rights granted to 90 Tour Italia were not essential in order to ensure safety during the World Cup.

Consequently, even if the principle of Article 36 of the Treaty could be applied to the present case, the world exclusive rights granted to 90 Tour Italia were disproportionate to the objective pursued and cannot therefore be justified by the need to maintain safety.

(117) With regard to package tours inclusive of tickets, strict control of ticket distribution was necessary. It was particularly important that a tour operator putting together such package tours should be able to make sure that the travel agencies distributing them downstream complied with the distribution conditions imposed by the tour operator.

(118) For this reason, the Commission considers it justified that travel agencies not controlled by the organizers, such as the agency which has brought the complaint in this case, should not have been able to acquire blocks of entrance tickets with a view to putting together package tour that would have been sold in a way that was not controlled.

(119) However, the Commission considers that a number of tour operators imposing the same distribution conditions on travel agencies authorized to sell their package tours could have competed on the market without jeopardizing spectator safety.

(120) The Commission notes that this possibility was acknowledged by the representatives of the local organizing committee during the hearing when they stated that any tour operators fulfilling the same criteria as 90 Tour Italia could have been selected.

## I. Article 85(3)

(121) The agreements in question were not notified to the Commission with a view to exemption under Article 85(3) of the EEC Treaty.

(122) In any case, the Commission considers that the agreements did not fulfil the conditions required for the granting of such exemption.

(123) Even if it had been considered that the agreements could contribute to improving the distribution of tickets and package tours, the Commission takes the view that the agreements imposed restrictions that were not indispensable to the attainment of the objectives pursued and, moreover, afforded the undertakings the possibility of eliminating competition in respect of a substantial part of the services in question.

## J. Effect on trade between Member States

(124) The contracts related to the exclusive distribution of package tours inclusive of tickets in the Community and the rest of the world, without any possibility of alternative sources of supply. The contracts thus appreciably affected trade between Member States, since, if they had not been concluded, trade on the market for such tours could have been expected to have been greater.

## K. Imposition of fines

(125) It must be borne in mind that this is the first time that the Commission has taken action on the distribution of tickets for a sporting event.
Furthermore, this case involved undoubted complicating factors in view of major safety aspects.
Lastly, the infringement came to an end with the completion of the 1990 World Cup.
Consequently, the Commission considers that fines should not be imposed on the parties to the agreements.

(126) However, the Commission considers that a Decision is necessary in order to clarify the legal position and prevent the same or any similar infringement from being committed in future. In accordance with the case law of the Court of Justice (Case 7/82, GVL v. Commission[135]), the Commission therefore has a legitimate interest in finding that the contracts infringed Article 85 of the Treaty,

## HAS ADOPTED THIS DECISION:

Article 1
FIFA, the FIGC, the local organizing committee Italia '90, CIT SpA, Italia Tour SpA and 90 Tour Italia SpA have infringed Article 85(1) of the EEC Treaty as regards the provisions of the contracts of 26 June 1987 and 11 February 1988 concluded between the local organizing committee Italia '90 and CIT SpA and Italia Tour SpA, on the one hand, and 90 Tour Italia SpA, on the other, which provided for the exclusive supply at world level to 90 Tour Italia SpA of ground entrance tickets for the purpose of putting together package tours to the 1990 World Cup. Such tickets formed part of a general system for the distribution of ground entrance tickets developed and implemented by the local organizing committee Italia '90 in accordance with the instructions of the FIGC and FIFA, after approval by FIFA, a system which prohibited the sale of tickets for the putting together of such package tours, thus making it impossible for other tour operators and travel agencies to find sources of supply other than 90 Tour Italia SpA.

Article 2
This Decision is addressed to:

---

[135] ECR 483 [1983].

- 90 Tour Italia SpA
  Via Laura Mantegazza, 75
  I-Roma,
  - Col Italia/Italia '90
  Via Po, 36
  I-00198 Roma,
- Compagnia Italiana Turismo spA
  Piazza della Repubblica 68
  I-00185 Roma,
- Federation internationale de football association
  PO Box 85
  Hitzigweg 11
  Ch-8030 Zurich,
- Federazione italiana gioco calcio
  Via Po 36
  I-00198 Roma,
  - Italia Tour SpA
  Piazzale Schuman 78
  I-Roma.

Done at Brussels, 27 October 1992. For the Commission
Leon Brittan
Vice-President

———

**2.4.6.    DRAFT NOTICE PURSUANT TO ARTICLE 19 (3) OF COUNCIL
REGULATION NO 17[136] CONCERNING A NOTIFICATION IN CASES
NO IV/33.145 – ITVA/FOOTBALL AUTHORITIES AND NO IV/33.245 –
BBC, BSB AND FOOTBALL ASSOCIATION, 3 APRIL 1993[137]**

1.   On 12 June 1989 and 6 July 1989 the English Football Association (FA) concluded
     agreements with the BBC and BSB respectively concerning television rights to
     football matches of which the FA holds the rights, superseding earlier agreements
     dated 23 November 1988. The agreements were notified to the Commission on 10
     July 1989, on behalf of BSB; 14 August 1989 on behalf of the BBC – together with
     an agreement between the BBC and BSB, the so-called coverage agreement dated
     23 November 1988, which covers the sharing of the rights between them and on 7
     September 1989, on behalf of the FA. The agreements are also in part the subject
     of a complaint, lodged by the Independent Television Association (ITVA) on 5
     April 1989.

**I.    The parties**
*1.    The Football Association*
2.   The (English) Football Association Limited (FA) is the governing body of the sport
     of association football in England. It is one of the four national football associa-
     tions in the United Kingdom – the other three being the Scottish Football Associa-
     tion, the Football Association of Wales and the (Northern) Irish Football
     Association, which are all affiliated members of FIFA and UEFA. The Football

---

[136]  OJ 13, 21-2-1962, p. 204.
[137]  OJ C 94, 3-4-1993, p. 6.

Association has as its object to promote the game of association football in every way by, for example, laying down rules and regulations of the game, affiliating clubs and associations, registering players or referees, etc. It itself organizes national matches – FA Cup and Charity Shield – and international matches, involving the England national team, to which it holds the television rights.

2.    *The BBC*
3.    The British Broadcasting Corporation (BBC) is the publicly founded television arid radio broadcasting organization in the United Kingdom. It provides two generalist channels, BBC 1 and BBC 2, which broadcast diversified programmes including a certain amount of sports.

3.    *BSB, now BSkyB*
4.    British Satellite Broadcasting was a new television company based in the United Kingdom which came into operation in April 1990. It provided via satellite several different channels, including one dedicated sports channel, for direct reception by viewers in the United Kingdom and Ireland with the necessary reception equipment. In November 1990, BSB merged with Sky Television, another satellite television company based in the United Kingdom and a subsidiary of News Corporation. The new company, called British Sky Broadcasting (BSkyB), operates five direct satellite channels, including Sky Sports, a dedicated sports channel for viewers in the United Kingdom and Ireland which recently has become a pay-TV channel.

4.    *ITVA*
5.    The complainant is the Independent Television Association Limited (ITVA), a trade association the members of which are the independent television -contractors to the Independent Broadcasting Authority (IBA). They are private companies, funded by advertising and providing television services at regional level, including traditionally a certain amount of sports such as football. The ITVA represents their collective interests throughout the United Kingdom. The ITV network is currently in a transitional period, after the 15 regional franchises were put out to tender, with the result that three of the companies will be replaced on 1 January 1993. At the same time there will be a structural change in that the regional companies will become directly responsible as individual broadcasters, instead of contractors to the IBA.

**II.    The agreements**
6.    In 1988 the BBC and BSB, which at that time had not yet come into operation, agreed to bid jointly for the rights held by the FA and to share the rights between them in such a way that each party would show a number of matches live, while the other would either not show these matches at all or would show only recorded highlights of them. However, both parties concluded separate agreements with the FA, dated 23 November 1988, which were subsequently superseded by the agreements dated 12 June 1989 and 6 July 1989, and an additional agreement between them called the coverage agreement, also dated 23 November 1988 which covers the sharing of the rights between them.

1.    *The agreements between the FA the BBC and BSB, now BSkyB*
7.    (i)    According to the agreements between the FA, the BBC and BSkyB, the FA grants them for five years (1988-1993 seasons) exclusive television rights to

all national and international matches of which the FA is the television rights owner, i.e. national matches of the national cups organized by the FA (Charity Shield and FA Cup, with the exception of the FA Cup final) and international matches involving the England national team and taking place in England, or taking place abroad if the FA in this case in some way or other acquires the television rights.

8.    (ii)    In addition, the agreements originally granted the BBC and BSB for the duration of the contract the exclusive permission to transmit football matches from abroad which matches pursuant to Article 14 of the Statutes of UEFA (and pursuant to the former Article 37 (a) of the FIFA Statutes which subsequently has been abolished by FIFA) can he shown on television in England only with the prior permission of the FA. This clause was the main subject of the complaint by ITVA.

9.    Article 14 of the UEFA Statutes, which concerns the cross-border broadcasting of football matches is also the subject of the complaint in question by ITVA and of further complaints by The European Sports Network (RESN) in Case No IV/33.742 − TESN/Football Authorities and by BSkyB (former BSB) in Case No IV/34.199 − BSkyB/Football Authorities and has been notified to the Commission in Case No IV/34.319 UEFA. According to Article 14 of the UEFA Statutes television right's to football matches cannot be sold from one country to the other, which means in practice that matches cannot be shown, without the association of each receiving country having given its consent to such transmission in its territory. Under the present revised version national associations can withhold such consent only if a domestic match is being played on the same day within that Association's territory.

10.    In line with its agreements with the BBC and BSB, the FA made it clear in a circular letter sent on 3 January 1989 to all national associations in membership with FIFA that it had granted the BBC and BSB exclusive permission to broadcast foreign football under the relevant FIFA and UEFA rules and that it would not allow the broadcasting of such matches by any other broadcaster in the United Kingdom.

11.    At the request of the Commission the clause granting exclusive, permission to broadcast foreign foothall matches, which in the Commission's view was not only contrary to Article 85 (1) of the Treaty but also an abuse of a dominant position by the FA within the meaning of Article 86 of the Treaty, has been removed from the agreements between the FA, the BBC and BSkyB. Pending the Commission's decision on Article 14 of the UEFA- Statutes the FA has undertaken to the Commission not to apply Article 14 in a manner which discriminates between on the one hand the BBC and BSkyB and on the other hand thirdparty broadcasters, such as the ITV companies, wishing to show foreign matches in England.

*2.    The coverage agreement between the BBC and BSB, now BSkyB*

12.    The coverage agreement sets out in detail which matches are to be broadcast by each of the parties in order to avoid simultaneous transmissions. It also provides that both parties shall make available to each other news exchange of each match they cover. Furthermore, the parties shall use their best efforts where appropriate jointly to acquire the rights for matches played outside England. Originally the agreements also provided that the parties should not unilaterally negotiate with the FA to extend or vary their rights and should not unilaterally enter into negotlations with ITVA in respect of the rights that ITVA has acquired to English league football. However, at the request of the Commission, the bans on unilateral negotia-

tions with the FA or with ITVA in respect of English league footbalt have been removed from the coverage agreement.

### III. The decision envisaged by the Commission
Following the abovementioned modifications the Commission proposes to take a favourable decision on the agreements notified. Before doing so, it invites all interested third parties to send their comments within one month of the date of publication of this notice, quoting the reference – IV/33.145 ITVA/Football Authorities and IV/33.245 – BBC, BSB and Football Association, to:
Commission of the European Communities,
Directorate-General for Competition,
Directorate for Restrictive Practices and Abuse of Dominant Position and other Distortions of Competition,
IV/B-4,
rue de la Loi 200,
B-1049 Brussels.

---

### 2.4.7.    COMMISSION DECISION RELATING A PROCEEDING PURSUANT TO ARTICLE 85 OF THE EEC TREATY (IV/32.150 – EBU/ EUROVISION SYSTEM), 11 JUNE 1993[138]

*The Commission of the European Communities,*

– Having regard to the Treaty establishing the European Economic Community,
– Having regard to Council Regulation No 17 of 6 February 1962, First Regulation implementing Articles 85 and 86 of the Treaty[139], as last amended by the Act of Accession of Spain and Portugal, and in particular Articles 4, 6 and 8 thereof,
– Having regard to the Commission Decision of 5 December 1988 to initiate proceedings in this case,
– Having regard to the application submitted on 3 April 1989 by the European Broadcasting Union for negative clearance, or for exemption pursuant to Article 85(3) of the EEC Treaty in respect of its internal provisions ('Statutes') and other regulations governing the acquisition of television rights to sports events, the exchange of sports programmes within the framework of Eurovision and contractual access to such programmes for third parties,
– Having published, pursuant to Article 19(3) of Regulation No 17, a summary[140] of the rules and the resultant cooperation under the Eurovision arrangements,
– Having given third parties concerned the opportunity to make known their views on the Commission's intention to grant an exemption, pursuant to Article 19(3) of Regulation No 17 and Commission Regulation No 99/63/EEC of 25 July 1963 on the hearings provided for in Article 19(1) and (2) of Regulation No 17[141],
– Having consulted the Advisory Committee on Restrictive Practices and Dominant Positions,
Whereas:

---

[138]  OJ L 179, 22-7-1993, p. 23-37. No longer in force.
[139]  OJ 13, 21-2-1962, p. 204.
[140]  OJ C 251, 5-10-1990, p. 2.
[141]  OJ 127, 20-8-1963, p. 2268.

## I. THE FACTS

(1)     On 3 April 1989 the European Broadcasting Union (EBU) notified to the Commission its provisions ('Statutes') and other rules governing the acquisition of television rights to sports events, the exchange of sports programmes within the framework of Eurovision and contractual access to such programmes for third parties (EBU model contract for the acquisition of Eurovision rights in a sports event, rules on sharing of transmission rights under Eurovision sports agreements − including relating rules − rules on the use of the Eurovision signal and rules on sub-licences to non-members). In conjunction with the notification it applied for negative clearance or, alternatively, exemption pursuant to Article 85(3) of the EEC Treaty.

### A.     The EBU organization

(2)     The EBU is an association of radio and television organizations set up in 1950 with headquarters in Geneva. It has no commercial aim. Its principal objects are: to support its active members in their task of serving the interests of the general public in the best possible manner, to support and defend in every domain the interests of its members and to assist its members in negotiations of any kind or negotiate at their request on their behalf; to promote cooperation between its members and with other broadcasting organizations or groups of such organizations and in particular to promote radio and television programme exchanges by all possible means; to prepare and take all measures designed to assist the development of broadcasting in all its forms.

(3)     Active membership of the EBU is open to broadcasting organizations or groups of such organizations which provide, in a country situated in the European broadcasting area, a service of national character and national importance. They must also be under an obligation to cover the entire national population and must, in practice, cover at least a substantial part thereof while using their best endeavours to achieve full coverage in due course; they must further be under an obligation to provide, and must actually provide, varied and balanced programming for all sections of the population, including a fair share of programmes catering for special/minority interests of various sections of the public irrespective of the ratio of programme-costs to audience, and must themselves produce or commission under their own editorial control a substantial proportion of the programmes broadcast.

(4)     A group of broadcasting organizations qualifies for EBU membership as a single member if it is a de jure or de facto association of broadcasting organizations from the same country, which individually or − as regional organizations − collectively qualify for EBU membership. Broadcasting organizations which qualify only collectively for membership must meet the specific membership requirements with regard to the respective broadcasting area for which they are licenced. A group may, in addition, include:

(a)     an organization which, under domestic law, assumes responsibility for coordination and management of national and international activities on behalf of and in institutional liaison with, the broadcasting organizations forming the group;

(b)     an organization whose main function is the operation of technical broadcasting or transmission facilities on a permanent basis on behalf of, and in institutional liaison with, the broadcasting organization forming the group;

(c)     broadcasting organizations which provide specialized programme services in coordination with, and in addition to, the other group members' services.

(5)     Those requirements limit active membership to broadcasters which have to fulfil a

particular public mission to which they are committed by national law and practice, irrespective of the form of organization or the method of financing. Such public mission-oriented broadcasters have to provide a broadcasting service in the public interest regardless of considerations of profitability. This is in particular reflected by their obligation to provide varied programming including cultural, educational, scientific and minority programmes without any commercial appeal and to cover the entire national population irrespective of the costs. They are allowed neither to concentrate irrespective of the costs. They are allowed neither to concentrate on mass-appeal programmes able to achieve high ratings and to generate advertising revenues nor to specialize in certain categories of programme nor to limit themselves to cost-effective coverage of densely populated areas The new, wholly commercial broadcasters which in recent years have been launched in several Member States usually fail to fulfil these conditions and accordingly are not admitted as members.

(6) Active membership carries an obligation to further the objectives of the EBU and to contribute actively to radio and television programme exchanges and other EBU activities. After its merger with its eastern European counterpart, Organisation Internationale de Radiodiffusion et Télévision (OIRT) (see recital 8), the EBU has 67 active members (including groupings of television and radio channels) in 47 countries situated in the European broadcasting area. Most of them are public service broadcasters, although there are also some private ones, which are nevertheless public mission-oriented. In most countries there is only one member, the exceptions within the EEC being Belgium, Denmark, France, Germany and the United Kingdom where there are several. Whereas the majority of members are wholly or partly financed by a licence-fee, a number rely in addition, or some even exclusively, on advertising revenue, which revenue is often subject to restrictions (ceilings on advertising revenue, maxima of advertising spots per hour or day, advertising only on weekdays or during certain hours of the day etc.). The members broadcast mainly via terrestrial frequencies, their respective reception areas – notwithstanding some overspill – being predominantly limited to the national territory. However, in recent years some of the members have also started to transmit via satellite and cable, not only to their own national territories but also to other, mainly neighbouring countries.

(7) Apart from active members there is a large number of associate members (currently 54) which do not take part in the Eurovision System. Associate membership is open to broadcasting organizations, or groups of such organizations, from countries outside the European Broadcasting Area which provide, in their respective countries, a broadcasting service of national character and national importance and which offer varied programming.

(8) Following the process of democratization in eastern Europe the EBU has merged with its east European counterpart OIRT and its members. The merger came into effect on 1 January 1993 and will involve substantial financial and technical aid provided by the EBU and its members to the new members from eastern Europe.

**B.    The market for the acquisition of television sports programmes**
*(a)    The development of the broadcasting sector*
(9) In recent years the deregulation of television broadcasting in some Member States, together with the introduction of satellite-to-cable television and – more recently – direct satellite television, has led to the establishment of a number of new, mostly commercial broadcasters. They operate on a regional, national or transnational level, their programmes being transmitted via terrestrial networks and/or via satel-

lite and cable. They are mainly financed by advertising – some also charge a subscription fee – and provide either a diversified range of programmes, including
sports, or a specialist service, such as sports, films, news, etc. Between 1984 and
1990, 31 new satellite channels and 25 new commercial terrestrial channels were
launched which resulted in significant gains in viewing share by commercial channels in a number of Member States, the situation varying from country to country –
for example, Belgium (Flemish community): VTM, 43% in 1991 (source: CIM);
Germany (West only): RTL plus and SAT1, 14,8% and 11,1% in 1991 (source:
GFK Television Research); Greece: Mega Channel and Antenna TV, 39,8% and
32,2% in 1991 (source: AGB Hellas); Italy: Canale 5, Italia 1 and Rete 4, 16,4%,
10,5% and 8,9% (source: Auditel); Netherlands: RTL-4, 23,3% in 1991 (source:
NOS KLO); Spain: Tele 5 and Antena 3, 13,8% and 8,9% (source: Ecotel).

(10)   Until recently there were in particular the following dedicated sports channels:
Eurosport, a pan-European satellite sports channel broadcast in four languages
throughout Europe, operated by a consortium of active EBU members and TF1
(Télévision française 1), likewise an active EBU member; The European Sports
Network TESN which, via its affiliates Screensport (United Kingdom), Sportkanal
(Germany), Sportnet (Netherlands) and TV Sport (France), likewise provided a
pan-European programmes service dedicated to sports and broadcast via satellite
and cable in four languages throughout Europe; Sky Sports, a satellite channel (direct to home) operated by BSkyB (British Sky Broadcasting), which is aimed at
viewers in the United Kingdom and Ireland only. A newly launched sports channel
in Germany, Deutsches Sportfernsehen, has existed since the beginning of 1993.
Eurosport and TESN have recently agreed to combine forces and to provide one
single programme service under the name 'Eurosport'. The relevant agreement
which has been notified to the Commission is being dealt with in Case No IV/
34.605 – Eurosport Mark III.

(11)   The broadcasting sector is thus in a state of transition, with commercial broadcasters entering the market or expanding their activities and gaining a significant audience share. The new commercial channels not only provide for technical
innovation (in particular in the cable and satellite field) and for a broader choice for
television viewers, they also enhance competition both to the benefit of viewers
and advertisers and to the benefit of sports organizers or other persons offering
television rights. As their audience share increases, the new commercial channels
are becoming considerable competitors to the traditional public broadcasters on
both the market for advertising and that for programme procurement. This is reflected by the steadily increasing advertising revenues of private broadcasters (for
example, SAT1 (Germany): rise from DM 22,4 million (1,2% of total West German television advertising expenditure) in 1986 to DM 653,9 million (28,9%) in
1991, in comparison ARD: fall from DM 1 102,2 million (58,4%) to DM 483,0
million (21,4%) in 1991 (source: Nielsen S& P Werbeforschung), and their increasing investments in attractive programme material (see, for example, in the
United Kingdom: BSkyB's acquisition, together with the BBC, of five-year exclusive coverage of Premier League football matches at a price of £ 304 million –
BSkyB's share in the price being about £ 190 million). In some countries, the national EBU members compete at a growing disadvantage vis-à-vis commercial
channels, which are in some cases backed by powerful media conglomerates, since
the various constraints arising from the EBU members' public mission and in particular the limitations on sponsorship and advertising to which they are subject in a
number of countries, often hamper their ability to buy and exploit programmes in a
commercially viable way.

(12)   A number of commercial channels have set up an association (Association of Com-
       mercial Television in Europe (ACT)) in order to represent their common interests
       and to promote cooperation in different areas including the production of sports
       programmes. The Commission notes with interest this development. At this stage it
       is clearly not in a position to evaluate how future developments in this area are to
       be assessed within the context of the Community competition rules.

*(b)    Particular characteristics of sports programmes*
(13)   At the moment most of the commercial broadcasters are trying to increase their
       share of widely popular sports programmes, which, together with the launching of
       dedicated sports channels, has led to a considerable increase in sports programming
       on television. Sports programmes covering widely popular sports or major interna-
       tional events are a very attractive programme item for both the traditional public
       broadcasters and the new generalist commercial channels which want to provide an
       attractive and balanced schedule of programmes in order to appeal to as wide an
       audience as possible. As far as partly or wholly advertising-financed channels –
       both commercial and public broadcasters – are concerned, the importance of cer-
       tain sports programmes arises from their attraction to advertisers, as described be-
       low. As far as public broadcasters are concerned the importance of sports
       programmes also follows from their public mission to provide a diversified
       programme for all sectors of the population, which traditionally includes a certain
       amount of both national and international sports events.
(14)   Sports programmes, in particular major international events such as Olympic
       Games, Football World Cup, international tennis tournaments etc., are often able to
       achieve high viewing figures, in particular between viewers with a high buying
       power (males aged between 16 and 50), which is essential for advertisers. Sports
       programmes are also generally considered to be particularly suited to carrying ad-
       vertisements, as is reflected by the amount of sponsorship involved. Furthermore,
       sport is a type of entertainment which to some extent transcends cultural bound-
       aries and is thus uniquely suitable for transnational satellite and cable television
       and for transnational advertising. Finally, sports programmes reach a readily identi-
       fiable audience which is a special target for certain important advertisers and can-
       not easily be reached by other programmes. As a result, there has been a
       considerable increase in the demand for sports programmes as a whole in recent
       years, and increased competition for television rights.
(15)   However, the attraction of sports programmes and hence the level of competition
       for the television rights varies according to the type of sport and the type of event.
       Mass sports like football, tennis or motor-racing generally attract large audiences,
       the preferences varying from country to country. By contrast, minority sports
       achieve very low ratings. International events tend to be more attractive for the au-
       dience in a given country than national ones, provided the national team or a na-
       tional champion is involved, while international events in which no national
       champion or team is participating can often be of little interest.
(16)   On the other hand, some outstanding international events such as the Football
       World Cup and European Football Championships, the Olympic Games and World
       and European Athletic Championships etc. generally achieve high viewing figures,
       the participation and performance of national teams of champions being less im-
       portant. Because of the high viewing figures and the prestige that the coverage of
       these events bestows on the broadcaster involved, competition for these rights is
       strong, whereas there is often little demand for rights to events in minority sports.
(17)   Sports programmes can be a rather expensive programme item, the costs and risks

associated with the broadcasting of sports events being considerable. In addition to the prices for the rights – which are low for less attractive sports and events but very high for mass-appeal events – the most important factor is the cost of production of the television signal (basic video and sound feed), which is usually very high. This applies in particular to tournaments or championships which take place over a number of days with several events staged at the same time. While only a fraction can be broadcast, most, if not all, of it must be covered in order to be able to broadcast a meaningful selection. The nature of the sport and the terrain on which it takes place may also increase the costs. Commentary costs and studio costs (editing, presentation) must be added to the costs for the production of the signal on the spot, as well as costs for the transport of the signal. Thus the costs of sports programmes are, on average, higher today than the costs for broadcasting a cinematographic film (taking into account the price for the television rights and the necessary processing of the material) or for big entertainment shows.

(18) Moreover, the broadcasting of sports programmes involves a number of risks. The television rights for a sports event must be acquired in advance of the event, but its attractiveness may change considerably depending on how the event evolves and on the actual participation and success of teams or participants appealing to national audiences. In addition, particular risks such as weather, boycotts etc., are involved.

*(c)* *Difference in approach to sports programming*

(19) According to whether sports programmes are more or less attractive to viewers and hence to advertisers and according to the costs and risks involved in the broadcasting of sports events, public mission-oriented broadcasters and purely commercial broadcasters often take a different approach to the broadcasting of sports events. Purely commercial broadcasters (with the exception of dedicated sports channels) are more interested in mass-appeal sports events which allow them to attract advertisers and/or to persuade viewers to subscribe to their service or to buy the reception equipment. Public mission-oriented broadcasters, by contrast, also have to cover minority sports or less attractive events, as by virtue of their public mission they also have to cater for minority interests. As a result, public mission-oriented channels normally show a broader range of sports then purely commercial channels.

(20) Furthermore, purely commercial broadcasters are less interested in events which require production efforts that are enormous compared to the broadcasting time devoted to the event. Public mission broadcasters, by contrast, are often prepared to cover an event in full (in terms of production of the signal) even if it can be broadcast only in short extracts, irrespective of cost/revenue considerations, because they consider the provision of extracts to be part of their public mission. Some new commercial channels, in particular some of the new satellite-to-cable channels whose market penetration is still low, often prefer to seek sub-licences for ready-made sports programmes produced by other broadcasters rather than to acquire full rights and produce the coverage themselves.

*(d)* *Television rights to sports events*

(21) Television rights to sports events are normally granted for a given territory, usually per country, on an exclusive basis. Exclusivity is as a general rule considered to be necessary in order to guarantee the value of a given sports programme, in terms of the viewing figures and advertising revenues which it can achieve. Exclusivity is generally granted for broadcasting by all technical means (terrestrial frequencies,

satellite-to-cable or direct satellite) without distinction between terrestrial rights and cable and satellite rights. The rights are often offered as packages and comprise all matches, rounds or competitions forming one event (championship, tournament, cup, league round etc.).

(22)   Television rights are normally held by the organizer of a sports event, who is able to control the access to the premises where the event is staged. In order to control the televising of the event and to guarantee exclusivity the organizer admits only one broadcaster (the so-called host-broadcaster, i.e. a broadcaster in the country where the event takes place) or in any case only a limited number of broadcasters to produce the television signal. Under their contract with the organizer they are not allowed to make their signal available to any third party who has not acquired the relevant television rights.

(23)   Organizers of widely popular sports events are often rather powerful national or international associations which are in a sort of monopoly situation with regard to television rights to certain events or certain types of sports, as there is usually a single national or international association for each sport.

(24)   Nevertheless, for many years prices for television rights to sports events were kept relatively low, as sports organizers were more concerned to secure television coverage in order to attract sponsorship and the widest promotion of their events through television exposure. In recent years, with increased competition for the rights, organizers have become more and more aware of the value of their rights and prices have increased considerably: for instance, the fee for the Eurovision rights paid by the EBU to the International Amateur Athletics Federation (IAAF) for the World Athletic Championships rose from US $ 6 million for the championships in Tokyo in 1991 to US $ 91 million for the two championships in Stuttgart 1993 and in Gothenburg 1995. The fee for the summer Olympics rose from US $ 90 million for the Barcelona Olympics in 1992 to US $ 250 million for the Atlanta Games in 1996. Increasingly, sports organizers have chosen to sell their rights via international rights agencies which have established themselves as intermediaries and deal with the marketing of the rights on purely commercial terms. These intermediates are either independent or are affiliated to commercial broadcasters in whose interests they acquire the rights. In so far as vertical integration between intermediaries and television channels is concerned the Commission is not, at this stage, in a position to evaluate to what extent developments in this area would fall under the Community competition rules. In order to maximize profits, the intermediaries attempt to 'unbundle' the rights by selling them country-by-country to individual broadcasters and by distinguishing between rights for live and for deferred transmissions, and rights for highlights only, and by selling those various rights separately. This has resulted in a further increase in prices.

(25)   Increased competition from private broadcasters, together with the birth of professional sports rights agencies, have meant that the television rights to certain major international events traditionally broadcast by the established public broadcasters have moved into the hands of new commercial channels. Examples of this include the rights to the Wimbledon Open Tennis Championship, the United States Open Tennis Tournament, the Masters Tennis Tournaments, the World Open Basketball Tournament, the World Ice-Hockey Championship, Formula One Motor Racing and the Paris-Dakar motor rally. At national level, EBU members are increasingly outbid for widely popular national events such as national football with, for example, the German public broadcasters having lost the television rights to their commercial competitors for a number of years. Some other sports organizers have nevertheless sought to maintain their relationship with public broadcasters, as they

can guarantee national coverage of their events. A number of organizers, indeed, consider a high-quality television coverage which reaches the entire national population to be a valuable service which not only contributes to the standing of the event and to the popularity of the sport concerned but also increases the value of advertising space in the stadium for advertisers.

## C. The Eurovision system

(26) All active members of the EBU are eligible to participate in an institutionalized exchange system for television programmes, including sports programmes via a European network known as Eurovision, and to participate in a system of joint acquisition of television rights to international sports events – the so-called Eurovision rights. Currently, all but three active members (Lebanon, Malta and Vatican) participate in the system. Furthermore, apart from single members, consortia consisting exclusively of active members from different countries which together provide a transnational programme service that is public mission-oriented and complementary to individual members' national channels are likewise eligible to participate in the system.

### (a) Joint acquisition and sharing of television rights

(27) The rules governing the acquisition of Eurovision rights provide that the television rights for international sports events are normally acquired jointly by all interested members, who then share the rights and the related fee between them. Whenever EBU members from two or more countries are interested in a specific sports event they request coordination from the EBU. As a result, negotiations are carried out on behalf of all interested members either by a member – sometimes assisted by the EBU – in the country where the event takes place or by the EBU itself. Once negotiations for Eurovision rights have commenced, and until they have been formally declared to have failed, members are required not to engage in separate negotiations for national rights. Only if joint negotiations have failed are members free to negotiate separately.

(28) The Eurovision rights, which normally exclude non-members, are acquired on behalf of the members who participate in the contract for their respective countries. All members participating in the agreement are entitled to the full benefit or the rights, regardless of the territorial scope of their activity and regardless of their technical means of broadcasting. However, members who compete for the same national audience (several members in one country or members broadcasting from their country into the country of another member in the same language) have to agree among themselves on the procedure for attributing or priority to one of them.

(29) Several members in one country usually agree to share the rights, for example by alternating transmission of the event. If no such procedure can be agreed upon, all the members concerned become entitled to non-exclusive rights with respect to the country or countries in question. Members which provide the coverage of an event (i.e. produce the signal) are, unless otherwise agreed, entitled to priority over foreign members aiming their broadcast at the same national audience.

(30) The joint acquisition of rights normally concerns only international sports events and not national events such as national football, where national EBU members buy the television rights individually on the market, thereby competing with each other in some countries. The percentage of television sports programmes the rights to which have been negotiated and acquired via the Eurovision System varies from country to country. In Germany and the United Kingdom those programmes accounted for 2% of all sports programmes broadcast on German and British televi-

sion in 1990. In France the percentage was about 6,6% in 1990. The total number of contracts for television sports rights negotiated via Eurovision amounted to 45 in 1992.

*(b)*     *The exchange of the signal*

(31)    For events which take place within the Eurovision area the coverage (television signal consisting of basic video and international sound-feed) is produced by a member in the country concerned and is available to all other members via the Eurovision programme exchange system. The Eurovision programme exchange system is based on reciprocity: whenever one of the participating members covers an event, in particular a sports event, which takes place on its own national territory and is of potential interest to other Eurovision members, it offers its coverage free of charge to all the other Eurovision members on the understanding that in return it will receive corresponding offers from all the other members in respect of events taking place in their respective countries. The originating member also provides the necessary infrastructure to other interested members such as commentary positions, etc.

(32)    Since in each country there is at least one EBU member providing and producing sports programmes, it can be taken for granted that essentially all events that are of potential interest beyond national boundaries will be covered (provided that the members have been able to acquire the rights) and will be available to the members throughout the Eurovision area. The reciprocity system does not take account of actual input and withdrawal by individual members. In essence, it amounts to a solidarity system under which the financially more powerful organizations from large countries support organizations from smaller countries with a view to ensuring a board flow of sports programmes to all parts of the Eurovision area.

(33)    If an event takes place outside the Eurovision area, and thus the coverage is produced by a non-EBU member, the members participating in a Eurovision agreement normally have to pay a fee for the use of that other broadcaster's signal, which fee they share between them. However, there are reciprocity agreements with equivalent broadcasting organizations in other areas under which the signal is in some cases made available free of charge to EBU members.

(34)    The transport of the signal from the point of origin to the transmission facilities in the individual countries where the event is to be transmitted, is effected via a network which links all Eurovision members with each other. The network consists of permanently leased terrestrial circuits (supplemented on an ad hoc basis by occasionally leased terrestrial links) as well as a certain number of terrestrial circuits owned by individual members. These terrestrial links total a length of approximately 18 000 km with over 60 points of injection (not taking into account the circuits of the new members from eastern Europe). In addition, the EBU leases some satellite circuits on a permanent basis and further satellite circuits on an ad hoc basis.

(35)    Finally, the Eurovision system also provides for administrative and technical coordination. Administrative coordination including programme coordination is carried out by the EBU's permanent services in Geneva or – for example, in the case of the Olympics – by special operation groups, with the object of coordinating the specific needs and desires of the different members and of achieving optimal coverage of as many competitions as possible. It involves, in particular, the planning of scheduling, including dealing with possible time-differences between the site of the event and the members' countries, the selection of competitions in cases where several competitions take place simultaneously, etc. Technical coordination is car-

ries out by the EBU's technical centre which deals in particular with technical planning, monitoring and quality control with regard to the signal itself.

## D.   The access scheme for non-members

(36)   At the request of the Commission, the EBU has revised its scheme of rules governing contractual access for non-members. Under the new scheme submitted on 26 February 1993, the EBU and its members undertake to grant non-member broadcasters extensive access to Eurovision sports programmes for which the rights have been acquired through collective negotiations. The terms and conditions of access are freely negotiated between the EBU (for transnational channels), or the member(s) in the country concerned (for national channels), and the non-member. However, the EBU and its members will in no circumstances grant less favourable access than is stipulated below.

(37)   Access for live transmissions is granted if the event is not broadcast live by the EBU member(s) in the country or countries concerned, except for those parts or competitions (particular disciplines, individual matches, rounds, etc.) which the member(s) have reserved for their own live transmission.

If an event (or, in the case of events lasting more than one day, a day of competition) is broadcast live by the EBU member(s) in the country or countries concerned – i.e. if the majority of the principal competitions constituting it are transmitted live – access is granted for deferred transmissions, beginning not earlier than one hour after the end of the event or the last competition of the day and not earlier than 10.30 p.m. local time (London time for pan-European channels). The different embargos (for events lasting not more than one day, embargo until four hours after the end of the first prime-time transmission (for national channels) or the last prime-time transmission (for transnational channels) of the EBU members in the countries concerned; and for events lasting more than one day, embargo until 2 a.m. following each day of competition) and additional restrictions concerning the volume and timing of transmissions (for events lasting more than one day, no transmissions during prime-time: Monday to Friday 6 a.m. to 9 a.m., 12 noon to 2 p.m., 6 p.m. to 1 a.m., Saturday and Sunday 12 noon to 1 a.m., and maximum volume of daily transmission of, for instance, 75 minutes for Summer Olympic Games or 25 minutes per match of the Football World Cup) contained in the previous sub-licensing scheme which was the subject of the Commission's notice of 5 October 1990, given pursuant to Article 19(3) of Regulation No 17, have been removed at the request of the Commission.

(38)   In addition, news access is granted. Except where national law or regulations provide otherwise, the EBU and its members grant access to two news items of up to 90 seconds each per event or day of competition – with the possibility of repeating one of such reports later the same day – which must be included in regularly scheduled general news bulletins, or in regularly scheduled general sports-news programmes of dedicated sports channels, within 24 hours.

(39)   The access fee (for access to the television rights and the television signal) has to be negotiated. For the routing of the signal, the non-member is free to make its own arrangements or may ask the EBU to route the signal via the Eurovision network. In that case the EBU will submit an estimate for the costs.

(40)   In the event of a dispute over the access fee where all other conditions of access have been agreed at the request of the non-member the matter will be submitted to arbitration by independent expert(s). The expert(s) will be nominated jointly by the parties. Failing agreement, nomination will be by the president of the competent Court of Appeal in the case of national arbitration (concerning access for national

channels) and by the president of the International Chamber of Commerce in the case of international arbitration (concerning access for pan-European channels). The expert(s) shall fix the access fee. The decision shall be final and binding.

The complete text of the scheme can be obtained by interested third parties from the EBU or from the national members.

**E.    The proceedings**

(41)    On 17 December 1987 the Commission received a complaint by Screensport (later TESN) concerning:

(i) the refusal of the EBU and its members to grant Screensport sub-licences to sports events;

and

(ii) a joint venture between a consortium of active EBU members and News International/Sky Channel establishing a television sports channel called Eurosport Mark I.

The second part of the complaint was the subject of separate proceedings in Case No IV/32.524 – Screensport/EBU members and of Commission Decision 91/130/ EEC[142]. The first part of the complaint was withdrawn following the agreement between Eurosport and TESN referred to above (recital 10).

(42)    On 12 December 1988 the Commission sent a first statement of objections to the EBU, declaring that the granting of an exemption to the rules governing the acquisition and the use of television rights to sports events within the framework of the Eurovision System could be envisaged provided that the EBU and its members accepted an obligation to grand non-members sub-licences for a substantial part of the rights in question and on reasonable terms. On 3 April 1989 the EBU notified its relevant rules to the Commission with the aim of obtaining negative clearance or an exemption and indicating that the EBU and its members were prepared to grant sub-licences to non-members. On 12 April 1990 the Commission received a second complaint by Still Moving Films, a United Kingdom-based company involved in the production of sports programmes, likewise concerning the EBU's sub-licensing policy. On 3 July 1990 the EBU adopted a sub-licensing scheme which had previously been the subject of discussions with the Commission.

(43)    On 5 October 1990 the Commission published a notice pursuant to Article 19(3) of Regulation No 17 in the Official Journal indicating its intention to grant an exemption pursuant to Article 85(3) of the EEC Treaty. Following the publication, the Commission received a number of criterial observations from third parties, including the complainants, mainly concerning the EBU sub-licensing scheme. As a result, the Commission on 18 and 19 December 1990 organized an oral hearing with all interested third parties, at which the sub-licensing scheme, which was found to be too restrictive, too bureaucratic and not workable in practice, was discussed in detail.

(44)    On the basis of the outcome of the hearing the Commission on 24 June 1991 sent a supplementary statement of objections, declaring that the sub-licensing scheme was not acceptable. Subsequently, the EBU on 8 November 1991 submitted a new scheme governing contractual access for non-members, in which most of the clauses of the previous sub-licensing scheme which had been criticized by third parties had been removed. After further amendments had been carried out at the request of the Commission, the final version of the scheme was submitted on 26 February 1993.

---

[142] OJ L 63, 9-3-1991, p. 32.

## II.     LEGAL ASSESSMENT
### A.     Article 85(1)
#### 1.     Agreements between or decisions by (an association of) undertakings

(45)    The EBU members are undertakings within the meaning of Article 85(1). This applies notwithstanding the fact that the majority of members are non-profit-making public institutions entrusted under national law with the task of providing programmes in the public interest. The functional concept of 'undertaking' under Article 85(1) covers any body carrying on activities of an economic nature regardless of its legal from and regardless of whether it has a commercial aim. Accordingly, the Court of Justice has ruled that public television broadcasting organizations are 'undertakings' within the meaning of Article 85(1) in so far as they exercise economic activities[143]. The acquisition of television rights to sports events and the granting of sub-licences for such programmes are clearly activities of an economic nature which are covered by Article 85(1).

(46)    The EBU statutory provisions and internal rules relating to the acquisition of television rights to sports events and the exchange of sports programmes within the framework of Eurovision and contractual access for third parties to such rights and programmes are decisions of an association of undertakings, while the case-by-case agreements of individual members concerning the negotiation, acquisition and sharing of the rights are agreements between undertakings within the meaning of Article 85(1).

#### 2.     Restriction of competition
*(a)     Restriction of competition between the EBU members*

(47)    The EBU rules governing the joint negotiation, acquisition and sharing of television rights to sports events and the related case-by-case agreements between the members have as their object and effect the restriction of competition between the members.

(48)    Without the cooperation within the framework of Eurovision, the EBU members would to some extent compete with each other for the acquisition of television rights to sports events. Although it is true that members from different countries usually acquire television rights only for their respective countries and do not, therefore, compete directly with each other for the rights, a competitive situation arises in two cases. First, there are five Member States where there are two or more EBU members (Belgium, France, Denmark, Germany, United Kingdom) which would normally compete with each other for television rights to international events, as they in fact do for rights to national events, which are not covered by Eurovision. Secondly, there is an increasing number of members who broadcast via satellite and cable into other members' countries and who, therefore, would normally have to acquire the rights for those countries in competition with the national members.

(49)    As a result of the joint negotiation and acquisition of the right within the framework of Eurovision this competition between the members is greatly restricted if not, in many cases, eliminated. Instead of bidding against each other, members participate in joint negotiations and agree among themselves the financial and other conditions for the acquisition of the rights as well as the way in which they share these rights. The restriction of competition exists notwithstanding the fact that the internal EBU rules governing the negotiation and acquisition of the rights are only recommendations and not legally binding. It follows both from the EBU

---

[143]  Case 155/73, Sacchi, [1974] ECR, p. 409.

statutes (Article 13 (4)) and from the nature of Eurovision as a solidarity system that members bind themselves to respect the common interest and to comply with the internal rules set up in this common interest. As a result, members who are interested in the acquisition of the rights do in fact participate in the joint negotiations, and engage in separate negotiations have officially been declared to have failed. These cases are very rare.

*(b)      Distortion of competition vis-à-vis non-EBU members*

(50)    On the other hand, competition vis-à-vis purely commercial channels, which are not admitted as members, is to some extent distorted. It is a disadvantage for those channels that they cannot participate in the rationalization and cost-savings achieved by the Eurovision system (as described in recitals 58 to 67), which renders the broadcasting of sports events more expensive and complicated for them.

(51)    Moreover, the joint negotiation and acquisition of the rights enable the EBU members to strengthen their market position to the disadvantage of their independent competitors. By combining their forces, the EBU members acquire a considerable market power which non-member channels often find difficult to equal. In particular, the fact that the EBU members bid jointly for the rights for a number of countries or the whole Eurovision area gives them an advantage, since international sports federations often prefer to dispose of the television rights for a large area in one transaction instead of becoming involved in negotiations with numerous national broadcasters. However, this advantage is increasingly being eroded by the entry into the market of international sports rights agencies which enable sports organizers to maximize profits by selling the rights country-by-country without involving themselves in various negotiations with individual broadcasters. This has facilitated rights acquisition by non-member channels, especially those commercial channels which are affiliated to sports rights agencies, as is reflected by the number of international events which in recent years have moved into the hands of commercial channels (see recital 25).

(52)    Some distortion of competition also results from the fact that consortia consisting of different EBU members and providing a transnational sports programme service participate in the joint acquisition system. This again strengthens the negotiating power of the EBU and its members vis-à-vis sports organizers, because in addition to their generalist channels they have the use of a transnational dedicated sports channels which can provide a 24-hour coverage of the sports events in question and ample opportunities for advertising and sponsorship without the programme constraints to which generalist channels are normally subject.

**3.      Effect on trade between Member States**

(53)    Trade between Member States is affected in that the Eurovision system concerns cross-border acquisition and use of television rights. This applies in particular to the joint acquisition and sharing of the rights between members from different countries and to the exchange of the related television signal between them.

**4.      Appreciability of the restriction of competition and the effect on trade between Member States**

(54)    The abovementioned restrictions have an appreciable impact on the market for the procurement of sports programmes. The overall programme procurement market is divided into separate markets for different programmes items, such as feature films, television films and series, shows and games, drama, documentaries, sports, etc. From the point of view of the broadcaster who is seeking programmes and/or

the relevant television rights, the different programme items are only to a limited extent interchangeable. In particular, sports programmes can be substituted by other programmes only to a limited extent.

(55)     This is demonstrated, first, by the existence of specialized sports channels, which shows that sports programmes are quite distinct from other programmes and have a special audience that justifies a dedicated sports channel. But also from the point of view of generalist channels, sports programmes have special characteristics and are a particularly important programme item. It may be true that feature films or popular television series ('soap operas') or games are able to attract similar or even higher viewing figures than major sports events and that a broadcaster, by scheduling another popular programme, is able to attract viewers away from sports programmes being shown on a competing network. Nevertheless, sports programmes are indispensable for every generalist channel, whether commercial or public. Sports programmes are considered to be part of the traditional programme-mix of a generalist channel and cannot be totally replaced by other programmes.

(56)     As far as partly or wholly advertising-financed broadcasters are concerned, this is also due to the attraction of sports programmes to advertisers and to the fact that sports programmes reach an audience which is a special target for certain advertisers and cannot be easily reached by other programmes. As far as public broadcasters are concerned this lack of substitutability also follows from their public mission to provide a diversified programme for all parts of the population, which traditionally includes a certain amount of sports events, both national and international. Public broadcasters consider it part of their public mission to show the most popular events which the entire general public wants to watch.

(57)     On the market for sports programmes and the related television rights the abovementioned restrictions are appreciable notwithstanding the fact that the Eurovision System concerns in practice only the broadcasting of international events and does not normally affect the broadcasting of national events. Although international events form only a relatively small proportion of all sports broadcasting, some of them – for example, the Olympic Games or Football World and European Cups – are of such widespread appeal, and of such economic importance, that their impact on the market is not adequately reflected by their expression as a mere percentage.

**B.       Article 85(3)**
**1.       Improvement in the production or distribution of 'goods'**
(58)     The Eurovision System provides for a number of benefits which relate to the joint acquisition and sharing of the rights as well as to the exchange of the signal and its transport on the common network and to the contractual access that will be granted to non-members. The various benefits provided by the Eurovision system and the underlying rules constitute a unified whole where each constituent element complements the others.

*(a)      The joint acquisition and sharing of the rights*
(59)     Joint negotiations and joint acquisition of the rights lead to an improvement in purchasing conditions. Firstly, they reduce the transaction costs which would be associated with a multitude of separate negotiations. They also guarantee that the negotiations are carried out by the most competent negotiator. This means either the national member in the country where the event takes place, which is familiar with local conditions, or the EBU itself, which has specialized staff experienced in

negotiations on an international level. That last practice benefits in particular smaller members who do not have the necessary specialized staff. The cooperation between the members and the coordination of their different interests by the negotiating member and/or the EBU further ensures that the specific interests and needs of all members are taken care of. In separate negotiations members, in particular members from small countries, would find it more difficult to secure contracts suitable for specific needs.

(60) The joint acquisition and the related sharing of the rights further leads to a programme coordination at national level. At national level the joint acquisition and the sharing of the rights by two or more members in the same country usually result in an alternation of the transmission of an event by the members concerned. In the case of events of major interest like the Olympic Games this sharing means that a quasi-permanent coverage can be guaranteed by the alternating members, whereby one of the members transmits the event while the other provides attractive alternatives. If, instead, one of the members had individually acquired the exclusive rights it could individually show much less of the event, given that public mission-oriented broadcasters cannot concentrate on sport but have to provide a diversified programme even at times when major sports events take place.

(61) Furthermore, at international level the sharing of the rights allows members from one country to broadcast into other members' countries, which facilitates cross-border broadcasting. According to the relevant EBU rules, all members participating in the joint acquisition of Eurovision rights are entitled to the full benefit of the rights regardless of the territorial scope of their activity and thus are free to use the rights for transnational purposes (with the exception of the exclusivity or priority granted to the member which produces the coverage). That means, in practice, that members who broadcast via satellite to cable or via a direct broadcasting satellite into other members' countries are free to do so without being obliged to acquire the relevant television rights for these countries. Pending the adoption of the Community directive on the coordination of certain rules concerning copyright and neighbouring rights applicable to satellite broadcasting and cable retransmission and its transposition into national legislation, without the Eurovision System each individual member engaged in transnational broadcasting would be obliged to acquire the television rights for all countries covered by its service (at least as far as broadcasting via satellite to cable is concerned; the situation for direct satellite broadcasting is not clear in all Member States). This would be not only very expensive, but also difficult to achieve, considering that television rights are usually granted country-by-country on an exclusive basis. The sharing of the rights under the Eurovision rules therefore facilitates cross-border activities of the participating members and thus contributes to the development of a single European broadcasting market.

(62) The participation of consortia providing a transnational dedicated sports channel leads to a further improvement. On the one hand, it enables EBU members participating in such a consortium to provide a broader range of sports programmes, including minority sports and sports programmes with educational, cultural or humanitarian content, that they cannot show on their national generalist channels. This is not only to the benfit of television viewers, who are offered a larger choice, but also in the interest of organizers of minority sports, which often find it difficult to secure television coverage and thereby attract interest in their events. On the other hand, a pan-European sports channel broadcasting a common programme service throughout Europe contributes to the development of a single European broadcasting market.

*(b)*     *The exchange of the television signal*

(63)     The joint acquisition and sharing of the rights is also a necessary element for the exchange of the television signal, which is the heart of the Eurovision System. The exchange of the television signal results in considerable rationalization and cost-savings in that it allows other members to use the originating member's signal free of charge. In particular, it provides members from smaller countries and their national audiences with programmes they would otherwise find it very difficult to afford in terms of production costs. In addition, the Eurovision System stimulates the production of television signals as a result of the reciprocity system. As a result of reciprocity and solidarity any EBU member will feel obliged to produce the television signal for events taking place in its country, even if it is not itself interested in the event (for instance if no national champion or team is participating), in order to enable other interested EBU members to show the event. This again leads to more sports programmes, in particular minority sports, being produced and shown on television than would be the case without the Eurovision system.

(64)     Furthermore, the administrative and technical coordination linked to the programme exchange and carried out by the EBU and the host broadcaster guarantee not only a high-quality signal but also an optimal adaptation to the different needs of the different members in terms of commentary facilities, selection of events in the case of a number of heterogenous or similar competitions or matches taking place at the same time (as in the case of the Olympics, athletic championships etc.), scheduling and presentation of the programmes, etc.

(65)     Finally, the Eurovision System provides for reliable transmission facilities by delivery of the signal via a common network. This common network, the costs of which are shared between the members, again provides for considerable rationalization and cost-savings. The long-term planning and coordination of delivery of the signal, which are carried out by the technical centre of the EBU in line with the requirements of the members which share the respective television rights between them, guarantee high-quality programmes for each of the participating members.

*(c)*     *The access scheme for non-members*

(66)     The possibility of contractual access for non-members not only reduces the restriction of competition against non-members but itself also provides for some improvements. Owing to the general increase in sports programmes on television, there is an increasing demand for second, deferred transmissions of major events. In particular, some satellite and cable channels whose technical potential is still low and who would hardly be able to afford the high costs for live or first-run rights and for the production of the signal may find it attractive to offer second, deferred transmissions. Such transmissions are now faciliated under the new access scheme. The setting-up of a common scheme of objective rules which are made public and available to all interested thrid-party channels, makes the access policy of the EBU and its members more transparent and predictable and facilities negotiations by third parties.

(67)     Furthermore, it is a special advantage for transnational channels that they can obtain access direct from the EBU instead of having to engage in separate negotiations with the members in each country which is covered by their services. Normally, transnational satellite-to-cable channels seeking access to sports programmes have to reach agreements with a number of different broadcasters who can the rights in the various countries covered by the transnational programme service. In view of the divergent circumstances and interests of the broadcasters concerned, this is very difficult if not, in some cases, impossible to

achieve. The EB access scheme, by contrast, provides transnational channels with one negotiator and uniform conditions for all the countries in question, which considerably facilities access by such channels.

**2.     Fair share of the resulting benefits for consumers**
(68)    Consumers, i.e. the television viewers, benefit from the Eurovision System in that the System enables the members to show more, and higher-quality, sports programmes – both widely popular sports and minority sports – than they would be able to do without the advantages of Eurovision. The Eurovision System enables in particular national members from smaller countries to provide their chair viewers with a broad range of international sports events with a commentary in their own language and tailored to their specific national interests. Moreover, given that the vast majority of members are non-profit-making public institutions, it is likely that the cost-savings they achieve are passed on to their viewers in that they use the money they save for the acquisition of other attractive programmes.

**3.     Indispensability of the restrictions**
(69)    The restrictions of competition as defined above are indispensable for the achievement of the improvements in question.

*(a)     Indispensability of the rules governing the joint negotiation and acquisition of the rights and contractual access for non-members*
(70)    The cost-savings and rationalization resulting from the Eurovision System cannot be obtained by a less restrictive arrangement. It is indeed necessary that members be required to refrain from separate negotiations once joint negotiations have commenced. The success of the joint negotiations would be put in jeopardy if individual members simultaneously engaged in separate negotiations for national or transnational rights. It has to be emphasized that members are free to engage in separate negotiations once the joint negotiations are declared to have failed. It is further necessary that members in every single case agree among themselves the financial and other conditions for the acquisition of the rights and the way they share these rights. As every sports event is different from the next and needs a different approach, it is inevitable that the conditions for the acquisition of the rights are agreed between the members on a case-by-case basis.
(71)    The access scheme for non-members, which at the request of the Commission has been substantially amended, likewise contains no restrictions which are not indispensable to the attainment of the objectives described above. The new scheme will limit the exclusivity of the rights acquired under Eurovision rights agreements and will provide access for non-members on reasonable terms both in relation to the time and scope of non-member transmissions and to the financial conditions. Earlier, more restrictive conditions have been substantially relaxed. This applies in particular to the restrictions on time, number and volume for non-member transmissions and the embargos. The remaining exclusivity for EBU members is necessary in order to allow them a fair return on their investments (rights fee, cost of production of the signal, etc.). It must be emphasized that EBU members are free to grant contractual access for their national territories on more favourable terms if they wish to do so. As regards the financial conditions, it is also important that any disputes will be determined by arbitration which will ensure reasonable prices.

*(b)     Indispensability of limiting participation to public mission-oriented broadcasters*
(72)    It is necessary that membership of the Eurovision System be limited to public mission-oriented broadcasters fulfilling certain objective criteria regarding the pro-

duction and variety of their programmes and the coverage of the national population. The programme exchange which is at the heart of Eurovision is based on reciprocity and solidarity without taking into account the actual input and output of the individual members. It is understood that each member will use its best endeavours with regard to any international event taking place in its country to negotiate and acquire the television rights on behalf of all interested members as well as to produce the signal and to make it available to them free of charge. Such a system can only work between public mission-oriented broadcasters who, regardless of cost-revenue considerations, provide the widest possible range of sports programmes as part of their public mission.

(73) It is in particular necessary that the participating members themselves produce a considerable part of their programmes, as opposed to some of the new commercial channels who rather rely on ready-made sports programmes. It is further essential that they provide diversifies programmes for all segments of the population, which means that, as far as sport is concerned, they also cater for minority sports regardless of whether there is a return on the investments involved.

(74) It is also vital that they cover the entire national population. On the one hand, this is necessary in order to ensure that the common network through which the Eurovision members are linked and through which the programme exchange takes place covers the whole Eurovision area and that all members bear a proportional share thereof. On the other hand, it could severely damage the image of the EBU as an organization of public mission-oriented broadcasters providing a programme srvice in the public interest if, because of the limited reception area of some of its members, parts of the national audiences were prevented from watching major events. This would not only incur the displeasure of the television viewers and of public opinion, as recent controversies in some Member States have shown where private channels with a limited reception area have acquired rights to mass-appeal events, thus preventing a part of the national population from watching these events, it would also weaken the position of the EBU members in negotiations with sports organizers, who often want to reach as large an audience as possible and are in some cases reluctant to sell their rights to broadcasters who reach only a part of the population.

(75) It must be emphasized that the new commercial channels, although they are normally not admitted as members, are nevertheless offered contractual access and thus can also benefit from the Eurovision System. In fact, some of the new commercial channels whose applications for membership have been rejected have nevertheless reached agreements concerning contractual access to certain events with the EBU and/or its members.

(76) It is also necessary that the participation of dedicated sports channels in the Eurovision System is limited to transnational (pan-European) channels which are operated by consortia consisting exclusively of active EBU members and which themselves fulfil a public mission. Purely commercial sports channels, operated by non-EBU members, could not be expected to respect the principles of reciprocity and solidarity which are at the heart of the Eurovision System (see recital 72) and which is, for instance, reflected by a complementarity in programmes between EBU-backed sports channels and EBU members' generalist channels.

**4. No possibility of eliminating competition**

(77) The rules governing the Eurovision System do not allow the participating members to eliminate competition for a substantial part of the products in question. Given that the joint negotiation and acquisition of television rights in practice con-

cern only international events and not national events, which are the majority of sports on television, the Eurovision System affects only a part of the market. Furthermore, it has to be taken into account that even for international events there is increasing competition outside the Eurovision System from independent broadcasters, who have in recent years acquired the rights for a number of events which had traditionally been broadcast by the EBU members.

**C.      Article 90(2)**

(78)    The applicability of Article 85 is not excluded by Article 90(2). Public mission broadcasters operating under statutory obligations assigned as them by an act of public authority may be entrusted with services of general economic interest[144]. However, there is no risk that the application of the competition rules could obstruct the performance of their particular task, i.e. the provision of varied and balanced programming for all sections of the population, including a certain amount of sport, and the acquisition of the relevant television rights.

(79)    Without the benefits of the Eurovision System as described above (recitals 58 to 67) the broadcasting of international sports events and the acquisition of the rights would certainly be more difficult and more costly, with the result that fewer events would be broadcast – in particular by smaller members from small countries. However, the mere fact that the accomplishment of the particular task is rendered more difficult is not sufficient for the undertaking to benefit from the derogation in Article 90(2). It follows from the clear wording that the accomplishment of the task has to be rendered impossible by the application of the competition rules. Accordingly, the Court has stated that television companies, in so far as in some Member States they are entrusted with services of general economic interest, have to abide by the competition rules provided that to do so is not demonstrably incompatible with the accomplishment of their task[145]. This is, at least for the time being, not the case.

**D.      Articles 6 and 8 of Regulation No 17**

(80)    In accordance with Article 6(1) of Regulation No 17, this Decision should be declared applicable from the day on which the amended scheme of rules governing contractual access for non-members was submitted, i.e. 26 February 1993.

(81)    Given the structure and development of the relevant market and the effect of the notified rules thereon, exemption should be granted pursuant to Article 8(1) of Regulation No 17 for five years.

(82)    In order to ensure contractual access for third parties to the television rights to sports events acquired within the framework of Eurovision such contractual access must be allowed under the agreements with the rights owners (sport organizers or rights agents). The EBU and its members, therefore, must be under an obligation to finalize only agreements which either allow the EBU and its members to grant access or allow the rights owners to grant access to third parties in accordance with the access scheme or, subject to the approval of the EBU, on more favourable conditions.

(83)    In order to assist the Commission during the exemption period in checking whether the conditions for exemption continue to be fulfilled and whether in particular the membership conditions and the rules on contractual access are applied in an appropriate, reasonable and non-discriminatory way, the EBU must be re-

---

[144] Case 155/73, Sacchi, [1974] ECR, p. 409.
[145] Case 155/73, Sacchi, [1974] ECR, p. 409.

quired to inform the Commission of all amendments and additions to the rules notified, of all arbitration procedures concerning disputes under the access scheme and of all decisions regarding applications for membership by third parties,

*Has adopted this decision:*

Article 1
Pursuant to Article 85(3) of the EEC Treaty the provisions of Article 85(1) are hereby declared inapplicable for the period 26 February 1993 to 25 February 1998, to the EBU's internal provisions ('Statutes') and other regulations concerning the acquisition of television rights to sports events, the exchange of sports programmes within the framework of Eurovision and contractual access to such programmes for third parties.

Article 2
The declaration of exemption contained in Article 1 shall be subject to the following obligations:
1. the EBU and its members shall collectively acquire television rights to sports events only under agreements which either allow the EBU and its members to grant access or allow the rights' owners to grant access to third parties in conformity with the access scheme or, subject to the approval of the EBU, on conditions more favourable to the non-member;
2. the EBU shall inform the Commission of any amendments and additions to the rules notified, of all arbitration procedures concerning disputes under the access scheme and of all decisions regarding applications for membership by third parties.

Article 3
This Decision is addressed to the:
European Broadcasting Union
Ancienne Route 17A
CH-1218 Grand-Saconnex (Geneva).
Done at Brussels, 11 June 1993.
For the Commission
Karel van Miert
Member of the Commission

———

**2.4.8.     EUROPEAN COURT OF JUSTICE, JUDGMENT OF THE COURT OF FIRST INSTANCE (SECOND CHAMBER), ALL WEATHER SPORTS BENELUX BV V COMMISSION OF THE EUROPEAN COMMUNITIES, CASE T-38/92, 28 APRIL 1994**[146]

Content of the Court's judgment
Acts of the institutions – Statement of reasons – Obligation – Scope – Decision applying the rules on competition – Decision relating to several addressees – Identification of the entity liable for an infringement – Inadequate statement of reasons – Possibility of characterizing the inadequacy as a mere error – Conditions
(EEC Treaty, Art. 190)

---

[146] ECR 1994, p. II-211.

## Summary

*If it relates to several addressees and there is a problem with regard to liability for the infringement, a decision taken in application of the competition rules in the Treaty must include an adequate statement of reasons with respect to each of the addressees, in particular those whom it identifies as having to bear liability for the infringement.*

*The statement of reasons must be especially detailed if during the administrative procedure the undertaking on which the final decision imposes a fine has advanced several reasons why it cannot be held liable for the infringement and the Commission has not clarified its position on this point.*

*In particular, for a Commission decision in a competition case, which in its statement of reasons merely identifies as the party committing an infringement the legal entity which existed prior to the date of the purchase of its assets by another undertaking, lawfully to be able to impute liability for that infringement to the purchaser of the undertaking, there must be no dispute as to the identity of the successor legal entity or as to the reality of the continuance by that entity of the activity, carried on by the undertaking in question, which gave rise to the proceedings.*

*The Commission cannot attribute an inadequacy, from the point of view of the requirements of the Treaty, in a statement of reasons to an error unless it establishes that error with sufficient certainty. That is not the case if it does not refer to such an error until the final stage of the procedure before the Community courts and has not notified a corrigendum in the proper form to the addressee of the decision.*

*That is all the more so where the alleged error relates, firstly, to the actual operative part of the contested decision and, secondly, to the very identity of the addressees, in other words, those who are ordered to pay the fine imposed, those being points on which scrupulous observance of the principle of legal certainty is essential.*

*There is no adequate statement of reasons if the operative part of a decision holds a company liable for an infringement, while identifying another company as having committed the infringement, solely on the ground that it has taken over the assets of a company which itself is not identified as having committed the infringement.*

## Parties

In Case T-38/92,

All Weather Sports Benelux BV, a company established under Netherlands law whose registered office is at Zoetermeer (Netherlands), represented by Paul Glazener, of the Rotterdam Bar, with an address for service in Luxembourg at the Chambers of Marc Loesch, 11 Rue Goethe, applicant, v Commission of the European Communities, represented by Berend-Jan Drijber, a member of its Legal Service, acting as Agent, with an address for service in Luxembourg at the office of Georgios Kremlis, a member of its Legal Service, Wagner Centre, Kirchberg, defendant,

Application for annulment of Commission Decision 92/261/EEC of 18 March 1992 relating to a proceeding pursuant to Article 85 of the EEC Treaty (IV/32.290 – Newitt/Dunlop Slazenger International and Others, Official Journal 1992 L 131, p. 32), in so far as it holds the applicant liable for an infringement of Article 85(1) of the EEC Treaty and imposes a fine on it,

The Court of First Instance of the European Communities (Second Chamber),
composed of: J.L. Cruz Vilaça, President, C.P. Briëët, A. Kalogeropoulos, D.P.M. Barrington and J. Biancarelli, Judges,
Registrar: H. Jung,
having regard to the written procedure and further to the hearing on 15 December 1993,
gives the following
Judgment

**Grounds of the judgment**

Facts and procedure

1.    The applicant company, All Weather Sports Benelux BV, a company incorporated
      under Netherlands law whose registered office is at Zoetermeer (Netherlands),
      was formed on 17 April 1989. It specializes in the marketing of sports goods.

2.    Also on 17 April 1989 the applicant concluded an agreement, with retroactive ef-
      fect as from 1 January 1989, by which it took over the activities relating to the
      import and wholesale of sports goods, together with the relevant assets, of All
      Weather Sports BV (hereinafter 'AWS'), a company incorporated under Nether-
      lands law whose registered office was also at Zoetermeer and which belonged to
      the Buehrmann-Tetterode Nederland BV group (hereinafter 'Buehrmann-
      Tetterode'), a company incorporated under Netherlands law whose registered of-
      fice was at Amsterdam. The assets thus acquired by the applicant included inter
      alia an exclusive distribution agreement, originally covering the Netherlands and
      subsequently extended to the whole of Benelux, for products of the Dunlop brand
      from the British company Dunlop-Slazenger International Ltd (hereinafter
      'DSIL'). DSIL gave notice to terminate the distribution agreement on 18 Septem-
      ber 1988 and it ended on 30 April 1989. The assets acquired also included rights
      relating to the distribution of the products of a sports brand belonging to All
      Weather Sports International BV (hereinafter 'AWS International'), a company in-
      corporated under Netherlands law engaging in commercial activities relating to
      sports goods, working closely together with AWS, having its registered office at
      Zoetermeer, like AWS, and also belonging to the Buehrmann-Tetterode Group.

3.    Following the transfer of assets on 17 April 1989, AWS and AWS International
      ceased their commercial activities and, after transferring their registered offices to
      Amsterdam and changing their names to BT Sports BV and BT Sports Interna-
      tional BV respectively, continued to exist for tax reasons, although they no longer
      carried on any commercial activities.

4.    On 29 May 1990 the Commission, after carrying out investigations at the offices
      of DSIL's exclusive distributors in the Netherlands, including an investigation at
      AWS on 3 November 1988, sent that company, under its former name of All
      Weather Sports BV and at its former registered office at Zoetermeer, a statement
      of objections relating to an infringement of Article 85(1) of the EEC Treaty. That
      statement of objections was drawn up as part of an infringement proceeding initi-
      ated by the Commission following a complaint by Newitt & Co. Ltd, a company
      incorporated under British law, a wholesaler and retailer of sports goods and a
      customer of DSIL, against DSIL for obstructing exports of its products from the
      United Kingdom to other Member States. The objections sent to AWS related to a
      number of concerted practices by it and DSIL with the aim of eliminating parallel
      exports of DSIL products to the Benelux countries, so as to ensure that its exclu-
      sive distributors, including AWS, had complete territorial protection.

5.    The statement of objections was responded to by a written reply filed on 31 July
      1990 on behalf of the applicant and the three companies BT Sports (formerly
      AWS), BT Sports International (formerly AWS International) and AWS Neder-
      land BV, the applicant's Netherlands subsidiary.

6.    At the hearing before the Commission on 5 October 1990 the applicant and the
      three other companies submitted a common defence.

7.    Both in their written reply to the objections and at the hearing on 5 October 1990,
      the four companies explained that because of the name used for the company to
      which the statement of objections had been notified, in other words AWS, the
      identity of the company addressed by the Commission was not clear, and for that

reason their replies and observations on the objections were made 'on behalf of all the companies to the extent that they must be addressees or are to be regarded as addressees of the statement of objections' (written observations of 31 July 1990, paragraph 2.1.3).

8.  With respect to identification of the company to which the statement of objections was addressed, and consequently the question of which company was to be held liable for the alleged infringement, each of the companies argued before the Commission that it could not be held liable for the infringement and that, since the undertaking carried on by AWS at the time of the alleged infringement no longer existed, the infringement proceedings had become devoid of purpose.

9.  On this point it was stated to the Commission that the Zoetermeer address to which the statement of objections had been sent was no longer that of AWS, but that of the applicant and its Netherlands subsidiary, AWS Nederland BV, that AWS now had its registered office at Amsterdam under its new name of BT Sports, that since the transfer of its assets on 17 April 1989 it no longer carried on any commercial activity, and that consequently it had ceased to exist as an undertaking within the meaning of Article 85 of the Treaty, as had BT Sports International (formerly AWS International). It was also stated that BT Sports and BT Sports International continued to exist as legal persons solely for tax reasons, that the Buehrmann-Tetterode group of which AWS and AWS International were subsidiaries could not be regarded as liable for the infringement, in view of the fact that when AWS carried on its activities, it enjoyed considerable autonomy in its commercial management.

10. With respect more particularly to the applicant company, that company essentially argued before the Commission that the mere fact that it had taken over the assets of the previous companies AWS and AWS International, a takeover which had moreover related to elements which were not necessary for carrying on its own commercial activities, was not sufficient for it to be identified with those two companies. It maintained in this respect that it was an entirely new company which did not carry on the activities formerly carried on by AWS in the economic sector in question, that the persons who had worked for AWS at the material time no longer worked in the undertaking, and that in any event the alleged infringements had ceased after the transfer of assets on 17 April 1989, given that the exclusive distribution agreement between AWS and DSIL had been rescinded by that date and had actually ended on 30 April 1989. Finally, the applicant stated to the Commission that while the agreement of 17 April 1989 provided for the assignment to the applicant of the contracts between AWS and DSIL, that was solely to ensure that during the period remaining before their expiry, which had nearly come to an end at the time of conclusion of the agreement for the transfer of assets, orders in progress would be carried out.

11. On being requested by the applicant and the other companies concerned in the infringement proceedings to clarify which undertaking was in fact the addressee of the statement of objections, the Commission, at the hearing of 5 October 1990, during which that question was again raised, postponed examination of it to a later stage.

12. On 21 December 1990 the applicant, in a letter from its lawyer to the Commission, again drew the Commission's attention to the question of liability for the infringement of which AWS was accused. That letter requested the Commission to reach a decision on that point before adopting any decision concluding the infringement proceedings.

13. In a letter of 7 August 1991 the Commission sent the applicant, in accordance with

Article 11 of Council Regulation No 17 of 6 February 1962, First Regulation implementing Articles 85 and 86 of the Treaty (Official Journal, English Special Edition 1959-1962, p. 87, hereinafter 'Regulation No 17'), a request for information on the turnover of AWS in 1988 and the turnover of Dunlop products by that company. On 18 March 1992 it adopted Decision 92/261/EEC relating to a proceeding pursuant to Article 85 of the EEC Treaty (IV/32.290 – Newitt/Dunlop Slazenger International and Others) (Official Journal 1992 L 131, p. 32). That decision states, in point 3 of its statement of reasons, that in 1989 'AWS was purchased by its management from the group Buehrmann-Tetterode Nederland BV, which controlled it, and took the name All Weather Sports Benelux BV'. The operative provisions are as follows:
'Article 1
Dunlop Slazenger International Ltd has infringed Article 85(1) of the EEC Treaty by applying in its business relations with its customers a general ban on exporting its products, designed to protect its exclusive distribution network, and by implementing, in respect of some of its products (tennis-balls, squash-balls, tennis-rackets and golfing equipment), various measures – refusal to supply, dissuasive pricing measures, marking and follow-up of exported products, buy-back of exported products and the discriminatory use of official labels – in order to ensure enforcement of the export ban.
All Weather Sports International BV has infringed Article 85(1) by urging and participating in the implementation of such measures in the Netherlands in respect of Dunlop products.
[...]
Article 2
A fine of ECU 5 000 000 is hereby imposed on Dunlop Slazenger International Ltd and a fine of ECU 150 000 on All Weather Sports Benelux BV (which has taken over the assets of All Weather Sports BV) in respect of the infringements referred to in Article 1. [...]'

14. In those circumstances the applicant brought the present application, which was received at the Registry of the Court of First Instance on 22 May 1992, against the Commission's decision.

15. The written procedure was completed on 13 November 1992, as the reply was filed out of time. On application by the applicant of 18 November 1992, and with the consent of the Commission, given on 24 November 1992, the written procedure was reopened by an order of the Court of First Instance (Second Chamber) of 10 December 1992, and was completed on 8 March 1993. Upon hearing the report of the Judge-Rapporteur, the Court (Second Chamber) decided to open the oral procedure; it asked the parties to reply to a number of questions and requested the applicant to produce certain documents. At the hearing on 15 December 1993 the parties presented oral argument and replied to the questions put by the Court.

**Forms of order sought**

16. The applicant claims that the Court should:
   (i) annul Article 2 of the Commission decision of 18 March 1992 (IV/32.290 – Newitt/Dunlop Slazenger International and Others), with respect to the applicant;
   (ii) order the defendant to pay the costs.

17. The Commission contends that the Court should:
   (i) dismiss the application as unfounded;
   (ii) order the applicant to pay the costs.

**Substance**

18. The applicant company states in its application that its challenge is directed only against the correctness of the administrative procedure before the Commission and of the manner in which the contested decision was adopted, in so far as it held it liable for the alleged infringement and imposed a fine, and against the criteria used by the Commission in fixing the amount of that fine.

19. In support of its application, the applicant company argues firstly that there was a breach of paragraph 1 in conjunction with paragraph 3 of Article 2 of Regulation No 99/63/EEC of the Commission of 25 July 1963 on the hearings provided for in Article 19(1) and (2) of Council Regulation No 17 (Official Journal, English Special Edition 1963-1964, p. 47). It submits that by imposing a fine on the company without having informed it directly of the objections, even though the statement of the objections raised in the procedure in question was notified after it had taken over the assets of AWS, and without having given it at least an opportunity to be heard on the question of liability for the infringement allegedly committed by AWS, the Commission infringed an essential procedural requirement. Secondly, the applicant contends that the Commission infringed Article 85(1) of the Treaty and Article 15(2) of Regulation No 17 in that the Commission held it liable for the alleged infringement and fined it on the basis of inappropriate grounds, or at least without having given it a proper statement of the reasons for the contested decision. Finally, the applicant argues, in the alternative, that the Commission infringed Article 15(2) of Regulation No 17 by applying incorrect criteria for determining the amount of the fine imposed.

20. The Court of First Instance considers that it should first examine the applicant company's plea that it was not given a sufficient statement of reasons for the contested decision and that the procedure whereby that decision was adopted was not proper.

The plea in law alleging the lack of an adequate statement of reasons for the decision

**Summary of the pleas in law and main arguments of the parties**

21. The applicant argues, firstly, that if a decision imposes a fine on an undertaking by reason of the conduct of another undertaking, the statement of reasons must demonstrate clearly to the undertaking in question why it is to be held liable for an infringement which is not its doing. It maintains that, contrary to the practice of the Commission, which has always provided detailed reasons in similar decisions, the contested decision does not provide it with a sufficient statement of reasons.

22. The applicant considers that the mere mention of the fact that it took over the assets of AWS does not constitute a statement of reasons for the decision sufficient to hold it liable for the infringement, given that such a takeover does not mean that the applicant can automatically be identified with AWS for the purposes of the application of Article 85 of the Treaty. Furthermore, it points out that the reason which, in the Commission's opinion, justified the decision to hold it liable for the infringement is stated only in the actual operative part of the contested decision and not in the statement of reasons, which contains only a single sentence referring to it, that sentence being a mere statement of fact, which is moreover incorrect in that the Commission states that AWS was purchased by its management, whereas in fact only the assets of that company were taken over, and that by the applicant company itself, whose shares were merely held at the time by the AWS management.

23. Secondly, the applicant company argues that the identity of the undertaking which

committed the infringement for which it was fined is not clear from the contested decision. It submits that in Article 1 of the operative part of the decision the Commission asserts that AWS International is liable for the infringement of Article 85(1) of the Treaty, although that company is not mentioned anywhere else in the decision, and that the Commission then fines the applicant in Article 2 of the operative part on the grounds that it took over the assets of AWS. In its opinion, if it is AWS International which is regarded by the Commission as having committed the infringement, the contested decision completely lacks reasons, both with respect to AWS International and with respect to the applicant, in that it is thus held liable for conduct which is not specified in the decision, simply because of its takeover of the assets of AWS. If, on the other hand, it is AWS which the Commission considers liable for the infringement, the reasons stated in the contested decision are in any event insufficient with respect to the applicant, since even if it is admitted that the mere takeover of the assets of AWS could be a reason for identifying the applicant with that company from the economic and legal points of view, the Commission in any case does not state that it is for that reason that a fine is imposed on it.

24.     The Commission argues that since the addressees of decisions relating to infringements of Article 85(1) of the Treaty are the economic entities constituted by undertakings, not companies as legal persons, and as in the present case, it shows by proper reasons that an undertaking has committed an infringement, it is not obliged in law to explain in its decision why that decision is addressed to a particular company within that undertaking. In the present case, the applicant company continued the activity of the undertaking which had previously been carried on by the two companies AWS and AWS International, following the takeover by the applicant of the assets of those companies under the agreement of 17 April 1989, that being a classic case of a transfer of an undertaking. It considers that in view of the fact that the takeover of assets and the ensuing transfer of an undertaking were neither wide-ranging nor complex, there was no need for a more detailed statement of reasons explaining why the applicant was liable for the infringement, in contrast to other cases in which it was obliged in its decisions to deal with detailed arguments on the liability for an infringement.

25.     Finally, in answer to the Court's question relating to the fact that in Article 1 of the operative part of the decision AWS International is referred to as having committed the infringement, whereas in Article 2 of the operative part AWS is referred to, the Commission explained that this confusion resulted from an error, and both companies should correctly have been mentioned in Article 1 of the operative part on the same basis, as both having committed the infringement, liability for which was imputed to the applicant, which took over their assets and continued carrying on the undertaking which they had previously carried on together. However, according to the Commission, that error has no effect on the validity of Article 2 of the operative part of the decision. The fact that AWS is not mentioned in Article 1 of the operative part does not give rise to any doubts as to its having committed the infringement, given that, firstly, that company is mentioned throughout the decision and, secondly, that it is clearly referred to, both in paragraph 3 of the grounds and Article 2 of the operative part, as the company whose assets were taken over by the applicant.

## Assessment by the Court

26.     The Court notes to begin with, firstly, that the statement of the reasons on which a decision having adverse effect is based must make it possible to carry out an effec-

tive review of its legality and must provide the party concerned with details sufficient to allow that party to ascertain whether or not the decision is well founded, and, secondly, that the adequacy of such a statement of reasons must be assessed in the context of the circumstances of the case, and in particular the content of the measure in question, the nature of the reasons relied on and the interest which addressees, or other persons to whom the measure is of direct and individual concern, within the meaning of the second paragraph of Article 173 of the Treaty, may have in obtaining explanations (see the judgments of the Court of Justice in Joined Cases 296 and 318/82 Netherlands and Leeuwarder Papierwarenfabriek v Commission [1985] ECR 809, Case 41/83 Italy v Commission [1985] ECR 873, and Joined Cases 172 and 226/83 Hoogovens Groep v Commission [1985] ECR 2831). It should also be noted that, in order to perform those functions, an adequate statement of reasons must disclose in a clear and unequivocal fashion the reasoning followed by the Community authority which adopted the measure in question (judgment of the Court of Justice in Case C-269/90 Technische Universitaet Muenchen [1991] ECR I-5469, paragraph 26). In addition, where, as in the present case, a decision taken in application of Article 85 or 86 of the Treaty relates to several addressees and raises a problem with regard to liability for the infringement, it must include an adequate statement of reasons with respect to each of the addressees, in particular those of them who according to the decision must bear the liability for the infringement.

27. In assessing, in the light of the requirements of the case-law mentioned above, whether adequate reasons were stated for the decision with respect to the applicant, it should be noted that it is established that during the administrative procedure before the Commission the applicant advanced several reasons why in its opinion it could not be held liable for the alleged infringement. It is also established that at that stage of the proceedings the Commission, despite thus being challenged, did not clarify its position on the question of liability for the alleged infringement. It follows that, in order for there to be an adequate statement of reasons with respect to the applicant, the contested decision must contain an even more detailed account of the grounds for holding the applicant liable for the infringement.

28. On this point, the Court finds that in this case the reasons given in the contested decision for the applicant's liability for the alleged infringement consist firstly of the statement in paragraph 3 of the account of facts that 'AWS was purchased by its management from the group Buehrmann-Tetterode Nederland BV, which controlled it, and took the name All Weather Sports Benelux BV', and secondly of the reference, in Article 2 of the operative part, to the fact that the applicant 'has taken over the assets of All Weather Sports BV'. The Court considers that it is thus necessary to examine whether the reasons stated in the decision justify its operative part, and whether the operative part is appropriate with respect to the applicant.

29. Firstly, with respect to paragraph 3 of the grounds for the decision, the Court finds that as justification for holding the applicant liable for the infringement, the decision, as stated above, merely notes the purchase of AWS and the fact that AWS then adopted the name of the applicant company, 'All Weather Sports Benelux BV'. That statement of reasons thus ignores the two points raised by the applicant, namely that the companies AWS and AWS International continue to exist as legal persons under the new names BT Sports and BT Sports International and that they form part of the Buehrmann-Tetterode group, as they did before the takeover of their assets.

30. The Court notes on this point that for a Commission decision, which in its state-

ment of reasons merely identifies as the party committing an infringement the legal entity which existed prior to the date of the purchase of its assets, lawfully to be able to impute liability for that infringement to the purchaser of the undertaking, there must be no dispute as to the identity of the legal entity which is the legal successor of the party committing the infringement, or as to the reality of the continuance by that entity of the activity, carried on by the undertaking in question, which gave rise to the proceedings (see the judgment of the Court of Justice in Joined Cases 29 and 30/83 CRAM and Rheinzink v Commission [1984] ECR 1679, paragraph 6 et seq.). That is not the case here, where the party which committed the infringement continues to exist as a legal person, as stated above, even though the economic activity which it carried on before the takeover of its assets is now carried on by a different legal entity.

31.  In those circumstances the Court considers that, faced with a serious specific challenge by the applicant as to the identity of the undertaking to be held liable for the infringement, the Commission cannot argue that the facts and law of the case were simple, and there was consequently no need for a more detailed statement of reasons, to justify the inadequacy of the reasons given for the contested decision, as disclosed by an examination of paragraph 3 of the reasons for the decision. It follows that since the operative part of the contested decision must be read in the light of the grounds supporting it, in particular the said paragraph 3 of the decision, that paragraph is not in itself justification for holding the applicant liable for the infringement.

32.  Secondly, assessing the appropriateness of the reasons stated with respect to the applicant in the actual operative part of the contested decision, the Court finds that, as the applicant submits, although the decision names AWS as the party which committed the infringement in its account of the facts, in Article 1 of the operative part, by contrast, it names AWS International as having committed the infringement, and in Article 2 of the operative part it holds the applicant liable for the infringements 'referred to in Article 1' on the grounds that the applicant has taken over the assets of AWS. However, Article 2 of the operative part cannot lawfully hold the applicant company liable for an infringement – which it is known not to have committed – as described in Article 1 of the operative part, solely on the ground that it has taken over the assets of a company which itself is not identified in Article 1 of the operative part as having committed the alleged infringement.

33.  Thirdly, the Commission also argued during the oral procedure that the disparity between the identity of the companies referred to in Articles 1 and 2 of the operative part was due to an error and Article 1 should have referred to AWS as well as to AWS International, since both those two companies were involved in the alleged infringement and it was AWS which was named in the statement of reasons for the decision as having committed the infringement.

34.  On this point, the Court considers that on the essential question of identifying the party committing the infringement or the addressees of the decision, even assuming that an alleged error can be accepted, the Commission must be able to establish it with sufficient certainty. That is not the case here, since, firstly, as stated above, that argument was put forward for the first time only at the final stage of the procedure and, secondly, the Commission failed to notify a corrigendum to the applicant in the proper form. That is all the more so in the present case where the alleged error relates firstly to the actual operative part of the contested decision, in other words the part of the act which directly determines the extent of the obligations imposed or rights conferred by the act in question on those concerned and,

secondly, the very identity of the addressees of the decision and hence the liability for the alleged infringement and the financial burden of the fine imposed, so that scrupulous observance of the principle of legal certainty is essential, that principle being a fundamental principle of the Community legal order (see, by analogy, the judgment of the Court of First Instance in Joined Cases T-79/89, T-84/89, T-85/89, T-86/89, T-89/89, T-91/89, T-92/89, T-94/89, T-96/89, T-98/89, T-102/89 and T-104/89 BASF and Others v Commission [1992] ECR II-315). The Commission's argument relating to an error affecting the contested decision can therefore not be accepted. In any event and in view of what has been stated above, that argument could not alter the Court's assessment of the statement of reasons for the challenged decision.

35.    It follows that the plea in law alleging that the Commission did not state reasons for the contested decision with respect to the applicant is well founded and must be upheld.

36.    Consequently, without it being necessary to consider the other pleas in law advanced in the application, Article 2 of the contested decision must be annulled in so far as it relates to the applicant company.

**Decision on costs**

**Costs**

37.    Under Article 87(2) of the Rules of Procedure, the unsuccessful party is to be ordered to pay the costs if they have been applied for in the successful party's pleadings. Since the applicant sought such an order, the Commission must be ordered to pay the costs.

**Operative part of the judgment**

On those grounds,
THE COURT OF FIRST INSTANCE (Second Chamber)
hereby:

1.    Annuls Article 2 of the operative part of Commission Decision 92/261/EEC of 18 March 1992 relating to a proceeding pursuant to Article 85 of the EEC Treaty (IV/32.290 – Newitt/Dunlop Slazenger International and Others) in so far as it holds the applicant liable for the infringements referred to in Article 1 of the operative part and imposes a fine on it;

2.    Orders the Commission to pay the costs.

———

**2.4.9.    EUROPEAN COURT OF JUSTICE, JUDGMENT OF THE COURT OF FIRST INSTANCE (FIRST CHAMBER), SCOTTISH FOOTBALL ASSOCIATION V COMMISSION OF THE EUROPEAN COMMUNITIES, CASE T-46/92, 9 NOVEMBER 1994**[147]

**Content of the Court's judgment**

1.    Actions for annulment of measures – Measures against which actions may be brought – Decision ordering information to be supplied pursuant to Article 11(5)

---

[147]    ECR 1994, p. II-1039.

of Regulation No 17 – Interest in bringing proceedings – Prior compliance with the contested decision – Not relevant

(EC Treaty, Art. 173, fourth para.; Council Regulation No 17, Art. 11(5))

2. Acts of the institutions – Statement of reasons – Obligation – Scope – Decision ordering information to be supplied pursuant to Article 11(5) of Regulation No 17

(EC Treaty, Art. 190; Council Regulation No 17, Art. 11(5))

3. Competition – Administrative procedure – Request for information – Powers of the Commission

(Council Regulation No 17, Art. 11(5))

## Summary

1. *The mere fact that in a procedure applying the competition rules the Commission requests information by way of a decision is liable to affect the legal situation of the undertaking concerned, for an undertaking faced with such a decision runs a higher risk of sanctions than one confronted with a 'mere' request for information. Consequently, even though it may be disposed in principle to reply to the questions addressed to it, the undertaking cannot be deprived of its legitimate interest in preventing the Commission from moving prematurely to the decision stage without first satisfying the criteria laid down by Article 11(5) of Regulation No 17.*

   *That interest in bringing proceedings still exists where the decision has already been complied with by its addressee at the time when the action for annulment is brought, since the action has no suspensory effect. Annulment per se of such a decision may also have legal consequences, in particular by obliging the Commission to take the measures needed to comply with the Court's judgment and by preventing it from repeating such a practice.*

2. *The purpose of the obligation to give reasons for an individual decision is to enable the Community judicature to review the legality of the decision and to provide the party concerned with an adequate indication as to whether the decision is well founded or whether it may be vitiated by some defect enabling its validity to be challenged; the scope of that obligation depends on the nature of the act in question and on the context in which it was adopted.*

   *Where a decision ordering information to be supplied is adopted pursuant to Article 11(5) of Regulation No 17 following an exchange of correspondence between the Commission and the undertaking concerned, repeating verbatim the request for information which formed the subject-matter of that correspondence, it cannot be argued that the decision contains any surprises and that a particularly detailed statement of reasons is consequently necessary.*

3. *Article 11 of Regulation No 17 lays down a two-stage procedure for the exercise by the Commission of its power to request an undertaking or association of undertakings to supply the information it considers necessary, the second stage of which, involving the adoption by the Commission of a decision specifying the information required, may only be initiated if the first stage, in which a request for information is sent, has been tried without success.*

   *As regards the point at which the Commission is entitled to take the view that the first stage has not succeeded, it should be noted that Regulation No 17 confers on the Commission wide powers of investigation and imposes on individuals the obligation to cooperate actively in the investigative measures. Given that obligation to cooperate actively, a passive reaction may in itself be enough to justify adoption of a formal decision under Article 11(5) of Regulation No 17 without the need for any manifest obstruction on the part of the undertaking concerned.*

**Parties**

In Case T-46/92,

The Scottish Football Association, a company incorporated under Scots law, established at Glasgow (United Kingdom), represented by Ian S. Forrester QC, of the Scots Bar, and Alasdair R.M. Bell, Solicitor, with an address for service in Luxembourg at the Chambers of Marc Loesch, 8 Rue Zithe, applicant, v Commission of the European Communities, represented by Julian Currall, of the Legal Service, acting as Agent, with an address for service in Luxembourg at the office of Georgios Kremlis, of the Legal Service, Wagner Centre, Kirchberg, defendant,

Application for the annulment of the Commission' s decision of 31 March 1992 relating to a procedure pursuant to Article 11(5) of Regulation No 17 of the Council of 6 February 1962, First Regulation implementing Articles 85 and 86 of the Treaty (IV/33.742 – TESN/ Football Authorities),

The Court of First Instance of the European Communities (First Chamber),

composed of: R. Schintgen, President, R. García-Valdecasas, H. Kirschner, B. Vesterdorf and K. Lenaerts, Judges,

Registrar: H. Jung,

having regard to the written procedure and further to the hearing on 12 July 1994,

gives the following

Judgment

**Grounds of the judgment**

Facts and procedure

1    The applicant is incorporated under Scots law in the form of a company limited by guarantee. It consists principally of football clubs and footballing bodies, and its function is to promote football in Scotland and to represent the interests of Scots clubs at all levels.

2    On 5 December 1991 the Commission sent to the applicant a letter based on Article 11 of Regulation No 17 of the Council of 6 February 1962, First Regulation implementing Articles 85 and 86 of the Treaty (OJ, English Special Edition 1959-1962, p. 87, hereinafter 'Regulation No 17'). In that letter, which reproduced the relevant extracts from Article 11 together with extracts from Article 15 of Regulation No 17, the Commission referred to a complaint made by The European Sports Network (TESN) and indicated its concern over the fact that the applicant appeared to be intending to prevent TESN from broadcasting Argentinian football matches in Scotland. The applicant had apparently contacted the Argentinian Football Association in that regard, in accordance with Article 47 of the rules of the Federation of International Football Associations (hereinafter 'FIFA'), which authorized FIFA' s Executive Committee to set up a new scheme of rules governing the international broadcasting of football matches. To the Commission' s knowledge, such a new scheme of rules had not yet been set up. It was therefore not clear on what legal basis the applicant' s inquiry to the Argentinian Football Association was made. The applicant was thus requested – 'in order to enable the investigation of this matter to be made in full knowledge of the facts and in their correct economic context' – to reply to the following questions:

'1.  On what legal basis was your inquiry to the Argentinian Football Association made?

2.  Are there any agreements between the National Associations in membership with FIFA governing the transmission of football matches from one country into the other, pending the setting up of a new scheme of rules under Article 47 of the FIFA statutes by the Executive Committee?

3. Are there any instructions by FIFA, its Executive Committee or any other of its legal or executive authorities relating to the application of Article 47, or the former Article 37, with respect to those transmissions, pending the setting up of a new scheme of rules?

4. Please provide copies of your correspondence with the Argentinian Football Association concerning the televising of Argentinian football by TESN.'

The time-limit for replying to those questions was fixed at four weeks. The Commission referred in that regard to Article 11(5) of Regulation No 17.

3    On 14 January 1992 the applicant replied as follows:

'...

We have received your enquiry with some surprise. It is well recognized in Scotland, and also in other countries, that the broadcasting of football matches on television can have a damaging effect on gates at live games. Our duty is to support and encourage football as a sport, both as a spectator sport and as a participative sport. Television is an excellent medium for promoting appreciation of, and support for, the game, but it can also, at the wrong time, damage the game, especially by reducing the numbers of those who would normally go to watch a football match.

For these reasons, this Association is not embarrassed to state that it has a policy, and will continue that policy, of trying to ensure a balance of control over the broadcasting in Scotland of televised football games when these could damage the overall interests of the Scottish football industry, professional, semi-professional and amateur.

Football associations around the world have similar concerns. We therefore regularly consult with each other as a matter of courtesy and within the framework of the game' s international governing bodies, to avoid clashes between television and the live game. We feel we do not need any 'legal basis' to justify writing to another football association reminding it of our mutual interest in balancing the benefit and the damage which can result from the televising of foreign matches.

We are not informed as to when FIFA will complete the planned revision of its rules on this topic.

Speaking frankly, we do not understand why Mr Barron is so jumpy about this matter, nor why the Commission should have intervened in such a peremptory fashion.

We are happy to meet you at any time to explain our views on the broad topic of television versus live game, but we honestly think that as to the Argentinian matter, the Commission need not be troubled about an exchange of correspondence between two fraternal associations about how the game should best be served. ...'

In the absence of any response from the Commission, the applicant wrote to it on 11 March 1992 to enquire whether its letter of 14 January had been received.

4    Thereafter the Commission sent to the applicant, by telefax of 31 March 1992, a decision bearing the same date – formal notification of which was received by the applicant a few days later ? relating to a procedure pursuant to Article 11(5) of Regulation No 17. In that decision, the Commission required the applicant to provide within two weeks from the date of notification the information requested in the letter of 5 December 1991, stating that if the applicant failed to do so it would be liable to periodic penalty payments of ECU 500 per day (Articles 1 and 2 and the Annex thereto). Article 3 of the decision states that an appeal against it may be made to the Court of First Instance pursuant to Articles 173 and 185 of the Treaty. In the preamble to the decision, the Commission sets out details of the complaint made by TESN (points 1 and 2), the purpose of the initial request for information

and the incomplete nature of the reply given by the applicant on 14 January 1992 (point 3), the need for the information requested for the purposes of the Commission's investigation (point 4), the time-limit considered by it to be appropriate for responding to the decision (point 6) and the amount of the periodic penalty payments to be imposed in the event of non-compliance (points 7 and 8).

5     On 15 April 1992 the applicant sent, by way of reply to that decision, a letter in which it emphasized the strong sense of injustice which it felt at the conduct of the Commission, which had not replied to either of the two letters sent to it by the applicant in January and March 1992, and stated as follows in response to the four questions asked in the decision:

1. Several legal bases could be cited to justify the applicant's correspondence with a fellow football association. The applicant's own charter called for it to promote football in Scotland in all its branches; writing to other associations formed part of the applicant's discharge of this duty. The applicant had asked the Argentinian Association that it be consulted, pursuant to Article 47 of the FIFA rules and in accordance with the practice regularly followed by football associations around the world, before Argentinian football matches were transmitted in Scotland. It was clear from the correspondence between the two football associations that the applicant did not seek to prohibit the televising in Scotland of Argentinian football.

2. The FIFA rules relating to the international use and broadcasting of televised football matches were currently under review. Until that revision was completed, the applicant (together with other national football associations all over the world) would continue to respect the established convention of consulting with fellow associations before televised transmissions went ahead.

3. The applicant was aware of no instruction by FIFA, its Executive Committee or any other legal or executive authority relating to the application of Article 47 (or the former Article 37) of the FIFA rules with respect to those transmissions.

4. The applicant annexed to its letter copies of the letters to the Argentinian association.

### Procedure and forms of order sought by the parties

6     Those were the circumstances in which, by application lodged at the Registry of the Court of First Instance on 10 June 1992, the applicant brought the present action.

7     After the action had been brought, the Commission confirmed, by letter sent to the applicant on 24 June 1992, that the answers given by the applicant in its letter of 15 April 1992 were sufficient to supply the information requested in its decision and that, consequently, the applicant had fully complied with the decision.

8     The written procedure before the Court of First Instance followed the usual course. The Commission did not, however, lodge a rejoinder. By a document lodged on 17 July 1992, the Commission raised an objection of inadmissibility. By order of the Court of First Instance (First Chamber) of 28 October 1992, the decision on that objection was reserved until final judgment. Upon hearing the report of the Judge-Rapporteur, the Court of First Instance (First Chamber) decided to open the oral procedure without any preparatory inquiry. On application by the applicant, the hearing fixed for 13 October 1993 was adjourned.

9     The oral procedure took place on 12 July 1994. The representatives of the parties made their oral submissions and gave their replies to the questions put by the Court.

10    The applicant claims that the Court should:
      (i)    dismiss the objection of inadmissibility raised by the Commission;
      (ii)   annul the decision addressed to it by the Commission on 31 March 1992;
      (iii)  take such further or different steps as justice may require;
      (iv)   order the Commission to pay the costs.
      The Commission contends that the Court should:
      (i)    reject the application as inadmissible;
      (ii)   in the alternative, dismiss it as unfounded;
      (iii)  order the applicant to pay the costs.

**Admissibility**

11    In support of its objection of inadmissibility, the Commission essentially main-
      tains that, in the particular circumstances of the case, the applicant no longer has
      an interest in pursuing the action, since it complied with the contested decision be-
      fore bringing its action, without ever challenging the Commission' s right to re-
      quest the information in question. Consequently, no purpose can now be served by
      annulling that decision. Moreover, the applicant suffered no substantive prejudice
      as a result of the decision; it did not challenge it before replying, although it was
      informed, in Article 3, of the appeal procedures open to it.

12    The applicant considers that, if an act is illegal, it remains illegal whether or not it
      is complied with. It is apparent from the fourth paragraph of Article 173 of the EC
      Treaty that it clearly has an interest in contesting a decision which is specifically
      addressed to it and which threatens it with periodic penalties where such a mea-
      sure was not necessary. Given that the Commission' s power to take decisions has
      been used in an abusive manner, the applicant considers that it has a legitimate in-
      terest in ensuring that such an abuse should not recur. The applicant further stated
      at the hearing that the contested decision came at a time when negotiations on tele-
      vised broadcasting of football matches had been entered into at European level,
      and were still proceeding, between the Commission and the national football asso-
      ciations; in bringing its action, the applicant was seeking, therefore, to protect it-
      self against the real risk that it might find itself confronted, in the framework of
      those negotiations, with further unjustified decisions of the same kind as that with
      which the present action is concerned.

13    Considering those circumstances, the Court finds, first, that the purely procedural
      complaints made by the applicant in relation to the decision are essentially that by
      going from the first stage of its investigation, involving a 'mere' request for infor-
      mation, to the second stage, in which that request was made by way of a decision,
      the Commission acted excessively and prematurely. As is apparent from Articles
      11(5), 15(1)(b) and 16(1)(c) of Regulation No 17, however, an undertaking or as-
      sociation of undertakings faced with such a decision runs a higher risk of sanctions
      than one confronted with a 'mere' request for information: it may be fined if it
      fails to provide the information requested 'within the time-limit fixed' and re-
      quired to pay periodic penalty payments so as to compel it to supply 'complete and
      correct' information. Consequently, the sole fact that the Commission requests in-
      formation by way of a decision is liable to affect the legal situation of the party
      concerned, which, even though it may be disposed in principle to reply to the
      questions addressed to it, cannot be deprived of a legitimate interest in preventing
      the Commission from moving prematurely to the decision stage without first satis-
      fying the criteria laid down by Article 11(5) of Regulation No 17.

14    That legal interest in bringing proceedings still exists even where the decision or-
      dering information to be supplied has already been complied with by its addressee

at the time when the action for annulment is brought, since that action has no suspensory effect. Furthermore, annulment per se of such a decision may have legal consequences, in particular by obliging the Commission to take the measures needed to comply with the Court' s judgment and by preventing the Commission from repeating such a practice (see the judgments of the Court of Justice in Case 53/85 AKZO Chemie v Commission [1986] 1965, paragraph 21, and Case 207/86 Apesco v Commission [1988] ECR 2151, paragraph 16). That is particularly so in the present case, given that, as the parties observed at the hearing, the negotiations at European level between the Commission and the national football associations on the televised broadcasting of football matches are still going on. So the applicant must expect to find itself faced with further requests from the Commission for information at any time. It therefore still has a legitimate interest in having the Community judicature make clear the legal conditions under which the Commission has power to act by way of decision in the matter.

15    It follows that the objection of inadmissibility raised by the Commission must be dismissed.

## Substance

16    The applicant advances five pleas in support of its application: breach of the obligation to state reasons laid down by Article 190 of the EC Treaty, breach of the principles of proportionality, good administration and good faith, and disregard of fundamental rights.

## The plea that the contested decision was not sufficiently reasoned
## Arguments of the parties

17    The applicant maintains that, contrary to Article 190 of the Treaty, the Commission failed to give an adequate statement of the reasons for the contested decision when it was particularly important in this case that it should fulfil its obligation in this regard. The Commission has omitted essential factual information. In particular, the decision makes no mention whatever of the letter of 11 March 1992, in which the applicant asked the Commission whether it had received its initial reply. The absence of any reference to that letter in the reasons given for the decision make it appear as though the applicant had embarked on a policy of intentional non-compliance designed to frustrate the Commission' s investigations. Lastly, contrary to what is stated in point 8 of the decision, the applicant did not 'refuse', in its letter of 14 January 1992, to supply the information requested: it replied to some of the questions and offered to discuss the whole matter.

18    The Commission states that it set out, in points 1 to 4, 6 and 8 of the contested decision, the main reasons which led it to adopt it. By referring to the original complaint, the decision was inviting a comparison between the questions asked in the letter of 5 December 1991 and the answers given in the letter of 14 January 1992. That comparison shows that the Commission had every reason to treat the letter of 14 January 1992 as a refusal to provide the information requested in complete form.

## Findings of the Court

19    It is settled case-law that the purpose of the obligation to give reasons for an individual decision is to enable the Community judicature to review the legality of the decision and to provide the party concerned with an adequate indication as to whether the decision is well founded or whether it may be vitiated by some defect enabling its validity to be challenged; the scope of that obligation depends on the

nature of the act in question and on the context in which it was adopted (see, for example, the judgment of the Court of Justice in Case C-181/90 Consorgan v Commission [1992] ECR I-3557, paragraph 14).

20    In the present case, the contested decision was adopted following an exchange of correspondence between the parties. It repeats verbatim the request for information which formed the subject-matter of that correspondence. It cannot therefore be argued that the decision contained any surprises for the applicant and that a particularly detailed statement of reasons was consequently necessary.

21    Next, as regards the grounds relied on by the Commission in the contested decision, it should be noted that, after summarizing the circumstances leading to the dispatch of its letter of 5 December 1991, in which it requested the applicant to supply the information in question, the Commission pointed out, in point 3, that the reply dated 14 January 1992 'failed to provide the information requested in complete form'. The Commission also stated in point 4 that the information requested, in particular the applicant's correspondence with the Argentinian Football Association, was necessary to assess the applicant's conduct in the light of Articles 85(1) and 86 of the EC Treaty. The parties agree that that correspondence was not produced in response to the 'mere' request for information addressed to the applicant by the abovementioned letter of 5 December 1991. In those circumstances, the Commission was not obliged to provide a more detailed explanation of the incomplete nature of the information provided.

22    It should be added that the applicant apparently understood the purpose of the contested decision since it provided, within the period of two weeks which it was allowed, a response which the Commission considered to be complete and satisfactory.

23    Finally, the applicant's complaint that the Commission failed to mention in the contested decision either its offer to discuss the matter or its request for confirmation of receipt of its first letter must be regarded as being of no consequence. That omission did not prevent the applicant from apprehending the import of the contested decision or from raising the grounds of challenging that decision open to it and does not hinder review by the Court. The Commission was not obliged, therefore, to discuss those matters in its statement of reasons for the decision.

24    Consequently, the Court considers that the contested decision is to be regarded as sufficiently reasoned for the purposes of Article 190 of the Treaty and that the plea of inadequate reasoning must be dismissed.

## The plea of breach of the principle of proportionality
## Arguments of the parties

25    The applicant essentially bases this plea on the assertion that in the factual circumstances of this case the Commission acted disproportionately and excessively in relation to the applicant's conduct by threatening it, in a formal decision, with the imposition of penalties when it could have achieved its objective by simply asking it, if necessary by telephone, to supplement the answers already given in its letter of 14 January 1992. As the Court of Justice held in its judgment in Case 8/55 Fédération Charbonnière de Belgique v High Authority [1954 to 1956] ECR 245, respect for the principle of proportionality is particularly important in cases which involve the imposition of penalties.

26    The applicant observes that the decisive issue in this case is whether an individual who attempts to reply to a request for information but who allegedly fails to answer satisfactorily can be threatened with financial penalties. The applicant is prepared to concede that this should be so in the case of a wilful and obstructive

refusal to cooperate. However, it should not be possible to take such a measure where an individual has tried to satisfy a request for information, has offered to meet the competent officials in order to discuss the matter, has sent a follow-up letter to the Commission and has, in response, been met with silence.

27    The Commission states in reply that it is clear even from the most superficial comparison of the questions in its letter of 5 December 1991 and the answers given in the applicant' s letter of 14 January 1992 that the applicant more or less ignored the second and third questions and, as to the other questions, gave the Commission to understand that the 'Argentinian matter' was not its business, whilst the offer to discuss generalities did not relate to the specific questions put to the applicant. The Commission concludes from this that it was justified in considering that its initial request for information had been refused. Faced with such a refusal, and given that Article 11 of Regulation No 17 only creates a two-stage procedure, it therefore acted lawfully and proportionately in going on to the second stage, involving a request for information by way of a decision, without more ado.

28    At the hearing the Commission made the further point that it had certain responsibilities towards TESN, which had submitted a complaint and which could have brought proceedings for failure to act. The applicant expressly acknowledged that the time-limits fixed by the Commission in the letter of 5 December 1991 and in Article 1 of the contested decision were adequate to enable a response to be given to the questions asked.

**Findings of the Court**

29    First, the plea advanced by the applicant does not concern the inherent legality of the request for information addressed to it, since the applicant does not challenge the Commission' s power to put to it the four questions concerned. Its sole complaint is that the Commission acted prematurely and excessively in adopting the decision threatening it with periodic penalties instead of continuing to exchange informal correspondence with it.

30    Next, as regards the question whether in adopting the contested decision in the circumstances of this case the Commission correctly applied Article 11 of Regulation No 17, it should be remembered that, according to the case-law of the Court of Justice, that article lays down, for the exercise by the Commission of its power to request the information it considers necessary, a two-stage procedure, the second stage of which, involving the adoption by the Commission of a decision specifying the information required, may only be initiated if the first stage, in which a request for information is sent, has been tried without success (Case 136/79 National Panasonic v Commission [1980] ECR 2033, paragraph 10).

31    As regards the ways in which the Commission should 'try' the first stage of the preliminary investigation procedure, the Court of Justice has held that Regulation No 17 confers on the Commission wide powers of investigation and imposes on the individuals concerned the obligation to cooperate actively in the investigative measures, which means that they must make available to the Commission all information relating to the subject-matter of the investigation (Case 374/87 Orkem v Commission [1989] ECR 3283, paragraphs 22 and 27). Consequently, the applicant' s argument that the contested decision could only have been justified if it had manifestly obstructed the Commission in carrying out its task must be rejected. Given that the individuals concerned have such an obligation to cooperate actively in the initial investigation procedure, a passive reaction may in itself justify the adoption of a formal decision under Article 11(5) of Regulation No 17.

32    It is in the light of those considerations that the responses which the applicant gave

in its letter of 14 January 1992 to the request for information of 5 December 1991 must therefore be considered. The Court observes in that regard that the applicant stated, in response to the first question, that it did not have to have any legal basis to justify writing to the Argentinian Football Association and, in response to the second question, that it did not have the information requested; instead of replying to the third question, it offered to give general oral explanations; and it did not provide at all the correspondence between the applicant and the Argentinian Football Association requested by the fourth question. In the Court's view, those responses cannot be regarded as active cooperation on the part of the applicant.

33    Furthermore, the applicant stated that 'we honestly think that as to the Argentinian matter, the Commission need not be troubled about an exchange of correspondence between two fraternal associations ...'. Considered objectively, that remark constitutes a polite but explicit refusal to cooperate with the Commission in the matter. In those particular circumstances, the Commission was under no obligation either to pursue lengthy informal correspondence or to engage in oral discussions with the applicant, which had provided only part of the information requested. It was entitled to proceed to the second stage of the preliminary investigation procedure, involving a request for information by way of a decision, and that step cannot be regarded as excessive.

34    It follows from all the foregoing considerations that the Commission correctly applied Article 11 of Regulation No 17 and that the plea of breach of the principle of proportionality must therefore be dismissed.

### The plea of breach of the principle of good administration
### Arguments of the parties

35    The applicant, which refers to the judgments of the Court of Justice in Case 179/82 Lucchini v Commission [1983] ECR 3083 and Joined Cases 96 to 102, 104, 105, 108 and 110/82 IAZ and Others v Commission [1983] ECR 3369, maintains that it could not have known that its letter of 14 January 1992 did not meet the Commission's request. Without any reaction from the Commission, which did not even reply to its letter of 11 March 1992, the contested decision should not have been adopted.

36    The Commission contests the relevance of the case-law cited by the applicant.

### Findings of the Court

37    As is clear from the findings set out above, the applicant's letter of 14 January 1992 did not contain all the information which the Commission considered necessary for its investigation. By stating that the Commission 'need not be troubled' about the correspondence requested, the applicant should have expected that the Commission might find such a response inadequate. The mere request, made in the letter of 11 March 1992, for confirmation that the first letter of 14 January 1992 had been received does not affect this conclusion of the Court. Consequently, the applicant should have expected adoption of a decision under Article 11(5) of Regulation No 17. There was therefore no breach of the principle of good administration.

### The plea of breach of the principle of good faith and disregard of fundamental rights

38    The applicant maintains that the Commission failed to respect the principle of good faith by acting in an arbitrary way. The Court has already found that the applicant did not actively cooperate with the Commission during the first stage of the investigation procedure. Consequently, the applicant has not shown that good

faith, capable of being breached by the Commission, existed. The same considerations apply to the plea of disregard of fundamental rights, in support of which the applicant claims that, by denying it a fair opportunity to respond to its 'mere' request for information, the Commission gave the first stage of the initial investigation procedure no realistic chance of success.

39    Consequently, those pleas, which in any event would appear to be simply repetitious, cannot be upheld either.

40    It follows that the action must be dismissed in its entirety.

**Decision on costs**

**Costs**

41    Under Article 87(2) of the Rules of Procedure, the unsuccessful party is to be ordered to pay the costs if they have been applied for in the successful party's pleadings. Since the applicant has been unsuccessful, it must be ordered to pay the costs, as applied for by the Commission.

**Operative part of the judgment**

On those grounds,
The Court of First Instance (First Chamber)
hereby:
1.    Dismisses the action;
2.    Orders the applicant to pay the costs.

———

**2.4.10.    COMMISSION DECISION RELATING TO A PROCEEDING PURSUANT TO ARTICLE 85 OF THE EC TREATY (IV/32.948 – IV/ 34.590: TRETORN AND OTHERS), 21 DECEMBER 1994**[148]

*The Commission of the European Communities,*

–    Having regard to the Treaty establishing the European Community,

–    Having regard to Council Regulation No 17 of 6 February 1962: First Regulation implementing Articles 85 and 86 of the Treaty[149], as last amended by the Act of Accession of Spain and Portugal, and in particular Articles 3 and 15 (2) thereof,

–    Having regard to the Commission decision of 14 May 1993 to initiate proceedings in this case,

–    Having given the undertakings concerned the opportunity to make known their views on the objections raised by the Commission, in accordance with Article 19(1) of Regulation No 17 and with Commission Regulation No 99/63/EEC of 25 July 1963 on the hearings provided for in Article 19(1) and (2) of Council Regulation No 17[150],

–    After consulting the Advisory Committee on Restrictive Practices and Dominant Positions,

Whereas:

---

[148]   OJ L 378 , 31-12-1994, p. 45-53.
[149]   OJ No 13, 21-2-1962, p. 204.
[150]   OJ No 127, 20-8-1963, p. 2268.

## A. THE FACTS

### I. THE PARTIES

(1)  Tretorn AB, (hereinafter referred to as 'Tretorn AB'), is a Swedish industrial company. It operates within the Community in the market in tennis balls, through its subsidiary Tretorn Sport Ltd, Ireland. For the year 1992, Tretorn AB's turnover was of about ECU 16,5 million.

(2)  Tretorn Sport Ltd, (hereinafter 'Tretorn'), is a subsidiary of Tretorn AB, manufacturing tennis balls. For the year 1992, Tretorn had a turnover of about ECU [. . .][151].

(3)  Formula Sport International Ltd (hereinafter 'Formula') was Tretorn's exclusive distributor in the United Kingdom until 1989.

(4)  Fabra SPA, (hereinafter 'Fabra'), was Tretorn's exclusive distributor in Italy until mid-1993.

(5)  Tenimport SA (hereinafter 'Tenimport'), was Tretorn's exclusive distributor in Belgium.

(6)  Zuercher AG, (hereinafter 'Zuercher'), is Tretorn's exclusive distributor in Switzerland.

(7)  Van Megen Tennis BV, (hereinafter 'Van Megen'), is Tretorn's exclusive distributor in the Netherlands.

### II. THE MARKET FOR TENNIS BALLS

(8)  The market is oligopolistic. Four producers share most (about 80%) of the Community market for first-grade balls:
   – Dunlop Slazenger International: 39%
   – (Dunlop 28%, Slazenger 11%),
   – Dunlop France: 19%,
   – Penn: 16%,
   – Tretorn: 11%.

These figures are estimated by Dunlop Slazenger International (1986): see Commission Decision 92/261/EEC, Newitt Dunlop Slazenger International and others[152]. The Commission has no reason to suppose that any significant change has taken place since. Tretorn sales are mainly orientated on Europe.

(9)  According to the producers, there are no major technological barriers to entry. Barriers are of an economic nature and include the production volumes necessary for profitability and the presence on the market of a small number of well-established enterprises with brand-name loyalty, the latter supported by sponsorship of major events and the system of national associations granting 'official ball' status to certain brands.

(10)  Although 'first-grade balls' are technically fully substitutable, brand loyalty leads to a much lower level of substitution than would be expected. Also, the cross-elasticity of demand is low.

### III. TRETORN'S DISTRIBUTION SYSTEM

(11)  Tretorn AB uses its own subsidiaries to distribute in Germany and Denmark, and in other Member States Tretorn AB or its subsidiary Tretorn set up a network of exclusive distributorships.

---

[151] In the published version of the Decision, some information has hereinafter been omitted, pursuant to the provisions of Article 21 (2) of Regulation No 17 concerning non-disclosure of business secrets.

[152] OJ L 131, 16-5-1992, p. 32.

## IV. THE BASIS OF THE OBJECTION

(12)    On the basis of the information available, the Commission carried out investiga-
        tions at the premises of various tennis ball companies, including those of Tretorn.
        This investigation uncovered documents and correspondence which show that
        Tretorn actively erected barriers against parallel imports of its products within the
        Community.

## V. GENERAL EXPORT BAN AND BARRIERS ERECTED BY TRETORN AGAINST PARALLEL IMPORTS

(13)    Since 1987 at least, Tretorn has, in concertation with its exclusive distributors
        within and outside the Community, introduced an export ban in its exclusive dis-
        tribution system and has set up a series of mechanisms aimed at implementing and
        reinforcing that ban.
(14)    Those mechanisms consisted of: systematic reporting and investigation of in-
        stances of parallel imports; marking of products to identify the origin of parallel
        imports; and suspension of supplies to specific markets to prevent actual or poten-
        tial parallel imports.
(15)    Generally, Tretorn's intention to implement all the above measures is evidenced
        by a fax, from Tretorn AB to Zuercher, its Swiss distributor, dated 6 June 1989. In
        that fax Tretorn AB stated:
        '. . . our policy is to protect each and every distributor from grey market imports.
        We have also . . . implemented many controls, designed new packages, refused
        several orders, etc., in order to keep this grey market business at a minimum.
        . . . we are always prepared to listen to new ideas and proposals re how to stop this
        business.'

### 1. Export ban

(16)    It appears from various documents that there was an agreement or a concerted
        practice between Tretorn and its distributor in the United Kingdom to prevent sup-
        ply to dealers likely to engage in parallel exports.
(17)    In a telex dated 13 February 1987 to Formula, Tretorn specifically warned For-
        mula against supplying to Newitt Ltd (hereinafter 'Newitt') of York. Tretorn also
        informed Formula that Dunlop Slazenger International Ltd (hereinafter 'DSI') had
        already stopped dealing with Newitt and had curtailed supplies to JJB (another,
        but smaller, possible parallel exporter).
(18)    Newitt was again singled out, along with JJB, at a meeting between Tretorn and
        Formula at Wellebourne on 18 February 1987. Tretorn stated that the relationship
        between Formula and Tretorn would be in jeopardy if balls supplied to Formula
        turned up as parallel imports in other European countries. Formula gave an assur-
        ance that it would not ship to any customer who would export.
(19)    In a fax of 17 April 1987, Tretorn informed Formula that cheap balls had appeared
        as parallels in certain retail outlets in Switzerland. According to the date codes
        they had all been shipped to Formula. By letter of 6 May 1987, Formula assured
        Tretorn that supply via Newitt would not be an issue again.
(20)    The fact that the general export ban was the result of an agreement between
        Tretorn and its distributors and not the result of unilateral action by Tretorn is evi-
        denced in part by the following correspondence:
        A letter of 7 November 1986 from Formula to Newitt; a telex of 20 January 1987
        from Formula to Newitt again; letters of 6 and 11 May 1987 from Formula to
        Tretorn.

In the letter of 7 November 1986, Formula informed Newitt that its 'immediate concern is to penetrate the United Kingdom market and not actively canvass export business, as this may well disturb Tretorn's existing network'.

In the telex of 20 January 1987, Formula informed Newitt that its distribution agreement with Tretorn AB prohibits exports to 'certain European countries' and suggests that Newitt 'clarify any potential export business'. In those cases, Formula will 'ship direct, where necessary, into those countries which do not conflict with Tretorn's established distribution network'.

In the letter of 11 May 1987, Formula informed Tretorn that an order from Newitt had been accepted on the basis that the balls were to be re-sold only on the United Kingdom market. The Formula invoice was marked 'For re-sale in United Kingdom-territory only'. In the same letter Formula promised not to supply Newitt any more.

(21)  Even with those assurances from Formula, which clearly show its participation in the agreement on the export ban, Tretorn was not confident that Formula would not sell to Newitt and took steps to change to another United Kingdom distributor (Tretorn's international note of 11 May 1987).

## 2. Reporting and investigating parallel imports

(22)  Tretorn itself or Tretorn's distribution network reported parallel importers wherever there was evidence of such imports.

(23)  Reference is made to the faxes of 6 June 1989 and 17 April 1987 respectively, quoted at paragraphs 15 and 19.

(24)  In July 1987, Van Megen informed Tretorn that Tretorn balls were 'again turning up' in Holland. Tretorn asked Van Megen to forward the code number to it to allow it to find out 'which country has shipped' (fax from Tretorn to Tretorn AB dated 16 July 1987).

(25)  In an internal Tretorn note dated 20 June 1988, Van Megen was said to have parallels from two different sources. He hoped to obtain date codes.

(26)  In a fax dated 15 November 1988, Fabra informed Tretorn that they had identified a parallel importer in Italy, Fabra having obtained an invoice from a customer who bought a carton of balls from the parallel importer. They asked Tretorn to comment. Tretorn answered by fax dated 21 November 1988, asking for information about the type of packaging and the original shipment. By telex dated 24 November 1988, Fabra answered those questions.

(27)  In a telex dated 5 December 1988, Fabra informed Tretorn of the name of another Italian parallel importer.

(28)  In a fax dated 10 January 1989, Tretorn AB's German subsidiary reported a 'German exporter' who had tried to purchase Tretorn balls. Tretorn Germany refused to sell the balls. The exporter expressed its intention to buy Tretorn balls direct from the USA. Tretorn Germany informed Tretorn AB, asking it to inform Tretorn and Tretorn USA so as to prevent any sales to this presumed parallel exporter.

(29)  The minutes of 22 February 1989 of a meeting between Fabra and Tretorn expressed Fabra's concern about cancelled orders due to parallel imports. It was decided that Fabra should inform Tretorn immediately of any deterioration in the situation.

(30)  In a fax dated 27 February 1989, Tenimport informed Tretorn that parallel exports were on their way to Italy via Belgium and expressed its concern about the significantly lower prices offered by Tretorn to other distributors.

(31)  Following Tenimport's fax dated 27 February 1989 Tretorn asked Fabra, in a telex dated 28 February 1989, for information concerning the parallel importer. The

telex stated that Tretorn was monitoring the situation in order to ensure that the parallel importer did not receive any parallel-imported balls. In a fax from Fabra to Tretorn of the same day, Fabra replied that they had not been able to trace the parallel importer, and Fabra therefore asked for more information.

(32)   In a fax dated 21 March 1989, Fabra identified and gave the address in France of a so-called 'parallel' and requested an investigation.

(33)   The minutes of a meeting held on 5 April 1989 state that 'both parties (are) concerned about parallel . . .' and Tretorn agreed with Fabra to share the costs of an investigation as to which of its customers in France was exporting to Italy.

(34)   In a fax dated 6 June 1989, Tretorn AB complained to its German subsidiary that balls intended for the United States Army in Germany had ended up in Switzerland, thereby causing Tretorn and its Swiss distributor 'great problems'. While informing Tretorn Germany that Tretorn AB's marketing contribution for these balls was cancelled, Mr Alven asked him to investigate to find out 'how this could have happened' and to see what steps should be taken.

## 3. Marking of products

(35)   The evidence in the Commission's possession indicates that Tretorn marked their tennis balls with date codes which would allow the origin of parallel imports to be traced. Numerous references to these codes and their use are found in Tretorn's correspondence. Moreover, Tretorn admits having used different packaging with a view to making parallel exports less attractive.

(36)   In a letter dated 13 April 1987, Zuercher informed Tretorn of parallel imports to Switzerland, and gave specific date codes, requesting Tretorn to take action.

(37)   In a fax dated 17 April 1987, Tretorn pointed out to Formula that date codes on balls which had been parallel-imported into Switzerland showed that the balls came from a shipment to Formula.

(38)   In a fax dated 15 May 1987 Tretorn informed Formula that date codes clearly show that balls shipped to Formula ended up in Switzerland as parallel imports, concluding that Formula was guilty for having sold to Newitt.

(39)   The minutes of a meeting between Tretorn and Fabra on 6 October 1988 show that Tretorn agreed to prepare a sticker to put on ball packs to show that Fabra was the Tretorn distributor. The minutes state that this device would allow the Fabra salesmen to identify parallel imports with the retailers.

(40)   In a letter dated 17 March 1989, Fabra gave Tretorn details of codes on packs of balls sold by parallel importers, clearly intending this as a means of identifying the origin of the balls.

(41)   In an internal Tretorn memorandum of 17 April 1989, it is stated that the colour of the packaging of Tretorn balls meant for the American market was changed so that it differed from the colour of the packaging of balls for the European market. Tretorn however did not believe that this would 'alleviate the problem' of the re-exports of balls from the USA to Europe which had increased at an 'unprecedented rate despite all the efforts to control/stop this by our American colleagues'.

(42)   The fax of 6 June 1989 quoted at paragraph 15 also makes reference to designing new packages as a measure to prevent parallel imports.

(43)   Likewise, in an undated market overview (presumably conducted in early 1988), Tretorn has stated that one of the ball types will be sold in tubes in Italy in order to combat parallels from France.
In an internal memorandum dated 23 August 1988, Tretorn also contemplated changing the names of the balls exported to the USA in order to make their reex-

portation to Europe more difficult. It considered however that 'judging from past experience in Switzerland this would not solve the problem'.

#### 4. Suspension of supplies to prevent parallel imports

(44)     As stated by Tretorn in the fax of 6 June 1989 quoted at paragraph 15, it appears that Tretorn or its distributors suspended supplies to different markets in order to prevent parallel imports.

(45)     Reference is made to the letters of 6 and 11 May 1987 quoted at paragraphs 19 and 20, and to the fax of 10 January 1989 cited at paragraph 28.

(46)     In an internal Tretorn memorandum dated 23 August 1988, it is recommended to stop supplies to the United States market because Tretorn USA were unable to prevent re-exportation. Balls shipped to the United States were turning up as parallel imports in the Netherlands and Switzerland. The United States balls buds were sold at half the price of the balls marketed in Switzerland by the Tretorn distributor, Zuercher.

(47)     In an internal memo of 2 November 1988, it is stated that Tretorn USA promised once again to do all they could to prevent parallel exports from the USA. They informed Tretorn that they had stopped a shipment in San Diego the week before.

(48)     In the same memo of 2 November 1988, Tretorn stated that a decision had been taken to stop shipments to the United States market if there were 'major problems' with parallel imports in the spring of 1989.

(49)     In a fax dated 6 February 1989 from Tretorn to Fabra giving the minutes of a meeting between those two parties, it is stated that Fabra had some problems with 'grey imports' from France and that Tretorn would do everything possible to stop these imports. Tretorn's memorandum to Fabra of 22 February 1989 makes it clear that shipments to France were actually suspended for February and March 1989 while investigations into parallel imports were carried out. Tretorn stated that the suspension ensured that there would be no more parallel trade.

(50)     In an internal memorandum of 17 April 1989 Tretorn suggested the immediate cessation of supplies to all mail order companies and certain large chain stores in the USA in order to try to prevent parallel imports into Europe.

### B. LEGAL ASSESSMENT

#### I. ARTICLE 85(1)

(51)     The general export ban and the barriers erected to parallel imports, as described above, should not be regarded as the result of unilateral action by Tretorn[153] but as an integral, although unwritten, parts of its distribution or sales agreements, or at least as the result of concerted action by Tretorn and its distributors.

The general export ban and the barriers had the direct object and effect of restricting competition, affecting trade between Member States and partitioning the common market. This, in fact, constitutes an obstruction of the achievement of a fundamental objective of the Treaty, the integration of the common market. It also allows Tretorn and its distributors to apply a differentiated price policy.

#### A. Agreements and/or concerted practices: restrictions of competition

#### 1. General Ban on Exports (paragraphs 15 and 16 to 21)

(52)     The fax dated 6 June 1989 from Tretorn to Zuercher, and the correspondence between Tretorn and Formula, in particular, show that Tretorn, in combination with

---

[153] 'Tretorn' must be understood in this part of the Decision as designating either Tretorn Sport Ltd or Tretorn AB.

its exclusive distributor for the United Kingdom, set up a distribution system providing for total territorial protection and therefore aimed at excluding all parallel trade.

This shows:

– that Tretorn's exclusive distribution arrangements include an unwritten undertaking by Tretorn to provide its distributors with absolute territorial protection,

– that sales agreements between Tretorn and its retailers and distributors include an unwritten condition of sale prohibiting them from exporting or supplying to any company likely to export.

(53)    The fax mentioned in paragraph 52 indicates that the agreement or concerted practice applies 'to protect each and every distributor from imports'. As was stated above, there is a Tretorn exclusive distributor in all Community countries, except Germany and Denmark, where Tretorn used its own subsidiaries as distributors.

(54)    Tretorn's determination to implement this agreement or concerted practice is evidenced by the minutes of a meeting between Tretorn and Formula Sport on 18 February 1987 (see paragraph 18).

(55)    Clearly the agreement or concerted practice was implemented not just by Tretorn, but also in particular by the United Kingdom distributor (see paragraph 20).

(56)    Those agreements or concerted practices between Tretorn and its exclusive distributors to prevent parallel trade and to monitor the implementation thereof, are specifically prohibited by Article 85(1).

**2. Reporting and investigating parallel imports (paragraphs 15 and 22 to 34)**

(57)    Tretorn's policy of preventing parallel imports was further implemented by its distributors by reporting to Tretorn instances of parallel imports.

(58)    This system of reporting and investigation in order to identify parallel importers and cut off supplies to them is clearly the result of an agreement or concerted practice between Tretorn and its distributors and reinforces the ban on parallel exports in breach of Article 85(1).

**3. Marking of products (paragraphs 15 and 35 to 43)**

(59)    The marking of products played an integral part in the implementation of Tretorn's policy to prevent parallel imports. Balls were marked with date codes and/or exclusive distributor stickers for the specific purpose of identifying the origins of parallel imports.

(60)    Clearly, Tretorn's distributors made use of this marking system when reporting on parallel importers.

(61)    This system of product-marking is also in agreement or concerted practice aimed at implementing and reinforcing the ban on parallel trade, thereby protecting Tretorn's distributors, contrary to Article 85(1).

**4. Suspension of supplies (paragraphs 15 and 44 to 50)**

(62)    As shown in paragraphs 44 to 50 Tretorn clearly suspended supplies to different markets in order to prevent parallel imports.

(63)    It is clear that the suspension of supplies was made in coordination with Tretorn's distributors, who asked Tretorn to take action when parallel imports turned up on their markets. These actions, which reinforced and implemented the ban on parallel trade, are clear examples of concerted practices contrary to Article 85(1).

**B. Effect on trade between Member States**

(64)    The ban on exports contained in the Tretorn distribution agreements has the direct

object of hampering trade between Member States. The ban is a general one, and affects trade throughout the Community, since Tretorn has distributors or subsidiaries in almost all Community countries. This results in a partitioning of the common market.

(65)    Tretorn's prevention of parallel exports from the Community and into Switzerland meant that only Tretorn could deliver its products to the Swiss market through its distributor Zuercher while others in the Community were excluded from any such exports. The impediment of parallel exports from the Community and into Switzerland affected trade between Member States since it prevented Swiss dealers from buying from one Member State and re-exporting to a second Member State.

Tretorn maintains in its replies that the situation is highly unlikely since the same opportunity for re-exportation does not arise, because the price of tennis balls in Switzerland is estimated to be 15 to 20% higher than in the Community.

Such an allegation is rejected on the grounds that it is likely that Swiss dealers would, in the absence of the restrictive practices, buy tennis balls at the lowest Community prices and resell them, even without physically shipping them to Switzerland, in Member States where the prices are higher.

The effect of the restrictive practices is therefore to maintain price differentials between Member States.

(66)    Tretorn's prevention of parallel exports from the USA and into Switzerland also had an appreciable effect on trade between Member States, since the price structure in Europe and in the USA made re-exportation into the Community highly probable.

## C. Main elements of Tretorn's and its distributors' position

(67)    Only Tretorn, Tenimport and Van Megen replied to the statement of objections. Formula became insolvent, whilst Zuercher considered that the Treaty did not apply. A hearing was held on 16 November 1993.

(68)    In the written and oral replies to the statement of objections, Tretorn generally denies that it had the intention of preventing parallel import or export, or that it had taken any measures having such an effect. Tretorn argues that even if some of the documents may suggest that Tretorn prevented parallel trade, the documents were formulated to pay 'lip service' to the distributors and that no actual measure has ever been taken.

Further, Tretorn maintains that it is the distributors who have taken the initiative leading to the contested actions.

This argument cannot be accepted.

Firstly, the documents referred to in paragraphs 13 to 50 demonstrate that Tretorn and its distributors have initiated a number of measures to create barriers to avoid parallel import or export and that Tretorn even penalized one of its own distributors for having sold to a parallel exporter.

As to Tretorn's intention, the wording of the correspondence to Tretorn's distributors and of internal Tretorn documents does not support the conclusion that Tretorn took measures merely to fall into line with the demands of the distributors.

Even assuming that Tretorn had not taken measures with a view to preventing parallel import or export, the system of distribution organized with its distributors resulted in a partitioning of the common market for Tretorn's tennis balls and the barriers set up resulted in encouraging the distributors to prevent parallel trade. This is acknowledged by Tretorn itself in its reply.

Tretorn also claims that, as far as Formula is concerned, the reason for preventing it from selling to parallel exporters was its bad performance in the United Kingdom territory. Even if this were true, it cannot constitute a justification. Besides, it is not the Commissions's place to evaluate the performance of Tretorn's distributors. The correspondence between Tretorn and Formula (see paragraphs 16 to 21) shows clearly that the aim of preventing parallel exports was to avoid the disruption of Tretorn's closed distribution system in other countries.

Finally, Tretorn also claims that it has itself delivered direct to dealers which Tretorn knew to be parallel importers. Even if this were the case, it does not alter the fact that the other hindrances to parallel exports or imports exercised by Tretorn constitute an infringement.

## Tenimport

(69)   Tenimport points out that the fax which is referred to by the Commission (see paragraph 30) must be understood in its context. Tenimport considers that Tretorn charged it the highest prices and that the object of the quoted fax was not to prevent parallel imports but to ask Tretorn to explain how some dealers could benefit from much lower prices.

Even if this interpretation of the text of the quoted fax were correct, the fact remains that the information given by Tenimport has resulted in measures taken by Tretorn and Fabra with a view to suppressing that source of parallel imports (see paragraph 31). Since the behaviour of Tenimport had the effect, even if it was not intended, of restricting competition and partitioning the common market, it constituted an infringement of Article 85(1).

## Van Megen

(70)   Van Megen explained that its object in reporting date codes to Tretorn was not to prevent parallel imports but to check whether Tretorn did not supply direct in its territory. It declares that it itself supplies companies that it knows to be parallel exporters.

Even if the interpretation given by Van Megen were correct, the fact remains that the information was given in the context of a ban on parallel exports of which Van Megen was well aware and it actively participated in identifying the source of the parallel imports with a view to suppressing it (see paragraphs 24 and 25).

## II. REGULATION (EEC) No 1983/83

(71)   Article 1 of Commission Regulation (EEC) No 1983/83[154] provides that exclusive distribution agreements are in general exempt from the prohibition in Article 85(1) if they fulfil the conditions set out in that Regulation.

The exclusive distribution system operated by Tretorn does not however qualify for block exemption as it includes an unwritten undertaking giving absolute territorial protection to Tretorn's distributors, and implementation of the system involved – as was stated above – agreement or concerted practices to prevent parallel imports. For that reason the system falls within Article 3 (d) of Regulation (EEC) No 1983/83.

## III. ARTICLE 85 (3)

(72)   The Tretorn distribution agreements were not notified to the Commission and do not therefore qualify for an individual exemption. The agreements would not have qualified for exemption even if they had been notified, because of the export bans

---

[154]   OJ L 173, 30-6-1983, p. 1.

involved in the agreements, which are not indispensable to the effectiveness of Tretorn's distribution system.

## IV. ARTICLE 3 OF REGULATION No 17

(73)   Pursuant to Article 3(1) of Regulation No 17 the Commission may, if it finds that there has been an infringement of Article 85, require by decision that the undertakings concerned bring such infringements to an end.

(74)   Tretorn should be required, in so far as it has not already done so, to terminate the export bans contained in its sales agreements and the absolute territorial protection involved in its distribution system. Tretorn and those of its abovementioned exclusive distributors which are still active, namely Tenimport, Zuercher and Van Megen should also be required to end the agreements or concerted practices described in paragraphs 13 to 50.

## V. ARTICLE 15 (2) OF REGULATION No 17

(75)   Pursuant to Article 15 (2) (a) of Regulation No 17 the Commission may, by decision, impose fines of from ECU 1 000 to 1 000 000 or a sum in excess thereof but not exceeding 10% of the turnover in the previous business year on undertakings which, either intentionally or negligently, infringe Article 85. In fixing the amount of the fine, regard shall be had both to the gravity and to the duration of the infringement.

(76)   Tretorn could not have been unaware that the export ban in its distribution system and conditions of sale infringed Article 85(1) and that it has always been the policy of the Commission and the Court of Justice, in their decisions, to regard such bans as particularly serious infringements. Tretorn and its relevant distributors could not also have been unaware that the same applies to the various concerted practices aimed at preventing parallel imports. Consequently, a fine is to be imposed on Tretorn and its relevant distributors (with the exception of Tenimport). The documents in the Commission's possession prove that the infringement was concerted between Tretorn and its subsidiary companies, Tretorn Sport in particular, and it is therefore appropriate to fine Tretorn AB and Tretorn Sport jointly and severally.

(77)   The infringement committed by Tretorn and its distributors go back at least to 1987 (see paragraphs 13 to 50). There is no reason to believe that the practices are terminated. However, for the purpose of the fine only the years 1987 to 1989 will be considered.

It should finally be mentioned that, during the course of the procedure, Tenimport collaborated with the Commission, confirming the existence of an unwritten but actual prohibition on exports. It considered that the recent cancellation of its distribution agreement with Tretorn could only be understood as meaning that Tenimport had not complied with that prohibition.

(78)   In determining whether to impose fines and at what level the Commission has taken into account the fact that some of Tretorn's distributors have taken a particularly active part in preventing parallel imports; but also that such participation was in other cases of a limited nature and has to be set in the context of Tretorn's general policy of prohibiting any export of its products. Moreover, the part played by Tenimport was of a less substantial nature and it is therefore justified in refraining from imposing a fine on that untertaking,

## HAS ADOPTED THIS DECISION:

Article 1

Tretorn Sport Ltd and Tretorn AB have infringed Article 85(1) of the EC Treaty by applying a general export ban to their distributors of tennis balls, implemented through monitoring measures and sanctions, through the reporting and investigation of parallel imports of tennis balls, the marking of tennis balls, and the suspension of supplies in order to prevent parallel imports and exports of tennis balls.

Formula Sport International Ltd has infringed Article 85(1) by participating in the implementation in the United Kingdom of the export ban and suspension of supplies in order to enforce Tretorn Sport Ltd's policy of preventing parallel imports and exports of tennis balls.

Fabra SPA has infringed Article 85(1) by participating in the implementation in Italy of the export ban and suspension of supplies through the reporting and investigation of parallel imports of tennis balls, the marking of tennis balls and the suspension of supplies in order to enforce Tretorn Sport Ltd's policy of preventing parallel imports and exports of tennis balls.

Tenimport SA has infringed Article 85(1) by participating in the export ban and the suspension of supplies, through the reporting of parallel imports to Tretorn with the effect that Tretorn and its Italian exclusive distributor took measures with a view to eliminating those imports.

Zuercher AG has infringed Article 85(1) by participating in the implementation in Switzerland of the export ban and suspension of supplies, through the reporting and investigation of parallel imports of tennis balls and the marking of tennis balls in order to enforce Tretorn Sport Ltd's policy of preventing parallel imports and exports of tennis balls.

Van Megen Tennis BV has infringed Article 85(1) by participating in the implementation in the Netherlands of the reporting and investigation of parallel imports in order to enforce Tretorn Sport Ltd's policy of preventing parallel imports and exports of tennis balls.

Article 2

A fine of ECU 600 000 is hereby imposed on Tretorn Sport Limited and Tretorn AB jointly and severally and fines of ECU 10 000 each on Formula Sport International Ltd; on Fabra SPA; on Zuercher AG; and on Van Megen Tennis BV, in respect of the infringements referred to in Article 1.

The fines shall be paid, in ecus, to the Commission of the European Communities, account No 310-0933000-43, Banque Bruxelles Lambert, Agence Européenne, Rond Point Schuman 5, B-1040 Brussels, within three months of notification of this Decision.

After the expiry of that period, interest shall automatically be payable at the rate charged by the European Monetary Institute on its ecu operations on the first working day of the month in which this Decision is adopted, plus three and a half percentage points.

Article 3

Tretorn Sport Ltd, Tretorn AB, Fabra SPA, Tenimport SA, Zuercher AG and Van Megen Tennis BV shall, in so far as they have not already done so, terminate the infringements referred to in Article 1. They shall refrain from adopting any other measures having equivalent effect.

Article 4

This Decision is adressed to:

Tretorn Sport Ltd
Industrial Estate
Portlaoise
IRL-County Laois

Tretorn AB
Roenowsweg 10 Box 931
S-25100 Helsingborg
Formula Sport International Limited
c/o Arthur Andersen
PO Box 55
1 Surrey Street
UK-London WC2R 2NT
Fabra SPA
Via Sansovino 243/60
I-10151 Torino
Tenimport SA
Rue des Cottages 73
B-1180 Bruxelles
Zuercher AG
Gewerbestrasse 18
CH-8800 Thalwil
Van Megen Tennis BV
Parmentierweg 5
NL-5657 EH-Eindhoven
This Decision shall be enforceable pursuant to Article 192 of the EC Treaty.

Done at Brussels, 21 December 1994.
For the Commission
Karel van Miert
Member of the Commission

———

## * 2.4.11. ANSWER ON BEHALF OF THE COMMISSION TO WRITTEN QUESTION E-459/96 BY PETER PEX (PPE) AND JAMES JANSSEN VAN RAAY (PPE), 12 APRIL 1996[155] *

Subject: Plans by the Royal Dutch Football Association (KNVB) to set up a separate sports channel

———

## 2.4.12. NOTICE PURSUANT TO ARTICLE 19(3) OF COUNCIL REGULATION NO 17[156] – CASE NO IV/F-1/33.55 – DANISH TENNIS FEDERATION, 9 MAY 1996[157]

A.     Introduction
1.     In April 1994, the Danish Tennis Federation (hereinafter 'DTF') notified to the Commission, in accordance with Article 4 of Council Regulation No 17, the text of an agreement, with a view to obtaining negative clearance or alternatively an exemption pursuant to Article, 85 (3) of the EC Treaty.
2.     The aim of the notified agreement is to create a ball sponsorship where distributors of tennis balls, in return for financial support, obtain a right to supply their products to official tennis tournaments in Denmark.

---

[155] Question of 29-2-1996; OJ C 217, 26-7-1996, p. 47.
[156] OJ 13, 21-2-1962, p. 204.
[157] OJ C 138, 9-5-1996, p. 6. (Text with EEA relevance).

In the notified agreement all manufacturers can become members of a ball pool if they fulfil certain objective criteria. A member of the ball pool will acquire the right to present himself as member of the ball pool, to use this titie and to use the ball pool logo. DTF will call for tenders among the members of the ball pool for the supply of products to DTF tournaments, and a member, who has been appointed supplier, will acquire the right to present himself as supplier' to DTF's tournaments and to identify his products as having been supplied to tournaments for which he has successfully bid.

3.  DTF is the largest central organization for tennis clubs in Denmark. DTF has seven unions under it and is a member of Dansk Idræts Forbund, which is the largest mother organization in Denmark organizing sports associations. One of DTF's functions is to organize national and international toumaments. In 1989 DTF had a total of 113.000 members.

B.  Background
4.  The case goes back to 17 November 1988 when a Danish parallel importer of tennis balls, PTD Sport, informed the Commission that it was encountering difficulties in selling tennis balls on the Danish market. PTD Sport claimed that this was the result of the 'DTF's Official Balls' selection system enforced by the DTF.
    (a) In 1986 and again in 1988, DTF entered into agreements with Hammergaard Hansen Sport A/S, LS Sport A/S – (formerly DS Sport) and Tretorn A/S, respectively distributors for Penn Slazenger and Tretorn tennis ball brands in Denmark. The agreements were for three-year periods. In return for financial support to DTF, the abovementioned sponsoring companies were accorded the right to attach a sticker to their packaging indicating that the balls were 'DTF's Official Balls' and reproducing the DTF's logo. The 'official sticker' should be physically attached to the packaging by the exclusive distributors in Denmark and not by the producers; it thereby ensured that the balls were distributed through the exclusive network of the sponsors participating in the agreement and thereby excluding all other manufacturers and distributors. This very effectively prohibited any parallel import of tennis balls for use in tournaments covered by the agreement.
    (b) In addition to attaching the sticker to the packaging the sponsors would be allowed to advertise the balls as 'selected by' or 'approved by' DTF. This and the fact that the sticker appeared on the packaging of the balls were believed to influence players to think that these balls were technically superior to other tournament balls which was not, in fact, the case.
    (c) DTF had furthermore explicitly prohibited the use of brands other than the selected brands and of parallel imported tennis balls by a notice in every edition of the DTF periodical 'tennis avisen'.
    (d) If a match within a tournament under the guidance of 'DTF was not played with a 'DTF's Official Ball', the match was declared lost for the party who suggested not to use the selected balls.
5.  After a preliminary examination, the Commission warned DTF in October 1990 that the agreements constituted an infringement of Articles 85 and 86 of the Treaty. DTF replied that it would amend its practices, but in fact DTF did not bring the infringement to an end. On 28 July 1992 the Commission therefore sent a formal statement of objections to DTF and the abovementioned producers and distributors.
6.  Following discussions with the Commission, DTF submitted a new agreement on 26 October 1992. DTF claimed the new agreement was in accordance with an

agreement entered into by the English Tennis Federation, which had been accepted by the Commission. The Commission still found some elements unsatisfactory. In January 1993 DTF informally submitted a revised agreement, which at first sight appeared to the Commission to be acceptable, but DTF did not officially notify until April 1994.

7.    In the notified agreement DTF has accepted to make in particular the following amendments as a result of the Commission's intervention:
    (a) The period:
        The notified agreement is now made for a one-year period.
    (b) The rights for a member of the ball pool and a member who has been appointed supplier:
        The use of the sticker with the term 'DTF's Official Ball' has been removed. The sticker was attached by the distributors, thereby ensuring that only the selected balls were used in the tournaments.

C.    Assessment of the new agreement

8.    In the Commission's opinion there are large differences between the two agreements.
    –  The notified agreement is now for a one-year period, so that new members of the ball pool, as well as old members, will have the possibility to bid for adoption as supplier of tennis balls to DTF's tournaments every year. DTF is obliged to accept the best bid subject only to verification of the type and quality of the tennis balls and other equipment and all manufacturers are able to become members of the ball pool.
    –  The right to supply 'DTF's Official Balls' by the use of an 'Official Sticker' and in that connection advertise balls as 'selected' and 'approved' has been replaced by the right to present oneself as supplier' and identify the products as having been supplied and being entitled to use a ball pool logo.
        The difference lies in the use of the word 'official', which implied selection and approval, thereby indicating that the 'DTF's Official Balls' were of a higher quality than other tennis balls, which, in fact, was not the case.

Since the measures adopted in order to exclude the utilization of tennis balls coming from parallel imports and to prevent other distributors from supplying tennis balls of other brands to DTF tournaments have thus been removed, the Commission is of the opinion that the notified agreement does not constitute an infringement.

D.    The Commission's intentions

9.    Since the main objections raised by the Commission have been met, the Commission intends to take a favourable decision in respect of the agreement notified on 18 April 1994, and to grant negative clearance.

Before doing so, however, the Commission invites interested parties to send their comments on the case within one month from the date of publication of this notice, quoting the reference IV/33.055 – Danish Tennis Federation, to the:

European Commission,
Directorate-General for Competition,
Directorate IV/F,
Rue de la Loi/Wetstraat 200
B-1049 Brussels.

———

**2.4.13.    EUROPEAN COURT OF JUSTICE, JUDGMENT OF THE COURT OF
FIRST INSTANCE (FIRST CHAMBER, EXTENDED COMPOSITION),
METROPOLE TÉLÉVISION SA AND RETI TELEVISIVE ITALIANE
SPA AND GESTEVISIÓN TELECINCO SA AND ANTENA 3 DE
TELEVISIÓN V COMMISSION OF THE EUROPEAN
COMMUNITIES, JOINED CASES T-528/93, T-542/93, T-543/93 AND
T-546/93, 11 JULY 1996**[158]

*Competition – Decisions of associations of undertakings – Agreements between undertakings – Exemption decision.*

**Content of the Court's judgment**
1.    *Actions for annulment – Natural or legal persons – Measures of direct and individual concern to them – Commission decision exempting under Article 85(3) of the Treaty the statutes of a trade association of radio and television organizations – Action brought by a competing television company excluded from the advantages resulting from membership of the association – Admissibility*
       *(EEC Treaty, Art. 173; Regulation No 17, Art. 19(3))*
2.    *Competition – Cartels – Prohibition – Exemption – Conditions – Indispensable nature of restrictions of competition – Membership conditions of a trade association of radio and television organizations – Prior consideration whether they are objective and sufficiently determinate so as to enable them to be applied uniformly in a non-discriminatory manner to all potential members – Duty of the Commission – Exemption based solely on fulfilment of a particular public mission – Not permissible*
       *(EEC Treaty, Arts 85(3)(a) and 90(2))*

**Summary**
1.    In so far as a Commission decision granting exemption under Article 85(3) of the Treaty to the statutes of a trade association of radio and television organizations enables a television company competing with that association and all its members in the common market to be excluded from the benefit of the competitive advantages arising out of membership of that association, it affects the competitive position of the company in question. Accordingly, that company must be classed as an interested third party within the meaning of the first sentence of Article 19(3) of Regulation No 17 and be entitled to be associated by the Commission with the administrative procedure for the adoption of the decision. In that same capacity, it has to be regarded as being individually concerned by the decision within the meaning of Article 173 of the Treaty.
       In this regard, it is irrelevant that the company merely attended the hearing held by the Commission without adopting any specific position or that it did not avail itself in this case of its procedural rights under Article 19(3). On the one hand, the procedural right provided for by Article 19(3) is not subject to any condition relating to the manner of its exercise. On the other, if the capacity to bring proceedings of specified third parties who enjoy procedural rights in the administrative procedure were made subject to their actually taking part in that procedure, this would be tantamount to introducing an additional condition of admissibility in the form of a compulsory pre-litigation procedure, which is not provided for in Article 173 of the Treaty.

---

[158]   ECR 1996, p. II-649.

*Moreover, the company in question is directly concerned by the decision where there is a direct causal link between the decision, which requires no implementing measure, and effects on the company's competitive position.*

2. *The grant by the Commission of an individual exemption pursuant to Article 85(3) of the Treaty supposes that the agreement or the decision by an association of undertakings fulfils all four conditions set forth in that provision. It is sufficient for one of the four conditions not to be met in order for exemption to have to be refused. In order to assess, more specifically, whether the restrictions of competition resulting from the membership rules of a trade association of radio and television organizations which afford competitive advantages to its members are indispensable within the meaning of the aforesaid provision, the Commission must first consider whether those membership rules are objective and sufficiently determinate so as to enable them to be applied uniformly and in a non-discriminatory manner vis-à-vis all potential active members. The indispensable nature of the restrictions in question cannot be correctly assessed unless that prior condition is fulfilled.*

   *In the same context, the Commission is not entitled to use as a criterion for granting exemption, without other justification, simply the fulfilment by the members of the association of a particular public mission defined essentially by reference to the mission of operating services of general economic interest referred to in Article 90(2) of the Treaty, inasmuch as that provision is not applicable. Whilst, in the context of an overall assessment, the Commission is entitled to base itself on considerations connected with the pursuit of the public interest in order to grant exemption under Article 85(3) of the Treaty, it must show that such considerations make it indispensable for the restrictions of competition entailed by the rules of the association to exist.*

## Parties

In Joined Cases T-528/93, T-542/93, T-543/93 and T-546/93,

Métropole Télévision SA, a company incorporated under French law, established in Paris, represented by Pierre Deprez, Philippe Dian and, at the hearing, by Didier Théophile, all of the Paris Bar, with an address for service in Luxembourg at the Chambers of Aloyse May, 31 Grand-Rue, applicant, Reti Televisive Italiane SpA, a company incorporated under Italian law, established in Rome, represented by Carlo Mezzanotte and Giovanni Motzo, of the Rome Bar, and Aurelio Pappalardo, of the Trapani Bar, and, at the hearing, by Massimo Merola, of the Trapani Bar, with an address for service in Luxembourg at the Chambers of Alain Lorang, 51 Rue Albert Ier, applicant, supported by Sociedade Independente de Comunicação SA (SIC), a company incorporated under Portuguese law, established at Linda-a-Velha (Portugal), represented by Carlos Botelho Moniz, of the Lisbon Bar, with an address for service in Luxembourg at the Chambers of Carole Kerschen, 31 Grand-Rue,

intervener, Gestevisión Telecinco SA, a company incorporated under Spanish law, established in Madrid, represented by Santiago Muñoz Machado, of the Madrid Bar, with an address for service in Luxembourg at the Chambers of Carlos Amo Quiñones, 2 Rue Gabriel Lippmann, and Antena 3 de Televisión, a company incorporated under Spanish law, established in Madrid, represented by Fernando Pombo Garcia, Ricardo Garcia Vicente, Emiliano Garayar Gutierrez and Maria Luisa Tierno Centella, of the Madrid Bar, with an address for service in Luxembourg at the Chambers of Claude Wassenich, 6 Rue Dicks, applicants, v Commission of the European Communities, represented:

−   in Case T-528/93, initially by Berend Jan Drijber, of its Legal Service, and Géraud de Bergues, a national civil servant seconded to the Commission, subsequently by Mr Drijber alone,

–    in Case T-542/93, by Berend Jan Drijber, of its Legal Service, assisted by Alberto Dal Ferro, of the Vicenza Bar,

–    in Cases T-543/93 and T-546/93, by Berend Jan Drijber and Francisco Enrique González Díaz, of its Legal Service,

and, at the hearing, by Guy Charrier, a national civil servant seconded to the Commission, acting as Agents, with an address for service in Luxembourg at the office of Carlos Gómez de la Cruz, of its Legal Service, Wagner Centre, Kirchberg, defendant,

supported

in Case T-528/93 by European Broadcasting Union, an association of broadcasting organizations governed by Swiss law, based in Geneva (Switzerland), represented by Hanns Ullrich, a university professor in Munich, with an address for service in Luxembourg at the Chambers of Jean Welter, 100 Boulevard de la Pétrusse,

in Case T-542/93 by Radiotelevisione Italiana SpA (RAI), a company incorporated under Italian law, established in Rome, represented by Patrizia Ferrara Ginsburg, of the Luxembourg Bar, Alessandro Pace and Gian Luigi Tosato, of the Rome Bar, with an address for service in Luxembourg at the Chambers of Ferrara Ginsburg, 31 Avenue Guillaume, and

in Cases T-543/93 and T-546/93 by Radiotelevisión Española (RTVE), a public body governed by Spanish law, established in Madrid, represented initially by Alfredo Sánchez-Bella Carswell, Rafael Aldama Caso and José Rivas Andrés, of the Madrid Bar, subsequently by Aldama Caso and Rivas Andrés, with an address for service in Luxembourg at the Chambers of Jean Welter, 100 Boulevard de la Pétrusse, interveners,

APPLICATION for annulment of Commission Decision 93/403/EEC of 11 June 1993 relating to a proceeding pursuant to Article 85 of the EEC Treaty (IV/32.150 – EBU/ Eurovision System, OJ 1993 L 179, p. 23),

*The Court of First Instance of the European Communities* (First Chamber, Extended Composition),

composed of: A. Saggio, President, H. Kirschner, A. Kalogeropoulos, V. Tiili and R.M. Moura Ramos, Judges,

Registrar: J. Palacio González, Administrator,

having regard to the written procedure and further to the hearing on 16 and 17 January 1996,

gives the following

Judgment

## Grounds of the judgment

Object of the proceedings

1    Métropole Télévision SA (hereinafter 'M6'), the applicant in Case T-528/93, is a general-coverage private television channel which was authorized by decision of 26 February 1987 by the competent French authority to operate a nationwide television service broadcast uncoded, terrestrially and over the air for a ten-year period.

2    Reti Televisive Italiane SpA (hereinafter 'RTI'), the applicant in Case T-542/93 and a company incorporated under Italian law, obtained from the competent Italian authority on 13 August 1992 three separate licences to broadcast, nationwide, television programmes produced by three broadcasters (Canale 5, Italia 1 and Retequattro), broadcast by a single State company and distributed by interconnected installations.

3    Gestevisión Telecinco SA (hereinafter 'Telecinco'), the applicant in Case T-543/ 93 and a company incorporated under Spanish law in March 1989, is authorized by the competent Spanish authority to operate a private television service in Spain for a ten-year period, which may be extended.

4     Antena 3 de Televisión (hereinafter 'Antena 3'), the applicant in Case T-546/93 and a company incorporated under Spanish law on 7 June 1988, was granted a licence by the competent Spanish authority to operate indirectly the State public television service for an initial period of ten years.

5     In these proceedings the applicants seek annulment of Commission Decision 93/403/EEC of 11 June 1993 relating to a proceeding pursuant to Article 85 of the EEC Treaty (IV/32.150 – EBU/Eurovision System, OJ 1993 L 179, p. 23, hereinafter 'the Decision'), the addressee of which is the European Broadcasting Union (hereinafter 'the EBU').

6     The Decision, which was adopted pursuant to Article 85(3) of the Treaty, declares the provisions of Article 85(1) inapplicable for the period 26 February 1993 to 25 February 1998:

      – to the EBU's internal provisions and other regulations concerning the acquisition of television rights to sports events;
      – the exchange of sports programmes within the framework of Eurovision;
      – contractual access to such programmes for third parties.

**The EBU and the Eurovision System**

7     The EBU is a non-profit-making trade association of radio and television organizations set up in 1950 with headquarters in Geneva (Switzerland). According to Article 2 of its Statutes, as amended on 3 July 1992, its objectives are to represent its members' interests in the field of programmes and in the legal, technical and other spheres and in particular to promote radio and television programme exchanges by all possible means – for example, Eurovision and Euroradio – and any other form of cooperation among its members and with other broadcasting organizations or groups of such organizations, and also to assist its active members in negotiations of all kinds and, when asked, to negotiate on their behalf. At the date of the Decision, the EBU had, after its merger with its eastern European counterpart, 67 active members in 47 countries situated in the European broadcasting area, most of them being public-sector broadcasters.

8     At the time when the EBU was set up, radio and television broadcasting services were provided in Europe almost entirely by public-sector organizations or by bodies entrusted with the operation of a public service and often enjoying a monopoly. In 1984, just before the development of television and broadcasting undertakings of a predominantly commercial character which marked the second half of the 1980s, the EBU for the first time admitted as a member a private television organization, the French company Canal Plus. In addition, in 1986 the EBU authorized the French television channel TF1 to remain an active member after it was privatized. During that period, as a result of important developments in technology in the audiovisual sector, that sector lost its original relatively uniform nature. New types of operator, of a national, regional or cross-frontier character, sometimes specializing in certain kinds of programmes (cultural, sports or musical) or financed by subscription ('pay' television), appeared on the market in order to exploit the distribution of television programmes by cable and satellite.

9     On 9 February 1988, the Statutes of the EBU were amended in order, according to the EBU itself, to 'limit the number of members of Eurovision in accordance with its objectives and mode of operation' which mark them out as a special group of broadcasters.

10    Article 3 of the Statutes, in the version of 3 July 1992, reads as follows:

      '§1    There are two categories of EBU members:

–    active members
–    associate members.

(...)

§3 Active membership of the EBU is open to broadcasting organizations or groups of such organizations from a member country of the International Telecommunication Union (ITU) situated in the European Broadcasting Area as defined by the Radio Regulations annexed to the International Telecommunication Convention, which provide in that country, with the authorization of the competent authorities, a broadcasting service of national character and national importance, and which furthermore prove that they fulfil all the conditions set out below:

(a)    they are under an obligation to cover the entire national population and in fact already cover at least a substantial part thereof, while using their best endeavours to achieve full coverage in due course;

(b)    they are under an obligation to, and actually do, provide varied and balanced programming for all sections of the population, including a fair share of programmes catering for special/minority interests of various sections of the public, irrespective of the ratio of programme cost to audience;

(c)    they actually produce and/or commission under their own editorial control a substantial proportion of the programmes broadcast.'

11    In order to take account of the rights acquired by the old members, the second paragraph of Article 21 of the EBU' s Statutes, as amended on 9 February 1988, provided that Article 3, also as amended, was not to affect the status of organizations which were already active members on 1 March 1988 when it entered into force, but did not meet all the requirements laid down therein. In the version of the Statutes of 3 July 1992, that provision appears in the second subparagraph of Article 6(1).

12    Eurovision constitutes the main framework for the exchange of programmes among the active members of the EBU. It has been in existence since 1954 and is one of the main objectives of the EBU. According to Article 3(6) of the Statutes, in the version of 3 July 1992, " Eurovision' is a TV programme exchange system organized and coordinated by the EBU, based on the understanding that members offer to the other members, on the basis of reciprocity, their news coverage of important events and their coverage of current affairs and of sports and cultural events taking place in their countries and of potential interest to other members, thereby enabling each other to provide a high quality service in these fields to their respective national audiences'. Eurovision members are active members of the EBU and consortia of such members. All active members of the EBU may participate in a system of joint acquisition and sharing of television rights (and of the costs relating thereto) to international sports events, which are referred to as 'Eurovision rights'.

13    Until 1 March 1988 the benefit of the services of the EBU and Eurovision was exclusively reserved to their members. However, when the Statutes were amended in 1988 a new paragraph (paragraph 6) was added to Article 3 providing that contractual access to Eurovision may be granted to associate members and non-members of the EBU.

14    It appears from the case-file that, since it was formed, M6 has submitted five applications to join the EBU as an active member (in 1987, 1988, 1990 and 1993). Its most recent application, lodged on 8 February 1993, was rejected by letter of 6

July 1993. That letter, from the Secretary General of the EBU, stated in particular that: 'In accordance with EBU internal guidelines relating to the interpretation of the criteria to be fulfilled in order to become a member, M6, as a commercial broadcasting organization, must be regarded prima facie (in the absence of proof to the contrary) as not satisfying the requirements for being an active member of the EBU. (...) It has certainly appeared to the [EBU Administrative] Council that since 1990 M6 has changed in a positive manner as regards both coverage and programming, but the Council has not found the proof needed in order to arrive at a contrary conclusion.'

15    By letter dated 27 March 1990, Antena 3 applied to join the EBU as an active member. On 4 April 1990 the EBU informed it that, in view of the need to adapt certain EBU rules, no new members would be admitted before early 1991. Eventually, its membership application was rejected by decision of the EBU Administrative Council, which was notified to the applicant by letter of 3 June 1991. That letter stated in particular that 'this decision is based on the fact that your organization does not fulfil the obligation that the applicant organization must cover the entire national population, which is specified in the first place in Article 3 § (3)(a) of the EBU Statutes as a condition for admission as an active member'.

16    In contrast, RTI and Telecinco have never applied to join the EBU.

**Facts**

17    Following a complaint from the television channel Screensport relating to the refusal of the EBU and its members to grant it sub-licences for the retransmission of sports events, on 12 December 1988 the Commission sent the EBU a first statement of objections, declaring that the granting of an exemption to the rules governing the acquisition and the use of television rights to sports events within the framework of the Eurovision System could be envisaged provided that the EBU and its members accepted an obligation to grant non-members sub-licences for a substantial part of the rights in question and on reasonable terms.

18    On 3 April 1989 the EBU notified to the Commission its rules on the acquisition of television rights to sports events, the exchange of sports broadcasts in the context of Eurovision and contractual access of third parties to such broadcasts, and at the same time sought negative clearance or, failing that, an exemption under Article 85(3) of the Treaty. Under those rules, third parties' contractual access to television rights in respect of sports events acquired by EBU members pursuant to agreements concluded within the framework of Eurovision took place through a scheme whereby the EBU or its members granted sub-licences enabling non-members to complete their own sports and news programmes in so far as they had not themselves acquired retransmission rights on the market. Under the so-called 'embargo' principle, non-members obtained, in principle, only the right to deferred retransmission.

19    By letter dated 18 July 1989 the Commission invited M6 to submit observations on the rules notified by the EBU governing contractual access of third parties to broadcasting rights acquired by the EBU and its members. On 15 February 1990 M6 expressed reservations about those rules and also criticized the discrimination to which it was allegedly subject in comparison with, in particular, other private channels which were active members of the EBU.

20    By letter dated 29 July 1989 the Commission informed the company controlling RTI (Fininvest) of the existence of the EBU/Eurovision System case and of the sub-licensing scheme which the EBU was preparing to adopt, and invited it to submit observations thereon within six weeks. On 29 January 1990 Fininvest submit-

ted critical observations. It observed in particular that the rules governing the grant of sub-licences were very general, which prevented it from subjecting them to serious evaluation.

21   On 3 July 1990 the EBU adopted a first sub-licensing scheme, which had previously been the subject of discussions with the Commission.

22   By Notice 90/C 251/02 of 5 October 1990 (OJ 1990 C 251, p. 2) pursuant to Article 19(3) of Council Regulation No 17 of 6 February 1962, First Regulation implementing Articles 85 and 86 of the Treaty (OJ, English Special Edition 1959-1962, p. 87, 'Regulation No 17'), the Commission announced its intention to take a decision under Article 85(3) of the Treaty on the rules notified to it by the EBU. After receiving critical observations from third parties, the Commission organized a hearing on 18 and 19 December 1990 attended by interested parties.

23   M6 submitted written observations to the Commission by letter dated 5 November 1990 in which it expressed 'the utmost reservations about the scheme for the grant of sub-licences to third parties in respect of EBU sports broadcasts, as described in No C 251/2 of the Official Journal of the European Communities'. M6 also took part in the hearing held on 18 and 19 December 1990.

24   RTI did not submit any written observations to the Commission. It did, however, attend the hearing on 18 and 19 December 1990.

25   By letter dated 5 November 1990 Telecinco submitted observations to the Commission on the EBU/Eurovision System case. It asked the Commission to reject the application for exemption under Article 85(3) of the Treaty as regards the rules notified. Telecinco also attended the hearing on 18 and 19 December 1990.

26   Antena 3 neither submitted written observations to the Commission nor attended the hearing held on 18 and 19 December 1990.

27   On 24 June 1991 the Commission sent the EBU a second statement of objections, declaring that the sub-licensing scheme 'was not acceptable'. Subsequently, on 8 November 1991, the EBU submitted a new scheme governing contractual access for non-members from which, according to the Commission, most of the clauses of the previous sub-licensing scheme that had been criticized by interested third parties had been removed.

28   The Commission adopted the Decision after, on 26 February 1993, the EBU had presented a new version of the rules of the sub-licensing scheme which had been revised in agreement with the Commission.

**The Decision**

29   The Decision finds that the object and effect of the internal provisions and other regulations of the EBU governing the joint negotiation, acquisition and sharing of television rights to sports events and the related case-by-case agreements between members of the EBU is greatly to restrict, if not, in many cases, eliminate, competition between them, contrary to Article 85(1) of the Treaty (points 47, 48 and 49). In addition, according to the Decision, the joint negotiation and acquisition of rights enable EBU members to strengthen their market position to the disadvantage of their independent competitors (point 51). The Decision further finds that the rules governing membership of the EBU (laid down in particular in Article 3(3) of its Statutes) distort to some extent competition vis-à-vis purely commercial channels, which are not admitted as active members (point 50). Lastly, it finds that trade between Member States is affected in that the Eurovision System concerns cross-border acquisition and use of television rights and that this applies in particular to the joint acquisition and sharing of the rights between members from different countries and to the exchange of the related television signal between them (point 53).

30      It considers nevertheless that the Eurovision System and the underlying rules pro-
        vide for a number of benefits within the meaning of Article 85(3) which relate to
        the joint acquisition and the sharing of rights as well as to the exchange of the sig-
        nal and its transport on the common network and to the contractual access granted
        to non-members (point 58).

31      The exemption granted is subject to two conditions. First, there is the obligation
        for the EBU and its members collectively to acquire television rights to sports
        events only under agreements which themselves embody one of the following two
        possibilities: either they allow the EBU and its members to grant access to televi-
        sion rights to third parties or they allow the rights' owners to grant access to third
        parties in conformity with the access scheme or, subject to the approval of the
        EBU, on conditions more favourable to the non-member (Article 2(1)). Secondly,
        the Decision lays down an obligation for the EBU to inform the Commission of
        any amendments and additions to the rules notified, of all arbitration procedures
        concerning disputes under the access scheme and of all decisions regarding appli-
        cations for membership by third parties (Article 2(2)).

**The course of the procedure**

32      M6, RTI, Telecinco and Antena 3 brought their actions by applications lodged at
        the Court Registry on 5, 16 and 18 October 1993 respectively.

33      On 25 January 1994 the Commission raised an objection of inadmissibility in Case
        T-546/93.

34      By applications lodged at the Court Registry on 9 February, 2 March and 10
        March 1994, the EBU, Radiotelevisione Italiana SpA ('RAI') and Radiotelevisión
        Española ('RTVE') sought leave to intervene in Cases T-528/93, T-542/93 and in
        the two cases T-543/93 and T-546/93, respectively, in support of the form of order
        sought by the defendant. Leave to intervene was granted by orders of the President
        of the Second Chamber of the Court of First Instance given on 28 March, 17 May
        and 6 May 1994 respectively.

35      By application lodged at the Court Registry on 10 March 1994, Sociedade
        Independente de Comunicação SA ('SIC') sought leave to intervene in Case T-
        542/93 in support of the form of order sought by RTI. Leave to intervene was
        granted by order of the President of the Second Chamber of the Court of First In-
        stance on 13 June 1994.

36      By order of 29 September 1994, the Court of First Instance (First Chamber, Ex-
        tended Composition) decided to reserve the objection raised by the Commission in
        Case T-546/93 until consideration of the substance.

37      The written procedure in Cases T-528/93, T-542/93, T-543/93 and T-546/93 ended
        respectively on 19 August 1994 when M6' s observations were lodged on the state-
        ment in intervention of the EBU, on 2 March 1995 when the Commission' s obser-
        vations were lodged on the document submitted by the intervener SIC, on 14
        August 1994 when Telecinco' s observations were lodged on the statement in in-
        tervention of RTVE, and on 9 March 1995 when the observations of the Commis-
        sion and the intervener RTVE were lodged on the documents submitted by Antena
        3 on 13 and 20 February 1995.

38      Following the close of the written procedure in each of the four cases and upon
        hearing the report of the Judge-Rapporteur, the Court (First Chamber, Extended
        Composition) decided to open the oral procedure and asked the Commission to an-
        swer two sets of questions in writing by way of measures of organization of proce-
        dure.

39      By order of the President of the First Chamber, Extended Composition, of 11
        April 1995, the cases were joined for the purposes of the oral procedure.

## Forms of order sought

40      In Case T-528/93, M6 claims that the Court should:
        – by way of preliminary measure, order the Commission to communicate the
          Statutes of the EBU and other rules governing the Eurovision System;
        – annul the Decision of 11 June 1993;
        – order the Commission and the EBU to pay the costs.
41      The Commission claims that the Court should:
        – dismiss the application for an injunction made by M6;
        – dismiss the latter' s application;
        – order the applicant to pay the costs.
42      In Case T-542/93, RTI claims that the Court should:
        – order the EBU to produce the preliminary draft agreement concluded between
          RAI and the Italian national olympic committee on the broadcasting of sports
          events;
        – annul the Commission' s Decision of 11 June 1993;
        – order the defendant to pay the costs.
43      The Commission claims that the Court should:
        – declare RTI' s application inadmissible;
        – in the alternative, dismiss its application for measures of inquiry as inadmis-
          sible and dismiss its application as unfounded;
        – order the applicant to pay the costs;
        – order the intervener SIC to pay the costs incurred by the Commission on ac-
          count of its intervention.
44      In Case T-543/93, Telecinco claims that the Court should:
        – declare the application admissible;
        – annul the Commission' s Decision of 11 June 1993 and, in general, take all
          such measures as the Court should deem necessary in order to reinstate the
          Community competition rules on the relevant market;
        – order the defendant to pay the costs;
        – order the intervener RTVE to pay its own costs.
45      The Commission claims that the Court should:
        – dismiss Telecinco' s application;
        – order the applicant to pay the costs.
46      In its application in Case T-546/93, Antena 3 claims that the Court should:
        – annul the Decision of 11 June 1993;
        – order the defendant to pay the costs.
47      In its observations on the objection of admissibility raised by the Commission,
        Antena 3 claims that the Court should:
        – declare the Commission' s objection unfounded and reserve consideration of
          the admissibility of the application until consideration of the substance;
        – in the alternative, declare the application admissible;
        – reserve the costs.
48      The Commission claims that the Court should:
        – declare Antena 3' s application inadmissible or, in the alternative, dismiss it as
          unfounded;
        – order the applicant to pay the costs.
49      SIC, intervening in support of the form of order sought by RTI in Case T-542/93,
        claims that the Court should:

- declare the application well founded and, accordingly, annul the Commission's Decision of 11 June 1993;
- order the defendant to pay the costs, including those incurred by the intervener.

50 The EBU, intervening in support of the form of order sought by the Commission in Case T-528/93, claims that the Court should:
- dismiss M6' s application;
- order the applicant to pay the costs, including those incurred by the intervener.

51 RAI, intervening in support of the form of order sought by the Commission in Case T-542/93, claims that the Court should:
- declare RTI' s application inadmissible;
- in the alternative, dismiss the application as unfounded;
- order the applicant to pay the costs, including those incurred by the intervener.

52 RTVE, intervening in support of the form of order sought by the Commission in Cases T-543/93 and T-546/93, claims that the Court should:
- dismiss the applications brought by Telecinco and Antena 3;
- order those applicants to pay the costs, including those incurred by the intervener.

## Admissibility
## Admissibility of the application in Case T-546/93 (Antena 3)
### Summary of the arguments of the parties

53 The Commission, essentially supported by RTVE, intervening, considers that Antena 3' s application is inadmissible on the ground that the Decision is not of direct and individual concern to the applicant within the meaning of Article 173 of the Treaty, as interpreted in settled case-law since Case 25/62 Plaumann v Commission [1963] ECR 95, at 107. Apart from the fact that it belongs to a general, abstract class comprising all television companies competing with the EBU or its active members for the acquisition of television rights in respect of international sports events, Antena 3 has not shown that it has any attribute peculiar to it or that there are circumstances differentiating it from all other persons and hence distinguishing it individually just as in the case of the addressee of the Decision, within the meaning of the aforementioned case-law.

54 First, the Decision does not rule on the legality of the application of the EBU' s membership rules to specific cases by its management organs. Consequently, the fact that Antena 3' s application for membership was rejected does not put it in a situation differentiating it from all other competitors of the EBU. Secondly, the fact that Antena 3 operates the essential public television service owned by the Spanish State does not confer on it any particular attribute capable of distinguishing it individually just as in the case of the addressee of the Decision. It is not the only television channel in Spain with that attribute and other European undertakings are in the same circumstances.

55 The Commission further observes that, unlike M6, RTI and Telecinco, Antena 3 did not submit observations following the publication made in accordance with Article 19(3) of Regulation No 17 and was not present at the hearing held by the Commission on 18 and 19 December 1990. The Commission recognizes that in principle, in the context of competition law, the fact that an undertaking to which a decision was not addressed participated in the administrative procedure which led to that decision is not the only factor capable of distinguishing it individually for the purposes of Article 173 of the Treaty. It considers, however, that in this case the only factor which would have been capable of distinguishing Antena 3 individually and making its application admissible would have been its participation

pursuant to Article 19(3) of Regulation No 17 in the procedure by which the Decision was adopted. If Antena 3 had exercised the procedural rights conferred on it by that provision, it would ipso facto have been distinguished individually just as in the case of the addressee of the Decision (Case 75/84 Metro v Commission [1986] ECR 3021, paragraphs 20 to 23).

56    Antena 3 argues that, even if the Decision could not be regarded as a decision rejecting the complaints made by it to the Commission pursuant to Article 3(2)(b) of Regulation No 17 on 27 February and 2 March 1992, the Decision is nevertheless of individual concern to it within the meaning of the Plaumann case-law, regardless of the fact that it did not voluntarily participate in the procedure by which the Decision was adopted.

57    The truly relevant question is not whether or not a party participated in the administrative procedure for the adoption of a decision, but to what extent such participation helps to put third parties which were not addressees of the Decision in what the judgment in Plaumann describes as 'circumstances in which they are differentiated from all other persons and [the decision] by virtue of these factors distinguishes them individually just as in the case of the person addressed'. In that respect, in Case 26/76 Metro v Commission [1977] ECR 1875, the Court of Justice took account, in order to hold that an applicant could bring an action against a Commission decision addressed to another person, not only of the fact that the applicant had made a complaint pursuant to Article 3(2)(b) of Regulation No 17, but also, among other things, of the fact that its application to join the distribution system at issue had been rejected. In Case 75/84 Metro v Commission, the Court held that the applicant had locus standi, not only because it had submitted observations pursuant to Article 19(3) of Regulation No 17, but also and in particular because its application to join the distribution system in question had been rejected.

58    In this case, Antena 3 belongs to a narrower class than that consisting of all the other television channels in a relationship of competition with the EBU or its members. It belongs to the perfectly identifiable class of persons who, prior to the adoption of the Decision, applied to join the EBU and Eurovision, whose applications were rejected in a discriminatory manner even though they fulfilled objectively the requirements laid down for membership, and who were consequently excluded from the system in question. The very content of the Decision contradicts the Commission's argument that the actual application of the EBU's membership rules is not the subject of the Decision. It emerges from point 83 of the Decision that the application of those rules 'in an appropriate, reasonable and non-discriminatory way' is a precondition for granting and maintaining the exemption granted under Article 85(3) of the Treaty. Moreover, by virtue of its particular attribute of operator of the 'essential public television service coming under the State', which was shared in Spain with the only Spanish member of the EBU, Antena 3 is differentiated from every other television channel. In those circumstances, its application should be declared admissible.

**Findings of the Court**

59    Under Article 173 of the Treaty, any natural or legal person may institute proceedings against a decision addressed to another person only if the decision in question is of direct and individual concern to the former. Since the Decision was addressed to the EBU, it must be considered whether Antena 3 fulfils the two conditions laid down by that provision.

60    According to settled case-law, provisions of the Treaty concerning the right of interested persons to bring an action must not be interpreted restrictively, and hence,

where the Treaty makes no provision, a limitation in that respect cannot be presumed to exist. Persons other than those to whom a decision is addressed may only claim to be individually concerned if that decision affects them by reason of certain attributes which are peculiar to them or by reason of circumstances in which they are differentiated from all other persons and by virtue of these factors distinguishes them individually just as in the case of the person addressed (see Plaumann v Commission, at 107, and Joined Cases T-447/93, T-448/93 and T-449/93 AITEC and Others v Commission [1995] ECR II-1971, paragraph 34).

61    In this case, Antena 3 is an undertaking competing with the EBU and with all its members within the common market. In the narrower context of the Spanish market, it is a direct competitor of RTVE, the only active member of the EBU operating on that market. It follows that the Decision affects its competitive position in so far as it enables Antena 3 to be excluded from the benefit of the competitive advantages arising out of membership of the EBU through the exempted rules of the EBU' s Statutes. Accordingly, Antena 3 must be classed as an interested third party within the meaning of the first sentence of Article 19(3) of Regulation No 17, as the Commission itself acknowledges. In that capacity, Antena 3 was therefore entitled to be associated by the Commission with the administrative procedure for the adoption of the Decision. In that same capacity, it has to be regarded as being individually concerned by the Decision within the meaning of Article 173 of the Treaty (see, by analogy, Case C-198/91 Cook v Commission [1993] ECR I-2487, paragraphs 24, 25 and 26, and Case C-225/91 Matra v Commission [1993] ECR I-3203, paragraphs 18, 19 and 20; see also to this effect the order in Case C-295/92 Landbouwschap v Commission [1992] ECR I-5003, paragraph 12).

62    No argument to the contrary can be derived from the fact that Antena 3 did not avail itself in this case of its procedural rights under Article 19(3) of Regulation No 17 and did not make written or oral observations during the administrative procedure for the adoption of the Decision. If the capacity to bring proceedings of specified third parties who enjoy procedural rights in the administrative procedure were made subject to their actually taking part in that procedure, this would be tantamount to introducing an additional condition of admissibility in the form of a compulsory pre-litigation procedure, which is not provided for in Article 173 of the Treaty (see Case T-96/92 Comité Central d' Entreprise de la Société Générale des Grandes Sources and Others v Commission [1995] ECR II-1213, paragraphs 35 and 36, and Case T-12/93 Comité Central d' Entreprise de la Société Anonyme Vittel and Others v Commission [1995] ECR II-1247, paragraphs 46 and 47).

63    Antena 3' s capacity to bring proceedings is also confirmed by the fact that it applied to join the EBU and its application was rejected before the Decision was adopted. That specific circumstance is also capable of distinguishing Antena 3 just as in the case of the addressee of the Decision, irrespective of whether or not the Decision rules on the legality of the application by the organs of the EBU of the membership rules exempted by the Decision to actual cases (see Case 26/76 Metro v Commission, paragraph 13, and Case 75/84 Metro v Commission, paragraphs 18 to 23).

64    Antena 3 is, moreover, directly concerned by the Decision. Suffice it to say on this point that there is a direct causal link between the Decision, which requires no implementing measure, and effects on Antena 3' s competitive position.

65    It follows from the foregoing that the application brought by Antena 3 must be declared admissible.

**Admissibility of the application in Case T-542/93 (RTI)**
**Summary of the arguments of the parties**

66    The Commission, supported by RAI, intervening, questions the admissibility of
      the application on the grounds that RTI failed, first, to submit written observations
      following the publication referred to in Article 19(3) of Regulation No 17 and,
      secondly, to make any comments on the case during the hearing held by the Com-
      mission on 18 and 19 December 1990.

67    In the first place, the aim of the publication provided for in Article 19(3) is to en-
      able the Commission to have available to it before it takes a decision all the factual
      and legal information to take a fully informed decision. To allow an action to be
      brought by an interested third party who has not availed himself of his procedural
      rights under Regulation No 17 and who has therefore, on his own initiative, not
      submitted written observations during the administrative proceedings would be
      tantamount to changing the nature of the action of the Community Court. The re-
      view carried out by the Court would no longer relate to compliance with the rights
      in question, but constitute an alternative procedure to the one provided for in the
      regulation. The only eventuality in which active participation by an interested
      third party might not be regarded as a necessary condition for exercising his right
      to bring judicial proceedings is where he was not aware of the existence of the
      procedure for reasons not attributable to him.

68    Secondly, the absence of any comments from RTI during the hearing on 18 and 19
      December 1990 is tantamount to acquiescence or, at the very least, to lack of inter-
      est on its part in the procedure, which means that the Decision cannot be regarded
      as being of individual concern to it.

69    Lastly, the application should be declared inadmissible by contrary inference from
      the judgment in Case T-2/93 Air France v Commission [1994] ECR II-323, para-
      graphs 44, 45 and 46. In this case, none of the three factors are present on which
      the Court made the admissibility of an application depend, namely active partici-
      pation of the applicant in the pre-litigation procedure, assessment by the Commis-
      sion expressly taking into account the applicant' s situation and active
      involvement of the applicant in the circumstances which were the subject of that
      assessment.

70    RTI observes in the first place that it is in a relationship of direct competition on
      the Italian market with the only Italian member of the EBU, RAI, as regards both
      the acquisition of television rights and the sale of advertising time. Consequently,
      that competitive relationship is not a general one. It is specifically influenced by
      the rules on the organization and functioning of the EBU.

71    Submission of observations following notice pursuant to Article 19(3) of Regula-
      tion No 17 and active participation in a hearing could, admittedly, support the idea
      that a third party is actually concerned by a procedure and even possibly form the
      basis for a presumption that it has a legitimate interest. However, they could in no
      case be elevated to the rank of a condition necessary for establishing an interest in
      bringing proceedings. In this regard, the judgment in Case 75/84 Metro v Commis-
      sion, paragraph 21, should be interpreted as meaning that participation in the ad-
      ministrative procedure constitutes an additional factor going to establish proof of a
      legitimate interest to bring legal proceedings and not a condition sine qua non for
      the existence of such an interest.

72    Consequently, since RTI has proved that it was in a position comparable to that of
      the addressee of the Decision, having regard to its particular effects on RTI' s indi-
      vidual situation, it is unnecessary to have recourse to the presumption resulting
      from participation in the pre-litigation procedure.

73    At the very least, contrary to the Commission' s assertions, participation in an administrative procedure could take the practical form of merely attending it. In this case, that RTI did not adopt a specific position or formulate critical assessments reflected the fact that, for objective reasons not attributable to it, RTI was unable to assess with the requisite precision the implications of a possible exemption decision at the time of publication pursuant to Article 19(3) of Regulation No 17. In any event, that attitude could not be equated with acquiescence, which, apart from the fact that acquiescence could be envisaged solely in respect of definitive measures against which judicial proceedings might lie, should result from express acceptance or from acts incompatible with the intention of seeking redress.

**Findings of the Court**

74    In this case, it cannot be contested that the Decision is of individual concern to RTI within the meaning of Article 173 of the Treaty.

75    As a television channel competing with the EBU and with all its members within the common market, and the only active member of the EBU in the narrower context of the Italian market, RTI is affected in its competitive position by the Decision in so far as it enables RTI to be excluded from the benefit of the competitive advantages arising out of membership of the EBU through the exempted rules of the EBU' s Statutes. Accordingly, RTI had the status of an interested third party within the meaning of Article 19(3) of Regulation No 17 and was therefore entitled to be associated by the Commission with the administrative procedure for the adoption of the Decision, a situation which distinguishes it individually just as in the case of the addressee of the Decision (see paragraph 61, above).

76    The mere fact that RTI simply attended the hearing organized by the Commission without adopting a specific position cannot call that conclusion in question. The procedural right provided for by Article 19(3) of Regulation No 17 is not subject to any condition relating to the manner of its exercise.

77    The Decision is, moreover, of direct concern to RTI, in the same way as it is to the applicant in Case T-546/93 (see paragraph 64, above).

78    It follows from the foregoing that RTI' s application must be declared admissible.

**Substance**

79    M6 raises four pleas for annulment alleging, first, infringement of the procedural rules for the adoption of the Decision, secondly, errors and shortcomings in the statement of reasons vitiating the Decision, thirdly, erroneous application of Article 85(3) of the Treaty and, fourthly, violation of Article 10 of the European Convention for the Protection of Human Rights and Fundamental Freedoms.

80    RTI raises four pleas. The first alleges infringement of essential procedural requirements, in so far as the Commission did not comply with the procedural rule laid down by Article 19(3) of Regulation No 17. The second plea alleges misuse of powers, in so far as the Commission exercised powers conferred on it by the Treaty with a view to safeguarding competition in order to regulate the sector concerned. The third plea alleges error of fact in assessing the circumstances warranting the application of Article 85(3). The fourth plea alleges erroneous application of Article 85(3) as a result of the alleged error of fact.

81    Telecinco raises six pleas, the first alleging infringement of essential procedural requirements, the second manifest error of fact, the third infringement of the Community competition rules, in particular Articles 85(3), 86 and 90 of the Treaty, the fourth infringement of the general principle of equality of undertakings, the fifth misuse of powers, and the sixth lack of competence of the Commission to adopt the Decision.

82      Antena 3 raises four pleas. In the first place, it alleges that the Decision is vitiated
        by a manifest error in assessing the factual circumstances. Secondly, the Decision
        interprets Article 90(2) of the Treaty manifestly erroneously and applies it incor-
        rectly. Thirdly, it interprets Article 85(3) manifestly erroneously and applies it in-
        correctly. Fourthly, the Decision is vitiated by a misuse of powers.

83      The Court considers that it should consider the plea common to the four applica-
        tions alleging essentially that Article 85(3) of the Treaty was erroneously inter-
        preted and incorrectly applied. It will be appropriate to consider the two limbs of
        that plea in succession: the first relates to the discriminatory nature of the EBU' s
        membership rules, which, it is argued, should have precluded exemption under Ar-
        ticle 85(3)(a); the second to the taking into account, for the purposes of the appli-
        cation of that provision, of the concept of particular public mission which,
        according to the Decision, members of the EBU have to fulfil.

**Plea alleging infringement of Article 85(3) of the Treaty**
**1. The EBU' s membership rules having regard to Article 85(3)(a) of the Treaty**
**Summary of the arguments of the parties**

84      All the applicants essentially submit that the examination which the Commission
        undertook in order to exempt the rules laying down the conditions for becoming
        an active member of the EBU, as set out in Article 3(3) of the association' s Stat-
        utes, involves errors of fact and law and omissions.

85      In the first place, the Decision wrongly finds that those rules reflect an essential
        difference between television channels which have to fulfil a particular public
        mission, such as the members of the EBU, and the new commercial television
        channels which, in general, do not fulfil the conditions laid down by those rules.
        However, according to M6 and Antena 3, it does not appear from the EBU' s Stat-
        utes that EBU members have to fulfil a particular public mission. This is therefore
        a new condition, added unjustifiably by the Decision. Taken together with the
        rules on the admission of new members laid down by Article 3(3) of the Statutes,
        that condition reinforces the discriminatory nature of the EBU and the Eurovision
        System, inasmuch as it enables the new channels to be debarred a priori from be-
        coming active members of the EBU on account of their commercial nature, even if
        they actually fulfil the conditions laid down by that provision for becoming active
        members. Their discriminatory nature is confirmed by Article 6(1) of the Statutes
        of the EBU, which overtly recognizes that not all members of that association ful-
        fil the membership conditions. The actual example of this is Canal Plus.

86      Secondly, the applicants submit that the Commission failed to carry out an objec-
        tive examination, both of the situation of the channels which are not members of
        the EBU and of that of its members in the light of the exempted membership rules.
        If it had done so, it would have been bound to find, first, that a number of non-
        member channels have characteristics identical to those of some members of the
        EBU, yet without having been admitted to that association, and, secondly, that
        some members of the EBU do not in fact fulfil the conditions laid down by Article
        3(3) of the Statutes. In that regard, RTI and Telecinco point out that the Italian leg-
        islation and the Spanish legislation impose on private television licensees particu-
        larly strict obligations as regards diversified programming and in-house
        production. Moreover, the limits on broadcasting advertising are the same for
        members and non-members of the EBU. In their view, this is sufficient to call in
        question the Commission' s finding that there are in those areas substantial differ-
        ences between the commercial channels and the channels affiliated to the EBU.

87      According to Antena 3, the omission to carry out that examination conflicts with

point 83 of the Decision, which requires the Commission to check during the exemption period whether the EBU membership conditions are applied in an appropriate, reasonable and non-discriminatory way. By granting the exemption, the Commission must have considered, without carrying out any prior examination, that that condition was fulfilled.

88 The Commission contends in response that, in the context of the Decision, the concept of particular public mission is intended simply to encapsulate the membership rules set out in the EBU' s Statutes and that, as a result, it cannot constitute an additional condition for active membership of that association. That concept denotes the obligations or burdens to which membership of the EBU is subject by virtue of Article 3(3) of its Statutes and does not merge in any case with the concept of a public undertaking or with the concept of an undertaking entrusted with the operation of services of general economic interest appearing in Article 90(2) of the Treaty.

89 Turning to the criticism of the content and scope of its examination of the EBU' s membership rules, the Commission submits, first, that, for the purposes of the application of Article 85(3), it was not under a duty to carry out a systematic examination of the implementation of those rules by the EBU itself. Consequently, it was legitimately entitled to adopt the Decision without examining the application of Article 3(3) of the Statutes of the EBU on a case-by-case basis.

90 More specifically, the Commission argues that it was not under a duty to prove that each of the members of the EBU fulfilled the conditions laid down by the relevant rules of its Statutes. The fact that, for historical reasons, a member of the EBU – such as Canal Plus – does not fulfil all the conditions laid down by Article 3(3) of the Statutes does not invalidate its analysis generally. The Commission unreservedly admits, however, that at present there may be private television channels which also fulfil the conditions in question. Lastly, it observes that it has never ruled on the question as to whether there is discrimination in favour of certain members of the EBU which do not entirely satisfy the membership criteria currently in force.

91 On the other hand, the Commission acknowledges that it is for it to supervise that the EBU membership rules exempted by the Decision are complied with by all interested parties. In this connection, it stresses that the Decision placed the EBU under an obligation to inform the Commission of all decisions regarding applications for membership by third parties. In the event that an application for membership of the EBU were to be unjustifiably refused, this would not lead to the annulment of the Decision. In fact, the Decision would be infringed by the EBU, its addressee.

92 EBU, intervening, considers that the decisions admitting members or refusing membership applications which it adopted pursuant to the membership rules at issue were rightly examined by the Commission, not in order to check that they were justified on a case-by-case basis, but in order to limit the cooperation group to what is necessary, or even indispensable, to secure the cohesion and functioning which will enable it to achieve its objectives. The sound functioning of the exempted system and the maintenance of substantial competition depends on the common denominator of members of the EBU, namely fulfilment of a particular public mission.

## Findings of the Court

93 Two observations should be made in limine. First, the grant by the Commission of an individual exemption supposes that the agreement or the decision by an asso-

ciation of undertakings fulfils all four conditions set forth in Article 85(3) of the Treaty. It is sufficient for one of the four conditions not to be met in order for exemption to have to be refused (Joined Cases 43/82 and 63/82 VBVB and VBBB v Commission [1984] ECR 19, paragraph 61; order in Case C-137/95 P SPO and Others v Commission [1996] ECR I-0000, paragraph 34; Case T-17/93 Matra Hachette v Commission [1994] ECR II-595, paragraph 104, and Case T-29/92 SPO and Others v Commission [1995] ECR II-289, paragraphs 267 and 286). Secondly, in cases such as this where the Community institutions have a power of appraisal in order to be able to fulfil their tasks, respect of the rights guaranteed by the Community legal order in administrative procedures is of even more fundamental importance; those guarantees include, in particular, the duty of the competent institution to examine carefully and impartially all the relevant aspects in the individual case (Case C-269/90 Technische Universitaet Muenchen [1991] ECR I-5469, paragraphs 14 and 26, and Case T-44/90 La Cinq v Commission [1992] ECR II-1, paragraph 86).

94    Next, it should be observed that, according to point 50 of the Decision, 'competition vis-à-vis purely commercial channels, which are not admitted as members, is to some extent distorted' by the EBU' s membership rules, since those channels cannot participate in the rationalization and cost savings achieved by the Eurovision System. According to point 72 et seq., the restrictions of competition caused by those membership rules are nevertheless indispensable within the meaning of Article 85(3)(a) of the Treaty.

95    In order to assess the legality of the Decision in this respect, the Court must first consider, as the Commission was under a duty to do, whether those membership rules (quoted in paragraph 10, above) are objective and sufficiently determinate so as to enable them to be applied uniformly and in a non-discriminatory manner vis-à-vis all potential active members in accordance with well-established case-law (see, for example, Case 26/76 Metro v Commission, paragraph 20). The indispensable nature of the restrictions of competition resulting from those rules cannot be correctly assessed unless that prior condition is fulfilled.

96    From reading the Decision the Court finds forthwith that the Commission omitted to carry out such an examination.

97    Next, it finds that the content of the three conditions laid down by Article 3(3) of the EBU' s Statutes relating to coverage of the population, to programming and to the production of the programmes broadcast is not sufficiently determinate. Since they refer essentially to unquantified quantitative criteria, they are vague and imprecise. Consequently, in the absence of further specification, they cannot form the basis for uniform, non-discriminatory application.

98    The fact that the EBU, as it stated at the hearing, has itself found it necessary to lay down, ex post facto, a note interpreting the first membership condition ('internal guideline' fixing the obligation to cover the population at 90%) confirms this assessment.

99    In these circumstances, the Commission should have concluded that it was not even in a position to assess whether the corresponding restrictions were indispensable within the meaning of Article 85(3)(a) of the Treaty. Consequently, it was not entitled to exempt them on that ground.

100    For the same reasons, the Commission is not in a position to check during the exemption period in accordance with point 83 of the Decision 'whether the conditions for exemption continue to be fulfilled and whether in particular the membership conditions (...) are applied in an appropriate, reasonable and non-discriminatory way'. Moreover, it admitted at the hearing that it had taken no action

on the information which it had received pursuant to Article 2(2) of the Decision relating to decisions taken by the EBU regarding applications for membership by third parties.

101 Furthermore, point 83 of the Decision shows that the Commission wrongly considered that it was dispensed from having to examine the implementation by the EBU of the contested membership rules as regards applications for membership from the new television channels before granting exemption. Indeed, the obligation which it undertook in that point of the Decision to check, as a condition for maintaining the exemption at issue, whether the membership conditions are applied in an appropriate, reasonable and non-discriminatory way, should have caused it to consider itself also bound to carry out such a check before granting exemption. Such an approach was necessary especially since the status of active member of the EBU is granted 'by decision of the General Assembly, which takes its decision on the basis of a proposal from the Administrative Council' (Statutes of the EBU, Article 3(12)), which means that applicants for membership of the EBU have to depend on decisions adopted by a body representing the active members of that association (see to this effect La Cinq v Commission, paragraph 89).

102 In follows from the foregoing that, by failing to examine first whether the membership rules were objective and sufficiently determinate and capable of uniform, non-discriminatory application in order next to assess whether they were indispensable within the meaning of Article 85(3)(a) of the Treaty, the Commission based its decision on an erroneous interpretation of that provision.

103 The first limb of the plea alleging violation of Article 85(3)(a) of the Treaty must therefore be upheld.

## 2. The concept of particular public mission having regard to Article 85(3)(a) of the Treaty
### Summary of the arguments of the parties

104 The applicants argue essentially that the concept of 'particular public mission' purported to be characteristic of members of the EBU, apart from being discriminatory, has nothing to do with the analysis which the Commission is empowered to carry out under Article 85(3) of the Treaty. The Decision was based on that concept in order to favour the undertakings, most of them public, which are members of the EBU by taking them outside the scope of Article 85(1) of the Treaty in breach of the principle of equal treatment. The Commission would not have granted the exemption if it had not recognized the member companies of the EBU, and them alone, as having that common characteristic.

105 It is also claimed that, through that concept, the Commission wrongly applied Article 85(3) in this case in order to grant a derogation under Article 90(2) of the Treaty, since the members of the EBU are not undertakings entrusted with the particular mission of operating services of general economic interest within the meaning of the latter provision.

106 In this regard, Telecinco submits that an undertaking can be regarded as carrying out a particular public mission only where a public authority legally imposes upon it missions or tasks that it would not otherwise assume voluntarily. Consequently, decisions voluntarily taken or obligations voluntarily assumed by television channels with regard to their geographical coverage, programming or in-house production cannot be regarded as aspects of a particular public mission assigned to those channels. In those circumstances, examination of the national legal rules to which the various television channels which are members of the EBU are subject would suffice in order to conclude that fulfilment of a particular public mission cannot be

regarded as being a characteristic common to all the members of the EBU and to them alone.

107    In this context, it is also complained that the Decision omitted to consider the privileged public funding (public aid, subsidies, authorizations to run budget deficits, etc.) which most EBU members enjoy. According to SIC, intervening, if specific burdens are possibly imposed on the members of the EBU by the public authorities, those authorities also grant them very specific compensations. Those compensations constitute a relevant aspect of this case which the Commission should have considered carefully and impartially.

108    The Commission observes that, whilst the competition rules of the Treaty have to be applied in the same manner to public undertakings and to private undertakings, this does not mean, however, that it is not entitled to take into consideration, in an exemption procedure under Article 85(3), the particular features of the economic sector in which the − public or private − undertakings operate and the burdens and obligations incumbent upon them, without prejudice to the specific provisions of Article 90(2). More specifically, it considers itself to be entitled to take into consideration under Article 85(3), in the context of a specific sector, the position of a group of undertakings in their relations as between themselves and with third parties, without for all that infringing the principle of equal treatment. Taking the particular features of an economic sector into account in that way does not mean, however, that, in another economic sector, an agreement or a restrictive practice with the same object should necessarily be granted an exemption.

109    Moreover, the Decision does not prejudge whether the members of the EBU may or may not be considered undertakings entrusted with the operation of services of general economic interest within the meaning of Article 90(2) of the Treaty.

110    In any event, the Decision is based only in the alternative on 'public mission', an expression which, in the context in which it is used, is merely a way of summarizing the conditions laid down by Article 3(3) of the EBU Statutes for active membership of that association. In this case, the Commission confined itself to assessing the positive effects of the decisions and agreements at issue and, in the alternative, to taking account, when examining whether they were indispensable, of the obligations to which membership of the EBU is subject.

111    Lastly, the Commission says that it did not carry out a detailed analysis of the alleged system of privileged funding of EBU members in the context of Article 85(3), because the appropriate setting for such an analysis would be Articles 92 and 93 of the Treaty. In any event, the applicants have not proved that the funding system is privileged.

112    RAI, intervening, points out that, by virtue of a consistent practice of the Commission, which was approved in particular in Case 26/76 Metro v Commission (paragraph 43), the assessments which it makes for the purpose of the application of Article 85(3) also take account of the aspects of the situation falling outside the sphere of competition, in particular socio-economic aspects. It is precisely the protection of pluralism, a task deemed essential in the context of the Community' s audiovisual policy, which makes it inevitable to assess the differences between television channels pursuing a public mission and purely commercial channels. In any event, the Decision is based primarily on the strictly economic benefits arising out of the exempted decisions and agreements.

113    RTVE, intervening, submits that the concept of 'public service' cannot be equated with 'public service obligation'. The latter concept is to be found in Community terminology in the expression 'service of general economic interest' appearing in Article 90(2) of the Treaty. However, the Decision never started out from the prin-

ciple that all members of the EBU are broadcasters entrusted with a mission of general economic interest involving their being subject to obligations under their statutes by virtue of an official act. It finds that some members of the EBU are in that situation, but merely takes as a factor distinguishing members of the EBU from commercial channels the formers' self-imposed decision to offer varied programmes necessarily including the less popular sports, irrespective of the ratio between their production cost and their profitability.

**Findings of the Court**

114   In the context of the supervisory jurisdiction normally exercised by the Court, it considers that it should also consider
      –   ex abundanti cautela, given that it has just found an infringement of Article 85(3) of the Treaty warranting the annulment of the Decision
      –   whether or not the concept of particular public mission, as employed in the Decision, constitutes a relevant factor which may be taken into consideration for the purposes of the application of Article 85(3), particularly as regards the condition set out under (a). If it is not such a factor, the Court will have to conclude that the Commission committed a manifest error of law in taking account of such a factor which may have distorted its assessment of the indispensable nature of the restrictions of competition for which it granted exemption (see La Cinq v Commission, paragraph 63, and Joined Cases T-163/94 and T-165/94 NTN Corporation and Koyo Seiko v Council [1995] ECR II-1381, paragraphs 113 and 114).

115   From simply reading the Decision, it must be held that, contrary to the Commission's assertion, the concept of particular public mission which it utilized proves to be a fundamental component of the statement of reasons of the Decision. According to the statement of reasons (points 5, 11, 19, 20, 45, 60, 72 and 74), fulfilment of a particular public mission enables broadcasters to become active members of the EBU and the constraints associated with such a mission are such as to justify the EBU's having a special status with regard to the competition rules. The concept of particular public mission, as defined by the Commission, is therefore the principal factor in defining the circle of beneficiaries of the exemption at issue.

116   According to the Decision, the particular public mission is characterized in particular by the 'obligation to provide varied programming including cultural, educational, scientific and minority programmes without any commercial appeal and to cover the entire national population irrespective of the costs' (point 5). The Decision therefore essentially takes over the elements of the particular mission of operating services of general economic interest provided for in Article 90(2) of the Treaty, as it has been interpreted by the Community Court, namely and in particular, operation 'on behalf of all users throughout the territory of the Member State concerned (...) irrespective of the specific situations or the degree of economic profitability of each individual operation' (see Case C-320/91 Corbeau [1993] ECR I-2533, paragraph 15). In order to hold that the condition relating to Article 85(3)(a) of the Treaty was fulfilled, the Commission therefore took account of factors falling within the field of application of Article 90(2) of the Treaty.

117   However, inasmuch as, according to the Decision itself (point 78), Article 90(2) is not applicable, factors coming essentially within the ambit of that article cannot in this case constitute a criterion for the application of Article 85(3) in the absence of other justification.

118   Admittedly, in the context of an overall assessment, the Commission is entitled to

base itself on considerations connected with the pursuit of the public interest in order to grant exemption under Article 85(3) of the Treaty. However, in the present
case it should have shown that such considerations required exclusivity of rights to
transmit sports events, which the Decision authorizes for the benefit of members
of the EBU, and that that exclusivity was indispensable in order to allow them a
fair return on their investments (point 71).

119    However, in its answer to a written question from the Court concerning the need
for such exclusivity, the Commission, referring to point 24 of the Decision, merely
stated that below a certain 'threshold' the acquisition of television rights to sports
events at very high prices 'is no longer economically justifiable' and that the 'concept of fair returns cannot be expressed as a precise figure' but corresponds instead to an 'overall financial equilibrium on the part of the broadcasters'.

120    It appears from those statements that the Commission did not base itself upon a
minimum amount of actual economic data, which might have consisted of figures
for the investments made by the members of the EBU in their economically different national contexts and of specific calculations establishing a ratio between those
investments and the income associated with the broadcasting of sports events. In
those circumstances, the Commission's statement of reasons in this regard is not
even amenable to review by the Community Court within the limits set by the
case-law.

121    In any event, the Commission would not be justified in taking into account, for the
purposes of exemption pursuant to Article 85(3), the burdens and obligations arising for the members of the EBU as a result of a public mission, unless it also examined, carefully and impartially, as the case-law cited above (at the end of
paragraph 93) requires it to do, the other relevant aspects of the case, such as the
possible existence of a system of financial compensation for those burdens and obligations, without prejudice to Articles 92 and 93 of the Treaty. The Commission
has, however, expressly stated that it was not necessary to examine the alleged
privileged funding of members of the EBU, on the ground that the only appropriate setting for such an examination would be Articles 92 and 93 of the Treaty.

122    Furthermore, by exempting membership rules which are not amenable to uniform,
non-discriminatory application (see paragraph 97, above), the Decision does not
preclude either broadcasters entrusted with a public mission recognized by the
competent national authorities from being deprived of the advantages resulting
from membership of the EBU or other broadcasters lacking that attribute from
continuing to benefit from those advantages.

123    It follows that, by using in this case as a criterion for granting exemption from the
rules of Article 85(1) of the Treaty simply fulfilment of a particular public mission
defined essentially by reference to the mission of operating services of general
economic interest referred to in Article 90(2) of the Treaty, the Commission based
its reasoning on a misinterpretation of Article 85(3) of the Treaty. That error of
law is likely to have distorted the assessment which it made of the indispensable
nature of the restrictions of competition for which it granted exemption.

124    The second limb of the plea alleging infringement of that provision must therefore
be upheld.

125    It follows from the considerations formulated with regard to the two limbs of the
plea examined that the Commission concluded on the basis of a misinterpretation
of Article 85(3) of the Treaty that the restrictions of competition for which it
granted exemption, in particular those resulting from the EBU's membership
rules, were indispensable within the meaning of that provision.

126    Consequently, the Decision must be annulled and it is unnecessary to rule on the

other pleas raised or to carry out the measures of inquiry requested by the applicants.

## Decision on costs
### Costs

127    Under Article 87(2) of the Rules of Procedure, the unsuccessful party is to be ordered to pay the costs if they have been applied for in the successful party' s pleadings.

128    Since the Commission has been unsuccessful and the applicants and SIC, intervening in Case T-542/93, claimed that it should pay their costs, it should be ordered to bear its own costs and pay those incurred by the applicants and SIC.

129    Since M6 claimed that the EBU should be ordered to pay the costs connected with its intervention in Case T-528/93, the EBU should be ordered to bear its own costs and to pay those incurred by M6 in connection with that intervention. Since RTI did not claim that RAI should be ordered to pay the costs connected with its intervention in Case T-542/93, RAI should be ordered only to bear its own costs. In the context of its intervention in Case T-543/93, RTVE must bear only its own costs in accordance with the form of order sought by Telecinco. Lastly, since Antena 3 did not claim that RTVE should be ordered to pay the costs connected with its intervention in Case T-546/93, that intervener must also bear only its own costs.

## Operative part of the judgment

On those grounds,

The Court of First Instance (First Chamber, Extended Composition) hereby:

1.    Annuls Commission Decision 93/403/EEC of 11 June 1993 relating to a proceeding pursuant to Article 85 of the EEC Treaty (IV/32.150 – EBU/Eurovision System);

2.    Orders the Commission to bear its own costs and to pay the costs incurred by the applicants and those incurred by the intervener Sociedade Independente de Comunicação SA;

3.    Orders Reti Televisive Italiane SpA to bear the costs incurred by it in connection with the intervention of Radiotelevisione Italiana SpA; orders Gestevisión Telecinco SA and Antena 3 de Televisión to bear the costs respectively incurred by them in connection with the interventions of Radiotelevisión Española;

4.    Orders the intervener European Broadcasting Union to bear its own costs and to pay the costs incurred by the applicant Métropole Télévision SA in connection with its intervention; orders the interveners Radiotelevisione Italiana SpA and Radiotelevisión Española to bear their own costs.

---

## 2.4.14. NOTIFICATION OF A LICENSING AGREEMENT FOR THE BROADCASTING OF DUTCH FOOTBALL MATCHES (CASE NO IV/36.33 – KNVB/SPORT 7), 7 AUGUST 1996[159]

1.    On 25 June 1996, having previously informed the Commission about preparatory agreements, pursuant to Article 4 of Council Regulation No 17[160], the Koninklijke Nederlandsche Voetbal Bond (KNVB) and the consortium, Sport 7, submitted to

---

[159] OJ C 228, 7-8-1996, p. 4. (Text with EEA relevance).

[160] OJ 13, 21-2-1962, p. 204.

the Commission a rights agreement. Under the rights agreement, the KNVB grant to Sport 7 the exclusive right to exploit their recording and television rights, in particular, to a certain number of matches from the PTT Telecompetitie (premier league), the Eerste Divisie (second division) the Amstel Cup (FA Cup) and to other football matches. The licence does not include broadcasting by radio, the pay-per-view right, nor the near video-on-demand right. The duration of the agreement is seven years.

2.  Sport 7 is a commercial television broadcaster which has as its objectives the broadcasting of sports events and related programming. It is envisaged that Sport 7 will be disseminated via the cable networks in the Netherlands commencing on 18 August 1996 and that viewers will pay a nominal fee for reception of Sport 7 which will be collected en behalf of Sport 7 by cable companies. Sport 7's activities include the packaging and broadcasting of programmes. Sport 7's shareholders are as follows: KNVB, Philips Electronics N-V, Internationale Nederlanden Groep NV, Endemol, NUON, Koninklijke PTT Netherland NV, Stichting Kabelbelangen, and De Telegraaf. The KNVB is an association under Dutch law whose membership includes professional and amateur football clubs which participate in KNVB organized leagues.

3.  Under the rights agreement, Sport 7 has the right to sell its exclusive rights as sublicences to third parties in the Netherlands and abroad. Negotiations for sub-licences have been concluded with the Nederlandse Omroep Stichting ( NOS) and with Nethold's subscription service, Filmnet. Further negotiations are taking place with other broadcasters.

4.  Under the rights agreement, prior to the expiry of the period of the exploitation of the rights, Sport 7 will make its bid for renewal of the rights. Following the making, of bids by third parties, Sport 7 will be given the opportunity to make the last bid. According to the notification (but not in the rights agreement) Sport 7 will not know the content of the bids made by third parties.

5.  Upon preliminary examination, the Commission finds th at t he notified agreement could fall within the scope of Regulation No 17. The Commission envisages that it may be necessary to impose obligations upon the parties to the agreement, including a requirement for a clear licensing policy known and applicable to all interested broadcasters.

6.  The Commission invites interested third parties to submit their possible observations on the proposed operation to the Commission. In accordance with Article 20 of Regulation 17, such observations will be protected by professional secrecy.
    Observations must reach the Commission not later than 10 days following the date of this publication. Observations can be sent to the Commission by fax (No (32 2) 296 98 04) or by post, under reference IV/36.033, to the following address:

    European Commission,
    Directorate-General for Competition (DG IV),
    Directorate C,
    Office 3/103,
    Avenue de Cortenberg/Kortenberglaan 150,
    B-1040 Brussels.

    ———

**2.4.15.    EUROPEAN COURT OF JUSTICE, JUDGMENT OF THE COURT OF FIRST INSTANCE (FOURTH CHAMBER), VAN MEGEN SPORTS GROUP BV V COMMISSION OF THE EUROPEAN COMMUNITIES, CASE T-49/95, 11 DECEMBER 1996**[161]

Competition – Article 85 of the EC Treaty – Proof of the infringement – Fine – Statement of the reasons for the decision

*Content of the Court's judgment*
1.    Competition – Agreements, decisions and concerted practices – Exclusivity agreements – Exemption – Exclusive distribution contract without an export ban – Existence of a concerted practice seeking to restrict parallel imports – Exclusion from the exemption
2.    Acts of the institutions – Statement of reasons – Obligation – Scope
      (EC Treaty, Art. 190)
3.    Competition – Fines – Amount – Commission's margin of discretion
      (Council Regulation No 17, Art. 15)
4.    Competition – Fines – Assessment in relation to the undertaking's own conduct – No penalty imposed on another trader – Irrelevant
      (Council Regulation No 17, Art. 15(2))

*Summary*
5.    *The provisions of Article 85(1) of the Treaty may in no circumstances be declared inapplicable to an exclusive distribution contract which does not in itself include a prohibition of re-exports of the products which are the subject of the contract, where the contracting parties are engaged in a concerted practice aimed at restricting parallel imports intended for an unauthorized dealer.*
6.    *The purpose of the obligation to give reasons for an individual decision is to enable the Community judicature to review the legality of the decision and to provide the party concerned with an adequate indication as to whether the decision is well founded or whether it may be vitiated by some defect enabling its validity to be challenged; the scope of that obligation depends on the nature of the act in question and on the context in which it was adopted. Each part of the decision must be read in the light of the others.*
      *Although under Article 190 of the Treaty the Commission is obliged to state the reasons on which its decisions are based and to mention the factual and legal elements which provide the legal basis for the measure and the considerations which have led to its adoption, it is not required to discuss all the issues of fact and law raised by every party during the administrative procedure.*
7.    *The fines which the Commission imposes in cases of breach of Article 85 et seq. of the Treaty constitute an instrument of its competition policy. The Commission must therefore be allowed a margin of discretion when fixing the amount of fines, in order that it may direct the conduct of undertakings towards compliance with the competition rules.*
8.    *Where an undertaking has by its conduct infringed Article 85(1) of the Treaty, it may not escape a penalty on the ground that another undertaking has not been fined, when the latter's circumstances are not even the subject of proceedings before the Community judicature.*

---

[161]  ECR 1996, p. II-1799.

**Parties**
**In Case T-49/95,**
Van Megen Sports Group BV, formerly Van Megen Tennis BV, a company incorporated under Netherlands law, established in Eindhoven (Netherlands), represented by Antonius Wouters Willems, Advocaat, Eindhoven, with an address for service in Luxembourg at the Chambers of Marc Loesch, 11 Rue Goethe,
applicant, v Commission of the European Communities, represented by Francisco Enrique González Díaz and Wouter Wils, of its Legal Service, acting as Agents, with an address for service in Luxembourg at the office of Carlos Gómez de la Cruz, Wagner Centre, Kirchberg,
defendant,

APPLICATION for annulment of Commission Decision 94/987/EC of 21 December 1994 relating to a proceeding pursuant to Article 85 of the EC Treaty (IV/32.948 – IV/34.590: Tretorn and others) (OJ 1994 L 378, p. 45),

THE COURT OF FIRST INSTANCE OF THE EUROPEAN COMMUNITIES
(Fourth Chamber),
composed of: K. Lenaerts, President, P. Lindh and J.D. Cooke, Judges,
Registrar: J. Palacio Gonzáález, Administrator,
having regard to the written procedure and further to the hearing on 22 October 1996,
gives the following
Judgment

**Grounds of the judgment**

**The facts of the case**
1.   The applicant, Van Megen Sports Group BV (whose name at the material time was Van Megen Tennis BV), a company incorporated under Netherlands law and established in Eindhoven (the Netherlands), is the exclusive distributor in the Netherlands of Tretorn Sports Ltd (hereinafter 'Tretorn'), a company incorporated under Irish law. Tretorn is a subsidiary of Tretorn AB, a company incorporated under Swedish law, which manufactures tennis balls.
     The administrative procedure before the Commission
2.   On 14 May 1993 the Commission, after carrying out an investigation at Tretorn's premises in July 1989, decided to initiate proceedings for infringement of Article 85(1) of the EEC Treaty; it subsequently sent a statement of objections to the applicant.
3.   On 13 August 1993 the applicant submitted written observations to the Commission on the statement of objections; it made oral observations at the hearing which took place on 16 November 1993.

**The contested decision**
4.   Following the administrative procedure the Commission adopted Decision 94/987/ EC of 21 December 1994 relating to a proceeding pursuant to Article 85 of the EC Treaty (IV/32.948 – IV/34.590: Tretorn and others) (OJ 1994 L 378, p. 45, hereinafter 'the Decision' or 'the contested decision').
     The Decision reads as follows:
     'Article 1
     Tretorn Sport Ltd and Tretorn AB have infringed Article 85(1) of the EC Treaty by applying a general export ban to their distributors of tennis balls, implemented

through monitoring measures and sanctions, through the reporting and investigation of parallel imports of tennis balls, the marking of tennis balls, and the suspension of supplies in order to prevent parallel imports and exports of tennis balls.

Formula Sport International Ltd has infringed Article 85(1) by participating in the implementation in the United Kingdom of the export ban and suspension of supplies in order to enforce Tretorn Sport Ltd's policy of preventing parallel imports and exports of tennis balls.

Fabra SPA has infringed Article 85(1) by participating in the implementation in Italy of the export ban and suspension of supplies through the reporting and investigation of parallel imports of tennis balls, the marking of tennis balls and the suspension of supplies in order to enforce Tretorn Sport Ltd's policy of preventing parallel imports and exports of tennis balls.

Tenimport SA has infringed Article 85(1) by participating in the export ban and the suspension of supplies, through the reporting of parallel imports to Tretorn with the effect that Tretorn and its Italian exclusive distributor took measures with a view to eliminating those imports.

Zuercher AG has infringed Article 85(1) by participating in the implementation in Switzerland of the export ban and suspension of supplies, through the reporting and investigation of parallel imports of tennis balls and the marking of tennis balls in order to enforce Tretorn Sport Ltd's policy of preventing parallel imports and exports of tennis balls.

Van Megen Tennis BV has infringed Article 85(1) by participating in the implementation in the Netherlands of the reporting and investigation of parallel imports in order to enforce Tretorn Sport Ltd's policy of preventing parallel imports and exports of tennis balls.

Article 2

A fine of ECU 600 000 is hereby imposed on Tretorn Sport Limited and Tretorn AB jointly and severally and fines of ECU 10 000 each on Formula Sport International Ltd; on Fabra SPA; on Zuercher AG; and on Van Megen Tennis BV, in respect of the infringements referred to in Article 1.

[...]

Article 3

Tretorn Sport Ltd, Tretorn AB, Fabra SPA, Tenimport SA, Zuercher AG and Van Megen Tennis BV shall, in so far as they have not already done so, terminate the infringements referred to in Article 1. They shall refrain from adopting any other measures having equivalent effect.'

5.    In the Decision the Commission found that since 1987 at least Tretorn had, in concertation with its exclusive distributors, introduced an export ban in its exclusive distribution system and had set up a series of mechanisms aimed at implementing and reinforcing that ban. Those mechanisms consisted of systematic reporting and investigation of instances of parallel imports, marking of products to identify the origin of parallel imports, and suspension of supplies to specific markets to prevent actual or potential parallel imports (points 13 and 14 of the Decision).

6.    With respect to the reporting and investigating of parallel imports, the Commission found that Tretorn itself or Tretorn's distribution network had reported parallel imports wherever there was evidence of such imports (point 22 of the Decision). A fax from Tretorn to Tretorn AB of 16 July 1987 showed that in July 1987 the applicant had informed Tretorn that Tretorn tennis balls were 'again turning up' in the Netherlands. Tretorn asked the applicant to forward the code number to it to allow it to find out 'which country [had] shipped' (point 24). In an

internal Tretorn memorandum of 20 June 1988 it was stated that the applicant had found parallel imports from two sources and hoped to obtain the date codes (point 25).

7.     With respect to the marking of products, the Commission found that the evidence in its possession indicated that Tretorn marked its tennis balls with date codes which would allow the origin of parallel imports to be traced. Numerous references to those codes and their use could be found in Tretorn's correspondence (point 35 of the Decision).

8.     During the procedure before the Commission, the applicant explained that its object in reporting date codes to Tretorn was not to prevent parallel imports but to check whether Tretorn was not supplying directly in its territory, and stated that it itself supplied companies which it knew to be parallel exporters. The Commission considered that 'even if the interpretation given by Van Megen were correct, the fact remain[ed] that the information [had been] given in the context of a ban on parallel exports of which Van Megen was well aware and it [had] actively participated in identifying the source of the parallel imports with a view to suppressing it [...]' (point 70 of the Decision).

9.     As to the imposition of fines on Tretorn's distributors, the Commission stated (point 78 of the Decision):
'In determining whether to impose fines and at what level the Commission has taken into account the fact that some of Tretorn's distributors have taken a particularly active part in preventing parallel imports; but also that such participation was in other cases of a limited nature and has to be set in the context of Tretorn's general policy of prohibiting any export of its products. Moreover, the part played by Tenimport was of a less substantial nature and it is therefore justified in refraining from imposing a fine on that undertaking.'

10.    Finally, according to point 77 of the contested decision, 'during the course of the procedure, Tenimport [...] confirm[ed] the existence of an unwritten but actual prohibition on exports. It considered that the recent cancellation of its distribution agreement with Tretorn could only be understood as meaning that Tenimport had not complied with that prohibition.'

## Procedure

11.    By application lodged with the Registry of the Court of First Instance on 21 February 1995, the applicant brought the present action.

12.    Upon hearing the report of the Judge-Rapporteur, the Court of First Instance (Fourth Chamber) decided to open the oral procedure without any preparatory measures of inquiry. The Court did, however, by letter of 4 October 1996, request the Commission to produce certain documents. The Commission did so, by letter lodged at the Registry on 9 October 1996.

13.    The parties presented oral argument and their replies to the Court's questions at the hearing on 22 October 1996.

## Forms of order sought by the parties

14.    The applicant, Van Megen Sports Group BV, claims that the Court should annul the Commission's decision.

15.    The defendant Commission contends that the Court should:
       –  dismiss the application;
       –  order the applicant to pay the costs.

## The claim for annulment of the contested decision

16.    Article 1 of the Decision charges the applicant with having participated in the implementation in the Netherlands in the reporting and investigation of parallel

imports of tennis balls in order to enforce Tretorn's policy of preventing parallel imports and exports. The pleas in law put forward by the applicant, which essentially seek annulment of Article 1 of the Decision and consequently also of Article 2, in so far as those articles concern the applicant, should be examined with respect to that charge.

Arguments of the parties

17.    The applicant submits in effect that in so far as it finds that the applicant participated in the reporting and investigating of parallel imports of tennis balls, the Decision is not based on sufficient evidence and lacks an adequate statement of reasons.

18.    It observes that since about 1985 it has had a monopoly of sales in the Netherlands of tennis balls manufactured in Ireland by Tretorn, but there is no written agreement confirming that exclusive right. Tretorn never imposed a ban on exports. Since the start of commercial relations between them, the applicant reported to Tretorn on two occasions only, in 1987 and 1988, that Tretorn tennis balls not supplied by the applicant were being offered for sale to its customers. It submits that it made those reports, by telephone, for two reasons. First, it wished to check whether the balls had not been supplied directly by Tretorn to customers in the Netherlands, since at that stage of their commercial relations it was afraid that Tretorn might not respect its obligation not itself to supply the applicant's customers in the applicant's territory. That obligation was consistent with Commission Regulation (EEC) No 1983/83 of 22 June 1983 on the application of Article 85(3) of the Treaty to categories of exclusive distribution agreements (OJ 1983 L 173, p. 1). Secondly, given that the applicant's customers could buy Tretorn tennis balls at prices considerably lower than those at which it could offer them, it had tried, by making those reports, to strengthen its position in negotiations with Tretorn, so as to obtain a better price.

19.    As to the fax of 16 July 1987, the applicant had been informed by telephone by some of its customers that Scapino BV (hereinafter 'Scapino'), a chain of shoe and clothes shops based in Assen (Netherlands), was selling tennis balls to consumers at a lower price than that applied by the applicant. Its customers had asked how that was possible and whether it was invoicing different prices to Scapino and to them. It had therefore contacted Tretorn to find out whether Tretorn did sometimes supply the Netherlands; this Tretorn denied. The fact that that does not appear in the fax is of no importance, since the fax was neither sent by nor addressed to the applicant, so that it could not have been aware of its content at the time. The wording of the fax should therefore not be given the importance attached to it by the Commission. The applicant states that it was asked to forward the date codes but was unable to find them. In any case, those codes would not have made it possible to determine from which country the tennis balls had been sent, since neither the manufacturer nor the importers have a tracking system. The code numbers on the packaging of the balls gave only the date of manufacture or shipment. Whether the balls were supplied to Germany, France or another country, all the balls manufactured during a given week were packaged in packaging bearing the same code. The codes were not mentioned on the invoices or packaging forms. Even if it could be ascertained that tennis balls came from a particular country, that would not make it possible to find out who had shipped the consignment in question. In the present case, it was easy to find out, for example, that the tennis balls purchased by Scapino came from France, because in France the packaging has to have text in French, something which the applicant pointed out in its telephone conversation with Tretorn. In any event, it was a matter of indifference to the ap-

plicant who had supplied Scapino with the balls. What mattered was to be able to pay for the balls the same price as the other distributors. The applicant found that Tretorn sold its tennis balls in France at a lower price than in the Netherlands. It discussed that with Tretorn and was eventually able to obtain better terms.

20.   The same happened in mid-1988. The applicant points out that the memorandum of 20 June 1988, like the fax of 16 July 1987, was not sent by it and that it was not aware of its content at the time.

21.   The applicant then states that it was not informed of any agreements or concerted practices between Tretorn and/or other distributors and that it never acted in concert with the latter with respect to stopping supplies to parallel importers and/or exporters. On the contrary, it supplied tennis balls to Scapino, knowing that Scapino was selling Tretorn tennis balls in the Netherlands obtained by parallel imports from France. Scapino was the only undertaking which engaged in the parallel importation of Tretorn balls into the Netherlands. The applicant did nothing to obstruct those activities. In this respect, it cites a letter from Scapino as evidence. Scapino's statements in that letter show that the applicant's communications to Tretorn did not constitute acts incompatible with Community competition law.

22.   In this connection, the two reports referred to in paragraph 18 above, the only evidence relied on by the Commission, do not show or do not sufficiently show that the applicant actively participated in obstructing parallel imports of Tretorn tennis balls within the Community. Since the applicant was not aware of the other agreements, practices or actions of Tretorn and/or the other distributors, those agreements, practices or actions cannot be imputed to it, and consequently cannot be used in argument against it. In the applicant's opinion, it is striking that in point 46 of the Decision the Commission mentions an internal Tretorn memorandum dated 23 August 1988 recommending stopping supplies to the United States market because tennis balls shipped there were turning up in the Netherlands as parallel imports, without asserting or establishing that that information came from the applicant.

23.   Moreover, the applicant observes that according to point 70 of the Decision it was well aware that the information given to Tretorn was given in the context of a ban on parallel imports, so that it 'actively participated in identifying the source of the parallel imports with a view to suppressing it'. It submits that that reasoning is wrong and does not follow from the facts. It asserts that two telephone reports in 10 years, in which it attempted to find out whether Tretorn was exporting directly to the Netherlands and to obtain better prices, cannot be regarded as 'active participation'. In the absence of other arguments by the Commission, the statement of reasons must consequently be considered inadequate.

24.   The Commission contends to begin with that the evidence it has to show that Tretorn infringed Article 85(1) of the Treaty is particularly solid and justifies the conclusion that Tretorn's conduct was not unilateral but was part of an agreement or concerted practice between it and its distributors. The Commission refers to points 16 to 50 of the Decision, and in particular point 15, where it quotes a passage from a fax of 6 June 1989 from Tretorn AB to Zuercher AG, which says that '[...] our policy is to protect each and every distributor from grey market imports. We have also [...] implemented many controls, designed new packages, refused several orders, etc., in order to keep this grey market business at a minimum.'

25.   It then asserts that it has sufficient evidence of the infringement committed by the applicant. The two pieces of evidence summarized in points 24 and 25 of the Decision, namely the fax of 16 July 1987 and the internal memorandum of 20 June

1988, fully warrant the conclusion that the applicant actively participated in the Netherlands in reporting and investigating parallel imports in order to implement Tretorn's policy.

26. On this point, the fax of 16 July 1987 shows that it was the applicant who telephoned Tretorn to inform it that Tretorn tennis balls not coming from the applicant had 'again' turned up on the Netherlands market. Tretorn thereupon asked the applicant to inform it of the code number, to enable it to find out 'which country [had] shipped' those products. The remainder of the text of the fax shows that Tretorn already had suspicions ('while I of course suspect our friends') as to the origin of the goods, namely the United Kingdom ('if it is the UK'), and that the request to the applicant to forward the code number was intended to obtain proof of those suspicions ('we must wait for proof').

27. The Commission considers that the reasons given by the applicant to explain its reports to Tretorn are unconvincing. First, the word 'again' leaves some doubt as to the applicant's assertion that its report was an isolated occurrence. Secondly, the fax makes no mention whatever of the applicant's being suspicious that Tretorn was itself supplying the Netherlands. Nor does it refer to attempts by the applicant to obtain a better price. It refers solely to an instance of parallel imports reported by the applicant and looked into by Tretorn and the applicant jointly. In particular, the sentence mentioning that the applicant had been asked to forward the code number in order to determine the country of origin leaves no doubt as to the applicant's actual participation in reporting and investigating cases of parallel imports.

28. The same conclusion follows from the internal memorandum of 20 June 1988. That memorandum shows that the applicant had reported that there were parallel imports from two sources and was evidently in the course of investigating the code numbers in order to identify those sources. The final sentence of the memorandum shows that the applicant hoped to find out the date codes within a few days.

29. The Commission rejects the applicant's argument that the fax and the internal memorandum have no evidential value. It observes that these are internal Tretorn documents, written by someone who was well-informed, in which certain practices of the applicant are reported, outside the context of any defence or justification before the Commission or the Court of First Instance. The fact that the documents come from a well-informed person who had no reason to falsify his description of the applicant's practices only confirms their probative force.

30. As to the applicant's argument relating to point 46 of the Decision (see paragraph 22 above), the Commission explains that, with regard to the applicant, it did not rely on the fact mentioned in point 46, but only on the two items of evidence referred to in points 24 and 25 of the Decision. It was thus unnecessary to refer to the applicant by name in point 46. Nevertheless, Tretorn could not have been informed except by the applicant that tennis balls supplied to the United States were appearing on the Netherlands market.

31. The Commission submits that the letter from Scapino does not contradict its evidence in any way. Rather, it follows from that letter that the applicant played a double game. The Commission notes that the letter was written recently in the context of the applicant's defence to the Commission's findings. There is no proof that it really was Scapino which benefited from parallel imports in 1987 and 1988, nor that it was the only parallel importer. Nor has it been established that Scapino was aware of the general context of the applicant's practices, in particular its contacts with Tretorn.

32. The Commission disputes the applicant's assertion that it is not possible to deter-

mine from the date codes from which country the tennis balls have been shipped. There is no doubt that the Tretorn manager knew what information could be deduced from the codes. The fact that he asked the applicant for the date codes in order to find out from them the country of origin of the tennis balls shows that the codes could indeed be used for that purpose.

33.     The Commission submits, finally, that contrary to the applicant's assertion, the Decision contains a sufficient statement of reasons. It refers on this point to its observations (see above).

**Findings of the Court**

34.     The applicant does not deny that Tretorn operated a system of exclusive distribution coupled with a prohibition of exports and with mechanisms intended to ensure that that prohibition was applied as effectively as possible. It acknowledges that it has been Tretorn's exclusive distributor in the Netherlands since 1985. It denies, on the other hand, that Tretorn imposed an export ban on it and that it participated in the reporting and investigating of parallel imports. Until the Commission initiated the infringement procedure, it had not even been aware of the ban on parallel exports.

35.     According to the case-law of the Court of Justice and the Court of First Instance, the provisions of Article 85(1) of the Treaty may not be declared inapplicable to an exclusive distribution contract which does not in itself include a prohibition of re-exports of the products which are the subject of the contract, where the contracting parties are engaged in a concerted practice aimed at restricting parallel imports intended for an unauthorized dealer (see Case 86/82 Hasselblad v Commission [1984] ECR 883 and Case T-43/92 Dunlop Slazenger v Commission [1994] ECR II-441, paragraph 88).

36.     In the present case, the Commission had relied on the following two documents, described in points 24 and 25 of the Decision, as proof that the applicant had taken part in the Netherlands in the reporting and investigating of parallel imports:
  –     a fax of 16 July 1987 from Mr M. of Tretorn to Mr A. of Tretorn AB:
        'I just had a phone call from Will Van Megen to advise that XL boxes of 4 again turning up in a major shoe chain in Holland.
        I have asked Will to forward the Code No. to [Mr O.] so that he can advise which country has shipped.
        While I of course suspect our friends, we must wait for the proof.
        If it is the UK, then obviously the shipment has been made to Holland in the past few weeks.'.
  –     Tretorn internal memorandum of 20 June 1988 from Mr M. to Mr O.:
        'Please ring Will Van Megen. He has parallel from 2 different sources. 1 Box of 4, made in Ireland, no date code yet. 2 Box of 4, USTA approved, no date code yet. He hopes to have date codes in a few days.'

37.     Those two documents from Tretorn have probative force. As the Commission rightly observed, they were written by a well-informed third party who had no reason to give false information. Moreover, they were written outside the context of any procedure for defence or justification before the Commission or this Court.

38.     Those two pieces of evidence clearly establish that the applicant participated in the reporting and investigating of parallel imports of tennis balls, for the purposes of applying Tretorn's policy. It is clear from the fax of 16 July 1987 that the applicant informed Tretorn of the existence of parallel imports of Tretorn tennis balls in the Netherlands, that it was not the first time that it gave Tretorn such information, and that it had been asked to provide the date codes which might enable Tretorn to

determine the country from which the balls came. As to the internal memorandum of 20 June 1988, that document shows that the applicant again informed Tretorn of the existence of parallel imports of Tretorn tennis balls in the Netherlands, that it had identified two different sources of those imports, and that it was investigating to obtain the date codes.

39. With respect to the Tretorn internal memorandum of 23 August 1988, mentioned at point 46 of the Decision, recommending the stopping of deliveries to the American market because tennis balls delivered there were reappearing in the Netherlands via parallel imports, it is sufficient to observe that the Commission did not rely on that document with regard to the applicant. Point 46 of the Decision comes under the heading 'Suspension of supplies to prevent parallel imports', under which the Commission mentions the measures adopted by Tretorn to deal with those imports. That document is thus relied on as against Tretorn, and not the applicant, in whose case the Commission rightly considered that it had sufficient evidence.

40. As to the date codes, the fax of 16 July 1987, the internal memorandum of 20 June 1988 and the other evidence relied on by the Commission in the Decision (see points 36 to 38 and 40) show beyond doubt that Tretorn could identify the origin of parallel imports from the date codes. That can be seen in particular from a fax of 17 April 1987 from Tretorn to Formula Sport International Ltd (see point 37), in which Mr M. of Tretorn stated: 'The date codes are all from the shipment to Formula.' It can also be seen from a fax of 15 May 1987, also from Tretorn to Formula Sport International Ltd, in which Mr M. states: 'We are sure of our facts/ date codes and the balls shipped to Formula ended up in Switzerland. [...] Formula is guilty so let's not have any more discussion.'

41. As for the letter from Scapino, that document does not in any way contradict the Commission's evidence. The applicant could not itself prevent the parallel imports by Scapino. Had it wished to prevent them, it would have had to contact Tretorn, so that that company might take the necessary measures for that purpose. Moreover, it was naturally in the applicant's interest to sell as many Tretorn tennis balls as possible, to Scapino amongst others. It should also be noted that Tretorn's policy was to prohibit exports. There is nothing before the Court to suggest that Scapino would have exported the Tretorn tennis balls supplied by the applicant. The applicant therefore did not infringe Tretorn's policy by selling the balls to Scapino, which, like the applicant, is a Netherlands undertaking. Tretorn thus had no interest either in asking the applicant to refuse to supply Scapino, even assuming that it had been informed of those sales.

42. The reasons given by the applicant to explain why it made reports to Tretorn cannot be accepted. If the applicant had wished to make those reports solely in order to find out whether Tretorn was making direct supplies to customers in the Netherlands and to strengthen its position in negotiations with Tretorn and thereby obtain a better price, it would not have needed to try to obtain the date codes of the tennis balls imported in parallel. It is thus apparent that it was in fact aware of Tretorn's policy of prohibiting parallel imports. It follows that the Commission was correct in finding, in point 70 of the Decision, that even if the interpretation given by the applicant was correct, 'the fact remains that the information was given in the context of a ban on parallel exports of which Van Megen was well aware and it actively participated in identifying the source of the parallel imports'.

43. The applicant cannot, finally, argue that its two telephone conversations with Tretorn cannot be described as active participation, since it was the applicant which took the initiative in contacting Tretorn, not vice versa. Moreover, it can be

seen from paragraph 38 above that the applicant made inquiries to obtain the date codes of the parallel imports. It follows that the applicant actively participated in Tretorn's policy.

44. It follows from the foregoing that the pleas in law alleging that the Commission did not adduce sufficient evidence and did not give an adequate statement of reasons for its decision must be rejected.

## The claim for annulment of the fine
### Arguments of the parties

45. The applicant submits, first, that the reasons stated for the amount of the fine, set out in point 78 of the Decision (see paragraph 9 above), are insufficient. It observes that the Commission does not indicate the degree to which each distributor participated in Tretorn's policy or the evidence it relied on to establish that participation. It points out that the same fine was imposed on four of the five distributors even though, in its opinion, the documents in the case made it clear enough that the 'contribution', whether conscious or not, of the various distributors varied greatly.

46. It states, secondly, that during the administrative procedure it argued that, assuming that it had infringed Article 85(1) of the Treaty, which it denied, a penalty should not be imposed on it, since its two telephone reports were isolated occurrences of secondary importance. The Commission failed to take account of that argument, although it expressly refrained from imposing a fine on Tenimport. The applicant had, however, put forward a comparable defence and its situation had been almost the same as Tenimport's. That the applicant never maintained that there was a ban on exports was attributable to the fact that such a ban had never been imposed on it.

47. The applicant does not accept the Commission's argument that it had doubts as to whether an infringement of the Treaty was imputable to Tenimport. The applicant considers that the remission of a fine for an infringement regarded as proven cannot depend on the extent of the doubts subsisting in the Commission's assessment.

48. The Commission considers that it gave sufficient reasons for the amount of the fine imposed on the applicant. As to the part played by the applicant in the infringement, that was determined in points 24, 25, 70 and 76 of the Decision. As regards the level of each fine imposed in relation to the others, the Commission took into account, in fixing them, as indicated in point 78 of the Decision, the degree to which each distributor had participated in the infringement. It also considered the part played by the various distributors 'in the context of Tretorn's general policy of prohibiting any export of its products'. Those considerations led it to impose a substantial fine, as a proportion of its turnover, on Tretorn alone. By contrast, it imposed on the distributors only a flat-rate fine of a small amount. The underlying idea of that decision was that Tretorn had been principally responsible, while the distributors' responsibility consisted merely in cooperating in the functioning of the system operated by Tretorn. The Commission states that since what was involved was cooperation in the functioning of one and the same system and the fines envisaged were moreover to be flat-rate fines of small amounts, it did not think it necessary to draw a distinction between the distributors.

49. However, an exception was made for the Belgian distributor, Tenimport, because the Commission considered that it did not have such strong evidence of its participation in implementing Tretorn's policy. The only document it had was a fax of 27 February 1989 from Tenimport to Tretorn. In that fax Tenimport complained of the 'incredible' price of the Tretorn tennis balls which transited through Belgium

to Italy and asked how such prices could be applied. The Commission concluded that the explanation given by Tenimport, namely that it was doing no more than negotiating prices with Tretorn, did not seem altogether improbable. On the other hand, the fax of 16 July 1987 and the internal memorandum of 20 June 1988 concerning the applicant made no mention of prices, but only of the appearance on the Netherlands market of tennis balls which did not come from the applicant and of cooperation between Tretorn and the applicant to find the source of those parallel imports. Those documents were thus quite different in content from the fax from Tenimport.

50.   The Commission rejects the applicant's argument that it put forward the same defence as Tenimport. As point 77 of the Decision shows, Tenimport confirmed at the hearing the existence of the infringement committed by Tretorn. Tenimport also cooperated with the Commission's investigations after that. Furthermore, it can be seen from point 77 that Tenimport had been penalized by Tretorn, which terminated the distribution agreement because Tenimport had refused to cooperate in the context of its system of export bans. In any event, it is not for the applicant to defend Tenimport, which has not lodged a complaint against the contested decision.

**Findings of the Court**

51.   It is settled case-law that the purpose of the obligation to give reasons for an individual decision is to enable the Community judicature to review the legality of the decision and to provide the party concerned with an adequate indication as to whether the decision is well founded or whether it may be vitiated by some defect enabling its validity to be challenged; the scope of that obligation depends on the nature of the act in question and on the context in which it was adopted (see, inter alia, Case T-46/92 Scottish Football Association v Commission [1994] ECR II-1039, paragraph 19). Moreover, since a decision constitutes a single whole, each of its parts must be read in the light of the others (see Case T-150/89 Martinelli v Commission [1995] ECR II-1165, paragraph 66).

52.   In the present case, the Commission clearly indicated in the Decision the degree to which each distributor participated in Tretorn's policy and the evidence on which it relied to establish that participation. As regards, more specifically, the applicant, the degree of its participation may be seen in particular from points 24, 25, 57, 70 and 76 to 78 and from the sixth paragraph of Article 1 of the Decision. The analysis as set out in paragraphs 36 to 44 above shows that the Commission provided adequate substantiation and reasons for its decision, in that it found that the applicant had participated in the reporting and investigating of parallel imports of Tretorn tennis balls in order to enforce Tretorn's policy.

53.   As to the amount of the fine, it should be pointed out that, according to the case-law, since fines constitute an instrument of the Commission's competition policy, that institution must be allowed a margin of discretion when fixing their amount, in order that it may direct the conduct of undertakings towards compliance with the competition rules (see Martinelli, cited above, paragraph 59).

54.   As may be seen from the first paragraph of Article 2 of the Decision, the Commission imposed flat-rate fines of small amounts on Tretorn's distributors. It should also be noted that the distributors all cooperated in the functioning of the same system. In such a situation the Commission is not obliged to distinguish between the various distributors or state reasons peculiar to each distributor for the amount of the fine imposed. Consequently, the Commission did not exceed the limits of its margin of discretion.

55. With reference to the applicant's argument that a penalty should not have been imposed on it because the two telephone reports were isolated occurrences of secondary importance, it follows from paragraph 43 above that the applicant's participation in Tretorn's policy had to be regarded as active. The Commission was therefore correct in taking no account of that argument. On this point, it should also be noted that, according to settled case-law, although under Article 190 of the Treaty the Commission is obliged to state the reasons on which its decisions are based and to mention the factual and legal elements which provide the legal basis for the measure and the considerations which have led to its adoption, it is not required to discuss all the issues of fact and law raised by every party during the administrative procedure (see, inter alia, Case T-149/89 Sotralentz v Commission [1995] ECR II-1127, paragraph 73).

56. Finally, the applicant's reliance on the fact that no fine was imposed on Tenimport can be of no assistance to its case. An applicant may not argue from such a circumstance in order himself to escape a penalty imposed for breach of Article 85 of the Treaty when the other undertaking's circumstances are not even the subject of proceedings before the Community judicature (see Joined Cases C-89/85, C-104/85, C-114/85, C-116/85, C-117/85 and C-125/85 to C-129/85 Ahlstroem and Others v Commission [1993] ECR I-1307, paragraph 197, and Dunlop Slazenger, cited above, paragraph 176).

57. The claim for annulment of the fine must consequently be rejected.

58. It follows from all the foregoing considerations that the application must be dismissed in its entirety.

**Decision on costs**
**Costs**
59. Under Article 87(2) of the Rules of Procedure, the unsuccessful party is to be ordered to pay the costs if they have been applied for in the successful party's pleadings. Since the applicant has been unsuccessful and the Commission has asked for costs, the applicant must be ordered to pay the costs.

**Operative part of the judgment**
On those grounds,
The Court of First Instance
(Fourth Chamber)
hereby:
1. Dismisses the application;
2. Orders the applicant to pay the costs.

———

**\* 2.4.16. COMMUNICATION DE LA COMMISSION ADOPTÉE SUR COMMUNICATION DE M.OREJA – DROITS EXCLUSIFS POUR LA TÉLÉDIFFUSION DES GRANDS ÉVÉNEMENTS SPORTIFS; H. DROIT COMMUNAUTAIRE; 5. DROIT D'ACCÈS DU PUBLIC A L'INFORMATION / ARTICLE 10 DE LA CONVENTION EUROPÉENNE DE SAUVEGARDE DES DROITS DE L'HOMME(CEDH); 6. POINT DE VUE DE LA COMMISSION, 4 FEBRUARY 1997[162]**

———

[162] SEC(1997) 174/9.

**2.4.17.    RESOLUTION OF THE EUROPEAN PARLIAMENT ON UEFA AND THE COCA-COLA CUP, 2 FEBRUARY 1998**[163]

*The European Parliament,*

A.    whereas the European Union must recognize the specific nature of sport and the autonomy of the sports movement,

B.    whereas in its resolution of 13 June 1997 on the role of the European Union in the field of sport ((OJ C 200, 30-6-1997, p. 252.)) Parliament insisted that 'solutions must be found [...] which, in practice, do not dissuade [...] medium-sized and small professional [...] clubs, from making significant efforts to [...] fulfil their educational and social role ",

C.    whereas there is currently a conflict between UEFA and the Premier League on the number of clubs allowed to participate in the first division championship,

D.    whereas the English Football League, which represents all the professional clubs, is in legal terms completely independent of the Premier League which is composed of only the professional clubs in the first division ('Premiership "),

E.    whereas the Coca-Cola Cup is organised by the Football League and not by the Premier League,

F.    whereas the Football League Cup winners used to qualify for the UEFA Cup (C3 Cup),

G.    whereas the UEFA decision to change the rules by not permitting the Football League Cup winners to qualify for the UEFA Cup is arbitrary, could be considered as related to the abovementioned conflict and could have considerable negative economic and social consequences for a great many English professional clubs, especially from the lower divisions,

H.    whereas this decision could also be considered as discriminatory, since winners of similar league cups organised in other European countries will continue to play in the UEFA Cup,

I.    whereas this decision is an infringement of Article 86 of the EC Treaty concerning abuse of a dominant position,

J.    whereas the economic activity generated by professional sport cannot be exempt from the provisions of Community law, and whereas this action will almost certainly have enormous financial consequences,

The European Parliament,

1.    Urges the Commission to deal with this problem as a matter of priority;

2.    Asks UEFA to reverse its decision in the light of the considerations above;

3.    Requests UEFA thereby to ensure that all the football leagues in the Member States are treated equally;

4.    Instructs its President to forward this resolution to the Commission, to the governments and parliaments of the Member States, UEFA and the English Football and Premier Leagues.

———

**\* 2.4.18.    ANSWER ON BEHALF OF THE COMMISSION TO WRITTEN QUESTION E-3980/97 BY KONSTADINOS KLIRONOMOS (PSE), 6 MARCH 1998**[164] **\***

Subject: Takeovers of football clubs

———

---

[163]  OJ C 34, 2-2-1998, p. 99.
[164]  Question of 14-1-1998; OJ C 310, 9-10-1998, p. 6.

**\* 2.4.19.  ANSWER ON BEHALF OF THE COMMISSION TO WRITTEN QUESTION E-466/98 BY ALLAN MACARTNEY (ARE), 25 MARCH 1998**[165] **\***

Subject: Competition rules and television rights for the European Football Championships in 2000

———

**\* 2.4.20.  THE COMMISSION CONDITIONALLY APPROVES SPONSORSHIP CONTRACTS BETWEEN THE DANISH TENNIS FEDERATION AND ITS TENNIS BALL SUPPLIERS, 15 APRIL 1998**[166]

———

**\* 2.4.21.  ANSWER ON BEHALF OF THE COMMISSION TO WRITTEN QUESTION E-1059/98 BY JOHN IVERSEN (PSE), 7 MAY 1998**[167] **\***

Subject: Competition rules in sport

———

**\* 2.4.22.  ANSWER ON BEHALF OF THE COMMISSION TO WRITTEN QUESTION E-1718/03 BY ANTOINE-FRANÇOIS BERNARDINI (PSE), 9 JULY 1998**[168] **\***

Subject: Compatibility of the players' agent licensing system

———

**\* 2.4.23.  ANSWER ON BEHALF OF THE COMMISSION TO WRITTEN QUESTION E-1815/98 BY JESSICA LARIVE (ELDR), 17 JULY 1998**[169] **\***

Subject: Inadequate European Commission reaction to World Cup 98 ticket sales

———

**\* 2.4.24.  ANSWER ON BEHALF OF THE COMMISSION TO WRITTEN QUESTION P-2361/98 BY ANGELA BILLINGHAM (PSE), 3 SEPTEMBER 1998**[170] **\***

Subject: UEFA rule on common ownership

———

**\* 2.4.25.  ANSWER ON BEHALF OF THE COMMISSION TO WRITTEN QUESTION E-2175/98 BY NIKITAS KAKLAMANIS (UPE), 15 SEPTEMBER 1998**[171] **\***

Subject: Exclusion of AEK football team from UEFA Cup

———

---

[165] Question of 27-2-1998; OJ C 304, 2-10-1998, p. 111.
[166] IP/98/355.
[167] Question of 6-4-1998; OJ C 402, 22-12-1998, p. 65.
[168] Question of 29-5-1998; OJ C 50, 22-2-1999, p. 77.
[169] Question of 11-6-1998; OJ C 13, 18-1-1999, p. 92.
[170] Question of 15-7-1998; OJ C 50, 22-2-1999, p. 143.
[171] Question of 10-7-1998; OJ C 31, 5-2-1999, p. 130.

**\* 2.4.26.  ANSWER ON BEHALF OF THE COMMISSION TO WRITTEN QUESTION P-3103/98 BY GRAHAM WATSON (ELDR), 28 OCTOBER 1998**[172] **\***

Subject: Purchase of Manchester United Football Club

———

**\* 2.4.27.  ANSWER ON BEHALF OF THE COMMISSION TO WRITTEN QUESTION E-3056/98 BY JOHN CUSHNAHAN (PPE), 29 OCTOBER 1998**[173] **\***

Subject: Breakaway super soccer league

———

**\* 2.4.28.  ANSWER ON BEHALF OF THE COMMISSION TO WRITTEN QUESTION E-3054/98 BY JOHN CUSHNAHAN (PPE), 4 NOVEMBER 1998**[174] **\***

Subject: Manchester United

———

**\* 2.4.29.  ANSWER ON BEHALF OF THE COMMISSION TO WRITTEN QUESTION E-2790/98 BY GRAHAM WATSON (ELDR), 16 NOVEMBER 1998**[175] **\***

Subject: European-wide leagues

———

**\* 2.4.30.  ANSWER ON BEHALF OF THE COMMISSION TO WRITTEN QUESTION E-3097/98 BY UMBERTO BOSSI (NI), 19 NOVEMBER 1998**[176] **\***

Subject: The monopoly enjoyed in Italy by CONI – football clubs and free competition

———

**\* 2.4.31.  REPLY ON BEHALF OF THE COUNCIL TO WRITTEN QUESTION E-3096/98 BY UMBERTO BOSSI (NI), 7 DECEMBER 1998**[177] **\***

Subject: The monopoly enjoyed in Italy by CONI – football clubs and free competition

———

[172] Question of 8-10-1998; OJ C 118, 29-4-1999, p. 180.
[173] Question of 8-10-1998; OJ C 135, 14-5-1999, p. 162.
[174] Question of 8-10-1998; OJ C 135, 14-5-1999, p. 161.
[175] Question of 17-9-1998; OJ C 135, 14-5-1999, p. 116.
[176] Question of 16-10-1998; OJ C 142, 21-5-1999, p. 83.
[177] Question of 19-10-1998; OJ C 118, 29-4-1999, p. 179-180.

**\* 2.4.32.   ANSWER ON BEHALF OF THE COMMISSION TO WRITTEN QUESTION E-3055/98 BY JOHN CUSHNAHAN (PPE), 11 DECEMBER 1998[178] \***

Subject: Manchester United

———

**2.4.33.   CASE NO IV/37.214 – DFB – CENTRAL MARKETING OF TV AND RADIO BROADCASTING RIGHTS FOR CERTAIN FOOTBALL COMPETITIONS IN GERMANY, 9 JANUARY 1999[179]**

1.      On 25 August 1998, the Commission received a notification from Deutscher Fußball-Bund (DFB) pursuant to Article 4 of Council Regulation No 17[180] by which DFB asks for a negative clearance or an exemption. The notification concerns the collective selling (or central marketing) of the television and radio broadcasting rights for the 'Bundesspiele' with participation of 'Lizenzligamannschaften'.

**Football competitions covered by DFB's central marketing**

2.      The term 'Bundesspiele' refers mainly to the matches of the first national football league ('Bundesliga'),the second national league ('2. Bundesliga') and of the national cup competition ('DFB-Vereinspokal').

'Lizenzligamannschaften' are professional football teams that participate in the Bundesliga or the 2. Bundesliga.

DFB is the German national football association and a member of UEFA, the 'Union des associations européennes de football'. The ordinary members of DFB are the five regional and 21 provincial (Länder)football associations; the 36 clubs participating in the two abovementioned professional leagues are extra-ordinary members of DFB. DFB is the only notifying party as it is of the opinion that the collective selling is based on decisions by an association of undertakings in the sense of Article 85(1) of the EC Treaty.

3.      The central marketing of the broadcasting rights is based on Article 3 of the DFB-Lizenzspielerstatut (LSpSt), which sets the rules for professional football in Germany. The LSpSt is adopted by the 'DFB-Beirat', an organ consisting mainly of the members of the Board (Vorstand) of DFB and the chairpersons of the member associations and several special DFB committees.

According to Article 3 of the LSpSt, it is the DFB which has the right to conclude contracts about the broadcasting on TV or radio (or other media) of Bundesspiele and of Internationale Wettbewerbsspiele' (i.e. matches of the German football clubs in international/UEFA competitions). The 'Liga-Ausschuß', an organ of the DFB with the task of representing the interests of the professional clubs, negotiates the contracts and the 'Vorstand' (Board) of DFB adopts them afterwards. DFB receives the revenues generated by these contracts and distributes them among the Lizenzligamannschaften.

**Football competitions not covered by DFB's central marketing**

4.      'Internationale Wettbewerbsspiele' are not concerned by the notification as the

---

[178]   Question of 8-10-1998; OJ C 142, 21-5-1999, p. 77.

[179]   OJ C 6, 9-1-1999, p. 10. (Text with EEA relevance).

[180]   OJ 13, 21-12-1962, p. 204/62.

rights for these matches are no longer sold collectively by DFB. Following a decision by the Bundesgerichtshof (BGH) on 11 December 1997, home matches of German clubs in the UEFA Cup and in the UEFA Cupwinners' Cup are commercialised individually by the clubs. The rights to the matches in the UEFA Champions League (except the qualification-round) are sold collectively by UEFA.

**Contracts concluded by DFB as part of central marketing**
5.      The three most important contracts that DFB has concluded concern:
–   the broadcasting rights for the matches of the Bundesliga and 2. Bundesliga on free TV in Germany and abroad (mostly deferred broadcasting of highlights and a limited amount of live coverage in Germany) (contractor: ISPR GmbH),
–   the pay-TV rights for Germany of a limited number of matches per round in the Bundesliga and the 2. Bundesliga for live broadcasting (contractor: UFA Sports GmbH),
–   the rights for the matches of the cup competitions (DFB-Vereinspokal and DFB-Ligapokal) and of the German representative teams (contractor: SportA GmbH).
The duration of these contracts is typicaliv two years with a possibility of extension.

**Arguments put forward by DFB in favour of the central marketing systems**
6.      DFB claims to be at least co-owner of ihe broadcasting rights together with the clubs, because it founded the competitions and delivers a wide range of organisational services for them. It argues that such a system of collective setting does not fall, therefore, within the scope of Article 85(1) of the EC Treaty.
In the opinion of DFB, the system of collective selling of the broadcasting rights and the redistribution of the generated funds aim at balancing advantages of financially stronger clubs in favour of weaker clubs (solidarity principle) in the interest of preserving competitive professional football in Germany.
All the funds generated by the collective selling of the TV rights for the two Bundesligen are distributed between the clubs participating in the Bundesliga and 2. Bundesliga (in a relation of 65:35 in 1996/97 and 68:32 in 1997/98), mostly in equal shares per club, with only a small amount depending on the performance of a club.
7.      In order to justify an exemption, DFB argues that central marketing rationalises distribution of the broadcasting rights; it serves solidarity between financially stronger and weaker clubs by distributing the revenues equally; and it supports amateur and youth football. In its opinion, collective selling is indispensable.
DFB objects to the proposal of a solidarity fund because of the conflict of interests between the different clubs and also because of tax reasons.
DFB disputes the existence of any effect on trade between Member States caused by its collective selling system because the situation is that the sports rights agencies are the ones that acquire the rights from DFB and later sell them to broadcasters in Germany and abroad.
According to DFB, the broadcasters or sports rights agencies are interested in purchasing the rights for the whole championship, and the prices are calculated accordingly.
In the view of DFB, the consumers, i.e. primarily the broadcasters hut also the viewers, are interested in the protection of a functioning championship competition and are allowed a fair share of the benefit resulting from collective selling. Furthermore, collective selling does not eliminate competition.

**Relevant market to be considered according to DFB**

8.   The notifying party defines the relevant product market as the one for the acquisition of broadcasting rights for sports events and the whole EEA as the relevant geographic market.

9.   On preliminary examination, the Commission finds that the notified rules could fall within the scope of Regulation No 17.

10.   The Commission invites interested third parties to submit their possible observations on the notified rules. In accordance with Article 20 of Regulation No 17, such observations will be protected by professional secrecy.

Observations must reach the Commission not later than 30 days following the date of this publication. Observations can be sent by fax (No (32-2) 296 98 04) or by post under reference IV/37.214 DFB to the following address:

European Commission,
Directorate-General for Competition (DG IV),
Directorate C,
Unit C-2: Media and music publishing,
Office C-150, 3/162,
Avenue de Cortenberg/Kortenberglaan 150,
B-1040 Brussels.

———

**2.4.34.   NOTE D'INFORMATION A LA COMMISSION – ORIENTATIONS PRELIMINAIRES SUR L'APPLICATION DES REGLES DE CONCURRENCE AU SECTEUR DU SPORT, 15 FEBRUARY 1999**

———

**2.4.35.   COMMISSION DECISION RELATING TO A PROCEEDING PURSUANT TO ARTICLE 85 OF THE EC TREATY (CASE NO IV/ 36.237 – TPS) (NOTIFIED UNDER DOCUMENT NUMBER C(1999) 387), 3 MARCH 1999[181]**

*The Commission of the European Communities,*

–   Having regard to the Treaty establishing the European Community,

–   Having regard to Council Regulation No 17 of 6 February 1962, First Regulation implementing Articles 85 and 86 of the Treaty[182], as last amended by the Act of Accession of Austria, Finland and Sweden, and in particular Articles 2, 6 and 8 thereof,

–   Having regard to the application for negative clearance and the notification for exemption submitted, pursuant to Articles 2 and 4 of Regulation No 17, on 18 October 1996, by Télévision Française 1, France Télévision Entreprises, France Télécom, Compagnie Luxembourgeoise de Télédiffusion, Métropole Télévision and Lyonnaise des Eaux, concerning the agreements creating the company Télévision par satellite,

–   Having regard to the summaries of the application and notification published[183] pursuant to Article 19(3) of Regulation No 17,

---

[181]   OJ L 90, 2-4-1999, pp. 6-22.
[182]   OJ 13, 21-2-1962, p. 204.
[183]   OJ C 65, 28-2-1998, p. 5.

–       After consulting the Advisory Committee on restrictive practices and dominant
        positions,
Whereas:

## I. THE FACTS
### A. Introduction

(1)     The parties first contacted the Commission in connection with this operation in the
        summer of 1996, with a view to notification under Council Regulation (EEC) No
        4064/89 of 21 December 1989 on the control of concentrations between undertak-
        ings[184], as last amended by Regulation (EC) No 1310/97[185]. However, having been
        informed by the Commission that Télévision par satellite (hereinafter referred to
        as 'TPS') was not a joint venture in the sense of an undertaking under the joint
        control of its members, on 18 October 1996 they notified the operation to the
        Commission and requested negative clearance and/or exemption pursuant to Regu-
        lation No 17.

(2)     The agreements creating the company were notified to the Commission by the
        abovementioned parties, namely Télévision Française 1 (hereinafter referred to as
        'TF1'), France Télévision Enterprises, France Télécom, Métropole Télévision
        (hereinafter referred to as 'M6'), Compagnie Luxembourgeoise de Télédiffusion
        (hereinafter referred to as 'CLT') and Lyonnaise des Eaux, now called Suez
        Lyonnaise des Eaux. TPS was set up in the form of a partnership (société en nom
        collectif) under French law with a view to launching and managing a digital plat-
        form for the distribution in France of satellite pay-TV programmes and services.
        The stated object of the company also permits its activities to be extended to other
        French-speaking areas in Europe.

(3)     On 13 March 1998 the parties informed the Commission of a change in the share-
        holder structure that had taken place after notification of the agreements. CLT had
        withdrawn from TPS and sold its shares to M6 Numérique and Lyonnaise Satel-
        lite, which now each hold 25% of the capital of TPS.
        At the time of notification, the ownership structure of TPS was as follows:
        [...]
        Following the withdrawal of Société pour le Numérique Francophone, the stakes
        held in TPS are distributed as follows:
        [...]
        TF1 Développement is wholly owned by TF1. The capital of France Télévision
        Entreprises is divided between France Télécom (66%) and France Télévision
        (34%), itself owned in equal proportions by the public television companies
        France 2 and France 3. M6 Numérique and Lyonnaise Satellite are wholly owned
        subsidiaries of M6 and Suez Lyonnaise des Eaux respectively.

(4)     On 27 July 1998 the parties also notified the Commission of an amendment which
        deleted the clause whereby the cable operators holding shares in TPS undertook to
        coordinate their programmes and services with those supplied by the digital plat-
        form. The scope of the non-competition clause was, at the Commission's request,
        spelt out by two amendments dated 17 September 1998, and a provision on pos-
        sible exclusive broadcasting of the 'Arte' and 'La Cinquième' channels was de-
        leted by another amendment dated 17 September 1998.

---

[184] OJ L 395, 30-12-1989, p. 1; corrected and republished in OJ L 257, 21-9-1990, p. 13.
[185] OJ L 180, 9-7-1997, p. 1.

## B. The parties
### 1. TF1

(5)     Télévision Française 1 (TF1) operates the first French television channel broadcast in clear via the terrestrial network. It has a broadcasting licence which was renewed in 1996. TF1 is also distributed by cable in the French-speaking parts of Belgium and in Luxembourg.

(6)     With a holding of 39%, the Bouygues group, which operates mainly in the construction and property development sectors, has, de facto, control of TF1.

(7)     TF1's main activity is the unencrypted broadcasting of general-interest television programmes. TF1 is also active via its subsidiaries in the advertising, production and services sectors, audiovisual and film production, the marketing of audiovisual rights, the broadcasting of two special-interest channels, and the production and distribution of derived products and services.

(8)     In 1996, the Bouygues group generated a worldwide turnover of ECU 11180,5 million, while that of TF1 was ECU 1475,8 million.

### 2. France Télévision

(9)     France Télévision is made up of France 2 and France 3, two limited companies wholly owned by the French State which operate the second and third French television channels broadcast by terrestrial transmission. In so doing, they are required to comply with the conditions and public-service obligations laid down by the law defining their activities. France 2 and France 3 programmes are broadcast in clear and are financed by television-licence revenues and advertising.

(10)    France 2 and France 3 broadcast general-interest programmes nationally. France 3 also broadcasts regional and local programmes. Both channels are also distributed by cable in Belgium and Luxembourg.

(11)    In addition to their general-interest broadcasting activities, the two channels are also involved, via various shareholdings and subsidiaries, in the following audiovisual activities: advertising production, audiovisual and film production, marketing of audiovisual rights, broadcasting of special-interest channels (cultural and educational), and the production and distribution of derived products and services.

(12)    In 1996, France 2 generated turnover of ECU 760,3 million, while that of France 3 was ECU 784,7 million.

### 3. France Télécom

(13)    France Télécom is the long-standing telecommunications operator in France. It was partially privatised in 1997, with 25% of its capital now being held by members of the public, institutional investors and its staff. France Télécom operates voice-telephony (fixed and mobile) services, public networks, terminals (telephones and fax machines, telephone exchanges), cable networks and telematic and multimedia services.

(14)    It owns the 'Viaccess' conditional access technology used by TPS and its rival platform AB-Sat.

(15)    In the cable distribution sector, France Télécom Cable, a subsidiary of France Télécom, operates a network of more than 1,2 million possible connections and has achieved a market penetration[186] of 23%. In terms of the number of subscribers, France Télécom Cable has a market share of around 29,5%.

(16)    In 1996, the France Télécom group generated a turnover of ECU 23049,13 million.

---

[186] The ratio of actual subscribers to the number of possible connections.

## 4. M6

(17) Métropole Télévision (M6) is a company governed by French law which received a broadcasting licence on 26 February 1987 to operate a national terrestrial channel. Its main shareholders are CLT and Suez Lyonnaise des Eaux. Its licence was renewed in 1996 with effect from 1 March 1997.

(18) M6 is also active in various branches of the audiovisual industry, including advertising production, cinema and audiovisual production, the marketing of rights to audiovisual programmes and films, the operation of special-interest channels, record, magazine and video production, and teleshopping.

(19) In 1996, M6 generated a turnover of ECU 315,93 million.

## 5. Suez Lyonnaise des Eaux

(20) As of October 1997, the capital of Suez Lyonnaise des Eaux was divided between the following shareholders: Electrafina (GBL) (10%), Crédit Agricole (7,6%), AXA-UAP (6,2%), CDC (4,5%), Saint-Gobain (4%), Cogema (3%) and staff (1,1%), the rest (63,6%) being in the hands of the general public.

(21) Suez Lyonnaise des Eaux is developing its activities in the areas of water distribution, cleansing, energy, public works, infrastructure concessions and financial services. It is also present in the communications sector, principally via M6, of which it holds 34,45% of the capital, and via its subsidiary Lyonnaise Communications, which operates a cable network in France with more than 1,5 million possible connections and has achieved a market penetration of 18,8%. In terms of the number of subscribers, Lyonnaise Communications has a share of around 26% of the French market.

(22) In 1996, its consolidated pro forma turnover was ECU 26394,52 million (the merger having taken place on 19 June 1997).

## C. The relevant markets
## 1. Product markets

(23) The notified operation chiefly affects the pay-TV market, that being the market on which TPS operates. As producer of some of the special-interest channels it distributes, TPS is also active on the market in the acquisition of broadcasting rights and the distribution and operation of special-interest channels.

(24) The market in technical services for pay-TV also has to be taken into account since the object of TPS includes the development, marketing, purchase and sale of all conditional access systems and the operation and marketing of subscriber management systems.

## 1.1. The pay-TV market

(25) As may be seen from Commission Decision 94/922/EC[187], and also from the Commission Decision of 7 October 1996 (Bertelsmann/CLT)[188] and from the Commission Decison 1999/153/EC (Bertelsmann/Kirch/Premiere)[189], pay-TV constitutes a product market that is separate from free-access television, whether the latter is financed wholly or partly by advertising revenues. Whereas in the case of free television there is a trade relationship between the broadcaster and the advertiser, in the case of pay-TV there is a trade relationship between the broadcaster and the

---

[187] OJ L 364, 31-12-1994, p. 1, at recitals 32 and 33; Case No 1V/M.779 – Bertelsmann/CLT of 7-10-1996; Case No IV/M.993 – Bertelsmann/Kirch/Premiere of 27-5-1998.

[188] OJ C 364, 4-12-1996, p. 3.

[189] OJ L 53, 27-2-1999, p. 1.

viewer as subscriber. The conditions of competition are accordingly different for the two types of television. Whereas in the case of free TV the audience share and the advertising rates are the key parameters, in the case of pay-TV the key factors are the shaping of programmes to meet the interests of the target groups, with the emphasis on the first transmission of feature films and sports coverage, and the level of subscriptions charged. Other features of pay-TV are the need for viewers to have a decryption module (decoder), the fact that it is marketed through a network of distributors or using a sales team, and the need for a subscriber management system and (in the case of the operator) for conditional access technology.

(26) The relevant product market of pay-TV cannot be subdivided into analog and digital pay-TV, as the Commission has already pointed out[190]. Digital pay-TV is only a further development of analog pay-TV. Although the two technologies currently coexist on satellite and cable in France, analog pay-TV is to be expected to be completely superseded by digital pay-TV in future. The case of CanalSatellite Analogique is instructive here: some of its subscribers having migrated to digital pay-TV, CanalSatellite decided to withdraw its analog 'bouquet' in October 1998, a little more than two and a half years after launching its digital bouquet. In any event, whether it uses analog or digital technology, pay-TV displays the same features: need for a conditional access system, same method of marketing, subscriber management, choice of programmes[191], etc.

(27) Pay-TV services can be delivered in France via terrestrial transmission, by satellite or by cable.

(28) Traditionally, the pay-TV services of Canal+ have been transmitted via terrestrial transmission. Today, the terrestrial Canal+ service still has by far the largest number of subscribers (around 3,5 million in September 1998), although the channel can also be received by satellite and cable. As in the case of satellite and cable transmission, terrestrial pay-TV offers programmes mainly based on feature films and sport, is marketed via a distribution network, uses a terminal associated with a decoding system and requires a subscriber management system.

(29) As far as cable is concerned, subscriptions to special-interest channels, whether analog or digital, are, as in the case of satellite transmission, marketed in the form of packages: a basic subscription and a set of options. The cable operators market most of the channels offered by the satellite platforms and offer a mix of the channels broadcast by CanalSatellite, TPS[192], AB-Sat and Canal+, which makes their content similar to what is offered by the satellite operators. It should also be pointed out that the satellite platforms each apply the same pricing policy throughout France and do not charge different rates according to whether or not they are operating in a cabled area.

(30) The penetration of cable is low in France: market penetration in the pay-TV sector, excluding the 'antenna service', which relays only the general-interest channels that are broadcast unencrypted, is a little more than 22% (number of actual subscribers/number of possible connections) and the overall level of penetration (number of cable subscribers/number of households with television) around 10%.

---

[190] OJ L 53, 2-2-1999, p. 1.

[191] A comparison of prices charged in 1996 shows that the subscription for Canal+ broadcast via analog terrestrial transmission (FRF 175) was similar to that charged for CanalSatellite Numérique (FRF 98 for the basic subscription plus FRF 55 for the cinema option plus FRF 30 for the music option).

[192] However, the NumériCâble network controlled by Canal+ does not carry the TPS cinema channels.

Furthermore, in cabled areas, where consumers have a choice between cable and satellite – in urban and suburban areas – satellite television is generally subject to a number of constraints (rules governing apartment buildings, municipal by-laws) relating to the installation of satellite dishes which are favourable to cable. These considerations do not, however, provide sufficient justification for treating cable and satellite as separate markets. The fact that the penetration of satellite in cabled areas is low or very low tends, on the contrary, to prove that, where cable pay-TV exists, it is a substitute for satellite pay-TV, with consumers preferring the convenience of cable connection to the formalities usually involved in the installation of a satellite dish. It can therefore be concluded that the French pay-TV market currently comprises the three methods of transmission: terrestrial, satellite and cable.

(31)     According to data provided by the French Conseil supérieur de l'audiovisuel, the three satellite bouquets (CanalSatellite, TPS and AB-Sat) accounted in June 1998 for 15% of subscribers in France, while 28% were served by cable and 57% by Canal+ broadcast via the terrestrial network.

### 1.2. The market in technical services for pay-TV

(32)     The operation of pay-TV requires a special technical infrastructure for encrypting broadcasts and enabling authorised viewers to decode them. To that end, a terminal has to be installed in each subscriber's home. In the case of digital pay-TV, the terminal usually combines functions for demodulating the satellite or cable signal, decompressing the digital signal, demultiplexing the different channels, unscrambling the encrypted signal and managing conditional access, together with a bank card interface.

(33)     The pay-TV operator must have a conditional access system allowing the transmission of encrypted data containing information on programmes subscribed to and on the subscribers entitled to receive those programmes, together with the television signals themselves. The system usually also comprises a smart card which is issued to the subscriber and is able to decipher the authorisation data and transfer them to the terminal.

### 1.3. The market in the acquisition of broadcasting rights, in particular for films and sporting events

(34)     It is universally acknowledged that films and sporting events are the two most popular pay-TV products. It is necessary to have the corresponding rights in order to put together programmes that are sufficiently attractive to persuade potential subscribers to pay for receiving television services. Films and sport are therefore pay-TV's loss leaders. There is no need for the purposes of this case to determine whether separate markets exist for film broadcasting rights and rights to broadcast sporting events.

(35)     As far as films are concerned, the rights acquired fall into the following categories: unencrypted TV broadcasting, pay-TV, pay-per-view, near video-on-demand and video-on-demand[193]. In accordance with the sequence of film distribution in France, rights to unencrypted terrestrial transmission may be exploited at the earli-

---

[193] Pay-TV refers to the encrypted transmission, by whatever means, of television programmes or channels which can be accessed on payment of a subscription.
Pay-per-view offers access to individual encrypted programmes, for which a charge is made per viewing, at a time scheduled by the operator. Near video-on-demand is a pay-per-view service accessible on several channels (multiplex); video-on-demand offers the consumer access to a programme, for which a charge is made per viewing, at a time chosen by the consumer.

est 36 months after a film's release for cinema showing, while pay-TV rights are accessible after 12 months, with shorter periods applying to co-productions. Pay-TV rights for satellite or cable transmission can be divided into 'first-window' and 'second-window' rights. This trend was launched by the major Hollywood studios but has not yet taken root among French producers/distributors. It should also be noted that no distinction is made according to whether the rights are to be exploited through analog or digital transmission.

(36)     Rights to sporting events are also broken down into rights for broadcasting in clear, pay-TV and pay-per-view.

**1.4. The market in the distribution and operation of special-interest channels**

(37)     Special-interest channels are essential for putting together pay-TV services. Although certain French or foreign general-interest channels are also distributed by cable or satellite, the fact remains that they do not constitute a category of programmes that are specific to pay-TV.

(38)     This market is enjoying rapid growth owing to the introduction of digital technology which, thanks to compression, enables a much higher number of channels and services to be distributed than analog technology.

(39)     Initially limited to a few channels produced for cable in France, this market now comprises more than 140 French, European and non-European special-interest channels transmitted by satellite and cable.

**2. Relevant geographic markets**

(40)     TPS currently markets its services only in France but may in future extend its coverage to other French-speaking countries in Europe, as provided for in the notified agreements. However, it is not necessary for the purposes of this case to determine whether the geographic market should be defined as the French market or the French-speaking European market.

(41)     The same applies to the market in technical services for pay-TV, which the Commission has already recognised in Decision 94/922/EC and in its decision regarding Bertelsmann/Kirch/Premiere[194] as being closely linked to the supply of pay-TV programmes.

(42)     As far as the market in the distribution of special-interest channels is concerned, although foreign channels are distributed in France, the fact remains that their inclusion in the satellite bouquets and in the range of programmes distributed via cable is negotiated and organised at most at national level.

(43)     As regards the geographic market for the acquisition of broadcasting rights, although rights can be sourced from anywhere in the world and some operators acquire rights for more than one territory at a time, it has to be borne in mind that broadcasting rights are still acquired mainly on a national basis or, at the most, by language area[195]. Thus, in Commission Decision 89/536/EEC the Commission noted that film broadcasting rights are usually granted for a given language version and broadcasting area. It is not necessary for the purposes of this case to determine whether the market for the acquisition of broadcasting rights should be defined as the French market or the French-speaking European market.

---

[194] OJ L 364, 31-12-1994, p. 1, at recitals 32 and 33; Case No IV/M.779 – Bertelsmann/CLT of 7 October 1996; Case No IV/M.993 – Bertelsmann/Kirch/Premiere of 27-5-1998. OJ L 53, 27-2-1999, p. 1.

[195] OJ L 284, 3-10-1989, p. 36.

## 3. Structure of the markets
### 3.1. The pay-TV market

(44)   The longest-established competitor on the French pay-TV market is Canal+.
       Launched in 1984, this pay-TV service is accessible chiefly via analog terrestrial
       transmission, but is also offered in a digital multiplexed version (Canal+ bleu,
       jaune and vert) broadcast by satellite and is transmitted in both analog and digital
       form on cable. Canal+ currently has a total of 4,3 million subscribers. Its program-
       ming, as a premium channel, focuses on exclusive first transmissions of feature
       films and top-quality sporting events. Canal+ enjoys a strong brand image in
       France and possesses highly developed know-how in the management of pay-TV
       services thanks to its long experience in the field.

(45)   The Canal+ group is also active in cable distribution since it controls the
       NumériCâble cable network, which has a share of around 21% of the cable market
       in France.

(46)   In 1992 CanalSatellite, a 70% controlled company by Canal+, launched a bouquet
       of analog pay-TV channels broadcast by satellite. A CanalSatellite Numérique ser-
       vice was launched in 1996. By the end of 1997, CanalSatellite Analogique still
       had around 100000 subscribers whereas CanalSatellite Numérique had already re-
       cruited 650000. CanalSatellite Analogique decided to cease operations in October
       1998. CanalSatellite Numérique had 900000 subscribers by the end of June 1998
       and expected to reach the figure of one million subscribers in the autumn of the
       same year.

(47)   In terms of numbers of subscribers, the Canal+ group, including the premium
       channel Canal+, CanalSatellite and the NumériCâble network, accounted for ap-
       proximately 70% of the French pay-TV market by 30 June 1998.

(48)   The Canal+ group is also active on several pay-TV markets outside France: Spain,
       Italy, the Nordic countries, French-speaking Belgium, Flanders, the Netherlands,
       Poland and Africa. The group has launched or is preparing to launch digital plat-
       forms alongside the premium channels in most of these countries. The group had a
       total of 10,3 million subscribers in Europe by 30 June 1998[196].

(49)   In April 1996, the AB group, whose main activity is programme production and
       the distribution of television rights, launched another bouquet on the French mar-
       ket composed of some 20 satellite pay-TV channels produced by the group. As at
       30 June 1998, this bouquet had 100000 subscribers. In March 1997 AB-Sat con-
       cluded a Simulcrypt agreement with CanalSatellite enabling subscribers to the two
       bouquets to receive both operators' programmes on a single digital terminal and
       with a single card. AB-Sat and CanalSatellite have also signed an agreement
       whereby some of AB-Sat's channels, and in particular the sports channel, are
       transmitted by CanalSatellite. An agreement was also concluded in July 1998 with
       TPS for the distribution of one of AB-Sat's channels as part of TPS's basic bou-
       quet and five more as an option.

(50)   TPS, for its part, had 457000 subscribers by 31 July 1998 and estimated that it
       would have 600000 by the end of the year.

(51)   On the pay-TV market, the largest cable operators, taking part in the 'Plan-Câble'
       launched by the French Government in 1982, are France Télécom, Lyonnaise
       Câble, both of which have stakes in TPS, and NumériCable, which is controlled by
       Canal+. As at 31 January 1998, France Télécom had 442000 subscribers (6,22%
       of the pay-TV market), Lyonnaise Communications had 439212 subscribers

---

[196] Satellifax, 24-7-1998.

(6,18% of that market) and Numéri-Câble 357210 (5,1%)[197]. Those three operators together hold around 80% of the cable market. The remaining 20% is shared between a number of smaller cable operators.

### 3.2. The market in technical services for pay-TV

(52)    The notified agreements allow TPS to develop and market conditional access systems and subscriber management systems. However, for its operations TPS has for the time being opted for the Viaccess conditional access system, in respect of which it has a licensing agreement with France Télécom, and it looks after its own subscriber management.

(53)    France Télécom, as the designer and owner of the Viaccess conditional access system (a digital version of the Eurocrypt system), is active on this market, where it competes with the Canal+ group, which owns the Mediaguard conditional access system and has developed the Mediasat digital terminal.

(54)    The Viaccess system is also used by AB-Sat, which has concluded a licensing agreement with France Télécom, and by the cable operator Lyonnaise Communications.

### 3.3. The market in the acquisition of broadcasting rights, in particular for films and sporting events

(55)    The TPS Agreement provides for the creation of movie channels, a pay-per-view service and companies to produce them[198]. Three movie channels and a children's channel, which broadcasts almost exclusively cartoon films, are currently produced by TPS Cinéma, a wholly owned subsidiary of TPS. Pay-per-view services (films and sporting events) are produced by the company Multivision, which is 78% controlled by TPS, alongside France Télécom and Suez Lyonnaise des Eaux.

(56)    Via its two subsidiaries which produce channels and services, TPS is therefore active on the market in the acquisition of television rights, particularly for films and sporting events.

(57)    As far as film rights are concerned, TPS has signed agreements with five large American studios for the acquisition of pay-TV and pay-per-view rights; however, in three of these cases the rights acquired are for 'second window' pay-TV (after broadcasting on Canal+). TPS also has pay-per-view rights to the Roland-Garros tennis tournament, to the European Champions League football matches and to some of the Coupe de France football championship matches.

(58)    Its main competitors in this field, and in particular in the purchase of film rights, are Canal+ and the special-interest channels in which Canal+ has a stake, notably via the Multithématiques company. The Canal+ group enjoys a particularly strong position on this market. As a premium channel that has built its reputation chiefly on first transmissions of quality feature films, Canal+ has signed contracts with five of the seven major Hollywood studios and with Polygram in order to obtain exclusive rights over the first transmission of their films on pay-TV. Canal+ is said to hold rights equivalent to around 87% of Hollywood's output, expressed in

---

[197] Avica publication, January 1998. These figures include only subscribers who have an individual contract with the cable operator and exclude subscribers to the 'antenna service'. The latter relays the channels broadcast in clear and does not constitute a pay-TV service proper since there is no direct relationship between the subscriber and the cable operator (the price of the service is billed along with the building maintenance charges).

[198] Traditionally, a company producing special-interest channels acquires broadcasting rights, devises programmes and manages and markets the channels it produces.

terms of box-office receipts[199]. It should also be mentioned that the price paid by Canal+, on the basis of its 4,3 million subscribers, constitutes the floor price in negotiations between distributors and purchasers of pay-TV rights.

(59)     The Canal+ group also owns the UGC DA/Canal+ DA film catalogue, which comprises some 4800 films as well as fiction films, cartoon films and documentaries.

(60)     As far as rights to sporting events are concerned, the Canal+ group has exclusive encrypted transmission and pay-per-view rights to the French football championship and to football championships in certain other European countries. It also has exclusive encrypted transmission and pay-per-view rights to Formula 1 racing. The exclusive rights to other sporting events held by Canal+ are sometimes limited (rights shared with unencrypted channels).

(61)     Although the AB group operates mainly in the programme production and rights distribution sector and owns a catalogue comprising more than 30000 hours of programmes[200], AB-Sat also uses the broadcasting rights acquisition market in order to purchase rights to fiction films and sporting events.

(62)     The general-interest channels are also active in this market, both for the purposes of acquiring rights to sporting events for their broadcasts in clear and with a view to acquiring rights to existing films or to new films, in particular through co-production in the case of French cinema films. The general-interest channels are above all very active in commissioning audiovisual works (TV series, television films, cartoon films and TV programmes)[201].

(63)     Of a total of 163 new French films produced in 1997, 73 were co-produced by the general-interest channels; Canal+ purchased in advance the pay-TV rights to 134 of those films[202] and TPS the rights to four[203].

(64)     As producers of special-interest channels, the members of TPS are also present on this market.

### 3.4. The market in the distribution and operation of special-interest channels

(65)     The market in the distribution and operation of special-interest channels is enjoying extremely rapid growth, particularly with the appearance of digital platforms.

(66)     Stakes in the long-standing channels, referred to as the 'cable channels', were held by the leading pay-TV operators: Canal+ and the three largest cable operators, namely Lyonnaise des Eaux, now Suez Lyonnaise des Eaux, Générale des Eaux and, to a lesser extent, France Télécom. Most of the unencrypted TV operators also had stakes in special-interest channels, although their holdings were more modest.

(67)     Since the emergence of satellite platforms, the companies involved in pay-TV all have holdings in special-interest channels operating on the market.

(68)     The stakes held in special-interest channels are fairly evenly distributed among the main players on this market. Canal+ is a major player, however, since it has hold-

---

[199] Opinion 98-A-14 delivered on 31 August 1998 by the Conseil de la concurrence concerning the takeover of Havas by Compagnie Générale des Eaux – Bulletin officiel de la concurrence, de la consommation et de la répression des fraudes of 7 October 1998.

[200] AB group presentation, September 1997.

[201] French legislation requires the general-interest channels to invest 15% of their turnover in commissioning audiovisual works filmed in French and to devote 3% of their turnover to developing the production of French-speaking and European cinema films.

[202] Canal+ is under the obligation to invest 9% of its turnover in the acquisition of cinema films made in French.

[203] CNC Info No 268, April 1998.

ings in the longest-standing channels which have achieved the best penetration of the cable market and have the largest number of subscribers[204].

(69)  Certain foreign companies are also active on this market: American channels such as CNN, ABC and NBC and recently Arabic-speaking channels distributed via TPS and certain cable networks. The Hollywood studios (Disney, Fox, Paramount, Universal) are also suppliers of special-interest channels, the distribution of which is usually negotiated and sometimes imposed as part of a package with film rights.

**D. The operation: the notified agreements**

(70)  Four agreements have been notified. The basic principles governing the operation of TPS are set out in the Agreement of 11 and 18 April 1996, subsequently expressed in more concrete and structured terms in the Associates' Pact, signed on 19 June 1996, and in the TPS and TPS Gestion ('TPSG') Articles of Association of the same date.

(71)  These agreements and the contractual clauses referred to below are valid for 10 years.

**1. Administration of TPS**

(72)  TPS's management is entrusted to a second company, TPSG, which has exactly the same shareholder structure as TPS.

(73)  TPSG is governed by a board of directors with 12 members, three of whom are appointed by TF1, three by France Télévision Entreprises and six by M6 Numérique and Lyonnaise Satellite. The board of directors has to give its prior approval to any decision concerning changes in the activities of TPS and TPSG, substantial modifications to TPS's development plan and operating forecast, the adoption of annual operating and investment budgets, the general policy on the composition of the digital services offered, pricing policy, etc. The board of directors decides by simple majority on any matters relating to TPS's commercial policy, and the chairman does not have a casting vote.

(74)  It has to be concluded from these provisions that the shareholders in TPS do not exercise joint control over the company's commercial policy.

(75)  In the event of sale of shares in TPS or in TPSG, a pre-emption procedure is set in motion in order to give preferential treatment to the initial partners.

**2. Aims of the TPS agreements**

(76)  Under the notified agreements, TPS's object is to devise, develop and distribute a range of programmes and services aimed at French-speaking television viewers in Europe, for which they are required to pay. This service is to be broadcast in digital mode by satellite and to be received directly by satellite dishes and cable networks. The company's object covers all operations which might be linked to this activity, including:
    – the purchase, sale, marketing, advertising and broadcasting of television programmes and services;
    – the purchase, hiring and supply of technical services necessary for routing and access to the digital service,
    – the development, marketing, purchase and sale of all conditional access systems, and the operation and marketing of subscriber management systems,
    – the negotiation of agreements concerning the production, co-production and creation of television programmes and services intended for TPS.

---

[204] Report by the Conseil supérieur de l'audiovisuel entitled 'La télévision a péage par satellite', August 1997.

**3. Contractual clauses**

**3.1. Non-competition clause (amendments to Article 11 of the Agreement of 11 and 18 April 1996 and Article 5.3 of the Associates' Pact of 19 June 1996: 'Exclusivity')**

(77)   Except for ongoing cases as at the date of conclusion of the agreements, and except for the sale of new programmes and services that are not under contract to TPS, the parties undertake not to become in any way involved, even indirectly, and for as long as they remain TPS shareholders, in companies engaged in or whose object is the distribution and marketing of a range of television programmes and services for payment which are broadcast in digital mode by satellite to French-speaking homes in Europe.

**3.2. Clause concerning TPS's programmes and services (Article 6 of the Agreement of 11 and 18 April 1996: 'Digital programmes and services')**

(78)   3.2.1. In order to supply TPS with the programmes it requires, the parties have agreed to give TPS first refusal in respect of the programmes or services which they themselves operate or over which they have effective control within the producing company, and in respect of the programmes and services which they produce. TPS is also entitled to final refusal or acceptance on the best terms proposed by competitors with regard to any programmes or services which its shareholders offer to third parties. If it accepts them, whether on exclusive terms or not, TPS will apply financial and contractual terms which are at least equivalent to those which the programmes and services could receive elsewhere.

(79)   As regards the acquisition of these channels and services, TPS will freely decide, on the basis of its own assessment, whether or not to agree to integrate them into its digital bouquet, either exclusively or non-exclusively; however, the parties underline their objective of having programmes and services in TPS's digital bouquet on an exclusive basis.

(80)   Since the general-interest channels are dealt with separately and in detail below, these provisions concern only the special-interest channels and television services controlled by the members of TPS.

(81)   3.2.2. A provision relating specifically to the general-interest channels (TF1, France 2, France 3 and M6) lays down that those channels are to be exclusively transmitted by TPS, which will meet the technical costs of transporting and broadcasting the programmes but will not pay any remuneration for them. The possibility of entrusting exclusive transmission of the Arte and La Cinquieme channels to TPS was also originally provided for in the agreements, but the relevant clauses have been deleted by the parties.

(82)   If, as a result of an external legislative or regulatory constraint, one of the general-interest channels were no longer exclusively transmitted by TPS, that channel would have to bear the satellite and transport costs.

**3.3. Clause concerning cable (Article 5 of the Agreement of 11 and 18 April 1996: 'Coordination with the cable service')**

(83)   The clause whereby the cable operators who hold shares in TPS undertook to give priority to including the programmes and services supplied by TPS on their networks, in particular its pay-per-view services, and to consult with each other on coordinating these programmes and services with those already on cable, has been deleted by the parties at the Commission's request. An amendment to the Agreement of 11 and 18 April 1996 was notified to the Commission on 27 July 1998.

**E. Observations by third parties**

(84)    A number of interested third parties have submitted observations in response to the notice published pursuant to Article 19(3) of Regulation No 17. Most comments relate to the clause concerning cable: these stressed that its application would weaken the independent channels. Given the small size of the cable sector in France and the position of the two cable operators who are shareholders in TPS and together hold 56% of the cable market, restricting the access of independent channels to their network would seriously threaten their viability.

(85)    As is indicated above, the parties to the TPS agreements have deleted the clause concerning cable: on 27 July 1998 they notified the Commission of an amendment deleting the clause with effect from 2 April 1998.

(86)    Certain third parties have also commented on the preferential right which the shareholders have granted to TPS in respect of the programmes and services they operate. Since the term 'programmes' can be interpreted extensively, the clause in question would have the practical effect of granting TPS a preferential right not only in respect of the national channels (which are the subject of a specific provision) and the special-interest channels and interactive services produced and operated by the parties, but also in respect of all the broadcasting rights held by the TPS shareholders. The preferential right over broadcasting rights would have a clear crowding-out effect on producers of special-interest channels who are not linked to TPS.

(87)    The Commission considers that the clause in question should be construed strictly and should be applied solely to the channels and television services produced and operated by TPS's shareholders. The broadcasting rights held by the members of TPS are therefore not covered by any preferential right granted to TPS. This interpretation has been confirmed by the parties to the agreements by letter of 9 October 1998.

(88)    As to the provision concerning exclusive transmission of the general-interest channels by TPS, interested third parties have stressed that the presence of those channels in the bouquet offered to subscribers confers a substantial competitive advantage. According to a survey carried out in January 1998 by Audicabsat-Médiamétrie, the general-interest channels traditionally attract by far the largest audience shares in France, namely 90% of viewers, all methods of transmission combined, and 75,1% of cable viewers. Moreover, the often poor reception of the terrestrial channels in a large number of homes (estimated by some sources at over 8 million) makes the possibility of receiving them in digital mode particularly attractive to the public. In areas where reception of terrestrial broadcasts is poor, there was therefore said to be a serious risk that competition might be eliminated in favour of TPS.

(89)    Lastly, some third parties have put forward the view that the composition of the TPS pool could give rise to competition problems. It should be pointed out in this connection that the project was only able to go ahead thanks to the presence of all the shareholders in TPS, who brought not only the financial capacity necessary for the investments needed to launch TPS and for covering the resulting losses, but also a great deal of experience and know-how essential for gaining a satisfactory market share.

(90)    The Commission has examined these observations, which confirmed comments it had previously received. The concerns voiced had already been discussed with the parties and had been taken into account by the Commission in its assessment of the notified agreements. Therefore, with the exception of the clause concerning cable, which has been deleted by the parties, the observations received have not

prompted the Commission to make any substantial change to its position on the notified agreements as announced in the abovementioned notice and presented below.

## II. LEGAL ASSESSMENT

### A. Application of Article 85(1) to the creation of TPS

(91)    Through the TPS agreements, the parties have set up a company that is not under the joint control of its shareholders. An agreement to set up a company does not, however, in itself constitute a restriction of competition within the meaning of Article 85(1).

(92)    Having received comments from third parties voicing concern at the risks of collusive behaviour between the members of TPS, and particularly the broadcasters with shares in it, the Commission nevertheless examined the impact of the creation of TPS on the relevant product markets, and concluded that there was no risk of coordination between the parties to the TPS agreements.

(93)    On the pay-TV market, the broadcasters who are members of TPS are not present outside TPS. They operate mainly on the unencrypted television market, where they have continued to compete fiercely since the creation of TPS. Neither are the two cable operators who are parties to the TPS agreements to be regarded as genuine competitors on the pay-TV market since they operate in different geographic areas, and the overlap between cable and satellite pay-TV is very small in France.

(94)    On the market in technical services for pay-TV, France Télécom is not for the time being in competition with any of the other TPS shareholders.

(95)    On the market in the acquisition of broadcasting rights, in particular for films and sporting events, where the unencrypted broadcasters with shares in TPS are extremely active in purchasing unencrypted broadcasting rights there is little risk of coordination as long as TV broadcasting in clear continues to account for the bulk of their activities and the resulting competition between them is maintained[205]. The members of TPS also acquire pay-TV rights as producers of special-interest channels. However, none of them produce or directly control movie channels; as far as sports channels are concerned, only TF1 holds shares in the Eurosport channel, alongside Canal+.

(96)    On the market in the distribution of special-interest channels, there is, admittedly, some competition between TPS shareholders and TPS itself in so far as they all have stakes of varying sizes in special-interest channels. As far as satellite transmission is concerned, however, the risk that they might coordinate their behaviour is now ruled out by the clause granting TPS a priority right to its shareholders' special-interest channels. As regards the distribution of special-interest channels

---

[205] Third parties voiced their concern to the Commission at the possibility of collusion between the broadcasters with shares in TPS as regards the acquisition of broadcasting rights, quoting the example of TCM. The company TCM was set up by some of the broadcasters with shares in TPS (TF1, M6 and CLT, which subsequently withdrew) when an overall agreement was concluded with Paramount. That agreement, which was vitally important to the creation of movie channels and therefore to the launch of TPS, provided for the purchase not only of pay-TV and pay-per-view rights, but also of unencrypted broadcasting rights, which were acquired by TCM with funds provided by its shareholders. The Commission sent the parties to the agreement setting up TCM, which was the subject of a separate investigation, a comfort letter stating that the agreement did not restrict competition provided that TCM's activities were confined to the conclusion of agreements essential to the operation of TPS; it took that view particularly because the parties undertook to place all the unencrypted broadcasting rights on the market and to resell them at market prices and without discrimination.

via cable, coordination between TPS shareholders, particularly on price, is hardly conceivable given the differences between the commercial value of the different channels: some channels are much longer established and more popular and consequently have a higher commercial value than more recently created and less well known channels. Price differentials range on average between FRF 6 and FRF 2 per month and per subscriber depending on the channel concerned, with subscriptions to movie channels costing up to FRF 20.

## B. Application of Article 85(1) to the contractual clauses

(97)    The following clauses are examined below:

(1) non-competition clause (Article 11 of the Agreement of 11 and 18 April 1996 and Article 5.3 of the Associates' Pact, as amended by the codicils dated 17 September 1998);

(2) clause granting TPS first refusal over programmes and services produced and distributed by its shareholders (Article 6 of the Agreement of 11 and 18 April 1996);

(3) clause in Article 6 of the Agreement of 11 and 18 April 1996 concerning the exclusive transmission of the general-interest channels in TPS's bouquet.

*1.      The non-competition clause, the scope of which was spelt out by the two amendments dated 17 September 1998, may be regarded as a restriction ancillary to the creation of TPS for the period deemed necessary to start up the company.*

(98)    TPS was chosen by its shareholders as the vehicle for penetrating the French pay-TV market. When TPS was launched, major doubts were raised as to its chances of success. The heavy investments required, the difficulty of establishing itself on a market dominated by an experienced operator possessing a strong subscriber base, the difficulties of gaining access to quality programmes, and major uncertainty surrounding consumer response to the provision of a wider range of pay-TV services made TPS a high-risk venture. Under these circumstances, it is logical for the parties to concentrate all their efforts on the project during the launch phase in order to enable this new operator to emerge on the pay-TV market.

(99)    The non-competition clause can therefore be regarded as ancillary to the creation of TPS during the platform's crucial launch phase and can therefore be deemed pro-competitive in that it contributes to the creation of a new entrant on the French pay-TV market during that period. On the basis of the data supplied by TPS on the amount of the investments necessary for launching the platform, forecasts regarding accumulated losses, the time and the number of subscribers needed to reach break-even point and the rate of cancellation of subscriptions, and the company's performance over the first 18 months, the length of the launch phase can be estimated at three years. Consequently, the clause does not fall within the scope of Article 85(1) during the first three years of its application.

*2.      The clause concerning programmes and services (Article 6 of the Agreement) requires the parties to give TPS first refusal in respect of all the special-interest channels and television services they operate or over which they have effective control within the producing company. They also undertake to give TPS final refusal or acceptance on the best market conditions in respect of any programmes or services which they offer to third parties, with TPS having the option of carrying those channels and services on an exclusive or non-exclusive basis.*

(100)   This provision comprises four different obligations: a right of first refusal for TPS, which binds the parent companies to TPS; a right of final refusal for TPS, which

also binds the shareholders to the company; the obligation on TPS to grant its shareholders the best market conditions should they accept a channel or a television service; and the right for TPS to distribute a channel or a service on an exclusive basis, a provision which binds the parties.

(101) The obligation on the members to give TPS first refusal over their special-interest channels might possibly be regarded as ancillary to the launch of the platform; this obligation, which is imposed for a period of ten years, nevertheless results in a limitation of the supply of special-interest channels and television services. In this respect, the clause in question falls within the scope of Article 85(1).

3.    *The provision appearing in Article 6 of the Agreement concerning the exclusive transmission of the general-interest channels (TF1, France 2, France 3 and M6) by TPS calls for special examination.*

(102) This provision grants TPS the exclusive right to broadcast the general-interest channels (also referred to as terrestrial channels) in encrypted form and digital mode by satellite, those channels also being retransmitted by the cable network, on which they are offered as part of the 'antenna service'.

(103) The general-interest channels traditionally attract the largest audience shares in France, namely 90% of viewers, if all methods of transmission are aggregated, and 75,1% of cable viewers.

(104) There is also potential demand for the general-interest channels broadcast in digital mode, which could largely be accounted for by a peculiarity concerning the reception of terrestrial broadcasts in France. Although broadcasting via terrestrial frequencies is by far the most common method of transmission, reception of the programmes is occasionally poor or even impossible in some areas of France. According to a survey conducted by Médiamétrie over the period November to December 1997[206], 9254000 of the 22330000 homes with a television set were located in areas where reception of the general-interest channels is poor. These figures are only indicative, however, because in addition to the four general-interest channels broadcast exclusively on TPS they also include Arte and La Cinquième, for which the initialisation rate is 80,6% of households, and the terrestrial Canal+ service, which approximately [...][207] households axe thought to receive in poor conditions.

(105) The attractiveness of the general-interest channels as part of TPS's bouquet was estimated in surveys carried out on behalf of the company: [...] of interviewees stated that they had decided to subscribe because of the presence of the general-interest channels.

(106) Consequently, although they do not constitute a separate programme category or a type of content that is essential for pay-TV, since the two other digital bouquets have been launched – with great success in the case of CanalSatellite – without offering them as part of the deal, the general-interest channels are undeniably important and attractive to viewers, to the sole benefit of TPS.

(107) The exclusive right to broadcast the four channels concerned for the duration of the agreements, namely 10 years, albeit limited to encrypted satellite transmission in digital mode, does constitute a restriction of competition since it denies TPS's competitors access to attractive programmes.

---

[206] Médiamétrie, bi-monthly initialisation survey, November of December 1997.

[207] Parts of this text have been edited to ensure that confidential information is not disclosed; those parts are enclosed in square brackets.

(108)   It therefore has to be concluded that Article 85(1) does apply to Article 6 of the Agreement of 11 and 18 April 1996.

(109)   The provision concerning possible exclusive broadcasting of the Arte and La Cinquième channels on TPS has not been applied since TPS has concluded a non-exclusive agreement with those channels. The parties furthermore deleted the provision in question by an amendment dated 17 September 1998.

## C. Effect on trade between Member States

(110)   The TPS agreements provide that the platform is aimed at serving all French-speaking homes in Europe: first in France, but subsequently in Belgium and Luxembourg as well. The range of services offered also includes a number of channels originating in other Member States. The TPS agreements will therefore have an appreciable effect on trade between Member States on the pay-TV market.

(111)   The market in the acquisition of television rights will also be affected by the creation of TPS insofar as the company, as a producer of special-interest channels, has to source programmes from European rightholders.

## D. Application of Article 85(3)

(112)   As demonstrated above, the provisions concerning programmes and services controlled by the members of TPS and the exclusive transmission of the general-interest channels on TPS are caught by Article 85(1) of the EC Treaty.

(113)   It is therefore necessary to examine whether the provisions fulfil the conditions for the application of Article 85(3).

**Improving the production and distribution of goods, and benefit for consumers**
**1. Improving the range of services on offer and increasing distribution and production**

(114)   By facilitating the successful launch of a new platform on the pay-TV market, the provisions concerning TPS's first refusal over the special-interest channels and television services produced or controlled by its members and its exclusive right to transmit the general-interest channels enable a new operator to emerge and increase the range of pay-TV services available to French viewers.

(115)   Furthermore, creation of a new platform automatically leads to the development of new special-interest channels and new services: TPS has produced four channels, its shareholders have created another four, and contracts have been concluded with foreign channels, and in particular Arabic-speaking channels, for broadcasting them on the platform. Both as regards the production of new channels, resulting in the purchase of rights and the making of programmes, and in broadcasting terms, the creation of TPS clearly has a positive impact on increasing the production and distribution of goods.

(116)   In general terms, the introduction of competition on the pay-TV market has the effect of stimulating operators, who endeavour to develop and further improve their range of programmes and services.

(117)   The increase in the number of special-interest channels also leads to an increase in the content available for cable distribution, since the channels broadcast as part of satellite packages are usually included in the range available on cable networks. Cable distribution is therefore also improved.

**2. Benefits for consumers**

(118)   By allowing a new operator to emerge, the abovementioned two provisions lead to an increase in the range of services on offer and to the development of new ser-

vices based on the use of a new technology, something which cannot but be beneficial to television viewers.

(119) Neither can it be disputed that the extremely keen competition that developed as soon as TPS was created between that platform and CanalSatellite/Canal+ has also benefited consumers. The first tangible result of that competition was special offers and advantageous financial conditions for subscribers: the subscription to CanalSatellite Numérique fell from FRF 153 for the basic service plus the movie channels plus the music programmes in 1996 to FRF 130 in early 1997, as part of a special offer valid for the first year's subscription for the basic service plus four movie channels plus Disney Channel, which was equivalent to the introductory subscription charge for the full TPS service during the same period; another result was a subscription to CanalSatellite's basic service for FRF 50 instead of FRF 98 per month for all Canal+ subscribers in the autumn of 1997. TPS's introductory offer (four months' free subscription) also prompted other promotions by CanalSatellite (such as a free satellite dish, also offered by TPS).

(120) TPS's market entry and the resulting competition has therefore had a beneficial effect on the prices and terms offered to final consumers.

## 3. Indispensable nature of the restrictions
### (a) Clause concerning TPS's channels and television services

(121) In order to secure a minimum content, and in particular a minimum number of special-interest channels, so that it could put together and market its bouquet, TPS had to have recourse to the channels and services produced or controlled by its shareholders. Channels such as LCI, Série Club, Teva and Festival were thus offered by the different TPS shareholders for inclusion in the bouquet.

(122) Without preferential access to those channels, TPS would have had to produce a large number of channels itself, which would have greatly increased the already extremely high costs of launching the platform, or else it would have had to look to other channels. However, the special-interest channels transmitted by CanalSatellite, which are among the best established on the French market, are covered by exclusivity terms and are therefore unavailable, at least for some time; furthermore, while it was theoretically possible to transmit channels produced by AB-Sat and wholly owned by it, that would have made no sense for two platforms being launched on the market at the same time, which needed to build a brand image and therefore to differentiate the range of channels they offered. It is therefore particularly important for TPS, as a new market entrant facing competition from a well-established first operator possessing attractive and plentiful programme content, to have priority access to its members' special-interest channels during the launch period so that it can create an identity for itself and ensure continuity in the services it offers during that period. In estimating the length of time during which TPS should be allowed to have such priority access, the Commission has taken into account the data and forecasts provided by the parties – such as the amount of investment necessary for launching TPS, forecasts regarding accumulated losses, the time and the number of subscribers needed to reach break-even point and the rate of cancellation of subscriptions – and the company's performance over the first 18 months of operations. This information, assessed in the light of current market conditions and the relative strengths of TPS, on the one hand, and of Canal+ and CanalSatellite, on the other, has led the Commission to take the view that the minimum period during which the priority access under consideration is to be deemed essential to TPS is three years.

**(b) Provision concerning exclusive transmission of the four general-interest channels**

(123)   As a new entrant facing an operator which had, at the time TPS was launched, 4,2 million subscribers to Canal+ and 350000 subscribers to CanalSatellite Analogique and had launched CanalSatellite Numérique in February 1996, TPS suffers from a considerable handicap in penetrating the market.

(124)   When acquiring pay-per-view rights to films and sporting events, TPS also has to contend with the strong position of Canal+.

(125)   In dealing with the American film makers, TPS is in a much weaker position than Canal+, which has been their sole partner for 12 years in France. TPS has succeeded in concluding an overall agreement with two studios and in negotiating the acquisition of TV rights for its movie channels, mainly for second showings of films that have already been broadcast on Canal+. The situation is even more one-sided in terms of the value of films (based on box-office figures in France), since Canal+ holds rights representing 85% of Hollywood's output, as compared with 15% for TPS.

(126)   It should also be stressed that the cost is very high for new entrants, since the price of pay-TV rights is determined by the number of subscribers, and Canal+'s current customer base of 4,3 million subscribers is taken into account by the distributors of film rights when determining the reference price in France.

(127)   AB-Sat has, for its part, as a producer and distributor of rights, a catalogue of over 30000 hours of programmes and has concluded partnership agreements with certain American studios. It should be noted here that AB-Sat has chosen not to launch a premium platform that would have competed head-on with CanalSatellite, based on exclusive first showings of films and top-quality sporting events, but has instead opted for a complementary range of services.

(128)   As regards sporting events and in particular football – an extremely popular sport in France according to a study by Eurostat – TPS has rights to broadcast 132 football matches per year, whereas CanalSatellite has the rights to the 242 matches played during the French football championship[208].

(129)   In order to put together an attractive choice which differs from that of its competitors and to circumvent the difficulty of acquiring rights to films and sporting events, TPS has relied on the exclusive presence of the general-interest channels in order to offer a wide range of programmes.

(130)   The exclusive transmission of the general-interest channels is the factor which differentiates TPS's package from the others. Given the reception problems with terrestrial broadcasts in certain areas of France, the inclusion of those channels gives TPS considerable consumer appeal in those areas.

(131)   Without the general-interest channels, TPS would have no chance of successfully penetrating the French pay-TV market and standing as a genuine alternative to Canal+/CanalSatellite, particularly in view of the fact that the range of films offered by TPS comprises fewer exclusive first showings than Canal+ and that CanalSatellite broadcasts exclusively most of the longest-established and best-known special-interest channels in France, therefore those which are capable of recruiting most subscribers. It should be mentioned in this connection that CanalSatellite also used to, and continues to, broadcast channels some of whose shareholders also hold stakes in TPS (LCI, Eurosport and Paris Première, which is not broadcast on TPS)[209].

---

[208] Opinion 98-A-14 delivered on 31 August 1998 by the Conseil de la concurrence concerning the takeover of Havas by Compagnie Générale des Eaux.

[209] Paris Première, whose main shareholder is Suez Lyonnaise des Eaux, is broadcast exclusively on CanalSatellite.

(132)   It should therefore be concluded that the exclusive transmission of the general-interest channels, by making the TPS package attractive to consumers and differentiating it from other services, is indispensable to its penetration of the French pay-TV market.

(133)   Nevertheless, the indispensable nature of the exclusivity will naturally diminish over time, as TPS recruits subscribers and gains experience in the pay-TV field that will enable it to improve its service, thereby meeting the expectations of its viewers and securing their loyalty and raising awareness of the service. The promising performance of TPS over its first 18 months of operation, in excess of its original forecasts (457000 subscribers in July 1998 as against an initial forecast of […]), confirm both the effectiveness of the exclusive presence of the four general-interest channels, as a differentiating factor and a loss leader, and TPS's ability to penetrate the market earlier than expected, admittedly in the face of competitors, Canal+ and CanalSatellite, the second of which has also achieved results beyond its initial forecasts.

(134)   The duration of the exclusive right to broadcast the general-interest channels, which was to run for 10 years according to the Agreement, was deemed excessive by the Commission, as TPS had to establish itself on the market before the end of that period. It is furthermore extremely important, if this new platform is quickly to gain a market share and act as an effective competitor, for it to be able to build up a subscriber base as quickly as possible, thanks in particular to the distinguishing feature conferred by the presence of the four general-interest channels. Although it is difficult to forecast precisely how the market and the companies operating on it will develop – as is shown by the fact that the performance of CanalSatellite and TPS is currently outstripping forecasts – the Commission has used a set of financial and commercial data in order to estimate how long TPS can reasonably enjoy an exclusive right to transmit the general-interest channels. In doing so it has taken account, inter alia, of data on the investments necessary for launching TPS and forecasts regarding accumulated losses, the time and the number of subscribers needed to reach break-even point and the rate of cancellation of subscriptions to that platform. This information was assessed in the light of current market conditions and the relative strengths of TPS, on the one hand, and of Canal+ and CanalSatellite, on the other. The Commission has come to the conclusion that the minimum period during which the exclusive right to broadcast the four general-interest channels is considered essential to TPS is three years.

**4. No elimination of competition in respect of a substantial part of the products in question**

(135)   Far from eliminating competition, the TPS agreements are pro-competitive. Development of the pay-TV market has been strongly stimulated, particularly through the emergence of keen competition between CanalSatellite and TPS, competition which would not have developed between CanalSatellite and AB-Sat: as mentioned earlier, given its programming policy AB-Sat is not in head-on competition with Canal+ and Canal-Satellite.

(136)   The results recorded on the pay-TV market demonstrate that competition is far from being eliminated: Canal+ succeeded in recruiting 100000 more subscribers in 1997, despite being considered by some observers to have reached its ceiling. For its part, CanalSatellite has completely outstripped its own forecasts: 900000 subscribers as at 30 June 1998 although it expected to reach that target only by […]. As at 31 May 1998, the total number of subscribers to Canal+, CanalSatellite Analogique and CanalSatellite Numérique and to the Numéri-Câble cable network accounted for around 70% of all pay-TV subscribers in France.

(137)   The number of cable subscribers is also continuing to increase: 358456 subscribers to NumériCâble in July 1998 (as compared with 235680 in May 1997); 504162 subscribers to France Télécom Câble (as against 258310 in May 1997); and 416665 subscribers to Lyonnaise Câble (as against 300156 in May 1997[210]). Clearly, development of satellite TV has had an extremely favourable knock-on effect on cable TV. The impact of large-scale advertising campaigns for satellite TV raises public awareness of the special-interest channels that are also available on cable.

(138)   There are consequently no grounds for taking the view that the creation of TPS could eliminate competition on the pay-TV market or on the markets for the purchase of TV rights or the distribution of special-interest channels; competition has, on the contrary, been strengthened on these markets by the entry of a new player.

**E. Duration of the exemption**

(139)   In accordance with Article 8 of Regulation No 17, a decision in application of Article 85(3) of the Treaty must be issued for a specified period. Pursuant to Article 6 of Regulation No 17, the date from which such a decision takes effect may not be earlier than the date of notification.

(140)   In line with those provisions, as regards the clause concerning the special-interest channels and television services set out in Article 6 of the Agreement of 11 and 18 April 1996 and to the provision concerning the exclusive transmission of the four general-interest channels on TPS, also set out in Article 6 of the Agreement of 11 and 18 April 1996, this Decision should take effect from the date of notification and for a launch period which is estimated by the Commission, on the basis of the data referred to in recitals 121 to 134, at three years. Since TPS began marketing its services in mid-December 1996, the exemption is granted until 15 December 1999,

**Has adopted this decision:**

Article 1

On the basis of the facts in its possession, the Commission has no grounds for action pursuant to Article 85(1) of the Treaty in respect of the creation of TPS by TF1, France Télévision Entreprises, M6 and Suez Lyonnaise des Eaux.

Article 2

The Commission has no grounds for action pursuant to Article 85(1) of the EC Treaty during the launch period, namely until 15 December 1999, in respect of the non-competition clause set out in the codicil amending Article 11 of the Agreement of 11 and 18 April 1998 and Article 5.3 of the Associates' Pact.

Article 3

In accordance with Article 85(3) of the EC Treaty, the provisions of Article 85(1) of the EC Treaty are hereby declared inapplicable, for the period from the date of notification to 15 December 1999, to the clause concerning TPS's special-interest channels and television services, set out in Article 6 of the Agreement of 11 and 18 April 1996, and to the provision concerning the exclusive transmission of the four general-interest channels on TPS, also set out in Article 6 of the Agreement of 11 and 18 April 1996.

---

[210]   Ecran Total magazine Nos 176 and 232.

Article 4

This Decision is addressed to:

(1)     Télévision Française 1 33, rue Vaugelas F – 75015 PARIS

(2)     France 2
        Maison France Télévision
        7, esplanade Henri de France F – 75907 PARIS CEDEX 15

(3)     France 3
        Maison France Télévision
        7, esplanade Henri de France F – 75907 PARIS CEDEX 15

(4)     France Télécom 6, place d'Alleray F – 75015 PARIS

(5)     Métropole Télévision 16, cours Albert 1er F – 75008 PARIS

(6)     Suez Lyonnaise des Eaux 72, avenue de la Liberté F – 92000 NANTERRE.

Done at Brussels, 3 March 1999.

For the Commission
Karel van Miert
Member of the Commission

––––

## 2.4.36.  NOTIFICATION OF A NUMBER OF AGREEMENTS CONCERNING THE EUROPEAN FOOTBALL LEAGUE (CASE NO IV/37.400 – PROJECT GANDALF), 13 MARCH 1999[211]

On 3 February 1999, the Commission received notification pursuant to Article 4 of Council Regulation No 17 of a number of agreements concerning the establishment and administration of a new European Football League (EFL). The EFL will comprise two main pan-European football competitions, the SuperLeague and the ProCup involving a total of 132 clubs from all territories covered by UEFA-affiliated associations. The competition will run for three years.

The notifying party is Media Partners International Limited (MPI) a member of the Media Partners Group. MPI has notified:

(a)     a standard form founder's club agreement to be signed between Parsifal Football Company Limited (FootballCo), a subsidiary of the Media Partners Group and the 18 Founder Clubs, and

(b)     a draft marketing agreement between FootballCo and EFL Properties BV, a special purpose vehicle to be incorporated to perform certain marketing functions in connection with the EFL, and which will be owned by the participating clubs.

The 18 founder clubs will commit themselves to participate in the EFL exclusively for a period of three years. Other participating clubs will qualify for one season only, based on their performance in their domestic league or cup competitions. All participating clubs will assign all intellectual property rights relating to the EFL competitions, including the EFL brand name, TV rights, merchandising rights, sponsorship, advertising, licensing, and multimedia rights to EFL Properties BV, which will therefore have the exclusive right to commercialise the EFL competition for a three-year period. Pursuant to the marketing agreement above, FootballCo will have the exclusive right to market the EFL's rights for three years.

The Commission invites interested third parties to submit their possible observations on the proposed operation.

––––

[211]  OJ C 70, 13-3-1999, p. 5. (Text with EEA relevance).

Observations must reach the Commission not later than 20 days following the date of this publication. Observations can be sent to the Commission by fax (No (32-2) 295 30 80) or by post under reference IV/37.400 – Project Gandalf to:

European Commission,
Directorate-General for Competition (DG IV),
Directorate D,
Office 5/131,
Avenue de Cortenberg/Kortenberglaan 150,
B-01040 Brussels.

———

**2.4.37.    CASE NO IV/37.398 – UEFA. CENTRAL MARKETING OF THE COMMERCIAL RIGHTS TO THE UEFA CHAMPIONS LEAGUE, 10 APRIL 1999[212]**

1.      On 1 February 1999, the Commission received an application and a notification from Union des Associations Européennes de Football (UEFA) pursuant to Articles 2 and 4 of Council Regulation No 17[213] by which UEFA asks for a negative clearance or an exemption of the central marketing of the commercial rights to the UEFA Champions League.

**The notifying party**

2.      UEFA is an association of European national football associations. UEFA currently has 51 members, 18 of which are located inside the territory of the European Union. Its Statutes are a decision of an association of undertakings within the meaning of Article 85(1) of the EC Treaty and Article 53(1) of the EEA Agreement. UEFA and the national football associations are undertakings notwithstanding the fact that they are non-profit-making bodies, since, apart from any cultural or social activities they may pursue, they are engaged in activities of an economic nature stich as the exploitation of the commercial rights to football events.

**The UEFA Champions League**

3.      The UEFA Champions League is a football tournament with the participation of the domestic league champions of each of the 51 UEFA member associations plus the runner-up of the domestic league championship from the eight member associations with the highest 'coefficient'. The 'coefficient' is calculated on the basis of the results achieved by football clubs from all the member associations in the traditional UEFA club competitions over the previous five seasons. The competition leading to the Champions League consists of two qualifying phases prior to the Champions League. The Champions League itself consists of matches by six groups with four teams each, the quarter-final matches, the semi-final matches and the final match.

**The organisation of the central marketing of the commercial rights to the UEFA Champions League**

4.      The commercial rights, which are referred to in the notification, are the television broadcasting rights, sponsorship rights, supplier rights, licensing rights and intel-

_____

[212] OJ C 99, 10-4-1999, p. 23. (Text with EEA relevance)
[213] OJ C 13, 21-12-1962, p. 204.

lectual property rights. UEFA only markets the commercial rights to the group stages and final phase of the Champions League. The national associations, their affiliated organisations or clubs mark-et the commercial rights to the qualifying phases. None of the other football events staged by UEFA are included in this procedure.

5.   The central marketing of the commercial rights is based on the Regulations for the UEFA Champions League (the Regulations), which set the rules lor participation in and organisation of the UEFA Champions League. UEFA's Executive Committee adopts the Regulations.

According to Article 1(6) of the Regulations, UEFA shall exploit the commercial rights for the UEFA Champions League and according to its Article 18(7) 'the President and Secretary General of UEFA shall be responsible for negotiations and the concluding of contracts pertaining to the exploitation of the commercial rights for the UEFA Champions League'.

Furthermore, according to Article 18(9), the revenues generated by the contracts concluded by UEFA are allocated as follows:

–   68,5% of the total amount is paid to the 24 clubs taking part in the UEFA Champions League (group matches),
–   21,5% is shared with 7,5% to UEFA's member associations, 9% to clubs that are eliminated in the qualifying phases of the UEFA Champions League and 5,5% is used for general budgetary and administrative purposes, and
–   10% of the total amount is used as a share for football related financial measures in accordance with the decision of the Executive Committee, such as youth football, players' training and education.

6.   In 1992, UEFA engaged Team Football Marketing AG, a Swiss marketing agency, to act for and on behalf of UEFA as a full service marketing agent for the exploitation of the commercial rights to the UEFA Champions League. In addition, UEFA employs various third parties to provide services in relation to the UEFA Champions League, such as stadium owners, graphics, signage and TV monitoring companies, research and photographic agencies, distributors of satellite TV signals, catering and insurance companies. The most important contracts that UEFA has concluded concern the broadcasting rights and the sponsorship rights. The duration of these contracts is typically up to three years.

**Arguments put forward by UEFA in favour of a negative clearance**

7.   UEFA considers that it is at least the co-owner of the commercial rights for the Champions League together with the clubs, because it has created the format and concept of the Champions League, which has established a brand identity that is entirely distinct from the identities of the competing clubs. UEFA is also responsible for a wide range of organisational services: the administration and regulation of the competition, the organisation of the match venues, the selection of service providers, insurance. UEFA also bears the financial risk for the success of the Champions League, as UEFA guarantees the participants a minimum amount irrespective of the revenues generated. UEFA argues that the notification therefore concerns the terms on which UEFA grants licences for its own property and that as long as these licences are not too long, the central marketing of the commercial rights does not fall within the scope of Article 85(1) of the EC Treaty.

UEFA moreover considers that the central marketing by UEFA of the commercial rights to the Champions League does not restrict competition to an appreciable extent, UEFA considers that the central marketing does not impede trade between Member States and the re-distribution of revenue by UEFA serves to enlarge the competitive base in European football. UEFA considers that the focus of major corporate investors on a small number of elite teams renders UEFA's redistribution role necessary to defend the interest of weaker clubs and associations.

**Arguments put forward by UEFA in favour of an exemption**

8.     In order to justify an exemption of the central marketing of the commercial rights for the UEFA Champions League, UEFA argues that:
  - the central marketing enables UEFA to maintain a distinctive UEFA Champions League brand; it rationalises the distribution of the commercial rights; it serves solidarity between financially stronger and weaker clubs through a redistribution of funds which contributes to the development of the sport by stimulating competition in European football and it supports amateur and youth football,
  - consumers benefit from a greater number and variety of football clubs competing at the top level of European club football and through UEFA's television policy to make the Champions League available principally on 'free' television,
  - without central marketing there would not be a distinctive UEFA Champions League brand and no distinctive product available to clubs, broadcasters, sponsors and spectators.

**UEFA's definition of the relevant market**

9.     UEFA defines the relevant product market as the market for the acquisition of commercial rights to sports events. The relevant geographic mark-et is considered to be EEA wide.

10.    On preliminary examination, the Commission finds that the notified rules could fall within the scope of Regulation No 17.

11.    The Commission invites interested third parties to submit their possible observations on the notified rules to the Commission. In accordance with Article 20 of Regulation No 17, such observations will be protected by professional secrecy.
       Observations must reach the Commission not later than 30 days following the date of this publication. observations can be sent by fax (32-2) 296 98 04) or by post under reference IV/37.398 – UEFA – central marketing of the commercial rights of the Champions League – to the following address:

European Commission
Directorate-General for Competition (DG IV)
Directorate C
Unit C-2: Media and music publishing
Office C-150, 3/158
Avenue de Cortenberg/Kortenberglaan 150
B-1040 Brussels

———

**\* 2.4.38.  COMMISSION APPROVES TICKETING ARRANGEMENTS FOR EURO 2000, 8 JUNE 1999**[214]

———

---

[214]  IP/00/591.

**\* 2.4.39. COMMISSION OPENS FORMAL PROCEEDINGS INTO FORMULA ONE AND OTHER INTERNATIONAL MOTOR RACING SERIES, 30 JUNE 1999**[215]

---

**2.4.40. COMMISSION DECISION RELATING TO A PROCEEDING UNDER ARTICLE 82 OF THE EC TREATY AND ARTICLE 54 OF THE EEA AGREEMENT (CASE IV/36.888 – 1998 FOOTBALL WORLD CUP) (NOTIFIED UNDER DOCUMENT NUMBER C(1999) 2295), 20 JULY 1999**[216]

*The Commission of the European Communities,*

–   Having regard to the Treaty establishing the European Community,
–   Having regard to the Agreement on the European Economic Area,
–   Having regard to Council Regulation No 17 of 6 February 1962, first Regulation implementing Articles 85 and 86 of the EC Treaty[217], as last amended by Regulation (EC) No 1216/1999[218], and in particular Article 15(2) thereof,
–   Having regard to the Commission Decision of 25 August 1998 to initiate a proceeding in this case,
–   Having given the undertaking concerned the opportunity to make known its views on the objections raised by the Commission, pursuant to Article 19(1) of Regulation No 17 and Commission Regulation No 99/63/EEC of 25 July 1963 on the hearings provided for in Article 19(1) of Regulation No 17[219],
–   After consulting the Advisory Committee on Restrictive Practices and Dominant Positions.

Whereas:

## I. THE FACTS
### A. SUBJECT OF THE DECISION
(1)   This Decision concerns arrangements relating to the sale to the general public in 1996 and 1997 of entry tickets for the 1998 Football World Cup finals tournament by the officially appointed local organising committee.

### B. THE CFO
(2)   The Comité français d'organisation de la Coupe du monde de football 1998 (CFO) was established as a non-profit making organisation on 10 November 1992 by the Fédération Française de Football (FFF) with the agreement of the Fédération Internationale de Football Association (FIFA), specifically for the purpose of carrying on all activities relating to the technical and logistical organisation of the 1998 World Cup finals tournament in France, in compliance with various operational constraints laid down by FIFA.

### C. TOURNAMENT
(3)   The 1998 World Cup finals tournament involved the participation of 32 football

---

[215]   IP/99/434.
[216]   OJ L 5, 8-1-2000, p. 55-74. (Text with EEA relevance).
[217]   OJ C 13, 21-2-1962, p. 204.
[218]   OJ L 148, 15-6-1999, p. 5.
[219]   OJ C 127, 20-8-1963, p. 2268.

teams representing countries from around the world. The tournament took place following the conclusion in 1997 of a preliminary qualifying competition involving the participation of 172 representative teams. Both Brazil, as winners of the previous tournament in 1994, and France, as host nation, were exempt from the requirement to qualify and as such did not take part in the preliminary qualifying competition.

(4)     In the first phase of the finals tournament, commencing 10 June 1998, teams were divided into eight groups of four teams each. The composition of those groups was determined by a 'group draw' which took place on 4 December 1997. Each team played a total of three matches against other teams in the same group.

(5)     Teams finishing either first or second in each of the eight first-phase groups qualified for the second-phase. The second phase therefore involved the participation of 16 teams, the first round of which was known as the 'Round of 16'. This was followed by four quarter-final matches, two semi-final matches, a match to determine the third and fourth-placed teams and, on 12 July 1998, the World Cup final itself.

(6)     Ten stadiums, each located in France, were used to host World Cup finals football matches. Each of a team's first-phase matches was played in a different stadium. According to the CFO, this guaranteed that each stadium would host at least two teams finishing top of their group in the first phase. In relation to second-phase matches, each of the 10 World Cup stadiums hosted at least one match taking place in the Round of 16 or one quarter final match.

## D. TICKETING ARRANGEMENTS

(7)     As holder of all rights relating to World Cup tournaments, FIFA establishes regulations outlining the general organisational framework of both preliminary and finals competitions. In relation to organisational arrangements relating to the 1998 Football World Cup finals tournament, FIFA established regulations providing that the CFO, subject to approval of the overall arrangements by FIFA[220], was responsible for all matters relating to the price, distribution, and sale of entry tickets for finals matches[221].

## E. TICKET DISTRIBUTION – GENERAL

(8)     In total, some 2666500 entry tickets were made available by the CFO for subsequent distribution either directly or through officially-appointed sales channels. Tickets were distributed as follows:
   –   28,12%, distributed by the CFO to the general public,
   –   23,33%, distributed by national football federations to the general public,
   –   6,58%, distributed by official tour operators to the general public worldwide,
   –   13,48%, distributed by the CFO to members of the 'Famille du Football Français'[222],
   –   13,15%, distributed by the CFO to sponsor organisations,
   –   7,51%, distributed by the CFO as Prestige/hospitality products principally to corporate bodies,
   –   4,07%, distributed by the CFO for miscellaneous purposes[223],
   –   2,86%, distributed by the CFO to public entities,
   –   0,70%, distributed to the handicapped,

---

[220]  Such approval did not, however, concern the arrangements at issue in this Decision.
[221]  Article 34 of FIFA Regulation 'Coupe du Monde de la FIFA 1998' of 31-5-1995.
[222]  Made up of football licence holders and club members in France.
[223]  For example, youth programmes.

- 0,20%, unsold.

(9)    Income derived from ticket sales represented 60% of total CFO receipts.

## F. TICKET SALES TO THE GENERAL PUBLIC

(10)    A total of 1547300 match tickets relating to all finals matches were made available exclusively for sale to the general public, representing 58,03% of all tickets distributed, and comprising ticket sales by the CFO (28,12%), by FIFA-affiliated national football federations (23,33%) and by officially appointed tour operators throughout the world (6,58%), including tour operators selling within Europe.

(11)    Tickets were sold to the general public either on an individual basis or as a package comprising five or six separate entry tickets marketed under the name 'Pass France 98'. This Decision concerns exclusively arrangements relating to the sale by the CFO in 1996 and 1997 of Pass France 98 and individual entry tickets for World Cup finals matches.

### Breakdown of sales

(12)    The general breakdown of ticket sales to the general public, which took place both before and after the group draw of 4 December 1997, can be summarised as follows.

Table 1
Sales of World Cup match tickets to the general public
[...]

### Timing of sales

(13)    The specific dates and sequence of ticket sales to the general public by each of the official distribution channels was:
27 November 1996 to 27 May 1997: 393200 tickets were sold direct by the CFO to members of the general public able to provide an address in France through Pass France 98. All Pass France 98 were sold by 27 May 1997;
18 September to 18 October 1997: applications from the general public able to provide an address in France could be lodged with the CFO for 181000 individual entry tickets relating to the opening match, quarter and semi-finals. third and fourth-place play-off and the final;
from 4 December 1997 (date of group draw): Following the group draw, individual entry tickets for finals matches were allocated to national football federations by FIFA. Ticket sales to the general public by national football federations relating to first-phase matches commenced shortly thereafter. The majority of second-phase ticket sales by national federations took place during the course of the tournament when the identities of teams participating in second-phase matches became known. A total of 622150 tickets relating to all finals matches were allocated in varying quantities to national football federations worldwide;
from 15 December 1997: individual tickets relating to finals matches were allocated to official tour operators authorised to sell tickets within the UEFA[224] zone (hereinafter referred to as 'European tour operators')[225]. Of the total number of entry tickets allocated to official tour operators worldwide, an initial allocation of ap-

---

[224] UEFA (l'Union des associations européennes de football) organises various football competitions in Europe. Its members include (inter alia) all national football federations in the EEA.
[225] Relating exclusively to matches involving the participation of at least one representative team based in the UEFA zone.

proximately 79150 entry tickets was made available by the CFO to European tour operators. Further entry tickets were made available by the CFO to European tour operators following the return at a later date of unsold tickets by national football federations. This additional allocation increased the total allocated to European tour operators by approximately 25%;

from 22 April 1998: 175500 entry tickets relating to first phase and round of 16 matches were sold direct by the CFO on an individual basis to the general public able to provide an address within the EEA.

Tickets sold 'blind' to the general public

(14)　Before the group draw of 4 December 1997 it was not possible to know the composition of the eight first-phase groups and hence the identities of teams participating in specific first-phase matches. For each first-phase match, therefore, only the date of the match and the venue at which it would take place was known. In relation to all second-phase knock-out matches, the identities of participating teams only became known following completion of the relevant matches in the round immediately preceding.

(15)　With the exception of the opening match, therefore, which was certain to involve the participation of Brazil as winners of the previous finals tournament in 1994, consumers purchasing entry tickets for first-phase matches before the group draw of 4 December 1997 did so on a so-called 'blind' basis, that is, at the time of purchase, the identities of teams participating in the matches concerned were not known.

(16)　In relation to sales of tickets relating to second-phase matches, consumers purchasing tickets before the completion of the relevant matches in the immediately preceding round also did so on a blind basis.

**Effect of the group draw of 4 December 1997**

(17)　The group draw of 4 December 1997, which allowed the general public to ascertain the identities of competing teams for all first-phase matches, had a profound effect in certain European countries on the level of interest in the tournament and, more particularly, on the demand for tickets relating to certain matches which the quotas reserved by FIFA for certain national football federations were unable to satisfy.

**G. DIRECT SALES BY THE CFO TO THE GENERAL PUBLIC**

**Sales of Pass France 98**

(18)　Pass France 98 comprised a group of five or six separate match tickets. Other than for matches taking place at three of the 10 World Cup stadiums, Pass France 98 entitled the holder to attend matches taking place at a single stadium involving all first-phase matches and a match in the round of 16[226]. First-phase and round of 16 matches took place over a period of between 13 and 20 days, depending on the venue in question.

(19)　In the event, Pass France 98 was marketed and sold exclusively by the CFO to members of the general public able to provide an address in France, such sales taking place well in advance of the group draw of 4 December 1997 and therefore

---

[226] Pass France 98 relating to matches taking place at the Saint-Denis stadium did not entitle the purchaser to attend the opening match of the tournament. Pass France 98 for matches taking place at the Lyons and Nantes stadiums allowed access only to all first-phase matches given that no round of 16 matches took place in those stadiums.

before the identities of teams participating in specific first-phase matches were known. Sales of Pass France 98 before the group draw were considered necessary by the CFO in order, on the one hand, to ensure as far as was possible that all first-phase and Round of 16 matches were played in front of capacity crowds regardless of the identities of participating teams and, on the other, to provide necessary financing for the CFO in the run-up to the tournament.

(20)     A total of 393200 blind entry tickets were sold by the CFO through Pass France 98 to the general public between 27 November 1996 and 27 May 1997, representing approximately 15% of the total number of tickets available for finals matches and 6% of the CFO's total ticketing income. While figures varied from stadium to stadium, between 71% and 91% of all Pass France 98 sold by the CFO were bought either by the general public living in the Département in which a host stadium was located or in the immediately surrounding Départements.

Sales of individual entry tickets

(21)     Individual entry tickets were sold to the general public by the CFO in two separate tranches.

First tranche (18 September to 18 October 1997)

(22)     In its first tranche of sales, the CFO invited the general public able to provide an address in France to apply for approximately 181000 match tickets relating to the opening match, quarter and semi-finals, the third and fourth-place play-off and the final.

(23)     Applications for those tickets had to be lodged with the CFO between 18 September 1997 and 18 October 1997. Following receipt of some 1043 million applications, a lottery draw took place on 19 December 1997 to determine the identities of successful applicants. Sales of individual entry tickets in 1997 represented approximately 7% both of total tickets available for finals matches and of the CFO's total ticketing income.

**Second tranche (from 22 April 1998)**

(24)     In a second tranche of sales commencing 22 April 1998, the CFO sold some 175500 individual entry tickets to the general public able to provide an address in the EEA, relating to all first-phase and round of 16 matches (other than the opening match). At the time of those sales, the identities of teams participating in all first-phase matches were known, while teams participating in each round of 16 match could be identified from a list of no more than eight teams participating in the first phase.

(25)     For reasons of security, no more than approximately 10% of entry tickets sold by the CFO in this second tranche could be assigned to supporters of teams participating in any given match, taking into account the limited number of seats which at that time remained available for sale to the non-neutral public (see recital 57). All remaining entry tickets were sold exclusively to 'neutral' spectators who could be allocated seats reserved specifically for that sector of the public.

(26)     Approximately 45% of entry tickets made available in this second tranche of sales were purchased by the general public in the EEA providing addresses outside France, while some 38% of all tickets sold were purchased by consumers from countries whose teams had qualified for the finals competition[227].

---

[227] As confirmed by the CFO in its letter of 4-6-1998 (Annex 3), responding to the Commission's formal request for information of 15-5-1998.

## H. TICKET SALES TO THE GENERAL PUBLIC BY OTHER DISTRIBUTION CHANNELS (EUROPEAN TOUR OPERATORS AND NATIONAL FOOTBALL FEDERATIONS)

(27)    European tour operators and national football federations sold all entry tickets distributed to them by the CFO on an individual basis after the group draw of 4 December 1997, when the identities of teams taking part in each first-phase match were known. As such, neither of those distribution channels sold Pass France 98 to the general public.

**Sales of individual entry tickets to the general public by European tour operators**
**Selection of tour operators**

(28)    Following meetings with the Commission in March 1997, the CFO submitted a notification on 11 June 1997 relating to its proposed system for the selection of tour operators authorised to sell entry tickets for finals matches in the UEFA zone (including, inter alia, all countries within the EEA). Given the stated urgency of the notification, and following an assessment by the Commission of the CFO's specific proposals, those arrangements were approved by way of comfort letter on 30 June 1997.

(29)    Although the notification outlined in broad terms the arrangements for the sale of entry tickets for finals matches generally, at no time was the Commission informed by the CFO of its intention to implement the arrangements at issue in this Decision.

(30)    On 24 November 1997 the CFO announced publicly, by way of a press release, that 17 tour operators had been appointed to sell tickets worldwide, of which five were granted the exclusive right to sell tickets in the UEFA zone.

**CFO sales to European tour operators**

(31)    European tour operators ordered the maximum number of tickets initially made available to them by the CFO, representing some 79150 in total. The CFO made additional allocations to European tour operators at a later date, thereby increasing this initial figure by approximately 25%.

**Orders of Pass France 98**

(32)    As distributor of all entry tickets to finals matches, the CFO offered European tour operators the opportunity to purchase 100 Pass France 98 relating to games taking place at each of the 10 World Cup stadiums. Taking all venues together, this amounted to a maximum offer to each European tour operator of some 5500 individual entry tickets. European tour operators were free to decide whether to order Pass France 98 before or after the group draw of 4 December 1997.

(33)    By the time of their appointment, and well after the conclusion of sales of Pass France 98 by the CFO, European tour operators had already confirmed to the CFO their intention to order the maximum number of tickets made available through Pass France 98 after the group draw of 4 December 1997, representing some 27500 entry tickets in total. That being so, and notwithstanding the fact that European tour operators could have ordered and sold match tickets for first-phase matches before the group draw, all such tickets were made available to the general public at a time when the identities of the teams participating in first-phase matches were known.

(34)    Each European tour operator was permitted to sell tickets making up Each Pass France 98 package on a desegregated, individual basis. In the event, European tour operators chose to sell all entry tickets allocated to them through Pass France 98 on such a basis.

**Orders of individual tickets**

(35)     In addition to orders of Pass France 98, the CFO offered European tour operators the opportunity to purchase entry tickets for first and second-phase matches on an individual basis. In the event, each of the five European tour operators ordered the maximum number of individual entry tickets initially made available by the CFO for first and second-phase matches. Taking orders by European tour operators together, a total of 33950 and 17700 individual entry tickets were ordered for first and second-phase matches respectively.

**Sales by European tour operators**

(36)     The majority of first and second-phase entry tickets offered for sale by European tour operators to the general public were marketed as part of a package, including, in addition to the ticket itself, the provision of other services, including access to hospitality facilities and, in relation to particular matches, the provision of accommodation and travel services as well. Prices therefore reflected both the charge for the ticket and that for the provision of additional services, thereby increasing significantly the overall cost to consumers wishing to purchase tickets from European tour operators. The decision of each European tour operator to package ticket sales with those of other services was taken independently and without any interference from the CFO.

**Sales of individual entry tickets to the general public by national football federations**

(37)     Individual match tickets sold by national football federations to the general public were distributed to those federations at the discretion of FIFA. FIFA reserved for itself an allocation of up to 20% of all available entry tickets (excluding hospitality boxes and prestige tickets) for subsequent distribution to national football federations. In the event, the CFO made some 25.2% of entry tickets available to FIFA for this purpose (representing 622150 tickets in total).

(38)     The overwhelming majority of tickets assigned by FIFA to national football federations were sold to the general public at a time when the identities of participating teams were known.

(39)     Of the 622150 entry tickets allocated to FIFA, those relating to first-phase matches were distributed to national football federations throughout the world after the group draw of 4 December 1997. At the same time FIFA distributed a small proportion of their allocation of tickets for second-phase matches to national football federations. Distribution by FIFA to national football federations of the significant majority of tickets for second-phase matches commenced only after the conclusion of the first phase of the competition on 26 June 1998 as and when the identities of teams involved in each stage of the second-phase became known.

(40)     National football federations therefore sold all tickets relating to first-phase matches after the group draw at a time when the identities of teams participating in those matches were known. Similarly, in relation to second-phase matches, national football federations receiving a significant allocation of entry tickets[228] were not in a position to sell most of those tickets to the general public until after the identities of participating teams became known.

(41)     Table 2 reflects, inter alia, approximate ticket allocations by FIFA to national football federations located within the EEA prior to the beginning of the finals tourna-

---

[228] Only federations whose teams qualified for second-phase matches received significant allocations of tickets. Such allocations could only take place after the identities of teams participating in second-phase matches became known.

ment on 10 June for all first and second-phase matches. Figures relating to second-phase entry tickets represent the maximum number which could have been sold by those federations to the general public on a blind basis[229]. For purposes of illustration only, the table includes details of FIFA ticket allocations to the French, English, Italian and Scottish football federations.

Table 2
FIFA allocations to EEA national football federations prior to the finals tournament
[...]

## I. CONDITIONS APPLYING TO THE GENERAL PUBLIC PURCHASING ENTRY TICKETS DIRECT FROM THE CFO
### CFO sales in 1996 and 1997

(42)    Before the group draw, the CFO sold 574200 entry tickets direct to the general public in 1996 and 1997, comprising sales of Pass France 98 (393200) and individual tickets relating to the opening match, quarter and semi-finals, third and fourth-place play-off and the final (181000). All such tickets, other than those relating to the opening match, were sold blind by the CFO.

(43)    In relation to those sales, the general public could purchase tickets subject to the condition that they provided a postal address in France to which the tickets could be delivered.

(44)    The CFO informed the Commission in January 1998[230] that the general public was not required to indicate French nationality or prove residence in France in order to purchase entry tickets sold direct by the CFO, and that the condition was imposed in order to facilitate their safe delivery. In June 1998[231], the CFO added to the reasoning for imposing such a condition by stating that the obligation was also imposed to ensure that entry tickets were sold only to 'neutral' spectators. This resulted from the CFO's decision to consider all members of the general public providing an address in France as 'neutral'[232].

(45)    The CFO derived no commercial advantage by requiring members of the general public wishing to purchase entry tickets in 1996 and 1997 to provide an address in France. Revenue from CFO sales of Pass France 98 and individual tickets in 1996 and 1997 represented some 8% of the CFO's overall turnover.
### CFO sales in 1998

(46)    In relation to sales of individual entry tickets from 22 April 1998, the CFO had originally intended to sell those tickets under arrangements similar to those already described. Following intervention by the Commission, however, the CFO undertook to sell 175500 entry tickets to the general public on condition that purchasers provided an address in the EEA[233].

---

[229] The figures do not therefore reflect FIFA's allocation of tickets made after the completion of the first phase of the competition on 26-6-1998.

[230] See CFO response of 27-1-1998 to the Commission's request for information of 15-1-1998.

[231] See CFO response of 4-6-1998 to the Commission's request for information of 15-5-1998.

[232] See point (b) at page 3 of the CFO's letter to the Commission of 11-6-1998.

[233] See Commission letter of 20 February 1998 to the CFO asking it to bring an end to what the Commission considered abusive practices under Article 82 of the EC Treaty.

## J. CONDITIONS APPLYING TO THE GENERAL PUBLIC PURCHASING ENTRY TICKETS FROM NATIONAL FOOTBALL FEDERATIONS AND TOUR OPERATORS

### National football federations

(47)    Although entry tickets were allocated to national football federations by FIFA, the CFO imposed conditions on those federations relating to their resale (conditions générales de vente). Those conditions included, inter alia, the requirement to make tickets available for sale to all members of the general public subject only to restrictions resulting from reasons of security. The CFO did not, however, seek to influence the commercial decisions taken by national football federations relating to the means by which such tickets were sold.

(48)    To the CFO's knowledge, only the English Football Federation restricted sales to the general public, choosing to offer tickets exclusively to members of a supporters' club in order to prevent their purchase by football hooligans.

### European tour operators

(49)    In relation to the sale of tickets by European tour operators, and at the request of the Commission following the submission of the CFO's notification in June 1997[234], the CFO implemented arrangements which permitted each to sell entry tickets throughout the EEA. Furthermore, the CFO allowed European tour operators to sell entry tickets in any manner they chose, and accordingly did not seek to influence any commercial decisions taken by them. The Commission is not aware that any European tour operator restricted the sale of tickets to the general public, either territorially or otherwise.

## K. MEANS OF RESERVING TICKETS SOLD BY THE CFO TO THE GENERAL PUBLIC IN 1996 AND 1997

(50)    Subject always to the requirement that a purchaser provided a postal address in France, the means by which the general public could purchase Pass France 98 and individual entry tickets direct from the CFO in 1996 and 1997 were as follows:

(a) written reservation (Pass France 98 and individual tickets): Pass France 98 and individual entry tickets could be reserved from the CFO in writing. For individual entry tickets sold by the CFO via the draw on 19 December 1997, the return of a special application form, available from branches of Credit Agricole in France, was obligatory;

(b) reservation by Minitel (Pass France 98 only): Pass France 98 could be reserved using the electronic Minitel system, available widely in France. The general public outside France could benefit from this means of reservation only by subscribing to the Minitel service through the Internet at an additional cost of FRF 350;

(c) reservation by telephone (Pass France 98 only): Pass France 98 could be reserved over the telephone. The telephone number provided for this purpose was not accessible to the general public wishing to call from outside metropolitan France;

(d) reservation through branches of Credit Agricole (Pass France 98 only): Pass France 98 could be reserved using Minitel services provided in 2500 branches of Credit Agricole located in France.

---

[234]  See recital 28.

## L. INFORMATION PROVIDED BY THE CFO TO THE GENERAL PUBLIC OVER THE WORLDWIDE WEB

(51)    On 6 May 1997 the CFO opened a website dedicated to providing information and advice to the general public in and outside France concerning, inter alia, the means by which entry tickets for finals matches could be obtained.

(52)    Information made available to consumers outside France stated expressly that tickets would not be sold by the CFO to members of the non-French public[235]. Those consumers were advised instead to contact either an authorised tour operator or their respective national football federation in order to purchase entry tickets for finals matches[236]. On 6 May 1997, when the website was opened, the overwhelming majority of Pass France 98 had already been sold by the CFO to the general public able to provide an address in France[237].

## M. SECURITY
### European Convention on Spectator Violence and Misbehaviour at Sports Events and in particular at Football Matches (1985)

(53)    The organisation of the World Cup raises issues relating to security which must be taken into account.

(54)    In this respect the CFO sought to implement a security policy which would give effect to the principles established by the European Convention on Spectator Violence and Misbehaviour at Sports Events and in particular at Football Matches (1985) (hereinafter referred to as 'the 1985 Convention'). The 1985 Convention requires that measures be taken to prevent or control violence or misbehaviour at sporting events. Such measures as referred to in the 1985 Convention include the effective segregation of rival groups of supporters and, in order to ensure such segregation, a strict control over the sale of match tickets[238]. The 1985 Convention does not, however, prescribe specific measures to be adopted in order to achieve such segregation and control.

(55)    The CFO also took note of guidelines agreed in 1996 by the Permanent Committee to the 1985 Convention relating specifically to the control of ticket sales for high-risk football matches. Those guidelines reiterate the importance of maintaining a strict control over ticket sales in order to ensure segregation of rival groups of supporters at football matches[239].

### Security considerations relating to purchasers of blind tickets

(56)    The CFO has informed the Commission of the opinion of experts who consider

---

[235] See Internet document <http://www.france98.com/english/tickets/faq.html> of 13-8-1998, at question 10. These arrangements were reaffirmed in various CFO press releases which indicated that CFO sales in 1996 and 1997 were aimed specifically at the general public resident in France.

[236] See Internet document <http://www.france98.com/english/tickets/out_france.html> of 31-8-1998.

[237] As of 1-4-1997, all Pass France 98 relating to matches taking place at eight of the is World Cup stadiums had been sold. Only a limited number of Category 1 Pass France 98 for matches taking place at the Montpellier and Saint-Etienne stadiums remained available for sale. All such remaining tickets were sold by 27-5-1997.

[238] See Article 3(4)(b) and (c), of the 1985 Convention.

[239] 'Recommandations relative à des lignes directrices pour le contrôle de la vente des billets lors de rencontres à haul risque (adoptée à la 5e réunion du Comité permanent de la convention européenne sur la violence les débordements de spectateurs lors de manifestations sportives et notamment de matches de football 1985)', Groupe de travail ad hoc sur les problèmes pratiques (Strasbourg, 14 novembre 1996).

that blind Pass France 98 and blind tickets generally are purchased by peaceful spectators who do not present a specific security risk. Conversely, the CFO considers that sales of entry tickets in relation to which the identities of participating teams are known attract supporters presenting a significantly greater security risk[240].

**Segregation of supporters by the CFO through ticket sales**
(57) With the provisions of the 1985 Convention in mind, the CFO sought to implement arrangements which ensured that supporters of teams participating in any given match were placed at opposing ends of any given stadium. Seats located in such areas were classified by the CFO as 'low risk'. Consequently. all tickets made available to national football federations whose teams took part in the tournament, and which were intended for resale to the general public, related to low-risk seats. As a general rule, seats which were not classified as low risk were reserved for 'neutral' spectators, who were deemed not to support either of the teams participating in a given match. For security purposes and in accordance with arrangements adopted by tournament organisers previously, the CFO considered members of the general public from the host nation (in this case France) as neutral spectators for the purposes of seat allocation for all finals matches.
CFO sales in 1996 and 1997
(58) In relation to blind sales to the general public of Pass France 98 and individual tickets by the CFO in 1996 and 1997, the CFO regarded as neutral spectators all consumers able to provide an address in France[241].

**CFO sales in 1998**
(59) For sales of individual entry tickets to the general public after 22 April 1998 relating to first-phase matches (those which therefore took place at a time when the identities of participating teams were known), the CFO distinguished between applicants whose addresses were located in one of the two countries whose representative team was participating in the match for which the ticket was required, and those whose addresses were located elsewhere within the EEA. Those in the former category were deemed to be supporters of one of the two participating teams and were accordingly attributed tickets relating to seats in the stadium reserved specifically for that group of supporter. Those in the latter category were deemed to be neutral spectators and as such were allocated seats reserved specifically for that group of public.

**Sales by European tour operators and national football federations**
(60) In relation to ticket sales by European tour operators, the CFO required each tour operator to provide it with information relating to the nationality of customers to whom tickets had been sold, as well as the team supported. In relation to ticket sales by national football federations, the CFO required each to retain information relating to the identity of each purchaser including his/her name, address, and details of the team supported.

**Other security measures**
(61) In addition to the abovementioned arrangements, the CFO took other measures to

---

[240] See CFO letter of 4-6-1998 (point 24), responding to the Commission's formal request for information of 15-5-1998.
[241] See letter from the CFO to the Commission dated 11-6-1998 (page 3, point (b)).

ensure, as far as was possible, the effective maintenance of security at football matches. Some 35500 match tickets remained deliberately unsold by the CFO in order to ensure, where appropriate, a strict separation of supporters of participating teams. Measures intended to prevent black-market ticket sales and to avoid the counterfeiting of tickets were also taken by the CFO in this context.

## N. ARGUMENTS OF THE CFO RELATING TO THE FACTS

(62)    During the course of the oral hearing the CFO suggested that the total number of tickets allocated to the general public included 359500 entry tickets sold specifically to members of the Famille du Football Français through Pass France 98 and 18550 entry tickets sold to handicapped spectators.

(63)    The Commission does not accept such a view. Individual consumers throughout the EEA were required to fulfil specific conditions in order to qualify as members of each of those groups which were different from those required of consumers to which this Decision refers. Thus, tickets made available to the general public cannot properly include Pass France 98 reserved specifically for sale to members of the Famine du Football Français and individual entry tickets reserved for sale to handicapped spectators. The Commission notes that the CFO had itself always distinguished between ticket sales to the general public and those to the Famille du Football Français and handicapped spectators in previous dealings with the Commission.

## II. LEGAL ASSESSMENT
## A. TERMS OF ARTICLE 82 OF THE EC TREATY AND ARTICLE 54 OF THE EEA AGREEMENT

(64)    Pursuant to Article 82 of the EC Treaty and Article 54 of the EEA Agreement, any abuse by an undertaking of a dominant position within the common market or in a substantial part of it shall be prohibited as incompatible with the common market in so far as it may affect trade between Member States. Such abuse may, inter alia, consist of direct or indirect imposing of unfair trading conditions or limiting markets to the prejudice of consumers.

## B. UNDERTAKING

(65)    Any entity carrying on activities of an economic nature, regardless of its legal form, constitutes an undertaking within the meaning of Article 82 of the EC Treaty and Article 54 of the EEA Agreement. An activity of an economic nature means any activity, whether or not profit-making, that involves economic trade. Given that it. was responsible for the distribution of over 2,6 million match tickets of which approximately 1,55 million were sold to the general public, the CFO was carrying out activities of an economic nature and as such is an undertaking for the purposes of Article 82 of the EC Treaty and Article 54 of the EEA Agreement.

## C. RELEVANT PRODUCT MARKETS

(66)    The relevant product market can be determined by considering the extent to which an undertaking's competitors, if they exist, are capable of constraining its behaviour and preventing it from acting independently of competitive pressures. In determining the scope of the relevant product market and the extent to which undertakings are able to act independently on such a market it is necessary to consider, inter alia, the manner in which consumers are likely to react to changes in the price of the product or service in question. In this context, a relevant product market will usually be limited to a single product or service if a small but signifi-

cant increase in the price of that product or service (for example, 10%) does not lead to any measurable change in consumer demand in favour of substitutable products or services.

(67) With regard to ticket sales by the CFO in 1996 and 1997 it is therefore necessary to consider the extent to which

(a) adequate substitutes existed for sales of World Cup match tickets to the general public,

(b) adequate substitutes existed for the sale in 1996 and 1997 by the CFO of blind Pass France 98 to the general public, and

(c) adequate substitutes existed for the sale in 1997 by the CFO of blind individual entry tickets to the general public.

## Substitutes for Football World Cup finals entry tickets

(68) The nature of the World Cup finals competition is such that an increase of at least 10% in the price of match tickets would not have resulted in a significant switch in demand by the general public to otherwise competing products. This is principally due to the following:

(a) The popularity of football throughout Europe and the world, over and above other sports

While other sports command strong regional interest from the general public, only football is able to generate a broad, sustained and loyal support on a European and worldwide scale. Furthermore, sports are different, and the general public interested in one will not necessarily be followers of others. Members of the general public seeking to attend World Cup finals matches are accordingly unlikely to have considered attendance at international events involving sports other than football as adequate substitutes, whether or not the price of tickets for World Cup football matches was increased by (at least) 10%.

(b) The significance of the Football World Cup finals competition, over and above other football tournaments

Football is played in many, if not all, European countries at both national and international level. At the national level, local teams usually play one another on a weekly basis from one year to the next. At the international level, the best players from each qualifying nation participate in the European Football Championships, the finals of which take place every four years. While both national and European tournaments are often well attended, however, only the finals competition of the Football World Cup provides the general public with an opportunity to watch and assess the best players and the best teams in the world in the course of a single tournament.

(c) The timing of the Football World Cup finals competition vis-à-vis other football competitions in Europe

Even if, in the minds of the general public, entry tickets for European Football Championship matches represented identical products to those of the finals competition of the Football World Cup, attendance at one cannot be considered as substitutable for attendance at the other, given that the tournaments take place two years apart.

(d) Evidence relating to demand for Football World Cup finals entry tickets vis-à-vis the available supply

Where the demand for match tickets significantly exceeds available supply, consumers are unlikely to change their behaviour in the event of a small but significant rise in the price of those tickets. Given that some 1043 million applications were made by the general public able to provide an address in

France for 181000 individual tickets sold by the CFO in 1997, it can be assumed that the demand generally for entry tickets would remain unaffected notwithstanding an increase in price of at least 10%.

Substitutes for the sale by the CFO to the general public of blind Pass France 98 in 1996 and 1997

(69)  Pass France 98 sold by the CFO in 1996 and 1997 related to matches for which the identities of participating teams were unknown. The demand for Pass France 98 was therefore limited to spectators who were not concerned to watch a particular team or teams, but who nevertheless wanted to attend a series of finals matches taking place in a single stadium. Such sales were in marked contrast to those by national football federations and European tour operators, who sold individual entry tickets after the group draw, at a time when interest in and demand for entry tickets for finals matches had increased significantly.

(70)  In view of the limited number of entry tickets made available on an individual basis at a much later date by each national football federation, members of the general public wishing to purchase blind Pass France 98 are unlikely to have regarded tickets sold by those federations as substitutable products for blind Pass France 98 sold direct by the CFO in 1996 and 1997.

(71)  In relation to sales by European tour operators, similar considerations apply. Furthermore, even if European tour operators had chosen to sell some or all of their limited allocation of tickets as Pass France 98, they are likely to have sold most if not all of those products with other services, thereby increasing significantly the price at which Pass France 98 could be obtained. That being so, the general public would not, at the time of CFO sales of Pass France 98 in 1996 and 1997, have considered the uncertain prospect of future sales by European tour operators as in any way substitutable for those sold earlier by the CFO[242].

**Substitutes for the sale by the CFO to the general public of blind individual entry tickets in 1997**

(72)  In relation to 181000 individual tickets sold by the CFO to the general public in 1997 for the opening match, quarter and semi-finals, third and fourth-place play-off and the final, only a very limited number of tickets for those high-profile matches were made available to all national football federations. Only those federations whose teams progressed from one stage of the second phase to another received significant additional allocations, most of which were sold to the general public wishing to support the participating teams. In view of this limited supply, consumers wishing to purchase tickets for those matches in 1997 are unlikely to have regarded national football federations as a suitable alternative source of supply to the CFO.

(73)  In relation to sales of second-phase entry tickets by European tour operators, similar considerations apply given the limited number of tickets made available to them. Furthermore, European tour operators sold most if not all of such tickets with other services, thereby increasing significantly the price at which they could be obtained. Consequently, the general public would not at the time of CFO sales of 181000 blind second-phase entry tickets in 1997, have considered the prospect

---

[242] Although no explanation is given, the CFO arrived at a similar conclusion in relation to ticket sales by European tour operators in its notification to the Commission of 11 June: '[Les tour-operateurs] forment un marché spécifique [...]. Le marche peut donc, selon le CFO, êêtre défini comme le marché de la vente de billets pour la Coupe du Monde 1998 par les professionnels du tourisme' (at section 6.1).

of ticket sales at a later date by European tour operators as in any way substitutable for those sold earlier by the CFO[243].

**Conclusion on the relevant product markets**

(74) On the basis of the foregoing analysis, the relevant product markets for the purposes of this Decision are:

(a) the market for the sale in 1996 and 1997 by the CFO to the general public of 393200 blind Pass France 98, and

(b) the market for the sale in 1997 by the CFO to the general public of 181000 blind individual entry tickets relating to the opening match, quarter and semi-finals, third-place play-off and the final.

**Arguments of the CFO relating to the relevant product markets**

(75) The CFO considers that the relevant product markets for the purposes of ticket sales to the general public for the 1998 World Cup finals competition are

(a) the market for sales of Pass France 98, and

(b) the market for sales of individual entry tickets by the CFO, national football federations and tour operators relating to all finals matches, whether sold blind or at a time when the identities of participating teams were known. This differs from the Commission's conclusion in so far as it makes no distinction between sales of individual entry tickets by the CFO in 1997 and those in 1998 by each of the three official distribution channels.

(76) The relevant markets as referred to in this Decision explicitly recognise the different characteristics of Pass France 98 vis-à-vis individual tickets. Nevertheless, the CFO's argument that blind sales of individual entry tickets by the CFO in 1997 are substitutable for sales by the CFO and other outlets at a later date is not accepted. The objective of defining relevant product markets is to identify the actual competitors of an undertaking that are capable of constraining the behaviour of that undertaking and of preventing it from behaving independently of effective competitive pressure. An analysis of the conditions under which sales took place of individual entry tickets relating to second-phase matches in 1997 by the CFO confirms that the CFO was able at that time to act in an environment free from any such competitive pressure. Those tickets related to prestigious matches for which the number of applications from consumers able to provide an address in France exceeded almost six times the available supply, notwithstanding the fact that the identities of participating teams were unknown at the time of sale[244]. In view of such demand levels, and because consumers are unlikely in 1997 to have considered national football federations and European tour operators as realistic alternative sources of supply, the CFO was clearly able to operate, in relation to its sale of such tickets, as a de facto monopolist free from any competitive pressure from other undertakings.

**D. RELEVANT GEOGRAPHIC MARKET**

(77) In view of the widespread demand for tickets throughout the EEA[245], the geographic market relating to the sale by the CFO to the general public of Pass France 98 and individual entry tickets in 1996 and 1997 comprises at least all countries

---

[243] See previous footnote.

[244] Blind sales of such tickets can be contrasted with those of tickets relating to first-phase matches which, in order to maximise the participation of supporters, were packaged as Pass France 98.

[245] Evidenced by the outcome of CFO sales to EEA countries from 22-4-1998 when 45% of tickets were sold to consumers outside France.

within the EEA. Notwithstanding the widespread demand for those tickets, the CFO's conditions of sale artificially limited sales to members of the general public either resident or able to provide an address in France.

**Arguments of the CFO relating to the scope of sales of Pass France 98**

(78)    In its response to the Commission's Statement of Objections and during the oral hearing, the CFO argued that, in relation to sales in 1996 and 1997 of Pass France 98, the requirement to provide a postal address in France had no effect on consumers outside France and that the geographic market did not, therefore, extend beyond France. According to the CFO, only the general public living close to World Cup stadiums would have wished to purchase Pass France 98, given the unknown identity of teams participating in matches to which those tickets gave entry as well as the constraints imposed by such a product on the purchaser (notably the requirement either to secure accommodation near a stadium for a significant period of time or to make as many return trips as were necessary between one's place of residence and the stadium in order to attend all matches).

(79)    In support of this argument, the CFO referred the Commission to evidence suggesting that between 71% and 91% of Pass France 98 were bought either by the general public living in the Département in which a host stadium was located or in the immediately surrounding Départements. The CFO also referred the Commission to the decision by European tour operators not to offer Pass France 98 to the general public, as well as those of national football federations not to package the sale of tickets into Pass France 98 type products, as evidence that demand outside France for Pass France 98 was non-existent and that the geographic market was therefore limited to residents local to World Cup stadiums in France.

(80)    The Commission rejects these arguments. In relation to sales of Pass France 98, it cannot be ruled out that a significant number of consumers outside France would have wished to purchase such tickets, given the Europe-wide interest that the finals competition generated. This is supported in part by an assessment of the purchasing habits of consumers outside France in relation to individual ticket sales for first phase and round of 16 matches by the CFO from 22 April 1998, which demonstrates that consumers outside France were not exclusively interested in watching matches involving the participation of their national team[246].

(81)    Had consumers outside France been given the opportunity to purchase Pass France 98 from the CFO, it is quite probable that a significant number would have chosen to make as many return trips as were necessary to allow them to watch all the matches to which Pass France 98 allowed access. While this applies notably to Pass France 98 sold for matches taking place in Lens, in view of its proximity to the Belgian border, it is reasonable to assume also that consumers in other countries would have been prepared to travel to other venues given the ease with which those venues could be accessed (stadiums located in Bordeaux and Toulouse, for example, were easily accessible to consumers from Spain while the stadium in Marseille was accessible to consumers from Italy).

(82)    Furthermore, and notwithstanding the statistics referred to by the CFO, it is entirely foreseeable that a significant number of consumers outside France might

---

[246] See recitals 25 and 26, while some 38% of individual entry tickets sold by the CFO after 22-4-1998 were purchased by the general public providing addresses outside France but in countries whose teams had qualified for the finals competition, only 10% of entry tickets sold after this date could be purchased by supporters of teams participating in any given match. As such, a significant proportion of the general public outside France were interested to attend matches not involving the participation of their national team.

have wished to make arrangements to stay in or near the town in which a host stadium was located for the duration of the first phase and (where necessary) Round of 16 competition, thereby combining guaranteed attendance at a series of finals matches with an extended stay in what is well known to be a popular destination for foreign visitors.

(83)    The decision by European tour operators to sell tickets distributed to them through Pass France 98 on a desegregated, individual basis cannot be interpreted as suggesting a lack of demand for Pass France 98 outside France. Such a practice, involving as it did the sale of individual tickets together with that of other services, was likely to have been motivated instead by a desire to maximise revenues which sales of Pass France 98 would not have achieved. In relation to sales by national football federations, the Commission does not consider their failure to sell Pass France 98-type products as relevant, given the nature of tickets allocated to them[247] and the lack of any economic incentive for them to do so.

## E. DOMINANT POSITION

(84)    The CFO represented the sole outlet for blind sales to the general public in 1996 and 1997 of Pass France 98 and individual entry tickets. As such, and in view of its ability to act independently and, therefore, free from competitive restraint, the CFO held a dominant position on the relevant markets.

### Responsibilities of the CFO as dominant undertaking on the relevant markets

(85)    In accordance with the case-law of the Court of Justice and the Court of First Instance of the European Communities, an undertaking in a dominant position has a special responsibility not to allow its conduct to impair undistorted competition on the common market. The actual scope of that special responsibility must be considered in the light of the specific circumstances of the case, reflecting a weakened competitive situation[248].

(86)    The scope of the parties' responsibility must therefore be considered in relation to the degree of dominance held by the parties and to any special characteristics of the market which might affect the competitive situation.

(87)    Taking particular account of the significant difference between the demand for and supply of Pass France 98 and individual tickets sold by the CFO to the general public in 1996 and 1997, the CFO was, as a de facto monopolist, under a prima facie obligation to ensure that entry tickets sold in 1996 and 1997 for finals matches were made available to the general public under non-discriminatory arrangements throughout the EEA, even though demand from consumers outside France for certain ticket products may have been relatively small as against the demand from the general public in France. While exceptions to this general principle may apply, each must be considered on its individual merits and in the light of an objective assessment of what is the minimum necessary to achieve the stated aims.

---

[247] Which would have made the bundling of anything other than a very small number of tickets into Pass France 98 type-products impossible.

[248] Judgment of the Court of First Instance in Case T/83/91 Tetra Pak II [1994] ECR II-755, at paragraphs 114 and 115. In Case 7/82 GVL [1983] ECR 483, the Court of Justice had previously acknowledged the scope of a monopolist's special responsibility in relation to discriminatory conduct on grounds of nationality or residence. The Court had stated (inter alia): 'Such a refusal [to manage rights] by an undertaking having a de facto monopoly to provide its services for all those who may be in need of them but who do not come within a certain category of persons defined by the undertaking on the basis of nationality or residence must be regarded as an abuse of a dominant position within the meaning of the first paragraph of Article 86 of the Treaty' (at paragraph 56).

## F. ABUSE

(88)   In view of
  (a) the conditions of sale which applied in relation to CFO sales of blind tickets in 1996 and 1997,
  (b) the sales information made available by the CFO on its official World Cup website and on which the general public outside France could have reasonably been expected to rely, and
  (c) the restrictive means made available to the general public outside France for reserving entry tickets, the CFO abused its dominant position on the relevant markets because its behaviour had the effect of imposing unfair trading conditions on residents outside France which resulted in a limitation of the market to the prejudice of those consumers.

### Requirement to provide a postal address in France

(89)   The general public outside France were free to purchase entry tickets direct from the CFO on condition that they provided a postal address in France to which the tickets could be delivered[249].

(90)   At the time of CFO sales of Pass France 98 and individual tickets, the general public resident in France had little difficulty in providing an address to which tickets could be delivered. However. only by entering into wholly arbitrary, impractical and exceptional arrangements[250] could most of the general public resident outside France have obtained tickets direct from the CFO in 1996 and 1997[251]. While it is questionable whether the general public outside France had ever been adequately informed that tickets could be purchased direct from the CFO, the effect of the requirement to provide a postal address in France was to discriminate specifically against the general public resident outside France, given that those resident in France were significantly better placed to meet that requirement.

(91)   This discrimination amounted in practice to an imposition by the CFO of unfair trading conditions on residents outside France and resulted in a limitation of the market to the detriment of those consumers in relation to CFO sales of 393200 tickets through Pass France 98 and 181000 tickets relating to the opening match, quarter and semi-finals, third and fourth-place play-off and the final, contrary to Article 82 of the EC Treaty and Article 54 of the EEA Agreement.

### Sales information provided by the CFO

(92)   From 6 May 1997 the CFO provided information on its official World Cup website relating to the means by which the general public in and outside France could obtain match tickets for the finals competition. Members of the general public resident outside France were advised to obtain tickets either from authorised tour operators or national football federations. No indication was given that entry tickets could be obtained direct from the CFO. Furthermore, information was provided to the effect that the CFO would not sell tickets direct to the non-French public, and that accordingly a non-French citizen visiting France and wishing to purchase entry tickets for finals matches would be obliged to contact a national football federation or tour operator.

---

[249]  Responding to the Commission's formal request for information of 15-1-1998.

[250]  Examples include use of poste restante or embassy services.

[251]  Given the emphasis which the CFO placed in its sales information on the requirement to be resident in France and the advice given to the general public that it would not supply to the non-French public, it is open to doubt whether residents abroad would have been permitted by the CFO to avail themselves of these alternatives in practice.

(93)  The effect of such advice was to limit the demand for blind CFO sales of individual tickets in 1997 either exclusively to French citizens or to the general public resident in France. Conversely, that advice would have deterred the non-French public or, at the very least, those not resident in France, from seeking to purchase individual entry tickets direct from the CFO. This resulted in a strict limitation of the market by the CFO to the prejudice of the general public resident outside France in relation to CFO sales of 181000 tickets for the opening match, quarter and semi-finals, third and fourth-place play-off and the final itself, contrary to Article 82 of the EC Treaty and Article 54 of the EEA Agreement.

**Channels available for reserving entry tickets direct from the CFO**

(94)  Of the different means by which tickets could be reserved by the general public from the CFO, only that of applying in writing was available to consumers resident outside France. Telephone reservations could be made only from within metropolitan France, while reservation by Minitel (an information system used by and designed specifically for those living in France) was available only to residents outside France via connection to the Internet, and then only at an additional cost of FRF 350. Similarly, ticket reservations through branches of Crédit Agricole could only be made in France.

(95)  Given the anticipated high level of demand for Pass France 98 in relation to their limited supply, the need to reserve tickets quickly would have been of paramount importance to the general public. Thus, consumers for whom the only means of reserving tickets was by written request would have been at a disadvantage vis-à-vis those who were able to avail themselves of other, quicker means of ticket reservation.

(96)  In relation to individual entry tickets sold direct by the CFO in 1997, the general public was required to submit applications between 18 September and 18 October 1997. Although such tickets were not allocated on a first-come-first-served basis, members of the general public resident in France were favoured over those resident elsewhere in the EEA, given that application forms were made available only through branches of Credit-Agricole based in France.

(97)  Consequently, the means by which Pass France 98 and individual tickets could be obtained direct from the CFO in 1996 and 1997 discriminated against the general public resident outside France.

**Arguments of the CFO as to abuse**

(98)  In its response to the Commission's Statement of Objections, the CFO argued that, on the basis of previous Commission practice and the case-law of the Court of Justice, the CFO could not have abused a dominant position, given that certain of the conditions necessary for the application of Article 82 of the EC Treaty[252] were not fulfilled.

**Conduct having an effect on the structure of competition**

(99)  The CFO argued that conduct in breach of Article 82 must affect the structure of competition in a given market to the detriment of a dominant undertaking's competitors, given that the provision is not intended to protect, in a direct manner, the interests of consumers[253]. The CFO contends therefore that its conduct does not

---

[252] All comments by the CFO in this regard are equally pertinent to the application of Article 54 of the EEA Agreement.

[253] In this context, the CFO argued that Article 82 must be read in the light of Article 3(g) of the EC Treaty, which requires that competition in the internal market is not distorted.

fall within the scope of Article 82, as the requirement to provide an address in France for ticket sales in 1996 and 1997 did not affect the structure of competition on the relevant markets.

(100)  The Commission rejects such an interpretation of Article 82. While the application of Article 82 often requires an assessment of the effect of an undertaking's behaviour on the structure of competition in a given market, its application in the absence of such an effect cannot be excluded. Consumers' interests are protected by Article 82, such protection being achieved either by prohibiting conduct by dominant undertakings which impairs free and undistorted competition or which is direct prejudicial to consumers. Accordingly, and as has been expressly recognised by the Court of Justice[254], Article 82 can properly be applied, where appropriate, to situations in which a dominant undertaking's behaviour direct prejudices the interests of consumers. notwithstanding the absence of any effect on the structure of competition.

**Commercial advantage**

(101)  The CFO argued that an undertaking abuses its dominant position only if it makes use of the opportunities arising out of its dominant position in such a way as to reap trading benefits which it would not have reaped if there had been normal and sufficiently effective competition. The CFO derived neither a financial nor competitive advantage by requiring consumers to provide an address in France for ticket sales in 1996 and 1997, and thus derived no trading benefits as a result of its actions.

(102)  The Commission rejects such an argument. While evidence that a dominant undertaking has secured for itself a financial or competitive advantage as a result of its actions may support a conclusion of abuse, it is not essential to a finding of abuse[255]. In this case, the effect of the CFO's behaviour was to discriminate against residents outside France, which indirect amounted to a discrimination against those consumers on grounds of nationality, contrary to fundamental Community principles. Such conduct cannot, in this case, be considered to fall outside the scope of Article 82 on the grounds that the CFO, as a dominant undertaking, failed to derive a commercial or other advantage from its actions.

**Limitation of markets**

(103)  The CFO contests the Commission's view that it abused its dominant position under Article 82(b) by limiting the market for sales of Pass France 98 and individual tickets to the prejudice of consumers outside France, for the following reasons:

(a)  Had European tour operators decided to sell Pass France 98 as foreseen by the CFO, no such limitation of the market would have occurred, since consumers outside France would have been able to obtain Pass France 98 without being required to provide an address in France. In relation to sales of individual tick-

---

[254]  Case 6/72 Continental Can [1973] ECR 215 at paragraph 26: The Court held that Article 82 'is not only aimed at practices which may cause damage to consumers directly, but also at those which are detrimental to them through their impact on an effective competition structure'.

[255]  For example, cases concerning excessive pricing require an assessment of the extent to which (if at all) a dominant undertaking charged a price which was excessive in relation to the economic value of the product or service. Hence, the extent to which that undertaking was able to obtain a commercial advantage, which it otherwise would not have been able to obtain under conditions of normal competition, must usually be determined before any conclusions concerning excessive pricing can be drawn.

ets, the CFO's conduct did not limit the market. since tickets were offered to the general public throughout the EEA at various times by each of the three distribution channels;

(b) According to the case-law of the Court of Justice[256], an undertaking abuses its dominant position through a limitation of the market under Article 82(b) only where it benefits from the absence of competitive pressure by failing to improve its performance which it would have otherwise been required to do. Given that the number of match tickets was necessarily limited and that CFO sales arrangements had no effect on the quality of the product consumed, the CFO argues that the existence of competitive pressure in the market would not have resulted in any such improvement in performance by the CFO, and that as such its conduct cannot be qualified as abusive under Article 82(b).

(104) The Commission rejects each of those arguments. As the dominant undertaking on the relevant product markets, the CFO was under an obligation not to artificially limit ticket sales, whether or not other economic operators could or did sell such tickets. In relation to the CFO's arguments concerning the scope of application of Article 82(b), the requirement to provide an address in France had the undeniable effect of limiting the geographic market for the sale of entry tickets by the CFO in 1996 and 1997 to the prejudice of consumers resident outside France. The implementation of those arrangements represents an abuse of the CFO's dominant position in accordance with the specific wording of Article 82(b), a conclusion which is in no way inconsistent with the case-law of the Court of Justice to which the CFO has referred[257]. The CFO's argument that it could not have improved its performance under conditions of competition is, therefore, irrelevant.

## G. SECURITY

(105) Ensuring effective security at football matches is essential and may, in particular circumstances, justify the implementation of special ticket sales arrangements by tournament organisers. Nevertheless, in order to determine whether and, if so, to what extent, security considerations may justly ticketing arrangements which would otherwise be deemed to infringe Community law, each set of arrangements must be considered on their individual merits in the light of an objective assessment of what is necessary to achieve reasonable security objectives.

### Security at football matches

(106) The principal concern of the CFO was to ensure, in compliance with the provisions of the 1985 Convention, that rival groups of supporters of teams participating in any given match were separated from one another in each of the World Cup stadiums.

(107) The CFO sought to achieve such a segregation through the allocation to national football federations whose teams were participating in a given match of tickets relating to seats located at opposite ends of the stadium. Thus, tickets reserved for rival groups of supporters were not sold blind by the CFO but were made available at a time when the identities of participating teams were known.

(108) Tickets sold blind by the CFO in 1996 and 1997 related to seats reserved for neutral spectators. The CFO sold such tickets exclusively to members of the general public able to provide an address in France, who were classified in relation to all

---

[256] Cases cited by the CFO: Case 41/90 Hofner [1991] ECR 1979 and Case 179/90 Merci [1991] 5889.

[257] See previous footnote.

matches as neutral spectators. The CFO has, however, previously referred the Commission to expert opinion which considers that consumers purchasing blind tickets generally are peaceful spectators who do not represent a specific security risk. Such an analysis appears reasonable, given that consumers purchasing such tickets are evidently doing so because they wish to attend a football match irrespective of the teams involved, and are not therefore motivated by their support for any particular team.

(109)   It follows therefore that any consumer, regardless of nationality, purchasing entry tickets on a blind basis should not, in principle, be regarded as a supporter of any particular team for purposes of security. Accordingly, such consumers should not, in principle, be subject to arrangements relating to the segregation of rival groups of supporters as envisaged under the 1985 Convention. The obligation to provide a postal address in France, imposed on consumers wishing to purchase blind tickets from the CFO in 1996 and 1997, was therefore excessive and failed to contribute in any material way to maintaining or improving security at football matches.

**Arguments of the CFO relating to security**

(110)   In its response to the Commission's Statement of Objections and during the oral hearing, the CFO sought to justify its discriminatory sales arrangements on security grounds. According to the CFO, if it had sold tickets in 1996 and 1997 to the general public throughout the EEA, supporters of participating teams are likely to have found themselves located in those parts of the stadium reserved for neutral spectators. That being so, the CFO considers that for the purposes of ticket sales in 1996 and 1997 it was unable to treat all spectators throughout the EEA as neutral without at the same time contravening the provisions of the 1985 Convention as well as the relevant guidelines, which required an effective separation of rival groups of supporters of participating teams.

(111)   The CFO also argued
    (a) that it was not possible to sell tickets on a blind basis in 1996 and 1997 and to determine the placement of ticket holders at a later date when the identities of participating teams were known, and
    (b) that no comparison could be made between CFO sales in 1996 and 1997 to the general public able to provide an address in France and CFO sales in 1998 to the general public able to provide an address within the EEA, given that sales in 1998 took place after the group draw when the identities of participating teams in first-phase matches were known.

(112)   The CFO's argument that it could not have treated all members of the general public in the EEA in 1996 and 1997 as neutral is rejected. The 1985 Convention refers specifically to the need to ensure an effective segregation of rival groups of supporters through (inter alia) a strict control over ticket sales. While the CFO considered it necessary to treat all members of the general public other than those able to provide an address in France as a potential rival supporter in 1996 and 1997 for the purposes of ticket sales, such a policy was excessive because it failed to take into account the generally peaceful nature of consumers purchasing tickets at a time when the identities of participating teams are not known. As the CFO has itself previously confirmed[258], consumers purchasing tickets on a blind basis would not have represented a specific security risk. Thus, the CFO was wrong to have considered members of the general public who were unable to provide an address

---

[258] See CFO letter of 4-6-1998 (point 24), responding to the Commission's formal request for information of 15-5-1998.

in France but who wished to purchase tickets from it in 1996 and 1997 as potential rival supporters for the purposes of security.

(113)  In any event, even if consumers purchasing tickets on a blind basis could properly have been considered to represent a specific security risk (which is not accepted by the Commission), it is unlikely in the extreme that anyone, having purchased a ticket on a blind basis (thereby entitling admission to that part of the stadium reserved specifically for the neutral public) and having by chance found himself attending a match involving the participation of his home team, would be located next to or within the vicinity of supporters of the opposing team, given that at the very least the latter must also have been fortunate enough, having purchased tickets on a blind basis, to find themselves also attending a match involving the participation of their home team in that part of the stadium reserved for the neutral public. Hence, any risk that the CFO might have breached the terms of the 1985 Convention by implementing non-discriminatory sales arrangements in 1996 and 1997 was, in statistical terms, insignificant.

(114)  In view of the above, the CFO's supposed inability to determine the siting of blind ticket holders after the identities of participating teams became known, as well as its contention that sales arrangements implemented in 1998 cannot be compared with those adopted previously, are irrelevant for the purposes of this Decision (see recital 111).

## H. SUBSTANTIAL PART OF THE COMMON MARKET

(115)  Since the CFO held a dominant position on the relevant markets, and since it determined the conditions under which consumers within the whole of the EEA could purchase Pass France 98 and individual tickets in 1996 and 1997, the CFO's dominant position extended to at least the whole of the EEA, and, accordingly, a substantial part of the common market for the purposes of Article 82 of the EC Treaty.

## I. EFFECT ON TRADE BETWEEN MEMBER STATES

(116)  In relation to ticket sales on the relevant product markets, the CFO imposed conditions of sale on the general public which had the effect of denying the overwhelming majority of residents outside France access to those markets. Thus, the requirement to provide an address in France for sales of Pass France 98 and individual entry tickets in 1996 and 1997 appreciably affected trade between Member States.

### Arguments of the CFO relating to effects on trade

(117)  The arguments put forward by the CFO concerning the effect of its conduct on trade between Member States are considered above in recitals 78 to 83.

## J. THE NOTIFICATION OF 11 JUNE 1997

(118)  In its response to the Statement of Objections, the CFO argued that as the general arrangements for the distribution of tickets were explained to the Commission at the time of the notification in June 1997, any objections relating to those arrangements should have been raised at the time. The CFO argues further that as no such objections were raised by the Commission it was entitled to assume that its general ticketing arrangements were in compliance with Community law. The CFO considers therefore that the Commission's decision to initiate proceedings against the CFO represented a breach of the principle of legitimate expectation as defined by the Court of Justice.

(119)  The Commission rejects the CFO's assertions in this regard. While it accepts that in the notification the CFO explained the means by which tickets would be sold through each of the officially appointed distribution channels, the Commission was not made aware, at the time, of the requirement obliging consumers to provide a postal address in France for CFO sales in 1996 and 1997[259]. Indeed, the CFO expressly told the Commission that Pass France 98, while intended principally for sale to football supporters and the local and regional public, would in fact be accessible to all[260].

(120)  Furthermore, an undertaking which notifies specific agreements or arrangements cannot, as a matter of principle, be permitted to argue at a later date that it was legitimately entitled to assume that agreements or arrangements which did not form part of the notification but which may have been communicated to the Commission at the time of the notification were in accordance with the competition provisions of the EC Treaty. As the CFO's notification concerned exclusively arrangements relating to the proposed system for the selection of tour operators authorised to sell entry tickets for finals matches in Europe, the Commission was under a legal obligation to consider those arrangements only, and cannot therefore be criticised at a later date for deciding to initiate proceedings in relation to other arrangements upon which it was not formally requested to take a view.

## K. FINES

(121)  In accordance with Article 15 of Regulation No 17, the Commission may, by decision, impose on an undertaking which either intentionally or negligently infringes Article 82 of the EC Treaty and Article 54 of the EEA Agreement, a fine of between EUR 1000 and EUR 1 million, or a sum in excess thereof but not exceeding 10% of the undertaking's turnover in the preceding business year.

(122)  The abusive conduct to which this Decision refers, the effect of which was to discriminate in favour of consumers able to provide an address in France, indirectly amounts to discrimination on grounds of nationality, since ticket sales were artificially and predominantly limited by the CFO to residents located within a single Member State. Such conduct represents a breach of fundamental Community principles.

(123)  The Commission notes that the ticketing arrangements as implemented by the CFO were similar to those adopted for previous World Cup finals tournaments, and that the issues raised in relation to the application of EC competition rules are of such a specific nature as not to enable conclusions to be easily drawn from previous Commission decisions or case-law of the Court of Justice. The Commission has therefore concluded that the CFO was not, at the time, aware that its sales arrangements in 1996 and 1997 were in breach of Community law.

(124)  The Commission acknowledges further that the CFO took positive steps to ensure, to the extent that it considered it necessary, that ticketing arrangements for the 1998 Football World Cup complied with Community and national law through formal and informal contacts with the Commission and competition authorities in France. The Commission notes also the decision taken by the CFO, at the former's request, to amend its sales arrangements in order to give consumers throughout the EEA the chance to reserve 175500 individual entry tickets directly from the CFO in 1998.

---

[259]  It should be noted further that at the time of the notification the CFO had already sold all Pass France 98 to the general public under the arrangements in question.

[260]  At section 4.1(ii) of the CFO's notification of 11-6-1997.

(125)   Every abuse of a dominant position should normally be penalised by a fine vary-
         ing in accordance with the gravity and duration of the infringement. In view of the
         foregoing arguments, however, the Commission considers it appropriate to impose
         only a symbolic fine on the CFO of EUR 1000. This does not, however, represent
         a policy to be adopted in all future similar cases,

## HAS ADOPTED THIS DECISION:

Article 1
The Comité français d'organisation de la Coupe du monde de football 1998 (CFO) has
infringed Article 82 of the EC Treaty and Article 54 of the EEA Agreement by applying
discriminatory arrangements in 1996 and 1997 relating to the sale to the general public of
entry tickets for World Cup finals matches. Those arrangements involved the imposition
of unfair trading conditions on consumers outside France which resulted in a limitation of
the market to the prejudice of those consumers in relation to the sale of 393200 tickets
through Pass France 98 and 181000 tickets relating to the opening match, quarter and
semi-finals, third and fourth-place play-off and the final.

Article 2
A fine of EUR 1000 is hereby imposed on the CFO in respect of the infringement referred
to in Article 1.

Article 3
The fine shall be paid in euro within three months of the date of notification of this Deci-
sion to the following account:
Account No 310-0933000-43
European Commission
Banque Bruxelles-Lambert
Agence Européenne
Rond Point Schuman/Schumanplein 5 B – 1040 Brussels.
After three months, interest shall automatically be payable at the rate applied by the Euro-
pean Central Bank to its repo operations on the first working day of the month in which
this Decision was adopted, plus 3,5 percentage points.

Article 4
This Decision is addressed to: Comité français d'organisation de la Coupe du monde de
football 1998 (CFO) 23-25 Rue de Berri F – 75008 Paris.
This Decision is enforceable pursuant to Article 256 of the EC Treaty.

Done at Brussels, 20 July 1999.

For the Commission
Karel Van Miert
Member of the Commission

———

## * 2.4.41.   COMMISSION STATEMENT ON PENDING COURT CASE
##             REGARDING FORMULA ONE, 26 JULY 1999[261]

———

---

[261]  IP/99/564.

**2.4.42.    COMMISSION DECISION RELATING TO A PROCEEDING UNDER ARTICLE 81 OF THE EC TREATY (IV/36.539 – BRITISH INTERACTIVE BROADCASTING/OPEN), 15 SEPTEMBER 1999**[262]

*The Commission of the European Communities,*

–    Having regard to the Treaty establishing the European Community,
–    Having regard to Council Regulation No 17 of 6 February 1962, First Regulation implementing Articles 85 and 86 of the Treaty[263], as last amended by Regulation (EC) No 1216/1999[264], and in particular Articles 6 and 8 thereof,
–    Having regard to the application for negative clearance and the notification for exemption submitted, pursuant to Articles 2 and 4 of Regulation No 17, on 13 June 1997,
–    Having regard to the summary of the application and notification published pursuant to Article 19(3) of Regulation No 17[265],

After consultation with the Advisory Committee for Restrictive Practices and Dominant Positions;
Whereas:

## I. THE FACTS
## A. INTRODUCTION

(1)     On 13 June 1997, the parties notified to the Commission the creation of a joint venture company, British Interactive Broadcasting Ltd (BiB, now named Open) and requested negative clearance and/or exemption pursuant to Regulation No 17. BiB's parent companies are BSkyB Ltd, BT Holdings Limited, Midland Bank plc and Matsushita Electric Europe (Headquarters) Limited.

(2)     BiB is to provide a new type of service, digital interactive television services, to consumers in the United Kingdom. This involves putting in place the necessary infrastructure and services to allow companies, such as banks, supermarkets and travel agents, to interact directly with the consumer. An important element of this infrastructure is a digital settop box. BiB will subsidise the retail selling price of digital satellite set-top boxes, satellite dishes and lownoise blocks[266] (LNBs).

(3)     The same infrastructure will be used by television companies, as it will allow them to integrate interactivity into their services: for instance, interactive advertisements and voting in quiz shows.

(4)     BiB will also provide certain services direct to the consumer, such as e-mail, 'walled garden' Internet access[267] and downloading of computer games. Its service is expected to begin in the autumn of 1999.

## B. THE PARTIES
### 1. BT Holdings Limited

(5)     BT Holdings Limited is a wholly-owned subsidiary of British Telecommunications plc (BT). BT is licensed to run certain telecommunications services in the

---

[262] 99/781/EC, OJ L 53,
[263] OJ 13, 21-2-1962, pp. 204-262.
[264] OJ L148, 15-6-1999, p. 5.
[265] OJ C 322, 21-10-1998, p. 6.
[266] A low-noise block converter (LNB) detects the signal relayed from the feed, converts it to an electrical current, amplifies it and lowers its frequency.
[267] The parties use this term to describe access to a limited amount of Internet content.

United Kingdom. It supplies telephone exchange lines to homes and businesses; local, trunk and international (to and from the United Kingdom) telephone calls and other telecommunications services and equipment for customers' premises.

## 2. British Sky Broadcasting Ltd

(6)     British Sky Broadcasting Ltd (BSkyB) is a wholly-owned subsidiary of British Sky Broadcasting Group plc. News Corporation owns 39,88% of the shares of BSkyB Group plc's shares.

(7)     BSkyB is a broadcaster of analogue pay television ('paytv') services delivered by the ASTRA satellites for directto-home (DTH) and cable reception in the United Kingdom and Ireland. BSkyB operates at both retail and wholesale levels in these areas. It launched a digital satellite pay-tv service on 1 October 1998 using the digital set-top box, satellite dish and low-noise block which BiB will subsidise. BSkyB Group is also active in the provision of conditional access services and other technical services necessary for pay television.

## 3. Midland Bank plc

(8)     Midland Bank plc is a public limited company authorised by the Bank of England to carry on a banking business. It is part of the HSBC group of companies and a direct subsidiary of the holding company, HSBC Holdings plc. Midland and the other companies in the HSBC group provide a range of banking and financial services in the United Kingdom and around the world.

## 4. Matsushita Electric Europe (Headquarters) Limited

(9)     Matsushita Electric Europe (Headquarters) Limited (Matsushita) is a wholly-owned subsidiary of Matsushita Electric Industrial Co. Ltd. (MEI). MEI is a designer, developer and manufacturer of electronic and electrical products and associated software and information technology for home, industrial and commercial uses. The MEI group operates world-wide and manufactures and/or trades through a number of subsidiaries in the United Kingdom and other Member States.

## C. THE RELEVANT MARKETS

(10)    BiB will be principally active on the digital interactive television services market and on the technical services market. Two of its parent companies, BSkyB and BT, are present in markets which are closely related to one or more of these markets.

## 1. Product markets
### (a) Digital interactive television services

(11)    The following services will form part of the BiB digital interactive television service: home banking, home shopping, holiday and travel services, down-loading of games, learning on-line, entertainment and leisure, sports, motor world, a limited collection of 'walled garden' Internet sites provided by a third party and e-mail and public services. BiB describes retailers which offer goods or services over its infrastructure as 'content providers'.

(12)    In the view of the Commission, the digital interactive television services market is a separate market.

(13)    In defining product markets, the most important factor is evaluation of demand substitutability. Given that digital interactive television services, such as those to be offered by BiB, are not currently available throughout the United Kingdom[268],

---

[268] However, commercial trials in limited areas are underway.

past data does not exist to evaluate the likely response of customers to a hypothetical small, non-transitory change in relative prices of BiB's services and possible substitutes[269]. Demand substitutability can also be assessed by comparing the characteristics of products or services in order to determine whether they are particularly suited to satisfy constant needs and are only to a limited extent interchangeable with other products or services[270].

(14)    The Commission contacted BiB's main prospective customers and the main companies in the industry to ask for their views about the boundaries of the relevant market and to obtain the necessary factual evidence to reach a conclusion. In this context, the Commission also has taken into account the fact that content providers' willingness to pay BiB to be part of its service, and their likely reaction to a small permanent increase in the price charged, will ultimately depend on the attitude of end-users. It is therefore the retail-demand substitutability for digital interactive television services which is determinant in defining the upstream market of the supply of digital interactive television services by service providers, such as BiB, to content providers.

(15)    Prospective content providers have confirmed to the Commission that it is the breadth of the package of services which will attract them to a digital interactive television services platform, as they believe that it is the availability of a broad range of services which will attract consumers[271]. In other words, such a range of services will increase the number of potential customers for the content providers' services. The television interface will also allow content providers access to a unique mass market for their products or services, reaching potentially almost 100% of British households.

(16)    End-user demand substitutability for a package of interactive services is distinguishable from demand substitutability of the individual services which form part of the package or from close alternative sources of supply for the customers of BiB's services such as highstreet retailing or interactive services via personal computers. The digital interactive television services and pay-television services are different markets.

(17)    As it explained in recitals 18 to 23, this conclusion is based on the different characteristics of the types of goods and services provided and on the consumers' views on their substitutability which mean that customers will not be in a position to switch easily to available alternative products and/or services or to suppliers located elsewhere. Market distinct from high-street retailing

(18)    Retailing services represent only one part of the typical package of services forming digital interactive television services. E-mail, downloading of computer games, limited Internet access and information services will also form part of the

---

[269] See Commission Notice on the definition of the relevant market for the purposes of Community competition law, (OJ C 372, 9-12-1997, p. 5).

[270] In its judgment of 26 November 1998, in Case C-7/97, Oscar Bronner GmbH Co. KG v Mediaprint [1998] ECR I-7791, the Court of Justice repeated the formula (paragraph 33) that 'the market for the product or service in question comprises all the products or services which in view of their characteristics are particularly suited to satisfy constant needs and are only to a limited extent interchangeable with other products or services (Case 31/80 L'Oréal v De Nieuwe AMCK [1980] ECR 3775, paragraph 25; Case C-62/86 AKZO v Commission [1991] ECR I-3359, paragraph 51)'.

[271] An operator explained that 'what seems clear [...] is that shopping is not a sufficient stand alone reason for customers to want to invest in the equipment for such services. The offer must be part of a larger offer, including entertainment and education, which again favours the BSkyB based channel as it is part of the wider digital relaunch of the network'.

package. There are economies of scope in the provision of such a package of services, because the infrastructure required for each of the individual services is the same. BiB will market this package of services and has entered into an agreement with BSkyB to this end. The promotion of an interactive service brand, distinct from that of the individual content providers, strongly suggests that BiB regards its own services as distinct from those of high-street retailing.

(19)   The characteristics of the retailing services of the type to be offered by BiB and high-street retailing are markedly different. For example, the range of products or services offered on-line by retailers is likely to be far more limited than what is available in high-street shops. This is most likely to be the case with perishable goods, such as food, or bulky goods where storage and delivery charges would be high. There will be a price difference between goods or services purchased in the high street and those obtained via a package of digital interactive television services, if only on account of the delivery charge. In terms of price, it seems that consumers would be willing to pay a premium for the convenience of home shopping[272].

(20)   It follows from the above that the market for digital interactive television services is separate from that for the traditional retailing of goods and services in high streets. Distinction between markets for digital interactive services available via televisions and those available via personal computers

(21)   Both the demand-substitutability test and differences in the characteristics of interactive services available via television sets and via personal computers lead to the conclusion that they are separate product markets. A small permanent increase in the price of such services available via televisions is unlikely to be constrained by the existence of services available on personal computers. While television sets are ubiquitous, in the United Kingdom only some 25% of households have a personal computer and fewer than half of these are equipped with a modem. Moreover, the relatively high cost of personal computers means that the switching cost for end-users would be high. The parties themselves have pointed out that consumer demand for services available via television is different from that for services delivered via personal computers. They point to differences both in purchase prices of televisions and personal computers and in their characteristics of use[273]. Digital interactive services delivered to televisions can also be distinguished from services delivered to personal computers by the fact that interactivity can be integrated into traditional broadcast entertainment channels.

(22)   This distinction is confirmed by the reaction of some retailers[274] who have said that they will target different customers using different brands belonging to the

---

[272] Binary Compass Enterprises Report, 1997, by David Reibstein and Sunil Gupta 'The online retail commerce report' rated price competition fourth in what was important to customers.

[273] The parties' statements coincide with independent analysis. See 'Regulating Communications: approaching convergence in the Information age' July 1998, policy document of British Departments of Trade and Industry and of Culture, Media and Sport at paragraphs 1.13-1.15: 'Traditional television and radio are likely to retain their strong and distinctive position because of their ubiquity, familiarity, low cost and ease of use. The environments of the living room (the traditional place for the TV) and the work room (the home of the PC) are generally quite distinct.' Furthermore, BiB will offer limited internet access via TV sets.

[274] 'We see BiB and the current Internet offers as being differing customer groups, rather than two ways to reach the same group'. 'mass market development on on-line retail requires a TV interface rather than a PC/internet channel which we see as being relatively limited for mass market apparel'. 'PC and TV delivered services are 'complementary''.

same group of companies when providing digital interactive services available via
television sets and personal computers[275].

**Market separate from pay television**

(23)    Finally, the demand for, and characteristics and intended use of, pay-television
services are largely different from those of digital interactive television services,
the former being largely entertainment services, the latter being largely transactional or informational services[276]. The business scope of interactive television
service providers such as BiB excludes forms of entertainment where viewing itself is the primary form of entertainment for the viewer, such as pay-television
channels. The digital interactive television services market is complementary to
and separate from, that for pay-television.

**(b) Pay-television**

(24)    Pay-television constitutes a product market separate from that for free-access television, namely advertisingfinanced television and television financed wholly or
partly through licence fees[277]. While, in the case of feeand advertising-financed
television, there is a trade relationship only between the programme supplier and
the advertising industry, in the case of pay-television there is a trade relationship
between the programme supplier and the viewer as subscriber. The conditions of
competition are accordingly different for the two types of television. Whereas in
the case of fee- and advertising-financed television the audience share and the advertising rates are the key parameters, in the case of pay-television the key factors
are the shaping of programmes to meet the interests of the target groups and the
level of subscriptions.

(25)    The Commission has stated in the past that there is no reason to distinguish between markets for analogue and digital pay television[278]. Digital pay-television is
only a further development of analogue pay-television and therefore does not constitute a separate relevant product market. Moreover, account should be taken of
the fact that in the next few years analogue broadcast paytelevision will be completely superseded by digital broadcast pay-television.

(26)    Pay-television is available to subscribers in the United Kingdom by various means
of transmission: digital terrestrial, satellite (analogue and digital) and cable (analogue, with digital cable services expected to start up in the near future). In the
United Kingdom, it is not appropriate to distinguish between pay-television markets on the basis of their mode of transmission. Paytelevision services provided by
one means of transmission act as a competitive constraint on their provision using
other means. Historical data shows this to be the case in respect of pay-television
delivered by satellite and cable. It is clear from end-user behaviour that the services are considered as substitutes. The composition of cable and satellite pay-

---

[275] This distinction is similar to the one made in the advertising markets in that different distribution mechanisms reach different target audiences. See Commission Decision 96/346/EC (IV/
M.553-RTL-Veronica-Endemol) (OJ L 134, 5-6-1996, p. 32, in particular recital 23).
[276] See Commission Decision 94/922/EC (IV/M.469-MSG Media Service) (OJ L 364, 31-12-
1994, p. 1, recital 38).
[277] See MSG Media Service, at paragraphs 32 and 33; Commission Decision 1999/153/EC (IV/
M993-Bertelsmann/Kirch/Premiere) (OJ L 53, 27-2-1999, p. 1, recital 18); Commission Decision
1999/242/EC (IV/36.237-TPS) (OJ L 90, 2-4-1999, p. 6).
[278] Bertelsmann/Kirch/Premiere, recital 18 and TPS.

television services is broadly similar[279] as is the price. BSkyB's penetration rate is [...] (*). Moreover, BSkyB's 'churn rate'[280] is [...] (*). Thus, the fact that satellite customers may have purchased a satellite set-top box and/or satellite dish does not create such a significant lock-in effect that switching between satellite and cable services is unlikely. There is no justification, either, for distinguishing a separate product market in respect of digital terrestrial pay television.

(27)    There is, therefore, a single pay-television market in the United Kingdom, with no distinction between analogue and digital, nor between modes of transmission.

**(c) Markets for the wholesale supply of films and sports channels for pay-television**

(28)    Experience has shown that, to be successful as a paytelevision operator, it is essential to include film and sports channels as part of the service[281]. BSkyB has itself identified 'movies and sports as key sales drivers'[282]. Pay-television operators' demand for particular channels reflects the demand of their subscribers. Pay-television channels composed of recently released films and live exclusive coverage of attractive sports events attract the largest viewing figures[283]. The subscriptions to such channels are the most expensive: while thematic or general interest paytelevision channels are supplied to customers as part of a package, film and sports channels are charged on an individual basis. For pay-television, the fact that sports and films programmes achieve very high viewing rates is crucial as it is a reflection of viewer's willingness to pay more for sports and films channels.

(29)    The wholesale price of acquiring film and sports channels is also far higher than that of other channels: small permanent increases in relative prices have been profitable. Taking the figures most favourable to BSkyB from BSkyB's wholesale price list (rate card) for the supply of its channels to cable operators, the cost to a cable operator of acquiring a single film or sport channel is at least seven times as much as the most expensive Sky basic channel[284]. This demonstrates that the

---

[279] In terms of premium film and sports channels, BSkyB's channels are available via both satellite and cable. Differences in the composition of the basic packages of service are not significant. (*) Parts of this text have been edited to ensure that confidential information is not disclosed; those parts are enclosed in square brackets and marked with an asterisk.

[280] 'Churn rate' represents the average number of customers who stop their subscription to a pay-television service over a given period of time.

[281] See Bertelsmann/Kirch/Premiere Decision, in particular recitals 34 and 48.

[282] BSkyB annual report 1997, page 3. See also conclusion in the The Director-General's Review of BSkyB's Position in the Wholesale Pay-TV Market, December 1996, point 2.18: 'We concluded that premium sports and movie channels were the main drivers of subscription to pay-TV. Without rights to high quality sports and/or movies there seems no way that competing broadcasters would be able to enter the market at the premium level'.

[283] In the United Kingdom in 1995, 44 of the top 50 satellite pay television programmes in terms of audience ratings were either films or sports. Sports programmes accounted for 27 of the top 50 programmes, films for 17 and other programmes for 6. Football alone accounted for 22 of the top 50 programmes, amongst which 14 of the top 20. Source: Cable and Satellite Express, 25 January 1996. The four top programmes ever on cable and satellite television in the United Kingdom were all sports programmes: the top programme was a football match, number two a boxing match, followed by two football matches. Source: New Media Markets, 21 March 1996. In the United Kingdom in 1997, 42 of the top 50 pay-television programmes available on cable and satellite were either films or sports. The top 10 programmes were all films or sports; films accounted for 26 of the top 50 programmes; and sports for 16. Source: Cable and satellite Express, 29 January 1998.

[284] [...](*).

wholesale supply of film and sports channels forms a separate market[285]. For the purposes of this case, it is not necessary to decide whether there are separate wholesale markets in respect of films and sports channels[286].

## (d) Technical services for digital interactive television services and pay television

(30)   The Commission has defined a product market for the wholesale provision of the technical services necessary for pay-television in a number of decisions[287]. These services essentially comprise the making available of settop boxes, the provision of conditional access services[288] including smart cards, subscriber management services[289] and possibly the services relating to accessing the electronic programme guide[290] and the writing of applications compatible with the application programming interface included in the settop box[291]. In addition, the provision of digital interactive television services also requires a system to allow financial transactions to be conducted in a secure environment. A transaction management system (TMS) forms part of this system. It is a software system for authorising and undertaking financial transactions, and connects to the on-line servers of the various content providers. The TMS also routes requests for payment to the 'merchant acquirer': merchant acquiring is the general processing of credit and debit card payments made through retailers and other vendors of goods and services.

(31)   There is a very large area of overlap between the technical services necessary for pay-television and the services necessary for digital interactive television such as the making available of set-top boxes or the electronic programme guide. For the latter, provision of conditional access services for non-broadcast (that is, on-line) data ('access control services') and transaction management services are needed.

(32)   The skills and technologies underlying each of the individual technical services necessary for pay-television and/or digital interactive television services are different in some aspects. Narrower product markets may, therefore, exist[292]. However, it is not necessary to determine this point for the purposes of this case. The

---

[285] See Commission Decision of 3 December 1998 (Case No IV/ M.1327 – NC/Canal+/CDPQ/ BankAmerica) (OJ C 233, 14-8-1999, p. 51).

[286] The British Office of Fair Trading concluded that films and sports each constitute separate wholesale programming supply markets for pay-television, in The Director-General's Review of BSkyB's Position in the Wholesale Pay-TV Market, December 1996.

[287] See for example, Bertelsmann/Kirch/Premiere, paragraphs 19, 20 and 21.

[288] Conditional access is the means by which only viewers who are authorised to watch a service are able to do so.

[289] Subscriber management services are necessary in order to collect subscriptions from viewers. This involves maintenance of information on subscribers so that they may be authorised and billed for the services which they view.

[290] An electronic programme guide (EPG) is a navigation system which lists channels and services and via which viewers are able to tune to different data signals, and thus to change channels or services.

[291] An application programming interface (API) allows applications to be written to run on a set-top box. In order to write applications compatible with the API embedded in a particular set-top box, authoring tools are also necessary.

[292] See Joint Oftel and DTI Notice and Consultation – July 1997, Chapter 3, paragraph 25: 'There can be very different supply and demand conditions surrounding the different (technical) services so that in principle they could be represented as separate product markets. However, in practice it is likely to be possible to exploit economies of scope (and possibly scale) in the SMS, SAS and customer management functions. There is also likely to be a close association between a particular encryption technology and the organisation of these associated administration services.'

relevant product market is therefore that for technical services necessary for digital interactive television services and for pay television[293].

### (e) Customer access infrastructure market for telecommunications and related services

(33) The demand from consumers for telecommunications services in the past was almost exclusively for voice telephony services, although more recently demand for data services, such as Internet access, has grown significantly. To provide these services, companies need infrastructure capable of bringing them into the home.

(34) The fact that telecommunications services, by definition, require two-way communication capability has imposed a constraint on the types of infrastructure that can be used for such services. Historically, that demand could only be fulfilled by a copper-based public switched telecommunications network, although in recent years alternative access mechanisms, such as cable TV networks and wireless networks, have developed.

(35) Cable television networks are capable of providing a range of services from basic telephony through ondemand services to full broadcast services.

(36) Wireless fixed networks are generally less costly to install than wire networks. However, the current generation of wireless networks in the UK have relatively limited bandwidth and cannot be used for the range of services that can be provided over cable. Wireless networks should probably not form part of the relevant product market, although the conclusions in this case would not be changed if wireless networks were to be included in the market definition.

(37) Digital mobile networks based on the GSM standard or on the DCS 1800 standard cannot provide the same range of services as copper or cable networks, although this may change in the medium to long term, with the introduction of the next generation mobile standard, the universal mobile telecommunications system (UMTS). At present, given the differing characteristics and prices for voice telephony services provided over fixed or wireless networks as compared with those services provided over digital mobile, the services constitute separate markets. In addition, given the very limited data transmission capacity of mobile networks at present, they cannot be regarded as substitutes at the infrastructure level.

(38) A market therefore exists for the provision of a customer-access telecommunications infrastructure. This market includes the traditional copper network of BT, and the cable networks of the cable operators.

(39) For present purposes it is not necessary to decide whether separate customer-access markets exist for callorigination and call-termination markets.

## 2. Geographic markets

(40) The United Kingdom is the geographic market in which all the abovementioned relevant markets should be assessed.

### (a) Digital interactive television services

(41) BiB is to operate in the United Kingdom. There is an extremely close relationship between the digital interactive television services to be provided by the joint venture and the digital pay-television services provided by BSkyB in the United Kingdom. Both kinds of service are adapted to the national taste. The transaction, information and services to be provided by BiB will all largely have national demand: the transaction services will be reliant on retailers with national or regional

---

[293] See MSG Media Service, recital (31)(f).

operations and will be priced in sterling. The information services will be largely related to national demand for information. The market for digital interactive services is national and in this case is limited to the United Kingdom.

### (b) Pay-television

(42)    Pay-television broadcasting markets are, largely for linguistic, cultural, licensing and copyright reasons, generally national or extend to single linguistic areas. In this case, whether the market is the United Kingdom or also covers Ireland, would make no difference to the legal assessment.

### (c) Wholesale supply of film and sport channels for pay-television

(43)    BSkyB owns most of the underlying programme rights, and supplies the channels in both the United Kingdom and Ireland. National preferences, in particular with regard to sporting events, would point to a national service market. However, in this case, whether the market is the United Kingdom or also covers Ireland, would make no difference to the legal assessment.

### (d) Technical services for pay-television and digital interactive television services

(44)    The same geographic market definition as in paytelevision applies to this market which the Commission has already recognised as being closely linked to the pay-television market[294].

(45)    The finding that this market is national in character is corroborated by the fact of there being a specific regulatory regime in the United Kingdom in the framework of the implementation of European Parliament and Council Directive 95/47/EC of 24 October 1995 on the use of standards for the transmission of television signals[295].

(46)    Pursuant to Directive 95/47/EC, implemented in the United Kingdom by statute law and by statutory instrument[296], suppliers of conditional access services for digital television broadcast services must supply conditional access on fair, reasonable and nondiscriminatory terms. In the United Kingdom, suppliers of such services must comply with the terms of the Conditional Access Class Licence, granted on 7 January 1997, pursuant to Section 7 of the Telecommunications Act 1984.

(47)    The obligations in Directive 95/47/EC relating to digital conditional access services are limited in scope to the provision of such services to 'broadcasters' for 'digital television services'. Neither of these terms is defined. However, conditional access will be used both for nonbroadcast services (such as on-line services) and for services other than television (such as digital radio). The United Kingdom regulatory regime refers to the provision of conditional access for these services as

---

[294]    MSG Media Service (OJ L 364, 31-12-1994); Bertelsmann/Kirch/Premiere.

[295]    OJ L 281, 23-11-1995, p. 51.

[296]    SI 1996/3151 – The Advanced Television Services Regulations 1996 – implements most of the provisions of the Directive. It came into force on 7 January 1997. The statutory instrument has been supplemented by guidelines from Oftel – the UK regulatory body charged with enforcing the statutory instrument – 'Digital Television and Interactive Services/Ensuring access on fair, reasonable and non-discriminatory terms. A statement issued by the Director-General for Telecommunications. Pricing of conditional access and access control services/Oftel Guidelines April 1999'. Article 2 (save the last paragraph) of the Directive dealing with transmission signals is implemented for broadcasters other than the BBC by Section 142 of the Broadcasting Act 1996, and regulated by the Independent Television Commission (ITC).

access control services. A class licence for the provision of access control services has been established by the Office of Telecommunications (Oftel) and the Department of Trade and Industry (DTI) which came into effect on 31 December 1997[297]. This licence extends the obligations of the television standards Directive by extending the rights granted to broadcasters to other service providers.

(48)    Access to electronic programme guides is regulated in the United Kingdom by both the Independent Television Commission (ITC) and Oftel. In 1997, the ITC issued a Code of Conduct on Electronic Programming Guides (EPG)[298], the object of which is to ensure that access to EPGs is granted on fair, reasonable and nondiscriminatory terms[299]. In particular, the code requires EPG providers to ensure that the EPG does not prevent or hinder viewers from accessing free-to-air services. The code further requires vertically integrated EPG providers, such as BSkyB, to treat television services of other broadcasters/service providers on an equal footing with its own, or connected, services when granting access. Oftel laid down similar principles[300] in its Guidelines to the Regulation of the Provision of Conditional Access for Digital Television Services[301]. Oftel considers the EPG to be part of the conditional access system in so far as it controls access by viewers to television services. It thus considers it to be a technical conditional access service within the scope of the Conditional Access Class Licence which implements the provisions of Directive 95/47/EC. There is consequently an obligation to offer such services on a fair, reasonable and non-discriminatory basis.

(49)    In any event, whether the market is the United Kingdom or also covers Ireland, would make no difference to the legal assessment.

**(e) Customer access infrastructure market for telecommunications and related services**

(50)    Finally, given the national nature of BT's former telecommunications monopoly, the national nature of the regulatory regime, and the national nature of demand for services to be delivered across the telecommunications infrastructure, the market for customer access infrastructure should also be regarded as national.

**3. Market structure**

**(a) Digital interactive television services**

(51)    The services to be provided by BiB are not yet provided on a significant scale in the British market[302].

(52)    There are a number of other projects under development or undergoing early deployment which would allow television sets to be used as display devices for viewing Internet-based content or content which is proprietary to the particular

---

[297] Telecommunications Class Licence, as revoked and re-issued on 31-12-1997, pursuant to section 7 of the Telecommunications Act 1984.

[298] A licensee found to be acting in a manner which impedes fair and effective competition is liable to directions and/or sanctions as set out in the Broadcasting Acts of 1990 and 1996, including the imposition of financial penalties and the revocation of its licence.

[299] ITC Code of Conduct on Electronic Programming Guides of 13-6-1997.

[300] The Guidelines list instances where Oftel believes that competitive neutrality would not be achieved. These include vertically integrated EPG providers that favour their own or connected television service by granting special terms of access, by the design of the EPG and/or by the listing of the television services provided.

[301] Oftel Guidelines: The Regulation of Conditional Access for Digital Television Services of 3-4-1997. Section 6. Electronic Programming Guides.

[302] Limited trials are under way.

service. Other, similar, services are therefore likely to be launched on the British market in the short to medium term[303].

(53)    Cable networks in the United Kingdom have two-way capability. For the moment, both digital satellite and digital terrestrial transmission are capable of only oneway communication. However, interactivity is made possible by the use of the public switched telecommunications network (PSTN) as a return path. In the short to medium term, it will be possible to provide such services using only the PSTN, as digital technology such as the 'Digital Subscriber Line' (DSL) family of technologies can be used to upgrade its capability.

(54)    The means of transmission employed can have an impact on the nature of the digital interactive television services provided. For example, capacity constraints on digital terrestrial transmission limit the number of services which can be provided. In addition, there is a regulatory limit, whereby only a maximum of 10% of digital terrestrial broadcast capacity can be used for non-programme services such as text or data[304]. There are no such technical or regulatory constraints on digital cable or digital satellite, which is the means of transmission which BiB will use. A broader range of services can therefore be provided via digital satellite than via digital terrestrial transmission. Although technically feasible in the context of analogue broadcasting, it is the digitisation of broadcasting that allows BiB to provide the particular range and type of services proposed.

## (b) Pay-television
Identity of pay-television operators in the United Kingdom

### Satellite
(55)    Satellite pay-television services are offered principally by BSkyB, although individual niche channels such as 'The Racing Channel' (dedicated to horse racing) and 'Zee TV' (Indian-language programming) are also provided via satellite. Subscriber numbers to BSkyB's pay-television service far outstrip those to individual niche channels[305].

(56)    BSkyB's satellite pay-television service is comprised, variously, of wholly-owned BSkyB channels, channels in which BSkyB has an interest, and third-party channels. BSkyB owns and operates 13 channels: six basic channels[306], six premium film and sports channels[307] and the pay-per-view channel, Sky Box Office. In addition, BSkyB operates 11 channels in joint ventures with third parties[308].

---

[303] For example, Microsoft's Web TV has announced trials of its service combining internet access with some of its own content. The three largest cable operators in the United Kingdom, Cable & Wireless, Telewest and NTL, also have plans to launch televisiondelivered services similar to that of BiB, although their plans also include provision of full access to the Internet from television sets. It is not yet clear whether interactive services will be offered via digital terrestrial television in the United Kingdom.

[304] Limit set by the Broadcasting Act 1996.

[305] In fact, the total number of subscribers to such satellite niche paytelevision channels is less than 5% of the number of subscribers to BSkyB's satellite pay-television service.

[306] BSkyB wholly-owned basic channels are: Sky 1, Sky News, Sky Sports News (launched in 1998), Sky Travel, Sky Soap and '.tv' (re-named in 1998, previously The Computer Channel). Source: BSkyB Group plc 1998 annual report.

[307] BSkyB wholly-owned premium channels are: Sky Premier, Sky Moviemax, Sky Cinema (relaunched in 1998, previously known as The Movie Channel, Sky Movies and Sky Movies Gold), Sky Sports 1, 2 and 3. Source: BSkyB Group plc 1998 annual report.

[308] Joint venture basic channels are: Nickelodeon (50 %), QVC (20 %), The Paramount Comedy Channel (25 %), Granada Plus, Granada Men and Motors and Granada Breeze (re-named in 1998,

(57)    On 1 October 1998, BSkyB launched a digital paytelevision service, in addition to its analogue service. Both the analogue and digital services distinguish between basic and premium channels[309]. However, while BSkyB offers a single analogue basic package of channels (the 'Sky Multi Channels Package' comprising 29 channels), it offers a number of different digital basic packages. In addition, the digital service offers a wider choice of premium services, including digital radio services. In total, BSkyB's digital pay-television service comprises some 200 channels.

(58)    Roughly [...] (*) % of BSkyB's analogue subscribers take premium film and sport channels in addition to basic channels.

(59)    BSkyB's analogue service is transmitted via the Astra satellites and is available to subscribers in the UK and Ireland. Satellite reception is possible in almost all areas of these countries. BSkyB's digital service is also transmitted via Astra satellites. However, it is not yet available in Ireland, although BSkyB intends to launch services there in the future.

**Cable**

(60)    A number of cable operators also supply pay-television services in the United Kingdom. Cable operators must bid for regional franchises in which they may offer services. In contrast to the situation in some other European countries, cable networks in the United Kingdom have been built to supply both television and telephony services. As at 1 July 1998, slightly more than 75%[310] of British television households were within an existing cable franchise. However, only some 48% of British television households were, in fact, passed by a cable network at that date[311]. Although the construction rate of cable operators has recently slowed[312], cable coverage of the United Kingdom is expected to reach more than 70% of the population over the next five years.

(61)    The three largest cable operators are Cable & Wireless Communications, Telewest and NTL. Both Telewest and NTL carry the Front Row pay-per-view channel[313], which is independent of BSkyB.

(62)    Cable operators in the United Kingdom offer both paytelevision and telephony services. This combination of services appears to be a major reason why subscribers take cable pay-television. In fact, only 17,9%[314] of subscribers to cable pay-television take cable paytelevision alone; the remainder are dual subscribers.

(63)    Various cable companies in the United Kingdom began digital pay-television services in the course of 1999 and others have announced their intention of doing so shortly.

---

previously Granada Good Life) (all 49,5 %), The History Channel (50 %), National Geographic Channel (50 %) and Music Choice (49 %). Joint venture premium channels: Playboy TV UK (30 %) and MUTV (Manchester United TV) (33,3 %). Source: BSkyB Group plc 1998 annual report.

[309]    Basic channels are supplied in the form of a package of channels. The customer cannot choose to subscribe to the individual channels comprised in the package, but must subscribe to the package as a whole. Premium channels are primarily films and sports channels, and are only available to customers who subscribe to basic services.

[310]    Financial Times New Media Markets, 17 September 1998, page 9.

[311]    Independent Television Commission News Release (82/98) of 16 September 1998.

[312]    The number of homes passed by cable increased by 3% in the quarter to 1 July 1998, as opposed to 17% over the previous nine months. Source: Cable Europe Volume 8, Issue 20, September 30, 1998.

[313]    Operated by a consortium of cable operators, including Telewest and NTL.

[314]    Financial Times New Media Markets, 17 September 1998, page 9.

**Digitalterrestrial**

(64)    Digital terrestrial pay-television services were launched by ONdigital (previously known as British Digital Broadcasting) on 15 November 1998. Capacity constraints prevent ONdigital from offering as many channels as BSkyB or cable operators. Initially, it will offer some 15 channels comprising both basic and premium channels.

(65)    ONdigital's parent companies will each supply certain channels, as will third parties. BSkyB will supply ONdigital with its premium film and sports channels under contract for the first [...] (*) years of its operation. It will also supply ONdigital with one of its basic channels. Market position of pay-television operators in the United Kingdom

(66)    As at 30 June 1998, roughly a quarter of domestic television households[315] in the United Kingdom subscribe to a pay-television service[316] in addition to paying a licence fee which entitles them to watch the five terrestrial free-to-air channels which are available there.

(67)    If the domestic subscribers to pay-television, according to BSkyB [...] (*)% subscribe to BSkyB and [...] (*)% to the various cable pay-television operators[317].

(68)    It should be noted, however, that the figures[318] for the number of cable pay-television subscribers published by the competent industry regulator in the United Kingdom, the Independent Television Commission (ITC), suggest that there are [...] (*) fewer cable pay-television subscribers than is suggested by BSkyB[319]. If these figures were relied upon, then BSkyB would have a market share of [...] (*)% as compared to [...] (*)% for all cable operators.

(69)    If again we use the ITC figures[320], the largest single cable pay-television operator, Cable & Wireless Communications, had 781 944 subscribers at 1 July 1998[321]. This equates to a market share of [...] (*) %.

(70)    Using figures provided by BSkyB for the period at end June 1998, all subscribers to cable pay-television take [...] (*). Moreover, some [...] (*)% of subscribers to cable pay-television subscribe to one or more BSkyB premium channel.

---

[315] It should also be noted that there are commercial subscribers to pay-television in addition to domestic subscribers. Commercial subscribers are typically hotels or pubs. Commercial subscribers are interested essentially in either premium film or premium sports channels. They do not normally subscribe to basic channels. By the end of June 1998, there was a total of [...]* commercial subscribers in the United Kingdom. Some [...]* of these subscribe directly to BSkyB's satellite pay-television service. The remainder subscribe to BSkyB's premium film and/or sports channels via a cable operator.

[316] There were some [...]* million such subscribers at this date. This figure reflects the addition of the total number of subscribers to BSkyB's satellite pay-television and the total number of subscribers to all cable pay-television operators. It does not take account of subscribers to 'niche' satellite pay-television channels. There are no figures available to clarify whether subscribers to such channels are also subscribers to BSkyB's service. If 'niche' subscribers were included, there would therefore be a risk of double counting. Source: BSkyB, response to request for information of 30 October 1998. The total number of domestic television households was 23,86 million: Source: Barb, quoted in New Media Markets, Volume 16, Number 33, 17 September 1998.

[317] Subscribers to BSkyB at the end of June 1998, [...]* million: source BSkyB, response to request for information of 9 November 1998. Subscribers to cable operators at the end of June 1998, [...]* million.

[318] In respect of the same period, i.e. at the end of June 1998.

[319] Independent Television Commission News Release (82/98) of 16 September 1998.

[320] BSkyB has not provided figures which distinguish between the various cable operators.

[321] Independent Television Commission News Release (82/98) of 16 September 1998.

(71)    There are significant barriers to entry in the paytelevision market. Entry into the pay-television market presupposes in the first place that transmission capacity is available. Owing to frequency shortages, no analogue capacity is available for terrestrial transmission. The digital terrestrial frequencies have already been allocated. There is no available capacity on the Astra analogue satellite transponders which BSkyB uses. Digital satellite transponder capacity on the Astra satellites is available. In terms of cable networks, franchises have been awarded which cover some 75% of television households in the United Kingdom. While these franchises have recently been made non-exclusive, the very significant costs of constructing such a network makes it highly unlikely that a second network operator would choose to build a cable network within an existing franchise area.

(72)    An entrant into the pay-television market also requires programmes, and above all, premium film and sports channels[322]. These are the basics around which other channels can be offered to subscribers. Providers of individual niche channels may be able to enter the market without such channels. As experience throughout the Community has shown, a pay-television platform provider is most unlikely to do so. As explained in recitals 73 to 81, BSkyB's position in this field is particularly strong. In the medium term, therefore, entry into the British pay-television market using digital satellite transmission independently of BSkyB appears a remote possibility.

**(c) Wholesale supply of channels for pay-television**

(73)    In 1996, the Office of Fair Trading (OFT) in the United Kingdom reviewed BSkyB's position in the wholesale pay-television market and found that it had more than 90% of the pay-television rights to first-run major films[323]. The OFT concluded that BSkyB held a 'very high market share'[324] in each of the separate markets for the wholesale supply of pay-television film and sports channels to cable operators. It further concluded that: 'BSkyB was dominant in the supply of sports channels in the United Kingdom Pay-TV market and was at that time the only provider of premium sports channels with the exception of one specialist channel (The Racing Channel)'[325].

(74)    In the light of its findings, the OFT imposed requirements on the terms and conditions under which BSkyB can supply its channels to cable operators. In particular, BSkyB may supply its channels only in accordance with terms which have previously been approved by the OFT[326].

(75)    The Commission's investigation has confirmed that there has been little evolution in the situation described by the OFT in 1996.

(76)    At present BSkyB has pay-television rights to first run major films under contracts with [...] (*) major Hollywood studios and [...] (*) larger independent studios. [...]

---

[322]  Bertelsmann/Kirch/Premiere, in particular recitals 34,48 and 49.

[323]  'BSkyB had long term rights contracts with the major Hollywood studios and with the larger independents which gave BSkyB Pay-TV rights to over 90% of first run major films' Paragraph 1.7 of 'The Director-General's Review of BSkyB's position in the wholesale Pay-TV market', December 1996.

[324]  The Director-General's Review of BSkyB's Position in the Wholesale Pay-TV Market, December 1996, point 1.2.

[325]  The Director-General's Review of BSkyB's Position in the Wholesale Pay-TV Market, December 1996, point 2.19.

[326]  Informal undertakings published in OFT press release No. 32/96 of 24 July 1996 and at appendix A to The Director-General's Review of BSkyB's Position in the Wholesale Pay-TV Market, December 1996.

(*) of BSkyB's pay-television rights contracts are 'output deals'. This means that they cover new product released by film studios[327]. Some also cover library films. In terms of means of transmission, BSkyB's contracts concern exclusive rights for [...] (*). The majority of the contracts continue for at least [...] (*) years from the launch of digital pay-television in 1998.

(77)    BSkyB's pay-per-view agreements are [...] (*). In other respects their terms vary: [...] (*).

(78)    BSkyB's major pay-television sports rights contracts include rights to almost all national league football, rugby football, cricket, golf and boxing. The contracts relate to [...] (*). As with films, the sports rights contracts generally cover [...] (*). In line with industry practice the duration of the agreements is shorter than for films. The precise duration of the agreements varies: the majority continue until [...] (*).

(79)    The extent and duration of BSkyB's exclusive film contracts and sports rights contracts prevent the emergence of any significant competition to BSkyB in the supply of pay-television film and sports channels in, at least, the medium term[328]. The fact that the rights contracts cover [...] (*) modes of transmission also means that BSkyB's retail pay-television competitors, the various cable operators and ONdigital, have no choice but to purchase BSkyB's film and sports channels if they are to offer such channels as part of their own services to subscribers.

(80)    BSkyB supplies both British cable operators and ONdigital with its premium film and sports channels, in addition to certain of its basic channels [...] (*)% of subscribers to cable pay-television take at least one of BSkyB's film or sports channels. On average, BSkyB wholly-owned basic and premium film and sports channels account for some [...] (*)% of total programming costs for cable operators. On average, acquisition of BSkyB film and sports channels accounts for some [...] (*)% of cable operators' total programming costs[329]. Again on average, between [...] (*)% of expenditure on film and sports channels is paid to BSkyB.

(81)    BSkyB's control of the pay-television rights to most major films and many of the most popular sports also means that BSkyB obtains revenue from its paytelevision competitors as both cable companies and ONdigital are dependent on BSkyB for the supply of such channels. In the medium term, any gain in market share of BSkyB's competitors on the pay-television market would, to a certain extent, be offset by increased revenue from the wholesale supply of film and sports channels.

**(d) Technical services necessary for pay-television and digital interactive television services**

(82)    The various cable operators and ONdigital each use different technical services to BSkyB.

(83)    BSkyB Group brings together a number of companies that deal with various aspects of these technical and administrative services[330]. Sky Subscribers Services

---

[327] Sometimes referred to as 'first run' or 'first release' rights.

[328] This has been recognised by independent analysts. See for example, page 23 of the Nat West Markets analysis of Digital Broadcasting 'Looking for Direction – UK Media Sector' October 1997: '[...] the fact is that BSkyB's movie contracts remain in place through the first three years of its transition to digital. There is simply no route to market for aspiring competitors in the initial stages of the development of digital services'. In fact, these contracts remain in place for some six years.

[329] [...](*)% of BSkyB's expenditure on programmes is accounted for by films and sports.

[330] Sky Subscribers Services Ltd (SSSL) and Satellite Encryption Services Ltd (SESL) are both wholly-owned subsidiaries of BSkyB Ltd. SSSL provides analogue conditional access and subscriber management services to BSkyB Ltd. SESL provides the same services to third party satellite

Ltd (SSSL) will provide Videoguard digital conditional access and access control services both to BSkyB Ltd and to third parties under the British regulatory regime, including BiB. BSkyB, through SSSL, has an exclusive licence for the United Kingdom and Ireland to use, and to offer to third parties, the Videoguard system developed by New International's wholly-owned subsidiary, News Data Systems[331].

(84)   As the parties themselves recognise, 'demand for set-top boxes is directly linked to demand for TV broadcasting since the only purpose of purchasing a set-top box is to access the broadcast TV market'[332]. It follows from this that the market position of a supplier of technical services is largely determined by the position on the pay-television market of the companies which use its services in their set-top boxes. BSkyB, through SSSL, therefore controls some [...] (*)% of installed set-top boxes in the United Kingdom.

(85)   BSkyB's position in the technical services market is also secured by its control of the content markets described at recitals 76 to 79[333].

**(e) Customer access telecommunications infrastructure market for telecommunications and related services**

(86)   BT is the former telecommunications monopolist in the United Kingdom. Its telecommunications network covers almost the whole of the United Kingdom. 86% of residential fixed lines in use were provided by BT[334]. The remainder were mainly provided by cable operators.

(87)   BT has made significant investments in digitising its network in recent years and now almost 100% of BT's exchanges are digital.

(88)   BT faces competition at both the infrastructure and service provision levels of its business. Looking only at residential services, BT competes with cable operators at both the infrastructure and the service level. In addition, BT competes at the service level with a number of operators who use BT's network to deliver services to consumers.

(89)   Cable operators' networks currently pass 48% of homes in the United Kingdom. This is expected to rise to 70 to 80% over the coming years. In areas covered by cable networks, cable operators attract an average of approximately one in four potential residential customers.

(90)   It is unclear whether there will be significant coverage of the United Kingdom by wireless fixed networks in the short to medium term. In the longer term, other forms of infrastructure may be used for telecommunications services in the United Kingdom. For example, power-line technology may allow data transmission over existing domestic electricity cables. There are also four digital mobile networks based on the GSM standard which provide almost complete coverage of the United Kingdom. At present, the data capacity of GSM networks is relatively limited, and voice services provided over GSM networks in the United Kingdom tend to be more expensive than those delivered over fixed lines.

---

direct-to-home pay-television broadcasters using ASTRA transponders. Sky In-Home Services Limited (SIHSL, formerly Tele-Aerials Satellite Limited) is also a wholly-owned subsidiary. SIHSL is involved in the sale and installation of analogue and digital satellite dishes.

[331] BSkyB Group has a similar exclusive licence in respect of its analogue conditional access system, VideoCrypt.

[332] Form A/B, p. 51.

[333] Bertelsmann/Kirch/Premiere, in particular at recital 108.

[334] For the period January to March 1998. Source: Oftel Market Information Update, November 1998.

(91)    The significant sunk costs involved in constructing a nation-wide telecommunica-
        tions customer access network make it very unlikely that a new entrant would do
        so. Indeed, despite the existence of the cable networks, BT continues to have a
        market share of some 86% of fixed residential telephony lines in use to receive
        services. Both as a result of the coverage of its network and as a result of its mar-
        ket share, other providers of residential telecommunications services use the BT
        network in order to terminate the majority of calls in the United Kingdom.

## D. THE OPERATION
### 1. The notified arrangements

(92)    The notification essentially comprised the joint venture agreement between the
        parties, together with its annexes. For present purposes, the most important of the
        annexed agreements is the marketing services agreement between BiB and BSkyB
        which provided details of the parties' plans with respect to subsidisation of BiB-
        compatible digital interactive set-top boxes, digital satellite dishes and low-noise
        blocks, [...] (*) and the conditions under which consumers were eligible to pur-
        chase it. Three further agreements between BiB and Midland were notified, con-
        cerning Midland's provision to BiB of a transaction management system,
        merchant acquiring services and Mondex cards respectively.

(93)    A number of related agreements were provided to the Commission for information
        purposes, although they do not form part of the notification. The most important of
        these are the agreements between BSkyB and Open TV concerning the application
        programming interface in BiB-compatible digital interactive set-top boxes, and
        that between BiB and Open TV concerning the authoring tools for that application
        programming interface.

### 2. Structure of joint venture

(94)    The shareholdings in BiB will be as follows: BSkyB 32,5 %, BT 32,5 %, Midland
        20% and Matsushita 15%. The Board will consist of 10 Directors: three appointed
        by BSkyB, three by BT, two by Midland and two by Matsushita.

(95)    BiB has been established for an indefinite duration. Certain major decisions, in-
        cluding material variations to the business plan, concerning BiB will require the
        consent of each shareholder whose interest in BiB is at least 10%[335]. For example,
        if BiB wished to subsidise set-top boxes for transmission means other than satel-
        lite, this would require the unanimous consent of the shareholders. BiB will be
        jointly controlled by its parent companies.

### 3. Scope and purpose of joint venture

(96)    BiB has been created in order to develop the infrastructure necessary for the provi-
        sion of digital interactive television services and to provide such services over that
        infrastructure. BiB will also provide technical services necessary for digital inter-
        active television services. The geographic scope of BiB's activities is limited to
        the United Kingdom.

### (a) Infrastructure for the provision of digital interactive television services

(97)    The BiB infrastructure has been developed specifically to provide digital interac-
        tive television services via satellite[336].

---

[335] Below this 10% threshold, a shareholder loses the right to Board representation and joint
control.

[336] Although the parties have indicated that they intend to enter negotiations with a view to making the BiB service available alongside the digital broadcast entertainment services transmitted on
digital terrestrial and digital cable in the United Kingdom.

(98)    BiB will provide the content providers with all the infrastructure necessary to pro-
        vide interactive services: a broadcast and on-line delivery system, conditional ac-
        cess and access control services, a system to allow financial transactions to be
        completed, a service-creation system and access to a digital interactive set-top
        box.

**Broadcast and on-line delivery system**

(99)    Digital satellite transponder capacity will be sub-leased from BSkyB. The up-link
        of broadcast content to the satellite will be provided by BT, as will the transmis-
        sion to the up-link site. The software for the broadcast server will be supplied by
        Oracle and will be based upon Oracle's standard packages. BT has entered into an
        agreement with Oracle for certain enhancements of the Oracle software. Access to
        the on-line system is through a network of access points throughout the United
        Kingdom (Point of Presence network). BT will contract with BiB to supply these
        services for an initial period of three years.

**Conditional access and access control services**

(100)   Essentially for reasons of copyright protection, both the content broadcast via sat-
        ellite and delivered on-line will be encrypted. This also prevents unauthorised sig-
        nals from corrupting set-top boxes. SSSL, BSkyB's whollyowned subsidiary, will
        supply BiB with both conditional access and access control services.

**System to allow financial transactions on platform**

(101)   The completion of transactions on the BiB infrastructure requires a secure envi-
        ronment such that consumers and content providers are willing to transact. BiB
        has contracted with Midland to provide a transaction management system (TMS).
        BiB has granted Midland a 10-year exclusivity in respect of the TMS. The TMS
        will interface with a merchant acquiring system. Midland will similarly supply
        merchant acquiring services to BiB content providers, on the basis of a 10-year ex-
        clusive contract. The present exclusivity is twofold as it affects both content pro-
        viders and consumers which will contract with BiB the use of BiB's platform or
        the provision of digital interactive television services.

(102)   Neither of these exclusive agreements prevents a different interactive services
        company which uses the BiB infrastructure to provide services from using differ-
        ent TMS and merchant acquiring services from those envisaged in the agreements.
        The BiB-subsidised set-top box also has a slot into which electronic payment
        cards, such as Mondex, can be slotted. The slot is standardised and will therefore
        accept alternative payment cards.

**Service creation system**

(103)   The interactive applications of content providers must be so written as to be com-
        patible with the application programming interface (API) of BiB subsidised set-
        top boxes. BiB will write applications for content providers on its digital
        interactive TV services platform, although content providers may also do so them-
        selves.

(104)   Broadcasters and interactive advertisers will also need authoring tools to write ap-
        plications compatible with the enhanced Open TV API, whether for purposes of
        'side-channels' or to carry out interactive transactions.

(105)   Under the Open Author Agreement between BiB and Open TV, BiB is granted a
        non-exclusive licence for the necessary authoring tools. The licence covers the
        United Kingdom and Ireland. Third parties can obtain the necessary authoring
        tools either from BiB or from Open TV direct.

**Digital interactive set-top box**

(106)  The most important element of the infrastructure from the point of view of the end consumer is a BiBcompatible digital interactive set-top box. Any telephone line can be used to access BiB services.

(107)  BSkyB, with input from the BiB parties, has specified a digital interactive set-top box, the Digibox, which embeds BSkyB's proprietary conditional access (CA) and access control (AC) systems and BSkyB has ordered such boxes from manufacturers. As the box does not contain a common interface, this means that it is tied to BSkyB's CA and AC systems. However, the Commission has imposed as a condition that BSkyB shall develop and operate Simulcrypt arrangements[337]. The box includes a digital satellite demodulator and has interface ports onto which digital cable, digital terrestrial and broadband telecommunications network sidecar demodulators can be attached. This means that BiBcompatible boxes could be used with all other transmission systems if appropriate sidecars were attached. The box will also include a modem and a standardised slot for electronic payment cards.

**Application Programming Interface**

(108)  The application programming interface (API) in the box is supplied by Open TV[338]. BSkyB has commissioned Open TV to develop enhancements to the Open TV 1.2 API. These enhancements allow the box to decode high quality still pictures broadcast via satellite (MPEG or JPEG) in addition to moving pictures (MPEG); the quality of sound via PSTN (on-line) is improved (G 729 audio) and finally they allow the API to 'talk' to the interface modules (such as alternative demodulator sidecars or games consoles).

(109)  The intellectual property rights for these enhancements will vest in Open TV. By virtue of clause 12.4 of the agreement between BSkyB and Open TV, Open TV undertook not to license these enhancements to any third party in the United Kingdom for two years from the launch date of BiB services. However, following the Commission's intervention, the parties have given up their veto over the licensing of the Open TV 1.2 API enhancements.

**Electronic Programme Guide**

(110)  BSkyB's specifications for the set-top box allow only one EPG to run, which is its own proprietary EPG. BiB will therefore have a menu position on the BSkyB EPG. As originally notified, Clause 4 of the joint venture agreement (JVA) had provided that BiB would be the exclusive provider of digital interactive TV services via the BSkyB EPG for a period of 10 years. Clause 4 also provided that if a subsidy-recovery mechanism was agreed between the parties and the relevant regulatory authorities, the exclusivity would be limited to 18 months. Following the Commission's intervention the parties have ended the exclusivity for BiB in respect of the BSkyB EPG.

**Subsidisation of set – top box, digital satellite dishand LNB: 'Boxpackages'**

(111)  BiB will subsidise 'box packages' with a view to reducing the retail selling price of such set-top boxes, dishes and LNBs to what the parties consider to be an affordable price below GBP 200 including VAT[339].

---

[337]  Condition No 6 of this Decision.

[338]  Formerly known as Thomson Sun Interactive.

[339]  The JVA originally provided that BiB would also subsidise the costs of installation of the box and installation or upgrade of a digital satellite dish in the consumer's home. However, subsidi-

(112)  BiB's largest business cost over the first 10 years of its operation will consist of subsidising the retail price of such box packages. The purchase of such packages both by customers who presently take BSkyB's analogue services and by new customers will be subsidised. BiB will pay a higher level of subsidy in respect of the former. The BiB Business Plan envisages that for a substantial number of years most of the subsidy will be directed towards existing BSkyB retail customers.

**(b) Sources of revenue of BiB**

(113)  BiB will have essentially three sources of revenue. First, it will charge content providers which form part of its own digital interactive service. Secondly, it will charge end-users for certain services which it will itself provide[340]. Thirdly, it will require all service providers which wish to access BiB-subsidised digital interactive set-top boxes to provide their own encrypted services to contribute to its historic and ongoing costs of subsidisation. Thus, BiB's main sources of revenue are derived at the wholesale level, rather than direct from end-users.

(114)  BiB proposes to recover contributions to both its historic and its ongoing subsidy costs from two sources. First, BiB expects to recover a proportion indirectly through its general charging mechanisms vis-à-vis content providers. Secondly, BiB proposes to recover subsidy contributions directly from all broadcasters or interactive services providers (including BiB's own services business and BSkyB) who intend to use the box, save for un-encrypted free-to-air broadcasters. All such users will require conditional access and/or access control from SSSL, and SSSL will, as part of its charges for conditional access/access control, levy a contribution to subsidy recovery, in respect of which it will be invoiced by BiB.

(115)  The parties' initial proposal was that (a) broadcasters would pay 5% of subsidy and interactive services providers would pay 95% and (b) third parties who were required to pay subsidy recovery would have to pay a substantial initial payment equivalent to their share of the unrecovered historic subsidy costs. The Commission has imposed as a condition the modification of the operation of the subsidy recovery mechanism[341].

**(c) Non-competition provisions**

(116)  The draft joint venture agreement, forwarded to the Commission on 14 July 1998, stated that for so long as the parties or any affiliate hold shares in BiB and two years thereafter, they would not:
  – provide and operate, or hold more than a 20% interest in a company which provides and operates, a platform for the provision of digital interactive television services in the United Kingdom via any transmission means; or
  – supply or license to any person the majority of the hardware, software and know-how for such a platform for the purpose of providing digital interactive television services in the United Kingdom via any transmission means.

(117)  This non-competitive obligation included digital interactive television services associated with video-ondemand entertainment services.

---

sation of installation costs was removed from the business scope of BiB in the agreements signed on 4 August 1998.

[340]  BiB's service will generally be available free to customers with the exception of down-loading of games, learning on-line and limited Internet access for which a separate fee may be charged.

[341]  Condition No 7 of this Decision.

## 4. Relationship with BSkyB's services

(118)   There is a close relationship between BiB and BSkyB's digital services. The respective infrastructures needed are largely complementary. This is particularly the case for the set-top box. The JVA[342] commits the parties to promote only digital satellite set-top boxes which are capable of receiving the BiB service for so long as BiB is subsidising set-top boxes. BSkyB may not therefore use a set-top box which is not compatible with BiB for its own digital pay-television service[343]. Indeed, the parties have stated that BiB's digital interactive television services' business would not be viable unless it were closely associated with traditional broadcast services, such as BSkyB's, with which consumers are more familiar[344].

(119)   Along the same lines BSkyB has agreed that the subscription price for its digital pay-television service will be no higher than that of similar analogue packages of satellite entertainment services[345]. It has also agreed to use reasonable endeavours to ensure that all programmes broadcast on BSkyB's analogue satellite service will be broadcast simultaneously on BSkyB's digital satellite service[346] and to spend a substantial amount of money on the marketing of its digital paytelevision services[347]. The close relationship between the two services is further reinforced by the provisions of the JVA requiring certain advertising of the BiB service to be integrated with BSkyB advertising[348] and committing BiB, in its early financial years, to spend a substantial proportion of its total marketing expenditure on advertising via digital television[349].

(120)   For the end-user, the two services are closely linked because purchase of the equipment necessary to receive the BSkyB service automatically gives access to that of BiB. Moreover, pursuant to the original marketing services agreement, it was a condition of purchase of a BiB subsidised set-top box that consumers subscribed to BSkyB's digital pay-television service for the minimum contract term of 12 months. The latter requirement has been removed.

## 5. Relationship with BT's services

(121)   The JVA[350] requires the parties to negotiate in good faith with a view to BT's and BiB's entering into an agreement under which BT will supply to BiB all BiB's telecommunications requirements for the period ending three years after BiB's launch.

(122)   Pursuant to clause 3.3 (A) of the JVA, the parties agree that a shareholder who wishes to provide digital interactive television services by means of a broadband system can do so only where it has given BiB a right of first refusal to provide such a service and BiB has not agreed to provide such a service on terms at least as favourable as those offered by a third party within six months of the offer or 31 March 1999, whichever is the later. This provision is of most relevance to BT.

---

[342]   Clause 20.4 of JVA.

[343]   However, BSkyB may promote any other set-top box where the purpose of such promotion relates to the use of such boxes in homes which already have a BiB subsidised set-top box.

[344]   Pages 47 and 49 of Form A/B.

[345]   Clause 19 of JVA.

[346]   Clause 19 of JVA.

[347]   Clause 20 of JVA.

[348]   Clause 17 of JVA.

[349]   Clause 18 of JVA.

[350]   Clause 8 of JVA.

## E. CHANGES MADE FURTHER TO THE COMMISSION'S INTERVENTION

(123) On the basis of the analysis carried out by the Commission, and of the comments received from third parties following the publication in the Official Journal of the European Communities of a first notice inviting third party comment[351] and then of a notice published pursuant to Article 19(3) of Regulation No 17, certain features of the notified agreements appeared to be incompatible with Community competition rules. The Commission informed the parties of its concerns. The changes to the notified agreements are set out in recitals 124 to 134. These are reflected in the new version of the JVA signed on 4 August 1998.

### (a) Non-competition provisions

(124) The non-competition provisions in the JVA have been amended to limit them to the business scope of BiB, namely digital interactive television services, including the provision of digital interactive television services associated with broadcast services. Thus, the proviso to the provision relating to digital interactive television services associated with video-on-demand entertainment services was deleted as it went beyond the business scope of BiB.

(125) The parties further amended the non-competition provision so that it applies only to shareholders with joint control. The non-competition provision continues to apply to a shareholder for a period of 12 months after that shareholder loses joint control, where that loss occurs within three years of the date of the exemption decision pursuant to Article 81(3) of the EC Treaty.

### (b) Legal separation

(126) The Commission was concerned that the combination in a single company of activities relating to the subsidisation of set-top boxes and the recovery of subsidies, together with the operation of services using the set-top box, would lead to a lack of transparency in the operation of the subsidy recovery mechanism which could allow the parties to confer benefits on their own downstream operations in comparison with third parties. In order to address this concern the structure of the joint venture itself has been modified. Two separate companies have been created[352] for BiB's subsidies of set-top boxes and the recovery of subsidy from third parties[353], and the creation and operation of BiB interactive services[354].

(127) The Board of each of these wholly-owned subsidiaries will consist of shareholder representatives only. No individual will be a member of both. Each of the companies will have its own operational management, responsible to its respective board. These management teams will both report to the chief executive officer of the BiB Group, who will be responsible for the management and performance of the whole BiB Group, and will report to the BiB Board. The two companies will publish annual audited accounts. Auditors will certify that all transactions between the two companies have been carried out at arms' length[355]. This new management structure ensures transparency and nondiscriminatory treatment between the two operations and responds to the Commission's concern.

### (c) Access to BiB-subsidised digital interactive settop boxes

(128) The parties have ended the exclusivity for BiB in respect of the BSkyB EPG. They

---

[351] OJ C 259, 26-8-1997, p. 3.
[352] Clause 2.2 of JVA.
[353] Marketing Contributions Co – 'McCo'.
[354] Platform Co.
[355] Clause 2.2 of JVA.

have also relinquished their veto over the licensing of the Open TV 1.2 API enhancements. The parties are seeking an agreement with Open TV to determine the
contribution which Open TV will levy on licences for the Open TV 1.2 API enhancements (and, where relevant, any updates) supplied to third parties, such levy
being based on the development costs of those enhancements.

(129)   The requirement that customers wishing to purchase a BiB-subsidised set-top box,
digital satellite dish and LNB must subscribe to BSkyB's pay-television service
has been removed. The only conditions governing purchase of such box packages
are now the following[356]. First, that the customer agrees to connect the set-top box
to a telephone line for a one-year period. Secondly, if Midland so requests pursuant to the Mondex agreement, arrangements will be made for the issue to the customer of a Mondex card and the opening of a feed bank account[357]. Thirdly,
customers agree to the installation of box packages by an installer approved by the
parties.

(130)   These amendments to the originally notified agreements address the Commission's concern that if competing providers of digital interactive services were
to be denied access to BiB-subsidised set-top boxes, or were to be granted access
on terms less favourable than BiB, then competition in the digital interactive television services market could be eliminated.

### (d) Commitments given by BSkyB in relation to the British regime

(131)   The regulatory requirements placed on BSkyB in relation to the supply of conditional access and access control services and in relation to access to its proprietary
electronic programme guide exist independently of its participation in the BiB
joint venture. In the course of the Commission's examination of BiB, BSkyB has
informed the Commission of how it intends to comply with the British regulatory
regime. The Commission considers as a fact basic to the making of the decision
the British regulatory obligations on BSkyB. If the relevant British authorities
were to bring an action against BSkyB for infringement of these obligations, the
Commission would consider this situation under Article 8(3)(a) of Regulation 17.

(132)   BSkyB has confirmed that its wholly-owned subsidiary, SSSL, will provide access
control services under the terms of the Telecommunications Services Class Licence (as granted on 31 December 1997 under Section 7 of the Telecommunications Act 1984) or any licence which supersedes the access control provisions of
the Telecommunications Services Class Licence.

(133)   BSkyB has further agreed that when requested to supply access control services
(within the meaning of the British regime), SSSL will comply with the obligations
to cooperate in advance of service launch set out in Regulation 11(4) to (8) of the
Advanced Television Services Regulations 1996, as if that Regulation applied to
such services[358]. Again, this prevents BSkyB from relying on a possible loophole
in the British regime.

(134)   The Conditional Access Class Licence prevents providers of digital conditional
access services from bundling the various services which constitute the conditional access services. It is unclear whether the British regulatory regime requires

---

[356] Marketing Contributions Services Agreement between McCo and BSkyB of 4 August 1998.

[357] Customers are not charged for this service, nor are they required to make any deposits on
such an account.

[358] And as if the reference to the 'primary duty' therein were references to the duty to provide
Access Control Services pursuant to the British Regime and references to 'technical services' were
to technical services within the said meaning of Access Control Services.

providers of such services to supply verification (digital signature) services separately. BSkyB [...] (*) is, in principle, willing to allow [...] (*) to sign its own interactive applications subject to [...] (*) meeting certain financial, technical and other criteria and subject to the agreement of commercial terms, including a condition that the third party takes responsibility for errors in its signing. BSkyB has agreed that it will offer such right [...] (*) on fair and reasonable terms[359] and on a nondiscriminatory basis (which shall include a requirement on such third parties to meet the technical, commercial and financial criteria as are required [...] (*)).

## F. THIRD PARTY OBSERVATIONS

(135)  Following the publication of a notice pursuant to Article 19(3) of Regulation No 17, interested third parties submitted observations to the Commission. Broadly speaking, third parties welcome the conditions that the Commission proposed to apply to BiB and under which an Article 81(3) exemption could be granted. Concerns expressed in these observations included: – the restrictions on competition between the participants in BiB are not indispensable
   – the duration of the exemption
   – the Commission should continue to monitor the joint venture over a number of years, in particular in the field of access to the local loop if there were a risk that BT might have an incentive to slow the development of broadband services in the UK because of its stake in BiB
   – BSkyB should be required to enter into negotiations with other interactive service providers who wish to add interactive enhancements to BSkyB programming.

(136)  The Commission carefully reviewed all third-party observations and concluded that concerns expressed therein have been addressed during the notification procedure. The conditions attached to this Decision take sufficient account of these concerns, and third-party observations have not therefore affected the Commission's substantive position as described in the Article 19(3) notice. However, in the interest of legal certainty the Commission has spelled out in greater detail in this Decision the scope of certain conditions imposed on the parties and the fulfilment of the four conditions which govern exemption under Article 81(3).

(137)  In addition, the Commission considered it necessary, as a result of third-party observations, to extend the scope of the condition on the availability of a clean-feed. The condition imposed in this Decision allows more flexibility to companies which distribute BSkyB's movies and/or sport programming with interactive applications. The distributor's option to remove or keep all of the icons[360] is extended, subject to an agreement for the carriage of BiB or BSkyB's services, to allow a situation where some of the icons remain on the screen whilst some of the icons are removed.

## II. LEGAL ASSESSMENT

(138)  The Commission has concluded that the notified arrangements as amended fall within the scope of Article 81(1) of the EC Treaty, but that subject to certain conditions, the criteria of Article 81(3) of the EC Treaty are met.

---

[359] Terms approved by the Director-General for Telecommunications will be presumed to be fair and reasonable.
[360] 'All-or-nothing' option in the Article 19(3) Notice.

## A. COOPERATIVE JOINT VENTURE

(139)   The joint venture has to be assessed under Regulation No 17 because there is a risk of coordination between the parent companies in the market of the joint venture and in neighbouring markets such as video-on-demand entertainment services.

## B. ARTICLE 81(1)

(140)   BSkyB and BT's participation in BiB results in an appreciable restriction of competition on the market for digital interactive television services. This restriction of competition affects trade between Member States. The creation of the BiB joint venture therefore falls within the ambit of Article 81(1). The Commission cannot give negative clearance to the agreements as requested by the parties in their notification.

### 1. Applicability of Article 81(1) to the creation of BiB
### (a) Digital interactive television services market

Restriction of competition between the parent companies – BSkyB and BT are potential competitors

(141)   Prior to the conclusion of the BiB joint venture, BT and BSkyB were potential competitors in the provision of digital interactive television services. Both have sufficient skills and resources to launch such services and both would be able to bear the technical and financial risks of doing so alone. The creation of BiB eliminates this potential competition. Given the market positions of BT and BSkyB in markets related to the one in which BiB will be active, the restriction of competition between them is appreciable.

(142)   The fact that BT is a potential competitor reflects a more general world-wide development in the telecommunications sector for operators to seek to expand the number and types of services provided over their networks. This diversification increases the return on the capital employed to build, or in the case of BT, maintain the network. More particularly, by virtue of the Digital Subscriber Line family of technologies, traditional copper-line telecommunications customer access infrastructure, such as that of BT, can be upgraded to allow for the provision of services such as those to be provided by BiB in addition to other services such as video telephony, video-on-demand and high-speed Internet access. One operator in the United Kingdom, Kingston Communications, has already committed itself to such an upgrade of its infrastructure[361]. In other European countries, trials are underway. BT has conducted extended residential trials[362]. The latest trial ran until March 1999. Some service providers will offer a range of services, including on-demand entertainment, news and information programming, home shopping and home banking.

(143)   The general tendency towards diversification of telecommunications operators to provide services similar to those of BiB has been accepted by the parties. Indeed, the parties themselves have stated that 'the main telecommunications operators (other than BT) could become competitors to BiB'[363]. The parties' claim that BT's competitors should be regarded as potential competitors, whereas BT itself should

---

[361]   Source: Inside Cable & Telecoms Europe, <http://www.insidecable. co.uk>, article of 14 December 1998, 'Kingston first to commit to ADSL in Europe'.

[362]   Source: Inside Cable & Telecoms Europe, <http://www.insidecable. co.uk>, article of 22 December 1998, 'BT's ADSL Trails -More Details'.

[363]   Form A/B, at page 77.

not, cannot be accepted. The joint venture agreement itself envisages that BT will upgrade its network to allow provision of services such as those to be provided by BiB[364].

(144) BSkyB is also a potential competitor in the provision of digital interactive television services. BSkyB has extensive experience in running a popular mass market television service. It is the digitisation of such services which allows digital interactive television services to be introduced. There are significant common costs in the technical services and infrastructure required for both. In the absence of BiB, BSkyB would have required a digital set-top box for its own pay-television business and would have subsidised its retail selling price itself[365]. The marginal cost increase in producing a set-top box capable of allowing interactivity is relatively small in comparison with the overall cost of the set-top box − the parties have estimated the marginal cost to be approximately GBP [...] (*)[366]. Given the common infrastructure costs, and given that subsidisation of settop boxes is BiB's largest single cost over the first [...] (*) years of its operation, the marginal cost increase of establishing an interactive service once the decision has been made to launch a digital television service is relatively small[367].

## 2. Applicability of Article 81(1) to contractual provisions

(145) The following contractual provisions and agreements restrict competition:
1. The non-competition provision between the parties contained in Clause 3.1 of the joint venture agreement, as amended at the demand of the Commission.
2. The parties' agreement that a shareholder who wishes to provide digital interactive television services by means of a broadband system may do so only where it has given BiB a right of first refusal to provide such a service and BiB has not agreed to provide such a service on terms at least as favourable as those offered by a third party within six months of the offer or 31 March 1999, whichever is the later[368].
3. The exclusive supply agreements between BiB and Midland Bank in respect of merchant acquiring and transaction management services.
4. The provisions of the JVA requiring certain advertising of the BiB service to be integrated with BSkyB advertising[369].
5. The commitment of the parties to promote only digital satellite set-top boxes which are capable of receiving the BiB service for so long as BiB is subsidising set-top boxes. However, BSkyB may promote any other set-top box where the purpose of such promotion relates to the use of such boxes in homes which already have a BiB-subsidised settop box and BSkyB agrees to spend a substantial amount of money on the marketing of its digital pay-television service[370].

---

[364] Clause 3.3 (A) of JVA, referred to at recital 119.

[365] ONdigital is subsidising the retail selling price of the digital settop boxes necessary for its service.

[366] Response of 8 August 1997 on behalf of BiB parties to request for information of 25 July 1997.

[367] For example, the total investment in BiB is GBP [...](*) million (of which BSkyB is in any event contributing [...](*) %). The peak annual cost of running the BiB services is GBP [...](*) million (in [...](*), of which approximately [...](*) is attributable to subsidisation of the set-top box.

[368] Clause 3.3 (A) of JVA.

[369] Clause 17 of JVA.

[370] Clause 20 of JVA.

6.  BSkyB's commitment that the subscription price for its digital pay-television service will be no higher than that of similar analogue packages of satellite entertainment services and its commitment to use reasonable endeavours to ensure that all programmes broadcast on BSkyB's analogue satellite service will be broadcast simultaneously on BSkyB's digital satellite service[371].

(146)  These clauses are directly related and necessary restrictions to the creation and operation of BiB with the exception of the prohibition in the non-competition clause on holding more than a 20% interest in a company competing with BiB, for the following reasons:

## (a) Non-competition provision

(147)  Subject to recital 149, the agreement amongst the parties not to compete in the provision of digital interactive television services is necessary for, and directly related to, the establishment of BiB, given the technical and financial risks involved in entering a new market, and the level of investment required. The uncertainty inherent in such a joint venture, and the need to ensure a stable base of operations in its early years, justify this non-competition clause.

(148)  The fact that the non-competition clause continues to apply to a shareholder for a period of 12 months after that shareholder loses joint control provided that the loss occurs within three years of the date on which this Decision takes effect, is justified as a protection for the joint venture and for the investors against a parent company withdrawing from the joint venture and taking unfair advantage of the know-how acquired during its participation in the joint venture in order to compete in the same market.

(149)  The Commission has examined the prohibition contained in the non-competition provision, which precludes the BiB parent companies from holding more than a 20% interest in a company competing with BiB. The clause is not limited to the acquisition of material influence but it does include the purchase of shares for investment purposes only. Therefore, this restriction cannot be considered directly related and necessary to the operation of the joint venture. The Commission needs to examine whether the clause fulfils the criteria set out in Article 81(3).

## (b) BiB's right of first refusal

(150)  This clause limits the scope of the non-competition provision. BiB's right does not go beyond the scope of activities which fall under the non-competition obligations between the parent companies. This provision is of particular relevance to BT, which could in the future be interested in the provision of digital interactive television services via broadband networks. BiB's right of first refusal shows the commitment of the parent companies to ensuring the success of BiB and of their investments.

## (c) Exclusive agreements between BiB and Midland Bank

(151)  Both a transaction management system and merchant acquiring services are essential parts of the infrastructure necessary for BiB Platform Co.'s service. Midland was willing to bear the full cost of developing the software necessary for the transaction management system, in return for a fee equivalent to a percentage of each transaction. This allowed BiB to reduce its initial capital requirements and to match its payments to income in an economically efficient manner. The financial risk of the development costs remains with Midland. However, a period of exclu-

---

[371]  Clause 19 of JVA.

sivity allows Midland the opportunity to recoup its initial investment, with no guarantee that it will do so. In terms of merchant acquiring services, Midland has undertaken to provide the services at an advantageous fixed rate to help with the establishment of BiB. Midland, on the other hand, requires a guarantee that BiB will not change suppliers once it is established.

Moreover, neither agreement prevents other providers of digital interactive services from seeking transaction management or merchant acquiring services from companies other than Midland. The exclusive agreements, which will play with regard to content providers and end-users using the BiB platform or contracting BiB services, thus constitute the necessary quid pro quo for Midland's willingness to incur up-front capital costs for the benefit of the operation of the joint venture. They are thus crucial to its participation in BiB and cannot be considered in isolation from the joint venture.

### (d) Commitments of the parent companies in markets related to BiB's (Clauses 17, 19 and 20 of the JVA)

(152)   These provisions are necessary to the establishment of BiB and to the penetration in the market of a new package of services. BSkyB will concentrate its efforts on the development of BiB's services. These obligations on BSkyB are intended to enable BiB to succesfully enter the new market. These clauses are necessary for and directly related to the operation of the joint venture.

### 3. Effect on trade between Member States

(153)   An agreement which may have an influence, direct or indirect, actual or potential, on the pattern of trade between Member States meets the criterion of effect on trade between Member States[372].

(154)   The BiB joint venture agreement limits the territory within which the parties will initially provide digital interactive television services to the United Kingdom, Isle of Man and Channel Islands. However, the service is technically capable of being provided in other European countries, although certain technical modifications due to continuing differences in currency would be required. The parties have stated that the difficulties of provision of the service in other countries are likely to decrease in the future[373].

(155)   BSkyB's analogue pay-television service is currently available via both satellite and cable in Ireland. It is likely that its digital service will be available there in the near future, at least via satellite. Given the absence of linguistic barriers, the presence of BSkyB, and the presence of certain retailers in both the United Kingdom and Ireland, it cannot be excluded that the BiB service, or a localised version, will be made available in Ireland. If BSkyB enters the pay-television markets in other Member States, the geographic scope of activity of BiB may be similarly extended thereafter.

(156)   However, even if this is not the case, the agreement affects the competitive structure for the provision of digital interactive television services throughout the United Kingdom[374]. As a result of this operation entry in the relevant market in the

---

[372]   See for example, Case 42/84 Remia v Commission [1985] ECR 2545.

[373]   'Over time it could be expected that some or all of [the] barriers to internationalising the service would decline. It is entirely feasible to envisage BiB and other transactional platform providers in different Member States developing in the medium term and expanding into other Member States.' (Form A/B, at page 49).

[374]   Cases 6 and 7/73 Commercial Solvents v Commission [1974] ECR 223 at paragraphs 30 to 35.

United Kingdom is made more difficult to other possible Community competitors. The latter is also applicable to the prohibition to the BiB's parent companies, in the non-competition provision, of holding more than a 20% interest in a competing company. Potential entrants in the digital interactive television services market in the United Kingdom cannot rely on the investments of BiB's parent companies. Finally, by establishing a prime mover with substantial advantages, BiB is likely to procure certain services from other non-British content providers[375]. There will thus be an effect on the flow of trade.

(157)   On the basis of recitals 153 to 156, the agreements are likely to affect trade between Member States.

## C. ARTICLE 81(3)

(158)   The notified agreements satisfy the criteria for an exemption set out in Article 81(3) of the EC Treaty, for the following reasons:

### 1. Improvement in distribution of goods and technical and economic progress

(159)   In developing the BiB joint venture, the parties have overcome the current technological limitations of both satellite broadcast technology and narrowband telecommunications customer access infrastructure. The former is, for the time being, capable of only one-way communication and could not alone provide interactive services of the type envisaged by BiB. The latter, while capable of the two-way communication inherent in telephony is not, at the moment, suitable for services which require a higher bandwidth. In combination, however, their use enables provision of a new form of service which had not been offered yet, available to the vast majority of consumers in the United Kingdom. Retailers of goods and services also obtain a new outlet for their products. The creation of the joint venture, therefore, contributes to an improvement in the distribution of goods and technical and economic progress[376].

(160)   The improvements attained as a result of this operation would not materialise without the prohibition set out in the non-competition provision on the holding or more than a 20% interest in a competing company. This clause eliminates the economic incentive for the parties to transfer to a competitor any ideas and strategies that are being developed by BiB. Such ideas and strategies are of enormous value in a new and fast-moving industry such as the digital interactive television services market: for instance, the right moment to launch the service and the modalities of entering the market; special offers, pricing structure, whether the set-top box should be offered free of charge to potential subscribers. These ideas and strategies, which have been first tested in BiB from the synthesis of the four parents' contributions, are not covered by the prohibition of the non-competition clause on the transfer of the greater part of the know-how to a competitor.

(161)   The digital interactive services could also be provided by upgrading BT's copper network. If the medium term effect of BT's participation in the joint venture were to be a reduction in its economic incentive in upgrading its narrowband telecommunications customer access infrastructure, the Commission's positive assessment of BiB's impact on technical and economic progress would require reconsideration in the light of the broader developments in the market. As was explained in

---

[375] Form A/B, at page 32.

[376] See Commission Decision 98/536/EEC (Case IV/31.734: Film purchased by German television stations) (OJ L 284, 3-10-1989, p. 36, at recital 49); Decision 90/25/EEC (Case IV/32.265 – Concordato Incendio) (OJ L 15, 19-1-1990, p. 25, at recital 25).

recital 86, BT owns the only such nation-wide infrastructure and has a very high market-share of fixed residential lines in use. If upgraded, it would provide an alternative national transmission mechanism for the provision of broadband interactive services. In addition, it could carry other services, such as video telephony, broadband internet access and video-on-demand. One telecommunications operator in the United Kingdom has already upgraded its network and it is being used for provision of BiB-type services. BT itself is conducting trials.

(162) Evaluation of the impact of BT's participation in BiB on the development of the customer access infrastructure market, and therefore on the services market using that infrastructure, is premature. If BT's commercial interest in maintaining and upgrading its exiting network were lessened as a result of its participation in BiB, then this would constitute a significant impediment to technical and economic progress. The result would depend, in part, on developments in the geographic coverage of broadband cable infrastructure in the United Kingdom.

## 2. Benefit to consumers

(163) Until recently, services comparable to those of BiB have been available only via the Internet and using personal computers as a display screen. However, the still limited penetration of personal computers in the United Kingdom has prevented such services from reaching the mass market. Almost all households in the United Kingdom possess a television set. Purchase of a BiB/ BSkyB digital set-top box would give them access to interactive services via television screens. The introduction of a new service of this type is of benefit to consumers.

(164) The benefits for the consumers resulting from this operation would not materialise if it were not for the prohibition, set out in the non-competition clause, on any holding of more than a 20% interest in a competing company. This clause prevents the parties from transferring to a competitor the ideas and strategies that are being developed by BiB in its new market and ensures the commitment of the parties to BiB and eventually to BiB's success in the market.

(165) In addition, the Commission has imposed a condition whereby the parties shall provide information both to end-users and to their agents for the sale of set-top boxes, that end-users need not subscribe to BSkyB's digital pay-television service as a condition of the purchase of a BiB-subsidised set-top box. The condition ensures both that the original requirement is not reintroduced at a later date and that end-users are provided with accurate information. Consequently, the condition ensures that consumers are given a choice either to acquire the set-top box with BSkyB's paytelevision package or to acquire it without subscribing to BSkyB's pay-television offer.

## 3. Indispensability

(166) BT and BSkyB have the necessary expertise to provide some form of interactive services individually. However, by cooperating together in BiB they are able to provide a better service and to do so more quickly. Their participation, together with Midland Bank and Matsushita, is thus indispensable to the creation of BiB, and to its ultimate establishment on a new market. BT has gained skills and experience in the course of its past interactive television trials in the development and integration of interactive multimedia services which it contributes to the joint venture. This is in addition to its expertise in the provision of telecommunications services which have been vital to the operation of the BiB telecommunications return path and its connections with the servers. BSkyB contributes its experience in settop box design and operation, together with its knowledge of consumer demand

for pay-television. Midland contributes expertise in the area of merchant acquiring and transaction management, and the integration of these services into the BiB infrastructure. Finally, Panasonic contributes its technical expertise, particularly in the area of set-top box design.

(167)  The prohibition to hold more than a 20% interest in a competing company is indispensable for this operation. The success of BiB would be jeopardised in case of a transfer to a competitor of the unique ideas and strategies, which are being developed by the parties in BiB.

## 4. Non-elimination of competition in respect of a substantial part of the products in question

(168)  Companies other than BiB, notably the various cable operators, have plans to launch digital interactive television services. The BiB parties have estimated that a subscriber base of at least one million subscribers is necessary to achieve the necessary scale for the provision of digital interactive television services. Following the consolidation in the United Kingdom cable industry, the cable networks of Cable & Wireless Communications, NTL and Telewest each have a reach of more than one million homes. NTL has already launched a commercial trial[377]. Cable operators have an advantage in the provision of such services as their cable networks have two-way capability. This allows them alone, or in cooperation with third parties, to use the network for interactive services. Other companies also have plans to introduce digital interactive television services, in particular WebTV and Videonet.

(169)  However, both BSkyB and BT have very important positions in the United Kingdom, in markets neighbouring and closely related to that in which the BiB joint venture will be active. Their positions in these markets are safeguarded, at least in the medium term, by the existence of barriers to entry. Both therefore possess a degree of market power which is central to the legal assessment of the impact of the elimination of potential competition between BT and BSkyB as a result of the creation of the BiB joint venture.

(170)  Accordingly, the Commission considered that the combination of the very significant market power of BT, and in particular of BSkyB in related markets, with that in which BiB will be active such as the customer access infrastructure market, the technical services for paytelevision and digital interactive services, the paytelevision market and the market for the wholesale supply of film and sport channels for pay-television, risked eliminating a substantial part of competition on the markets for digital interactive television services[378]. The conditions set out in this Decision should ensure that this risk does not materialise and that, in particular, competition to BT comes from the cable networks, that third parties are ensured sufficient access to BiB's subsidised set-top boxes and to BSkyB's films and

---

[377] NTL is testing the service of Yes Television on its cable network in Cardiff until Summer 1999. Research is being carried out on the possibilities of a full-scale launch. Yes Television offers entertainment and music on demand, along with news and information services, travel services, educational services and home shopping. Source: Inside Cable & Telecoms Europe, <http:// www.inside-cable.co.uk>, article of 11 January 1999, 'Cardiff gets UK's first interactive TV'.

[378] In this respect the parties' revised business plan provided to the Commission on 12 August 1997 is illuminating. It was based on the assumption that little competition would emerge on the digital interactive television services market: 'BiB is the sole provider of digital television interactive services, as defined in the joint venture agreement, to both BSkyB subscribers and to [...](*)% of cable subscribers'.

sport channels and that set-top boxes other that BiB's set-top box can be developed in the market, so that the digital interactive television services remain open to competition.

(171) Even given the prohibition in the non-competition clause, preventing BiB's parent companies from holding more than a 20% interest in a competing company, there is no chance that competition will be eliminated as a result of the creation of BiB. The conditions imposed upon the parties ensure that the relevant market will remain open and that BiB will face significant competition. The conditions imposed on the parties can be summarised as follows:

**(a) Competition from the cable networks**

(172) In the customer access infrastructure market and in the corresponding telecommunication and interactive services markets that can be provided via this infrastructure, the most significant competition facing BT comes from the actual and potential owners of the cable networks who can compete with BT in the provision of telecommunication services and with BiB in the provision of digital interactive services. BT provided 86% of residential fixed lines in use and is the only telecommunication operator in the United Kingdom with a network which covers almost the whole of the country: consequently, it is important to safeguard and encourage competition coming from the cable segment. If BT were to expand its cable interests and at the same time participate in the operation of BiB, BT would not have an incentive to develop, through its cable networks, digital interactive television services of the kind to be provided by BiB, and it would not have an incentive to facilitate third parties to compete with BiB in the provision of these digital interactive television services via its cable networks. Therefore, it is a condition of exemption that BT has agreed not to expand its existing cable television interests in the United Kingdom. The Commission notes that it has further agreed to divest itself of its existing interests. This will allow competition in the provision of broadband cable infrastructure to develop independently of BT throughout the United Kingdom and to counterbalance the restrictive effects of the combination of BT and BSkyB in BiB.

**(b) Third party access to BiB-subsidised set-top boxes**

(173) BiB is to subsidise the set-top box which will be used both for its own service and for BSkyB's digital paytelevision service. BSkyB and BiB together control the access of competing digital interactive television services and pay-television operators to those boxes. BSkyB's control is ensured by its position on the technical services market – that is, by the supply of conditional access and access control services. BiB controls access by means of the operation of the subsidy recovery mechanism which requires all providers of encrypted services to contribute to its historic and ongoing subsidy costs as part of their conditional access and access control payments.

(174) Third party access to BiB-subsidised set-top boxes is important because of the market position of BSkyB. BSkyB has a market share of some [...] (*)% in the paytelevision market. In theory, competitors to BiB and BSkyB which wished to provide services using digital satellite could launch a competing set-top box. However, the capital costs of establishing a competing infrastructure, combined with the general reluctance of consumers to acquire more than one set-top box, makes this unlikely. This conclusion is reinforced by BSkyB's control of film and sports. In practice, therefore, they are more likely to seek access to BiB/BSkyB's existing

set-top box infrastructure[379]. This has been the case in respect of analogue pay-television services in the United Kingdom. There is no reason to presume that it will be different in respect of digital services, where the investment costs of establishing a set-top box infrastructure are even larger.

(175) If competing providers of digital interactive services were to be denied access to BiB-subsidised set-top boxes, or were to be granted access on terms less favourable than BiB and/or BSkyB, then a substantial part of competition on the downstream services markets would be eliminated. Legal separation of BiB

(176) Pursuant to the amended joint venture agreements (JVA)[380] BiB will establish legally separate companies for BiB's activities in respect of the subsidisation of settop boxes and the recovery of monies from third party users of the box and the creation and operation of the BiB interactive services. Each company will have separate management and each will publish annual audited accounts. In addition, it has been imposed as a condition of exemption that auditors shall certify that all transactions between the two companies have been carried out at arm's length, in accordance with the principles set out in the OECD transfer pricing guidelines. This should ensure transparency and nondiscriminatory treatment between the two operations, and prevent the subsidy mechanism from being used as an artificial barrier to entry on the market for digital interactive television services.

**Operation of subsidy recovery mechanism**

(177) The Commission has imposed a condition on the operation of the subsidy recovery mechanism which seeks to ensure that it is transparent and nondiscriminatory. The operation of the subsidy recovery mechanism also falls to be regulated by the United Kingdom authorities pursuant to Directive 95/47/EC and to national measures. The Commission considers that compliance with the condition will be presumed where the parties comply with the British arrangements.

(178) According to the condition, third parties will have an option either to pay an initial sum, or to pay subsidy contributions on an ongoing basis. The subsidy contributions will be related to usage of the box – meaning the number of conditional access cards issued or the number of access control authentications. This condition ensures that a smaller operator will not pay the same as a larger operator in order to facilitate market entrance.

(179) BiB Platform Co., as an operating provider for digital interactive services, will contribute to subsidy recovery in the same way as its competitors. These payments will form part of its cost base to be covered through its charges to content providers. BSkyB will also contribute to subsidy recovery in the same way as other paytelevision operators.

**Supply of technical services to third parties**

(180) First, the Commission has imposed a condition that BSkyB shall offer to develop and operate Simulcrypt arrangements with interested parties subject to appropriate commercial agreements. This should ensure that users of other conditional access systems will be in a position, should they so choose, to address customers who own BiB digital satellite set-top boxes.

(181) Secondly, downstream service providers which wish to use BiB-subsidised set-top boxes, and those which do use the boxes, require information about the technical specifications of the set-top box, including proposed changes to the specifications.

---

[379] See Bertelsmann/Kirch/Premiere, at recital 56.
[380] Clause 2 of the JVA.

In the absence of such information, they would be unable to develop their own services and to continue to up-date them in response to any changes to the specifications of the set-top box. The Commission has therefore imposed a condition that such information be provided to interested parties[381]. It now appears likely that the majority of the relevant information will be held by BSkyB. However, this position may change. To ensure that there is no gap in the parties' duty to provide relevant information to third parties, information provision conditions are imposed on both BSkyB and BiB McCo.

### (c) Third party access to BSkyB's pay-television channels

(182) BSkyB's channels are supplied both to cable operators and to the digital terrestrial operator, ONdigital. The channels are then offered to subscribers as part of the latter's own pay-television service. However, they act only as distributors of the channels and must distribute them without modification of their content. They may not add, or indeed remove, any elements without BSkyB's consent. The parties have indicated that it is their intention, subject to the conclusion of the necessary agreements, to make the BiB service available to end-users via cable networks or digital terrestrial television.

(183) BiB's cable and digital terrestrial competitors will not be able to place interactive links in the most popular paytelevision channels in the United Kingdom. This would only be possible if both technical[382] and commercial obstacles were overcome. They would require them to reach an agreement with a competitor, BSkyB, which has significant market power in upstream markets and an incentive to foreclose the downstream digital interactive television services market.

(184) It is, therefore, necessary to impose a condition on BSkyB's wholesale supply of its film and sports channels to its cable and digital terrestrial competitors. BSkyB will be obliged to offer to distribute its film and sports channels either with or without ('clean-feed') interactive applications, at the choice of the purchaser on a nondiscriminatory basis. This prevents BSkyB from bundling interactivity at the wholesale supply level with its channels to the detriment of both competitors to BiB on the digital interactive television services market and its own competitors in pay-television. BiB's competitors would not be able to integrate their own interactive services into these channels. However, they would be able to do so in respect of channels which are not owned by BSkyB. [...] (*) it would also be possible for BiB's competitors to negotiate agreements for the use of their different interactive services in respect of film payper- view services[383]. Thus competition with BiB will not be eliminated.

---

[381] The parties have raised with the Commission as a possible means of complying with this condition the use of a website, parts or all of which may be password protected, for the provision of the non-disclosure agreement and/or the supplemental technical agreement and/or the technical information. The Commission considers that this is one of the ways in which the parties could fulfil this condition. However, the choice of mechanism is a matter appropriately left to the parties.

[382] Both cable operators and ONdigital use different set-top boxes and interactive technology to BSkyB/BiB. Evidence provided by BSkyB and third parties indicated that although it would be possible in theory to re-author in real-time the interactive elements in BSkyB's film and sports channels so that they would function with these different technologies, doing so would have cost and timing implications for the competing cable and/or digital terrestrial operators, making this option at best significantly less attractive, and at worst impossible.

[383] NTL and Telewest operate the Front Row pay-per-view service which is independent of BSkyB.

### (d) Contribution to the development of alternative set-top boxes

(185) It is a condition of exemption that BSkyB limits the exercise of its veto rights in the joint venture agreement to the extent that it will be obliged in certain circumstances to support any proposal to subsidise other set-top boxes as part of an agreement for carriage of the BiB service on cable and/or digital terrestrial television. Given that companies requesting BiB to subsidise other set-top boxes would in practice be competitors of BSkyB on its core market, this condition is intended to address BSkyB's conflict of interest in its decisions as a BiB shareholder and its interests as a paytelevision operator. This should ensure that BiB as a commercial company is free to take decisions in relation to BSkyB's competitors on commercial grounds, and is not limited by BSkyB's other commercial interests.

### (e) Anti-avoidance

(186) Given both the complex nature of the arrangements between the parties, and the ongoing development of the BiB joint venture itself, it is conceivable that conditions imposed on one party could be avoided by actions of other parties or BiB itself. This applies in particular to the conditions relating to the information to the retailers that there is no requirement that a purchaser of a BiB set-top box should take out a subscription to any pay-television services, the subsidy recovery mechanism and the provision of information to third party users of the set-top box. This condition is intended to prevent this.

### 5. Conclusion

(187) The Commission concludes that the BiB transactions meet all four conditions for an individual exemption pursuant to Article 81(3) of the EC Treaty.

### D. DURATION OF THE EXEMPTION AND CONDITIONS

(188) Pursuant to Article 8 of Regulation No 17 a decision in application of Article 81(3) of the EC Treaty has to be issued for a specified period and conditions and obligations may be attached thereto. Pursuant to Article 6 of Regulation No 17 the date from which such a decision takes effect cannot be earlier than the date of notification.

(189) In this case, this Decision takes effect from the date on which all of the changes to the arrangements referred to in recitals 124 to 134 were made, and the conditions set out in this Decision were fulfilled. Therefore, the relevant date is 4 August 1998.

(190) As for the duration of the exemption decision, the Commission has examined BiB's business plan, the joint venture agreements and the conditions prevailing on the United Kingdom market, in order to ascertain what would be the minimum period for which BiB would need the support of its parent companies, in the form permitted by this Decision, to establish itself as a viable business in the new market of the digital interactive television services. There is no doubt that the present operation entails a significant financial risk for the shareholders, who will invest significant resources in a new market with a considerable degree of uncertainty as to the response of United Kingdom consumers to the new digital services proposed. The parties predicted that BiB would not make an operating profit until [...] (*) and the shareholders would not receive back their initial cash investment until [...] (*). This prediction is confirmed by the Business Plan of the parties. The Commission considers a period of seven years to be sufficient and appropriate in the special circumstances of the United Kingdom market [...] (*). The contractual clauses described in recitals 145 to 152 which are directly related and necessary to

the creation and operation of BiB are exempted for the same period of seven years. The prohibition in the non-competition provision, which has been assessed under Article 81(1) and (3), is also exempted for a seven-year period which is the period considered necessary for [...] (*).

(191) The most crucial requirements to safeguard competition are attached as conditions, owing to the need to prevent an elimination of effective competition on the market for digital interactive television services. Strict compliance with these require- ments is so important that the Commission must ensure immediate consequences in the event of a breach.

(192) However, the principle of proportionality requires that far-reaching legal, financial and commercial consequences do not ensue from occasional or individual mis- takes whose effects on the market are negligible. As a matter of principle, for an exemption to be based on certain conditions, those conditions must be proportion- ate to the competition concern. Trivial breaches of conditions should not inevita- bly lead to the ending of any exemption. The Commission considers that in relation to the subsidy recovery mechanism and the requirements to provide infor- mation, it is appropriate to distinguish between trivial and material breaches of these conditions. The Commission considers that the concept of breach as used in Article 3 will allow national authorities and national courts to determine whether a condition has been materially breached.

(193) Accordingly, infringements of Conditions Nos 7, 8 and 9 cannot be considered to breach a condition attached to this Decision unless such infringements fulfil the criteria set out in Article 3.

(194) The Commission has expressed its concerns about the impact of BT's participation in BiB on the development of the customer access infrastructure market. However, the Commission concluded that this evaluation is premature. The Commission therefore may consider it necessary to conduct a review of BT's participation in the joint venture in the medium term. If it were proved that such participation was impeding the supply of services using broadband customer access infrastructure in the United Kingdom, the Commission might consider this fact to be relevant pur- suant to Article 8(3) of Regulation No 17,

## HAS ADOPTED THIS DECISION:

### Article 1
Pursuant to Article 81(3) of the EC Treaty and subject to Article 2 of this Decision, the provisions of Article 81(1) of the EC Treaty area hereby declared inapplicable, for a pe- riod of seven years from 4 August 1998 to:
(a)     the joint venture agreement for the creation of a joint venture company, British In- teractive Broadcasting Ltd (now named Open) by BSkyB Limited, BT Holdings Limited, Midland Bank plc and Matsushita Electric Europe (Headquarters) Lim- ited as notified on 13 June 1997 and amended on 4 August 1998;
(b)     all the related agreements notified to the Commission for the creation of British Interactive Broadcasting Ltd set out in Annex I to this Decision.

### Article 2
The exemption set out in Article 1 of this Decision shall be subject to the following condi- tions:

*Condition No 1: (Legal separation of BiB box and services operations – auditors)*
The auditors who are required to certify on an annual basis that the marketing contribu-

tion activities of McCo. have been undertaken at arms' length to the activities of BiB Services Co. will interpret the term 'arms' length' in accordance with the transfer pricing guidelines.

*Condition No 2: (Information on the removal of subscription tie between BiB boxes and BSkyB services)*

A.    The BiB Parties will procure that retailers who sell digital interactive reception equipment with the benefit of marketing contributions and installers of such equipment are informed in writing that there is no requirement that a purchaser of such equipment should take out a subscription to any pay-television services and that services other than BSkyB's services will be available via the BiB box including those non-subscription services which are transmitted via digital satellite for reception on BiB boxes. The BiB Parties will further require that purchasers of equipment benefiting from marketing contributions are advised in writing at the point of sale that there is no such requirement and that services other than BSkyB's services will be available via the BiB box including those non-subscription services which are transmitted via digital satellite for reception on BiB boxes.

B.    BSkyB will put in place written procedures, of which it will provide copies to the Commission, to ensure that all of its analogue customers, when offered a subscription to BSkyB's digital satellite services ('Sky Digital Subscription'), are informed clearly in writing (by notice approved in writing by the Commission) that there is no requirement for them to take out a Sky Digital Subscription in order to be eligible to purchase a BiB box and that services other than BSkyB's services will be available via the BiB box including those non-subscription services which are transmitted via digital satellite for reception on BiB boxes.

C.    BSkyB will put in place written procedures, of which it will provide copies to the Commission, to ensure that its agents for the sale of Sky Digital Subscriptions who also sell BiB boxes are informed clearly in writing that there is no requirement on the purchaser to take out a Sky Digital Subscription in order to be eligible to purchase a BiB box and that services other than BSkyB's services will be available via the BiB box including those non-subscription services which are transmitted via digital satellite for reception on BiB boxes.

*Condition No 3: (Availability of a clean feed)*

Where movies and/or sports programming (but not advertising time paid for by parties other than BSkyB or BiB) on any of BSkyB's movies and/or sports channels includes on-screen representations directing the viewer to BiB's digital interactive television services and/or BSkyB's enhanced movies and/or sports television services, BSkyB will give distributors of such channels, on a non-discriminatory basis, an option either:

(i)    where the distributor is also a distributor of BiB's digital interactive television services and/or BSkyB's enhanced movies and/or sports television services (as the case may be), to receive a signal for the channel(s) which include(s) the on-screen representation and interactive applications (authored in BSkyB's chosen technology) directing the viewer to such of BiB's digital interactive television services and/or BSkyB's enhanced movies and/or sports television services as the distributor is carrying, or

(ii)   to receive a signal for the channel(s) such that the onscreen representations directing the viewer to such of BiB's digital interactive television services and/or BSkyB's enhanced movies and/or sports television services as the distributor is not carrying may not be viewed by means of, at the distributor's option, either:

(a) (where delivery of the channel is by satellite) a signal which includes the on-screen representations within a part of the signal which is transmitted separately from the main television picture; or

(b) (where delivery of the channel is by landline) a signal which does not include the on-screen representations or, at the distributor's option, includes them within a part of the signal which is transmitted separately from the main television picture[384];

or such other means as is agreed by the parties. This is subject in any such case to the distributor bearing any costs incurred in the development and ongoing provision of any such solution, including, where relevant, the costs relating to the installation, operation and maintenance of a landline and any related equipment necessary to provide the feed by landline.

*Condition No 4: (Divestiture of cable)*

A.    BT shall not buy or seek any broadband cable television franchises in the United Kingdom beyond its existing holdings, and shall dispose of any such franchises acquired in the course of any other transaction. This undertaking shall however not restrict BT from providing broadcast services (should BT be permitted to do so in the future), broadband services or broadband interactive services (including for the avoidance of doubt in competition with the franchises in Westminster and Milton Keynes) over its own networks.

B.    With effect from the date of this Decision (the 'Exemption Decision') to divest itself of its broadband cable television franchises in Westminster and Milton Keynes (together 'the Businesses') on the following basis:

(i)    BT shall use its best efforts to arrange for the sale of the Businesses, at fair market value, within [...] (*) months of the Exemption Decision;

(ii)   BT shall maintain the Businesses in legally separate entities and shall operate them in a manner which enables it to maintain, as far as possible, their viability, marketability and value pending sale and final disposal;

(iii)  prior to the sale of the Businesses, BT shall separately manage and hold separate the Businesses from the other businesses of BT in the United Kingdom Structural changes to the Businesses, until the date of such sale, shall not be undertaken by BT until after BT shall have informed the Commission of any such proposed change and the Commission shall not have explicitly opposed such proposed additional change in writing within two weeks of receiving BT's notice of change;

(iv)   BT shall, as soon as reasonably practicable after receipt of the Commission's Decision, submit to the Commission a list of three nominations of accountancy firms, investment banks or similar undertakings. One such firm or bank or other body shall be appointed, subject to the approval of the Commission, as an independent expert. Such expert shall, if the Commission so requests, report to the Commission on whether or not BT is complying with subparagraph (iii).

C.    If the Businesses have not been sold within the deadline set out in subparagraph B(i), BT shall appoint, subject to the approval of the Commission, a trustee in relation to the Businesses (such trustee may be the expert appointed in accordance with subparagraph B(iv) above). The terms of appointment shall be such that the trustee shall use his best efforts to sell the Businesses at fair market value within

---

[384] BSkyB shall have the right to refuse a request for delivery by landline only where this is approved by a suitable British regulator.

[...] (*) months of the Exemption Decision or on such other terms as may be agreed between BT and the Commission.

D.    If the trustee has not sold the Businesses in accordance with paragraph C, the trustee shall be obliged to sell the Businesses for the best possible price they are reasonably able to obtain within [...] (*) months of the Exemption Decision. (The remaining terms and conditions of the trustee's appointment shall continue to apply.)

E.    BT or, where relevant, the trustee shall notify the Commission in writing of the identity of the proposed purchaser of the Business. If, within ten working days of receipt of such notification the Commission has not informed BT or the trustee in writing to the contrary, the proposed purchaser shall be deemed to be acceptable to the Commission.

*Condition No 5: (Veto rights)*
A.    BSkyB will vote in favour of any resolution of BiB to authorise its subsidiary which is responsible for promotional activities by means of marketing contributions for the subsidisation of set-top boxes ('McCo.') to provide marketing contributions or similar financial contributions in respect of sales of digital interactive set-top boxes where such resolution, where relevant including the proposed means of financing and any other consequent changes, has been recommended by the Chief Executive Officer of BiB and unanimously agreed to by the other BiB partners.

B.    This condition will apply subject to the following criteria being met:
   (i)    the relevant digital set-top boxes are capable of receiving and running all of BiB's interactive services either in Open TV or reauthored format;
   (ii)   the operator(s) to whom it is proposed to provide marketing contributions or similar financial contributions in respect of sales of digital interactive set-top boxes have undertaken to make capacity available for BiB's interactive services for a period equivalent to that for which BiB has secured transponder capacity;
   (iii)  in the event that each of the three other BiB shareholders has a commercial interest in such a proposal (independently of their respective interest in BiB), BiB's auditors providing an opinion that the proposal is not, when taken as a whole, significantly less favourable than the provision of marketing contributions in respect of sales of BiB boxes set out in the BiB Business Plan. The auditor may take into account all factors which appear to the auditor to be relevant, including the balance of risk and reward to be derived from such proposal as compared to that to be derived from the provision of marketing contributions in respect of BiB boxes;
   (iv)   the proposal (a) does not require BSkyB to commit funding to BiB or McCo. in addition to that which it has already committed pursuant to the JVA; (b) is not funded through revenues which would otherwise be available for distribution to BSkyB as distributable profits; and (c) does not result in BSkyB losing joint control of BiB, in the event that the other shareholders commit additional funding to BiB and BSkyB does not; and
   (v)    the proposal does not reduce the funds contemplated as available within the agreed business plan for use as marketing contributions towards DTH digital interactive set-top boxes.

*Condition No 6: (Conditional access and Simulcrypt)*
A.    BSkyB and Sky Subscribers Services Limited ('SSSL') confirm that SSSL will of-

fer to develop and to operate Simulcrypt arrangements with all conditional access providers who administer access to non-SSSL digital television decoders in the United Kingdom. This offer to develop and operate Simulcrypt arrangements will remain open for the duration of the exemption.

B.  SSSL will (and BSkyB will procure that it will) confirm in writing its offer to develop Simulcrypt arrangements within 21 days of a written request from a conditional access provider made in the required manner.

C.  SSSL will (and BSkyB will procure that it will) use all reasonable endeavours to procure that Simulcrypt arrangements are operational within 12 months of the relevant request or within such other timescale as is agreed between the parties and to this end BSkyB and SSSL will cooperate fully with the conditional access provider (and its technology provider, if different).

D.  In the event that BSkyB/SSSL is unable to meet these deadlines, a reasoned request for an extension must be submitted to OFTEL at least one month before the expiry of the deadline, which extension must be granted unless the inability to comply with such time frame is due primarily or exclusively to culpability on the part of BSkyB or SSSL. OFTEL will inform in writing the Commission of its reasons to accept or reject the request for the extension at least two weeks before adopting its decision. If the Commission does not object to OFTEL's proposal within a period of two weeks, it will be understood that the Commission accepts this proposal.

E.  This condition is subject to:

(i)  the conditional access provider who wishes to operate a Simulcrypt arrangement (and its technology provider, if different) cooperating fully with SSSL, and if appropriate, SSSL's technology provider, News Digital systems Limited (NDS), in developing a Simulcrypt arrangement between the NDS technology administered by SSSL and the conditional access system employed by the conditional access provider and agreeing fair and reasonable commercial terms for such development;

(ii)  the conditional access provider agreeing with SSSL fair and reasonable commercial terms for ongoing arrangements relating to the operation of the Simulcrypt arrangement, including, without limitation, arrangements for the cross carriage of necessary data; and

(iii)  the security of the conditional access provider's system not being compromised such that it creates a threat to the security of the system used by SSSL.

*Condition No 7: (Subsidy recovery)*

A.  The BiB Parties confirm that McCo. will carry out its activities in the United Kingdom for the recovery of marketing contributions under arrangements with SSSL and, as relevant, other conditional access and access control providers each of which is, or will at the relevant time be, subject to the British regime.

B.  The recovery of marketing contributions by McCo. shall be permitted provided that the following conditions shall apply:

(i) recovery in respect of marketing contributions will be made via:

(a)  charges to customers for broadcast conditional access services (including BSkyB); and

(b)  charges to customers for access control services (including BiB's subsidiary which carries out the business of an interactive service platform operator 'Services Co.')and such charges will be made on a fair, reasonable and non-discriminatory basis;

(ii) the subsidy recovery element of any conditional access and access control charges will be based on a charge per card entitled (conditional access) or per authentication (access control) basis which may vary over time provided that:

(a) different charges may be made for different classes of conditional access and access control usage, so long as such differentiation does not distort, prevent or restrict competition within or between members of any of the following classes of purchasers of conditional access or access control services or between such classes: broadcasters, retailers of broadcast services, BiB Services Co. and its competitors, competitors to BiB Services Co. inter se, and any other class of purchasers of conditional access or access control services which may from time to time emerge;

(b) different options taking account of bulk purchases of conditional access and/or access control services may be offered on a non-discriminatory basis;

(iii) recovery will be made:

(a) in accordance with a scheme (or schemes) allocating recovery charges on an objective basis between customers for broadcast conditional access services and customers for access control services on each of which the Director-General for Telecommunications has:

– been consulted, and

– had prior notice of at least 30 days of the form of the scheme which is put into practice, and

– raised no objection to that form of scheme being put into practice or

(b) as otherwise required by the Director-General for Telecommunications from time to time, or

(c) as determined in the resolution of any dispute:

– by a court of competent jurisdiction, or

– by a competent national authority, or

– by a procedure contemplated by Directive 95/47/EC or the British regime or any other relevant national legislation or regulation implementing the same or any relevant national legislation or regulation governing the provision of access control services, or – under an appropriate and independent arbitration procedure which the BiB Parties will procure is made available to third parties.

C. Compliance with this condition shall be presumed where the BiB Parties have operated in accordance with the British regime.

D. References in this condition to the Director-General for Telecommunications shall be read as references to such regulator or regulatory body as from time to time is entrusted with the regulation of the British regime.

*Condition No 8: (Provision of information by McCo.)*

A. The BiB Parties shall procure that McCo. shall not in any way discriminate between BiB Services Co. and any other interested party in connection with:

(i) the dissemination of technical information within its responsibility;

(ii) the dissemination of changes to technical information within its responsibility which would affect the ability of interested parties to utilise the features of BiB for such purpose.

B. Where a company within the BiB Group receives a request in the required manner from an interested Party which is not within its responsibility but is within the responsibility of another party, it will provide within ten working days the name and address of each person whom it believes could supply such technical information and forward the request to such person or persons.

*Condition No 9: (Provision of information by BSkyB)*
BSkyB shall take the following steps in relation to the dissemination of technical information regarding the functional features of BiB boxes:

(a) within ten working days of the date or receipt of a request made in the required manner from an interested party, BSkyB or SSSL will make available to such interested party a non-disclosure agreement;

(b) within ten working days of the date of receipt in the required manner of a non-disclosure agreement executed by such interested party, BSkyB will make available to such interested party a list of technical information, which shall specify any item which requires the execution of a supplemental technical agreement, should such party wish to have access to it;

(c) within ten working days of the date of receipt of a request made in the required manner, BSkyB will make available copies of any item of technical information requested by any interested party who has received a list of technical information in accordance with the provision of paragraph (b) above. Where access to a particular item requires execution of a supplemental technical agreement, time shall run from the date of receipt in the required manner of the relevant executed supplemental technical agreement, which shall be made available to the interested party within ten working days of the relevant request;

(d) BSkyB will advise affected parties if the BiB box specification changes immediately after it advises manufacturers of BiB boxes;

(e) BSkyB will advise affected parties of any functional change:
 (i) as regards the intention to introduce such functional change, immediately after completion of the technical specification and before testing together with an estimate of the time at which the change will be implemented;
 (ii) as regards any alterations to the intentions and estimated timings referred to above, immediately after deciding to make such alterations;
 provided that if any information falling within the first exclusion in the definition of functional change is information which will affect the ability of affected parties to deliver broadcast and/or interactive services through BiB boxes such information will be advised to them as soon as reasonably practicable;

(f) BSkyB shall procure that SSSL complies with the provisions of paragraphs (a) to (e) with regard to technical information within its sphere of responsibility;

(g) where BSkyB or any member of the BSkyB Group receives a request in the required manner from an interested party for technical information which is not within its responsibility, but is within the responsibility of another party, it will provide within ten working days the name and address of each person whom it believes could supply such technical information and forward the request to such person or persons.

*Condition No 10: (Anti-avoidance)*
A. The BiB parties will ensure that no other member of the BiB Group does anything which would, if carried out by McCo., be a breach of the requirements set out in Conditions Nos 2(A), 7 and 8 or which has the effect of avoiding the effect of any such requirement.

B. Breaches of the abovementioned requirements shall not be a breach of this condition unless they would have been a breach of a condition set out in any of Conditions Nos 2, 7 and 8.

## Article 3

Breaches of Conditions Nos 7, 8 and 9 set out in Article 2 or, where relevant, breaches of the British regime shall not be considered an infringement of those conditions unless, in relation to the achievement overall of the objects of those conditions:

(a)     such breaches have been clear and serious; or

(b)     such breaches have had serious and material adverse affects on a third party; or

(c)     such breaches have resulted in irreparable and serious damage to a third party; or

(d)     although the individual breaches are minor, there have been several breaches demonstrating a persistent failure properly to comply, provided that, if a breach is shown to exist in a contractual term used in more than one contract or in a commonly used commercial practice, only one breach shall be considered to have occurred, irrespective of the number of such contracts or examples of such practice; or

(e)     where such breaches relate to interested parties who are currently providing services using BiB boxes, the breaches have been of long duration, no regard being made to the duration of any dispute resolution procedure, and provided that in the case of a breach shown to exist in a contractual term, time shall run for the purpose of this indent only when the circumstances to which the term relates have arisen and for so long as they continue.

## Article 4

For the purpose of the conditions set out in Article 2, the terms used shall be construed in accordance with the definitions set out in Annex II to this Decision.

## Article 5

This Decision is addressed to:

BT Holdings Limited
Newgate Street
London EC1A 7AJ
United Kingdom

Midland Bank plc
27-32 Poultry
PO Box 648
London EC2P 2BX
United Kingdom

British Sky Broadcasting Limited
Grant Way
Isleworth
Middlesex TW7 5QD
United Kingdom

Matsushita Electric Europe (Headquarters) Limited
Furzeground Way
Stockley Park
Uxbridge
Middlesex UB11 1DD
United Kingdom

Done at Brussels, 15 September 1999.
For the Commission
Karel VAN MIERT
Member of the Commission

## ANNEX I
### List of notified agreements and chronology of their provision to Commission

1.      In the notification the parties referred to a number of different agreements, not all of which were supplied with the notification. In response to a request for clarification from the Commission, the parties stated in a letter of 6 August 1997 that the following 16 agreements were notified:

1. The joint venture agreement and its annexes
2. EPG content design, look and feel
3. Start-up costs
4. Business plan and annual operating plan and budget
5. Agreed form completion board/extraordinary general meeting resolutions
6. Agreed form taste and ethics policy
7. Memorandum and Articles of Association
8. Box specification
9. Transponder capacity term sheet
10. Marketing services agreement
11. Technology transfer and licensing agreement
12. Content provider terms
13. Initial commitments agreement
14. Digital terrestrial television commitments – deleted in agreements of 4 August 1998
15. Subordinated loan agreement
16. Funding loan agreement.

2.   By letter of 30 March 1998, the parties provided the Commission with final drafts of 3 more agreements, dated 27 March 1998, which they requested form part of the notification:

    1. Transaction management system agreements, (between BiB and Midland)
    2. Merchant acquiring agreement (between BiB and Midland)
    3. Mondex agreements (between BiB and Midland).

3.   By letter of 14 July 1998, the parties provided the Commission with a revised draft of the joint venture agreement itself, dated 6 May 1998, without its annexes. Some of the amendments were made to address the Commission's concerns.

4.   By letter of 25 September 1998, the parties provided the Commission with copies of the joint venture agreement and its annexes which were completed by the parties on 4 August 1998. The digital terrestrial television commitments agreement (referred to above at point 14) was deleted from the completed agreements, while the marketing services agreement (referred to above at point 10) was subdivided into two separate agreements: the marketing contributions services agreement and the advertising and promotional services agreement. Two new agreements were signed, namely a loan agreement and the marketing contributions recovery agreement.

5.   An incorrect version of one of the completed agreements concerning the payment of subsidy was provided at that time. The correct version was provided to the Commission on 9 November 1998 in response to a request for information.

## ANNEX II

'Affected party': means any interested party who is at the relevant time delivering broadcast and/or interactive services through BiB boxes (or who is committed to do so and is preparing to commence such services) and who has current non-disclosure agreement.

'Another party': means another member of the BSkyB Group, a member of the BiB Group, a BiB Party or a third party.

'BiB box' or 'BiB boxes' means digital interactive set-top boxes sold with the benefit of marketing contributions provided by BiB.

'BiB box specification': means British Sky Broadcasting STB Specification Issue 3.00 of 30 July 1997, British Sky Broadcasting STB Specification V3.0 Errata V5.0 and British Sky Broadcasting STB Technical Guidelines Version V1.2 of 23 October 1997 as updated and amended from time to time.

'BSkyB Group': means British Sky Broadcasting Group plc.

'Conditional access provider': means a person who is licensed to provide conditional access services pursuant to the class licence granted by the Secretary of State on 7 January 1997 under Section 7 of the Telecommunications Act 1984 for the running of telecommunications systems for the provision of conditional access services.

'Functional change': means information which is intended to be implemented to become technical information and which comprises software intended to be downloaded into BiB boxes for the delivery of broadcast and/or interactive services, but excluding:

- downloads to address problems affecting the operation of software already in BiB boxes,
- downloads related to security of BiB boxes or to the security of any conditional access system or access control system utilised for broadcasts and/or interactive services accessible through BiB boxes.

'Interested partiy': means any broadcaster, cable operator, telecommunications operator, digital terrestrial television platform operator or satellite direct to home platform operator, whether for broadcast only or for interactive services or for any combination thereof, including BiB Services Co.

'Marketing contributions': means the subsidy which BiB will provide for BiB boxes, as set out in Clause 16 of the JVA and the marketing services agreement.

'Non-disclosure agreement': means the standard form confidentiality agreement, which BSkyB or SSSL may require an interested party to enter into before making available a list of technical information to that interested party and which must be current in the event that an affected party or an interested party is to have access to any information the subject of Condition No 9.

'Non-SSSL digital television decoders': means decoders which do not contain the conditional access technology employed by SSSL.

'Purpose': means, in respect of any interested party, the purpose of utilising the features of BiB boxes to deliver broadcast services, whether or not interactive, through BiB boxes and no other purpose.

'Request': means a written request for any item or items of technical information or for a list of technical information in either case for the purpose.

'Required manner': means in respect of any request or other communication by an interested party or conditional access provider:

- to BSkyB: a registered letter sent to BSkyB's registered office addressed to the head of regulatory affairs,
- to BiB: a registered letter sent to BiB's registered office addressed to the compliance officer.

'Simulcrypt': means the use of the European common scrambling algorithm in two populations of digital television decoders, each population containing a different conditional access technology, in order to facilitate the ability of retailers of digital television services using either of such conditional access technologies to opt to offer their services to consumers via digital television decoders containing the other conditional access technology (subject to such other population of decoders containing the requisite level of functionality for the type of services proposed to be offered by such retailer) together with the associated synchronisation of the two technologies required to implement such process.

'Supplemental technical agreement': means any appropriate licensing agreement which BSkyB or SSSL may require in relation to the release of a specific item of technical information.

'Technical information': means information about the current functional technical characteristics of BiB boxes, including the BiB box specification, which is the subject of completed technical specifications in written and/or diagrammatic form, but excluding:

- information, including information in relation to proprietary technology, which it is essential for a conditional access services supplier or access control services supplier and/or any of its technology suppliers to maintain in strict confidence in order to protect the security and integrity of its systems, or of the conditional access services or access control services which it supplies or intends to supply and/or its ability to provide a secure and confidential service to each of its customers, and
- information which any member of the BiB Group, BSkyB or SSSL has a statutory duty or obligation under any regulatory licence binding upon it or SSSL to maintain in confidence, and
- information which any member of the BiB Group, BSkyB or SSSL is contractually bound to maintain in confidence and has no right to divulge to third parties, and
- information required exclusively for the purpose of manufacturing a box, and
- in respect of SSSL, any information which does not relate to the operational and functional aspects of BiB boxes, which arise from the design of the conditional access or access control system or from the design of the electronic programme guide, and, for the avoidance of doubt, the above definition of technical information does not include creative information about the manner in which the functional technical characteristics of BiB boxes may be utilised for broadcasting and interactive applications.

'Transfer pricing guidelines': means the OECD transfer pricing guidelines for multinational enterprises and tax administrations, as updated from time to time.

'British regime': means the British regime for conditional access and access control services, which incorporates the British implementation of the relevant parts of Directive 95/47/EC of the European Parliament and of the Council, namely:

- the Advanced Television Services Regulations 1996 (as amended) (SI 1996 Nos 3151 and 3197), and
- the Conditional Access Services Class Licence granted on 7 January 1997 pursuant to Section 7 of the Telecommunications Act 1984, and
- the Telecommunications Class Licence ('TSL') as revoked and re-issued on 31 December 1997 pursuant to Section 7 of the Telecommunications Act 1984, and
- any re-enactment, re-issue or amendment of the above or any of them, provided that the reference in Condition No 15 to Regulation 11(4)-(8) of the Advanced Television Services Regulations 1996 is to that Regulation as in force at the date of publication of the Article 19(3) Notice/Decision.

By way of explanation, the British regime contains provisions for the resolution by the Director-General for Telecommunications of disputes in a number of ways.

---

### * 2.4.43. ANSWER ON BEHALF OF THE COMMISSION TO WRITTEN QUESTION E1577/99 BY CARLES-ALFRED GASÒLIBA I BÖHM (ELDR), 8 OCTOBER 1999[385] *

Subject: System for the distribution of tickets for the European Cup final held in Barcelona on 26 May 1999

---

### * 2.4.44. COMMISSION LAUNCHES FORMAL PROCEEDINGS ON FIFA RULES GOVERNING PLAYERS' AGENTS, 21 OCTOBER 1999[386]

---

[385] Question of 1-9-1999; OJ C 27 E, 29-1-2000, p. 137.
[386] IP/99/782.

**\* 2.4.45.  ANSWER ON BEHALF OF THE COMMISSION TO WRITTEN QUESTION P-2127/99 BY BART STAES (VERTS/ALE), 3 DECEMBER 1999[387] \***

Subject: Upholding the law of competition in the canvassing for sponsors for EURO 2000

———

**2.4.46.  LIMITS TO APPLICATION OF TREATY COMPETITION RULES TO SPORT: COMMISSION GIVES CLEAR SIGNAL [MOUSCRON CASE], 9 DECEMBER 1999[388]**

*The Commission has adopted two decisions demonstrating the limits to the application of the EC Treaty's competition rules to sport. It highlights three key aspects of the Commission's policy in this sector: (i) the Commission recognises the regulatory powers of sports organisations as regards the non-economic aspects linked to the specific nature of the sport, (ii) the rules of sports organisations that are necessary to ensure equality between clubs, uncertainty as to results, and the integrity and proper functioning of competitions are not, in principle, caught by the Treaty's competition rules; (iii) the Commission investigates only cases that have a Community dimension and significantly affect trade between Member States.*

The first decision (the Mouscron case) rejects once and for all a complaint lodged by the Communauté Urbaine de Lille against UEFA. The Commission takes the view that the UEFA Cup rule to the effect that each club must play its home match at its own ground ('at home and away from home' rule) is a sports rule that does not fall within the scope of the Treaty's competition rules. In its opinion, there is no Community interest that would justify looking more closely into whether UEFA has abused any dominant position it might have by applying exceptions to that rule without taking account of the integration that exists between certain frontier regions.

The other decision, which was taken following a notification made by UEFA on 14 October 1999, allows publication in the Official Journal of the European Communities of a notice calling on interested third parties to submit their observations on the UEFA rule book entitled 'Integrity of UEFA Club Competitions: Independence of the clubs' (ownership of more than one club). The Commission's preliminary view is that the rule in question, which does not allow more than one club belonging to the same owner to take part in the same competition, could also fall outside the Treaty's competition rules. Before confirming this view by adopting an exemption decision, it must ascertain whether there are not less restrictive means of ensuring the integrity of competitions where more than one club belongs to the same owner. The Commission hopes that the observations of interested third parties will provide it with the information necessary to settle this question.

Commissioner Mario Monti emphasised, upon adoption of these two important decisions, that they would contribute to achieving one of the objectives set by the Commission for this sector, namely to draw over time a dividing line between the practices of sports organisations that fall outside the competition rules and prohibited practices. A third category, namely practices that may be exempted, will also be identified on a case-by-case basis.

'This guideline for applying the competition rules to sport will make it possible to create a framework that provides the world of sport with the legal certainty which it quite legitimately seeks', declared Mr. Monti.

---

[387] Question of 18-11-1999; OJ C 225 E, 8-8-2000, p. 56.
[388] IP/99/965.

The Mouscron case stems from a complaint lodged against UEFA with the Commission on 31 December 1997 by the Communauté Urbaine de Lille. The complaint challenged UEFA's decision not to allow the UEFA Cup game between Excelsior Mouscron (the football club of a Belgian town located near the French border) and FC Metz to be held at the ground of Lille Métropole. As a result, the Communauté Urbaine de Lille was unable to hire out the stadium to Excelsior Mouscron. UEFA based its decision on the UEFA Cup rules, which stipulate among other things that every club must play its home match at its own ground, except in a number of very exceptional circumstances.

The Commission considers that the 'at home and away from home' rule and the exceptions to that rule (which do not rule out the possibility of the host club playing its home match in its opponent's country) is needed to ensure equality between clubs. It argues, therefore, that, by adopting this rule and the exceptions to it, UEFA has exercised its legitimate right of selfregulation as a sports organisation in a manner which cannot be challenged by the Treaty's competition rules.

However, when it comes to applying the exceptions laid down, UEFA has introduced a further condition that prevents a club from playing its home match in its opponent's country. In the Commission's view, there is not sufficient Community interest in examining more closely whether this further condition and its application could constitute examples of improper exercise of UEFA's regulatory powers that might significantly affect trade between Member States. The lack of any Community interest is justified by the fact that the probability of establishing that Article 82 of the Treaty (which prohibits abuses of dominant positions) has been infringed is reduced for three reasons in particular: (i) this case must be assessed within the context of the national geographical organisation of football in Europe, which is not called into question by Community law; (ii) the case is the only one that has been brought to the Commission's notice and is an isolated case that gave rise to a dispute in the past; (iii) the investigatory measures needed would be disproportionate to the probability of establishing that an infringement had taken place.

———

**2.4.47. COMMUNICATION MADE PURSUANT TO ARTICLE 19(3) OF COUNCIL REGULATION NO 17 CONCERNING REQUEST FOR NEGATIVE CLEARANCE OR FOR EXEMPTION PURSUANT TO ARTICLE 81(3) OF THE EC TREATY (CASE NO 37.632 – UEFA RULE ON 'INTEGRITY OF THE UEFA CLUB COMPETITIONS: INDEPENDENCE OF CLUBS', 17 DECEMBER 1999[389]**

## I. THE FACTS
## 1. THE NOTIFICATION

1. On 14 October 1999 the Union des Associations Européennes de Football (UEFA) applied for negative clearance or, failing this, for exemption pursuant to Article 81(3) of the EC Treaty in respect of the rule named 'Integrity of the UEFA club competitions: independence of the clubs'.

2. UEFA is an association which has its seat in Nyon, Switzerland. It is the governing body responsible for European football. Membership of UEFA is open to all Eurpean national football associations. UEFA currently consists of 51 members associations, eighteen of which are located inside the territory of the European Union.

   As a rule, there is a single association in each Member State of the EU and EEA, which organises the sport at national level. An exception is the United Kingdom,

---

[389] OJ C 363, 17-12-1999, p. 2 (Text with EEA relevance).

where for historical reasons England, Wales, Scotland and Northern Ireland each have their own association.

As the confederation of FIFA (Fédération Internationale de Football Association) for Europe, UEFA regulates football throughout Europe. UEFA also organises and conducts international football competitions and international tournaments at European level. Until the 1998/1999 European football season, UEFA has organised three main club competitions: the Chamnpions' league, the Cup Winners Cup and the UEFA Cup. Recently, UEFA has cancelled the Cup Winners' Cup. Therefore, from the 1999/2000 season on, only the Champions' league (giving access to a great number of clubs) and the UEFA Cup will be organised.

## 2. THE NOTIFIED RULE

3.     The notified rule was adopted by the UEFA Executive Committee on 19 May 1998. On 24 November 1998, an Extraordinary Conference of the Presidents of UEFA Member Associations adopted unanimously a Resolution in which the associations confirmed their 'unqualified support for the UEFA rule, and the sporting principles which underlie it'.

4.     The rule named 'Integrity of the UEFA club competitions: independence of the clubs' provides as follows:

'A. General Principle

It is of fundamental importance that the sporting integrity of UEFA club competitions be protected. To achieve this aim, UEFA reserves the right to intervene and take appropriate action in any situation in which it transpires that the same individual or legal entity is in a position to influence the management, administration and/or sporting performance of more than one team participating in the same UEFA club competition.

B.   Criteria

With regard to admission to the UEFA club competitions, the following criteria are applicable in addition to the respective competition regulations.

1.     No club participating in a UEFA club competition may, either directly or indirectly:

(a)     hold or deal in the securities or shares of any other club, or

(b)     be a member of any other club, or

(c)     be involved in any capacity whatsoever in the management, administration and/or sporting performance of any other club, or

(d)     have any power whatsoever in the management, administration and/or sporting performance of any other club participating in the same UEFA club competition.

2.     No person may at the same time, either directly or indirectly, be involved in any capacity whatsoever in the management, administration and/or sporting performance of more than one club participating in the same UEFA club competition.

3.     In the case of two or more clubs which are under common control, only one may participate in the same competition. In this connection, an individual or legal entity has control of a club where he/she/it:

(a)     holds a majority of the shareholders' voting rights, or

(b)     has the right to appoint or remove a majority of the members of the administrative, management or supervisory body, or

(c)     is a shareholder and alone controls a majority of the shareholders' voting rights pursuant to an agreement entered into with other shareholders of the club in question.

4. The Committee of the UEFA Club Competitions will take a final decision with regard to the admission of clubs to these competitions. It furthermore reserves the right to act vis-à-vis clubs which cease to meet the above criteria in the course of ongoing competition.'

5. The UEFA Club Competitions Committee defined the criteria for selecting the club which may participate in the competition, when two or more clubs under 'common control' are put forward to play in a UEFA competition. The selection criteria provides as follows:

'Admission Criteria

If two or more clubs are affected by the new regulations to safeguard the integrity of the UEFA club competitions, the Committee for the UEFA club competitions shall apply the following criteria in sequence, to determine which club is admitted to the competition in question:

A. Admission of a club

    I.    UEFA Club Coefficient (cumulative coefficient of the last five seasons):
          The club with the highest club coefficient is admitted to the UEFA competition in question.

    II.   UEFA National Association Coefficient (cumulative coefficient of the last five seasons):
          If two or more clubs have the same club coefficient (see I above), the current UEFA coefficient of the respective national associations is taken into consideration. The club whose association has the highest coefficient is admitted to the UEFA club competition in question.

    III.  Drawing of lots
          If two or more clubs also have the same national association coefficient (see II above), a decision is taken by the drawing of lots.

B. Filling of vacant place

The national association of a club which is not admitted to a UEFA club competition under the above criteria may fill the place thus rendered vacant with another of its clubs. As a rule, this vacant place should go to the club which finished the domestic league championship immediately below the club that is not admitted (for the UEFA Champions league and UEFA Cup). In the UEFA Cup Winners' Cup, the domestic cup runner-up or, if necessary, one of the semi-finalists, can be entered instead of the team not admitted. The Committee for the UEFA Club Competitions has the right to confirm the admission of the replacement club.'

6. In conclusion the rule establishes that: 1. no club should have a financial or management interest in another club which participates in the same UEFA competition; 2. no person should be involved in the management of more than on club participating in the same UEFA competition and 3. no person or company may control more than one club participating in the same UEFA competition.

## 3. THE UEFA ARGUMENTS FOR NEGATIVE CLEARANCE

7. According to UEFA the rule: 1. is designed to preserve the integrity of competition and the uncertainty of outcome in the international club competitions it organises, 2. seeks to achieve this objective by avoiding the 'conflict of interests' which would result if an individual or a company was able to influence the sporting performance of two (or more) teams participating in the same competition and which might lead to the manipulation of results. 3. is not concerned with economic or commercial activities but is concerned with football as a sport, 4. the rule falls

outside the scope of the competition provisions of the EC Treaty because it pursues a sporting objective; the rule does not restrict competition but even if it was held to restrict competition on the market for ownership interests in football clubs capable of taking part in UEFA competitions, the rule whould not still violate Article 81 of the EC Treaty as it is needed for the proper functioning of sporting competition.

8.     In this last respect UEFA considers in line with the award pronounced on 20 August 1999 by the Court of Arbitration for Sport in case CAS 98/200 AEK Athens and Slavia Prague/UEFA, point 150) that the actual effect of the rule is to place some limitation on mergers between European high level football clubs, and thus it preservers or even enhances economic competition between club owners and economic and sporting competition between clubs. On the basis of the same CAS award (point 154) UEFA also point out, that contrary to other types of business, in the sports business consumer welfare requires that numerous clubs remain on the market and achieve the highest possible economic and sporting balance between them. Furthermore, UEFA refers to Paragraph 107 of the Opinion of Advocate-General Alber in case C-176/96, Lehtonen (delivered on 22 June 1999). Here Mr Alber reminds, on the basis of the case law of the Court of Justice, that EC competition rules shall not be assessed in the abstract and that they are always depending of the economic conditions in the relevant markets. Rules restricting freedom of action which by their effect are necessary to the creation of competition on the relevant market, can therefore be compatible with Articles 81 and 82 of the EC Treaty, so long as they are necessary and appropriate to attain this objective.

9.     In the submission of UEFA, the rule is a balanced and proportionate measure to ensure that competition is genuine and is seen to be genuine because it does not prevent investment in clubs (from other than clubs participating in UEFA competitions or owners of such clubs), but simply prohibits clubs under common control from playing in the same UEFA competition.

       Moreover, according to UEFA, the definition of 'control', based on EU law[390], constitutes the minimum regulatory measure necessary to ensure that the public is fully confident in the integrity of the competitions it organises. UEFA mentions also that any investor may acquire a shareholding of up to 50% in any two or more European football clubs participating in UEFA competitions without ever being affected by the rule in question, provided that the investor is not a club or a person involved in the management, administration and/or sporting performance of another club participating in UEFA competitions. Furthermore, UEFA stresses that several sporting bodies and some state legislators have issued stricter regulations to deal with the same issue.

## II. THE COMMISSION'S INTENTION

10.    The Commission considers that the notified rule can be qualified as a decision of an association of undertakings or an agreement between associations of undertakings inside UEFA, in the meaning of Article 81 of the EC Treaty. Taking into account what the Court of Justice has recognised in the Bosman Case as legitimate objectives[391] in the view of the considerable social importance of football in the Community, the Commission considers that the restrictions imposed by the rule may escape to the prohibition laid down in Article 81(1) of the Treaty. In order to establish whether this preliminary conclusion can be upheld or not, the Commis-

---

[390]  In particular, Council Directive 88/627/EC of 12-12-1988 (OJ L 342, 17-12-1998, p. 62).
[391]  Judgement of 15-12-1995, case C-415/93, [1995] ECR I-4921, point 106.

sion has to know if such restrictions are limited to what is necessary to preserve the integrity of the UEFA club competitions and to ensure the uncertainty as to results. In other words, the Commission must confirm whether there are or not less restrictive means to achieve the same objective.

11. In this view, the Commission invites third parties to send their observations within one month of the publication of this notice to the following address, quoting the reference 'COMP/37.632 — UEFA rule on the protection of integrity of competitions':

———

**\* 2.4.48.   ANSWER ON BEHALF OF THE COMMISSION TO WRITTEN QUESTION P-2548/99 BY THERESA ZABELL (PPE-DE), 11 JANUARY 2000**[392] **\***

Subject: Monopoly purchasing practices in Olympic sailing classes

———

**2.4.49.   COMMISSION DECISION DECLARING A CONCENTRATION TO BE COMPATIBLE WITH THE COMMON MARKET (CASE NO IV/M.037 — B SKY B/KIRCH PAY TV) ACCORDING TO COUNCIL REGULATION (EEC) NO 4064/89, 21 MARCH 2000**[393]

To the notifying parties
Dear Sirs,

Subject: Case No COMP/JV.37 — BSkyB / KirchPayTV
Notification of 22 December 1999 pursuant to Article 4 of Council Regulation (EEC) No 4064/89

1. On 22 December 1999, the Commission received a notification of a proposed concentration pursuant to Article 4 of Council Regulation (EEC) No 4064/89[394] (the 'Merger Regulation') by which British Sky Broadcasting Group plc ('BSkyB') would acquire 24% of KirchPayTV GmbH & Co. KGaA ('KirchPayTV') from Kirch Vermögensverwaltungs GmbH & Co. KG, holding company for the Kirch-Gruppe ('Kirch').

2. On 13 January 2000, the notification was declared incomplete. The parties subsequently provided the requested information. Consequently, the notification was declared complete on 7 February 2000.

3. The parties submitted commitments designed to eliminate the competition concerns identified by the Commission during the first part of the investigation, in accordance with Art. 6(2) of the Merger Regulation. In light of these commitments, the Commission has concluded that the notified operation falls within the scope of Council Regulation (EEC) No 4064/89 and does not raise serious doubts as to its compatibility with the common market.

---

[392] Question of 16-12-1999; OJ C 219 E, 1-8-2000, p. 180.
[393] OJ C 110, 15-4-2000, p. 45.
[394] OJ L 395, 30-12-1989, p. 1; corrigendum: OJ L 257, 21-9-1990, p. 13; as last amended by Regulation (EC) No 1310/97, OJ L 180, 9-7-1997, p.1; corrigendum: OJ L 40, 13-2-1998, p. 17.

## I. THE PARTIES

4.      BSkyB is quoted on the London and New York Stock Exchanges and is owned as to 39.72% by News International Television Limited ('News International').

5.      BSkyB's principal business is, through its British Sky Broadcasting Ltd subsidiary, broadcasting analogue and digital television services via satellite and cable in the UK and Ireland and via digital terrestrial television in the UK. BSkyB also supplies its own pay-TV channels for retail to its satellite subscribers and wholesale for cable and terrestrial operators in UK and Ireland. A small amount of the programming on these channels is also produced by BSkyB.

6.      BSkyB has an interest in the British Interactive Broadcasting joint venture, which provides digital interactive television services to consumers in the United Kingdom via its subsidiary, Open.

7.      BSkyB also provides conditional access and customer management services via its subsidiaries Satellite Encryption Services Ltd. ('SESL') and Sky Subscribers Services Ltd. ('SSSL'). It also subleases some of its spare satellite transponder capacity on the Astra satellite system, which is used by broadcasters whose channels are broadcast unencrypted throughout Europe.

8.      The News Corporation Ltd. ('News') has not been notified as a party to the concentration but it has acknowledged, based on the Judgement of the Court of First Instance in Kesko Oy v Commission[395], that it has sufficient influence over BSkyB to be taken into account for the purposes of Article 2 of the Merger Regulation. News International is an affiliate of News, the international multimedia group with interests in television broadcasting, film production and distribution, books, newspapers, magazines, data processing and media access control. News International's German interest are limited to a 66% interest in a German free to air channel, TM3, which it is currently negotiating to sell, and ownership of some German broadcasting rights, including those for the UEFA Champions League football matches.

9.      KirchPayTV operates pay-TV services in Germany and Austria and has a 40% interest in a Swiss pay-TV service. KirchPayTV provides a bouquet of its own channels, through its 'Premiere' operation. This consists of premium movies, live sports events and thematic pay-TV channels. It is offered in programme packages via cable or satellite transmission for a monthly subscription fee. Premiere has recently launched Premiere World, a digital, multi-channel pay TV operation that combines the activities of KirchPayTV's former pay-TV services, Premiere and DF1. The programming packages of Premiere World consist of both KirchPayTV channels and a few third party channels. Some of these channels – Discovery and Krimitel – are joint ventures in which Kirch has an interest via MultiChannel GmbH.

10.     KirchPayTV is wholly owned by the holding company of Kirch. Kirch is an audio-visual media group of companies ultimately owned and controlled by Dr. Leo Kirch. It is active in particular in the fields of commercial television, rights trade (fiction), sports rights trade, film and TV production and post-production, business TV, pay TV, TV channel production, technical services for digital broadcasting and encryption technology.

11.     Kirch controls BetaResearch GmbH ('BetaResearch'), the company that has developed the conditional access system which is used by KirchPayTV. BetaResearch has granted licences for its conditional access system to both BetaDigital GmbH ('BetaDigital') and to Deutsche Telekom AG ('Telekom') (for

---

[395] Case T-22/97 Kesko Oy v Commission, 15-12-1999, paragraphs 137-140.

its cable operations). BetaResearch has also developed the d-box decoder.

12.     KirchPayTV operates the technical platform for digital satellite television via its subsidiary BetaDigital. BetaDigital is a technical service provider that offers play-out services such as data compression, multiplexing, encryption, and satellite-up-link to affiliates, including Premiere, and third parties. BetaDigital has leased transponder capacity on the Astra satellites from SES. BetaDigital provides its encryption services on the basis of a technology licence for conditional access technology from BetaResearch.

## II. THE OPERATION

13.     The net effect of the proposed operation will be a change in control of KirchPayTV, from sole control by Kirch to joint control with BSkyB after the proposed operation is given effect. The basic structure of the proposed transaction is the acquisition of 24% of KirchPayTV in return for EUR 510 million and a 4,3% interest in BSkyB for KirchPayTV.

## III. CONCENTRATION

14.     The proposed operation constitutes a concentration within the meaning of Article 3(1)(b) of the Merger Regulation and is a full function joint venture for the purposes of Article 3(2) of the Merger Regulation.

### Joint control

15.     Under the proposed concentration BSkyB will invest in KirchPayTV which is a Kommanditgesellschaft auf Aktien, a partnership with general partners and holders of limited partners' shares. Kirch, via a holding company, is currently the sole general partner of KirchPayTV. BSkyB's investment will create a second general partner, BSkyB General Partner. This arrangement gives BSkyB and Kirch joint control of KirchPayTV.

16.     BSkyB has a right to at least two seats (or one third) on the KirchPayTV Supervisory Board, comprising at least six members. The other members will be selected by Kirch. This arrangement will be revised when the initial public offer of shares ('IPO') in KirchPayTV occurs, which is expected before the end of 2003.

17.     Until the IPO, BSkyB's approval will be needed for KirchPayTV, or any subsidiary of KirchPayTV, to take or perform a range of decisions relating to: [...]

18.     By virtue of these rights of approval BSkyB will have the ability to exercise decisive influence over the strategic direction of KirchPayTV. Therefore, BSkyB and Kirch will have joint control over KirchPayTV notwithstanding the fact that BSkyB has control over less than 50% of the shares and only one third of the board.

19.     BSkyB and Kirch will jointly control KirchPayTV within the meaning of Article 3 (1) (b) of the Merger Regulation.

### Autonomous economic entity acting on a lasting basis

20.     KirchPayTV is already a fully functioning economic entity and will continue to operate on a long term basis in pay-TV. KirchPayTV has had and will continue to have the necessary financial resources, personnel and other assets, including broadcasting rights, to provide pay-TV in the German market. It will therefore perform on a lasting basis all the functions of an autonomous economic entity within the meaning of Article 3(2) of the Merger Regulation.

## IV. COMMUNITY DIMENSION

21.    The combined world-wide turnover of the undertakings concerned is more than EUR 5 000 million (Kirch: EUR [...]billion, BSkyB: EUR 2,49 billion).

22.    Each of them has an aggregate Community-wide turnover in excess of EUR 250 million (Kirch: EUR [...] billion, BSkyB: EUR 2,48 billion), but they do not achieve more than two-thirds of their aggregate Community-wide turnover within one and the same Member State. The notified operation therefore has a Community dimension.

## V. COMPETITIVE ASSESSMENT
### A. The relevant markets
### 1. Pay-TV

**Product market**

23.    Pay-TV constitutes a relevant product market separate from that for free-to-air or free-access television (free TV), i.e.advertising-financed private television and public television financed through fees and partly through advertising.[396]

24.    While, in the case of advertising-financed television, there is a trade relationship only between the programme supplier and the advertising industry, in the case of pay-TV there is a trade relationship between the programme supplier and the viewer as subscriber. In view of these trade relationships, the conditions of competition are accordingly different for the two types of television. Whereas in the case of advertising-financed television the audience share and the advertising rates are the key parameters, in the case of pay-TV the key factors are the shaping of programmes to meet the interests of the target groups of viewers and the level of subscriptions.

25.    The fact that subscribers are prepared to pay considerable sums for pay-TV indicates that the latter is a distinguishable product with specific extra utility. As digitalisation continues to spread, there could admittedly, with the passage of time, be a certain convergence between pay-TV and free TV. However, this possible future development is not enough now to justify the conclusion that pay-TV and free TV are part of the same market.

26.    The Commission has stated in the past that there is no reason to distinguish between markets for analogue and digital pay television[397]. Digital pay-TV is only a further development of analogue pay-TV and therefore does not constitute a separate relevant product market. Moreover, account should be taken of the fact that in the next few years analogue broadcast pay-TV will be completely superseded by digital broadcast pay-TV. Under Premiere's business plan, analogue subscriptions will be gradually transformed into digital ones, so that by 2002 the only subscribers will be digital ones.

27.    Television signals can be broadcast by terrestrial transmitter, satellite or cable. Pay-television is available to subscribers in Germany by two different means of transmission: satellite (analogue and digital) and cable (analogue and digital).

---

[396] See Commission Decision 94/922/EC, MSG Media Service (OJ L 364, 31-12-1994, p. 1), paragraphs 32 and 33; Commission Decision 1999/153/EC, Bertelsmann/Kirch/Premiere (OJ L 53, 27-2-1999, p. 1), paragraph 18; Commission Decision 1999/242/EC, TPS (OJ L 90, 2-4-1999, p. 6), paragraph 25; Commission Decision 1999/781/EC, British Interactive Broadcasting/Open (OJ L 312, 6-12-1999, p. 1), paragraph 24.

[397] See Bertelsmann/Kirch/Premiere, paragraph 18; TPS, paragraph 26; British Interactive Broadcasting/Open, paragraph 25.

**Geographic market**

28.     Despite the fact that in certain niche markets channels are broadcast throughout
        Europe, television broadcasting is still generally organised on a national basis. As
        the Commission has already stated in a number of decisions[398], owing primarily to
        different regulatory regimes, language barriers, cultural factors and other different
        conditions of competition prevailing in the individual Member States, the markets
        for the organisation of television are national in nature.

29.     Germany is accordingly the relevant geographic market for pay-TV. The Commis-
        sion came to the same conclusion in the Bertelsmann/Kirch/Premiere case and the
        MSG Media Service case, although it indicated in the second Decision that, bear-
        ing in mind the lack of any language barrier, a market might in future be assumed
        to exist for German language pay-TV[399]. The Commission's investigation in the
        Bertelsmann/Kirch/Premiere case brought to light a number of reasons for consid-
        ering that the relevant geographic market for pay-TV extends beyond Germany
        and, in view of the lack of any language barrier, comprises the entire German-
        speaking area. This question can, however, be left open for the purposes of this
        case, as the competition assessment of the concentration would be the same even
        on the assumption of a market encompassing the whole of that region.

## 2. Digital interactive television services

**Product market**

30.     KirchPayTV will be active in the near future on the digital interactive television
        services market. In defining product markets, the most important factor is evalua-
        tion of demand substitutability.[400] However, given that digital interactive televi-
        sion services, such as those which are likely to be offered by KirchPayTV, are not
        currently available in Germany, past data does not exist to evaluate the likely re-
        sponse of customers to a hypothetical small, non-transitory change in relative
        prices of KirchPayTV's services and possible substitutes. Nevertheless demand
        substitutability can also be assessed by comparing the characteristics of products
        or services in order to determine whether they are particularly suited to satisfy
        constant needs and are only to a limited extent interchangeable with other products
        or services.[401]

31.     Typically the following retail services seem likely to be offered to viewers on digi-
        tal interactive television: home banking, home shopping, holiday and travel ser-
        vices, down-loading of games, learning on-line, entertainment and leisure etc.[402]
        However, the operators of digital interactive television will typically not be the
        suppliers of the goods and services purchased by consumers. Rather they will pro-

---

[398] See MSG Media Service, paragraph 46; Commission Decision 96/346/EC, RTL/Veronica/
Endemol, (OJ L 134, 5-6-1996, p. 32), paragraph 25, Bertelsmann/Kirch/Premiere, paragraph 23;
British Interactive Broadcasting/Open, paragraph 42.

[399] See MSG Media Service, paragraph 51.

[400] See Commission Notice on the definition of the relevant market for the purposes of Community competition law (OJ C 372, 9-12-1997, p. 5).

[401] In its judgement of 26-11-1998, in Case C-7/97, Oscar Bronner GmbH Co. KG v Mediaprint
[1998] ECR I-7791, the Court of Justice repeated the formula (paragraph 33) that 'the market for the
product or service in question comprises all the products or services which in view of their characteristics are particularly suited to satisfy constant needs and are only to a limited extent interchangeable
with other products or services (Case 31/80 L'Orééal v De Nieuwe AMCK [1980] ECR 3775, paragraph 25; Case C-62/86 AKZO v Commission [1991] ECR I-3359, paragraph 51)'.

[402] See British Interactive Broadcasting/Open, paragraph 11.

vide a 'platform' through which vendors, otherwise known as 'content providers', will promote and sell their goods and services. Thus, for the operators of digital interactive television services, the primary source of demand, and income, will be from 'content providers' who wish to offer goods and services to consumers through digital interactive television.

32.    The demand from 'content providers' for access to the 'platform' provided by operators of digital interactive television is likely to be determined by how popular the 'platform' and all the services it carries is with final consumers. The more consumers the digital interactive service has, the more powerful the attraction of the 'platform' for content providers. Conversely the attractiveness of the 'platform' to final consumers will be determined by the range and types of services they can find on it. In particular the Commission has already recognised that pay TV, whilst being in a separate market, is likely to be a 'driver' for digital interactive television services.[403] This is because pay TV offers premium and exclusive programmes which enables digital interactive services operators who carry this service to attract a high number of above average income viewers.

**– Digital interactive services distinguishable from alternative sources of supply**

33.    The Commission has already held that the demand substitutability of final consumers for digital interactive services (access to the 'the platform') is likely to be distinguishable from alternative sources of supply such as e.g. high-street retailing.

34.    As explained below this conclusion is based on the different characteristics of the types of goods and services that will be provided.

**– Market separate from high street retailing**

35.    Retailing services represent only one part of the typical package of services forming digital interactive television services. E-mail, downloading of computer games, limited Internet access and information services will also form part of the package. There are economies of scope in the provision of such a package of services, because the infrastructure required for each of the individual services is the same.

36.    The characteristics of the retailing services of the type likely to be offered by KirchPayTV and those of high-street retailing will be markedly different. For example, the range of products or services that is likely to be offered on-line by retailers will probably be very different from that available in high-street shops. This is most likely to be the case with perishable goods, such as food, or bulky goods where storage and delivery charges would be high. There will almost certainly be a price differential between goods or services purchased in the high street and those obtained via a package of digital interactive television services. In terms of price, it seems that consumers may even be willing to pay a premium for the convenience of home shopping.[404]

37.    It follows from the above that the market for digital interactive television services is separate from that for the traditional retailing of goods and services in high streets.

---

[403] 'The Development Of The Market For Digital Television In The European Union' COM (1999) 540 Final.

[404] Binary Compass Enterprises Report, 1997, by David Reibstein and Sunil Gupta 'The online retail commerce report' rated price competition fourth in what was important to customers.

**– Distinction between markets for digital interactive services available via televisions and those available via personal computers.**

38.     Both the demand-substitutability test and differences in the characteristics of inter-active services available via television sets and via personal computers lead to the conclusion that they are at this stage separate product markets. A small permanent increase in the price of such services available via television is unlikely to be con-strained by the existence of services available on personal computers. While tele-vision sets are ubiquitous, far fewer households have a personal computer; fewer still have a modem. Moreover, the relatively high cost of personal computers means that the switching cost for end-users would be high. Digital interactive ser-vices delivered to television can also be distinguished from services delivered to personal computers by the fact that interactivity can be integrated into traditional broadcast entertainment channels.

39.     As the Commission found in the British Interactive Broadcasting/Open case, re-tailers are also likely to target different customers using different brands belonging to the same group of companies when providing digital interactive services avail-able via television sets and personal computers.

**– Market Separate from but linked and complementary to pay TV**

40.     Finally, the demand for, and characteristics and intended use of, pay-TV services are largely different from those of digital interactive television services, the former being largely entertainment services, the latter being largely transactional or infor-mational services. Typically the business scope of digital interactive television ser-vice providers excludes forms of entertainment where viewing itself is the primary form of entertainment for the viewer, such as pay-television channels. However, as already noted, pay-TV is likely to be a 'driver' for interactive services. Thus, in summary, the digital interactive television services market will be complementary to and separate from that for pay-TV.

**Geographic market**

41.     Digital interactive television services will operate on a national basis. The kinds of service offered will be determined by the national taste and national demand: the transaction services are likely to be reliant on retailers with national or regional operations. The information services will be largely related to national demand for information and will be in German. The market for digital interactive services can therefore, in the foreseeable future, be seen as national and limited to Germany. However, for the purposes of this case the exact definition of the relevant geo-graphic market can be left open.

**3. The market for the acquisition of broadcasting rights, in particular for films and sporting events**

**Product market**

42.     It is universally accepted that films and sporting events are the two most popular pay-TV products. It has been acknowledged by the Commission in a previous De-cision[405] that it is necessary to have the corresponding rights in order to put to-gether programmes that are sufficiently attractive to persuade potential subscribers to pay for receiving television services. Films and sport are therefore pay-TV's 'drivers'. There is no need for the purposes of this case to determine whether sepa-

---

[405]  See TPS, paragraph 34.

rate markets exist for film broadcasting rights and rights to broadcast sporting events.

43.    As far as films are concerned, the rights for pay-TV are available separately from those for other broadcasting 'windows', such as free to air and pay-per-view. Pay-TV rights may be exploited prior to free to air broadcasting rights. No distinction is made according to whether the rights are to be exploited through analogue or digital transmission.

44.    Rights to sporting events are also broken down into rights for broadcasting in clear, pay-TV and pay-per-view.

**Geographic market**

45.    With regard to the geographic market for the acquisition of broadcasting rights, although rights can be sourced from anywhere in the world and some operators acquire rights for more than one territory at a time, it has to be borne in mind that broadcasting rights are still acquired mainly on a national basis or, at the most, by language area.[406] Thus the Commission has noted that film broadcasting rights are usually granted for a given language version and broadcasting area.[407] In this case the markets are those for the rights for the UK, Ireland and Germany. It is not necessary for the purposes of this case to determine whether the market for the acquisition of broadcasting rights should be defined as the German market or the German-speaking market.

46.    In the case of some sporting events, however, the rights are acquired on an exclusive basis for the whole European territory and, regardless of the technical means of transmission, to be thereafter re-sold per country. These major sport events, such as the Olympic Games, have a pan-European interest from the viewers' perspective. Accordingly, there could be a separate geographic market for pan-European sports rights, although it is not necessary to precisely define the market for the purposes of this case.

**B. Dominance**
**1. Pay-TV**

47.    KirchPayTV holds 95% of Premiere Medien GmbH & Co. KG (hereafter: 'Premiere'). It offers the analogue pay-TV channel 'Premiere' and (since October 1999) the digital pay-TV bouquet 'Premiere World', consisting of 22 programme channels. This bouquet also includes channels from other providers like Multi-théématiques (Canal+) and Universal Studios. Premiere World is broadcast both by satellite and through the broadband cable network of Telekom and offers various packages of channels (for movies, sports, family/children channels etc.) as well as pay-per-view services.

48.    KirchPayTV has, through Premiere, virtually a monopoly in the provision of pay-TV services in Germany. In December 1999, Premiere had around 2,1 million subscribers of which around 1,1 million had subscribed to the digital format.

49.    A number of third parties have claimed that the notified operation will strengthen the dominant position of KirchPayTV in the German pay-TV market by providing it with a badly needed influx of financial resources and know-how. It is also argued that the operation will eliminate BSKyB as a potential competitor in Germany.

---

[406] Commission Decision 89/536, Filmeinkauf deutscher Fernsehanstalten, OJ L 284, 3-10-1989, p. 36.
[407] See Filmeinkauf deutscher Fernsehanstalten, paragraph 25.

**Influx of financial resources and know-how**

50. The parties themselves acknowledge that KirchPayTV is in need of 'an injection of significant resources' to develop its business. They have estimated the total investment required by KirchPayTV at [...], with accrued losses standing at [...]. According to its notification, KirchPayTV has, however, been unable to raise the funds it needs on the open market. In addition to money, BSkyB will add a wealth of marketing and distribution know-how which, it has been suggested to the Commission by certain operators in the market, KirchPayTV crucially lacks.

Given the significant costs of operating in this market, particularly the need to digitalise services over the next few years, the Commission has serious doubts as to whether KirchPayTV would have been able to maintain its position on the pay-TV market in Germany in the absence of this operation. For instance, failure to modernise its pay-TV services according to market expectations, or an inability to maintain its control over the content necessary for pay-TV, could significantly improve the conditions for entry by a third party in the medium term. As specified by Article 2(1)(b) of the Merger Regulation, the economic and financial power of the parties are factors which the Commission must take into account when assessing the effects on competition of a concentration. It also has to be noted that the Commission has, in a number of decisions, held that the addition of greater financial resources as a result of a concentration can lead to the creation or strengthening of a dominant position.[408]

51. Based on the facts available to it, the Commission concludes that this operation raises serious doubts as to the compatibility of the concentration with the common market as it reinforces KirchPayTV's dominant position on the market for pay-TV in Germany.

**Elimination of potential competition**

52. Neither BSkyB nor News and/or any affiliated company of News are active on the German pay-TV market. They are not actual competitors to KirchPayTV.

53. However a number of third parties have argued that BSkyB, in combination with News, is the most likely entrant on the German pay-TV market. This is based primarily on the following reasons:

   – BSkyB is the biggest operator of pay-TV services in the UK and Ireland and one of the biggest operators of pay-TV services in Europe and has experience in running a technical platform for pay-TV.
   – Germany is an attractive, large market and pay-TV is underdeveloped.
   – News has acquired the pay-TV rights to the UEFA Champions League for Germany.
   – News has access to other rights via the Fox Entertainment Group, one of the world's largest producers of films and TV shows (Hollywood film studio Twentieth Century Fox).
   – TM3, in which News German Television Holding GmbH owns a 66% interest, has asked for and was granted in December 1999 broadcasting licenses for six thematic channels from the Bavarian media authority.

54. Based on the facts available to it the Commission has, however, come to the conclusion that neither BSkyB nor any other company is likely to enter the German pay-TV market in the short to medium term.

---

[408] See for example Commission Decision 97/816/EC, Boeing/McDonnell Douglas (OJ L 336, 8-12-1997, p. 16), paragraphs 53 and 72; Commission Decision M.196, Volvo/Procordia (OJ C 281, 19-10-1993), paragraph 12; Commission Decision M.139, VIAG/EB Bruehl (OJ C 333, 24-12-1991), paragraph 18.

55.     There are four main reasons for this.

**– Strength of the free TV market in Germany**
56.     The German pay-TV market is difficult to develop because there is a strong mar-
        ket for free TV in Germany. Pay-TV and free TV are separate markets, as has al-
        ready been explained. There is, nevertheless some interaction between them. The
        more varied and attractive the programmes offered by the free broadcasters, the
        less incentive there is for viewers to subscribe to pay-TV as well. The existence of
        this interaction is borne out by the slow pace of development of pay-TV in Ger-
        many in comparison to France or the United Kingdom, which is doubtless due pri-
        marily to the more varied programmes on offer in Germany from free TV.[409]
57.     Due to the offer from over 30 channels, consumers in Germany have not shown a
        strong desire to subscribe to pay-TV. Out of around 27,5 million households that
        can be reached either by cable or by satellite, only 2,1 million have taken a pay-
        TV subscription (to Premiere). One third party has indicated that an operator will
        need 3,5 million subscribers to 'break-even'. Indeed independent studies have
        shown that KirchPayTV, despite being the sole supplier in this market, will con-
        tinue to make significant losses until 2003.

**– Kirch's control over the decoder infrastructure and encryption technology used in
Germany**
58.     The operation of pay-TV requires a special technical infrastructure which makes it
        possible to encrypt the television signals and to decrypt them for the authorised
        viewer. In order to receive pay-TV, a decoder (set-top box) is installed in the
        viewers' homes.
59.     In addition to a decoder base, pay-TV requires a system of conditional access.
        This system includes the transmission of encrypted data, which contain informa-
        tion on the programmes or packages of programmes subscribed to and on the en-
        titlement of the pay-TV subscribers to receive the programmes, together with the
        television signal, and possibly smart cards which are made available to the viewer
        and are able to decipher the encrypted authorisation data and transfer them to the
        decoder.[410]
60.     Pay-TV services can be supplied to viewers in Germany in one of two ways: either
        via the cable network or by satellite. For the supply of cable television, network
        levels 3 and 4 are of particular importance. The distribution network from the
        cable head-end to the boundary of a given plot of land (network level 3) is oper-
        ated in Germany almost exclusively by Telekom. Telekom is also by far the big-
        gest provider of the network infrastructure between that boundary and the junction
        boxes of TV households (network level 4). As a consequence, Telekom has the
        preponderant share of the cable network market.[411] It is MSG MediaServices
        GmbH ('MSG'), a subsidiary of Telekom, that operates the technical cable plat-
        form for pay-TV.[412]

---

[409]  See Bertelsmann/Kirch/Premiere, paragraph 87.
[410]  See Bertelsmann/Kirch/Premiere, paragraphs 19 and 20; Commission Decision 1999/154/
EC, Deutsche Telekom/BetaResearch (OJ L 53, 27-2-1999, p. 31), paragraphs 16 and 17.
[411]  See Deutsche Telekom/BetaResearch, paragraph 26.
[412]  Under the brand 'MediaVision', MSG has as its main offer 'Premiere World'. In addition,
MSG also offers as a basic package the digital free TV bouquets of the public broadcasters ARD and
ZDF, digital radio programmes and an Electronic Programme Guide (EPG). Currently, it is furthermore possible to subscribe to 5 thematic channels and 8 foreign language channels.

61.  For the provision of technical services for digital signal transmission over cable networks, Telekom exclusively uses BetaResearch access technology which is currently only decipherable by the d-box decoder. This technology and the d-box are controlled by Kirch and are of a proprietary nature. This means that any potential competitor wishing to supply services using the cable can only do so after acquiring a license for the encryption technology from BetaResearch. It would then try to use Kirch's d-box to reach viewers. However, this would mean that that the potential entrant would depend on its direct competitor, Kirch.

62.  To avoid BetaResearch technology, and thereby potential interference from its direct competitor Kirch, a potential entrant could attempt to enter using its own technical infrastructure. Given the exclusive use of Beta technology on the cable, the new entrant would therefore have to enter through satellite transmission. However from the point of view of the pay-TV operator the transmission of programmes by satellite is not comparable to cable, at least in Germany. A TV supplier who broadcasts his programmes exclusively via satellite direct to the home would fail to reach two-thirds of all households not receiving television solely from land-based transmitters. In particular, households in large apartment blocks in Germany cannot, as a rule, be reached by satellite, as there is usually a clause in the lease restricting the use of satellite dishes. In addition there are also considerable differences between the costs borne by a pay-TV operator per viewing household which make cable transmission much more profitable than by satellite.[413]

63.  The potential new entrant would also have to persuade consumers to buy or rent its decoder, as well as a receiver dish if they did not already have one. The UK market has shown that consumers are unlikely to buy/rent such equipment unless it is subsidised heavily. This represents an enormous cost, as BSkyB is currently showing with the introduction of digital and interactive television in the UK. Thus entry through satellite alone in Germany is unlikely.

64.  In summary, an undertaking wishing to enter the market will be obliged to use Kirch's technical infrastructure. In doing so it will be reliant on Kirch, its direct competitor. This makes entry, particular in a loss making market, seem unlikely.

**– Lack of access to content**

65.  Any operator wishing to enter the pay TV market in Germany would have to offer programmes which are attractive to German viewers.

66.  As far as programme rights are concerned, Kirch is the leading German supplier of feature films and entertainment programmes for television. In its decision in MSG Media Service the Commission noted that Kirch had at its disposal a stock of about 15 000 movies of all types and 50 000 hours of television programmes, and also had extensive production activities in the area of movies and television.[414] In the years 1995 to 1997, Kirch has concluded exclusive output deals for pay-TV rights with numerous film studios, including almost all the Hollywood majors, and has thereby acquired a commanding position in the area of programming.[415] These long-term output deals include license agreements of pay-TV broadcasting rights to current and future theatrical motion pictures with Columbia Tri-Star, Universal Studios, Paramount/Viacom, Walt Disney/Buena Vista, Warner Bros., MGM, Polygram, Twentieth Century Fox, and Dreamworks. The finishing dates of these contracts vary between [...]. In 1997, Twentieth Century Fox, a News affiliate, has

---

[413]  See Deutsche Telekom/BetaResearch, paragraphs 20 and 21.
[414]  See MSG Media Service, paragraph 76.
[415]  See also Bertelsmann/Kirch/Premiere, paragraph 36.

licensed all its pay-TV output to Premiere with a term of [...]. As a result of the output deals concluded by Kirch for pay-TV rights in particular, Premiere enjoys a de facto monopoly in premium films for pay-TV. Thus it appears that there is little film content available for a potential entrant in the German market.

67.     With regard to sports rights, Kirch owns or controls the pay-TV rights to many live sports events including the German football Bundesliga, Formula One Grand Prix races, boxing, tennis, ice hockey, golf, handball, athletics, American sports, and wrestling events. This reduces significantly the amount of sports rights that would be available to a potential new entrant.

**– Need for considerable financial resources**
68.     While it is correct that BSkyB is a successful pay-TV operator in the UK and Ireland and has access to the technology and some of the content required to develop a successful pay-TV business, it has to be noted that BSkyB is forced to invest heavily in the upgrading of its new digital pay-TV service in the UK, due to growing competition from cable operators and terrestrial pay-TV operators. At the same time, it has significant commitments to the roll-out of the British Interactive Broadcasting/Open platform for digital interactive television services in the UK.

69.     Entry into the German pay-TV market would need the investment of large amounts of capital. As BSkyB faces enormous but necessary costs in the UK, it is unlikely that it will have access to the resources necessary to enter a difficult and loss-making new market in the short to medium term, even with the backing of News.

70.     In conclusion, the Commission takes the view that, in the short to medium term, BSkyB, with or without News' backing, is not a potential entrant into the German pay-TV market. This assessment is in line with previous Commission Decisions.[416]

**– News' alleged preparations to enter the pay TV market**
71.     Despite these difficulties, at least one third party has maintained that News International, through its own actions, has shown that it is a potential entrant. It is argued that that News' purchase, in 1999, of the German broadcast rights to the UEFA Champions League for four years, as well as the application by TM3 for licenses for six digital channels, shows News intended to enter the market.

72.     The Commission does not share this analysis of the facts. It notes that the deal between UEFA and News included the free TV as well as pay TV rights for Germany. The Commission's investigations have shown that, soon after the deal with UEFA, the pay-TV rights were in fact offered, for the full four year duration, to Premiere. Subsequently TM3 began to exploit the free TV rights itself. The acquisition of the pay TV rights cannot therefore be taken as an indication that News envisaged entering the German pay-TV market. Had it done so, the offer to Kirch would not have been made. As far as the broadcasting licenses for TM3 are concerned, an application was made to the Bayerische Landesanstalt für Neue Medien (BLM). In December 1999, the BLM granted these licences after the Direktorenkonferenz der Landesmedienanstalten[417] and the Kommission zur Er-

---

[416] See MSG Media Service, paragraph 75; Bertelsmann/Kirch/Premiere, paragraph 50; Deutsche Telekom/BetaResearch, paragraph 29.

[417] See Press release 29/99 of the 'Direktorenkonferenz der Landesmedienanstalten (DLM)' of 8-12-1999

mittlung der Konzentration im Medienbereich[418] had agreed. However the Commission understands that the application for the licences indicates that the channels were designed to be thematic free TV channels.[419]

## 2. Digital interactive television services

73.     Digital interactive television services are not, as yet, available in Germany. However, a number of operators, including KirchPayTV[420], Bertelsmann, ARD, UPC and Primacom group have announced plans to launch interactive services in the near future. There are no indications that BSkyB intended to independently enter this market in the short to medium term.

74.     However, the installation of a technical infrastructure for the transmission of digital interactive television services requires major investment. Potential entrants must have the resources not only to develop the advanced technology necessary to provide such services but also to promote and, almost certainly, subsidise the rental or sale of digital decoders to consumers. The costs, as shown by the experience of BiB/Open, are significant.

75.     Potential entrants have indicated to the Commission that they would only make the required investment if there were corresponding opportunities for market penetration. In its current form, however, the proposed concentration is likely to significantly reduce the possibility of entry by third parties. This is because it will enable KirchPayTV to enter the market before, or at the same time, as any other operator. As explained below, the entry of KirchPayTV into this market at an early stage is likely to significantly raise barriers to entry for other potential suppliers by establishing the d-box as the standard decoder in Germany. Given the proprietary technology on which the box is based, such an entry is likely to create a dominant position.

KirchPayTV lacks the resources to enter digital interactive television services market

76.     According to the parties, KirchPayTV is in need of 'an injection of significant resources' to develop its business. The parties have estimated the total investment required by KirchPayTV at [...], with accrued losses standing at [...]. According to its notification, KirchPayTV has been unable to raise the funds it needs on the open market. Given the significant costs of entry into this market, it seems unlikely that KirchPayTV would be able to finance its entry into this market, at least in the short to medium term. These financial constraints are very significantly reduced by the proposed operation.

77.     Third party comments suggest that, as a consequence of the financial obstacles it faces, KirchPayTV lacks the necessary know-how to enter this market in the immediate future. The vast majority of 'd-boxes' in current use are unable to provide digital interactive television services. Whilst KirchPayTV is in the process of launching a new box, the Commission's investigation has indicated that the new box may not be equipped to provide a full range of digital interactive television services. For example, there is some indication that BetaResearch has not completed the development stage for software which will allow services such as data broadcasting, tele banking, home shopping and video-on-demand to be supplied through the new d-box. Similarly, independent market testing of the box indicates

---

[418] See Press release 12/99 of the 'Kommission zur Ermittlung der Konzentration im Medienbereich (KEK)' of 15-12-1999.

[419] See Press release 90/1999 of the BLM of 16-12-1999.

[420] See KirchPayTV Offering Memorandum of 31-8-1999.

that the new box may not be capable, at the least for the time being, of supporting typical digital features such as videotext display, electronic programming guides with colour graphics and moving previews, or Dolby Digital technology. Like other potential entrants into the German market, KirchPayTV also lacks marketing know-how or experience of running digital interactive television services. The absence of this knowledge raises the already significant risks of entering this market. BSkyB, on the other hand, is the only broadcaster in Europe with direct experience of the digital interactive television services market. Through the BiB/Open joint venture it has successfully launched these services in the UK. Its box, known as the Digibox, is technologically advanced, being able to support the full range of digital interactive television services. It will therefore be in the position, and will have the incentive after the merger, to provide its German daughter company with the requisite know how and marketing experience required to successfully enter the market.

### Creation of a dominant position

78.     In itself entry into a new market by a firm dominant on a closely related one, does not automatically lead to the creation of a dominant position. However, in this case the entry of KirchPayTV into digital interactive television services risks foreclosing the market to other potential entrants by significantly raising the barriers to entry. It should be recalled that the demand from 'content providers' for access to an operator's digital interactive television 'platform' is likely be determined by the popularity of the 'platform' with final consumers whilst the attractiveness of the 'platform' to final consumers will be determined by the range and types of services they can find on it. It has already been noted that pay-TV is likely to be an important 'driver' for digital interactive television services. As a result of its monopoly position on the pay TV market, KirchPayTV will be the only undertaking in Germany able, in the foreseeable future, to offer pay-TV in combination with digital interactive television services. This is likely to mean that consumers will choose KirchPayTV as it will allow them access, through the d-box, to both interactive services and pay-TV without the cost or inconvenience of having two boxes. As a result the d-box will become the standard decoder in Germany for interactive services, as well as pay-TV. The position of the d-box is buttressed by the decision of Telekom to provide technical services for digital transmission of TV programmes on its broadband cable network exclusively using Beta technology. Telekom has announced that it is selling its cable assets and the first sale is currently being finalised. Nonetheless the situation is likely to remain the same in the short to medium term as the process of divesting the cable has only just commenced and the Commission understands that Beta technology will continue to be used as the main technical service technology.

79.     In itself even this would not necessarily lead to the creation of a dominant position for KirchPayTV on the market for digital interactive television services if other operators were able to supply digital interactive television services through the d-box. However, it should be recalled that the d-box is a 'closed' decoder which operates with a proprietary technology developed by BetaResearch. This means that a third party operator wishing to reach customers using the d-box must seek a licence from BetaResearch. In granting licenses, BetaResearch would have no interest in exposing its sister company, KirchPayTV, to competition on the market for digital interactive television services. BetaResearch would therefore have an incentive to use its licensing policy to hamper other service providers access to the market – with regard to this point the Commission notes that in their submissions,

a number of third parties have claimed that their plans to develop services have already been frustrated by BetaResearch. In addition to requiring a license, third parties wishing to operate new digital interactive television services are currently obliged to submit their plans in advance to BetaResearch to ensure their compatibility with the system. This means that BetaResearch would have access to information on competitors of its sister company KirchPayTV which, potentially, could be very sensitive commercially.

80.    Thus there are serious doubts that the proposed concentration will be compatible with the common market as it will lead to the creation of a dominant, if not monopoly, position on the market for digital interactive television services for KirchPayTV.

### 3. The market for the acquisition of broadcasting rights, in particular for films and sporting events

81.    By virtue of its dominant position in the pay-TV market, and as indicated by its extensive rights library, Kirch dominates the market for the acquisition of broadcasting rights, in particular for films and sporting events, in Germany. It has long term exclusive agreements with all of the major Hollywood studios and the German rights holders for many major sports[421].

82.    Kirch is also active as a purchaser of pan-European rights to sporting events which can be sublicensed in several European territories.[422] Kirch has control of such rights as the Football Championships for 2002 and 2006; and Wimbledon (European-wide without Great Britain).

83.    BSkyB dominates the pay-TV market in the UK, having over 50% of the subscription revenue on the retail market and being the leading wholesale supplier of pay-TV channels. By virtue of this buying power it also dominates the market for acquisition of broadcasting rights, in particular for films and sport. It has agreements with most of the major studios which give it control of the pay-TV rights for almost all first run films and rights to leading sports events, including the UK's Premier League football.[423] Through its controlling shareholder,[424] News International, it also controls the German pay-TV and free to air rights for Champions League football, and has bid for the some pan-European sports event rights. News International's interests in German free to air TV[425] led to it acquiring some other free to air rights in Germany. However, its free to air interests are in the process of being divested.

84.    Third parties have expressed the concern that as Kirch is the only buyer of pay-TV rights for Germany the concentration will provide the means and incentive to use this power in related markets, to benefit itself or BSkyB. It is argued that this

[421] These pay-TV rights include: German football league, Formula One, Tennis-ATP Super-9-Series, ATP-Championships and US Open; US Golf PGA-Tour ; Golf PGA-Tour Europe

[422] KirchMedia holds 50% of the capital of the sports agency ISPR, as well as the entire capital of Taurus Sport GmbH which is active in the field of sports rights and which holds interests in the sports rights agencies CWL (95%) and Prisma (80%).

[423] In 1996, the Office of Fair Trading in the United Kingdom found that BSkyB had more than 90% of the pay-television rights to first-run major films and that, 'BSkyB was dominant in the supply of sports channels in the United Kingdom Pay-TV market and was at that time the only provider of premium sports channels with the exception of one specialist channel.' (The Director-General's Review of BSkyB's Position in the Wholesale Pay-TV Market, December 1996, point 2.19).

[424] As defined in Article 117 of BSkyB's Articles of Association.

[425] News International had a 49% interest in VOX and holds a 66% interest in TM3, two small free to air channels.

would take the form of tying the acquisition of German pay-TV rights to those for other broadcasting windows (free to air, internet, pay-per view) or other territories (the UK, Ireland, Italy) and that their joint resources would allow the parties to outbid other bidders. It is also alleged that they will engage in joint buying of pan-European sports events rights, a point which is addressed under Article 2(4).

85.    Kirch already has the strength to engage in tied buying for different windows, if it wished to, by virtue of its dominance of pay-TV and extensive free-TV interests in Germany. The addition of BSkyB does not significantly strengthen that position.

86.    The same applies to the argument about added resources to outbid other purchasers. Kirch has no need to offer higher bids for German pay-TV rights as it already has all these rights in long term agreements and is the only bidder when they come up for renewal. If Kirch and BSkyB buy together for the UK and Germany the amount they have available to bid for the joint rights would be substantially the same as they had separately. There is no indication that in buying the joint rights they would offer more than they would offer separately for the individual rights.

87.    On the issue of tying rights for different territories, it has been argued, however, that the concentration could strengthen BSkyB's dominant position on the pay-TV market in the UK. The concentration could provide Kirch with the means to make the acquisition of the rights for Germany conditional on BSkyB obtaining the rights for the other territory. It is suggested that Kirch would use its dominant position in the German pay-TV market to oblige rights holders, such as the Hollywood studios, to only supply the rights for the UK and Ireland to BSkyB. Kirch would threaten not to buy the German pay-TV rights, unless such an agreement was made. Although this does not alter Kirch's buying power it does increase that of BSkyB, who would not have to outbid the competing pay-TV operations in the UK.

88.    Such an arrangement, however, would face a number of practical hurdles, such as the fact that the output deals for film rights, as well as those for sports rights, are usually under exclusive contract for long periods and the chances of these contracts ending at a similar time for two or more territories is low, making such activities difficult to co-ordinate. Such behaviour would also run the risk of rights holders, such as the film studios, developing their own film channels which would reduce the control of Kirch over premium film content, thus lowering the barriers to entry to the pay-TV market in the medium term.

89.    In addition there would have to be a motive for Kirch to take the risk when the benefit would go only to BSkyB in the UK and Ireland. Kirch's 4% shareholding in Sky, who is the only party to directly benefit from tied buying, would not seem to be a sufficient incentive for Kirch to engage in such behaviour, especially with the risk of losing control over pay-TV rights.

## C. Co-ordination of competitive behaviour
### 1. Definition of a candidate market for co-ordination
90.    The market for pan-European sports events broadcasting rights is an upstream market to that in which the joint venture operates. Both parents , through Kirch's sports agencies and News International, are active in this market, which is defined in paragraph 46.

### 2. Assessment under Article 2(4)
91.    The concern is that the parties will jointly bid for pan-European sports rights, where they previously competed, and that they will preferentially sell the territorial rights to each other. For such collusion to be caught under Article 2(4), the

parents' incentives to co-ordinate under Article 81(1) and causality between the creation of the JV and a co-ordination of the competitive behaviour of the parents must be established. Some incentive to engage in such behaviour may exist separately from the concentration, namely the attempt to reduce costs in one of the most expensive areas for pay-TV operator, the acquisition of sports rights. There is therefore a lack of causality with regard to the potential collusion. Joint bidding could be done without the framework of the concentration and the concentration does not facilitate this process. Accordingly there are no Article 2(4) aspects in this case.

## VI. COMMITMENTS

92.     On the basis of the above assessment the Commission had serious doubts about the compatibility of the concentration with the common market. These doubts relate to the strengthening of a dominant position on the pay-TV market in Germany resulting from the influx of financial resources from BSkyB and the creation of a dominant position on the market for digital interactive television services.

93.     In view of these and third party concerns, the parties offered commitments, which are set out at Annex 1 and which form an integral part of this decision, notwithstanding any additional statutory or other legal obligations to which the parties are currently subject or to which they may be subject in the future. The first set of commitments concerns the market for the acquisition of broadcasting rights. The Commission notes these commitments, though it is of the view that they are not necessary to address serious doubts about the compatibility of the concentration.

94.     The second set of commitments relate to the technological platform for pay-TV and interactive services. The creation or strengthening of KirchPayTV's dominant position due to the influx of resources and know-how is sufficiently compensated for by these commitments. They lower the barriers to entry on the pay-TV market and prevent KirchPayTV from leveraging its dominance on this market into the market for digital interactive television services. These commitments therefore eliminate the serious doubts with regard to a creation or strengthening of a dominant position resulting from the proposed concentration.

## VII. CONCLUSION

95.     For the above reasons, the Commission decides not to oppose the notified operation and to declare it compatible with the common market and with the EEA Agreement, subject to the condition of full compliance with the commitments given to the Commission on 25 February 2000 (as amended on 20 March 2000) which are set out in the Annex. This decision is adopted in application of Article 6(1)(b) of Council Regulation (EEC) No 4064/89.

For the Commission,

## ANNEX 1

Case No. Comp/jv.37 – BSkyB/Kirchpaytv
Proposed undertakings by parties
The parties propose the following undertakings in the context of an agreement that the above case would not, if the undertakings are agreed, proceed to a second stage.
References in these undertakings to Kirch shall include all entities controlled or jointly controlled by Kirch VermöögensVerwaltungs GmbH & Co. KG ('Kirch') or its successors.

These undertakings do not affect in any way statutory, or any other legal obligations which the parties are currently or in the future will be under.

Each of the undertakings below will remain in force as long as BSkyB and Kirch have joint control over KirchPayTV within the meaning of Art. 3 MCR and will expire when joint control no longer exists.

Each of the relevant Kirch company, News and/or BSkyB, as the case may be, will submit to arbitration before the 'Arbitrator' in relation to any dispute with a third party regarding the implementation of these undertakings.

The burden of proof for any refusal to meet a request by a third party pursuant to these undertakings rests with Kirch, News and/or BSkyB, as the case may be. The proof must be provided to the Arbitrator within the time limits set by the Arbitrator.

The parties will propose an arbitration process to the Commission within two weeks of the Decision. The arbitration process shall comprise the process to be used and the appointment of the Arbitrator(s). The Commission shall decide within one month whether they approve the proposed arbitral process. If the Commission does not approve the arbitral process, the parties shall have a further fourteen days to propose alternatives and the Commission a further month to give its final approval. If the Commission does not approve any process proposed by the parties it may lay down the arbitral process itself.

The Arbitrator may decide all matters relating to these undertakings arising between the parties or any of them and a third party. The arbitral process shall be for the benefit of third parties for the purpose of procuring that the parties achieve full compliance, and make good any non-compliance, with the undertakings vis-a-vis third parties. In reaching a decision the Arbitrator shall take full account of any prior decision by any other arbitrator, court or regulatory body on matters covered by these undertakings relevant to the dispute before him. Decisions of the Arbitrator shall be final and binding on all persons submitting to arbitration. Nothing in the arbitral process shall affect the powers of the Commission to take decisions in relation to the undertakings in accordance with its powers under the Merger Regulation and the Treaty.

* Technology

Access to Kirch's technical platform by interested third parties

1.  Kirch agrees to procure that the relevant Kirch company will offer to all interested third parties, on a fair, reasonable and non-discriminatory basis, technical services (either individually or together) enabling the interested third parties' digitally-transmitted services, (including interactive services), where supported by Kirch's technical platform, to be received by viewers authorised by means of digital decoders administered by such Kirch company. Kirch will not preclude other existing or future third party licensees who administer access to digital decoders containing Kirch technology from offering technical services. Technical services shall mean any of encryption services, subscriber authorisation services, EPG access and any other service or part thereof which is of a technical nature where failure to provide such a part means that the interested third party's digitally transmitted services could not be displayed to viewers as intended by the third party using the full functionality supported by the platform.

2.  Kirch agrees that the relevant Kirch company will keep separate financial accounts regarding its activities as a provider of technical services for each technical service separately, which shall be audited on an annual basis as part of its annual audit by an audit firm of international standing. Kirch will deliver copies of such accounts to the Arbitrator and the Commission if and when either of them so requests.

Kirch will make available at its premises said accounts for inspection by interested third parties within two weeks of receipt of a written request. The Arbitrator shall be entitled to call for and the relevant Kirch parties will submit all necessary information, including the transfer pricing and other terms of supply for each technical service separately within Kirch Group to enable the Arbitrator to evaluate any claim that the terms offered by the Kirch party are discriminatory. The Arbitrator may at its discretion make available said transfer pricing for technical services to any third party in an arbitration instituted pursuant to these undertakings subject to such third party entering into an appropriate confidentiality undertaking, which if not agreed, shall be determined by the Arbitrator.

3.    Kirch agrees, subject to performance by the offeree of its services of the condition below, to co-operate when requested by the offeree to ensure that the offeree is in a position to take full advantage of the performance by the relevant Kirch company of its duty under 1 above. This duty includes the duty to disclose information (within one month of receipt of a request in writing) concerning the conditional access system and the technical services referred to in 1 to the offeree in order to enable the offeree to take full advantage of the performance by the relevant Kirch company of its duty under 1 above including ensuring that the offeree is not placed at a disadvantage when compared to other offerees, or to other Kirch entities who themselves are conditional access customers of the relevant Kirch company.

The condition mentioned above is that the offeree has provided the relevant Kirch company with the necessary information to enable the relevant Kirch company to comply with its duty in 1 above and has given the relevant Kirch company an undertaking in writing that information supplied to the offeree pursuant to the above shall be kept confidential and shall (together with all copies thereof) be returned to the relevant Kirch company should the offeree no longer require that the relevant Kirch company perform its duty under 1. above in relation to him.

Kirch agrees to provide information about technical up-grades to the d-box functionality at the same time as it supplies the technical specification to manufacturers of the d-box, or, if earlier, at the time that the corresponding software download is ready for downloading to the base of d-box decoders. Kirch shall fulfil this obligation by placing a notice on its web-site announcing the intention to introduce such an up-grade and information will be provided to interested third parties requesting such information within ten days of receipt of appropriate confidentiality undertakings from such interested third parties.

Kirch agrees to make available within two weeks of receipt of a written request from interested third parties a list of technical services and the prices of each technical service from time to time offered by Kirch on its platform.

\* Access of third party applications to Kirch's d-box system

\* 4.    (a) Kirch confirms that all the information relating to the API necessary to develop applications based on the API of the d-box 1 has been disclosed and, within two weeks of a request in writing, is available to interested third parties

      (b) Kirch agrees that any third party who wishes to supply an application (service) to the users of the d-box (whichever version) via the API will not (subject to agreeing fair, reasonable and non-discriminatory commercial terms for its use) be required to obtain a technical authorisation or approval by the relevant Kirch company provided that such third party and its technology provider (if different) shall have guaranteed, and assumed liability, to the relevant Kirch company that the application is compatible and does not interfere with, any functionality of the d-box, or offerings or applications of any other party. The technology provider must be duly qualified. The third party as well as the technology provider (if different) must be solvent and each shall have obtained adequate insurance.

(c) If the third party submits its application to testing by the relevant Kirch company and if the testing shows that the application is compatible with and does not interfere with any functionality of the d-box, then the application shall be permitted to run on Kirch's d-box base without further liability. Testing shall be to no higher standards than those applied to the testing of other applications, including Kirch's own. The testing shall be undertaken on reasonable commercial terms and within a reasonable time scale, such time scale to be agreed between the relevant Kirch company and the third party within 1 month of receipt of a written request together with the necessary information to evaluate a realistic time-scale for testing and in the absence of agreement within such month, within such time-scale as is determined by the Arbitrator. Kirch undertakes to provide adequate resources to perform such testing and to permit it to be done in the same timeframe as provided for other equivalent applications, including Kirch's own.

(d) The personnel within Kirch who have access to or knowledge of any such application submitted for testing shall not be involved in any programme content or software development activities of Kirch, and will be under strict contractual confidentiality obligations not to disclose any information on the application or its existence to any other Kirch entity or use the information for anything other than testing purposes.

(e) Should an independent entity be willing to undertake the testing of applications for third parties and thereafter assume full liability for applications tested by it and take out adequate insurance therefor, Kirch will, on reasonable commercial terms, support the establishment of such institution by providing all necessary information and support in order to facilitate an efficient and sufficient testing environment. Applications tested by such independent entity will be permitted to run on the d-box without further testing.

* Interoperability of applications

5. (a) Kirch agrees to procure that the relevant Kirch company will implement the application programming interface (API) as standardised by the Digital Video Broadcasting Group (DVB) and known as DVB Multimedia Home Platform (MHP) into the integrated receiver decoder (IRD) known under the trade name 'd-box' or any successor IRDs. Kirch agrees to procure that the relevant Kirch company will use all reasonable endeavours to ensure that the implementation of the MHP API will be operational within 9 months after the adoption and publication by ETSI of the technical specifications of the MHP API as standardised by the DVB or within12 months from the submission by the DVB to ETSI of such technical specification for publication, whichever is earlier, unless Kirch demonstrates that any delay is due to reasons beyond Kirch's control.

(b) Kirch undertakes that any extensions or plug-ins developed or deployed by Kirch will maintain the openness of the MHP interface so that no additional licences for developing applications to run on MHP would be required from Kirch. Once the MHP API software is operational, Kirch undertakes without further delay to download the MHP API software into all boxes which have sufficient storage capacity to do so, which shall include all d-boxes known as d-box 2.

(c) Kirch will not occupy the memory of its d-box or any of its successors with applications that are not necessary for the functionality of the digital services offered by Kirch at that time.

* Interoperability of competing technical platforms

6.    Kirch agrees to procure that the relevant Kirch company will offer to develop and to operate Simulcrypt arrangements (including the provision of the necessary coding information) with all digital conditional access providers in the German speaking territories who request the same, on reasonable commercial terms. Kirch will use all reasonable endeavours to procure that Simulcrypt arrangements are operational as soon as possible, or within such time-scale as is agreed by the parties to the Simulcrypt arrangement, such time scale to be agreed within 1 month of receipt of a written request together with the necessary information to evaluate a realistic time-scale, and in the absence of agreement within such month, within such time-scale as is determined by the Arbitrator. To this end the relevant Kirch company will co-operate fully with the conditional access provider (and its technology provider, if different).

This condition is subject to:

(a) the conditional access provider who wishes to operate a Simulcrypt arrangement (and its technology provider, if different) co-operating, as far as objectively necessary, with the relevant Kirch company, and if appropriate, such company's technology suppliers, in developing a Simulcrypt arrangement between Kirch's digital conditional access technology and the conditional access technology employed by the conditional access provider and agreeing fair and reasonable commercial terms for such development;

(b) the conditional access provider agreeing with the relevant Kirch company fair and reasonable commercial terms for ongoing arrangements relating to the operation of the Simulcrypt arrangement, including, in particular, arrangements for the cross carriage of necessary data; and

(c) the security of the conditional access provider's system not being compromised such that it creates an objective threat to the security of the system used by the relevant Kirch company.

* Access to Kirch Pay TV services by other technology platforms

7.    In the event that an interested third party notifies Kirch in writing that it intends to establish or has established a technical platform on cable or via the same digital satellite system as is used by Kirch Pay TV which allows or will allow viewers in German speaking territories to access pay TV services via digital television decoders other than the d-box, Kirch agrees to procure that, Kirch Pay TV offers, at the request of such platform provider, to retail its pay TV services directly to subscribers via Simulcrypt arrangements to digital television decoders other than the d-box and directly to administer their subscriptions and address their smart cards on such platform, provided that:

(a) such Simulcrypt arrangements are offered to Kirch Pay TV on fair, reasonable and non-discriminatory terms;

(b) Such platform displays at least equivalent technical functionality as Kirch Pay TV's own technical platform, thereby enabling Kirch Pay TV's services to be offered to viewers with identical functionality to Kirch Pay TV's own digital satellite offering; and

(c) Such platform is technically secure and the platform provider commits to guarantee such security on an unlimited liability basis related to income losses by Kirch in its subscription services and liability to third parties and with adequate insurance in the event of a security breach.

Kirch will not discriminate in terms of retail price between the customers receiving via such platform and the customers receiving via its own platform subject to it not incurring additional costs for such distribution and subject to (a) above.

* The use of Kirch's technology by competing platforms

8.    Kirch agrees to procure that the relevant Kirch company will offer licenses for the d-box network (operating system, conditional access system and API) on a reasonable and non-discriminatory basis to all interested third parties who wish to operate a digital technical platform in German speaking territories and who request such a licence. Such offer will be made within 1 (one) month after receiving a written request for a license together with the information necessary to enable the relevant Kirch company to construct such offer. To the extent that the relevant Kirch company controls the technology, Kirch undertakes that any third party licensee, will be offered, on reasonable commercial terms, a license to the software which is at least equal in scope to those offered to any Kirch controlled entity.

Kirch agrees to make available on written request by interested third parties term sheets including licensing fees and conditions for standard technology, where Kirch is in a position to grant licences for this technology to third parties.

* Production of 'multiple system' boxes

–     (a) Kirch agrees to procure that the relevant Kirch company will grant manufacturing licenses for the production of the d-box to interested manufacturers of IRDs or comparable hardware in a non-discriminatory manner and under terms and conditions which are customary in and normally applied by the industry. It shall do so within 1 (one) month after receiving a written request for a license together with the information necessary to enable the relevant Kirch company to grant such a licence or, if the granting of the manufacturing license objectively requires more than 1 (one) month, within such timeframe as to be agreed within 1 (one) month after the receipt of the request between the relevant Kirch company and the interested party or, in the absence of an agreement, within such timeframe as to be determined by the Arbitrator. Kirch undertakes that it will not, in licensing manufacturers to manufacture d-box decoders which include Kirch's conditional access system, preclude the manufacturers from including in such decoders a third party's conditional access system, or capability for a third party's conditional access system to be attached to such decoder, and furthermore Kirch undertakes that it will not refuse to supply subscribers with its Pay TV services based solely on the fact that they wish to subscribe using a d-box which contains such capability.

–     (b) Kirch will not impose any other licence restrictions on manufacturers which would prevent them from manufacturing such a box which contains additional conditional access system(s).

The above undertakings are subject to such third party's conditional access system not affecting in any way Kirch's conditional access system or adversely affecting its operating system within the d-box or the applications running on the box, or in any way compromising the security of either system.

* Transition to digital of analogue subscribers

10. Kirch agrees to offer a d-box to every subscriber who is not in default of its subscription that requests a d-box in place of its analogue box within three months of such request and to change the subscriber's subscription accordingly (subject to the subscriber signing a new digital subscription agreement).

* Limitation on Kirch for additional cable capacity

11. Kirch Pay TV agrees that it will not apply for further digital cable capacity in Germany prior to 31st December 2000.

Rights acquisition.

1. Each of News and BSkyB agree that, in bidding for programming rights for exploitation on a pay TV basis in the UK and Eire, they will not impose upon the rights holder as a condition of their bids, that the rights holder must grant the pay TV programming rights for the German territory to Kirch; and Kirch agrees that, in bidding for programming rights for exploitation on a pay TV basis in the German territory, it will not impose on the rights holder as a condition of its bid a condition that the rights for the UK and Eire be sold to BSkyB or News.

2. In the event that News or BSkyB on the one hand, or Kirch on the other, acquires rights for the exploitation via pay TV of a major live international sports event on a multi-national basis, each of News and BSkyB agree that they will not give to Kirch the status of preferred bidder for such rights in respect of Germany, and Kirch agrees that it will not give to either of BSkyB or News the status of preferred bidder for such rights with respect to the UK and Republic of Ireland (in the case of BSkyB), or such territories within which News undertakes broadcasting activities (in the case of News), in all cases by granting a right of first negotiation, first refusal or first offer or a right of last matching offer or other rights with similar effect.

3. None of News or BSkyB on the one hand, or Kirch on the other, will agree to refrain from bidding for TV rights to major live international sports events for exploitation via pay TV in one or more Member States where such agreement is given in return for valuable consideration (which shall include, without limitation, a reciprocal agreement) from either News or BSkyB (in the case of Kirch) and from Kirch (in the case of News or BSkyB).

4. Kirch, News and BSkyB agree that Kirch and News or Kirch and BSkyB, as the case may be, will not bid jointly for multi-national TV rights to major live international sports events for exploitation via pay TV in one or more Member States unless, in respect of any particular sports event, another bidder or bidders for such rights include(s) (or is/are reasonably believed by the parties to include):
   a) a group of bidders with TV interests in several Member States bidding, directly or indirectly, for rights (either jointly, or where one or more bidders bid on behalf of others) for several Member States; or

b) a single bidder with TV interests in several Member States who is bidding, directly or indirectly, for rights for several Member States.

For the purpose of this undertaking 'several' Member States means two or more, save that UK and Eire count as one, and Germany and Austria count as one.

Submitted on February 25th 2000 as amended 20th March 2000
KirchPayTV GmbH & Co. KGaA ('Kirch Pay TV')
Kirch VermögensVerwaltungs GmbH & Co. KG ('Kirch')
British Sky Broadcasting Group plc. ('BSkyB')
The News Corporation Limited ('News')

———

**\* 2.4.50.  ANSWER ON BEHALF OF THE COMMISSION TO WRITTEN QUESTION E-396/00 BY DORIS PACK (PPE-DE), 27 MARCH 2000[426] \***

Subject: FIBT TV rights

———

**\* 2.4.51.  ANSWER ON BEHALF OF THE COMMISSION TO WRITTEN QUESTION E-397/00 BY DORIS PACK (PPE-DE), 28 MARCH 2000[427] \***

Subject: FIBT advertising rights on bobsleighs, helmets and competitors' clothing

———

**\* 2.4.52.  ANSWER ON BEHALF OF THE COMMISSION TO WRITTEN QUESTION E-432/00 BY GIORGOS KATIFORIS (PSE), 4 APRIL 2000[428] \***

Subject: Commission dispute with the International Automobile Federation

———

**\* 2.4.53.  COMMISSION READY TO LIFT IMMUNITY FROM FINES TO TELEFÓNICA MEDIA AND SOGECABLE IN SPANISH FOOTBALL RIGHTS CASE, 12 APRIL 2000[429]**

———

**2.4.54.  COMMISSION DECISION RELATING TO A PROCEEDING PURSUANT TO ARTICLE 81 OF THE EC TREATY (CASE IV/32.150 – EUROVISION), 10 MAY 2000[430]**

*The Commission of the European Communities,*

– Having regard to the Treaty establishing the European Community,
– Having regard to the Agreement on the European Economic Area and in particular Article 53 thereof,
– Having regard to Council Regulation No 17 of 6 February 1962, first Regulation implementing Articles 85 and 86 of the Treaty[431], as last amended by Regulation

---

[426] Question of 15-2-2000; OJ C 303 E, 24-10-2000, p. 188.
[427] Question of 15-2-2000; OJ C 330 E, 21-11-2000, p. 151.
[428] Question of 23-2-2000; OJ C 330 E, 21-11-2000, p. 157.
[429] IP/00/372.
[430] OJ L 151 , 24-6-2000, p. 18-41. (Text with EEA relevance).
[431] OJ 13, 21-2-1962, p. 204.

(EC) No 1216/1999[432], and in particular Articles 6 and 8 thereof,
–  Having regard to the application for negative clearance and the notification for exemption submitted, pursuant to Articles 2 and 4 of Regulation No 17, on 3 April 1989, as supplemented on 27 August 1996,
–  Having published summaries of the application and notification[433] pursuant to Article 19(3) of Regulation No 17,
–  After consulting the Advisory Committee for Restrictive Practices and Dominant Positions,
Whereas:

## I. THE FACTS
## 1. INTRODUCTION

(1)  On 3 April 1989 the European Broadcasting Union (EBU) applied for negative clearance or for exemption pursuant to Article 81(3) of the EC Treaty in respect of its internal rules and regulations governing the acquisition of television rights to sporting events, the exchange of sports programmes within the framework of Eurovision and contractual access to such programmes for third parties.

(2)  On 11 June 1993 the Commission adopted Decision 93/403/EEC[434] pursuant to Article 81(3) of the EC Treaty granting a conditional exemption to the notified EBU provisions until 25 February 1998. The exemption was subject to the scheme for sub-licensing by the EBU to third parties of the jointly acquired television rights to sporting events and to the obligation to inform the Commission of any amendments to the rules notified, of all arbitration procedures under the scheme for EBU non-members' access to Eurovision sports programmes[435] and of all decisions regarding applications for membership by third parties.

(3)  On 11 July 1996 the Court of First Instance annulled the Commission's decision following an application by a number of European television channels[436].

(4)  The EBU appealed against the Court of First Instance's judgment before the Court of Justice. The Commission is supporting the EBU's appeal which is still pending.

(5)  On 27 August 1996 the Guidelines of Interpretation of Criteria for EBU Active Membership (dated 12 August 1992) were submitted by the EBU to the Commission. The membership rules and the Guidelines of Interpretation were amended on 3 April 1998 by the EBU.

(6)  The Commission published a summary of the agreements notified in the Article 19(3) notice of 5 October 1990 and in a second Article 19(3) notice of 1 September 1999.

## 2. THE EUROPEAN BROADCASTING UNION[437]

(7)  The EBU is an association of radio and television organisations set up in 1950 with headquarters in Geneva. The association is a non-profit-making association. However, to attain its objectives, it may pursue activities of a commercial nature.

---

[432] OJ L 148, 15-6-1999, p. 5.
[433] OJ C 251, 1990, p. 2 and OJ C 248, 1-9-1999, p. 4.
[434] OJ L 179, 22-7-1993, p. 23.
[435] See Annex I.
[436] Metropole télévision SA and Reti Televisive Italiane SpA and Gestevisión Telecinco SA and Antena 3 de Televisión v Commission of the European Communities, Joined Cases T-528/93, T-542/93, T-543/93 and T-546/93. [1996] ECR II – 649.
[437] For a detailed description of the EBU organisation, see paragraphs 2 to 5 of the Article 19(3) notice of 5-10-1990 and paragraphs 7 to 13 of the Article 19(3) notice of 1-9-1999.

The objectives of the EBU are to serve the interests of its members in the programming, legal, technical and other fields. In particular, the EBU will coordinate and support television programme exchanges among its active members, in the framework of Eurovision, and will promote co-productions and any other form of cooperation among its members and with other broadcasting organisations or groups of such organisations. The EBU will assist its active members in negotiations of all kinds and, when asked, negotiate on their behalf. Solidarity is the EBU's guiding precept.

(8)     There are two categories of EBU members: active members and associate members. Only active members can be Eurovision members. Associate members are from countries outside the European Broadcasting Area. Associate members do not belong to Eurovision and thus have no access to Eurovision sports rights, beyond contractual access in the same way as non-members. They do, however, participate in the work of the professional association.

## A. The EBU's conditions for active membership

(9)     The conditions for active membership of the EBU are set out in Article 3(3) of the EBU's Statutes as interpreted by the Guidelines of Interpretation of Criteria for Active Membership. Both Articles 3(3) of the Statutes and the Guidelines were amended on 3 April 1998 by the EBU. Active membership of the EBU is open to broadcasting organisations, or groups of such organisations, which provide, in a country situated in the European broadcasting area, a service of national character and national importance. They must cover virtually all of the national radio and/or television households and must all be under an obligation to provide, and actually provide, varied and balanced programming for all sections of the population. Finally, they themselves must produce a substantial proportion of the programmes broadcast. According to Article 3(3) of its Statutes, the EBU applies the following criteria to assess requests for membership.

(a) Technical coverage: 98% of the national radio and/or television households are in a position and technically equipped to receive the entirety of their major radio and/or television programme service with satisfactory technical quality.

(b) Programme obligations: varied and balanced programming for all sections of the population in the context of television sports programming means that a minimum should be attained:

–       between 7 a.m. and 1 a.m., plus any live coverage between 1 a.m. and 7 a.m., programming should include at least 200 hours of sports programming per year,

–       sports programming should include at least 12 different categories of sport, of which at least eight have a total annual transmission time of more than three hours.

(c) Own production: the production by the EBU's members at their own cost and under their own editorial control of a substantial proportion of the programmes broadcast means an own production of at least 30% of the totality of the programmes broadcast.

(10)    In addition, the last subparagraph of Article 3(6) expressly requires the EBU's Administrative Council to ensure compliance with the membership rules. The Administrative Council must ensure at all times that participation in the joint acquisition and sharing of sports rights in the framework of Eurovision remains strictly limited to those organisations which fully comply with the conditions laid down in Article 3(3) of the EBU Statutes and in the Guidelines for Interpretation.

(11)    Finally, Article 3(15) provides for the possibility of recourse to arbitration for ap-

plicants. An organisation whose application for active membership has not been successful has the possibility of recourse to arbitration in Geneva in accordance with the Swiss arbitration concordat. The same right to arbitration applies where a non-member whose application for membership was not successful questions the Administrative Council's assessment that a given member in the same country is entitled to participate in the joint acquisition and sharing of sports rights.

(12)    Since 1998, the EBU has a set of rules concerning the continuing participation of former Eurovision members in existing sport programmes[438]. In accordance with these rules, the entirety of the former member's rights will be offered in its country market and on the same financial terms as to the former member, first, to another existing Eurovision member and, in case of lack of success, to non-members (including at the end the former Eurovision member). The new rightowners will be bound by the 1993 EBU scheme on non-members' access to Eurovision sports programmes. Therefore, the new rightowners are subject to the sub-licensing obligations and the access of third parties to the jointly acquired sports rights is also guaranteed.

(13)    The EBU has 68 active members in 49 countries situated in the European broadcasting area and 50 associate members in 30 countries outside the area.

## 3. THE NOTIFIED ARRANGEMENTS: THE EUROVISION SYSTEM

(14)    The notified arrangements are the 'Eurovision system', that is, the rules which govern within the EBU and the Eurovision/Sports system:
(1) the joint acquisition of sport television rights
(2) the sharing of the jointly acquired sport television rights
(3) the exchange of the signal for sporting events
(4) the access scheme for non EBU members to Eurovision sports rights and
(5) the sub-licensing rules relating to exploitation of Eurovision rights on pay-TV channels.

(15)    The notification does not include radio matters.

(16)    Eurovision is a TV programme exchange system organised and coordinated by the EBU, based on the understanding that members offer to other members, on a reciprocal basis, their news coverage of important events and their coverage of current affairs and of sports and cultural events taking place in their countries and of potential interest to other members, thereby enabling members to provide a high quality service in these fields to their respective national audiences. In addition, in the framework of Eurovision, EBU active members participate in the joint acquisition and sharing of sports rights.

A. Joint acquisition of sport television rights

(17)    Television rights for international sporting events are normally acquired jointly by all interested members on an exclusive basis.

(18)    The joint acquisition of rights normally concerns only international sporting events and not national events such as national football, where national EBU members buy the television rights individually on the market, thereby competing with each other in some countries.

(19)    Whenever EBU members from two or more countries are interested in a specific sporting event they request coordination from the EBU. As a result, negotiations

---

[438] The Commission was informed of these rules on 7-12-1998. The rules were first applied to Canal+. The EBU changed the membership rules on 3-4-1998 with the result that Canal+ can no longer participate in the Eurovision/sports system. The full text of these rules has been published by the EBU on the internet <http:/www.ebu.ch>.

are carried out on behalf of all interested members either by a member – sometimes assisted by the EBU- in the country where the event takes place or by the EBU itself. Once negotiations for Eurovision rights have commenced, and until they are formally declared to have failed, members are required not to engage in separate negotiations for national rights. Only if joint negotiations have failed are members free to negotiate separately.

**B. Sharing of the jointly acquired sport television rights**
(20)   The Eurovision rights are acquired on behalf of the members who participate in the contract for their respective countries. Once the exclusive rights have been acquired, all members participating in the agreement share the rights and are entitled to the full benefit of the rights, regardless of the territorial scope of their activity and regardless of the technical means of broadcasting. However, members who compete for the same national audience (several members in one country or members broadcasting from their country into the country of another member in the same language) have to agree among themselves on the procedure for attribution of priority to one of them.
(21)   Several members in one country usually agree to share the rights, for example by alternating transmission of the event. If no such procedure can be agreed on, all the members concerned become entitled to non-exclusive rights with respect to the country or countries in question. Members which provide the coverage of an event (i.e. produce the signal) are, unless otherwise agreed, entitled to priority over foreign members aiming their broadcast at the same national audience.

**C. The exchange of the signal**
(22)   For events which take place within the Eurovision area the coverage (television signal consisting of basic video and international sound-feed) is produced by a member in the country concerned and is available to all other members via the Eurovision programme exchange system. The Eurovision programme exchange system is based on reciprocity: whenever one of the participating members covers an event, in particular a sporting event, which takes place on its own national territory and is of potential interest to other Eurovision members, it offers its coverage free of charge to all the other Eurovision members on the understanding that in return it will receive corresponding offers from all the other members in respect of events taking place in their respective countries. The originating member also provides the necessary infrastructure to other interested members such as commentary positions.
(23)   Since in each country there is at least one EBU member providing and producing sports programmes, it can be taken for granted that essentially all events that are of potential interest beyond national boundaries will be covered (provided that the members have been able to acquire the rights) and will be available to the members throughout the Eurovision area. The reciprocity system does not take account of actual input and withdrawal by individual members. In essence, it amounts to a solidarity system under which the financially more powerful organisations from large countries support organisations from smaller countries with a view to ensuring a broad flow of sports programmes to all parts of the Eurovision area.
(24)   If an event takes place outside the Eurovision area, and thus the coverage is produced by a non-EBU member, the members participating in a Eurovision agreement normally have to pay a fee, which they share between them, for the use of that other broadcaster's signal. However, there are reciprocity agreements with equivalent broadcasting organisations in other areas under which the signal is in some cases made available free of charge to EBU members.

(25) The transport of the signal from the point of origin to the transmission facilities in the individual countries where the event is to be transmitted, is effected via a network which links all Eurovision members with each other. The network consists of permanently leased terrestrial circuits (supplemented on an ad hoc basis by occasionally leased terrestrial links) as well as a certain number of terrestrial circuits owned by individual members. In addition, the EBU leases some satellite circuits on a permanent basis and further satellite circuits on an ad hoc basis.

(26) The Eurovision system also provides for administrative and technical coordination. Administrative coordination including programme coordination is carried out by the EBU's permanent services in Geneva or, for example, in the case of the Olympics, by special operation groups, with the object of coordinating the specific needs of the different members and of achieving optimal coverage of as many competitions as possible. It involves, in particular, the planning of scheduling, including dealing with possible time differences between the site of the event and the members' countries and the selection of competitions in cases where several competitions take place simultaneously. Technical coordination is carried out by the EBU's technical centre which deals, in particular, with technical planning, monitoring and quality control with regard to the signal itself.

(27) The parties made some changes to the notified arrangements. These changes, which are part of the notified Eurovision system, are the 1993 and the 1999 access schemes for non-members.

**D. The access scheme for non-EBU members to Eurovision sports rights (1993)**

(28) Under the scheme submitted to the Commission on 26 February 1993, the EBU and its members undertake to grant non-member broadcasters extensive access to Eurovision sports programmes the rights for which have been acquired on an exclusive basis through collective negotiations. The 1993 scheme grants live and deferred transmission rights to third parties of jointly acquired Eurovision sports rights. In particular the non-EBU members have significant access to the unused rights, i.e. for the transmission of sporting events which are not transmitted by, or of which only a minor part are transmitted by an EBU member. The terms and conditions of access are freely negotiated between the EBU (for transnational channels), or the member(s) in the country concerned (for national channels), and the non-member. However, the EBU and its members will in no circumstances grant less favourable access than stipulated in recitals 29 to 33.

(29) Access for live transmissions is granted if the event is not broadcast live by the EBU member(s) in the country or countries concerned, except for those parts or competitions (particular disciplines, individual matches, rounds, etc.) which the member(s) have reserved for their own live transmission.

(30) If an event (or, in the case of events lasting more than one day, a day of competition) is broadcast live by the EBU member(s) in the country or countries concerned, i.e. if the majority of the principal competitions constituting it are transmitted live, access is granted for deferred transmissions, beginning not earlier than one hour after the end of the event or the last competition of the day and not earlier than 10.30 p.m. local time (London time for pan-European channels).

(31) Except where national law or regulation provides otherwise, the EBU and its members grant access to two news items of up to 90 seconds each per event or day of competition, with the possibility of repeating one such report later the same day, which must be included in regularly scheduled general news bulletins, or in regularly scheduled general sports-news programmes of dedicated sports channels within 24 hours.

(32)    The access fee (for access to the television rights and the television signal) has to be negotiated. For routing the signal, the non-member is free to make its own arrangements or may ask the EBU to route the signal via the Eurovision network. In that case the EBU will submit an estimate for the costs.

(33)    In the event of a dispute over the access fee where all other access conditions have been agreed at the request of the non-member the matter will be submitted to arbitration by independent expert(s). The expert(s) will be nominated jointly by the parties. Failing agreement, nomination will be by the President of the competent Court of Appeal in the case of national arbitration (concerning access for national channels) and by the President of the International Chamber of Commerce in the case of international arbitration (concerning access for pan-European channels). The expert(s) shall fix the access fee. The decision shall be final and binding.

(34)    The complete text of the scheme can be obtained by interested third parties from the EBU or from the national members. It has also been published by the EBU on the Internet: http://www.ebu.ch and it is attached at Annex I.

**E. The sub-licensing rules relating to exploitation of Eurovision rights on pay-TV channels (1999)**

(35)    As an addition to the general rules on EBU non-members' access to Eurovision Sport Programmes adopted on 24 February 1993, the EBU has adopted, and submitted to the Commission on 26 March 1999, a set of sub-licensing rules relating to exploitation of Eurovision rights on pay-TV channels.

(36)    Pursuant to the 1999 rules, when an EBU member transmits part of a sporting event on its national general programme channel and part on its pay-TV channel:
   – a non-EBU member has all rights stemming from the 1993 rules for the broadcasting on its free-to-air or pay-TV channels, live or deferred. In addition:
   – A non-EBU member has the right to transmit on its pay-TV channel identical or comparable competitions to those presented on the EBU member's pay-TV channel.

(37)    The full text of those rules has been published by the EBU on the Internet: http://www.ebu.ch, and is attached at Annex II to this Decision.

**4. THE RELEVANT MARKET**
**4.1. Product market**

(38)    The EBU considers that the relevant market for the assessment of the case is the market for the acquisition of the television rights to important sporting events in all disciplines of sport, irrespective of the national or international character of the event. The EBU is only active in the acquisition of television rights to sporting events of pan-European interest[439].

(39)    The Commission shares EBU's view that sports programmes have particular characteristics; they are able to achieve high viewing figures and reach an identifiable audience, which is a special target for certain important advertisers.

(40)    However, contrary to what the EBU suggests, the attraction of sports programmes and hence the level of competition for the television rights varies according to the type of sport and the type of event. Mass sports like football, tennis or motor-racing generally attract large audiences, the preferences varying from country to country. By contrast, minority sports achieve very low ratings. International events

---

[439] Sporting events of a pan-European interest include for example: the Olympic Games, the Football World cup, the European football Championships, the World and European Athletic Championships; Wimbledon, the US and French tennis Opens, the NBA basketball.

tend to be more attractive for the audience in a given country than national ones, provided the national team or a national champion is involved, while international events in which no national champion or team is participating can often be of little interest. In the last 10 years, with increased competition in the television markets, the prices for television rights to sporting events have increased considerably (see recitals 50 to 58 ), this is particularly true with regard to outstanding international events such as the Football World Cup or the Olympic Games.

(41) The preferences of viewers determine the value of a programme to advertisers and pay-TV broadcasters[440]. In free-to-air television we cannot directly observe viewers' reactions to changes in the price of broadcasts, and hence we cannot directly observe evidence on the price elasticities of demand. This is also true for pay-TV since pay-TV contracts usually involve monthly or annual payments for bundles of channels, but not individual prices for each programme. However, if we observe that sports broadcasts achieve the same or similar sized audiences whether or not they are competing with simultaneously broadcast sporting events, there is strong evidence that those events could determine the subscribers' or advertisers' choice of a certain broadcaster.

(42) Indeed, data on viewer behaviour, among major sporting events, shows that for at least some sporting events which have been analysed such as the summer Olympics, the winter Olympics, the Wimbledon Finals and the Football World Cup viewing behaviour does not appear to be influenced by the coincidence of other major sporting events being broadcast simultaneously, or nearly simultaneously. That is, viewing figures for the major sporting events appear to be largely independent of whatever other major sports are broadcast at a similar time[441]. Therefore, the offer of such sporting events could influence the subscribers or advertisers to such an extent that the broadcaster would be inclined to pay much higher prices.

(43) In conclusion, the Commission's investigation shows that the market definition proposed by the EBU is too large and that there is a strong likelihood that there are separate markets for the acquisition of some major sporting events, most of them international.

(44) However, it is not necessary for the purposes of this case to exactly define the relevant product markets. Taking into account the present structure of the market and the sub-licensing sets of rules granting access to non-EBU members to the Eurovision Sport Programmes these agreements do not raise competiton con-

---

[440] In the same way that customer substitutability determines the upstream market of the supply of digital interactive television services by service providers to content providers as the Commission has decided in Decision 1999/781/EC, Case 36.539, British Interactive Broadcasting/Open (OJ L 312, 6-12-1999, p. 1).

[441] When major sporting event A is broadcast simultaneously with another major sporting event B, event A achieves (on average) the same audience as it does when event B is not available. For instance, there is evidence that the elasticity of demand in the UK for the Wimbledon finals with respect to the World Cup Football is very small, and probably zero. World Cup Football viewers do not appear to watch Wimbledon Finals, even when the world cup is not available. The same can be said with regard to the Premier League Football broadcast by BSkyB in relation to the top 30/40 most viewed sport programmes in free-to-air TV in the UK. The test indicates that viewers of Premier League matches do not substitute to other major sporting events when broadcast on the same day. Source: 'Market definition in European sports broadcasting and competition for sports broadcasting rights' by Market Analysis Ltd, a study for the Directorate-General for Competiton of the European Commission, October 1999.

cerns, even on the basis of markets for the acquisition of particular sporting events such as the summer Olympics.

(45)   As explained in recital 41, the acquisition of exclusive TV rights to certain major sporting events has a strong impact on the downstream television markets in which the sporting events are broadcast as part of the broadcasters' offer to viewers and/ or subscribers.

## 4.2. Geographic market

(46)   Some sporting events rights are acquired on an exclusive basis for the whole European territory and, regardless of the technical means of transmission, to be resold thereafter per country, which others are acquired on a national basis. The kind of major sporting event rights for which the EBU bids, which have a pan-European interest from the viewers' perspective, such as the Olympic Games, will normally fall within the first category of European licences.

(47)   Nevertheless, irrespective of the scope of the licences, as explained in recitals 38 to 45, the preferences of viewers can significantly vary from country to country depending on the type of sport and the type of event and, therefore, the conditions of competition for the television rights can vary accordingly.

(48)   With regard to the downstream markets affected by the present notification, the free-to-air and pay-TV broadcasting markets should be considered, largely for linguistic, cultural, licensing and copyright reasons, generally national or extending to single linguistic areas.

(49)   However, for the purposes of this case it is not necessary to define the relevant geographic market exactly. Taking into account the present structure of the market and the sub-licensing rules granting non-EBU members access to the Eurovision sport programmes, these agreements do not raise competition concerns even on the basis of national markets for the acquisition of sports rights, nor for the downstream markets of free-to-air and pay-TV broadcasting.

## 5. MARKET STRUCTURE

(50)   In the Community markets, competition between terrestrial broadcasters has increased everywhere, and a significant number of new cable and satellite companies have entered the broadcasting markets in the last 10 years. The number of broadcasting companies and broadcasting channels in the Community's five biggest television markets (Germany, France, United Kingdom, Italy and Spain) doubled or tripled between 1982 and 1997. The new national free-to-air broadcasters are obviously interested in spending large sums for attractive sporting events to increase the prestige of their channels. In addition, pay-TV broadcasters, particularly in France, the United Kingdom and Spain have discovered that having attractive sporting events is an enormously motivating factor in recruiting subscribers, in particular young males with disposable income. Consequently, the capacity devoted to sports broadcasts has increased dramatically in recent years and this growth has come principally from non-EBU broadcasters[442].

(51)   Television rights to sporting events are granted for a given territory, normally on an exclusive basis. Exclusivity is generally granted for broadcasting by all technical means (satellite, cable, terrestrial). Exclusivity is considered necessary by the broadcasters in order to guarantee the value of a given sports programme, in terms of the viewing figures and advertising revenues which it can achieve. The rights

---

[442] See diagram showing this evolution since 1990 at Annex III.

are often offered as packages and comprise all matches, rounds or competitions forming one event (championship, tournament, cup, league round).

(52) Television rights are normally held by the organiser of a sporting event, who is able to control access to the premises where the event is staged. In order to control the televising of the event and to guarantee exclusivity the organiser admits only one broadcaster (the host, broadcaster, i.e. a broadcaster in the country where the event takes place) or, in any case, only a limited number of broadcasters to produce the television signal. Under their contract with the organiser they are not allowed to make their signal available to any third party who has not acquired the relevant television rights. Organisers of widely popular sporting events are often rather powerful national or international associations which are in an extremely strong situation with regard to television rights to certain events or certain types of sports, as there is usually a single national or international association for each sport.

(53) As a result of the new entrants and the increased capacity devoted to sports broadcasts, there are fierce bidding contests to obtain valuable sports broadcasting rights. The effect of that seems to be a transfer of profits away from downstream broadcasters and towards upstream rights owners[443]. The prices of the TV rights for sporting events have therefore increased sharply.

(54) In this context, the EBU has lost significant market share in the relevant markets for the last ten years.

(55) With regard to the acquisition of exclusive television rights to certain major sporting events, the EBU's position has been effectively attacked by the big European media groups[444], in particular those with interests in both generalist and pay-TV channels, and by the international brokers[445]. The best example of this trend is that the EBU was unsuccessful in the bidding for the 2002 and 2006 Football World Cups. In 1987 the EBU paid GBP 215 million to show the 1990, 1994 and 1998 football World Cups. In 1997 the Kirch Group paid GBP 1,37 billion for the world rights to the next three World Cups, a sixfold increase. The EBU bid was 78% of the winning bid for these worldwide rights[446]. The EBU has also not acquired or has lost a very significant number of other important sporting events in the last few years because of higher competitive offers such as the Formula One Motor Racing, the Motor Cycling Grand Prix World Championships since 1998, the Athletics Grand Prix Meetings (Golden Four), the Gymnastics World Championships, the Ski World Cup races in Italy, Norway, France, Slovenia, Spain, Sweden, USA and Canada, the Basketball World Championships and European Championships from 1999, Wimbledon (since 1988), US Open (since 1985), Masters Final (since 1987), Grand Slam Cup (since 1990), the Davis Cup Final tennis tournaments, the Rugby World Cup and the Paris to Dakar rally.

(56) However, the EBU remains in a strong market position in the acquisition of major international sporting events with a very strong appeal for European viewers in respect of which the rights owners still insist that the events must not be broadcast on pay television. In addition, the EBU still has a unique one-stop-shop position, which guarantees the organisers the widest possible viewing audience in Europe. Thus, the EBU holds the rights for the summer Olympic Games in Sydney (2000),

---

[443] See Annex IV table 'The costs of the European rights to the Olympics for the EBU from 1984 to 2008': Source: market analysis, report of October 1999.

[444] Kirch, Mediaset, Bertelsmann, BSkyB, Canal+.

[445] ISL, IMG, ISPR, Team or UFA.

[446] Source: market analysis report of October 1999.

Athens (2004) and the 2008 summer Olympic Games, the winter Olympic Games in Salt Lake City (2002) and the 2006 winter Olympic Games, the UEFA Cup Finals (1998-2000), Roland Garros (1998 to 1999), Australian tennis Open (1998 to 2000) and the FIS Alpine and Nordic World Championships (1999-2005). The EBU also has contracts for world and European championships in other categories such as athletics, basketball, biathlon, boxing, cycling, equestrian events, fencing, gymnastics, judo, rowing, skating, swimming, table tennis, volleyball, weight-lifting and wrestling.

(57)   It is particularly relevant that the European television rights for the Olympic Games have always been sold to the EBU. However, it is also worth noting that in the latest round of bidding the EBU bought the rights to all games between 2000 and 2008 for a total of USD 1,44 billion. News Corporation had bid USD 2 billion for the same rights. This reflects a policy of the IOC of keeping the most important events available on free TV but the trend resulting from the entrance of new players and the impact on EBU's market power is confirmed by the higher bid made by News Corporation for the rights to the Olympic Games between 2000 and 2008.

(58)   The market position of the EBU members in the free-to-air market in their respective national territories has also undoubtedly declined as a result of the sharp increase in new broadcasting companies entering the market. With regard to the pay television market, the EBU members are now starting to enter the market, normally through a still very limited number of thematic channels. Well established pay-TV operators such as Canal+, BskyB and Kirch hold very strong market positions in some European countries with very valuable sports rights.

## 6. THIRD PARTY OBSERVATIONS

(59)   In its notice of 5 October 1990, pursuant to Article 19(3) of Regulation No 17, the Commission indicated its intention to grant an exemption pursuant to Article 81(3) of the EC Treaty. A number of third parties addressed critical opinions to the Commission on the notified agreements, mainly concerning the EBU sub-licensing scheme. As a result, on 18 and 19 December 1990, the Commission organised an oral hearing with all interested third parties, at which the sub-licensing scheme, which was found to be too restrictive, was discussed in detail.

(60)   As a result of the third parties' comments and the Commission's intervention, the EBU submitted a new scheme to the Commission on 26 February 1993, governing contractual access for non-members.

(61)   On 1 September 1999, the Commission published a second notice pursuant to Article 19(3) of Regulation No 17 and received further observations from interested third parties. The main concerns expressed in those observations were:
       (a) the conditions for active membership of the EBU as set out in Article 3 of the EBU's Statutes are not sufficiently objective and transparent within the meaning of the judgment of the Court of First Instance of 11 July 1996[447]. Those membership rules and the joint acquisition of sports rights by the EBU fall under Article 81(1) of the EC Treaty and cannot be exempted pursuant to Article 81(3) of the EC Treaty,
       (b) the product market definition proposed by the EBU[448] is too broad.

(62)   The Commission has carefully reviewed all observations from third parties and

---

[447] Metropole télévision SA and Reti Televisive Italiane SpA and Gestevisión Telecinco SA and Antena 3 de Televisión v Commission of the European Communities, Joined Cases T-528/93, T-542/93, T-543/93 and T-546/93. [1996] ECR II - 649.

[448] The market for important sporting events in all disciplines of sports and irrespective of the national or international character of the event.

concluded that the concerns expressed therein have been addressed during the notification procedure. In particular:

(a) with regard to the EBU membership rules and the joint acquisition of sports rights by the EBU the Commission has taken into account the third parties' concerns in the assessment below,

(b) with regard to the question of product market definition, the Commission has taken this into account in recitals 38 to 49.

## II. THE ASSESSMENT

(63) The Commission has concluded that the notified arrangements fall within the scope of Article 81(1) of the EC Treaty and Article 53(1) of the EEA Agreement, but that subject to the conditions and obligations set out in Article 2 of this Decision and following the changes made as a result of the Commission's intervention, the criteria of Article 81(3) of the EC Treaty and Article 53(3) of the EEA Agreement are met.

## 1. ARTICLE 81(1) OF THE EC TREATY AND ARTICLE 53(1) OF THE EEA AGREEMENT

### A. Agreements between or decisions by an association of undertakings

(64) The EBU members are undertakings within the meaning of Article 81(1) of the EC Treaty and Article 53(1 ) of the EEA Agreement. The Court of Justice has ruled, in particular in Case 155/73 Sacchi[449], that public television broadcasting organisations are 'undertakings' within the meaning of Article 81(1) in so far as they exercise economic activities. The acquisition of television rights to sporting events and the granting of sub-licences for such programmes are clearly activities of an economic nature which are covered by Article 81(1) of the EC Treaty and Article 53(1) of the EEA Agreement.

(65) The notified EBU internal rules and regulations governing the Eurovision system are decisions of an association of undertakings within the meaning of Article 81(1) of the EC Treaty and Article 53(1) of the EEA Agreement.

### B. The EBU's membership rules

(66) The Court of First Instance, in its judgment of 11 July 1996, annulled Commission Decision 93/403/EEC. The Court of First Instance assessed whether the membership rules were objective and sufficiently determinate so as to enable them to be applied uniformly and in a non-discriminatory manner vis-à-vis all potential active members. The Court of First Instance found that the Commission had omitted to carry out such an examination when exempting those rules. It did not comment on the restrictive nature of the membership rules.

(67) The Commission recognises that Decision 93/403/EEC, because of its ambiguous drafting, gave grounds to the interpretation by the Court of First Instance that the Commission had considered the EBU's membership rules to be restrictive of competition and had exempted them, which was actually not the case[450]. Indeed, the conditions for active membership of the EBU set out in Article 3(3) of the EBU Statutes were not even notified to the Commission by the EBU; only the 'Eurovision system' was notified.

(68) The Commission continues to consider that the membership rules of a professional

---

[449] [1974] ECR 409.

[450] See in particular recital 50 and the obligation imposed on the EBU in Article 2 of Decision 93/403/EEC.

association of broadcasters cannot in themselves restrict competition within the meaning of Article 81(1) of the EC Treaty. It has to be remembered that many other organisations and associations in Europe, with economic activities in the market, have internal rules establishing conditions for membership comparable to those of the EBU[451]. There can be no obligation on such associations under Article 81(1) of the EC Treaty to accept members against their will. This is in particular true for associations like the EBU with a market position which does not allow them to eliminate competition (see recitals 100 to 103). Third parties wishing to create similar associations are free to do so.

(69)    The Commission finds that it is a completely separate issue whether within such an association, restrictions of competition might have been agreed. These possible restrictions will be assessed separately in recitals 71 to 80.

(70)    The Commission notes that the EBU membership rules which were in force at the time of the Decision 93/403/EEC annulled by the Court of First Instance, have been substantially amended. Indeed, the EBU transmitted to the Commission, on 27 August 1996, the Guidelines of interpretation of criteria for EBU active membership which were adopted on 12 August 1992. The 1992 Guidelines already contained a quantified criterion on the population coverage condition and detailed explanations on the programme and own production obligations. The membership rules and the Guidelines of Interpretation were again amended on 3 April 1998[452] by the EBU. The result is that the conditions set out in the membership rules were further quantified[453].

## C. Restriction of competition between the EBU members as a result of the notified agreements

(71)    The EBU rules governing the joint acquisition and sharing of television rights to sporting events and the use of the Eurovision signal have as their object and effect the restriction of competition between members.

## C.1. The joint acquisition of rights

(72)    The EBU rules governing the joint acquisition of television rights to sporting events on an exclusive basis have as their object and effect the restriction of competition between members.

(73)    As a result of the EBU statutes (Article 13(4)) and from the nature of Eurovision as a solidarity system, the EBU members bind themselves to jointly acquire television rights to sporting events. Therefore, the joint acquisition of rights within the framework of Eurovision restricts and, in many cases, eliminates competition between the participants in the Eurovision system. Instead of bidding against each other, members participate in joint negotiations and agree among themselves the financial and other conditions for the acquisition of rights. The restriction of competition exists notwithstanding the fact that the internal EBU rules governing the negotiation and acquisition of rights are only recommendations and not legally binding. As already stated, it follows from both the EBU Statutes (Article 13(4)) and from the nature of Eurovision as a solidarity system that members bind them-

---

[451] For an example of an association orgnaising fairs, see Commission Decision 77/722/EEC of 7-11-1977 in Case 'BPICA' (OJ L 299, 299, 23-11-1977, p. 18).

[452] The amended Article 3 of the EBU Statutes and the amended Guidelines of interpretation have been published by the EBU on the internet: http:/www.ebu.ch. See also recitals 9 to 13 describing the EBU organisation.

[453] See paragraphs 95 and 97 of the Court of First Instance's judgment.

selves to respect the common interest and to comply with the internal rules set up in this common interest. There is therefore pressure on the individual members to engage in joint negotiations. Members who are interested in acquiring the rights do, in fact, participate in the joint negotiations, and negotiate separately only once those joint negotiations have officially been declared to have failed. These cases are very rare.

(74)   Without the joint acquisition of rights within the framework of Eurovision, the EBU members would, in principle, compete with each other for the acquisition of television rights to sporting events. In particular, there are Member States with two or more EBU members, which would normally compete with each other for television rights to international events for broadcasting at national level[454]. Furthermore, there are EBU members which broadcast via satellite and cable into other member's countries and which, therefore, would normally have to acquire the rights for those countries in competition with the national members[455].

(75)   In addition, when considering the obligation for the EBU-members to jointly acquire the rights at issue it has to be taken into account that those rights are in general sold on an exclusive basis (see recitals 50 to 58). Under those circumstances, the obligation on the EBU-members to acquire jointly could have a particularly harmful effect in the market. In fact, non-EBU members would not, in principle, have access to those rights at all. That is why the EBU submitted the 1993 and 1999 sub-licensing schemes, following the Commission's intervention.

## C.2. The sharing of the Eurovision rights

(76)   The Eurovision rights are shared between the EBU members participating in the joint acquisition of the rights for a specific sporting event. All members participating in the agreement are entitled to the full benefit of the rights regardless of the territorial scope of their activity and regardless of their technical means of broadcasting. However, members which compete for the same national audience (several members in one country or members broadcasting from their country into the country of another member in the same language) have to agree among themselves on the procedure for attributing priority to one of them.

(77)   The Eurovision system notified provides that several members in one country are meant to agree to share the rights, for example by alternating transmission of the event. If no such procedure can be agreed on, there exists the theoretical possibility that all the members concerned become entitled to broadcast the rights with respect to the country or countries in question without taking into account the other members' programming. However, the solidarity principle which forms the basis for the Eurovision system creates a strong incentive for the members to agree on the sharing of the rights. Indeed, in practice the rights are almost always shared among the members. Finally, members which provide coverage of an event (i.e. produce the signal) are, unless otherwise agreed, entitled to priority over foreign members aiming their broadcast at the same national audience.

(78)   Therefore, the rules on the sharing of rights restrict competition because the EBU members have to agree among themselves on the procedure for sharing the rights. In their absence the EBU members would compete for the same national audience, in particular when there is more than one member in one country.

---

[454]  France, Denmark, Germany, United Kingdom, Finland.

[455]  According to the relevant EBU rules, all members participating in the joint acquisition of Eurovision rights are entitled to the full benefit of the rights regardless of the territorial scope of their activity.

### C.3. The exchange of the Eurovision signal

(79)    For events which take place within the Eurovision area the coverage (television signal consisting of basic video and international sound-feed) is produced by a member in the country concerned and is available to all other members via the Eurovision programme exchange system. The Eurovision programme exchange system is based on reciprocity: whenever one of the participating members covers an event, in particular a sporting event, which takes place on its own national territory and is of potential interest to other Eurovision members, it offers its coverage free of charge to all the other Eurovision members on the understanding that, in return, it will receive corresponding offers from all the other members in respect of events taking place in their respective countries. The originating member also provides the necessary infrastructure to other interested members such as commentary positions.

(80)    Therefore, the rules on the exchange of the Eurovision signal restrict competition because they might oblige one member to offer the transmission signal to another member of the EBU free of charge.

### D. Effect on trade between Member States

(81)    The Eurovision system concerns cross-border acquisition and use of television rights within the Community. This applies in particular to the joint acquisition of the rights by members from different Member States. The notified agreements will affect trade between Member States.

### E. Appreciability of the restrictions of competition and the effect on trade between Member States

(82)    Many of the international sporting events addressed by the Eurovision system, such as the Olympic Games, are of such widespread appeal and of such economic importance, that any restriction on the acquisition, sharing or exchange of the Eurovision signal of the corresponding television rights among the European broadcasters is appreciable for the purposes of Article 81(1) of the EC Treaty and Article 53(1) of the EEA Agreement.

(83)    The best example of the economic importance and therefore the appreciability of the joint acquisition of rights by the EBU is the last bid for the rights for the Olympic Games between 2000 and 2008 which were bought by the EBU for a total of USD 1,44 billion. News Corporation had bid USD 2 billion for the same rights. There is no question as to the appeal for European viewers of such a sporting event.

### 2. ARTICLE 81(3) OF THE EC TREATY AND ARTICLE 53(3) OF THE EEA AGREEMENT

### A. Improvement in the production or distribution of goods and promotional technical and economic progress

### A.1. The joint acquisition of rights

(84)    The joint acquisition of rights in the framework of the Eurovision system improves the distribution of television services and promotes technical and economic progress.

(85)    Without the joint acquisition of rights the EBU members and in particular the smaller members would have more difficult access to the relevant television rights to sporting events.

(86)    Indeed, the joint acquisition reduces the transaction costs, which would be associated with a multitude of separate negotiations, improving the purchasing condi-

tions. In addition, it is guaranteed that the negotiations are carried out by the most competent negotiator. This means either the national member in the country where the event takes place, which is familiar with local conditions, or the EBU itself, which has specialised staff experienced in negotiations on an international level. Therefore, the smaller members without such specialised staff benefit in particular in the context of the acquisition of rights for major international events. In the context of the joint negotiations the specific interests and needs of the participants in the joint acquisition are taken care of. In separate negotiations members, in particular members from small countries, would find it more difficult to secure contracts suitable for specific needs.

(87)   Therefore, as a result of this joint acquisition more sporting events are broadcast by a larger number of broadcasters. The resulting better coverage of the sporting events improves distribution.

### A.2. The sharing of the Eurovision rights

(88)   Without the Eurovision rules which lead to the sharing of rights and the alternation of the transmission of an event by the members concerned, there would be less coverage of the event in question. Indeed, when at national level two or more members in the same country or members broadcasting from their country into the country of another member in the same language participate in the joint acquisition, there will usually be an alternation of the transmission of an event by the members concerned. This sharing means that the alternating members can guarantee quasi-permanent coverage of the sporting event in question, for example of the Olympic Games.

(89)   Therefore, distribution is improved as a result of the EBU's internal rules which govern the sharing of the Eurovision rights.

### A.3. The exchange of the Eurovision signal

(90)   As a result of the reciprocity and solidarity principles of the Eurovision system as set out in the EBU statutes, any EBU member will be obliged to produce free of charge the television signal for events taking place in its country, even if it is not itself interested in the event, in order to enable other interested EBU members to show the event. This leads to more sports programmes being produced and shown on television. Therefore, distribution is improved.

### B. Benefit to consumers
### B.1. The joint acquisition of rights

(91)   As a result of the joint acquisition of rights, the participants in the Eurovision system can show more and higher quality, sports programmes, both popular sports and minority sports, to European television viewers. In particular, national participants in the joint acquisition from smaller countries can provide their chair viewers with a broad range of international sporting events with a commentary in their own language and tailored to their specific national interests.

### B.2. The sharing of the Eurovision rights

(92)   The sharing of the Eurovision rights benefits European television viewers because as explained at recital 88 when, at national level, there is an alternation of the Eurovision rights (between two or more members in the same country or members broadcasting from their country into the country of another member in the same language), there will usually be a quasi-permanent coverage of the sporting event in question.

### B.3. The exchange of the Eurovision signal

(93)    Since in each country there is at least one EBU member providing and producing sports programmes, it can be taken for granted that essentially all events that are of potential interest beyond national boundaries will be covered and will be available to the members and their television viewers through the Eurovision area. This is to the benefit of consumers.

### C. Indispensability

(94)    The Eurovision rules governing the joint acquisition, the sharing of the rights and the exchange of the signal are, technically and economically, interdependent matters which are based on the principle of solidarity between the Eurovision participants. Therefore, if EBU members were forced to negotiate separately for television rights, were not to agree on the sharing of the rights or were not to offer the signal free of charge, the solidarity system would be jeopardised and with it all the objectives in terms of improvement of distribution and benefits to consumers.

### C.1. The joint acquisition of rights

(95)    The joint acquisition of rights by the participants in the Eurovision system is indispensable for the achievement of the objectives described.

(96)    It is necessary for members to be required to refrain from separate negotiations once joint negotiations have commenced. The success of the joint negotiations would be put in jeopardy if individual members, and in particular the larger ones, simultaneously engaged in separate negotiations for national or transnational rights. It must be emphasised that EBU members are free to engage in separate negotiations once the joint negotiations are declared to have failed.

(97)    It is necessary under the Eurovision system for all members wishing to acquire the rights to be included within the joint negotiations. Otherwise Eurovision could not find a place at the negotiating table where the rights to the top sporting events are sold and the improvements in distribution described could not be brought about.

### C.2. The sharing of the Eurovision rights

(98)    The agreements on the sharing of the Eurovision rights between the participants in the joint acquisition do not contain restrictions which are not indispensable to the attainment of the aforementioned objectives. These sharing agreements, in particular in domestic situations (with more than one member in the same country alternating the broadcast of the sporting event in question) or members broadcasting from their country into the country of another member in the same language, are indispensable to attain the maximum possible coverage of sporting events to the benefit of the European viewers.

### C.3. The exchange of the Eurovision signal

(99)    The agreements on the exchange of the Eurovision signal do not contain restrictions which are not indispensable to the attainment of the objectives. The free exchange between the members of the Eurovision signal is an expression of the reciprocity and solidarity principles which form the basis for the Eurovision system and which improve the coverage of sports events to the benefit the European television viewers. It is in particular indispensable for the smaller members which sometimes could not afford the costs of production and the fee for the use of other broadcasters' signal.

## D. Non-elimination of competition in respect of a substantial part of the products in question

### D.1. The joint acquisition of rights

(100)  The joint acquisition of the rights in the framework of the Eurovision system will not eliminate competition in respect of a substantial part of the rights in question.

(101)  It should be recalled, first, that the EBU in principle only acquires international events and not national events, which are the majority of the sports events shown on television, secondly, that there is increasing competition outside the Eurovision system from media groups and brokers and, thirdly, that EBU's market position has been declining for the last 10 years[456]. From this perspective, the jointly acquired Eurovision rights can hardly eliminate competition to a substantial extent.

(102)  However, the Commission was concerned that some of the jointly acquired rights affect sporting events, for instance the Olympic Games, of particular economic and popular importance, which could constitute a separate market on their own and rights to which are exclusively held by the Eurovision members.

(103)  To address these concerns the EBU has modified the notified agreements to include a set of sub-licensing rules which make sure that non-EBU members have extensive access to the Eurovision sports rights. This counterbalances the restrictive effects of the joint acquisition of the sports rights. The schemes will provide extensive live and deferred transmission access for non-members on reasonable terms.

D.2. The sharing of the Eurovision rights

(104)  The restriction arising from the sharing of the Eurovision rights cannot eliminate competition given the current market structure and considering that non-EBU members will be able to participate in the broadcast of the sporting events in question following the EBU sub-licensing schemes.

### D.3. The exchange of the Eurovision signal

(105)  The restriction stemming from the exchange of the Eurovision signal cannot eliminate competition given the current market structure. The economic disadvantage for non-EBU members of not having access to the free signal exchanged in the framework of the Eurovision system is of limited economic impact and cannot eliminate competition between broadcasters.

### E. The access scheme for non-EBU members

(106)  The scheme includes the general rules on EBU non-members' access to Eurovision sport programmes adopted on 2 February 1993 and the rules relating to exploitation of Eurovision rights on pay-TV channels adopted on 26 March 1999[457]. Both sets of rules have to be read together, as the 1999 scheme applies as an obligation additional to the 1993 scheme

### (i) The 1993 sub-licensing rules

(107)  Under the scheme submitted to the Commission on 26 February 1993, the EBU and its members undertake to grant non-member broadcasters extensive access to Eurovision sports programmes for which the rights have been acquired through collective negotiations. The 1993 scheme grants live and deferred transmission rights to third parties of jointly acquired Eurovision sports rights. The 1993 sub-licensing rules were adapted to a situation in the market in which the EBU mem-

---

[456]  See Annex III.
[457]  See Annexes II and III.

bers did not enter the pay-TV field via thematic channels. Indeed, the 1993 scheme was sufficient to grant extensive access to non-EBU members in a context in which the EBU members' activities in the broadcast of sporting events took place exclusively in the framework of generalist channels broadcasting in free-to-air television.

### (ii) The 1999 sub-licensing rules

(108)  First, as an introduction to this scheme, it is useful to recall the evolution of the European television market which led to the EBU members entering the thematic channels' segment. In each European country, television started as a national public service operation on one channel. This channel offered generalist programming. Then second channels were established, normally but not always offered by the same broadcaster. These second channels, while also offering generalist programming, tried to differentiate themselves from the first channel; usually, whereas mass appeal programming of all genres (news, sports, entertainment and so forth) was more concentrated on the first channel, the second channel specialised more in programming catering for minority interests. Then, in the late 1980s, commercial television started. Again, there would normally be one or two generalist channels with mass appeal programming, and further commercial channels which looked more specifically for niches in the market. Then came transnational programme channels (such as TVS, Eurosport, Euronews and NBC). Then, as a logical further development, came specialised (thematic) channels, especially in the fields of news, sport, music, films and children's programming. These channels may be pan-European (such as MTV, Eurosport, Euronews) or national (linguistic area) such as Kinderkanal. While some of these channels are still essentially advertising-financed, others are offered as pay-TV, and sometimes even pay-per-view television. Digital technology offers the technical potential for more and more such channels, and the large majority (if not the totality) of such further channels will certainly be both thematic (in terms of programming) and pay-TV (in terms of financing). Therefore, in the late 1990s when the possibilities for technical delivery were exploding and as a consequence, a multitude of different channels were offered and audiences were becoming more and more fragmented, the EBU members had to adapt and to diversify its programming offer accordingly with thematic channels. In this context, the 1999 access scheme became necessary in order to ensure that the joint acquisition origin of the EBU's rights would not unfairly place other pay-TV competitors at a disadvantage.

(109)  The 1999 scheme was submitted as part of the notified agreements by the EBU in order to reflect the changes in the pay-TV market and to ensure that competition would not be eliminated in that field. The 1999 scheme relating to pay-TV establishes a stricter sub-licensing regime for the EBU. Pursuant to the 1999 EBU rules applicable to competing pay-TV channels, a non-EBU member has the right to transmit, on its pay-TV channel, identical or comparable competitions to those presented on the EBU member's pay-TV channel arising from Eurovision rights. This places the non-EBU pay-TV operators on an equal footing with the EBU members with regard to those jointly acquired sports rights used in the pay-TV field.

(110)  Finally, it must be emphasised that EBU members are free to grant contractual access for their national territories on more favourable terms if they wish to do so. As regards the financial conditions, it is also important that any disputes will be determined by arbitration which will ensure reasonable prices.

# 3. DURATION OF THE EXEMPTION, CONDITIONS AND OBLIGATIONS

## 3.1. Duration of the exemption, starting date for exemption

(111)  Pursuant to Article 8 of Regulation No 17, a decision in application of Article 81(3) of the EC Treaty is to be issued for a specified period and conditions and obligations may be attached thereto. Pursuant to Article 6 of Regulation No 17, the date from which such a decision takes effect cannot be earlier than the date of notification.

(112)  In this case, this decision takes effect from 26 February 1993 when the EBU submitted to the Commission the access scheme for non EBU members to Eurovision sports rights and consequently all four conditions pursuant to Article 81(3) of the EC Treaty and Article 53(3) of the EEA Agreement were met. Afterwards, the market conditions changed and in 1999 additional sub-licensing rules were needed to reflect those changes in the market. However, during the period 1993 to 1999, the 1993 sub-licensing rules were sufficient to respond to the market situation. To conclude, the agreements should be exempted from 26 February 1993.

## 3.2. Duration of exemption, length of the exemption period

(113)  The Commission has explained in this Decision the structure and development of the relevant market which clearly marks a decline in the EBU's market position. On the other hand, the Commission considers it necessary to ensure that the joint acquisition of rights to particularly important sporting events takes place under conditions which respect the relevant competition rules and grant sufficient access to non-EBU members. Among those particularly important sporting events, the most relevant are undoubtedly the Olympic Games and, in particular, the summer Olympic Games. It is, therefore, appropriate to take the moment at which the rights for the next summer Olympic Games will be offered in the market as a reference for the length of the exemption period in order to allow the Commission to reassess the competition situation at that time and make sure that the EBU's position will not eliminate competition if a change in the market structure occurs. The EBU has already acquired the rights for the 2008 summer Olympic Games. The negotiations for the 2012 Olympic Games will take place, following settled practice, six years in advance, i.e. in 2006. It is, therefore, appropriate to grant the present exemption until 31 December 2005.

(114)  In conclusion, given the structure and development of the relevant market and the effect of the notified rules thereon, exemption is granted pursuant to Article 8(1) of Regulation No 17 from 26 February 1993 until 31 December 2005. Regarding the European Economic Area Agreement, the exemption pursuant to Article 53(3) starts on 1 January 1994, date of entry into force of that Agreement.

## 3.3. Conditions and obligations

## 3.3.1. Conditions

(115)  In order to ensure contractual access for third parties to the television rights to sporting events acquired within the framework of Eurovision, such contractual access must be allowed under the agreements with the rights owners (sports organisers or rights agents). It is therefore a condition of the exemption that the EBU and its members only conclude agreements which allow the EBU and its members to grant access to third parties in accordance with the access scheme for non EBU members to Eurovision sports rights and the sub-licensing rules relating to the exploitation of Eurovision rights on pay-TV channels or, subject to the approval of the EBU, on more favourable conditions.

### 3.3.2. Obligations

(116)  In order to assist the Commission during the exemption period in checking whether the rules on contractual access for non-EBU members to Eurovision sports rights and the sub-licensing rules relating to the exploitation of Eurovision rights on pay-TV channels are applied in an appropriate, reasonable and non-discriminatory manner, the EBU must be under an obligation to inform the Commission of all amendments and additions to the access schemes and of all arbitration procedures concerning disputes under the access schemes[458],

## HAS ADOPTED THIS DECISION:

Article 1

Pursuant to Article 81(3) of the EC Treaty and Article 53(3) of the EEA Agreement and subject to Article 2 of this Decision, the provisions of Article 81(1) of the EC Treaty are hereby declared inapplicable from 26 February 1993 until 31 December 2005 and the provisions of Article 53(1) of the EEA Agreement are hereby declared inapplicable from 1 January 1994 until 31 December 2005, to the following notified agreements:

(a)    the joint acquisition of sport television rights;
(b)    the sharing of the jointly acquired sport television rights;
(c)    the exchange of the signal for sporting events;
(d)    the access scheme for non EBU members to Eurovision sports rights;
(e)    the sub-licensing rules relating to the exploitation of Eurovision rights on pay-TV channels.

Article 2

The declaration of exemption contained in Article 1 shall be subject to the following conditions and obligations:

(a)    The condition
       The EBU and its members shall collectively acquire television rights to sporting events only under agreements which allow the EBU and its members to grant access to third parties in conformity with the access scheme for non EBU members to Eurovision sports rights of 24 February 1993 and the sub-licensing rules relating to the exploitation of Eurovision rights on pay-TV channels of 26 March 1999 or, subject to the approval of the EBU, on conditions more favourable to the non-member.

(b)    The obligation
       The EBU shall inform the Commission of any amendments and additions to the access scheme for non EBU members to Eurovision sports rights of 24 February 1993 and the sub-licensing rules relating to the exploitation of Eurovision rights on pay-TV channels of 26 March 1999. In addition, the EBU shall inform the Commission of all arbitration procedures concerning disputes under the access scheme for non-EBU members to Eurovision sports rights of 24 February 1993 and the sub-licensing rules relating to the exploitation of Eurovision rights on pay-TV channels of 26 March 1999.

Article 3

This Decision is addressed to: European Broadcasting Union Ancienne Route 17A CH – 1218 Grand-Saconnex ( Geneva ).

Done at Brussels, 10 May 2000.

---

[458]  (28) See Annexes I and II.

For the Commission
Mario Monti
Member of the Commission

## ANNEX I

## EBU NON-MEMBERS' ACCESS TO EUROVISION SPORTS PROGRAMMES

I.    Principle

The EBU and its members undertake to grant non-member broadcasters extensive access to Eurovision sports programmes the rights for which have been acquired via collective negotiations, in accordance with the terms and stipulations set out below and on a non discriminatory basis.

II.   Access requests

Broadcasters providing a pan-European programme service shall submit their requests to the EBU.

All other broadcasters shall submit their requests to the EBU member(s) in the country in or from which they broadcast.

III.  Scope of access

Access can be granted for the entire geographical area covered by the Eurovision contract.

Access is in principle granted on a non-exclusive basis, but it may also be granted on an exclusive basis vis-a-vis other non-members of Eurovision.

The contract concluded with a non-member stipulates the number of transmissions granted and the period for which the rights are acquired. It may also oblige the non-member to credit on-screen the organisation(s) which granted the access.

IV.   Conditions of access

The terms and conditions of access are freely negotiated between the EBU or the member(s) in the country concerned and the non-member. However, the EBU and its members will in no circumstances grant less favourable access than stipulated below.

1. Live transmission

    1.1.    Transnational channels

        If an event is not transmitted live by any of the members of Eurovision to any of the audiences at which the programme service of a non-member transnational channel is normally aimed, the latter may transmit the event live, except for those parts or competitions which any such member has reserved for its own live transmission.

    1.2.    National channels

        If an event is not transmitted live by an EBU member in a given country, a non-member in that country may transmit the event live, except for those parts or competitions which the member has reserved for its own live transmission.

    1.3.    Definition of live transmission

        An event is considered to be transmitted live if the majority of the principal competitions constituting it are transmitted live.

        Where for a given event two or more television signals are available simultaneously, live transmission shall be considered to be given if for the majority of the time during which the principal competitions take place the Eurovision member transmits live.

2. Deferred transmission

    2.1.    Where a non-member channel may not, pursuant to point 1, transmit live, it may nevertheless make a deferred transmission of the entire event or of the day's competitions, or a summary thereof, not earlier than one hour after the end of the event or of the last competition of the day, provided that such transmission shall not commence before 10.30 p.m. local time (London time for pan-European channels).

However, if such a channel does not take advantage of the possibility offered it to transmit live, it cannot make a deferred transmission until after the end of the presentation of a summary by the EBU member(s) concerned.

2.2. Subject to points 2.1 and 3.1, dedicated sports channels may re-broadcast the event an unlimited number of times, in whole or in summary form, such re-broadcasts to take place within 90 days of the opening day of the event.

3. Financial conditions

3.1. The global fee for access to the Eurovision programme is to be negotiated with the EBU or with the national member(s) concerned. The access fee shall duly reflect the fact that the programme is aimed at the same audience. In assessing the overall commercial value of the programme, all the relevant factors of the specific case shall be taken into account (in particular the rights fee paid by EBU or the member(s) concerned; the cost of production of the signal; any additional costs incurred by the EBU member(s) (such as Eurovision coordination costs, special EBU operations group costs, etc.) the results of which are also to the benefit of the non-member; the number of households reached by the programme service; the language(s) of the programme service; the targeted audience's specific interest in the particular programme; the timing, number and duration of the transmission(s)).

3.2. For routing the signal, the non-member is free to make its own arrangements. At the non-member's request, the EBU can assume responsibility for routing the signal via its own network. In such cases, the EBU will submit an estimate for the cost of routing the signal to the non-member's premises, plus transmission coordination and supervision.

4. News access

Except where national law or regulation provides otherwise, the following provisions shall apply:

Per event or day of competition the non-member is entitled to transmit up to two news reports of up to 90 seconds each, with the possibility of repeating once one such report. These news reports must be included, within 24 hours, in regularly scheduled general news bulletins or in regularly scheduled general sports news programmes of dedicated sports channels.

Non-members shall pay a fee based on the number of minutes transmitted. Tariffs shall be mutually agreed, country by country, between the member and non-member; such tariffs shall apply for news access to sports programmes granted by either party.

For pan-European services, the fee will be based on the average rate applied for countries within the European Economic Community.

5. Arbitration

5.1. In the event of a dispute over the access fee where all other access conditions have been agreed, at the request of the non-member the matter will be submitted to arbitration by an independent expert or, if both parties agree, by three such experts. If the transmission is carried out prior to arbitration the fee must be paid before the transmission subject to review by arbitration.

5.2. The expert will be nominated jointly. In the case of an arbitration board, each party nominates one expert and the two nominated experts will jointly nominate a third. Failing agreement, nomination will be by the President of the competent Court of Appeals in the case of national arbitration and by the President of the International Chamber of Commerce in the case of international arbitration.

5.3. Arbitration will be carried out in the city where the organisation granting the access has its headquarters. Unless otherwise agreed between the parties, the law and the language of the country of arbitration will apply. However, where EBU grants access to an organisation operating a transnational programme service with headquarters in an EC country, the law and the language of the latter country shall apply.

5.4. The expert(s) shall not be bound by any procedural rules. However, the parties' right to make both oral and written presentations to the expert(s) shall be guaranteed.

5.5. The expert(s) shall fix the access fee in accordance with the criteria listed in point 3.1. The decision of the expert(s) shall be final and binding and shall take effect as a provision of the parties' agreement.

5.6. The parties shall bear their own individual costs and share the costs of the arbitration equally between them.

6. Reciprocity

For all sports programmes for which a non-member has the contractual capacity to grant access to other broadcasters, the non-member is expected to grant such access to interested EBU members on conditions comparable to those outlined above.

## ANNEX II

Sub-licensing rules relating to the exploitation of Eurovision rights on pay-TV channels
The following rules shall apply, as an obligation additional to the general rules on EBU non-members' access to Eurovision sports programmes adopted on 24 February 1993, when collectively acquired rights are to be exploited on a member's own pay-TV channel.

(i) If a Eurovision member intends to use Eurovision sports programming on its own pay-TV channel (pay-per-view, pay-per-channel or, subject to point (v), a channel which is part of a digital bouquet or of a basic cable package), it shall offer competing pay-TV channels in the same pay-TV category and in the same country the possibility to do the same.

To do the same means

- identical embargo, if any, to that applying to the member's own pay-TV channel,
- identical competitions to those presented on the member's own pay-TV channel (e.g. eliminary round matches, mixed-doubles tournament, everything up to the quarter-finals, etc.). Where the member presents a mix of competitions which take place simultaneously, or at least partially overlap in time, the non-member may choose to present its own mix, unless instead it prefers to cover the entirety of one given competition, or
- comparable/equivalent competitions to those presented on the member's own pay-TV channel (e.g. of 10 matches available for presentation on a pay-TV channel, the member would retain five matches for its own channel and offer

five equivalent matches to the competing pay-TV channel). If the non-member is not satisfied that 'equivalence' has been given, it shall be entitled to demand the rights for identical competitions,
  — identical volume of broadcast time as that offered on the member's own pay-TV channel (e.g. a maximum of two hours per day).
(ii)    The member remains free to offer the non-member more favourable conditions.
(iii)   The fee to be paid by the non-member shall fairly reflect the terms on which the rights were obtained by the Eurovision member, taking into account in particular the complementary nature of the rights, the volume and timing of the broadcast and which of the three pay-TV categories referred to in point (i) the channel operates in, as well as the number of its subscribers and the amount of its monthly subscription or per-view fee.
The same pricing policy shall apply where a member grants a non-member the right of pay-TV coverage, without itself exercising that right.
In case of a dispute over the fee, the matter shall be submitted to arbitration, in accordance with point 5 of the general rules on EBU non-members' access to Eurovision sports programmes.
(iv)    The member shall announce any possibility under the foregoing paragraphs for non-members' pay-TV channels sufficiently in advance of the event, but in no case later than
  — three months before Olympic Games, World and European Football Championships and World Athletics Championships, and
  — two months before any other events.
(v)     Channels which are part of a digital bouquet (basic package) or a basic cable package are not subject to the foregoing rules if the same programme service is simultaneously broadcast, in analogue or digital mode, for free-to-air reception in the same country.
In the case of a pan-European sports channel, the same shall apply where the service is broadcast, with at least one sound commentary in one of the major European languages, for free-to-air reception throughout the European Broadcasting Area, and where for the convenience of the respective local audience the same service is simultaneously made available as part of a digital bouquet or a basic cable package with a local sound commentary.

## ANNEX III

Hours of sports broadcasting in Europe
[...]

## ANNEX IV

The costs of the European rights to the Olympics for the EBU
[...]

---

## * 2.4.55. ANSWER ON BEHALF OF THE COMMISSION TO WRITTEN QUESTION P-1542/00 BY MARGRIETUS VAN DEN BERG (PSE), 6 JUNE 2000[459] *

Subject: Sponsorship for Euro 2000

---

[459] Question of 10-5-2000; OJ C 46 E, 13-2-2001, p. 201.

**2.4.56.   COMMISSION DECISION DECLARING A CONCENTRATION TO BE COMPATIBLE WITH THE COMMON MARKET (CASE NO IV/M.1978 – TELECOM ITALIA / NEWS TELEVISION / STREAM) ACCORDING TO COUNCIL REGULATION (EEC) NO 4064/89, 29 JUNE 2000[460]**

Brussels, 29.06.2000
SG(2000)D/104578
To the notifying parties:
Dear Sirs,

Subject: Case No COMP/M. 1978 – Telecom Italia/News Television/Stream
Notification of 25.5.2000 pursuant to Article 4 of Council Regulation No 4064/89

1.  The notification concerns the proposed acquisition by Telecom Italia (TI) and the British News Television ('News') of joint control of Stream.

2.  After examination of the notification, the Commission has concluded that the notified operation falls within the scope of application of Council Regulation No. 4064/89 and does not raise serious doubts as to its compatibility with the common market and with the functioning of the EEA Agreement.

**I. THE PARTIES**

3.  Telecom Italia is the leading telecommunications operator in Italy providing the full range of telecommunication services.

4.  News is a subsidiary of News International plc (which is controlled by News Corporation Limited) is a UK based company. The News group is active in printing and publishing of national newspapers in the UK, development and sale of conditional access software, warehousing, transportation, and the provision of satellite television in the UK and Republic of Ireland, the production and distribution of filmed entertainment, television broadcasting, books, newspapers, magazines, insert publishing and data processing.
    Stream has been acting as an operator of satellite and cable digital pay-TV in Italy since 1998.

**II. THE OPERATION**

5.  Before the present concentration the shares of Stream were divided among TI (35%), News (35%), Cecchi Gori Group FINMAVI S.p.A. (CGG) (18%) and S.D.S. -Società Diritti Sportivi S.r.l. (SDS).
    Following a capital increase from 400 billion to 940 billion Italian lira, which increased the shareholding of the parties to 41, 7% each, TI and News on the one hand and SDS and CGG on the other hand agreed on the transfer of the remaining shares of SDS and CGG to TI and News respectively. As a result, TI and News will each have a 50% stake in Stream.

**III. CONCENTRATION**

6.  The operation involves the acquisition of joint control by TI and News. Stream is an existing company. It will continue to perform on a lasting basis all the functions of an autonomous economic entity.

---

[460] OJ C 066, 15-3-2002, p. 14.

## IV. COMMUNITY DIMENSION

7.    The undertakings have a combined aggregate worldwide turnover in excess of EUR 5 billion. (TI: [...], News:[...]. TI and News have each a Community wide turnover of more than EUR 250 Million (TI: [...], News:[...]. They do not achieve more than two-thirds of their aggregate Community-wide turnover within one and the same Member State. The notified operation therefore has a Community dimension.

## V. COMPETITIVE ASSESSMENT

**Pay-TV-market**

8.    The present operation concerns the market for pay-TV, which the Commission has regarded to be distinct from the free-access-TV, which – in contrast to pay-TV – is financed by public fees or/and advertising rates and offers a more general program mix whereas pay-TV has to meet more specified consumer-preferences to persuade potential viewers to pay extra fees[461]. However, as the present case does not raise competition concerns even in the narrowest possible market of pay-TV, the product market can be left open.

9.    The pay-TV is still a national market due to language differences throughout the Community which continue to hinder a wide expansion of television channels outside their home countries and distinct cultural and political interests of the respective national audience, which have to be taken into account by the TV-operators when designing a program-mix[462].

10.   In Italy the pay-TV market is still at a very early stage of its development being only penetrated to a degree of approximately [5-15%]% of all Italian households. There are two operators active – Telepiù and Stream, with Stream holding a share of [15 – 25] of the market in terms of subscribers by the end of 1999 ([...] subscribers) and Telepiù, which is controlled by Canal+, accounting for [75 – 85] of the market ([...]subscribers by the end of December 1999). In terms of turnover Telepiù even holds marketshares of approximately [...]%, leaving only [...]% to Stream.

11.   The increase of the shareholding of the parties to the concentration does not lead to an addition of market shares. However, due to the activities of the parent companies in upstream markets the proposed concentration will have vertical effects.

**Transmission-capacity**

12.   According the information given in the notification, Telecom Italia (through its subsidiary Telespazio) provides [75 – 85]% of transmission capacity (in terms of turnover) needed for pay-TV on the Italian market, which – as the parties suggest – comprises cable as well as satellite capacity. Disaggregating transmission capacity, 82 % account for satellite capacity, which leaves 18% to cable capacity. As regards satellite capacity, Telecom Italia provides [75 – 85]% by its subsidiary Telespazio. As far as cable services are concerned, Telecom Italia – as the owner of the only existing cable network in Italy – accounts even for 100% of the capacity. Thus, independent from the product market definition, the Telecom Italia-concern is the main supplier of transmission capacity for pay-TV.

13.   As a consequence of the proposed merger, Telepiù will have to acquire the needed transmission capacity from a parent of its main competitor Stream. Nevertheless, at the present stage of the market, the proposed concentration does not give suffi-

---

[461] OJ L 53/ 1, 27-2-99 – Bertelsmann/Kirch/Premiere.
[462] More detailed, see Kirch/Richemont/Telepiù OJ C 225 of 1-8-1994.

cient evidence for foreclosure effects to the detriment of Stream's competitors.

14. Satellite capacity is transmitted via transponders, which form part of the satellite and are owned by the Satellite consortium (here: the Eutelsat Consortium, in which 48 nation participate). The Eutelsat Consortium allotes the transponders to its members. Customers wanting to lease transponder capacity, have to address the single members of the consortiums. They cannot acquire directly from the Consortium.

15. In Italy 15 digital transponders are used for the transmission of pay-TV-services, Telepazio subleases 11 transponders, three account for British Telecom and 1 for Slovenian PTT. Telepiù uses in total 8 transponders for the transmission of pay-TV, out of which only 4 are leased from Telespazio. The duration of the underlying contracts are linked to the commercial lifetime of the satellite, which is expected to be at least 12 years from the beginning of the contract onwards. Thus, Telepiù's position as regards its dependance on transmission capacity should not be worsened as a consequence of the proposed merger. In addition to that, the contract of Telepiù contains an English clause, thus balancing a prospective incentive for Telespazio to discriminate against Telepiù. In any case, Telepiù can demand transmission capacity from each of the 48 members of the Eutelsat consortium.

16. As to the Italian cable network as a second source of transmission capacity, it is developed only to a minor extent and has not played a significant role for the emerging of the pay-TV-market by now. Only Stream has connected some of its customers ([...] in total by the end of April 2000, i.e. [0-10]% of all pay-TV subscribers) by cable. (Telepiù, however, has just settled a contract on the deliverance of cable capacity with Telecom Italia to cover some blind spots, which occur with the satellite supply). The further development of the cable is, nevertheless, difficult to predict. In fact, the 'Socrates Project', which formed the framework which led to the set up of the existing cable network and initially aimed at the connection of all 20 Mio Italian households, had been interrupted in 1998, due to the high costs of the project and the related economic risks. It is not foreseeable whether or when the Italian cable network, which connects 1 Mio of the Italian households at present, will be further extended. It is also not certain that it will be Telecom Italia, who takes the initiative. As the current cable network is not widespread and as considerable investments would be necessary during the start-up phase of such an expansion, it is conceivable that a third party will have to take over the cable. It must also be noted that the Commission is just developing a regulatory framework for communications infrastructure and associated services to secure fair and non-discriminatory access to telecommunication networks: As regards access to cable TV-networks, an 'obligation to negotiate access' on a cable TV operator with significant market power for delivery of broadband services with the possibility of a National Regulatory Authority's intervention when commercial negotiation fails is foreseen[463].

## Set-top-boxes and conditional-access-technology

17. The parties state that Telecom Italia through its subsidiary Italtel participate by a share of [35 – 45]% in the sale of set-top-boxes in Italy. Given that in 1999 Italtel sold about 99% of its set-top-boxes to Stream, the proposed concentration will have no market effects beyond the relationship of the involved parties. It is therefore not necessary to decide, whether set-top-boxes are a separate market (as the

---

[463] See: COM (1999) 539:Towards a new framework for Electronic Communications infrastructure and associated services – The 1999 Communications Review, page 30 , paragraph 4.2.4.

parties suggest) or whether they form part of the market for technical and administrative services for pay-TV. Neither has to be decided, whether the geographic market is not only national.

18.    Foreclosure effects to the detriment of Stream's competitors on the pay-TV market cannot be predicted, either, because of the fact, that – as from April 2000 – News – through the NDS group plc, in which it holds a 80% stake – provides Stream with the CA-technology NDS. To fulfil the requirements of Directive 95/47/EC on the use of standards for transmission of television signals and its Italian implementation, Stream is expected to adopt the symulcrypt option to ensure that viewers can receive digitally-transmitted services of different broadcasters by means of a single decoder. Streams competitor Telepiù uses the CA-technology SECA, belonging to the same group as Telepiù, and Irdeto. As neither NDS in the market of CA-technology nor Stream in the market of pay-TV has a dominant position in Italy this vertical effect of the operation will not lead to foreclosure effects

**Broadcasting rights**

19.    In line with previous Commissions decisions the acquisition of broadcasting rights for Pay TV channels constitutes a separate product market within the wider one for Pay TV.[464] There are two distinct categories of products in this sector. The first one, referred to as 'premium' offer, regards major sporting events and first television screenings of recent movies bearing the higher attraction on users. The second package, called 'basic' offer, includes different products, such as news, music programs, general culture programs or second wind movies, that, although not particularly attractive in themselves, usually contribute to the general programme-mix.

20.    At the present stage of Pay-TV's development, the market for broadcasting rights can be regarded as national for a number of reasons. Firstly, TV programs are nationally restricted and transmitted only in the relevant national language. Secondly, the range of programmes available and the programme mix are clearly determined by the cultural differences and the specific preferences of the relevant audience. Accordingly, broadcasting rights are generally granted for one or more specified countries or language regions. However, the geographic definition of the market can be left open for the future since neither a narrower nor a greater dimension of the market for the acquisition of broadcasting rights would entail the creation or the strengthening of a dominant position as a result of the proposed operation.

21.    With respect to major sporting events, the operation doesn't lead to the addition of market shares. Stream owns long term exclusive broadcasting rights of approximately 40% of the Italian Football League matches (7 teams out of 18) whereas Telepiu' which is the current leading operator in the Italian Pay TV sector, holds the exclusive rights for the encrypted transmission of approximately 60 % of the Italian Football League matches (11 teams out of 18 playing in the Premier League).

22.    As regards other premier products there are not significant conglomerate aspects to this concentration. Stream has acquired the broadcasting rights for the distribution of the leading children channel ('Fox Kids') produced by the 20th Century Fox, a company controlled by News Television, and, up to the present time, has

---

[464] British Interactive Broadcasting/Open (BiB), case IV/36.539 OJ L312 of 6-12-99 and also MSG Media Service, case IV/M.469 OJ L364, 31-12-1994, p.1.

mainly entered agreements concerning broadcasting rights for second wind movies. The sector is therefore still dominated by Telepiu` which has concluded output deal agreements with all the USA majors producers (Buena Vista-Disney, Columbia, Paramount, 20th Century Fox, Time Warner) and holds long-term exclusive pay-TV and pay-per view rights on all the movies released by the quoted producers. In 1998 Telepiu` had the broadcasting rights of [70- 80]% of the most profitable premier movies. Following the market investigation and due to the broad range of suppliers, it does not appear that the vertical integration between Stream and the 20th Century Fox or other companies belonging to the Newscorp Investments Group could prospectively foreclose the acquisition of broadcasting rights by Telepiu` and hinder the competition in this sector.

## VI. CONCLUSION

23.   For the above reasons, the Commission has decided not to oppose the notified operation and to declare it compatible with the common market and with the EEA Agreement. This decision is adopted in application of Article 6(1)(b) of Council Regulation (EEC) No 4064/89.

For the Commission,
(Signed) Mario Monti

——

## * 2.4.57.   COMMISSION WITHDRAWS THREAT OF FINES AGAINST TELEFÓNICA AND SOGECABLE, BUT PURSUES EXAMINATION OF THEIR JOINT FOOTBALL RIGHTS, 23 NOVEMBER 2000[465]

——

## * 2.4.58.   COMMISSION WELCOMES PROGRESS TOWARDS RESOLVING THE LONG-RUNNING FIA/FORMULA ONE CASE, 26 JANUARY 2001[466]

——

## * 2.4.59.   ANSWER ON BEHALF OF THE COMMISSION TO WRITTEN QUESTION P-71/01 BY GLYN FORD (PSE), 15 FEBRUARY 2001[467]

Subject: TV rights relating to football

——

## 2.4.60.   REFERENCE FOR A PRELIMINARY RULING BY THE HOF VAN BEROEP TE GENT BY JUDGMENT OF THAT COURT OF 3 JANUARY 2001 IN THE CASES OF S. MONNIER AGAINST GOVAN SPORTS N.V., E. VAN ANKEREN AGAINST GOVAN SPORTS N.V., GOVAN SPORTS N.V. AGAINST P. JACOBS, AND GOVAN SPORTS N.V. AGAINST D. D'HONDT (CASES C-9, 10, 11 AND 12/01), 24 FEBRUARY 2001[468]

Reference has been made to the Court of Justice of the Hof van Beroep te Gent (Court of Appeal, Ghent), received at the Court Registry on 10 January 2001, for a preliminary rul-

---

[465] IP/00/1352.
[466] IP/01/120.
[467] Question of 18-1-2001; OJ C 174 E, 19-6-2001, p. 251.
[468] OJ C 61, 24-2-2001, p. 10.

ing in the cases of S. Monnier against Govan Sports N. V. (C-9/01), E. Van Ankeren against Govan Sports N. V. (C-10/01), Govan Sports N. V. against P. Jacobs (C-11/01) and Govan Sports N. V. against D. D'Hondt (C-12/01) on the following question:

Do the provisions of the Treaty concerning the free provision of services preclude a statutory prohibition on providing employment procurement services for paid sportspersons (whether or not they are professionals) and/or does the holding of a monopoly on the provision of such services for such sportspersons by the Vlaamse Dienst voor Arbeidsbemiddeling(Flemish Employment Procurement Service) constitute an abuse of a dominant positiono. Do the provisions of the Royal Decree of 28 November 1975 thus infringe the provisions of Community law, and in particular Articles 86 and 90(1) of the EC Treaty, in so far as that Royal Decree confers the exclusive right to procure employment for paid (professional or non-professional) sportspersons on a public employment agency, in so far as that statutory provision also renders the actual pursuit of such activities by private employment agencies impossible by maintaining in force a statutory provision under which such activities are prohibited and non-observance of that provision renders the agreements concerned void, and in so far as the procurement activities concerned may extend to the nationals or to the territory of other Member States?

## * 2.4.61. ANSWER ON BEHALF OF THE COMMISSION TO WRITTEN QUESTION P-357/01 BY BART STAES (VERTS/ALE), 14 MARCH 2001[469] *

Subject: UEFA rules in contravention of European Treaties

## 2.4.62. EUROPEAN COURT OF JUSTICE, JUDGMENT OF THE COURT OF FIRST INSTANCE (FOURTH CHAMBER), MÉTROPOLE TÉLÉVISION SA V COMMISSION OF THE EUROPEAN COMMUNITIES, CASE T-206/99, 21 MARCH 2001[470]

*Competition – Rejection of a complaint – Compliance with a judgment of the Court of First Instance annulling an exemption decision of the Commission – Duty to state reasons – Obligations in relation to the investigation of complaints.*

### Content of the Court's judgment

1.  *Actions for annulment – Judgment annulling a measure – Effects – Obligation to adopt measures to comply with the judgment – Scope – Regard to be had to both the grounds and the operative part of the judgment*
    *(Art. 233 EC)*
2.  *Actions for annulment – Judgment annulling a measure – Effects – Annulment of a Commission decision granting an exemption under Article 81(3) EC – Possibility of the Commission going back on its position concerning the application of Article 81(1) EC – Conditions*
    *(Arts 81(1) EC, 230 EC and 233 EC)*
3.  *Acts of the institutions – Statement of reasons – Obligation – Scope – Decision applying the competition rules*
    *(Art. 253 EC; Council Regulation No 17, Art. 3)*

---

[469] Question of 6-2-2001; OJ C 235 E, 21-8-2001, p. 184.
[470] ECR 2001, p. II-1057.

4. *Competition – Administrative procedure – Examination of complaints – Obligations of the Commission*
   *(Council Regulation No 17, Art. 3; Commission Regulation No 99/63, Art. 6)*

5. *Competition – Administrative procedure – Examination of complaints – Assessment of the seriousness of the alleged interferences with competition and the persistence of their consequences – Practices having ceased – Duty of the Commission to ascertain whether anti-competitive effects continue*
   *(Council Regulation No 17, Art. 3)*

**Summary**

1. *When the Community judicature annuls an act of an institution, that institution is required, under Article 233 EC, to take the measures necessary to comply with the judgment. In that connection, in order to comply with the judgment and to implement it fully, the institution is required to observe not only the operative part of the judgment but also the grounds which led to the judgment and constitute its essential basis, inasmuch as they are necessary to determine the exact meaning of what is stated in the operative part. It is those grounds which, on the one hand, identify the precise provision held to be illegal and, on the other, indicate the specific reasons which underlie the finding of illegality contained in the operative part and which the institution concerned must take into account when replacing the annulled measure.*
   *( see para. 35 )*

2. *Where, in a judgment annulling a Commission decision granting an exemption under Article 81(3) EC, the Court of First Instance does not rule on the application of Article 81(1) EC, the annulling judgment cannot have the effect of preventing the Commission from going back on its position concerning the application of Article 81(1) EC. Such a change of position does, however, require a statement of reasons.*
   *It is not for the Court of First Instance, in the context of an action for the annulment of an exemption decision brought pursuant to Article 230 EC, to raise of its own motion the plea concerning application of Article 81(1) EC.*
   *(see paras 41-42)*

3. *The statement of reasons on which a decision adversely affecting a person is based must, first, be such as to enable the person concerned to ascertain the matters justifying the measure adopted so that, if necessary, he can defend his rights and verify whether the decision is well founded and, secondly, enable the Community judicature to exercise its power of review as to the legality of the decision. In that connection, the Commission is not obliged, in stating the reasons for the decisions which it takes to ensure the application of the competition rules, to adopt a position on all the arguments relied on by the persons concerned but need only set out the facts and legal considerations which are of decisive importance in the context of the decision.*
   *( see para. 44 )*

4. *In the context of investigating applications submitted to the Commission pursuant to Article 3 of Regulation No 17, although the Commission cannot be compelled to conduct an investigation, the procedural safeguards provided for by Article 6 of Regulation No 99/63 oblige it nevertheless to examine carefully the factual and legal particulars brought to its notice by the complainant in order to decide whether they disclose conduct of such a kind as to distort competition in the common market and affect trade between the Member States.*
   *Although the Commission is not obliged to investigate each of the complaints*

*lodged with it, once it decides to proceed with an investigation, it must, in the absence of a duly substantiated statement of reasons, conduct it with the requisite care, seriousness and diligence so as to be able to assess with full knowledge of the case the factual and legal particulars submitted for its appraisal by the complainants.*
*( see paras 58-59 )*

5. *When examining complaints, the Commission is required to assess in each case how serious the alleged interferences with competition are and how persistent their consequences are. That obligation means in particular that it must take into account the duration and extent of the infringements complained of and their effect on the competition situation in the Community.*
*Therefore, in deciding to dismiss a complaint of practices allegedly contrary to the Treaty, the Commission cannot rely solely on the fact that those practices have ceased, without having ascertained whether anti-competitive effects still continue.*
*( see paras 64-65 )*

**Parties**
In Case T-206/99,
Métropole Télévision SA, established in Paris (France), represented by D. Théophile, Avocat, with an address for service in Luxembourg, applicant, v Commission of the European Communities, represented by K. Wiedner and B. Mongin, acting as Agents, with an address for service in Luxembourg, defendant,
APPLICATION for the annulment of the Commission's decision of 29 June 1999 rejecting the complaint lodged by Métropole Télévision on 5 December 1997,

*The Court of First Instance of the European Communities* (Fourth Chamber),
composed of: V. Tiili, President, R.M. Moura Ramos and P. Mengozzi, Judges,
Registrar: G. Herzig,
having regard to the written procedure and further to the hearing on 27 September 2000, gives the following
Judgment

**Grounds of the judgment**
**Facts**
1    The European Broadcasting Union (EBU) is a non-profit-making trade association of radio and television organisations set up in 1950 with headquarters in Geneva (Switzerland). According to Article 2 of its Statutes, as amended on 3 July 1992, its objectives are to represent its members' interests in the field of programmes and in the legal, technical and other spheres and in particular to promote radio and television programme exchanges by all possible means – for example, Eurovision and Euroradio – and any other form of cooperation among its members and with other broadcasting organisations or groups of such organisations, and also to assist its active members in negotiations of all kinds and, when asked, to negotiate on their behalf.
2    The Statutes of the EBU had already been amended on 9 February 1988, in order to limit the number of members of Eurovision in accordance with its objectives and its method of operation, those members being defined as a particular group of broadcasters.
3    Article 3 of the Statutes, in the version of 3 July 1992, reads as follows:
    1    There are two categories of EBU members:
        – active members
        – associate members.
        ...

3 Active membership of the EBU is open to broadcasting organisations or groups of such organisations from a member country of the International Tele-communication Union (ITU) situated in the European Broadcasting Area as defined by the Radio Regulations annexed to the International Telecommuni-cation Convention, which provide in that country, with the authorisation of the competent authorities, a broadcasting service of national character and national importance, and which furthermore prove that they fulfil all the conditions set out below:

(a) they are under an obligation to cover the entire national population and in fact already cover at least a substantial part thereof, while using their best endeavours to achieve full coverage in due course;

(b) they are under an obligation to, and actually do, provide varied and bal-anced programming for all sections of the population, including a fair share of programmes catering for special/minority interests of various sections of the public, irrespective of the ratio of programme cost to au-dience;

(c) they actually produce and/or commission under their own editorial con-trol a substantial proportion of the programmes broadcast.

4 Article 6 of the Statutes, in the version of 3 July 1992, reads as follows:

1 Any member no longer fulfilling the conditions described in Article 3 shall cease to be a member of the EBU by decision of the Administrative Council, which will have immediate effect, subject to a ratifying decision by the follow-ing General Assembly taken by a majority of at least three-quarters of the votes that may be cast by those present, if members holding together at least three-quarters of the totality of EBU votes are present or represented.

However, this shall not apply to members which on 1 March 1988 did not meet all the requirements laid down in Article 3[3] (as entered into force that day). For such members, the membership conditions laid down in the previous ver-sion of Article 3 continue to be applicable.

...

5 Eurovision constitutes the main framework for the exchange of programmes among the active members of the EBU. It has been in existence since 1954 and is one of the main objectives of the EBU. According to Article 3(6) of the Statutes, in the version of 3 July 1992, 'Eurovision' is a television programme exchange system organised and coordinated by the EBU, based on the understanding that members offer to the other members, on the basis of reciprocity, ... their coverage of sports and cultural events taking place in their countries and of potential interest to other members, thereby enabling each other to provide a high quality service in these fields to their respective national audiences. Eurovision members are active members of the EBU as well as consortia of such members. All active members of the EBU may participate in a system of joint acquisition and sharing of television rights (and of the costs relating thereto) to international sports events, which are referred to as Eurovision rights.

6 Until 1 March 1988, the benefit of the services of the EBU and Eurovision was exclusively reserved to their members. However, when the Statutes were amended in 1988, a new paragraph (paragraph 6) was added to Article 3 providing that con-tractual access to Eurovision may be granted to associate members and non-mem-bers of the EBU.

7 Following a complaint of 17 December 1987 from the television channel Screensport, the Commission investigated the compatibility of the rules governing that system of joint acquisition and sharing of television rights to sports events

with Article 85 of the EC Treaty (now Article 81 EC). The complaint related in particular to the refusal of the EBU and its members to grant it sub-licences for the retransmission of sports events. On 12 December 1988, the Commission sent the EBU a statement of objections concerning the rules governing the acquisition and use of television rights to sports events within the framework of the Eurovision System, which are generally exclusive in nature. The Commission declared itself willing to envisage an exemption in favour of those rules on condition that the EBU and its members accepted an obligation to grant non-members sub-licences for a substantial part of the rights in question and on reasonable terms.

8   On 3 April 1989, the EBU notified the Commission of its Statutes and other rules on the acquisition of television rights to sports events, the exchange of sports broadcasts in the context of Eurovision and contractual access of third parties to such broadcasts, with a view to obtaining negative clearance or, failing that, an exemption under Article 85(3) of the Treaty.

9   After EBU had agreed to relax the rules for obtaining sub-licences for the broadcasts in question, the Commission adopted Decision 93/403/EEC of 11 June 1993 relating to a proceeding pursuant to Article 85 of the EEC Treaty (OJ 1993 L 179, p. 23), whereby it granted an exemption under Article 85(3) (the exemption decision).

10   That decision was annulled by the judgment of the Court of First Instance in Joined Cases T-528/93, T-542/93, T-543/93 and T-546/93 Métropole Télévision and Others v Commission [1996] ECR II-649 (the judgment of 11 July 1996).

11   Since 1987, Métropole Télévision (M6) has lodged an application to join the EBU six times. Each time, its application has been rejected on the ground that it did not fulfil the membership conditions laid down by the EBU's Statutes. Following the last refusal of the EBU, on 2 June 1997, M6 filed a complaint with the Commission, complaining of EBU's practices towards it, and in particular of the systematic a priori refusal of its applications for admission.

12   By decision of 29 June 1999 (the contested decision), the Commission dismissed the applicant's complaint.

## Procedure and forms of order sought

13   The applicant brought this action by application lodged at the Registry of the Court of First Instance on 15 September 1999.

14   Upon hearing the report of the Judge-Rapporteur, the Court of First Instance (Fourth Chamber) decided to open the oral procedure. In the context of measures of organisation of procedure, the Commission was asked to produce certain documents and reply in writing to two questions.

15   The parties presented oral argument and replied to the questions put to them orally by the Court at the hearing on 27 September 2000.

16   The applicant claims that the Court should:
   – annul the contested decision;
   – order the Commission to pay the costs.

17   The Commission contends that the Court should:
   – dismiss the application;
   – order the applicant to pay the costs.

## Law

### Preliminary observations

18   In its complaint, the applicant made essentially two claims. In the first, it complained of the fact that the EBU continued to invoke against it the former admis-

sion criteria under its Statutes in breach of the judgment of 11 July 1996 annulling the exemption decision. Taking the view that those admission criteria could no longer be applied, the applicant requested the Commission to take all necessary steps to put an end to the EBU's practices, and in particular to order the latter to give it access to the television rights to sports events acquired by the EBU on behalf of its members within the Eurovision framework, and to give it access to news pictures within the framework of the system for exchanging such pictures called News Access/EBU, on the same conditions as those enjoyed by rival undertakings, namely live retransmission.

19    In its second claim, the applicant complained of the acquired rights clause laid down in Article 6 of the EBU Statutes (see paragraph 4 above), allowing that association to impose on the applicant conditions for joining that its members did not fulfil. In that respect, M6 complained, in particular, of the situation of CANAL+ and certain subsidiaries of television channels which were members of the EBU, such as Eurosport and LCI, which benefited from the EBU's system of joint acquisition without fulfilling the criteria which the EBU imposed on the applicant for joining.

20    In the contested decision, the Commission rejected the complaint because, first, it considered that it did not have the necessary legal powers to order the EBU to grant M6 live access to television rights for sporting events acquired by the association on behalf of its members, and, secondly, it did not share the opinion of M6 as to the scope of the judgment of 11 July 1996. In that respect, the Commission stated:

The Court of First Instance did not as such express a view as to the applicability of [Article 81(1) EC] to the membership rules, any more than did the Commission, as is proved by the wording of Article 1 of the exemption decision of 11 June 1993, which is limited to granting exemption for the system of acquiring television rights for sporting events; to the exchange of sports broadcasts in the context of Eurovision and contractual access of third parties to such broadcasts. That Article 1 does not at any time refer to the membership rules, which are therefore not at issue. The Commission considers that the former membership rules of the EBU do not fall within the scope of [Article 81(1) EC]; that is to say the criteria are not in themselves restrictions on competition. (Point 5.1.)

21    Thirdly, concerning the applicant's second claim, the Commission made the following observation:

It should be noted that CANAL+ does not participate in the EBU's joint acquisition group for sports rights. (Point 6.)

22    The applicant makes two pleas in law in support of its action. The first, its main argument, alleges infringement of the Treaty and of the rules concerning its application. The second, in the alternative, alleges misuse of powers.

**The plea alleging infringement of the Treaty and of the rules concerning its application**

**Arguments of the parties**

23    The applicant argues that the Commission has misread the judgment of 11 July 1996 and the complaint lodged by it, and that, therefore, the defendant has infringed the obligation placed upon it by Article 233 EC to take all necessary measures to comply with an annulling judgment. It argues, in that respect, that the Court of First Instance did indeed rule on the applicability of Article 81(1) EC to the membership rules and that, moreover, it considered that the Commission had not justified the exemption granted.

24     Contrary to what the Commission claims, the applicant does not consider that the judgment of 11 July 1996 gives it automatic access to the EBU. Since the Court of First Instance held that the membership criteria could not be relied upon against third parties, the question of the applicant's membership became secondary, since the EBU no longer had the right to rely on its Statutes in order to hold that the applicant could not benefit from the Eurovision system. In those circumstances, what was discussed in the complaint concerned equal access of third parties to television rights for sporting events acquired through Eurovision, the applicant declaring itself willing to bear all charges falling upon EBU members. Therefore, the Commission's argument that it did not have the power to order the EBU to accept M6's membership application was irrelevant, because that was not the applicant's aim.

25     The applicant further argues that the Commission gives an incomplete answer to the main head of claim in its complaint. The Commission did not express a view on the discrimination which M6 claims to have suffered by reason of the presence within the EBU of CANAL+, which has never fulfilled the membership criteria, and of the participation of that channel in the Eurovision system until the 1998 World Cup. The applicant argues that Article 6 of the Statutes of the EBU is essentially anti-competitive in that it allows a television channel like CANAL+ to benefit from television rights for sporting events acquired within the Eurovision framework over a period of 15 years without ever fulfilling the minimum requirements for becoming a member of the EBU.

26     The Commission argues that the aim of the applicant's complaint was to claim the ability to join the EBU without having to fulfil the existing membership criteria. The complaint was not limited to the question of access to the Eurovision system but concerned the whole of the advantages linked to the status of EBU member. The Commission therefore considers that it correctly interpreted the complaint by holding that the applicant was claiming to benefit from live access to television rights for sporting events acquired by the EBU on behalf of its members.

27     In those circumstances, the Commission maintains that it had to reject that complaint, because, even if the membership rules contained in the Statutes had to be regarded as an independent restriction on competition contrary to Community law, the Commission did not have the legal means to order the EBU to grant M6 live access to the television rights acquired by the association. Moreover, even if the judgment of 11 July 1996 had to be interpreted as meaning that the EBU membership rules were wrongly exempted by the Commission, compliance with the judgment required those rules to be amended so as to meet the requirements imposed by the Court of First Instance, but that does not mean that the membership criteria no longer exist or that the applicant has an automatic right to be a member of the EBU. The Commission considers that the EBU complied with the judgment of 11 July 1996 by making successive amendments to its membership rules, the last being dated 3 April 1998.

28     In any event, the question of the Commission's exercise of its power to issue a direction should arise only if the former membership rules could be regarded as restrictive and it were established that they were exempted, which is not the case. In that respect, the Commission argues that neither it nor the Court of First Instance have stated a formal position as to the restrictive character of the membership rules contained in the Statutes.

29     As regards the exemption decision taken by the Commission, Article 1 of that decision shows that it concerned the provisions in the Statutes and the rules applying to the Eurovision system, as notified by the EBU. The only provisions concerned

were those governing the joint acquisition and subsequent sharing of television rights for sports broadcasts within the framework of Eurovision and the rules governing contractual access by third parties to those broadcasts.

30    By contrast, the Commission submits that the three conditions for joining the EBU contained in Article 3(3) of the Statutes does not form the subject-matter of the exemption. That conclusion is deduced from four circumstances: first, from the content of the notification made by the EBU in order to obtain negative clearance and in the alternative an exemption pursuant to Articles 2 and 6 of Council Regulation No 17 of 6 February 1962: First Regulation implementing Articles 85 and 86 of the Treaty (OJ, English Special Edition 1959-1962, p. 87). The notification concerned not the conditions for joining but the joint acquisition of programmes and detailed provisions concerning sub-licences, the only mention of those conditions in the notification being designed to specify the context of the EBU's application; second, from the heading of the exemption decision (Eurovision system); third, from the fact that that decision had not contained any elaboration of the membership conditions demonstrating that they constituted an independent cause of restriction upon competition, and, fourth, from the wording of Article 1 of the operative part of the decision, which referred only to the mechanism governing the acquisition of television rights, without making any reference to the membership rules.

31    The Commission therefore maintains that the conditions in which EBU members jointly acquire exclusive rights are at the heart of the present case and that the membership rules do not fall within that joint acquisition system. Similarly, it maintains that there is no contradiction in excluding the membership criteria contained in the Statutes from the scope of the exemption and obliging the EBU to inform the Commission of all decisions taken on membership applications. The Commission had, rightly, put in place a mechanism for keeping track of the policy for admission to the Eurovision system pursued by the EBU in order to be aware of the number of members of that body and detect any possible monopolisation of the sector.

32    As for the judgment of 11 July 1996, that was based on the premiss that the Commission had taken the view that the membership rules were restrictive of competition and had been exempted. However, the Commission had not stated any view on the application of Article 81 EC to those rules. The latter did not, in themselves, constitute restrictions on competition covered by Article 81(1) EC.

33    It therefore concludes that all the applicant's arguments based on the annulment by the Court of First Instance of a decision exempting the membership rules fail entirely, since that exemption was never applied for, could therefore never have been granted and therefore, finally, could never have been annulled.

34    As for the argument that the Commission did not reply to the complaint of discrimination which the applicant draws from the presence of CANAL+ in the EBU, the Commission maintains that the membership rules are not restrictive and that there is no cause to censure them. In any event, at the time the applicant's complaint was examined, CANAL+ no longer had access to the joint acquisition system for television rights.

## Findings of the Court

35    It should be noted as a preliminary observation that, when the Court of First Instance annuls an act of an institution, that institution is required, under Article 233 EC, to take the measures necessary to comply with the Court's judgment. In that connection, both Community courts have held that, in order to comply with their

judgments and to implement them fully, the institution is required to observe not only the operative part of the judgment but also the grounds which led to the judgment and constitute its essential basis, inasmuch as they are necessary to determine the exact meaning of what is stated in the operative part. It is those grounds which, on the one hand, identify the precise provision held to be illegal and, on the other, indicate the specific reasons which underlie the finding of illegality contained in the operative part and which the institution concerned must take into account when replacing the annulled measure (Joined Cases 97/86, 99/86, 193/86 and 215/86 Asteris v Commission [1988] ECR 2181, paragraph 27; Case T-224/95 Tremblay v Commission [1997] ECR II-2215, paragraph 72).

36    As regards the interpretation of the judgment of 11 July 1996, it should be noted that, at paragraph 94, the Court held: ... according to point 50 of the [exemption] decision, 'competition vis-à-vis purely commercial channels, which are not admitted as members, is to some extent distorted' by the EBU's membership rules, since those channels cannot participate in the rationalisation and cost savings achieved by the Eurovision System. According to point 72 et seq., the restrictions of competition caused by those membership rules are nevertheless indispensable within the meaning of Article 85(3)(a) of the Treaty.

37    In order to assess whether the conditions set out in Article 85(3) of the Treaty were fulfilled, the Court first examined the three conditions imposed on channels wishing to join the EBU: the obligation to cover the entire national population, the obligation to provide varied and balanced programming for all sections of the population, and the obligation to produce a substantial proportion of the programmes broadcast themselves. It then stated that, in accordance with settled case-law, the Commission had to examine whether those membership rules were objective and sufficiently determinate so as to enable them to be applied uniformly and in a non-discriminatory manner vis-à-vis all potential active members (see, for example, Case 26/76 Metro v Commission, paragraph 20). The Court added: The indispensable nature of the restrictions of competition resulting from those rules cannot be correctly assessed unless that prior condition is fulfilled (paragraph 95 of the judgment of 11 July 1996).

38    It then held that: the content of the three conditions laid down by Article 3(3) of the EBU's Statutes relating to coverage of the population, to programming and to the production of the programmes broadcast is not sufficiently determinate. Since they refer essentially to unquantified quantitative criteria, they are vague and imprecise. Consequently, in the absence of further specification, they cannot form the basis for uniform, non-discriminatory application (paragraph 97 of the judgment of 11 July 1996).

39    The Court of First Instance concluded that the Commission was wrong to refrain from carrying out an examination of the application of the three membership criteria in the case in question and held that the Commission should have concluded that it was not even in a position to assess whether the corresponding restrictions were indispensable within the meaning of Article 85(3)(a) of the Treaty. Consequently, it was not entitled to exempt them on that ground (paragraph 99 of the judgment of 11 July 1996).

40    It therefore follows from the judgment of 11 July 1996 that, as the EBU's membership rules were not sufficiently determinate in content, they were not capable of being applied uniformly and without discrimination and could not therefore benefit from an exemption under Article 81(3) EC.

41    However, contrary to what the applicant maintains, the Court did not rule on the application of Article 81(1) EC to the membership criteria. In paragraph 94 of the

judgment of 11 July 1996, the Court merely found that the Commission had held in the exemption decision that the membership rules restricted competition, but did not give a ruling on that qualification. In the action for annulment brought against the exemption decision, the application of Article 81(1) EC to the membership rules was not raised by the applicants. Since that is a plea which goes to the substantive legality of a decision, it was not for the Court to raise it of its own motion in an action for annulment brought pursuant to Article 230 EC (see, to that effect, Case C-367/95 P Commission v Sytraval and Brink's France [1998] ECR I-1719, paragraph 67).

42    In those circumstances, the judgment of 11 July 1996 cannot have the effect of preventing the Commission from going back on its position concerning the application of Article 81(1) EC to the EBU's membership rules. Such a change of position did, however, require a statement of reasons.

43    In that respect, and in so far as the insufficiency or lack of reasoning constitutes an infringement of essential procedural requirements within the meaning of Article 230 EC and is a plea of public policy which the Community judicature must raise of its own motion (Sytraval, paragraph 67), it needs to be examined whether sufficient reasons are stated for such an adoption of position.

44    For that purpose, it should be recalled that, according to consistent case-law, the statement of reasons on which a decision adversely affecting a person is based must, first, be such as to enable the person concerned to ascertain the matters justifying the measure adopted so that, if necessary, he can defend his rights and verify whether the decision is well founded and, secondly, enable the Community judicature to exercise its power of review as to the legality of the decision. In that connection, the Commission is not obliged, in stating the reasons for the decisions which it takes to ensure the application of the competition rules, to adopt a position on all the arguments relied on by the persons concerned but need only set out the facts and legal considerations which are of decisive importance in the context of the decision (see, for example, Case T-5/93 Tremblay v Commission [1995] ECR II-185, paragraph 29).

45    The Commission maintains that the position taken in the contested decision, that the former membership rules of the EBU do not fall within the scope of [Article 81(1) EC]; that is to say the criteria are not in themselves restrictions on competition is a mere confirmation of the position adopted in the exemption decision inasmuch as, in the latter, it had never sought to cover the EBU's membership rules but only the system of joint acquisition of television rights. In those circumstances, it is necessary to examine the exemption decision and determine to what extent the EBU's membership rules are covered by it.

46    In that regard, it should first be noted that in point 50 of the exemption decision, under the heading A. Article 85(1); 2. Restrictions on competition; b) Distortion of competition vis-à-vis non-members of the EBU, the Commission stated as follows:
      The membership rules do to some extent distort competition vis-à-vis purely commercial channels, which are not admitted as members. The inability of those channels to participate in the rationalisation and cost savings achieved by the Eurovision System ... makes the broadcasting of sporting events more costly and complicated for them.

47    Next, in points 72 to 74, under the heading B. Article 85(3); 3. Indispensable nature of the restrictions; b) Indispensability of limiting participation to public service broadcasters, the Commission stated:
      It is necessary that participation in the Eurovision system in the capacity of mem-

ber be limited to public service broadcasters which meet certain objective criteria concerning the production and diversity of their programmes and coverage of the national population ... It is necessary, in particular, that the participating members themselves produce a significant proportion of their programmes ... It is also vital that they cover the whole of the national population.

48     Moreover, in point 83 of the exemption decision, the Commission required the EBU, in order to be able to verify whether the conditions for exemption [were] always fulfilled and whether, in particular, the membership conditions [were] applied in an appropriate, reasonable and non-discriminatory manner, to keep the Commission informed of any amendment of or addition to the notified rules, any arbitration procedure concerning differences arising within the framework of the access system, and of any decision concerning membership applications by third parties.

49     Finally, the operative part of that decision, which, according to settled case-law, is indissociably linked to the statement of reasons for it and must be interpreted in the light of the grounds for the latter (Case C-355/95 P TWD v Commission [1997] ECR I-2549, paragraph 21), provides that the provisions of Article 85(1) are declared inapplicable ... to the provisions in the Statutes and other rules of the EBU governing the acquisition of television rights for sporting events, to the exchange of sports broadcasts within the framework of Eurovision, and to contractual access by third parties to those broadcasts.

50     The term provisions in the Statutes, interpreted in the light of the grounds for the exemption decision referred to in paragraphs 46 to 48 above, necessarily covers the EBU's membership rules which are defined in Article 3(3) of the Statutes. That interpretation is, moreover, borne out by point 58 of the exemption decision, where it is stated that the various advantages provided by the Eurovision system and its underlying rules form a whole of which the constituent elements are complementary.

51     It therefore follows from a reading of the exemption decision as a whole that, contrary to what it claims, the Commission considered in 1993 that the EBU's membership rules were restrictive of competition and that they could be exempted from the application of Article 85(1) of the Treaty.

52     Moreover, none of the arguments raised by the Commission is capable of calling that conclusion into question. Even if the heading of a decision were relevant in determining its scope, it is sufficient to note that the heading of the exemption decision contains the words EBU/Eurovision system and not, as the Commission claims, merely the words Eurovision system. Furthermore, concerning the subject-matter of the application for negative clearance or exemption submitted by the EBU and on the basis of which the Commission adopted the exemption decision, it is also sufficient to note that the membership rules were notified in point 1 of Title III of that application.

53     In those circumstances, the dismissal of the applicant's complaint on the ground that the former membership rules of the EBU do not fall within the scope of [Article 81(1) EC]; that is to say the criteria are not in themselves restrictions on competition constitutes a substantial change in the Commission's position which it has not in any way justified. It follows that the statement of reasons for the contested decision does not allow the applicant to ascertain the grounds on which its complaint was dismissed and that the Commission has not therefore complied with its obligation under Article 253 EC.

54     That lack of reasoning is all the more serious if the contested decision is placed in its context and, in particular, if it is interpreted in the light of the correspondence

exchanged between the EBU and the applicant concerning the latter's application for membership. It emerges from that correspondence, and in particular from the letters of 20 December 1996 and 8 May and 3 June 1997, that the EBU's membership rules and, more particularly, the consequences of the annulment by the Court of First Instance of the exemption which those rules previously enjoyed, are at the heart of the difference between the applicant and the EBU, in relation to which the Commission was led to take a position. Therefore, the Commission could not remove the EBU's membership conditions from the argument without putting forward grounds enabling the applicant to understand such a decision.

55   It follows that the contested decision must be annulled for insufficient statement of reasons.

56   In its second claim, the applicant argues that the Commission did not reply to the part of the complaint concerning the discrimination which it suffered from the EBU vis-à-vis some of its members.

57   It should be noted that, according to consistent case-law, where the Commission has a power of appraisal in order to carry out its duties, respect for the rights guaranteed by the Community legal order in administrative procedures is all the more fundamental. Those guarantees include, in particular, the duty of the competent institution to examine carefully and impartially all the relevant aspects of the individual case (Case C-269/90 Technische Universität München [1991] ECR I-5469, paragraph 14; Case T-44/90 La Cinq v Commission [1992] ECR II-1, paragraph 86).

58   Thus, in the context of investigating applications submitted to the Commission pursuant to Article 3 of Regulation No 17, the Court of First Instance has held that although the Commission cannot be compelled to conduct an investigation, the procedural safeguards provided for by Article 6 of Regulation No 99/63 oblige it nevertheless to examine carefully the factual and legal particulars brought to its notice by the complainant in order to decide whether they disclose conduct of such a kind as to distort competition in the common market and affect trade between the Member States (see Case T-7/92 Asia Motor France v Commission [1993] ECR II-669, paragraph 35, and the judgments referred to therein).

59   Lastly, although in accordance with the case-law of the Court of First Instance cited above the Commission is not obliged to investigate each of the complaints lodged with it, in contrast, once it decides to proceed with an investigation, it must, in the absence of a duly substantiated statement of reasons, conduct it with the requisite care, seriousness and diligence so as to be able to assess with full knowledge of the case the factual and legal particulars submitted for its appraisal by the complainants (Asia Motor France v Commission, cited above, paragraph 36).

60   It is in the light of those considerations that it needs to be assessed whether the contested decision contains an appropriate examination of the factual and legal particulars submitted for the Commission's appraisal.

61   In point 5 of the complaint, the applicant states that Article 5 of the EBU's Statutes expressly provided, in the 1988 version, that any member which did not fulfil the conditions imposed in order to become an active member of the EBU ceased to belong to that association. However, to take account of the rights acquired by former members, Article 21 of the Statutes provided that Article 3(2) (now Article 3(3) in the 1992 version) of the Statutes would not be applicable to bodies which, at the time of its entry into force on 1 March 1988, were already active members and did not fulfil all the membership conditions laid down by that latter provision.

The applicant states that, in the 1992 version of the EBU's Statutes, the content of Article 21, cited above, appears in Article 6.

62      It then states that a company which was a member of the EBU before 1 March 1988 could retain that capacity even if it had never satisfied the membership conditions notified to the Commission. The applicant thus points out in its complaint that thanks to that article, CANAL+ remained an active member of the EBU even though that channel never fulfilled the membership criteria before they were annulled by the Court of First Instance, in particular as to the coverage of national territory, which does not exceed 72%. According to the applicant, the situation of CANAL+ was the most striking example of the competitive disadvantage which it suffered, especially if one bears in mind that the EBU's main complaint against [the applicant] was always that it did not offer sufficient coverage of the national population.

63      At the hearing, the Commission stated that CANAL+ no longer formed part of the Eurovision system but that it continued to enjoy rights previously acquired.

64      It should be remembered that, when examining complaints, the Commission is required to assess in each case how serious the alleged interferences with competition are and how persistent their consequences are. That obligation means in particular that it must take into account the duration and extent of the infringements complained of and their effect on the competition situation in the Community.

65      In deciding to dismiss a complaint of practices allegedly contrary to the Treaty, the Commission cannot therefore rely solely on the fact that those practices have ceased, without having ascertained whether anti-competitive effects still continue (see, to that effect, Case C-119/97 P UFEX v Commission [1999] ECR I-1341, paragraphs 92 to 96).

66      In this case, the Commission refused to examine the part of the complaint concerning the EBU's treatment of CANAL+, giving as its reason the mere fact that the practices allegedly contrary to the Treaty had ceased in that CANAL+ no longer formed part of the Eurovision system, thereby omitting in this case to assess the possible persistence of anti-competitive effects and their impact on the market in question, consequently infringing the obligations upon it when examining a complaint for infringement of Article 81 EC.

67      It follows from the whole of the above that the contested decision must be annulled on the grounds that, first, the Commission infringed its obligation to state reasons under Article 253 EC, and, second, it infringed the obligations which it has when dealing with complaints of infringements of competition law.

68      There is therefore no need to examine the alternative plea of misuse of powers.

**Decision on costs**
**Costs**
69      Under Article 87(2) of the Rules of Procedure of the Court of First Instance, the unsuccessful party is to be ordered to pay the costs if they have been applied for in the successful party's pleadings. Since the Commission has been unsuccessful, it must, in accordance with the form of order sought by the applicant, be ordered to pay the costs.

**Operative part of the judgment**
On those grounds,
The Court of First Instance (Fourth Chamber),
hereby:

1.  Annuls the Commission's decision of 29 June 1999, rejecting the complaint of Métropole Télévision SA of 5 December 1997;
2.  Orders the Commission to pay the costs.

———

**\* 2.4.63. ANSWER ON BEHALF OF THE COMMISSION TO WRITTEN QUESTION E-146/01 BY MARGRIETUS VAN DEN BERG (PSE), 2 APRIL 2001[471] \***

Subject: Sale of television broadcasting rights for sporting events

———

**\* 2.4.64. ANSWER ON BEHALF OF THE COMMISSION TO WRITTEN QUESTION E-403/01 BY TOINE MANDERS (ELDR), WARD BEYSEN (ELDR), GRAHAM WATSON (ELDR), ELSPETH ATTWOOLL (ELDR) AND OLE ANDREASEN (ELDR), 9 APRIL 2001[472] \***

Subject: Complaint about abuse of UEFA's position

———

**2.4.65. COMMISSION DECISION RELATING TO A PROCEEDING PURSUANT TO ARTICLE 81 OF THE EC TREATY AND ARTICLE 53 OF THE EEA AGREEMENT (CASE 37.576 UEFA'S BROADCASTING REGULATIONS), 19 APRIL 2001[473]**

*The Commission of the European Communities,*

–   Having regard to the Treaty establishing the European Community,
–   Having regard to the Agreement on the European Economic Area,
–   Having regard to Council Regulation No 17 of 6 February 1962, first Regulation implementing Articles 85 and 86 of the Treaty[474], as last amended by Regulation (EC) No 1216/1999[475], and in particular Article 2 thereof,
–   Having regard to the application for negative clearance and the notification with a view to an exemption registered on 19 July 1999, as amended on 5 April 2000 pursuant to Articles 2 and 4(1) of Regulation No 17,
–   Having regard to the summary of the notification[476] published pursuant to Article 19(3) of Regulation No 17,
–   Having consulted the Advisory Committee on Restrictive Practices and Dominant Positions,

Whereas:

**1. FACTS**
(1)   This decision relates to the rules of the Union des Associations Européennes de Football (UEFA) which regulate the broadcasting of football matches. The rules

---

[471] Question of 31-1-2001; OJ C 235 E, 21-8-2001, p. 127.
[472] Question of 15-2-2001; OJ C 340 E, 4-12-2001, p. 21-22.
[473] OJ L 171 , 26-6-2001, p. 12-28 (Text with EEA relevance).
[474] OJ 13, 21-2-1962, p. 204.
[475] OJ L 148, 15-6-1999, p. 5.
[476] OJ C 121, 29-4-2000, p. 14.

are the 'Regulations governing the implementation of Article 47 of the UEFA statutes, 2000 edition' (broadcasting regulations), which implement Article 47 of UEFA's Statutes. Within the territories of UEFA's member associations, the broadcasting regulations enable national football associations to block a very limited number of hours during which football may not be broadcast on television. The object of the broadcasting regulations is to provide national football associations with a limited opportunity to schedule domestic football fixtures at times when they are not liable to be disrupted by the contemporaneous broadcasting of football to the detriment of stadium attendance and amateur participation in the sport.

(2)     UEFA is an international organisation of 51 national football associations. It has its seat in Nyon in Switzerland. Membership of UEFA is open to all European national football associations. As a rule, there is a single association in each Member State of the EEA, which organises the sport at national level, except for the United Kingdom, where for historical reasons England, Wales, Scotland and Northern Ireland each have their own association. Recognised as the European confederation by FIFA (Fédération Internationale de Football Association), UEFA is the governing body for European football. UEFA also organises international football competitions and tournaments at European level such as the UEFA European Football Championships, the UEFA Champions League and the UEFA Cup.

(3)     UEFA first introduced broadcasting rules in 1988. These rules, which were notified to the Commission on 19 May 1992[477], were amended on several occasions over the years and have been the subject of complaints from a number of broadcasters[478]. The complainants found that the rules restricted competition, a concern that was shared by the Commission. The Commission sought to find, with the parties, an amicable solution that would also be compatible with EC competition law. A mediator was appointed in 1994 who concluded in 1996 that a compromise solution could not be found.

(4)     On 16 July 1998, the Commission therefore issued a statement of objections finding that the broadcasting regulations applicable at that time infringed Article 81(1) of the EC Treaty and Article 53(1) of the EEA Agreement and that they were not eligible for exemption under Article 81(3) of the EC Treaty and Article 53(3) of the EEA Agreement.

(5)     In its reply to the statement of objections on 15 October 1998, UEFA presented a proposal for new broadcasting regulations. Based on this proposal, UEFA adopted new broadcasting regulations on 2 July 1999 replacing the ones, which had been the subject of the statement of objections and notified them to the Commission on 19 July 1999. At that occasion UEFA also withdrew its notification of 1992.

(6)     Having examined UEFA's new broadcasting regulations of 2 July 1999, the Commission considered that further amendments were necessary. By letter of 14 Feb-

---

[477] Registered as Case IV/C-2/34.319.

[478] The complainants were originally: Case IV/33145 – Independent Television Association Limited (ITVA), complaint of 5-4-1989; Case IV/33734 – Gestevision, complaint of 24-10-1990; Case IV/34199 – British Sky Broadcasting Limited (BSkyB), complaint of 28-1-1992; Case IV/34784 – Channel Four Television, complaint of 13-7-1993; Case IV/34790 – Canal+ SA, complaint of 16-7-1993; Case IV/34948 – Telepiù srl., complaint of 13-12-1993; Case IV/35001 – CWL Telesport, complaint of 16-2-1994; Case IV/35048 – Telecinco SA, complaint of 22-3-1994; Case IV/37350 – Association of Commercial Television in Europe (ACT); complaint of 16-12-1998; Case IV/37461 – Channel 5 Broadcasting Limited, complaint of 6-4-1999.

ruary 2000, the Commission insisted that UEFA should further reduce the scope for national associations to block the broadcasting of football. In particular, Article 3(3) of the broadcasting regulations and its application gave rise to difficulties. Article 3(3) required national associations to provide proof that the hours blocked according to Article 3(1) actually correspond to the main domestic fixture schedule. The reason for the difficulty was that the broadcasting regulations did not define the main domestic fixture schedule precisely. This made verification of the national associations' compliance with the obligation to block hours corresponding only to the main domestic fixture schedule very difficult.

(7)    The Commission therefore requested UEFA to clearly define the main domestic fixture schedule. It also requested the introduction of a clear and unambiguous rule that the blocked hours should correspond to the main domestic fixture schedule. The Commission insisted that the main domestic fixture schedule is traditionally played during one day of the weekend, Saturday or Sunday. A football match lasts 2 x 45 minutes with a 15 minutes break in the middle, in total nearly two hours. The Commission therefore only accepted that national associations were authorised to block hours on Saturday or Sunday and only for two and a half hours, which gives spectators sufficient time for transport to and from the stadiums and to watch the football match in the stadiums without being concerned about missing football on TV. The Commission requested these amendments because the presence of a clear rule regarding the main domestic fixture schedule together with a strict enforcement of the requirement of the provision of proof by the national associations, eliminates the problem of excessive blocking of hours. Moreover, the Commission found that the close link with the main domestic fixture schedule, which is a static schedule, means that national football associations would block the same hours from year to year and provide stable conditions for the broadcasting of football.

(8)    UEFA accepted the Commission's request and informed the Commission by letter of 5 April 2000 of the amendment of Article 3 of the broadcasting regulations in accordance with the Commission's request. The letter of 5 April 2000 also constituted a formal notification of the amendment of Article 3. According to Article 9 of the broadcasting regulations, they were approved by the UEFA Executive Committee on 31 March 2000 and came into force on 1 August 2000.

### 1.1. UEFA's rules on the broadcasting of football
### 1.1.1. 2000 Edition of UEFA's Statutes

(9)    The substantive UEFA rules on broadcasting are found in the broadcasting regulations. UEFA's Executive Committee issues these broadcasting regulations on the basis of Article 47(2) of UEFA Statutes. This Article empowers the UEFA Executive Committee to issue regulations implementing the rights of UEFA and member associations, pursuant to Article 47(1), to authorise the broadcasting of football: '1. UEFA and the Member associations shall have the exclusive rights to authorise audio-visual and sound broadcasting transmissions, as well as any other use and dissemination by picture and sound, either live or recorded, in whole or as excerpts, of matches which come within their jurisdiction. 2. The Executive Committee shall issue regulations governing the implementation of these rights.'

### 1.1.2. The broadcasting regulations of 31 March 2000

(10)   The purpose of the broadcasting regulations is to ensure that spectators are not deterred from attending local football matches of any kind and/or participating in

matches at amateur and/or youth level on account of transmissions[479] of football matches which may create competition with these matches[480]. Since some of the national associations do not fear this possible negative effect from broadcast football, the broadcasting regulations do not oblige national associations to block hours within their territories. However, the national associations are obliged to observe the blocked hours of other national associations when selling their broadcasting rights to football events into the territories of national associations which have actually blocked hours[481].

(11)    According to Article 3(1), each member association may decide that the broadcasting of football be prohibited within its territory for two and a half hours on a Saturday or on a Sunday. The prohibition applies only to intentional transmissions[482]. Pursuant to Article 3(3), these two and a half hours must correspond to the main domestic fixture schedule of the member association. The main domestic fixture schedule is defined in Article 3(4) as being the time when the majority (i.e. 50% or more) of the weekly football matches in the top two domestic leagues in the country are played. These matches can be either amateur or professional. The main domestic season begins with the first match of the national league championship and ends with the last match of the national league championship. For the avoidance of any doubt, any prohibition of football pursuant to Article 3(1) may apply only during the football season as notified to UEFA. The requirement that the national associations should only block hours during the season when football is actually played in their territory means that, if for instance, football is not played during the winter season in a given country for climatic reasons, that national football association cannot prohibit the broadcasting of football on television during that period.

(12)    If the Member Associations decide to use the possibility of blocking the broadcasting of football within their territory, Article 3(2) obliges the national associations to adopt such a decision at the latest one month before the beginning of its domestic season. Any modification of the blocked hours can only be decided upon with effect from the following football season and at least one month before that new season begins. Pursuant to Article 3(3), all decisions of the national football associations concerning blocked hours must be reported to UEFA in writing at the time of the decision which publishes relevant information[483]. The national associations must, according to Article 3(5), at the latest one month before the beginning of the domestic football season, provide UEFA with a copy of the relevant domestic fixture lists) which justifies the selected blocked hours and specifies the beginning and the end of the domestic football season. Should the Member Association fail to inform UEFA within the time-limit of its decision regarding 'blocked hours', no restriction will apply to television broadcasts of football during that season for that Member Association.

(13)    The provisions regarding blocked periods do not apply to the transmission of football during non-sporting programmes, such as news programmes which may in-

---

[479] Article 1(2) of the broadcasting regulations refers to 'Any transmission or reproduction of a football match by any actual or future transmission technique (including, but not limited to Internet)'.

[480] Article 2(1) of the broadcasting regulations.

[481] Article 5 of the broadcasting regulations.

[482] UEFA defines the notion 'intentional broadcast' as meaning broadcasts which are specifically produced for a given territory, e.g. in terms of language and/or content.

[483] UEFA has published such information on its Internet home home page: <http://www.uefa.com/>.

clude short (recorded) excerpts of football matches pursuant to Article 3(6)[484].

(14)    A few select football matches can be broadcast during the blocked periods[485]. Member associations must notify UEFA at least 45 days in advance of the dates and kick-off times of the matches to be exceptionally broadcast during blocked hours[486]. Given the exceptional character of the matches falling within the scope of this provision, it only finds extremely limited practical application[487]. If a Member Association allows the broadcast of a match, including those falling within the above categories, it cannot object to the incoming transmission of any other match played in the territory of another football association.

(15)    The national associations are required not to discriminate against football from other countries and these broadcasting regulations apply equally to transmissions of domestic and foreign matches[488]. It is the responsibility of the national football associations to ensure that all parties adhere strictly to the provisions contained in the broadcasting regulations[489]. UEFA's Control and Disciplinary Body may impose disciplinary measures or directives on member associations, which are found to be in breach of the broadcasting regulations. In addition, UEFA may impose administrative measures according to the current taxation systems agreed on by the member associations[490].

### 1.2. Comments submitted by interested third parties

(16)    The Commission published a notice in the Official Journal of the European Communities pursuant to Article 19(3) of Regulation No 17[491] which prompted reactions from seven interested third parties. The gist of the comments submitted by the complainants and interested third parties may be summarised as follows:

(17)    While they acknowledged[492] that the broadcasting regulations of 31 March 2000 are an improvement compared to earlier versions, third parties continue to consider that they restrict competition within the meaning of Article 81(1) of the EC

---

[484] UEFA has clarified this to mean news magazines, entertainment, and biographical and retrospective programmes that may include short excepts of football matches.

[485] Article 4(2) of the broadcasting regulations:
1. matches involving the senior national representative team;
2. matches required to be broadcast live according to national legislation; and
3. any other match of national importance.

[486] Article 4(3) of the broadcasting regulations.

[487] During the 1999/2000 season only three national associations applied the exception in respect of nine matches. For the 2000/2001 season, no national association has notified any match (on 18-10-2000).

[488] Article 2(2) of the broadcasting regulations.

[489] Article 5 of the broadcasting regulations.

[490] Article 7 of the broadcasting regulations.

[491] OJ C 121, 29-4-2000, p. 14. Only ACT, Canal+, Gestevision Telecinco SA, Channel Four Television and Channel 5 Braodcasting Limited maintained their complaints after having been invited by letter to react to the notice in the Official Journal pursuant to Article 19(3) of Regulation No 17. The remaining complainants, who have not come forward, are therefore considered to have lost their status as complainants.

[492] As illustrated by Canal+'s website in August 2000 where Canal+ stated that it is no less than 'world-news' that Canal+ is now able to broadcast live English Premier League in Denmark on Saturday afternoon, which has been blocked for more than 30 years. Canal+ attributes this new development to several years of dialogue with DBU, UEFA and the EU, which has lead to less restrictive broadcasting rules. Canal+ will therefore broadcast live Premier League football on Saturday, Sunday and Monday.

Treaty and Article 53(1) of the EEA Agreement, and claim that UEFA has not provided evidence to justify an exemption pursuant to Article 81(3) of the EC Treaty and Article 53(3) of the EEA Agreement, i.e. UEFA has not shown that there is a negative impact from the televising of football on stadium attendance or on amateur participation in the sport. It is argued that the broadcasting regulations should not apply to pay-TV, owing to the still low number of subscribers and consequently the low impact of pay-TV.

(18)    Moreover, it is argued that the broadcasting regulations make the acquisition of live broadcasting rights to football more risky since national associations only have to decide on blocked hours one month before the beginning of the football season. It is considered to be a particular problem since broadcasters are required to contract in respect of future years when there is no guarantee that football associations will not switch their main fixtures and relevant blackout period from one period to another.

(19)    British broadcasters argue that they face a particular problem due to the fact that there are four national associations in the United Kingdom who are not obliged to coordinate their blocking of hours and who could each block separate hours, thereby making the broadcasting of football in the United Kingdom very difficult. There is also concern that British broadcasters will not be able to benefit from Article 4 which serves to attenuate the restriction in Article 3 by providing for an exception to the blocked hours in respect of games of national importance. British broadcasters argue that since each of the four areas in the United Kingdom has individual interests and although one national association may give dispensation from the blocked hours for the broadcasting of a match, this dispensation will not apply to the other national associations rendering broadcasting impossible in those other areas.

(20)    Some broadcasters argue that technological developments will mean that broadcasters will soon broadcast to all of Europe. In the worst case, broadcasters will have to comply with different local blocked hours in several different jurisdictions, making transnational broadcasts cumbersome. Moreover, new services delivered via the Internet, TV on demand, pay-per-view-TV and other multimedia services would also be affected by the broadcasting regulations. Unlike traditional television, broadcasts of football matches via the Internet could be received on demand around the clock and not just during the programme hours. They argue that the reception of Internet transmission is geographically unlimited. Thus, they argue, in order to comply with the broadcasting regulations, an Internet service provider would have to observe all different blocked periods of all member associations. Consequently, the provider would have to lock the broadcasts during the blocked periods of each member association and unlock the broadcasts during the free periods. It is not economically sensible for Internet providers to follow this procedure. In addition, it is detrimental to the technical progress of multimedia services in Europe and would severely restrict the development of broadcasting sports by means of new services such as the Internet.

## 2. LEGAL ASSESSMENT
### 2.1. The relevant product market
#### 2.1.1. UEFA's submission

(21)    UEFA did not offer any definition of relevant product markets in its notification. UEFA only stated that the broadcasting rules have 'an effect on football and on broadcasting'.

### 2.1.2. Potentially affected markets

(22)    The Commission considers that the following markets could potentially be affected by UEFA's broadcasting regulations:
–    the upstream market(s) for the acquisition of free-TV and pay-TV broadcasting rights,
–    the downstream markets on which broadcasters compete for audiences, for advertising revenue dependent on audience rates, and for pay-TV subscribers.

(23)    The Commission moreover considers that Internet transmission rights and Internet content services could potentially be affected by UEFA's broadcasting regulations. However, at this stage, streaming of video feeds on the Internet is not a real alternative or supplement to television broadcasting of football matches. The technology for the transmission of video streams over the Internet for consumers is still immature and the economic value is still rather limited. The Commission does not know of any service that provides live full coverage streaming of football matches, or intends to provide such a service in the near future. There is consequently no service at this stage for which the broadcasting regulations could imply an appreciable restriction. Although this situation may change in the future if the necessary transmission capacity becomes widely available, it is not currently necessary for the purpose of this decision to consider Internet rights to football more closely, nor is it necessary to consider retailing of Internet content services or advertising in connection therewith.

### 2.1.3. The upstream market for the acquisition of broadcasting rights to football events

(24)    Viewer preferences are decisive for all types of broadcasters in their programme acquisition policy and thus determine the value of a programme to broadcasters[493]. The Commission notes that all broadcasters are actual or potential consumers of broadcasting rights to football events and that football is equally important to them all whatever the market[494]. Public service broadcasters acquire programmes in order to obtain a wide following in accordance with their public service obligations. Free-to-air broadcasters that are financed fully or partially by advertising revenues buy programmes to attract large audiences and they sell the opportunity to get exposure to this audience to advertisers. Pay-TV operators buy programmes to entice people to subscribe to their services.

(25)    While all broadcasters compete for broadcasting rights to football events, the trend is that more and more live full-length coverage broadcasting rights are sold to pay-TV broadcasters and that free-TV broadcasters acquire rights for deferred coverage or highlights of football matches. The reason is that pay-TV broadcasters are generally able to afford to pay more for the broadcasting rights than free-TV broadcasters as the latter have stronger budgetary restraints. Although in previous decisions[495] the Commission has defined pay-TV as a separate market, it is not necessary for the purpose of this case to analyse the free-TV or pay-TV markets

---

[493] In a similar way as the consumers' substitutability determines the upstream market of the supply of digital interactive television services by service providers to conent providers as the Commission decided in its decision of 15-9-1999 – Case 36.539 – British Interactive Broadcasting/Open (OJ L 312, 6-12-1999, p. 1).

[494] Commission Decision of 20-9-1995, RTL/Veronica/Endemol (OJ L 134, 5-6-1996), p. 32) and Commission Decision of 3-3-1999, TPS (OJ L 90, 2-4-1999, p. 6).

[495] See the following Commission Decisions:
Commission Decision of 2-8-1994 (ICV/M.410 – Kirch/Richmond/Telepiù) (OJ C 225, 13-8-1994, p. 3),

separately to measure the effects of the broadcasting regulations on the broadcasting market, since all types of broadcasting of football fall within the scope of the broadcasting regulations.

(26)     The ambit of the market for broadcasting rights can be delimited by the number of programmes that can achieve a desired purpose. Substitutability can therefore be tested by analysing to what extent other programmes achieve this purpose. If a specific type of programme can regularly attract high audience numbers, specific audiences or provide a brand image, which cannot be achieved by other programmes, then it may be considered that these programmes constitute a separate relevant market as there are no programmes which place a competitive restraint on the rights holders' ability to determine the price of these TV rights.

(27)     Hitherto, the Commission has not defined broadcasting rights to football events as constituting a separate relevant product market. Recently, in the TPS case, the Commission found that it is universally acknowledged that films and sporting events are the two most popular pay-TV products and it suggested that there might exist a separate market for rights to broadcast sports events[496]. In the Eurovision[497] case, the Commission found that there could be separate markets for the acquisition of some major sport events which do not take place regularly but from time to time, most of them international, such as the football World Cup. The Commission found that sports programmes have particular characteristics; they are able to achieve high viewing figures and reach an identifiable audience which is especially targeted by certain advertisers. The Commission concluded however, that it is not necessary for the purposes of this case to exactly define the relevant product markets.

(28)     The Commission's investigation in the present case has gathered evidence that there may exist a separate market for broadcasting rights to football events. The Commission has also found some evidence suggesting the existence of a separate market for the broadcasting rights to football events that do not take place regularly throughout every year such as the football World Cup and which are not substitutable with broadcasting rights to regular football events. In any event, the Commission considers that the restrictions of competition created by the UEFA broadcasting regulations would not be appreciable even on a market defined as narrow as the market for the broadcasting of football events played regularly throughout every year and which would in practice mainly concern national first and second league and cup events as well as the UEFA Champions League and UEFA Cup.

(29)     Although the Commission's investigation has identified a number of elements that suggest the existence of this market and which are explained below, it is not necessary for the purposes of this case to exactly define the relevant product markets.

---

Commission Decision 94/922/EC of 9-11-1994 (IV/M.469 – MSG media Service) (OJ L 364, 31-12-1994, p. 1),

Commission Decision of 3-8-1999 (COMP/M.1574 – Kirch/Mediaset) (OJ C 255, 8-9-1999, p. 3),

Commission Decision of 21-3-2000 (COMP/JV.37 – BSkyB/KirchPay TV), (OJ C 110, 15-4-2000, p. 45),

Commission Decision in RTL/Veronica/Endemol: see previous footnote.

Commission Decision in TPS (OJ L 90, 2-4-1999, p. 6).

Commission Decision of 12-5-2000 (IV/32.150 – Eurovision), OJ L 151, 24-6-2000, p. 18).

[496]   Commission Decision in TPS (OJ L 90, 2-4-1999, p. 6).

[497]   Commission Decision in Eurovision (OJ L 151, 24-6-2000, p. 18).

### 2.1.3.1. Brand image

(30)    Football is important to broadcasters owing to its ability to act as a developer of a brand image of a channel. Football has a distinct high profile among desirable viewers and it generally provides high audience figures. Football produces events which take place regularly throughout most of the year[498] and viewers are attracted not only to one match but also to the tournament as a whole. Football tournaments therefore provide guaranteed viewership for long periods. Football helps to induce viewers to regularly make an appointment to view a particular channel and to associate it with football. This contributes to developing a channel's brand image.

(31)    The development of a brand image is increasingly important in a Television industry where the number of channels among which viewers can choose increases rapidly and in which products are generally homogenised[499]. With a wider choice available to viewers, it becomes increasingly difficult for Television channels to attract and maintain audience loyalty. Branding encourages audiences to schedule their viewing habits to make appointments to view a particular channel. However, such loyalty is achieved only by offering a 'differentiated' product including eye-catching programmes and by strongly associating the channel with these programmes. If a channel usually broadcasts certain programmes such as the UEFA Champions League, viewers will develop the habit of screening that channel as their first port of call in determining their viewing choices. The creation of a brand loyalty to a channel encourages viewers to use the channel as a 'point of reference' for their viewing. This has beneficial effects on other programmes transmitted by the channel.

(32)    While the ability to build up brand loyalty to a particular channel is important to all types of channels, it is not least important for advertising funded Television channels. They must be able to present audiences to advertisers for all its broadcasts, otherwise it will not be able to sell its advertising space. Football is particularly attractive in that respect, because it has a wide following with continuously high audience figures. Viewers wanting to watch a particular match may often switch to that channel well in advance of the match and may 'hang on' after the match to see whether the following broadcast is interesting. It is suggested that in some cases this is reflected in the advertising rates that are high not only in the advertising slots immediately before and after the match but also in respect of the programmes that are broadcast before and after the match.

(33)    The Commission's investigation has confirmed that the development of a brand image is important for broadcasters in determining whether to acquire football rights[500]. Broadcasters consider that football enables them to create a brand image without which their channels would not be able to develop. The availability of alternative programming does not alter their interest in, or demand, for broadcasting

---

[498] For example, in England, the Premiership commences in August and ends in May. There are about 380 games played of which full live broadcasts of 60 take place.

[499] In its answer 2d of 26-11-1999 to the Commission's request for information, VMM (Vlaamse Media Maatschappij) states that: 'The acquisition (and broadcasting) of sports rights (programmes) is, in general not a profitable investment as such. However, the broadcasting of sports programmes, especially popular sport such as football and cycling, are important for the image and the branding of the channel'.

[500] In its answer 2k of 15-11-1999 to the Commission's request for information of 20-9-1999, RTL considers that 'The actual prices for football rights are so high that they cannot be covered by the revenues generated with football programming'. If such rights are still acquired anyway, it is for branding purposes.

rights to football events[501]. Richard Russell Associates have described sport as a 'driver' for BSkyB's 10-year old business[502].

(34)    One of the particular values of football in brand-building is its regularity. Unlike many other sporting events, football is characterised by tournaments which are played regularly throughout most of the year. Football, unlike other sports, therefore allows broadcasters to achieve high viewing figures on a regular, sustained and continuous basis[503]. Although there are league events for other sports, these are generally not as numerous and regular and whilst such sports may produce large audience figures, they do not achieve the same continued viewing figures as football. This is of a significant value for the branding of a channel, since it can only be achieved over a sustained period[504].

(35)    The quest for a brand image is so strong that broadcasters in certain circumstances do not mind losing money on individual programmes if the programme is of such quality that it can pull viewers to the channel. For some broadcasters, football could be considered as a kind of loss leader[505].

(36)    These features of the broadcasting rights to football make broadcasters willing to pay higher prices for broadcasting rights to football events than for any other events, including the most exceptional sporting events such as the Olympic Games and Formula One[506]. The table in Annex I shows that in the years from 1992 to 1996, 14 of the top 21 sports rights deals in Europe in terms of money paid concerned football. ONdigital states that 'Football rights are the most expensive of any sport [...]'[507]. The total expenditure on sports as a whole has seen substantial

---

[501]    ONdigital in its reply 2j of 23-11-1999 to the Commission's request for information of 20-9-1999: 'Our interest in football is not affected by the availability of other film, series, game shows or other content again, because of the unique market position football holds in the United Kingdom and partly because football is likely to appeal to a different market segment'.
NOS in its reply of 16-11-1999 to the Commission's request for information of 21-9-1999 considers that: 'Only to a limited exent NOS' interest in football is affected by the availability of Television rights for other sports because it is the No 1 sports in the Netherlands [...] football plays a key role in NOS' sports programming [...] providing other sports broadcasts by NOS with an audience they would not normally attract.' In reply 3e, NOS states that: '[...] football is a unique product in a 'league of its own'. No other sport has audience figures/market share that come close to those of football [...] enhance the image of NOS'.

[502]    Richard Russell Associates, 'Sports television: The ever changing face', 16 February 1999, pp. 10 and 12.

[503]    For example, in England, the Premiership commences in August and ends in May. There are about 380 games played of which full live broadcasts of 60 take place.

[504]    This conclusion is justified by broadcasters' responses to Article 11 letters; in particular replies of Eurosport, RTBF, VMM, VRT, France 2 and 3, and NOS.

[505]    In its reply 2k of 26-11-1999 to the Commission's request for information of 21-9-1999 VMM states that 'Actually, acquisition of TV rights for sport (especially football) is not a profitable operation as such [...] However, the branding of VMM's channels will be the decisive parameter for deciding the acquisition of TV rights for football games'. For instance, ONdigital, which has recently acquired the television rights to the UEFA Champions League and provides these rights on a promotional basis free to subscribers, states in its reply 2d of 23-11-1999 to the Commission's request for information of 20-9-1999 that 'In the early stages of platform growth building the subscriber base is considered to be more important than pure profit'. Further in its reply 2l of 23-11-1999 to the Commission's request for information of 20-9-1999, ONdigital states that 'ONdigital believes that the brand image and value attached to its consumer offer is directly by the sports content available on the platform'.

[506]    Kagan Euro TV Sports, 26-7-1996.

[507]    ONdigital in its reply 2e of 23-11-1999 to the Commission's request for information of 20-9-1999.

increases in the recent periods. Football accounted for the single highest proportion of television channels total sports expenditure. The European average was 44,6%[508]. The high percentage dedicated to the acquisition of football rights reflects the importance which broadcasters attach to football compared to the acquisition of the broadcasting rights to other sporting events.

### 2.1.3.2. A particular audience

(37)    Broadcasters wish to attract audiences. Broadcasters will therefore seek to have a balanced schedule with a range of different programmes in order to reach the widest possible audience. Catering to a wide audience is part of the public service remit for public service broadcasters. Pay-TV broadcasters wish to cater to the tastes of as many people as possible in order to sell subscriptions. For commercial broadcasters the reason is that they generally sell 'packages' of advertising slots spread across various programmes instead of individual slots during particular programmes[509]. Producers wishing to advertise during the Premier League, for example, will therefore also purchase slots during other types of programmes. This reflects the optimum strategy for an advertiser whose aim is to reach as large a proportion of its potential customers as possible, which is best done by showing adverts across a range of carefully selected programmes, each one of which will be watched by a different group of potential customers[510]. The fact that football is a regular and frequent event, which attracts high viewing figures, enhances the value of football programmes as part of an advertising package, because it allows the advertiser to make frequent contact with a potential customer with a distinct profile.

(38)    In deciding on a 'package', advertisers will not randomly pick programmes during which to show their adverts. The profile or type of audience, which a programme attracts, is of crucial importance to advertisers. This reflects the raison d'être of advertising: companies essentially advertise in order to attract new customers or to maintain existing ones. In order for an advert to fulfil this purpose, those who have at least a potential interest in the product being shown must see it[511].

(39)    Not all types of viewers are of equal value to broadcasters (and advertisers). Some people watch more television than others do. People have different spending powers and patterns. Amongst the most sought-after target audience are men with an above-average spending power and who are in the age group of 16 and 35, because that group is generally considered to have a less fixed spending pattern compared to older people. They are therefore more likely to try new products and services. The problem for broadcasters and advertisers is that this group contains a

---

[508]  Kagan Euro TV Sports, 26-7-1996.

[509]  ITV's reply 6f of 12-11-1999 to the Commission's request for information of 10-9-1999.

[510]  Thus, a football boot producer will, for example, reach a larger number of potential buyers by showing one advert during the final of a football tournament, when 'aficionados' are likely to be watching, and another during a feature film, when the weekend player may be watching, than showing two adverts during the football final. In this way a larger number of potential buyers will be contacted.

[511]  For example, whilst a breakfast cereal producer may have a less specific target audience, a meat producer is unlikely to wish to place an advert during a programme dedicated to vegetarian issues, even if this programme is very popular. Thus if broadcasters wish to have the business of meat producers, they can not only show programmes about vegetarianism, they must also televise programmes which are watched by people who are at least willing to eat meat (even if the programmes attract fewer viewers).

high proportion of 'light viewers'[512], who do not, as a rule, watch much television[513]. It is therefore much harder for advertisers to pass on their message to this target group via television advertising compared to other groups of the population such as women aged 55 or over, who on average watch a great deal more television. The attractiveness and elusiveness of the target group make programmes watched by them of significant value to broadcasters and they are thus keen to have programmes which attract this target audience.

(40)    The Commission's investigation has shown that football is the programme which seems to be the most effective tool for addressing this particular group of the population. Two thirds of the viewers are male and in the appropriate age groups[514]. As a result, broadcasters are able to charge higher rates for advertising in connection with football compared to other programmes, and the price of advertising slots during the transmission of football is higher than during the transmission of other sports. For instance, the Premier League and the UEFA Champions League allow British broadcasters to charge premiums of between 10 and 50% depending on the teams involved and the stage of the tournament[515].

(41)    The attraction of programmes and hence the level of competition for the broadcasting rights to them varies according to the type of sport and the type of event. Mass sports like football generally attract large audiences. By contrast, minority sports achieve very low ratings. International events tend to be more attractive for the audience in a given country than national ones, provided the national team or a national champion is involved, while international events in which no national champion or team is participating can often be of minor interest[516]. In most Member States, football constantly achieves the highest audience figures. In 1997, football accounted for 21 of the top 25 European sports broadcast. The popularity of football is also expressed in the number of hours dedicated to the broadcast of sport. Between 1996-1997, the number of hours dedicated to football transmission was 13936. The second most transmitted sport was tennis which achieved less than half this at 5115 hours[517]. These figures led the authors of Kagan Euro TV Sports to comment that 'the TV sports hours breakdown illustrates soccer's posi-

---

[512] Channel 5's reply 5c of 19-11-1999.

[513] For example in 1998, in the United Kingdom, television-viewing per day reached 81% of the adult population aged 16 and over. This group also watched on average 241 minutes of television per day. In contrast in the same period, television only reached 73% of the 16 to 34-year-old population. This group only watched a total of 182 minutes of television per day.

[514] For example Young & Rubicam Europe, reply 2e of 21-10-1999 to the Commission's request for information of 8-10-1999: product 'categories targeting female consumers are unlikely to advertise in sports programmes'. McCann-Erikson's reply 4a of 3-11-1999 to the Commission's request for information of 8-10-1999. Channel 5, reply 5c. ITV stated in its reply 5c of 12-11-1999 to the Commission's request for information of 10-9-1999 that the audiences to the UEFA Champions League 'are more male in profile than the average, younger than the average and more upmarket than the average.' McCann-Erikson's reply 2e of 3-11-1999 to the Commission's request for information of 8-10-1999 supports this. RTL considers in its reply 6d(i) of 15-11-1999 to the Commission's request for information of 20-9-1999 that it 'would lose advertising revenue if it substituted the UEFA Champions League by other football events or other sports events. Even if the viewer profile would be the same, the viewing times for these events would be much less because these sports events are less attractive'.

[515] McCann-Erikson's reply 3a of 3-11-1999 to the Commission's request for information of 8-10-1999.

[516] Recital 40 of the Eurovision decision (OJ L 151, 24-6-2000, p. 18).

[517] Kagan Euro TV Sports, 26-7-1996, p. 8.

tion as the most valuable sport to cover '[518]. Such views are also expressed in the replies to Article 11 letters: for example ONdigital states that 'In the United Kingdom Premier League football viewing consistently manages to attract audiences in the millions, outperforming all other seasonal sporting fixtures '[519].

### 2.1.3.3. Conclusion regarding the upstream market

(42)    In conclusion, the Commission's investigation shows that there is a likelihood that there is a separate market for the acquisition of broadcasting rights to football events played regularly throughout every year and which would in practice mainly involve national first and second league and cup events as well as the UEFA Champions League and UEFA Cup. A segmentation could be undertaken in respect of football events that do not take place on a regular basis throughout the year, such as the Football World Cup[520], since the latter does not constitute an equally regular source of programming for broadcasters. However, since even on the market for the acquisition of broadcasting rights of football events played regularly throughout every year, as mentioned above, the UEFA broadcasting regulations do not appreciably restrict competition, it is not necessary for the purposes of this case to exactly define the relevant product markets.

### 2.1.4. The downstream markets on which broadcasters compete for advertising revenue dependent on audience rates and pay-TV subscribers

(43)    As was explained above, the acquisition of broadcasting rights to football events has a strong impact on the downstream television markets in which the football events are broadcast as part of the broadcasters' competition for advertisers and/or subscribers. The broadcasting regulations do not restrict broadcasters' ability to compete for advertisers and/or subscribers. It is therefore not necessary to establish whether there are separate markets confined to the broadcasting of football events on the downstream markets because the broadcasting regulations do not raise competition concerns even on the narrowest market.

### 2.2. The relevant geographic market

(44)    The UEFA broadcasting regulations reflect the fact that the market for broadcasting rights to football events is national since such broadcasting rights are generally sold on a national basis – even for pan-European events such as the UEFA Champions League.

(45)    Also, the downstream television markets can be viewed as national or regional in scope, in particular for cultural and linguistic reasons[521].

### 2.3. Article 81(1) of the EC Treaty and Article 53(1) of the EEA Agreement

(46)    Article 81(1) of the EC Treaty and Article 53(1) of the EEA Agreement prohibits as incompatible with the common market all agreements between undertakings, decisions by associations of undertakings and concerted practices which may affect trade between Member States and the Contracting Parties to the EEA Agreement and which have as their object or effect the prevention, restriction or

---

[518]    Kagan Euro TV Sports, 26-7-1996, p. 163.

[519]    ONdigital in its reply 2i of 23-11-1999 to the Commission's request for information of 20-9-1999.

[520]    Recitals 42 and 43 of the Eurovision decision (OJ L 151, 24-6-2000, p. 18).

[521]    See Commission decision of 7-10-1996, Bertelsmann/CLT (OJ C 364, 4-12-1996, p. 3), Commission decision of 20-9-1995, RTL/Veronica/Endemol (OJ L 134, 5-6-1996, p. 32) and Commission decision of 3-3-1999, TPS (OJ L 90, 2-4-1999, p. 6).

distortion of competition within the common market and within the territory covered by the EEA Agreement.

### 2.3.1. Agreements between undertakings and decisions by associations of undertakings

(47)    The Court of Justice has ruled that, having regard to the objectives of the Community, sports are subject to Community law only in so far as they constitute an economic activity within the meaning of Article 2 of the Treaty[522]. Professional football clubs engage in economic activities[523] and they are undertakings within the meaning of Article 81(1) of the EC Treaty and Article 53(1) of the EEA Agreement. Individual national football associations are consequently associations of undertakings within the meaning of Article 81(1) of the EC Treaty and Article 53(1) of the EEA Agreement. They are also undertakings in so far as they themselves engage in economic activity[524]. UEFA is therefore an association of associations of undertakings and it is itself an undertaking to the extent it is engaged in economic activities such as the selling of the commercial rights to UEFA tournaments. UEFA, the national associations and the member football clubs are therefore undertakings within the meaning of Article 81(1) of the EC Treaty and Article 53(1) of the EEA Agreement, notwithstanding the fact that some of these entities are non-profit making bodies and apart from any cultural or social activities they may pursue.

(48)    The broadcasting regulations are laid down in the internal rules of UEFA. The competent organs of UEFA have adopted these regulations. This is a decision of an association of associations of undertakings within the meaning of Article 81(1) of the EC Treaty and Article 53(1) of the EEA Agreement[525].

---

[522] See judgments of the Court of 12-12-1974, Case 36/74, Walrave v Union cycliste internationale, [1974] ECR 1405, paragraph 4, of 14-7-1976, Case 13/76, Donà v Mantero, [1976] ECR 1333, paragraph 12, of 15-12-1995, Case C-415/93, URBSF v Bosman, [1995] ECR I-4921, paragraph 73, of 11-4-2000, Cases C-51/96 and C-191/97, Christelle Deliège v Ligue Francophone de Judo et Disciplines Asbl and Others [2000] ECR I-2549, paragraphs 41 and 42, and of 13-4-2000, Case C-176/96, Jyri Lehtonen and Others v Fédération Royale Belge des Sociétés de Basket-ball ASBL (FRBSB), [2000] ECR I-2681, paragraphs 32 and 33.

[523] For example selling tickets, transferring players, distributing merchandising articles, concluding advertising and sponsorship contracts, selling broadcasting rights, etc. The size of the undertaking does not matter and the concept of 'undertaking' does not presuppose a profit-making intention. See opinion of Advocate-General Lenz in Case C-415/93, URBSF v Bosman, [1995] ECR I-4921, paragraph 255 referring to the judgment in Joined Cases 209 to 215 and 218/78, Van Landewyck v Commission [1980] ECR 3125, paragraph 88.

[524] Opinion of Advocate-General Lenz in Case C-415/93, URBSF v Bosman, [1995] ECR I-4921, paragraph 256. See also Commission Decision of 27-10-1992 relating to a proceeding under Article 85 of the EEC Treaty (IV/33.384 and IV/33.378 – Distribution of package tours during the 1990 World Cup) (OJ L 326, of 12-11-1992, p. 31) paragraph 49 ('[...] FIFA is an entity carrying on activities of an economic nature and constitutes an undertaking within the meaning of Article 85 of the EEC Treaty') and paragraph 53 ('The [Federazione Italiana Gioco Calcio = the national Italian football association] also carries on activities of an economic nature and is consequently an undertaking within the meaning of Article 85 of the EEC Treaty') and judgment of the Court of First Instance of 9-11-1994 in Case T-46/92, Scottish Football Association v Commission, [1994] ECR II-1039, from where it can be concluded that the Scottish Football Association is an undertaking or an association of undertakings within the meaning of Articles 81 and 82. See also Joined Cases C-51/96 and C-1291/97, Christelle Deliège v Ligue Francophone de Judo et Disciplines Asbl and Others, reference given above, at paragraphs 52 to 57.

[525] If they were categorised as agreements between undertakings, this would not change the situation since Article 81 of the EC Treaty and Article 53(1) of the EEA Agreement apply in the same

## 2.3.2. The broadcasting regulations do not restrict competition appreciably

(49)   According to UEFA, the broadcasting regulations provide national associations with a limited possibility for scheduling their domestic football fixtures at times that do not coincide with football on television. UEFA argues that while this may sometimes result in situations where broadcasters are unable to broadcast football when they wish, the broadcasting regulations do not result in any appreciable restriction of competition, because the period when the broadcasting of football may be restricted is extremely limited in scope and time.

(50)   From the outset, the Commission notes that the broadcasting regulations may not be considered as having any anti-competitive object within the meaning of Article 81(1) of the EC Treaty or Article 53(1) of the EEA Agreement. The object is not to restrict in a commercial sense broadcasters' possibilities of acquiring broadcasting rights to football events or to restrict broadcasters' possibilities of competing for advertising revenues or subscribers. The object is to promote the development of football and the variety of the competition.

(51)   Nevertheless, the broadcasting regulations may under certain circumstances potentially result in situations where broadcasters are unable to broadcast football events live when they wish. This is caused by the fact that the national associations are obliged to ensure that, when broadcasting rights from their territories are sold into a territory with blocked hours, these blocked hours are respected and that the football events in issue are not actually broadcast during these hours. However, this effect of the broadcasting regulations cannot be qualified as constituting an appreciable restriction of competition within the meaning of Article 81(1) of the EC Treaty or Article 53(1) of the EEA Agreement.

(52)   The Commission has reached the following conclusion, taking the features of the UEFA broadcasting regulations into account.

(a) The broadcasting regulations make it possible for the national football associations to block the intentional broadcasting of football within their own territories no more than two and a half hours on either a Saturday or a Sunday.

(b) These blocked hours must correspond strictly to the main domestic fixture schedule as defined by the broadcasting regulations, which is the time when the majority (i.e. 50% or more) of the weekly football matches in the top two domestic leagues in the country are played.

(c) This requirement prevents arbitrary decisions as to when to block hours, and the blocking of hours in any excessive manner or when no football is played, such as during holiday periods.

(d) If the main domestic fixture schedule is spread out too much, so that 50% or more of the weekly football matches in the top two domestic leagues in the country are not played on Saturdays or Sundays, the national football associations cannot block any hours.

(e) The close link to the main domestic fixture schedule also provides that the blocked hours will largely remain the same over the years. Furthermore, once the blocked hours have been fixed, the national football associations have no further influence on their application through any authorisation procedures. On this basis, the national associations and broadcasters are able to schedule football events well in advance to take place at hours not conflicting with broadcast games – a feature which is important for the rescheduling of football matches for broadcasting purposes. This feature is designed to meet broadcast-

---

way to both those forms of coordination. See opinion of Advocate-General Lenz in Case C-415/93, URBSF v Bosman, [1995] ECR I-4921, paragraph 258.

ers' concerns about the risk they may incur from the fact that football associations could switch their main fixtures and relevant blackout period from one period to another. The perceived risk stems from the fact that broadcasters are often required to contract for broadcasting rights in respect of future years.

(f) If national football associations allow the broadcasting of football events during the blocked hours within their territories, they can not object to the broadcasting of any other football event.

(g) The blocked periods do not apply to the transmission of non-sporting programmes, which may include short (recorded) excerpts of football matches.

(53) In analysing the market, the Commission has taken note that for the 2000/2001 season only 10 out of 21 national football associations have applied the broadcasting regulations and blocked hours (six on Saturday and four on Sunday), as can be seen in the table in Annex II. While three of four national football associations in the United Kingdom[526] have introduced blocked hours, they have, as in the past, done so in a coordinated manner. British broadcasters' concern, namely that there are four national football associations in the United Kingdom which are not obliged by the broadcasting regulations to coordinate their blocking of hours which could lead to each national football association blocking separate hours and thus making the broadcasting of football in the United Kingdom technically more difficult (but technically still possible) because the broadcaster would have to replace its football transmission with some other programme, is therefore theoretical and unfounded in practice.

(54) Another concern pointed out by British broadcasters is that they would not be able to benefit from a single British national football association applying Article 4 which is an attenuation of the restriction in Article 3 by providing for an exception to the blocked hours in respect of games of national importance[527]. They argue that each of the four national football associations in the United Kingdom have individual interests and although one national association may give dispensation from the blocked hours for the broadcasting of a match, this dispensation will not apply to the other national associations, thus rendering broadcasting impossible in those areas. The Commission notes that Article 4 is advantageous for broadcasters because it provides for an exception from the blocking and diminishes the blocked hours applicable in respect of certain, however infrequent, football matches. The provision provides that a football match can be broadcast during blocked hours where there would otherwise be a ban against the broadcasting of football. Moreover, application of the dispensation has the effect that the member association that applies the provision must also accept the transmission of any other match in its territory during the same period. Article 4 thus provides an advantage to the general rule by attenuation of the restriction in Article 3. Furthermore, none of the UEFA national football associations apply the provision in the 2000/2001 season. During the 1999/2000 season where there were significantly more blocked hours, the provision was only applied in respect of nine football matches. The English and the Scottish Football Associations applied the provision three times. One time was in respect of the same hours. It is therefore considered that the provision,

---

[526] The existence of four associations in the United Kingdom has historical reasons.

[527] The possibility of derogating from the blocked hours provided for by Article 4 of the broadcasting regulations is coherent with the approach in Article 3(a)(1) of Council Directive 89/552/EEC (OJ L 298, 17-10-1989, p. 23), which aims at ensuring that a substantial proportion of the public is not deprived of the possibility of following such events via live live coverage or deferred coverage.

which provides a dispensation possibility from the blocked hours, has little practical importance.

(55) Broadcasters further argue that the broadcasting regulations pose problems in respect of transfrontier broadcasts. Broadcasters argue that technological developments will mean that broadcasters will soon broadcast to all of Europe. Broadcasters will therefore have to comply with different local blocked hours in several different jurisdictions making transnational broadcasts more cumbersome. While it is correct that broadcasters must comply with the blocked hours in the territories into which they broadcast intentionally, it is currently considered that this fact does not make the possible restrictions caused by the broadcasting regulations appreciable. The Commission has not learnt of any cases where the effects of the broadcasting regulations have caused problems. For the purposes of the broadcasting regulations, 'intentional transmission' is defined as a situation in which a broadcaster transmits in the local language. Where pan-European broadcasters transmit as encrypted television services, there is the possibility of cutting out the countries for which blocked hours apply. In free-to-air transmission, pan-European channels such as Eurosport have the possibility of not transmitting football with commentary in a given language in order to avoid the application of the regulations. That a differentiation between countries is possible is illustrated by the example of Eurosport which already 'tailors' programming for regional or local audiences. Furthermore, Eurosport as the only pan-European sports channel available in all Member States of the EU and the EEA does, in general, as far as national European leagues are concerned, not use live rights, but broadcasts this football deferred. Since the broadcasting regulations apply only to intentional transmissions as defined above and since most broadcasters transmit intentionally only into the territory of a single national football association, the problem does not seem to be significant or appreciable at this stage. If these facts change in the future, the Commission may have to review the situation.

(56) Broadcasters finally express concern about the impact of the broadcasting regulations on new services delivered via the Internet. In contrast to traditional television, broadcasts of football matches via the Internet could be received on demand round the clock and, more importantly, the reception of Internet broadcasts is geographically unlimited. Thus, in order to comply with the broadcasting regulations, an Internet service provider would have to observe all the different blocked periods of all member associations and the provider would have to lock the broadcasts during the blocked periods to users in each member association and unlock the broadcasts during the free periods. While technically possible for an Internet service provider, it is not economically sensible for Internet providers to follow this procedure and such a requirement could act as a barrier to the development of new, innovative services. However, the Commission shares the view of one of the third parties that have commented that the technology for the transmission of video streams over the Internet is still immature and the economic value of such services is still rather negligible. The Commission's current view is therefore that it cannot establish that the broadcasting regulations appreciably restrict the possibilities of providing football video streams over the Internet. The Commission does not know of a service that provides live full coverage streaming of football matches or intends to provide such a service in the near future. However, this view may change in the future: in particular, if developments are brought to the attention of the Commission which indicate that the broadcasting regulations have become a barrier to the development of new Internet services, it will reconsider this Decision in the light of these new circumstances.

(57)  With these facts in mind, the Commission has examined the fixtures for the first and second division football leagues in a number of the national football associations. The Commission has taken note that the traditional fixed fixtures – which according to the broadcasting regulations have to correspond to the blocked hours – vary in the different countries (see table in Annex II) and that the fixtures are increasingly spread – in particular in the leagues from the big football nations (e.g. England, France, Germany, and Spain) that have a foreign market outside their domestic market. In most of those leagues matches are played over several days of the week and at different and varying hours. The combination of the various fixtures will therefore only rarely result in situations where broadcasters would be prevented from broadcasting football of a particular origin and thus the acquisition of broadcasting rights of that origin[528]. Therefore, while broadcasters may not always be able to broadcast a particular match live, there are nevertheless plenty of other opportunities to broadcast other matches live from the same particular tournament. If a broadcaster wishes to broadcast live football from a particular country or tournament, it is consequently not, or only very rarely, prevented from doing so because of the broadcasting regulations. In addition, broadcasters also have the opportunity to broadcast live football matches from other national or pan-European tournaments, which are played at different times. Consequently, regardless of the existence of the broadcasting regulations, broadcasters are always able to acquire commercially interesting broadcasting rights to football events.

(58)  In addition, it should not be forgotten that broadcasters often also rely on the broadcasting of excerpts and highlights on a deferred basis in sports magazines programmes, etc. These programmes can easily be programmed so that they do not clash with blocked hours. Moreover, news coverage in non-sporting programmes is not blocked by the broadcasting regulations.

(59)  Since the Commission has found that the broadcasting regulations have no appreciable restrictive effect on the broadcasting market, it is not necessary for the purpose of this Decision to substantiate whether and to what extent there is a negative impact on stadium attendance and amateur participation in the sport due to the televising of football no matter whether it is on free-TV, pay-TV or streaming via the Internet.

(60)  The present decision does not in any way prejudice the assessment of the joint selling of broadcasting rights to football events under Article 81(1) of the EC Treaty and Article 53(1) of the EEA Agreement.

(61)  On the basis of these facts, the Commission has reached the conclusion that the UEFA broadcasting regulations cannot be considered to constitute an appreciable restriction of competition within the meaning of Article 81(1) of the EC Treaty and Article 53(1) of the EEA Agreement in this market,

## HAS ADOPTED THIS DECISION:

### Article 1
On the basis of the facts in its possession the Commission has no grounds for action under Article 81(1) of the EC Treaty and Article 53(1) of the EEA Agreement in respect of Article 47 of UEFA's Statutes as implemented by the broadcasting regulations.

---

[528] For example Canal+ is broadcasting English Premier League football into Denmark on Saturdays, Sundays and Mondays.

**Article 2**
This Decision is addressed to: Union des Associations Européennes de Football Route de Genève 46 CH – 1260 Nyon 2

Done at Brussels, 19 April 2001.

For the Commission
Mario Monti
Member of the Commission

**ANNEX I**

Top 21 European sports deals during 1992 to 1996 (Source: Kagan Euro TV Sports, 26 July 1996.)
[...]

**ANNEX II**

Broadcasting regulations (Article 3): Decision on 'blocked hours' by the national associations
(2000/2001 season – All local time)
[...]

———

**\* 2.4.66.  COMMISSION CLEARS UEFA'S NEW BROADCASTING REGULATIONS, 20 APRIL 2001**[529]

———

**2.4.67.  ACTION BY LAURENT PIAU AGAINST COMMISSION OF THE EUROPEAN COMMUNITIES, CASE T-121/01, 31 MAY 2001**[530]

An action against the Commission of the European Communities was brought before the Court of First Instance of the European Communities on 31 May 2001 by Laurent Piau, residing in Nantes, France, represented by Marguerite Fauconnet and Pierre Thielen, Avocats, with an address for service in Luxembourg.
The applicant claims that the Court should:
–     Declare that the Commission failed to adopt the necessary measures within a reasonable time following the applicant's complaint on the basis of Article 3 of Regulation No 17;
–     Declare that the Commission is obliged to take the necessary measures within one month against the party complained against in the applicant's complaint pursuant to Regulation No 17;
–     Order the defendant to pay the costs.
Pleas in law and main arguments
The applicant states that on 23 March 1998 he lodged a complaint with the Commission of the European Communities, arguing that the rules applied by Fédération International de Football Association (FIFA) to the activity of player's agent were contrary to Community law, in particular Articles and 81 EC (COMP/37.124 Piau/FIFA). The Commission

———

[529]  IP/01/583.
[530]  OJ C 227, 11-8-2001, p. 31.

made a thorough investigation and on 19 October 1999 sent FIFA a statement of complaints. On 24 February 2000 the parties presented their views orally. On 31 January 2001 the applicant, since he had not received any statement of position, called on the Commission to respond. To this day, almost three years after the complaint was made, the Commission has not taken a clear, explicit position on the problem submitted to it by the applicant.

The applicant considers that the Commission's inaction is contrary to the Treaty and to Regulation No 17, since it is allowing an infringement of Article 81(1) of the Treaty to continue, although it has all the evidence available to adopt the necessary measures.

———

**2.4.68.  NOTICE PUBLISHED PURSUANT TO ARTICLE 19(3) OF COUNCIL REGULATION NO 17 CONCERNING CASES COMP/35.163 – NOTIFICATION OF FIA REGULATIONS, COMP/36.638 – NOTIFICATION BY FIA/FOA OF AGREEMENTS RELATING TO THE FIA FORMULA ONE WORLD CHAMPIONSHIP, COMP/36.776 – GTR/FIA AND OTHERS, 13 JUNE 2001**[531]

1.    THE CASES

On 22 July 1994, the Fédération Internationale de l'Automobile (FIA) notified its regulations to the Commission under Regulation 17[532]. Subsequently, the agreement between FIA and International Sportsworld Communicators Ltd (ISC) relating to the marketing of broadcasting and media rights to certain FIA championships (except formula one) was also notified (Case COMP/35.613). The commercial arrangements relating to the FIA Formula One World Championship were notified separately (Case COMP/36.638 – FIA/FOA) by the FIA and Formula One Administration Limited ('FOA') on 5 September 1997.

The Commission published notices[533] summarising the notified agreements and inviting third party comments.

In 1997 and 1998, the Commission received three complaints concerning these notifications. The complaints were lodged by: (i) the AE TV Cooperation GmbH (Case COMP/36.520 and Case COMP/37.319), a television company whose complaint focused mainly on the European Truck Racing Cup; (ii) the GTR Organisation (Case COMP/36.776), which organised and promoted an international series for 'Grand Touring' (GT) cars. All three complaints were subsequently withdrawn, and the cases closed.

On 29 June 1999, the Commission issued a Statement of Objections. The parties submitted their written responses to the Statement of Objections in February 2000.

On 26 April 2000, the FIA and FOA submitted several proposals to modify substantially the notified arrangements in order to meet the concerns expressed by the Commission in the Statement of Objections. Subsequently, the parties filed further submissions, the latest on 12 January 2001. This notice describes the FIA rules and the commercial arrangements between FIA, FOA and ISC which will result from the above-mentioned proposals, modifications and submissions by the parties.

---

[531] OJ C 169, 13-6-2001, p. 5-11 (Text with EEA relevance).
[532] OJ 13, 21-2-1962, p. 204.
[533] OJ C 361, 27-11-1997, p. 7 related to Case COMP/35.163 and Case COMP/36.638.

2.     THE PARTIES

FIA was founded in France as a non-profit-making association. It has at present more than 162 members (29 from EU countries). These are national automobile clubs, associations, and national motor sport federations (ASNs). The FIA members organise and regulate motor sport in their respective territories. ISC is a company founded by Mr Bernie Ecclestone. Its principal activity was the marketing of television rights to FIA international series other than F1. In spring 2000, Mr Ecclestone sold the company to Mr David Richards and ISC is now charged with the promotion of the FIA World Rally Championship and the FIA Regional Rally Championships.

FOA/FOM, companies controlled by Mr Ecclestone, are engaged in the promotion of the FIA Formula One Championship. The term FOA/FOM, for the purposes of this notice, includes FIA Formula 3000 International Championship Limited, an Ecclestone family trust interest, which is engaged in the promotion of the FIA F3000 Championship. The 1998 Concorde Agreement provides that FOA is the Commercial Rights Holder to the FIA Formula One Championship. FOA is thus responsible for televising and generally commercialising the Championship. On 28 May 1999, FOA changed its name to Formula One Management Limited (FOM) which manages the rights. The commercial rights themselves were taken over by an associated company, now also named FOA.

3.     PRODUCTS/SERVICES

These cases concern the following services and products: (a) the organisation of cross-border motor sport series; (b) the promotion of such series; (c) the certification/licensing of motor car sport events' organisers and participants; (d) the broadcasting rights of the FIA Formula One Championship.

4.     THE NOTIFIED ARRANGEMENTS

4.1.   The FIA rules

The rules, which are the subject of the notification, comprise five sets of documents[534] :

   (i)     The Statutes of the FIA, ('the Statutes')

The Statutes are the principal constitutional document of FIA. They record the objectives of FIA; the persons eligible to become members; the rights and obligations attaching to membership; the role of FIA and its members in relation to motor sport; the structure and the organs of FIA and its sources of income.

FIA operates through a General Assembly; a Committee consisting of the FIA World Council for Touring and the Automobile and the FIA World Motor Sport Council; a Senate; the specialised Motor Sport Commissions; an International Court of Appeal; a Secretariat; and any other permanent or temporary commission or sub-commission which the Committee decides to set up.

   (ii)    The International Sporting Code of the FIA and its Appendices, ('the Code')

The Code is the document by which FIA lays down rules for the organisation and the conduct of motor sport events. It is administered by a number of different organs of the FIA, in particular the World Mo-

---

[534] The complete text of these documents is published every year by the FIA and can be found on FIA homepage <www.FIA.com>.

tor Sport Council. The Code and the General Prescriptions (see below) detail the sporting/technical rules under which the relevant motor sports events are to be conducted. The Code contains various appendices, which lay down very detailed specifications for vehicles, driver's equipment, approval of circuits, etc.

The Code takes effect as an agreement among the members of FIA. It confers on the ASNs power to issue licences to various classes of participants in motor sport competitions (drivers, manufacturers and organisers). By accepting a licence, the licence holder accepts to be contractually bound by the provisions of the Code and the provisions for its enforcement in accordance with the FIA statutes.

The main provisions of the Code as notified are:
– in accordance with Article 108 of the Code, any person wishing to be eligible to participate, as a competitor or as a driver, in any competition is required to make an application for a licence to the relevant ASN and to pay the appropriate fees,
– all international competitions are required to be entered on the international sporting calendar recording all international events to be held during the year. Article 47 states that no licence holder may participate in an international event if it is not entered on the FIA calendar and that no one may take part in such an event if he does not possess an FIA licence. Initially, entry on the calendar was at the discretion of FIA. If a participant does not comply with these provisions, FIA may withdraw his licence thereby excluding him from any event authorised by FIA. For instance, Article 58 states that in the case of non-compliance, any person or group which organises a competition or takes part therein will have their licence withdrawn. Article 118 provides that 'any person who shall enter for, drive in, officiate at, or in any manner whatsoever take part in a prohibited competition will be suspended by the ASN which has issued them with their licence',
– the version of Article 24 initially notified provided that no international series could be organised without the written approval of FIA which approval was conditional on the respect of FIA's rights of ownership concerning the televising of international championships.

(iii)  The General Prescriptions applicable to all FIA championships, challenges, trophies and cups ('the General Prescriptions')
The General Prescriptions set out the detailed sporting and technical rules under which FIA motor sport series are to be conducted. The initial notification included a provision according to which all filming and moving picture rights pertaining to any FIA World Championship are vested in FIA. In 1997, FIA submitted to the Commission a new version of this General Prescription which provided that this rule applied not only to all FIA championships but also to any international series authorised by FIA. In 1998, FIA again modified the rule in order to reduce its scope solely to FIA series.

(iv)  The Regulations of FIA International Championships
Each FIA International Championships has its own set of sporting and technical rules which are published in the FIA Yearbook of Automobile Sport.

(v)   Information contained in the FIA Yearbook and the FIA Bulletin
      The FIA Yearbook and the FIA Bulletin include regulations and infor-
      mation on drag racing, the annual international sporting calendar,
      organisers of events, advertising in automobile sport, international cir-
      cuits and hill-climb courses and long distance rallies.

4.2.  The notified agreements
      The notified arrangements also consisted of the following agreements: the
      Concorde Agreement, the Formula One Agreement, a number of promoters
      contracts, a number of Broadcasting Agreements relating to the FIA Formula
      One World Championship and the FIA-ISC Agreement concerning the FIA
      World and Regional Rally Championships.
      The Concorde Agreement as originally notified was agreed on 5 September
      1996 and was for a period of five years from 1 January 1997. On 27 August
      1998, the parties notified the 1998 Concorde Agreement which replaces the
      earlier agreement and runs from 1 January 1998 until 31 December 2007. The
      agreement is between FIA, all of the Formula One teams and FOA, the latter
      being designated as the commercial rights holder. The agreement sets out
      terms for the organisation and running of the FIA Formula One World Cham-
      pionship and the voting structure for its control, by reference to other agree-
      ments, contracts, FIA rules and regulations.
      In the Concorde Agreement, the teams recognise FIA's exclusive property in
      the FIA Formula One Championship, including in particular the trade marks,
      the right to the title thereof and responsibility for its organisation (clause 1.1).
      The teams undertake to participate each year for the duration of the agreement
      (clauses 5.3 and 5.2) and not to participate in any other race, competition, ex-
      hibition or championship for open wheel single seat cars other than formula
      one or a race for cars complying with a current FIA Formula (for instance,
      Formula 3000) (clause 5.2).
      Clause 4.1(b) defines FIA rights as all rights that are or become lawfully
      vested in and held by or on behalf of FIA including all rights granted by the
      teams. The teams grant to FIA on an exclusive basis the rights in, and ancillary
      to, their performance, the performance of all cars, machines, equipment and
      persons connected to the teams (including the drivers) as well as the rights in
      the formula one events (clause 4.2(a) and (b)). According to clause 4.10, the
      teams have no rights to the championship elements, i.e. to any film footage of
      the relevant events and any official timing information, intellectual property
      rights, trade names, logos or other indicia owned by or on behalf of and/or
      vested in FIA and/or FOA. However, the teams retain certain rights such as the
      right to produce and market their own merchandise as well as computer games
      (clause 4(d)).
      FIA and FOA undertake to the formula one teams (clause 5.4(d)(ii)), that the
      championship will be shown free to air where there are suitable broadcasters
      prepared to do this. FIA warrants that all FIA rights will be granted to FOA for
      exploitation in order to make payments to the teams as provided by schedule 5
      of the agreement (clause 5.5)[535]. FOA also undertakes to each team that it will
      enter into Grand Prix contracts with the promoters who are to host a formula

---

[535] The Concorde Agreement sets out the obligations on FOA to pay certain amounts to all
teams to reflect their contribution to the FIA Formula One World Championship. FOA agrees to pay
each team a sum calculated by reference to, inter alia, FOA's gross revenues from exploitation of the
TV rights.

one Grand Prix during the term of the 1998 Concorde Agreement (clause 5.4(c)). FIA undertakes to enter a Grand Prix event on the FIA calendar only where the promoters have entered into a Grand Prix Contract with FOA (clause 11.2(a)).

The Formula One Agreement is between FIA and FOM (then called FOCA Administration Limited) (the latter has now novated its rights to FOA). It is dated 19 December 1995, took full effect on 1 January 1997 and is effective until 2010. FOA acquires from FIA for 14 years all of FIA's commercial rights to the FIA Formula One World Championship, including the such right as the FIA has to exploit the sound and moving picture rights to the Championship. FOA agrees to reward FIA and all teams to reflect their contribution to the championship. FIA and FOA mutually undertake to use their best endeavours to maintain the FIA Formula One World Championship as the premier world championship for racing cars and the only FIA world championship for single seater open wheeled racing cars.

The Grand Prix contracts between FOA and local promoters are drafted in accordance with the terms of schedule 4 to the Concorde Agreement. The agreements typically run for five years. They relate to the promotion of a Grand Prix event and govern the commercial and financial management of such Grand Prix. The promoter assigns to FOA all copyright, intellectual property rights and other rights which it may have now or in the future in any media (clause 23.3). Under clause 27, the promoters undertake to ensure that during the term of the contract no race for open wheeled cars other than the Grand Prix or a race in the Formula 3000 Championship will take place on the circuit.

The Broadcasting Agreements have been concluded by FOA with 60 broadcasters worldwide. For each Grand Prix, FOA contracts with a broadcasting company in the host country to serve as host broadcaster, who is responsible for the production of moving images of the Grand Prix and making a signal – the 'international feed' – available to non-host broadcasters. Some of the agreements provided for a discount of 33% on the price paid by the broadcaster if the broadcaster agreed not to broadcast any open wheeler racing other than formula one. There are two categories of broadcasting agreements. For free-access television, contracts are typically concluded with one broadcaster in a territorially defined area and with certain limited exclusivity granted. They have a duration of between one and five years except for a small number which are for 10 years. For pay television, FOA has entered into pay TV contracts for the 'supersignal' – a service provided by FOA using state-of-the-art digital technology to produce six separate channels. The duration of these agreements is up to 11 years.

The FIA/ISC Agreement became effective on 27 August 1996 and expires on 31 December 2010. Under this agreement, FIA granted ISC for 14 years the exclusive broadcasting rights to 18 FIA championships for ISC's own use and benefit. ISC also submitted copies of agreements it had concluded with organisers of events and with broadcasters. In April 2000, an Ecclestone family trust sold the entire share capital of ISC to a conglomerate led by Mr David Richards who informed the Commission that prior to the transaction, FIA had modified its contract with ISC which now only holds the rights to the FIA World Rally and Regional Rally (European, African, etc.) Championships.

5.    MODIFICATIONS AND UNDERTAKINGS BY THE PARTIES
The Commission's Statement of Objections issued in June 2000 made the prelimi-

nary assessment that FIA had a 'conflict of interest' in that it was using its regulatory powers to block the organisation of races which competed with the events promoted or organised by FIA (i.e. those events from which FIA derived a commercial benefit). Moreover, for a certain period of time, FIA may have been abusing a dominant position under Article 82 of the EC Treaty by claiming the TV rights to motor sport series it authorised. An analogous situation was created in formula one by the imposition of certain clauses in the Concorde Agreement. Finally, certain notified contracts appeared to contravene Article 81 and/or Article 82 of the EC Treaty in that they raised further the barriers to entry for a potential entrant: the promoters' contracts prevented circuits used for formula one from being used for races which could compete with formula one for a period of 10 years; the Concorde Agreement prevented the teams from racing in any other series comparable to formula one; the agreements with broadcasters placed a financial penalty on them if they showed motor sports that competed with F1 series. Certain agreements between FOA and broadcasters appeared to restrict competition within the meaning of Article 81 of the EC Treaty by granting the latter exclusivity in their territories for excessive periods of time.

Although the parties do not agree with the Commission's Objections, they have nevertheless agreed to modify significantly certain of their arrangements.

The modifications have the following objectives:
- to establish a complete separation of the commercial and regulatory functions in relation to the FIA Formula One World Championship and the FIA World Rally Championship where new agreements are proposed which place the commercial exploitation of these championships at arm's length,
- to improve transparency of decision making and appeals procedures, and to create greater accountability,
- to guarantee access to motor sport to any person meeting the relevant safety and fairness criteria,
- to guarantee access to the international sporting calendar and ensure that no restriction is placed on access to external independent appeals,
- to modify the duration of free-to-air broadcasting contracts in relation to the FIA Formula One World Championship.

In order to achieve a more complete separation between sporting and commercial matters and in order to increase transparency, FIA proposes that Mr Ecclestone relinquish his seat on the FIA Senate and his role as FIA Vice-President for Promotional Affairs. FIA proposes to make Mr Ecclestone an honorary Vice-President of FIA. FIA is also prepared to stipulate that the representative of the formula one commission should not participate in any decision in the FIA World Motor Sport Council regarding the authorisation of any series which is a potential rival.

Moreover, FIA will be prepared in principle to participate in the sporting management and attach the FIA's name to a series where the series' organiser wishes to form a partnership with FIA, where an organiser promotes the definitive competition in a particular discipline, where that organiser demonstrably properly manages that competition and where the discipline itself is sufficiently popular and developed.

On 28 June 2000 and 5 October 2000, FIA modified the International Sporting Code as follows:
- Article 2 – addition of a positive affirmation that the purpose of the code is to facilitate motor sport and that the code will never be enforced so as to prevent or impede a competition or the participation of a competitor, save where FIA concludes that this is necessary for the safe, fair or orderly conduct of motor sport,

- Articles 17, 58, 84, 113, 118 - addition of a provision stating that FIA will state reasons for refusing any entry to an international event, for any withdrawal of a licence which arises as a consequence of a rule breach, if an international licence for a track or autodrome is refused, if a licence to an applicant who does not meet the relevant criteria is refused and in the event of FIA being called upon to adjudicate upon a disagreement between ASNs upon the imposition of certain penalties,
- Article 24 - deletion of a reference to the FIA rights of ownership to the media rights in championships as described in the general prescriptions,
- Article 47 - insertion of a positive affirmation that any applicant who qualifies for a licence within the terms of the code shall be entitled to such a licence and that any refusal of a licence shall be reasoned,
- Article 63 - insertion of a positive affirmation that the holders of organiser's licences who apply for organiser's permits shall be entitled to those permits provided that the relevant criteria are met,
- Article 74 - insertion of a positive affirmation that any refusal of an entry will be reasoned and deletion of a provision stating that no appeal is available in the event of the refusal of an entry,
- Article 165 - insertion of a positive affirmation that FIA will notify and state reasons to the persons upon whom sentence is passed in the event of a decision to suspend or disqualify,
- Article 169 - insertion of the positive declaration 'without prejudice to any right to appeal any decision' and removal of the statement that any appellant may incur disqualification in the event of such an appeal,
- Article 189 - insertion of a positive declaration that judgments of FIA's Court of Appeal shall be reasoned,
- Article 191 - in relation to the publication of judgments, insertion of the statement 'without prejudice to any right of appeal' and removal of the statement that any appellant may incur disqualification in the event of such an appeal. FIA proposes to introduce a new sub Article (Article 191(b)) in the International Sporting Code which states: 'For the avoidance of doubt, nothing in the code shall prevent any party from pursuing any right of action which it may have before any Court or Tribunal',
- Article 204 - removal of a cross-reference to the general prescriptions which claims ownership of the media rights to FIA's championships,
- Annex G - insertion of a guarantee that provided an event complies in all respects with the provisions of the code FIA will enter it onto the calendar. FIA proposes to incorporate a new Article 5 to Annex G of the International Sporting Code as follows: 'Where two applications are received for the same date in the calendar and the Calendar Commission determines that it would be contrary to the interests of the sport to grant both and where no negotiated solution is possible, the event which has a longer history of holding its event on the day in question shall take precedence',
- Article 27 of the general prescriptions - deletion of this article which incorporated a claim by FIA to ownership of the media rights and replacement with an affirmation that the organiser of an event shall ensure that media coverage is fair and impartial.

The parties have also modified their commercial arrangements in the following manner:
- 1998 Concorde Agreement

By letter dated 28 July 2000 from FIA to the signatory teams to the Concorde

Agreement and to FOM (formerly named FOA), FIA unilaterally waived its right to enforce the provision in clause 5.2 of that Agreement which bound the teams not to participate in any other race, competition, exhibition or championship for open wheeler single seat cars. FOA did the same by a letter dated 1 September 2000 to the signatory teams to the Concorde Agreement and FIA. By its letter of 28 July 2000, FIA unilaterally waived its rights in relation to clause 27 of the promoters contracts between the commercial rights holder and the promoters.

Moreover, FIA intends to waive its right to enforce clause 4.2 of the Concorde Agreement. However this waiver is expressly without prejudice to:

- the right of FOA to use images of the teams and cars in computer games,
- the right of FOA to use images of the teams and cars for promotional material as defined in Article 4.3 of the Concorde Agreement (such as photographs for posters, tickets, etc.), and
- the teams' agreement and consent to FOA continuing to film, broadcast and otherwise exploit footage containing images or representations of the teams and drivers to the extent that any such agreement and consent might be necessary under any national laws.
- Grand Prix contracts with the promoters

By letter dated 13 September 2000 to every promoter in the European Union whose contract contained a clause 27 provision, FOA unilaterally waived its rights in relation to this clause.

- FIA/FOA Agreement dated 19 December 1995

The main proposed amendments to the FIA/FOA Agreement dated 19 December 1995 between FIA and FOA aim at deleting any reference to FIA favouring the FIA Formula One Championship or to FIA endorsing a Grand Prix (over other events) and at guaranteeing that no provision in the agreement would prevent FIA from performing its regulatory functions.

Upon expiry of the abovementioned agreement with FOA, FIA proposes to enter into a 100-year agreement with a commercial rights holder for the marketing of FIA rights in relation to the formula one championship. All rights to organise and receive revenues from the championship will be transferred to this company for a fixed fee. FOA will not be automatically named as successor to the existing agreement. The draft agreement provides for the separation of commercial and regulatory functions in relation to formula one, allows FIA to use its logos etc. for regulatory purposes, acknowledges FIA as the sole regulator of the championship and does not contain any provision requiring FIA to favour this specific championship over others.

FIA proposes to adopt a similar approach to the FIA World Rally Championship (FIA/ISC Agreement) and to any other commercially viable FIA series. FIA will enter into arms'-length commercial agreements which will provide for fixed payments to be made to FIA removing thus any incentive for FIA to discriminate in favour of any series for commercial purposes.

- FOA broadcasting contracts

FOA has removed from its standard form TV contract the provision whereby broadcasters were afforded a discount of the rights fee payable if they did not broadcast any other form of open wheeler racing and by letters dated 14 August 2000 to the two broadcasters in the European Union whose contracts contained such a clause FOA unilaterally waived its rights in relation to it. Where exclusive rights have been granted in relation to terrestrial television, FOA is now limiting the duration of these contracts to a maximum of five years in the case of host broadcasters; and to a maximum of three years in all other cases.

FOA undertakes to notify comparable rival broadcasters when exclusive free to air broadcasting arrangements for a given territory expire and to invite them to apply. FOA has agreed to consider applications for broadcast rights on a non-discriminatory basis.

6. ASSESSMENT

The proposed changes to the regulatory framework and to the commercial arrangements appear to the Commission to introduce sufficient structural remedies minimising the risk of possible future abuse and to set the basis for a healthy competitive environment in economic activities related to motor sport. The Commission considers that, inter alia, the following elements are of particular relevance to this assessment.

The new rules introduce a separation of commercial and regulatory activities in motor sport, which FIA intends to make effective, inter alia, through the appointment as from 2010 of a 'commercial rights holder' for 100 years, for each of the FIA Formula One and FIA World Rally Championships, in exchange of one-off fixed fee, payable at the outset.

Minimum standards of safety are essential to the proper functioning of motor sport and it is appropriate for FIA to impose rules on participants in and organisers of motor sport events in order to guarantee the maintenance of those standards. In the absence of binding rules, organisers of and participants in motor sport events might be tempted to overlook certain essential safety requirements in an effort to reduce costs.

The modified rules provide that and the Commission has been assured that the FIA rules will never be enforced so as to prevent or impede a competition or the participation of a competitor, save for reasons inherently linked to FIA's regulatory role of maintaining safety standards. FIA has guaranteed that its licensing and disciplinary rules only be enforced to ensure a minimum level of safety at motor sport events (Article 2 FIA code). The reformed rules appear to provide satisfactory guarantees for a new regulatory environment where the FIA's licensing powers and the code's sporting and technical rules will be applied in an objective, non-discriminatory and transparent manner. The FIA will not object to the establishment of new events and the participation of circuits, teams and drivers in them, provided that the essential provisions contained in the code have been complied with. The FIA has in this respect confirmed that all those complying with the rules of the code will have their events listed on the international calendar as a matter of right.

FIA's submissions have confirmed the availability of legal challenge against FIA decisions both within the FIA structure and before national courts. Access to external independent appeals has been guaranteed in the FIA rules. As mentioned above, the FIA has agreed to insert a new clause clarifying that anyone who is subject to FIA decisions can challenge them before the national courts.

The new regulatory environment removes the previously identified obstacles to intra-brand as well as inter-brand competition. Competing events and series within the formula one discipline (and with other motor sport disciplines) will be possible. The reforms also create the possibility of increased inter-brand competition. New disciplines can be created, and events and series in potentially competing disciplines can be approved. FIA will have neither the commercial incentive nor the regulatory power to limit the type and number of events it authorises, other than on the basis of objective criteria.

The notified agreements as amended will remove those barriers which had prevented in the past the use of FIA licensed products and circuits or the participation of FIA licensees in different disciplines or in competing events in the same discipline. The proposed changes to the notified agreements will, for example, result in the availability of racetracks in Europe for rival series to use, even if these circuits already host FIA Formula One championship events.

The modified Concorde Agreement establishes the organisational structure of the FIA Formula One Championship and provides for the commercial arrangements aiming at marketing the series. As motor sport and especially formula one is a particularly complex technical activity requiring important investments in technological research and development, it is indispensable for all participants to agree on the way the series are organised. In this sport, for instance, all teams participate in all events at the same time. However, it is impossible to market the individual rights of each team participating in a race. As FIA, FOA, the teams, the drivers, the manufacturers and the local organiser or promoter may all have rights in the event, some arrangement between all of them for the sale of rights, especially the broadcasting rights, appears to be indispensable. The Concorde Agreement provides for FOA to be the commercial rights holder for the FIA Formula One World Championship and to negotiate on behalf of the teams and FIA the organisation of the races with the local promoters and the sale of broadcasting rights with broadcasters. These arrangements do not appear to affect prices or output in the market to any significant degree. Individual formula one events do not compete with each other as they are not broadcast at the same time. Moreover all formula one events are available for broadcasting.

Moreover, due to the complex technicalities of this particular sport, the Concorde Agreement allows more efficient marketing of formula one series and guarantees that free to air will be the principal way of transmission to viewers.

All provisions in the notified agreements whereby FIA compelled licence holders to surrender to FIA their broadcasting rights have been removed. The agreements no longer contain any rule or mechanism which would allow FIA to appropriate all media rights to a given championship.

The broadcasting arrangements for formula one, as amended, will bring periods of exclusivity granted to individual broadcasters to a length that does not exceed what seems reasonable in view of the nature of the rights and the obligations and investments undertaken by broadcasters, given the specific features of the sport. The pricing policy applied to contracts no longer penalises broadcasters who choose to broadcast open wheeler racing events other than formula one. The possibility of intra-brand competition to formula one brought about by the new regulatory environment constitutes a further element in the Commission's favourable assessment of the amended broadcasting arrangements.

7.   CONCLUSION

The modifications and undertakings of the parties described above substantially alter the legal and economic context as compared to that described by the Commission in its Statement of Objections. The Commission now intends to take a favourable view in respect of the notified agreements. Before adopting a favourable opinion, the Commission invites third parties to send their observations within one month of the publication of this notice by mail to the following address or by fax to the following number quoting the reference Case COMP/35.163 FIA or COMP/36.638 FIA/FOA:

European Commission Directorate-General for Competition
Directorate C

Rue de la Loi/Wetstraat 200 B – 1049 Brussels Fax (32-2) 296 98 04.

If a party considers that its observations contain business secrets, it must indicate the passages which in its opinion ought not to be disclosed on the ground that they contain business secrets or other confidential material, and state the reasons. If the Commission does not receive a request with reasons it will assume that the observations do not contain any confidential information.

---

**\* 2.4.69.   ANSWER ON BEHALF OF THE COMMISSION TO WRITTEN QUESTION E-1097/01 BY BART STAES (VERTS/ALE), 14 JUNE 2001**[536] **\***

Subject: Violation of European Treaties by UEFA rules

---

**\* 2.4.70.   ANSWER ON BEHALF OF THE COMMISSION TO WRITTEN QUESTION E-967/01 BY RICHARD CORBETT (PSE), 19 JUNE 2001**[537] **\***

Subject: Restrictive practices for sports equipment

---

**2.4.71.   EUROPEAN COURT OF JUSTICE, ORDER OF THE COURT (FOURTH CHAMBER), STÉPHANE MONNIER V GOVAN SPORTS NV, EDWIN VAN ANKEREN V GOVAN SPORTS NV, GOVAN SPORTS NV V PASCAL JACOBS AND GOVAN SPORTS NV V DANNIE D'HONDT, JOINED CASES C-9/01 TO C-12/01, 19 JUNE 2001**[538]

(references for a preliminary ruling from the Hof van Beroep te Gent)[539]

Article 104(3) of the Rules of Procedure — Activity of procuring employment for professional sportsmen

In Joined Cases C-9/01 to C-12/01: references to the Court under Article 234 EC from the Hof van Beroep te Gent (Court of Appeal, Ghent), Belgium, for a preliminary ruling in the proceedings pending before that court between Stéphane Monnier and Govan Sports NV, Edwin van Ankeren and Govan Sports NV, Govan Sports NV and Pascal Jacobs, and Govan Sports NV and Dannie D'Hondt – on the interpretation of Article 59 of the EC Treaty (now, after amendment, Article 49 EC), Articles 86 and 90(1) of the EC Treaty (now Articles 82 EC and 86(1) EC) — the Court (Fourth Chamber), composed of: A. La Pergola, President of the Chamber, D.A.O. Edward and C.W.A. Timmermans (Rapporteur), Judges; D. Ruiz-Jarabo Colomer, Advocate General; R. Grass, Registrar, has made an order on 19 June 2001, in which it rules:

*Public employment procurement offices are subject to the prohibition in Article 86 of the EC Treaty (now Article 82 EC), provided that the application of that provision does not frustrate the specific function entrusted to them. A Member State which prohibits any ac-*

---

[536]   Question of 6-4-2001; OJ C 340 E, 4-12-2001, p. 169-170.

[537]   Question of 30-3-2001; OJ C 340 E, 4-12-2001, p. 135.

[538]   OJ C 254, 1-9-2001, p. 2. (Provisional translation; the definitive translation will be published (2001/C 245/04) in the European Court Reports).

[539]   OJ C 61 of 24-2-2001, p. 10.

*tivity of mediation and intervention between the seeking and offering of employment which is not carried on by those offices infringes Article 90(1) of the EC Treaty (now Article 86(1) EC) if it creates a situation in which public employment procurement offices are necessarily put in a position where they contravene the provisions of Article 86 of the Treaty. That is the case in particular where the following conditions are met:*

- *the public employment procurement offices are manifestly unable to satisfy demand on the labour market for the kind of activities concerned;*
- *the actual carrying on of employment procurement activities by private agencies is rendered impossible by the maintenance in force of provisions of law which prohibit those activities on pain of criminal and administrative penalties;*
- *the procurement activities in question are to extend to the nationals or the territory of other Member States.*

———

**\* 2.4.72. COMMISSION OPENS PROCEEDINGS AGAINST UEFA'S SELLING OF TV RIGHTS TO UEFA CHAMPIONS LEAGUE, 20 JULY 2001**[540]

———

**2.4.73. EUROPEAN COURT OF JUSTICE, JUDGMENT OF THE COURT OF FIRST INSTANCE (THIRD CHAMBER), MÉTROPOLE TÉLÉVISION (M6), SUEZ-LYONNAISE DES EAUX, FRANCE TÉLÉCOM AND TÉLÉVISION FRANÇAISE 1 SA (TF1) V COMMISSION OF THE EUROPEAN COMMUNITIES, CASE T-112/99**[541]**, 18 SEPTEMBER 2001**

*Actions for annulment – Competition – Pay television – Joint venture – Article 85 of the EC Treaty (now Article 81 EC) – Article 85(1) of the Treaty – Negative clearance – Ancillary restrictions – Rule of reason – Article 85(3) of the Treaty – Exemption decision – Duration.*

**Parties**
Métropole télévision (M6), established in Neuilly sur Seine (France), Suez-Lyonnaise des eaux, established in Nanterre (France), France Télécom, established in Paris (France), represented by D. Théophile, lawyer, with an address for service in Luxembourg, and Télévision française 1 SA (TF1), established in Paris, represented by P. Dunaud and P. Elsen, lawyers, with an address for service in Luxembourg, applicants, v Commission of the European Communities, represented by E. Gippini Fournier and K. Wiedner, acting as Agents, with an address for service in Luxembourg, defendant, supported by CanalSatellite, established in Paris, represented by L. Cohen-Tanugi and F. Brunet, lawyers, with an address for service in Luxembourg, intervener,
APPLICATION for annulment of Articles 2 and 3 of Commission Decision 1999/242/EC of 3 March 1999 relating to a proceeding pursuant to Article 85 of the EC Treaty (IV/ 36.237 – TPS) (OJ 1999 L 90, p. 6),

*The Court of First Instance of the European Communities*
(Third Chamber), composed of: J. Azizi, President, K. Lenaerts and M. Jaeger, Judges, Registrar: D. Christensen, Administrator, having regard to the written procedure and further to the hearing on 18 January 2001, gives the following Judgment

---

[540] IP/01/1043.
[541] ECR 2001, p. II-2459.

**Grounds of the judgment**

**General background to the case**

**A. Description of the operation**

1.    This case relates to Commission Decision 1999/242/EC of 3 March 1999 relating to a proceeding pursuant to Article 85 of the EC Treaty (Case No IV/36.237 – TPS) (OJ 1999 L 90, p. 6) ('the contested decision') concerning the creation of Télévision par satellite (hereinafter 'TPS'), whose object is to devise, develop and broadcast, in digital mode by satellite, a range of television programmes and services, against payment, to French-speaking television viewers in Europe (point 76 of the contested decision).

2.    TPS, which was set up in the form of a partnership (société en nom collectif) under French law by six major companies active in the television sectors (Metropole television (M6), Télévision française 1 SA (TF1), France 2 and France 3) or in the telecommunication and cable distribution sectors (France Telecom and Suez-Lyonnaise des Eaux) is a new entrant on markets that are very much dominated by a long-standing operator, namely Canal+ and its subsidiary CanalSatellite.

**B. The relevant markets and their structure**

3.    According to the contested decision, the main product market affected by the creation of TPS is the pay-TV market (points 23 and 24 of the contested decision). The operation also affects the market in the acquisition of broadcasting rights and the marketing of special-interest channels.

4.    As regards the relevant geographic market, the Commission stated in the contested decision that at the time when the decision was adopted, those various markets had to be assessed on a national basis, so that in the present case the markets were confined to France (points 40 to 43 of the contested decision).

**1. The pay-TV market in France**

5.    According to point 25 of the contested decision, this market constitutes a product market that is separate from free-access television (also referred to as 'television in clear'). Unlike in the latter market, in which the trade relationship is between the broadcaster and the advertiser, in the case of pay-TV there is a trade relationship between the broadcaster and the viewer as subscriber. The conditions of competition are therefore different on those two markets.

6.    The contested decision also states that, when the decision was adopted, the pay-TV market comprised three methods of transmission (terrestrial, satellite and cable) and that those three different transmission methods did not constitute separate markets (point 30 of the contested decision).

7.    The longest-established competitor on the French pay-TV market is Canal+, which enjoys a strong brand image and highly developed know-how in the management of pay-TV (point 44 of the contested decision). The Canal+ group also operates in the cable distribution sector through its control of the NumériCâble network. Moreover, through its subsidiary CanalSatellite, Canal+ offers a bouquet of digital pay-TV satellite channels (hereinafter 'the digital bouquet') (point 46 of the contested decision). According to the contested decision, 'in terms of numbers of subscribers, the Canal+ group, including the premium channel Canal+, CanalSatellite and the NumériCâble network, accounted for approximately 70% of the French pay-TV market by 30 June 1998'.

8.    Another operator on the pay-TV market, AB-Sat, was launched in April 1996 by the French AB group, whose main activity is programme production and the distri-

bution of television rights. AB-Sat had 100 000 subscribers at the end of June 1998 (point 49 of the contested decision).

9.  Finally, TPS had 457 000 subscribers at the end of July 1998 and estimated that it would have 600 000 by the end of that year (point 50 of the contested decision).

**2. The market for the acquisition of broadcasting rights, in particular with regard to films and sport**

10. Since films and sport are the two most popular pay-TV products, the acquisition of broadcasting rights for such programmes is necessary in order to put together a sufficiently attractive range of programmes to convince potential subscribers to pay for receiving television services (point 34 of the contested decision).

11. According to the contested decision, the main competitors of TPS on that market, in particular in the purchase of rights to broadcast French and American films and sporting events, are Canal+ and the special-interest channels in which Canal+ has a stake (point 58 of the contested decision). The Commission also explains in the contested decision that 'the Canal+ group enjoys a particularly strong position on this market' and that AB-Sat and the general channels are also present on it (ibidem).

**3. The market in the distribution and operation of special-interest channels**

12. According to the contested decision, special-interest channels are essential for putting together attractive pay-TV services and the market in the distribution and operation of special-interest channels is enjoying rapid growth in France, particularly with the appearance of digital technology (points 37 to 39 and 65 to 69 of the contested decision).

13. As regards the market structure, the contested decision states: 'since the emergence of satellite platforms, the companies involved in pay-TV all have holdings in special-interest channels operating on the market. The stakes held in special-interest channels are fairly evenly distributed among the main players on this market. Canal+ is a major player, however, since it has holdings in the longest-standing channels which have achieved the best penetration of the cable market and have the largest number of subscribers' (points 67 and 68 of the contested decision).

**C. The notification and the notified agreements**

14. The parties first contacted the Commission in connection with this operation in the summer of 1996, with a view to notification under Council Regulation (EEC) No 4064/89 of 21 December 1989 on the control of concentrations between undertakings (OJ 1990 L 257, p. 13, as last amended by Council Regulation (EC) No 1310/97 of 30 June 1997 (OJ 1997 L 180, p. 1)) (point 1 of the contested decision). However, having been informed by the Commission that TPS was not a joint venture in the sense of an undertaking under the joint control of its members, on 18 October 1996 they notified the operation to the Commission and requested negative clearance and/or exemption pursuant to Regulation No 17 of the Council of 6 February 1962, First Regulation implementing Articles 85 and 86 of the Treaty (English Special Edition, Series I (1959-1962) p. 87) (ibidem).

15. Four agreements were notified. The basic principles governing the operation of TPS are set out in the Agreement of 11 and 18 April 1996 (hereinafter 'the Agreement'); they were expressed in more concrete and structured terms in the subsequent Associates' Pact signed on 19 June 1996 and in the TPS and TPS Gestion Statutes of the same date (point 70 of the contested decision). The agreements were concluded for a period of 10 years (point 71 of the contested decision).

16.     Three clauses contained in those agreements were the subject of the Commission's attention in the contested decision. They are, first, the non-competition clause, second, the clause relating to special-interest channels and, third, the exclusivity clause.

## 1. The non-competition clause

17.     This clause is included in Article 11 of the Agreement and Article 5.3 of the Associates' Pact and, at the Commission's request, its scope was defined by a supplementary agreement of 17 September 1998. It specifies as follows:
        'Except for ongoing cases as at the date of conclusion of the agreements, and except for the sale of new programmes and services that are not under contract to TPS, the parties undertake not to become in any way involved, even indirectly, and for as long as they remain TPS shareholders, in companies engaged in or whose object is the distribution and marketing of a range of television programmes and services for payment which are broadcast in digital mode by satellite to French-speaking homes in Europe' (point 77 of the contested decision).

## 2. The clause relating to special-interest channels

18.     Article 6 of the Agreement (under the heading 'Digital programmes and services') and Article 5.4 of the Associates' Pact cited above, provide that TPS has a right of priority and a right of final refusal with regard to the production of special-interest channels and television services by its shareholders. The clause is worded as follows:
        In order to supply TPS with the programmes it requires, the parties have agreed to give TPS first refusal in respect of the programmes or services which they themselves operate or over which they have effective control within the producing company, and in respect of the programmes and services which they produce. TPS is also entitled to final refusal or acceptance on the best terms proposed by competitors with regard to any programmes or services which its shareholders offer to third parties. If it accepts them, whether on exclusive terms or not, TPS will apply financial and contractual terms which are at least equivalent to those which the programmes and services could receive elsewhere.
        As regards the acquisition of these channels and services, TPS will freely decide, on the basis of its own assessment, whether or not to agree to integrate them into its digital bouquet, either exclusively or non-exclusively; however, the parties underline their objective of having programmes and services in TPS's digital bouquet on an exclusive basis' (points 78 and 79 of the contested decision).

## 3. The exclusivity clause

19.     Lastly, Article 6 of the Agreement provides that the general-interest channels (M6, TF1, France 2 and France 3, are to be broadcast exclusively by TPS (point 81 of the contested decision). TPS is to meet the technical costs of transporting and broadcasting the programmes but will not pay any remuneration for them (ibidem).

## D. The contested decision

20.     On 3 March 1999, the Commission adopted the contested decision.
21.     As is apparent from Article 1 of that decision, the Commission considered that on the basis of the facts in its possession it had no grounds for action pursuant to Article 85(1) of the EC Treaty (now Article 81(1) EC) in respect of the creation of TPS.

22. On the other hand, with regard to the contractual clauses described in paragraphs 17 to 19 above, the Commission concluded that:
   – with regard to the non-competition clause, there were no grounds for action in respect of that clause for the period of three years, namely until 15 December 1999 (Article 2 of the contested decision);
   – with regard to the exclusivity clause and the clause relating to special-interest channels, those provisions could benefit from an exemption under Article 85(3) of the Treaty for a period of three years, namely until 15 December 1999 (Article 3 of the contested decision).

**Procedure and forms of order sought**

23. By application lodged at the Registry of the Court of First Instance on 10 May 1999, the applicants brought the present action.
24. By document lodged at the Registry of the Court on 5 November 1999, CanalSatellite sought leave to intervene in these proceedings in support of the form of order sought by the Commission.
25. By order of 31 January 2000 the President of the Third Chamber of the Court granted leave to intervene and agreed in part to the request, lodged by the applicants, for confidential treatment of some information in the application and the annexes thereto.
26. The intervener lodged its statement in intervention on 24 March 2000. The Commission, TF1 and M6 lodged their observations on that statement on 4, 5 and 8 May 2000 respectively.
27. Upon hearing the report of the Judge-Rapporteur, the Court of First Instance (Third Chamber) decided to open the oral procedure. As measures of organisation of procedure pursuant to Article 64 of its Rules of Procedure, the Court requested the parties to reply to certain written questions. They complied with that request within the prescribed period.
28. The parties presented oral argument and replied to the Court's questions at the hearing on 18 January 2001.
29. The applicants claim that the Court should:
   – annul Articles 2 and 3 of the contested decision;
   – order the Commission and the intervener jointly and severally to pay the costs.
30. The Commission and the intervener contend that the Court should: – dismiss the action;
   – order the applicants to pay the costs.

**Law**

**A. Admissibility of the action**

**Arguments of the parties**

31. The Commission, supported by the intervener, claims that the applicants' action is inadmissible. It states that it is settled law that the applicants may only contest measures which are capable of producing binding legal effects affecting their interests. It also observes that, as is apparent from the Court's judgments in Case T-138/89 NBV and NVB v Commission [1992] ECR II-2181, paragraph 31, and in Joined Cases T-125/97 and T-127/97 Coca-Cola v Commission [2000] ECR II-1733, paragraph 79, only the operative part of the measure is capable of producing legal effects and, therefore, of adversely affecting such interests. The grounds for the decision in question, on the other hand, are open to review by the Community judicature only to the extent to which, as grounds for an act adversely affecting a person's interests, they constitute the necessary support for its operative part.

32.　According to the Commission, the operative part of a decision granting negative clearance and an exemption, such as that contested in the present action, does not adversely affect its addressee. The applicants' action for annulment is therefore inadmissible.

33.　The Commission considers that this conclusion is all the more necessary because, since 15 December 1999, the contested decision has exhausted all the legal effects which it produced. The present case is therefore of purely theoretical interest.

34.　The applicants dispute that the present action is inadmissible. They observe that the contested decision has binding legal effects which affect their interests (judgment in Case 60/81 IBM v Commission [1981] ECR 2639, paragraph 9) because the negative clearance and exemption are granted for only a period of three years. They observe, moreover, that in the judgment in Joined Cases T-374/94, T-375/94, T-384/94 and T-388/94 European Night Services and Others v Commission [1998] ECR II-3141, which also concerned an action for annulment of an exemption decision brought by the persons to whom that exemption was granted, the actions were held admissible.

**Findings of the Court**

35.　It is settled law that any measure which produces binding legal effects such as to affect the interests of an applicant by bringing about a distinct change in his legal position is an act or decision which may be the subject of an action under Article 173 of the EC Treaty (now, after amendment, Article 230 EC) for a declaration that it is void (IBM v Commission, cited above, paragraph 9, Joined Cases C-68/94 and C-30/95 France and Others v Commission [1998] ECR I-1375, paragraph 62, Case T-87/96 Assicurazioni Generali and Unicredito v Commission [1999] ECR II-203, paragraph 37, and Coca-Cola v Commission, cited in paragraph 27 above, paragraph 77).

36.　Thus, any natural or legal person may bring an action for annulment of a decision of a Community institution which does not allow, in whole or in part, a clear and precise request from that person which falls within the competence of that institution (see, to that effect, as regards a request based on Article 3(2)(b) of Regulation No 17, Case 26/76 Metro v Commission [1977] ECR 1875, paragraph 13). In such a situation the total or partial rejection of the request produces binding legal effects capable of affecting the interests of its maker.

37.　It is necessary to establish, in the light of those principles, whether the present action for annulment is admissible.

38.　In the present case, the applicants notified to the Commission the agreements relating to the creation of TPS and the restrictions which they considered to be ancillary to that operation, with a view to obtaining, under Article 2 of Regulation No 17, negative clearance for the entire duration of those agreements, that is to say for a period of 10 years, or, failing that, to obtaining an individual exemption for the same period under Article 4(1) of that regulation.

39.　It is apparent from the operative part of the contested decision that both the negative clearance relating to the non-competition clause (Article 2) and the individual exemption relating to the exclusivity clause and to the clause on special-interest channels (Article 3) are granted only for a period of three years.

40.　It follows from that limitation on the duration of the negative clearance and of the exemption provided for in Articles 2 and 3 that the applicants benefit only for a much shorter period than that with which they initially reckoned in terms of legal certainty resulting from such decisions. Moreover, the applicants have claimed, without contradiction by the Commission in that regard, that this factual situation also affected the calculation of the profitability of the investments underlying the conclusion of the notified agreements.

41.    That part of the operative part of the decision therefore produces binding legal effects capable of affecting the applicants' interests.

42.    It is of little importance in that regard that the applicants might possibly, following a new notification of the restrictions at issue, obtain a new negative clearance or exemption for a period that is less, equal, or even greater than that initially granted. Since they do not already enjoy the legal certainty which they would have enjoyed if the negative clearance and exemption provided for in Articles 2 and 3 of the contested decision had been granted for a period of 10 years, their interests are definitely affected by that part of the operative part of the contested decision.

43.    Lastly, unlike in the applications in the cases which gave rise to the judgments in NBV and NVB v Commission and Coca-Cola v Commission, cited in paragraph 31 above, the action for annulment brought by the applicants is aimed at the operative part and not the grounds of the contested decision. In the form of order sought by the applicants, they seek annulment of Articles 2 and 3 of the operative part of the contested decision. Furthermore, although it is true that in the judgment in NBV and NVB v Commission, cited above (paragraph 32), the Court held that a decision to grant negative clearance 'satisfie[d] the applicant and, by its very nature, [could] neither change his legal position nor adversely affect his interests', it must be observed that in the case giving rise to that judgment the negative clearance had been issued for a period which corresponded to that sought by the interested parties. On the other hand, as has been observed above, in the present case the negative clearance was granted for only a period of three years, whereas the applicants had requested that it be granted for a period of 10 years.

44.    It follows from the foregoing that the action is admissible.

## B. Merits

45.    The Court will first examine the pleas for annulment of Article 3 of the contested decision, that is to say, those relating to the exclusivity clause and the clause on special-interest channels. The Court will then examine the plea directed at Article 2 of the contested decision, concerning the non-competition clause.

## 1. The pleas for annulment of Article 3 of the contested decision

46.    With regard to Article 3 of the contested decision, the applicants rely on two pleas, alleging infringement of Article 85(1) and (3) of the Treaty. In the first plea, they submit that the Commission infringed Article 85(1) of the Treaty in that the exclusivity clause and the clause relating to the special-interest channels do not constitute restrictions of competition within the meaning of that provision and, in the alternative, that those agreements must be classified as restrictions that are ancillary to the creation of TPS. In the second plea the applicants submit that the Commission infringed Article 85(3) of the Treaty in that it did not correctly apply the criteria for exemption under that provision and committed an error of assessment with regard to the duration of the exemption.

## (a). The first plea: infringement of Article 85(1) of the Treaty

(i)    *The principal submission: the exclusivity clause and the clause relating to the special-interest channels do not constitute restrictions of competition within the meaning of Article 85(1) of the Treaty*

47.    The applicants submit that, in reaching its conclusion in the contested decision that the exclusivity clause and the clause relating to the special-interest channels con-

stitute restrictions of competition within the meaning of Article 85(1) of the Treaty, the Commission relied on incorrect assessments and misapplied that provision.

48. The Commission, supported by the intervener, disputes that those two objections are well founded.

## – The existence of incorrect assessments
## Arguments of the parties

49. The applicants state that in order to find that the exclusivity clause restricted competition the Commission tried to show, in points 102 to 107 of the contested decision, that the general-interest channels were attractive to viewers and that the effect of this clause was to deprive competitors of TPS of access to such programmes. According to the applicants, that finding is based on incorrect assessments.

50. They submit, first, that the Commission's finding that the attractiveness of the general-interest channels offered by TPS is explained by the existence of 'shadow zones' in France, that is to say zones in which reception by antenna of those channels is poor or deficient, is incorrect. The figures in the survey by Médiamétrie in November/December 1997 relating to the bi-monthly follow-up of initialisation ('the Médiamétrie survey') cited by the Commission are incorrect and do not take account of the fact that almost everyone in France receives TF1, France 2 and France 3 under good conditions. In support of that assertion, the applicants submitted at the hearing that, first, the Médiamétrie survey did not explain the methodological principles on which it had been drawn up and, second, that the broadcasting quality of television programmes from French television channels was checked every five years by the Conseil supérieur de l'audovisuel in the course of the licensing or licence extension procedure.

51. Second, the applicants observe that, contrary to what is indicated by the Commission in the contested decision, it is apparent from the market surveys that television viewers opt for TPS more on account of the wealth of programmes offered than the reception in digital quality of the general-interest channels.

52. Third, the applicants submit that the Commission's assertion that the two 'digital bouquets' (CanalSatellite and AB-Sat) were able to be launched successfully without exclusive broadcasting of the general-interest channels is irrelevant in this case. They observe that CanalSatellite benefited from a number of exclusive rights to films and sporting events when it was launched and still has exclusive rights to broadcast the Canal+ channel and that AB-Sat is established on a different market segment.

53. Lastly, the applicants state that, contrary to the Commission's finding in the contested decision, the fact that the four general-interest channels, which account for 90% of all television viewers and around 75% of cable television viewers, are broadcast exclusively by TPS does not necessarily mean that the access of competitors to the programmes of those channels is restricted. They observe that the market in television in clear and the market in pay-TV are two separate markets, so that there cannot be such a link of cause and effect. Furthermore, it is not certain that, if the four general-interest channels had not entered into commitments upon the creation of TPS, they would have agreed to participate in another digital bouquet. They note, moreover, that, as is shown by the situation in the other European countries, in which a single operator has a monopoly on the pay-TV market, a new entry onto the pay-TV market in France is no longer possible.

54. The Commission, supported by the intervener, disputes that its finding that the ex-

clusive right to broadcast the four general-interest channels constitutes a restriction of competition is based on erroneous assessments.

## Findings of the Court

55. The factual evidence on which the applicants rely in order to show that the Commission's finding that the exclusivity clause restricts competition is based on erroneous assessments, is either incorrect or irrelevant.

56. First, in the absence of any supporting cogent evidence, it is not possible to agree with the applicants' assertion that the figures in the Médiamétrie survey relating to the existence of 'shadow zones' in France, reproduced in point 104 of the contested decision, are incorrect and that almost all television viewers in France receive TF1, France 2 and France 3 in good conditions.

57. The intervener explained at the hearing, without being contradicted by the applicants, that Médiamétrie is the only market research institute which draws up viewer surveys in France and that those surveys are the reference point for all French television channels, which use them in particular in order to calculate their advertising income.

58. Moreover, contrary to the applicants' assertion, the controls carried out every five years by the Conseil supérieur de l'audiovisuel in the course of the licensing or license extension procedure do not prove that those figures are incorrect. As the applicants also accepted at the hearing, the control by the Conseil only relates to the broadcasting quality of the television channels and not the quality of the reception of those channels by French television viewers.

59. It should also be pointed out that the existence of large shadow zones in France, as shown by the Médiamétrie survey, appears to be confirmed by the market survey produced by the applicants, since it is apparent from that study that [...] % of persons questioned subscribed to TPS 'in order to receive the national channels correctly'.

60. Furthermore, the Commission clearly stated in the contested decision that the figures published in the Médiamétrie survey were, for it, 'only indicative [...] because in addition to the four general-interest channels broadcast exclusively on TPS they also include Arte and La Cinquième, for which the initialisation rate is 80.6% of households, and the terrestrial Canal+ service, which approximately [...][542] households are thought to receive in poor conditions' (point 104 of the contested decision).

61. Second, the fact that according to the various market surveys commissioned by TPS (in particular the BVA survey) the reason why persons have subscribed to TPS is above all the richness of the range on offer and not the possibility of also receiving the general-interest channels, as the applicants submit, does not invalidate the Commission's finding. Since the programmes of the general-interest channels enrich what is offered by TPS, those channels contribute to the attractiveness of that offer. Furthermore, as has been found in paragraph 59 above, it is apparent from the same market surveys that a significant proportion of persons questioned stated that they had decided to subscribe to TPS in order to receive the general-interest channels correctly.

62. Third, as regards the applicants' argument that it is irrelevant in the present case that CanalSatellite and AB-Sat were able to be launched on the market without the exclusive right to broadcast the general-interest channels, it must be pointed out that this factor was put forward by the Commission in order to show that the gen-

---

[542] Confidential data omitted.

eral-interest channels 'do not constitute a separate programme category or a type of content that is essential for pay-TV' (point 106 of the contested decision). Although it is true that this factor becomes of relatively secondary importance in regard to determining whether the exclusivity clause restricts competition, it nevertheless establishes that this clause is not objectively necessary for the creation of TPS, so that it cannot be regarded as an ancillary restriction (see, to this effect, paragraph 118 et seq. below).

63.     Finally, it is necessary to reject the factual arguments submitted by the applicants in order to prove that the exclusivity clause does not have the effect, contrary to the Commission's finding in the contested decision, of denying 'TPS' competitors access to attractive programmes'.

64.     It is in fact manifest that, as only TPS is authorised to transmit the general-interest channels owing to the exclusive rights which it enjoys, the competitors of TPS are denied access to the programmes which are considered attractive by numerous French television viewers.

65.     Furthermore, the applicants have not adduced any evidence to support their assertion that it is possible that the general-interest channels would refuse to be broadcast as part of the other digital bouquets.

66.     In the light of the foregoing, the applicants have not showed that the Commission relied on erroneous assessments in concluding that the exclusivity clause restricted competition within the meaning of Article 85(1) of the Treaty.

67.     That objection must therefore be rejected.

**– Misapplication of Article 85(1) of the Treaty (failure to apply a rule of reason)**
**Arguments of the parties**

68.     The applicants submit that the Commission should have applied Article 85(1) of the Treaty in the light of a rule of reason rather than as an abstract rule. Under a rule of reason, an anti-competitive practice falls outside the scope of the prohibition in Article 85(1) of the Treaty if it has more positive than negative effects on competition on a given market. They submit that the existence of a rule of reason in Community competition law has already been confirmed by the Court of Justice (Case 258/78 Nungesser and Eisele v Commission [1982] ECR 2015 and Case 262/81 Coditel and Others [1982] ECR 3381, paragraph 20). They also assert that, contrary to the Commission's submission, those two judgments are relevant in the present case because the creation of TPS also took place in conditions and on a market that are wholly peculiar.

69.     The applicants submit that the application of a rule of reason would have shown that Article 85(1) of the Treaty did not apply to the exclusivity clause and to the clause relating to the special-interest channels. They observe that, as follows implicitly from the reasoning adopted by the Commission in regard to Article 85(3) of the Treaty, those clauses, rather than restricting competition on the pay-TV market in France, in fact favour such competition as they allow a new operator to gain access to a market which was dominated until then by a single operator, CanalSatellite and its parent company Canal+ (the service offered by AB-Sat not really being a competitor, but rather complementary to that of Canal+).

70.     According to the applicants, the line of reasoning that Article 85(1) of the Treaty does not apply to the exclusivity clause and the clause relating to the special-interest channels is all the more compelling in the light of the case-law of the Court of Justice. It is apparent from that case-law that, first, a clause granting exclusive sales rights must be the subject of an economic assessment and is not necessarily caught by Article 85(1) of the Treaty (Case 56/65 Société technique minière

[1966] ECR 235) and that, second, an exclusive right granted with a view to penetrating a new market is not caught by the prohibition laid down in that article (Nungesser and Eisele v Commission, cited in paragraph 68 above, and Société technique minière, cited above; more generally, on the scope of Article 85(1) and (3) of the Treaty, Case C-399/93 Oude Luttikhuis and Others [1995] ECR I-4515, paragraph 10, and Case T-77/94 VGB and Others v Commission [1997] ECR II-759, paragraph 140, and European Night Services and Others v Commission, cited in paragraph 34 above, paragraph 136).

71. The Commission disputes that it infringed Article 85(1) of the Treaty by not applying a rule of reason, as suggested by the applicants, when examining the compatibility with that provision of the exclusivity clause and of the clause relating to the special-interest channels.

**Findings of the Court**

72. According to the applicants, as a consequence of the existence of a rule of reason in Community competition law, when Article 85(1) of the Treaty is applied it is necessary to weigh the pro and anti-competitive effects of an agreement in order to determine whether it is caught by the prohibition laid down in that article. It should, however, be observed, first of all, that contrary to the applicants' assertions the existence of such a rule has not, as such, been confirmed by the Community courts. Quite to the contrary, in various judgments the Court of Justice and the Court of First Instance have been at pains to indicate that the existence of a rule of reason in Community competition law is doubtful (see Case C-235/92 P Montecatini v Commission [1999] ECR I-4539, paragraph 133 ('[...] even if the rule of reason did have a place in the context of Article 85(1) of the Treaty'), and Case T-14/89 Montedipe v Commission [1992] ECR II-1155, paragraph 265, and in Case T-148/89 Tréfilunion v Commission [1995] ECR II-1063, paragraph 109).

73. Next, it must be observed that an interpretation of Article 85(1) of the Treaty, in the form suggested by the applicants, is difficult to reconcile with the rules prescribed by that provision.

74. Article 85 of the Treaty expressly provides, in its third paragraph, for the possibility of exempting agreements that restrict competition where they satisfy a number of conditions, in particular where they are indispensable to the attainment of certain objectives and do not afford undertakings the possibility of eliminating competition in respect of a substantial part of the products in question. It is only in the precise framework of that provision that the pro and anti-competitive aspects of a restriction may be weighed (see, to that effect, Case 161/84 Pronuptia [1986] ECR 353, paragraph 24, and Case T-17/93 Matra Hachette v Commission [1994] ECR II-595, paragraph 48, and European Night Services and Others v Commission, cited in paragraph 34 above, paragraph 136). Article 85(3) of the Treaty would lose much of its effectiveness if such an examination had to be carried out already under Article 85(1) of the Treaty.

75. It is true that in a number of judgments the Court of Justice and the Court of First Instance have favoured a more flexible interpretation of the prohibition laid down in Article 85(1) of the Treaty (see, in particular, Société technique minière and Oude Luttikhuis and Others, cited in paragraph 70 above, Nungesser and Eisele v Commission and Coditel and Others, cited in paragraph 68 above, Pronuptia, cited in paragraph 74 above, and European Night Services and Others v Commission, cited in paragraph 34 above, as well as the judgment in Case C-250/92 DLG [1994] ECR I-5641, paragraphs 31 to 35).

76. Those judgments cannot, however, be interpreted as establishing the existence of a

rule of reason in Community competition law. They are, rather, part of a broader trend in the case-law acording to which it is not necessary to hold, wholly abstractly and without drawing any distinction, that any agreement restricting the freedom of action of one or more of the parties is necessarily caught by the prohibition laid down in Article 85(1) of the Treaty. In assessing the applicability of Article 85(1) to an agreement, account should be taken of the actual conditions in which it functions, in particular the economic context in which the undertakings operate, the products or services covered by the agreement and the actual structure of the market concerned (see, in particular, European Night Services and Others v Commission, cited in paragraph 34 above, paragraph 136, Oude Luttikhuis, cited in paragraph 70 above, paragraph 10, and VGB and Others v Commission, cited in paragraph 70 above, paragraph 140, as well as the judgment in Case C-234/89 Delimitis [1991] ECR I-935, paragraph 31).

77.    That interpretation, while observing the substantive scheme of Article 85 of the Treaty and, in particular, preserving the effectiveness of Article 85(3), makes it possible to prevent the prohibition in Article 85(1) from extending wholly abstractly and without distinction to all agreements whose effect is to restrict the freedom of action of one or more of the parties. It must, however, be emphasised that such an approach does not mean that it is necessary to weigh the pro and anticompetitive effects of an agreement when determining whether the prohibition laid down in Article 85(1) of the Treaty applies.

78.    In the light of the foregoing, it must be held that, contrary to the applicants' submission, in the contested decision the Commission correctly applied Article 85(1) of the Treaty to the exclusivity clause and the clause relating to the special-interest channels inasmuch as it was not obliged to weigh the pro and anti-competitive aspects of those agreements outside the specific framework of Article 85(3) of the Treaty.

79.    It did, however, assess the restrictive nature of those clauses in their economic and legal context in accordance with the case-law. Thus, it rightly found that the general-interest channels presented programmes that were attractive for subscribers to a pay-TV company and that the effect of the exclusivity clause was to deny TPS' competitors access to such programmes (points 102 to 107 of the contested decision). As regards the clause relating to the special-interest channels, the Commission found that it resulted in a limitation of the supply of such channels on that market for a period of 10 years (point 101 of the contested decision).

80.    This objection must therefore be rejected.

(ii)    *The alternative claim, alleging that the exclusivity clause and the clause relating to the special-interest channels are ancillary restrictions*

**– Arguments of the parties**

**The concept of an ancillary restriction**

81.    As regards the concept of an ancillary restriction, the applicants refer to the Commission's XXIVth Report on competition policy, 1994 (page 120, paragraph 166), according to which 'restrictions [of competition] in the context of joint ventures' are 'restrictions only imposed on the parties or the joint venture (not on third-parties) which are objectively necessary for the successful functioning of the joint venture and thus by their very nature inherent in the operation concerned [...]'.

82.    The applicants also refer to the Commission's Notice of 16 February 1993 con-

cerning the assessment of cooperative joint ventures pursuant to Article 85 of the EEC Treaty (OJ 1993 C 43, p. 2, 'the notice on cooperative joint ventures'), in which the Commission stated that agreements 'which are directly related to the [joint venture] and necessary for its existence must be assessed together with the [joint venture]. They are treated under the rules of competition as ancillary restrictions if they remain subordinate in importance to the main object of the [joint venture]' (point 66).

83. The applicants further observe that it is clear from the notice on cooperative joint ventures, first, that an exclusive operating license granted to the joint venture without time-limit was regarded as indispensable for its creation and operation and second, that the theory of ancillary restrictions will, in general, be applied in the case of a joint venture which undertakes new activities in respect of which the parent companies are neither actual nor potential competitors (point 76 of the notice on cooperative joint ventures).

84. According to the applicants, the Commission's actual decisions show that those principles have been faithfully applied.

85. The applicants state that in Commission Decision 94/895/EC of 15 December 1994 relating to a proceeding pursuant to Article 85 of the EC Treaty and Article 53 of the EEA Agreement (IV/34.768 – International Private Satellite Partners) (OJ 1994 L 354, p. 75, point 61) the Commission took the view that clauses restricting competition had to be regarded as ancillary where they are indispensable to the joint venture and do not exceed what the creation and operation of the joint venture requires (see also Commission Decision 97/39/EC of 18 December 1996 relating to a proceeding under Article 85 of the EC Treaty and Article 53 of the EEA Agreement (Case IV/35.518 – Iridium) (OJ 1997 L 16, p. 87, point 48 et seq.) and, with regard to concentrations, the Commission Decision of 6 April 1995 declaring a concentration compatible with the common market on the basis of Regulation No 4064/89 (IV/M.564 – Havas Voyages/American Express) (OJ 1995 L 117, p. 8)).

86. The applicants submit, moreover, that the decisions and judgments cited by the Commission are, in general, irrelevant to the present case.

87. They state that the judgment in Pronuptia (cited in paragraph 74 above) and the judgment in Case 42/84 Remia v Commission [1985] ECR 2545 relate to the criteria for the application of Article 85(1) and (3) of the Treaty but make no reference to the problem of ancillary restrictions. They observe, next, that Commission Decision 87/100/EEC of 17 December 1986 relating to a proceeding under Article 85 of the EEC Treaty (IV/31.340 – Mitchell/Cotts/Sofiltra) (OJ 1987 L 41, p. 31, paragraph 23) does not add anything new. As to Commission Decision 90/410/EEC of 13 July 1990 relating to a proceeding under Article 85 of the EEC Treaty (IV/32.009 – Elopak/Metal Box – Odin) (OJ 1990 L 209, p. 15, point 31) that decision, in the applicants' opinion, confirms rather than contradicts the principle prominent in the decisions to which they have referred.

88. Lastly, the applicants submit that, contrary to the submission of the Commission and the intervener, classification of a clause as an ancillary restriction should not be by way of abstract analysis of the restriction but requires in-depth analysis of the market.

89. The applicants submit, moreover, that the Commission carried out such an examination in the contested decision. They also state that all the decisions and judgments cited by the intervener illustrate the fact that the market context is taken into account when classifying 'ancillary restrictions'. Thus, in the judgment in Remia v Commission, cited in paragraph 87 above, the Court of Justice refused, in the light

of the circumstances of the case, to classify a non-competition clause for a period exceeding four years as an ancillary restriction. In Commission Decision 1999/329/EC of 12 April 1999 relating to a proceeding pursuant to Articles 85 and 86 of the EC Treaty and Articles 53 and 54 of the EEA Agreement (Cases No IV/D-1/30.373 – P & I Clubs, IGA and No IV/D-1/37.143 – P & I Clubs, Pooling Agreement (OJ L 125, p. 12) it was decided, after an examination of the prices and terms of sale on the reinsurance market, that the joint purchase of reinsurance was, in the case in point, an ancillary restriction. In Commission Decision 1999/574/EC of 27 July 1999 relating to a proceeding under Article 81 of the EC Treaty and Article 53 of the EEA Agreement (Case IV/36.581 – Télécom développement) (OJ L 218, p. 24, 'the Télécom développement Decision') the Commission carried out an assessment of the economic and competitive position of Télécom développement on the market for voice telephony and concluded that the clauses notified were to be classified as ancillary restrictions. Lastly, in Decision 97/39 the Commission decided to classify the clauses notified to it as ancillary restrictions, again in the light of the specific conditions of that case.

90.    The Commission, supported by the intervener, disputes that the concept of an ancillary restriction should be interpreted in the manner suggested by the applicant.

**The consequences of classification as an ancillary restriction**

91.    The applicants submit that it is apparent from both the Commission's publications and its previous decisions that the commitments classified as ancillary restrictions must be treated in the same way as the main operation.

92.    The applicants point out that in its XXIVth Report on competition policy the Commission stated that ancillary restrictions are not 'assessed separately under Article 85(1) of the Treaty if the joint venture itself does not infringe Article 85(1) or is exempted under Article 85(3). While ancillary restrictions are normally only accepted for a limited period of time, in the context of joint ventures they are usually allowed for the whole duration of the joint venture.' Likewise, they observe that in the notice on cooperative joint ventures the Commission stated that 'if a [joint venture] does not fall within the scope of Article 85(1), then neither do any additional agreements which, while restricting competition on their own, are ancillary to the [joint venture] in the manner described above' (point 67) and that they 'must be assessed together with the [joint venture]' (point 66).

93.    The applicants also submit that the Commission has applied those principles in its previous decisions. Thus, in point 62 of Decision 94/895 the Commission took the view that, inasmuch as the joint venture did not fall within the scope of Article 85(1) of the Treaty, then neither did the clauses at issue (see also Decision 97/39, point 48).

94.    The Commission states that, although it is true that the legal consequence of applying the concept of an ancillary restriction is to cause contractual clauses that are a priori restrictive of competition and capable of affecting trade between Member States to an appreciable extent to fall outside the scope of Article 85(1), that does not mean that those clauses necessarily benefit from negative clearance for the same period as the main operation. As is apparent from the judgment in Remia v Commission, cited in paragraph 87 above, and from the contested decision, the duration of a restriction may be an essential criterion for determining whether or not it is ancillary.

**Classification of the exclusivity clause as an ancillary restriction**

95.    The applicants submit that there is no doubt that the Commission should have classified the exclusivity clause as an ancillary restriction.

96. They state that, in the light of the dominant position of Canal+, in particular in the market for broadcasting rights for French and American films, that exclusivity was the only means of entering the pay-TV market in France and of remaining on it by retaining an attractive range of programmes. The wholly peculiar nature of that advantage is also clear from the fact that it was granted to TPS by its shareholders, without payment on either side, in order to ensure its success on the market.

97. According to the applicants, the Commission's main argument to show that the exclusivity clause is not ancillary, namely that the creation of a venture that is active in the digital satellite TV sector would be conceivable even if it did not have the exclusive right to broadcast the four general-interest channels, is incorrect. They state that they did not have – and still have only very few – exclusive rights to broadcast films and sporting events when they decided to create TPS, so that their only competitive weapon was (and still is) the exclusive right to broadcast the general-interest channels. That clause is therefore directly linked to the creation of TPS and is necessary for its proper functioning.

98. The Commission disputes that it committed an error of assessment in not classifying the exclusivity clause as an ancillary restriction.

### Classification of the clause relating to the special-interest channels as an ancillary restriction

99. The applicants submit that the Commission committed an error of assessment in failing to classify the clause relating to the special-interest channels as an ancillary restriction.

100. They state that the Commission did not in fact take account of the fact that this clause was indispensable to the creation and operation of TPS, in as much as that privileged access to the channels and programmes of its shareholders and the right of last refusal was the only means by which TPS could secure its acquisition of special-interest channels, having regard in particular to the especially strong position of the Canal+ group on the market in those channels.

101. The applicants submit that it is appropriate to refer to Commission Decision 1999/573/EC of 20 May 1999 relating to a proceeding under Article 81 of the EC Treaty (Case IV/36.592 – Cégétel + 4) (OJ 1999 L 218, p. 14, 'the Cégétel Decision') and to the Télécom Développement Decision. Those decisions relate to competitive situations that are quite similar to the present case (markets dominated by a long-standing operator) and in those decisions the Commission's analysis related to clauses comparable to the clause relating to the special-interest channels, the clause at issue in the Télécom développement Decision providing for preferential access to an infrastructure and, in the Cégétel Decision, the clause providing for preferential purchasing by the joint venture from its shareholders. The applicants observe that, unlike in the present case, the Commission did not hesitate to classify those clauses as ancillary restrictions and to treat them in exactly the same way as the joint venture (see also Decision 1999/329).

102. The Commission disputes that it has committed an error of assessment in not classifying the clause relating to the special-interest channels as an ancillary restriction.

### – Findings of the Court

103. It is necessary, first of all, to define what constitutes an 'ancillary restriction' in Community competition law and point out the consequences which follow from classification of a restriction as 'ancillary'. It is then necessary to apply the principles thereby established to the exclusivity clause and to the clause relating to the

special-interest channels in order to determine whether, as the applicants' assert, the Commission committed an error of appraisal in not classifying those commitments as ancillary restrictions.

### The concept of 'ancillary restriction'

104.    In Community competition law the concept of an 'ancillary restriction' covers any restriction which is directly related and necessary to the implementation of a main operation (see, to that effect, the Commission Notice of 14 August 1990 regarding restrictions ancillary to concentrations (OJ 1990 C 203, p. 5, hereinafter 'the notice on ancillary restrictions', point I.1), the notice on cooperative joint ventures (point 65), and Articles 6(1)(b) and 8(2), second paragraph, of Regulation No 4064/89).

105.    In its notice on ancillary restrictions the Commission rightly stated that a restriction 'directly related' to implementation of a main operation must be understood to be any restriction which is subordinate to the implementation of that operation and which has an evident link with it (point II.4).

106.    The condition that a restriction be necessary implies a two-fold examination. It is necessary to establish, first, whether the restriction is objectively necessary for the implementation of the main operation and, second, whether it is proportionate to it (see, to that effect, Remia v Commission, cited in paragraph 87 above, paragraph 20; see also points II.5 and II.6 of the notice regarding ancillary restrictions).

107.    As regards the objective necessity of a restriction, it must be observed that inasmuch as, as has been shown in paragraph 72 et seq. above, the existence of a rule of reason in Community competition law cannot be upheld, it would be wrong, when classifying ancillary restrictions, to interpret the requirement for objective necessity as implying a need to weigh the pro and anti-competitive effects of an agreement. Such an analysis can take place only in the specific framework of Article 85(3) of the Treaty.

108.    That approach is justified not merely so as to preserve the effectiveness of Article 85(3) of the Treaty, but also on grounds of consistency. As Article 85(1) of the Treaty does not require an analysis of the positive and negative effects on competition of a principal restriction, the same finding is necessary with regard to the analysis of accompanying restrictions.

109.    Consequently, as the Commission has correctly asserted, examination of the objective necessity of a restriction in relation to the main operation cannot but be relatively abstract. It is not a question of analysing whether, in the light of the competitive situation on the relevant market, the restriction is indispensable to the commercial success of the main operation but of determining whether, in the specific context of the main operation, the restriction is necessary to implement that operation. If, without the restriction, the main operation is difficult or even impossible to implement, the restriction may be regarded as objectively necessary for its implementation.

110.    Thus, in the judgment in Remia v Commission, cited in paragraph 87 above (paragraph 19), the Court of Justice held that a non-competition clause was objectively necessary for a successful transfer of undertakings, inasmuch as, without such a clause, 'and should the vendor and the purchaser remain competitors after the transfer, it is clear that the agreement for the transfer of the undertaking could not be given effect. The vendor, with his particularly detailed knowledge of the transferred undertaking, would still be in a position to win back his former customers immediately after the transfer and thereby drive the undertaking out of business.'

111.    Similarly, in its decisions, the Commission has found that a number of restrictions

were objectively necessary to implementing certain operations. Failing such restrictions, the operation in question 'could not be implemented or could only be implemented under more uncertain conditions, at substantially higher cost, over an appreciably longer period or with considerably less probability of success' (point II.5 of the notice regarding ancillary restrictions; see also, for example, Decision 90/410, point 22 et seq.)

112. Contrary to the applicants' claim, none of the various decisions to which they refer show that the Commission carried out an analysis of competition in classifying the relevant clauses as ancillary restrictions. On the contrary, those decisions show that the Commission's analysis was relatively abstract. Thus point 77 of Decision 1999/329 states as follows:
'Actually, a claim-sharing arrangement cannot function properly without at least one level of cover to be offered being agreed by all its members. The reason is that no member would be willing to share claims brought to the pool by other clubs of a higher amount than the ones it can bring to the pool.'

113. Where a restriction is objectively necessary to implement a main operation, it is still necessary to verify whether its duration and its material and geographic scope do not exceed what is necessary to implement that operation. If the duration or the scope of the restriction exceed what is necessary in order to implement the operation, it must be assessed separately under Article 85(3) of the Treaty (see, to that effect, Case T-61/89 Dansk Pelsdyravlerforening v Commission [1992] ECR II-1931, paragraph 78).

114. Lastly, it must be observed that, inasmuch as the assessment of the ancillary nature of a particular agreement in relation to a main operation entails complex economic assessments by the Commission, judicial review of that assessment is limited to verifying whether the relevant procedural rules have been complied with, whether the statement of the reasons for the decision is adequate, whether the facts have been accurately stated and whether there has been a manifest error of appraisal or misuse of powers (see, to that effect, with regard to assessing the permissible duration of a non-competition clause, Remia v Commission, cited in paragraph 87 above, paragraph 34).

**Consequences of classification as an ancillary restriction**
115. If it is established that a restriction is directly related and necessary to achieving a main operation, the compatibility of that restriction with the competition rules must be examined with that of the main operation.

116. Thus, if the main operation does not fall within the scope of the prohibition laid down in Article 85(1) of the Treaty, the same holds for the restrictions directly related and necessary for that operation (see, to that effect, Remia v Commission, cited in paragraph 87 above, paragraph 20). If, on the other hand, the main operation is a restriction within the meaning of Article 85(1) but benefits from an exemption under Article 85(3) of the Treaty, that exemption also covers those ancillary restrictions.

117. Moreover, where the restrictions are directly related and necessary to a concentration within the meaning of Regulation No 4064/89, it follows from both Article 6(1)(b) and Article 8(2), second subparagraph, of that regulation that those restrictions are covered by the Commission's decision declaring the operation compatible with the common market.

**Classification of the exclusivity clause as an ancillary restriction**
118. It is necessary to examine, in the light of the principles set out in paragraphs 103

to 114 above, whether in the present case the Commission committed a manifest error of assessment in not classifying the exclusivity clause as a restriction that was ancillary to the creation of TPS.

119.    The applicants submit that the exclusivity clause is ancillary to the creation of TPS as the clause is indispensable to allow TPS to penetrate the pay-TV market in France because TPS does not enjoy any exclusive rights to films and sporting events of the first rank.

120.    It must, however, be observed, first of all, that the fact that the exclusivity clause would be necessary to allow TPS to establish itself on a long-term basis on that market it is not relevant to the classification of that clause as an ancillary restriction.

121.    As has been set out in paragraph 106 above, such considerations, relating to the indispensable nature of the restriction in the light of the competitive situation on the relevant market, are not part of an analysis of the ancillary nature of the restrictions. They can be taken into account only in the framework of Article 85(3) of the Treaty (see, in that regard, Pronuptia, cited in paragraph 74 above, paragraph 24, and Dansk Pelsdyravlerforening v Commission, cited in paragraph 113 above, paragraph 78).

122.    Next, it must be observed that although, in the present case, the applicants have been able to establish to the requisite legal standard that the exclusivity clause was directly related to the establishment of TPS, they have not, on the other hand, shown that the exclusive broadcasting of the general-interest channels was objectively necessary for that operation. As the Commission has rightly stated, a company in the pay-TV sector can be launched in France without having exclusive rights to the general-interest channels. That is the situation for CanalSatellite and AB-Sat, the two other operators on that market.

123.    Even if the exclusivity clause was objectively necessary for the creation of TPS, the Commission did not commit a manifest error of assessment in taking the view that this restriction was not proportionate to that objective.

124.    The exclusivity clause is for an initial period of 10 years. As the Commission finds in point 134 of the contested decision, such a period is deemed excessive as 'TPS [has] to establish itself on the market before the end of that period'. It is quite probable that the competitive disadvantage of TPS (principally with regard to access to exclusive rights to films and sporting events) will diminish over time (see, to that effect, point 133 of the contested decision). It cannot, therefore, be ruled out that the exclusive broadcasting of the general-interest channels, although initially intended to strengthen the competitive position of TPS on the pay-TV market might ultimately allow it, after some years, to eliminate competition on that market.

125.    Moreover, the exclusivity clause is also disproportionate in so far as its effect is to deprive TPS' actual and potential competitors of any access to the programmes that are considered attractive by a large number of French television viewers (see, to that effect, the judgment in Oude Luttikhuis and Others, cited in paragraph 70 above, paragraph 16). This excessiveness of the commitment is also reinforced by the existence of 'shadow zones'. The television viewers living in those zones who wish to subscribe to a pay-TV company which also broadcasts the general-interest channels can turn only to TPS.

126.    It must therefore be held that the Commission did not commit a manifest error of assessment in not classifying the exclusivity clause as a restriction that was ancillary to the creation of TPS.

127.    That limb of the applicants' argument must, therefore, be rejected.

**Classification of the clause relating to the special-interest channels as an ancillary restriction**

128. It is also necessary to examine, in the light of the principles set out in paragraphs 103 to 114 above whether, in the present case, the Commission committed a manifest error of assessment in not classifying the clause relating to the special-interest channels as an ancillary restriction.

129. In that regard, it must be pointed out that in the contested decision (point 101) the Commission stated:

'The obligation on the members to give TPS first refusal over their special-interest channels might possibly be regarded as ancillary to the launch of the platform; this obligation, which is imposed for a period of 10 years, nevertheless results in a limitation of the supply of special-interest channels and television services. In this respect, the clause in question falls within the scope of Article 85(1).'

130. It is clear from point 101 of the contested decision that the main reason why the Commission refused to classify the clause as an ancillary restriction was that it had a negative impact on the situation of third parties over quite a long period.

131. The applicants, despite having the burden of proof in that regard, have not adduced any evidence to invalidate that assessment.

132. They merely assert that on account of the exclusivity policy operated by CanalSatellite, the special-interest channels operated or created by them are the only channels to which TPS has access, so that the clause at issue is indispensable for its survival. Even accepting that such an assertion is correct, a consideration of that kind relating to the competitive situation of TPS cannot be taken into account for the purpose of classifying that clause as an ancillary restriction. As explained in paragraphs 107 to 112 above, the objectively necessary nature of the clause is established without reference to the competitive situation.

133. Furthermore, as the market for the operation of special-interest channels is enjoying rapid growth (point 65 of the contested decision), the Commission did not commit a manifest error of assessment in taking the view that the obligation on the shareholders of TPS, for a period of 10 years, to offer their special-interest channels first to TPS exceeded what was necessary for the creation of TPS.

134. Finally, as the Commission has correctly submitted, the applicants are wrong in referring to the decisions in Cégétel and Télécom développement inasmuch as those decisions relate to different factual situations. Thus, the situation of TPS cannot be compared to that of a new entrant on a market dominated by a company with a long-standing monopoly and which requires access to essential infrastructure. Canal+ does not enjoy a long-standing monopoly on the market for the operation of the special-interest channels and entry onto that market does not require access to essential infrastructure. Furthermore, in the Cégétel and Télécom développement decisions, the effect of the clauses considered was not to deprive third-parties of any possibility of access to the services of the shareholders. It was merely a question of preferential treatment.

135. It must therefore be held that the Commission did not commit a manifest error of assessment in not classifying the clause relating to the special-interest channels as a restriction that was ancillary to the creation of TPS.

136. That part of the applicants' alternative argument must therefore be rejected.

*(iii) Conclusion*

137. In the light of the foregoing, the present plea must be rejected as unfounded.

**(b) The second plea: infringement of Article 85(3) of the Treaty**
*(i) The argument alleging misapplication of the criteria for exemption laid down in Article 85(3) of the Treaty Argument of the parties*

138.    The applicants submit, first, that the Commission infringed Article 85(3) of the Treaty by taking into account, when applying that provision, assessments relating to competition on the pay-TV market which, they claim, fall within the scope of Article 85(1).

139.    They observe, next, that according to the case-law (judgment in Joined Cases T-528/93, T-542/93, T-543/93 and T-546/93 Métropole télévision and Others v Commission [1996] ECR II-649, paragraph 114), the factors taken into account by the Commission in applying Article 85(3) of the Treaty must be relevant and relate to that article. According to the applicants, instead of examining whether the exclusivity clause and the clause relating to the special-interest channels, which it had held to be contrary to Article 85(1) of the Treaty, satisfied the conditions for exemption laid down in Article 85(3), the Commission in fact analysed whether the creation of TPS on the market satisfied those conditions.

140.    The Commission disputes that it misapplied the exemption criteria laid down in Article 85(3) of the Treaty.

**Findings of the Court**

141.    As regards the applicants' argument that the Commission is under an obligation, when applying Article 85(1) of the Treaty rather than Article 85(3) of the Treaty, to weigh the pro and anti-competitive effects of a restriction, the Court refers to the findings set out in paragraph 72 et seq. above.

142.    As regards the question whether the Commission correctly verified whether the conditions for exemption were satisfied with respect to the exclusivity clause and the clause relating to the special-interest channels, it must be observed, first, that, contrary to the applicants' assertion, the Commission examined whether those conditions were satisfied with regard to each of those clauses.

143.    Thus, with regard to the condition that there should be a contribution to the improvement of production or distribution of goods or promotion of technical or economic progress, the Commission found that this condition was satisfied inasmuch as 'by facilitating the successful launch of a new platform on the pay-TV market [the exclusivity clause and the clause relating to the special-interest channels] enable a new operator to emerge and increase the range of pay-TV services available to French viewers' (point 114 of the contested decision).

144.    Those clauses also benefit consumers inasmuch as they led to 'an increase in the range of services on offer and to the development of new services based on the use of new technology' (point 118 of the contested decision) and 'extremely keen competition that developed as soon as TPS was created between that platform and CanalSatellite/Canal+' (point 119 of the contested decision).

145.    As to the indispensability of the clauses at issue, the Commission found, in particular, that 'without preferential access to those [special-interest] channels, TPS would have had to produce a large number of channels itself, which would have greatly increased the already extremely high costs of launching the platform' (point 122 of the contested decision) and that 'the exclusive transmission of the general-interest channels, by making the TPS package attractive to consumers and differentiating it from other services, is indispensable to its penetration of the French pay-TV market' (point 132 of the contested decision).

146.    It is true that, as regards the fourth condition laid down by Article 85(3) of the Treaty, the requirement that there be no possibility of eliminating competition in

respect of a substantial part of the products in question, the Commission did not explicitly refer to the exclusivity clause and the clause relating to the special-interest channels. It merely found that 'far from eliminating competition, the TPS agreements are pro-competitive' (point 135 of the contested decision). It is, however, implicit from the Commission's analysis that, in reaching that conclusion, it took account of those clauses and found that they were indispensable to the success of TPS.

147. Second, it is appropriate to point out that, even though the Commission rightly considered that the exclusivity clause and the clause relating to the special-interest channels could not be regarded as restrictions ancillary to the creation of TPS for the reasons set out in paragraphs 118 to 137 above, those restrictions are, however, directly linked to that operation. The analysis of whether the various conditions laid down by Article 85(3) of the Treaty were satisfied had therefore to be made in the light of the main operation to which those clauses were attached.

148. It must also be observed that the applicants' argument in that regard is contradictory. They assert that the Commission should have regarded those clauses as restrictions ancillary to the creation of TPS and, on the other hand, that it should have verified, without reference to the main operation, whether the conditions laid down in Article 85(3) of the Treaty were satisfied in regard to them.

149. That contradiction is due to a misinterpretation of the concept of 'ancillary restriction'. According to the applicants, where a restriction cannot be classified as an ancillary restriction, it must necessarily be analysed separately. However, as has been pointed out in paragraph 147 above, such a view does not take account of the fact that when certain restrictions directly linked to an operation cannot be classified as ancillary restrictions because they are not objectively necessary or not proportionate to the achievement of the main operation, they nevertheless remain inextricably linked to that operation. It is, therefore, normal that they should be analysed by taking into account the economic and legal context of that transaction.

150. That part of the applicants' argument must, therefore, be rejected.

*(ii) The argument alleging erroneous assessment of the duration of the individual exemption*
*Arguments of the parties*

151. The applicants submit that the Commission committed an error of assessment in taking the view in the contested decision that the duration of the exemption in respect of the exclusivity clause had to be fixed at three years. The grounds put forward by the Commission namely that the restriction is indispensable for TPS only during the launch period and its indispensability will lessen over time inasmuch as TPS will be able to sign up subscribers, gain experience in the pay-TV sector and so improve its offer, are erroneous.

152. They state that the indispensability of the exclusivity will not diminish but, quite to the contrary, will increase, having regard to the unassailable positions which the Canal+ group holds on the market. They observe that without exclusive rights to transmit the general-interest channels the viability of TPS is in danger.

153. The applicants consider that it is necessary to refer to the Cégétel decision, in which an exclusive distribution clause for certain telephony services was exempted for a period of 10 years, in particular on the ground that Cégétel would not be able to make the investments in those telecommunication services pay until an extremely long period had expired.

154. The applicants also submit that the Commission committed an error of assessment in restricting to three years, that is to say to the launch period, the duration of the

exemption for the clause relating to the special-interest channels. They submit that this clause is indispensable not merely during the launch period, as the Commission asserts, but also throughout the period of operation of TPS inasmuch as that clause is, for TPS, the only means of securing its supply of special-interest channels.

155.    The Commission disputes that it committed an error of assessment in fixing the exemption period at three years.

**Findings of the Court**

156.    It must be observed, first, that it is settled law that the exercise of the Commission's powers under Article 85(3) of the Treaty necessarily involves complex evaluations on economic matters, which means that judicial review of those evaluations must confine itself to an examination of the relevance of the facts and of the legal consequences which the Commission deduces from them (see, in particular, the judgment in Case 56/64 and 58/64 Consten and Grundig v Commission [1966] ECR 382 and Matra Hachette v Commission, cited in paragraph 74 above, paragraph 104).

157.    That principle applies especially with regard to the Commission's determination of the period during which a restriction is considered indispensable (Remia v Commission, cited in paragraph 87 above, paragraph 34).

158.    Second, it must be observed that in Matra Hachette v Commission, cited in paragraph 74 above (paragraph 104), the Court held that 'it is incumbent upon notifying undertakings to provide the Commission with evidence that the conditions laid down by Article 85(3) are met (judgment in Joined Cases 43/82 and 63/82 VBVB and VBBB v Commission [1984] ECR 19), an obligation which, in the proceedings before the Court, must be assessed in the light of the onus which falls on the applicant to provide information to challenge the Commission's appraisal'.

159.    However, the applicants merely assert that the Commission committed an error of assessment inasmuch as, according to them, the indispensability of the exclusivity will increase rather than diminish, having regard to the unassailable positions held by the Canal+ group on the market. As to the clause relating to special-interest channels, they submit that it is necessary in order to secure the supply to TPS of channels of that type. They do not, however, adduce any cogent evidence to show that this assertion is correct, an assertion which, moreover, does not take account of changes in the market. Lastly, the applicants do not dispute any of the facts on the basis of which the Commission took the view that the indispensability of those clauses would necessarily diminish over time and held that three years was the minimum period during which they were indispensable for TPS (point 134 of the contested decision).

160.    Third, it must be observed that the applicants are wrong in referring to the Cégétel decision. As the Commission correctly states, only the exclusive distribution of certain products was the subject of an exemption in that decision and the distribution of those products was merely a small part of Cégétel's activities, whereas the exclusive right to transmit the general-interest channels is an essential element of the services offered by TPS.

161.    It must therefore be found that the Commission did not commit a manifest error of assessment in limiting the period of exemption to three years.

162.    That part of the applicants' argument must therefore be rejected.

*(iii) Conclusion*

163.    In the light of the foregoing, the present plea must be rejected as unfounded.

**2. The plea relating to Article 2 of the contested decision, alleging infringement of the principle of legal certainty**
**Arguments of the parties**

164.   The applicants submit that, by issuing a negative clearance for a period limited to three years on the ground that the non-competition clause could be classified as a restriction ancillary to the creation of TPS only during the launch period, the Commission did not comply with the rules which it had set out in its XXIVth Report on competition policy. They observe that the Commission stated in that document, which is binding on it, that 'in the context of joint ventures, [the ancillary restrictions] are usually allowed for the whole duration of the joint venture' (page 120, point 166).

165.   According to the applicants, it is clear from the case-law (Case T-7/89 Hercules Chemicals v Commission [1991] ECR II-1711, and Case T-9/89 Hüls v Commission [1992] ECR II-499) that by failing to observe that rule in the present case the Commission infringed the principle of legal certainty.

166.   The applicants observe that the Commission's position in the present case is all the more open to criticism because that rule is still current, as is apparent from the Cégétel and Télécom Développement decisions. In those decisions two non-competition clauses were classified as ancillary restrictions and were treated in the same way as the joint venture.

167.   The Commission disputes that it infringed the principle of legal certainty or committed an error of assessment in taking the view that the non-competition clause was an ancillary restriction only during the launch period, that is to say during the first three years.

**Findings of the Court**

168.   In the first place, it must be observed that it is apparent from the extract from the XXIVth Report on competition policy cited by the applicants, namely that 'the ancillary restrictions are usually allowed for the whole duration of the joint venture' and from the specific context in which it is found (the analysis of the establishment of five joint ventures in the research and development sector) that the part of the report in which that extract is found does not lay down strict rules which the Commission is alleged to have imposed on itself with regard to classification of an agreement as an ancillary restriction. It is more in the nature of a simple description of a number of principles which the Commission normally follows when assessing certain clauses which it considers to be ancillary to a main operation.

169.   Contrary to the applicants' assertion, the present case cannot therefore be compared to the case which gave rise to the judgment in Hercules Chemicals v Commission, cited in paragraph 165 above. In that case the Commission had in fact made known, through its annual report on competition policy, a number of rules which it had imposed on itself relating to access to the file in competition proceedings.

170.   It is also apparent from the extract from the XXIVth Report on competition policy cited by the applicants that the extract merely reproduces, almost literally, the principles set out by the Commission in paragraph 67 of the notice on cooperative joint ventures. However, as that notice makes clear, it has only indicative value as regards the way in which the Commission will apply the theory of ancillary restrictions in practice.

171.   It follows that the applicants cannot rely on the above extract in order to prove that the Commission infringed the principle of legal certainty in regard to them.

172.   In the light of the foregoing, the present plea must be rejected as unfounded.

173.    As all the pleas on which the applicants rely are unfounded, the application must
        be dismissed.

**Decision on costs**

**Costs**

174.    Under Article 87(2) of the Rules of Procedure, the unsuccessful party is to be or-
        dered to pay the costs if they have been applied for in the successful party's plead-
        ings. Since the applicants have been unsuccessful and the Commission has applied
        for costs, they must be ordered to pay the costs of the Commission and of the in-
        tervener in addition to bearing their own.

**Operative part of the judgment**

On those grounds,
*The Court of First Instance*
(Third Chamber),
hereby:
1.    Dismisses the application;
2.    Orders the applicants to bear their own costs and to pay those incurred by the
      Commission and by the intervener.

––––

**2.4.74.    EUROPEAN COURT OF JUSTICE, ORDER OF THE COURT IN
             FIRST INSTANCE, LAURENT PIAU V COMMISSION OF THE
             EUROPEAN COMMUNITIES, CASE T- 121/01, 19 SEPTEMBER
             2001**[543]

(Action for failure to act – Communication under Article 6 of Regulation No 2542/98 –
Taking of position bringing infringement to an end – No need to adjudicate)
(Language of the case: French)
In Case T-121/01: Laurent Piau, residing in France, represented by M. Fauconnet, lawyer,
with an address for service in Luxembourg, against Commission of the European Communities (Agent: E. Gippini Fournier) – application for a declaration that the Commission
refrained, contrary to the Treaty, from ruling on a complaint concerning alleged infringements of Article 81 EC the Court of First Instance (First Chamber), composed of B.
Vesterdorf, President, N.J. Forwood and H. Legal, Judges; H. Jung, Registrar, made an
order on 19 October 2001, the operative part of which is as follows:
1.    There is no need to adjudicate on the action.
2.    The parties shall bear their own costs.

––––

**2.4.75.    EUROPEAN COURT OF JUSTICE, JUDGMENT OF THE COURT OF
             FIRST INSTANCE (SECOND CHAMBER), MÉTROPOLE
             TÉLÉVISION (M6) V COMMISSION OF THE EUROPEAN
             COMMUNITIES, CASE T-354/00, 25 OCTOBER 2001**[544]

*Competition – Rejection of a complaint – Objection of inadmissibility – Decision confirm-
ing a contested decision within the prescribed period – Inadmissibility*

––––––––––––

[543]    OJ C 31, 2-2-2002, p. 23; OJ C 227, 11-8-2001.
[544]    ECR 2001, p. II-3177.

**Parties**

In Case T-354/00,

Métropole télévision SA (M6), established in Paris (France), represented by D. Théophile, lawyer, with an address for service in Luxembourg, applicant, v Commission of the European Communities, represented by K. Wiedner and B. Mongin, acting as Agents, with an address for service in Luxembourg, defendant,

Application for the annulment of the Commission's decision of 12 September 2000 rejecting the complaint lodged by the applicant on 6 March 2000,

*The Court of First Instance of the European Communities* (Second Chamber), composed of: R.M. Moura Ramos, President, J. Pirrung and A.W.H. Meij, Judges, Registrar: H. Jung, makes the following Order

**Grounds of the judgment**

**Facts and background to the case**

1      The European Broadcasting Union (EBU) is a non-profit-making trade association of radio and television organisations which was set up in 1950 and has its headquarters in Geneva (Switzerland). According to Article 2 of its Statutes, as amended on 3 July 1992, the objectives of the EBU are to represent the interests of its members in the programme, legal, technical and other fields, and in particular to promote radio and television programme exchanges by all possible means, such as Eurovision and Euroradio, and any other form of cooperation, among its members and with other broadcasting organisations or groups of such organisations, and to assist its active members in negotiations of any kind or itself negotiate at their request and on their behalf.

2      Eurovision constitutes the main framework for programme exchanges between active members of the EBU. It has been in existence since 1954 and provides the principal means by which the EBU pursues its objectives. Article 3(6) of the EBU Statutes, as amended on 3 July 1992, states: Eurovision is a TV programme exchange system organised and coordinated by the EBU, based on the understanding that members offer to the other members, on a basis of reciprocity, ... their coverage of ... sports and cultural events taking place in their countries and of potential interest to other members, thereby enabling each other to provide a high quality service in these fields to their respective national audiences. Eurovision members are active members of the EBU and consortia consisting of active EBU members. All active members of the EBU may participate in a system of the joint acquisition and sharing of television rights (and of the costs relating thereto) to international sports events, which are referred to as Eurovision rights.

3      In order to become an active member a broadcasting body must meet the conditions laid down in Article 3(3) of the Statutes (the membership criteria). Those conditions concern, in particular, the level of national coverage, and the nature and funding of the programming.

4      Until 1 March 1988, the benefit of the services of the EBU and Eurovision was exclusively reserved for their members. However, when the EBU's Statutes were amended in 1988 a new paragraph (paragraph 6) was added to Article 3 providing that contractual access to Eurovision may be granted to associate members and non-members of the EBU.

5      Following a complaint made by Screensport on 17 December 1987, the Commission investigated the compatibility of the rules governing that system of joint ac-

quisition and sharing of television rights to sports events with Article 81 EC. The complaint related in particular to the refusal of the EBU and its members to grant sub-licences for sports events. On 12 December 1988 the Commission sent the EBU a statement of objections concerning the rules governing the acquisition and use of television rights to sports events within the framework of the Eurovision system, which are generally exclusive in nature. The Commission declared itself willing to envisage an exemption in favour of those rules on condition that sub-licences should be granted to non-members, for a substantial share of the rights in question and on reasonable terms.

6      On 3 April 1989 the EBU notified the Commission of its Statutes and other rules on the acquisition of television rights to sports events, the exchange of sports broadcasts in the context of Eurovision and contractual access by third parties to such broadcasts, with a view to obtaining negative clearance or, failing that, an exemption under Article 81(3) EC.

7      After the EBU agreed to relax the rules for obtaining sub-licences for the broadcasts in question, the Commission adopted Decision 93/403/EEC of 11 June 1993 relating to a proceeding pursuant to Article [81] of the EEC Treaty (OJ 1993 L 179, p. 23), whereby it granted an exemption under Article 81(3) (the first exemption decision).

8      That decision was annulled by the Court of First Instance in Joined Cases T-528/93, T-542/93, T-543/93 and T-546/93 Métropole télévision and Others v Commission [1996] ECR II-649 (the judgment of 11 July 1996).

9      Since 1987 Métropole télévision (M6) has lodged an application to join the EBU six times. Each time its application has been rejected on the ground that it did not fulfil the membership criteria laid down in the EBU Statutes. Following the EBU's last refusal, M6 filed a complaint with the Commission on 5 December 1997, complaining of the EBU's practices towards it and, in particular, of the systematic a priori refusal of its applications for admission.

10     On 3 April 1998 the EBU amended Article 3(3) of its Statutes, adding in particular a condition regarding the applicant channel's independence from any sports rights agencies in competition with the EBU; it also adopted new rules interpreting those criteria (the new membership criteria). Those new rules were notified to the Commission on the same day.

11     By decision of 29 June 1999 the Commission rejected the applicant's complaint.

12     The Court of First Instance, in a judgment of 21 March 2001, annulled that decision on the grounds that the Commission had infringed its obligation to state reasons and the obligations which it had when dealing with complaints (Case T-206/99 Métropole télévision v Commission [2001] ECR II-1057).

13     Meanwhile, on 6 March 2000, M6 filed a further complaint with the Commission in which it sought a declaration by the Commission that the new EBU membership criteria restricted competition and could not be granted an exemption under Article 81(3) EC.

14     On 10 May 2000 the Commission adopted a further exemption decision [Decision 2000/400/EC relating to a proceeding pursuant to Article 81 of the EC Treaty (OJ 2000 L 151, p. 18)] in which it declared, in particular, under Article 81(3) EC that the provisions of Article 81(1) of the EC Treaty were inapplicable from 26 February 1993 until 31 December 2005 to notified agreements relating to the joint acquisition of sport television rights, the sharing of the jointly acquired sport television rights, the exchange of the signal for sporting events, the access scheme for non-EBU members to Eurovision sports rights, and the sub-licensing rules relating to the exploitation of Eurovision rights on pay-TV channels (Article 1). The

exemption decision was subject to a condition and an obligation (Article 2).

15      In that decision the Commission stated with regard to the membership criteria:

    67.    The Commission recognises that [the first exemption decision], because of its ambiguous drafting, gave grounds to the interpretation by the Court of First Instance that the Commission had considered the EBU's membership rules to be restrictive of competition and had exempted them, which was actually not the case. Indeed, the conditions for active membership of the EBU set out in Article 3(3) of the EBU Statutes were not even notified to the Commission by the EBU; only the 'Eurovision system' was notified.

    68.    The Commission continues to consider that the membership rules of a professional association of broadcasters cannot in themselves restrict competition within the meaning of Article 81(1) of the EC Treaty. It has to be remembered that many other organisations and associations in Europe, with economic activities in the market, have internal rules establishing conditions for membership comparable to those of the EBU. There can be no obligation on such associations under Article 81(1) of the EC Treaty to accept members against their will. This is in particular true for associations like the EBU with a market position which does not allow them to eliminate competition ... . Third parties wishing to create similar associations are free to do so.

    69.    The Commission finds that it is a completely separate issue whether within such an association, restrictions of competition might have been agreed. These possible restrictions will be assessed separately in recitals 71 to 80.

16      On 13 July 2000 M6 brought an action against that decision. It was registered at the Registry of the Court of First Instance as Case T-185/00.

17      By letter of 12 September 2000 (the contested decision) the Commission rejected the complaint of 6 March 2000 as follows:

I find that your complaint contains the same terms and arguments as the complaint you made on 5 December 1997, which was rejected by the Commission in its decision of 29 June 1999. You brought an action against that decision on 15 September 1999. The questions raised in the complaint are therefore now being referred to the Court of First Instance, which will be called upon to consider the various arguments put forward.

There is no change in the current circumstances from those which prevailed in December 1997 to justify a further complaint by M6.

Lastly, on 13 July 2000 you brought an action in the Court of First Instance against the decision of 10 May 2000 exempting the EBU's joint acquisition system. In that action you also raised the matter of the conditions for admission to and participation in the EBU's system, as you did in both complaints, using the same arguments.

In view of all those factors and of the repetitive nature of your complaint of 6 March last, that complaint is totally redundant and has no practical effect as regards the matters submitted for adjudication by the Court of First Instance.

There is therefore no reason to pursue the inquiry.

## Procedure and forms of order sought

18      By application lodged at the Registry of the Court of First Instance on 23 November 2000 the applicant brought the present action.

19      By separate document lodged at the Registry of the Court of First Instance on 21 December 2000 the Commission raised an objection of inadmissibility against the application under Article 114 of the Rules of Procedure of the Court of First Instance.

20    The applicant lodged its observations on that objection on 12 February 2001.

21    By document lodged at the Registry of the Court of First Instance on 17 April 2001, the EBU applied for leave to intervene in this case in support of the form of order sought by the defendant.

22    In its objection of inadmissibility the Commission claims that the Court should:
      – declare the application inadmissible;
      – order the applicant to pay the costs.

23    In its observations on the objection of inadmissibility the applicant contends that the Court should:
      – declare the application admissible;
      – order the Commission to pay the costs.

24    By letter of 5 April 2001 the Court of First Instance requested the applicant to inform it whether it considered it appropriate to continue the proceedings, in view of the fact that if the contested decision were to be annulled the Commission might in that case be obliged to adopt a position on the new membership criteria, and that the Commission had already adopted such a position in Decision 2000/400, which has been contested by the applicant in Case T-185/00.

25    The applicant replied to the Court by fax of 19 April 2001. In its reply it gave two reasons for considering it appropriate to continue the proceedings in this case. First, in Decision 2000/400 the Commission did not adopt a position on all the points raised in the applicant's complaint of 6 March 2000 and, in particular, on the complaints made by the applicant that the new membership criteria could not be given an exemption under Article 81(3) EC. It states in that regard that since the Commission does not deal with these points in its decision of 10 May 2000, termination of these proceedings would deprive M6 of a reply to the main arguments it has put forward.

26    Second, the applicant contends that, since its application is based on infringement of certain procedural rules for dealing with complaints, it is still in its interest for that infringement to be censured by a judgment of the Court of First Instance.

**Admissibility**

27    Under Article 113 of its Rules of Procedure the Court of First Instance may at any time of its own motion consider whether there exists any absolute bar to proceeding with an action, including, as the Court has consistently held, the conditions for the admissibility of an action for annulment, and is to give its decision in accordance with Article 114(3) and (4) (see, in particular, order of the Court of First Instance in Case T-100/94 Michailidis and Others v Commission [1998] ECR II-3115, paragraph 49 and the case-law cited). The Court of First Instance is not therefore bound solely by the defendant's pleas in law in the objection of inadmissibility.

28    In the present case the Court considers it has obtained sufficient information from the documents in the case and has decided, pursuant to that article, to adjudicate without further steps in the proceedings.

29    It is settled case-law that a natural or legal person may, pursuant to the fourth paragraph of Article 230 EC, contest only measures producing binding legal effects such as to affect the interests of that person by bringing about a distinct change in his legal position (Case T-64/89 Automec v Commission [1990] ECR II-367, paragraph 42, and order of the Court of First Instance in Case T-235/95 Goldstein v Commission [1998] ECR II-523, paragraph 37).

30    It is therefore necessary to consider whether the contested decision affects the interests of the applicant by bringing about a distinct change in its legal position.

That must be the case in order for the applicant to establish an interest in having the contested measure annulled.

31 Before taking the contested decision, the Commission adopted Decision 2000/400, the provisions of which were referred to in paragraph 15 above. In that decision the Commission considered that the EBU membership criteria did not fall within the scope of Article 81(1) EC because the membership rules of a professional association of broadcasters cannot in themselves restrict competition within the meaning of Article 81(1) of the EC Treaty and found that it was a completely separate issue whether within such an association, restrictions of competition might have been agreed.

32 As the Commission, in the contested decision, simply referred to the position it had already adopted clearly and expressly in its Decision 2000/400, the contested decision constitutes an act which merely confirms Decision 2000/400 (see Case 26/76 Metro v Commission [1977] ECR 1875, paragraph 4).

33 As regards whether it is possible to contest a confirmatory act, the applicant cites the case-law to the effect that an action for the annulment of a confirmatory decision is inadmissible only if the confirmed decision has become final vis-à-vis the person concerned without any action having been brought before the Court within the prescribed period. Where, as in the present case, the applicant contested the confirmed decision within the prescribed period, he would be entitled to contest either the confirmed decision or the confirmatory decision or both (judgment of the Court of Justice in Joined Cases 193/87 and 194/87 Maurissen and European Public Service Union v Court of Auditors [1989] ECR 1045, paragraph 26 and judgment of the Court of First Instance in Case T-64/92 Chavane de Dalmassy and Others v Commission [1994] ECR-SC I-A-227 and II-723, paragraph 25).

34 It is true that the concept of a confirmatory act has been developed in case-law in particular in order to prevent the bringing of an action which would have the effect of causing expired limitation periods to begin to run again (see, in particular, Case T-188/95 Waterleiding Maatschappij v Commission [1998] ECR II-3713, paragraph 108). Consequently, in situations where there has been no such circumvention of the time-limits for bring an action, the Community judicature has on some occasions acknowledged the admissibility of claims directed against both a confirmed decision and a confirmatory decision in the same action.

35 That solution cannot, however, be applied where as in the present case the confirmed decision and the confirmatory decision are contested in two separate actions and the applicant can defend his point of view and put his arguments in the first action.

36 That conclusion cannot be invalidated by any of the arguments the applicant has put forward to establish that it was the complaint of 6 March 2000 alone which caused the Commission to adopt a position on the new membership criteria and that therefore the contested decision contained a new element capable of providing binding legal effects of a nature such as to affect the interests of the applicant by bringing about a distinct change in its legal position.

37 It is clear from the correspondence the applicant sent the Commission, which is on the file, in particular the letters of 16 July 1997 and 21 April and 11 December 1998, that at the time of the administrative procedure relating to Decision 2000/400 the applicant had already drawn the Commission's attention to the new EBU membership criteria and to the fact that in its view the changes which had been made did not enable a reply to be given to the criticisms made by the Court of First Instance in its judgment of 11 July 1996 and so did not enable the Commission to exempt those criteria. Therefore, when the Commission adopted Decision

2000/400 it considered that the EBU membership criteria, including the new criteria, did not restrict competition, and it did so in full knowledge of the applicant's position with regard to those membership criteria.

38  Furthermore, since the Commission considered in Decision 2000/400 that the membership criteria, including the new criteria, did not fall within the scope of Article 81(1) EC, it cannot be accused of failing to deal with the question whether the new membership criteria could be granted an exemption under Article 81(3) EC. In those circumstances, the applicant's argument that it retains an interest in this action because the Commission did not, in Decision 2000/400, cover all the points raised in its complaint of 6 March 2000 is wholly unfounded.

39  Moreover, the question whether the membership criteria restrict competition and whether the Commission can grant the Eurovision system an exemption by disregarding criteria which enable a television channel to access that system as a member, lies at the very heart of the issues raised by the applicant in Case T-185/00 in relation to Decision 2000/400.

40  Lastly, the argument seeking to justify the admissibility of this action, based on an interest of the applicant in having infringements allegedly committed by the Commission in dealing with the complaints censured must be rejected. Since the Commission, in the contested decision, merely referred to the position it had already adopted in an earlier decision, which had been contested by the applicant, the pleas raised by the applicant against the contested decision cannot in themselves justify bringing a further action before the Court of First Instance.

41  It follows that the application must be dismissed as inadmissible.

42  Since the present application is inadmissible and the Court has granted the form of order sought by the defendant there is no need to adjudicate on the EBU's application for leave to intervene.

**Decision on costs**
**Costs**
43  Under Article 87(2) of the Rules of Procedure, the unsuccessful party is to be ordered to pay the costs if they have been applied for in the successful party's pleadings. Since the applicant has been unsuccessful, it must be ordered to pay the costs, as applied for by the Commission.

**Operative part of the judgment**
On those grounds,
The Court of First Instance (Second Chamber)
hereby orders:
1.  The application is dismissed as inadmissible.
2.  The applicant is ordered to pay the costs.
3.  There is no need to adjudicate on the application made by the European Broadcasting Union for leave to intervene.

———

**\* 2.4.76.  ANSWER ON BEHALF OF THE COMMISSION TO WRITTEN QUESTION E-2523/01 BY FREDDY BLAK (GUE/NGL), 26 OCTOBER 2001[545] \***

Subject: Infringement by FIFA of EU competition rules

———

[545] Question of 19-9-2001; OJ C 93 E , 18-4-2002, p. 148.

**\* 2.4.77.   COMMISSION CLOSES ITS INVESTIGATION INTO FORMULA ONE AND OTHER FOUR-WHEEL MOTOR SPORTS, 30 OCTOBER 2001**[546]

———

**\* 2.4.78.   ANSWER ON BEHALF OF THE COMMISSION TO WRITTEN QUESTION P-2967/01 BY ARLENE MCCARTHY (PSE), 16 NOVEMBER 2001**[547] **\***

Subject: UEFA Champions League commercial contracts inventigation and implications for the FA Premier League

———

**\* 2.4.79.   ANSWER ON BEHALF OF THE COMMISSION TO WRITTEN QUESTION E-3137/01 BY GLYN FORD (PSE), 3 DECEMBER 2001**[548] **\***

Subject: Fine on French football authorities with regard to World Cup tickets

———

**\* 2.4.80.   ANSWER ON BEHALF OF THE COMMISSION TO WRITTEN QUESTION E-3474/01 BY CHARLES TANNOCK (PPE-DE), 18 FEBRUARY 2002**[549] **\***

Subject: The application of Competition Policy with regard to collective sale of broadcasting rights to football matches

———

**\* 2.4.81.   ANSWER ON BEHALF OF THE COMMISSION TO WRITTEN QUESTION E-3370/01 BY TOINE MANDERS (ELDR), 11 MARCH 2002**[550] **\***

Subject: Licences for football clubs

———

**2.4.82.   COMMISSION EUROPÉENNE, BRUXELLES, LE 16 AVRIL 2002 [PLAYERS' AGENTS]**

Recommandé avec accusé de reception

Objet: Affaire COMP [...]
[...]

**1. Introduction**
1.     En 1998, [...] a déposé, auprès de la Commission, une plainte au titre de l'article 3 du règlement 17/62 contre la Fédération Internationale de Football Association (ci-après FIFA). Cette plainte considère que le règlement de la FIFA gouvernant

---

[546] IP/01/1523.
[547] Question of 18-10-2001; OJ C 160 E, 4-7-2002, p. 52.
[548] Question of 14-11-2001; OJ C 160 E, 4-7-2002, p. 60.
[549] Question of 8-1-2002; OJ C 172 E, 18-7-2002, p. 69.
[550] Question of 6-12-2001; OJ C 160 E, 4-7-2002, p. 104.

l'activité des agents de joueurs contrôle et restreint l'accès à la profession d'agents de joueurs par les sanctions applicables aux joueurs et aux clubs désirant travailler avec des agents non licenciés FIFA et par une obligation financière non fondée et un examen aux modalités opaques et non vérifiables.

2.  Le 3 août 2001, M. Pons au nom de M. Schaub a communiqué à [...] que la Commission conformément à l'article 6 du règlement (CE) no. 2842/98, du 22 décembre 1998,[551] envisageait de considérer que les éléments en sa possession ne justifiaient pas de donner une suite favorable à sa demande.

3.  Cette conclusion provisoire était en particulier fondée sur le fait que la Commission estime qu'il n'existe pas un intérêt communautaire suffisant qui justifierait de poursuivre la procédure contre la FIFA concernant le règlement sur les agents de joueurs, dans la mesure où les dispositions restrictives les plus importantes faisant l'objet de la plainte sont, à présent abrogées, et que le caractère obligatoire de la licence -dont le caractère restrictif est fortement amoindri du fait de l'aménagement de modalités d'examen transparentes et objectives et de la suppression de l'exigence d'une caution- pourrait être justifié. En tout état de cause, s'il s'avérait, dans le futur, que l'objectif visé pourrait être atteint sans la réglementation de la FIFA en cause, par exemple du fait de la réglementation de la profession par les Etats membres, ou parce que la profession d'agent de joueurs était en mesure de s'auto-réglementer en garantissant un niveau de professionnalisme et d'intégrité élevé de ses membres, la Commission se réserve le droit de réexaminer le règlement en question et notamment le caractère obligatoire de la licence FIFA.

4.  Par lettre du 28 septembre 2001, que le conseil de [...] a adressée à M. Pons, [...] a présenté des observations au sujet de la position préliminaire de la Commission. [...] conteste le fait que le nouveau règlement mette fin aux dispositions restrictives qui faisaient l'objet de sa plainte et notamment pour les raisons suivantes:
    (1) Le caractère obligatoire de la licence subsiste;
    (2) L'examen laisse encore une marge de man uvre à la FIFA et aux fédérations nationales pour rejeter un candidat de façon arbitraire;
    (3) L'assurance telle que prévue dans le règlement pose problème;
    (4) Le code de déontologie vise à renforcer le contrôle de la FIFA sur les agents de joueurs;
    (5) Le nouveau règlement fixe la rémunération des agents de joueurs,
    (6) Le contrat-type encadre de façon indue l'activité des agents de joueurs;

5.  [...] estime par ailleurs que la Commission n'a pas suffisamment justifié pourquoi le nouveau règlement serait susceptible de remplir les conditions de l'article 81 paragraphe 3 du traité CE. Par ailleurs, [...] constate que la Commission n'a pas exigé une notification de la part de la FIFA. En dernier lieu, [...] estime que la Commission a écarté sans motivation l'application de l'article 82 dans cette affaire.

## 2. Les faits
## 2.1. Les parties

6.  La FIFA est une association au sens de l'article 60 du code civil suisse qui a été fondée le 21 mai 1904. Elle a son siège à Zurich. Ses membres sont les associations nationales. Elles sont actuellement au nombre de 203. La FIFA a, notamment, pour objet (article 2 des Statuts):
    (1) de promouvoir le jeu du football d'association par tous les moyens à sa disposition;

---

[551] OJ L 354, 30-12-1998, p. 18.

(2) contrôler tous les types d'association de football en adoptant des mesures pour empêcher des violations aux Statuts et règlements de la FIFA ou des 'Règles du Jeu' telles qu'établies par l'''International Football association Board' pour empêcher l'introduction d'autres méthodes ou pratiques dans le jeu et pour le protéger d'abus;

(3) fournir, par moyen de réglementations, des principes qui permettent de régler les conflits susceptibles de survenir entre ou à l'intérieur des associations nationales.

7.   [...] souhaite exercer la profession d'agent de joueurs.

## 2.2.   Les arguments [...]

8.   Selon la plainte du 23 mars 1998 et la lettre en date du 4 novembre 1998, les arguments du plaignant peuvent se résumer comme suit. Premièrement, la profession de foi de la FIFA (l'objectif de moraliser cette profession) ne peut justifier pourquoi elle refuse aux joueurs la possibilité de choisir un agent de joueurs qui n'a pas la licence FIFA. En second lieu, l'examen prévu par le règlement FIFA ne présente pas les garanties d'équité et d'égalité entre les citoyens européens, n'a pas de procédure d'appel, les connaissances nécessaires en matière de transferts et de droit des contrats pour se présenter à l'examen ne sont pas définies et floues. Enfin, le principe et le montant de la caution exigée ne sont pas justifiés.

## 2.3.   Le Règlement gouvernant l'activité des agents de joueurs

9.   L'article 17 du Règlement d'application des statuts de la FIFA prévoit que
the use of agents or other intermediaries in the transfer of players is prohibited.
The executive Committee shall, however, if it deems necessary draw up stringent regulations authorising the licencing of players' Agents under certain conditions.

10.  Le Comité Exécutif de la FIFA, se basant sur l'article 17 alinéa 2 du Règlement d'application des statuts de la FIFA a adopté le 20 mai 1994 un règlement gouvernant l'activité des agents de joueurs. Il a été modifié le 11 décembre 1995 et est entré en vigueur le 1er janvier 1996. Suite à la présente procédure la FIFA a adopté un nouveau règlement le 10 décembre 2000 qui est entré en vigueur le 1er mars 2001. La FIFA a, en date du 3 avril 2002 par la circulaire 803 (jointe en annexe), amendé les articles 2 et 6 du règlement du 10 décembre 2000.

11.  Le règlement gouverne l'activité des agents de joueurs qui agissent dans le cadre de transferts de joueurs au sein d'une même association nationale ou d'une association nationale à une autre.

## 2.4.   Les principaux arguments de la FIFA

12.  La FIFA soutient qu'elle n'est pas une entreprise quand elle adopte des règlements comme celui en cause. Dans ce contexte, la FIFA n'exerce pas une activité économique mais agit comme une autorité réglementaire.

13.  Selon la FIFA, le règlement n'impose pas de limite quant au nombre d'agents mais exige un minimum de standards de qualité. Le règlement s'apparente à un système de distribution sélective que la Cour a par ailleurs accepté[552] lorsque la sélection est faite sur base non discriminatoire, les critères qualitatifs ne vont pas au-delà de ce qui est nécessaire et tous les candidats qui conviennent sont admis. En outre, à l'instar de la décision de la Commission IMA[553], le règlement de la

---

[552] Arrêt du 11 décembre 1980, Affaire C31/80 NV L'Oréal et SA L'Oréal contre PVBA 'De nieuwe AMCK', Recueil 1980, p. 3775.

[553] Décision de la Commission du 7 avril 1999. JO L 106 du 23 avril 1999.

FIFA est nécessaire pour assurer l'impartialité, la compétence, l'intégrité, la responsabilité des agents de joueurs.

14.  La FIFA n'a pas notifié son règlement car elle estime qu'il ne relève pas de l'article 81. L'objectif du règlement est d'améliorer les services des agents et de protéger les intérêts des joueurs et des clubs.

## 3.  Appréciation juridique
### 3.1  Les modalités du nouveau règlement
3.1.1  L'examen

15.  Suite à l'adoption du nouveau règlement, l'examen prend désormais la forme d'un questionnaire à choix multiples. Tout candidat obtenant le nombre de point minimum requis est considéré comme ayant réussi l'examen. Les dates d'examen sont les mêmes à l'échelle mondiale. Les griefs d'arbitraire et d'opacité qui faisaient l'objet de la plainte initiale disparaissent du fait de l'organisation d'un examen écrit au corrigé sans subjectivité (une seule réponse bonne par question). 15 questions sur 20 seront identiques à l'échelle mondiale, les cinq autres testant les spécificités nationales, ceci répond également au grief d'inégalité entre les candidats selon leur lieu d'examen. Un système d'appel à deux niveaux est également prévu dans le nouveau règlement ce qui répond au grief d'absence d'appel.

16.  Dans les commentaires du 28 septembre 2001, le plaignant indique que le fait d'exiger deux ans de résidence dans un pays pour pouvoir participer à l'examen est contraire à la liberté d'établissement à l'intérieur de la Communauté. La FIFA a supprimé l'exigence de deux ans de résidence pour les ressortissants de l'Union Européenne par sa circulaire 803 du 3 avril 2002 qui a amendé le règlement en cause.

17.  le plaignant estime également que la notion de 'parfaite réputation' exigée par la FIFA n'est pas définie et l'arbitraire est toujours de mise. Il faut tout d'abord rappeler que le préambule du règlement gouvernant l'activité des agents de joueurs stipule que chaque association nationale est tenue d'établir, sur base des dispositions suivantes, son propre règlement relatif aux agents de joueurs.(..) Ce règlement doit satisfaire aux principes ci- dessous énoncés. Lors de l'établissement de leur règlement, les associations nationales doivent respecter les Statuts et Règlements de la FIFA de même que la législation nationale et les traités internationaux. Le règlement de la FIFA doit donc être 'transposé' par chaque association nationale selon les principes qui y sont définis. C'est ainsi que l'article 2 paragraphe 2 du règlement FIFA prévoit que le requérant doit être de parfaite réputation. L'association nationale décide si les exigences préalables sont remplies conformément à la législation nationale du pays concerné. La définition de la parfaite réputation et les exigences qui en découlent en droit national doivent faire l'objet de la transposition nationale du règlement. En France l'activité d'agent sportif est encadrée par la loi no. 2000/627 du 6 juillet 2000 dite loi sur le sport. Son article 7 stipule les condamnations pénales qui empêchent un candidat ou un agent d'obtenir ou de détenir une licence. La Fédération Française de Football (FFF) a indiqué à la FIFA que le règlement de la FFF serait de toute évidence à la fois compatible avec la loi française et le règlement FIFA.

18.  le plaignant fait également remarquer que les agents licenciés FIFA n'ont pas à repasser l'examen mais doivent simplement échanger leur licence, ce qui serait contraire aux principes d'équivalence des diplômes en droit communautaire. Les directives sur la reconnaissance des diplômes s'appliquent uniquement aux personnes qui sont déjà pleinement qualifiées dans un Etat membre pour exercer

une profession donnée et qui souhaitent exercer la même profession dans un autre Etat membre qui réglemente cette profession. Le cas d'espèce des agents de joueurs n'entre pas du tout dans ce cas de figure.

### 3.1.2 L'assurance

19. le plaignant estime de nouveau que le texte n'est pas suffisamment précis, notamment sur le point de savoir qui fixera la somme maximum couverte par l'assurance et comment. La réponse à cette question se trouvera dans la transposition du dit règlement comme indiqué au paragraphe 16. En outre, [...] considère que la solution de l'assurance responsabilité civile professionnelle telle que prévue par le règlement n'est pas satisfaisante parce que l'agent ne peut choisir librement ni·sa compagnie d'assurance, ni l'étendue de la garantie, que celle ci est fonction du chiffre d'affaires, que la compagnie doit se soumettre aux règlements de la FIFA et que l'association nationale peut refuser la compagnie choisie par l'agent.

20. Selon le plaignant, l'agent ne peut choisir l'étendue de la garantie. Le nouveau règlement prévoit que la garantie doit couvrir tous les risques susceptibles de résulter de l'activité de médiation. Cette exigence est nécessaire pour que les joueurs et les clubs puissent obtenir un dédommagement rapide et direct en évitant de longues procédures devant les tribunaux nationaux. C'est pourquoi, la FIFA requiert une couverture des risques mentionnés. Cette exigence n'apparaît pas disproportionnée par rapport aux risques couverts par exemple par les assurances professionnelles des professions libérales. Rien n'empêche l'agent de souscrire une garantie plus étendue pour couvrir d'autres risques. Le fait que le montant de la garantie soit fonction du chiffre d'affaires de l'agent n'est pas problématique en soi et semble être une pratique usuelle pour les assurance professionnelles des professions libérales[554]. Le chiffre d'affaires pour une activité de médiation est une bonne indication des risques encourus et un critère objectif. Il faut, cependant, noter que bien que cet argument soit avancé dans les commentaires de [...], il n'est pas expliqué pourquoi cet aspect pose problème. En ce qui concerne les allégations selon lesquelles, le contrat d'assurance doit contenir une référence au dit règlement qui contraint la compagnie d'assurance à accepter les dites règles et l'association nationale examinera le contenu de la police d'assurance et pourrait la refuser, le règlement ne prévoit en aucune manière ce que le plaignant indique. Il n'y a pas la référence en cause et l'agent doit simplement transmettre une copie de la police d'assurance à l'association nationale. Cette dernière a, en effet, besoin de les répertorier dans le cas d'un éventuel litige ultérieur.

21. En tout état de cause, selon les polices d'assurances envoyées par la FIFA, plusieurs agents ont déjà souscrit des polices d'assurance responsabilité civile professionnelle dans plusieurs Etats membres de la Communauté dont la France sans difficulté. Ces compagnies d'assurance n'ont pas soulevé ces problèmes quant à la prétendue obligation de se soumettre aux règlements de la FIFA et ont conclu des contrats d'assurance en bonne et due forme. D'ailleurs cette référence ne figure dans aucune des polices dont la Commission dispose. Par ailleurs, la FIFA a modifié la rédaction de cet article dans sa circulaire 803 qui a amendé le règlement en cause afin que les polices d'assurance présentées par les agents de joueurs souscrites auprès de compagnies d'assurances d'un des pays de l'EEE, même s'il est différent de celui dans lequel l'agent a passé son examen soient acceptées par les fédérations nationales de l'EEE.

---

[554] La prime d'assurance responsabilité civile professionnelle des architectes et ingénieurs-conseils, par exemple, est fonction du montant des honoraires perçus.

3.1.3   Le code de déontologie

22.   le plaignant s'interroge sur les critères qui seront utilisés par l'association nationale ou la FIFA pour définir les infractions à ce code pompeusement baptisé de déontologique. Comme le Tribunal l'a rappelé dans son arrêt IMA du 28 mars 2001[555], il ne peut être admis que des règles organisant l'exercice d'une profession, par le seul fait qu'elles seraient qualifiées de 'déontologiques' par les organismes compétents, échapperaient par principe au champ d'application de l'article 81, paragraphe 1, CE. Seul un examen au cas par cas permet d'apprécier la validité d'une telle règle au regard de cette disposition du traité, notamment en tenant compte de son impact sur la liberté d'action des membres de la profession et sur l'organisation de celle-ci, ainsi que sur les bénéficiaires des services en cause.

23.   Les principes énoncés dans le code de déontologie sont très généraux et n'imposent aucune obligation disproportionnée aux agents. Ces obligations sont la conscience professionnelle, la transparence, la sincérité, la gestion juste des intérêts et l'établissement d'une comptabilité. Ces obligations sont clairement au bénéfice des clients des agents de joueurs.

3.1.4   La fixation de la rémunération de l'agent de joueurs

24.   le plaignant considère qu'avec le nouveau règlement, l'agent ne peut appliquer ni le principe (rémunération en fonction du salaire brut, primes exclues), ni le montant de rémunération qu'il souhaite au détriment des clients. L'article 12 paragraphe 4 stipule que la rémunération d'un agent de joueurs mandaté par un joueur sera calculée en fonction du salaire de base brut réalisé par le joueur aux termes du contrat de travail négocié par l'agent (soit sans tenir compte de toutes prestations supplémentaires telles que voiture et logement de fonction, primes de matches, primes de réussite et autres avantages). L'article 12 paragraphe 7 indique qu 'en cas de désaccord sur le montant de rémunération, l'agent a droit à 5% du salaire de base négocié.

25.   En ce qui concerne le premier point, le salaire brut est un critère objectif et transparent pour fixer la commission des agents de joueurs. En ce qui concerne le second point, il s'agit d'un mécanisme visant à régler les différends entre joueurs et agents. Rien n'empêche les agents de négocier une rémunération inférieure, ce que les joueurs ne refuseront pas.

3.1.5   Le contrat-type

26.   le plaignant estime que l'envoi pour enregistrement d'une copie du contrat signé entre un joueur et un agent à l'association nationale concernée est une atteinte à la vie privée. Sans se prononcer sur le bien fondé ou non de cet argument, il faut noter qu'il ne s'agit pas d'un problème qui est susceptible d'être appréhendé par les règles de concurrence communautaire. En tout état de cause, cette exigence semble justifiée par le fait que l'association nationale doit vérifier qu'un contrat a bien été signé par une personne habilitée et que le contrat type a été utilisé.

**3.2   Le caractère obligatoire de la licence et les justifications possibles pour une exemption**

27.   [...] estime que le caractère obligatoire de la licence est une restriction de concurrence et que la Commission n'a pas suffisamment justifié pourquoi le nouveau règlement serait susceptible de remplir les conditions de l'article 81 paragraphe 3

---

[555] Affaire T-144/99 Institut des mandataires agréés près l'Office européen des brevets contre Commission. Rec. 2001 page II-1087.

du traité CE. Tout d'abord, il est important de rappeler que suite à l'instruction préalable menée par ses services, la Commission avait en effet considéré dans sa communication des griefs que le caractère obligatoire de la licence pouvait constituer une barrière à l'entrée.

28. Les conclusions de la Commission ont été réexaminées à la lumière des observations soumises par les différentes parties intéressées. En cela, quatre considérations ont été particulièrement prises en considération. D'une part, l'objectif visé par cette exigence de protection des clients de cette profession, i.e. les joueurs et les clubs, contre des agents non qualifiés. La carrière des joueurs professionnels est courte et un transfert mal négocié peut aisément en compromettre la suite. Le système des licences pour les agents de joueurs impose en fait des restrictions qualitatives, bien plus que quantitatives, à l'exercice de la profession d'agent de joueurs. Ces restrictions peuvent dans certains cas être compatibles avec le droit de la concurrence lorsqu'elles sont encadrées par des garanties de non-discrimination, d'objectivité et de proportionnalité[556]. L'intervention de représentants de joueurs lors de l'audition par la voix de la FIFPro a par ailleurs montré l'attachement des joueurs eux-mêmes à ce caractère obligatoire de la licence. Il s'avère d'autre part que les agents de joueurs ne forment pas, pour le moment, un corps professionnel suffisamment organisé pour être capable d'établir eux- mêmes des règles déontologiques pour la profession. Enfin, le recours aux seules règles des droits nationaux, là où elles existeraient, paraît clairement aléatoire et inadapté à une activité par nature transfrontalière. En revanche, une entité internationale telle que la FIFA semble à même de mettre en place et d'administrer une réglementation efficace de cette profession.

29. Considérant le fait que les restrictions de concurrence relevées dans la communication des griefs ont par ailleurs été éliminées par l'entrée en vigueur du nouveau règlement, l'exigence d'une licence pour les agents de joueurs, si elle devait être considérée comme une restriction de concurrence, pourrait probablement bénéficier (au moins pendant une certaine période permettant l'évaluation du nouveau règlement) d'une exemption en vertu de l'article 81, paragraphe 3, ce qui en vertu de la jurisprudence de la Cour, justifie la prise de position adoptée par la Commission[557]. En effet l'objectif de protection des joueurs et de moralisation du milieu sportif, bien qu'il ne justifie aucune exclusion de principe du champ d'application du droit de la concurrence des règles s'y rattachant, devrait néanmoins être pris en compte dans l'application de l'article 81 paragraphe 3 du traité. La jurisprudence a déjà considéré que des 'restrictions' répondant à un objectif légitime, comme par exemple celui d'assurer de façon proportionnée le maintien d'un équilibre entre clubs, en préservant une certaine égalité des chances et l'incertitude des résultats (arrêt Lehtonen)[558] ou d'encourager le recrutement et la formation des jeunes joueurs (cf. conclusions de M. Lenz dans Bosman)[559], pourraient être justifiées au regard des règles du traité relatives aux libertés fondamentales. Elles pourraient également, dans un raisonnement analogue, bénéficier d'une exemption au titre de l'article 81 paragraphe 3 du traité.[560] Il faut

---

[556] Cf. par analogie la jurisprudence en matière de distribution sélective, arrêt de la Cour du 25 octobre 1977, *Metro contre Commission*, 26/76, Rec. p. 1875.

[557] Ordonnance de la Cour du 16 septembre 1997, *Koelman contre Commission*, C-59/96 P , point 42

[558] Arrêt du 13 avril 2000, aff. C-176/96, *Lehtonen*, Rec. p. I-268.

[559] Arrêt du 15 décembre 1995, aff. C-415/93, *Bosman*, Rec. p. I-4921.

[560] Voir à cet égard les conclusions de M. Lenz dans l'affaire C-413/93, *Bosman*, point 278.

toutefois s'assurer que ces restrictions sont indispensables pour atteindre les
objectifs recherchés ce qui implique qu'elles soient proportionnées à ces objectifs.
Un code de conduite que l'agent pourrait signer sur une base volontaire a souvent
été évoqué comme un moyen moins restrictif pour moraliser la profession.
Compte tenu de l'absence d'organisation au sein de cette profession et des risques
encourus par les joueurs qui ont une carrière professionnelle très courte, ce moyen
n'est pas suffisant pour atteindre l'objectif visé. En tout état de cause, s'il
s'avérait, dans le futur, que l'objectif visé pourrait être atteint sans la réglementation de la FIFA en cause, par exemple du fait de la réglementation de la profession par les Etats membres, ou parce que la profession d'agent de joueurs était
en mesure de s'auto-réglementer en garantissant un niveau de professionnalisme et
d'intégrité élevé de ses membres, la Commission se réserve le droit de réexaminer
le règlement en question et notamment le caractère obligatoire de la licence FIFA.

### 3.3    L'absence de notification

30.    Le règlement 17/62 n'impose pas aux entreprises la notification des accords
tombant dans le champ de l'article 81 paragraphe 1 du traité. Cependant la Commission ne peut accorder une exemption qu'aux accords remplissant les conditions
de l'article 81 paragraphe 3 et qui ont été notifiés. Par ailleurs, il est possible à la
Commission de rejeter une plainte sur le fondement que l'accord en question
pourrait bénéficier d'une exemption, ainsi qu'indiqué dans l'ordonnance de la
Cour du 16 septembre 1997 dans l'affaire Casper Koelman contre Commission[561]
la circonstance qu'un accord ou une pratique concertée, à supposer même qu'une
infraction à l'article 81, paragraphe 1, du traité puisse être établie, aurait pu bénéficier d'une exemption au titre de l'article 81 paragraphe 3, si une telle possibilité
s'était présentée, motive à suffisance le rejet d'une plainte à son encontre qui ne se
prononce pas sur l'existence ou l'inexistence d'une infraction à l'article 81
paragraphe 1.

### 3.4    L'article 82 du traité

31.    le plaignant indique que la Commission aurait dû instruire cette affaire au titre de
l'article 82 du traité. Il faut cependant noter que la plainte de 1998 ne contenait
aucune référence à cet article. Par ailleurs, les commentaires du 28 septembre
2001 sont flous quant au marché sur lequel la FIFA aurait une position dominante
et à l'abus qui serait allégué. En effet, il y est indiqué que ce droit exclusif que
s'est octroyé la FIFA est constitutif d'un monopole au sens de l'article 82 dans la
mesure où ce droit est exploité de manière abusive puisque toute concurrence n'est
pas pratiquement, mais totalement éliminée. ( ) La part de marché détenu par la
FIFA est totale. Ce marché comprend tous les services qui ont pour objet de
satisfaire une demande déterminée à savoir: le conseil dans la gestion de la
carrière professionnelle d'un joueur de football. Or, la FIFA n'est pas active sur le
marché du conseil.

### 4.    Conclusion

32.    En conclusion, la Commission considère, compte tenu de ce qui a été exposé qu'il
n'existe pas un intérêt communautaire suffisant qui justifierait de poursuivre la
procédure contre la FIFA concernant le règlement sur les agents de joueurs, dans
la mesure où:
(1) les dispositions restrictives les plus importantes faisant l'objet de la plainte

---

[561] Affaire C-59/96/P Rec. 1997 page I-4809.

sont à présent aujourd'hui abrogées, et que le caractère obligatoire de la licence – dont le caractère restrictif est fortement amoindri du fait de l'aménagement de modalités d'examen transparentes et objectives et de la suppression de l'exigence d'une caution – pourrait être justifié.

(2) Les arguments soulevés par le plaignant dans ses commentaires suite à l'envoi de la communication au titre de l'article 6 du traité ne permettent pas de constater des éléments restrictifs de concurrence dans le nouveau règlement qui ne seraient pas justifiables dans le cadre d'une demande d'exemption au titre de l'article 81 paragraphe 3.

(3) L'article 82 ne trouve pas application dans le cas d'espèce tel qu'explicité par le plaignant.

33. Pour ces raisons, je vous communique que la décision finale de la Commission est de rejeter la demande de constatation d'infraction que vous lui avez soumise le [ ] 1998 conformément à l'article 3 paragraphe 2 du règlement no.17 du Conseil du 6 février 1962.

34. Un recours contre cette décision peut être formé devant le Tribunal de première instance des Communautés Européennes au titre de l'article 230 du traité CE. Ces recours, conformément à l'article 242 du traité CE, n'ont pas d'effet suspensif, sauf si le Tribunal ordonne le sursis à exécution.

Veuillez croire, [ ], à l'assurance de ma considération distinguée.
Fait à Bruxelles, le 16 avril 2002

Pour la Commission
Mario Monti
Membre de la Commission
(signé)

---

## * 2.4.83. COMMISSION CLOSES INVESTIGATIONS INTO FIFA RULES ON PLAYERS' AGENTS, 18 APRIL 2002[562]

---

## * 2.4.84. COMMITTEE ON CULTURE, YOUTH, EDUCATION, THE MEDIA AND SPORT – PUBLIC HEARING 'SPORTS AND AUDIOVISUAL RIGHTS', 18 APRIL 2002

---

## * 2.4.85. ANSWER ON BEHALF OF THE COMMISSION TO WRITTEN QUESTION P-894/02 BY FREDDY BLAK (GUE/NGL), 30 APRIL 2002[563] *

Subject: Unfair terms of competition in football

---

## * 2.4.86. COMMISSION WELCOMES UEFA'S NEW POLICY FOR SELLING THE MEDIA RIGHTS TO THE CHAMPIONS LEAGUE, 3 JUNE 2002[564]

---

[562] IP/02/585.
[563] Question of 20-3-2002; OJ C 309 E, 12-12-2002, p. 57.
[564] IP/02/806.

**\* 2.4.87.  THE APPLICATION OF THE EU'S COMPETITION RULES TO SPORTS, 5 JUNE 2002**[565]

———

**2.4.88.  ACTION BY LAURENT PIAU AGAINST COMMISSION OF THE EUROPEAN COMMUNITIES, CASE T- 121/01, 14 JUNE 2002**[566]

An action against the Commission of the European Communities was brought before the Court of First Instance of the European Communities on 14 June 2002 by Laurent Piau, residing in Nantes (France), represented by Marguerite Fauconnet, lawyer.
The applicant claims that the Court should:
–   annul the decision of the Commission of 15 April 2002;
–   order the Commission to pay the cost.

Pleas in law and main arguments
On 23 March 1998, the applicant lodged a complaint with the Commission arguing that the rules applied by FIFA to players' agents were contrary to Community law. That complaint was registered by the Commission which then carried out a thorough investigation. Having heard no more as to progress on his case, the applicant on 31 January 2001 placed the on notice and on 31 May 2001 brought an action for failure to act (Case T- 121/00 OJ 2001 C 227, p. 30). On 3 August 2001 the Commission wrote to the applicant informing him of its intention not to uphold his complaint.
After receiving the applicant's comments, the Commission rejected the applicant's complaint in view of the fact that the most restrictive provisions were repealed after proceedings were initiated. In the present case, the applicant contests that decision.
In support of his application, the applicant alleges, first, manifest error of assessment of the facts and of the law.
According to the applicant, the Commission's statement that most restrictive of the provisions of FIFA's rules have been repealed is wrong.
Furthermore, other aspects of the rules have not been correctly assessed either.
Moreover, the applicant alleges inadequate statement of reasons for the decision. According to the applicant, the Commission did not investigate the complaint on the basis of Article 82 of the EC Treaty and did not provide reasons for the rejection of that part of the complaint. According to the applicant, FIFA holds a dominant position in the market in football and abuses its position in the related market in services linked to player transfers.
The applicant further alleges error of assessment in that, in his view, FIFA's rules do not comply with Article 81 of the EC Treaty and that those rules cannot benefit from an exemption under Article 81(3).
The applicant also claims that the Commission infringed Article 49 of the EC Treaty. In his view, the Commission does ties was brought before the Court of First Instance of the not have the power implicitly to confer a power to lay down rules on the awarding of diplomas on FIFA.

———

**\* 2.4.89.  COMMISSION CLOSES INVESTIGATIONS INTO UEFA RULE ON MULTIPLE OWNERSHIP OF FOOTBALL CLUBS, 27 JUNE 2002**[567]

———

---

[565]  MEMO/02/127.
[566]  OJ C 219, 14-9-2002, p. 21.
[567]  IP/02/942.

**\* 2.4.90. ANSWER ON BEHALF OF THE COMMISSION TO WRITTEN QUESTION E-1912/02 BY ROBERT GOEBBELS (PSE), 31 JULY 2002[568] \***

Subject: FIFA and UEFA's de facto monopoly

———

**\* 2.4.91. COMMISSION REJECTS COMPLAINT AGAINST INTERNATIONAL OLYMPIC COMMITTEE BY SWIMMERS BANNED FROM COMPETITIONS FOR DOPING, 9 AUGUST 2002[569]**

———

**2.4.92. NOTICE PUBLISHED PURSUANT TO ARTICLE 19(3) OF COUNCIL REGULATION NO 17 CONCERNING CASE COMP/C.2/37.398 – JOINT SELLING OF THE MEDIA RIGHTS OF THE UEFA CHAMPIONS LEAGUE ON AN EXCLUSIVE BASIS, 17 AUGUST 2002[570]**

**1. THE NOTIFICATION**

1. On 1 February 1999 the 'Union des Associations Européennes de Football' (UEFA) applied for a negative clearance under Article 81(1) of the EC Treaty or, failing this, an exemption under Article 81(3) of the EC Treaty in respect of its arrangements for the joint selling of the commercial rights of the UEFA Champions League[571].

2. UEFA is a society registered in the register of companies under the terms of the Swiss Civil Code. Its headquarters is located in Switzerland. As the European confederation recognised by Fédération Internationale de Football Association (FIFA), UEFA is the governing body for European football. UEFA membership is open to all national football associations in the European Continent. UEFA is thus an association of national football associations. Currently, UEFA's membership comprises 52 national football associations. 21 of these member associations are located in the EEA[572]. UEFA organises a number of football tournaments in addition to the UEFA Champions League.

3. The notified arrangement provides that UEFA is granted the exclusive right to sell the commercial rights of the UEFA Champions League. This excludes clubs from taking independent commercial actions regarding the exploitation of these rights. Consequently, UEFA negotiates and concludes contracts pertaining to the exploitation of the commercial rights of the UEFA Champions League. UEFA's commercial policy is to sell the TV rights in a single package on an exclusive basis to a single broadcaster per Member State.

4. Several third parties submitted observations on the notified arrangements. These observations added no new arguments in favour of the notified arrangement to those submitted by UEFA in its notification. These relate essentially to solidarity, the social and economic aspects of sport, and the balance in sport competition between rich and poor clubs and associations. Several third parties argued against

---

[568] Question of 2-7-2002; OJ C 92 E, 17-4-2003, p. 115-116.

[569] IP/02/1211.

[570] OJ C 196, 17-8-2002, p. 3-5 (Text with EEA relevance)

[571] TV broadcasting rights, sponsorship, suppliership, licensing and IPR.

[572] In the UK there are four UEFA member associations: England, Wales, Scotland and Northern Ireland.

joint selling. They essentially argue that joint selling leads to higher prices, and less football on TV. They also argue that UEFA's solidarity measures are inefficient, insufficient and conducted in a non-transparent way.

5.   On 19 July 2001, the Commission issued a statement of objections finding that the notified arrangement for the joint selling of the TV broadcasting rights restrict competition pursuant to Article 81(1) of the EC Treaty and that they were not eligible for exemption under Article 81(3). Even though UEFA may be regarded as a co-owner of the commercial rights of the UEFA Champions League, joint selling still restricts competition on the horizontal level by preventing clubs from taking independent commercial action in respect of their rights. UEFA's joint selling arrangement also restricts competition on the vertical level, because UEFA's commercial policy is to grant an exclusive license to a single broadcaster in each Member State covering all TV rights of the UEFA Champions League. The combination of the two restrictions reinforces their restrictive effect.

6.   The arrangements restrict competition in the upstream market for the acquisition of TV rights of football. This market is closely linked with the downstream television markets where free-TV broadcasters compete for advertisers and pay-TV broadcasters compete for subscribers: the restrictions therefore affect the downstream markets as well. Football is in most countries the driving force not only for the development of pay-TV services but it is also an essential programme item for free TV broadcasters.

7.   The statement of objections found that any possible efficiencies and benefits that joint selling could provide in the broadcasting market are negated by the commercial policy pursued by UEFA. This is because all TV rights of the UEFA Champions League are sold to a single broadcaster in each territory for several years in a row on an exclusive basis. Consequently, only a single large broadcaster in each territory is able to acquire the TV rights of the UEFA Champions League. The statement of objections concluded that the combination of these restrictions has a negative effect on the structure of the downstream TV broadcasting markets since football is in most countries a driving force for the development of the TV markets. The restrictions therefore enhance media concentration and hamper competition between broadcasters. If one broadcaster holds all relevant football TV rights in a Member State, it will become extremely difficult for competing broadcasters to establish themselves in that market due to the inability to acquire interesting content.

8.   On 16 November 2001, UEFA submitted its formal reply to the statement of objections and on 8 January 2002 it presented a preliminary outline of a possible new commercial policy. Subsequently, on 12 March 2002 UEFA presented a rights segmentation table for the exploitation of not only the TV rights but also all the media rights of the UEFA Champions League, including radio, television, Internet, UMTS and physical media rights (such as DVD, VHS, CD Rom, etc.). Based on the principles in this proposal, on 13 May 2002 UEFA notified a new commercial policy designed to remedy the infringements that were the subject of the statement of objections. The Commission's preliminary view is that the competition concerns that were expressed in the statement of objections will be remedied by UEFA's new commercial policy.

## 2.   THE NOTIFIED AGREEMENT

9.   The notified new revised UEFA Champions League joint selling arrangement may be summarised in the following manner[573] :

---

[573]  The notified documents explaining UEFA's new commercial policy is displayed on UEFA's official web <http://www.UEFA.com>.

2.1.     Television broadcasting rights

10.     UEFA will award the TV rights of the UEFA Champions League following a public invitation to broadcasters to bid. The TV rights contracts shall be concluded for a period not exceeding three UEFA Champions League seasons.

11.     UEFA will offer its TV rights in several smaller packages (the precise format of which may vary depending on the structure of the TV market in the particular Member State in which the rights are being offered).

12.     Subject to the above, UEFA will have the exclusive right to sell two main live rights packages (free or pay-TV) each comprising two matches per match night (UEFA Champions League matches are currently played Tuesday and Wednesdays). The first package will usually include first and third pick per match day and the second package second and fourth pick. These two packages would cover 61 matches out of a total of 157.

13.     UEFA will likewise have the exclusive right to sell the remaining matches for live pay-TV/pay-per-view exploitation. However, if UEFA has not managed to sell the rights within one week after the draw for the First Group stage of the competition, UEFA will lose its exclusive right to sell these TV rights. Thereafter, the individual home clubs participating in a given match will also be able to sell the rights of their matches for live pay-TV/pay-per-view exploitation. The right of UEFA and the individual football clubs to sell these matches will be subject to picks one to four made by the broadcasters having bought the main live packages. While these rights may not be bundled together with the rights of other clubs thus creating an alternative UEFA Champions League programming offer, football clubs may under certain circumstances combine their TV rights with a view to make a regional offering. Any purchaser of these rights from UEFA (or the clubs, as the case may be) will be obliged to show the matches live.

14.     UEFA will in addition have the exclusive right to sell a highlight package covering all matches of the UEFA Champions League available as of 22.45 on each match night.

15.     As of Thursday midnight (i.e. one day after the last match of the match week), both UEFA and the football clubs can exploit the deferred TV rights. UEFA exploitation shall be related to action from the whole UEFA Champions League; the individual football clubs exploitation shall be in relation to matches in which they participate, it must be 'club branded' and must not be bundled with rights of other clubs to create a competing UEFA Champions League programming offer, save once again that football clubs may under certain circumstances combine their TV rights with a view to make a regional offering.

16.     UEFA will have the exclusive right to sell live TV rights outside the EEA area. Deferred rights available to clubs are subject to the same rules both inside and outside the EEA area.

2.2.     Internet

17.     Both UEFA (in respect of all matches) and the clubs (in respect of matches in which they participate) will have a right to provide video content on the Internet as of midnight on the night of the match. This content will be based on the raw feed produced for television. UEFA will apply a revenue sharing system in respect of the income generated from the raw feed or the Internet content. UEFA intends to build a service that will produce UEFA Champions League content for streaming of moving pictures on the Internet. This service can be exploited both via uefa.com and via the football clubs' web-sites. Clubs may acquire the raw feed from UEFA or they may participate in the UEFA service. Clubs may customise

and edit the content for the purposes of creating a club focused and club branded product. Clubs will pay a fee for the UEFA Internet service and/or the raw feed. This fee shall be both transparent and fair, reasonable and non-discriminatory and submitted to an arbitration system to solve possible disputes.

18. Both UEFA (in respect of all matches) and the clubs (in respect of matches in which they participate) may likewise offer streaming of live audio rights. UEFA will establish a revenue sharing mechanism from the income generated from uefa.com.

2.3. Wireless 3G/UMTS product
19. Both UEFA (in respect of all matches) and the clubs (in respect of matches in which they participate) will have a right to provide audio/video content via UMTS services. This content will be based on the raw feed produced for television. UEFA will apply a revenue sharing system in respect of the income generated from the raw feed or the UMTS content. UEFA intends to build a 3G/UMTS wireless product that will be based on an extensive video database to be developed by UEFA. UEFA will offer the rights on an exclusive or non-exclusive basis to operator(s) with an UMTS licence, initially for a period of four years and subsequently for periods of three years. Clubs may acquire the raw feed from UEFA or they may participate in the UEFA service. The clubs may customise and edit the content for the purposes of creating a club focused and club branded product. This product may not consist solely or mostly of UEFA Champions League content and must include other club-related multimedia content as well. Clubs will pay a fee for the UEFA wireless service and/or the raw feed. This fee shall be both transparent and fair, reasonable, and non-discriminatory and submitted to an arbitration system to solve possible disputes.

2.4. Physical media rights
20. Both UEFA and the football clubs are entitled to exploit the physical media rights (DVD, VHS, CD Rom, etc.) to archive material from the previous UEFA Champions League season with an embargo of 48 hours after the final. While UEFA's rights extend to all action in the UEFA Champions League, the rights of the football clubs are limited to action in which the football clubs are participating.

2.5. Radio broadcasting rights and Internet audio
21. Both UEFA and the clubs may sell licenses to live radio broadcasting of UEFA Champions League football matches on a non-exclusive basis.

**THE COMMISSION's INTENTIONS**
22. On the basis of the foregoing, the Commission intends to take a favourable view in respect of UEFA's revised joint selling arrangement. Before adopting a favourable opinion, the Commission invites third parties to send their observations within one month of the publication of this notice to the following address quoting the reference Case 37.398 – Joint selling of the TV rights to the UEFA Champions League on an exclusive basis:

European Commission Directorate-General for Competition
Office J-70 0/18
B – 1049 Brussels Fax (32-2) 295 01 28.

**2.4.93. EUROPEAN COURT OF JUSTICE, JUDGMENT OF THE COURT OF FIRST INSTANCE (FIRST CHAMBER, EXTENDED COMPOSITION), MÉTROPOLE TÉLÉVISION SA (M6) (T-185/00), ANTENA 3 DE TELEVISIÓN, SA (T-216/00), GESTEVISIÓN TELECINCO, SA (T-299/00) AND SIC – SOCIEDADE INDEPENDENTE DE COMUNICAÇÃO, SA (T-300/00) V COMMISSION OF THE EUROPEAN COMMUNITIES, JOINED CASES T-185/00, T-216/00, T-299/00 AND T-300/00, 8 OCTOBER 2002[574]**

*Competition – Decision granting exemption – Television rights – Eurovision system – Article 81(1) and (3) EC – Manifest error of assessment.*

**Parties**

In Joined Cases T-185/00, T-216/00, T-299/00 and T-300/00,

Métropole télévision SA (M6), established in Neuilly-sur-Seine (France), represented by D. Théophile, lawyer, with an address for service in Luxembourg, applicant in Case T-185/00, Antena 3 de Televisión SA, established in Madrid (Spain), represented by F. Pombo García, E. Garayar Gutiérrez and R. Alonso Pérez-Villanueva, lawyers, with an address for service in Luxembourg, applicant in Case T-216/00, Gestevisión Telecinco SA, established in Madrid, represented by S. Muñoz Machado and M. López-Contreras Gonzalez, lawyers, with an address for service in Luxembourg, applicant in Case T-299/00, SIC – Sociedade Independente de Comunicação SA, established in Linda-a-Velha (Portugal), represented by C. Botelho Moniz, lawyer,

applicant in Case T-300/00, supported by Deutsches SportFernsehen GmbH (DSF), established in Ismaning (Germany), represented by K. Metzlaff, lawyer, with an address for service in Luxembourg, intervener in Case T-299/00, and by Reti Televisive Italiane Spa (RTI), established in Rome (Italy), represented by G. Amorelli, lawyer, with an address for service in Luxembourg, intervener in Case T-300/00, v Commission of the European Communities, represented, in Case T-185/00, by K. Wiedner and B. Mongin, acting as Agents; in Cases T-216/00 and T-299/00, by K. Wiedner and É. Gippini Fournier, acting as Agents, assisted by J. Rivas Andrés, lawyer; and in Case T-300/00, by K. Wiedner and M. França, acting as Agents, with an address for service in Luxembourg, defendant, supported by Union européenne de radio-télévision (UER), established in Grand-Saconnex (Switzerland), represented by D. Waelbroeck and M. Johnsson, lawyers, with an address for service in Luxembourg, intervener in Cases T-185/00, T-216/00, T-299/00 and T-300/00, and by Radiotelevisión Española (RTVE), established in Madrid, represented by J. Gutiérrez Gisbert, lawyer, with an address for service in Luxembourg, intervener in Cases T-216/00 and T-299/00,

Application for annulment of Commission Decision 2000/400/EC of 10 May 2000 relating to a proceeding pursuant to Article 81 of the EC Treaty (Case IV/32.150 – Eurovision) (OJ 2000 L 151, p. 18),

*The Court of First Instance of the European Communities* (Second Chamber, Extended Composition),

composed of: R.M. Moura Ramos, President, V. Tiili, J. Pirrung, P. Mengozzi and A.W.H. Meij, Judges,

Registrar: B. Pastor, Principal Administrator,

having regard to the written procedure and further to the hearing on 13 and 14 March 2002,

gives the following

Judgment

---

[574] ECR 2002, p. II-3805.

**Grounds of the judgment**
**The European Broadcasting Union and the Eurovision system**

1    The European Broadcasting Union (EBU) is a professional non-profit association
     of radio and television organisations set up in 1950 and with its headquarters in
     Geneva (Switzerland). In accordance with Article 2 of its Statutes as amended on
     3 July 1992, the objectives of the EBU are to represent the interests of its members
     in the field of programming and in legal, technical and other areas, and in particu-
     lar to promote the exchange of radio and television programmes by all means – for
     example, Eurovision and Euroradio – and any other form of cooperation among its
     members and with other broadcasting organisations or their associations, as well
     as to assist its active members in negotiations of all kinds and, when asked, to ne-
     gotiate on their behalf.

2    Eurovision constitutes the main framework for the exchange of programmes
     among the active members of the EBU. It has been in existence since 1954 and is
     one of the main objectives of the EBU. According to Article 3(6) of the EBU Stat-
     utes, in the version of 3 July 1992, ''Eurovision' is a television programme ex-
     change system organised and coordinated by the EBU, based on the understanding
     that members offer to the other members, on the basis of reciprocity, ... their cov-
     erage of sports and cultural events taking place in their countries and of potential
     interest to other members, thereby enabling each other to provide a high quality
     service in these fields to their respective national audiences.' Eurovision members
     include active members of the EBU as well as consortia of such members. All ac-
     tive members of the EBU may participate in a system of joint acquisition and shar-
     ing of television rights (and of the costs relating thereto) to international sports
     events, which are referred to as 'Eurovision rights'.

3    To become an active member, a broadcasting organisation must satisfy the condi-
     tions relating, inter alia, to national coverage and to the nature and financing of
     programming (hereinafter 'the membership conditions').

4    Until 1 March 1988, the benefit of EBU and Eurovision services was exclusively
     reserved to their members. However, when the Statutes of the EBU were amended
     in 1988, a new paragraph (in the current version, paragraph 7) was added to Ar-
     ticle 3, providing that contractual access to Eurovision may be granted to associ-
     ated members as well as non-members of the EBU.

**Applicants**

5    Métropole télévision (M6) is a company incorporated under French law, which
     operates a national television service broadcast free-to-air via a land radio relay
     channel as well as by cable and satellite.

6    Since 1987, M6 has lodged an application to join the EBU six times. Each time, its
     application has been rejected on the ground that it does not fulfil the membership
     conditions laid down by the EBU Statutes. Following the last refusal of the EBU,
     M6 filed a complaint with the Commission on 5 December 1997, complaining of
     EBU's practices towards it, and in particular the refusal of its applications for ad-
     mission. By decision of 29 June 1999, the Commission dismissed the applicant's
     complaint. The Court of First Instance, in its judgment in Métropole télévision v
     Commission (Case T-206/99 [2001] ECR II-1057), annulled that decision to reject
     the complaint on the grounds that the Commission infringed its obligations to state
     reasons and the obligations it has when dealing with complaints.

7    Meanwhile, on 6 March 2000, M6 filed a new complaint with the Commission,
     asking it to declare the EBU's membership conditions as amended in 1998 anti-
     competitive and not qualifying for an exemption under Article 81(3) EC. By letter

of 12 September 2000, the Commission dismissed that complaint. The applicant brought an action for annulment of that dismissal. That action was held inadmissible by order of the Court of First Instance in Case T-354/00 M6 v Commission [2001] ECR II-3177.

8     Antena 3 de Televisión SA (hereinafter 'Antena 3') is a company governed by Spanish law set up on 7 June 1988, which has been granted by the competent Spanish authority a concession indirectly to operate the public television service.

9     On 27 March 1990. Antena 3 lodged an application to join the EBU. By letter of 3 June 1991, Antena 3 was notified of the decision by the EBU's administrative council to refuse that application.

10    Gestevisión Telecinco SA (hereinafter 'Telecinco') is a company governed by Spanish law which operates a terrestrial television channel with national coverage, broadcast free-to-air. In accordance with Spanish national law, that undertaking is one of three private operators to which the Spanish authorities granted a 10-year concession in 1989 to operate indirectly the public television service. The concession for Telecinco was renewed for an additional 10 years.

11    SIC – Sociedade Independente de Comunicação SA (hereinafter 'SIC') is a company governed by Portuguese law whose purpose is to carry out television-related activities and which has, since October 1992, operated one of the main national television stations broadcast free-to-air in Portugal.

**Background to the proceedings**

12    In response to a complaint of 17 December 1987 by the company Screensport, the Commission examined the rules governing the Eurovision system of joint acquisition and sharing of sport television rights to see whether they were compatible with Article 81 EC. The complaint related, in particular, to the refusal by the EBU and its members to grant sub-licences for sporting events. On 12 December 1988, the Commission sent the EBU a statement of objections referring to the rules governing the acquisition and use, within the Eurovision system, of television rights for sporting events, which are generally exclusive. The Commission stated that it was prepared to consider an exemption for those rules, on the condition that a requirement to grant sub-licences to non-members be laid down for a substantial portion of the rights in question, under reasonable conditions.

13    On 3 April 1989, the EBU notified to the Commission the provisions of its Statute and other rules governing the acquisition of television rights to sporting events, the exchange of sports programmes within the framework of Eurovision and contractual access to such programmes for third parties, in order to obtain negative clearance or, alternatively, an exemption pursuant to Article 81(3) EC.

14    After the EBU revised its rules to make it possible to obtain sub-licences for the broadcasts in question ('the 1993 access scheme for non-members of the EBU', hereinafter the 'sub-licensing scheme'), the Commission adopted, on 11 June 1993, Decision 93/403/EEC relating [to] a proceeding pursuant to Article [81] of the EEC Treaty (IV/32.150 – EBU/Eurovision System) (OJ 1993 L 179, p. 23), under which it granted an exemption pursuant to Article 81(3). That decision was annulled by judgment of the Court of First Instance in Joined Cases T-528/93, T-542/93, T-543/93 and T-546/93 Métropole Télévision and Others v Commission [1996] ECR II-649.

15    Subsequently, upon request by the Commission, the EBU adopted and submitted to the Commission, on 26 March 1999, rules granting access to Eurovision rights operated on pay-channel television (the 'sub-licensing rules of 1999 relating to the exploitation of Eurovision rights on pay-TV channels of 26 March 1999', herein-

after 'the sub-licensing rules').

16    On 10 May 2000, the Commission adopted Decision 2000/400/EC relating to a
      proceeding pursuant to Article 81 of the EC Treaty (Case IV/32.150 – Eurovision)
      (OJ 2000 L 151, p. 18, hereinafter 'the contested decision'), by which the Com-
      mission granted a new exemption pursuant to Article 81(3).

17    In Article 1 of the contested decision, the Commission declared that, pursuant, in-
      ter alia, to Article 81(3) EC, the provisions of Article 81(1) EC are inapplicable
      from 26 February 1993 until 31 December 2005 to the following notified agree-
      ments:
      (a)    the joint acquisition of sport television rights;
      (b)    the sharing of the jointly acquired sport television rights;
      (c)    the exchange of the signal for sporting events;
      (d)    the sub-licensing scheme;
      (e)    the sub-licensing rules.

18    The sub-licensing scheme and the sub-licensing rules together constitute the ac-
      cess scheme for third parties to the Eurovision system.

19    In connection with the sub-licensing scheme, the contested decision states:
      '[T]he EBU and its members undertake to grant non-member broadcasters exten-
      sive access to Eurovision sports programmes the rights for which have been ac-
      quired on an exclusive basis through collective negotiations. ... [That scheme]
      grants live and deferred transmission rights to third parties of jointly acquired
      Eurovision sports rights. In particular the non-EBU members have significant ac-
      cess to the unused rights, i.e. for the transmission of sporting events which are not
      transmitted by, or of which only a minor part are transmitted by, an EBU member.
      The terms and conditions of access are freely negotiated between the EBU (for
      transnational channels), or the member(s) in the country concerned (for national
      channels), and the non-member ...' (paragraph 28 of the contested decision).

20    In connection with the sub-licensing rules, the contested decision specifies that a
      non-member of the EBU may buy television rights in order to broadcast on its
      pay-TV channel sports competitions which are identical or comparable to those
      presented by the members of Eurovision on their own pay-TV channels. The fee to
      be paid by the non-member is to fairly reflect the terms on which the rights were
      obtained by the Eurovision member (Annex II (iii) to the contested decision).

21    The declaration of exemption contained in Article 1 of the contested decision is
      subject to a condition and an obligation. The condition requires the EBU and its
      members collectively to acquire television rights to sporting events only under
      agreements which allow them to grant access to third parties in conformity with
      the access scheme or, subject to the approval of the EBU, on conditions more
      favourable to the non-member. The obligation requires the EBU to inform the
      Commission of any amendments and additions to the access scheme and of all ar-
      bitration procedures concerning disputes under the access scheme (Article 2 of the
      contested decision).

**Procedure and forms of order sought**

22    M6, Antena 3, SIC and Telecinco brought their actions by applications lodged at
      the Registry of the Court of First Instance on 13 July, 21 August and 18 and 19
      September 2000, respectively.

23    By applications lodged at the Registry of the Court of First Instance on 5, 17 and
      26 January 2001, the EBU and Radiotelevisión Española (hereinafter 'RTVE')
      sought leave to intervene, the former in Cases T-185/00, T-216/00, T-299/00 and
      T-300/00 and the latter in Cases T-216/00 and T-299/00, in support of the forms of

order sought by the defendant. Those applications were granted by orders of the President of the Fourth Chamber of the Court of First Instance on 7 February, 29 March and 7 May 2001.

24 By letter of 22 February 2001, SIC lodged at the Registry of the Court of First Instance a request for confidentiality for parts of the application. The Court granted that request by order of the President of the Fourth Chamber of 30 April 2001.

25 By applications lodged at the Registry of the Court of First Instance on 7 March and 13 March 2001, Deutsches SportFernsehen GmbH (DSF) and Reti Televisive Italiane Spa (RTI) sought leave to intervene in Cases T-299/00 and T-300/00 respectively in support of the forms of order sought by the applicant. Those applications were granted by orders of the President of the Fourth Chamber of the Court of First Instance on 7 May and 7 June 2001.

26 Owing to a change in the composition of the Chambers of the Court of First Instance as of 20 September 2001, the Judge-Rapporteur was assigned to the Second Chamber and the present cases were therefore assigned to that Chamber.

27 By decision of the Court of First Instance of 20 February 2002, the cases were referred to a Chamber composed of five judges.

28 By order of 25 February 2002, the President of the Second Chamber (Extended Composition) joined the four cases for the purposes of the oral procedure and the judgment, pursuant to Article 50 of the Rules of Procedure of the Court of First Instance.

29 Upon hearing the report of the Judge-Rapporteur, the Court of First Instance (Second Chamber, Extended Composition) decided to open the oral procedure. Within the framework of the measures of organisation of procedure, he invited the parties to produce certain documents and to provide written responses to certain questions.

30 The oral arguments of the parties and their responses to the Court's questions were heard at the hearing on 13 and 14 March 2001.

31 In Case T-185/00, M6 claims that the Court should:
    – annul the contested decision;
    – order the Commission to pay the costs;
    – order the EBU to pay the costs of its intervention.

32 In Case T-216/00, Antena 3 claims that the Court should:
    – order the Commission to add several documents to the file;
    – annul the contested decision;
    – order the Commission to pay the costs;
    – order the interveners to pay the costs of their interventions.

33 In Case T-299/00, Telecinco claims that the Court should:
    – annul the contested decision;
    – order the Commission to pay the costs.

34 In Case T-300/00, SIC claims that the Court should:
    – order the Commission to produce certain documents;
    – annul the contested decision;
    – order the Commission to pay the costs;
    – order the EBU to pay the costs of its intervention.

35 In the four joined cases, the Commission contends that the Court should:
    – dismiss the applications;
    – order the applicants to pay the costs.

36 DSF, intervener in support of the form of order sought by Telecinco in Case T-299/00, claims that the Court of First Instance should annul the contested decision.

37    RTI, intervener in support of the form of order sought by SIC in Case T-300/00, claims that the Court should:
      – annul the contested decision;
      – order the Commission to pay the costs, including those of the intervener.
38    The EBU, intervener in the four cases in support of the form of order sought by the Commission, claims that the Court should:
      – dismiss the applications;
      – order the applicants to bear the costs of their interventions.
39    The RTVE, intervener in Cases T-216/00 and T-299/00 in support of the form of order sought by the Commission, claims that the Court should:
      – dismiss the application;
      – order the applicants to bear the costs of their intervention.

## Law
### Preliminary observations

40    The applicants put forward seven pleas altogether in support of their action. The first plea, raised in the four cases, relates to infringement of the obligation to comply with the judgments of the Court of First Instance. The second plea, put forward in Cases T-216/00 and T-300/00, relates to an error as to the facts and an infringement of the obligation to provide a statement of reasons. The third plea, raised in all the cases, alleges misapplication of Article 81(1) EC. The fourth plea, raised in the four cases, concerns infringement of Article 81(3) EC. The fifth plea, raised in all the cases, is based on errors in law relating to the material and temporal scope of the contested decision. The sixth plea, raised in Case T-216/00, relates to infringement of the principle of sound administration. Finally, the seventh plea, raised in all the cases, alleges misuse of powers.

41    It is appropriate to analyse first the fourth plea, raised in all four cases, concerning infringement of Article 81(3) EC.

42    By that plea, the applicants claim that the Eurovision system does not satisfy any of the criteria for exemption laid down in Article 81(3) EC, in particular the absence of the possibility of eliminating competition in respect of a substantial part of the products in question. Further, the submissions put forward by M6 as regards the discriminatory nature of the sub-licensing scheme and the indispensable character of that discrimination should be amended, inasmuch as, by those arguments, M6 is essentially claiming that the sub-licensing scheme does not guarantee access for non-member channels to the rights acquired by the EBU, thereby leading to compartmentalisation of the market for televised rebroadcasting rights and, as a result, the elimination of competition in that market.

### The fourth plea, concerning infringement of Article 81(3) EC as regards the criterion relating to the absence of the possibility of eliminating competition in respect of a substantial part of the products in question
#### Arguments of the parties

43    The applicants claim that the Commission misapplied Article 81(3)(b) EC in the present case, for two main reasons.

44    First, the Commission did not exactly define either the product market or the geographic market in question. In the absence of a definition of the relevant market, the Commission's conclusion that the agreements notified do not afford the undertakings benefiting from the exemption the possibility of eliminating competition in respect of a substantial part of the products in question can have no basis of reference. Without a preliminary definition it is impossible to determine whether the

guarantees offered by the third party access scheme to the Eurovision system satisfy the condition in Article 81(3)(b) EC.

45    In addition, inasmuch as the contested decision accepts that major international sporting events, such as the Olympic Games or major football championships, constitute autonomous markets, the Commission should have concluded that, within those markets, the Eurovision system eliminates any competition.

46    Second, as regards the guarantees provided by the third-party access scheme to the Eurovision system which, according to the contested decision, makes it possible to avoid eliminating competition in the market, the applicants consider that if the Commission had correctly analysed the product market, it would have noted that the third-party access scheme could not avoid eliminating from competition general channels such as the applicants. First, that scheme in fact only authorises deferred transmission of sports programmes and, second, it does not really work in the case of general channels which, like the applicants, compete against EBU members.

47    The Commission, supported by the EBU, contends that it is settled practice for it to leave open the definition of the relevant product market or geographic market when, on the basis of the narrowest possible definition of the market, no problem of restriction on competition arises.

48    In the present case, the Commission considers it clear that the agreements notified affect trade between Member States (paragraph 81 of the contested decision) and that they restrict competition (paragraph 71 of the contested decision). However, the Commission considers that on the narrowest definition of the product market, such as the market for the acquisition of transmission rights for specific sporting events like the summer Olympics, and taking account of the structure of the market and all the rules governing sub-licensing for access to Eurovision sports programmes by broadcasting organisations which are not EBU members, the notified agreements do not give rise to any restriction on competition.

49    The Commission considers that, in the light of the narrowest possible definition of the market, the restrictive effects of the notified agreements have been resolved by the amendment of the agreements and by the conditions imposed by the Commission (relating to the third-party access scheme to the Eurovision system). There is therefore no need to define more precisely the markets concerned.

50    As regards the third-party access scheme to the Eurovision system, the Commission, supported by the EBU and RTVE, points out that following the changes made to that scheme, live transmission rights which are not used by EBU members are made available to their competitors. The access to deferred transmission rights imposed by the Commission was also greatly enlarged. That scheme functioned in practice and a number of competitors of EBU members had recourse to it for both live and deferred transmissions, as well as for the transmission of extracts. In short, as a result of that scheme, it was not possible to eliminate competition in a substantial part of the market, even by defining the market as narrowly as the transmission rights for the summer Olympics.

### Findings of the Court

51    In light of the arguments of the parties, the terms of the contested decision should first be set out as they relate to the definition of the market to which the notified agreements refer. In that regard, the contested decision specifies, in paragraphs 38 to 49:

'4.1. Product market

The EBU considers that the relevant market for the assessment of the case is the market for the acquisition of the television rights to important sporting events in all disciplines of sport, irrespective of the national or international character of the event. The EBU is only active in the acquisition of television rights to sporting events of pan-European interest.

The Commission shares the EBU's view that sports programmes have particular characteristics; they are able to achieve high viewing figures and reach an identifiable audience, which is a special target for certain important advertisers.

However, contrary to what the EBU suggests, the attraction of sports programmes and hence the level of competition for the television rights varies according to the type of sport and the type of event. Mass sports like football, tennis or motor-racing generally attract large audiences, the preferences varying from country to country. By contrast, minority sports achieve very low ratings. International events tend to be more attractive for the audience in a given country than national ones, provided the national team or a national champion is involved, while international events in which no national champion or team is participating can often be of little interest. In the last 10 years, with increased competition in the television markets, the prices for television rights to sporting events have increased considerably ...; this is particularly true with regard to outstanding international events such as the Football World Cup or the Olympic Games.

The preferences of viewers determine the value of a programme to advertisers and pay-TV broadcasters. ... However, if we observe that sports broadcasts achieve the same or similar sized audiences whether or not they are competing with simultaneously broadcast sporting events, there is strong evidence that those events could determine the subscribers' or advertisers' choice of a certain broadcaster.

Indeed, data on viewer behaviour, among major sporting events, show that for at least some sporting events which have been analysed, such as the summer Olympics, the winter Olympics, the Wimbledon Finals and the Football World Cup, viewing behaviour does not appear to be influenced by the coincidence of other major sporting events being broadcast simultaneously, or nearly simultaneously. That is, viewing figures for the major sporting events appear to be largely independent of whatever other major sports are broadcast at a similar time. Therefore, the offer of such sporting events could influence the subscribers or advertisers to such an extent that the broadcaster would be inclined to pay much higher prices.

In conclusion, the Commission's investigation shows that the market definition proposed by the EBU is too large and that there is a strong likelihood that there are separate markets for the acquisition of some major sporting events, most of them international.

However, it is not necessary for the purposes of this case to exactly define the relevant product markets. Taking into account the present structure of the market and the sub-licensing ... rules granting access to non-EBU members to Eurovision sport programmes, these agreements do not raise competition concerns, even on the basis of markets for the acquisition of particular sporting events such as the summer Olympics.

...

4.2. Geographic market

Some sporting events rights are acquired on an exclusive basis for the whole European territory and, regardless of the technical means of transmission, are to be re-sold thereafter per country, [while] others are acquired on a national basis. The kind of major sporting event rights for which the EBU bids, which have a pan-European interest from the viewers' perspective, such as the Olympic Games, will normally fall within the first category of European licences.

Nevertheless, irrespective of the scope of the licences ... the preferences of viewers can significantly vary from country to country depending on the type of sport and the type of event and, therefore, the conditions of competition for the television rights can vary accordingly.

With regard to the downstream markets affected by the present notification, the free-to-air and pay-TV broadcasting markets should be considered, largely for linguistic, cultural, licensing and copyright reasons, generally national or extending to single linguistic areas.

However, for the purposes of this case it is not necessary to define the relevant geographic market exactly. Taking into account the present structure of the market and the sub-licensing rules granting non-EBU members access to the Eurovision sport programmes, these agreements do not raise competition concerns even on the basis of national markets for the acquisition of sports rights, nor for the downstream markets of free-to-air and pay-TV broadcasting.'

52    It follows from the contested decision, and particularly those passages reproduced in the preceding paragraph, that the Commission's position with respect to defining the markets concerned may be summarised as follows: the Eurovision system gives rise to effects in two distinct markets, that of the acquisition of television rights, where the EBU is in competition with other large European multimedia groups (the upstream market), and that of the transmission of purchased sports rights, where EBU members are competing, for each country or linguistic area, with other television channels, for the most part national.

53    As regards the upstream market, the Commission admits that 'there is a strong likelihood' (in English, which is the only authentic text) that there are separate markets for the acquisition of rights to some major international sporting events which are normally acquired for the whole European territory. Concerning the downstream market, even if the Commission does not make it clear as regards the definition of the product market, its analysis nevertheless shows that, with respect to the preference of television viewers and their influence on the value of programmes for announcers and pay-TV companies, a specific market for the transmission of major sporting events exists. That market, which according to the Commission is subdivided into a free-to-air TV market and a pay-TV market, is generally limited to the national territory or to a homogeneous linguistic area.

54    None the less, the Commission considered it unnecessary to define exactly either the product market or the geographic market affected by the Eurovision system, since even if the narrowest possible market is taken as a reference point – that is, the market for acquiring rights to certain sporting events such as the Olympic Games – the Commission takes the view that the Eurovision system, given the structure of the market and the third-party access scheme to the system, does not give rise to competition concerns.

55    Second, the Commission states, in paragraphs 100 to 103 of the contested decision, relating to the non-elimination of competition in respect of a substantial part of the products in question as regards the joint acquisition of rights, that despite the fact that the EBU is facing increasing competition from media groups and brokers, 'the Commission was concerned that some of the jointly acquired rights affect sporting events, for instance the Olympic Games, of particular economic and popular importance, which could constitute a ... market ... exclusively held by the Eurovision members'. It goes on:

'To address these concerns the EBU has modified the notified agreements to include a set of sub-licensing rules which make sure that non-EBU members have extensive access to the Eurovision sports rights. This counterbalances the restrictive effects of the joint acquisition of the sports rights. The schemes will provide extensive live and deferred transmission access for non-members on reasonable terms.'

56    Moreover, as regards the restriction arising from the sharing of Eurovision rights between EBU members competing for the same audience, the Commission concludes, in paragraph 104 of the contested decision, that there will be no elimination of competition 'given the current market structure and considering that non-EBU members will be able to participate in the broadcast of the sporting events in question following the EBU sub-licensing schemes'.

57    It thus appears from the contested decision that, even if the Commission did not consider it necessary exactly to define the product market concerned, it nevertheless assumed the existence of a market consisting entirely of certain major international sporting events, such as the Olympic Games, in order to verify whether the Eurovision system complies with the conditions for exemption provided for in Article 81(3) EC. Therefore, the absence of such an exact definition has not, in the present case, affected the Commission's analysis of whether the Eurovision system satisfies the condition for exemption laid down in Article 81(3)(b) EC and, consequently, that part of the applicants' reasoning must be held to have no bearing on the issue.

58    Second, it should be determined whether and, if necessary, to what extent the defendant made a manifest error of assessment when applying the relevant condition for exemption in concluding that, even in a market made up of specific international sporting events, the third-party scheme for access to the Eurovision system made it possible to compensate for restrictions on competition in relation to third parties and thus to avoid competition being eliminated to their detriment.

59    Before analysing that scheme, it is necessary first to set out the structure of the markets at issue and the restrictions on competition to which the Eurovision system gives rise.

60    As far as the structure of the markets is concerned, the contested decision indicates, inter alia, that television rights to sporting events are granted for a given territory, normally on an exclusive basis. That exclusivity is considered necessary by broadcasters in order to guarantee the value of a given sports programme in terms of viewing figures and advertising revenues (paragraph 51 of the contested decision).

61    Television rights are normally held by the organiser of a sporting event, who controls access to the premises where the event is staged. In order to control the televising of the event and to guarantee exclusivity, the organiser admits only one broadcaster or a limited number of broadcasters to produce the television signal. Under their contract with the organiser, they are not allowed to make their signal available to any third party who has not acquired the relevant television rights (paragraph 52 of the contested decision).

62    The Commission observes that the EBU has lost significant market share in the relevant markets over the past 10 years. With regard to the acquisition of television rights to certain sporting events, the EBU has faced competition from the big European media groups as well as from international brokers. The EBU has also lost a large number of important sporting events during the past years as the result of higher competitive offers (paragraphs 54 and 55 of the contested decision). However, the EBU remains in a strong market position in the acquisition of rights to major international sporting events with a very strong appeal for European viewers, in respect of which the rights owners still insist that the events must not be broadcast on pay television. In addition, the EBU still has a unique one-stop-

shop position, which guarantees the organisers the widest possible viewing audience in Europe. The fact that the European television rights for the Olympic Games have always been sold to the EBU is of particular importance (paragraphs 55 to 57 of the contested decision).

63    As regards the effects of the Eurovision system on competition, the contested decision shows (paragraphs 71 to 80) that there are two types of restrictions. First, the joint acquisition of television rights to sporting events, their sharing and the exchange of signal restricts or even eliminates competition among EBU members which are competitors on both the upstream market, for the acquisition of rights, and for the downstream market, for televised transmission of sporting events. In addition, that system gives rise to restrictions on competition as regards third parties since those rights, as set out in paragraph 75 of the contested decision, are generally sold on an exclusive basis, so that EBU non-members would not in principle have access to them.

64    While it is true that the purchase of televised transmission rights for an event is not in itself a restriction on competition likely to fall under Article 81(1) EC and may be justified by particular characteristics of the product and the market in question, the exercise of those rights in a specific legal and economic context may none the less lead to such a restriction (see, by analogy, Case 262/81 Coditel v Ciné-Vog Films [1982] ECR 3381, paragraphs 15 to 17).

65    In that vein, the Commission states, in paragraph 45 of the contested decision, that 'the acquisition of exclusive TV rights to certain major sporting events has a strong impact on the downstream television markets in which the sporting events are broadcast'.

66    In addition, it appears from the analysis of the documents in the case and the arguments of the parties that the acquisition of transmission rights to a major international sporting event such as the Olympics or the football World Cup cannot fail to affect strongly the market in sponsorship and advertising, which is the main source of revenue for television channels which broadcast free-to-air, since those programmes attract a very wide audience.

67    Moreover, as pointed out by SIC, the effects which restrict competition for third parties as a result of the Eurovision system are accentuated, first, by the level of vertical integration of the EBU and its members, which are not merely purchasers of rights but also television operators which broadcast the rights purchased, and second, by the geographic extent of the EBU, whose members broadcast in all the countries of the European Union. As a result, when the EBU acquires transmission rights for an international sporting event, the access to that event is in principle automatically precluded for all non-member operators. By contrast, the situation appears to be different when the transmission rights for sporting events are acquired by an agency which buys those rights in order to resell them, or when they are bought by a media group which only has operators in certain Member States, since that group will tend to enter into negotiations with operators in other Member States in order to sell those rights. In that case, despite the exclusive purchase of the rights, other operators still have the opportunity to negotiate their acquisition for their respective markets.

68    In light of those facts – that is, the structure of the market, the position of the EBU in the market for certain international sporting events and the level of vertical integration of the EBU and its members – there is reason to determine whether the scheme for third-party access to the Eurovision system makes it possible to counterbalance the restrictions on competition affecting those third parties and thus to avoid their exclusion from competition.

69    Before that analysis is made, it should be noted that the contested decision indicates (inter alia, in paragraphs 106 to 108) that, when the Commission concluded, in paragraphs 103 and 104 of the contested decision (see paragraphs 55 and 56 above) that restrictions on competition resulting from the Eurovision system are compensated for by a series of sub-licensing rules, it was referring to the full scheme for access by third parties to the Eurovision system, which includes the sub-licensing scheme and the sub-licensing rules (see paragraph 18 above). However, as the applicants are television channels which transmit free-to-air, only the sub-licensing scheme is likely to counterbalance the restrictions on competition of which they complain. Therefore, the Court's analysis will apply only to that scheme.

70    In paragraph 107 of the contested decision, the Commission states that, under the sub-licensing scheme, 'the EBU and its members undertake to grant non-member broadcasters extensive access to Eurovision sports programmes for which the rights have been acquired through collective negotiations ...'. According to the Commission, '[t]he 1993 scheme grants live and deferred transmission rights to third parties of jointly acquired Eurovision sports rights'. In addition, in paragraph 28 of the contested decision, it is suggested in that regard that 'the non-EBU members have significant access to the unused rights, i.e. for the transmission of sporting events which are not transmitted by, or of which only a minor part are transmitted by, an EBU member'.

71    As is apparent from Annex I to the contested decision, the sub-licensing scheme, applicable to free-to-air television channels, provides that sub-licences may be granted for live and deferred transmissions. Live transmissions (Annex I, Part IV(1)) are stipulated only for residual transmissions, that is, for transmissions of those competitions or parts of competitions which are not reserved for live transmission by EBU members, since an 'event is considered to be transmitted live if the majority of the principal competitions constituting it are transmitted live' (Annex I, Part IV(1.3)). Therefore, an EBU member need only reserve the live transmission of the majority of the competitions of an event for non-members competing for the same market to be refused sub-licences for live transmission of the entire event, including competitions in that event which no EBU member will transmit live.

72    The answers given by SIC to the questions posed by the Court of First Instance indicate that, in application of that rule, the Portuguese public operator (RTP-Radiotelevisão Portuguesa SA, hereinafter 'RTP'), an EBU member, refused to sell SIC sub-licences for the live broadcast of 1994 World Cup matches, including for matches that RTP did not intend to broadcast, on the ground that RTP intended to broadcast live the majority of the matches in that competition, that is, 47 matches out of 52.

73    However, even if it proves necessary, for reasons linked to exclusive transmission rights for sporting events and the guarantee of their economic value (see paragraph 60 above), for EBU members to reserve for themselves live transmission of the programmes acquired by the EBU, none of these reasons justifies their being able to extend that right to all the competitions which are part of the same event, even when they do not intend to broadcast all those competitions live.

74    In addition, as a result of the joint application of the sub-licensing scheme (applicable to channels which transmit free-to-air) and the sub-licensing rules (applicable to pay-TV channels), even when an EBU member transmits less than the majority of the competitions of a sporting event but nevertheless broadcasts the remaining competitions of that event on its pay-TV channel, the non-member of

EBU has access only to deferred transmission, unless it itself is a pay-TV channel – in which case, under the sub-licensing rules, it may purchase sub-licences for live transmissions of competitions identical or comparable to that being transmitted by the EBU member.

75 As a result, as the documents in the case make clear, in particular the correspondence between M6 and the Groupement de radiodiffuseurs français de l'union européenne de radio-télévision (GRF) and the correspondence between SIC and the RTP, the opportunity for non-members of the EBU to transmit the main sporting events live is rendered inoperative to the extent that EBU members can themselves either transmit the events live or make use, under the sub-licensing scheme, of a right of reserve which also applies to events which they do not intend to transmit live.

76 Those restrictions are all the more severe in view of the fact that, as these proceedings show, generally only live transmission is of real interest to the applicants, which are general television channels transmitting free-to-air with national coverage, since televised broadcasts of sporting competitions – at least the most important of them – are able to attract a wide audience and thereby justify their economic cost only as long as the result of those competitions remains unknown and, therefore, only if the broadcast is live. The deferred broadcast of sporting events, by contrast, is of no real interest in economic terms for general television channels, such as the applicants, whose financing depends exclusively on broadcast publicity and sponsorship.

77 Added to those restrictions – at least in the case of France, where several television channels are EBU members – are questions of a practical nature which make it difficult for non-members to have access both to the 'direct' purchase of sub-licences and to the purchase in auction of EBU rights which have not been used by its members (that was the case for the television transmission rights for the Sydney Olympic Games on French television). Those difficulties are in essence linked to the fact that television channels which are not members of the EBU do not have available to them sufficiently early the information they need in order to set up the technical facilities necessary, first, to televise transmissions of sporting events and, second, to adapt both their programming and their public information so as to attract large enough audiences to justify the investment.

78 Thus, following the request by M6 by letter of 18 January 1996 that it be notified of the events of the Atlanta Olympic Games (July 1996) which it could broadcast, it was not until a discussion on 7 June 1996 that the GRF informed it, in very vague terms, that the French members of the EBU were going to broadcast those games live for 15 hours a day and that, as a result, access by M6 to direct transmissions 'might possibly apply to a few football matches or events of little interest, such as softball'.

79 In the light of all the preceding considerations, the first conclusion to be made is that, contrary to what the Commission contends, the sub-licensing scheme does not guarantee that live transmission rights which are not used by EBU members are made available to their competitors.

80 As regards the possibility of acquiring sub-licences to cover deferred events or to provide roundups of these, and keeping in mind the fact that those modes of transmission are of limited interest for general channels which transmit free-to-air with national coverage, it is clear that this possibility is also subject to several restrictions. First, competitions the rights for which have been purchased by the EBU may not be broadcast until, at the earliest, one hour after the end of the event (the one-hour embargo) or of the last competition of the day, but never before 22.30

local time. Second, as is clear from the documents included in the file by the applicants, in reality, the members of the EBU, in any case in the countries where the applicants operate, impose even stricter conditions on embargo times and the editing of programmes.

81    Lastly, the scheme under analysis enables non-members of the EBU to purchase the rights to transmit news commentaries (two per event or per day of competition, of 90 seconds each), called 'News Access'. However, as pointed out by the applicants, that opportunity is always guaranteed them in the countries where they operate, independently of the sub-licensing scheme. In Spain and Portugal, the option to broadcast roundups of sporting events for public information is guaranteed under the constitutional right to information. In France, that opportunity exists under the code of good conduct which applies to French television channels.

82    In answer to the questions put by the Court of First Instance as to what information led the Commission to state that the scheme for third-party access to Eurovision rights, in force for channels transmitting free-to-air since 1993, gives 'extensive possibilities for live and deferred transmissions for non-members under reasonable conditions', the Commission placed on the file a list issued by the EBU which sets out the sub-licences granted up until 13 May 1997. Nevertheless, far from confirming the statements by the Commission and the EBU as regards the scheme for third-party access to the Eurovision system, the data in that list invalidate them. They show that while in certain States, such as The Netherlands, Sweden and Norway, EBU members appear to grant sub-licences to competing television channels, in other Member States the granting of sub-licences remains extremely restricted, limited to the sub-licences granted to regional television channels which operate in narrowly limited markets, as in Spain (that is, moreover, confirmed by the list of sub-licences which RTVE has provided in the context of its intervention), or to sub-licences which are for the most part limited to the transmission of news commentaries for public information ('News Access'), as in Italy or Germany. For the countries where two of the applicants operate, France and Portugal, no sub-licence is mentioned.

83    All the information provided to the Court of First Instance thus goes to show that, contrary to what the Commission concludes in the contested decision, the sub-licensing scheme does not guarantee competitors of EBU members sufficient access to rights to transmit sporting events held by the latter on the basis of their participation in that purchasing association. Apart from a few exceptions, nothing in the rules or mode of implementation of the scheme enables competitors of EBU members to obtain sub-licences for the live broadcast of unused Eurovision rights. In reality, the scheme merely permits the acquisition of sub-licences to transmit roundups of competitions under extremely restrictive conditions.

84    That conclusion is not invalidated by the argument put forward by the EBU to the effect that the proof of the proper functioning of the scheme for access by third parties to the Eurovision system is the absence of recourse to the arbitration procedures which it provides for. First, that argument proves incorrect, inasmuch as the correspondence between SIC and the RTP shows that those operators had recourse to arbitration, at least in relation to the purchase of sub-licences for the 1994 world football championships. In addition, recourse to arbitration is foreseen in the scheme analysed only for disputes concerning the price of sub-licences, which implies that the parties will resort to it only when they agree on all the other conditions of access (see Annex I, Part IV(5.1) and Annex II(iii) to the contested decision). Therefore, the failure to use that procedure cannot show that the sub-licensing scheme allows genuine access to the programmes acquired by the EBU.

85    It follows from all the preceding considerations that the Commission made a manifest error of assessment in the application of Article 81(3)(b) EC in determining that, even if a product market limited to certain major international sports events exists, the sub-licensing scheme guarantees access for third parties which are competitors of the EBU's members to Eurovision rights and consequently avoids the elimination of competition in that market.

86    Since the Commission's decision to grant individual exemption assumes that the agreement or the decision of the association of undertakings satisfies all four conditions laid down in Article 81(3) EC and that an exemption must be refused if any of the four conditions is not met (see, inter alia, Joined Cases 56/64 and 58/64 Consten and Grundig v Commission [1966] ECR 299, 347 and Case T-17/93 Matra Hachette v Commission [1994] ECR II-595, paragraph 104), the contested decision must be annulled without there being any need to rule on the other pleas put forward or to deal with the requests for production of documents made by the applicants in Cases T-216/00 and T-300/00.

**Decision on costs**
**Costs**
87    Under Article 87(2) of the Rules of Procedure, the unsuccessful party must be ordered to pay the costs if they have been applied for in the successful party's pleadings.

88    Since the Commission has been unsuccessful and the applicants, as well as the RTI, the intervener in Case T-300/00, have applied for costs, the Commission must be ordered to pay its own costs and to bear the costs incurred by the applicants and the RTI. Since DSF has not applied for the Commission to be ordered to pay the costs of its intervention in Case T-299/00, that intervener must bear its own costs.

89    Since Antena 3 has claimed that the EBU and RTVE should be ordered to bear the costs of their interventions in Case T-216/00, the EBU and RTVE must be ordered to pay their own costs as well as those incurred by Antena 3 in its intervention. Since M6 and SIC have requested that the EBU be ordered to pay the costs of its intervention in Cases T-185/00 and T-300/00, the EBU must be ordered to pay its own costs as well as those incurred by M6 and SIC in their interventions. As Telecinco did not request that the EBU and RTVE be ordered to pay the costs of their interventions in Case T-299/00, those interveners need only pay their own costs in that case.

**Operative part of the judgment**
On those grounds,
The Court of First Instance (Second Chamber, Extended Composition),
hereby:
1.    Annuls Commission Decision 2000/400/EC of 10 May 2000 relating to a proceeding pursuant to Article 81 of the EC Treaty (IV/32.150 – Eurovision);
2.    Orders the Commission to pay its own costs, together with those of the applicants and of the intervener Reti Televisive Italiane Spa;
3.    Orders DSF Deutsches SportFernsehen GmbH to bear the costs of its intervention;
4.    Orders the intervener Union européenne de radio-télévision to bear its own costs, together with those incurred by Métropole télévision SA, Antena 3 de Televisión SA and SIC – Sociedade Independente de Comunicação SA for their interventions;

5.    Orders the intervener Radiotelevisión Española to bear its own costs, together with
      those incurred by Antena 3 de Televisión SA for its intervention;
6.    Orders Gestevisión Telecinco SA to bear the costs it incurred in connection with
      the intervention of the Union européenne de radio-télévision and of Radio-
      televisión Española.

___

### 2.4.94.  ACTION BROUGHT BY DAVID MECA-MEDINA AND IGOR MAJCEN AGAINST THE COMMISSION OF THE EUROPEAN COMMUNITIES, CASE T-313/02, 11 OCTOBER 2002[575]

An action against the Commission of the European Communities was brought before the
Court of First Instance of the European Communities on 11 October 2002 by David
Meca-Medina, residing in Barcelona (Spain), and Igor Majcen, residing in Ljubljana
(Slovenia), represented by J.-L. Dupont, lawyer.
The applicants claim that the Court should:
–    annul the Commission's decision notified to the applicants on 5 August 2002 reject-
     ing the complaint of 31 May 2001 against the International Olympic Committee;

*Pleas in law and main arguments*
By the contested decision, the Commission rejected the complaint lodged by the applicants, who are professional swimmers, that certain practices and rules of the International
Olympic Committee (IOC) concerning the fight against doping were contrary to European
competition law. The applicants objected, in particular, to the fact that, in connection with
the detection of the substance nandrolone, the IOC continues to apply a maximum level
which has now been found to lack scientific merit.
They claim that the Commission manifestly erred in fact and in law in finding that, with
respect to anti-doping rules, the IOC is not an undertaking for the purposes of Community
law. It is clear that the IOC cannot be treated in the same way as a public institution providing social security services and that it does not exercise the prerogatives of a public
authority.
Moreover, the rules in question affect the conduct of all athletes on the market for the
sports which the applicants perform.
In addition, the applicants claim that the Commission committed a manifest error of assessment in finding that, in the present case, the limitation on the freedom of athletes is
not a restriction of competition within the meaning of Article 81 EC, on the ground that
such a limitation is inherent in the organisation and smooth running of competitive sport.
The Commission's findings constitute a manifest misapplication of the criteria laid down
by the Court of Justice in paragraph 97 of the judgment in *Wouters*[576] and the restrictive
effects of the IOC rules in question are clearly not inherent in the pursuit of the praisewor-
thy aims of the campaign against doping.
According to the applicants, it is for the Commission – in accordance with the 'necessity
test' and/or the 'proportionality test' – to declare that a rule which has been proven to
have no scientific basis can in no way satisfy the requirements of such tests.
Finally, the Commission's assessment is manifestly incorrect in so far as it fails to
recognise Article 49 EC as having any direct horizontal effect. It must be found that, since
they do not satisfy a 'test of necessity', the contested IOC rules also infringe Article 49
EC.

___

[575]  OJ C 305, 7-12-2002, p. 62.
[576]  Case C-309/99 Wouters [2002] ECR I-1577.

**\* 2.4.95.  ANSWER ON BEHALF OF THE COMMISSION TO WRITTEN QUESTION P-2664/02 BY ROBERT GOEBBELS (PSE), 12 NOVEMBER 2002[577] \***

Subject: Neutral effect of competition law on the live broadcasting rights to sports events

———

**\* 2.4.96.  COMMISSION OPENS PROCEEDINGS INTO JOINT SELLING OF MEDIA RIGHTS TO THE ENGLISH PREMIER LEAGUE, 20 DECEMBER 2002[578]**

———

**\* 2.4.97.  ANSWER ON BEHALF OF THE COMMISSION TO WRITTEN QUESTION E-3522/02 BY BART STAES (VERTS/ALE), 29 JANUARY 2003[579] \***

Subject: Television rights relating to Champions League matches – dispute as to what constitutes news gathering and what is covered by copyright

———

**\* 2.4.98.  COMMISSION CLEARS TICKETING ARRANGEMENTS FOR THE ATHENS OLYMPIC GAMES, 23 MAY 2003[580]**

———

**\* 2.4.99.  ANSWER ON BEHALF OF THE COMMISSION TO WRITTEN QUESTION P-1994/03 BY PIETRO-PAOLO MENNEA (PPE-DE), 10 JULY 2003[581] \***

Subject: Television rights

———

**2.4.100.  FINAL REPORT OF THE HEARING OFFICER IN CASE COMP/C2/ 37.398 – UEFA CHAMPIONS LEAGUE (PURSUANT TO ARTICLE 15 OF COMMISSION DECISION (2001/462/EC, ECSC) OF 23 MAY 2001 ON THE TERMS OF REFERENCE OF HEARING OFFICERS IN CERTAIN COMPETITION PROCEEDINGS (OJ L 162, 19-6-2001, P. 21)), 15 JULY 2003[582]**

The draft decision in this case gives rise to the following observations on the right to be heard:

On 19 February 1999 UEFA (Union des Associations Europééennes de Football) notified to the Commission its Regulation concerning the joint selling of the commercial rights to the UEFA Champions League.

On 19 July 2001 a statement of objections was sent to UEFA. UEFA responded on 16

---

[577] Question of 23-9-2002; OJ C 155 E, 3-7-2003, p. 38-39.
[578] IP/02/1951.
[579] Question of 28-11-2002; question not yet published in the OJ.
[580] IP/03/738.
[581] Question of 4-6-2003; question not yet published in the OJ.
[582] OJ C 269, 8-11-2003, p. 29. Text with EEA relevance.

November 2001 following an extension of the deadline to reply. No oral hearing took place in this case. A non-confidential version of the statement of objections was sent to a number of interested third parties in this case. Their observations in non confidential form were sent to UEFA.

Following discussions with the relevant Commission service, UEFA notified a new joint selling arrangement to the Commission on 13 May 2002.

On 17 August 2002 the Commission published a notice pursuant to Article 19(3) of Regulation 17/62 setting out the main elements of the new arrangement, stating its intention to take a favourable view on this arrangement and inviting comments. Comments were received from a number of third parties as well as the German National Competition Authority. Further modifications were subsequently made to the agreement.

On 5 May 2003 the Commission informed UEFA of its intention to attach a condition to the proposed exemption decision, attaching the condition proposed, and inviting UEFA to comment. UEFA responded on 15 May 2003.

In the light of the above I conclude that the rights to be heard in this case have been respected.

Brussels, 15 July 2003.
Karen Williams

——

### 2.4.101. COMMISSION DECISION RELATING TO A PROCEEDING PURSUANT TO ARTICLE 81 OF THE EC TREATY AND ARTICLE 53 OF THE EEA AGREEMENT (COMP/C.2-37.398 – JOINT SELLING OF THE COMMERCIAL RIGHTS OF THE UEFA CHAMPIONS LEAGUE), 23 JULY 2003[583]

*The Commission of the European Communities,*

–    Having regard to the Treaty establishing the European Community,
–    Having regard to the Agreement on the European Economic Area,
–    Having regard to Council Regulation No 17 of 6 February 1962, First Regulation implementing Articles 85 and 86 of the Treaty[584], as last amended by Regulation (EC) No 1/2003[585], and in particular Articles 6 and 8 thereof,
–    Having regard to the application for negative clearance submitted by UEFA on 1 February 1999 pursuant to Article 2 of Regulation No 17 and the notification with a view to obtaining an exemption submitted by UEFA on 1 February 1999 on 1 February 1999 and as amended on 13 May 2002 pursuant to Article 4 of Regulation No 17,
–    Having regard to the Commission decision of 18 July 2001 to initiate proceedings in this case,
–    Having given the undertakings concerned the opportunity[586] to make known their views on the objections raised by the Commission pursuant to Article 19(1) of Regulation No 17 and Commission Regulation (EC) No 2842/98 of 22 December

---

[583]    OJ L 291, 8-11-2003, p. 25-55. (Text with EEA relevance.) (notified under document number C(2003) 2627).

[584]    OJ 13, 2-2-1962, p. 204/62.

[585]    OJ L 1, 4-1-2003, p. 1.

[586]    OJ C 196, 17-8-2002, p. 3.

1998 on the hearing of parties in certain proceedings under Articles 85 and 86 of the Treaty[587],

– After consulting the Advisory Committee on Restrictive Practices and Dominant Positions,

– Having regard to the final report of the Hearing Officer in this case[588],

Whereas:

## 1. INTRODUCTION

(1) This Decision relates to the rules, regulations and all implementing decisions taken by Union des Associations Européennes de Football (UEFA) and its members concerning the joint selling arrangement regarding the sale of the commercial rights[589] of the UEFA Champions League, a pan-European club football competition. The Regulations of the UEFA Champions League provide UEFA, as a joint selling body, with the exclusive right to sell certain commercial rights of the UEFA Champions League on behalf of the participating football clubs. The joint selling arrangement restricts competition among the football clubs in the sense that it has the effect of co-ordinating the pricing policy and all other trading conditions on behalf of all individual football clubs producing the UEFA Champions League content. However, the Commission considers that such restrictive rules can be exempted in the specific circumstances of this case. UEFA's joint selling arrangement provides the consumer with the benefit of league focused media products from this pan-European football club competition that is sold via a single point of sale and which could not otherwise be produced and distributed equally efficiently.

## 2. PARTIES

(2) UEFA is a company, registered in the register of companies under the terms of the Swiss civil code, with its headquarters located in Nyon, Switzerland[590]. UEFA is an association of national football associations. Its membership comprises national football associations situated in the European continent[591]. Currently, UEFA has 51 members; 21 of these member associations are located in the EEA[592].

(3) UEFA is the regulatory authority of European football. UEFA has the sole jurisdiction to organise or abolish international competitions in Europe in which member associations and/or their football clubs participate. Other international competitions or tournaments require the approval of UEFA[593] except for those organised by Fédération internationale de football association (FIFA). UEFA organises a number of European football tournaments in addition to the UEFA Champions League.

(4) UEFA's congress is the supreme controlling organ of UEFA. Each national football association has one vote at the congress[594]. The congress adopts UEFA's stat-

---

[587] OJ L 354, 30-12-1998, p. 18.

[588] OJ C 269, 8-11-2003.

[589] Media rights (radio, television, Internet and UMTS), sponsorship, suppliership, licensing and IPRs.

[590] Article 1 of UEFA's Statutes (Edition 2000).

[591] Article 5 of UEFA's Statutes.

[592] In the United Kingdom, there are four UEFA member associations: England, Wales, Scotland and Northern Ireland.

[593] Article 48 of UEFA's Statutes.

[594] Article 18 of UEFA's Statutes.

utes. It elects the president[595] and the Executive Committee[596]. The Executive Committee consists of the president and 13 members who must hold office within a national member association[597]. The Executive Committee manages UEFA, except to the extent it has delegated responsibility to the Chief Executive Officer[598] whom it also appoints[599]. The Executive Committee draws up the regulations governing the conditions for participation in and the staging of UEFA competitions, including the Regulations of the UEFA Champions League. It is a condition for entry into the UEFA Champions League competition that each member association and/or football club affiliated to a Member Association agrees to comply with the statutes and regulations and decisions of the competent UEFA organs[600].

**3.        THE NOTIFIED AGREEMENT**
**3.1.      The UEFA Champions League**
*3.1.1.    The origins of the UEFA Champions League*
(5)        The UEFA Champions League is UEFA's most prestigious club competition. Originally created as the European Champion Clubs' Cup prior to the 1955/1956 season, the competition changed format and name in time for the 1992/1993 season. The UEFA Champions League is open to each national football association's domestic club champions, as well as the clubs, which finish just behind them in the domestic championship table. The number of clubs that can be entered by an association depends on the football association's position in UEFA's coefficient ranking list. Including the qualifying stages, a total of 96 football clubs participate in the UEFA Champions League.

*3.1.2.    The UEFA Champions League format*
(6)        The UEFA Champions League format applicable at the time of the notification[601] consisted of two qualifying phases prior to the UEFA Champions League. The UEFA Champions League itself consisted of the group matches and a final knockout phase of quarter-finals, semi-finals and a final. The UEFA Executive Committee decided on 10 and 11 July 2002 to replace the second group stage with a knockout phase as from the 2003/2004 season. With the elimination of the second group stage, there will be a total of 125 matches and a total of 13 match days in the 2003/2004 UEFA Champions League format.
(7)        In the 2003/2004 season the competition consists of the following phases. 80 football clubs participate in three initial qualifying rounds playing a total of 160 matches, which is required to find 16 qualifiers to join the top 16 automatic qualifiers playing in the UEFA Champions League. The UEFA Administration seeds football clubs for the qualifying rounds and the group stage in accordance with the club rankings established at the beginning of the season. These rankings are drawn up on the basis of a combination of the national associations' coefficient and the football clubs' individual performance in the UEFA club competitions during the same period. For the qualifying rounds, a draw between the same number of seeded and unseeded football clubs determines the pairings. For the third qualify-

---

[595] Article 13(1)(f) of UEFA's Statutes.
[596] Article 13(1)(g) of UEFA's Statutes.
[597] Article 21 of UEFA's Statutes.
[598] Article 23(2) of UEFA's Statutes.
[599] Article 24(1)(e) of UEFA's Statutes.
[600] Article 49 of UEFA's Statutes.
[601] Regulations for the UEFA Champions League 1998/1999.

ing round the UEFA administration is empowered to form groups in accordance with set principles. For the purpose of the draw, the 32 football clubs involved in the UEFA Champions League group stage are seeded into eight groups of four in accordance with the aforementioned rankings. All matches are played according to UEFA's match calendar. The venues, dates and kick-off times of all qualifying matches must be confirmed and communicated to the UEFA administration by the national associations of the football clubs concerned.

(8) Member associations and their affiliated organisations or football clubs sell the media rights of these three qualifying rounds themselves. UEFA does not participate in the selling of these rights and UEFA consequently does not undertake organisational and administrative responsibilities other than conducting the draw procedure and appointing referees and a 'match delegate' to oversee sporting/disciplinary standards. UEFA is not involved in the selection or appointment of third party service providers to provide services that are required in connection with a match. Nor is UEFA involved in production of full audio visual match coverage for each match or appointment of commercial partners: sponsors, suppliers, or licensees.

(9) The football clubs have not extended the joint selling arrangement to these three qualifying rounds and the manner in which these rights are sold are therefore not relevant for the purposes of this decision. It would appear that the UEFA and football clubs have decided not to extend the joint selling arrangement to these matches as demand for such early stage qualifying matches is rather low and of a local nature. The matches that will take place between small and big clubs due to UEFA's seeding system are without pan-European cross-border appeal. Demand is typically from broadcasters of the two countries of the football clubs. It would moreover greatly increase the costs for UEFA to maintain the consistency of branding and presentation of the UEFA Champions League if it were to include all the qualifying matches in the joint selling concept (more than 100 matches). UEFA would have to make site surveys and visits to all the additional match venues. It would have to ensure compliance with all standard UEFA Champions League broadcaster facilities. It would have to make sure 'clean' stadia would be provided for the UEFA Champions League commercial partners and so forth. UEFA would have to monitor all the other obligations, which clubs must meet for participation in the UEFA Champions League. This would explain the fact that UEFA and the football clubs do not find it efficient to sell those media rights jointly or indispensable to restrict football clubs in their individual marketing.

(10) The qualifying-phase matches are played according to a knockout system with each club playing each opponent twice in home and away matches. The team which scores the greater aggregate of goals in the two matches qualifies for the next stage (second qualifying round, third qualifying round or the UEFA Champions League group stage, as applicable). The football clubs defeated in the first and second qualifying rounds are eliminated from the competition. The 16 clubs defeated in the third qualifying round are entitled to play in the first round of the current UEFA Cup.

(11) Beginning in September these 32 football clubs then contest the group stage, comprising eight groups of four clubs. The winners and runners-up from these eight groups, in total 16 football clubs, then advance to a second knockout phase on a home and away basis. The surviving football clubs contest the quarter-finals. For the quarter-final (8 clubs) and semi-final stage (4 clubs), the clubs play two matches against each other on a home and away basis, with the team scoring the

greater aggregate of goals qualifying for the next round. The two winners of the two semi-finals play in the final, which is staged as a single match.

(12)	The games are played on Tuesday or Wednesday nights from September with the final played in May. As a rule, matches in the UEFA Champions League kick off at 20.45 hours central European time. The UEFA Champions League therefore avoids clashing with the fixtures of domestic leagues, which are mostly played weekends, and the UEFA Cup, which is mostly played on Thursdays.

### 3.1.3.	*UEFA's role in the UEFA Champions League*

(13)	UEFA has the organisational and administrative responsibility for the UEFA Champions League. UEFA conducts the draw procedure and approves the participants. UEFA appoints referees, match delegates and referee observers and covers their expenses. It is the disciplinary body supervising and enforcing all aspects of the competition. UEFA selects and appoints a wide range of third party service providers to provide services that are required in connection with a match[602].

(14)	Television Event and Media Marketing AG (TEAM), an independent marketing company, assists UEFA in the implementation and follow-up of the commercial aspects of the UEFA Champions League. As an agent under UEFA's control and responsibility, TEAM conducts negotiations with the commercial partners. The agreements are signed and executed by UEFA, which assumes all legal responsibilities.

(15)	UEFA arranges for the production of full audio visual match coverage for each match. UEFA's broadcast partners act as host-broadcaster for the matches within their territory. UEFA assumes the responsibility towards the broadcasters if any match should be cancelled or postponed.

(16)	In addition to media operators, UEFA has three types of commercial partners: sponsors, suppliers[603], and licensees[604].

### 3.1.4.	*The football clubs' role in the UEFA Champions League*

(17)	The participating football clubs provide a team of football players and the stadium. UEFA has no direct contacts with the stadium owners. The football clubs are obliged to follow the guidelines set out by UEFA and act under UEFA's supervision. They are responsible for fulfilling safety and security requirements. The football clubs also provide facilities for the press, hospitality areas, offices, working areas and seats for UEFA's commercial partners. UEFA appoints a 'Venue Team' that carries out a 'site survey' to ensure that the stadium is equipped to stage an UEFA Champions League match.

---

[602] The range of services that UEFA arranges include: product development, sales, after sales services and client relations with broadcasters, sponsors, suppliers, licensees and participating clubs, media services (booking of commercial spots and broadcast sponsorship throughout the world), legal services, television production services, auditing and monitoring of UEFA Champions League television programs throughout the world, research services, operational implementation of the commercial concept, hospitality services, financial and administrative services, and statistical and information services (competition analysis).

[603] For example there is a computer and telecommunications supplier, which provides technical support to the broadcast graphics service and, in return, receives on-screen credits in all the European live match broadcasts and during the highlights programme.

[604] The UEFA Champions League licensing concept allows for selected companies to produce high-quality products related to the UEFA Champions League, for example, UEFA Champions League video games, UEFA Champions League videos or UEFA Champions League CD-ROM football encyclopaedias.

**3.2. The notification**

(18) UEFA notified the rules, regulations and implementing decisions regarding its joint selling arrangement to the Commission on 19 February 1999. The notification included standard rights agreements for conclusion with television broadcasters, sponsors and suppliers. The Commission issued a statement of objections on 18 July 2001, which stated that the notified joint selling arrangement relating to the sale of the television broadcasting rights infringed Article 81(1) of the Treaty and Article 53(1) of the EEA Agreement. It also stated that the joint selling arrangement was not eligible for exemption under Article 81(3) of the Treaty and Article 53(3) of the EEA Agreement.

(19) The statement of objections concluded that the notified joint selling arrangement prevented the individual football clubs participating in the UEFA Champions League from taking independent commercial action in respect of the TV rights and excluded competition between them in individually supplying TV rights to interested buyers. The effect of such joint selling arrangement was the restriction of competition. The implication for third parties is that they only have a single source of supply. The statement of objections moreover found that the possible efficiencies and benefits that the joint selling arrangement could provide for the TV broadcasting market were negated by the commercial policy pursued by UEFA. The reason was that UEFA sold the free-TV and pay-TV rights on an exclusive basis in a single bundle to a single TV broadcaster per territory for several years in a row. Since the broadcasting rights agreements covered all TV rights of the UEFA Champions League, it made it possible for a single large broadcaster per territory to acquire all TV rights of the UEFA Champions League to the exclusion of all other broadcasters. It also left a number of rights effectively unexploited. Such a broad exclusivity did not have any beneficial effects on the TV broadcasting market and was not in line with the Helsinki Report on Sport[605].

(20) In most countries football is not only the driving force for the development of pay-TV services but is also an essential programme item for free-TV broadcasters. Joint selling of free-TV and pay-TV rights combined with wide exclusive terms therefore has significant effects on the structure of the TV broadcasting markets as it can enhance media concentration and hamper competition between broadcasters. If one broadcaster holds all or most of the relevant football TV rights in a Member State, it is extremely difficult for competing broadcasters to establish themselves successfully in that market.

**3.3. UEFA's amendment of the notification**

(21) UEFA replied to the statement of objections on 16 November 2001. On 8 January

---

[605] See also point 4.2.1.3 of the Report from the Commission to the European Council with a view to safeguarding current sports structures and maintaining the social function of sport within the Community framework – The Helsinki Report on Sport – of 10-12-1999:
'Any exemptions granted in the case of the joint sale of broadcasting rights must take account of the benefits for consumers and of the proportional nature of the restriction on competition in relation to the legitimate objective pursued. In this context, there is also a need to examine the extent to which a link can be established between the joint sale of rights and financial solidarity between professional and amateur sport, the objectives of the training of young sportsmen and women and those of promoting sporting activities among the population. However, with regard to the sale of exclusive rights to broadcast sporting events, it is likely that any exclusivity which, by its duration and/or scope, resulted in the closing of the market, would be prohibited.'

2002 UEFA submitted an outline of a new joint selling arrangement. Subsequently, on 12 March 2002, UEFA presented a rights segmentation table for the exploitation of not only the TV broadcasting rights but, also, all the other media rights of the UEFA Champions League. These include rights for radio, television, Internet, universal mobile telecommunications system (UMTS) and physical media such as DVD, VHS, CD-ROM, etc.

(22)    UEFA's proposal for a new joint selling arrangement means a reduction of UEFA's exclusive right to sell the UEFA Champions League media rights. The new joint selling arrangement would allow also the football clubs to sell on a non-exclusive basis in parallel with UEFA certain media rights relating to action in which they are participating. UEFA's proposal also implies an unbundling of the media rights by splitting them up into several different rights packages that would be offered for sale in separate packages to different third parties.

(23)    UEFA's proposal for a new joint selling arrangement was the subject of several meetings between UEFA and the Commission and it was modified in a number of points at the request of the Commission. Subsequent to the introduction of these modifications, the Commission's preliminary view was that the competition concerns as expressed in the statement of objections would be remedied by UEFA's proposal. The Commission therefore intended to take a favourable view in respect of UEFA's proposal, which UEFA notified to the Commission on 13 May 2002. However, the Commission's preliminary approval was subject to giving third parties the opportunity to comment on the proposal following the publication of a notice pursuant to Article 19(3) of Regulation No 17.

(24)    That notice was published in the Official Journal of the European Communities on 17 August 2002 and prompted reactions from a number of interested third parties. The third party comments, which are summarised below in section 5, resulted in the Commission requesting UEFA to make further amendments in its joint selling arrangement. UEFA agreed to amend its joint selling arrangement in most respects, but not all. At a meeting on 4 April 2003 UEFA was informed that the Commission intended to attach conditions to the exemption decision. It was subsequently notified thereof by letter dated 5 May 2003, in which UEFA was invited to communicate its position on the Commission's intention to impose a condition. UEFA indicated in its reply of 15 May 2003 that it could accept the Commission's intention.

### 3.4. UEFA's amended joint selling arrangement
(25)    UEFA proposes, as a general principle, that media rights contracts be concluded for a period not exceeding three UEFA Champions League seasons.

*3.4.1.  TV broadcasting rights*
3.4.1.1. Football matches subject to joint selling
(26)    As already explained in recital 9, UEFA's joint selling arrangement does not apply to the three initial qualifying rounds prior to the UEFA Champions League. The individual football clubs sell the TV broadcasting rights of those matches individually. This involves 80 football clubs playing 160 matches. UEFA's joint selling arrangement applies only to the UEFA Champions League group stage and final knockout phases. The joint selling arrangement therefore applies to a total of 32 football clubs playing a total of 125 matches during a total of 13 match days from September to May. In UEFA's terminology, a match day consists of two calendar days (currently Tuesday and Wednesday).

3.4.1.2. Tendering procedure

(27)     The award of the rights contracts follows an 'invitation to tender' giving all quali-
         fied broadcasters an equal opportunity to bid for the rights in the full knowledge of
         the key terms and conditions.

(28)     UEFA will, from time to time, publish criteria on the standards which broadcasters
         must satisfy for televising the UEFA Champions League. A 'qualified broad-
         caster' is a television broadcast organisation that holds a television broadcast li-
         cence for the relevant territory and that has the appropriate infrastructure,
         resources and standing to broadcast UEFA Champions League programming.
         Contracts for the award of the rights are advertised on the UEFA website
         (www.uefa.com) at appropriate times and all qualified broadcasters in the contract
         territory are entitled to request the invitation to bid documentation. All rights
         packages are, in principle, put on the market at the same time.

(29)     The invitation to bid documentation contains relevant details of all rights packages
         together with key terms and conditions and an explanation of the information
         which interested parties must provide with their bid. All qualified broadcasters are
         entitled to request a presentation to explain the various rights packages on offer
         and the sales process. All qualified broadcasters must be given a reasonable time
         limit in which to submit their bids.

(30)     UEFA has indicated that it will evaluate the bids in accordance with a number of
         objective criteria, including in particular the following:
         (a)   price offered for the rights package or packages;
         (b)   acceptance by the bidder of all relevant broadcast obligations;
         (c)   level of audience penetration of the bidder in the contract territory;
         (d)   proposed method of delivery or transmission;
         (e)   proposed promotional support offered for the UEFA Champions League;
         (f)   production capability and host broadcast expertise;
         (g)   combination of rights packages offered in the contract territory;
         (h)   balance between free and pay television.

(31)     Negotiations may take place with individual bidders on the basis of offers re-
         ceived. The content of all offers remains confidential.

3.4.1.3. Rights packaging

(32)     UEFA will offer its TV rights in several smaller packages on a market-by-market
         basis. The precise format may vary depending on the structure of the TV market in
         the Member State in which the rights are being offered.

(33)     UEFA will have the exclusive right to sell two main live rights packages for free-
         TV or pay-TV each comprising two matches per match night[606]. UEFA Champi-
         ons League matches are currently played Tuesdays and Wednesdays. The
         packages will usually include two picks per match day. These two packages would
         cover 47 matches out of a total of 125. Consequently, when the competition has
         reached the final stages the two main live packages will absorb all TV rights of the
         UEFA Champions League.

(34)     UEFA will likewise initially have the exclusive right to sell the remaining
         matches[607]. UEFA has decided to sell them for live pay-TV/pay-per-view exploita-
         tion. However, if UEFA has not managed to sell the rights within one week after
         the draw for the group stage of the UEFA Champions League, UEFA will lose its

---

[606] Referred to as package 1 and 2 and also as the Gold and Silver packages in UEFA's rights
segmentation table.
[607] Referred to as package 4 in UEFA's rights segmentation table.

exclusive right to sell these TV rights. Thereafter, UEFA will have a non-exclusive right to sell these TV rights in parallel with the individual home clubs participating in the match[608]. UEFA's rights segmentation means that the football clubs selling the live TV rights comprised by package 5 individually are restricted to sell these only to pay-TV or pay-per-view exploitation.

(35)    The right of UEFA and the individual football clubs to sell these remaining matches will be subject to picks made by the broadcasters having bought the main live packages 1 and 2.

(36)    UEFA will moreover have the exclusive right to sell a highlight package covering all matches of the UEFA Champions League available as of 22.45 on each match night[609].

(37)    Football clubs exploiting UEFA Champions League footage individually must present the footage in a club-focused manner and relating only to matches in which they are participating. Broadcasters who exploit the TV rights which are sold by the individual clubs are not allowed to package such rights into a single product which would appear as an UEFA Champions League branded product. In particular regarding live TV rights, UEFA defines an UEFA Champions League branded programme as one consisting of more than two live UEFA Champions League matches per day.

(38)    As of Thursday midnight, that is to say, one day after the last matches of the match week the football clubs can exploit the deferred TV rights in parallel with UEFA. UEFA exploitation must be related to action from the whole UEFA Champions League competition. The individual football clubs' exploitation must be related only to matches in which they participate. The individually sold matches must be 'club branded' and must not be bundled with rights of other clubs to create an alternative UEFA Champions League branded product. In this context UEFA accepts programmes with delayed TV rights on club channels containing 100% UEFA Champions League content. Regarding club magazine programmes, UEFA defines a programme as UEFA Champions League branded, when it contains more than 50% UEFA Champions League content. In general programming, a programme should not contain more than 30% UEFA Champions League content to avoid being defined as UEFA Champions League branded. Where an entire match is shown on a delayed basis (that is to say, the full 90 minutes) on a club magazine programme or in general programming then the respective 50% and 30% rule would not apply and the programme could consist mostly or entirely of that single match.

(39)    UEFA will have the exclusive right to sell live TV rights outside the EEA. Deferred rights available to clubs are subject to the same rules both inside and outside the EEA.

### 3.4.2.  Internet rights

(40)    Both UEFA (in respect of all matches) and the football clubs (in respect of matches in which they participate) will have a right to provide video content on the Internet one and a half hours after the match finishes, that is to say, as from midnight on the night of the match. Live streaming will not be made possible because of the technical development of the Internet at this stage, which does not permit the maintenance of a satisfactorily high quality. This will of course change over time, making it necessary to revisit the embargo in the foreseeable future.

---

[608]  Referred to as package 5 in UEFA's rights segmentation table.
[609]  Referred to as package 3 in UEFA's rights segmentation table.

(41) UEFA will offer 'competition specific' or 'UEFA branded' products whereas the football clubs will offer 'club specific' or 'club branded' products. For Internet rights UEFA accepts club channel programmes containing 100% UEFA Champions League content. Club magazine programmes may contain no more than 50% UEFA Champions League content without being defined as a UEFA Champions League branded product. In general programming the maximum permissible UEFA Champions League content is 30% of the programme. Where an entire match is shown on a delayed basis (that is to say, the full 90 minutes) on a club magazine programme or in general programming then the respective 50% and 30% rule would not apply and the programme could consist mostly or entirely of that single match.

(42) Both UEFA and the football clubs may choose to provide their services themselves or via Internet service providers. The content will be based on the raw feed produced for television. UEFA intends to build a service that will produce UEFA Champions League content for streaming of moving pictures on the Internet. This service can be exploited both via 'www.uefa.com' and via the football clubs' websites. UEFA will offer technical expertise and know-how in the new media area to clubs.

(43) Clubs may acquire the raw feed from UEFA or they may participate in the UEFA service. Clubs may customise and edit the content for the purposes of creating a club focused and club branded product. UEFA will apply its principle of financial solidarity by redistributing the revenues from new media. However, for the initial three-year period (seasons 2003/2004 to 2005/2006), football clubs will not pay any solidarity fee for the raw feed but only technical costs, a situation, which will be reviewed at the end of the second season (2004/2005). Any fee must be transparent and fair, reasonable and non-discriminatory and submitted to an arbitration system to solve possible disputes. UEFA will establish a revenue sharing mechanism from the income generated from 'www.uefa.com'.

### 3.4.3. *Wireless 3G/UMTS rights*

(44) Both UEFA (in respect of all matches) and the clubs(in respect of matches in which they participate) will have a right to provide audio/video content via UMTS services available maximum 5 minutes after the action has taken place (technical transformation delay). This content will be based on the raw feed produced for television. UEFA will apply a revenue sharing system in respect of the income generated from the raw feed or the UMTS content.

(45) UEFA intends to build a 3G/UMTS wireless product that will be based on an extensive video database to be developed by UEFA. UEFA will offer the rights on an exclusive or non-exclusive basis to operator(s) with an UMTS licence, initially and exceptionally for a period of four years and subsequently for periods of three years.

(46) Clubs may acquire the raw feed from UEFA or they may participate in the UEFA service. The clubs may customise and edit the content for the purposes of creating a club focused and club branded product. This product may not consist solely or mostly of UEFA Champions League content and must include other club-related multimedia content as well. Clubs will pay a fee for the UEFA wireless service and/or the raw feed. This fee must be transparent and fair, reasonable, and non-discriminatory and submitted to an arbitration system to solve possible disputes.

### 3.4.4. *Physical media rights*

(47) Both UEFA and the football clubs are entitled to exploit the physical media rights

of DVD, VHS, CD-ROM, and so forth to archive material from the previous UEFA Champions League season with an embargo of 48 hours after the final. While UEFA's rights extend to all action in the UEFA Champions League, the rights of the football clubs include only action in which they participate.

### 3.4.5. *Audio rights*

(48) Both UEFA (in respect of all matches) and the football clubs (in respect of matches in which they participate) may sell licences to live radio broadcasting of UEFA Champions League football matches on a non-exclusive basis.

### 3.4.6. *Other commercial rights*

(49) UEFA also jointly sells other commercial rights relating to the UEFA Champions League which associate third parties with the UEFA Champions League brand such as sponsorship rights, suppliership rights, licensing rights and other intellectual property rights.

#### 3.4.6.1. Sponsorship rights

(50) UEFA has a UEFA Champions League sponsorship package, which comprises traditional elements of event sponsorship with programme sponsorship and commercial airtime in the event broadcasts. Sponsors purchase a defined package of event rights including, among others, elements such as perimeter boards, sponsor logo identification on backdrops, tickets, advertisement in each match day programme, sponsor identification on tickets, use of official designations and the UEFA Champions League logo.

(51) In addition, media rights are available to sponsors, which consist, among others, of the broadcast sponsorship rights for up to two sponsors per programme, billboards in the opening and closing sequences of the UEFA Champions League programmes as well as 'break-bumpers'[610]. They also get an option to purchase commercial airtime in and around UEFA Champions League programmes through UEFA.

#### 3.4.6.2. Suppliership rights

(52) In addition to the sponsorship rights, the UEFA Champions League concept allows for four supplier packages. For example there is a computer and telecommunications supplier, which provides technical support to the broadcast graphics service and, in return, receives on-screen credits in all the European live match broadcasts and during the highlights programme.

#### 3.4.6.3. Licensing rights

(53) The UEFA Champions League licensing concept allows for selected companies to produce high quality products related to the UEFA Champions League, for example, UEFA Champions League video games, UEFA Champions League videos or UEFA Champions League CD-ROM football encyclopaedias.

#### 3.4.6.4. Other intellectual property rights

(54) UEFA is the registered holder of various categories of intellectual property right such as trademark and design rights for example, the UEFA Champions League

---

[610] A 'break-bumper' is an editorial graphic element at the beginning and end of a commercial break, which is used to separate the match programme from commercial spots. It normally includes UEFA Champions League and sponsor identification.

'Starball' logo, which is the recognised trademark of the UEFA Champions League along with the UEFA Champions League music. The UEFA Champions League logo, name, and the trophy have been protected as trademarks. The official music, which was commissioned by UEFA, forms part of the UEFA Champions League competition. This anthem is always played with the television opening and closing sequences as well as during the countdown to kick-off in all UEFA Champions League stadiums around Europe. UEFA holds the copyright in the music. Clubs, which qualify for the UEFA Champions League, may use the orthographic, musical and artistic forms developed in connection with the UEFA Champions League logo for non-commercial promotional purposes for the duration of the competition.

## 4.   THE RELEVANT MARKET
### 4.1.   Product markets
*4.1.1.   UEFA's submission*
(55)   UEFA submits that although the UEFA Champions League is a very important sport event, it does not constitute a separate relevant product market. UEFA argues that it is part of a much wider market with a large number of sports events in addition to the UEFA Champions League, which allow broadcasters, sponsors and suppliers to achieve the same commercial objective, such as the national club football leagues. In addition, there are other prestigious and quality sports events on the market. Furthermore, non-sport content, in particular, popular films, soap operas and comedy shows can also attract very sizeable audiences. UEFA moreover argues that the Commission should differentiate between UEFA Champions League matches involving domestic clubs and UEFA Champions League matches not involving domestic clubs. UEFA also submits that the free-TV market and the pay-TV market constitute distinct relevant product markets.

*4.1.2.   The markets*
(56)   The Commission considers that the following markets are relevant to an assessment of the effects of the joint selling arrangements:
   (a)   the upstream markets for the sale and acquisition of free-TV, pay-TV and pay-per-view rights;
   (b)   the downstream markets on which TV broadcasters compete for advertising revenue depending on audience rates, and for pay-TV/pay-per-view subscribers;
   (c)   the upstream markets for wireless/3G/UMTS rights, Internet rights and video-on-demand rights, which are emerging new media markets at both the upstream and downstream levels that parallel the development of the markets in the pay-TV sector;
   (d)   the markets for the other commercial rights namely sponsorship, suppliership and licensing.

*4.1.3.   The upstream market for the acquisition of TV broadcasting rights of football events played regularly throughout every year*
(57)   Viewer preferences are decisive for all types of broadcasters in their content acquisition policy as they determine the value of programmes to broadcasters[611]. All

---

[611] In a similar way as the customer substitutability determines the upstream market for the supply of digital interactive TV services by service providers to content providers, see Commission Decision 1999/781/EC in Case IV/36.539 British Interactive Broadcasting/Open (OJ L 312, 6-12-1999, p. 1).

broadcasters are actual or potential buyers of TV broadcasting rights of football events and football is equally important to all broadcasters whichever the market they operate in[612]. Broadcasters acquire programmes in order to attract large audiences whether they are financed fully or partially by advertising revenues (to sell the opportunity to advertisers to get exposure to the audience) or not (to comply with their public service obligations). Pay-TV operators buy programmes to entice people to subscribe to their services.

(58)     The characteristics of programmes that can achieve a desired purpose can delimit the ambit of the market for the acquisition of TV broadcasting rights. Substitutability can therefore be tested by analysing the extent to which other programmes achieve this desired purpose. If a specific type of content can regularly attract high audience numbers, specific audiences or provide a certain brand image, which cannot be achieved by means of other content, it may be considered that such content constitutes a separate relevant product market. Consequently, there are no other programmes which place a competitive restraint on the rights holders' ability to determine the price of these TV broadcasting rights.

(59)     The Commission's investigation of the situation throughout the Community has gathered evidence suggesting the existence of a separate market for the acquisition of TV broadcasting rights of football events that are played regularly throughout every year. That conclusion represents an expansion of the conclusions reached in previous cases.

(60)     In the TPS case[613] the Commission found that it is universally acknowledged that films and sporting events are the two most popular pay-TV products and it suggested that a separate market might exist for rights to broadcast sports events. The Commission found that sports programmes have particular characteristics; they are able to achieve high viewing figures and reach an identifiable audience, which is especially targeted by certain advertisers. However, the Commission did not adopt a precise definition of the market in that case.

(61)     In the case regarding UEFA's Broadcasting Regulations[614], the Commission's investigation suggested the likelihood of the existence of a separate market for the acquisition of TV broadcasting rights of football events played regularly throughout every year. This definition would, in practice, mainly involve national first and second league and cup events as well as the UEFA Champions League and the UEFA Cup. It was suggested that a distinction could be made between football events that do not take place on a regular basis throughout the year. The reason is that the latter do not constitute an equally regular source of programming for broadcasters. Although the decision found that all elements were present for the definition of a separate market for the TV broadcasting rights of football events played regularly throughout every year, the Commission did not actually define the relevant product market in that case.

(62)     The Commission's market investigation in the case regarding the merger of the sports rights trading subsidiaries, Sport+ SNC and UFA Sports GmbH with the Groupe Jean-Claude Darmon SA[615] demonstrated that although sports broadcasting rights may constitute a distinct field from other television programming, that

[612] Commission Decision IV/M.553 – RTL/Veronica/Endemol (OJ L 134, 5-6-1996, p. 32) and Commission Decision 1999/242/EC – TPS (OJ L 90, 2-4-1999, p. 6).

[613] Commission Decision 1999/242/EC – TPS (OJ L 90, 2-4-1999, p. 6).

[614] Commission Decision 2001/478/EC – UEFA Broadcasting Regulations (OJ L 171, 26-6-2001, p. 12).

[615] Commission Decision COMP/M.2483 – Canal+/RTL/GJCD/JV (IP 01/1579).

market ought to be further subdivided into other separate product markets and that, at least within the EEA, football broadcasting rights may not be regarded as substitutes to other sports broadcasting rights. The Commission therefore concluded that there is a separate market for the acquisition and resale of football broadcasting rights to events that are played regularly throughout every year. In practice this involves matches in the national leagues (primarily the first division) and cups, the UEFA Champions League and the UEFA Cup. It was concluded that events that take place more intermittently are not part of that market definition[616].

(63)    In the present case, the Commission also considers that the relevant product market can appropriately be defined as the market for the acquisition of TV broadcasting rights of football events played regularly throughout every year. This definition would in practice mainly include national First and second division and cup events as well as the UEFA Champions League and UEFA Cup. The TV rights of football events create a particular brand image for a TV channel and allow the broadcaster to reach a particular audience at the retail level that cannot be reached by other programmes. In pay-TV football is a main driver of the sale of subscriptions. As regards free TV, football attracts a particular consumer demographic and hence advertising, which cannot be attracted with other types of programming.

4.1.3.1. Channel brand image

(64)    Football is important to broadcasters due to its ability to act as a developer of a brand image of a channel. Football has a distinct high profile among desirable viewers. Football generally provides high audience figures and produces events which take place regularly throughout most of the year[617]. Viewers are attracted not only to one match but also to the tournament as a whole. Football tournaments, not least those that are branded such as the UEFA Champions League, therefore guarantee viewership for long periods and induce viewers regularly to make an appointment to view a particular channel, which they associate with football. This contributes to developing the brand image of a channel.

(65)    The development of a brand image is increasingly important in a TV industry where the number of channels among which the viewers can choose increases rapidly and where products are generally homogenised[618]. With a wider choice available to viewers, it becomes increasingly difficult for a TV channel to attract and maintain audience loyalty. Branding therefore encourages audiences to schedule their viewing habits to make appointments to view a particular channel. However, such loyalty may be achieved only by offering a 'differentiated' product including eye-catching programmes and by strongly associating the channel with those

---

[616] In the same manner the Commission stated in the Newscorp/Telepiù case, that there exists a separate market for the acquisition of exclusive broadcasting rights for football events played every year where national teams participate (the national league, primarily first division and cups, the UEFA Champions League and the UEFA Cup). Commission Decision COMP/M.2876 – Newscorp/Telepiù, (IP/03/478).

[617] For example, in Germany the Bundesliga commences in August and ends in May. There are 306 games played in the tournament, which are all broadcast live throughout the season.

[618] Vlaamse Media Maatschappij state in an answer of 26-11-1999 to the Commission's request for information that: 'The acquisition (and broadcasting) of sports rights (programmes) is, in general not a profitable investment as such. However, the broadcasting of sports programmes, especially popular sports such as football and cycling, are important for the image and the branding of the channel.'

programmes. If a channel usually broadcasts certain programmes, such as the UEFA Champions League, which is in itself a strongly branded event, viewers may develop a habit of screening that channel as their first port of call in determining their viewing choices. The creation of a brand loyalty to a channel encourages viewers to use the channel as a 'point of reference' for their viewing. This has beneficial effects on other programmes broadcast by the channel.

(66)    While the ability to build up brand loyalty to a particular channel is important to all types of channels, it is especially important for advertising-funded TV channels. They must be able to present audiences to advertisers for all their broadcasts otherwise they will not be able to sell their advertising space. Football is particularly attractive in that respect, because it has a wide following with continuously high audience figures. Viewers wanting to watch a particular match may often switch to that channel well in advance of the match and some of them may 'hang on' after the match to see whether the following broadcast is interesting. In some cases this is reflected in the advertising rates that are high not only in the advertising slots immediately before and after the match but also in respect of the programmes that are broadcast before and after the match.

(67)    The Commission's investigation has confirmed that the development of a brand image is of particular importance for broadcasters when determining whether or not to acquire football rights[619]. Broadcasters consider that football enables them to create a brand image without which their channels would not be able to develop. The availability of alternative programming does not alter their interest in or demand for broadcasting rights of football events[620].

(68)    One of the particular values of football for broadcasters in brand building is its regularity. Unlike many other sport events, football is characterised by national and European tournaments which are played regularly throughout most of the year. The UEFA Champions League is one of the most recognised among those tournaments with a strongly developed own brand. Football, unlike other sports, therefore allows broadcasters to achieve high viewing figures on a regular, sustained and continuous basis if they can get access to these rights. Although there are league events for other sports and whilst such sports may produce large audience figures, they do not achieve the same continued viewing figures as football. This is of significant value for the branding of a channel, since it can only be achieved over a sustained period.

(69)    The quest for a brand image is so strong that broadcasters in certain circumstances

---

[619] RTL considers in its answer of 15-11-1999 to the Commission's request for information that 'The actual prices for football rights are so high that [...] they cannot be covered by the revenues generated with football programming.' If such rights are still acquired anyway, it is reasonable to think that this is because of branding purposes.

[620] NOS in its reply of 16-11-1999 to the Commission's request for information of 21-9-1999 considers that: 'Only to a limited extent NOS' interest in football is affected by the availability of TV rights for other sports [...] because it is the No 1 sports in the Netherlands [...] football plays a key role in NOS' sports programming [...] providing other sports broadcasts by NOS with an audience they would not normally attract.' NOS also states that: '[...] football is a unique product in 'a league of its own'. No other sport has audience figures/market share that come close to those of football [...] enhance the image of NOS.' ONdigital in its reply of 23-11-1999 to the Commission's request for information of 20-9-1999: 'Our interest in football is not affected by the availability of other film, series, game shows or other content again, because of the unique market position football holds in the United Kingdom and partly because football is likely to appeal to a different market segment.' Richard Russell Associates have described sport as a 'driver' for BSkyB's 10-year old business in 'Sports Television: The ever changing face', 16 February 1999, pp. 10 and 12.

do not mind losing money on individual programmes if they are of such a quality that they can pull viewers to the channel. For some broadcasters football could be considered as a kind of loss leader, because they may be willing to invest more in acquiring the TV rights than they can, strictly speaking, hope to recuperate looking at the possible revenues that they can make from the individual broadcasts in isolation[621].

(70)   These features of the TV rights of football have the consequence that the prices which broadcasters are willing to pay for those rights exceed all other prices, including events such as Formula One[622]. ONdigital states that 'Football rights are the most expensive of any sport [...]'[623] The total expenditure on sports as a whole has recently seen substantial increases. Football accounted for the single highest proportion of TV channels' total sports expenditure[624]. The European average was 44,6% in 1998[625]. The high percentage dedicated to the acquisition of TV rights of football represents the importance which broadcasters attach to football compared to the acquisition of the broadcasting rights to other sporting events.

4.1.3.2. A particular audience

(71)   In order to attract the widest possible audiences, broadcasters will seek to have a balanced schedule with a range of different programmes. Catering to a wide audience is part of the public service remit for public service broadcasters. Pay-TV broadcasters wish to cater to the tastes of as many people as possible in order to sell subscriptions. For commercial free-TV broadcasters the reason for having a balanced schedule is that they generally sell 'packages' of advertising slots spread across various programmes instead of individual slots during particular programmes[626]. Producers wishing to advertise during for example, the UEFA Champions League will also purchase slots during other types of programmes. This reflects the optimum strategy for an advertiser whose aim is to reach as large a proportion of its potential customers as possible. Showing adverts across a range of carefully selected programmes, each one of which will be watched by different

---

[621] In its reply of 26-11-1999 to the Commission's request for information of 21-9-1999 Vlaamse Media Maatschappij states that 'Actually, acquisition of TV rights for sport (especially football) is not a profitable operation as such [...]. However [...] the branding of VMM's channels will be the decisive parameter for deciding the acquisition of TV rights for football games.' For instance ONdigital, which has acquired the pay-TV rights to the UEFA Champions League and provided these rights on a promotional basis free to subscribers, states in its reply of 23-11-1999 to the Commission's request for information of 20-9-1999 that 'In the early stages of platform growth building the subscriber base is considered to be more important than pure profit.' Further in its reply ONdigital states that 'ONdigital believes that the brand image and value attached to its consumer offer is directly affected by the sports content available on the platform.'

[622] Kagan Euro TV Sports, 26-7-1996.

[623] ONdigital's reply of 23-11-1999.

[624] According to Kagan's 'European media sports rights', April 1999, football took the major share of the total rights expenditure in most Member States in 1998 (the share of the nearest rival is in brackets): Austria 32,4% (skiing 11,3%); Belgium 53,6% (cycling 9,5%); Denmark 45,4% (handball 13,2%); Finland 32,1% (ice hockey 16,9%); France 37,8% (motor racing 9,3%); Germany 42% (tennis 6,6%); Greece 43,3% (basketball 41,4%); Ireland 47% (horse racing 13,1%); Italy 65,2% (motor racing 7,4%); Netherlands 54,5% (motor racing 9,3%); Portugal 44,3% (motor racing 11,8%); Spain 51,6% (basketball 10,1%); Sweden 39,5% (ice hockey 19,1%); United Kingdom 51,6% (rugby 11,7%).

[625] Kagan's 'European media sports rights' April 1999.

[626] ITV's reply of 12-11-1999 to a request for information of 10-9-1999.

potential customer groups, is the best way to do this[627]. The fact that football is a regular and frequent event, which attracts high viewing figures, enhances the value of football programmes as part of an advertising package, because it allows the advertiser to make frequent contacts with a potential customer with a distinct profile.

(72)    In deciding on a 'package', advertisers will not randomly pick programmes during which to show their adverts. The profile of the audience, which a programme attracts, will be a crucial factor to be taken into account. This reflects the 'raison d'être' of advertising: companies essentially advertise in order to attract new customers or to keep the existing ones. In order for an advert to fulfil this purpose those who have at least a potential interest in the product being shown must see it[628].

(73)    Not all types of viewers are of equal value to broadcasters (and advertisers). Some people watch more TV than others do. People have different spending powers and patterns. Amongst the most sought-after viewers are men with an above-average spending power and who are in the age groups of 16 to 20 and 35 to 40, because those groups are generally considered to have a less fixed spending pattern compared to older people. They are therefore more likely to try new products and services. The problem for broadcasters and advertisers is that these groups contain a high proportion of 'light viewers' of television[629], who do not, as a rule, watch much television. It is therefore much harder for advertisers to get their message through to these target groups via television advertising compared to other groups of the population, for example, women aged 55 or over, who on average watch a great deal more television. The attractiveness, and elusiveness, of the target group make programmes watched by them of significant value to broadcasters that are keen to have programmes that attract this audience.

(74)    The Commission's investigation of the situation in the Member States has shown that football, which is a mass attractive sport with high viewing figures, is the programme, which seems to be the most effective tool to address this particular group of the population. Two-thirds of the viewers are male and in the appropriate age groups[630].

---

[627] Thus a football boot producer will, for example, reach a larger number of potential buyers by showing one advert during the final of a football tournament, when 'aficionados' are likely to be watching, and another during a feature film, when the weekend player may be watching, than showing two adverts during the football final. In this way a larger number of potential buyers will be contacted.

[628] For example, whilst a producer of breakfast cereals may have a broader target group, a meat producer is unlikely to wish to place an advert during a programme dedicated to vegetarian issues, even if this programme is very popular. Thus if broadcasters wish to have the business of meat producers, they can not only show programmes about vegetarianism, they must also televise programmes which are watched by people who are at least willing to eat meat (even if the programmes attract fewer viewers).

[629] Channel 5's reply of 19-11-1999.

[630] RTL considers in its reply of 15-11-1999 to the Commission's request for information of 20-9-1999 that it 'would lose advertising revenue if it substituted the UEFA Champions League by other football events or other sports events. Even if the viewer profile would be the same, the viewing times for these events would be much less because these sports events are less attractive.' Young & Rubicam Europe states in its reply of 21-10-1999 to the Commission's request for information of 8-10-1999: product 'categories targeting female consumers are unlikely to advertise in sports programmes.' Channel 5's reply: 'These (football) audiences are more male in profile than the average, younger than the average, and more upmarket than the average.' ITV stated in its reply of 12-11-1999 to the Commission's request for information of 10-9-1999 that the audiences to the UEFA

(75)    A result of football being a tool to reach a hard-to-get-to audience is that broadcasters are able to charge higher rates for advertising in connection with football compared to other programmes. The price of advertising slots during the transmission of football is higher than during the transmission of other sports, for example, the UEFA Champions League allows broadcasters to charge premiums of between 10 to 50% depending on the teams involved and the stage of the tournament[631].

(76)    The attraction of programmes and hence the level of competition for the TV rights to them varies according to the type of sport and the type of event. Mass sports like football generally attract large audiences. By contrast, minority sports achieve very low ratings. In most Member States football constantly achieves the highest audience figures. In 1997, football accounted for 21 of the top 25 European sports broadcasts. The popularity of football for viewers is also expressed in the number of hours dedicated to the broadcast of sport. Between 1996 and 1997, the number of hours dedicated to football transmission was 13939. The second most transmitted sport was tennis which achieved less than half this at 5115 hours[632]. These figures led the authors of Kagan to comment that 'the TV sports hours breakdown illustrates soccer's position as the most valuable sport to cover'[633]. Kagan confirms its findings in its 2002 report, where it states that: 'Soccer is by far the most popular programming on TV in Western Europe, where it made up a massive 79% of total sports programming in 2000'[634].

4.1.3.3. Conclusion regarding the upstream market

(77)    The Commission's investigation shows that there are no programmes which place a competitive restraint on the ability of the holder of the TV rights to football events being played regularly throughout every year to determine the price of these TV rights. TV rights to other sports events or other types of programmes such as feature films do not put a competitive restraint on the holder of the TV rights to such football events. Including such rights in the market definition would make the definition too wide. In other words, there is no substitutability between the TV rights to football and the TV rights to other types of programmes.

(78)    Some have suggested that narrower market definitions may exist, such as for matches involving only national clubs. Assuming that such market definitions were correct, they would nevertheless not substantially alter the market share of UEFA. As such it is not necessary to consider such alternative market definitions for the purposes of this case.

(79)    The Commission therefore concludes that there is a separate market for the acquisition of TV broadcasting rights to football which is played regularly throughout every year. This definition would, in practice, mainly involve matches in national league and cup events as well as the UEFA Champions League and UEFA Cup.

*4.1.4.    The downstream markets on which broadcasters compete for advertising revenue depending on audience rates and pay-TV subscribers*

(80)    The acquisition of TV broadcasting rights of football events is closely linked with

---

Champions League 'are more male in profile than the average, younger than the average and more upmarket than the average.' McCann-Erikson's reply of 3-11-1999 to the Commission's request for information of 8-10-1999 supports this.

[631] McCann-Erickson's reply of 3-11-1999 to a Commission request for information of 8-10-1999.

[632] Kagan Euro TV Sports, 26-7-1996, page 8.

[633] Kagan Euro TV Sports, 26-7-1996, page 163.

[634] Kagan World Media, 2002, page 3.

the downstream television markets in which the football events are broadcast as an important element of the TV broadcasters' competition for advertisers on free-TV, which depends on viewer interest/ratings and/or pay-TV subscribers, who may in particular be enticed into subscribing to a TV channel by means of football.

*4.1.5.   The upstream and downstream markets for the acquisition of media rights for new media (wireless 3G/UMTS and Internet) of football*

(81)   UEFA's joint selling arrangement is not limited to TV rights, but also covers all other forms of media rights to the UEFA Champions League. Although not addressed in the Commission's statement of objections, they were included in UEFA's amendments to the notified new joint selling arrangement.

(82)   Regarding the new media rights such as wireless and Internet content rights, these markets are very much in their infancy. This is largely due to the fact that these technologies are currently at an early stage of development and also to the lack of infrastructure, which is presently available to deliver those services to the consumers. Therefore, there is no clear empirical evidence on which to base market definitions. It is nevertheless possible to draw some conclusions, however broad, which would permit a realistic appraisal of the restrictive effect of UEFA's joint selling arrangement on those new media markets.

(83)   First, content rights will be necessary for the development of the new services, in the same way as content rights are necessary for TV broadcasting services, where football content is being used to entice consumers to take up pay-TV subscriptions and to attract advertisers to TV channels. As these new services allow increasingly narrowly targeted forms of content delivery, it will be possible to identify and supply narrower customer demands than is the case with current media delivery systems. As such, it is likely that relatively narrow upstream content markets will emerge, given the ability to supply narrow downstream markets. It is therefore likely that football content rights, in relation to TV broadcasting, will also constitute a separate relevant product market in relation to new media and that football content will have a similar function. It is likely that new media operators will wish to acquire football content to attract advertisers and subscribers.

(84)   Secondly, it is likely that each different form of exploitation will provide a specific service to specific consumers. On-demand services delivered via wireless mobile devices or via the Internet will not compete with live TV broadcasting. Likewise mobile clip services will not compete with television highlights packages[635].

(85)   It is therefore likely that new media markets will emerge at both the upstream and downstream levels, which parallel the development of markets in the pay-TV sector.

*4.1.6.   The upstream and downstream markets for the other commercial rights – sponsorship, suppliership and product licensing*

(86)   UEFA jointly sells a number of other commercial rights related to the UEFA Champions League such as sponsorship, suppliership and product licensing. These commercial rights are likely to form part of wider product markets for commercial advertising. However, since it is not likely that UEFA's sale of these commercial rights would appreciably restrict competition, it is not necessary for the purposes of this case to exactly define the scope of the relevant product markets.

---

[635]  See Commission Decision Comp/JV.48 – Vodafone/Vivendi/Canal+ (Vizzavi).

## 4.2. The geographic markets

(87) UEFA submits that the geographic scope of the affected markets is essentially national in character because of cultural factors and national audience preferences.

### 4.2.1. The geographic scope of the upstream market

(88) Media rights to football events like the UEFA Champions League are normally sold on a national basis. This is due to the character of distribution, which is national due to national regulatory regimes, language barriers, and cultural factors. The Commission therefore considers the geographic scope of the upstream markets for the media rights to be national.

(89) The geographic scope of the relevant product markets for the other commercial rights could be wider than national as the sponsors, etc., associate themselves with the UEFA Champions League as such and not with individual football clubs. However, since it is not likely that UEFA's joint selling arrangement regarding these commercial rights would appreciably restrict competition, it is not necessary for the purposes of this case to define exactly the geographic scope of the relevant product markets.

### 4.2.2. The geographic scope of the downstream market

(90) The reasons for defining the geographic scope of the upstream markets as national, such as varying regulatory regimes, language barriers, and cultural factors, are also decisive in the downstream market. A pay-TV broadcaster normally only sells subscriptions to viewers in a certain territory. TV advertising is normally adapted to fit the tastes and languages of a certain territory. The same would seem to apply to new media services. The Commission therefore considers the geographic scope of the downstream markets to be national or at least confined to linguistic regions.

## 5. THIRD-PARTY OBSERVATIONS

(91) The Commission published a notice in the Official Journal of the European Communities pursuant to Article 19(3) of Regulation No 17, which prompted reactions from a number of interested third parties.

(92) The football associations welcome the compromise. G14, a European economic interest grouping whose 18 founding members are leading European football clubs, in particular considers that the achievement of a segmentation of media rights in separate windows addresses in a satisfactory manner the objections raised by the Commission. G14 moreover considers that the mix of joint and individual sales strikes the right balance between solidarity and protection of the consumer and the freedom of individual clubs. G14 therefore supports the compromise solution and the new marketing model while emphasising that the implementation should involve active participation of the parties concerned within the decision-making bodies of UEFA.

(93) Some pay-TV broadcasters are concerned that the reorganisation of the UEFA Champions League media rights sales system will increase competition in the TV broadcasting markets and that it therefore does not take account of the current economic reality for pay-TV in Europe. The reduction of exclusivity through the splitting up into several packages and short embargoes reduce the value for broadcasters. They consider that a sport event only has value when it is held in exclusivity by one broadcaster. The segmentation of rights, which the Commission strives for, risks reducing the value of the event and could lead to more (too much) football on TV and viewers having to buy several subscriptions. They also fear competition from Internet/UMTS and wish for more restrictions imposed on new

media rights, inter alia, with longer embargoes, which would hold back the development of these new media.

(94)    Other free-TV broadcasters are positive to the opportunities created by the new solution and note, inter alia, that whether the package solution will further the opportunity for more than one free-TV broadcaster to broadcast UEFA competitions will have to be proved in practice. They note that the UEFA Cup already allows more than one free-TV broadcaster to broadcast UEFA competitions. A free-TV broadcaster states that it is unable to determine on the basis of the facts provided whether the new system would, in practice, alleviate the concerns risen in the statement of objections. It is however, concerned about the reduced level of exclusivity created by the packaging. The third package of live rights is of no real value to broadcasters as the national games by definition will be included in the Gold and Silver packages.

(95)    One sport rights agency congratulates UEFA and the Commission for having agreed on a compromise that generally accepts the principle of joint selling. It considers that this principle guarantees the attraction of the product and the 'UEFA Champions League' brand as being in the consumers' interest and is best fitted to reconcile all the different interests at stake. However, it regrets the deviation from the joint selling principle created by package 5, as this may negatively influence the UEFA Champions League brand.

(96)    Other sport rights agencies are not convinced that the compromise solves the issues objected to by the Commission regarding the TV broadcasting rights to football events, which represent 15 to 40% of the value of broadcasting rights to regular football events. They argue that a joint selling arrangement is not necessary to establish the UEFA Champions League as a brand. Nor do they consider that solidarity or that a single point of sale are relevant arguments under Article 81(3). They further argue that the compromise is likely to serve as a model for other football competitions, including for the UEFA Cup. They consider that packages 1 and 2 will contain all commercially valuable matches whereas matches contained in package 5 have very little commercial value. Only UEFA can market a wireless and Internet service covering the whole UEFA Champions League. In addition, football clubs are restricted in marketing club branded and related services. They are therefore concerned that clubs may not create a product competing with the UEFA Champions League. Finally, they point out that clubs must pay a fee for the raw feed and that Internet rights are available only at midnight.

(97)    A telecommunications operator that has interests in free-TV, Internet and wireless welcomes the Commission's initiative of opening the market for the sale of the UEFA Champions League media rights. It considers that packages 1 and 2 should be unbundled allowing broadcasters to bid for single matches and that, at least, a broadcaster should be prevented from bundling the two packages. It also argues that the same package should be sold to both a free-TV and a pay-TV broadcaster. It furthermore considers that TV broadcasters should be allowed to resell the rights to ISPs and wireless providers.

(98)    Internet services providers would like to have live rights. They consider that the embargo is too long for deferred exploitation and that Internet and TV are two distinct markets. They regret that deferred rights are reserved for UEFA and the football clubs and that Internet service providers are excluded from competing for the rights.

(99)    Only one national competition authority has submitted comments to the Commission. It considers that the compromise does not resolve the problems identified in the statement of objections and as such does not qualify for exemption. It consid-

ers that on the horizontal level the UEFA arrangement remains restrictive of competition as UEFA continues to maintain the exclusive right to sell all matches. In respect of the vertical level the new commercial model does not alleviate competition concerns, as the two main packages are still effectively only within the reach of large broadcasters. It moreover considers that the football clubs' sale of package 5 to pay-TV/pay-per-view is an illusion as in Germany there is only one pay-per-view broadcaster.

(100) Finally, radio broadcasters query how UEFA is able to sell radio rights in view of the right of information of the public. They argue that the right of the public to have access to information cannot be considered as a market like TV.

(101) UEFA was informed that, on the basis of the third party comments, the Commission had identified certain issues where a modification of the compromise would be required. The issues raised by the third party comments were discussed with UEFA in a number of meetings and gave rise to an exchange of correspondence following which UEFA agreed to amend its joint selling arrangement to accommodate those comments. The modifications relate, in particular, to restrictions imposed on football clubs' individual sale of media rights (for example, bundling, field of use restrictions) and achieving a more equitable balance between and mix of joint and individual selling. Also Internet service providers are granted better access to content.

## 6. APPLICATION OF ARTICLE 81 OF THE TREATY AND ARTICLE 53 OF THE EEA AGREEMENT

### 6.1. Jurisdiction

(102) In this case, the Commission is the competent authority to apply both Article 81(1) of the Treaty and Article 53(1) of the EEA Agreement on the basis of Article 56 of the EEA Agreement, since UEFA's joint selling arrangement has an appreciable effect on competition in the common market as well as on trade between Member States.

### 6.2. Article 81(1) of the Treaty and Article 53(1) of the EEA Agreement

(103) Article 81(1) of the Treaty prohibits as incompatible with the common market all agreements between undertakings, decisions by associations of undertakings and concerted practices, which may affect trade between Member States and which have as their object or effect the prevention, restriction or distortion of competition within the common market.

(104) Article 53(1) of the EEA Agreement (which is modelled on Article 81(1) of the Treaty) contains a similar prohibition. However, the reference in Article 81(1) of the Treaty to 'trade between Member States' is replaced by a reference to 'trade between contracting Parties' and the reference to competition 'within the common market' is replaced by a reference to competition 'within the territory covered by the [...] (EEA) Agreement'.

### 6.3. Agreements or decisions between undertakings and associations of undertakings

(105) The Court of Justice has ruled that, having regard to the objectives of the Community, sport is subject to Community law to the extent it constitutes an economic activity within the meaning of Article 2 of the Treaty[636].

---

[636] See judgments of the Court of Justice in Case 36/74, Walrave v Union Cycliste Internationale, [1974] ECR 1405, paragraph 4; Case 13/76, Donà v Mantero, [1976] ECR 1333, paragraph 12;

(106)   Football clubs engage in economic activities[637] and they are undertakings within the meaning of Article 81(1) of the Treaty and Article 53(1) of the EEA Agreement. The membership of the national football associations consists of those football clubs. The national football associations are therefore associations of undertakings within the meaning of Article 81(1) of the Treaty and Article 53(1) of the EEA Agreement. The national football associations are also undertakings themselves in so far as they engage in economic activities[638]. The members of UEFA are the national football associations. UEFA is therefore both an association of associations of undertakings as well as an association of undertakings. UEFA is moreover an undertaking in its own right as it also engages directly in economic activities.

(107)   Notwithstanding the fact that some of these entities are non-profit making bodies, UEFA, the national football associations and the football clubs are all undertakings within the meaning of Article 81(1) of the Treaty and Article 53(1) of the EEA Agreement.

(108)   Article 81(1) of the Treaty and Article 53(1) of the EEA Agreement are applicable to associations of undertakings in so far as:

- the activities of the association or of the undertakings belonging to the association are calculated to produce the results which Article 81(1) of the Treaty and Article 53(1) of the EEA Agreement aim to suppress[639], and/or
- the association intended to and did coordinate the conduct of its members on the market[640].

(109)   The Regulations of the UEFA Champions League constitute a decision taken by

---

Case C-415/93, URBSF v Bosman, [1995] ECR I-4921, paragraph 73; Joined Cases C-51/96 and C-191/97, Christelle Deliège v Ligue francophone de judo et disciplines associées ASBL, Ligue belge de judo ASBL, Union Européenne de judo (C-51/96) and François Pacquée (C-191/97) [2000] ECR 2549, paragraphs 41 and 42; Case C-176/96, Jyri Lehtonen and Castors Canada Dry Namur-Braine ASBL v Fédération royale belge des sociétés de basket-ball ASBL (FRBSB), [2000] ECR 2681 paragraphs 32 and 33.

[637] For example, selling tickets, transferring players, distributing merchandising articles, concluding advertising and sponsorship contracts, selling broadcasting rights, etc. The size of the undertaking does not matter and the concept does not presuppose a profit-making intention. See opinion of Advocate General Lenz in Case C-415/93, URBSF v Bosman, [1995] ECR I-4921, paragraph 255 referring to the judgment in Joined Cases 209 to 215 and 218/78, Van Landewyck v Commission [1980] ECR 3125, paragraph 88.

[638] Opinion of Advocate General Lenz in Case C-415/93, URBSF v Bosman, [1995] ECR I-4921, paragraph 256. Commission Decision 92/521/EEC − Distribution of package tours during the 1990 World Cup, OJ L 326, 12-11-1992, p. 31, paragraph 49: '[...] FIFA is an entity carrying on activities of an economic nature and constitutes an undertaking within the meaning of Article 85 of the EEC Treaty' and paragraph 53: 'The (Federazione Italiana Gioco Calcio = the national Italian football association) also carries on activities of an economic nature and is consequently an undertaking within the meaning of Article 85 of the EEC Treaty'. Judgment in Case T-46/92, Scottish Football Association v Commission, [1994] ECR II-1039, from where it can be concluded that the Scottish Football Association is an undertaking or an association of undertakings within the meaning of Article 81 and 82. See also joined Cases C-51/96 and C-191/97, Christelle Deliège v Ligue Francophone de Judo et Disciplines ASBL and Others, [2000] ECR 2681 paragraphs 52-57, Case T-513/93 Consiglio Nazionale degli Spedizionieri Doganali v Commission of the European Communities ECR [2000] II-1807.

[639] Joined Cases 209 to 215 and 218/78 Fedetab, 1980 [ECR] 3125 at paragraph 88.

[640] Case 45/85 Sachversicherer at paragraph 32.

an association of associations of undertakings within the meaning of Article 81(1) of the Treaty and Article 53(1) of the EEA Agreement[641].

(110) The Regulations of the UEFA Champions League provide the regulatory basis for the manner in which the commercial rights of the UEFA Champions League are sold. UEFA's Executive Committee adopts the Regulations of the UEFA Champions League. UEFA's Congress, the membership of which consists of the national football associations of which the football clubs are members, appoints the Executive Committee. The Regulations of the UEFA Champions League are binding on the national football associations and on the football clubs. The football clubs playing in the UEFA Champions League, which are co-owners of the commercial rights of the UEFA Champions League, confirm the binding nature of the UEFA Statutes, the Regulations of the UEFA Champions League and other decisions relevant to the competition taken by the competent bodies of UEFA, referred to in the entry form, which they sign when they sign up for participation in the UEFA Champions League.

(111) In agreement with the aforementioned competent bodies of UEFA, associations and football clubs, UEFA adopted a new joint selling arrangement regarding the UEFA Champions League media rights, the content of which is summarised above under sections 1.4 to 1.6.

(112) UEFA will, in the future, conclude rights contracts with third parties on the basis of the principles enshrined in the notified joint selling arrangement. The vertical rights agreements with television broadcasters that were originally notified are no longer applicable following the introduction of the new joint selling arrangement and will therefore not be addressed in this Decision.

## 6.4. Restriction of competition

(113) The notified joint selling arrangement grants UEFA the exclusive right to sell jointly certain commercial rights on behalf of the football clubs participating in the UEFA Champions League. This includes media rights that relate to the UEFA Champions League as a whole and involving action from all matches of the UEFA Champions League. Those media rights, which are listed in section 1.6 above, relate to all types of media rights and are not restricted to the rights for specific markets. As such, the restrictive effects of UEFA's joint selling arrangement are capable of manifesting themselves on any of the markets where the rights could be used.

(114) UEFA's joint selling arrangement has the effect that through the agreement to jointly exploit the commercial rights of the UEFA Champions League on an exclusive basis through a joint selling body, UEFA, prevents the individual football clubs from individually marketing such rights. This prevents competition between the football clubs and also between UEFA and the football clubs in supplying in parallel media rights to the UEFA Champions League to interested buyers in the upstream markets. This means that third parties only have one single source of supply. Third-party commercial operators are therefore forced to purchase the relevant rights under the conditions jointly determined in the context of the invitation to bid, which is issued by the joint selling body. This means that the joint selling body restricts competition in the sense that it determines prices and all other trad-

---

[641] If the Statutes were categorised as an agreement between undertakings, this would not change the situation since Article 81(1) of the Treaty and Article 53(1) of the EEA Agreement apply in the same way to both categories. See Case C-415/93, URBSF v Bosman, [1995] ECR I-4921 at paragraph 46.

ing conditions on behalf of all individual football clubs producing the UEFA Champions League content. In the absence of the joint selling agreement the football clubs would set such prices and conditions independently of one another and in competition with one another. The reduction in competition caused by the joint selling arrangement therefore leads to uniform prices compared to a situation with individual selling.

(115) UEFA's joint selling arrangement also has the effect that certain restrictions are imposed on football clubs in respect of the exploitation of those commercial rights that they have not granted to UEFA for joint selling, but which are exploited by themselves individually. The restrictions imposed on individual football clubs concern in particular:

(a) a restriction on football clubs' individual selling of live TV rights, which restricts them to selling such live rights only to pay TV/pay-per-view broadcasters and prevents the sale of such rights to free-TV broadcasters (package 5 of the rights segmentation table);

(b) embargoes on the exploitation of deferred media rights, in particular TV and Internet rights, (packages 6, 7 and 12 of the rights segmentation table);

(c) a limitation on the bundling of individually sold live and deferred media rights restricting the football clubs from selling their individually sold media rights to end-users (broadcasters) which would exploit those rights as a UEFA Champions League focused product (packages 5, 6, 11 and 12 of the rights segmentation table).

(116) UEFA's joint selling arrangement therefore restricts competition in the upstream markets not only between football clubs but also between UEFA and the football clubs in supplying commercial rights to interested buyers. In addition, the notified joint selling arrangement has an impact on the downstream broadcasting markets as football events are an important element of TV broadcasters' competition for advertisers or for subscribers for pay-TV and pay-per-view services. Such an arrangement has as its effect the restriction of competition. It is therefore also caught by the prohibition in Article 81(1) of the Treaty and Article 53(1) of the EEA Agreement[642].

*6.4.1. Scope of the present procedure*

(117) Under the new sales policy the media rights are no longer all offered to a single operator but are split up into a large number of smaller rights packages. It is not the object of the present procedure to ascertain whether individual rights contracts between UEFA and a broadcaster would restrict competition within the meaning of Article 81(1) of the Treaty and Article 53(1) of the EEA Agreement. Nor is it possible to ascertain in the context of the present procedure whether competition would be restricted if a single operator acquired several packages of rights. This decision will therefore not deal with the individual rights contracts concluded by UEFA with third parties and does not in any way prejudice their evaluation under Community competition law.

**6.5. Applicability of Article 81(1) of the Treaty or Article 53(1) of the EEA Agreement**

*6.5.1. League rights and individual football clubs' rights*

(118) For each individual football match played in the UEFA Champions League, the

---

[642] See chapter 5 (in particular chapter 5.3.1.2) of the Commission's guidelines on the applicability of Article 81 to horizontal cooperation agreements (OJ C 3, 6-1-2001, p. 2).

two participating football clubs may claim ownership to the commercial rights. This is because it would be difficult to deny that an individual home club, as user of the football ground, has the right to deny admission to media operators wishing to record those matches. Likewise, it would be difficult to deny that the visiting club, as a necessary participant in the football match, should have some influence as to whether the match should be recorded and, if so, how and by whom.

(119)   Looking at a whole football tournament, it would seem that each football club would have a stake in the rights in the different constellations in which they play but their ownership could not be considered to extend beyond that. Therefore, there are in a football tournament a large number of individual ownership constellations that are independent of one another. The fact that football clubs play in a football tournament does not mean that ownership extends to involve all matches in the tournament. Nor does it mean that ownership is inter-linked to an extent where it must be held that all clubs have an ownership share in the whole league as such and in each individual match.

(120)   UEFA argues that it is UEFA's intellectual efforts and organisational responsibility that have created a football league with its own brand image distinct from that of the participating football clubs. Therefore, without any joint selling arrangement, no commercial rights would be available at all. UEFA argues that it is the owner of the UEFA Champions League property rights due to the tasks it undertakes. To the extent UEFA is selling its own property, Article 81(1) of the Treaty and Article 53(1) of the EEA Agreement are inapplicable. According to UEFA, the case therefore does not concern the joint selling arrangement but the terms on which the rights are sold to third parties. UEFA consequently argues that as long as these terms do not restrict competition, there is no infringement of Article 81(1) of the Treaty or Article 53(1) of the EEA Agreement.

(121)   UEFA moreover argues that if UEFA cannot be considered as the sole owner of the property rights, it should be considered a 'co-owner' of the rights. Therefore, according to UEFA, the notified joint selling arrangement is fundamentally different from any conventional joint selling arrangement in which the individual undertakings pool individually owned rights which they sell jointly, as UEFA, in this case, also exploits its own property rights. UEFA is stresses its view on the property rights situation with reference to the situation in the individual Member States[643].

---

[643] In a reply of 16 February 2001 to the Commission's request for information of 15-11-2000, UEFA explains the situation regarding ownership to the TV rights in the EEA States is as follows: In Austria, the home club is recognised as the owner of the TV rights. Belgian legislation does not determine ownership to the TV rights to football. Danish legislation does not determine ownership, but in a concrete case the Danish competition authorities have allegedly stated that they consider that the TV rights of a match played in the Danish National Championship belong to the Danish Football Association, as the owner of the tournament, and the home club of the specific match jointly. English legislation is silent about the matter. The Finnish clubs are the owners to the TV rights to the matches of the Finnish club competitions. In France it is the club participating in the European tournament, which is the owner. In Germany, the clubs are the owners of the rights and the organiser, UEFA, could be considered to be a co-owner. According to Greek and Italian legislation the clubs are the owners of the TV rights. Luxembourg legislation is silent about the matter. Dutch case-law (under appeal) gives the ownership of the TV rights to the home club. In Northern Ireland, according to the Irish Football Association, the association owns the rights to the national league (no legal source quoted), however, the clubs themselves sell the TV rights to matches in European competitions. Portuguese legislation does not regulate the matter. In the Republic of Ireland it seems that the

(122) The Commission takes note of the fact that there is no common uniform concept in the EEA Member States regarding the ownership of the property media rights to football events nor is there any Community or EEA law concept[644]. It is true that if UEFA were the sole owner of the rights in a Member State no horizontal restriction of competition would occur from UEFA selling the commercial rights. However, on the basis of the information submitted by UEFA, UEFA can at best be considered as a co-owner of the rights, but never the sole owner. The question of ownership is for national law and the Commission's appreciation of the issue in this case is without prejudice to any determination by national courts.

(123) The Commission therefore proceeds on the basis that there is co-ownership between the football clubs and UEFA for the individual matches, but that the co-ownership does not concern horizontally all the rights arising from a football tournament. It is not considered necessary for the purpose of this case to quantify the respective ownership shares.

(124) It suffices to note that there are multiple owners of the media rights to the UEFA Champions League. An agreement between the three owners (the two football clubs and UEFA) which are indispensable to produce one unit of output (the licence to broadcast one match) would not be caught by Article 81(1) of the Treaty and Article 53(1) of the EEA Agreement. However, since the agreement regarding UEFA's joint selling arrangement extends beyond that, Article 81(1) of the Treaty and Article 53(1) of the EEA Agreement apply to the arrangement.

*6.5.2. The special characteristics of sport*

(125) UEFA is of the opinion that it is not appropriate to evaluate the relationship between football clubs with a 'free play of competition' test, as football clubs are not truly independent competitors. UEFA considers that this test may be valid to evaluate the merits of an agreement between independent business entities that would compete with one another under normal circumstances.

(126) Furthermore according to UEFA, Article 81(1) of the Treaty and Article 53(1) of the EEA Agreement are not applicable because the structure and operation of the UEFA Champions League serves to promote and not to restrict competition in European football. UEFA considers that the model of financial solidarity helps to maintain a balance between clubs and to encourage recruitment of young players, which serves to promote competition in European football. As a result of the financial policies implemented by UEFA, competition between clubs in Europe is enhanced and the number of competitors on the market is increased.

(127) The Court of Justice has ruled that, having regard to the objectives of the Commu-

---

national association is the owner of the TV rights, but the TV rights to the European competitions are disposed of without interference from the football association. No information regarding the legislative situation in Scotland has been given. Reference is only made to the bylaws of the Scottish Football Association which claim ownership to the rights. Spanish legislation has not taken a position on the ownership issue. The clubs in the First and Second Division sell the rights individually. Swedish legislation is silent about the matter. No information has been submitted regarding the legal situation in Wales.

The Commission has asked the national football association in Iceland, Liechtenstein and Norway directly: In Iceland and Liechtenstein it is the clubs participating in the European competitions, which are considered as the owner. In Norway the individual clubs seem to be recognised as the owner of the TV rights.

[644] Article 295 of the Treaty provides that: 'The Treaty shall in no way prejudice the rules in Member States governing the system of property ownership.'

nity, sport is subject to Community law to the extent it constitutes an economic activity within the meaning of Article 2 of the Treaty[645].

(128) UEFA and the football clubs are economic competitors in selling commercial rights (property rights and media rights) to football matches. If there were no joint selling arrangement these parties would be selling the rights individually and in competition with one another.

(129) In fact, the object of the notified agreement is not the organisation of the UEFA Champions League but the sale of the commercial rights of the UEFA Champions League. The Commission is aware that some form of cooperation among the participants is necessary to organise a football league and that there is, in this context, certain interdependence among clubs. This interdependence between all clubs does not, however, extend to all activities of the UEFA Champions League participants. Clubs already compete in the areas of sponsorship, stadium advertising and merchandising. Clubs also compete for players. Consequently, the decision of an association of associations of undertakings to sell the commercial rights jointly on behalf of its members, which is an area in which the clubs are economic competitors, is not necessary in terms of Article 81(1) of the Treaty and Article 53(1) of the EEA Agreement to stage a football league. These provisions are therefore applicable to such an arrangement. Any need to take the specific characteristics of sport into account, such as the possible need to protect weaker clubs through a cross-subsidisation of funds from the richer to the poorer clubs, or by any other means, must be considered under Article 81(3) of the Treaty and Article 53(3) of the EEA Agreement.

(130) According to UEFA, its joint selling arrangement is a prerequisite for the existence of the UEFA Champions League. UEFA would not organise the UEFA Champions League without its joint selling arrangement and without being able to redistribute the revenues. UEFA considers that the joint selling arrangement does not impede trade between Member States and that the redistribution of revenue by UEFA serves to enlarge the competitive base in European football. In UEFA's view, its financial policy pursues objectives that have been recognised by the Court of Justice in the Bosman case[646], that is to say, the objective of maintaining a balance between clubs by preserving a certain degree of equality, and encouraging the recruitment of players.

(131) The Commission fully endorses the specificity of sport, as expressed for example in the declaration of the European Council in Nice in December 2000. On that occasion the Council encouraged the mutualisation of part of the revenue from the sales of TV rights, at the appropriate levels, as beneficial to the principle of solidarity between all levels and areas of sport. However, while UEFA's interest in the commercial aspects is understandable, it has not demonstrated that a joint selling arrangement is an indispensable prerequisite for the redistribution of revenue. The UEFA Cup demonstrates that a pan-European football competition can exist

---

[645] See judgments in Case 36/74, Walrave v Union Cycliste Internationale, [1974] ECR 1405, paragraph 4; Case 13/76, Donà v Mantero, [1976] ECR 1333, paragraph 12; Case C-415/93, URBSF v Bosman, [1995] ECR I-4921, paragraph 73; Joined Cases C-51/96 and C-191/97, Christelle Deliège v Ligue francophone de judo et disciplines associées ASBL, Ligue belge de judo ASBL, Union Européenne de judo (C-51/96) and François Pacquée (C-191/97), [2000] ECR 2549, paragraphs 41-42; Case C-176/96, Jyri Lehtonen and Castors Canada Dry Namur-Braine ASBL v Fédération royale belge des sociétés de basket-ball ASBL (FRBSB), [2000] ECR 2681 paragraphs 32-33.

[646] Case C-415/93, URBSF v Bosman, [1995] ECR I-4921.

without a joint selling arrangement for the sale of the TV rights, as in this case the individual football clubs are selling the TV rights individually. There are also national examples of this in Spain, Italy and Greece. A redistribution of revenue can be undertaken in other ways without being linked to any joint selling arrangement. It can be implemented through a taxation system or through voluntary contributions. Article 81(1) of the Treaty and Article 53(1) of the EEA Agreement are therefore applicable to such a joint selling arrangement. In any event it is more appropriate to consider any such argument under Article 81(3) of the Treaty and Article 53(3) of the EEA Agreement.

### 6.5.3. *Appreciability of the restriction on competition*

(132)   In assessing the appreciability of the restrictions of competition, the Commission notes that premium sports, in particular football, are regarded as one of the main drivers of television. UEFA sold the UEFA Champions League TV rights for more than CHF 800 million in 1999 (EUR 526 million). In the 1999/2000 season in a Community-wide average, the UEFA Champions League accounted for around 20% of the money paid for TV rights of football events by broadcasters[647]. Bearing in mind that football accounts for the single highest proportion of TV channels' sports expenditure[648], the Commission considers that the effect of UEFA's joint selling arrangement is to bring about an appreciable restriction of competition in the broadcasting market.

### 6.6.   Effect on trade between Member States

(133)   Article 81(1) of the Treaty is aimed at agreements which might harm the attainment of a single market between the Member States, whether by partitioning national markets, or by affecting the structure of competition within the common market. Similarly, Article 53(1) of the EEA Agreement is directed at agreements that undermine the achievement of a homogeneous European Economic Area.

(134)   The commercial rights of the UEFA Champions League are sold throughout the EEA. UEFA's joint selling arrangement therefore affects trade between Member States. If the media rights were sold by the individual football clubs or on a non-exclusive basis, it would change the flow of trade in the TV rights.

(135)   The UEFA Champions League is the most prestigious pan-European club football tournament, involving 32 of the best European clubs. The agreement establishing the joint selling arrangement between the football clubs participating in the UEFA Champions League has an appreciable effect on trade between Member States.

### 7.   ARTICLE 81(3) OF THE TREATY AND ARTICLE 53(3) OF THE EEA AGREEMENT

(136)   In evaluating the restrictions of competition created by UEFA's joint selling ar-

---

[647] This figure is calculated on the basis of the acquisition of domestic and UEFA tournaments. Source: A study commissioned by UEFA from Oliver & Ohlbaum Associates, London.

[648] According to Kagan's 'European media sports rights', April 1999, football took the major share of the total rights expenditure in most Member States in 1998 (the share of the nearest rival is in brackets): Austria 32,4% (skiing 11,3%); Belgium 53,6% (cycling 9,5%); Denmark 45,4% (handball 13,2%); Finland 32,1% (ice hockey 16,9%); France 37,8% (motor racing 9,3%); Germany 42% (tennis 6,6%); Greece 43,3% (basketball 41,4%); Ireland 47% (horse racing 13,1%); Italy 65,2% (motor racing 7,4%); Netherlands 54,5% (motor racing 9,3%); Portugal 44,3% (motor racing 11,8%); Spain 51,6% (basketball 10,1%); Sweden 39,5% (ice hockey 19,1%); United Kingdom 51,6% (rugby 11,7%).

rangement pursuant to the criteria for exemption set out in Article 81(3) of the Treaty and Article 53(3) of the EEA Agreement, the Commission has considered the benefits generated by the restrictive arrangement. Where the benefits are such as to offset the restrictive effects, then an exemption under Article 81(3) of the Treaty and Article 53(3) of the EEA Agreement is justified.

(137) The assessment required under Article 81(3) of the Treaty and Article 53(3) of the EEA Agreement is therefore whether the benefits generated by the notified joint selling arrangement outweigh the negative effects that it deploys, namely:

(a) the grant by the football clubs to UEFA of the exclusive right to sell certain of the commercial rights relating to the UEFA Champions League;

(b) the restrictions agreed to by the football clubs in selling their commercial rights individually.

(138) Article 81(3) of the Treaty and Article 53(3) of the EEA Agreement provide that the provisions of Article 81(1) of the Treaty and Article 53(1) of the EEA Agreement respectively may be declared inapplicable to any agreements between undertakings which contribute to improving the production or distribution of goods or to promoting technical or economic progress, while allowing consumers a fair share of the resulting benefit, and which do not impose on the undertakings concerned restrictions which are not indispensable to the attainment of these objectives, nor afford such undertakings the possibility of eliminating competition in respect of a substantial part of the products in question. The following sections contain an assessment in relation to each of those four conditions.

## 7.1. Improvement in production or distribution and/or promoting technical or economic progress

(139) UEFA considers that its joint selling arrangement facilitates the business operations of UEFA's commercial partners by creating a single point of sale. The creation of a single point of sale is of particular interest for an international tournament such as the UEFA Champions League, because this tournament involves a great number of football clubs from many different countries. In addition to the practical difficulties that may create, there is moreover the issue that the ownership structures vary from Member State to Member State with the possibility of the presence of multiple different co-owners of the media rights to each match. Furthermore, there is dispersed demand from broadcasters who are likewise of different nationalities and operating in many different national markets.

(140) Moreover, UEFA argues that the creation of a single point of sale is a prerequisite for the existence of the UEFA Champions League product. Since no individual club knows before the start of the season how far it will get in the tournament it could not sign a commercial agreement with a broadcaster giving the broadcaster any certainty that the football clubs will make it to the very end of the UEFA Champions League season. This provides an element of uncertainty for broadcasters. Similarly, joint selling of the rights by UEFA allows sponsors and other suppliers to receive a uniform package for the duration of the competition guaranteeing them media exposure for the entire period of the event, which allows them to structure their advertising budgets accordingly.

(141) UEFA also considers that its joint selling arrangement enables UEFA to maintain the uniform excellence and consistency of the 'product' at a level and quality which it would not be possible to achieve if the media rights were handled on an ad hoc basis by individual football clubs selling the media rights to a succession of different operators. This is essential for the maintenance of the distinctive UEFA Champions League brand, which is of particular interest to UEFA's commercial partners.

(142)  UEFA finally argues that UEFA's financial solidarity model supports the development of football from the grass roots upwards. It improves production and stimulates the development of the sport in the smaller countries. This results in a more competitive base for the future of European football allowing even the smallest and financially weakest football clubs to compete with the biggest and strongest football clubs.

### 7.1.1. *Single point of sale of a league product*

(143)  Joint selling of the media rights of a football tournament provides an advantage for media operators, football clubs and viewers since it leads to the creation of a single point of sale for the acquisition of a packaged league product.

(144)  The advantages of a single point of sale are attractive in the context not only of a national football tournament, but also of an international competition where the difficulties in selling the rights are greater and where the efficiencies of joint selling may be particularly high. The creation of a single point of sale is of particular interest for an international tournament such as the UEFA Champions League, because this tournament involves a great number of football clubs from many different countries. In addition to the practical difficulties that may create, there is moreover the issue that the ownership structures vary from Member State to Member State. Furthermore, there is dispersed demand from broadcasters who are likewise of different nationalities and operating in many different national markets.

(145)  Joint selling moreover allows the creation of packages of UEFA Champions League rights. This allows media operators to provide coverage to consumers of the league as a whole and over the course of an entire season. The creation of a single point of sale facilitates the existence of the UEFA Champions League product in view of the hybrid character of the UEFA Champions League which is a combination of a league and a knock-out competition where only a limited number of football clubs reach the final stages of the competition. Therefore, an individual club could not enter into a commercial agreement, which would give a broadcaster any guarantee of being able to plan its programme schedule for the whole UEFA Champions League season right to the final round. The joint selling of the TV rights solves this problem, as the broadcaster does not buy the rights of particular football clubs, but the right to broadcast the matches which are played on certain days.

(146)  The benefits of this packaged approach are evident in every match week when rights to the entire UEFA Champions League allow a comprehensive highlights programme to be produced which offers the possibility of showing the most interesting bits of the action of the match days/week in question.

(147)  The benefits are also evident in respect of live coverage. Joint selling provides media operators and consumers with an overview of the whole UEFA Champions League, benefiting, for example, those viewers who have a general interest in the UEFA Champions League as a whole. By ensuring that clubs grant rights to UEFA, which are then licensed to media operators, UEFA can offer a complete package of rights to such operators. This package currently includes, for example, the first pick of matches played on each match day. It is obviously impossible to know at the start of the season which matches will be most interesting throughout the course of the season. The package therefore provides media operators with an opportunity to purchase, and then sell to consumers, a distinct and valuable media service, with guaranteed coverage of the most interesting matches throughout the whole season.

(148) It is conceivable that media operators could put such a package together even without joint selling. However, this would require the acquisition of significantly more rights than is currently the case. For a media operator to create the same end product in the context of individual sale of all media rights would risk being significantly less efficient, involving more acquisition and transaction costs[649]. The only guarantee of an equally interesting selection of matches would be if one media operator were to buy all of the rights available individually either before the start of the football season or consecutively as the football season develops depending on the performance of the football clubs.

(149) In addition, instead of having to conduct negotiations with football clubs throughout the 51 different UEFA member territories with the communication difficulties and transaction costs that is likely to entail, broadcasters can acquire the league media rights packages from the original rights holders though a single outlet. Also in this respect, joint selling therefore reduces the transaction complexity and costs for broadcasters. Broadcasters can establish predictable commercial, technical and programming plans for a whole football season, which enhances the selling of advertising slots and subscriptions. It enables advertisers to build a campaign around the TV coverage of a league and is instrumental in securing broadcast sponsorship.

(150) Joint selling reduces broadcasters' financial risk. In a situation with individual selling of the media rights by the football clubs they risk a reduction in the value of the rights acquired from an individual club if that club performs badly in the league. Joint selling therefore allows a higher level of investment in the league product leading to more innovative match coverage such as better general presentation in both the stadium and the studio.

(151) Even in respect of competitions where the media rights are sold by the individual clubs, the rights are generally aggregated and packaged in later levels of the transaction chain by intermediaries such as sports agents or by the broadcasters creating clearing houses or joint exploitation bodies. A certain level of packaging or aggregation of the individual rights therefore seems optimal or even necessary for an efficient exploitation of the media rights of a football tournament.

(152) Viewers benefit from being offered multiple forms of coverage of the UEFA Champions League. The viewer is interested in having a choice between various forms of broadcasts of the matches of a league. A viewer is likely to wish to have a choice of being able to watch a match live in its total length and also to be informed about several matches in brief on a delayed basis at several different times. The viewer wants to gain information not only about a single match but also about all matches on a given match day. A jointly sold packaged league product is more likely to provide viewers with the product desired as a broadcaster cannot simply acquire the rights to a single match but also needs rights to provide a certain coverage of the other matches of the league on every match day[650].

(153) Football clubs benefit from the sale of the commercial rights via a single point of sale/joint selling agency. The football clubs avoid having to build up own commercial departments of the magnitude that is necessary to deal with the complexity of developing a commercial policy and executing the rights deals in a large number of countries. It is likely that it would be extremely difficult for many football clubs to be able to build up such commercial departments and it is therefore likely

---

[649] ITV, in its reply of 12-5-1999 to the Commission's notice (OJ C 99, 10-4-1999, p. 23) states that joint selling by a central selling body '[...] also significantly reduces the transaction complexity for broadcasters.'

[650] Taurus Holding in a letter dated 22-1-2002.

that an outsourcing of such function would be necessary in any circumstances. It would seem that the individual football clubs could more easily carry out such a task in respect of national competitions, as the national market would be much more easily accessible in terms of language, culture, communication and commercial transparency.

### 7.1.2. *Branding*

(154)   UEFA's second argument that it is able to create and maintain the uniformity and consistency in quality of a UEFA Champions League product via its joint selling arrangement is not without merit. These are factors that contribute to establishing the reputation of a brand, which is associated with a uniform and high quality TV coverage underpinned by a homogeneous presentation which increases the attractiveness for the viewer[651]. These are also factors that attract the best football clubs who want to participate in this particular international tournament. The UEFA Champions League has, in fact, become the most prestigious pan-European club football tournament with the participation of the very best European football clubs.

(155)   Among the factors underlying the success of the UEFA Champions League and distinguishing it from other tournaments are the specific tasks undertaken by UEFA including the 'dressing-up' of the stadium facilities, the recording of the match and the on-screen presentation, on-screen signage, music, etc.

(156)   Furthermore, the organisational steps undertaken by UEFA and the joint selling of the league media products provide benefits for broadcasters in terms of a common and consistent look to the on-screen presentation of the matches by all partner broadcasters throughout the UEFA Champions League season. This is of benefit to viewers as they are able immediately to recognise a UEFA Champions League branded media product associated with quality football, which in turn stimulates viewers' interest and demand.

(157)   UEFA's joint selling of packages of media rights to broadcasters leads to more objectivity in the media coverage of the UEFA Champions League. It provides coverage of the league in a manner that protects the league media product and the brand better than in a situation where one football club would be presented with a favourable bias to the detriment of other clubs and the league brand[652]. This improves the coverage of and the interest in the UEFA Champions League brand, thereby improving the production and the distribution of the UEFA Champions League media product.

### 7.1.3. *Football clubs' individual sale of live TV rights unsold by the joint selling body*

(158)   UEFA's exclusive right to sell the live TV rights comprised by package 4 of the rights segmentation table becomes a non-exclusive right one week after the draw for the first round for the UEFA Champions League, which normally takes place in August. Following that cut-off date, where UEFA fails to sell such rights, the football clubs will have an opportunity to offer such rights to the pay-TV/pay-per-view market on a non-exclusive basis in parallel with UEFA. These are the rights referred to in package 5 of the rights segmentation table.

(159)   The philosophy behind the Commission's insistence in giving the football clubs an opportunity for individual sale of such live TV rights is twofold. First, the efficiencies and benefits of joint selling can be argued where the joint selling body fails to

---

[651]   KrichMedia in a letter dated 17-9-2002 in reply to the Article 19(3) notice.
[652]   Taurus Holding in a letter dated 22-1-2002.

find demand in the market for such rights. Secondly, maintaining competition between UEFA and the football clubs in bringing such rights to the market helps to avoid rights to the UEFA Champions League remaining unused, where there is demand for them. Football clubs should therefore also be able to meet demand from free-TV broadcasters. For example, a risk of unused rights is likely to occur in territories where there are no pay-TV/pay-per-view broadcasters or where the existing pay-TV/pay-per-view broadcasters have already satisfied their demand with the Gold or Silver rights packages. In such cases, only free-TV broadcasters seem likely as potential buyers of such rights and there are no efficiencies in preventing them from potentially acquiring such rights. This decision should therefore be made subject to the condition that the provision in package 5 of the rights segmentation table restricting football clubs from selling live TV rights to free-TV broadcasters does not apply where there is no reasonable offer from any pay-TV broadcaster.

### 7.1.4. Football clubs' individual sale of deferred media rights

(160) The amended joint selling arrangement provides that a number of additional types of deferred TV rights, as well as new media rights, will be exploited not only by UEFA but also by the individual clubs in parallel. However, these additional media rights are made available for exploitation by UEFA and the football clubs only after some embargoes introduced to secure products for which there is much viewer interest and to establish the reputation of the UEFA Champions League brand, which is strictly associated with a uniform and high quality TV coverage, underpinned by a homogeneous presentation. Consequently, deferred TV rights are available as of midnight one day after the last of the games of the relevant match week. Archive rights are available 48 hours after the final. Given the current development of the Internet and to ensure that the UEFA Champions League Internet product remains a quality product, these rights are available 1 1/2 hour after the game. This will of course change over time, making it necessary to revisit the embargo in the foreseeable future.

(161) Under these circumstances, the Commission considers that the negative effects arising from the joint selling arrangement are outweighed by the increased amount of content made available for a wider distribution, thereby promoting technical or economic progress of the media content itself and the new media carriers distributing them.

### 7.1.5. Enhancing the focus of the respective UEFA Champions League and football clubs' brands

(162) Football clubs exploiting UEFA Champions League footage individually will present the footage in a club-focused manner and relating only to action in which they are participating. Football clubs or the broadcasters exploiting the media rights in question[653] cannot package the rights from several football clubs into a single product which would appear as an UEFA Champions League branded product. In particular regarding live TV rights, UEFA defines as an UEFA Champions League branded product as one consisting of more than two live UEFA Champions League matches per day. Regarding delayed TV rights and Internet rights, UEFA would accept programmes containing 100% UEFA Champions League content on a club channel. However, UEFA defines a UEFA Champions League

---

[653] The bundling limitation logically does not apply to the whole sale level, as there is no risk that viewers would experience any brand confusion caused by a bundling at that level.

branded programme as one presented as a club magazine programme, which contains more than 50% UEFA Champions League content. In general programming, the maximum permissible UEFA Champions League amounts to 30% of the programme. Where an entire match is shown on a delayed basis (that is to say, the full 90 minutes) on a club magazine programme then the 50% rule would not apply and the programme could consist mostly or entirely of that single match. Similarly, if a whole match were broadcast in general programming on a channel, then the 30% rule would not apply in that situation.

(163)   The definitions of UEFA Champions League branded products will optimise the global interaction between UEFA Champions League branded and club branded products. The provisions regarding branding are aimed at furthering the development of the UEFA Champions League brand as being a unique independent quality labelled football media product distinguished from club branded products existing in parallel with the UEFA Champions League branded products. The definitions are designed to ensure that club rights do not metamorphose into a product which could be confused with the UEFA Champions League. This contributes to safeguarding the identity and reputation of the UEFA Champions League product, as the UEFA Champions League brand in many circumstances serves as a vehicle and a platform for exposure and promotion of the individual football clubs within and outside the EEA. This will be of benefit, in particular, to smaller clubs with less well-known brands in a wider geographic area who are likely to get broader television exposure through this means.

### 7.1.6. Solidarity

(164)   In its notification, UEFA advanced as a justification for exemption the issue of financial solidarity. UEFA argues that its financial solidarity model supports the development of European football by ensuring a fairer distribution of revenue. The solidarity model could therefore be said to improve production and to stimulate the development of the sport[654].

(165)   The Commission understands that it is desirable to maintain a certain balance among the football clubs playing in a league because it creates better and more exciting football matches, which could be reflected in/translate into better media rights. The same applies to the education and supply of new players, as the players are a fundamental element of the whole venture. The Commission recognises that a cross-subsidisation of funds from richer to poorer may help achieve this. The Commission is therefore in favour of the financial solidarity principle, which was also endorsed by the European Council declaration on sport in Nice in December 2000[655].

(166)   However, the Commission found that the efficiencies and the consumer benefits created by the originally notified joint selling arrangement in 1999 did not outweigh the negative impact of the restrictions of competition inherent in that system.

(167)   The Commission nevertheless considers that it is not necessary for the purpose of this procedure to consider the solidarity argument any further. An exemption, under Article 81(3) of the Treaty and Article 53(3) of the EEA Agreement, of the

---

[654]   Case 26/76 Metro v Commission [1977] ECR 1975, Case 42/84 Remia v Commission [1985] ECR 2545 and Cases 56 and 58/64 Consten & Grundig v Commission [1966] ECR 299.

[655]   'The European Council thinks that moves to encourage the mutualisation of part of the revenue from such sales, at the appropriate levels, are beneficial to the principle of solidarity between all levels and areas of sport.'

new and amended joint selling arrangement is justified because of the creation of a branded league product which is sold in packages via a single point of sale.

### 7.1.7.  *Conclusion regarding improvement in production or distribution and/or promoting technical or economic progress*

(168)   The Commission accepts that the decision of the football clubs and UEFA regarding the joint selling arrangement improves production and distribution of the UEFA Champions League within the meaning of Article 81(3) of the Treaty and Article 53(3) of the EEA Agreement by enabling the creation of a quality branded content product and by providing an advantage for media operators, football clubs and viewers, since it leads to the creation of a single point of sale for the acquisition of a packaged league product. However, since no such benefits arise from the restriction of football clubs' freedom to sell live TV rights under package 5 to other broadcasters than pay-TV/pay-per-view broadcasters, this decision should be subject to a condition, which will enable football clubs to sell their live TV rights to free-TV broadcasters, where there is no reasonable offer from any pay-TV broadcaster.

### 7.2.   Fair share of the benefit to consumers

(169)   The Commission considers that UEFA's joint selling arrangement provides consumers with a fair share of the benefits, which are in particular created by the single point of sale as explained above under section 7.1.1.

(170)   The Commission considers that the creation of a UEFA Champions League packaged content, which is available from a single point of sale, is a genuine benefit, which flows from UEFA's joint selling arrangement. Media operators, as consumers of football content, get more efficient and easier access to this unique content which is in addition carrying the UEFA Champions League quality brand label.

(171)   UEFA's joint selling arrangement therefore creates efficiencies, which allow media operators to invest more in new improved production and transmission technologies, quality television coverage, quality production and presentation, etc. It is also likely to lead to a more intensive and innovative exploitation of the rights to the benefit of the consumer. The sale of the UEFA Champions League media rights in separate packages by means of a public bidding procedure should enhance the possibility for more broadcasters, including small and medium-sized companies, to obtain UEFA Champions League content. The UEFA Champions League joint selling arrangement also ensures that companies interested in new media and deferred media rights and archives will have the opportunity to bid for such content rights.

(172)   The Commission also considers that viewers get access to better quality media coverage of the UEFA Champions League product allowing them to watch all premium matches of every match day over the course of the entire season which are of particular interest to them. Viewers also benefit from a facilitation of access to deferred media content and archive material, which may be of special interest to them.

(173)   However, as indicated in section 3.4.1.3, the Commission considers that the restriction in package 5 of the rights segmentation table limiting football clubs to selling such TV rights to pay-TV/pay-per-view broadcasters does not lead to an improvement in production or distribution and/or the promotion of technical or economic progress. In addition, no benefits to consumers are likely to arise from such restrictions. In fact, the main justification put forward by UEFA to justify the restriction was linked to UEFA's fear that in the absence of the restriction, there

would be a risk of severe economic devaluation of the main rights packages. It is difficult to see how such restriction designed to maintain or raise prices and to remove content from free-TV broadcasters could be regarded as enhancing consumer benefits.

## 7.3.    Restrictions that are indispensable

*7.3.1.   Indispensability of restrictions to create a league product sold via a single point of sale*

(174)   The Commission notes that media rights of sport competitions most often are aggregated in some form at some level of the exploitation chain before they are offered to the viewer. The Commission is neutral as to who undertakes this task. The Commission notes that UEFA could have a legitimate interest in creating a UEFA Champions League focused product, separate from any interest that any other operators may have in creating aggregated products based on UEFA Champions League footage. The interests may overlap, but would not always coincide. UEFA could therefore not necessarily rely on broadcasters, sport rights agents or others to create a UEFA Champions League focused product on its behalf. If UEFA wishes to ensure the benefits for itself, its members and its supporters of a UEFA Champions League media product, it would appear indispensable for UEFA to take a role in ensuring the production of such product. Under the notified joint selling arrangement UEFA is therefore able to ensure the production of a quality product, which represents the UEFA Champions League in an objective and independent manner.

(175)   Secondly, it would appear that the complexity of producing such a product through individual sales by the clubs could compromise the quality and availability of a UEFA Champions League product, and could be less efficient for media operators, in particular since the UEFA Champions League is a pan-European football tournament involving participants from many different countries. As a practical matter, an interesting UEFA Champions League media product would have to encompass matches of interest to consumers throughout the season. As it is impossible to predict accurately at the start of the season which matches will still be of interest at the end of the season, it would not be possible for media operators to buy those matches in advance. The alternative – buying a significant number of matches from a number of different clubs – would be inefficient and still not guarantee success. Media products of football leagues are generally aggregated into a media product covering the league as a whole. The Commission accepts that such aggregation seems indispensable to present a worthwhile product that interests viewers. The Commission will therefore simply have to examine the terms on which the aggregation takes place, not the identity of the body performing the task.

(176)   Thirdly, it also seems indispensable that clubs are not able to sell on their own behalf precisely the same rights as those that are included in the jointly sold UEFA Champions League package. Where the same intellectual property is in the hands of two different sellers, it is likely that the combined revenue from the two possible sales would be significantly less than that which would be received were there only to be one seller. This is because a media operator would be less interested in rights which are available to all of its competitors, as there would be a reduced possibility to distinguish its product from those products of its competitors.

(177)   In other words, it does not seem possible to alter the arrangements in such a way that the clubs grant UEFA a non-exclusive licence to all of their media rights

while at the same time maintaining the improvements and efficiencies referred to in the first requirement of Article 81(3) of the Treaty and Article 53(3) of the EEA Agreement. However, where the joint selling body has failed to sell the aggregated media rights – the media rights sold by UEFA being a composite product – the rights of the joint selling body should not remain exclusive, but the individual co-owners should have an opportunity to test market demand for their individual rights. It would moreover not be indispensable for the proper functioning of the joint selling body if any further restrictions were to be imposed on the football clubs when selling those rights individually[656].

(178)  The Commission also accepts that it is indispensable for UEFA to have the exclusive right to sell the UEFA Champions League live and delayed TV rights outside Europe as it provides the likelihood of a wider and more efficient distribution of the UEFA Champions League. UEFA is, in principle, able to present a product of much wider appeal than any individual football clubs would be able to do.

(179)  It is therefore likely that a centrally packaged product, identifiable as a UEFA Champions League product and focused not on one individual football club but on the UEFA Champions League as a whole, is most efficiently produced through joint selling. UEFA's role in coordinating this work through the mechanism of joint selling is indispensable to the provision to consumers of a UEFA Champions League media product.

(180)  The Commission therefore accepts that the restrictions of competition in UEFA's joint selling arrangement are indispensable within the meaning of Article 81(3) of the Treaty and Article 53(3) of the EEA Agreement to provide the efficiencies and improvements leading to consumer benefits, as long as the joint selling body is able to find demand for the jointly sold media rights.

### 7.3.2.  *Individual football clubs' sale of own media rights*

(181)  It is a feature of European football that clubs typically participate in a number of different leagues, cups and tournaments over the course of a season. A successful UEFA Champions League team, for example, will also participate in national leagues and cups.

(182)  Each individual football club has a group of supporters which is particularly interested in the fate and actions of that particular club. Consequently, there is demand for club-related items including club-related media products. Clubs already carry out a large number of commercial activities aimed at providing their fans with targeted services.

(183)  For the football fan with an interest in one particular club, regardless of the tournament in which the club is participating, UEFA's new joint selling arrangement provides good opportunities to follow the club. While UEFA's joint selling arrangement is focused on the development of the UEFA Champions League brand, it nevertheless also allows clubs to pursue their relationship with their own fans.

(184)  The football clubs are subject to limited restrictions in selling their media rights individually. However, these restrictions are considered to be indispensable for the functioning of UEFA's joint selling arrangement.

(185)  UEFA's joint selling arrangement provides that the clubs may address their fans with live television if UEFA has not managed to sell those live rights. Football clubs may furthermore address their fans via deferred television, mechanical reproduction media, Internet, UMTS, etc.

---

[656] On this point see also section 3.4.3.2.

(186)    The live TV rights, which could be sold by the football clubs[657], concern the football matches which are not picked by the broadcasters that have bought the Gold
and Silver live television packages or sold by UEFA as part of package 4 of the
rights segmentation table. The rights that are referred to in packages 4 and 5 cover
the same matches. In order to improve the chances of these residual rights finding
a buyer, it is considered indispensable for UEFA, as the joint selling body, to be
given a first exclusive right to sell those live TV rights.

(187)    If the joint selling body, UEFA, fails to sell the rights in package 4 within one
week after the draw for the group stage of the UEFA Champions League, UEFA
loses its exclusive right to sell them. After this cut-off date both the football clubs
holding the live TV rights to the matches in question also have an opportunity to
sell those rights (referred to as package 5 in the rights segmentation table) on a
non-exclusive basis in competition with UEFA.

(188)    However, UEFA's rights segmentation means that the football clubs are restricted
to selling the residual live TV rights to pay-TV or pay-per-view broadcasters. The
Commission considers that this is a restriction imposed on the football clubs,
which is not indispensable for the attainment of the objectives set out in Article
81(3) of the Treaty and Article 53(3) of the EEA Agreement. Once the joint selling body has proven inefficient in selling the residual rights in question at the cut-
off date it cannot be considered indispensable to the proper operation of the joint
selling arrangement and to the attainment of the resulting benefits that the football
clubs are prevented from selling those rights to free-TV broadcasters where there
is no reasonable offer from any pay-TV broadcaster. This would be likely to occur
in territories where there are no pay-TV/pay-per-view broadcasters or where the
existing pay-TV/pay-per-view broadcasters have already satisfied their demand
with the Gold or Silver rights packages.

(189)    This decision should therefore be made subject to the condition that, to the extent
there is no reasonable offer from any pay-TV/pay-per-view broadcaster, the restriction imposed by the joint selling arrangement under package 5 in the rights
segmentation table, aimed at preventing football clubs from selling their live TV
rights to free-TV broadcasters, shall not apply.

(190)    The embargoes that are imposed on the exploitation of deferred media rights and
which apply equally to rights sold jointly by UEFA as well as the rights sold individually by the football clubs, are indispensable to enhance focus on the league
product and in particular the highlights product[658] covering the UEFA Champions
League in its entirety. The embargoes contribute to creating a product for which
there is much viewer interest and to establishing the reputation of the UEFA
Champions League brand, which is closely associated with uniform and high quality TV coverage underpinned by a homogeneous presentation, which affects the
acceptance by the viewer. As regards the embargoes imposed on the exploitation
of the Internet rights, the need to maintain such embargoes for quality reasons
will, of course, change over time with the development of Internet technologies.

(191)    Moreover, football clubs exploiting UEFA Champions League footage individually must present the footage in a club-focused manner and relating only to action
in which they are participating. Football clubs or bodies to whom they cede their
media rights are not allowed to package the rights from several football clubs into
a single product which would appear as an alternative UEFA Champions League
branded product. In particular regarding live TV rights, such a product is defined

---

[657] Package 5 of the rights segmentation table.
[658] Package 3 of the rights segmentation table.

as one consisting of more than two live UEFA Champions League matches per match day. Regarding delayed TV rights and Internet rights, UEFA would accept programmes containing 100% UEFA Champions League content on a club channel. However, UEFA defines a UEFA Champions League branded programme as one presented as a club magazine programme which contains more than 50% UEFA Champions League content. In general programming, the maximum permissible UEFA Champions League could amount to 30% of the programme. Where an entire match is shown on a delayed basis (that is to say, the full 90 minutes) on a club magazine programme then the 50% rule would not apply and the programme could consist mostly or entirely of that single match. Similarly, if a whole match were to be broadcast in general programming on a channel then the 30% rule would not apply in that situation

(192) The Commission accepts that provisions regulating the possibilities for third parties to bundle media rights sold by the individual football clubs are indispensable to preserve the integrity and branding of the jointly sold UEFA Champions League media rights. However, following receipt of the comments in reply to the notice published pursuant to Article 19(3) of Regulation No 17, the Commission requested clarifications of the rules, which lead to a reduction of their scope and intensity. It therefore has become possible for a single broadcaster to exploit two individually sold live matches contemporaneously. The Commission considers that opening up this possibility is likely to render the impact of the restriction so marginal that it will not be felt by the end-users of the rights, the broadcasters, as the rights available for any single broadcaster would be sufficient to satisfy existing demand from broadcasters for this type of residual matches. Likewise, regarding deferred rights, it has become possible to broadcast a whole match irrespective of the definition of a UEFA Champions League branded programme.

## 7.4. No elimination of competition

(193) Commercial rights are available from a number of football tournaments which fall within the scope of the relevant markets. For example, according to UEFA, the TV rights of UEFA Champions League represent on average only 20% of the rights in the relevant market. Since new media rights affect emerging markets, it is not yet possible to ascertain the position of the UEFA Champions League content in those markets. However, it is not likely to be more significant than its position in the traditional TV rights markets. The media rights of the UEFA Champions League are therefore just one possibility for media operators wishing to acquire content concerning football events taking place regularly throughout every year.

(194) Moreover, jointly sold media rights of the UEFA Champions League are split up into several different rights packages, which are offered for sale in a competitive bidding procedure open to all interested media operators. This allows several media operators to acquire media rights of the UEFA Champions League from UEFA.

(195) Finally both UEFA and the football clubs sell certain categories of UEFA Champions League media rights on a non-exclusive basis. Interested buyers therefore have several possible sources of supply from the owners of such rights.

(196) The joint selling of the media rights of the UEFA Champions League by UEFA is therefore unlikely to eliminate competition in respect of a substantial part of the media rights in question.

## 7.5. Conclusion

(197) In the light of the foregoing, it can be concluded that the cumulative conditions of

Article 81(3) of the Treaty and Article 53(3) of the EEA Agreement are fulfilled and an exemption can therefore be granted in respect of the joint selling arrangement.

## 8. CONDITIONS AND DURATION OF EXEMPTION

(198) Under Article 8(1) of Regulation No 17, conditions may be attached to a declaration of exemption. In this case, the clause of the joint selling arrangement preventing football clubs from individually selling live TV rights to free-TV broadcasters is a restriction on competition which does not satisfy all the conditions of Article 81(3) of the Treaty and Article 53(3) of the EEA Agreement. Such a restriction cannot be considered as improving the production or distribution of goods or promoting technical or economic progress, while allowing consumers a fair share of the resulting benefit, and not imposing on the undertakings concerned restrictions which are not indispensable to the attainment of those objectives.

(199) The exemption should therefore be subject to the condition that football clubs must not be prevented from selling their live TV rights to free-TV broadcasters where there is no reasonable offer from any pay-TV broadcaster. The Commission considers that no reasonable offer would exist, in particular, when there is no offer from any pay-TV broadcaster, which is comparable to the offer from the free-TV broadcaster.

(200) Pursuant to Article 8(1) of Regulation No 17, a decision in application of Article 81(3) of the Treaty and Article 53(3) of the EEA Agreement is to be issued for a specified period. The notified joint selling arrangement works with cycles of contract periods of three years. It is therefore appropriate to define the duration of this exemption accordingly and to let the joint selling arrangement operate for two contract periods. Exemption should therefore be granted pursuant to Article 8(1) of Regulation No 17 from 13 May 2002, the date of notification of the last version of the joint selling arrangement, until 31 July 2009.

## 9. CONCLUSION

(201) It is concluded that UEFA's joint selling arrangement leads to the improvement of production and distribution by creating a quality branded league focused product sold via a single point of sale. Moreover consumers receive a real fair share of the benefits deriving from it. Furthermore, the restrictions inherent in UEFA's joint selling arrangement are indispensable for achieving these benefits, save for the provision prohibiting individual football clubs from selling live TV rights to free-TV broadcasters. Finally, it is concluded that the joint selling of the media rights to the UEFA Champions League by UEFA is unlikely to eliminate competition in respect of a substantial part of the media rights in question. It is therefore appropriate to grant an exemption pursuant to Article 81(3) of the Treaty and Article 53(3) of the EEA Agreement, subject to a condition,

**Has Adopted this Decision:**

**Article 1**

1. Pursuant to Article 81(3) of the Treaty and Article 53(3) of the EEA Agreement, the provisions of Article 81(1) of the Treaty and Article 53(1) of the EEA Agreement are declared inapplicable from 13 May 2002 until 31 July 2009 to the amended version of UEFA's joint selling arrangement in respect of the media rights to the UEFA Champions League, as described in this Decision.

2. The exemption in paragraph 1 shall be subject to compliance with the condition

that the restriction prohibiting football clubs from selling live TV rights to free-TV broadcasters shall not apply where there is no reasonable offer from any pay-TV broadcaster.

**Article 2**
On the basis of the facts in its possession there are no grounds under Article 81(1) of the Treaty and Article 53(1) of the EEA Agreement for action by the Commission in respect of UEFA's joint selling arrangement for sponsorship, suppliership and IPR licensing relating to the UEFA Champions League.

**Article 3**
This Decision is addressed to:
Union des Associations Européennes de Football Route de Genève, 46 1260 Nyon 2 Switzerland

Done at Brussels, 23 July 2003.
For the Commission
Mario Monti
Member of the Commission

———

**\* 2.4.102. NEW MARKETING SYSTEM FOR BUNDESLIGA BROADCASTING RIGHTS, 24 JULY 2003**[659]

———

**\* 2.4.103. ANSWER ON BEHALF OF THE COMMISSION TO WRITTEN QUESTION E-2260/03 BY MARGRIETUS VAN DEN BERG (PSE), 22 AUGUST 2003**[660] **\***

Subject: European licensing system for professional football clubs

———

**\* 2.4.104. ANSWER ON BEHALF OF THE COMMISSION TO WRITTEN QUESTION E-2671/03 BY TOINE MANDERS (ELDR), 17 OCTOBER 2003**[661] **\***

Subject: Action Plan for European Professional Football

———

**2.4.105. NOTICE PUBLISHED PURSUANT TO ARTICLE 19(3) OF COUNCIL REGULATION NO 17 IN CASE COMP/C.2/37.214 – JOINT SELLING OF THE MEDIA RIGHTS TO THE GERMAN BUNDESLIGA, 30 OCTOBER 2003**[662]

**1.    THE NOTIFICATION**

1.    On 25 August 1998 the German Football Federation (Deutsche Fußballbund

---

[659] IP/03/1106.
[660] Question of 27-6-2003; question not yet published in the OJ.
[661] Question of 27-8-2003; question not yet published in the OJ.
[662] OJ C 261, 30-10-2003, p. 13-15 (Text with EEA relevance).

(DFB)) applied for negative clearance or, failing this, an individual exemption under Article 81(3) of the EC Treaty in respect of the joint selling (or central marketing) of television and radio broadcasting rights and rights to other technical forms of exploitation[663] for matches in the first and second national football divisions ('Bundesliga' and '2. Bundesliga' respectively).

2.      DFB is the German national football association. The League Association ('Ligaverband') is a member of the DFB. The members of the League Association are the professional clubs and companies in the first and second divisions ('the clubs'). The DFL (German Football League) conducts the operational business of its only shareholder, the League Association. Following the original notification, the DFB's application has been amended several times on account of internal structural reform and the setting-up of the League Association in 2001. The League Association adopted the DFB's amended notification as its own on 19 February 2003.

3.      According to the DFB's articles of incorporation, the League Association is entitled to organise the professional league football competitions leased by the DFB and to exploit them exclusively in its own name[664]. This prevents the clubs, which are at least coowners of the broadcasting rights, from making independent commercial use of those rights.

4.      The firm Infront Buli GmbH (Infront), still trading as BULI Vermarktungs GmbH (BULI), acquired almost all of the centrally sold rights by contract signed on 28 June 2002. At the time, BULI was a subsidiary of KirchMedia GmbH and Co. KGaA. It is no longer part of the Kirch group and its shares are now held by independent investors. As owner of the rights, Infront grants sublicences for television and other types of coverage of league matches.

5.      The notified arrangement is permissible under German domestic law[665].

6.      After the originally notified arrangement was published, the Commission received comments from a number of third parties. The German and United Kingdom competition authorities took the view that central marketing constituted a restriction of competition and was not essential for club solidarity. Some of the larger clubs shared this view. However, the associations argued that only the notified arrangement allowed overall representation of the sports competition, its effective marketing and the necessary solidarity between clubs. Television broadcasters essentially agreed, stressing that they as users were interested in acquiring broadcasting rights for all matches, and that this would be more difficult if the rights were sold individually. A similar view was taken by sports-rights agents, which also felt that there was no distortion of competition on the other side of the market and no ap-

---

[663] The joint selling right covers all types of broadcasting right: free-TV, pay-TV and pay-per-view TV terrestrial broadcasting, cable or satellite broadcasting; live or deferred broadcasting; showing of the entire event, of extracts or of compiled highlights; and radio. It also covers rights for all kinds of existing and future technical facilities such as UMTS, the internet or business-TV.

[664] The marketing of international club competitions is not covered. The selling of rights to UEFA Champions League games is thus covered by the decision of 23-7-2003 on the joint selling of the media rights of the UEFA Champions League on an exclusive basis (IP/03/1105).

[665] Under Section 31 of the German Law against Restraints of Competition, Section 1 of the same Law, which prohibits anticompetitive agreements, does not apply to the central marketing of rights to television broadcasting of sports competitions organised according to by-laws, by sports associations which, in the performance of their socio-political responsibilities, are committed also to promoting youth and amateur sports activities and which fulfil this commitment by allocating an adequate share of the income from the central marketing of these television rights.

preciable effect on trade within the meaning of Article 81(1) of the EC Treaty.

7.    In the Commission's view, the central marketing system in place to date is incompatible with Article 81. It restricts competition on the upstream market for the acquisition of television rights for football matches played regularly and the corresponding rights for mobile telecommunications and internet broadcasting. It also restricts competition on the downstream television markets for free-TV and pay-TV and on the downstream markets where mobile telecommunications and internet providers compete for customers. Under the existing system, the first- and second-division clubs have no right to exploit their German football league games or to act as independent suppliers. Moreover, central marketing, together with the exclusive selling of all rights to one broadcaster, means that only a few broadcasters, or other content users have a chance of participating in the market.

8.    The total exclusion of the clubs from marketing their matches is not necessary to achieve efficiency gains for content providers and clubs or other benefits of joint selling on media markets. Moreover, the duration and extent of the exclusive rights granted to date by the DFB/League Association to a single broadcaster cancel out any possible benefits. They strengthen the tendencies towards concentration in the media industry. The arrangement as originally notified also acts as a barrier to the development of football coverage via the new media, such as the internet and mobile telecommunications. Bundling together the sale of television rights and the sale of rights in respect of the new media discourages broadcasters from fully developing the markets in the new media because they wish to protect their traditional branch of business.

9.    In these circumstances, the League Association and the DFL presented the Commission on 10 June 2003 with a new plan which significantly amends the originally notified arrangement. In future, the League Association will market centrally packages of broadcasting rights under established and transparent rules. In addition, clubs will be able to sell certain rights individually. The Commission has come to the provisional conclusion that the new arrangement allays its concerns.

## 2.    NEW MARKETING MODEL PROPOSED BY THE PARTIES

### 2.1.    Central marketing

2.1.1.  Award procedures

10.    The rights will be offered in several packages via a transparent and non-discriminatory procedure. The public invitation to tender will be published four weeks before the start of the procedure. Tenderers will then have a further four weeks within which to bid for one or more packages. The rights will be awarded by the League Association or an authorised independent agent. An arbitration panel will be set up to handle disputes over the award procedure. The contracts to be concluded with the agent and the sublicence holders may not cover more than three seasons.

2.1.2.  Television

11.    Live broadcasts of first- and second-division matches will be offered in two packages. Package 1 includes the main match days of the two leagues (Saturday and Sunday), which can be broadcast in parallel and in full. Package 2 covers the other match days for both leagues (Sunday and Friday) with possible parallel broadcasting in full. Both packages also entitle the successful bidder to broadcast matches on the other days through a conference channel and can, in addition, include the right to deferred first-highlights coverage on pay-TV.

12.    A third package comprises live broadcasting rights to at least two first-division matches and to deferred first-highlights coverage on free-TV. A fourth package covers live second-division matches as well as deferred first-highlights coverage on free-TV. Secondary and tertiary exploitation rights are offered in a fifth package. Packages 3 to 5 can be awarded to several operators.

2.1.3.  Internet, mobile communications and other
13.    Package 6 covers live and/or deferred internet broadcasting of first- and second-division matches, in the form of extracts or in full. The right to deferred exploitation (without priority) is also included. This package will be specified in more detail by the League Association in the tender procedure and can be awarded to several operators. A seventh package comprises deferred highlights coverage and can also be awarded to several operators.

14.    Package 8 comprises live and/or near-live and/or deferred broadcasting rights for first- and/or second-division matches via mobile phones, whether in the form of extracts or in full. This package will be specified in more detail by the League Association in the tender procedure and can be awarded to several mobile communications operators. In this case, the League Association can ensure that the offers are mutually consistent as regards content. Package 9 comprises deferred mobile phone broadcasting rights in respect of extracts of first- and/or second-division matches.

15.    All other media rights not covered by packages 1 to 9 or by the exploitation rights of the clubs are combined in a further package that includes audio and moving picture rights for public productions, advertising and production of picture/sound carriers for end consumers (video, CD, DVD) and for computer-aided game and player analysis. This package can be awarded to several operators with variations in content.

## 2.2.    Rights marketed by the clubs
Under the new system, the clubs have the following exploitation rights.

2.2.1.  Television
16.    Every club can sell its home games to a free-TV broadcaster 24 hours after the match for one-off free-TV broadcasting of the full match.

2.2.2.  Internet, mobile telecommunications and other
17.    Every club can show a summary (not more than 30 minutes) of its home and away matches on its own internet website two hours after the end of the match. After 24 hours, the entire match can be shown. In the case of audio reporting via the internet, clubs can provide live, full coverage of home and away matches. Internet exploitation can also be assigned exclusively to a third party by way of 'outsourcing', but the presentation of the matches must be recognisably linked to the club.

18.    Every club can sell to a mobile communications provider the rights to coverage of its home matches on mobile networks within the EEA. During a match, an unlimited number of one-minute deferred clips are allowed. Up to two hours after the end of the match, two-minute clips may be transmitted. After two hours, the entire match can be broadcast via mobile phone.

19.    Every club can sell unlimited rights to freely receivable radio coverage of its home matches after the end of the game. Live coverage may not exceed ten minutes per half.

20.     Clubs are also entitled to show limited moving picture coverage of their own matches (the match in progress or past matches) in the stadium (ten seconds of pre-goal play per goal during the match; three minutes of past play from the match in progress; three minutes from other matches in the current season). In addition, they are entitled to use moving picture material for advertising (30 seconds per match, where this does not interfere with the rights of other clubs or players), club-related picture/sound carriers (video, CD, DVD) for end-consumers or for their own computer-aided game and player analysis.

2.2.3.  Rules for individual selling
21      The above rights may not be sold in such a way as to allow a user to produce a product which runs counter to the interests of the DFB and the League Association or of the holders of rights packages 1 to 9 in a uniform product or which undermines the benefits of branding and central marketing (one-stop shop). Where clubs individually sell exploitation rights, therefore, they may not bundle together more than two matches. For the same reason, coverage of a league match based on rights sold by the clubs may not exceed 30% of the total coverage of a programme. However, if the coverage is broadcast via a club's broadcasting platform ('club-TV'), 100% of the programme can be league-related. If club matches are broadcast via the platform of a third party (e.g. 'Club-TV Magazine' or 'Club-Radio Show'), league coverage can take up 50% of the programme.

## 2.3.   No unused rights
22.     According to the parties' amended proposal, unused rights may be exploited by the clubs. However, the league association remains entitled to parallel, non-exclusive marketing of the corresponding package.
        –   This applies when the League Association has failed to sell certain rights covered by the joint selling procedure. If, on completion of the fourth fixture of the season, no agreement has been concluded with a user for one of the above packages as defined, the clubs themselves, from the fifth fixture until the end of the season, may exploit the rights from the unused package in respect of their home games. The conditions outlined in Section 2.2.3 must be met.
        –   Clubs are also entitled to sell rights where the holder of those rights, for no objective reason, fails to use them, i.e. where on more than two match days in a season he does not exploit the number of matches allocated to him or does not do so in the form (live, near live, deferred) or to the extent laid down. The rights holder must immediately inform the League Association so that the clubs can be informed and use their rights.

## 2.4.   Transitional phase
23.     The amendments relating to television will enter into force on 1 July 2006. All other amendments will apply from 1 July 2004. These transitional phases will allow successive account to be taken of competition concerns, without interfering with the smooth operation of the first and second divisions of the Bundesliga.
24.     The licensing agreements to be concluded are not covered by the marketing model outlined above. The Commission reserves the rights to scrutinise them separately in the light of Community law, especially if several of the centrally marketed packages comprising exclusive rights are acquired in combination by a single operator.

## 3. THE COMMISSION'S INTENTIONS

25. The amended arrangement is likely to bring benefits for consumers which out-weigh the competition concerns. The Commission therefore intends to take a favourable view of the amended arrangement notified. However, before doing so, it invites interested third parties to submit their comments within one month of the publication of this notice to the following address, quoting the reference 'Case No 37.214 − Joint selling of the media rights to the German Bundesliga': European Commission Directorate-General for Competition

---

## * 2.4.106. COMMISSION REACHES PROVISIONAL AGREEMENT WITH FA PREMIER LEAGUE AND BSKYB OVER FOOTBALL RIGHTS, 16 DECEMBER 2003[666]

---

## 2.4.107. EUROPEAN COMMISSION [ENIC/ UEFA] [NO DATE]

Brussels,
D(2002) /ENIC plc

For the attention of
[...]

**Subject: Case COMP/37 806: ENIC/ UEFA**

Dear Sir,

### I. Introduction

1. [...]
2. On 18 February 2000, you lodged a complaint pursuant to Article 3(2) of Regulation 17/62 against the 'Union des Associations Européennes de Football' (UEFA) as regards its rule on 'Integrity of the UEFA Club competitions: Independence of clubs' (the UEFA rule). The UEFA rule was the subject of a communication[667] made pursuant to Article 19(3) of Council Regulation 17/62, concerning a request by UEFA for negative clearance or for exemption pursuant to Article 81(3). Your complaint challenges the compatibility of the UEFA rule with Articles 81 and 82 of the EC Treaty.
3. On 23 January 2002, Mr. Pons on behalf of Mr. Schaub informed you that the Commission, according to Article 6 of Regulation (EC) 2842/98 of 22 December 1998[668] intended to consider that there were insufficient grounds for acting on your application.
4. This preliminary conclusion was in particular based on the fact that the Commission considers that the contested rule seems to be inherent to the very existence of the UEFA clubs competitions and does not lead to a limitation on the freedom of action of clubs and investors that goes beyond what is necessary to ensure its legitimate aim of protecting the uncertainty of the results and giving the public the

---

[666] IP/03/1748.
[667] Published on 17-12-1999, OJ C 363.
[668] OJ L 354, 30-12-1998, p.18.

right perception as to the integrity of the UEFA competitions with a view to ensure their proper functioning. Thus, the rule cannot be qualified as a restriction of competition and therefore falls outside the scope of Article 81(1) of the EC Treaty. Furthermore, in adopting the rule UEFA does not appear to have abused any possible dominant position.

5.    By letter of 15 March 2002, you submitted a reply to the Article 6 letter. Your reply focuses upon the following claims:

    (1)    The object of the contested rule is in fact to distort competition. The Commission makes no reference to an UEFA internal memorandum attached as annex 22 to the complaint. An important motive for UEFA in introducing the rule was to maintain its grip on the economic activities.

    (2)    ENIC produced body of evidence that the public will not perceive a risk of match-fixing if clubs sharing a common owner meet in competition. More over from an economic point of view it will be unwise to fix matches.

    (3)    The rule has negative effects as shown in the NERA report attached to the complaint. The rule has led to a reduction in investment in small and medium size clubs.

    (4)    The rule goes beyond what is necessary to achieve any legitimate objectives. There is no consideration, in the Article 6 letter of the nature or the scope of the rule and of the concept of control it defines and no analysis of possible alternatives.

    (5)    ENIC considers that Article 82 applies in this case.

## II. THE FACTS

### 1. The parties

6.    UEFA is a confederation of FIFA that has the responsibility to promote football in Europe and to organise and conduct international competitions and international tournaments at European level. UEFA currently consists of 51 member associations, eighteen of which are located inside the territory of the European Union (one per Member State except in the United Kingdom where there exist four).

7.    ENIC plc is a public limited company, listed on the London Stock Exchange. It consists of three divisions: entertainment, sport and media. ENIC currently owns stakes in five clubs – Glasgow Rangers FC in Scotland (25,1%), FC Basel in Switzerland (50%), Vicenza Calcio in Italy (99,9%), Slavia Praga in the Czech Republic (96,7%), AEK Athens in Greece (47%) and recently in Tottenham Hotspur in England (29.9%). Its Media arm has also been involved in sports, namely through the delivery of betting services.

### 2. The UEFA rule

8.    The rule establishes that:

    (1) *no club* participating in a UEFA club competition may, either directly or indirectly:

        (a)    Hold or deal in the securities or shares of any other club, or

        (b)    Be a member of any other club, or

        (c)    Be involved in any capacity whatsoever in the management, administration and/or sporting performance of any other club, or

        (d)    Have any power whatsoever in the management, administration and/or sporting performance of any other club.

    (2) *no person* may at the same time, either directly or indirectly be involved in any capacity whatsoever in the management, administration and/or sporting performance of more than one club participating in the same UEFA competition. And

(3) In the case of two or more clubs which are under common control, only one may participate in the same UEFA club competition. In this connection, an individual or legal entity has control of a club where he/she/it

    (a)    Holds a majority of the shareholders' voting rights, or

    (b)    Has the right to appoint or remove a majority of the members of the administrative, management or supervisory body, or

    (c)    Is a shareholder and alone controls a majority of the shareholders' voting rights pursuant to an agreement entered into with other shareholders of the club in question.

9.    The rule provides for selection criteria to apply when two or more clubs under common control are put forward to play in a UEFA competition. The rule was adopted by the UEFA Executive Committee on 19 May 1998 and on 24 November 1998. An Extraordinary Conference of the Presidents of UEFA Member associations unanimously adopted a Resolution in which the associations confirmed their 'unqualified support for the UEFA rule and the sporting principles which underline it'.

### 3. The complaint: ENIC arguments

*ENIC's legitimate interest*

10.    ENIC justifies its legitimate interest in lodging the complaint because it has been directly and materially affected by the operation of the UEFA rule and it is likely to continue to suffer irreparable damage in the future.

*The relevant market and some ancillary markets*

11.    In support of its complaint, ENIC defines the relevant market as the market for capital investment in football clubs in Europe. It also identifies a number of other ancillary markets in which, allegedly, the UEFA rule actually or potentially produces appreciable restrictions and distortions of competition. According to ENIC the first market is characterised on the demand side by football clubs seeking capital and/or investment and on the supply side by individuals or corporations interested in investing in a European football club. Football clubs are competing in this market for access to capital. ENIC seems here to rely on the market definition followed by the Court of Arbitration for Sport (CAS) in its arbitral award dated 20 August 1999 in Case CAS 98/200 − AEK Athens and Slavia Prague v UEFA but the demand side for ENIC is the supply side for CAS and vice-versa. In fact, the relevant market defined by the CAS is 'the market for ownership interests in football clubs capable of taking part in UEFA competitions' which includes in the supply side the potential sellers of ownership interests (point 133). CAS considered this narrow market 'because of the peculiarities of the football sector, investment in football clubs does not appear to be interchangeable with investments in other businesses, or even in other leisure businesses' (point 135).

12.    However, in a report prepared by National Economic Research Associates (NERA) which ENIC sent to the Commission in December 2000 to further clarify the market definition, it is argued that whether the UEFA rule distorts competition in the market for the supply of capital to football clubs 'for the purposes of assessing the competitive impact of the rule' the relevant market should be defined as 'the supply of club football in the EU' without giving details about the definition of such a market.

13.    The ancillary markets are, according to ENIC: the market for players; the sponsorship market; the football merchandising market; the media rights market and the market for gate revenues.

*The UEFA rule does not fall outside Article 81(1) of the Treaty, rather it violates Article 81(1) and does not fulfil the conditions of 81(3)*

14.     ENIC stresses that the UEFA rule is not a rule of the game, for example one defining the number of players in a team or the size or the shape of the ball. Even if the UEFA rule is purely concerned with non-economic activities, given its clear economic impact it cannot fall within the so-called 'sporting exception', confirmed by the case law of the Court of Justice with regard to the Treaty's provisions on the free movement of persons and services.

15.     On the basis of the arguments below, ENIC sustains that the introduction and the maintenance in force of the UEFA rule infringes Articles 81 of the EC Treaty because it is a decision of an association of undertakings which appreciably restricts and distorts competition in the market for capital investment in football clubs and in a number of ancillary markets. The rule both actually and potentially prevents, restricts and distorts competition by: (1) preventing and restricting investment in European clubs; (2) changing the nature, intensity and patterns of competition between commonly-controlled clubs and those having other ownership structures; (3) enhancing the economic imbalance between football clubs leading to increasing market dominance of a few clubs over the majority of smaller and medium sized clubs with the result of decreasing uncertainty in the outcome of the matches. Furthermore, in the market for players, clubs excluded from UEFA competitions will lose a competitive edge on the transfer market and will be deprived of reputation and substantial revenues needed to retain and attract top class players. Similarly, the loss of opportunity to participate in UEFA competitions will have an economic impact on gate revenues and on sponsorship, merchandising and media rights arrangements.

16.     In ENIC's opinion, even if these restrictions were indispensable for attaining the legitimate objectives pursued they would not be proportionate and therefore they could not escape the application of Article 81(1) of the Treaty. ENIC states that the UEFA *a priori* assumption that multi-ownership increases the risk of match fixing or creates such a perception was not demonstrated by any evidence and therefore there is no objective justification for the rule. The 'dominant purpose of the UEFA rule was to preserve UEFA's monopoly control over European football competitions'[669]. Even if there was a public perception issue to be addressed, the absolute prohibition for commonly owned teams competing in the same competition is not the least restrictive means to protect concerns arising from public perception. A clear example of a less restrictive alternative would be a regulatory system which would allow the football regulator to analyse a specific common-owned club's participation in a competition on a case by case basis, allowing scrutiny of all interests. For instance, one solution could be the common owner taking no further part in the administration of one of the clubs until the participation of both clubs in the competition comes to an end. Therefore, ENIC stresses that the rule does not fulfil the criteria for an exemption set out in Article 81(3) because it is disproportionate to any legitimate aim which it may seek to address and is neither necessary nor appropriate to achieve the aims of preserving sporting integrity and uncertainty of outcome of matches and as such is not indispensable to the achievement of certain pro-competitive objectives.

---

[669]   In support of this allegation ENIC makes reference to its annex 22 of the complaint which is an internal UEFA memorandum of 25 February 1998 where some doubts were expressed *inter alia* about the probability of a media group to take advantage of ENIC's groundwork and create a European league with the ENIC clubs.

17.　A report prepared by Deloitte & Touche, produced before the CAS and another one prepared by NERA contain further discussion of the possible direct and indirect effects of the UEFA rule. They stress on one hand the advantages of multi-club ownership as a key source of capital for clubs which significantly improves sporting success and commercial activity. On the other hand they focus on the restrictions and distortions of competition resulting from the UEFA rule on the 'European market for professional football', which is not the same market as defined in the complaint, and on the ancillary markets (the same as identified in the complaint). The restrictions on investors and on clubs are described in a similar way as in the complaint.

*The rule violates Article 82 of the Treaty*

18.　Moreover, ENIC argues that UEFA has abused its dominant position in the Common Market, contrary to Article 82 by introducing a rule that is without sufficient objective basis to justify its anti-competitive effect. UEFA is the only body that organises European competitions and therefore holds a dominant position in the European football market and in other ancillary football markets. Equally, UEFA and its member associations – which themselves normally enjoy monopoly power in their respective countries – enjoy joint dominance by virtue of their economic links and in particular through the obligation of those member associations to comply with the UEFA Statutes, regulations and decisions made under them. This position of dominance and the ability to control entry in competitions requires UEFA and its member associations to show that the rules they adopt are objectively justified, precise and non-discriminatory in application, necessary and proportionate to the aims thought to be achieved. The contested rule constitutes an abuse of dominant position because it restricts competition, is an unnecessary and disproportionate means of achieving the objective of protecting the integrity of UEFA competitions and unfairly discriminates between clubs, placing those which have common owners at a competitive disadvantage.

*Summary of ENIC's arguments*

19.　To sum up according to ENIC, the UEFA rule cannot be qualified as a sporting rule and it appreciably restricts investment in European football clubs' stocks which has an economic impact not only in the relevant market but also in some ancillary markets. This restriction cannot be exempted because it is not indispensable to attain the legitimate aim of avoiding the risk of match fixing or of creating such a perception. The UEFA rule constitutes also an abuse of a dominant position because it restricts competition and it is not proportionate to the objective of protecting the integrity of UEFA competitions.

**4. UEFA comments on the complaint**

20.　UEFA considers, as it states in the notification, that 'the rule at issue is a valid sporting rule which is not covered by the competition provisions of the EC Treaty'. According to UEFA the contested rule is inherent in the nature of sport and does not violate either the competition provisions or the free movement provisions of the EC Treaty. Contrary to ENIC, UEFA argues that even if a rule has economic consequences it still can fall outside Article 81(1) of the Treaty and therefore can be covered by a 'sporting exception', provided it is necessary for the organisation of sport or it can be justified on non-economic (sporting) grounds. Thus, UEFA's claim is that an analogy with the case law relating to the free move-

ment of persons and services should be made. In support of its position UEFA refers to the CAS arbitral award above mentioned and to the Lehtonen[670] and
Deliège[671] judgements of the Court of Justice.

21. The UEFA statement that the rule at issue is necessary to meet the public believe
that the teams are really trying to win and therefore is 'inherent in the nature of
sports' was confirmed by the CAS when it stated that 'the crucial element of integrity in football is the public's perception of the authenticity of results' and that
'the most important requirement for football is not honesty in itself or authenticity
of results in itself but rather the public perception of such honesty and such authenticity'. According to the CAS 'it is not enough that competing athletes, coaches or managers are in fact honest; the public must perceive that they try their
best to win and, in particular, that clubs make management or coaching decisions
based on the single objective of their club winning against any other club. This
particular requirement is inherent in the nature of sports'.

22. UEFA concludes from the Lethonen and Deliège judgements that rules that are inherent in conduct and/or organisation of sporting events do not, in themselves, infringe Community law and that the responsibility in adopting such rules remains
that of the sporting organisations. Therefore, UEFA considers that it has the responsibility to take appropriate measures to protect the integrity of competition
without having 'a legal duty to divine the least restrictive alternative to protect integrity of competition'. In the views of UEFA, it is not either for the European
Commission to assess whether there are less restrictive alternatives, since that
would mean that the Commission would end up as the *de facto* regulator for sport.
UEFA recognises that the notified rule should be consistent with the principle of
proportionality but considers that 'this does not mean that the rule would be necessarily illegal in the sole event that somebody conceives a less restrictive alternative to achieve the same objective'.

23. Furthermore, UEFA stresses that the contested rule can neither provoke irreparable loss and damage on ENIC or other potential investors, nor does it have the
inevitable effect of deterring investors from making future investments in European football. UEFA supports this position by citing some statements of ENIC to
the press following the CAS arbitral award where ENIC confirmed 'its commitment to maintaining its position within the European sports community as this position is not dependent on the holding of majority interests in football clubs. Of the
five investments currently held only two holdings are in excess of 50%' and ENIC
affirmed that it 'continued maximising the value of the investments in the clubs'
which was evidenced by the recent acquisition of a significant shareholding in
AEK Athens[672]. UEFA states that there is no evidence to suggest that the rule has
impeded investment in football clubs. UEFA illustrates this statement with some
examples that show that corporate investment has continued in football clubs even
in countries where rules to protect the sporting integrity of the competition are
even more restrictive than the UEFA rule. In any case UEFA concludes that even
if the rule had such economic effects it could not nevertheless be declared illegal
because it is designed to protect the integrity of sporting competition and it is a
proportionate measure for the attainment of that goal. For UEFA it is a rule designed to prevent ' a clear conflict of interests situation occurring and goes to en-

---

[670] Case C-176/96 *Lehtonen* [2000] ECR.
[671] Joint cases C-51/96 and C-191/97 [2000] ECR.
[672] It should be added that ENIC has also since the complaint was lodged acquired a 29.9%
stake in the Premiership club Tottenham Hotspur.

sure that competition is genuine' and there was not an 'ulterior motive' for the adoption of the rule, contrary to what ENIC suggests.

24.    As to the alleged abuse of dominant position UEFA simply says that the adoption of a measure aiming to protect the integrity of competition cannot be qualified as abusive conduct. As to the less restrictive alternative means suggested by ENIC, UEFA sustains that they are not viable and refers to the CAS's opinion which considered the rule as proportionate to the aim of protecting public confidence in the authenticity of results and that it was not necessary to test the rule against any conceivable alternative because judges should not substitute for legislators.

## III. LEGAL ASSESSMENT

### 1. Applicability of Article 81(1) of the Treaty
*Undertakings or associations of undertakings*
25.    According to the Court of Justice, 'the concept of an undertaking encompasses every entity engaged in an economic activity, regardless of the legal status of the entity and the way it is financed'.[673]
26.    The practice of sport is subject to EC law only in so far as it is an economic activity[674]. Professional football clubs are undertakings within the meaning of Article 81(1) of the Treaty. A football club, through its team, supplies sporting entertainment by playing matches against other clubs, usually in the context of a championship. These events are made available against payment (admission fees and/or radio and television broadcasting rights, sponsorship, advertising, merchandising, etc.) on several markets. As clubs are engaged in economic activity and are undertakings within the meaning of Article 81(1) of the Treaty, it follows that national associations grouping clubs together may be considered associations of undertakings within the meaning of the same provision[675]. UEFA, which groups together national football associations at European level, is an association of associations of undertakings.[676] The fact that, as well as the professional clubs, a large number of amateur clubs also belong to the national associations makes no difference to their status as associations of undertakings or to UEFA's status as an association of associations of undertakings. UEFA can also be qualified as an undertaking for certain activities such as the organisation of European club competitions.

*Decision*
27.    The UEFA rule on 'Integrity of the UEFA club competitions: independence of clubs' is a decision taken by an association of associations of undertakings[677] within the meaning of Article 81(1) of the Treaty, as it was drawn up by UEFA Executive Committee.

---

[673]  Case C-41/90 *Höfner v Macroton* [1991] ECR I- 1979.

[674]  Case 36/74 *Walrave et al. v Association Union Cycliste Internationale et al* [1974] ECR 1405.

[675]  Case T-513/93 *CNSD v Commission,* [2000]ECR, paragraph 39

[676]  Case 71/74 *FRUBO* [1975]ECR, p.563. See also Opinion of Advocate-General Lenz in Case C-415/93,*URBSF v Bosman* [1995 ]ECR I-4921,paragraph 256; Commission Decision of 19-4-2001 relating to a proceeding pursuant to Article 81 of the EC Treaty and Article 53 of the EEA Agreement (Case 37.576 UEFA's broadcasting regulations) *Official Journal L 171 , of 26-06-2001 p .0012/0028.*

[677]  See Case T-25/95 *S.A. Cimenteries CBR v.Commission* [2000] ECR, paragraph 1325.

*Restriction of competition*

28.    In order to assess whether an agreement is caught by the prohibition contained in Article 81(1) of the Treaty it is necessary to consider whether, taking account of the economic context in which it is to be applied, its *object* or *effect* is to restrict or distort in an appreciable manner competition within the common market and whether it is possible to foresee with a sufficient degree of probability that it may have an influence – direct or indirect, actual or potential – on the pattern of trade between Member States[678].

29.    The *object* of the contested rule is not to distort competition. On the basis of the information in its possession the Commission considers that the main purpose of the rule is to protect the integrity of the competition and to avoid conflicts of interests that may arise from the fact that more than one club controlled by the same owner or managed by the same person play in the same competition. It is motivated by the need to protect integrity of sporting UEFA competitions. It aims to ensure the uncertainty of the outcome and to guarantee that the consumer has the perception that the games played represent honest sporting competition between the participants, as consumers may suspect that teams with a common owner will not genuinely compete.

30.    In your reply of 15 March, you stated that the Article 6 letter made no reference to certain sentences extracted from the UEFA internal memorandum attached as annex 22 to the complaint where you alleged that the object of the Rule was to preserve UEFA's lucrative marketing rights and control over pan-European competitions. This is not correct since there was a clear reference to this memorandum in the Article 6 letter in footnote 2. The memorandum in question amounts to the minute of a meeting between UEFA and ENIC where the latter presented its structure as well as its strategy and aims. After this presentation, there is a section about ENIC's and UEFA's discussion on multiple involvement in clubs versus clean competition. The memorandum goes on with the comments from UEFA on the pros and cons of ENIC's approach. The selection of quotations you mentioned in your reply are taken from the list of possible problems, risks and questions. The reading of the memorandum, contrary to what you argue, does not shows that the objective of UEFA is to preserve its position in the economic sphere, but that the main focus of the discussion was on *clean competition*.

31.    However, the simple fact that the UEFA rule may not have as its object a restriction of competition is not sufficient to consider that it falls outside of the scope of application of Article 81(1) of the Treaty. It is also necessary to assess whether the *effect* of the rule is restrictive and if so, whether this effect is inherent in the pursuit of the objective of the rule which is to ensure the very existence of credible pan European football competitions. The rule may limit the freedom to act of clubs or their owners.

32.    As the Court of Justice recently stated in the Wouters case[679], not every agreement between undertakings or any decision of an association of undertakings which restricts the freedom of action of the parties or of one of them necessarily falls within the prohibition laid down in Article [81(1)] of the Treaty. For the purposes of application of that provision to a particular case, account must first of all be taken of the overall context in which the decision of the association of undertakings was taken or produces its effects. More particularly, account must be taken of its objectives, which are here connected with the need to make rules relating to

---

[678] Case C-56-65, *Société Technique Minière* [1966] ECR, p. 337
[679] Case C-309/99, *Wouters*, judgment of 19-2-2002, ECR 2002, p. I-1577, points 97 and 110.

organisation, qualifications, professional ethics, supervision and liability, in order to ensure that the ultimate consumers of legal services and the sound administration of justice are provided with the necessary guarantees in relation to integrity and experience (see, to that effect, Case C-3/95 Reisebüro Broede [1996] ECR I-6511, paragraph 38). It has then to be considered whether the consequential effects restrictive of competition are inherent in the pursuit of those objectives. (...) a national regulation such as the 1993 Regulation adopted by a body such as the Bar of the Netherlands does not infringe Article [81(1)] of the Treaty, since that body could reasonably have considered that that regulation, despite the effects restrictive of competition that are inherent in it, is necessary for the proper practice of the legal profession, as organised in the Member State concerned.

33. Thus the question to answer in the present case is whether the consequential effects of the rule are inherent in the pursuit of the very existence of credible pan European football competitions. Taking into account the particular context in which the rule is applied, the limitation on the freedom to act that it entails is justified and cannot be considered as a restriction of competition. Without the UEFA rule, the proper functioning of the market where the clubs develop their economic activities would be under threat, since the public's perception that the underlying sporting competition is fair and honest is an essential precondition to keep its interest and marketability. If UEFA competitions were not credible and consumers did not have the perception that the games played represent honest sporting competition between the participants, the competitions would be devalued with the inevitable consequence over time of lower consumer confidence, interest and marketability. Without a solid sporting foundation, clubs would be less capable of extracting value from ancillary activities and investment in clubs would lose value.

34. In your reply of 15 March 2002, you firstly indicated that the rule has negative effects as shown in the NERA report attached to the complaint and the rule has led to a reduction in investment in small and medium size clubs. As previously mentioned, a rule may fall outside the scope of Article 81(1) despite possible negative effects that are inherent in it for the pursuit of an objective such as the integrity of pan European football competitions.

35. Moreover, the rule does not prevent capital investment in football clubs. It is limited to prohibiting more than one club with the same ownership, management or control from participating in the same UEFA competition. Accordingly, investors or managers remain free to take control of or manage whatever number of clubs they want if they accept the risk that should more than one of these clubs qualify for the same UEFA competition, only one would play. In addition, contrary to what ENIC stated UEFA confirmed that point 2 of the rule concerning the protection of integrity of the UEFA club competitions does not apply to accountants and auditors of the clubs provided they remain independent of the relevant clubs.

36. The *ratio* of the rule is manifest: if two or more clubs participating in the same contest are under control of or managed by one single entity, there is cause for concern that in a given situation the existence of opposing interests which underlies any sport competition will not be apparent. For instance, should two clubs under joint control or ownership meet at a certain stage of the competition, the public's perception of the authenticity of the result would be jeopardised. In the present case, for example, ENIC's business interests in the field of the provision of betting services could be seen by some as an obstacle to the development of fair competition on the pitch. Secondly, the UEFA rule does not limit the freedom of action of investors that have shares in clubs below the level that gives them con-

trol over the club, because clubs with such ownership structure remain free to play in the same UEFA competition. Thirdly, in some Member States national associations have adopted rules, even stricter than the UEFA rule, in order to attain the same objective. In England the mere holding of shares in another club would be prohibited. Even though the English rule provides for an exception if the Board of the League gave its written consent, in practice such an exception has never been granted. The Scottish, French, German, Spanish and Portuguese Leagues have rules designed to ensure that clubs remain independent. Accordingly, the UEFA rule seems to constitute a prolongation of the national rules and their natural corollary. In the United States, the four major League sports (Basket ball, American football, ice hockey and Base ball) all have similar provisions.

37. Fourthly, a voluntary code of conduct which you see as a less restrictive mean does not seem to be, in this particular context, an alternative to the contested rule. As there is a possibility that some clubs would not comply with it, there will be in the public a general suspicion that clubs with the same owner or manager do not play a fair game. In order to achieve the same aim its substance would have to be the same and it would have to be binding. Furthermore, any regulatory system which would allow the football regulator to analyse a specific common-owned club's participation on a case by case basis only, would not enable clubs (or spectators) to know in advance whether or not they would be likely or able to participate in a UEFA competition and would not be a workable alternative to the UEFA rule either. In addition, a case-by-case evaluation would by its very nature leave scope for discretion and it may be difficult for the governing body to disregard considerations, such as the significance of investments already made or the prestige of the clubs concerned, which would have no place in such an analysis.

38. In your reply of 15 March 2002 you stated that UEFA is about to introduce for the 2004/2005 season a system of auditing each club qualifying for UEFA competitions and therefore the case by case analysis of clubs ownership should be workable. However, it should be noted that responsibility for implementing the new Licensing System will be with each national football association, not with UEFA itself. The national associations act as 'licensors' and decide whether clubs have satisfied the licence conditions. Only in exceptional circumstances would UEFA take over the function of 'licensor' (for example, if a national association refused to comply with its obligations as licensor according to the UEFA licensing system). The UEFA Club Licensing System does not contain any common provisions concerning multiple ownership of clubs because various national associations in Europe have established their own national rules which deal with, *inter alia*, protecting sporting integrity and guarding against conflicts of interests. These national rules will remain valid. At the same time, UEFA's rule protecting the integrity of the UEFA club competitions remains a requirement (in addition to holding a valid club licence) which clubs must satisfy in order to be eligible to participate in a UEFA club competition. UEFA will verify that this rule has been complied with once clubs which have qualified for each of the three single UEFA club competitions (on the basis of their sporting performance) are known. UEFA cannot therefore examine issues of multiple ownership during the licensing process since at that time it will not be known whether a club has qualified for a UEFA club competition. Instead, it will be more logical and efficient for UEFA to examine this matter at the time when individual clubs are being admitted to the UEFA club competitions in question.

39. On the basis of the above, the limitation on the freedom to act therefore merely constitutes the effect of the application of a rule which is deemed necessary and

proportionate to the need to maintain the public's confidence in the fairness and authenticity of the game, the absence of which would have the effect of rendering, in the long term, any competition impossible.

40.     You also added that UEFA has shown a lack of concern in the past towards the public perception of football competitions in Europe and in particular in Greece where corruption and match-fixing would be widespread. The rule on multiple ownership does not have as objective to solve any outstanding issue on the integrity of football competitions in general, but to adress the specific issue of 'clean' football in pan European football competitions.

41.     Therefore, the rule cannot be qualified as a restriction of competition under Article 81(1) of the Treaty because its object is not to restrict competition and that the limitation of freedom of action of clubs and investors that it entails is inherent to the very existence of the UEFA competitions.

42.     In any case the rule does not seem to go beyond what is necessary to ensure its legitimate aim – to ensure the uncertainty of the outcome and to guarantee that the consumer has the perception that the games played represent honest competition between the participants with a view to ensure a proper functioning of the UEFA competitions and of the markets developed around them in order to keep fans and spectators interested in the sporting competition.

43.     In conclusion, taking into account the aim of the rule and its context, on the basis of a settled case-law[680] related to the application of Article 81(1) of the Treaty, the UEFA rule seems to fall outside Article 81(1) of the Treaty provided it is applied in an objective and non-discriminatory manner.

## 2. Applicability of Article 82 of the Treaty

44.     ENIC alleges that UEFA alone or jointly with national associations enjoys a dominant position both in the market for the organisation of the UEFA competitions and in other related markets.

45.     UEFA, which groups together national football associations at European level, is an association of associations of undertakings.

46.     If one were to assume that UEFA enjoys a dominant position in whatever market, the fact that UEFA has adopted such a rule does not appear to constitute in itself an abuse of dominant position. In your reply of 15 March, you stated that the rule is abusive in that it discriminates between clubs and because ENIC was faced with the choice of either one of its clubs being excluded or either being forced to sell part of its shareholding. There is no evidence that the rule in question is applied in a discriminatory manner to clubs liable to take part in competitions organised by UEFA.

47.     Contrary to your submission, there is no evidence that such a rule is disproportionate to its ends. On the basis of the facts and arguments known to the Commission at this time, it is not plausible that the use of a provision less stringent would achieve the aims which are sought by UEFA, i.e. to ensure that the sport is perceived by consumers as being honest (see paragraphs 33 and 34 above). The Commission therefore finds no evidence of any abuse of a dominant position.

## IV – CONCLUSION

48.     In conclusion the Commission considers that there are insufficient grounds for act-

---

[680] Case 26/76 *Metro v Commision*, [1977] ECR p. 1875, paragraphs 20-22, Case 161/84 *Pronuptia* [1986] ECR p. 353, paragraphs 14-27, Case T-112/99 *Metropole Television and others v Commission*, ECR 2001, p. II-2459, paragraphs 107.

ing on your complaint. This is based on the reasons mentioned above and which can be summarised as follows:

(a) The object of the contested rule (a decision by an association of associations of undertakings) is not to distort competition,

(b) Its possible effect on the freedom of action of clubs and investors is inherent to the very existence of credible UEFA competitions and,

(c) In any case, it does not lead to a limitation on the freedom of action of clubs and investors that goes beyond what is necessary to ensure its legitimate aim of protecting the uncertainty of the results and giving the public the right perception as to the integrity of the UEFA competitions with a view to ensure their proper functioning

Therefore the rule cannot be qualified as a restriction of competition and therefore falls outside the scope of Article 81(1) of the EC Treaty.

Furthermore the rule does not lead to the application of Article 82.

49.   For these reasons, I inform you that the final decision of the Commission is to reject your complaint of 18 February 2000 pursuant to Article 3 paragraph 2 of Council Regulation 17 of 6 February 1962.

50.   An action challenging this Decision may be brought before the Court of First Instance of the European Communities in accordance with Article 230 of the EC Treaty. Such actions shall not, pursuant to Article 242 of the EC Treaty, have suspensory effect unless the Court otherwise orders.

Yours faithfully

Done in Brussels,
For the Commission
Mario Monti
Member of the Commission

———

## 2.5.    CUSTOMS*

* 2.5.1.    EUROPEAN COURT OF JUSTICE, OPINION OF MR ADVOCATE GENERAL ROZÈS, GUSTAV SCHICKEDANZ KG V OBERFINANZDIREKTION FRANKFURT AM MAIN, CASE 298/82, 6 OCTOBER 1983[681]

———

* 2.5.2.    EUROPEAN COURT OF JUSTICE, JUDGMENT (FIRST CHAMBER), GUSTAV SCHICKEDANZ KG V OBERFINANZDIREKTION FRANKFURT AM MAIN, CASE 298/82, 5 APRIL 1984[682]

———

* 2.5.3.    EUROPEAN COURT OF JUSTICE, OPINION OF MR ADVOCATE GENERAL LENZ, SPORTEX GMBH & CO. V OBERFINANZDIREKTION HAMBURG, CASE 253/87, 4 MAY 1988[683]

———

* 2.5.4.    EUROPEAN COURT OF JUSTICE, JUDGMENT (FIRST CHAMBER), SPORTEX GMBH & CO. V OBERFINANZDIREKTION HAMBURG, CASE 253/87, 21 JUNE 1988[684]

———

* 2.5.5.    EUROPEAN COURT OF JUSTICE, OPINION OF ADVOCATE GENERAL ALBER, SKATTEMINISTERIET V SPORTGOODS A/S, CASE C-413/96 , 16 DECEMBER 1997[685]

———

* 2.5.6.    EUROPEAN COURT OF JUSTICE, JUDGMENT (FIFTH CHAMBER), SKATTEMINISTERIET AND SPORTGOODS A/S, CASE C-413/96, 24 SEPTEMBER 1998[686]

———

---

*    The full texts of documents which are marked with an asterisk (*) are not incorporated in the book itself, but are freely accessible on the website of the ASSER International Sports Law Centre, at <www.sportslaw.nl> – documentation.

[681] ECR 1984, p. 1840.
[682] ECR 1984, p. 1829.
[683] ECR 1988, p. 3351.
[684] ECR 1988, p. 3351.
[685] ECR 1998, p. I-5285.
[686] ECR 1998, p. I-5285.

# 2.6. DIPLOMAS*

**\* 2.6.1.** **EUROPEAN COURT OF JUSTICE, OPINION OF ADVOCATE GENERAL MANCINI, UNION NATIONALE DES ENTRAÎNEURS ET CADRES TECHNIQUES PROFESSIONNELS DU FOOTBALL (UNECTEF) V GEORGES HEYLENS AND OTHERS, CASE 222/86, 18 JUNE 1987[687]**

———

**\* 2.6.2.** **EUROPEAN COURT OF JUSTICE, JUDGMENT, UNION NATIONALE DES ENTRAÎNEURS ET CADRES TECHNIQUES PROFESSIONNELS DU FOOTBALL (UNECTEF) V GEORGES HEYLENS AND OTHERS, CASE 222/86, 15 OCTOBER 1987[688]**

———

**\* 2.6.3.** **ANSWER ON BEHALF OF THE COMMISSION TO WRITTEN QUESTION E-3176/95 BY SPALATO BELLERÉ (NI), AMEDEO AMADEO (NI) AND CRISTIANA MUSCARDINI (NI), 8 JANUARY 1995[689]**

Subject: Physiotherapists and sports masseurs

———

**\* 2.6.4.** **ANSWER ON BEHALF OF THE COMMISSION TO WRITTEN QUESTION E-3856/98 BY CRISTIANA MUSCARDINI (NI), 23 FEBRUARY 1999[690]**

Subject: Freedom of movement for sports coaches

———

**\* 2.6.5.** **ANSWER ON BEHALF OF THE COMMISSION TO WRITTEN QUESTION E-899/99 BY CRISTIANA MUSCARDINI (NI), 4 MAY 1999[691]**

Subject: Freedom of movement for sports coaches

———

---

   \* The full texts of documents which are marked with an asterisk (\*) are not incorporated in the book itself, but are freely accessible on the website of the ASSER International Sports Law Centre, at <www.sportslaw.nl> – documentation.
   [687] ECR 1987, p. 4097.
   [688] ECR 1987, p. 4097.
   [689] Question of 29-11-1995; OJ C 79, 18-3-1996, p. 56.
   [690] Question of 4-1-1999; OJ C 207, 21-7-1999, p. 136-137.
   [691] Question of 8-4-1999; OJ C 341, 29-11-1999, p. 148.

**\* 2.6.6     ANSWER ON BEHALF OF THE COMMISSION TO WRITTEN QUESTION E-3976/00 BY CRISTIANA MUSCARDINI (UEN), 27 FEBRUARY 2001**[692]

Subject: Monopoly in sports and recognition of diplomas in sports training

———

**\* 2.6.7.     ANSWER ON BEHALF OF THE COMMISSION TO WRITTEN QUESTION E-1424/01 BY CRISTIANA MUSCARDINI (UEN), 5 JULY 2001**[693]

Subject: Freedom to engage in sports professions

———

---

[692] Question of 20-12-2000; OJ C 174 E, 19-6-2001 p. 205-206.
[693] Question of 17-5-2001; OJ C 350 E, 11-12-2001, p. 152.

# 2.7.    DISCRIMINATION*

**\* 2.7.1.    EUROPEAN COURT OF JUSTICE, OPINION OF ADVOCATE GENERAL WARNER, B.N.O. WALRAVE AND L.J.N. KOCH V ASSOCIATION UNION CYCLISTE INTERNATIONALE, KONINKLIJKE NEDERLANDSCHE WIELREN UNIE AND FEDERACIÓN ESPAÑOLA CICLISMO, CASE 36-74, 24 OCTOBER 1974[694] \***

———

**2.7.2.    EUROPEAN COURT OF JUSTICE, JUDGMENT, B.N.O. WALRAVE AND L.J.N. KOCH V ASSOCIATION UNION CYCLISTE INTERNATIONALE, KONINKLIJKE NEDERLANDSCHE WIELREN UNIE ET FEDERACIÓN ESPAÑOLA CICLISMO, CASE 36-74, 12 DECEMBER 1974 [695]**

Reference for a preliminary ruling: Arrondissementsrechtbank Utrecht – Netherlands

to the Court under Article 177 of the EEC Treaty by the,
in the action pending before that court between

**Content of the Court's judgment**

1.    *Community law – scope – sport – limitation to economic activities*
2.    *Discrimination based on nationality – prohibition – scope – work or service (EEC treaty, articles 48 and 59)*
3.    *Discrimination based on nationality – prohibition – scope – sport – composition of sporting teams – exclusion (EEC treaty, articles 7, 48 and 59)*
4.    *Discrimination based on nationality – prohibition – scope – extension to acts not emanating from public authorities (EEC treaty, articles 7, 48 and 59)*
5.    *Discrimination – prohibition – nature – territorial scope – locality – discretionary powers of national court (EEC treaty, articles 7, 48 and 59)*
6.    *Services – free provision – restrictions – abolition – direct effect (EEC treaty, article 59, first paragraph)*

**Summary**

1.    *The practice of sport is subject to community law only in so far as it constitutes an economic activity within the meaning of article 2 of the treaty.*
2.    *The prohibition of discrimination based on nationality in the sphere of economic activities which have the character of gainful employment or remunerated service covers all work or services without regard to the exact nature of the legal relationship under which such activities are performed.*

---

\*    The full texts of documents which are marked with an asterisk (\*) are not incorporated in the book itself, but are freely accessible on the website of the ASSER International Sports Law Centre, at <www.sportslaw.nl> – documentation.

[694]    ECR 1974, p. 1405.
[695]    ECR 1974, p. 1405.

3.     *The prohibition of discrimination based on nationality does not affect the composition of sport teams, in particular national teams, the formation of which is a question of purely sporting interest and as such has nothing to do with economic activity.*

4.     *Prohibition of discrimination does not only apply to the action of public authorities but extends likewise to rules of any other nature aimed at regulating in a collective manner gainful employment and the provision of services.*

5.     *The rule on non-discrimination applies to all legal relationships which can be located within the territory of the community by reason either of the place where they are entered into or of the place where they take effect.*

6.     *The first paragraph of article 59, in any event in so far as it refers to the abolition of any discrimination based on nationality, creates individual rights which national courts must protect.*

## Parties

In Case 36/74

Reference to the Court under Article 177 of the EEC Treaty by the Arrondissements-rechtbank (District Court) Utrecht, for a preliminary ruling in the action pending before that court between

1.     Bruno Nils Olaf Walrave
2.     Longinus Johannes Norbert Koch

And

1.     Association Union Cycliste Internationale
2.     Koninklijke Nederlandsche Wielren Unie
3.     Federacion Espanola Ciclismo

## Subject of the case

On the interpretation of articles 7, 48 and 59 of the EEC treaty and the provisions of regulation (EEC) no 1612/68 on freedom of movement for workers within the community (OJ l 257 of 19-10-1968, p. 2),

## Grounds of the judgment

1.     By order dated 15 May 1974 filed at the court registry on 24 May 1974, the Arrondissementsrechtbank Utrecht referred under article 177 of the EEC treaty various questions relating to the interpretation of the first paragraph of article 7, article 48 and the first paragraph of article 59 of the EEC treaty and of regulation no 1612/68 of the council of 15 October 1968 (OJ l 257, p. 2) on freedom of movement for workers within the community.

2.     The basic question is whether these articles and regulation must be interpreted in such a way that the provision in the rules of the Union Cycliste Internationale relating to medium-distance world cycling championships behind motorcycles, according to which 'l'entraineur doit être de la nationalité de coureur' (the pacemaker must be of the same nationality as the stayer) is incompatible with them.

3.     These questions were raised in an action directed against the union cycliste internationale and the Dutch and Spanish cycling federations by two Dutch nationals who normally take part as pacemakers in races of the said type and who regard the aforementioned provision of the rules of UCI as discriminatory.

4.     Having regard to the objectives of the community, the practice of sport is subject to community law only in so far as it constitutes an economic activity within the meaning of article 2 of the treaty.

5.     When such activity has the character of gainful employment or remunerated service it comes more particularly within the scope, according to the case, of articles 48 to 51 or 59 to 66 of the treaty.

6.     These provisions, which give effect to the general rule of article 7 of the treaty, prohibit any discrimination based on nationality in the performance of the activity to which they refer.

7.     In this respect the exact nature of the legal relationship under which such services are performed is of no importance since the rule of non-discrimination covers in identical terms all work or services.

8.     This prohibition however does not affect the composition of sport teams, in particular national teams, the formation of which is a question of purely sporting interest and as such has nothing to do with economic activity.

9.     This restriction on the scope of the provisions in question must however remain limited to its proper objective.

10.     Having regard to the above, it is for the national court to determine the nature of the activity submitted to its judgment and to decide in particular whether in the sport in question the pacemaker and stayer do or do not constitute a team.

11.     The answers are given within the limits defined above of the scope of community law.

12.     The questions raised relate to the interpretation of articles 48 and 59 and to a lesser extent of article 7 of the treaty.

13.     Basically they relate to the applicability of the said provisions to legal relationships which do not come under public law, the determination of their territorial scope in the light of rules of sport emanating from a world-wide federation and the direct applicability of certain of those provisions.

14.     The main question in respect of all the articles referred to is whether the rules of an international sporting federation can be regarded as incompatible with the treaty.

15.     It has been alleged that the prohibitions in these articles refer only to restrictions which have their origin in acts of an authority and not to those resulting from legal acts of persons or associations who do not come under public law.

16.     Articles 7, 48, 59 have in common the prohibition, in their respective spheres of application, of any discrimination on grounds of nationality.

17.     Prohibition of such discrimination does not only apply to the action of public authorities but extends likewise to rules of any other nature aimed at regulating in a collective manner gainful employment and the provision of services.

18.     The abolition as between member states of obstacles to freedom of movement for persons and to freedom to provide services, which are fundamental objectives of the community contained in article 3 (c) of the treaty, would be compromised if the abolition of barriers of national origin could be neutralized by obstacles resulting from the exercise of their legal autonomy by associations or organizations which do not come under public law.

19.     Since, moreover, working conditions in the various member states are governed sometimes by means of provisions laid down by law or regulation and sometimes by agreements and other acts concluded or adopted by private persons, to limit the prohibitions in question to acts of a public authority would risk creating inequality in their application.

20.     Although the third paragraph of article 60, and articles 62 and 64, specifically relate, as regards the provision of services, to the abolition of measures by the state, this fact does not defeat the general nature of the terms of article 59, which makes no distinction between the source of the restrictions to be abolished.

21.   It is established, moreover, that article 48, relating to the abolition of any discrimination based on nationality as regards gainful employment, extends likewise to agreements and rules which do not emanate from public authorities.

22.   Article 7(4) of regulation no 1612/68 in consequence provides that the prohibition on discrimination shall apply to agreements and any other collective regulations concerning employment.

23.   The activities referred to in article 59 are not to be distinguished by their nature from those in article 48, but only by the fact that they are performed outside the ties of a contract of employment.

24.   This single distinction cannot justify a more restrictive interpretation of the scope of the freedom to be ensured.

25.   It follows that the provisions of articles 7, 48 and 59 of the treaty may be taken into account by the national court in judging the validity or the effects of a provision inserted in the rules of a sporting organization.

26.   The national court then raises the question of the extent to which the rule on non-discrimination may be applied to legal relationships established in the context of the activities of a sporting federation of world-wide proportions.

27.   The court is also invited to say whether the legal position may depend on whether the sporting competition is held within or outside the community.

28.   By reason of the fact that it is imperative, the rule on non-discrimination applies in judging all legal relationships in so far as these relationships, by reason either of the place where they are entered into or of the place where they take effect, can be located within the territory of the community.

29.   It is for the national judge to decide whether they can be so located, having regard to the facts of each particular case, and, as regards the legal effect of these relationships, to draw the consequences of any infringement of the rule on non-discrimination.

30.   Finally, the national court has raised the question whether the first paragraph of article 59, and possibly the first paragraph of article 7, of the treaty have direct effects within the legal orders of the member states.

31.   As has been shown above, the objective of article 59 is to prohibit in the sphere of the provision of services, inter alia, any discrimination on the grounds of the nationality of the person providing the services.

32.   In the sector relating to services, article 59 constitutes the implementation of the non-discrimination rule formulated by article 7 for the general application of the treaty and by article 48 for gainful employment.

33.   Thus, as has already been ruled (judgment of 3 December 1974 in case 33/74, Van Binsbergen) article 59 comprises, as at the end of the transitional period, an unconditional prohibition preventing, in the legal order of each member state, as regards the provision of services — and in so far as it is a question of nationals of member states — the imposition of obstacles or limitations based on the nationality of the person providing the services.

34.   It is therefore right to reply to the question raised that as from the end of the transitional period the first paragraph of article 59, in any event in so far as it refers to the abolition of any discrimination based on nationality, create individual rights which national courts must protect.

**Decision on costs**

35.   The costs incurred by the commission of the european communities, which has submitted observations to the court, are not recoverable.

36.   Since these proceedings are, in so far as the parties to the main action are con-

cerned, a step in the action pending before the national court, costs are a matter for that court.

## Operative part of the judgment

On those grounds,
The court
In answer to the questions referred to it by the Arrondissementsrechtbank Utrecht, hereby rules:

1.  Having regard to the objectives of the community, the practice of sport is subject to community law only in so far as it constitutes an economic activity within the meaning of article 2 of the treaty.
2.  The prohibition on discrimination based on nationality contained in articles 7, 48 and 59 of the treaty does not affect the composition of sport teams, in particular national teams, the formation of which is a question of purely sporting interest and as such has nothing to do with economic activity.
3.  Prohibition on such discrimination does not only apply to the action of public authorities but extends likewise to rules of any other nature aimed at collectively regulating gainful employment and services.
4.  The rule on non-discrimination applies in judging all legal relationships in so far as these relationships, by reason either of the place where they are entered into or of the place where they take effect, can be located within the territory of the community.
5.  The first paragraph of article 59, in any event in so far as it refers to the abolition of any discrimination based on nationality, creates individual rights which national courts must protect.

———

**2.7.3.   EUROPEAN COURT OF JUSTICE, OPINION OF ADVOCATE GENERAL TRABUCCHI, GAETANO DONÀ V MARIO MANTERO, CASE 13-76, 6 JULY 1976[696] \***

———

**2.7.4.   EUROPEAN COURT OF JUSTICE, JUDGMENT OF THE COURT (FIRST CHAMBER), GAETANO DONÀ V MARIO MANTERO, CASE 13-76, 14 JULY 1976[697]**

## Content of the Court's judgment

1.  *Discrimination based upon nationality – prohibition – matches between professional sportsmen – exclusion – infringement of Articles 48 to 51 or 59 to 66 of the EEC Treaty – restrictions in the case of matches for reasons which are not of an economic nature – permissibility – jurisdiction of the national court*
    *(EEC Treaty, Articles 7, 48 to 51, 59 to 66)*
2.  *Workers – freedom of movement – services – freedom to provide – discrimination – abolition – direct effect – individual rights – protection by national courts*
    *(EEC Treaty, Article 48, first paragraph of Article 59, third paragraph of Article 60).*

---

[696] ECR 1976, p. 1343.
[697] ECR 1976, p. 1333.

**Summary**
1.      *Rules or a national practice, even adopted by a sporting organization, which limit the right to take part in football matches as professional or semi-professional players solely to the nationals of the state in question, are incompatible with Article 7 and, as the case may be, with Articles 48 to 51 or 59 to 66 of the Treaty, unless such rules or practice exclude foreign players from participation in certain matches for reasons which are not of an economic nature, which relate to the particular nature and context of such matches and are thus of sporting interest only. It is for the national court to determine the nature of the activities submitted to its judgment and to take into account Articles 7, 48 and 59 of the Treaty, which are mandatory in nature, in order to judge the validity or the effects of a provision inserted into the rules of a sporting organization.*
2.      *Article 48 on the one hand and the first paragraph of Article 59 and the third paragraph of Article 60 of the Treaty on the other – the last two provisions at least in so far as they seek to abolish any discrimination against a person providing a service by reason of his nationality or the fact that he resides in a member state other than that in which the service is to be provided – have a direct effect in the legal orders of the member states and confer on individuals rights which national courts must protect.*

**Parties**
In case 13/76,
Reference to the court under Article 177 of the EEC Treaty by the Giudice Conciliatore, Rovigo, for a preliminary ruling in the action pending before that court between
Gaetano Donà
and
Mario Mantero
**Subject of the case**
On the interpretation in particular of Articles 7, 48 and 59 of the EEC Treaty,

**Grounds of the judgment**
1.      By order of 7 February 1976, received at the court registry on 13 February 1976, the Giudice Conciliatore, Rovigo, referred to the court under Article 177 of the EEC Treaty various questions concerning the interpretation of Articles 7, 48 and 59 of that Treaty.
2.      The first two questions ask whether Articles 7, 48 and 59 of the Treaty confer upon all nationals of the member states of the community the right to provide a service anywhere in the community and, in particular, whether football players also enjoy the same right where their services are in the nature of a gainful occupation.
3.      Should the answer to these two questions be in the affirmative, the third question asks the court essentially to rule whether the abovementioned right may also be relied on to prevent the application of contrary rules drawn up by a sporting federation which is competent to control football on the territory of a member state.
4.      in case the first three questions should be answered in the affirmative, the fourth question asks the court whether the right in question may be directly invoked in the national courts and whether the latter are bound to protect it.
5.      these questions have arisen in the context of an action between two Italian nationals over the compatibility of the abovementioned Articles of the Treaty with certain provisions of the rules of the Italian football federation, under which only players who are affiliated to that federation may take part in matches as profes-

sional or semi-professional players, whilst affiliation in that capacity is in principle only open to players of Italian nationality.

6.   (1) Article 7 of the Treaty provides that within the scope of application of the Treaty, any discrimination on grounds of nationality shall be prohibited.

As regards employed persons and persons providing services, this rule has been implemented by Articles 48 to 51 and 59 to 66 of the Treaty respectively and by measures of the community institutions adopted on the basis of those provisions.

7.   as regards workers in particular, Article 48 provides that freedom of movement shall entail the abolition of any discrimination based on nationality between workers of the member states as regards employment, remuneration and other conditions of work and employment.

8.   under the terms of Article 1 of regulation no 1612/68 of the council of 15 October 1968 on freedom of movement for workers within the community, (OJ English special edition 1968 (II), p. 476), any national of a member state shall, irrespective of his place of residence, ' have the right to take up an activity as an employed person, and to pursue such activity, within the territory of another member state '.

9.   as regards freedom to provide services within the community, Article 59 provides that the restrictions existing in this field shall be abolished in respect of nationals of member states who are established in a state of the community other than that of the person for whom the services are intended.

10.  under the third paragraph of Article 60 the person providing a service may, in order to do so, temporarily pursue his activity in the state where the service is provided, under the same conditions as are imposed by that state on its own nationals.

11.  the result of the foregoing is that any national provision which limits an activity covered by Articles 48 to 51 or 59 to 66 of the Treaty to the nationals of one member state alone is incompatible with the community rule.

12.  (2) having regard to the objectives of the community, the practice of sport is subject to community law only in so far as it constitutes an economic activity within the meaning of Article 2 of the Treaty.

This applies to the activities of professional or semi-professional football players, which are in the nature of gainful employment or remunerated service.

13.  where such players are nationals of a member state they benefit in all the other member states from the provisions of community law concerning freedom of movement of persons and of provision of services.

14.  however, those provisions do not prevent the adoption of rules or of a practice excluding foreign players from participation in certain matches for reasons which are not of an economic nature, which relate to the particular nature and context of such matches and are thus of sporting interest only, such as, for example, matches between national teams from different countries.

15.  this restriction on the scope of the provisions in question must however remain limited to its proper objective.

16.  having regard to the above, it is for the national court to determine the nature of the activity submitted to its judgment.

17.  (3) as the court has already ruled in its judgment of 12 December 1974 in Walrave v Union Cycliste Internationale (Case 36/74 (1974) ECR 1405), the prohibition on discrimination based on nationality does not only apply to the action of public authorities but extends likewise to rules of any other nature aimed at collectively regulating gainful employment and services.

18.  it follows that the provisions of Articles 7, 48 and 59 of the Treaty, which are mandatory in nature, must be taken into account by the national court in judging the validity or the effects of a provision inserted in the rules of a sporting organization.

19.	the answer to the questions referred to the court must therefore be that rules or a national practice, even adopted by a sporting organization, which limit the right to take part in football matches as professional or semi-professional players solely to the nationals of the state in question, are incompatible with Article 7 and, as the case may be, with Articles 48 to 51 or 59 to 66 of the Treaty unless such rules or practice exclude foreign players from participation in certain matches for reasons which are not of an economic nature, which relate to the particular nature and context of such matches and are thus of sporting interest only.

20.	(4) as the Court has already ruled in its judgments of 4 December 1974 in case 41/74 (Van Duyn v Home Office (1974) ECR 1337) and 3 December 1974 in case 33/74 (van Binsbergen v Bestuur van de Bedrijfsvereniging voor de Metaalnijverheid (1974) ECR 1299) respectively, Article 48 on the one hand and the first paragraph of Article 59 and the third paragraph of Article 60 of the Treaty on the other – the last two provisions at least in so far as they seek to abolish any discrimination against a person providing a service by reason of his nationality or of the fact that he resides in a member state other than that in which the service is to be provided – have a direct effect in the legal orders of the member states and confer on individuals rights which national courts must protect.

## Decision on costs

Costs

21.	The costs incurred by the Commission of the European Communities, which has submitted observations to the court, are not recoverable, and as these proceedings are, in so far as the parties to the main action are concerned, in the nature of a step in the action pending before the Giudice Conciliatore, Rovigo, the decision as to costs is a matter for that court.

## Operative part of the judgment

On those grounds,

The court

In answer to the questions referred to it by the Giudice Conciliatore, Rovigo, by order of 7 February 1976, hereby rules:

1.	Rules or a national practice, even adopted by a sporting organization, which limit the right to take part in football matches as professional or semi-professional players solely to the nationals of the state in question, are incompatible with Article 7 and, as the case may be, with Articles 48 to 51 or 59 to 66 of the Treaty, unless such rules or practice exclude foreign players from participation in certain matches for reasons which are not of an economic nature, which relate to the particular nature and context of such matches and are thus of sporting interest only.

2.	Article 48 on the one hand and the first paragraph of Article 59 and the third paragraph of Article 60 of the Treaty on the other – the last two provisions at least in so far as they seek to abolish any discrimination against a person providing a service by reason of his nationality or the fact that he resides in a member state other than that in which the service is to be provided – have a direct effect in the legal orders of the member states and confer on individuals rights which national courts must protect.

## 2.7.5.    REPORT DRAWN UP ON BEHALF OF THE COMMITTEE ON WOMENS RIGHTS ON WOMEN IN SPORT, 30 JUNE 1987[698]

Rapporteur: Mrs. Hedy d'Ancona

At its sitting of 8 May 1985, the European Parliament referred the motion for a resolution tabled by Mrs Squarcialupi and others on a European Charter of Womens Rights in Sport (Doc. B 2-215/85) pursuant to Rule 47 of the Rules of Procedure to the Committee on Womens Rights as the committee responsible and to the Committee on Youth, Culture, Education, Information and Sport for an opinion.

At its meeting of 27 September 1985, the Committee on Womens Rights decided to draw up a report and appointed Miss Brookes Rapporteur.

The committee considered the draft report at its meeting of 28/29 April 1986 and of 23/24 March 1987. At the last meeting it adopted the motion for a resolution as a whole unanimously.

The following took part in the vote; Mrs d'Ancona, Chairman; Mrs Cinciari-Rodano, fist Vice-Chairman; Mrs Brookes, rapporteur; Mrs Braun-Moser, Mr Coimbra-Martins, Mrs Daly, Mrs Garcia-Arias, Mrs van den Heuvel (deputising for Mrs Crawley), Mrs Lenz, Mrs Lizin (deputising for Mrs Tonque), Mr Pordea (deputising for Mrs Lehideux), Mrs Schmidbauer, Mrs Schmit, Mrs Squarcialupi (deputising for Mrs Trupia), Mrs van Dijk, Mrs van Hemeldonck, Mrs Vayssade.

The opinion of the Committee on Youth, Culture, Education, Information and Sport is attached.

The report was tabled on 1 April 1987.

On 18 May 1987, in view of the resignation of the rapporteur Miss Brookes, the Committee decided to appoint its chairman, Mrs. d'Ancona, as rapporteur.

The deadline for tabling amendments to this report will be indicated in the draft agenda for the part-session at which it will be debated.

CONTENTS
A.    Motion fir a resolution
B.    Explanatory statement
ANNEX I
–    letter of questionnaire in connection with the report on women in sport
–    list of bodies from whom submissions were received in answer to this letter, with a brief summary of contents
ANNEX II
–    female participation at Olympic Games
ANNEX III
–    Motion for a resolution (Doc. B 2-215/85)
Opinion of the Committee on Youth, Culture, Education, Information and Sport (PE 107.500/def.)

The Committee on Womens Rights hereby submits to the European Parliament the following motion for a resolution, together with explanatory statement:

---

[698]  Doc. A 2-32/87/corr.

## A. Motion for a resolution on Women in sport

[...]

## Explanatory statement

*Background*
The committee having decided to draw up a report on women in sport, the rapporteur sent out a letter of questionnaire to sporting and womens organisations throughout the Community. The text of this letter is attached in annex, with a brief summary of the submissions received. The rapporteur wishes to take this opportunity of thanking all those who took the time to answer her questions and sent her their observations.

*Introduction*
The fundamental premise of equal treatment and anti-discrimination legislation is that the individual should be treated in terms of her/his personal capacity and qualilties, and not by reference to gender. This principle should apply by extension to sport.

Case I
A good example of the absurdity of sex discrimination in sport was reported in 'The Guardian' (2 March 1983). Dr Fiona Pixley was selected by Oxford University to play water polo against Cambridge. A member of Australia's international side, she was picked on merit for a team hitherto consisting entirely of men. The Amateur Swimming Association ruled that as the match would be in public, special dispensation was required to allow her to compete but could not be granted in time. Thus, despite her undoubted ability and for no other reason than her sex, Dr. Pixley was denied the chance to take part.[699]

Case II
Angela Lezziero, 13, plays ice-hockey in Strasbourg and is one if the stars of the local team. When her annual club subscription was due for renewal last year, she was informed by the club that she was no longer on the team, the reason given being the regulations of the Fédération française des sports de glace which stipulate that 'persons of the female sex are not permitted to take part in competitions'. Following legal action by her parents, this regulation was overruled, and Angela is playing again.

Case III
The 1986 show-jumping champion is Gail Creenaugh, from Canada, who won her title at Aachen in July 1986. Show-jumping is a discipline in which women and men compete in identical tests – in this case, all the finalists rode the horses of each of the competitors.

*Attitudes and Expectations*
'Even today it is still very common for sport to be seen as a male activity and one which naturally lends itself to masculine abilities, attitudes and expectations'.
'For example, it would not be considered abnormal for a woman to show a strong aversion to sport, but the same attitude in a boy or a man would be cause for concern.'[700]
It is clear from the data received in connection with this report that more men than women

---

[699] Quoted from 'Sex Discrimination in Sport' by David Pannick.
[700] 'Determinismes de la Pratique Sportive Féminine' – L. Willem et al. Université Catholique de Louvain, Institut d'Education Physique.

practise sport, that there is a higher level of sporting involvement among working women than among housewives, that mare car-owners than non car-owners regularly participate in sporting activities, and that, in general, the highest levels of participation are to be found among the well-educated and in high-income brackets.

Here we can see differing rates of participation by sex, and also by socio-economic standing. As well as reflecting the most obvious facets of access to sport, this clearly illustrates the pre-conceived social roles of women and men which tend to conform to a more traditional stereotype among lower-income families.

'Women are often doubly and trebly burdened by family and professional commitments.[701]

*People practice sports for different reasons*
Many of the submissions received emphasised that women tended to seek relaxation and social contact in their sporting activities, whereas competition and performance figured more prominently in male motivations.

The growing awareness in recent years of the health benefits ard general well-being to be gained from regular exercise goes a long way towards explaining the growth of movement/dance/fitness groups aimed mainly at women.

This tendency is of course reinforced by the stereotyped notion that grace should be an important element of womens sport.

The fact that peoples' motivations and reasons for taking up a sport or leisure activity are different, does not imply that some are more or less valid than others.

Indeed, if sport over the centuries had been an activity associated with women and from which men had been excluded, we might well find that strength and muscle-power were despised while grace and lightness were the most admired sporting attributes.

Traditional attitudes and opposition to womens sport tended to be based on myths which, although now scientifically disproven, continue in many cases to hold sway. In fact, female athletes can increase their strength beyond that of the average man of similar age not in training. As regards the myths surrounding pregnancy and sport, many female athletes have recorded best performances in the early stages of pregnancy, shorter labour and less complications at childbirth, and improved performances afterwards.

*Example*
'I know that an Olympic athlete is an idol for youth ... an example with a very strong influence on young people'.[702]

The exemplary value of excellence is also true for women − perhaps more so in the area of sport from which they have been so long excluded, and where traditional attitudes militate against equal access and full recognition of their achievements.

When Nawal, El Mentawakal, from Morocco, won the gold medal for the 400m hurdles at the 1984 Games in Los Angeles she was the first Arab woman and also the first African woman athlete to do so. Her victory was not just a personal triumph − it had an enormous symbolic significance for her country and particularly for women of her country.

This was immediately illustrated in her native city of Casablanca which built a stadium and three running tracks. Prior to Nawal's victory, few Moroccan women jogged − now thousands of girls and women have taken up this sport. And, in acknowledgement of the importance of her individual exploit, the King of Morocco declared that all girls born on that day should be named Nawal.

---

[701] Submission received from Deutscher Sportbund.

[702] Svetla Otzedtova-Guenova, Bulgarian gold medalist in the double sculls, Montreal Olympics 1976.

The importance of exemplary role models is felt at all levels of society; this is equally true of women in sport. The growing presence of women in sport and the results obtained in different sporting events are important factors in influencing society's image of women, and womens own image of themselves and their role in society.

*Media*
'... women(professional golfers) are no longer considered worthy of live TV coverage by the BBC, hence attracting only modest sponsorship deals ...' (The Sunday Telegraph – 13 July 1986)
A detailed analysis[703] of coverage of womens sport in the Belgian press has revealed a generally low level of reporting of womens events. In one paper it was found that 95.3% column inches were devoted to male sport, 4.7% only to womens, the ratio for photographs being identical. In reporting on womens sports, commentary was minimal – often only the results were given. Sports journalists (mainly male) interviewed, were overwhelmingly in favour of an aesthetic image of female sport.
Many submissions received have asserted that the emphasis in media reporting of women athletes on physical appearance, personal-/family life, rather than on the sporting achievement per se, results in a negative image of female sport. The generally low level of media coverage also results in lower levels of sponsorship making it difficult to organise and promote womens events.
The Dutch Emancipatieraad quotes a study which 'discovered that, television-owners went in for more sport than non-television owners. Not only was this re-assuring, but it also showed that, in order to stimulate emancipation in sport, it was necessary for the media to give much more attention to women in sport.'
Quite apart from the responsibility of the media to report what is actually happening (women do play football, rugby, cricket, as well as pursuing more graceful activities such as gymnastics, skating and dancing), should they adopt a policy of 'equal 'treatment' of womens and mens sport, we would
immediately have a situation where girls and women would have a wider and more genuinely representative range of sporting role models to imitate.

*Discrimination*
Many submissions received pointed out that, even where legal equality in society had been achieved on paper, there was often a de facto inequality with regard to access to facilities at sports clubs.
Certainly, in Britain and in Ireland, anti-discrimination legislation does not apply to private clubs. This is clear in traditionally male-dominated sports where women members may not have equal access at all times to the playing area and social facilities.
An interesting way of bringing pressure to bear in such cases is illustrated in a letter received from Ireland's Minister of State for Womens Affairs, with reference to the Golfing Union of Ireland (GUI) whose constitution stated that a golf club or association which gave women full rights to attend or vote at Annual or special general meetings could not be a member of the Union. When the GUI applied to Cospoir (the National Sports Council) for a grant in 1985, it was informed that such assistance could not be made while its constitution contained a clause that was clearly discriminatory against women. The Minister of State concludes that 'there is little doubt that this action was influential in persuading the GUI to amend the offending clause'.
The magnitude of the attitudinal problem was also underlined in the submission received from Greece's General Secretariat for Equality, which referred to 'the still existing diffi-

---

[703] Déterminismes de la Pratique Sportive féminine' p. 231 et seq.

culties and conditions of mentality', and stated that 'there are no legal restrictions concerning participation of girls and women in certain athletics although, in practice, they exist'.

## Separate Provision

Attitudes with regard to the necessity for/advisability of separate provision for women and girls in sports are quite varied. It was widely felt that organisation of 'women only' sport facilitated participation by women who felt embarrassed about bodies and sporting capabilities, or where modesty was an issue (e.g. teenage girls, women from ethnic minorities).

Similarity, older women were found to take part more easily in these circumstances. In general, it was felt that many girls and women lacked confidence which could be gained in a 'women only' environment and would then help them to participate in an integrated situation.

David Pannick argues in favour of separate sporting events for women for two reasons – firstly, to compensate for the unequal opportunities of the past with regard to access events, facilities, training, etc., and secondly, by analogy with organised by reference to weight or age.

The opposite view point put by Belgium's Secretary of State for the Environment and Social Development who felt that separate facilities were unnecessary because they would slow down womens integration in sport, and also believed women find greater satisfaction in sporting activities as a result of mixed events.

## Education

Sport is universally recognised as an important vehicle for development of the individual personality, as well as many of the social skills necessary in day-to-day living (team sports).

It is in the gymnasium and on the playing field that young people learn to accept victory or defeat with equanimity, learn those qualities of assertiveness, self-confidence and self-reliance, and cooperation with others, which will help them to succeed in professional life.

*Or do they?* The Deutscher Sportbund points out that 'a survey showed that for girls more emphasis is placed on 'feminine' types of sport such as dance and gymnastics, while boys play more team games such as football, handball, basketball ... school-girls have less experience of asserting themselves in competitive situations and of the team spirit ... On the whole it can be assumed that traditional sport instruction reinforces sex-linked differences in sport.'

Schools have traditionally recognised the importance of sport for young people ... as long as those young people were young men. Whereas equal treatment may be preached, too often stereotyped attitudes still prevail among teachers and parents as to what constitutes suitable sporting or athletic activity for girls, or even as to its necessity. It is interesting to note that submissions received from Ireland[704] and Greece[705] – two generally traditionalist countries – emphasised the necessity for 'awareness-raising' among teachers and parents, and indeed were able to quote positive results when such action was undertaken.

Many teenage girls feel unsure of themselves physically, and use menstruation as an excuse to drop out of school sports altogether. Rather than unquestioningly accepting this, parents and teachers should explain that exercise can help to alleviate period pain. Also changing and showering facilities should be such as to cater for teenage modesty.

---

[704] IRL – Department of Education, Sport and Youth Section.
[705] EL – Ministry to the Presidency, General Secretariat for Equality.

*Teaching*

The Belgian situation, where the majority of those teaching Physical Education at primary
school level are women (3:2), with this ratio being reversed at secondary school level, can
reasonably be assumed to reflect a general tendency. It is therefore extremely important
that physical education trainee teachers be made aware of the importance of encouraging
girls to be more actively involved in sport, male trainee PE teachers in particular.

The major Belgian study already referred to points out that 'since the entire female population has to pass through several levels of compulsory education, it would seem logical
that access to sporting activity should be encouraged most in this area.'[706]

'The most important aspect of the connection between sport in and out of school is that it
is hoped that taking part in a sport at school will encourage people to continue with a
sporting activity after leaving school.'[707]

*Leisure*

'Sport as a primary activity is promoted as being a vital ingredient in assisting relaxation,
decreasing stress levels and providing a necessary counterbalance to jobs which are of a
sedentary nature. This same reasoning applies equally to women and not only to those
working but also to those coping with the different stresses and challenges of mother-
hood.'[708]

Many more people have a sporting activity than are members of sports clubs and associations, thus demonstrating the importance of recreational sport.

In a number of countries (Germany, Ireland, Greece, Belgium), specific campaigns have
been organised to encourage women to take up sporting activities. In Great Britain, the
Sports Council decided against such a specific campaign, but has actively promoted
projects aimed at encouraging women to become more involved. For example, a pilot
project run by the Cambridgeshire Federations of Womens Institutes was successful in introducing many women to new sporting activities, and resulted, in many cases, in regular
participation by these women.

This project demonstrated the importance of the provision of creche facilities so that
mothers of young children were enabled to take part. Other important lessons that were
learned included the importance of a good relationship with the local press so that such
initiatives were presented in a sympathetic light, and the value of short introductory
courses.

A special project in Birmingham, promoting 'women only' swimming and aimed primarily at women of ethnic minorities (for many of whom the absence of men from the pool
was a deciding factor in enabling them to participate), resulted not only in participation by
local women from the Asian community, but has had the incidental and unforeseen side-
effect of stimulating social contacts between women from differing ethnic backgrounds.
Here again the crucial importance of childcare facilities was underlined.

Projects such as these, while increasing female participation in sports and leisure activities, also result in a more efficient daytime use of sports and leisure facilities. This can
also extend to elderly and retired people, the majority of whom are women, well as the
unemployed. According to the Dutch Social and Cultural Planning Bureau, 'the unemployed who take up a sport devote considerably more time to it than those in the other

---

[706] Déterminismes de la Pratique Sportive féminine – L. Willem et al., Université Catholique de
Louvain, Institut d'Education Physique.

[707] NL – Sociaal en Cultureel Planbureau (Social and Cultural Planning Bureau).

[708] Mary Glen Haig, member of the International Olympic Committee, President – Amateur
Fencing Association (GB).

(social) groups ... The unemployed ... gave sport and recreation as one of the last things they would give up if they had to make economies.'
Such projects and courses, to introduce women to sport or encourage them to take up again a sporting activity dropped on leaving school, apart from the beneficial effects for the individual, can also lead to families practising a sport together as a family leisure activity.

*Competition*
Many of the submissions spoke of different rules for qualifying levels for the same sports, when played by women and men, quite apart from the covert discrimination already referred to with regard to access to playing areas and facilities.
It must surely be clear that, should all obstacles, both overt and covert, to participation by women all sports at all levels, be immediately abolished, *nobody could aspire to a place in a sport or on a team which she/he did not fully deserve through, personal talent, qualifications and level of training.*
'The benefits, satisfactions, frustrations and rewards of competitive sport are not dependent on sex. They are human experiences which provide both men and women with enjoyment and challenges. These opportunities should never be restricted to one sex.'[709]
The Olympic Games are probably the best, and undoubtedly the most visible, example of the growth of participation by women in sport at a world level (see Annex II). At the Olympic Games in Paris in 1900, there were 11 women athletes taking part, compared with one thousand and seventy seven men. In Moscow, in 1980, women numbered one thousand hundred and seventy seven out of a total of seven thousand one hundred and nineteen competitors.
Womens performances and results at the Olympics have improved at a remarkable rate over the years, and, in many disciplines, the gap between female and male results is narrowing all the time (see Annex II). This is particularly true in long-distance events (e.g. swimming) where the greater female capacity for endurance is most clearly demonstrated. However, it must be remembered that the earliest female performances recorded might well, in many instances, have been preceded by virtually no training or proper preparation. In general, women have not had access to a comparable level of coaching or facilities or training.
The simple (and purely factual) assertion of the improved performance of women athletes, with results which would often have won the same mens events some thirty or even less years ago, does not in fact address the central issue which is *the entitlement of every sportswoman to practice on her own terms the sport of her choice to the level of her ability.*
Comparison of womens results and performances with mens are spurious, and manifest society's failure to accept womens sporting aspirations and achievements for themselves.

*Representation*
Amateur sports organisations are, in the main, run by volunteers. There is a very low level of female presence in the management of these organisations, reflecting the traditional male dominance of sporting activities.
Given the increased levels of participation by female athletes at Olympic level, it is astonishing to note the low numbers of women represented on national Olympic committees.
Women are also notably absent from coaching and refereeing, even of womens sports.
A number of submissions suggested that this phenomenon reflected a general lack of confidence on the part of many women who might well be active 'in the background'. It is

---

[709] Déterminismes de la Pratique Sportive féminine.

essential that sports organisations and federations be made aware of the necessity to better represent the women in their midst, both at management/organisational level, and in the actual sporting activity, through greater numbers of female coaches and referees.

Whereas for too long, women have been kept on the sidelines and have had little or no say in the organisation of sporting activities, it is imperative that their general level of representation be improved, and that, above all, they be involved in decisions concerning womens sport.

*Handicapped*

In general, where sport facilities receive financial aid from the State, such facilities must be accessible to handicapped people. Obviously, mere facility of access will not be sufficient to ensure a higher level of use by the handicapped, and special efforts must be made by the medical, and paramedical personnel who come into contact with the handicapped, to promote the benefits to be gained from regular exercise and sporting activity, which also widens social contact.

The development of competitive sports and parallel Olympic games for the handicapped has played an important part in promoting acceptance of the fact that the handicapped can play a full role in society.

Attention must be drawn to the particular problems of handicapped girls and women, for whom, over and above the physical aspect of their disability, incapacity or deformity can be a psychological problem. Given the social pressures on women to attractive, handicapped women tend to be inordinately aware of and embarrassed by bodily deformity.

Those working with the handicapped, particularly where sport (swimming etc.) being used for re-education or therapy, should be particularly sensitive to psychological problems caused by the perceived loss of personal attractiveness.

*Conclusions*

'The arguments about equality of opportunity in sport are fundamentally similar to those about equality of opportunity elsewhere and are fully deserving of serious attention.'[710]

It is clear that 'women' are not a homogeneous group and that no one solution will miraculously inspire them to take up or start regularly practising a sport. This human need for variety will mean the promotion of polyvalent sports centres, the organisation of introductory courses to many different sporting activities.

The current popularity of health-giving activities and leisure activities can and should be harnessed so that people, in general, and more women in particular, may be encouraged to try or take up again some form of sport.

Studies carried out in the Netherlands show that 'in future, women can be expected to participate in sport to a greater extent than now.'[711]

*'It is assumed that a boy who is not exposed to sport opportunities is deprived. We must begin to make the same assumptions for girls'.*[712]

**Annex I**

–　　　Letter of questionnaire in conrection with the report on women in sport

---

[710] Mary Glen Haig, member of the International Olympic Committee, President – Amateur Fencing Association (GB).

[711] NL: Emancipatieraad.

[712] Donna de Varona, U.S., Olympic swimming champion (2 gold medals, Tokyo, 1964), holder of 18 world records.

–   List of bodies from whom submissions were received in answer to this letter, with a brief summary of contents.


European Parliament,
Committee on Womens Rights
Secretariat

Dear Madam,
The European Parliament's Committee on Womens Rights has decided to draft a report on women in sport and has appointed Miss Beata Brookes (European Democrat, United Kingdom) rapporteur.
It is the rapporteur's intention to treat the subject under the headings of -
    Sport as education
    Sport as leisure
    Sport as competition
    Sport as employment
    Sport and the handicapped.
In order to present in her report as full a picture as possible of the situation of women in sport throughout the Member States of the European Community, the rapporteur would appreciate any information your organisation could provide in answer to the following questions:
(a)  *Sport as education*
    –   What is the role of sport in schools?
    –   Are the same sports opportunities available to boys and girls?
(b)  *Sport as leisure*
    –   Please comment on the availability of sports facilities for leisure, and the rate of usage of such facilities by clubs, individuals, etc.
(c)  *Sport as competition*
    –   Are all sporting competitions open to boys and girls, men and womeno.
    –   Do the same conditions of eligibility, rules of competition, etc. apply?
    –   What is the situation with regard to mixed competitions, and/or separate events reserved to one sex?
(d)  *Sport as employment*
    –   What are the comparative rates of employment of men and women in professions associated with sport – physical education teachers, sports coaches, umpires, referees, etc.?
    –   Please comment on the training facilities availabte to such professions notably with regard to equal access by men and women to these professions and to the necessary training
(e)  *Sport and the handicapped*
    –   Please comment on the availability of sports facilities suitable for use by handicapped people, the rate of usage of such facilities, the Level of organisation, assistance ... necessary to enable handicapped people to participate in sport (presence of monitors etc.)
Your comments would also be appreciated with regard to the *legal situation* – whether there are any legal obstacles to participation by girls/women in certain sports, and your organisation's feelings with regard to the concept of equal opportunities and equal treatment of men and women in sport. Finally, does your organisation consider that there are arguments in favour of separate facilities and events for women and girls; if so, please comment.

Please forward your submission to:-
Miss Cliodhna Dempsey
Committee on Womens Rights: Secretariat
European Parliament
L – 2929 Luxembourg
by 15 may 1986.

Thank you in anticipation of your contribution to this report.
Yours faithfully,
Cliodhna Dempsey

### I.      Belgium
(a)      Université Catholique de Louvain
Institut d'Education Physique
1 Place P. de Coubertin
B – 1348 Louvain-la-Neuve
(Contact: Mrs Lydie Willem)
–      a detailed study of womens sporting practice in Belgium under biological, psychological and social aspects, and analysis of womens sport as reported by media;
(b)      Nationale Vrouwen Raad
Louizalaan 183
B -1050 Brussel
(Contact: Mrs Lily Boeykens)
–      letter mainly concerning sport at school with interesting comments on the way in which 'social skills are stimulated through team sports';
–      also note from Dr. Pouliart, of the NVR Health Committee, stressing life-long benefits of sport, notably improved mobility and independence of the elderly;
(c)      Secrétaire d'Etat à l'Environnement et à l'Emancipation Sociale,
Rue de la Loi 56
B – 1040 Bruxelles
(Contact: Mrs Miet Smet)
–      answers to questionnaire, and statistics for rates of female/mate participation in different sports;
(d)      Ministère de la Communauté française
Direction générale du sport et du tourisme
Galerie Ravenstein 4-27
B – BRUXELLES
(Contact: Mr D Brons)
–      survey of participation in sport broken down per region, sex, age-group, socio-professional status.

### II.      Denmark

### III.      Germany
(a)      A.K.T. Aktion Klartext
Gleichsteltung der Frauen in der Medien
Am Ehrenkamp 15
D – 4800 BIELEFELD

(Contact: Mrs Hilde Junker-Seeliger)
  - report on seminar on 'Women in Sport – Women and Sports Reporting' calling for better reporting in the media of womens sport;
(b)   Deutscher Sportbund
      Otto Fleck Schneise 12
      Postfach 710263
      D – 6000 Frankfurt
      (Contact: Mrs Ursula Voigt)
  - interesting comments on differenciation between types of sport for boys and girls at school and the perpetuation of traditional attitudes, and lack of equal access to competitive sport; analysis oF membership of sports clubs by social class – attitudes and expectations.

## IV.   Greece
Ministry to the Presidency
General Secreriat for Equality
2 Mousseou Street
Plaka
EL – 105.55 Athens
(Contact: Mrs Chryssanthi Laiou-Antoniou)
  - interesting comment on the introduction of special awareness programmes for parents and emphasis on the importance of sport for 'physical and mental health'.

## V.   France
Centre national d'information sur les droits de la femme CNIDF – Diffusion
B.P. 3000
F-75500 PARIS Cedex
  - Number 31 of the magazine 'Citoyennes à part entière' (May 1984) contains an article on womens sporting participation in France, with useful statistical material, and lists prominent French sportswomen.

## VI.   Spain

## VII.   Ireland
(a)   Department of Education
      Sport and Youth Section Hawkins House (Floor 11)
      IRL – DUBLIN 2
      (Contact: Mrs Pauline Gildea)
  - General statement on the situation in Ireland with particular reference to efforts to promote women in sporting pursuits;
(b)   Minister of State for Womens Affairs
      Department of the Taoiseach
      Government Buildings
      IRL – Dublin 2
      (Contact: Mrs Nuala Fennell, T.D.)
  - description of the process whereby the Golfing Union of Ireland was recently obliged to revise its constitution, so as not to discriminate against women, in order to qualify for grant assistance from Cospoir (National Sports Council).

**VIII.    Italy**
(a)      Unione Italiana Sport Popolare
         Via Francesco Carrara 24
         I – 00196 Roma

         (Contact: Mrs Gigliola Venturini)
         –    Charter of Womens Rights in sport calling for
              –    the right to be different
              –    the right to physical integrity and respect for differences
              –    the right to equal opportunities
              –    the right to information
(b)      Commissione Nazionale per la realizzazione della parità fra uomo e donna
         Palazzo Chigi
         Piazza Colerera 37
         I – 00187 Roma
         –    statement that full participation of women in sport is still hampered by ex-
              istence of prejudices and discrimination, and suggested course of action to
              overcome this.

**IX.     Luxembourg**

**X.      Netherlands**
(a)      Emancipatieraad
         Lutherse Burgwal 10
         NL – 2512 CB Den Haag
         (Contact: Mrs Joke Huisman
         –    article on changing rates of male/female participation in sport in relation to
              sociological context
(b)      Sociaal en Cultureel Planbureau
         J.C. van Markenlaan 3
         Postbus 37
         NL – 2280 AA Rijswijk
         –    extracts from sociological study of sport and leisure, indicating rates of
              participation and analysing motivations.

**XI. Portugal**

**XII. United Kingdom**
(a)      Amateur Fencing Association
         The de Beaumon Centre
         83 Penham Road
         West Kensington
         GB – London W14 9SP
         (Contact: Mrs Mary Glen Haig, C.B.E.)
         –    excellent article on women in sport stating, inter alia, that 'the arguments
              about equality of opportunity in sport are fundamentally similar to those
              about equality of opportunity elsewhere and are fully deserving of serious
              attention';
(b)      Womens Sport Foundation
         c/o Centre for GEOED
         Sheffield City Polytechnic

Collegiate Crescent
GB – Sheffield S 10
(Contact: Mrs Celia Brackenridge)
– comments on factors, mainly attitudinal, accounting for a lesser presence
   of women in sport;
(c)    The National Council of Women of Great Britain
       34 Lower Sloane Street
       GB – London SW1W 8BP
       (Contact: Mrs Mary Mayne)
       – brief comment on education aspect stating 'there has been a tendency to
          spend more on boys' sports and more on their teams, however, this is be-
          ginning to be challenged';
(d)    The Sports Council
       16 Upper Woburn Place
       GB – London WC1H OPQ
       (Contact: Mrs Elizabeth Dendy)
       – answers to questionnaire, interesting explanation of why this body decided
          not to launch a specific campaign on women and sport, and a series of ex-
          cellent reports[713];
(e)    National Union of Teachers
       Hamilton House
       Mabledon Place
       GB – London WC1H 9BD
       (Contact: Mrs Jean Farrall)
       – extract from the Schools Council report 'Sit on the Sidelines and Watch the
          Boys Play' which emphasises development of social skills through sport
          and how detrimental it is that this is not sufficiently available to girls.

## XIII.    Other sources
(a)    Council of Europe
       – moist notably, report on seminar on 'the greater involvement of women in
          sport' (Dublin, autumn 1980) and resolution on greater participation by
          women in sport, adopted by the Council of Ministers at Palma in April
          1981;
(b)    I.O.C. (International Olympic Committee)
       Château de Vidy
       CH – 1007 Lausanne
       (Contact: Mrs Marie-Hélène Roukhadze)
       – the December 1985 issue of its magazine 'Olympic Message' was devoted
          to women in sport, in a series of excellent aticles
(c)    U.K. Womens Institutes
       (throughout Wales)
       – many brief answers to the questionnaire

---

[713] Notably on 'Women and Leisure', 'Sport and Recreation for Women and Girls', 'Women
and Sport', (report on a seminar held at the University of Leeds in October 1985), an 'all-women
issue' of 'Sport and Leisure' (the magazine of the Sports Council), and a report of a special project
in Birmingham on 'Swimming Provision for Women'.

**Annex II – Female Participation at Olympic Games**[714]

[Figures 1-4]

**Annex III**

*The European Parliament,*

A.    having regard to the resolutions of the Committee on Women's Rights and the
      Committee of Inquiry into the Situation of Women in Europe,
B.    whereas in the European Community, women experience great difficulty in engag-
      ing and establishing themselves in sports which are still traditionally considered as
      being men's preserves,
C.    whereas 1985 has been designated World Youth Year by the United Nations,

1.    Requests Member States to draft, as soon as possible, a European Charter of
      Women's Rights in Sport, based on that drawn up by the women's national coordi-
      nation section of the UISP – Italian Union of Sport – incorporating the following
      rights:
      a.    Right to physical integrity to prevent physiological or psychological manipu-
            lation or damage and insinuations that the results achieved by women com-
            petitors were due to male physical attributes,
      b.    Right to equal opportunities to remove from the statutes and regulations of
            sports associations any tendency to sexual discrimination and to ensure equal
            career and work opportunities in the field of sport (trainers, referees, etc.)
      c.    Right to a more equitable distribution of economic resources between sports
            practised by men and by women and greater equality in plans for the promo-
            tion of sports activities by public bodies and private financiers,
      d.    Right to proper information on the results achieved by women in sport and on
            sportswomen in general so as to give greater emphasis to real sporting value
            and to avoid limiting information on sportswomen to references to their pri-
            vate lives and items in the so-called gossip columns,
      e.    Right to an equal sports education allowing boys and girls to receive physical
            education together at school.
2.    Instructs its President to forward this resolution to the Commission, the Council,
      the Governments of Member States and all European sports federations.


**Opinion (pursuant to Rule 101 of the Rules of Procedure) of the Committee on
Youth, Culture, Education, Information and Sport**

Draftsman: Mrs Larive-Groenendaal

At its meeting of 29 January 1986 the committee decided to draw up an opinion on the
motion for a resolution by Mrs Squarcialupi and others on a European Charter of
Women's Rights in Sport (Doc. B 2-215/85) which had been referred to it on 8 May 1985.
At its meeting of 20 March 1986, the committee appointed Mrs Larive-Groenendaal
draftsman. It considered the draft opinion at its meetings of 25 November 1986 and 4
February 1987.

---
[714] 'Olympic Message' December 1985.

It adopted the draft opinion unanimously at the latter meeting.
The following took part in the vote: Mrs Lemass, chairman; Mr Papapietro, vice-chairman; Mrs Larive-Groenendaal, draftsman; Mr Hahn, Mr Kilby (deputizing for Miss Brookes), Mr Coimbra Martins and Mr McMillan-Scott.

The Committee on Youth, Culture, Education, information and Sport, asked to deliver an opinion for the Committee on Women's Rights on the motion for a resolution on a European Charter of Women's Rights in Sport (Doc. B 2-215/85), believes that encouraging women to take part in sport is part of the legitimate demand for opportunities for men and women and for the abolition of discrimination between men and women on the grounds of sex.
However, the Committee on Youth, Culture, Education, Information and Sport deems it important to emphasise those aspects of the promotion of sport for women which most closely concern the areas falling within its terms of reference: culture, education and information.

*Sport and culture*
Recent developments in sporting activities, sport as leisure or as a profession, reflect a development in life-styles and socio-cultural behaviour in industrialized societies. Greater life expectancy and progress in medicine, the reduction of working time and the introduction of paid leave have given rise to a concept of leisure within which sport plays an increasingly important role.
Participation in sport has been slowly democratized and is gradually becoming a cultural phenomenon on the same basis as cinema or television. For its part, professional sport has acquired the status of entertainment, the impact of which is increased by coverage on radio and TV and in the specialist and general press. Finally, sport is associated not only with the idea of health but also with a hedonistic cult of the body.
Apparently, women play less sport than men, and to do so have to overcome obstacles which are socio-cultural rather than physiological in origin.

*Cultural obstacles to women participating in sport*
The first and most obvious obstacle derives from the place of women in society. Whether she is considered primarily as the mother of a family responsible for bearing and bringing up children, or is obliged to work for economic reasons, or has chosen to pursue a profession, generally speaking, a woman has a much greater social burden to bear than a man and has less leisure.
However, the major obstacle to women taking part in sport lies in the deep-rooted conception of sport as a properly masculine activity, naturally suited to the capabilities, attitudes and interests of men.
For this reason, there are still many people who cannot accustom themselves to women's playing sports which hitherto formed an exclusively male preserve, such as football, cricket and rugby. It was not until the 1984 Olympic Games that women were finally allowed to run the marathon, although it has been medically proven that women have more stamina than men.
Sport was long regarded as dangerous for women's health. In the course of time, this notion was proved by medical science to be false, and its erroneous nature was demonstrated by the achievements of women taking part in competitive sports.
On the other hand, there are those who regard sport as beneficial for women on the grounds that it improves their capacity to bear children.
This notion gives to a rise to a number of equally erroneous attitudes which are more particularly evident in field of education and information.

## Sport and education

In most of the Member States of the Community, sport at school is too often considered to be of secondary importance, at best an hour of intellectual relaxation, at worst an hour wasted. Even where sport is properly valued as an instrument of personal development (health, physical shape, stamina, suppleness and, indirectly, self-confidence) and social development (introdution to the idea of life in groups, teams, responsibility, openness towards the outside world), all too frequently the amount and types of sport played still vary according to sex. While a boy should play contact sports or team sports, it is considered 'natural' for girls to be directed towards sports which allow them to express their femininity more freely (dancing, gymnastics, etc.). We feel this distinction derives from the basic idea which we criticized above. Just as much as little boys, little girls need this training for life in society which sport represents, and they must therefore not be prevented from playing the sports they wish to, even those considered to be boys' sports.

## Sport and information

Competitive sports occupy an increasingly important place in the media, although it is noticeable that coverage of women's sports is generally limited to the publication of resuits. This is true of both specialist and non-specialist newspapers and periodicals, and of radio and television.

The reasons most often given for this deplorable state of affairs are that women's sporting performances are inferior to men's, that men's sports are more spectacular and that there are, after all, more sportsmen than sportswomen.

Such attitudes are bound to create a vicious circle. Sports which receive media coverage have a greater chance of attracting the support of sponsors, with the result that more funds are available and better training facilities can be afforded. Sportsmen thus enjoy a privileged position. This is one of the reasons why it is impossible to compare the relative performances of men and women in sport. Moreover, comparatively speaking, women have only just begun to play sport professionally, and in many sports, they still lack the technical support and training enjoyed by their male colleagues.

There are, fortunateiy, some exceptions. The interest shown in women's tennis, for example, is encouraging. The battles in the Navratilova Evert-Lloyd final demonstrated that a ladies' singles match can be just as gripping as Boris Becker's straight-sets victory over Kevin Curran at Wimbtedon in 1985. In the case of tennis, women players have fought to be recognized as men's equals by demanding the same prize money and the recognition of their professional value by the competition organizers and by sponsors.

We are not aiming to pass judgment on the value of men's or women's amateur or professional sport as such. What is at stake is the importance of the participation in sport is recognized on the same terms as men's. If the star syndrome acts as an encouragement for boys to play sport, the emergence of women champions represent more than an incentive for women, it has a symbolic importance for the role of women in society, it provides them with a sense of their own worth and may help them to become equal members of society.

## Conclusions

The committee

–        whereas participation in sport is as vital for women as for men, for both body and mind,

–        whereas the obstacles to women playing sport are primarily cultural and social,
–        whereas participation in sport at any level gives women an opportunity to prove that they are not trapped in the social role traditionally imposed on them by society,

1.      Considers it unacceptable that certain sports organizations discriminate on the ba-
        sis of sex, with the result that women often have no say at all or play only a subor-
        dinate role in the administration of clubs and associations, and certain facilities
        (such as rules, changing rooms, etc.) are arranged for the benefit of men only; and
        calls on the Member States to exert pressure on these organizations − through their
        subsidization policy, in particular − so as to bring this discrimination to an end;
2.      Criticizes the fact that the media and sponsors devote relatively little attention to
        women's sport, thereby involuntarily perpetuating obsolescent notions about the
        insignificant role of women;
3.      Considers it vital that provision be made to enable women to take part in a variety
        of sports, for example, by publicizing in schools the opportunities for playing
        sports, improving access to sports facilities and taking account of women's spe-
        cific needs, such as creches and child-minding facilities;
4.      Recommends the setting-up of courses aimed specifically at women, in the fields
        of coaching, sport for young people and the training of women games teachers;
5.      Considers it essential that boys and girls should have equal opportunities to take
        part in sport on the same terms, both in school and as an extracurricular activity,
        and at all stages of their development;
6.      Hopes for general recognition that physical exercise and sport are of great impor-
        tance for the physical and mental education of both boys and girls so that more
        attention is given to the subject in schools;
7.      Calls for the encouragement at Community level of exchanges of girls and boys
        involved in sport;
8.      Calls on the Commission to set a good example in the sporting events organized
        under its auspices through a judicious choice of sports, by encouraging the partici-
        pation of women and by giving publicity to sportswomen;
9.      Considers that sport must be taken into account when measures are taken at Com-
        munity level to promote equal treatment of men and women.

                                        ——

**2.7.6.    RESOLUTION OF THE EUROPEAN PARLIAMENT ON WOMEN IN
            SPORT, 14 OCTOBER 1987**[715]

*The European Parliament,*

–       having regard to the motion for a resolution by Mrs Squarcialupi and others on a
        European Charter of Women's Rights in sport (Doc. B2-215/85),
–       having regard to the work of the Council of Europe, notably the European Charter
        on Sport for All, and the resolution on greater participation by women in sport,
        adopted respectively by the Conference of European Ministers responsible for
        sport, in Brussels in March 1981, and in Palma in April 1981,
–       having regard to its resolution of 11 June 1986 on violence against women[716],
–       having regard to the report of the Committee on Women's Rights and the opinion
        of the Committee on Youth, Culture, Education, Information and Sport (Doc. A2-
        32/87/corr.),

A.      whereas the basis of equal treatment policy is the principle that the individual

---

[715]   OJ C 305, 16-11-1987, p. 62.
[716]   OJ C 176, 14- 7-1986, p. 73.

should be treated in terms of personal capacity and qualities, and not by reference to gender,

B.     given the growing awareness in recent years of the health benefits and general well-being to be gained from regular exercise, and the benefits of creating a healthier population,

C.     whereas sport is practised increasingly as a means of gaining self-awareness ' enriching personality, and rediscovering movement, play and the competitive spirit, whilst accepting one's personal limitations,

D.     whereas sport can be important in the development of the personality and of social skills,

E.     whereas young children involved in competitive sports are subjected to excessively rigorous training programmes, and whereas this applies notably to young girls,

F.     whereas women are also increasingly using hormones to improve their performance,

G.     in view of the growing importance of leisure in modern society,

H.     whereas more men than women practise sport, and more women in paid employment than women working at home, hence making the active promotion of increased participation by women in sport a necessary part of equal opportunities policy,

I.     whereas measures must be taken in legislation and attempts must be made to change mental attitude to overcome the image of sport as a traditionally male preserve, to which women are allowed access only if they adapt themselves to methods, habits and mental attitudes oriented towards men,

## Legislation

1.     Considers that to tackle the question of women in sport the value of women's differing physiology, function, aptitude and psychology must be acknowledged and female identity safeguarded;

2.     Calls on those few Member States which allow the exemption of sporting activities from the scope of equal opportunities and anti-discrimination legislation to remove this exemption, so that equal opportunities for women may be promoted in sport as in all other areas of life;

3.     Therefore calls on all national and international Olympic sports federations to draw up their rules to comply with Community and national laws on equality, the first priority being equal access to sport for all citizens, regardless of sex or social conditions, ensuring equal rights for all members;

4.     Calls on authorities at national, regional and local levels, to bring pressure to bear on such organizations to amend such discriminatory provisions, notably by refusing grants to sporting clubs and organizations which discriminate against women;

5.     Considers, therefore, that in the sphere of sport too a policy of positive action and redistribution of financial resources is needed to encourage women to take part in sport;

6.     Calls for greater attention to be given in scientific research to the subject of women in all fields now involved in the development of sporting activity;

7.     Urges the authorities to ban the use of hormones in sport, in so far as they have not already done so, and to introduce appropriate measures to check that the ban is observed;

## Role of the media

8.     Notes and deplores the generally low level of coverage by the media of women in

sport, which results in lower levels of sponsorship of women's sporting events making them more difficult to organize and promote; further notes that many women feel that this low level of coverage results in a negative image of female sport;

9. Recognizes the power of the media to influence public attitudes and considers that fuller coverage by the media of sportwomen, in particular the special contribution made by women, would result, not only in more accurate reporting on sporting activities in general, but in promoting a fairer image of women, participating at all levels of life;

10. Considers that the public image of women in sport largely originates in the media and reflects society's ideas about women and men; further recognizes that competitive sport has traditionally been the preserve of men, with women's participation traditionally being restricted to more passive pastimes; believes that media coverage of women in sport reflects these traditions and that the current emphasis in sports reporting on competition, strength and physical dominance as a measure of excellence may contribute to problems of violence and hooliganism at some sporting events;

11. Considers that media coverage of women's sports events is often inferior to that of men's events (it is presented by men and is often less sport-focused, male presenters often compare female sports participants in terms of traditional concepts of feminity referring to their physical appearance and private lives rather than their sporting achievements) and believes that less sexist and less heterosexist sports coverage, promoting more positive information and imagery of women in sport would be of great benefit in encouraging women's participation in sport and in society in general;

12. Considers that media coverage of sport reinforces the idea that sport is for the young and physically fit and believes that attention should be given to finding ways of persuading women that age need not limit their scope for participating in sport;

13. Calls on the Commission to encourage, through special action programmes, a greater involvement of the mass media in sports events, thus changing attitudes and providing rolemodels for girls and women who wish to practise a sport;

14. Calls on the Commission, in the context of 1988 – Year of Cinema and Television, to coordinate
    (a) the organization of a Women's Sports Week from 7 to 13 March 1988, coinciding with International Women's Day on 8 March, with events in each Member State, and
    (b) full media publicity and coverage of these events;

15. Calls on the Commission to bear in mind participation by women when selecting sporting events for sponsorship and to encourage women to take part;

**Education and therapy**

16. Calls for fuller recognition by the education authorities of the Member States of the equal importance for girls and boys of physical education, not only for their physical development and well-being, but also as a means of developing the qualities which will help them to succeed in adult and professional life;

17. Urges that reporting of women's sports and competitions should place particular emphasis on the fact that women's sporting achievements should be assessed according to their own standards and qualifications and should not merely be seen only in relation to those of men;

18. Further calls on the education authorities to ensure that those training to be physi-

cal education teachers, particularly male trainees, be fully aware of these aspects of physical education, and of the importance of encouraging girls to be more actively involved in sport whilst acknowledging their difference; teachers should, in particular, discourage boys from adopting negative attitudes to girls' participation in traditionally male sports such as football;

19.    Points out the necessity for teachers and parents to be especially concerned by the problems of teenage girls who may feel unsure of themselves physically and to whom the physical and psychological benefits of regular exercise should be fully explained;

20.    Calls on those Member States where it is not common practice to encourage educational and local authorities to cooperate, with a view to facilitating the use of school sporting facilities by the public outside school hours;

21.    Calls for special attention to be given to the provision of sports facilities in schools and training centres for physically and mentally handicapped girls and women;

22.    Considers that the same facilities should be given to elderly women;

23.    Calls on medical and paramedical personnel who come into contact with the handicapped to greatly encourage them to practise sport by emphasizing the benefits to be gained from regular exercise and sporting activity, which also widens social contact;

24.    Considers in this respect that such personnel should develop a particularly strong response to. the problems of handicapped girls and women for whom incapacity or deformity can present an important psychological problem;,this should be borne in mind most especially where sport is used as therapy;

25.    Considers furthermore that more determined promotion of physical education at schools, particularly for girls, is an important preparation for the constructive use of leisure time and personal fulfilment, ever-growing aspects of modern life;

## Sports and leisure facilities

26.    Calls attention to the positive results of projects designed to reintroduce women to sport but asks national authorities to ensure that all leisure centres, whether State-financed or private, should provide adequate facilities for the practice of sports by both men and women, especially the handicapped and elderly women;

27.    Calls for women and women's teams not to take second place to men's teams in the use of sports facilities;

28.    Further notes that such projects, as well as resulting in increased participation by women of all age groups in sports and leisure activities, also lead to more efficient daytime use of sports and leisure facilities;

29.    Calls on national governments and local authorities to ensure that sports and leisure facilities include purpose-built, properly staffed creche facilities, and organize special sports sessions for mothers and children where appropriate;

30.    Urges national and local authorities to ensure that sports and leisure facilities are subsidized where necessary, to ensure that the low-paid or unwaged are not excluded because of cost;

31.    Calls on national and local governments to ensure that all sports and leisure facilities are adequately served by public transport so as to ensure that women are not discriminated against by not having access to a car;

32.    Urges organizers of sports and leisure facilities to actively encourage women's participation by:
    –    encouraging women's centres and women's groups to promote and organize sport and recreational activities,
    –    encouraging the formation of leagues, coaching classes and facilities for women in sports which are traditionally male-dominated,

- promoting women-only activities with female coaching staff,
- encouraging female membership of all sports associations,
- increasing women's awareness of the opportunities available for sport and leisure through appropriate marketing and communication channels e.g. Women's press, shops, libraries, nurseries, newsletters and leaflets specifically aimed at women,
- organizing events such as women's days of sport with activities in sports and leisure centres where women can try new sports which are traditionally viewed as 'male';

33.  Recognizes the particular problems faced by ethnic minority women and urges national and local authorities to ensure that facilities at sports and leisure centres take account of their needs and provide a suitable environment to encourage them to participate, and further urges all relevant authorities to develop and implement anti-racist policies;

**Competition**

34.  Considers it self-evident that no-one could aspire to a place in a sport or on a team which she/he did not fully deserve through personal talent, qualifications and level of training, and therefore calls for the amendment of sports regulations which may present obstacles to equal treatment of sportswomen and men;

**Representation**

35.  Calls on sport organizations and federations to ensure better representation of women at management and organization level, and on amateur sport governing bodies and the Olympic Committee, and in sporting activities by increased training and use of female coaches and referees;

36.  Considers it of the utmost importance that women be involved in decisions concerning women's sports and that women's representation on all bodies which discuss and promote sport and leisure should be increased;

37.  Considers that society should accept the right of each individual to practise on her/his own terms the sport of her/his choice to the level of her/his ability, and that all obstacles to such fulfilment should be abolished;

38.  Calls for further research to be undertaken to identify existing barriers to greater participation by women in sport and urges national governments, local authorities and sports organizers to suggest ways in which these barriers can be removed;

39.  Calls urgently on sports organizations and federations to ensure that training takes place under strict medical supervision so as to prevent young children from being subjected to excessive strain;

40.  Instructs its President to forward this resolution to the Commission, the Council, the governments of the Member States, and the Council of Europe.

———

**\* 2.7.7.    ANSWER ON BEHALF OF THE COMMISSION TO WRITTEN QUESTION NO 1868/90 BY MR MARC GALLE (S), 2 OCTOBER 1990[717] \***

Subject: Discrimination on grounds of nationality in amateur sport (Royal Belgian Tennis Federation)

———

[717] Question of 20-7-1990; OJ C 63, 11-3-1991, p. 43.

**\* 2.7.8.    ANSWER ON BEHALF OF THE COMMISSION TO WRITTEN QUESTION E-2773/95 BY TONY CUNNINGHAM (PSE), 7 FEBRUARY 1996[718] \***

Subject: Rugby's Union discrimination against League players

———

**2.7.9.    RESOLUTION OF THE EUROPEAN PARLIAMENT ON THE NON-PARTICIPATION BY WOMEN FROM CERTAIN COUNTRIES AT THE OLYMPIC GAMES, 4 JULY 1996[719]**

*The European Parliament,*

–       having regard to the United Nations Convention on the Elimination of All Forms of Discrimination Against Women (CEDAW) and the European Convention for the Protection of Human Rights and Fundamental Freedoms,
–       having regard to the Final Declaration and Platform for Action adopted in September 1995 in Beijing at the United Nations Fourth World Conference on Women: Action for Equality, Development and Peace,
–       having regard to the Olympic Charter which declares that all forms of discrimination based on reasons of race, religion, political opinion, sex or other are contrary to the Olympic movement (Rule 3, Chapter 1),

A.       whereas the Olympic Games open on 19 July 1996 in Atlanta,
B.       whereas women's rights are human rights; whereas full implementation of the human rights of women and of the girl child is an inalienable, integral and indivisible part of all human rights and fundamental freedoms,
C.       whereas 35 mainly Islamic countries nominated only men for participation in the previous Olympic Games,
D.       whereas this situation has been condemned by the Atlanta Plus Committee,
E.       whereas the dress code for women in many of these countries prohibits sporting activities even if women's participation is not forbidden as such, thus leading to the same result, namely non-participation,
F.       whereas the Olympic Games have always been considered as one of the few universal gatherings of people of all nations, irrespective of cultures, religions or race, apart from nations with declared apartheid; whereas participation in sporting activities and international competitions is an excellent opportunity, irrespective of background, for young people to meet and exchange views, thus fostering mutual understanding and peace,
G.       whereas denying competition to women discourages them as a whole from taking part in sports and is thus prejudicial to their health, given that the World Health Organisation (WHO) recognises sport as a means of preventing or limiting various serious illnesses,
H.       whereas to bar women from participation borders on 'gender discrimination' and is, therefore, a violation of human rights,
I.       whereas for many years the European Parliament, international institutions and the International Olympic Committee steadfastly and effectively campaigned against the apartheid suffered by blacks in South Africa,

---

[718] Question of 12-10-1995; OJ C 137, 8-5-1996, p. 2-3.
[719] OJ C 211 , 22-7-1996, p. 36.

1. Condemns the prohibition of some governments which prevents women from participating in the Olympic Games;
2. Strongly advises against European Union support or cooperation, whether material, financial or in any other form, with countries which effectively implement 'gender discrimination" by barring female citizens from participating in the Olympic Games;
3. Observes that the example mentioned above is part of a more general discrimination which affects women in certain Islamic countries;
4. Asks the Council to call for a ban on participation in future Olympic Games of countries which exercise 'gender discrimination";
5. Recalls that sport and politics have seldom been separate issues, despite frequent claims to the contrary;
6. Asks the Commission and Council to work actively in all fora possible for the Olympic Games and other international sporting events to be open to all with full regard to equal participation of men and women;
7. Instructs its President to forward this resolution to the Council, the Commission, the governments of the Member States, the United Nations and the International Olympic Committee.

———

## * 2.7.10. ANSWER ON BEHALF OF THE COMMISSION TO WRITTEN QUESTION E-1017/96 BY JESSICA LARIVE (ELDR), 4 JULY 1996[720] *

Subject: European day against racism and for fair play

———

## * 2.7.11. OPINION OF THE COMMITTEE OF THE REGIONS ON 'EQUAL OPPORTUNITIES FOR GIRLS AND BOYS IN LEISURE ACTIVITIES AND ESPECIALLY IN EU YOUTH AND SPORT PROGRAMMES, 20 NOVEMBER 1997[721]

———

## * 2.7.12. ANSWER ON BEHALF OF THE COMMISSION TO WRITTEN QUESTION E-3570/97 BY CRISTIANA MUSCARDINI (NI), 15 DECEMBER 1997[722] *

Subject: Serious case of racial discrimination against two Italian citizens by Belgian sports authorities.

———

## * 2.7.13. ANSWER ON BEHALF OF THE COMMISSION TO WRITTEN QUESTION E-3858/98 BY NIKITAS KAKLAMANIS (UPE), 16 MARCH 1999[723] *

Subject: FIBA decision concerning basketball

———

[720] Question of 26-4-1996; OJ C 305, 15-10-1996, p. 38.
[721] OJ C 64 , 27-2-1998 p. 81.
[722] Question of 13-11-1997; OJ C 158, 25-5-1998, p. 151.
[723] Question of 4-1-1999; OJ C 297, 15-10-1999, p. 108.

**\* 2.7.14.  ANSWER ON BEHALF OF THE COMMISSION TO WRITTEN QUESTION E-1592/99 BY GLYN FORD (PSE), 12 OCTOBER 1999**[724] **\***

Subject: Discrimination against footballers

———

**\* 2.7.15.  ANSWER ON BEHALF OF THE COMMISSION TO WRITTEN QUESTION E-1651/99 BY NELLY MAES (VERTS/ALE), 4 NOVEMBER 1999**[725] **\***

Subject: Discrimination in connection with pigeon racing in the border regions of Belgium and the Netherlands

———

**\* 2.7.16.  ANSWER ON BEHALF OF THE COMMISSION TO WRITTEN QUESTION E-2333/99 BY BART STAES (VERTS/ALE), 28 JANUARY 2000**[726] **\***

Subject: Measures for the benefit of disabled people who practise sport and use IT networks

———

**\* 2.7.17.  ANSWER ON BEHALF OF THE COMMISSION TO WRITTEN QUESTION E-2511/99 BY MARÍA SORNOSA MARTÍNEZ (PSE) AND MARÍA VALENCIANO MARTÍNEZ-OROZCO (PSE), 14 FEBRUARY 2000**[727] **\***

Subject: Infringement of the principle of sex equality in chess tournaments within the European Union

———

**\* 2.7.18.  ANSWER ON BEHALF OF THE COMMISSION TO WRITTEN QUESTION E-2621/99 BY ISIDORO SÁNCHEZ GARCÍA (ELDR), 28 FEBRUARY 2000**[728] **\***

Subject: Bringing the rules of the Spanish Swimming Federation allowing no more than two non-Spanish players to play in the national water polo league into line with Community law

———

**\* 2.7.19.  ANSWER ON BEHALF OF THE COMMISSION TO WRITTEN QUESTION E-2526/00 BY ARMANDO COSSUTTA (GUE/NGL), 5 OCTOBER 2000**[729] **\***

Subject: Discrimination against disabled people in Rotterdam

———

[724] Question of 1-9-1999; OJ C 219 E, 1-8-2000, p. 11.
[725] Question of 22-9-1999; OJ C 170 E, 20-6-2000, p. 63.
[726] Question of 13-12-1999; OJ C 225 E, 8-8-2000, p. 104.
[727] Question of 22-12-1999; OJ C 225 E, 8-8-2000, p. 154.
[728] Question of 12-1-2000; OJ C 280 E, 3-10-2000, p. 86.
[729] Question of 2-8-2000; OJ C 89 E, 20-3-2001, p. 198.

**\* 2.7.20.  ANSWER ON BEHALF OF THE COMMISSION TO WRITTEN QUESTION E-2554/00 BY CRISTIANA MUSCARDINI (UEN), 5 OCTOBER 2000**[730] **\***

Subject: Safeguarding the rights of the disabled and events in Rotterdam

———

**\* 2.7.21.  ANSWER ON BEHALF OF THE COMMISSION TO WRITTEN QUESTION E-2207/00 BY ILDA FIGUEIREDO (GUE/NGL), 17 OCTOBER 2000**[731] **\***

Subject: Discrimination in the Luxembourg Football Federation

———

**\* 2.7.22.  ANSWER ON BEHALF OF THE COMMISSION TO WRITTEN QUESTION P-3172/00 BY GERARDO GALEOTE QUECEDO (PPE-DE), 30 OCTOBER 2000**[732] **\***

Subject: Obstacles to the contracting of non-EU workers by sports clubs

———

**\* 2.7.23.  ANSWER ON BEHALF OF THE COMMISSION TO WRITTEN QUESTION E-4133/00 BY RAINER WIELAND (PPE-DE), 19 FEBRUARY 2001**[733] **\***

Subject: Right of an Israeli national to play in German handball leagues

———

**\* 2.7.24.  REPLY ON BEHALF OF THE COUNCIL TO WRITTEN QUESTION E-4132/00 BY RAINER WIELAND (PPE-DE), 14 MAY 2001**[734] **\***

Subject: Right of an Israeli national to play in German handball leagues

———

**\* 2.7.25.  ANSWER ON BEHALF OF THE COMMISSION TO WRITTEN QUESTION E-3074/01 BY CARLOS BAUTISTA OJEDA (VERTS/ALE), 21 DECEMBER 2001**[735] **\***

Subject: Discrimination in Spain against disabled pilots

———

**\* 2.7.26.  ANSWER ON BEHALF OF THE COMMISSION TO WRITTEN QUESTION P-1044/02 BY THERESA ZABELL (PPE-DE), 7 MAY 2002**[736] **\***

Subject: Sporting licences

———

[730] Question of 28-7-2000; OJ C 89 E, 20-3-2001 p. 199-200.
[731] Question of 3-7-2000; OJ C 113 E, 18-4-2001, p. 71.
[732] Question of 4-10-2000; OJ C 151 E, 22-5-2001, p. 86.
[733] Question of 16-1-2001; OJ C 187 E, 3-7-2001, p. 143.
[734] Question of 16-1-2001; OJ C 235 E, 21-8-2001, p. 76.
[735] Question of 12-11-2001; OJ C 147 E, 20-6-2002, p. 89.
[736] Question of 3-4-2002; OJ C 52E, 6-3-2003, p. 27-28.

**\* 2.7.27.  EUROPEAN COURT OF JUSTICE, OPINION OF ADVOCATE GENERAL STIX-HACKL, DEUTSCHER HANDBALLBUND EV V MAROS KOLPAK, CASE C-438/00, 11 JULY 2002[737] \***

---

**\* 2.7.28.  ANSWER ON BEHALF OF THE COMMISSION TO WRITTEN QUESTION E-2133/02 BY BARTHO PRONK (PPE-DE), 12 SEPTEMBER 2002[738] \***

Subject: Discrimination against international football referees on grounds of age

---

**\* 2.7.29.  REPLY ON BEHALF OF THE COUNCIL TO WRITTEN QUESTION E-1865/02 BY BRIAN CROWLEY (UEN), 16-19 DECEMBER 2002[739]**

Subject: Special Olympics 2003 and creating an inclusive sporting environment

---

**2.7.30.  WRITTEN DECLARATION OF THE EUROPEAN PARLIAMENT ON DISCRIMINATION AGAINST A MINORITY SPORT BY CATHERINE GUY-QUINT, COLETTE FLESCH, FREDDY BLAK, BRIAN SIMPSON AND TERENCE WYNN, 14 APRIL 2003[740]**

*The European Parliament,*

–    having regard to Rule 51 of the Rules of Procedure,
–    noting that the report by the French Commission of Inquiry into sport during the Occupation, dated 19 March 2002, has not been published,
–    noting that the university curriculum for future teachers of physical education and sport in France does not include rugby league,
–    noting that rugby league clubs' access to certain municipal facilities is often made difficult if not impossible, because of the existence of Article 616 (formerly Article 412) in the by-laws and regulations of the French Rugby (Union) Federation, which stipulates that a loan made by the Federation for the improvement of a municipal stadium reserves the stadium for the exclusive use of rugby union,

1.    Calls on the French Government:
–    to publish the report by the Commission and make it widely available to the general public;
–    to incorporate rugby league as a sport into the university curriculum for trainee teachers of physical education and sport;
–    to make municipal stadiums available to all sportsmen and take the necessary steps to repeal Article 616 (formerly Article 412) of the by-laws and regulations of the French Rugby (Union) Federation, this article being contrary to democratic rights since it allows a governing body to enjoy, at little expense, the exclusive right to public facilities to the detriment of other users;

---

[737]  ECR 2003, p. I-04135
[738]  Question of 17-7-2002; OJ C 110 E, 8-5-2003, p. 32-33.
[739]  Question of 28-6-2002; OJ C 92 E, 17-4-2003, p. 103.
[740]  7/2003.

2.      Instructs its President to forward this declaration, together with the names of the
        signatories, to the French Government.

———

**2.7.31.   EUROPEAN COURT OF JUSTICE, JUDGMENT (FIFTH CHAMBER),
            DEUTSCHER HANDBALLBUND EV V MAROS KOLPAK, CASE
            C-438/00, 8 MAY 2003**[741]

*External relations – Association Agreement between the Communities and Slovakia – Ar-
ticle 38(1) – Free movement of workers – Principle of non-discrimination – Handball –
Limitation on the number of professional players having the nationality of non-member
countries who may play on a team in the league of a sports federation*

In Case C-438/00,
Reference to the Court under Article 234 EC by the Oberlandesgericht Hamm (Germany)
for a preliminary ruling in the proceedings pending before that court between

Deutscher Handballbund eV and Maros Kolpak,

on the interpretation of Article 38(1) of the Europe Agreement establishing an association
between the European Communities and their Member States, of the one part, and the
Slovak Republic, of the other part, approved on behalf of the Communities by Decision
94/909/ECSC, EEC, Euratom of the Council and the Commission of 19 December 1994
(OJ 1994 L 359, p. 1),

The Court (Fifth Chamber),
composed of: D.A.O. Edward, acting for the President of the Chamber, A. La Pergola
(Rapporteur), P. Jann, S. von Bahr and A. Rosas, Judges,
Advocate General: C. Stix-Hackl,
Registrar: L. Hewlett, Principal Administrator,
after considering the written observations submitted on behalf of:
– Deutscher Handballbund eV, by P. Seydel, H.J. Bodenstaff and R. Jersch, Rechtsan-
wälte,
– the German Government, by W.-D. Plessing and B. Muttelsee-Schön, acting as Agents,
– the Spanish Government, by R. Silva de Lapuerta, acting as Agent,
– the Italian Government, by U. Leanza, acting as Agent, assisted by D. Del Gaizo,
avvocato dello Stato,
– the Commission of the European Communities, by M.-J. Jonczy, D. Martin and H.
Kreppel, acting as Agents,

–       having regard to the Report for the Hearing,
–       after hearing the oral observations of Deutscher Handballbund eV, represented by
        R. Jersch; of Mr Kolpak, represented by M. Schlüter, Rechtsanwalt; of the Greek
        Government, represented by V. Pelekou and S. Spyropoulos, acting as Agents; of
        the Spanish Government, represented by R. Silva de Lapuerta; of the Italian Gov-
        ernment, represented by G. Aiello, avvocato dello Stato; and of the Commission,
        represented by M.-J. Jonczy and H. Kreppel, at the hearing on 20 June 2002,
–       after hearing the Opinion of the Advocate General at the sitting on 11 July 2002,
        gives the following

---

[741] ECR 2003, p. I-04135.

**Judgment**

1.     By order of 15 November 2000, received at the Court on 28 November 2000, the Oberlandesgericht (Higher Regional Court) Hamm referred for a preliminary ruling under Article 234 EC a question on the interpretation of Article 38(1) of the Europe Agreement establishing an association between the European Communities and their Member States, of the one part, and the Slovak Republic, of the other part, signed in Luxembourg on 4 October 1993 and approved on behalf of the Communities by Decision 94/909/ECSC, EEC, Euratom of the Council and the Commission of 19 December 1994 (OJ 1994 L 359, p. 1) ('the Association Agreement with Slovakia').

2.     That question has been raised in a dispute between Deutscher Handballbund eV (the German Handball Federation) ('the DHB') and Mr Kolpak concerning the issue of a professional player's licence.

**The Association Agreement with Slovakia**

3.     Article 1(2) of the Association Agreement with Slovakia states that the aims of the Agreement are, *inter alia*, to provide an appropriate framework for political dialogue between the Parties, allowing the development of close political relations between them, to promote the expansion of trade and harmonious economic relations between the Parties in order to foster dynamic economic development and prosperity in the Slovak Republic, and to provide an appropriate framework for the Slovak Republic's gradual integration into the Communities, that country's ultimate objective being, according to the final recital in the preamble to that Agreement, accession to the Communities.

4.     With regard to the case in the main proceedings, the relevant provisions of the Association Agreement are to be found in Title IV thereof, entitled 'Movement of workers, establishment, supply of services'.

5.     Article 38(1) of the Association Agreement, which features in Title IV, Chapter I, entitled 'Movement of workers', provides:
'Subject to the conditions and modalities applicable in each Member State:
     – treatment accorded to workers of Slovak Republic nationality legally employed in the territory of a Member State shall be free from any discrimination based on nationality, as regards working conditions, remuneration or dismissal, as compared to its own nationals,
     – the legally resident spouse and children of a worker legally employed in the territory of a Member State, with the exception of seasonal workers and of workers coming under bilateral agreements within the meaning of Article 42, unless otherwise provided by such agreements, shall have access to the labour market of that Member State, during the period of that worker's authorised stay of employment.'

6.     Article 42 of the Association Agreement, which features in the same chapter, states:
     '1.   Taking into account the labour market situation in the Member State, subject to its legislation and to the respect of rules in force in that Member State in the area of mobility of workers:
          – the existing facilities for access to employment for Slovak Republic workers accorded by Member States under bilateral agreements ought to be preserved and if possible improved,
          – the other Member States shall consider favourably the possibility of concluding similar agreements.
     2.   The Association Council shall examine granting other improvements in-

cluding facilities of access for professional training, in conformity with rules and procedures in force in the Member States, and taking account of the labour market situation in the Member States and in the Community.'

7.    Article 59(1) of the Association Agreement, which appears in Title IV, Chapter IV, entitled 'General provisions', provides:
'For the purpose of Title IV of this Agreement, nothing in the Agreement shall prevent the Parties from applying their laws and regulations regarding entry and stay, work, labour conditions and establishment of natural persons, and supply of services, provided that, in so doing, they do not apply them in a manner as to nullify or impair the benefits accruing to any Party under the terms of a specific provision of this Agreement. ...'

## The national rules

8.    The DHB adopted the Spielordnung (federal regulations governing competitive games) ('the SpO'), Rule 15 of which, in the version in force on the date of the order for reference, provided as follows:
'(1)  The letter A is to be inserted after the licence number of the licences of players
(a)   who do not possess the nationality of a State of the European Union (EU State),
(b)   who do not possess the nationality of a non-member country associated with the EU whose nationals have equal rights as regards freedom of movement under Article 48(1) of the EC Treaty,
(c)   ...
(2)  In teams in the federal and regional leagues, no more than two players whose licences are marked with the letter A may play in a league or cup match.
...
(5)  The marking of a licence with the letter A is to be cancelled from 1 July of the year if the player's country of origin becomes associated within the meaning of Paragraph 1(b) by that date. The DHB shall publish and continually update the list of the States correspondingly associated.'

## The dispute in the main proceedings and the question submitted for preliminary ruling

9.    Mr Kolpak, who is a Slovak national, entered in March 1997 into a fixed-term employment contract expiring on 30 June 2000 and subsequently, in February 2000, entered into a new fixed-term contract expiring on 30 June 2003 for the post of goalkeeper in the German handball team TSV Östringen eV Handball, a club which plays in the German Second Division. Mr Kolpak receives a monthly salary. He is resident in Germany and holds a valid residence permit.

10.   The DHB, which organises league and cup matches at federal level, issued to him, under Rule 15 of the SpO, a player's licence marked with the letter A on the ground of his Slovak nationality.

11.   Mr Kolpak, who had requested that he be issued with a player's licence which did not feature the specific reference to nationals of non-member countries, brought an action before the Landgericht (Regional Court) Dortmund (Germany) challenging that decision of the DHB. He argued that the Slovak Republic is one of the non-member countries nationals of which are entitled to participate without restriction in competitions under the same conditions as German and Community players by reason of the prohibition of discrimination resulting from the combined provisions of the EC Treaty and the Association Agreement with Slovakia.

12.      The Landgericht ordered the DHB to issue Mr Kolpak with a player's licence not marked with an A on the ground that, under Rule 15 of the SpO, Mr Kolpak was not to be treated in the same way as a player who was a national of a non-member country. The DHB appealed against that decision to the Oberlandesgericht Hamm.

13.      The Oberlandesgericht takes the view that the reference to Article 48 of the EC Treaty (now, after amendment, Article 39 EC) by Rule 15(1)(b) of the SpO must be construed as meaning that this latter provision covers only players who enjoy complete equality of treatment *vis-à-vis* Community nationals in respect of free movement of workers. According to this interpretation, Mr Kolpak is not entitled to be issued with a licence which does not contain the limitations resulting from the addition of the letter A, as such general equality of treatment does not feature in the association agreements concluded with the countries of Eastern Europe and the Mediterranean Basin, which include the Association Agreement with Slovakia.

14.      The Oberlandesgericht accordingly asks whether Rule 15(1)(b) of the SpO is contrary to Article 38 of the Association Agreement. If that were so, and if the latter provision were to have direct effect in regard to individuals, Mr Kolpak would be entitled to be issued with an unrestricted licence.

15.      In the opinion of the Oberlandesgericht, the DHB breaches the prohibition in Article 38 of the Association Agreement with Slovakia through its refusal to issue Mr Kolpak with an unrestricted licence on the ground of his nationality.

16.      In that regard, the Oberlandesgericht Hamm observes that Mr Kolpak's contract, which is governed by Rule 15 of the SpO, is an employment contract, as that player undertakes thereby, in return for a fixed monthly salary, to provide sporting services, as an employee, in connection with training and matches organised by his club and that this constitutes his main professional activity.

17.      The Oberlandesgericht also takes the view that the provisions of Rule 15(1)(b) and 15(2) of the SpO, read together, give rise to inequality of treatment in regard to working conditions. Mr Kolpak is already lawfully employed within the territory of the Federal Republic of Germany, in which he is resident, he holds a valid residence permit, he is not, under German legislation, subject to any obligation to obtain a work permit, and he is no longer personally affected by any barrier to employment, even an indirect one; all that notwithstanding, he does not, by reason of the above provisions, enjoy the same opportunities as others to participate in official matches as part of his professional activity.

18.      Thus, according to the Oberlandesgericht, the prohibition of discrimination set out in Article 38 of the Association Agreement with Slovakia applies on condition that the proviso contained therein relating to the conditions and modalities in force in each Member State does not preclude this. In that regard, the Oberlandesgericht considers that such conditions and modalities are constituted solely by legal rules of a general character and not by rules involving the application of working conditions that differ according to the nationality of the worker. It thus tends to the view that the rules drawn up by the DHB, within the framework of the autonomy which associations are recognised as having, do not form part of those conditions and modalities. If the contrary were true, the prohibition of discrimination contained in the Association Agreement would serve no purpose.

19.      The Oberlandesgericht Hamm further takes the view that Article 38 of the Association Agreement with Slovakia, in the same way as Article 48 of the Treaty, is a directly applicable provision inasmuch as, regard being had to its wording and to the purpose and nature of the Agreement, it contains a clear and precise obligation which is not subject, in its implementation or its effects, to the operation of any further measure. According to the Oberlandesgericht, Article 38 of the Association

Agreement also has effects *vis-à-vis* third parties inasmuch as it does not apply solely to measures taken by the authorities but also extends to rules applying to employees that are collective in nature.

20. The Oberlandesgericht concludes that it is faced with an infringement of the prohibition of discrimination arising under Article 38 of the Association Agreement with Slovakia which should have the effect of rendering Rule 15(1)(b) of the SpO inapplicable to Mr Kolpak.

21. In those circumstances, the Oberlandesgericht Hamm has decided to stay the proceedings and to refer the following question to the Court for a preliminary ruling:
   'Is it contrary to Article 38(1) of the Europe Agreement establishing an association between the European Communities and their Member States, of the one part, and the Slovak Republic, of the other part – Final Act – if a sports federation applies to a professional sportsman of Slovak nationality a rule that it has adopted under which clubs may field in league and cup matches only a limited number of players who come from countries not belonging to the European Communities?'

**The question submitted for preliminary ruling**

22. By its question the Oberlandesgericht Hamm is asking, essentially, whether the first indent of Article 38(1) of the Association Agreement with Slovakia is to be construed as precluding the application to a professional sportsman who is a Slovak national and is lawfully employed by a club established in a Member State of a rule drawn up by a sports federation in that State under which clubs are authorised, during league or cup matches, to field only a limited number of players from non-member countries that are not parties to the Agreement on the European Economic Area ('the EEA').

23. In order to reply to the question, as thus reformulated, it is necessary first of all to examine whether the first indent of Article 38(1) of the Association Agreement with Slovakia can be invoked by an individual before a national court and then, if the answer to that question is in the affirmative, whether that provision can be invoked in regard to a rule drawn up by a national sports federation such as the DHB. Finally, it will be necessary to establish the scope of the principle of non-discrimination which that provision lays down.

*The direct effect of the first indent of Article 38(1) of the Association Agreement with Slovakia*

24. It should be noted at the outset that, in paragraph 30 of its judgment in Case C-162/00 *Pokrzeptowicz-Meyer* [2002] ECR I-1049, the Court has already recognised the first indent of Article 37(1) of the Europe Agreement establishing an association between the European Communities and their Member States, of the one part, and the Republic of Poland, of the other part, signed in Brussels on 16 December 1991 and approved on behalf of the Communities by Decision 93/743/Euratom, ECSC, EC of the Council and the Commission of 13 December 1993 (OJ 1993 L 348, p. 1) ('the Association Agreement with Poland'), as having direct effect.

25. It is to be observed, first, that the wording of the first indent of Article 38(1) of the Association Agreement with Slovakia and that of the first indent of Article 37(1) of the Association Agreement with Poland is identical.

26. Second, those two Association Agreements do not differ in regard to their objectives or the context in which they were adopted. Each has, according to the final recital in the preamble and Article 1(2), the aim, *inter alia*, of establishing an association to promote the expansion of trade and harmonious economic relations be-

tween the contracting parties so as to foster dynamic economic development and prosperity in the Slovak Republic and in the Republic of Poland respectively, in order to facilitate those countries' accession to the Communities.

27. That being so, just as Article 58(1) of the Association Agreement with Poland does not preclude the first indent of Article 37(1) of that Agreement from having direct effect (see *Pokrzeptowicz-Meyer*, cited above, paragraph 28), so Article 59(1) of the Association Agreement with Slovakia does not preclude the first indent of Article 38(1) of that Agreement from having direct effect, given the similarity of the provisions in question.

28. Furthermore, as with the first indent of Article 37(1) of the Association Agreement with Poland, implementation of the first indent of Article 38(1) of the Association Agreement with Slovakia is not subject to the adoption by the Association Council, set up by that Agreement, of additional measures to define the detailed rules governing its application (*Pokrzeptowicz-Meyer*, paragraph 29).

29. Finally, just as in the case of Article 37(1) of the Association Agreement with Poland, the words '[s]ubject to the conditions and modalities applicable in each Member State' in Article 38(1) of the Association Agreement with Slovakia cannot be interpreted in such a way as to allow Member States to make the application of the principle of non-discrimination set out in that provision subject to conditions or discretionary limitations inasmuch as such an interpretation would render that provision meaningless and deprive it of any practical effect (*Pokrzeptowicz-Meyer*, paragraphs 20 to 24).

30. In those circumstances, the first indent of Article 38(1) of the Association Agreement with Slovakia must be recognised as having direct effect, with the result that Slovak nationals who invoke it are entitled to rely on it before national courts of the host Member State.

*The question whether the first indent of Article 38(1) of the Association Agreement with Slovakia applies to a rule laid down by a sports federation*

31. As a preliminary point, it should be observed that, in regard to Article 48(2) of the Treaty, it follows from paragraph 87 of the Court's judgment in Case C-415/93 *Bosman* [1995] ECR I-4921 that the prohibition of discrimination laid down in that provision applies to rules laid down by sporting associations which determine the conditions under which professional sportsmen can engage in gainful employment.

32. In that connection, the Court pointed out, in paragraph 84 of *Bosman*, cited above, that working conditions in the different Member States are governed sometimes by provisions laid down by law or regulation and sometimes by agreements and other acts concluded or adopted by private persons, and that, if the scope of Article 48 of the Treaty were to be confined to acts of a public authority, there would therefore be a risk of creating inequality in its application.

33. With regard to the first indent of Article 38(1) of the Association Agreement with Slovakia, in order to determine whether that provision applies to a rule drawn up by a sports federation such as the DHB, it is necessary to examine whether the Court's interpretation of Article 48(2) of the Treaty may be transposed in this case to the above provision of the Association Agreement with Slovakia.

34. The Court has stated in this regard, in paragraphs 39 and 40 of *Pokrzeptowicz-Meyer*, that, although the first indent of Article 37(1) of the Association Agreement with Poland does not lay down a principle of free movement for Polish workers within the Community, whereas Article 48 of the Treaty establishes for the benefit of Member State nationals the principle of free movement for workers,

it follows from a comparison of the aims and context of the Association Agreement with Poland, on the one hand, with those of the EC Treaty, on the other hand, that there is no ground for giving to the first indent of Article 37(1) of that Association Agreement a scope different from that which the Court has recognised Article 48(2) of the Treaty as having.

35.     In that context, the Court stated in paragraph 41 of *Pokrzeptowicz-Meyer* that the first indent of Article 37(1) of the Association Agreement with Poland establishes, in favour of workers of Polish nationality, once they are lawfully employed within the territory of a Member State, a right to equal treatment as regards conditions of employment of the same extent as that conferred in similar terms by Article 48(2) of the Treaty on Member State nationals.

36.     It follows from the foregoing and from the reasoning set out in paragraphs 25 to 30 of this judgment that the interpretation of Article 48(2) of the Treaty adopted by the Court in *Bosman* and referred to in paragraphs 31 and 32 of the present judgment may be transposed to the first indent of Article 38(1) of the Association Agreement with Slovakia.

37.     That being so, it must be concluded that the first indent of Article 38(1) of the Association Agreement with Slovakia applies to a rule drawn up by a sports federation such as the DHB which determines the conditions under which professional sportsmen engage in gainful employment.

*The scope of the principle of non-discrimination set out in the first indent of Article 38(1) of the Association Agreement with Slovakia*

38.     According to the DHB and the Greek, Spanish and Italian Governments, the scope of the non-discrimination clause contained in Article 38 of the Association Agreement with Slovakia is not intended to place on an entirely equal footing workers who are nationals of the Slovak Republic and workers who are nationals of the Member States of the European Union. The free movement of workers provided for in Article 48 of the Treaty, as applied within the area of sport by the *Bosman* judgment, can, they argue, benefit only Community nationals or nationals of an EEA Member State.

39.     Furthermore, all the parties which submitted observations to the Court agree that the prohibition of discrimination on grounds of nationality, set out in the first indent of Article 38(1) of the Association Agreement with Slovakia, applies only to workers of Slovak nationality who are already lawfully employed in the territory of a Member State and solely with regard to conditions of work, remuneration or dismissal.

40.     On this point, the DHB and the Greek, Spanish and Italian Governments argue that the rule contained in Rule 15(1)(b) and 15(2) of the SpO relates to access of Slovak nationals to employment. Article 38(1) of the Association Agreement with Slovakia, they submit, cannot therefore preclude the application of such a rule.

41.     Against this, Mr Kolpak, the German Government and the Commission submit that the facts in point in the main proceedings come within the first indent of Article 38(1) of the Association Agreement with Slovakia inasmuch as Mr Kolpak is not seeking access to the German labour market but is already lawfully working in Germany pursuant to domestic law and is suffering, in that connection, discrimination in working conditions by reason of the SpO.

42.     In that regard, it must be observed, first, that, according to the wording of the first indent of Article 38(1) of the Association Agreement with Slovakia, the prohibition of discrimination on grounds of nationality laid down in that provision applies only to workers of Slovak nationality who are already lawfully employed in the

territory of a Member State and solely with regard to conditions of work, remuneration or dismissal. In contrast to Article 48 of the Treaty, that provision does not therefore extend to national rules concerning access to the labour market.

43.   According to the order for reference, Mr Kolpak is lawfully employed as a goalkeeper under a contract of employment signed with a second-division German club, has a valid residence permit and does not, under national law, require a work permit in order to exercise his profession. It thus appears that he has already had lawful access to the labour market in Germany.

44.   In that context, with more particular regard to the question whether a rule such as that laid down in Rule 15(1)(b) and 15(2) of the SpO constitutes a working condition, it is necessary to point out that, in *Bosman*, the dispute in the main proceedings related to, *inter alia*, similar nationality rules or clauses drawn up by the Union of European Football Associations (UEFA).

45.   It follows from paragraph 120 of the judgment in *Bosman* that clauses of that kind concern not the employment of professional players, on which there is no restriction, but the extent to which their clubs may field them in official matches, and that participation in such matches is the essential purpose of their activity.

46.   It follows that a sports rule such as that in issue in the main proceedings relates to working conditions within the meaning of the first indent of Article 38(1) of the Association Agreement with Slovakia inasmuch as it directly affects participation in league and cup matches of a Slovak professional player who is already lawfully employed under the national provisions of the host Member State.

47.   hat being so, in order to establish whether the first indent of Article 38(1) of the Association Agreement with Slovakia precludes the application of a rule such as that laid down in Rule 15(1)(b) and 15(2) of the SpO, it remains to determine whether that rule involves discrimination prohibited by that provision of the Association Agreement.

48.   In that regard, it must be observed, first, that, so far as Article 48(2) of the Treaty is concerned, it follows from paragraph 137 of *Bosman* that that provision precludes the application of rules laid down by sporting associations under which, in competition matches which they organise, football clubs may field only a limited number of professional players who are nationals of other Member States.

49.   With regard to the interpretation of the first indent of Article 38(1) of the Association Agreement with Slovakia, it follows from paragraphs 25 to 30, 34, 35 and 44 of the present judgment that that provision introduces for the benefit of workers of Slovak nationality, on condition that they are lawfully employed in the territory of a Member State, a right to equal treatment as regards working conditions having the same scope as that which, in similar terms, nationals of the Member States are recognised as having by virtue of Article 48(2) of the Treaty, and that the rule in issue in the case in the main proceedings is similar to the nationality clauses in point in *Bosman*.

50.   That being so, the interpretation of Article 48(2) of the Treaty applied by the Court in *Bosman* and set out in paragraph 48 of the present judgment can be transposed to the first indent of Article 38(1) of the Association Agreement with Slovakia.

51.   Thus, the first indent of Article 38(1) of the Association Agreement with Slovakia precludes any application to Mr Kolpak of a rule such as that laid down in Rule 15(1)(b) and 15(2) of the SpO in so far as that rule gives rise to a situation in which Mr Kolpak, in his capacity as a Slovak national, although lawfully employed in a Member State, has, in principle, merely a limited opportunity, in comparison with players who are nationals of Member States or of EEA Member States, to participate in certain matches, that is to say, league and cup matches of

the German federal or regional leagues, which constitute, moreover, the essential purpose of his activity as a professional player.

52. That interpretation cannot be called in question by the DHB's argument that the rule laid down in Rule 15(1)(b) and 15(2) of the SpO is justified on exclusively sporting grounds, as its purpose is to safeguard training organised for the benefit of young players of German nationality and to promote the German national team.

53. Admittedly, in paragraph 127 of *Bosman*, the Court pointed out that, in paragraphs 14 and 15 of its judgment in Case 13/76 *Donà* v *Mantero* [1976] ECR 1333, it had recognised that the Treaty provisions on the free movement of persons do not preclude rules or practices excluding foreign players from certain matches for reasons which are not economic in nature, which relate to the particular nature and context of such matches and are thus of sporting interest only, such as matches between national teams from different countries.

54. In paragraph 128 of *Bosman*, however, the Court stated that nationality clauses do not concern specific matches between teams representing their countries but apply to all official matches between clubs and thus to the essence of the activity of professional players.

55. In that context, the Court pointed out that a football club's links with the Member State in which it is established cannot be regarded as any more inherent in its sporting activity than are its links with its locality, town or region. Even though national championships are played between clubs from different regions, towns or localities, there is no rule restricting the right of clubs to field players from other regions, towns or localities in such matches. Moreover, in international competitions participation is limited to clubs which have achieved certain sporting results in their respective countries, without any particular significance being attached to the nationalities of their players (*Bosman*, paragraphs 131 and 132).

56. Regard being had to that case-law, the discrimination arising in the present case from Rule 15(1)(b) and 15(2) of the SpO cannot be regarded as justified on exclusively sporting grounds inasmuch as it follows from those rules that, during matches organised by the DHB, clubs are free to field an unlimited number of nationals of EEA Member States.

57. Furthermore, no other argument capable of providing objective justification for the difference in treatment between, on the one hand, professional players who are nationals of a Member State or of an EEA Member State and, on the other, professional players who are Slovak nationals, resulting from Rule 15(1)(b) and 15(2) of the SpO and affecting the working conditions of the latter, has been put forward in the observations submitted to the Court.

58. It follows that the answer to the question submitted for preliminary ruling must be that the first indent of Article 38(1) of the Association Agreement with Slovakia must be construed as precluding the application to a professional sportsman of Slovak nationality, who is lawfully employed by a club established in a Member State, of a rule drawn up by a sports federation in that State under which clubs are authorised to field, during league or cup matches, only a limited number of players from non-member countries that are not parties to the EEA Agreement.

## Costs

59. The costs incurred by the German, Greek, Spanish and Italian Governments and by the Commission, which have submitted observations to the Court, are not recoverable. As these proceedings are, for the parties to the main proceedings, a step in the action pending before the national court, the decision on costs is a matter for that court.

**On those grounds,**
**The Court (Fifth Chamber),**
in answer to the question referred to it by the Oberlandesgericht Hamm (Germany) by order of 15 November 2000, hereby rules:

The first indent of Article 38(1) of the Europe Agreement establishing an association between the European Communities and their Member States, of the one part, and the Slovak Republic, of the other part, signed in Luxembourg on 4 October 1993 and approved on behalf of the Communities by Decision 94/909/ECSC, EEC, Euratom of the Council and the Commission of 19 December 1994, must be construed as precluding the application to a professional sportsman of Slovak nationality, who is lawfully employed by a club established in a Member State, of a rule drawn up by a sports federation in that State under which clubs are authorised to field, during league or cup matches, only a limited number of players from non-member countries that are not parties to the Agreement on the European Economic Area.

---

**\* 2.7.32.   COMMITTEE ON WOMEN'S RIGHTS AND EQUAL OPPORTUNITIES, REPORT ON WOMEN AND SPORT, 21 MAY 2003**

Rapporteur: Geneviève Fraisse[742]

---

**2.7.33.   RESOLUTION OF THE EUROPEAN PARLIAMENT ON WOMEN AND SPORT, 5 JUNE 2003**[743]

*The European Parliament,*

–   having regard to Articles 3 and 141 of the Treaty establishing the European Community,
–   having regard to Articles 21 and 23 of the Charter of Fundamental Rights of the European Union,
–   having regard to the declaration on sport annexed to the Treaty of Amsterdam,
–   having regard to the declaration by the European Council in Nice of 7, 8 and 9 December 2000 on the specific characteristics of sport and its social function in Europe, of which account should be taken in implementing common policies,
–   having regard to the statement by the European Council meeting in Lisbon on 23 and 24 March 2000, aimed at making it easier to reconcile working and family life, in particular by improving child-care provision,
–   having regard to United Nations Convention on the Elimination of All Forms of Discrimination Against Women of 18 December 1979,
–   having regard to the declaration and platform for action adopted by the Fourth United Nations World Conference on Women held in Beijing from 4 to 15 September 1995 and the 'Beijing+5' resolution seeking to implement the declaration and platform for action, adopted by the United Nations General Assembly on 10 June 2000,
–   having regard to its resolution of 14 October 1987 on women in sport[744],

---

[742]   A5-0167/2003.
[743]   A5-167/2003.
[744]   OJ C 305, 16-11-1987, p. 62.

–   having regard to its resolution of 4 July 1996 on the non-participation by women from certain countries at the Olympic Games[745],
–   having regard to its resolution of 13 June 1997 on the role of the European Union in the field of sport[746],
–   having regard to the resolution of 17 December 1999 of the Council of Ministers for Youth on the non-formal education dimension of sporting activities in the European Community youth programmes[747],
–   having regard to its resolution of 7 September 2000 on the report from the Commission to the European Council 'With a view to safeguarding current sports structures and maintaining the social function of sport within the Community framework, The Helsinki Report on Sport'[748],
–   having regard to the conclusions of the Conference of Ministers for Sport held under the Belgian Presidency on 12 November 2001,
–   having regard to the European Sports Charter and Code of Sports Ethics of the Council of Europe, as revised in 2001,
–   having regard to the International Charter of Physical Education and Sport adopted by the General Conference of UNESCO at its 20th session on 21 November 1978 in Paris,
–   having regard to the declaration adopted by the Third International Conference of Ministers and Senior Officials responsible for Physical Education and Sport held in Punta del Este (Uruguay) from 30 November to 3 December 1999 (MINEPS III) under the auspices of UNESCO,
–   having regard to Article 2(5) of the Olympic Charter as amended in 1994,
–   having regard to the IOC World Conferences on Women and Sport held in Lausanne in 1996 and Paris in 2000,
–   having regard to the Brighton Declaration adopted at the First International Conference on 'Women, Sport and the Challenge of Change' from 5 to 8 May 1994,
–   having regard to the call for action 'Reaching out for Change' adopted at the Second International Conference on Women and Sport held in Windhoek on 22 May 1998,
–   having regard to the conferences held by the European Women and Sport network in Stockholm, Athens, Helsinki and Berlin respectively from 1996 to 2002,
–   having regard to the Council of Europe resolution of March 2002 on the prevention of sexual harassment and abuse of women, young people and children in sport,
–   having regard to the Charter of Olympus of 23 September 2001 and the Cultural Olympiad 2001-2004 launched by the Greek Ministry of Culture to mark the Olympic Games in Athens and aimed at renewing the basic Olympic ideals uniting sport and culture,
–   having regard to European Parliament and Council Directive 2002/73/EC amending Council Directive 76/207/EEC on the implementation of the principle of equal treatment for men and women as regards access to employment, vocational training and promotion, and working conditions[749],
–   having regard to Decision No 291/2003/EC of the European Parliament and of the

---

[745]  OJ C 211, 22-7-1996, p. 36.
[746]  OJ C 200, 30-6-1997, p. 252.
[747]  OJ C 8, 12-1-2000, p. 5.
[748]  OJ C 135, 7-5-2001, p. 274.
[749]  OJ L 269, 5-10-2002, p. 15.

Council of 6 February 2003 establishing the European Year of Education through Sport 2004[750],

–   having regard to the Declaration of Thessaloniki and the conclusions of the Conference on 'Women and Sports: Old and New Stereotypes' held by the Greek Presidency of the European Union on 7 and 8 March 2003,

–   having regard to Rule 163 of its Rules of Procedure,

–   having regard to the report of the Committee on Women's Rights and Equal Opportunities (A5-0167/2003),

A.   having regard to the declaration by the European Council in Nice of December 2000 stipulating that the Community must take account of the specific characteristics and the social, educational and cultural functions of sport, and whereas sport has had a democratic role since antiquity,

B.   whereas sport is one of the main cultural activities among Europeans; whereas in the European Union 29.5% of men, as opposed to 16% of women, and 63% of young men aged 15 to 24, as compared to 37% of young women of that age, say that they regularly take part in physical or sporting activity,

C.   whereas access to the practice of sport is a right and whereas sport is a means of self-expression and fulfilment, as well as a force for citizenship and solidarity; whereas the regular practice of sport improves physical and mental health,

D.   having regard to the strong disparities in access to sports activities between women and men and also between women themselves, based on social background and conditions of employment which may act as an obstacle to leisure and sports opportunities,

E.   whereas physical activity and sport represent an ideal form of rehabilitation and, equally, a means of social integration for the physically or mentally disabled, and whereas, in particular, steps must be taken to ensure that disabled persons of both sexes can exercise to the full their right to participate in all forms of sport at their level and in keeping with their own needs,

F.   whereas it is important to make available sporting activities which correspond to women's needs at every stage of their lives, in particular for pregnant women and young mothers, along with the provision of advice concerning sports suited to their condition; and whereas similar advice should be given to the elderly (women and men), suggesting sporting activities which are beneficial to their mental and physical health,

G.   whereas physical education in schools, which are a force for democratising sport, but also a forum for social reproduction, has a crucial influence on whether people take part in sporting activity in later life,

H.   whereas, in this connection, the downgrading of physical education and of the importance of coeducation in sport in the school curriculum of the countries of the enlarged Europe is a cause for concern,

I.   whereas sport provides a release for girls and women of all ages, a means of achieving success and emancipation, as well as in some cases a way of challenging social and cultural constraints; whereas, however, participation by migrant women and girls in sports is below average,

J.   whereas, although the legal prohibitions on women's access to sports have been removed, women still participate to a lesser extent than men in sports, are more prominently represented in some sports than others, and remain under-represented in sports administration and decision-taking,

---

[750] OJ L 43, 18-2-2003, p. 1.

K.     whereas women are under-represented among sports licence holders and in official competitions and make little use of institutionalised sports venues (clubs and associations), preferring mostly to pursue informal physical activities related to fitness and leisure,

L.     whereas sport is a forum where sexual identities are represented and sports continue to be firmly divided in line with gender-based stereotypes where dominant models of masculinity and femininity are reproduced, but may also be subverted,

M.     whereas, when they take part in sports, girls and boys must face the challenge of forging equality based on an acceptance of physical differences; whereas adolescence, with the onset of puberty, is a time when many girls give up sports activities, particularly those from disadvantaged backgrounds,

N.     having regard to the importance of highlighting the performances of top-level sportswomen, who should serve as a role model for young girls,

O.     whereas top-level women athletes are workers and, as such, are covered by Community employment law, in particular the abovementioned Directive 2002/73/EC,

P.     whereas top-level sportswomen do not enjoy equal treatment vis-à-vis their male counterparts with regard to income and financial resources (bursaries, subsidies, sponsors), nor as regards vocational reintegration,

Q.     whereas the status of top-level athlete gives sportsmen and sportswomen economic and social rights, while providing them with a professional environment; whereas in some European countries women still suffer from discrimination with regard to this status and the conditions for achieving it,

R.     whereas participation by women athletes in international competitions has increased, although technical and medical staff, as well as referees and officials, are still mostly men (at the Sydney Olympic Games women accounted for 38% of the athletes, 8% of technical staff and 4% of medical staff),

S.     whereas top-level sport poses a threat to the health of athletes, particularly women, who are vulnerable, for instance, to the 'female athlete triad', of eating disorders, irreversible amenorrhea and osteoporosis,

T.     whereas special attention should be paid to measures aimed at preventing and combating harassment and sexual abuse in the world of sport,

U.     having regard to the poor media coverage given to women's sport and the socially discriminating and sexually stereotyped reporting found in the media,

V.     having regard to the Brighton Declaration of 1994, the substantial work performed by the International Working Group on Women and Sport (IWG) and the European Women and Sport network (EWS),

W.     whereas the implementation of an integrated approach to gender equality in Community policies and actions in the field of sport is not backed up by sufficient human and financial resources nor by the necessary supervisory and monitoring mechanisms,

**Developing a structure for tackling the question of 'women and sport'**

1.     Declares that women's sport is an expression of the right to equality and the freedom of all women to take control of their bodies and participate in sports publicly, regardless of nationality, age, disability, sexual orientation or religion;

2.     Stresses that the goal of equal opportunities is to overcome barriers between so-called 'masculine' and 'feminine' sports and that the aim is to encourage all sports to be open to both sexes and enable all girls and boys to engage in the physical activity of their choice;

3.     Calls on the Member States and the European Union to guarantee women and men

equal access to sporting activities at all levels and at all stages of life, regardless of social background, particularly in the case of the mentally or physically disabled, who should be encouraged to take part in sport and physical activity;

4.    Calls on the European Convention to provide a legal basis for sport in the future Treaty of the Union, recognising its cultural, educational and social functions and including a reference to equal access for women and men to participation in sports and related responsibilities;

5.    Calls on the Commission to support the promotion of women's sports in Community programmes and actions, while also raising awareness in the sporting world and the Member States and disseminating best practice;

6.    Proposes that participation in sport by girls and women be included as an operational objective in the future Community framework strategy on gender equality for 2006-2010;

7.    Calls on the Member States, NGOs and other organisations to submit 'women and sport' projects in the context of the forthcoming call for submissions under the Community framework strategy on gender equality for 2001-2005, which will focus on the elimination of sexist stereotypes, particularly in sport;

8.    Calls on the Commission to incorporate rules to combat discrimination in sport in the new gender discrimination outside the scope of the Work Directive, based on Article 13 of the Treaty;

9.    Calls on the Commission to undertake a wide-ranging study into the position of women in sport, as suggested at the Conference of Sports Ministers held on 12 November 2001, and in the process to submit, inter alia, statistics on the general position of women in sport and information on gender budgeting;

10.   Calls on the European Union to provide support for the functioning of the European Women and Sport (EWS) network;

11.   Calls on the European Union to examine the health issue, social concerns and educational challenges relating to women's participation in sport, notably in the context of its sixth framework research programme;

12.   Hopes that the European Year of Education through Sport will provide an opportunity to examine the importance of sports coeducation in schools and calls on the Commission and the Member States to give clear priority to projects encouraging women to participate in sport;

13.   Calls on Eurostat to devise indicators and produce European statistics on male and female participation in sport at all levels;

14.   Calls on government authorities to systematically take account of gender equality in their sports policies, particularly in the granting of subsidies;

15.   Calls on the Commission and the Member States to include the issue of 'women and sport' in bilateral and cooperation agreements with third countries; calls on Parliament to include the issue of 'women and sport' in interparliamentary discussions and Euro-Mediterranean meetings;

16.   Is considering sending a delegation from its Committee on Women's Rights and Equal Opportunities to the EWS European Conference on 23-25 April 2004 in Paris and the IGW International Conference on 11-14 May 2006 in Kumamoto;

**Developing sport in schools and sport for leisure**

17.   Calls on the Member States to restore the important role of physical and sporting education in the school curriculum and to use it as an educational performance indicator;

18.   Calls on the Member States to carry out a study of the quantitative and qualitative

participation of girls and boys in sports within and outside schools and to provide the necessary resources to increase the participation of girls in sports and physical activities;

19. Calls on the Member States and competent authorities to provide physical education teachers with training on the issues of coeducation and gender by including these aspects in their curriculum, and to make parents aware of the blinkered attitudes produced by stereotypes;

20. Stresses the importance of the possibility of sports coeducation for children from nursery and primary school onwards; calls on schools, clubs, associations and regional authorities to develop pilot projects in this area;

21. Calls on the Member States to develop policies for the social integration of young people through sport, including girls among their target group, and to use Objective 3 of the Structural Funds for this purpose;

22. Calls on government and regional authorities to promote and to provide girls and boys with a broad range of school and extracurricular sporting activities;

23. Emphasises that every possible effort must be made to enable women to practise sport and physical activity and to give them better access to sports facilities by providing special courses and timetables, childcare facilities and decent transport services for sports centres;

24. Calls on sports associations to include in their statutes the principle of equal access to sport for women and men, to implement an action plan to promote women in their discipline, to carry out gender mainstreaming training and to earmark a budget heading for women's amateur sport, proposing mixed participation or introducing women's sections;

25. Calls on the Member States and competent authorities to ensure that sports coaches at all levels are properly trained and qualified and to include the gender dimension in their training courses;

26. Calls on government authorities, businesses and the two sides of industry to encourage sport activities at the workplace, in particular through collective agreements, and, more specifically, to develop measures designed to facilitate access to sport for women in precarious employment and women in difficulty, given the complexity of reconciling work, family life and leisure;

## Ensuring equal rights in top-level sport

27. Calls on the Member States and the sports movement to abolish the distinction between male and female disciplines in top-level sports recognition procedures;

28. Calls on national federations and their supervisory authorities to give women and men equal access to the status of top-level athlete, ensuring that they enjoy the same rights as regards income, training and supervision, medical back-up, access to competitions, social welfare, vocational training and active social reintegration at the end of their sports careers;

29. Calls on government and sports authorities to ensure the elimination of direct and indirect discrimination suffered by female athletes in their work;

30. Calls on businesses to step up their efforts to sponsor top-level sportswomen, seeking to enhance their image and promote women's sport as a whole;

31. Calls on the media to provide balanced coverage of male and female sport and to represent women in sport in a non-discriminatory manner;

32. Proposes that, when Directive 89/552/EEC[751] on 'Television without Frontiers' is amended, Article 3a concerning the broadcasting of major sports events should

---

[751] OJ L 298., 17-10-1989, p. 23.

give the Member States the possibility of including the gender dimension in the broadcasting of such events;

33.    Urges sportswomen to organise themselves in order to defend their sporting, economic and social rights and to bring cases of discrimination and harassment to the competent authorities or before the courts;

34.    Calls for the forthcoming Olympic Games in Athens to be exemplary and calls on the IOC to ensure mixed representation in all national teams;

**Protecting the health of female athletes**

35.    Urges sports federations and trainers to show the utmost vigilance as regards guidelines and conditions for the practice of sport and to inform top-level sportswomen, particularly young women, of the effects of intensive training, use of doping substances or neglect of dietary rules on their physical, physiological, sexual and reproductive health;

36.    Stresses that, in order to protect the health of female athletes, special training is needed for medical and paramedical staff, together with the inclusion of more women in medical and paramedical teams;

37.    Emphasises the need to carry out special gender-specific studies on the impact of sport on the health of athletes;

38.    Considers it important for female athletes to be given psychological support to enable them to come to terms with the changes in their physical appearance or to deal with questions regarding their femininity; believes that account of these aspects must be taken in training for coaches;

39.    Stresses that sportswomen enjoy inalienable rights as regards sexuality and reproduction and calls for any breach of these freedoms to be penalised;

40.    Urges Member States and sports federations to adopt measures for the prevention and elimination of sexual harassment and abuse in sport by enforcing the legislation on sexual harassment at work, to inform athletes and their parents of the risks of abuse and the means of legal action available to them, to provide sports organisations' staff with specific training and to ensure that criminal and disciplinary provisions are applied;

**Greater participation by women in decision-making**

41.    Notes that the participation of women in decision-making in sport faces the same barriers as in the political and economic sphere and that affirmative action is needed;

42.    Calls on Member States and regulatory authorities to make the recognition and subsidising of sports associations and authorities conditional upon the adoption of statutory provisions ensuring equal representation of women and men at all levels and for all decision-making posts;

43.    Calls on sports organisations and authorities to promote women's participation in refereeing and adjudication and to establish mixed representation on medical committees and selection committees;

44.    Calls on sports organisations to introduce training and counselling programmes for women athletes to help them find employment, in particular as coaches, technical staff and managers;

45.    Calls on the sports movement to comply with the IOC target for women's participation in decision-making (20% of women in management structures by 31 December 2005) and to increase it to 30% over the next 10 years;

46.     Instructs its President to forward this resolution to the Council, the Commission and the parliaments of the Member States.

———

**\* 2.7.34.  ANSWER ON BEHALF OF THE COMMISSION TO WRITTEN QUESTION E-1558/03 BY CLAUDE MORAES (PSE), 25 JUNE 2003**[752]

Subject: Soccer and racism

———

**2.7.35.  COMMISSION EUROPÉENNE, LE 15 JUILLET 2003**

Direction Genérale Justice et Affaires Intérieures
Direction A – Circulation des personnes, citoyenneté, droits fondamentaux
Unité A5: Citoyenneté, Charte des Droits Fondamentaux, Racisme et Xénophobie, Programme Daphné

Bruxelles, le 15 juillet 2003

Maître,
Je fais référence à votre courrier du 12 mars 2002, enregistrée sous le numéro SG(O2) A/ 2871 et à ma réponse du 11 juillet 2002 ref. JAI/A5/AH D(2002)4176.
Comme je vous avais informé dans ma lettre du 11 juillet 2002, les services de la Commission ont pris contact avec les autorités espagnoles à ce sujet par lettre du 3 juillet 2002. Dans cette lettre ils ont pris la position que le Règlement de la Fédération Royale de Football espagnole semble, à première vue, contraire à l'article 12 du traité CE. Les autorités espagnoles ont répondu en date du 22 août 2002 contestant l'incompatibilité du Règlement en objet avec le droit communautaire.
Les services de la Commission estiment que la pratique d'un sport en qualité d'amateur constitue un avantage social au sens de l'article 7.2 du Règlement 1612/68 relatif à la libre circulation des travailleurs à l'intérieur de la Communauté[753]. Les ressortissants des Etats membres, lorsqu'ils se déplacent dans un autre Etat membre devraient donc se voir reconnaître le droit d'avoir accès aux activités sportives, en tant que joueurs amateurs, dans les mêmes conditions que les ressortissants nationaux. Ce droit résulte directement du règlement 1612/68 pour les travailleurs salariés et les membres de leur famille, et de l'article 43 du traité CE pour les travailleurs non salariés et les membres de leur famille. La Cour, par le biais de l'interprétation du concept de citoyenneté inscrit à l'article 17 du traite CE, a étendu le droit à l'égalité de traitement en matière d'octroi d'avantages sociaux aux étudiants et aux inactifs résidant légalement dans l'Etat membre d'accueil (arrêt du 20 septembre 2001, Grzelczyk, C-184/99, Rec. p I-6193).
Eu égard à cette jurisprudence, les restrictions établies par une réglementation d'une fédération sportive à la pratique d'un sport amateur pour des étudiants d'autres Etats membres devraient dès lors être considérées comme contraires aux articles 12 et 17 du traité CE lorsque de telles restrictions ne sont pas imposées aux étudiants nationaux.
Citoyenne de l'Union, résidant légalement en Espagne, votre cliente, Mlle [...] devrait donc pouvoir se prévaloir directement du principe de l'interdiction de discrimination en raison de la nationalité de l'article 12 du traité CE pour Pouvoir participer à des compétitions de football comme joueuse amateur dans les même conditions qu'un

---

[752]  Question of 28-4-2003; OJ C 280E, 21-11-2003, p. 167.
[753]  JO L 257, 19-10-1968, p. 19.

ressortissant espagnol. Il vous appartient d'invoquer directement l'article 12 du traité CE devant les autorités, voire les tribunaux espagnols compétents, au cas où votre droit serait contesté par la fédération de football,

La Commission va procéder à l'examen des réglementations des fédérations sportives dans tous les Etats membres afin de vérifier leur compatibilité avec le principe de nondiscrimination. A l'issue de cet examen, la Commission se prononcera sur l'opportunité d'entamer une procédure d'infraction à l'encontre des Etats membres dans lesquels existeraient de telles réglementations discriminatoires.

Veuillez croire, Maître, à l'assurance de ma considération distinguée.

Alain Brun
Chef d'Unité

---

**\* 2.7.36.  REPLY ON BEHALF OF THE COUNCIL TO WRITTEN QUESTION E-1557/03 BY CLAUDE MORAES (PSE), 29 SEPTEMBER 2003**[754]

Subject: Soccer and racism

---

**\* 2.7.37.  ANSWER ON BEHALF OF THE COMMISSION TO WRITTEN QUESTION E-3000/03 BY GENEVIÈVE FRAISSE (GUE/NGL), 30 OCTOBER 2003**[755]

Subject: Follow-up to the 'women's sport' resolution adopted by the European Parliament on 5 June 2003

---

[754] Question of 28-4-2003; question not yet published in the OJ.
[755] Question of 2-10-2003; question not yet published in the OJ.

## 2.8.   DOPING*

* **2.8.1.   ANSWER ON BEHALF OF THE COMMISSION TO WRITTEN QUESTION NO 1856/87 BY SIR JACK STEWART-CLARK (ED-GB), 1 MARCH 1988**[756]

Subject: European Community action on drug-taking in sport

———

* **2.8.2.   ANSWER ON BEHALF OF THE COMMISSION TO WRITTEN QUESTION NO 346/90 BY SIR JAMES SCOTT-HOPKINS (ED), 3 APRIL 1990**[757]

Subject: Drugs in sport

———

* **2.8.3.   RESOLUTION OF THE COUNCIL AND OF THE REPRESENTATIVES OF THE GOVERNMENTS OF THE MEMBER STATES, MEETING WITHIN THE COUNCIL ON COMMUNITY ACTION TO COMBAT THE USE OF DRUGS, INCLUDING THE ABUSE OF MEDICINAL PRODUCTS, PARTICULARLY IN SPORT, 3 DECEMBER 1990**[758]

———

* **2.8.4.   DECLARATION BY THE COUNCIL AND THE MINISTERS FOR HEALTH OF THE MEMBER STATES, MEETING WITHIN THE COUNCIL ON ACTION TO COMBAT THE USE OF DRUGS, INCLUDING THE ABUSE OF MEDICINAL PRODUCTS, IN SPORT, 4 JUNE 1991**[759]

———

* **2.8.5.   ANSWER ON BEHALF OF THE COMMISSION TO WRITTEN QUESTION NO 1314/91 BY MR LUIGI VERTENATI (S), 5 SEPTEMBER 1991**[760]

Subject: Use of anabolic substances in sport

———

* **2.8.6.   RESOLUTION OF THE COUNCIL AND OF THE REPRESENTATIVES OF THE GOVERNMENTS OF THE MEMBER STATES, MEETING WITHIN THE COUNCIL ON A CODE OF CONDUCT AGAINST DOPING IN SPORT, 8 FEBRUARY 1992**[761]

———

---

*    The full texts of documents which are marked with an asterisk (*) are not incorporated in the book itself, but are freely accessible on the website of the ASSER International Sports Law Centre, at <www.sportslaw.nl> – documentation.

[756] Question of 18-12-1987; OJ C 160, p. 15.

[757] Question of 26-2-1990; OJ C 259, 15-10-1990, p. 27.

[758] OJ C 329, 31-12-1990, p. 4-5.

[759] OJ C 170, 29-06-1991 p. 1.

[760] Question of 24-6-1991; OJ C 323, 13-12-1991, p. 26.

[761] OJ C 44, 19-2-1992, p. 1-2.

**\* 2.8.7.**      **ANSWER ON BEHALF OF THE COMMISSION TO WRITTEN QUESTION NO. 1446/92 BY MRS ANNE ANDRÉ (LDR), 23 JULY 1992**[762]

Subject: European code of conduct to combat the use of drugs in sport

———

**\* 2.8.8.**      **RESOLUTION OF THE EUROPEAN PARLIAMENT ON SPORT AND DOPING, 27 APRIL 1994**[763]

———

**\* 2.8.9.**      **ANSWER ON BEHALF OF THE COMMISSION TO WRITTEN QUESTION P-1514/95 BY NIELS SINDAL (PSE), 19 JUNE 1995**[764]

Subject: Sport and doping

———

**\* 2.8.10.**      **ANSWER ON BEHALF OF THE COMMISSION TO WRITTEN QUESTION E-2592/95 BY AMEDEO AMADEO (NI), 16 NOVEMBER 1995**[765]

Subject: Sport and doping

———

**\* 2.8.11.**      **ANSWER ON BEHALF OF THE COMMISSION TO WRITTEN QUESTION E-471/96 BY GIAN BONIPERTI (UPE) AND ANTONIO TAJANI (UPE), 7 MAY 1996**[766]

Subject: The use of anabolic steroids

———

**\* 2.8.12.**      **ANSWER ON BEHALF OF THE COMMISSION TO WRITTEN QUESTION E-1262/96 BY FREDDY BLAK (PSE), 18 JULY 1996 AND 31 OCTOBER 1996**[767]

Subject: Athletes as employees

———

**\* 2.8.13.**      **ANSWER ON BEHALF OF THE COMMISSION TO WRITTEN QUESTION E-2906/98 BY GIANNI TAMINO (V), 9 DECEMBER 1998**[768]

Subject: Drug-taking in sport

———

---

[762] Question of 16-6-1992; OJ C 289 , 5-11-1992, p. 58.
[763] OJ C 205, 6-5-1994, p. 484.
[764] Question of 22-5-1995, OJ C 213, 17-8-1995, p. 62.
[765] Question of 27-9-1995, OJ C 56, 26-2-1996, p. 28.
[766] Question of 9-2-1996; OJ C 217, 26-7-1996, p. 50.
[767] Question of 24-5-1996; OJ C 305, 15-10-1996, p. 71.
[768] Question of 2-10-1998; OJ C 142, 21-5-1999, p. 55.

**\* 2.8.14.   ANSWER ON BEHALF OF THE COMMISSION TO WRITTEN QUESTION E-3183/98 BY MARIE-NOËLLE LIENEMANN (PSE), 11 DECEMBER 1998**[769]

Subject: Sport and drugs

———

**\* 2.8.15.   RESOLUTION OF THE EUROPEAN PARLIAMENT ON URGENT MEASURES TO BE TAKEN AGAINST DOPING IN SPORT, 17 DECEMBER 1998**[770]

———

**\* 2.8.16.   ANSWER ON BEHALF OF THE COMMISSION TO WRITTEN QUESTION E-5/99 BY ALEXANDROS ALAVANOS (GUE/NGL), 11 MARCH 1999**[771]

Subject: Consequences of doping for athletes' health

———

**\* 2.8.17.   ANSWER ON BEHALF OF THE COMMISSION TO WRITTEN QUESTION E-175/99 BY AMEDEO AMADEO (NI), 15 MARCH 1999**[772]

Subject: Combating the use of drugs in sport

———

**\* 2.8.18.   ANSWER ON BEHALF OF THE COMMISSION TO WRITTEN QUESTION P-1119/99 BY BÁRBARA DÜHRKOP (PSE), 7 MAY 1999**[773]

Subject: Commission's anti-doping programme

———

**\* 2.8.19.   ANSWER ON BEHALF OF THE COMMISSION TO WRITTEN QUESTION P-1611/99 BY GRAHAM WATSON (ELDR), 5 OCTOBER 1999**[774]

Subject: The use of Nandrolone

———

**\* 2.8.20.   COMMUNICATION TO THE COMMISSION – THE FIGHT AGAINST DOPING IN SPORT: PROPOSAL BY THE INTERNATIONAL OLYMPIC COMMITTEE FOR A WORLD ANTI-DOPING AGENCY, 13 OCTOBER 1999**[775]

———

[769] Question of 27-10-1998; OJ C 182, 28-6-1999, p. 49.
[770] OJ C 98, 9-4-1999, p. 291.
[771] Question of 19-1-1999; OJ C 289, 11-10-1999, p. 129.
[772] Question of 11-2-1999; OJ C 325, 12-11-1999, p. 80.
[773] Question of 20-4-1999; OJ C 370, 21-12-1999, p. 167-168.
[774] Question of 7-9-1999; OJ C 27 E, 29-1-2000, p. 149.
[775] Communication from Mrs Reding to the Commission.

**\* 2.8.21. COMMUNICATION FROM THE COMMISSION TO THE COUNCIL, THE EUROPEAN PARLIAMENT, THE ECONOMIC AND SOCIAL COMMITTEE AND THE COMMITTEE OF THE REGIONS ON A COMMUNITY SUPPORT PLAN TO COMBAT DOPING IN SPORT, 1 DECEMBER 1999**[776]

---

**\* 2.8.22. ANSWER ON BEHALF OF THE COMMISSION TO WRITTEN QUESTION P-428/00 BY PIETRO-PAOLO MENNEA (ELDR), 8 MARCH 2000**[777]

Subject: Inclusion of a symbol on medicine packages showing which medicaments contain banned substances

---

**\* 2.8.23. REPLY ON BEHALF OF THE COUNCIL TO WRITTEN QUESTION P-2818/99 BY PIETRO-PAOLO MENNEA (ELDR), 10/11 APRIL 2000**[778]

Subject: Enactment of Community criminal legislation to combat doping

---

**\* 2.8.24. COMMISSION'S CALL FOR PROPOSALS – PILOT PROJECT FOR CAMPAIGNS TO COMBAT DOPING IN SPORT IN EUROPE, 16 APRIL 2000**[779]

---

**\* 2.8.25. ANSWER ON BEHALF OF THE COMMISSION TO WRITTEN QUESTION E-1100/00 BY GRAHAM WATSON (ELDR), 22 MAY 2000**[780]

Subject: The use of Nandrolone

---

**\* 2.8.26. OPINION OF THE ECONOMIC AND SOCIAL COMMITTEE ON THE COMMUNICATION FROM THE COMMISSION TO THE COUNCIL, THE EUROPEAN PARLIAMENT, THE ECONOMIC AND SOCIAL COMMITTEE AND THE COMMITTEE OF THE REGIONS: COMMUNITY SUPPORT PLAN TO COMBAT DOPING IN SPORT, 24 MAY 2000**[781]

---

[776] COM(1999) 643 final.
[777] Question of 11-2-2000; OJ C 303 E, 24-10-2000, p. 191.
[778] Question of 10-1-2000; OJ C 303 E, 24-10-2000, p. 116.
[779] OJ C 116, 26-4-2000, p. 13.
[780] Question of 7-4-2000; OJ C 46 E, 13-2-2001, p. 123.
[781] OJ C 204 , 18-7-2000, p. 45-50.

**\* 2.8.27.  OPINION OF THE COMMITTEE OF THE REGIONS ON A
COMMUNICATION FROM THE COMMISSION TO THE COUNCIL,
THE EUROPEAN PARLIAMENT, THE ECONOMIC AND SOCIAL
COMMITTEE AND THE COMMITTEE OF THE REGIONS ON A
COMMUNITY SUPPORT PLAN TO COMBAT DOPING IN SPORT,
15 JUNE 2000**[782]

———

**\* 2.8.28.  OPINION OF THE COMMITTEE ON THE ENVIRONMENT, PUBLIC
HEALTH AND CONSUMER POLICY FOR THE COMMITTEE ON
CULTURE, YOUTH, EDUCATION, THE MEDIA AND SPORT ON THE
COMMUNICATION FROM THE COMMISSION TO THE COUNCIL,
THE EUROPEAN PARLIAMENT, THE ECONOMIC AND SOCIAL
COMMITTEE AND THE COMMITTEE OF THE REGIONS ON A
COMMUNITY SUPPORT PLAN TO COMBAT DOPING IN SPORT,
21 JUNE 2000**[783]

Draftsman: Mihail Papayannakis

———

**\* 2.8.29.  REPORT OF THE COMMITTEE ON CULTURE, YOUTH,
EDUCATION, THE MEDIA AND SPORT ON THE COMMISSION
COMMUNICATION TO THE COUNCIL, THE EUROPEAN
PARLIAMENT, THE ECONOMIC AND SOCIAL COMMITTEE AND
THE COMMITTEE OF THE REGIONS ON COMMUNITY SUPPORT
PLAN TO COMBAT DOPING IN SPORT, 17 JULY 2000**[784]

Rapporteur: Teresa Zabell

———

**\* 2.8.30.  RESOLUTION OF THE EUROPEAN PARLIAMENT ON THE
COMMISSION COMMUNICATION TO THE COUNCIL, THE
EUROPEAN PARLIAMENT, THE ECONOMIC AND SOCIAL
COMMITTEE AND THE COMMITTEE OF THE REGIONS ON
COMMUNITY SUPPORT PLAN TO COMBAT DOPING IN SPORT,
7 SEPTEMBER 2000**[785]

———

**\* 2.8.31.  ANSWER ON BEHALF OF THE COMMISSION TO WRITTEN
QUESTION E-1966/00 BY JOSÉ RIBEIRO E CASTRO (UEN),
19 SEPTEMBER 2000**[786]

Subject: The scandal of doping in the former GDR

———

---

[782]  OJ C 317, 6-11-2000, p. 63.
[783]  COM(1999)643.
[784]  COM(1999) 643.
[785]  OJ C 135, 7-9-2000, p. 270; A5-203/2000.
[786]  Question of 21-6-2000; OJ C 81 E, 13-3-2001, p. 120-121.

**\* 2.8.32. CONCLUSIONS OF THE COUNCIL AND THE REPRESENTATIVES OF THE GOVERNMENTS OF THE MEMBER STATES, MEETING WITHIN THE COUNCIL ON COMBATING DOPING, 4 DECEMBER 2000**[787]

**\* 2.8.33. ANSWER ON BEHALF OF THE COMMISSION TO WRITTEN QUESTION E-3200/00 BY MARIO MAURO (PPE-DE), 15 DECEMBER 2000**[788]

Subject: International body's discrimination of a sports company which has actively fought doping

———

**\* 2.8.34. REPLY ON BEHALF OF THE COUNCIL TO WRITTEN QUESTION E-3199/00 BY MARIO MAURO (PPE-DE), 26 FEBRUARY 2001**[789]

Subject: International body's discrimination of a sports company which has actively fought doping

———

**\* 2.8.35. COMMISSION'S CALL FOR PROPOSALS – PILOT PROJECT FOR CAMPAIGNS TO COMBAT DOPING IN SPORT IN EUROPE, 1 MAY 2001**[790]

———

**\* 2.8.36. ANSWER ON BEHALF OF THE COMMISSION TO WRITTEN QUESTION P-3135/02 BY GLYN FORD (PSE), 18 NOVEMBER 2002**[791]

Subject: Prescription-only medicines and racing pigeons

———

**\* 2.8.37. ANSWER ON BEHALF OF THE COMMISSION TO WRITTEN QUESTION E-3830/02 BY MICHL EBNER (PPE-DE), 25 FEBRUARY 2003**[792]

Subject: Medication – drugs abuse

———

**\* 2.8.38. ANSWER ON BEHALF OF THE COMMISSION TO WRITTEN QUESTION E-700/03 BY BART STAES (VERTS/ALE), 14 APRIL 2003**[793]

Subject: Doping in amateur sport

———

---

[787] OJ C 356, 12-12-2000, p. 1.
[788] Question of 12-10-2000; OJ C 151 E, 22-5-2001, p. 92.
[789] Question of 16-10-2000; OJ C 163 E, 6-6-2001, p. 59.
[790] OJ C 130, 1-5-2001, p. 8.
[791] Question of 28-10-2002; OJ C 137 E, 12-6-2003, p. 162-163.
[792] Question of 9-1-2003; OJ C 155 E , 3-7-2003 p. 194-195.
[793] Question of 10-3-2003; OJ C 242 E, 9-10-2003, p. 164-165.

# 2.9. EDUCATION / YOUTH*

* 2.9.1. **ANSWER ON BEHALF OF THE COMMISSION TO WRITTEN QUESTION E-2105/95 BY AMEDEO AMADEO (NI), 24 OCTOBER 1995**[794]

Subject: Sports activities

___

* 2.9.2. **OPINION OF THE COMMITTEE OF THE REGIONS ON INTERACTION BETWEEN EDUCATION OF YOUNG PEOPLE AND SPORT – A PROPOSAL FOR UNION-LEVEL ACTIONS TO PROMOTE THE POSITIVE EFFECTS OF SPORT IN EUROPE, 13 JUNE 1996**[795]

___

* 2.9.3. **ANSWER ON BEHALF OF THE COMMISSION TO WRITTEN QUESTION E-3594/97 BY CRISTIANA MUSCARDINI (NI), 6 JANUARY 1998**[796]

Subject: The umpteenth example of discrimination against an Italian citizen

___

* 2.9.4. **RESOLUTION OF THE COUNCIL AND OF THE MINISTERS FOR YOUTH MEETING WITHIN THE COUNCIL ON THE NON-FORMAL EDUCATION DIMENSION OF SPORTING ACTIVITIES IN THE EUROPEAN COMMUNITY YOUTH PROGRAMMES, 17 DECEMBER 1999**[797]

___

* 2.9.5. **ANSWER ON BEHALF OF THE COMMISSION TO WRITTEN QUESTION E-188/01 BY TOINE MANDERS (ELDR), 26 MARCH 2001**[798]

Subject: Young footballers and child labour

___

* 2.9.6. **ANSWER ON BEHALF OF THE COMMISSION TO WRITTEN QUESTION P-1334/01 BY THERESA ZABELL (PPE-DE), 12 JUNE 2001**[799]

Subject: Special arrangements for sportsmen and sportswomen

___

---

\* The full texts of documents which are marked with an asterisk (\*) are not incorporated in the book itself, but are freely accessible on the website of the ASSER International Sports Law Centre, at <www.sportslaw.nl> – documentation.

[794] Question of 18-7-1995; OJ C 9, 15-1-1996, p. 17.
[795] OJ C 337 , 11-11-1996, p. 60.
[796] Question of 13-11-1997; OJ C 134, 30-4-1998, p. 176.
[797] OJ C 8, 12-1-2000, p. 5.
[798] Question of 1-2-2001; OJ C 187 E, 3-7-2001.
[799] Question of 26-4-2001; OJ C 318 E, 13-11-2001, p. 236.

**\* 2.9.7.    ANSWER ON BEHALF OF THE COMMISSION TO WRITTEN
QUESTION E-1712/01 BY MARGRIETUS VAN DEN BERG (PSE),
31 JULY 2001**[800]

Subject: Trafficking in young footballers

———

**\* 2.9.8.    COMMISSION – PROPOSAL FOR A DECISION OF THE EUROPEAN
PARLIAMENT AND OF THE COUNCIL ESTABLISHING THE
EUROPEAN YEAR OF EDUCATION THROUGH SPORT 2004,
16 OCTOBER 2001**[801]

———

**\* 2.9.9.    ANSWER ON BEHALF OF THE COMMISSION TO WRITTEN
QUESTION E-2636/01 BY MARGRIETUS VAN DEN BERG (PSE),
16 NOVEMBER 2001**[802]

Subject: A European approach to trafficking in young footballers

———

**\* 2.9.10.   OPINION OF THE ECONOMIC AND SOCIAL COMMITTEE ON THE
PROPOSAL FOR A DECISION OF THE EUROPEAN PARLIAMENT
AND OF THE COUNCIL ESTABLISHING THE EUROPEAN YEAR OF
EDUCATION THROUGH SPORT 2004, 24 APRIL 2002**[803]

———

**\* 2.9.11.   OPINION OF THE COMMITTEE OF THE REGIONS ON THE
PROPOSAL, FOR A DECISION OF THE EUROPEAN PARLIAMENT
AND OF THE COUNCIL ESTABLISHING THE EUROPEAN YEAR OF
EDUCATION THROUGH SPORT 2004, 15 MAY 2002**[804]

———

**\* 2.9.12.   ANSWER ON BEHALF OF THE COMMISSION TO WRITTEN
QUESTION E-1921/02 BY CHRISTOPHER HEATON-HARRIS
(PPE-DE), 14 AUGUST 2002**[805]

Subject: Child protection in sport

———

**\* 2.9.13.   ANSWER ON BEHALF OF THE COMMISSION TO WRITTEN
QUESTION E-2101/02 BY TOINE MANDERS (ELDR), 23 SEPTEMBER
2002**[806]

Subject: Obesity

———

[800] Question of 14-6-2001; OJ C 364 E, 20-12-2001, p. 186-189.
[801] OJ C 25 E , 29-1-2002, p. 531-535.
[802] Question of 2-10-2001; OJ C 134 E, 6-6/2002, p. 67-68.
[803] OJ C 149, 21-6-2002, p. 17-23.
[804] OJ C 278, 14-11-2002, p. 23.
[805] Question of 3-7-2002; OJ C 137 E, 12-6-2003, p. 38.
[806] Question of 16-7-2002; OJ C 28 E, 6-2-2003, p. 185-186.

**\* 2.9.14. DECISION OF THE EUROPEAN PARLIAMENT AND OF THE COUNCIL ESTABLISHING THE EUROPEAN YEAR OF EDUCATION THROUGH SPORT 2004, 6 FEBRUARY 2003**[807]

---

**\* 2.9.15. ANSWER ON BEHALF OF THE COMMISSION TO WRITTEN QUESTION E-3899/02 BY SÉRGIO MARQUES (PPE-DE), 18 FEBRUARY 2003**[808]

Subject: European Year of Education through Sport

---

**\* 2.9.16. JOINT DECLARATION BY THE COUNCIL AND THE REPRESENTATIVES OF THE GOVERNMENTS OF THE MEMBER STATES MEETING WITHIN THE COUNCIL ON THE SOCIAL VALUE OF SPORT FOR YOUNG PEOPLE, 5 MAY 2003**[809]

---

**\* 2.9.17. COMMISSION'S CALL FOR PROPOSALS – DG EAC 04/03 – EUROPEAN YEAR OF EDUCATION THROUGH SPORT 2004, 28 MAY 2003**[810]

---

**\* 2.9.18. ANSWER ON BEHALF OF THE COMMISSION TO WRITTEN QUESTION E-1718/03 BY CHRISTOPHER HEATON-HARRIS (PPE-DE), 16 JULY 2003**[811]

Subject: Child protection in sport

---

**\* 2.9.19. ANSWER ON BEHALF OF THE COMMISSION TO WRITTEN QUESTION E-2064/03 BY BART STAES (VERTS/ALE), 31 JULY 2003**[812]

Subject: Harmonisation of the status of sportsmen and women from third countries

---

[807] OJ L 43, 18-2-2003, p. 1-5.
[808] Question of 14-1-2003; OJ C 155 E, 3-7-2003, p. 202-203.
[809] OJ C 134, 7-6-2003, p. 5.
[810] OJ C 126, 28-5-2003, p. 40.
[811] Question of 14-5-2003; question not yet published in the OJ.
[812] Question of 11-6-2003; OJ C 11E, 15-1-2004, p. 247-248.

## 2.10.   FREE MOVEMENT FOR WORKERS*

### * 2.10.1.   REPORT ON BEHALF OF THE COMMITTEE ON LEGAL AFFAIRS AND CITIZENS' RIGHTS ON THE FREEDOM OF MOVEMENT OF PROFESSIONAL FOOTBALLERS IN THE COMMUNITY, 1 MARCH 1989[813]

Reporter: Mr James L. Janssen van Raay

———

### 2.10.2.   RESOLUTION OF THE EUROPEAN PARLIAMENT ON THE FREEDOM OF MOVEMENT OF PROFESSIONAL FOOTBALLERS IN THE COMMUNITY, 11 APRIL 1989[814]

*The European Parliament,*

– having regard to motions for resolutions Docs. 2-1167184, 2-1582184, B2-1541/86, B21547/86, B2-81/87, B2-112/87, B2-234/87, B2-620187 and B2-1837/87,
– having regard to the report of the Committee on Legal Affairs and Citizens' Rights and the opinions of the Committee on Social Affairs and Employment and the Committee on Youth, Culture, Education, Information and Sport (Doc. A2-415/88),

A.   whereas ten Member States of the European Community have private-law football leagues that hold a monopoly over professional football, operating at European level within UEFA and at international level within FIFA and as the only recognized employers,

B.   whereas professional footballers are employees who have formed officially recognized trade unions in all ten countries and an international organization, Fifpro, and whereas they, like any other employee in the Community, should enjoy the protection of European law and benefit, in particular, from the provisions guaranteeing freedom of movement and prohibiting discrimination,

C.   whereas UEFA and some national football associations are in breach of national and European law insofar as they impose on players under contract a system of indefinite extensions of contract which precludes them from joining any other club of their choice at the end of their contract, unless the freedom to enter into an new contract is severed by payment of a transfer fee, on penalty of international suspension,

D.   whereas sport is an integral part of national culture and identity whose diversity adds to the richness of European culture and builds friendships among peoples,

E.   whereas UEFA and some national football associations have limited the number of foreign players including nationals of the Member States of the EC to a maximum of two or three per team,

F.   whereas UEFA unilaterally broke off negotiations with the Commission,

---

* The full texts of documents which are marked with an asterisk (*) are not incorporated in the book itself, but are freely accessible on the website of the ASSER International Sports Law Centre, at <www.sportslaw.nl> – documentation.

[813] A 2-415/88, 05 1-3-1989.
[814] OJ C 120, 16-5-1989, p. 33.

G.  whereas the ban by UEFA on English football teams playing in Europe is an inhibiting factor on the players involved, preventing them from displaying their skills,

H.  seeking to encourage local football teams and the talent of local youngsters,

1.  Regards the system of the payment of transfer fees in its present form as a latter-day version of the slave trade, a violation of the freedom of contract and the freedom of movement guaranteed by the Treaties and a contravention of Article 85 of the EEC Treaty;

2.  Believes that the present unilateral ban on English football teams by UEFA is without legal base and is contrary to the free movement of people;

3.  Is of the opinion that the present ban on English football teams by UEFA ' not allowing football players to display their skills at Community level;

4.  Considers the restriction on the number of foreign players entitled to play for a professional football team to be a proscribed discrimination on grounds of nationality, a contravention of freedom of movement pursuant to Article 48 of the EEC Treaty and a violation of Article 85 of the EEC Treaty, insofar as nationals of the Member States of the European Community are concerned;

5.  Regards this interpretation as being confirmed by the rulings of the Court of Justice[815];

6.  Calls on the Commission to initiate legal proceedings against UEFA on the grounds that their unilateral action against English teams by banning them from playing football at European level is contrary to the EEC Treaty;

7.  Stresses that achieving freedom of movement for all professions would highlight one of the freedoms enshrined in the Treaties and expects that, as existing restrictions are overcome, the popularity of sport and games will considerably enhance awareness of these principles;

8.  Recognizes that, since professional footballers can integrate fully into clubs of any nationality, the links and the identification of a club with a town or region would not be undermined, even if the number of players from other EC Member States increased;

9.  Takes the view that there is no threat to the development of future generations of players, given the mutual exchange of footballers and the large number of teams, particularly in the amateur sector, and is convinced that the clubs' directors and spectators will preserve the identity of teams without any difficulty;

10.  Insists that the nationality principle should be retained for national teams, in accordance with the abovementioned rulings of the Court of Justice[816] since this relates to a basic characteristic and is not a question of professional football as such but rather one of national pride and identity;

11.  Takes the view that it would not be appropriate to institute proceedings against the Member States pursuant to Article 169 of the EEC Treaty, given that football clubs are organizations covered by private law; does not believe, however, that this exempts the clubs from the direct applicability of Article 48 of the EEC Treaty;

12.  Calls on the Commission to institute proceedings pursuant to Article 85 of the EEC Treaty against UEFA and/or the national football associations, as well as individual clubs in the Community, in an endeavour to abolish the transfer fee system and gradually increase the number of foreign nationals of Member States

---

[815] Case 36174, Walrave, [1974] ECR, 1405 et seq; Case 13176, Donà v.Mantero.
[816] Case 36174, Walrave, [1974] ECR, 1405 and 1418.

entitled to play for any particular team, until complete freedom of movement is obtained;

13. Acknowledges the benefit to the clubs, however, of a controlled phasing-out of the system, the possibility of compensation for investment in apprenticeship and training − though this may be requested only while the apprenticeship is still in progress − and certain safeguards to allow clubs and spectators to identify with the teams;

14. Calls on the Commission to persuade UEFA and the national football associations to accept such a solution and, failing this, to use every remedy to enforce the application of Community law;

15. Takes the view that the transfer fee system and the rules of foreign players applied by national football associations in the Community contravene the ban on discrimination laid down in Article 48 of the EEC Treaty;

16. Calls on the Commission, as guardian of the Treaties, to take legal steps against these rules;

17. Takes the view that the Commission should use every remedy available to it under the Treaty to ensure complete freedom of movement by means of binding measures whose date of entry into force and duration are clearly defined;

18. Instructs its President to forward this resolution and the report of its committee to the Commission.

---

**2.10.3. EUROPEAN COURT OF JUSTICE, ORDER OF THE COURT, JEAN-MARC BOSMAN V COMMISSION OF THE EUROPEAN COMMUNITIES, CASE C-117/91 R, 27 JUNE 1991[817]**

*Application for interim measures − Conditions as to admissibility − Admissibility of the main application − Lack of relevance − Limits*
*(EEC Treaty, Arts 185 and 186; Rules of Procedure, Art. 83(1))*

*Although the issue of the admissibility of the main application should not, in principle, be examined in proceedings relating to an application for interim measures, so as not to prejudge the substance of the case, none the less, if the the manifest inadmissibility of the main application is pleaded, it is for the judge hearing the application for interim measures to establish that the main application reveals prima facie grounds for concluding that there is a certain probability that it is admissible.*

*Parties*
In Case C-117/91 R,
Jean-Marc Bosman, represented by J.-L. Dupont, L. Misson and M.-A. Lucas, of the Liège Bar, with an address for service in Luxembourg at the Chambers of E. Korn, 21 Rue de Nassau, applicant, v Commission of the European Communities, represented by J.-C. Séché, Legal Adviser, E. Traversa, a member of its Legal Service, and T. Margellos, a senior lecturer at the University of Picardy, on secondment to the Commission, acting as Agents, with an address for service in Luxembourg at the office of G. Berardis, a member of the Legal Service, Wagner Centre, Kirchberg, defendant,
Application for interim measures, in particular the suspension of the application of a decision adopted by the Commission on 17 April 1991 regarding an agreement between the Commission and the Union of European Football Associations (UEFA),

---

[817] ECR 1991, p. I-3353.

The President of the Court of Justice
makes the following

*Order*
*Grounds*
1 By application lodged at the Court Registry on 23 April 1991, Mr Jean-Marc
 Bosman, a professional football player, applied under the second paragraph of Article 173 of the EEC Treaty for the annulment of a decision adopted by the Commission on 17 April 1991, as set out in the Commission' s press release IP()1)316
 of 18 April 1991, regarding an agreement between the Commission and the Union
 of European Football Associations (hereinafter referred to as "the UEFA") on nationality clauses applicable to national championships and the system of transfer
 fees applicable to the transfer of professional players from one club to another.
 Pursuant to Article 178 and the second paragraph of Article 215 of the EEC
 Treaty, the applicant further sought damages for the harm caused to him by the
 decision.
2 It is clear from the press release to which the applicant refers that negotiations between the UEFA and the Vice-President of the Commission, Mr Bangemann, acting in pursuance of the powers conferred on him by the Commission, led to an
 amicable arrangement regarding the nationality clauses, whereby national football
 associations were required from the 1992/1993 season onwards to allow at least
 three non-national players, together with two non-national players actively engaged in their profession in the host country without interruption for five years, to
 be fielded in first-division matches played in national championships; the scheme
 was to be extended, not later than the end of the 1996/1997 season, to the other
 divisions in which professional players operate. The press release also states that,
 as far as contractual bonds between clubs and professional players are concerned,
 the first step has been taken regarding transfers, an agreement having emerged at
 that stage of negotiations, to accept the principle according to which any professional player is at liberty to play for another club upon the expiry of his contract,
 irrespective of the usual negotiations between the transferring club and the purchasing club concerning the fees to be paid to the former. The press release states
 in conclusion that the issue of a "standard contract" between clubs and professional players will require further discussion with all parties concerned.
3 By a separate document, also lodged at the Court Registry on 23 April 1991, the
 applicant submitted an application under Articles 185 and 186 of the EEC Treaty
 for interim measures, seeking in the first place to have the application of the contested decision suspended. The applicant also asks the Court to order the Commission to publicize the suspension by issuing a press release, to draw the release
 officially to the attention of both the Cour d' Appel, Liège, before which proceedings have been brought between the applicant and the Football Club de Liège, and
 the Union Royale Belge des Sociétés de Football Association, and also to forward
 to the Belgian court a copy of the arrangement reached with the UEFA together
 with the Commission' s decision approving it. Lastly, the applicant asks that the
 Commission be directed to order the UEFA to issue to the applicant a document
 certifying that he is provisionally entitled to hire out his services to any club established within the Community and to be fielded by such club in official matches
 without any obligation on its part to pay fees to his former club.
4 The Commission submitted written observations on the application for interim
 measures on 23 May 1991 and on 28 May 1991 a separate document, pursuant to
 Article 91(1) of the Rules of Procedure, in which it raised a preliminary objection

of inadmissibility regarding the main proceedings. It requested the Court to give a decision on that objection without proceeding to consider the substance of the case.

5    The Commission contends that the applicant' s request to the Court is manifestly inadmissible on the ground that the measure the annulment of which is sought is not a "decision" but an informal transitional arrangement. The Commission states that the contested measure is not to be regarded as an implied "decision" on the complaint submitted by the applicant against, amongst others, the UEFA for infringement of Articles 85 and 86 of the EEC Treaty. Even on the assumption that it is indeed a "decision", it was not addressed to the applicant and is not of direct and individual concern to him; it affects him only by virtue of his objective status as a professional football player. Lastly, the claim for damages is, according to the Commission, inadmissible because the measure in question has no binding legal effects and thus cannot render the Commission liable to the applicant.

6    It should be pointed out that under Article 83(1) of the Rules of Procedure an application for the suspension of the application of any measure or for other interim relief is admissible only if the Court is already seised of an action in which the applicant challenges the measure whose suspension is sought, or of a case to which the applicant is a party and to which the requested interim measures refer. An application for suspension or other interim relief cannot therefore be upheld if the main action to which the application relates is inadmissible.

7    It is, admittedly, established case-law that, in principle, the issue of the admissibility of the main application should not be examined in proceedings relating to an application for interim measures, so as not to prejudge the substance of the case (see most recently the order of the President of the Court in Case 160/88 R Fedesa v Council [1988] ECR 4121); however, according to that same case-law, if it is the manifest inadmissibility of the main application that is pleaded, it is for the judge hearing the application for interim measures to establish that the main application reveals prima facie grounds for concluding that there is a certain probability that it is admissible.

8    In that connection it should be observed that the suspension and the other interim measures sought relate to the application for annulment and that, prima facie, there is nothing in the documents before the Court to justify the conclusion that that application is admissible.

9    Accordingly, at this stage of the proceedings, the application for interim measures must be dismissed.

*Operative part*
On those grounds,
The President
hereby orders:
1.    The application for interim measures is dismissed;
2.    The costs are reserved.
Luxembourg, 27 June 1991.

———

### 2.10.4.    EUROPEAN COURT OF JUSTICE, ORDER OF THE COURT, JEAN-MARC BOSMAN V COMMISSION OF THE EUROPEAN COMMUNITIES, CASE C-117/91, 4 OCTOBER 1991[818]

*Procedure – Intervention – Interested persons – Dispute relating to the validity of a deci-*

---
[818] ECR 1991, p. I-4837.

*sion applying the rules on competition − Complainant undertaking − Undertaking to which the decision was addressed failed to bring an independent action − Procedural rights*
*(Statute of the Court of Justice of the EEC, Art. 37)*

1.   *Action for annulment − Measures open to challenge − Definition − Measures having binding legal effects − Noting by the Commission of conduct contemplated by a private association*
     *(EEC Treaty, Art. 173)*

2.   *Action for damages − Action brought against the Commission on the basis of a measure having no legal effect − Inadmissibility*
     *(EEC Treaty, Art. 178 and second para. of Art. 215)*

1.   Only measures, the legal effects of which are binding on, and capable of affecting the interests of, the applicant by bringing about a distinct change in his legal position may the subject of an application for annulment.

     That is not the position where it is clear from a press release distributed by the Commission that it confined itself on the one hand to taking formal notice of the amendments which a private association coordinating professional football at the European level proposed to make to its rules in order to facilitate the movement of professional footballers within the Community and, on the other hand, the plans envisaged in relation to the question of transfer of players, for in so doing the Commission neither adopted any unilateral decision having legal effects with regard to third parties nor entered into any contract or agreement capable of being challenged before the Court.

2.   An action seeking compensation for damage caused by the alleged unlawfulness of a measure adopted by an institution is inadmissible where that measure has no legal effect.

**Parties**

In Case C-117/91,

Jean-Marc Bosman, represented by J.-L. Dupont, L. Misson and M.-A. Lucas, of the Liège Bar, with an address for service in Luxembourg at the Chambers of E. Korn, 21, Rue de Nassau,

applicant, v Commission of the European Communities, represented by Jean-Claude Séché, Legal Adviser, Enrico Traversa, a member of its Legal Service, and T. Margellos, a senior lecturer at the University of Picardy, on secondment to the Commission, acting as Agents, with an address for service in Luxembourg at the office of Roberto Hayder, a representative of its Legal Service, Wagner Centre, Kirchberg, defendant,

Application for the annulment of a decision allegedly adopted on 17 April 1991 by the Commission in relation to an agreement between the Commission and the Union of European Football Associations and for compensation for the damage caused by that decision,

*The Court,*

composed of: O. Due, President, G.F. Mancini, T.F. O' Higgins, J.C. Moitinho de Almeida, G.C. Rodríguez Iglesias and M. Díez de Velasco (Presidents of Chambers), Sir Gordon Slynn, C.N. Kakouris, R. Joliet, F.A. Schockweiler, F. Grévisse, M. Zuleeg and P.J.G. Kapteyn, Judges,

Advocate General: C.O. Lenz,

Registrar: J.-G. Giraud,

after hearing the Advocate General,

makes the following

*Order*

*Grounds*

1      By application lodged at the Court Registry on 23 April 1991, Mr Jean-Marc Bosman, a professional footballer, brought an action under the second paragraph of Article 173 of the EEC Treaty for the annulment of a decision adopted by the Commission on 17 April 1991, as set out in particular in the Commission's press release IP(91)316 of 18 April 1991, regarding an agreement between the Commission and the Union of European Football Associations (hereinafter referred to as "UEFA") on nationality clauses applicable to national championships and the system of transfer fees applicable to the transfer of professional players from one club to another. Pursuant to Article 178 and the second paragraph of Article 215 of the EEC Treaty, the applicant further sought compensation for the damage caused to him by that decision.

2      It is apparent from the press release to which the applicant refers that following conversations between the Vice-President of the Commission, Mr Bangemann, acting in pursuance of the powers conferred on him by the Commission, and the UEFA, the latter agreed to amend its rules so that, as from the 1992/93 season, at least three non-national players, together with two non-national players actively engaged in their profession in the host country without interruption for five years, would be allowed to be fielded in the first-division matches played in national championships – the scheme being extended to other divisions in which professional players operate, not later than the end of the 1996/97 season. The press release also notes that, as far as contractual bonds between clubs and professional players are concerned, a first step has been taken regarding transfers, an agreement having emerged, at that stage of negotiations, to accept the principle according to which any professional player is at liberty to play for another club upon the expiry of his contract, irrespective of the usual negotiations between the transferring club and the purchasing club concerning the fees to be paid to the former. The press release states in conclusion that the question of a "standard contract" between clubs and professional players will require more detailed discussions with all parties concerned.

3      By a separate document, also lodged at the Court Registry on 23 April 1991, the applicant submitted an application under Articles 185 and 186 of the EEC Treaty for interim measures. By order of 27 June 1991 the President of the Court dismissed that application.

4      By a separate document lodged at the Court Registry on 28 May 1991 the Commission raised an objection of inadmissibility pursuant to Article 91(1) of the Rules of Procedure, on which it requested the Court to give a decision without proceeding to consider the substance of the case.

5      On 1 July 1991, Mr Bosman submitted his written observations on the objection of inadmissibility pursuant to Article 91(2) of the Rules of Procedure.

6      The Court considered that it had sufficient information from the parties' written observations and, pursuant to Article 91(3) of the Rules of Procedure, decided to give a decision without an oral procedure.

*The claim for annulment*

7      In support of its objection to the admissibility of the application for annulment the Commission alleges that it is directed against a non-existent measure or at least one that cannot produce legal effects. The contested measure is an informal transitional arrangement recording the progress achieved towards complete liberalization of the regulations of national football federations and the UEFA.

8     The Commission states in particular that the contested measure does not have the content which the applicant attributes to it. It cannot be regarded as an implied "decision" on the complaint submitted by the applicant against, amongst others, the UEFA for infringement of Articles 85 and 86 of the EEC Treaty, since the investigation of that complaint is still in progress. Since no agreement has been notified by the UEFA, the contested measure cannot be regarded as a decision of exemption pursuant to Article 85(3) of the Treaty or as a negative clearance pursuant to Article 2 of Regulation No 17 of the Council of 6 February 1962, the first regulation implementing Articles 85 and 86 of the Treaty (Official Journal English Special Edition 1959-1962, p. 87).

9     According to the Commission, even on the assumption that there is a "decision", it was not addressed to the applicant and is not of direct and individual concern to him; it affects him only by reason of his objective status as a professional football player.

10    Mr Bosman, on the other hand, considers that the contested measure does have binding legal effect capable of affecting his interest in so far as it alters his legal position. The measure in question cannot be characterized as non-existent, since Community measures are presumed to be valid. Nor is it an informal arrangement, since it affects the legal position of third parties, or a preparatory measure, because the very terms of the agreement between the Commission and UEFA demonstrate its definitive nature.

11    The applicant maintains in particular that the contested measure may be regarded as a measure relating to the application of the rules on competition contained in the Treaty since it involves the implied rejection of a complaint made to the Commission on 20 November 1990 by Mr Bosman on the incompatibility with Article 85 of nationality clauses and the mechanisms for the transfer of footballers, or as a decision of exemption adopted pursuant to Article 85(3) of the Treaty or as a negative clearance pursuant to Article 2 of Regulation No 17. If that were not so, it could be a measure reinforcing the effects of an agreement contrary to Article 85 of the Treaty, a communication relating to Article 48 of the Treaty or a measure by which the Commission waives its powers under Article 169 of the Treaty.

12    Mr Bosman alleges that the measure is of direct concern to him within the meaning of Article 173 of the Treaty since it in no way implies any implementing measure on the part of the Member States. The measure is also of individual concern to him in so far as it constitutes a reply to the complaint which he had made to the Commission and to the information which he had given to it on his opposition to an agreement. The Commission had decided to reopen negotiations with the UEFA following the action brought by Mr Bosman before the Belgian courts and the resolution of his personal case was a subject of a clause in the agreement. Mr Bosman is the only player in the Community engaged in legal proceedings with his federation and the Commission decision could affect the outcome of the proceedings in his case. Finally, his situation is individual to himself by reason of the specific nature and seriousness of the damage suffered.

13    In order to determine whether the present action is admissible the Court must consider, as a preliminary point, the nature of the contested measure. The Court has consistently held that only measures, the legal effects of which are binding on, and capable of affecting the interests of, the applicant by bringing about a distinct change in his legal position may be the subject of an application for annulment (see Case 60/81 IBM v Commission [1981] ECR 2639).

14    That is not the position with regard to the contested measure. It is clear from the very terms of the press release cited by the applicant and the other documents

which he has produced to the Court that on conclusion of the negotiations which took place between the Vice-President of the Commission and the UEFA on the position of professional footballers in the Community the Commission confined itself on the one hand to taking formal notice of the amendments which the UEFA proposed to make to its rules in order to facilitate the movement of players within the Community and on the other hand the plans envisaged in relation to the question of the transfer of players. It thus neither adopted any unilateral decision having legal effects with regard to third parties nor entered into any contract or agreement, of whatever nature, with the UEFA which was capable of being reviewed by the Court.

15    It follows from those findings that the contested measure is not capable of being the subject of an application for annulment and that the action must be dismissed as inadmissible.

*The claims for damages*

16    The Commission considers that the action for damages is inadmissible on the ground that the informal arrangement in question has not yet been finalized and that in any event it has no legal effect. Furthermore the damage alleged by the applicant is merely contingent.

17    Mr Bosman, on the other hand, considers that the action is admissible since the Commission' s measure has legal effects and the damage is genuine and present.

18    In that respect, it should be pointed out that Mr Bosman alleges he has suffered several distinct disadvantages which must be considered separately. It is therefore necessary to consider the admissibility of the claims for damages in relation to the various disadvantages cited.

19    Mr Bosman states that he has been placed in danger of losing his case before the Belgian courts and that the equilibrium of the proceedings has been upset; he also risks losing his present employment and being faced with a restriction of the employment market on which he should be able to offer his services. Those adverse effects are the result of the fault committed by the Commission in adopting the decision of 17 April 1991, alleged by the applicant to be unlawful, and which is also the subject of his claim for annulment.

20    As found above, that measure has no legal effect. The Court has already held (see the order in Case C-50/90 Sunzest (Europe) and Sunzest (Netherlands) v Commission [1991] ECR I-2917) that an action for damages seeking compensation for damage caused, in the applicant' s view, solely by the unlawfulness of a measure adopted by an institution is inadmissible where that measure has no legal effect.

21    The claim based on the second paragraph of Article 215 of the Treaty must therefore be dismissed as inadmissible.

22    It is therefore necessary to apply Article 91(4) of the Rules of Procedure and to declare the action inadmissible in its entirety.

*Decision on costs*

Costs

23    Under Article 69(2) of the Rules of Procedure, the unsuccessful party is to be ordered to pay the costs. Since the applicant has been unsuccessful, he must be ordered to pay the costs.

*Operative part*

On those grounds,

*The Court*
hereby orders:
1.    The application is dismissed as inadmissible;
2.    The applicant is ordered to pay the costs.
Luxembourg, 4 October 1991.

———

**\* 2.10.5.    EUROPEAN COURT OF JUSTICE, OPINION OF ADVOCATE
GENERAL LENZ, UNION ROYALE BELGE DES SOCIÉTÉS DE
FOOTBALL ASSOCIATION ASBL V JEAN-MARC BOSMAN, ROYAL
CLUB LIÈGEOIS SA V JEAN-MARC BOSMAN AND OTHERS AND
UNION DES ASSOCIATIONS EUROPÉENNES DE FOOTBALL
(UEFA) V JEAN-MARC BOSMAN, CASE C-415/93, 20 SEPTEMBER
1995**[819]

———

**2.10.6.    EUROPEAN COURT OF JUSTICE, JUDGMENT, UNION ROYALE
BELGE DES SOCIÉTÉS DE FOOTBALL ASSOCIATION ASBL V
JEAN-MARC BOSMAN, ROYAL CLUB LIÈGEOIS SA V JEAN-MARC
BOSMAN AND OTHERS AND UNION DES ASSOCIATIONS
EUROPÉENNES DE FOOTBALL (UEFA) V JEAN-MARC BOSMAN,
CASE C-415/93, 15 DECEMBER 1995**[820]

Reference for a preliminary ruling: Cour d'appel de Liège – Belgium. Freedom of movement for workers – Competition rules applicable to undertakings Professional footballers
– Sporting rules on the transfer of players requiring the new club to pay a fee to the old
club – Limitation of the number of players having the nationality of other Member States
who may be fielded in a match.

1.    *Procedure – Request for measures of inquiry – Request made after the close of the
       oral procedure – Conditions for admissibility
       (Rules of Procedure of the Court of Justice, Arts 59(2) and 60)*
2.    *Preliminary rulings – Jurisdiction of the Court – Limits – Manifestly irrelevant
       questions and hypothetical questions referred in circumstances in which a useful
       answer is precluded – Jurisdiction to reply to questions raised in the context of
       declaratory proceedings permitted under national law
       (EEC Treaty, Art. 177)*
3.    *Community law – Scope – Sport as an economic activity – Included
       (EEC Treaty, Art. 2)*
4.    *Freedom of movement for persons – Workers – Treaty provisions – Conditions of
       application – Existence of an employment relationship – Employer not an under-
       taking – Not relevant
       (EEC Treaty, Art. 48)*
5.    *Freedom of movement for persons – Workers – Treaty provisions – Scope – Rules
       governing business relationships between employers but affecting the terms of em-
       ployment of workers – Included
       (EEC Treaty, Art. 48)*

---

[819]  ECR 1995, p. I-4930.
[820]  ECR 1995, p. I-4921.

6.      *Freedom of movement for persons – Workers – Freedom of establishment – Free-*
        *dom tp provide services – Treaty provisions – Scope – Sporting activity – Limits*
        *(EEC Treaty, Arts 48, 52 and 59)*

7.      *Freedom of movement for persons – Workers – Treaty provisions – Scope – Limi-*
        *tation in order to respect the diversity of national cultures as required by Article*
        *128 of the EC Treaty – Not possible*
        *(EEC Treaty, Art. 48; EC Treaty, Art 128(1))*

8.      *Community law – Principles – Fundamental rights – Freedom of association – Im-*
        *plications – Right of sporting associations to lay down rules likely to restrict free-*
        *dom of movement for professional sportsmen – Excluded*
        *(Single European Act, preamble; Treaty on European Union, Art. F(2)).*

9.      *Community law – Principles – Principle of subsidiarity – Scope – Restriction on*
        *the exercise of rights conferred on individuals by the Treaty – Excluded*

10.     *Freedom of movement for persons – Workers – Treaty provisions – Scope – Rules*
        *aimed at regulating gainful employment in a collective manner but not emanating*
        *from a public authority – Included*
        *(EEC Treaty, Art. 48)*

11.     *Freedom of movement for persons – Workers – Restrictions justified on grounds of*
        *public policy, public security or public health – Grounds which may be relied on*
        *by any private individual or public body*
        *(EEC Treaty, Art. 48)*

12.     *Freedom of movement for persons – Workers – Treaty provisions – Scope – Rules*
        *laid down by sporting associations which determine the terms on which profes-*
        *sional sportsmen can engage in gainful employment – Included*
        *(EEC Treaty, Art. 48)*

13.     *Freedom of movement for persons 0 Workers – Treaty provisions – Scope – Pro-*
        *fessional sportsman who is a national of a Member State and has entered into a*
        *contract of employment with a club in another Member State with a view to exer-*
        *cising gainful employment in that State – Included*
        *(EEC Treaty, Art. 48)*

14.     *Freedom of movement for persons – Workers – Rules laid down by sporting asso-*
        *ciations making the recruitment of a professional sportsman by a new employer in*
        *another Member State subject to the payment of a fee by the new employer to the*
        *old employer – Not permissible – Justification – None*
        *(EEC Treaty, Art. 48)*

15.     *Freedom of movement for persons – Workers – Equal treatment – Rules laid down*
        *by sporting associations limiting the participation of players who are nationals of*
        *other Member States in certain competitions – Not permissible – Justification –*
        *None*
        *(EEC Treaty, Art. 48)*

16.     *Commission – Powers – Power to give guarantees concerning the compatibility of*
        *specific practices with the Treaty – None unless specifically conferred – Power to*
        *authorize practices contrary to the Treaty – None*

17.     *Preliminary rulings – Interpretation – Temporal effects of judgments ruling on in-*
        *terpretation 0 Retroactive effect – Limits – Legal certainty – Power of assessment*
        *of the Court*
        *(EEC Treaty, Art. 177)*

1.      A request for the Court to order a measure of inquiry under Article 60 of the Rules
        of Procedure, made by a party after the close of the oral procedure, can be admit-
        ted only if it relates to facts which may have a decisive influence and which the

party concerned could not put forward before the close of the oral procedure.

2.  In the context of the cooperation between the Court of Justice and the national courts provided for by Article 177 of the Treaty, it is solely for the national court before which the dispute has been brought, and which must assume responsibility for the subsequent judicial decision, to determine in the light of the particular circumstances of the case both the need for a preliminary ruling in order to enable it to deliver judgment and the relevance of the questions which it submits to the Court. Consequently, where the questions submitted by the national court concern the interpretation of Community law, the Court of Justice is, in principle, bound to give a ruling.

    Nevertheless, in order to determine whether it has jurisdiction, the Court should examine the conditions in which the case was referred to it by the national court. The spirit of cooperation which must prevail in the preliminary-ruling procedure requires the national court, for its part, to have regard to the function entrusted to the Court of Justice, which is to assist in the administration of Justice in the Member States and not to deliver advisory opinions on general or hypothetical questions.

    That is why the Court has no jurisdiction to give a preliminary ruling on a question submitted by a national court where it is quite obvious that the interpretation of Community law sought by that court bears no relation to the actual facts of the main action or its purpose or where the problem is hypothetical and the Court does not have before it the factual or legal material necessary to give a useful answer to the questions submitted to it.

    Questions submitted by a national court called upon to decide on declaratory actions seeking to prevent the infringement of a right which is seriously threatened are to be regarded as meeting an objective need for the purpose of settling the dispute brought before that court, even though they are necessarily based on hypotheses which are, by their nature, uncertain, if it holds them to be admissible under its interpretation of its national law.

3.  Having regard to the objectives of the Community, sport is subject to Community law in so far as it constitutes an economic activity within the meaning of Article 2 of the Treaty, as in the case of the activities of professional or semi-professional footballers, where they are in gainful employment or provide a remunerated service.

4.  It is not necessary, for the purposes of the application of the Community provisions on freedom of movement for workers, for the employer to be an undertaking; all that is required is the existence of, or the intention to create, an employment relationship.

5.  Rules governing business relationships between employers in a sector of activity fall within the scope of the Community provisions relating to freedom of movement for workers if their application affects the terms of employment of workers.

    That is true of rules relating to the transfer of players between football clubs which, although they govern the business relationships between clubs rather than the employment relationships between clubs and players, affect, because the employing clubs must pay fees on recruiting a player from another club, players opportunities for finding employment and the terms under which such employment is offered.

6.  The Community provisions concerning freedom of movement for persons and freedom to provide services do not preclude rules or practices in sport which are justified on noneconomic grounds which relate to the particular nature and context of certain competitions. Such a restriction on the scope of the provisions in ques-

tion must remain limited to its proper objective and cannot, therefore, be relied upon to exclude the whole of a sporting activity from the scope of the Treaty.

7.    Freedom of movement for workers, guaranteed by Article 48 of the Treaty, is a fundamental freedom in the Community system and its scope cannot be limited by the Community's obligation to respect the national and regional cultural diversity of the Member States when it uses the powers of limited extent conferred upon it by Article 128 (1) of the EC Treaty in the field of culture.

8.    The principle of freedom of association, enshrined in Article 11 of the Convention for the Protection of Human Rights and Fundamental Freedoms and resulting from the constitutional traditions common to the Member States, is one of the fundamental rights which, as the Court has consistently held and as is reaffirmed in the preamble to the Single European Act and in Article F(2) of the Treaty on European Union, are protected in the Community legal order.

      However, rules likely to restrict freedom of movement for professional sportsmen, laid down by sporting associations, cannot be seen as necessary to ensure enjoyment of that freedom by those associations, by the clubs or by their players, nor can they be seen as an inevitable result thereof.

9.    The principle of subsidiarity, even when interpreted broadly to the effect that intervention by Community authorities in the area of organization of sporting activities must be confined to what is strictly necessary, cannot lead to a situation in which the freedom of private associations to adopt sporting rules restricts the exercise of rights conferred on individuals by the Treaty.

10.   Article 48 of the Treaty not only applies to the action of public authorities but extends also to rules of any other nature aimed at regulating gainful employment in a collective manner.

      The abolition as between Member States of obstacles to freedom of movement for persons would be compromised if the abolition of State barriers could be neutralized by obstacles resulting from the exercise of their legal autonomy by associations or organizations not governed by public law. Furthermore, if the scope of Article 48 were confined to acts of a public authority there would be a risk of creating inequality in its application, inasmuch as working conditions in the different Member States are governed sometimes by provisions laid down by law or regulation and sometimes by agreements and other acts concluded or adopted by private persons.

11.   There is nothing to preclude individuals from relying, to justify restrictions on freedom of movement for workers which they may be alleged to have set up, on the grounds of public policy, public security or public health permitted by Article 48 of the Treaty. Neither the scope nor the content of those grounds of justification is in any way affected by the public or private nature of the restrictive rules in support of which they are adduced.

12.   Article 48 of the Treaty applies to rules laid down by sporting associations which determine the terms on which professional sportsmen can engage in gainful employment.

13.   The situation of a professional footballer who is a national of a Member State and, by entering into a contract of employment with a club in another Member State with a view to exercising gainful employment in that State, has accepted an offer of employment actually made within the meaning of Article 48(3)(a) of the Treaty, cannot be classified as purely internal and therefore not covered by Community law.

14.   Article 48 of the Treaty precludes the application of rules laid down by sporting associations, under which a professional footballer who is a national of one Mem-

ber State may not, on the expiry of his contract with a club, be employed by a club of another Member State unless the latter club has paid to the former club a transfer, training or development fee.

Such rules, even though they do not differ from those governing transfers within the same Member State, are likely to restrict the freedom of movement of players who wish to pursue their activity in another Member State by preventing or deterring them from leaving the clubs to which they belong even after the expiry of their contracts of employment with those clubs.

Nor are they an adequate means of achieving such legitimate aims as maintaining a financial and competitive balance between clubs and supporting the search for talent and the training of young players, since those rules neither preclude the richest clubs from securing the services of the best players nor prevent the availability of financial resources from being a decisive factor in competitive sport, thus considerably altering the balance between clubs, the fees provided for in those rules are by nature contingent and uncertain and are in any event unrelated to the actual cost of training borne by clubs and the same aims can be achieved at least as efficiently by other means which do not impede freedom of movement for workers.

15. Article 48 of the Treaty precludes the application of rules laid down by sporting associations under which, in matches in competitions which they organize, football clubs may field only a limited number of professional players who are nationals of other Member States.

Such rules are contrary to the principle of the prohibition of discrimination based on nationality as regards employment, remuneration and conditions of work and employment and it is of no relevance that they concern not the employment of such players, on which there is no restriction, but the extent to which their clubs may field them in official matches, since, in so far as participation in such matches is the essential purpose of a professional player's activity, a rule which restricts that participation obviously also restricts the chances of employment of the player concerned.

Nor can those rules, which do not concern specific matches between teams representing their countries but apply to all official matches between clubs, be justified for reasons which are not of an economic nature and are of sporting interest only, such as: preserving the traditional link between each club and its country, since a football club's links with the Member State in which it is established cannot be regarded as inherent in its sporting activity; creating a sufficient pool of national players to provide the national teams with top players to field in all team positions, since, whilst national teams must be made up of players having the nationality of the relevant country, those players need not necessarily be registered to play for clubs in that country; or maintaining a competitive balance between clubs, since there are no rules limiting the possibility for richer clubs to recruit the best national players, thus undermining that balance to just the same extent.

16. Except where such powers are expressly conferred upon it, the Commission may not give guarantees concerning the compatibility of specific practices with the Treaty and in no circumstances does it have the power to authorize practices which are contrary to the Treaty.

17. The interpretation which the Court, in the exercise of the jurisdiction conferred upon it by Article 177 of the Treaty, gives to a rule of Community law clarifies and where necessary defines the meaning and scope of that rule as it must be, or ought to have been, understood and applied from the time of its coming into force. It follows that the rule as thus interpreted can, and must, be applied by the courts even to legal relationships arising and established before the judgment ruling on

the request for interpretation, provided that in other respects the conditions for bringing before the courts having jurisdiction an action relating to the application of that rule are satisfied.

It is only exceptionally that the Court may, in application of the general principle of legal certainty inherent in the Community legal order, be moved to restrict the opportunity for any person concerned to rely upon the provision as thus interpreted with a view to calling in question legal relationships established in good faith. Such a restriction may be allowed only by the Court, in the actual judgment ruling upon the interpretation sought.

Since the specific features of the rules laid down by the sporting associations for transfers of players between clubs of different Member States, together with the fact that the same or similar rules applied to transfers both between clubs belonging to the same national association and between clubs belonging to different national associations within the same Member State, may have caused uncertainty as to whether those rules were compatible with Community law, overriding considerations of legal certainty militate against calling in question legal situations whose effects have already been exhausted.

It must therefore be held that the direct effect of Article 48 of the Treaty cannot be relied upon in support of claims relating to a fee in respect of transfer, training or development which has already been paid on, or is still payable under an obligation which arose before, the date of this judgment, except by those who have brought court proceedings or raised an equivalent claim under the applicable national law before that date.

In Case C-415/93,

Reference to the Court under Article 177 of the EEC Treaty by the Cour d'appel, Liège, Belgium, for a preliminary ruling in the proceedings pending before that court

between Union Royale Belge des Sociétés de Football Association ASBL and Jean-Marc Bosman,

between Royal Club Liégois SA and Jean-Marc Bosman, SA d'Économie Mixte Sportive de l'Union Sportive du Littoral de Dunkerque, Union Royale Belge des Sociétés de Football Association ASBL, Union des Associations Européennes de Football (UEFA), and

between Union des Associations Européennes de Football (UEFA) and Jean-Marc Bosman,

on the interpretation of Articles 48, 85 and 86 of the EEC Treaty,

**THE COURT,**

composed of: G.C. Rodriguez Iglesias, President, C.N. Kakouris, D.A.O. Edward and G. Hirsch (Presidents of Chambers), G.F. Mancini (Rapporteur), J.C. Moitinho de Almeida, P.J.G. Kapteyn, C. Gulmann, J.L. Murray, P. Jann and H. Ragnemalm, Judges,

Advocate General: C.O. Lenz,

Registrars: R. Grass, Registrar, and D. Louterman-Hubeau, Principal Administrator, after considering the written observations submitted on behalf of: Union Royale Belge des Sociétés de Football Association ASBL, by G. Vandersanden and J.-P. Hordles, of the Brussels Bar, and by R. Rasir and F. Moïses, of the Liège Bar, ' Union des Associations Européennes de Football (UEFA), by I.S. Forrester QC, Mr Bosman, by L. Misson, J.-L. Dupont, M.-A. Lucas and M. Franchimont, of the Liège Bar, the French Government, by H. Duchène, Foreign Affairs Secretary in the Legal Directorate of the Ministry of Foreign Affairs, and C. de Salins, Assistant Director in the same directorate, the Italian Government, by Professor L. Feffari Bravo, Head of the Legal Service in the Ministry of Foreign Affairs, assisted by D. Del Gaizo, Avvocato dello Stato, the Commission of the European Communities, by F.E. González Diaz, of its Legal Service, G. de Bergues, a national official placed at the disposal of its Legal Service, and Th. Margellos, of the Athens Bar,

having regard to the Report for the Hearing, after hearing the oral observations of Union Royale Belge des Sociétés de Football Association ASBL, represented by F. Mo;ises, J.-P. Hordies and G. Vandersanden; of Union des Associations Européennes de Football, UEFA, represented by I.S. Forrester and E. Jakhian, of the Brussels Bar; of Mr Bosman, represented by L. Misson and J.-L. Dupont; of the Danish Government, represented by P. Biering, Kontorchef in the Ministry of Foreign Affairs, acting as Agent; of the German Government, represented by E. Roeder, Ministerialrat in the Federal Ministry of the Economy; of the French Government, represented by C. de Salins and P. Martinet, Foreign Affairs Secretary in the Legal Directorate of the Ministry of Foreign Affairs, acting as Agents; of the Italian Government, represented by D. Del Gaizo; and of the Commission, represented by F.E. González Díaz, G. de Bergues and M. Wolfcarius, of its Legal Service, at the hearing on 20 June 1995,
after hearing the Opinion of the Advocate General at the sitting on 20 September 1995, gives the following

## Judgment

1.  By judgment of 1 October 1993, received at the Court on 6 October 1993, the Cour d'Appel (Appeal Court), Liège, referred to the Court for a preliminary ruling under Article 177 of the EEC Treaty a set of questions on the interpretation of Articles 48, 85 and 86 of that Treaty.
2.  Those questions were raised in various proceedings between (i) Union Royale Belge des Sociétés de Football Association ASBL ('URBSFA') and Mr Bosman, (ii) Royal Club Liégois SA ('RC Liège') and Mr Bosman, SA d'Économie Mixte Sportive de l'Union Sportive du Littoral de Dunkerque ('US Dunkerque'), URBSFA and Union des Associations Européennes de Football (UEFA) ('UEFA') and, (iii) UEFA and Mr Bosman.

## The rules governing the organization of football

3.  Association football, commonly known as 'football', professional or amateur, is practised as an organized sport in clubs which belong to national associations or federations in each of the Member States. Only in the United Kingdom are there more than one (in fact, four) national associations, for England, Wales, Scotland and Northern Ireland respectively. URBSFA is the Belgian national association. Also dependent on the national associations are other secondary or subsidiary associations responsible for organizing football in certain sectors or regions. The associations hold national championships, organized in divisions depending on the sporting status of the participating clubs.
4.  The national associations are members of the Fédération Internationale de Football Association ('FIFA'), an association governed by Swiss law, which organizes football at world level. FIFA is divided into confederations for each continent, whose regulations require its approval. The confederation for Europe is UEFA, also an association governed by Swiss law. Its members are the national associations of some 50 countries, including in particular those of the Member States which, under the UEFA Statutes, have undertaken to comply with those Statutes and with the regulations and decisions of UEFA.
5.  Each football match organized under the auspices of a national association must

be played between two clubs which are members of that association or of secondary or subsidiary associations affiliated to it. The team fielded by each club consists of players who are registered by the national association to play for that club. Every professional player must be registered as such with his national association and is entered as the present or former employee of a specific club.

**Transfer rules**

6.     The 1983 URBSFA federal rules, applicable at the time of the events giving rise to the different actions in the main proceedings, distinguish between three types of relationship: affiliation of a player to the federation, affiliation to a club, and registration of entitlement to play for a club, which is necessary for a player to be able to participate in official competitions. A transfer is defined as the transaction by which a player affiliated to an association obtains a change of club affiliation. If the transfer is temporary, the player continues to be affiliated to his club but is registered as entitled to play for another club.

7.     Under the same rules, all professional players' contracts, which have a term of between one and five years, run to 30 June. Before the expiry of the contract, and by 26 April at the latest, the club must offer the player a new contract, failing which he is considered to be an amateur for transfer purposes and thereby falls under a different section of the rules. The player is free to accept or refuse that offer.

8.     If he refuses, he is placed on a list of players available, between 1 and 31 May, for 'compulsory' transfer, without the agreement of the club of affiliation but subject to payment to that club by the new club of a compensation fee for 'training', calculated by multiplying the player's gross annual income by a factor varying from 14 to 2 depending on the player's age.

9.     1 June marks the opening of the period for 'free' transfers, with the agreement of both clubs and the player, in particular as to the amount of the transfer fee which the new club must pay to the old club, subject to penalties which may include striking off the new club for debt.

10.     If no transfer takes place, the player's club of affiliation must offer him a new contract for one season on the same terms as that offered prior to 26 April. If the player refuses, the club has a period until 1 August in which it may suspend him, failing which he is reclassified as an amateur. A player who persistently refuses to sign the contracts offered by his club may obtain a transfer as an amateur, without his club's agreement, after not playing for two seasons.

11.     The UEFA and FIFA regulations are not directly applicable to players but are included in the rules of the national associations, which alone have the power to enforce them and to regulate relations between clubs and players.

12.     UEFA, URBSFA and RC Liège stated before the national court that the provisions applicable at the material time to transfers between clubs in different Member States or clubs belonging to different national associations within the same Member State were contained in a document entitled Principles of Cooperation between Member Associations of UEFA and their Clubs, approved by the UEFA Executive Committee on 24 May 1990 and in force from 1 July 1990.

13.     That document provides that at the expiry of the contract the player is free to enter into a new contract with the club of his choice. That club must immediately notify the old club which in turn is to notify the national association, which must issue an international clearance certificate. However, the former club is entitled to receive from the new club compensation for training and development, to be fixed, failing agreement, by a board of experts set up within UEFA using a scale of multiplying factors, from 12 to 1 depending on the player's age, to be applied to the player's gross income, up to a maximum of SFR 5.000.000.

14.   The document stipulates that the business relationships between the two clubs in respect of the compensation fee for training and development are to exert no influence on the activity of the player, who is to be free to play for his new club. However, if the new club does not immediately pay the fee to the old club, the UEFA Control and Disciplinary Committee is to deal with the matter and notify its decision to the national association concerned, which may also impose penalties on the debtor club.

15.   The national court considers that in the case with which the main proceedings are concerned URBSFA and RC Liège applied not the UEFA but the FIFA regulations.

16.   At the material time, the FIFA regulations provided in particular that a professional player could not leave the national association to which he was affiliated so long as he was bound by his contract and by the rules of his club and his national association, no matter how harsh their terms might be. An international transfer could not take place unless the former national association issued a transfer certificate acknowledging that all financial commitments, including any transfer fee, had been settled.

17.   After the events which gave rise to the main proceedings, UEFA opened negotiations with the Commission of the European Communities. In April 1991, it undertook in particular to incorporate in every professional player's contract a clause permitting him, at the expiry of the contract, to enter into a new contract with the club of his choice and to play for that club immediately. Provisions to that effect were incorporated in the Principles of Cooperation between Member Associations of UEFA and their Clubs adopted in December 1991 and in force from 1 July 1992.

18.   In April 1991, FIFA adopted new Regulations governing the Status and Transfer of Football Players. That document, as amended in December 1991 and December 1993, provides that a player may enter into a contract with a new club where the contract between him and his club has expired, has been rescinded or is to expire within six months.

19.   Special rules are laid down for 'non-amateur' players, defined as players who have received, in respect of participation in or an activity connected with football, remuneration in excess of the actual expenses incurred in the course of such participation, unless they have reacquired amateur status.

20.   Where a non-amateur player, or a player who assumes non-amateur status within three years of his transfer, is transferred, his former club is entitled to a compensation fee for development or training, the amount of which is to be agreed upon between the two clubs. In the event of disagreement, the dispute is to be submitted to FIFA or the relevant confederation.

21.   Those rules have been supplemented by UEFA regulations 'governing the fixing of a transfer fee', adopted in June 1993 and in force since 1 August 1993, which replace the 1991 'Principles of Cooperation between Member Associations of UEFA and their Clubs'. The new rules retain the principle that the business relationship between the two clubs are to exert no influence on the sporting activity of the player, who is to be free to play for the club with which he has signed the new contract. In the event of disagreement between the clubs concerned, it is for the appropriate UEFA board of experts to determine the amount of the compensation fee for training or development. For non-amateur players, the calculation of the fee is based on the player's gross income in the last 12 months or on the fixed annual income guaranteed in the new contract, increased by 20% for players who have played at least twice in the senior national representative team for their country and multiplied by a factor of between 12 and 0 depending on age.

22     It appears from documents produced to the Court by UEFA that rules in force in other Member States also contain provisions requiring the new club, when a player is transferred between two clubs within the same national association, to pay the fonner club, on terms laid down in the rules in question, a compensation fee for transfer, training or development.

23.    In Spain and France, payment of compensation may only be required if the player transferred is under 25 years of age or if his former club is the one with which he signed his first professional contract, as the case may be. In Greece, although no compensation is explicitly payable by the new club, the contract between the club and the player may make the player's departure dependent on the payment of an amount which, according to UEFA, is in fact most commonly paid by the new club.

24.    The rules applicable in that regard may derive from the national legislation, from the regulations of the national football associations or from the terms of collective agreements.

**Nationality clauses**

25.    From the 1960s onwards, many national football associations introduced rules ('nationality clauses') restricting the extent to which foreign players could be recruited or fielded in a match. For the purposes of those clauses, nationality is defined in relation to whether the player can be qualified to play in a country's national or representative team.

26.    In 1978, UEFA gave an undertaking to Mr Davignon, a Member of the Commission of the European Communities, that it would remove the lin-iitations on the number of contracts entered into by each club with players from other Member States and would set the number of such players who may participate in any one match at two, that limit not being applicable to players established for over five years in the Member State in question.

27.    In 1991, following further discussions with Mr Bangemann, a Vice-President of the Commission, UEFA adopted the '3 + 2' rule per'tting each national association to limit to three the number of foreign players whom a club may field in any first division match in their national championships, plus two players who have played in the country of the relevant national association for an uninterrupted period of five years, including three years as a junior. The same limitation also applies to UEFA matches in competitions for club teams.

**Facts of the cases before the national court**

28.    Mr Bosman, a professional footballer of Belgian nationality, was employed from 1988 by RC Liège, a Belgian first division club, under a contract expiring on 30 June 1990, which assured him an average monthly salary of BFR 120.000, including bonuses.

29.    On 21 April 1990, RC Liège offered Mr Bosman a new contract for one season, reducing his pay to BFR 30.000, the minimum permitted by the URBSFA federal rules.
       Mr Bosman refused to sign and was put on the transfer list. The compensation fee for training was set, in accordance with the said rules, at BFR 11.743.000.

30.    Since no club showed an interest in a compulsory transfer, Mr Bosman made contact with US Dunkerque, a club in the French second division, which led to his being engaged for a monthly salary in the region of BFR 100.000 plus a signing-on bonus of some BFR 900.000.

31.    On 27 July 1990, a contract was also concluded between RC Liège and US Dun-

kerque for the temporary transfer of Mr Bosman for one year, against payment by US Dunkerque to RC Liège of a compensation fee of BFR 1.200.000 payable on receipt by the Fédération Française de Football ('FFF') of the transfer certificate issued by URBSFA. The contract also gave US Dunkerque an irrevocable option for full transfer of the player for BFR 4.800.000.

32.  Both contracts, between US Dunkerque and RC Liège and between US Dunkerque and Mr Bosman, were however subject to the suspensive condition that the transfer certificate must be sent by URBSFA to FFF in time for the first match of the season, which was to be held on 2 August 1990.

33.  RC Liège, which had doubts as to US Dunkerque's solvency, did not ask URBSFA to send the said certificate to FFF. As a result, neither contract took effect. On 31 July 1990, RC Liège also suspended Mr Bosman, thereby preventing him from playing for the entire season.

34.  On 8 August 1990, Mr Bosman brought an action against RC Liège before the Tribunal de Première Instance (Court of First Instance), Liège. Concurrently with that action, he applied for an interlocutory decision ordering RC Liège and URBSFA to pay him an advance of BFR 100.000 per month until he found a new employer, restraining the defendants from impeding his engagement, in particular by requiring payment of a sum of money, and referring a question to the Court of Justice for a preliminary ruling.

35.  By order of 9 November 1990, the judge hearing the interlocutory application ordered RC Liège and URBSFA to pay Mr Bosman an advance of BFR 30.000 per month and to refrain from impeding Mr Bosman's engagement. He also referred to the Court for a preliminary ruling a question (in Case C-340/90) on the interpretation of Article 48 in relation to the rules governing transfers of professional players ('transfer rules').

36.  In the meantime, Mr Bosman had been signed up by the French second-division club Saint-Quentin in October 1990, on condition that his interlocutory application succeeded. His contract was terminated, however, at the end of the first season. In February 1992, Mr Bosman signed a new contract with the French club Saint-Denis de la Réunion, which was also terminated. After looking for further offers in Belgium and France, Mr Bosman was finally signed up by Olympic de Charleroi, a Belgian third division club.

37.  According to the national court, there is strong circumstantial evidence to support the view that, notwithstanding the 'free' status conferred on him by the interlocutory order, Mr Bosman has been boycotted by all the European clubs which might have engaged him.

38.  On 28 May 1991, the Cour d'Appel, Liège, revoked the interlocutory decision of the Tribunal de Première Instance in so far as it referred a question to the Court of Justice for a preliminary ruling. But it upheld the order against RC Liège to pay monthly advances to Mr Bosman and enjoined RC Liège and URBSFA to make Mr Bosman available to any club which wished to use his services, without it being possible to require payment of any compensation fee. By order of 19 June 1991, Case C-340/90 was removed from the register of the Court of Justice.

39.  On 3 June 1991, URBSFA, which, contrary to the situation in the interlocutory proceedings, had not been cited as a party in the main action before the Tribunal de Première Instance, intervened voluntarily in that action. On 20 August 1991, Mr Bosman issued a writ with a view to joining UEFA to the proceedings which he had brought against RC Liège and URBSFA and bringing proceedings directly against it on the basis of its responsibility in drafting the rules as a result of which he had suffered damage. On 5 December 1991, US Dunkerque was joined as a

third party by RC Liège, in order to be indemnified against any order which might be made against it. On 15 October and 27 December 1991 respectively, Union Nationale des Footballeurs Professionnels ('UNFP'), a French professional footballers' union, and Vereniging van Contractspelers ('VVCS'), an association governed by Netherlands law, intervened voluntarily in the proceedings.

40.    In new pleadings lodged on 9 April 1992, Mr Bosman amended his initial claim against RC Liège, brought a new preventive action against URBSFA and elaborated his claim against UEFA. In those proceedings, he sought a declaration that the transfer rules and nationality clauses were not applicable to him and an order, on the basis of their wrongful conduct at the time of the failure of his transfer to US Dunkerque, against RC Liège, URBSFA and UEFA to pay him BFR 11.368.350 in respect of the damage suffered by him from 1 August 1990 until the end of his career and BFR 11.743.000 in respect of loss of earnings since the beginning of his career as a result of the application of the transfer rules. He also applied for a question to be referred to the Court of Justice for a preliminary ruling.

41.    By judgment of 1 1 June 1992, the Tribunal de Première Instance held that it had jurisdiction to entertain the main actions. It also held admissible Mr Bosman's claims against RC Liège, URBSFA and UEFA seeking, in particular, a declaration that the transfer rules and nationality clauses were not applicable to him and orders penalizing the conduct of those three organizations. But it dismissed RC Liège's application to join US Dunkerque as a third party and indemnifier, since no evidence of fault in the latter's performance of its obligations had been adduced. Finally, finding that the examination of Mr Bosman's claims against UEFA and URBSFA involved considering the compatibility of the transfer rules with the Treaty, it made a reference to the Court of Justice for a preliminary ruling on the interpretation of Articles 48, 85 and 86 of the Treaty (Case C269/92).

42.    URBSFA, RC Liège and UEFA appealed against that decision. Since those appeals had suspensive effect, the procedure before the Court of Justice was suspended. By order of 8 December 1993, Case C-269/92 was finally removed from the register following the new judgment of the Cour d'Appel, Liège, out of which the present proceedings arise. 43 No appeal was brought against UNFP or VVCS, who did not seek to intervene again on appeal.

43.    In its judgment ordering the reference, the Cour d'Appel upheld the judgment under appeal in so far as it held that the Tribunal de Première Instance had jurisdiction, that the actions were admissible and that an assessment of Mr Bosman's claims against UEFA and the URBSFA involved a review of the lawfulness of the transfer rules. It also considered that a review of the lawfulness of the nationality clauses was necessary, since Mr Bosman's claim in their regard was based on Article 18 of the Belgian Judicial Code, which permits actions 'with a view to preventing the infringement of a seriously threatened right', and Mr Bosman had adduced factual evidence suggesting that the damage which he fears ' that the application of those clauses may impede his career will in fact occur.

44.    The national court considered in particular that Article 48 of the Treaty could, like Article 30, prohibit not only discrimination but also non-discriminatory barriers to freedom of movement for workers if they could not be justified by imperative requirements.

45.    With regard to Article 85 of the Treaty, it considered that the FIFA, UEFA and URBSFA regulations might constitute decisions of associations of undertakings by which the clubs restrict competition between themselves for players. Transfer fees were dissuasive and tended to depress the level of professional sportsmen's pay. In

addition, the nationality clauses prohibited foreign players' services from being obtained over a certain quota. Finally, trade between Member States was affected, in particular by the restriction of players' mobility.

46. Furthermore, the Cour d'Appel thought that URBSFA, or the football clubs collectively, might be in a dominant position, within the meaning of Article 86 of the Treaty and that the restrictions on competition mentioned in connection with Article 85 might constitute abuses prohibited by Article 86.

47. The Cour d'Appel dismissed UEFA's request that it ask the Court of Justice whether the reply to the question submitted on transfers would be different if the system permitted a player to play freely for his new club even where that club had not paid the transfer fee to the old club. It noted in particular that, because of the threat of severe penalties for clubs not paying the transfer fee, a player's ability to play for his new club remained dependent on the business relationships between the clubs.

48. In view of the foregoing, the Cour d'appel decided to stay the proceedings and refer the following questions to the Court of Justice for a preliminary ruling: 'Are Articles 48, 85 and 86 of the Treaty of Rome of 25 March 1957 to be interpreted as:
    – prohibiting a football club from requiring and receiving payment of a sum of money upon the engagement of one of its players who has come to the end of his contract by a new employing club;
    – prohibiting the national and international sporting associations or federations from including in their respective regulations provisions restricting access of foreign players from the European Community to the competitions which they organize?'

49. On 3 June 1994, URBSFA applied to the Belgian Cour de Cassation (Court of Cassation) for review of the Cour d'appel's judgment, requesting that the judgment be extended to apply jointly to RC Liège, UEFA and US Dunkerque. By letter of 6 October 1994, the Procureur Général (Principal Crown Counsel) to the Cour de Cassation informed the Court of Justice that the appeal did not have suspensive effect in this case.

50. By judgment of 30 March 1995, the Cour de Cassation dismissed the appeal and held that as a result the request for a declaration that the judgment be extended was otiose. The Cour de Cassation has forwarded a copy of that judgment to the Court of Justice. The request for measures of inquiry

51. By letter lodged at the Court Registry en 16 November 1995, UEFA requested the Court to order a measure of inquiry under Article 60 of the Rules of Procedure, with a view to obtaining fuller information on the role played by transfer fees in the financing of small or medium-sized football clubs, the machinery governing the distribution of income within the existing football structures and the presence or absence of alternative machinery if the system of transfer fees were to disappear.

52. After hearing again the views of the Advocate General, the Court considers that that application must be dismissed. It was made at a time when, in accordance with Article 59(2) of the Rules of Procedure, the oral procedure was closed. The Court has held (see Case 77/70 *Prelle v Commission* [1971] ECR 561, paragraph 7) that such an application can be admitted only if it relates to facts which may have a decisive influence and which the party concerned could not put forward before the close of the oral procedure. 54 In this case, it is sufficient to hold that UEFA could have submitted its request before the close of the oral procedure. Moreover, the question whether the aim of maintaining a balance in financial and

competitive terms, and in particular that of ensuring the financing of smaller clubs, can be achieved by other means such as a redistribution of a portion of football takings was raised, in particular by Mr Bosman in his written observations.

## Jurisdiction of the Court to give a preliminary ruling on the questions submitted

53. The Court's jurisdiction to give a ruling on all or part of the questions submitted by the national court has been challenged, on various grounds, by URBSFA, by UEFA, by some of the governments which have submitted observations and, during the written procedure, by the Commission.

54. First, UEFA and URBSFA have claimed that the main actions are procedural devices designed to obtain a preliminary ruling from the Court on questions which meet no objective need for the purpose of settling the cases. The UEFA regulations were not applied when Mr Bosman's transfer to US Dunkerque fell through; if they had been applied, that transfer would not have been dependent on the payment of a transfer fee and could thus have taken place. The interpretation of Community law requested by the national court thus bears no relation to the actual facts of the cases in the main proceedings or their purpose and, in accordance with consistent case-law, the Court has no jurisdiction to rule on the questions submitted.

55. Secondly, URBSFA, UEFA, the Danish, French and Italian Governments and, in its written observations, the Commission have claimed that the questions relating to nationality clauses has no connection with the disputes, which concern only the application of the transfer rules. The impediments to his career which Mr Bosman claims arise out of those clauses are purely hypothetical and do not justify a preliminary ruling by the Court on the interpretation of the Treaty in that regard.

56. Thirdly, URBSFA and UEFA pointed out at the hearing that, according to the judgment of the Cour de Cassation of 30 March 1995, the Cour d'appel did not accept as admissible Mr Bosman's claims for a declaration that the nationality clauses in the URBSFA regulations were not applicable to him. Consequently, the issues in the main proceedings do not relate to the application of nationality clauses and the Court should not rule on the questions submitted on that point. The French Government concurred in that conclusion, subject however to verification of the scope of the judgment of the Cour de Cassation.

57. As to those submissions, it is to be remembered that, in the context of the cooperation between the Court of Justice and the national courts provided for by Article 177 of the Treaty, it is solely for the national court before which the dispute has been brought, and which must assume responsibility for the subsequent judicial decision, to determine in the light of the particular circumstances of the case both the need for a preliminary ruling in order to enable it to deliver judgment and the relevance of the questions which it submits to the Court. Consequently, where the questions submitted by the national court concern the interpretation of Community law, the Court of Justice is, in principle, bound to give a ruling (see, inter alia, Case C-125/94 *Aprile v Amministrazione delle Finanze dello Stato* [1995] ECR I-2919, paragraphs 16 and 17).

58. Nevertheless, the Court has taken the view that, in order to determine whether it has jurisdiction, it should examine the conditions in which the case was referred to it by the national court. The spirit of cooperation which must prevail in the preliminary-ruling procedure requires the national court, for its part, to have regard to the function entrusted to the Court of Justice, which is to assist in the administration of justice in the Member States and not to deliver advisory opinions on general or hypothetical questions (see, inter alia, Case C-83/91 *Meilicke v ADV/ORGA*

[1992] ECR I-487 1, paragraph 25). That is why the Court has held that it has no jurisdiction to give a preliminary ruling on a question submitted by a national court where it is quite obvious that the interpretation of Community law sought by that court bears no relation to the actual facts of the main action or its purpose (see, inter alia, Case C-143/94 *Furlanis v ANAS* [1995] ECR I-3633, paragraph 12) or where the problem is hypothetical and the Court does not have before it the factual or legal material necessary to give a useful answer to the questions submitted to it (see, inter alia, Meilicke, cited above, paragraph 32).

59.   In the present case, the issues in the main proceedings, taken as a whole, are not hypothetical and the national court has provided this Court with a clear statement of the surrounding facts, the rules in question and the grounds on which it believes that a decision on the questions submitted is necessary to enable it to give judgment.

60.   Furthermore, even if, as URBSFA and UEFA contend, the UEFA regulations were not applied when Mr Bosman's transfer to US Dunkerque fell through, they are still in issue in the preventive actions brought by Mr Bosman against URBSFA and UEFA (see paragraph 40 above) and the Court's interpretation as to the compatibility with Community law of the transfer system set up by the UEFA regulations may be useful to the national court.

61.   With regard more particularly to the questions concerning nationality clauses, it appears that the relevant heads of claim have been held admissible in the main proceedings on the basis of a national procedural provision permitting an action to be brought, albeit for declaratory purposes only, to prevent the infringement of a right which is seriously threatened. As is clear from its judgment, the national court considered that application of the nationality clauses could indeed impede Mr Bosman's career by reducing his chances of being employed or fielded in a match by a club from another Member State. It concluded that Mr Bosman's claims for a declaration that those nationality clauses were not applicable to him met the conditions laid down by the said provision.

62.   It is not for this Court, in the context of these proceedings, to call that assessment in question. Although the main actions seek a declaratory remedy and, having the aim of preventing infringement of a right under threat, must necessarily be based on hypotheses which are, by their nature, uncertain, such actions are none the less permitted under national law, as interpreted by the referring court. Consequently, the questions submitted by that court meet an objective need for the purpose of settling disputes properly brought before it.

63.   Finally, the judgment of the Cour de Cassation of 30 March 1995 does not suggest that the nationality clauses are extraneous to the issues in the main proceedings. That court held only that URBSFA's appeal against the judgment of the Cour d'appel rested on a misinterpretation of that judgment. In its appeal, URBSFA had claimed that that court had held inadmissible a claim by Mr Bosman for a declaration that the nationality clauses contained in its regulations were not applicable to him. However, it would appear from the judgment of the Cour de Cassation that, according to the Cour d'appel, Mr Bosman's claim sought to prevent impediments to his career likely to arise from the application not of the nationality clauses in the URBSFA regulations, which concerned players with a nationality other than Belgian, but of the similar clauses in the regulations of UEFA and the other national associations which are members of it, which could concern him as a player with Belgian nationality. Consequently, it does not appear from the judgment of the Cour de Cassation that those latter nationality clauses are extraneous to the main proceedings.

64.     It follows from the foregoing that the Court has jurisdiction to rule on the questions submitted by the Cour d'appel, Liège.

### Interpretation of Article 48 of the Treaty with regard to the transfer rules

65.     By its first question, the national court seeks in substance to ascertain whether Article 48 of the Treaty precludes the application of rules laid down by sporting associations, under which a professional footballer who is a national of one Member State may not, on the expiry of his contract with a club, be employed by a club of another Member State unless the latter club has paid to the former a transfer, training or development fee. Application of Article 48 to rules laid down by sporting associations.

66.     It is first necessary to consider certain arguments which have been put forward on the question of the application of Article 48 to rules laid down by sporting associations.

67.     URBSFA argued that only the major European clubs may be regarded as undertakings, whereas clubs such as RC Liège carry on an economic activity only to a negligible extent. Furthermore, the question submitted by the national court on the transfer rules does not concern the employment relationships between players and clubs but the business relationships between clubs and the consequences of freedom to affiliate to a sporting federation. Article 48 of the Treaty is accordingly not applicable to a case such as that in issue in the main proceedings.

68.     UEFA argued, inter alia, that the Community authorities have always respected the autonomy of sport, that it is extremely difficult to distinguish between the economic and the sporting aspects of football and that a decision of the Court concerning the situation of professional players might call in question the organization of football as a whole. For that reason, even if Article 48 of the Treaty were to apply to professional players, a degree of flexibility would be essential because of the particular nature of the sport.

69.     The German Government stressed, first, that in most cases a sport such as football is not an economic activity. It further submitted that sport in general has points of similarity with culture and pointed out that, under Article 128(1) of the EC Treaty, the Community must respect the national and regional diversity of the cultures of the Member States. Finally, referring to the freedom of association and autonomy enjoyed by sporting federations under national law, it concluded that, by virtue of the principle of subsidiarity, taken as a general principle, intervention by public, and particularly Community, authorities in this area must be confined to what is strictly necessary.

70.     In response to those arguments, it is to be remembered that, having regard to the objectives of the Community, sport is subject to Community law only in so far as it constitutes an economic activity within the meaning of Article 2 of the Treaty (see Case 36/74 *Walrave v Union Cycliste Internationale* [1974] ECR 1405, paragraph 4). This applies to the activities of professional or semi-professional footballers, where they are in gainful employment or provide a remunerated service (see Case 13/76 *Donà v Mantero* [1976] ECR 1333, paragraph 12).

71.     It is not necessary, for the purposes of the application of the Community provisions on freedom of movement for workers, for the employer to be an undertaking; all that is required is the existence of, or the intention to create, an employment relationship.

72.     Application of Article 48 of the Treaty is not precluded by the fact that the transfer rules govern the business relationships between clubs rather than the employment relationships between clubs and players. The fact that the employing clubs must

pay fees on recruiting a player from another club affects the players' opportunities for finding employment and the terms under which such employment is offered.

73. As regards the difficulty of severing the economic aspects from the sporting aspects of football, the Court has held (in *Donà*, cited above, paragraphs 14 and 15) that the provisions of Community law concerning freedom of movement of persons and of provision of services do not preclude rules or practices justified on non-economic grounds which relate to the particular nature and context of certain matches. It stressed, however, that such a restriction on the scope of the provisions in question must remain limited to its proper objective. It cannot, therefore, be relied upon to exclude the whole of a sporting activity from the scope of the Treaty.

74. With regard to the possible consequences of this judgment on the organization of football as a whole, it has consistently been held that, although the practical consequences of any judicial decision must be weighed carefully, this cannot go so far as to diminish the objective character of the law and compromise its application on the ground of the possible repercussions of a judicial decision. At the very most, such repercussions might be taken into consideration when determining whether exceptionally to limit the temporal effect of a judgment (see, inter alia, Case C-163/90 *Administration des Douanes v Legros and Others* [1992] ECR I-4625, paragraph 30).

75. The argument based on points of alleged similarity between sport and culture cannot be accepted, since the question submitted by the national court does not relate to the conditions under which Community powers of limited extent, such as those based on Article 128(1), may be exercised but on the scope of the freedom of movement of workers guaranteed by Article 48, which is a fundamental freedom in the Community system (see, inter alia, Case C- 19/92 *Kraus v Land Baden-Wuerttemberg* [1993] ECR I-1663, paragraph 16).

76. As regards the arguments based on the principle of freedom of association, it must be recognized that this principle, enshrined in Article 11 of the European Convention for the Protection of Human Rights and Fundamental Freedoms and resulting from the constitutional traditions common to the Member States, is one of the fundamental rights which, as the Court has consistently held and as is reaffirmed in the preamble to the Single European Act and in Article F(2) of the Treaty on European Union, are protected in the Community legal order.

77. However, the rules laid down by sporting associations to which the national court refers cannot be seen as necessary to ensure enjoyment of that freedom by those associations, by the clubs or by their players, nor can they be seen as an inevitable result thereof.

78. Finally, the principle of subsidiarity, as interpreted by the German Government to the effect that intervention by public authorities, and particularly Community authorities, in the area in question must be confined to what is strictly necessary, cannot lead to a situation in which the freedom of private associations to adopt sporting rules restricts the exercise of rights conferred on individuals by the Treaty.

79. Once the objections concerning the application of Article 48 of the Treaty to sporting activities such as those of professional footballers are out of the way, it is to be remembered that, as the Court held in paragraph 17 of its judgment in Walrave, cited above, Article 48 not only applies to the action of public authorities but extends also to rules of any other nature aimed at regulating gainful employment in a collective manner. 83 The Court has held that the abolition as between Member States of obstacles to freedom of movement for persons and to freedom to provide services would be compromised if the abolition of State barriers could be neutral-

ized by obstacles resulting from the exercise of their legal autonomy by associations or organizations not governed by public law (see *Walrave*, cited above, paragraph 18).

80. It has further observed that working conditions in the different Member States are governed sometimes by provisions laid down by law or regulation and sometimes by agreements and other acts concluded or adopted by private persons. Accordingly, if the scope of Article 48 of the Treaty were confined to acts of a public authority there would be a risk of creating inequality in its application (see *Walrave*, cited above, paragraph 19). That risk is all the more obvious in a case such as that in the main proceedings in this case in that, as has been stressed in paragraph 24 above, the transfer rules have been laid down by different bodies or in different ways in each Member State.

81. UEFA objects that such an interpretation makes Article 48 of the Treaty more restrictive in relation to individuals than in relation to Member States, which are alone in being able to rely on limitations justified on grounds of public policy, public security or public health.

82. That argument is based on an false premiss. There is nothing to preclude individuals from relying on justifications on grounds of public policy, public security or public health. Neither the scope nor the content of those grounds of justification is in any way affected by the public or private nature of the rules in question.

83. Article 48 of the Treaty therefore applies to rules laid down by sporting associations such as URBSFA, FIFA or UEFA, which determine the terms on which professional sportsmen can engage in gainful employment.

Whether the situation envisaged by the national court is of a purely internal nature.

84. UEFA considers that the disputes pending before the national court concern a purely internal Belgian situation which falls outside the ambit of Article 48 of the Treaty. They concern a Belgian player whose transfer fell through because of the conduct of a Belgian club and a Belgian association.

85. It is true that, according to consistent case-law (see, inter alia, Case 175/78 *Regina v Saunders* [1979] ECR 1129, paragraph 11; Case 180/83 *Moser v Land Baden-Wuerttemberg* [1984] ECR 2539, paragraph 15; Case C-332/90 *Steen v Deutsche Bundespost* [1992] ECR I-341, paragraph 9; and Case C-19/92 *Kraus*, cited above, paragraph 15), the provisions of the Treaty concerning the free movement of workers, and particularly Article 48, cannot be applied to situations which are wholly internal to a Member State, in other words where there is no factor connecting them to any of the situations envisaged by Community law.

86. However, it is clear from the findings of fact made by the national court that Mr Bosman had entered into a contract of employment with a club in another Member State with a view to exercising gainful employment in that State. By so doing, as he has rightly pointed out, he accepted an offer of employment actually made, within the meaning of Article 48(3)(a).

87. Since the situation in issue in the main proceedings cannot be classified as purely internal, the argument put forward by UEFA must be dismissed.

**Existence of an obstacle to freedom of movement for workers**

88. It is thus necessary to consider whether the transfer rules form an obstacle to freedom of movement for workers prohibited by Article 48 of the Treaty.

89. As the Court has repeatedly held, freedom of movement for workers is one of the fundamental principles of the Community and the Treaty provisions guaranteeing that freedom have had direct effect since the end of the transitional period.

90. The Court has also held that the provisions of the Treaty relating to freedom of

movement for persons are intended to facilitate the pursuit by Community citizens of occupational activities of all kinds throughout the Community, and preclude measures which might place Community citizens at a disadvantage when they wish to pursue an economic activity in the territory of another Member State (see Case 143/87 *Stanton v INASTI* [1988] ECR 3877, paragraph 13, and Case C-370/90 *The Queen v Immigration Appeal Tribunal and Surinder Singh* [1992] ECR I-4265, paragraph 16).

91. In that context, nationals of Member States have in particular the right, which they derive directly from the Treaty, to leave their country of origin to enter the territory of another Member State and reside there in order there to pursue an economic activity (see, inter alia, Case C-363/89 *Roux v Belgium* [1991] ECR I-273, paragraph 9, and Singh, cited above, paragraph 17).

92. Provisions which preclude or deter a national of a Member State from leaving his country of origin in order to exercise his right to freedom of movement therefore constitute an obstacle to that freedom even if they apply without regard to the nationality of the workers concerned (see also Case C-10/90 *Masgio v Bundesknappschaft* [1991] ECR I-1119, paragraphs 18 and 19).

93. The Court has also stated, in Case 81/87 *The Queen v H.M. Treasury and Commissioners of Inland Revenue ex parte Daily Mail and General Trust plc* [1988] ECR 5483, paragraph 16, that even though the Treaty provisions relating to freedom of establishment are directed mainly to ensuring that foreign nationals and companies are treated in the host Member State in the same way as nationals of that State, they also prohibit the Member State of origin from hindering the establishment in another Member State of one of its nationals or of a company incorporated under its legislation which comes within the definition contained in Article 58. The rights guaranteed by Article 52 et seq. of the Treaty would be rendered meaningless if the Member State of origin could prohibit undertakings from leaving in order to establish themselves in another Member State. The same considerations apply, in relation to Article 48 of the Treaty, with regard to rules which impede the freedom of movement of nationals of one Member State wishing to engage in gainful employment in another Member State.

94. It is true that the transfer rules in issue in the main proceedings apply also to transfers of players between clubs belonging to different national associations within the same Member State and that similar rules govern transfers between clubs belonging to the same national association.

95. However, as has been pointed out by Mr Bosman, by the Danish Government and by the Advocate General in points 209 and 210 of his Opinion, those rules are likely to restrict the freedom of movement of players who wish to pursue their activity in another Member State by preventing or deterring them from leaving the clubs to which they belong even after the expiry of their contracts of employment with those clubs.

96. Since they provide that a professional footballer may not pursue his activity with a new club established in another Member State unless it has paid his former club a transfer fee agreed upon between the two clubs or determined in accordance with the regulations of the sporting associations. the said rules constitute an obstacle to freedom of movement for workers.

97. As the national court has rightly pointed out, that finding is not affected by the fact that the transfer rules adopted by UEFA in 1990 stipulate that the business relationship between the two clubs is to exert no influence on the activity of the player, who is to be free to play for his new club. The new club must still pay the fee in issue, under pain of penalties which may include its being struck off for

debt, which prevents it just as effectively from signing up a player from a club in another Member State without paying that fee.

98.     Nor is that conclusion negated by the case-law of the Court cited by URBSFA and UEFA, to the effect that Article 30 of the Treaty does not apply to measures which restrict or prohibit certain selling arrangements so long as they apply to all relevant traders operating within the national territory and so long as they affect in the same manner, in law and in fact, the marketing of domestic products and of those from other Member States (see Joined Cases C-267191 and C-268/91 *Keck and Mithouard* [1993] ECR I-6097, paragraph 16).

99.     It is sufficient to note that, although the rules in issue in the main proceedings apply also to transfers between clubs belonging to different national associations within the same Member State and are similar to those governing transfers between clubs belonging to the same national association, they still directly affect players access to the employment market in other Member States and are thus capable of impeding freedom of movement for workers. They cannot, thus, be deemed comparable to the rules on selling arrangements for goods which in Keck and Mithouard were held to fall outside the ambit of Article 30 of the Treaty (see also, with regard to freedom to provide services, Case C-384/93 *Alpine Investments v Minister van Financiën* [1995] ECR 11/41, paragraphs 36 to 38).

100.    Consequently, the transfer rules constitute an obstacle to freedom of movement for workers prohibited in principle by Article 48 of the Treaty. It could only be otherwise if those rules pursued a legitimate aim compatible with the Treaty and were justified by pressing reasons of public interest. But even if that were so, application of those rules would still have to be such as to ensure achievement of the aim in question and not go beyond what is necessary for that purpose (see, inter alia, the judgment in *Kraus*, cited above, paragraph 32, and Case C-55/94 *Gebhard* [1995] ECR I-4165, paragraph 37). Existence of justifications.

101     First, URBSFA, LTEFA and the French and Italian Governments have submitted that the transfer rules are justified by the need to maintain a financial and competitive balance between clubs and to support the search for talent and the training of young players.

102.    In view of the considerable social importance of sporting activities and in particular football in the Community, the aims of maintaining a balance between clubs by preserving a certain degree of equality and uncertainty as to results and of encouraging the recruitment and training of young players must be accepted as legitimate.

103.    As regards the first of those aims, Mr Bosman has rightly pointed out that the application of the transfer rules is not an adequate means of maintaining financial and competitive balance in the world of football. Those rules neither preclude the richest clubs from securing the services of the best players nor prevent the availability of financial resources from being a decisive factor in competitive sport, thus considerably altering the balance between clubs.

104.    As regards the second aim, it must be accepted that the prospect of receiving transfer, development or training fees is indeed likely to encourage football clubs to seek new talent and train young players.

105.    However, because it is impossible to predict the sporting future of young players with any certainty and because only a limited number of such players go on to play professionally, those fees are by nature contingent and uncertain and are in any event unrelated to the actual cost borne by clubs of training both future professional players and those who will never play professionally. The prospect of receiving such fees cannot, therefore, be either a decisive factor in encouraging

recruitment and training of young players or an adequate means of financing such activities, particularly in the case of smaller clubs.

106. Furthermore, as the Advocate General has pointed out in point 226 et seq. of his Opinion, the same aims can be achieved at least as efficiently by other means which do not impede freedom of movement for workers.

107. It has also been argued that the transfer rules are necessary to safeguard the world-wide organization of football.

108. However, the present proceedings concern application of those rules within the Community and not the relations between the national associations of the Member States and those of non-member countries. In any event, application of different rules to transfers between clubs belonging to national associations within the Community and to transfers between such clubs and those affiliated to the national associations of nonmember countries is unlikely to pose any particular difficulties. As is clear from paragraphs 22 and 23 above, the rules which have so far governed transfers within the national associations of certain Member States are different from those which apply at the international level.

109. Finally, the argument that the rules in question are necessary to compensate clubs for the expenses which they have had to incur in paying fees on recruiting their players cannot be accepted, since it seeks to justify the maintenance of obstacles to freedom of movement for workers simply on the ground that such obstacles were able to exist in the past.

110. The answer to the first question must therefore be that Article 48 of the Treaty precludes the application of rules laid down by sporting associations, under which a professional footballer who is a national of one Member State may not, on the expiry of his contract with a club, be employed by a club of another Member State unless the latter club has paid to the former club a transfer, training or development fee.

**Interpretation of Article 48 of the Treaty with regard to the nationality clauses**

111. By its second question, the national court seeks in substance to ascertain whether Article 48 of the Treaty precludes the application of rules laid down by sporting associations, under which, in matches in competitions which they organize, football clubs may field only a limited number of professional players who are nationals of other Member States.

**Existence of an obstacle to freedom of movement for workers**

112. As the Court has held in paragraph 87 above, Article 48 of the Treaty applies to rules laid down by sporting associations which determine the conditions under which professional sports players may engage in gainful employment. It must therefore be considered whether the nationality clauses constitute an obstacle to freedom of movement for workers, prohibited by Article 48.

113. Article 48(2) expressly provides that freedom of movement for workers entails the abolition of any discrimination based on nationality between workers of the Member States as regards employment, remuneration and conditions of work and employment.

114. That provision has been implemented, in particular, by Article 4 of Regulation (EEC) No 1612/68 of the Council of 15 October 1968 on freedom of movement for workers within the Community (OJ, English Special Edition, 1968(II), p. 475), under which provisions laid down by law, regulation or administrative action of the Member States which restrict by number or percentage the employment of foreign nationals in any undertaking, branch of activity or region, or at a national level, are not to apply to nationals of the other Member States.

115.    The same principle applies to clauses contained in the regulations of sporting associations which restrict the right of nationals of other Member States to take part, as professional players, in football matches (see the judgment in *Donà*, cited above, paragraph 19).

116.    The fact that those clauses concern not the employment of such players, on which there is no restriction, but the extent to which their clubs may field them in official matches is irrelevant. In so far as participation in such matches is the essential purpose of a professional player's activity, a rule which restricts that participation obviously also restricts the chances of employment of the player concerned.

**Existence of justifications**

117.    The existence of an obstacle having thus been established, it must be considered whether that obstacle may be justified in the light of Article 48 of the Treaty.

118.    URBSFA, UEFA and the German, French and Italian Governments argued that the nationality clauses are justified on non-economic grounds, concerning only the sport as such.

119.    First, they argued, those clauses serve to maintain the traditional link between each club and its country, a factor of great importance in enabling the public to identify with its favourite team and ensuring that clubs taking part in international competitions effectively represent their countries.

120.    Secondly, those clauses are necessary to create a sufficient pool of national players to provide the national teams with top players to field in all team positions.

121.    Thirdly, they help to maintain a competitive balance between clubs by preventing the richest clubs from appropriating the services of the best players.

122.    Finally, UEFA points out that the '3 + 2' rule was drawn up in collaboration with the Commission and must be revised regularly to remain in line with the development of Community policy.

123.    It must be recalled that in paragraphs 14 and 15 of its judgment in *Donà*, cited above, the Court held that the Treaty provisions concerning freedom of movement for persons do not prevent the adoption of rules or practices excluding foreign players from certain matches for reasons which are not of an economic nature, which relate to the particular nature and context of such matches and are thus of sporting interest only, such as, for example, matches between national teams from different countries. It stressed, however, that that restriction on the scope of the provisions in question must remain limited to its proper objective.

124.    Here, the nationality clauses do not concern specific matches between teams representing their countries but apply to all official matches between clubs and thus to the essence of the activity of professional players.

125.    In those circumstances, the nationality clauses cannot be deemed to be in accordance with Article 48 of the Treaty, otherwise that article would be deprived of its practical effect and the fundamental right of free access to employment which the Treaty confers individually on each worker in the Community rendered nugatory (on this last point, see Case 222/86 *Unectef v Heylens and Others* [1987] ECR 4097, paragraph 14).

126.    None of the arguments put forward by the sporting associations and by the governments which have submitted observations detracts from that conclusion.

127.    First, a football club's links with the Member State in which it is established cannot be regarded as any more inherent in its sporting activity than its links with its locality, town, region or, in the case of the United Kingdom, the territory covered by each of the four associations. Even though national championships are played between clubs from different regions, towns or localities, there is no rule restrict-

ing the right of clubs to field players from other regions, towns or localities in such matches.

128. In international competitions, moreover, participation is limited to clubs which have achieved certain results in competition in their respective countries, without any particular significance being attached to the nationalities of their players.

129. Secondly, whilst national teams must be made up of players having the nationality of the relevant country, those players need not necessarily be registered to play for clubs in that country. Indeed, under the rules of the sporting associations, foreign players must be allowed by their clubs to play for their country's national team in certain matches.

130. Furthermore, although freedom of movement for workers, by opening up the employment market in one Member State to nationals of the other Member States, has the effect of reducing workers' chances of finding employment within the Member State of which they are nationals, it also, by the same token, offers them new prospects of employment in other Member States. Such considerations obviously apply also to professional footballers.

131. Thirdly, although it has been argued that the nationality clauses prevent the richest clubs from engaging the best foreign players, those clauses are not sufficient to achieve the aim of maintaining a competitive balance, since there are no rules limiting the possibility for such clubs to recruit the best national players, thus undermining that balance to just the same extent.

132. Finally, as regards the argument based on the Commission's participation in the drafting of the '3 + 2' rule, it must be pointed out that, except where such powers are expressly conferred upon it, the Commission may not give guarantees concerning the compatibility of specific practices with the Treaty (see also Joined Cases 142/80 and 143/80 *Amministrazione delle Finanze dello Stato v Essevi and Salengo* [1981] ECR 1413, paragraph 16). In no circumstances does it have the power to authorize practices which are contrary to the Treaty.

133. It follows from the foregoing that Article 48 of the Treaty precludes the application of rules laid down by sporting associations under which, in matches in competitions which they organize, football clubs may field only a limited number of professional players who are nationals of other Member States.

### Interpretation of Articles 85 and 86 of the Treaty

134. Since both types of rule to which the national court's question refer are contrary to Article 48, it is not necessary to rule on the interpretation of Articles 85 and 86 of the Treaty.

### The temporal effects of this judgment

135. In their written and oral observations, UEFA and URBSFA have drawn the Court's attention to the serious consequences which might ensue from its judgment for the organization of football as a whole if it were to consider the transfer rules and nationality clauses to be incompatible with the Treaty.

136. Mr Bosman, whilst observing that such a solution is not indispensable, has suggested that the Court could limit the temporal effects of its judgment in so far as it concerns the transfer rules.

137. It has consistently been held that the interpretation which the Court, in the exercise of the jurisdiction conferred upon it by Article 177 of the Treaty, gives to a rule of Community law clarifies and where necessary defines the meaning and scope of that rule as it must be, or ought to have been, understood and applied from the time of its coming into force. It follows that the rule as thus interpreted can, and

must, be applied by the courts even to legal relationships arising and established before the judgment ruling on the request for interpretation, provided that in other respects the conditions for bringing before the courts having jurisdiction an action relating to the application of that rule are satisfied (see, inter alia, Case 24/86 *Blaizot v University of Liège and Others* [1988] ECR 379, paragraph 27).

138.    It is only exceptionally that the Court may, in application of the general principle of legal certainty inherent in the Community legal order, be moved to restrict the opportunity for any person concerned to rely upon the provision as thus interpreted with a view to calling in question legal relationships established in good faith. Such a restriction may be allowed only by the Court, in the actual judgment ruling upon the interpretation sought (see, inter alia, the judgments in *Blaizot*, cited above, paragraph 28, and Legros, cited above, paragraph 30).

139.    In the present case, the specific features of the rules laid down by the sporting associations for transfers of players between clubs of different Member States, together with the fact that the same or similar rules applied to transfers both between clubs belonging to the same national association and between clubs belonging to different national associations within the same Member State, may have caused uncertainty as to whether those rules were compatible with Community law.

140.    In such circumstances, overriding considerations of legal certainty militate against calling in question legal situations whose effects have already been exhausted. An exception must, however, be made in favour of persons who may have taken timely steps to safeguard their rights. Finally, limitation of the effects of the said interpretation can be allowed only in respect of compensation fees for transfer, training or development which have already been paid on, or are still payable under an obligation which arose before, the date of this judgment.

141.    It must therefore be held that the direct effect of Article 48 of the Treaty cannot be relied upon in support of claims relating to a fee in respect of transfer, training or development which has already been paid on, or is still payable under an obligation which arose before, the date of this judgment, except by those who have brought court proceedings or raised an equivalent claim under the applicable national law before that date.

142.    With regard to nationality clauses, however, there are no grounds for a temporal limitation of the effects of this judgment. In the light of the *Walrave* and *Donà* judgments, it was not reasonable for those concerned to consider that the discrimination resulting from those clauses was compatible with Article 48 of the Treaty.

**Costs**

143.    The costs incurred by the Danish, French, German and Italian Governments and the Commission of the European Communities, which have submitted observations to the Court, are not recoverable. Since these proceedings are, for the parties to the main proceedings, a step in the action pending before the national court, the decision on costs is a matter for that court.

On those grounds,

*The Court,*

in answer to the questions referred to it by the Cour d'Appel, Liège, by judgment of 1 October 1993, hereby rules:

–       Article 48 of the EEC Treaty precludes the application of rules laid down by sporting associations, under which a professional footballer who is a national of one Member State may not, on the expiry of his contract with a club, be employed by a club of another Member State unless the latter club has paid to the former club a transfer, training or development fee.

– Article 48 of the EEC Treaty precludes the application of rules laid down by sporting associations under which, in matches in competitions which they organize, football clubs may field only a limited number of professional players who are nationals of other Member States.

– The direct effect of Article 48 of the EEC Treaty cannot be relied upon in support of claims relating to a fee in respect of transfer, training or development which has already been paid on, or is still payable under an obligation which arose before, the date of this judgment, except by those who have brought court proceedings or raised an equivalent claim under the applicable national law before that date.

———

\* 2.10.7.  NOTE DE LA DG 4 PRÉSENTÉE À LA COMMISSION: CONSÉQUENCES DE L'ARRÊT BOSMAN; AFFAIRE C 415/93 DE LA COUR DE JUSTICE, 1 FEBRUARY 1996[821]

———

\* 2.10.8.  SPORT AND FREE MOVEMENT, BOSMAN CASE, BACKGROUND SITUATION ON THE EUROPEAN COURT'S DECISION IN THE BOSMAN CASE, 2 FEBRUARY 1996[822]

———

\* 2.10.9.  ANSWER ON BEHALF OF THE COMMISSION TO WRITTEN QUESTION E-3647/95 BY CRISTIANA MUSCARDINI (NI) AND AMEDEO AMADEO (NI), 9 FEBRUARY 1996[823]

Subject: Effects of the Bosman judgment

———

\* 2.10.10.  ANSWER ON BEHALF OF THE COMMISSION TO WRITTEN QUESTION P-163/96 BY LUIGI MORETTI (ELDR), 21 FEBRUARY 1996[824]

Subject: Italy's failure to comply with the Court of Justice judgment on freedom of movement for people employed in the sports sector

———

\* 2.10.11.  ANSWER ON BEHALF OF THE COMMISSION TO WRITTEN QUESTION P-371/96 BY MILAN LINZER (PPE), 8 MARCH 1996[825]

Subject: Further Commission action following the Bosman ruling

———

---

[821]  SEC(1996)212/1.

[822]  SEC(1996)212, Consequences of the Bosman Judgment, Memorandum from Commissioners Van Miert, Flynn and Oreja.

[823]  Question of 12-1-1996; OJ C 109, 15-4-1996, p. 58.

[824]  Question of 26-1-1996; OJ C 112, 17-4-1996, p. 70.

[825]  Question of 9-2-1996; OJ C 173, 17-6-1996, p. 50.

**\* 2.10.12.  ANSWER ON BEHALF OF THE COMMISSION TO WRITTEN QUESTION E-480/96 BY PER GAHRTON (V), 10 APRIL 1996**[826]

Subject: Implications of the Bosman case for international football

———

**\* 2.10.13.  ANSWER ON BEHALF OF THE COMMISSION TO WRITTEN QUESTION P-647/96 BY FRANCIS DECOURRIÈRE (PPE), 12 APRIL 1996**[827]

Subject: Judgment of the Court of Justice of the European Communities – Bosman case (C-415/93) – of 15 December 1995

———

**\* 2.10.14.  ANSWER ON BEHALF OF THE COMMISSION TO WRITTEN QUESTION E-3937/97 BY GORDON ADAM (PSE), 30 JANUARY 1998**[828]

Subject: Player transfer restrictions imposed by the British Ice Hockey Association Ltd (BIHA) and the International Ice Hockey Federation (IIHF)

———

**2.10.15.  EUROPEAN COURT OF JUSTICE, JUDGMENT, ERMANNO AGOSTINI AND EMANUELE AGOSTINI V LIGUE FRANCOPHONE DE JUDO ET DISCIPLINES ASSOCIÉES ASBL AND LIGUE BELGE DE JUDO ASBL, CASE C-9/98, 8 JULY 1998**[829]

Reference for a preliminary ruling from the Tribunal de Première Instance, Namur
Reference for a preliminary ruling – Inadmissibility

**Summary of the Order**
*Preliminary rulings – Admissibility of reference – Questions put without sufficient information on the factual and legislative context – Questions put in a context which excludes a useful reply (EC Treaty, Art. 177; EC Statute of the Court of Justice, Art. 20)*

*In order to reach an interpretation of Community law which will be of use to the national court, it is essential that the national court define the factual and legislative context of the questions li is asking or, at the very least, explain the assumptions of fact on which these questions are based. The information provided in orders for reference not only enables the Court usefully to reply but also gives the Governments of the Member States and other interested parties the opportunity to submit observations pursuant to Article 20 of the EC Statute of the Court.*

*Consequently, a request from a national court which does not describe the factual context of the dispute or the assumptions of fact on which it is based, or explain the national legislative context, or the precise reasons which have prompted it to consider the interpretation of Community law and deem it necessary to refer questions to the Court for a*

---

[826]  Question of 1-3-1996; OJ C 297, 8-10-1996, p.6.
[827]  Question of 8-3-1996; OJ C 217, 26-7-1996, p. 87.
[828]  Question of 12-12-1997; OJ C 187, 16-6-1998, p. 97.
[829]  ECR 1998, p. I-4263.

*preliminary ruling, is manifestly inadmissible, in that it does not enable the Court to give a useful interpretation of Community law.*

REFERENCE to the Court under Article 177 of the EC Treaty by the Tribunal de Première Instance de Namur (Belgium) for a preliminary ruling in the proceedings pending before that court between

Ermanno Agostini, Emanuele Agostini, and Ligue Francophone de judo et Disciplines Associées ASBL, Ligue Belge de judo ASBL, on the interpretation of Articles 6, 48 and 59 of the EC Treaty, Regulation (EEC) No 1612/68 of the Council of 1-5 October 1968 on freedom of movement for workers within the Community (OJ, English Special Edition 1968(II), p. 475) and Council Directive 73/148/EEC of 21 May 1973 on the abolition of restrictions on movement and residence within the Community for nationals of Member States with regard to establishment and the provision of services (OJ 1973 L 172, p. 14),

THE COURT,
composed of: G.C. Rodriguez Iglesias, President, C. Gulmann, H. Ragnemalm, M. Wathelet and R. Schintgen (Presidents of Chambers), G.F. Mancini (Rapporteur), J.C. Moltinho de Almeida, P.J.G. Kapteyn, J.L. Murray, D.A.O. Edward, J.-P. Puissochet, G. Hirsch, P. Jann, L. Sevón and K. M. Ioannou, Judges.
Advocate General: G. Cosmas,
Registrar: R. Grass,

after hearing the Opinion of the Advocate General,
makes the following

Order

1.  By order of 5 January 1998, received at the Court on 15 January 1998, the Tribunal de Première Instance (Court of First Instance), Namur, referred to the Court for a preliminary ruling under Article 177 of the EC Treaty several questions on the interpretation of Articles 6, 48 and 59 of that Treaty, Regulation (EEC) No 1612/68 of the Council of 15 October 1968 on freedom of movement for workers within the Community (OJ, English Special Edition 1968(II), p. 475) and Council Directive 73/148/EEC of 21 May 1973 on the abolition of restrictions on movement and residence within the Community for nationals of Member States with regard to establishment and the provision of services (OJ 1973 L 172, p. 14).

2.  That order was made in proceedings between Ermanno and Emanuele Agostini and the Ligue Francophone de judo et Disciplines Associées ASBL and the Ligue Belge de judo ASBL.

3.  Since it considered that the dispute before it raised questions of interpretation of a number of Community provisions, the national court referred the following questions to the Court for a preliminary ruling:

    'Is it consistent or not with the Treaty of Rome, in particular Articles 6, 48 and 59 ei seq. thereof, and with Regulation No 1612/68 and Council Directive 73/148 to prohibit a national of a Member State of the European Union from taking part in a sporting competition, whether as a professional, semi-professional or amateur, on the ground that the person in question does not possess the nationality of the Member State on whose territory the competition is organised, where it is known that that person is the child of workers who are established in that Member State and has himself acquired the status of worker on the territory of that Member State?

Must the answer to that question be different in the case of taking part in a competition to find the national champion of the Member State concerned?

Further, may the person in question claim the right to be treated in the same way as nationals of that State with respect to the teams selected by the national sports federation of the Member State concerned for participation in major international tournaments and competitions such as the European or World Championships or the Olympic Games, or may the national federations reserve such selection for their nationals exclusively?'

4.      It must be observed at the outset that in order to reach an interpretation of Community law which will be of use to the national court, it is essential that the national court define the factual and legislative context of the questions it is asking or, at the very least, explain the assumptions of fact on which those questions are based (see, in particular, joined Cases C-320/90 to C-322/90 *Telemarsicabruzzo and Others v Circostel and Others* [1993] ECR I-393, paragraph 6, and the orders in Case C-157/92 *Banchero* [1993] ECR I-1085, paragraph 4; Case C-66/97 *Banco de Fomento e Exterior v Pechim and Others* [1997] ECR I-3757, paragraph 7; and Joined Cases C-128/97 and C-137/97 *Testa and Modesti* [1998] ECR I-2181, paragraph 5).

5.      It should be pointed out that the information provided in orders for reference not only enables the Court usefully to reply but also gives the Governments of the Member States and other interested parties the opportunity to submit observations pursuant to Article 20 of the EC Statute of the Court (order in Banco di Fomento e Exterior, paragraph 8).

6.      In the present case, the order for reference does not contain sufficient information to meet those requirements. The national court merely asks the questions without giving any information whatever on their basis. It does not describe the factual context of the dispute or the assumptions of fact on which it is based, nor does it explain the national legislative context, nor the precise reasons which have prompted it to consider the interpretation of Community law and deem it necessary to refer questions to the Court for a preliminary ruling.

7.      On the contrary, the court expressly states that it is 'not addressing the facts at present, nor indeed the law'.

8.      In those circumstances the Court is unable to give a ruling, in the absence of any information at all on the applicants' professional, semi-professional or amateur status, the nature of the competitions which are the subject of the main proceedings, the rules of selection for and participation in those competitions, or the applicable national legislation.

9.      Thus the information in the order for reference, by not referring precisely enough to the factual and legal situations addressed by the national court, does not enable the Court to give a useful interpretation of Community law.

10.     In those circumstances it must be held, pursuant to Articles 92 and 103(1) of the Rules of Procedure, that the questions referred to the Court for a preliminary ruling are manifestly inadmissible.

Costs

11.     Since these proceedings are, for the parties to the main proceedings, a step in the action pending before the national court, the decision on costs is a matter for that court.

On those grounds,

THE COURT
hereby orders:
The request for a preliminary ruling submitted by the Tribunal de Première
Instance de Namur by order of 5 January 1998 is inadmissible.

Luxembourg, 8 July 1998.

R. Grass, Registrar
G.C. Rodriguez Iglesias, President

———

**\* 2.10.16. EUROPEAN COURT OF JUSTICE, OPINION OF ADVOCATE
GENERAL ALBER, JYRI LEHTONEN AND ASBL CASTORS
CANADA DRY NAMUR-BRAINE V ASBL FÉDÉRATION ROYALE
BELGE DES SOCIÉTÉS DE BASKET-BALL AND ASBL BASKET
LIGA – LIGUE BASKET BELGIUM, CASE C-176/96, 22 JUNE 1999**[830]

———

**\* 2.10.17. ANSWER ON BEHALF OF THE COMMISSION TO WRITTEN
QUESTION E-2188/99 BY KONSTANTINOS HATZIDAKIS (PPE-DE),
31 JANUARY 2000**[831]

Subject: Review of the Bosman ruling

———

**2.10.18. EUROPEAN COURT OF JUSTICE, JUDGMENT OF THE COURT
(SIXTH CHAMBER),JYRI LEHTONEN, CASTORS CANADA DRY
NAMUR-BRAINE ASBL AND FÉDÉRATION ROYALE BELGE DES
SOCIÉTÉS DE BASKET-BALL ASBL (FRBSB), CASE C-176/96,
13 APRIL 2000**[832]

**Content of the Court's judgment**

1. *Preliminary rulings – Admissibility – Need to provide the Court with sufficient details of the factual and legal context*
   *(EC Treaty, Art. 177 (now Art. 234 EC))*
2. *Community law – Scope – Sport as an economic activity – Included*
   *(EC Treaty, Art. 2 (now, after amendment, Art. 2 EC))*
3. *Freedom of movement for persons – Workers – Treaty provisions – Scope – Sporting activity – Limits*
   *(EC Treaty, Art. 48 (now, after amendment, Art. 39 EC))*
4. *Freedom of movement for persons – Workers – Freedom of establishment – Freedom to provide services – Treaty provisions – Scope – Rules aimed at regulating gainful employment in a collective manner but not emanating from a public authority – Included*
   *(EC Treaty, Arts 48, 52 and 59 (now, after amendment, Arts 39 EC, 43 EC and 49 EC))*

---

[830] ECR 2000, p. I-2681.
[831] Question of 29-11-1999; OJ C 225 E, 8-8-2000, p.70.
[832] ECR 2000, p. I-2681.

5.      *Freedom of movement for persons – Workers – Definition – Professional sports-*
        *man who is a national of a Member State and has entered into a contract of em-*
        *ployment with a club in another Member State with a view to exercising gainful*
        *employment in that State*
        *(EC Treaty, Art. 48 (now, after amendment, Art. 39 EC))*
6.      *Freedom of movement for persons – Workers – Rules laid down by sporting asso-*
        *ciations of a Member State making the participation of professional players from*
        *another Member State in certain competitions subject to compliance with transfer*
        *deadlines – Not permitted in the absence of objective justification*
        *(EC Treaty, Art. 48 (now, after amendment, Art. 39 EC))*

**Summary**
1.      The need to provide an interpretation of Community law which will be of use to
        the national court makes it necessary that the national court define the factual and
        legal context of the questions it is asking or, at the very least, explain the factual
        circumstances on which those questions are based. Those requirements are of par-
        ticular importance in certain areas, such as that of competition, where the factual
        and legal situations are often complex. The information provided in decisions
        making references must not only enable the Court to reply usefully but also give
        the governments of the Member States and other interested parties the opportunity
        to submit observations pursuant to Article 20 of the Statute of the Court of Justice.
        It is the Court's duty to ensure that that opportunity is safeguarded, bearing in
        mind that, by virtue of the abovementioned provision, only the decisions making
        references are notified to the interested parties.
        ( see paras 22-23 )
2.      Having regard to the objectives of the Community, sport is subject to Community
        law in so far as it constitutes an economic activity within the meaning of Article 2
        of the Treaty (now, after amendment, Article 2 EC). That is the case with the ac-
        tivities of professional basketball players, where they work as paid employees or
        provide services for remuneration and those activities are effective and genuine
        activities and not such as to be regarded as purely marginal and ancillary.
        ( see paras 32, 43-44 )
3.      The Treaty provisions concerning freedom of movement for persons do not pre-
        clude rules or practices in the field of sport excluding foreign players from certain
        matches for reasons which are not of an economic nature, which relate to the par-
        ticular nature and context of such matches and are thus of sporting interest only,
        as in the case of matches between national teams from different countries. That
        restriction on the scope of those provisions must, however, remain limited to its
        proper objective, and may not be relied on to exclude all sporting activity from the
        scope of the Treaty.
        ( see para. 34 )
4.      The Community provisions on freedom of movement for persons and freedom to
        provide services not only apply to the action of public authorities but extend also
        to rules of any other nature aimed at regulating gainful employment and the provi-
        sion of services in a collective manner. The abolition as between Member States of
        obstacles to freedom of movement for persons and freedom to provide services
        would be compromised if the abolition of State barriers could be neutralised by
        obstacles resulting from the exercise of their legal autonomy by associations or
        organisations not governed by public law.
        ( see para. 35 )
5.      A professional basketball player who is a national of a Member State must be re-

*garded as a worker within the meaning of Article 48 of the Treaty (now, after amendment, Article 39 EC) where, having entered into a contract of employment with a club in another Member State with a view to exercising gainful employment in that State, he thereby accepts an offer of employment actually made, within the meaning of Article 48(3)(a) of the Treaty.*
*( see para. 46 )*

6. *Article 48 of the EC Treaty (now, after amendment, Article 39 EC) precludes the application of rules laid down in a Member State by sporting associations which prohibit a basketball club from fielding players from other Member States in matches in the national championship, where they have been transferred after a specified date, if that date is earlier than the date which applies to transfers of players from certain non-member countries, unless objective reasons concerning only sport as such or relating to differences between the position of players from a federation in the European zone and that of players from a federation not in that zone justify such different treatment.*
*( see para. 60 and operative part )*

## Parties

In Case C-176/96,
Reference to the Court under Article 177 of the EC Treaty (now Article 234 EC) by the Tribunal de Première Instance, Brussels, for a preliminary ruling in the proceedings pending before that court between
Jyri Lehtonen,
Castors Canada Dry Namur-Braine ASBL
and
Fédération Royale Belge des Sociétés de Basket-ball ASBL (FRBSB),
intervener:
Ligue Belge – Belgische Liga ASBL,
on the interpretation of Articles 6, 48 of the EC Treaty (now, after amendment, Articles 12 EC and 39 EC), 85 and 86 of the EC Treaty (now Articles 81 EC and 82 EC),
THE COURT (Sixth Chamber),
composed of: R. Schintgen, President of the Second Chamber, acting as President of the Sixth Chamber, G. Hirsch and H. Ragnemalm (Rapporteur), Judges,
Advocate General: S. Alber,
Registrar: L. Hewlett, Administrator,
after considering the written observations submitted on behalf of:
– Mr Lehtonen and Castors Canada Dry Namur-Braine ASBL, by L. Misson and B. Borbouse, of the Liège Bar,
– Fédération Royale Belge des Sociétés de Basket-ball ASBL (FRBSB), by J.-P. Lacomble and G. Tuts, of the Liège Bar,
– Ligue Belge – Belgische Liga ASBL, by F. Tilkin, of the Liège Bar,
– the German Government, by E. Röder, Ministerialrat in the Federal Ministry of Economic Affairs, and Sabine Maass, Regierungsrätin in that ministry, acting as Agents,
– the Greek Government, by V. Kontolaimos, Deputy Legal Adviser in the State Legal Service, and P. Mylonopoulos, Deputy Legal Adviser in the Special Legal Service, European Law Section, Ministry of Foreign Affairs, acting as Agents,
– the French Government, by M. Perrin de Brichambaut, Director of Legal Affairs in the Ministry of Foreign Affairs, and A. de Bourgoing, Chargé de Mission in the Legal Department of that ministry, acting as Agents,
– the Italian Government, by Professor U. Leanza, Head of the Legal Service in the

Ministry of Foreign Affairs, acting as Agent, assisted by D. Del Gaizo, Avvocato dello Stato,
– the Austrian Government, by M. Potacs, of the Federal Chancellor's Office, acting as Agent,
– the Commission of the European Communities, by M. Wolfcarius and F.E. González-Díaz, of its Legal Service, acting as Agents,
having regard to the Report for the Hearing,
after hearing the oral observations of Mr Lehtonen and Castors Canada Dry Namur-Braine ASBL, represented by L. Misson and B. Borbouse; Fédération Royale Belge des Sociétés de Basket-ball ASBL (FRBSB), represented by J.-P. Lacomble and F. Herbert, of the Brussels Bar; the Danish Government, represented by J. Molde, Head of Division in the Ministry of Foreign Affairs, acting as Agent; the Greek Government, represented by M. Apessos, Legal Agent in the State Legal Council, acting as Agent; the Spanish Government, represented by N. Díaz Abad, Abogado del Estado, acting as Agent; the French Government, represented by C. Chavance, Foreign Affairs Adviser in the Legal Department of the Ministry of Foreign Affairs, and C. Bergeot, stagiaire in that department, acting as Agents; the Italian Government, represented by D. Del Gaizo; and the Commission, represented by M. Wolfcarius and E. Gippini-Fournier, of its Legal Service, acting as Agent, at the hearing on 29 April 1999,
after hearing the Opinion of the Advocate General at the sitting on 22 June 1999,
gives the following Judgment

## Grounds of the judgment

1. By order of 23 April 1996, received at the Court on 22 May 1996, the Tribunal de Première Instance (Court of First Instance), Brussels, hearing an application for interim relief, referred to the Court for a preliminary ruling under Article 177 of the EC Treaty (now Article 234 EC) a question on the interpretation of Articles 6, 48 of the EC Treaty (now, after amendment, Articles 12 EC and 39 EC), 85 and 86 of the EC Treaty (now Articles 81 EC and 82 EC).

2. That question was raised in proceedings between Mr Lehtonen and Castors Canada Dry Namur-Braine ASBL (hereinafter 'Castors Braine) and Fédération Royale Belge des Sociétés de Basket-ball ASBL (hereinafter 'the FRBSB) and Ligue Belge – Belgische Liga ASBL (hereinafter 'the BLB) concerning the right of Castors Braine to field MrLehtonen in matches in the first division of the Belgian national basketball championship.

## Rules on the organisation of basketball and on transfer periods

3. Basketball is organised at world level by the International Basketball Federation (FIBA). The Belgian federation is the FRBSB, which governs both amateur and professional basketball. The BLB, which consisted on 1 January 1996 of eleven of the twelve basketball clubs in the first division of the Belgian national championship, has the objective of promoting basketball at the highest level and representing top-grade Belgian basketball at national level, in particular in the FRBSB.

4. In Belgium the national men's first division basketball championship is divided into two stages: a first stage in which all clubs take part, and a second stage which includes only the best-placed clubs (play-off matches to decide the national title) and the clubs at the bottom of the league table (play-off matches to decide which clubs will stay in the first division).

5. The FIBA rules governing international transfers of players apply in their entirety to all the national federations (Rule 1(b)). For national transfers, the national federations are recommended to take the international rules as guidance and draw up

their own rules on transfers of players in the spirit of the FIBA rules (Rule 1(c)). Those rules define a foreign player as a player who does not possess the nationality of the State of the national federation which has issued his licence (Rule 2(a)). A licence is the necessary authorisation given by a national federation to a player to allow him to play basketball for a club which is a member of that federation.

6.    Rule 3(c) of the FIBA rules prescribes generally that, for national championships, clubs are not allowed, after the deadline fixed for the zone in question as defined by FIBA, to include in their teams players who have already played in another country in the same zone during that season. For the European zone the deadline for the registration of foreign players is 28 February. After that date it is still possible for players from other zones to be transferred.

7.    Under Rule 4(a) of the FIBA rules, when a national federation receives an application for a licence for a player who has previously been licensed in a federation of another country, it must, before issuing him with a licence, obtain a letter of release from that federation.

8.    According to the FRBSB rules, a distinction must be drawn between affiliation, which binds the player to the national federation, registration, which is the link between the player and a particular club, and qualification, which is the necessary condition for a player to be able to take part in official competitions. A transfer is defined as the operation by which an affiliated player obtains a change of registration.

9.    Rule 140 et seq. of the FRBSB rules concern transfers between Belgian clubs of players affiliated to the FRBSB, which may take place during a defined period in each year, which in 1995 ran from 15 April to 15 May and in 1996 from 1 to 31 May of the year preceding the championship in which the club in question takes part. No player may be registered with more than one Belgian club in any one season.

10.    In the version applicable at the material time, Rule 244 of the FRBSB rules stated: 'Players who are not registered with the club or who are suspended may not be fielded. This prohibition also applies to friendly matches and tournaments.

...

Any contravention will be punished by [a] fine ...

Foreign or professional players (Law of 24 February 1978) who join after 31 March of the current season will no longer be qualified to play in competition, cup, and play-off matches of the current season.

11.    Rule 245(4) stated:
'Players of foreign nationality, including EU nationals, are qualified only if they have completed the formalities relating to affiliation, registration and qualification. They must in addition comply with the FIBA rules to obtain a licence.

**The main proceedings**

12.    Mr Lehtonen is a basketball player of Finnish nationality. During the 1995/1996 season he played in a team which took part in the Finnish championship, and after that was over he was engaged by Castors Braine, a club affiliated to the FRBSB, to take part in the final stage of the 1995/1996 Belgian championship. To that end the parties on 3 April 1996 concluded a contract of employment for a remunerated sportsman, under which Mr Lehtonen was to receive BEF 50.000 net per month as fixed remuneration and an additional BEF 15.000 for each match won by the club. That engagement had been registered with the FRBSB on 30 March 1996, the player's letter of release having been issued on 29 March 1996 by the federation of origin. On 5 April 1996 the FRBSB informed Castors Braine that if FIBA did

not issue the licence the club might be penalised and that if it fielded Mr Lehtonen it would do so at its own risk.

13.    Despite that warning Castors Braine fielded Mr Lehtonen in the match of 6 April 1996 against Belgacom Quaregnon. The match was won by Castors Braine. On 11 April 1996, following a complaint by Belgacom Quaregnon, the competition department of the FRBSB penalised Castors Braine by awarding to the other club by 20-0 the match in which Mr Lehtonen had taken part in breach of the FIBA rules on transfers of players within the European zone. In the following match, against Pepinster, Castors Braine included Mr Lehtonen on the team sheet but in the end did not field him. The club was again penalised by the award of the match to the other club. As it ran the risk of being penalised again each time it included Mr Lehtonen on the team sheet, or even of being relegated to the lower division in the event of a third default, Castors Braine dispensed with the services of Mr Lehtonen for the play-off matches.

14.    On 16 April 1996 Mr Lehtonen and Castors Braine brought proceedings against the FRBSB in the Tribunal de Première Instance, Brussels, sitting to hear applications for interim relief. They sought essentially for the FRBSB to be ordered to lift the penalty imposed on Castors Braine for the match of 6 April 1996 against Belgacom Quaregnon, and to be prohibited from imposing any penalty whatever on the club preventing it from fielding Mr Lehtonen in the 1995/1996 Belgian championship, on pain of a monetary penalty of BEF 100.000 per day of delay in complying with the order.

15.    By agreement of 17 April 1996, the parties to the main proceedings agreed to submit 'agreed submissions by which they would seek a reference to the Court of Justice for a preliminary ruling, the dispute between them being frozen pending the Court's judgment. In those circumstances, the penalties imposed would be maintained, fines would not be imposed on Castors Braine, and Castors Braine would not field Mr Lehtonen in the play-off matches, all rights of the parties being otherwise reserved.

16.    At the hearing on 19 April 1996, the BLB applied for leave to intervene in support of the FRBSB and the parties lodged their agreed submissions.

**The question referred for a preliminary ruling**

17.    In her order of 23 April 1996, the judge of the Tribunal de Première Instance, Brussels, hearing applications for interim relief considered first that there was nothing to prevent her from referring a question to the Court of Justice. She then found that, at the date on which the proceedings were brought, the condition of urgency was indisputably satisfied, since Castors Braine wished to field Mr Lehtonen in forthcoming championship matches. Finally, she took note of the agreement between the parties to enable a reference to be made to the Court, under the terms of which Castors Braine would not field Mr Lehtonen during the current championship, while the FRBSB undertook for its part to suspend all penalties.

18.    In those circumstances the Tribunal de Première Instance, Brussels, after allowing the BLB's application to intervene, stayed proceedings and referred the following question to the Court for a preliminary ruling:
       'Are the rules of a sports federation which prohibit a club from playing a player in the competition for the first time if he has been engaged after a specified date contrary to the Treaty of Rome (in particular Articles 6, 48, 85 and 86) in the case of aprofessional player who is a national of a Member State of the European Union, notwithstanding the sporting reasons put forward by the federations to justify those rules, namely the need to prevent distortion of the competitions?

**Jurisdiction of the Court to answer the question and admissibility of the question**

19. It may be noted to begin with that, as the Court held in Case 338/85 *Pardini* v *Ministero del Commercio con l'Estero* [1988] ECR 2041, paragraph 11, and Case C-159/90 *Society for the Protection of Unborn Children Ireland* v *Grogan* [1991] ECR I-4685, paragraph 12, a national court is empowered to make a reference to the Court for a preliminary ruling under Article 177 of the Treaty only if a dispute is pending before it in the context of which it is called on to give a decision which could take into account the preliminary ruling. Conversely, the Court has no jurisdiction to hear a reference for a preliminary ruling when at the time it is made the procedure before the court making it has already been concluded.

20. In the present case, after the Tribunal de Première Instance had taken note of the agreement between the parties, it decided to refer a question to the Court for a preliminary ruling, while reserving its decision on the remainder of the case. It follows that it will still have to rule on the lawfulness from the point of view of Community law of the penalties imposed on Castors Braine and on the possible consequences of those penalties. On that occasion it will be called on to give a decision in which the Court's ruling will necessarily have to be taken into account. Consequently, it cannot be argued that that court, in the context of the procedure for applications for interim relief, is not entitled to refer a question to the Court for a preliminary ruling and that the Court has no jurisdiction to answer it.

21. The Italian Government and the Commission contest the admissibility of the question, on the ground that the order for reference does not contain a sufficient account of the legal and factual context of the main proceedings.

22. According to settled case-law, the need to provide an interpretation of Community law which will be of use to the national court makes it necessary that the national court define the factual and legal context of the questions it is asking or, at the very least, explain the factual circumstances on which those questions are based. Those requirements are of particular importance in certain areas, such as that of competition, where the factual and legal situations are often complex (see, in particular, Joined Cases C-320/90 to C-322/90 *Telemarsicabruzzo and Others* [1993] ECR I-393, paragraphs 6 and 7, Case C-67/96 *Albany International* v *Stichting Bedrijfspensioenfonds Textielindustrie* [1999] ECR I-5751, paragraph 39, and Joined Cases C-115/97 to C-117/97 *Brentjens' Handelsonderneming* v *Stichting Bedrijfspensioenfonds voor de Handel in Bouwmaterialen* [1999] ECR I-6025, paragraph 38).

23. The information provided in decisions making references must not only enable the Court to reply usefully but also give the governments of the Member States and other interested parties the opportunity to submit observations pursuant to Article 20 of the EC Statute of the Court of Justice. It is the Court's duty to ensure that that opportunity is safeguarded, bearing in mind that, by virtue of the abovementioned provision, only the decisions making references are notified to the interested parties (see *inter alia* the order in Case C-458/93 *Saddik* [1995] ECR I-511, paragraph 13, and the judgments in *Albany International*, paragraph 40, and *Brentjens' Handelsonderneming*, paragraph 39).

24. In the main proceedings, it appears, first, from the observations submitted by the parties, the Governments of the Member States and the Commission pursuant to Article 20 of the EC Statute of the Court of Justice that the information in the order for reference enabled them properly to state their position on the question put to the Court, in so far as it concerns the Treaty rules on freedom of movement for workers.

25. Furthermore, although the Italian Government may have considered that the infor-

mation provided by the national court did not enable it to take a position on whether, in the main proceedings, Mr Lehtonen is to be regarded as a worker within the meaning of Article 48 of the Treaty, it must be observed that that Government and the other interested parties were able to submit observations of the basis of that court's statements of fact.

26.     Moreover, the information in the order for reference was supplemented by the material in the case-file forwarded by the national court and the written observations submitted to the Court. All that material, which was included in the Report for the Hearing, was brought to the notice of the Governments of the Member States and the other interested parties for the purposes of the hearing, at which they had an opportunity, if necessary, to amplify their observations (see also, to that effect, *Albany International*, paragraph 43, and *Brentjens' Handelsonderneming*, paragraph 42).

27.     Second, the information provided by the national court, supplemented as far as necessary by the above material, gives the Court sufficient knowledge of the factual and legal context of the main proceedings to enable it to interpret the Treaty rules relating to the principle of the prohibition of discrimination on grounds of nationality and on freedom of movement for workers with respect to the situation which is the subject of those proceedings.

28.     In so far as the question put concerns the competition rules applicable to undertakings, on the other hand, the Court considers that it does not have enough information to give guidance as to the definition of the market or markets at issue in the main proceedings. Nor does the order for reference show clearly the character and number of undertakings operating on that market or markets. In addition, the information provided by the national court does not enable the Court to make meaningful findings as to the existence and volume of trade between Member States or as to the possibility of that trade being affected by the rules on transfers of players.

29.     The order for reference therefore does not contain sufficient information to satisfy the requirements described in paragraphs 22 and 23 above, as far as the competition rules are concerned.

30.     Accordingly, the Court should answer the question referred in so far as it relates to the interpretation of the Treaty rules on the principle of the prohibition of discrimination on grounds of nationality and on freedom of movement for workers. The question is inadmissible, however, in so far as it relates to the interpretation of the competition rules applicable to undertakings.

**Substance**
31.     In the light of the above, the national court's question must be understood as essentially asking whether Articles 6 and 48 of the Treaty preclude the application of rules laid down in a Member State by sporting associations which prohibit a basketball club from fielding players from other Member States in matches in the national championship, where the transfer has taken place after a specified date.

*Scope of the Treaty*
32.     It should be noted, as a preliminary point, that, having regard to the objectives of the Community, sport is subject to Community law in so far as it constitutes an economic activity within the meaning of Article 2 of the EC Treaty (now, after amendment, Article 2 EC) (see Case 36/74 *Walrave* v *Union Cycliste Internationale* [1974] ECR 1405, paragraph 4, and Case C-415/93 *Union Royale Belge des Sociétés de Football Association and Others* v *Bosman and Others* [1995] ECR I-4921, paragraph 73). The Court has also acknowledged that sport has con-

siderable social importance in the Community (see *Bosman*, paragraph 106).

33. That case-law is also supported by Declaration No 29 on sport annexed to the Final Act of the conference which adopted the text of the Treaty of Amsterdam, which emphasises the social importance of sport and calls on the institutions of the European Union *inter alia* to give special consideration to the particular characteristics of amateur sport. In particular, that declaration is consistent with the above case-law, in that it concerns situations where sport constitutes an economic activity.

34. The Treaty provisions concerning freedom of movement for persons do not preclude rules or practices excluding foreign players from certain matches for reasons which are not of an economic nature, which relate to the particular nature and context of such matches and are thus of sporting interest only, as in the case of matches between national teams from different countries. The Court has, however, stated that that restriction on the scope of the Treaty must remain limited to its proper objective, and may not be relied on to exclude therefrom the whole of a sporting activity (see Case13/76 *Donà* v *Mantero* [1976] ECR 1333, paragraphs 14 and 15, and *Bosman*, paragraphs 76 and 127).

35. As to the character of the rules at issue in the main proceedings, it follows from *Walrave*, paragraphs 17 and 18, and *Bosman*, paragraphs 82 and 83, that the Community provisions on freedom of movement for persons and freedom to provide services not only apply to the action of public authorities but extend also to rules of any other nature aimed at regulating gainful employment and the provision of services in a collective manner. The abolition as between Member States of obstacles to freedom of movement for persons and freedom to provide services would be compromised if the abolition of State barriers could be neutralised by obstacles resulting from the exercise of their legal autonomy by associations or organisations not governed by public law.

36. In those circumstances, it must be stated that the Treaty, in particular Articles 6 and 48, may apply to sporting activities and to rules laid down by sports associations, such as those at issue in the main proceedings.

*The principle of prohibition of discrimination on grounds of nationality*

37. According to settled case-law, Article 6 of the Treaty, which lays down as a general principle that there shall be no discrimination on grounds of nationality, applies independently only to situations governed by Community law for which the Treaty lays down no specific rules prohibiting discrimination (see, *inter alia*, Case C-179/90 *Merci Convenzionali Porto di Genova* v *Siderurgica Gabrielli* [1991] ECR I-5889, paragraph 11, and Case C-379/92 *Peralta* [1994] ECR I-3453, paragraph 18).

38. As regards workers, that principle has been implemented and specifically applied by Article 48 of the Treaty.

*Existence of an economic activity and whether Mr Lehtonen is a worker*

39. In the light of the foregoing and of the arguments presented at the hearing, it must be ascertained whether a basketball player such as Mr Lehtonen may carry on an economic activity within the meaning of Article 2 of the Treaty, and, more particularly, whether he may be regarded as a worker within the meaning of Article 48 of the Treaty.

40. In the context of the judicial cooperation between national courts and the Court of Justice in connection with references for a preliminary ruling, it is for the national court to establish and evaluate the facts of the case (see, *inter alia*, Case 139/85

*Kempf* v *Staatssecretaris van Justitie* [1986] ECR 1741, paragraph 12) and for the Court of Justice to provide the national court with such interpretative information as may benecessary to enable it to decide the dispute (Case C-332/88 *Alimenta* v *Doux* [1990] ECR I-2077, paragraph 9).

41.     It must be pointed out, first, that the order for reference describes Mr Lehtonen as a professional basketball player. He and Castors Braine produced to the Court the contract of employment as a remunerated sportsman, mentioned in paragraph 12 above, under which he was to be paid a fixed monthly remuneration and bonuses.

42.     Next, with respect to the concepts of economic activity within the meaning of Article 2 and worker within the meaning of Article 48 of the Treaty, it must be observed that these concepts define the scope of one of the fundamental freedoms guaranteed by the Treaty and, as such, may not be interpreted restrictively (see, to that effect, Case 53/81 *Levin* v *Staatssecretaris van Justitie* [1982] ECR 1035, paragraph 13).

43.     With respect more specifically to the former concept, it is settled case-law (*Donà*, paragraph 12, and Case 196/87 *Steymann* v *Staatssecretaris van Justitie* [1988] ECR 6159, paragraph 10) that work as a paid employee or the provision of services for remuneration must be regarded as an economic activity within the meaning of Article 2 of the Treaty.

44.     However, as the Court held *inter alia* in *Levin*, paragraph 17, and *Steymann*, paragraph 13, those activities must be effective and genuine activities and not such as to be regarded as purely marginal and ancillary.

45.     As to the concept of worker, it must be borne in mind that, according to settled case-law, it may not be interpreted differently according to each national law but has a Community meaning. It must be defined in accordance with objective criteria which distinguish the employment relationship by reference to the rights and duties of the persons concerned. The essential feature of an employment relationship is that for a certain period of time a person performs services for and under the direction of another person, in return for which he receives remuneration (see, in particular, Case 66/85 *Lawrie-Blum* v *Land Baden-Württemberg* [1986] ECR 2121, paragraphs 16 and 17).

46.     It appears from the findings of fact made by the national court and from the documents produced to the Court that Mr Lehtonen had entered into a contract of employment with a club in another Member State with a view to exercising gainful employment in that State. As he has rightly submitted, he thereby accepted an offer of employment actually made, within the meaning of Article 48(3)(a) of the Treaty.

*Existence of an obstacle to freedom of movement for workers*

47.     Since a basketball player such as Mr Lehtonen must be regarded as a worker within the meaning of Article 48 of the Treaty, the Court must consider whether the rules on transfer periods referred to in paragraphs 6 and 9 to 11 above constitute an obstacle to freedom of movement for workers, prohibited by that article.

48.     It is true that stricter transfer deadlines apply to players coming from other Belgian basketball clubs.

49.     Those rules are nevertheless liable to restrict the freedom of movement of players who wish to pursue their activity in another Member State, by preventing Belgian clubs from fielding in championship matches basketball players from other Member States where they have been engaged after a specified date. Those rules consequently constitute an obstacle to freedom of movement for workers (see, to that effect, *Bosman*, paragraphs 99 and 100).

50.    The fact that the rules in question concern not the employment of such players, on which there is no restriction, but the extent to which their clubs may field them in official matches is irrelevant. In so far as participation in such matches is the essential purpose of a professional player's activity, a rule which restricts that participation obviously also restricts the chances of employment of the player concerned (see *Bosman*, paragraph 120).

*Existence of justifications*

51.    The existence of an obstacle to freedom of movement for workers having thus been established, it must be ascertained whether that obstacle may be objectively justified.

52.    The FRBSB, the BLB and all the governments which submitted observations to the Court submit that the rules on transfer periods are justified on non-economic grounds concerning only sport as such.

53.    On this point, it must be acknowledged that the setting of deadlines for transfers of players may meet the objective of ensuring the regularity of sporting competitions.

54.    Late transfers might be liable to change substantially the sporting strength of one or other team in the course of the championship, thus calling into question the comparability of results between the teams taking part in that championship, and consequently the proper functioning of the championship as a whole.

55.    The risk of that happening is especially clear in the case of a sporting competition which follows the rules of the Belgian first division national basketball championship. The teams taking part in the play-offs for the title or for relegation could benefit from late transfers to strengthen their squads for the final stage of the championship, or even for a single decisive match.

56.    However, measures taken by sports federations with a view to ensuring the proper functioning of competitions may not go beyond what is necessary for achieving the aim pursued (see *Bosman*, paragraph 104).

57.    In the main proceedings, it appears from the rules on transfer periods that players from a federation outside the European zone are subject to a deadline of 31 March rather than 28 February, which applies only to players from federations in the European zone, which includes the federations of the Member States.

58.    At first sight, such a rule must be regarded as going beyond what is necessary to achieve the aim pursued. It does not appear from the material in the case-file that a transfer between 28 February and 31 March of a player from a federation in the European zone jeopardises the regularity of the championship more than a transfer in that period of a player from a federation not in that zone.

59.    However, it is for the national court to ascertain the extent to which objective reasons, concerning only sport as such or relating to differences between the position of players from a federation in the European zone and that of players from a federation not in that zone, justify such different treatment.

60.    In the light of all the foregoing, the answer to the national court's question, as reformulated, must be that Article 48 of the Treaty precludes the application of rules laid down in a Member State by sporting associations which prohibit a basketball club from fielding players from other Member States in matches in the national championship, where they have been transferred after a specified date, if that date is earlier than the date which applies to transfers of players from certain non-member countries, unless objective reasons concerning only sport as such or relating to differences between the position of players from a federation in the European zone and that of players from a federation not in that zone justify such different treatment.

**Costs**

61.    The costs incurred by the Danish, German, Greek, Spanish, French, Italian and
Austrian Governments and by the Commission, which have submitted observations to the Court, are not recoverable. Since these proceedings are, for the parties
to the main proceedings, a step in the proceedings pending before the national
court, the decision on costs is a matter for that court.

On those grounds,
THE COURT (Sixth Chamber),
in answer to the question referred to it by the Tribunal de Première Instance, Brussels, by
order of 23 April 1996, hereby rules:
Article 48 of the EC Treaty (now, after amendment, Article 39 EC) precludes the application of rules laid down in a Member State by sporting associations which prohibit a basketball club from fielding players from other Member States in matches in the national
championship, where they have been transferred after a specified date, if that date is earlier than the date which applies to transfers of players from certain non-member countries,
unless objective reasons concerning only sport as such or relating to differences between
the position of players from a federation in the European zone and that of players from a
federation not in that zone justify such different treatment.

Schintgen
Hirsch
Ragnemalm Delivered in open court in Luxembourg on 13 April 2000.
R. Grass
J.C. Moitinho de Almeida
Registrar
President of the Sixth Chamber

———

**\* 2.10.19.   ANSWER ON BEHALF OF THE COMMISSION TO WRITTEN
QUESTION E-1561/00 BY GLYN FORD (PSE), 27 JUNE 2000[833]**

Subject: Amendment of the Bosman ruling

———

**\* 2.10.20.   REPLY ON BEHALF OF THE COUNCIL TO WRITTEN QUESTION
P-1528/00 BY JOSÉ RIBEIRO E CASTRO (UEN), 18/19 SEPTEMBER
2000[834]**

Subject: The 'Bosman case' – revision of the EC Treaty and addition of a protocol on professional football or sport in general

———

**\* 2.10.21.   ANSWER ON BEHALF OF THE COMMISSION TO WRITTEN
QUESTION P-2949/00 BY TOINE MANDERS (ELDR), 18 OCTOBER
2000[835]**

Subject: Transfer fees for professional sportsmen

———

[833] Question of 18-5-2000; OJ C 46 E, 13-2-2001, p. 202-203.
[834] Question of 10-5-2000; OJ C 72 E, 6-3-2001, p. 70
[835] Question of 11-9-2000; OJ C 113 E, 18-4-2001.

**\* 2.10.22.    ANSWER ON BEHALF OF THE COMMISSION TO WRITTEN QUESTION E-3006/00 BY GLYN FORD (PSE), 6 NOVEMBER 2000**[836]

Subject: Football

———

**\* 2.10.23.    ANSWER ON BEHALF OF THE COMMISSION TO WRITTEN QUESTION P-3562/00 BY TOINE MANDERS (ELDR), 14 DECEMBER 2000**[837]

Subject: Transfer system for professional football players

———

**\* 2.10.24.    ANSWER ON BEHALF OF THE COMMISSION TO WRITTEN QUESTION E-3569/00 BY ISIDORO SÁNCHEZ GARCÍA (ELDR), 12 JANUARY 2001**[838]

Subject: Guarantees regarding the freedom of movement of foreign sportsmen and women in transfer procedures

———

**\* 2.10.25.    ANSWER ON BEHALF OF THE COMMISSION TO WRITTEN QUESTION P-4077/00 BY MARIO MANTOVANI (PPE-DE), 29 JANUARY 2001**[839]

Subject: Football transfers

———

**\* 2.10.26.    OUTCOME OF DISCUSSIONS BETWEEN THE COMMISSION AND FIFA/UEFA ON FIFA REGULATIONS ON INTERNATIONAL FOOTBALL TRANSFERS, 5 MARCH 2001**[840]

———

**\* 2.10.27.    ANSWER ON BEHALF OF THE COMMISSION TO WRITTEN QUESTION E-31/01 BY BARTHO PRONK (PPE-DE), 20 MARCH 2001**[841]

Subject: Transfer system

———

**2.10.28.    EUROPEAN COURT OF JUSTICE, OPINION OF ADVOCATE GENERAL STIX-HACKL, TIBOR BALOG V ROYAL CHARLEROI SPORTING CLUB ASBL (RCSC), CASE C-264/98, 29 MARCH 2001**

Reference for a preliminary ruling from the Tribunal de première instance, Charleroi, Belgium

---

[836] Question of 26-9-2000; OJ C 136 E, 8-5-2001, p. 155-156.
[837] Question of 10-11-2000; OJ C 163 E, 6-6-2001, p. 164.
[838] Question of 17-11-2000; OJ C 163 E, 6-6-2001, p. 166.
[839] Question of 20-12-2000; OJ C 174 E, 19-6-2001, p. 229.
[840] IP/01/314.
[841] Question of 18-1-2001; OJ C 235 E, 21-8-2001, p. 97-98.

Competition rules applicable to undertakings – Professional footballers – Sporting regulations on the transfer of players – Payment of compensation when players are transferred – Transfers of players who are nationals of third countries – Transfers between the EEA and third countries

## I. Introduction
## A. The problem

1. The present case[842] concerns – once again – the relationship between professional sport and competition law[843], and specifically – again not for the first time[844] – the significance of the rule against cartels for the transfer rules in football. Unlike previous sports cases before the Court, however, the question referred for a preliminary ruling relates exclusively to the prohibition of cartels and the transfer of third-country nationals, third countries meaning States which are neither Member States nor contracting parties to the EEA Agreement.

## B. Organisation of football and rules on transfers

2. Football is organised by a series of federations and associations which may be thought of as forming a pyramid. At international level the responsible body is FIFA (Fédération Internationale de Football Association), an association governed by Swiss law, which functions as a sort of umbrella association. At European level UEFA (Union des Associations Européennes de Football) operates, whose members include in particular the national associations of the Member States and the EEA Contracting States. The individual clubs form national associations, in Belgium URBSFA (Union Royale Belge des Sociétés de Football Association). These organisations govern both professional and amateur football.

## 1. Rules of FIFA

3. FIFA's transfer rules, which were adapted following the Bosman judgment, consist essentially of the Regulations for the Status and Transfer of Players ('the Regulations') of 1997 and the so-called Circulaire No 616 ('Circular No 616').
4. The preamble to the Regulations states, in paragraphs 2 and 3:
   '2. The principles outlined under Art. 12, 13, 30, 31, 32 and 36 and under Chapters I, II, III, VII, VIII and X of these regulations are also binding at national level.
   3. Each national association is obliged to provide a system for transfers effected within its own association and for them to be governed by appropriate regulations which should be approved by FIFA.'
5. Article 7 of the Regulations lays down that a player cannot be registered to play until the new association receives an international transfer certificate issued by the former association. The certificate may be refused if the player has not fulfilled his contractual obligations, or if there are certain disputes over the transfer. In certain cases the new association may, after a period of 60 days from the request to the former association for issue of a transfer certificate issue a provisional transfer

---

[842] The increasing importance of sport, *inter alia* from the legal point of view, is shown, for example, by the 'Declaration on the specific characteristics of sport and its social function in Europe, of which account should be taken in implementing common policies' taken note of by the European Council in Nice.

[843] See Joined Cases C-51/96 and C-191/97 *Deliège* [2000] ECR 1-2549 and Case C-176/96 *Lehtonen* [2000] ECR I-2681.

[844] Case C-415/93 *Bosman* [1995] ECR I-4921.

certificate. During that 60-day period the player may not play in official matches for the new club.

6.    Article 12 of the Regulations determines, in several paragraphs, the principles of the transfer of players from one association to another:

'1.    A non-amateur player shall only be free to conclude a contract with another club if

(a)    his contract with his present club has expired or will expire within six months; or

(b)    his contract with his present club has been rescinded by one party or the other for valid reasons; or

(c)    his contract with his present club has been rescinded by both parties after mutual agreement.

2.    The player's new contract may not include anything which would interfere with the proper completion of his existing contract. If a player wishes to enter a new contract within six months before the expiry of his existing contract (see §1(a) above), he is permitted to enter only one new contract during that period.

[...]

4.    A player may not be transferred during the period of validity of his contract unless the three parties involved – the club he is leaving, the player himself, the club he is joining – all concur.'

7.    Article 13 of the Regulations provides as follows, in paragraphs 1 and 2:

'1.    A club wishing to engage the services of a player who is at present under contract with another club shall, before commencing any negotiations with that player, be obliged to inform this club in writing of its interest.

2.    For any confirmed violation of the foregoing obligation, the offending club will be subject to a fine of at least CHF 50 000.'

8.    Article 14 of the Regulations contains the core provisions on the payment of compensation for training and/or development:

'1.    If a non-amateur player concludes a contract with a new club, his former club shall be entitled to compensation for training and/or development.

2.    If an amateur player concludes a contract with a new club which he joins in a non-amateur capacity, his former club shall be entitled to compensation for his development.

[...]

8.    This article does not apply to the transfer of a player *who is a proven national of a country that is a member of the European Union (EU) or the European Economic Area (EEA)* if the transfer involves two national associations in member countries of the EU or the EEA and if the player's employment contract with his former club has validly expired from the point of view of both parties (that is, if the fixed period of the contract has terminated or if both parties have *mutually agreed* either to curtail or rescind the contract with immediate effect).'

9.    Article 15(1) of the Regulations prescribes that the amount of compensation mentioned in Article 14 is to be agreed upon between the two clubs involved. Any agreement on compensation made between a player and his former club or between a third party and the former club is to be disregarded.

10.   Article 16 of the Regulations governs the jurisdiction of FIFA in the event that the two clubs cannot reach agreement within 30 days on the amount of compensation. The committees responsible for deciding the dispute are specified in Article 17.

11.   Circular No 616 sets out certain decisions of the FIFA Executive Committee on

the status of players. Thus, *inter alia*, the date from which players who are not nationals of an EEA Contracting State are to be given equal treatment with players who are nationals of an EEA Contracting State is postponed from 1 April 1994 to 1 April 1999. It is also laid down that unilateral termination by a player is regarded as a breach of Article 12(1) of the Regulations, so that the national association is entitled to refuse the international transfer certificate under Article 7 of the Regulations.

**2.     UEFA**

12.     The transfer rules drawn up by UEFA relate essentially to the basis of calculation of the compensation for training and/or development.

**3.     Belgium (URBSFA)**

13.     Since the FIFA Regulations with respect to compensation for training and/or development within a Member State now contain only a recommendation, the mandatory requirements are determined by the regulations of the national association concerned, in the present case URBSFA.

The URBSFA regulations apply to transfers between clubs which belong to that national association, in other words transfers of players within a Member State. To take part in matches organised by URBSFA, players must be registered.

14.     For transfers of professional footballers on expiry of their contract, Article IV/85 is material. It provides that, if the player or his club does not renew the contract, the player is to be placed on a transfer list which is then published. Article IV/85 further determines a formula for calculating the amount of the transfer fee, the starting point being the gross income of the player in question, multiplied by an age factor. The URBSFA system also includes rules on free transfers and on classification as an amateur if no transfer takes place.

**II.     Facts and main proceedings**

15.     Mr Tibor Balog, a Hungarian national born on 1 March 1966, was employed from 1993 as a professional football player by Royal Charleroi Sporting Club (RCSC); his last contract expired on 30 June 1997. On 21 April 1997 RCSC sent him the draft of a new contract for one season, which he turned down. Mr Balog submits that he approached various football clubs abroad, in particular in France and Norway, with a view to being transferred, but the clubs did not pursue negotiations because RCSC, in accordance with Article IV/85 of the URBSFA regulations, demanded a transfer compensation of several million Belgian francs. He then contacted managers, whose approaches for the purpose of a transfer were likewise unsuccessful for the same reasons. In December 1997 Mr Balog was engaged by an Israeli club. No compensation was sought from that club, since the transfer was limited to the 1997/98 season and he was to return to RCSC after its expiry. On 1 April 1998 the representative of Mr Balog called on RCSC to acknowledge in particular that RCSC could not demand any transfer compensation or fee from a possible future employer. On 6 April 1998 RCSC refused to do so. On 16 April 1998 it sent Mr Balog a new offer of a contract, which was not accepted. On 23 April 1998 Mr Balog brought proceedings for interim relief in the Tribunal de première instance de Charleroi.

16.     Mr Balog sought an order requiring RCSC to refrain from any conduct, in particular the assertion of a claim for a 'transfer fee', with the intent or effect of directly or indirectly exercising pressure on or obstructing his freedom of contract or that of any club interested in employing him as a professional footballer. Secondly, Mr

Balog sought an order requiring RCSC to pay him a monthly amount of BEF 45 000 until an enforceable decision of the court on the substance of the case, unless he were able in the meantime to find employment with a gross remuneration at least equivalent thereto. In the alternative, he asked the court to make the interim order sought and refer a question to the Court of Justice for a preliminary ruling, with the proceedings being stayed.

17. On 2 July 1998 the national court ordered interim measures, while reserving a decision on the monthly payment. On 6 October 1998 FIFA became a party to the proceedings before that court.

### III.   The question referred for a preliminary ruling

18. By order of 2 July 1998 the Tribunal de première instance de Charleroi referred the following question to the Court for a preliminary ruling:
'Is it compatible with Article 85 of the Treaty of Rome and/or with Article 53 of the Agreement on the European Economic Area for a football club established in the territory of a Member State of the European Union to claim, on the basis of the rules and circulars of the national and international federations (URBSFA, UEFA, FIFA), payment of a 'transfer sum' on the occasion of the engagement of one of its former players, a professional footballer of non-Community nationality who has reached the end of his contract, by a new employer established in the same Member State, in another Member State of the European Union or the European Economic Area, or in a non-member country?'

19. It is apparent from the question referred that it relates only to certain aspects in connection with transfers. First, it relates only to transfers of players on expiry of a contract, not to the legal position for a transfer before a contract expires. Further, it does not concern possible prohibitions of transfers of players below a specified age limit or during the season. Nor has the Court been asked questions on related problems such as the maximum length of a contract and the right of a player to terminate a contract unilaterally.
The submissions of the parties will be discussed below only in so far as appears necessary for the purposes of the argument.

### IV.   Admissibility of the reference
### A.   Submissions of the parties

20. The Italian Government regrets that the national court has not adequately described the facts of the main proceedings. Moreover, the facts described in the order for reference are not material to the case, as Mr Balog has presumably not received any offers since returning from his Israeli club. The question referred is therefore purely hypothetical.

21. The Commission submits that the Court of Justice has no jurisdiction if the action before the national court has already terminated. It may be inferred from Belgian procedural law, first, that the judge making the order for reference cannot decide on the substance, and, second, that it is doubtful whether the proceedings for interim measures are still pending at all before the national court, so that the answer to the question could still be taken into account by that court.

### B.   Opinion
### 1.   Account of facts concerning the main proceedings

22. It is settled case-law that an interpretation of Community law which will be of use to the national court is possible only if that court defines the factual and legal context of the questions it is asking, or at the very least explains the assumptions of

fact on which those questions are based. That is especially the case in certain areas, such as that of competition law, which are characterised by complex factual and legal situations.[845]

23.     It must be pointed out, first, that the documents in the case provide a detailed account of the transfer rules applied.[846]

24.     Further, it may be seen from the observations submitted by the Governments of numerous Member States and the Commission pursuant to Article 20 of the Statute of the Court of Justice that they were able, on the basis of the information in the order for reference, to comment usefully on the question referred[847], even on individual elements of Article 85(1) of the EC Treaty (now Article 81(1) EC).

25.     As the Court held in two other cases concerning professional sport, in the context of judicial cooperation in the preliminary ruling procedure, it is for the national court to establish and evaluate the facts of the case and for the Court of Justice to provide the national court with such guidance on interpretation as may be necessary to enable it to decide the dispute.[848]

26.     The application of the provisions of Community law, as interpreted by the Court of Justice, to a specific case remains the task of the national court. It follows from this division of functions that it is not the Court of Justice that needs to know all the facts, but the national court which has to appraise them.[849]

27.     The absence of individual items of information does not therefore make it impossible for the Court to give a useful answer to the question referred.[850] Having regard to the very general nature of the questions referred[851], the Court has sufficient information to provide a helpful answer.

28.     It should be noted, moreover, that in the *Bosman* case, in which the factual context was not described by the national court in substantially more detail, the Court held that the question referred was admissible. It did not exclude the competition rules from admissibility, as in other cases[852] concerning professional sport.

29.     In view of those circumstances, therefore, it may be taken that the factual and legal context of the main proceedings has been sufficiently described.[853] The Court thus has enough information in this respect to interpret the Community rules on competition with reference to the facts which form the subject-matter of these proceedings.[854]

---

[845] See the requirements in Joined Cases C-51/96 and C-191/97 *Deliège* [2000] ECR 1-2549, paragraph 30, and Case C-176/96 *Lehtonen* [2000] ECR I-2681, paragraph 22.

[846] See Case C-67/96 *Albany* [1999] ECR I-5751, paragraph 42.

[847] See the corresponding requirements in Case C-67/97 *Albany* [1999] ECR I-5751, paragraph 40, and Joined Cases C-115/97, C-116/97 and C-117/97 *Brentjens'* [1999] ECR I-6025, paragraph 39.

[848] Joined Cases C-51/96 and C-191/97 *Deliège* [2000] ECR 1-2549, paragraph 50, and Case C-176/96 *Lehtonen* [2000] ECR I-2681, paragraph 40.

[849] Case 320/88 *Shipping and Forwarding Enterprise Safe* [1990] ECR I-285, paragraph 11, and Joined Cases C-115/97, C-116/97 and C-117/97 *Brentjens'* [1999] ECR I-6025, paragraph 42 et seq.

[850] Case C-56/99 *Gascogne* [2000] ECR I-3079, paragraph 30.

[851] See Joined Cases C-58/95, C-75/95, C-112/95, C-119/95, C-123/95, C-135/95, C-140/95, C-141/95, C-154/95 and C-157/95 *Gallotti and Others* [1996] ECR I-4345, paragraph 9.

[852] Joined Cases C-51/96 and C-191/97 *Deliège* [2000] ECR 1-2549, paragraph 40, and Case C-176/96 *Lehtonen* [2000] ECR I-2681, paragraph 30.

[853] On this condition, see Joined Cases C-320/90, C-321/90 and C-322/90 *Telemarsicabruzzo and Others* [1993] ECR 1-393, paragraph 6 et seq.

[854] Case C-67/96 *Albany* [1999] ECR I-5751, paragraph 44.

**2.** **Whether the proceedings for a reference are pending**

30. According to the judgment in *Pardini*, 'a national court or tribunal is not empowered to bring a matter before the Court by way of a reference for a preliminary ruling unless a dispute is pending before it in the context of which it is called upon to give a decision capable of taking into account the preliminary ruling. Conversely, the Court of Justice has no jurisdiction to hear a reference for a preliminary ruling when at the time it is made the procedure before the court making it has already been terminated.'[855]

31. As the Commission too observes, the proceedings before the national court have not yet been terminated, in so far as a decision is still to be made on the monthly payment to Mr Balog. The condition that the preliminary ruling must be capable of being taken into account is also fulfilled, as the national court has indicated that the content of the examination of the interim measure depends on the interpretation of Article 85 of the EC Treaty (now Article 81 EC).

32. Accordingly, the reference for a preliminary ruling is admissible.

**V.** **Applicability of Article 85 of the EC Treaty (now Article 81 EC)**

33. In the written procedure, several parties referred to Article 37 of the Europe Agreement with Hungary, which contains a prohibition on discrimination against workers. Since that provision is not the subject of the reference and there is no other reason for which it might be necessary for answering the question referred, the Court has no occasion to consider it further. That some of the parties have included Article 37 of the Europe Agreement with Hungary in their observations on answering the national court's question makes no difference. To answer such a – supplementary – question would be incompatible with the function entrusted to the Court by Article 177 of the EC Treaty (now Article 234 EC) and with its duty to ensure that the Governments of the Member States and the other parties concerned are given an opportunity to submit observations under Article 20 of the EC Statute of the Court of Justice.[856] The examination must therefore be limited to the applicability of Article 85 of the EC Treaty (now Article 81 EC).
Since Article 53 of the Agreement on the European Economic Area is modelled on Article 85 of the EC Treaty (now Article 81 EC), there is no need in the context to consider that provision separately below.

34. Under Article 85 of the EC Treaty (now Article 81 EC), all agreements between undertakings, decisions by associations of undertakings and concerted practices which may affect trade between Member States and which have as their object or effect the prevention, restriction, or distortion of competition within the common market are incompatible with the common market and prohibited.

35. The transfer regulations at issue must therefore be examined below by reference to the individual elements of Article 85(1) of the EC Treaty (now Article 81 EC). It does not appear appropriate to look at the transfer regulations separately according to different transfer directions, or only in relation to nationals of third countries, even though the question referred is confined to them. Against such an approach is the fact that all the transfer rules at issue are not only connected with each other but also form part of a complex transfer system. Since parts of a system are, according to the Court's case-law[857], to be treated as a whole, or as the aspects not

---

[855] Case 338/85 *Pardini* [1988] ECR 2041, paragraph 11.

[856] Case C-412/96 *Kainuun Liikenne and Pohjolan Liikenne* [1998] ECR I-5141, paragraph 24.

[857] Case 23/67 *Brasserie de Haecht* [1967] ECR 407, at p. 416, and Case 99/79 *Lancôme* [1980] ECR 2522, paragraph 24. See also Case 22/79 *SACEM* [1979] ECR 3275, paragraph 12, according

addressed expressly in the question referred ought to be taken into account as concomitant circumstances, the transfer regulations will basically, apart from certain aspects, not be examined below by means of such a differentiated approach.

**A.    Undertakings or associations of undertakings**

36.    It must first be considered whether the associations are to be categorised as associations of undertakings and the individual clubs as undertakings within the meaning of Article 85 of the EC Treaty (now Article 81 EC). The first point to look at here is whether the clubs or associations in question carry on an economic activity.

*Submissions of the parties*

37.    Mr Balog points in this connection to the position of the players, who act as providers of services. In the opinion of the Finnish and French Governments and the Commission, the clubs, at any rate the professional clubs, are to be regarded as undertakings for the purposes of competition law because they carry on specific economic activities, such as the exploitation of sporting events by the award of broadcasting rights, by sponsorship agreements or advertising contracts. The Italian Government, however, draws attention to the fact that not only sports clubs but also referees, for example, belong to the national associations, and says that they are therefore not associations of undertakings. FIFA stresses that it is a grouping of national associations and does not itself pursue economic objectives.

*Opinion*

38.    As regards FIFA's submission that the present proceedings concern sporting rather than economic aspects, it must be pointed out that only activities which are purely social, artistic or sporting do not come under Community competition law.

39.    According to what is now settled case-law of the Court, the practice of sport comes under competition law, however, in so far as it constitutes an economic activity within the meaning of Article 2 of the EC Treaty (now Article 2 EC).[858] It follows that, in addition to sporting activities, the rules laid down by sports associations are also not outside the scope of the EC Treaty.[859]

40.    The relationship between sport and Community law is also underscored by Declaration No 29 on sport, annexed to the Final Act of the conference at which the text of the Treaty of Amsterdam was decided. In that declaration, the bodies of the European Union are called on *inter alia* to give special consideration to the particular characteristics of amateur sport. That declaration shows that the conference assumed, first, that Community law applies in principle to the practice of sport in so far as it is an economic activity, but wishes for its particular characteristics to be taken into account. Second, it does not relate in that respect to professional sport, with which the present proceedings are, however, concerned.

41.    Since sport can in practice function only within fixed rules[860], Community law

---

to which individual contracts are not to be assessed in isolation but in the light of the activity of the undertaking as a whole.

[858] Joined Cases C-51/96 and C-191/97 *Deliège* [2000] ECR 1-2549, paragraph 41, Case C-176/96 *Lehtonen* [2000] ECR I-2681, paragraph 32, Case 36/74 *Walrave and Koch* [1974] ECR 1405, paragraph 4, and Case C-415/93 *Bosman* [1995] ECR I-4921, paragraph 73.

[859] Joined Cases C-51/96 and C-191/97 *Deliège* [2000] ECR 1-2549, paragraph 48, and Case C-176/96 *Lehtonen* [2000] ECR I-2681, paragraph 36.

[860] As said in the Opinion of Advocate General Alber in Case C-176/96 *Lehtonen* [2000] ECR I-2681, point 68.

does not preclude regulations which are exclusively of sporting interest.[861] These include sporting rules in the strict sense, in particular rules of play, such as the length of a match or the number of players in a team. However, the transfer rules at issue here go beyond such sporting rules in the strict sense.[862]

42. The rules on competition do not provide for a general exclusion of sport. The Court has indeed held that certain agreements 'by virtue of their nature and purpose' fall outside the prohibition of cartels, but that related to agreements between management and labour in the context of collective negotiations.[863]

43. The transfer regulations, in the version material to the present case, were not the result of negotiations between management and labour, however, nor do they have the effect of improving players' working conditions, which is what matters according to the case-law.[864]

44. Since the transfer regulations thus do not *per se* fall outside the scope of Article 85(1) of the EC Treaty (now Article 81(1) EC), the first element of that provision of the Treaty must be considered below.

45. The concept of an undertaking, according to the Court's case-law, covers 'every entity engaged in an economic activity, regardless of the legal status of the entity and the way in which it is financed'.[865] Whether an entity takes the form of a capital company or a club cannot therefore be of relevance.

46. Contrary to FIFA's submissions, the aims of the entity in question are not material either. It cannot thus make any difference that the clubs pursue essentially unquantifiable aims such as sociability, prestige or a higher position in the table. It is the activities actually embarked on which are and remain decisive. Finally, according to Community competition law it is also not a condition that activities are carried on with a view to making a profit.[866]

47. As the Court held in a judgment concerning professional sport[867], in the context of sporting activities a number of closely related services are provided, which may come under the freedom to provide services even if individual services are not paid for by those for whom they are performed.

48. A further indication that the clubs are undertakings is their financial resources. Thus clubs more and more finance themselves from their market activities, and no longer from members' subscriptions and other methods usual for clubs.

49. The statutes of FIFA, in particular Article 52 (as its predecessor), show that FIFA takes a share of receipts, namely the receipts of the associations. They have to pay FIFA a share of the gross receipts. Those gross receipts, according to Article 11 of the Regulations Governing the Application of the Statutes, 1996 version, include receipts from 'ticket sales, advertising rights, rights for television and radio broadcasts, and film and video rights etc'.

50. UEFA is also involved in this system. As a confederation, it receives, under Ar-

---

[861] Case 36/74 *Walrave and Koch* [1974] ECR 1405, paragraph 8.

[862] The transfer rules thus do not have the 'intrinsic sporting nature' described by Beloff, 'The sporting exception in EC competition law', *European Cur-rent Law* 1999, p. xvi (xix et seq.).

[863] See Case C-67/96 *Albany* [1999] ECR I-5751, paragraph 60, Joint Cases C-115/97 to C-117/97 *Brentjens'* [1999] ECR I-6025, paragraph 57, and Case C-219/97 *Bokken* [19991 ECR I-6121, paragraph 47.

[864] See on this point merely Case C-67/96 *Albany* [1999] ECR I-5751, paragraph 62 et seq.

[865] Case C-41/90 *Höfner and Elser* [1991] ECR 1-1979, paragraph 21.

[866] Joined Cases 209/78 to 215/78 and 218/78 *van Landewyck and Others v Commission* [1980] ECR 3125, paragraph 88.

[867] Joined Cases C-51/96 and C-191/97 *Deliège* [2000] ECR 1-2549, paragraph 56.

ticle 11(4) of the said application regulations, 1% of the gross receipts of matches played on the territory of the confederation between national associations belonging to the confederation.

51.     For the individual clubs, the economic aspect of their activity is also shown by the economic value of the transfer fees themselves. They even appear in the clubs' accounts.[868]

52.     Other sources of income of the individual clubs, besides the receipts mentioned in the above application regulations, are receipts from the sale of articles to fans or from sponsorship agreements.

53.     That professional clubs are to be regarded as undertakings is especially evident, finally, with respect to those clubs which are quoted on the stock exchange in the form of public limited companies.

54.     As regards the view taken by the Finnish and French Governments that the training of players is not an economic activity, it should be observed that the training of players by a professional club is ultimately probably directed to an economic aim, whether of improving match results and hence increasing receipts or of 'transferring' the trained players on the best possible terms. This is a form of occupational training and development similar to that in service undertakings, which ultimately benefits the undertaking too. It therefore relates in that respect to economic activities.

55.     Professional footballers perform remunerated work[869] for their club. That activity enables the clubs to organise a sporting event which can be attended by the public and transmitted by television broadcasters and may be of interest to advertisers and sponsors.[870] The clubs thus make use of players' services in order to be able to carry on their economic activity.

56.     With respect to the international and national associations, it must be said that their independent status as undertakings has also already been legally determined by Community institutions. Cases to be emphasised here are those in which an association concluded agreements for the sale of tickets[871] or the grant of television rights[872] on the occasion of world championships or cup ties. In these and comparable cases the clubs and associations even themselves expressly or tacitly acknowledge that they are carrying on an economic activity.

57.     That the national and international associations are also associations of undertakings may follow from the fact that their members have the character of undertakings. If it is assumed that the national associations are associations of undertakings, then UEFA and FIFA – apart from being undertakings themselves – could even be classified as groupings of associations of undertakings.[873]

58.     Even if it is assumed that only some of the activities of the associations and clubs are economic, that makes no difference to their character of undertakings.[874] That

---

[868] Trivellato, 'Spunti di rifflessione su C.O.N.I. e ordinamento sportivo', *Diritto e societá* 2000, p. 61 (80).

[869] Case 13/76 *Doná* [1976] ECR 1333, paragraph 12.

[870] Joined Cases C-51/96 and C-191/97 *Deliège* [2000] ECR 1-2549, paragraph 57, and Opinion of Advocate General Alber in Case C-176/96 *Lehtonen* [2000] ECR I-2681, point 102.

[871] See, for instance, the Commission Decision of 27 October 1992, OJ 1992 L 326, p. 31; compare also the Commission Decision of 20 July 1999, OJ 2000 L 5, p. 55.

[872] See on this point the judgment of the Court of First Instance in Case T-46/92 *Scottish Football Association* [1994] ECR II-1039.

[873] Case 71/74 *FRUBO* [19751 ECR 563.

[874] See on this point, for example, Emmerich in Immenga/Mestmäcker, paragraph 19 on Article 85(1).

would apply even if a national association also exercises functions of public authority.[875]

59. Transfer regulations concern the engagement and fielding of players, that is, their activity for a club and their playing in matches, and are therefore connected with the economic activity of the clubs.

60. The conclusion must therefore be that institutions such as professional clubs can – at least for the application of the Community competition rules[876] – be regarded as undertakings. FIFA, and also UEFA, and the national associations may, depending on the factual situation, be classified either as undertakings themselves or as associations of undertakings or groupings of associations of undertakings.

61. It makes no difference to that assessment that amateur clubs also belong to the national associations, in so far as the associations are at least formed by economically active clubs.[877]

## B. Agreements between undertakings or decisions of associations of undertakings

62. The next point to consider is whether the transfer regulations are based on agreements between undertakings or decisions of associations of undertakings.

*Submissions of the parties*

63. With respect to the nature of the transfer regulations, Mr Balog refers to the Opinion of Advocate General Lenz in the *Bosman* case, according to which all the elements of Article 85 of the EC Treaty (now Article 81 EC) are fulfilled. FIFA states essentially that the transfer regulations are part of the regulation of the sport and consequently are not agreements or decisions.

64. The Italian Government for its part takes the view that the regulations of sporting associations are neither agreements nor decisions but have normative effect like acts of the public authorities. Thus many Member States confer legislative powers on sporting associations. The ensuing restrictions of competition accordingly do not derive from the free will of the associations but are imposed by the State.

65. The Commission, on the other hand, classifies the transfer regulations – if they reflect the wishes of the members – as agreements or, like the French Government, as decisions.

*Opinion*

66. Transfer regulations are to be classified, depending on their origin, as an agreement between undertakings or a decision of an association of undertakings. The latter applies to the FIFA transfer regulations, for instance. The 'Regulations for the Status and Transfers of Players' were issued by the executive committee of FIFA. That they have the character of a decision is shown by the fact that the committee based the regulations on Article 57 of the FIFA Statutes then in force, that is, acted on the basis of the federation's statues, which are to be regarded as a collective legal act.

---

[875] Thus the Bundesanstalt für Arbeit, which was concerned in Case C-41/90 *Höfner and Elser* [1991] ECR 1-1979, paragraph 21 et seq., also exercised functions of public authority.

[876] Case C-55/96 *Job Centre* [1997] ECR I-7119, paragraph 25.

[877] That the membership of amateur clubs makes no difference in this respect has already been pointed out by Advocate General Lenz in his Opinion in Case C-415/93 *Bosman* [1995] ECR I-4921, point 256, Advocate General Cosmas in his Opinion in Joined Cases C-51/96 and C-191/97 *Deliège* [2000] ECR 1-2549, point 104, and Advocate General Alber in his Opinion in Case C-176/96 *Lehtonen* [2000] ECR I-2681, point 103.

67.    As also appears from the written observations of the Finnish Government, more-
       over, it makes no difference in law – apart from procedural law and liability for
       conduct – whether the transfer regulations are to be assessed as agreements or as
       decisions, since both are covered by Article 85(1) of the EC Treaty (now Article
       81(1) EC).[878]

68.    The transfer regulations are also to be categorised as legally binding, as the parties
       have not disputed. Whether the FIFA transfer regulations are also binding for na-
       tional transfers or merely constitute a recommendation is of no legal significance
       here, in that, according to the Court's case-law, non-binding instructions also
       come under Article 85(1) of the EC Treaty (now Article 81(1) EC) if they are vol-
       untarily complied with at least by several members who form a substantial part of
       the market.[879] That would be the case if the instructions were followed, for ex-
       ample, by some large national associations and hence by the clubs affiliated to
       them, such as the 'G-14' (group of the largest clubs in Europe).

69.    In response to the Italian Government's submission on the public authority charac-
       ter of regulations of sports associations, it should be observed that that is probably
       the case in some Member States only and such regulations, as the Italian Govern-
       ment itself concedes, may also be of a private law character.

70.    The transfer regulations at issue of the associations are in this respect altogether an
       expression of the free will of the relevant associations and are not imposed by the
       State. That in several Member States certain legal consequences may in certain
       circumstances be attached to the regulations adopted by international associations
       or the relevant national association need not be considered further here.

71.    As for regulations of sporting associations which are to be attributed to the State, it
       should be pointed out that such measures too may be covered by Community law,
       in particular if they prescribe, facilitate or magnify the effect of anticompetitive
       conduct.[880] Such regulations of sports associations would then have to be exam-
       ined in the light of Article 10 EC in conjunction with Article 81 EC. But even in
       such cases the undertakings could be liable for their conduct if, for instance, they
       made use of their residual discretion in a manner contrary to Community law.

## C.    Relevant market

72.    Even if the determination of the relevant market in the context of Article 85 of the
       EC Treaty (now Article 81 EC) does not have the same importance as in the con-
       text of Article 82 EC, the examination of possible interferences with competition
       presupposes such a determination.[881] It must be emphasised that the definition of
       the relevant market can also be done by the Court itself.[882] Before the interference
       with competition can be examined, then, the market affected by it should be ascer-
       tained.

---

[878] Advocate General Lenz therefore did not assign them to either alternative in his Opinion in
Case C-415/93 *Bosman* [1995] ECR I-4921, point 258.
    [879] Joined Cases 209/78 to 215/78 and 218/78 *van Landewyck and Others v Commission* [1980]
ECR 3125, paragraphs 86 and 89.
    [880] Case C-2/91 *Meng* [1993] ECR I-5751, paragraph 14, Case C-267/86 *Van Eycke* [1988] ECR
4769, paragraph 16, and Joined Cases 209/84 to 213/84 *Asjes* [1986] ECR I-1425, paragraphs 72 and
76.
    [881] Case C-234/89 *Delimitis* [1991] ECR I-935, paragraph 15 et seq.
    [882] See on this point the very thorough consideration in Case C-234/89 *Delimitis* [1991] ECR I-
935, paragraph 16 et seq.; compare also Case C-18/93 *Corsica Ferries* [1994] ECR I-1783, paragraph 41, and Case 247/86 *Alsatel v Novasam* [1988] ECR 5987, paragraph 15.

*Submissions of the parties*

73. FIFA submits that the players are to be regarded not as providers of services but as workers. They are therefore not undertakings, and so there cannot be a market for the purposes of competition law. The French Government stresses the particular features of sport and points in this connection to the difficulties of defining the market; it does not regard the contest between clubs as the relevant market.

*Opinion*

74. The materially relevant market must be determined first. It cannot be seriously disputed that in the field of professional sport certain particular features prevail which distinguish it from other branches of the economy. But that alone does not mean that there cannot be a market, or even several markets, in this sector too.

75. FIFA is correct in saying that professional footballers are employees rather than self-employed providers of services. For the examination required in this case of the transfer regulations at issue in the light of competition law, however, what matters most is the relationship between the former and new clubs, not the contractual relations between a player and his club, although certain clauses concerning transfers, such as a right to give notice, might also be found in the contract between the player and the club.

76. To define the relevant market for the transfer regulations at issue, it is first, necessary to distinguish several markets, three altogether. It must be emphasised that these markets are interconnected. That is shown by the fact that restrictions on an upstream market affect the downstream markets.

77. The first market, in which both individual clubs and national and international associations act as undertakings, is the market in which they exploit their performances. It is thus a market in secondary goods, including such things as the exploitation of broadcasting rights for matches.

78. Upstream of that market is another, second market, namely that in which the performances which are exploited are produced. This is the market in which the typical product of professional sport is produced: a sporting contest. Production takes place complementarily by two clubs playing against each other, with external factors such as spectators and sponsors also intervening. The contest is essentially a joint production of the clubs.[883] There are certain particular features. Thus this market lives very much on the standard of the teams and the uncertainty of the result. That presumes a certain, but not perfect and constant, balance of the teams, as otherwise every match would end in a draw. Equally unsatisfactory, of course, would be an extreme difference in the standard of play of the two opposing teams.

79. Production of the product, that is, the playing of a football match, takes place according to its own rules, essentially the rules of play. But since professional football does not consist of the staging of individual isolated matches, but primarily of league championships, special methods of organisation are necessary. In the case of leagues, the production process takes place in several phases because of the number of contests to be staged.

80. Typical of professional football here is the relegation system, which not only makes it possible for the individual clubs to be promoted to the higher league, but may also lead to a club being relegated to the inferior league. This circumstance, that is, the fact that the leagues are interconnected, means that the markets may not be strictly demarcated according to leagues.

81. In this connection the importance of transfers of players becomes clear. The clubs

---

[883] Fleischer, 'Absprachen im Profisport', *Wirtschaft und Wettbewerb* 1996, p. 473, 476.

thus endeavour − sometimes literally at all costs − to avert relegation, in particular by 'buying' good players.

82.   In practice the first and second markets, that is, the exploitation market and the contest market, may even coincide temporally, in particular where matches are transmitted live. However, that does not change the fact that in law there are two separate markets.

83.   In this second market a particularity of sporting contests may be seen, namely that 'production' of the product is very labour-intensive. As well as the players, trainers, physiotherapists and others also play a decisive part. As the Commission rightly stated, the performances of the players form the essential element of football events, with the players forming the most important production factors for producing the 'sporting contest' product.

84.   Although sporting contests cannot be carried out by one club alone, but only by several clubs, nevertheless − contrary to the view expressed by the Italian Government − there is no 'single entity'. This particularity of this sport does not change the fact that the individual clubs are undertakings. That the clubs are not to be regarded as a unit is shown precisely by their behaviour in connection with transfers of players, where the different interests of the individual clubs are especially clearly visible. It follows from the independence of the clubs that there is thus no question of 'internal' competition within a conglomerate.[884]

85.   The circumstance that the production factor 'professional footballer' consists of human beings is moreover not a particularity of professional sport but a characteristic of many branches of the economy in the service sector, and merely shows the high rank of 'human resources'. As the Court has already recognised, human labour too can be the subject of economic activity.[885]

86.   In this respect the players as production factors form one of the most important sources of supply for the individual clubs. The latter then encounter each other as purchasers and suppliers of players in another market, namely the market in sources of supply. This is upstream of the second market, that of the organising of contests. On the demand side here is the club which wants to recruit new players, and so for that club it is a question of acquisition. In this connection it is therefore not the players who act as purchasers or suppliers, as FIFA considers and as the Italian Government rightly denies.

87.   On this − third − market in sources of supply the clubs, in the same sort of way as in the contests market, have opposing interests which are expressed in the fight for the best players.[886] The importance for a club of the acquisition of good players may even lead in practice to several clubs using transfers as an instrument of control, by considering which player could be 'sold' to which club without the other club thereby becoming a danger to them.

88.   For the sake of completeness, it should also be pointed out that, so far as may be seen, the supply of and demand for professional footballers of third-country nationality do not form a separate material market. That there is no separate market would presumably be confirmed by a market analysis from the point of view of both the supplying and purchasing clubs.

---

[884] Streinz, 'Die Auswirkungen der europäischen Gesetzgebung auf den Sport', in: Tokarski, *EU-Recht und Sport*, 1998, p. 11 (56).

[885] Case C-41/90 *Höfner and Elser* [1991] ECR 1-1979, paragraph 21.

[886] T. van der Burg, 'Een gelijk speelveld voor het voetbal', *Economisch statistische berichten 2000*, p. 714 (716); see also Carmen Camba Costenla, 'Las cuestiones pendientes despues de la sentencia Bosman', *Revista de Administración Pública*, núm. 148, 1999, p. 249 (256).

89.    The Italian Government questioned the substitutability of players, in that their performances are too individual, in the same way as artistic performances. It may at any rate be assumed to begin with that what is concerned is the comparability of playing performance and not the individual characteristics of the players as persons.

90.    In favour of the substitutability of players is the transfer system as such, in particular where it provides for schematic formulae for calculating the amount of transfer fees. Further, the functional exchangeability of players should be seen in connection with what actually happens in the market. Thus practice shows that what matters is the 'sporting value' of the player. The starting point here is primarily the price level, that is, the transfer sum, of the footballer's playing performances, his age and previous success (e.g. objectivised according to the standard of his previous club) probably also being taken into account, and the intended purpose, generally the function of the player (e.g. attacker). Differentiations are thus altogether appropriate. That demand is not so narrowly restricted is shown by the circumstance that a club which is unable to engage a particular player then, after the failure of the transfer, engages another player, possibly a less expensive one. From the point of view of the recruiting club the essential point is the best possible way of meeting a particular need.

91.    An argument for such exchangeability is, finally, that the human capital of the individual players is not related to a specific club[887], as they could also perform for another club.

92.    The three markets are indeed closely connected, but must be distinguished precisely for the correct definition of the market relevant in this case. The relevant market for the transfer regulations is therefore the market which is formed by the supply of and demand for players, hence the acquisition market, as the French and Italian Governments have correctly indicated. However, that does not exclude the possibility of possible interferences with competition having an effect on the downstream markets.

93.    On the geographically relevant market in this case, it need only be said that it covers the territory of all the associations in which the transfer regulations which are the subject-matter of the case are applied.

### D.    Restriction of competition
*Submissions of the parties*

94.    Mr Balog specifies two adverse effects of the transfer regulations: the wages of players are kept at a low level and barriers to access to the market are erected. With respect to the geographical scope of competition law, Mr Balog is of the view that both transfers within a Member State and transfers from a Member State to a third country are covered. This is because the latter bring the club a transfer payment, unlike transfers within the EEA. On the other hand, transfer payments for transfers from a third country to the EEA do not affect competition between clubs within the EEA. Rather, they promote trade between Member States. Mr Balog also points out that transfer payments are not essential for the transfer of a player after his contract has expired.

95.    In FIFA's view, the transfer regulations do not restrict competition, but at most have the effect that the competitive situation is preserved. They are therefore competitively neutral, and are rules that are necessary for the organisation of the sport.

---

[887] Parensen, 'Die Fußball-Bundesliga und das Bosman-Urteil', in: Tokarski, *EU-Recht und Sport,* 1998, p. 70 (92).

The Finnish Government expresses the view that the transfer regulations affect the engagement of players. That applies also to transfers from third countries towards the EEA. The French Government concentrates, in its observations on adverse effects on competition, essentially on the Opinion of Advocate General Lenz in the *Bosman* case and on the difficulties of defining the market.

*Opinion*
## 1. Basic observations
96.   From the point of view of its effect, the transfer system which is the subject of these proceedings combines the right of the former club to retain the player with a right to compensation. Under the FIFA regulations, a transfer of a player presupposes in principle an agreement between the former and new clubs, including agreement on the amount of the transfer fee.

97.   The restrictive effect intervenes *inter alia* in particular in that the FIFA regulations provide, in the event of failure of the clubs to agree, for a special procedure and a decision by certain committees.

98.   As the Commission rightly submits, the clubs are therefore not free, in certain cases, to engage players without a transfer payment or for a smaller payment than that demanded. In a large number of cases it is precisely the amount of the fee demanded which prevents a player's transfer. The clubs' access to their sources of supply is thereby restricted. The transfer system at issue reduces the choice available to the clubs in respect of players who might be recruited by them.

99.   The transfer system with its uniform machinery within FIFA thus replaces the free play of the market forces of supply and demand on the acquisition market, in so far as it consists in sharing sources of supply within the meaning of Article 85(1)(c) of the EC Treaty (now Article 81(1)(c) EC).

100.   Since transfer fees are to be paid on a change of clubs even in cases where the player's contract has expired, the system contributes to preserving this competitive situation. Contrary to FIFA's submissions, however, even the mere maintenance of the competitive situation counts as an effect on competition within the meaning of Article 85 of the EC Treaty (now Article 81 EC).

101.   In examining interferences with competition, the situation including the interferences must be compared with the situation without those interferences.[888] That comparison shows that the transfer system at issue deprives the purchasing clubs of opportunities which they could have in the absence of the interferences.

102.   The transfer system, in particular the rules on transfer payments, thus prevent clubs from developing their economic activity[889] on the downstream markets. The clubs are prevented from raising the quality of their sporting performance and thereby also making that performance more exploitable. That affects especially small, economically weaker clubs. They are scarcely in a position to engage better qualified, that is, more expensive players.[890] At the same time the system strengthens the position of economically strong clubs, because they can obtain the better players for themselves.

103.   Furthermore, the transfer system at issue affects the players as well. The clubs clearly react to the high transfer fees by depressing the level of pay of the employ-

---

[888] Case 56/65 *Société Technique Minière (LTM)* [1966] ECR 235, at p. 250.

[889] Compare, with respect to a rule on transfer deadlines, Advocate General Alber in his Opinion in Case C-176/96 *Lehtonen* [2000] ECR I-2681, point 105.

[890] Bastianon, 'La libera circolazione dei calciatori e il diritto della concorrenza alla luce della sentenza Bosman', *Rivista di diritto sportivo* 1996, p. 508 (529).

ees concerned, that is, the players.[891] Players probably receive from their new club and employer smaller real remuneration than corresponds to their marginal product.[892] Paying smaller remuneration can yield the clubs a special return. The transfer system thus works to the detriment of third parties, namely the players, in this respect. They would obviously earn more without the transfer system. In addition, on expiry of his contract a club might offer a player poorer conditions because the club has the power of refusing consent to a transfer. That would particularly affect players to whom another club offers the possibility of a more favourable contract.

104. The rise in players' wages following the changes to the transfer regulations after the *Bosman* judgment clearly demonstrates the negative effects of transfer regulations on competition.

105. As to the comments made by several of the parties on the effect on competition of transfers from or to third countries outside the EEA, it should be pointed out that the national court's question relates only to transfers to a third country. The effects within the Community or the EEA as the case may be, necessary for Community or EEA competition law to be applicable, are present at any rate where the new club concerned regularly takes part in competitions within the EEA. In this connection it may be noted that this applies to some clubs based in third countries, clubs whose national associations belong to UEFA.

106. However, there may also be effects within the Community or the EEA if clubs compete with each. other in the acquisition market, that is, the recruitment of players. Moreover, Mr Balog rightly points out that competition within the EEA is affected by transfers to a third country, in so far as such transfers are more attractive to the former club than transfers within the EEA, because of the transfer fee to be expected.

**2.    Necessity of the transfer regulations**

107. The question to be examined below is to what extent the transfer regulations at issue are essential for the functioning of professional football. If that is the case, the restrictions of competition associated with them would be permissible under the Court's case-law[893] as 'ancillary restrictions'.

108. In the context of such an examination of proportionality, possible purposes of the transfer system should be looked at first, in particular the maintenance of the financial and sporting equilibrium for the benefit of small clubs, and compensation for costs of training.

109. In the *Bosman* case the Court expressly recognised certain aims connected with the transfer system. These include 'maintaining a balance between clubs by preserving a certain degree of equality and uncertainty as to results' and 'encouraging the recruitment and training of young players'.[894]

110. As regards the maintenance of a balance, the Court concluded in that judgment, however, that 'the application of the transfer rules is not an adequate means of maintaining financial and competitive balance in the world of football. Those rules

---

[891] Advocate General Lenz in his Opinion in Case C-415/93 *Bosman* [1995] ECR I-4921, point 263.

[892] Fleischer, 'Absprachen im Profisport', *Wirtschaft und Wettbewerb* 1996, p. 475; compare T. van der Burg, 'Een gelijk speelveld voor het voetbal', *Economisch statistische berichten 2000*, p. 716.

[893] Case 56/65 *Société Technique Minière (LTM)* [1966] ECR 235, at p. 250, and Case C-250/92 *Gøttrup-Klim v DLG* [1994] ECR I-5641, paragraph 31 et seq.

[894] Case C-415/93 *Bosman* [1995] ECR I-4921, paragraph 106.

neither preclude the richest clubs from securing the services of the best players nor prevent the availability of financial resources from being a decisive factor in competitive sport, thus considerably altering the balance between clubs.'[895]

111.  As regards promoting young players, the Court found that the specific form taken by the transfer system neither encourages recruitment and training of young players nor is an adequate means of financing such activities.[896]

112.  Finally, the Court pointed out that the aims purportedly pursued could 'be achieved at least as efficiently by other means.[897] That is shown, for instance, by examples in countries where the transfer systems were remodelled after the *Bosman* judgment and the standard of playing performances has even improved.

113.  The essential elements of the transfer system which was the basis of the *Bosman* judgment still typify the transfer system which is the subject of the present proceedings, such as the bases for ascertaining the amount of transfer fees. Consequently, the assessment the Court made then is still correct today.

114.  Although it is not the Court's function to develop transfer rules which-satisfy the requirements of Community law, certain alternatives may be pointed to. The elements of rules on the transfer of players which are necessary for the functioning of professional sport may perfectly well be retained.

115.  The question of the necessity of payments on the occasion of the transfer of a player depends essentially on the size of the payment and hence on the basis of calculation. Objective criteria are thus needed, which ought to be based primarily on the costs of training. The contribution of the player concerned to the economic success of the club should also be taken into account, however.

116.  Other possible objective factors are the remaining length of the contract, the salary paid hitherto, the age and the level of play of the professional footballer concerned. Further, it would be possible for the transfer fee to be shared by all the clubs which the player in question played for, which might include amateur clubs. A formula for sharing would have to be determined.

117.  It must be considered in principle whether the system could not be recast in such a way that transfer fees are payable only on the first transfer away from the club which trained the player.[898] Another alternative would be the setting up of a fund system. This could be based on a solidarity fund.[899] The fund might have *inter alia* the function of reimbursing the training costs in the place of the new club. It could be financed essentially from receipts from the sale of tickets and the exploitation of transmission rights. The receipts could be shared out according to a specified formula between the clubs and the association to which the fund might be affiliated. This solution would correspond essentially to the 'nursery system'. In such a system young players develop in smaller clubs – training places[900] -, that is, they are recruited and trained by them. This is financed by strong teams as buyers of the players, with the transfer fee being paid not to the former club only as in the transfer system at issue, but to the 'system'.

---

[895] Case C-415/93 *Bosman* [1995] ECR I-4921, paragraph 107.

[896] Case C-415/93 *Bosman* [1995] ECR I-4921, paragraph 109.

[897] Case C-415/93 *Bosman* [1995] ECR I-4921, paragraph 110.

[898] On this requirement, see Advocate General Lenz in his Opinion in Case C-415/93 *Bosman* [1995] ECR I-4921, point 239.

[899] On such an alternative, see van den Brink, 'EC Competition Law and the Regulation of Football: Part II', *European Competition Law Review* 2000, p. 420 (425).

[900] Cited after Lee, 'The Bosman Case', *Fordham International Law Journal* 1996, p. 1255 (1313, footnote 569 with further references).

118. In order to bring the regulations on transfers of players into conformity with the competition rules, methods other than the transfer system are also available, however. Thus provisions on a transfer to a new club might be laid down at contractual level, whether in the individual contracts of players with their (former) clubs or in the form of a collective agreement.

## 3. Appreciable effect

119. According to settled case-law[901] the prohibition in Article 85 of the EC Treaty (now Article 81 EC) catches only appreciable interferences with competition within the common market. That criterion does not, however, require that the interference actually has appreciable effects; instead, potential effects[902] suffice. Foreseeability with a sufficient degree of probability[903] of appreciable adverse effects is enough.

   Since the threshold of appreciability is very low[904], no special study of the market share of the transfers affected by the transfer regulations is needed.

120. An indication of the great importance of the transfer regulations for competition is the strong position and importance of the clubs and associations on the various markets.[905]

121. As the situation appears according to the parties' submissions – subject to the findings of the national court -, it may be taken that there is an appreciable effect, simply on the basis of the proportion of third-country nationals in the supply market of professional footballers altogether.

122. The present case has the particular feature that the main emphasis of the regulations at issue which interfere with competition lies essentially in a system which applies worldwide. FIFA comprises all the over 200 national associations, to which the individual football clubs of the countries concerned in turn belong. All sources of supply are thus in principle brought into the transfer system, although there are some national differences. The circumstance that as a consequence of the *Bosman* judgment certain transfers were excluded from the system at issue does not change the appreciable effect of the interferences, since the alternative possibilities for clubs which wish to recruit players nevertheless remain restricted.

## 4. Concluding remarks

123. Finally, the suggestion made at the hearing by the Italian Government that the Court should examine the applicability of Article 85(3) of the EC Treaty (now Article 81(3) EC) should be addressed. In relation to the possibility provided for in that provision of exempting certain agreements and decisions, it need only be said that such an exemption presupposes a corresponding application to the Commission and can only be granted by the Commission. It is therefore unnecessary to consider whether the conditions for an exemption would be satisfied in the present case.

124. On the basis of all the above considerations, it must therefore be concluded that

---

[901] I mention only the leading judgment in Case 56/65 *Société Technique Minière (LTM)* [1966] ECR 235, at p. 250.

[902] Case 19/77 *Miller* [1978] ECR 131, paragraph 15, Joined Cases 142/84 and 156/84 *BAT and Reynolds v Commission* [1987] ECR 4487, paragraph 54, and Case C-7/95 *Deere v Commission* [1998] ECR I-3111, paragraph 77.

[903] Case 99/79 *Lancôme* [1980] ECR 2522, paragraph 23.

[904] In Case 19/77 *Miller* [1978] ECR 131 it was a share of turnover of c. 5%.

[905] Case 99/79 *Lancôme* [1980] ECR 2522, paragraph 24.

the transfer regulations at issue have the effect of interfering with competition in the relevant market.

## E.     Effect on trade between Member States

*Submissions of the parties*

125.     With regard to Mr Balog's view on the question of effect on trade, reference is made to his submissions in connection with the geographical scope of competition law. FIFA adopts the position that transfers of nationals of third countries within a Member State do not come under Article 85 of the EC Treaty (now Article 81 EC). Transfers to a third country are not covered because clubs from third countries do not regularly take part in competitions within the EEA. Transfers of third-country nationals from a third country for their part are not covered because third-country nationals account for only a small proportion of players. The Finnish Government comments only on transfers towards the EEA, and considers that the first acquisition of a player by a club in the EEA should be covered. In the opinion of the French Government, the transfer regulations, because of their transitional nature and the small number of players With thirdcountry nationality, have no appreciable effect on trade. The Commission submits, finally, that the transfer regulations at issue affect trade between Member States. That is true of transfers within a Member State and from or to a third country.

*Opinion*

126.     According to settled case-law of the Court, if a decision or agreement 'is to be capable of affecting trade between Member States, it must be possible to foresee with a sufficient degree of probability, on the basis of a set of objective factors of law or of fact, that they may have an influence, direct or indirect, actual or potential, on the pattern of trade between Member States in such a way as to cause concern that they might hinder the attainment of a single market between Member States'.[906]

127.     As the Finnish Government rightly emphasised, the concept of trade is interpreted broadly in competition law, as the Court has consistently held.[907] It comprehends the placement of employees and the provision of services[908], and hence the supply of and demand for professional football players.

128.     Further, the transfer regulations at issue do not have an effect on trade only if and when they have actual consequences for trade between Member States. The mere likelihood of affecting trade suffices. That there is such a likelihood is strongly suggested by the circumstance that associations to which clubs from several Member States belong are concerned.[909]

129.     There is an effect on trade between Member States not only when transfers actually take place between Member States, but presumably also where the economic activities of the clubs and associations on the downstream markets are the object of trade between the Member States.[910] In this connection the Commission men-

---

[906] Case C-306/96 *Javico* [1998] ECR I-1983, paragraph 16; see also Case 5/69 *Völk* [1969] ECR 295, paragraph 5/7, and Case 56/65 *Société Technique Minière (LTM)* [1966] ECR 235, at p. 249.

[907] Case 155/73 *Sacchi* [1974] ECR 409 relating to television rights, and Case 172/80 *Züchner* [19811 ECR 2021, paragraph 18.

[908] Case C-55/96 *Job Centre* [1997] ECR I-7119, paragraph 37.

[909] Beloff/Kerr/Demetriou, *Sports Law,* 1999, paragraph 6.35.

[910] See Case 123/83 *BNIC v Clair* [1985] ECR 391, paragraph 29.

tions some telling examples which demonstrate the international interlacement, even going beyond the Member States, such as the participation of clubs in international contests, the supporters who travel abroad, the awarding of transmission rights to foreigners and cooperation with foreign sponsors.

130. That the transfer regulations at issue are capable of affecting trade may also be deduced from the fact that by their nature they obstruct the exercise of fundamental freedoms.[911]

131. Even if it is assumed that the transfer regulations merely maintain trade flows, that may also be an interference, if further penetration of the market is thereby prevented.[912]

132. As regards appreciability, transfers within a Member State and transfers to a third country must be considered separately.

133. With respect to transfers within a Member State, their capability of affecting trade between Member States follows from the fact that cross-frontier transfers are affected[913] in so far they are more frequently resorted to in order to avoid the burden of paying transfer fees. That could be done by means of a so-called triangular deal, where a player is loaned for a short period to a club in another Member State and then 're-imported' by another national club.[914] Assuming that the transfer system does not apply to those cross-frontier transfers, such transfers would then be 'exempt'.

134. With respect to transfers with third countries, it should be remembered here too that the national court's question relates only to transfers to a third country. The transfer regulations at issue have effects, in such cases too, on trade between Member States[915], in that the demand for players is thereby diverted. If intra-Community transfers are possible without payment of a transfer fee, then such transfers will increase in proportion to transfers to third countries.

135. As for effect on competition, so also for effect on trade between Member States, Article 85 of the EC Treaty (now Article 81 EC) covers only appreciable interferences.

136. Since the transfers to third countries concerned in the present case are exports, as it were, the starting point must be the proportion of total transfers made up by such transfers.[916]

137. While FIFA submits that transfers to third countries do not affect trade appreciably, it must be pointed out to begin with that a breakdown according to individual transfer directions does not appear appropriate. But even if looked at in isolation, in view of the background which has been described, it may be taken that the regulations in relation to transfers to third countries are surely at least capable of having an appreciable effect on trade. Empirical proof does not appear to be needed in this respect.[917]

---

[911] Compare, on rules on transfer deadlines, the Opinion of Advocate General Alber in Case C-176/96 *Lehtonen* [2000] ECR I-2681, point 104.

[912] Case C-35/96 *Commission v Italy* [1998] ECR I-3851, paragraph 45 et seq.

[913] Joined Cases 56/84 and 58/84 *Consten and Grundig* [1966] ECR 299, at p. 341 et seq.

[914] This effect is pointed out by Carmen Camba Costenla 'Las cuestiones pendientes despues de la sentencia Bosman', *Revista de Administración Pública*, núm. 148, 1999, p. 262.

[915] On exports to non-member countries, see Joined Cases C-89/85, C-104/85, C-114/85, C-116/85, C-117/85 and C-125/85 to C-129/85 *Ahlström and Others v Commission [1993]* ECR 1-1307, paragraph 141 et seq.

[916] Case 319/82 *Ciments et Bétons* [1983] ECR 4173, paragraph 9.

[917] But it should not be concealed that the figures for transfers to third countries given by the Commission appear to support this empirically.

## VI.    Temporal limitation of the effects of the judgment

*Submissions of the parties*

138.    In his written observations Mr Balog addressed the possibility that the Court might limit temporally the effects of its judgment and provide for transitional periods. At the hearing he amended this, in view of the time which had passed in the meantime, to the effect that he now proposes a limitation like that adopted by the Court in *Bosman,* that is, an exception for transfer payments on the basis of obligations which have arisen before the judgment to be given in the present case.

139.    FIFA likewise, in its written observations, suggested a temporal limitation of the effects. This should indeed also correspond essentially to the solution: adopted by the Court in the *Bosman* case, but with respect to transfers of third country nationals it should also cover obligations which have arisen between delivery of the judgment in *Bosman* and the date of the judgment in the present case.

140.    Both Mr Balog and FIFA wish, however, to exclude from this temporal limitation those persons who brought legal proceedings or made an equivalent claim under the applicable national law before the *Bosman* judgment or before the judgment in the present case.

*Opinion*

141.    According to the case-law of the Court, 'it is only exceptionally that the Court may, in application of the general principle of legal certainty inherent in the Community legal order, be moved to restrict for any person concerned the opportunity of relying upon a provision which it has interpreted with a view to calling in question legal relationships established in good faith [...] Two essential criteria must be fulfilled before such a limitation can be imposed, namely that those concerned should have acted in good faith and that there should be a risk of serious difficulties.'[918]

142.    On the question of good faith, that is, the protection of the expectations of the persons concerned, it must be said that the present case has certain particular points which the Court did not answer either in the judgment in *Bosman* or in other judgments relating to professional sport[919]: the application of the competition rules and the legal position specifically in relation to nationals of third countries.

143.    The absence of interpretative judgments of the Court on those points on the basis of references for preliminary rulings could admittedly argue in favour of good faith, but that circumstance alone is not decisive. The Commission plays an essential part in this connection.[920] Precisely on the basis of the Commission's conduct, associated in particular with intensive correspondence and numerous meetings, the associations and clubs concerned must surely have assumed that the transfer regulations in their present form might not be compatible with Community law.

144.    Since in the present case there is no good faith in this respect, there is no need to go on to consider whether serious difficulties might be expected. Financial consequences which the clubs could suffer if professional footballers concerned were, like Mr Balog, to make corresponding claims with effect for the past, which could

---

[918]    Case C-372/98 *Cooke* [2000] ECR I-08683, paragraph 42, and the oases cited there.

[919]    Joined Cases C-51/96 and C-191/97 *Deliège* [2000] ECR 1-2549 and Case C-176/96 *Lehtonen* [2000] ECR I-2681.

[920]    On the significance of the Commission, see Case C-437/97 *EKW and Wein & Co* [2000] ECR I-0000, paragraph 58, and Case C-372/98 *Cooke* [2000] ECR I-08683, paragraph 44 et seq.

upset the financial balance of numerous clubs[921], cannot in themselves constitute a justification.[922]

145.    In the light of the above, there is thus no occasion to limit the effects of the judgment temporally.

**VII.    Conclusion**

146.    On the basis of the above considerations, I propose that the Court give the following answer to the national court's question:

It is not compatible with Article 85(1) of the EC Treaty (now Article 81(1) EC) and/or Article 53 of the Agreement on the European Economic Area for a football club established in a Member State of the European Union to demand payment of a 'transfer sum', as provided for by the regulations and circulars of the national and international associations (URBSFA, UEFA, FIFA) in the versions in force at the material time, on the engagement of one of its former employees, a professional footballer of non-Community nationality who has reached the end of his contract, by a new employer who is established in the same Member State, in another Member State of the European Union or of the European Economic Area, or in a third country.

---

**\* 2.10.29.    REPLY ON BEHALF OF THE COUNCIL TO WRITTEN QUESTION E-4132/00 BY RAINER WIELAND (PPE-DE), 14 MAY 2001[923]**

Subject: Right of an Israeli national to play in German handball leagues

---

**\* 2.10.30.    ANSWER ON BEHALF OF THE COMMISSION TO WRITTEN QUESTION E-1136/01 BY CHRISTOPHER HEATON-HARRIS (PPE-DE), 28 MAY 2001[924]**

Subject: Football Transfer Fee

---

**\* 2.10.31.    ANSWER ON BEHALF OF THE COMMISSION TO WRITTEN QUESTION E-1051/01 BY GLYN FORD (PSE), 18 JUNE 2001[925]**

Subject: Transfer of footballers – Free movement of persons

---

**\* 2.10.32.    ANSWER ON BEHALF OF THE COMMISSION TO WRITTEN QUESTION P-2997/01 BY TOINE MANDERS (ELDR), 22 NOVEMBER 2001[926]**

Subject: Football: undesirable effects of the new transfer system

---

[921] Case C-262/88 *Barber* [1990] ECR I-1889, paragraph 44, concerning occupational pension schemes.

[922] Compare Joined Cases C-367/93 to C-377/93 *Rodgers and Others* [1995] ECR I-2229, paragraph 48.

[923] Question of 16-1-2001; OJ C 235 E, 21-8-2001, p. 76.

[924] Question of 10-4-2001; OJ C 318 E, 13-11-2001, p. 212.

[925] Question of 5-4-2001; OJ C 340 E, 4-12-2001, p. 156-157.

[926] Question of 22-10-2001; OJ C 205 E, 29-8-2002. p. 19.

**\* 2.10.33.   ANSWER ON BEHALF OF THE COMMISSION TO WRITTEN QUESTION P-1324/02 BY HELLE THORNING-SCHMIDT (PSE), 3 JUNE 2002**[927]

Subject: Danish Football Association (DBU) rules on non-EU citizens

——

**\* 2.10.34.   COMMISSION CLOSES INVESTIGATIONS INTO FIFA REGULATIONS ON INTERNATIONAL FOOTBALL TRANSFERS, 5 JUNE 2002**[928]

——

**\* 2.10.35.   ANSWER ON BEHALF OF THE COMMISSION TO WRITTEN QUESTION E-3066/02 TERENCE WYNN (PSE), 22 NOVEMBER 2002**[929]

Subject: Motor racing events and EU law

——

**\* 2.10.36.   ANSWER ON BEHALF OF THE COMMISSION TO WRITTEN QUESTION E-3456/02 BY CHRISTOPHER HEATON-HARRIS (PPE-DE), 7 JANUARY 2003**[930]

Subject: Recognition of motor racing licences within the EU

——

**\* 2.10.37.   ANSWER ON BEHALF OF THE COMMISSION TO WRITTEN QUESTION P-531/03 BY THERESA ZABELL (PPE-DE), 12 MARCH 2003**[931]

Subject: International participation licence for motor rallies in the EU

——

**\* 2.10.38.   ANSWER ON BEHALF OF THE COMMISSION TO WRITTEN QUESTION P-1814/03 BY MARIO BORGHEZIO (NI), 20 JUNE 2003**[932]

Subject: Mario Cipollini's arbitrary disqualification from the Tour de France

——

**2.10.39.   COMMISSION EUROPÉENNE: AFFAIRE COMP/36 726-SPORT ET LIBERTÉS/FIFA [NO DATE]**

Messieurs,

---

[927] Question of 2-5-2002; OJ C 229 E , 26-9-2002, p. 204-205.
[928] IP/02/824.
[929] Question of 25-10-2002; OJ C 192 E, 14-8-2003, p. 94.
[930] Question of 6-12-2002; OJ C 192 E, 14-8-2003, p. 116.
[931] Question of 18-2-2003; OJ C 192 E, 14-8-2003, p. 196-197.
[932] Question of 20-5-2003; question not yet published in the OJ.

**Introduction**

1.  Le 24 octobre 1997, Me [...], au nom et pour le compte de Sport et Libertés ASBL (ci-après SL), a saisi la Commission d'une demande de constatation d'infraction à l'article 81 et/ou 82 du Traité, en vertu de l'article 3 du règlement 17/62, contre la Fédération Internationale de Football Association (ci-après FIFA) et l'Union Royale des Sociétés de Football Association (ci-après URBSFA).

2.  Cette plainte met en cause la compatibilité, avec les articles 81 et 82 du Traité, des dispositions de la Circulaire no. 616 de la FIFA, du 4 juin 1997 en ce qu'elles interdisent la résiliation unilatérale par le joueur du contrat qui le lie à un club (point 2) et qu'elles prévoient le maintien, jusqu'au 1er avril 1999, des indemnités de transfert pour les transferts internationaux, à l'intérieur de l'EEE, de joueurs non-communautaires en fin de contrat. La plainte conteste également l'influence que l'URBSFA aurait eu sur l'adoption de ces mesures.

3.  Le 12 novembre 2001, M. Pons au nom de M. Schaub a communiqué à SL que la Commission conformément à l'article 6 du règlement (CE) no. 2842/98, du 22 décembre 1998,[933] envisageait de considérer que les éléments en sa possession ne justifiaient pas de donner une suite favorable à sa demande.

4.  Cette conclusion provisoire était en particulier fondée sur le fait que la Commission estime qu'elle avait donné suite aux aspects essentiels de la plainte et qu'en raison des engagements reçus de la FIFA il n'existait pas un intérêt communautaire qui justifierait de poursuivre la procédure d'application de l'article 81 ouverte contre la FIFA, le 14 décembre 1998, afin d'adopter une décision négative sur l'existence d'une infraction pour le passé. En outre, les griefs que SL a formulé contre l'URBSFA n'ont pas été poursuivis puisque les éléments portés à sa connaissance n'ont pas fait apparaître que les comportements de ces organisations, si confirmés, étaient de nature à fausser le jeu de la concurrence à l'intérieur du marché commun et à affecter le commerce entre Etats membres plus que ce que les règles FIFA en cause le faisait déjà et que ces aspects pourraient être portés à la connaissance de l'autorité nationale de concurrence ou d'un tribunal national.

5.  A ce jour et bien que le délai d'un mois à compter de la réception de la lettre au titre de l'article 6 du règlement (CE) no. 2842/98, du 22 décembre 1998 pour soumettre des commentaires soit largement dépassé, aucun commentaire n'est parvenu à la Commission.

**La position de Sports et Libertés**

6.  Les arguments de SL pour justifier la violation des articles 81 et 82 du Traité se limitent aux deux paragraphes suivants:

    *'En effet, cette circulaire, par son point 2, a pour objet et pour effet de neutraliser des lois nationales qui, telle que la loi belge du 24 février 1978 relative au contrat d'emploi du sportif rémunéré, autorisent le sportif professionnel à rompre unilatéralement son contrat moyennant le paiement d'une indemnité fixée par la loi. La circulaire a donc pour effet de compartimenter les marchés nationaux et de rendre plus malaisés les échanges entre Etats membres.*

    *En ce qui concerne le point 1 de la circulaire 616, la réintroduction d'un système précédemment aboli en raison de sa contrariété au droit européen de la concurrence, même à titre transitoire, sans autorisation préalable de la Commission européenne, est contraire aux articles 85 et/ou 86 du Traité de Rome. Cette réintroduction affecte directement les membres professionnels de 'Sport et Libertés'*

---

[933] JO L 354, 30-12-1998, p.18.

*n'ayant pas la nationalité d'un des Etats membres et se trouvant en fin de contrat'.*

7.    Pour plus de détails, SL renvoie 'aux arguments développés par Monsieur Van Miert dans l'interview écrite qu'il a accordée, le 30 juin 1997, à ce propos, à la 'Gazzetta dello Sport''. À noter que cette interview ne faisait aucune référence à une application éventuelle de l'article 82 du Traité aux comportements de la FIFA invoqués dans la plainte en question.

**Suite donnée par la Commission aux griefs à l'égard de l'article 81 du Traité**
Premières mesures d'instruction de l'affaire
8.    Sans approfondir la question de savoir si SL a un intérêt légitime au sens de l'article 3 paragraphe 2 du règlement no.17/62, étant donné que cette association a déposé la plainte non pas en tant qu'entreprise ou consommateur mais en tant qu'organisation qui a pour objet d'assurer la défense des droits des sportifs amateurs et professionnels, la Commission a quand même entamé des mesures d'instruction à l'égard des pratiques dénoncées. Ces mesures étaient destinées à obtenir une connaissance des faits dans leur contexte économique et juridique et à examiner s'il était justifié d'engager une procédure d'application de l'article 81 CE.

**Appréciation des griefs contre l'URBSFA**
9.    Sur la base des données recueillies, les services de la Commission ont constaté que les règles FIFA étaient à l'origine des questions soulevées dans la plainte. Dans le contexte d'une répartition efficace des compétences de la Commission, en tant que responsable de la mise en œuvre et de l'orientation de la politique de concurrence pour servir l'intérêt général, il a été considéré que la charge de travail nécessaire pour démontrer l'influence de l'URBSFA et de la Ligue professionnelle belge dans l'adoption des mesures de la FIFA mises en cause était disproportionnée par rapport à la probabilité d'établir l'existence d'une infraction par ces deux organisations. En examinant attentivement les éléments de fait et de droit portés à sa connaissance, ces éléments n'ont pas fait apparaître des comportements restrictifs qui pourraient amener la Commission à obtenir des résultats différents de ceux qu'elle obtiendrait en donnant uniquement suite à vos griefs contre la FIFA. Pour ces raisons, faute d'intérêt communautaire suffisant, la Commission n'a pas poursuit les mesures d'instruction nécessaires à établir les infractions présumées concernant l'URBSFA. Ces aspects de la plainte pourraient, si nécessaire, être appréciées par l'autorité nationale en matière de concurrence ou par un tribunal national en raison de leur compétence pour appliquer directement l'article 81, paragraphe 1 du Traité.

**Appréciation des griefs contre la FIFA**
*La communication des griefs*
10.    Les mesures d'instruction entamées par la Commission ont permis d'envoyer à la FIFA la communication des griefs du 14 décembre 1998, dont vous avez reçu copie.
11.    La communication des griefs adressée à la FIFA, tout en dépassant la portée de votre plainte, contient une appréciation juridique des griefs que vous avez soulevés, en particulier, de la compatibilité avec l'article 81 CE des dispositions de la circulaire no. 616 de la FIFA du 4 juin 1997 en ce qu'elles interdisent la résiliation unilatérale par le joueur du contrat qui le lie à un club (point 2) et qu'elle prévoit le maintien, jusqu'au 1er avril 1999, des indemnités de transfert

pour les transferts internationaux, à l'intérieur de l'EEE, de joueurs non-communautaires en fin du contrat (point 1). Cette dernière restriction n'existe plus et votre plainte est donc devenue sans objet à cet égard.

12. Dans la communication des griefs, la Commission estime que les dispositions de la FIFA qui interdisent de façon absolue la résiliation unilatérale d'un contrat de travail, alors même que le joueur aurait rempli les obligations prévues par le droit national applicable constituent une violation tant à l'article 39 (qui devrait être attaquée devant un tribunal national) qu'à l'article 81 du Traité.

13. La FIFA est une association d'associations d'entreprises car elle regroupe sur le plan mondial les associations nationales qui, à leur tour, regroupent les clubs qui sont des entreprises au sens de l'article 81 paragraphe 1 du Traité. La circonstance qu'en plus des clubs professionnels, de nombreux clubs amateurs font partie des associations nationales ne change rien ni à leur qualification d'association d'entreprises ni à celle d'association d'associations d'entreprises. Le football professionnel est, en effet, une activité économique. Un club de football, par le biais de son équipe, produit un spectacle sportif en disputant des rencontres avec d'autres clubs. Ces spectacles sont vendus sur plusieurs marchés.

14. Le point 2 de la circulaire no. 616 de la FIFA est une décision d'association d'associations d'entreprises qui a pour objet et pour effet de limiter les sources d'approvisionnement des clubs en matière de joueurs au sens de l'article 81 paragraphe 1 sous c). La concurrence entre clubs est entravée sur le marché de la production et de la vente du spectacle sportif de football des premières ligues ou divisions. Cette règle de la FIFA substitue au régime normal de l'offre et de la demande un mécanisme uniforme qui prive les clubs d'exploiter les opportunités qui s'offriraient à eux dans des conditions normales de concurrence. En l'absence de cette règle de la FIFA, les clubs pourraient engager des joueurs qui auraient résilié leur contrat unilatéralement selon les conditions établies par le droit national applicable ou prévues dans leurs contrats.

15. Les entraves ainsi créées aux opportunités des clubs pour constituer leurs équipes, limitent les chances de remporter les succès nécessaires pour occuper les premières places dans le 'ranking' des compétitions et pour attirer un plus grand nombre de spectateurs. Ces entraves semblent susceptibles d'affecter le courant d'échanges de joueurs et des activités économiques générées par le spectacle sportif qui évolueraient d'une façon différente en l'absence des restrictions.

16. L'interdiction absolue de résiliation unilatérale semble constituer, à elle seule, c'est-à-dire, même en l'absence d'autres limitations aux transferts internationaux de joueurs professionnels, une restriction sensible susceptible d'affecter de manière sensible les échanges entre Etats membres. Elle a pour conséquence de rendre uniquement possibles les transferts internationaux sous contrat d'un commun accord entre les trois parties concernées (club de départ, joueur et club d'accueil) – soumis selon les règles FIFA en vigueur au paiement d'indemnités de transfert arbitraires – ainsi que les transferts internationaux en fin de contrat, qui ne sont plus soumis au paiement d'indemnités, à l'intérieur de l'EEE. En pratique cette règle a, semble-t-il, servi à contourner l'arrêt *Bosman*. Les contrats sont devenus plus longs et les transferts ne se font presque plus en fin de contrat.

17. Comme vous le savez, la communication des griefs ne se cantonnait pas au domaine restreint faisant l'objet de votre plainte, visant la circulaire no. 616 de la FIFA (interdiction de la résiliation unilatérale par le joueur du contrat qui le lie à un club et maintien jusqu'au 1 avril 1999 des indemnités de transfert pour les joueurs non communautaires faisant l'objet d'un transfert à l'intérieur de l'EEE en fin de contrat). Au contraire, l'enquête de la Commission portait sur le système de

transferts *dans sa totalité*, dans la mesure où des règles restrictives émanant de la FIFA ou inspirées par celle-ci demeuraient d'application dans *quatre situations* relatives aux transferts internationaux pouvant avoir une incidence sur le commerce entre Etats membres et non couvertes par l'arrêt *Bosman* (voir notamment point 52 de la communication des griefs). La procédure engagée par la Commission concernait également l'obligation imposée par la FIFA aux associations nationales de mettre en œuvre des systèmes *nationaux* de transferts (voir point 59 de la communication des griefs), ainsi que des dispositions accessoires au système (interdiction de s'adresser aux tribunaux ordinaires: points 60 et 61 de la communication des griefs). Toutefois, ces aspects étant étrangers à votre plainte, il n'en sera plus question ci-après, sauf à des fins d'information.

18.   Vous avez eu l'opportunité de vous prononcer par écrit sur la communication des griefs et de participer à l'audition orale qui s'est tenue le 23 juin 1999.

**La suite donnée à l'affaire après la communication des griefs**

19.   Comme vous le savez, la FIFA, tout en contestant juridiquement les griefs formulés par la Commission, a manifesté également son intention d'introduire des modifications aux règles de transferts contestées et de mettre en vigueur des nouvelles règles compatibles avec le droit communautaire, au cours du 1er semestre de 2000.

20.   Après une période raisonnable d'attente et en l'absence de propositions concrètes de la FIFA, les services de la Commission ont continué d'instruire l'affaire en vue de faire adopter par la Commission une décision d'interdiction des dispositions réglementaires de la FIFA contestées. Cependant, cette voie était vue comme l'arme ultime de la Commission pour amener la FIFA à amender son règlement de 1997 et ses circulaires interprétatives de façon à les rendre compatibles avec le droit communautaire. La Commission était consciente que l'interdiction du système international de transferts dans son ensemble sans qu'une alternative moins restrictive était mise en place pour protéger notamment la formation donnée par les petits clubs n'était pas la meilleure solution.

21.   Le 26 avril 2000, la FIFA a fait parvenir aux services de la Commission un document indiquant des 'pistes de réflexion en matière de transferts'. Ce document a été discuté entre les services de la Commission concernés et les représentants de cette organisation, le 3 mai 2000.

22.   Le 16 juin 2000, le Commissaire Monti a informé la FIFA que la procédure ouverte contre elle, poursuivait son cours normal conduisant à proposer à la Commission l'adoption d'une décision négative. Il invitait, en même temps, cette organisation à lui présenter des propositions concrètes ou à notifier des nouvelles règles de transfert.

23.   Par lettre du 26 juillet 2000, M. Monti a rejeté une demande de la FIFA de suspendre la procédure qui conduirait à l'adoption d'une décision négative, tout en restant à sa disposition pour la recherche de nouvelles règles de transfert compatibles avec le droit communautaire.

**Les discussions avec la FIFA, UEFA, FIFPro**

24.   Le 31 août 2000, la FIFA a annoncé, pour la première fois publiquement, son intention d'apporter des modifications à ses règles de transfert afin de les rendre compatibles avec le droit communautaire. Elle a également annoncé la création d'un groupe de travail composé de représentants de l'UEFA, des associations nationales, des ligues et des joueurs professionnels.

25.   Le 8 septembre 2000, M. Monti a reçu les représentants de la 'task-force' issue de

ce groupe de travail chargée d'élaborer des propositions concrètes. La FIFA s'est engagée à présenter ces propositions, le 31 octobre 2000, au plus tard.

26.  Les propositions parvenues à M. Monti n'ont pas eu le soutien des représentants des joueurs. Le 22 novembre 2000, elles ont fait l'objet d'une première réunion avec les services de la Commission où toutes les parties représentées au groupe de travail FIFA/UEFA ont participé. Ces propositions étaient à plusieurs égards positives. Toutefois, elles ne donnaient pas de réponse à tous les griefs que la Commission avait communiqués à la FIFA et notamment au grief concernant l'interdiction de résiliation unilatérale par le joueur qui constitue l'objet essentiel de votre plainte.

27.  Les services de la Commission ont demandé la clarification de certains aspects essentiels des propositions que la FIFA a présentées, le 31 octobre 2000. Une réunion s'est tenue le 13 décembre 2000 où les représentants de la FIFPro ont également participé. Une troisième réunion technique s'est tenue le 20 décembre 2000. Les propositions sorties de cette réunion représentaient un progrès significatif par rapport aux propositions du 31 octobre 2000.

28.  Le 10 janvier 2001, les services de la Commission ont reçu un 'non-paper' de la FIFA dont les propositions étaient très proches de pouvoir être considérées comme compatibles avec le droit communautaire.

29.  La FIFA a toutefois retiré ce document quelques jours après, afin de régler le conflit qu'il avait provoqué entre cette organisation d'une part et l'UEFA, certaines ligues et le G-14, d'autre part. Une quatrième réunion technique du 24 janvier 2001 s'est traduite par un recul significatif par rapport aux propositions issues de la réunion du 20 décembre 2000 et également au 'non-paper' de la FIFA.

30.  Afin de faire progresser les discussions, les Commissaires Monti, Diamantopoulou et Reding ont décidé d'inviter les Présidents de la FIFA et de l'UEFA à une réunion qui a eu lieu le 14 février 2001.

31.  Cette réunion a permis d'aboutir à un accord de principe sur les éléments essentiels à prendre en compte pour l'amendement du règlement de la FIFA de 1997 sur le statut et le transfert des joueurs de façon à le rendre compatible avec le droit communautaire (voir communiqué de presse IP/01/FIFA du 14 février 2001). Une date butoir pour terminer les discussions entre la Commission et les organisations sportives en cause a également été fixée d'un commun accord.

**Le résultat des discussions**

32.  Plusieurs réunions au niveau technique ont encore eu lieu jusqu'à ce que, le 5 mars 2001, les Commissaires Monti, Diamantopoulou et Reding concluent les discussions avec les présidents de la FIFA et de l'UEFA. Le résultat final s'est traduit par un engagement du Président de la FIFA de modifier le Règlement de 1997 sur la base des principes généraux suivants:

(a)  Dans les cas de transferts de joueurs de moins de 23 ans, un système de compensation de la formation doit être mis en place en vue de promouvoir et rémunérer la formation donnée par les clubs, notamment par les petits clubs.

(b)  Création de mécanismes de solidarité qui permettront de redistribuer une partie significative des revenus aux clubs concernés par la formation du joueur, y inclus les clubs amateurs.

(c)  Transferts internationaux de joueurs de moins de 18 ans autorisés sous certaines conditions objectives; les autorités du football établiront et mettront en place un code de conduite visant à garantir que tant la formation sportive que l'éducation scolaire sont fournies au jeune.

(d)  Création d'une période de transferts par saison sportive et d'une période de

transferts supplémentaire au milieu de la saison, limitée à des cas exceptionnels; limitation du nombre de transferts à un par joueur et par saison.

(e)  Fixation de la durée des contrats minimum – 1 an – et maximum – 5 ans.

(f)  Contrats protégés pendant les 3 premières années avant les 28 ans et pendant
les 2 premières années après les 28 ans.

(g)  Afin de préserver la régularité et le bon fonctionnement des compétitions, les
ruptures unilatérales de contrat sont uniquement possibles à la fin de la saison
sportive.

(h)  Si un contrat est rompu unilatéralement, soit par un joueur soit par un club,
une compensation financière peut être payée.

(i)  Pendant la période protégée, dans le cas de ruptures unilatérales sans juste
cause ou juste cause sportive, des sanctions sportives proportionnées peuvent
être infligées aux joueurs, clubs ou agents de joueurs.

(j)  Création d'un système d'arbitrage effectif, rapide et objectif dont les
membres sont choisis en nombre égal par les joueurs et les clubs et avec un
président indépendant.

(k)  L'arbitrage est volontaire et n'empêche pas le recours aux tribunaux
ordinaires.

## Position de la Commission compte tenu des nouvelles règles adoptées par la FIFA

33.  Les nouvelles règles adoptées par le Comité exécutif de la FIFA, le 5 juillet 2001,
semblent être en mesure de donner une réponse satisfaisante au grief que vous
avez formulé portant sur le point 2 de la circulaire no. 616 de la FIFA du 4 juin
1997.

34.  En effet, ces règles FIFA basées sur les principes que cette organisation s'est
engagée, le 5 mars 2001, de mettre en œuvre, ne pourront plus interdire la
résiliation unilatérale par le joueur de son contrat de travail. La résiliation pour
juste cause ou juste cause sportive est prévue. En dehors de ces deux situations et
afin de garantir l'intégrité des compétitions – objectif légitime reconnu par la Cour
de Justice dans l'arrêt Lehtonen[934] – la résiliation unilatérale sera uniquement possible à la fin de la saison sportive. Par ailleurs, toujours dans le même souci,
durant une période de deux ans pour les joueurs de moins de 28 ans et d'un an
après qu'il atteint 28 ans, la résiliation unilatérale du fait d'un joueur pourra
donner lieu à une suspension. A l'issue de la troisième ou de la deuxième année du
contrat, selon le cas, l'imposition d'une suspension sera exceptionnelle, au cas où
le joueur n'aurait pas donné un préavis dans un délai approprié. Si la résiliation
unilatérale est le fait du club, celui-ci ne pourra procéder à l'engagement d'un
nouveau joueur pendant un certain temps. La suspension du joueur ne pourra pas
dépasser 4 mois. Ce n'est qu'en cas de récidive ou d'absence de préavis que la
suspension pourra aller jusqu'à 6 mois. La résiliation unilatérale pourra donner
lieu à une compensation financière, destinée à sanctionner le manquement à une
obligation contractuelle, et qui devra respecter, en premier lieu, le droit national
applicable.

35.  La mise en œuvre de l'engagement de la FIFA donnée le 5 mars 2001 par
l'adoption des nouvelles règles qui sont en vigueur depuis le 1er septembre 2001
vient mettre fin aux infractions visées par votre plainte. Il n'existe plus
d'interdiction absolue de résiliation unilatérale et les joueurs et/ou les clubs
peuvent depuis le 5 juillet 2001 prévoir dans leurs contrats la possibilité de
résiliation selon les nouvelles règles. Toutefois, la persistance éventuelle des effets

---

[934]  Arrêt de la Cour de Justice du 13 avril 2000, affaire C-176/96.

des infractions pour un certain temps pourrait avoir lieu en raison de la continuité de contrats signés selon les anciennes règles FIFA au cas où les organes arbitraux de la FIFA continueraient de régler selon les anciennes règles les conflits éventuels résultant de contrats signés avant le 1er septembre. Étant donné que la circulaire no. 769 de la FIFA du 24 août 2001 indique clairement (point 8) que les conflits résultant de contrats signés selon les anciennes règles seront réglés par les dispositions procédurales du nouveau règlement, il est très peu probable que les effets restrictifs résultant d'anciens contrats persistent. D'autres facteurs contribuent encore à diminuer cette probabilité, à savoir: (1) le fait que l'arbitrage sera dorénavant volontaire, ce qui veut dire que les joueurs et les clubs ne pourront plus se voir interdire de s'adresser aux tribunaux ordinaires; (2) que la nouvelle Chambre de règlement des litiges créée au sein de la Commission du statut du joueur est un organe paritaire et (3) qu'il en est de même pour le Tribunal Arbitral du Football, l'organe d'appel. Ces aspects viennent d'être renforcés par le communiqué de presse commun de la FIFA et de la FIFPro du 31 août 2001 qui annonce un accord entre ces deux organisations à propos de la participation de la FIFPro à la mise en place du nouveau règlement de la FIFA sur les transferts des joueurs et confirme que les joueurs seront bien représentés tant au niveau de la Chambre de règlement des litiges que du nouveau Tribunal Arbitral du Football.

36.  Les limitations à la résiliation unilatérale introduites par les nouvelles dispositions résumées au point 31, en abrogeant celles qui faisaient l'objet de votre plainte, semblent trouver une justification à l'égard de l'article 39 du Traité pour des raisons impérieuses d'intérêt général. De l'avis de la Commission, elles pourraient constituer une entrave à la liberté de circulation des joueurs, mais celle-ci pourrait être justifiée par un objectif légitime déjà reconnu par la Cour de justice dans l'arrêt Lehtonen – assurer la stabilité des équipes afin de garantir la régularité des compétitions et l'intégrité des championnats – et les moyens utilisés pour atteindre cet objectif sont proportionnés[935].

37.  Elles semblent ne plus constituer des restrictions de concurrence sensibles au titre de l'article 81 paragraphe 1 du Traité, notamment en raison de sa portée limitée. A supposer même que ces limitations soient susceptibles de constituer des restrictions de concurrence au sens de l'article 81 paragraphe 1 du Traité, la Commission considère que ces règles, rempliraient les conditions de l'article 81 paragraphe 3 pour les raisons ci-dessous[936].

38.  Elles contribuent à améliorer la production et la distribution du spectacle sportif de football car l'intégrité des compétitions sera préservée et les équipes resteront stables pendant toute une saison sportive. L'interdiction de résiliation unilatérale d'un contrat tant par le joueur que par le club pendant toute une saison sportive semble indispensable pour assurer l'objectif en cause. Si les joueurs pouvaient partir à n'importe quel moment d'un championnat, la valeur sportive de telle ou telle équipe serait sensiblement modifiée au cours du championnat, la concurrence entre clubs serait faussée et le bon déroulement du championnat dans son en-

---

[935] Arrêt de la Cour de Justice du 13 avril 2000, affaire C-176/96.

[936] Or, '[l]a circonstance qu'un accord ou une pratique concertée, à supposer même qu'une infraction à l'article 85, paragraphe 1, du traité soit établie à son égard, aurait pu bénéficier d'une exemption au titre de l'article 85, paragraphe 3, du traité, si une telle possibilité s'était présentée à la Commission, motive à suffisance le rejet d'une plainte à son encontre' (Ordonnance de la Cour du 16 septembre 1997, aff. C-59/96 P, Koelman contre Commission, Rec. p. I-4809, point 42; Arrêt du Tribunal de première instance du 9 janvier 1996, affaire T-575/93, Koelman contre Commission, Rec. p.II-1, point 40).

semble serait compromis. Cette restriction ne donne pas aux clubs la possibilité d'éliminer la concurrence sur le marché de la production et de la vente du spectacle sportif de football du fait qu'ils peuvent engager les joueurs qu'ils veulent à la fin de la saison sportive et pour des cas exceptionnels (par exemple, le remplacement de joueurs blessés) ils peuvent le faire durant la période de transferts d'hiver qui, en tout cas, doit avoir une portée très limitée. Les consommateurs, c'est-à-dire les spectateurs et les fans du spectacle de football, retirent également un bénéfice équitable de ces restrictions car la préservation de l'intégrité des compétitions rend le spectacle plus équitable et intéressant et les fans peuvent s'identifier pour plus longtemps avec une équipe stable.

39. La protection des contrats pendant une période de durée limitée qui se traduit par des sanctions correspondant notamment à la suspension du joueur pendant une période de 4 mois à 6 mois (dans des cas de récidives) semble indispensable pour garantir la construction d'une équipe. Un club a besoin d'un temps minimum pour construire son équipe. Si un joueur pouvait rompre unilatéralement son contrat dès la première année et être transféré à la fin de la saison vers un autre club, sans aucune sanction autre que la compensation financière, son club d'origine n'aurait pas de possibilité de construire convenablement son équipe. Les sanctions visent donc à démotiver les joueurs de rompre unilatéralement leurs contrats pendant les deux premières années pour permettre l'existence d'équipes stables. En raison des spécificités du secteur en cause la durée de la période protégée et des sanctions semble être proportionnée aux objectifs légitimes qu'elles visent à atteindre.

**Conclusion**

40. En conclusion, la Commission considère, compte tenu de ce qui a été exposé qu'il n'existe pas un intérêt communautaire suffisant qui justifierait de poursuivre la procédure dans la mesure où:

contre la FIFA, elle a donné suite aux aspects essentiels de votre plainte et qu'elle estime qu'en raison des engagements reçus de la FIFA, il n'existe plus un intérêt communautaire que justifie de poursuivre la procédure d'application de l'article 81 ouverte contre la FIFA, le 14 décembre 1998, afin d'adopter une décision négative. L'article 3 du règlement no.17 ne vous confère pas, en tant que plaignant, le droit d'obtenir une décision de la Commission au sens de l'article 249 du Traité, quant à l'existence ou non d'une infraction à l'article 81 du Traité et encore moins quant à l'existence d'une telle infraction pour le passé. La Commission a amené la FIFA à modifier les règles cadre qui doivent être prises en compte lors de la signature ou de la résiliation d'un contrat entre un club et un joueur professionnel. La FIFA ne va pas continuer à appliquer les anciennes règles aux conflits résultant d'anciens contrats. Dans ces conditions la Commission considère qu'il n'y a pas un intérêt communautaire qui justifie de continuer à poursuivre la procédure d'autant plus que, d'une part, la FIFA et la FIFPro ont conclu, le 31 août 2001, un accord sur la mise en place des nouvelles règles sur les transferts qui assure notamment la participation des représentants de la FIFPro dans les organes de décision sur le règlement des litiges et que, d'autre part, les joueurs, les clubs ou les associations nationales pourront dorénavant porter les conflits à ce sujet à l'appréciation des tribunaux nationaux sans avoir à craindre des représailles des organes de la FIFA ou de l'UEFA.

Contre l'URBSFA, les éléments portés à sa connaissance n'ont pas fait apparaître que les comportements de cette organisation étaient de nature à fausser le jeu de la concurrence à l'intérieur du marché commun et à affecter le commerce entre Etats membres plus que ce que les règles FIFA en cause le faisait déjà. Pour cette raison, développée au point 9, la Commission considère qu'il n'y a pas un intérêt communautaire suffisant pour donner suite à ces griefs, car les mesures d'instruction nécessaires seraient disproportionnées par rapport à l'importance de l'infraction alléguée. Ces aspects pourraient être portés à la connaissance de l'autorité nationale en matière de concurrence ou d'un tribunal national.

Le grief visant le point 1 de la circulaire no. 616 (point 29 supra) n'a plus d'objet car la disposition n'est plus en vigueur.

Vous n'avez avancé aucun argument justifiant l'application de l'article 82 du Traité au cas d'espèce, aspect que vous pouvez, toutefois, porter devant une juridiction nationale.

41. Pour ces raisons, je vous communique que la décision finale de la Commission est de rejeter la demande de constatation d'infraction que vous lui avez soumise, le 24 octobre 1997, conformément à l'article 3 paragraphe 2 du règlement no.17 du Conseil du 6 février 1962.

42. Un recours contre cette décision peut être formé devant le Tribunal de première instance des Communautés Européennes au titre de l'article 230 du traité CE. Ces recours, conformément à l'article 242 du traité CE, n'ont pas d'effet suspensif, sauf si le Tribunal ordonne le sursis à exécution.

Veuillez croire, Messieurs, à l'assurance de ma considération distinguée.

Fait à Bruxelles, le
Pour la Commission
Mario MONTI
Membre de la Commission

Copie Me [...]

———

## 2.11.   FREEDOM OF ESTABLISHMENT*

### * 2.11.1.   ANSWER ON BEHALF OF THE COMMISSION TO WRITTEN QUESTION E-1691/00 BY JONAS SJÖSTEDT (GUE/NGL), 5 JULY 2000[937]

Subject: Commission's examination of ban on Swedish professional boxing

———

---

* The full texts of documents which are marked with an asterisk (*) are not incorporated in the book itself, but are freely accessible on the website of the ASSER International Sports Law Centre, at <www.sportslaw.nl> – documentation.

[937] Question of 29-5-2000; OJ C 72 E, 6-3-2001, p. 101.

## 2.12.   FREEDOM TO PROVIDE SERVICES*

**\* 2.12.1.   ANSWER ON BEHALF OF THE COMMISSION TO WRITTEN QUESTION E-2105/97 BY JEAN-PIERRE BÉBÉAR (PPE), 9 SEPTEMBER 1997**[938]

Subject: The Evin Law and restrictions on freedom of movement

----

**\* 2.12.2.   ANSWER ON BEHALF OF THE COMMISSION TO WRITTEN QUESTION E-3832/97 BY JEAN-PIERRE BÉBÉAR (PPE), 3 FEBRUARY 1998**[939]

Subject: The Evin Law and restrictions on freedom of movement

----

**\* 2.12.3.   REPLY ON BEHALF OF THE COUNCIL TO WRITTEN QUESTION E-3098/98 BY UMBERTO BOSSI (NI), 20 AND 21 DECEMBER 1998**[940]

Subject: Professional relations among professional soccer players

----

**\* 2.12.4.   ANSWER ON BEHALF OF THE COMMISSION TO WRITTEN QUESTION E-3099/98 BY UMBERTO BOSSI (NI), 7 JANUARY AND 2 AUGUST 1999**[941]

Subject: Professional relations among professional soccer players

----

**\* 2.12.5.   EUROPEAN COURT OF JUSTICE, OPINION OF ADVOCATE GENERAL COSMAS, CHRISTELLE DELIÈGE V LIGUE FRANCOPHONE DE JUDO ET DISCIPLINES ASSOCIÉES ASBL, LIGUE BELGE DE JUDO ASBL, UNION EUROPÉENNE DE JUDO AND FRANÇOIS PACQUÉE, JOINED CASES C-51/96 AND C-191/97, 18 MARCH 1999**[942]

----

**2.12.6.   EUROPEAN COURT OF JUSTICE, JUDGMENT, QUESTORE DI VERONA V DIEGO ZENATTI, CASE C-67/98, 21 OCTOBER 1999**[943]

*Freedom to provide services – Restrictions – National legislation reserving for certain bodies the right to take bets on sporting events – Justification – Protection of consumers*

---

* The full texts of documents which are marked with an asterisk (*) are not incorporated in the book itself, but are freely accessible on the website of the ASSER International Sports Law Centre, at <www.sportslaw.nl> – documentation.

[938] Question of 23-6-1997; OJ C 82, 17-3-1998, p. 29.
[939] Question of 28-11-1997; OJ C 187, 16-6-1998, p. 66.
[940] Question of 19-10-1998; OJ C 135, 14-5-1999, p. 167.
[941] Question of 16-10-1998; OJ C 27 E, 29-1-2000, p. 10.
[942] ECR 2000, p. I-2549.
[943] ECR 1999, p. I-7289.

*and maintenance of order in society (EC Treaty, Art. 59 (now, after amendment, Art. 49 EC)*

*National legislation which reserves for certain bodies the right to take bets on sporting events and which thus prevents operators in other Member States from taking bets, directly or indirectly, constitutes an obstacle to the freedom to provide services even if it applies without distinction.*
*However, in so far as such legislation does not entail any discrimination on grounds of nationality, it can be justified where its objectives are to protect consumers and to maintain order in society. Although it does not totally prohibit the taking of bets on sporting events but reserves it for certain bodies under certain circumstances, determination of the scope of the protection which a Member State intends providing in its territory in relation to lotteries and other forms of gambling falls within the margin of appreciation enjoyed by the national authorities. It is for those authorities to appraise whether, in the context of the aim pursued, it is necessary to prohibit activities of that kind, totally or partially, or only to restrict them and to lay down more or less rigorous procedures for controlling them. In those circumstances, the mere fact that a Member State has chosen a system of protection different from that adopted by another Member State cannot affect the appraisal as to the need for and proportionality of the provisions adopted. They must be assessed solely in the light of the objectives pursued by the national authorities of the Member State concerned and of the level of protection which they are intended to ensure.*

**In Case C-67/98,**
Reference to the Court under Article 177 of the EC Treaty (now Article 234 EC) by the Consiglio di Stato (Italy) for a preliminary ruling in the proceedings pending before that court between
Questore di Verona
and
Diego Zenatti
on the interpretation of the provisions of the EC Treaty concerning the freedom to provide services,

**The Court,**
composed of- G.C. Rodríguez Iglesias, President, J.C. Moitinho de Almeida, D.A.O. Edward, R. Schintgen (Presidents of Chambers), P.J.G. Kapteyn, J.-P. Puissochet (Rapporteur), G. Hirsch, P. Jann and H. Ragnemalm, Judges,
Advocate General: N. Fennelly,
Registrar: L. Hewlett, Administrator,
after considering the written observations submitted on behalf of:
–       the Italian Government, by Professor U. Leanza, Head of the Department of Contentious Diplomatic Affairs, Ministry of Foreign Affairs, acting as Agent, assisted by D. Del Gaizo, Avvocato dello Stato,
–       Mr Zenatti, by R. Torrisi Rigano, of the Catania Bar, and A. Pascerini, of the Bologna Bar,
–       the German Government, by E. Röder, Ministerialrat in the Federal Ministry of the Economy, and C.-D. Quassowski, Regierungsdirektor in the same ministry, acting as Agents,
–       the Spanish Government, by N. Díaz Abad, Abogado del Estado, acting as Agent,
–       the Portuguese Government, by L.l. Femandes, Director of the Legal Service of the Directorate-General for the European Communities of the Ministry of Foreign Affairs, and M.L. Duarte, Legal Adviser in the same directorate, and A.P. Barros,

Legal Coordinator in the gaming department of Santa Casa da Misericórdia de Lisboa, acting as Agents,
- the Finnish Government, by H. Rotkirch, Ambassador, Head of the Legal Affairs Department in the Ministry of Foreign Affairs, and T. Pynnä, Legal Adviser in the same Ministry, acting as Agents,
- the Swedish Government, by E. Brattgård, Departmental Adviser in the Ministry of Foreign Affairs, acting as Agent,
- the Norwegian Government, by J. Bugge-Mahrt, Deputy-Director General in the Ministry of Foreign Affairs, acting as Agent,
- the Commission of the European Communities, by M. Patakia and L. Pignataro, of its Legal Service, acting as Agents,

having regard to the Report for the Hearing, after hearing the oral observations of the Italian Government, represented by D. Del Gaizo, Mr Zenatti, represented by R. Torrisi Rigano and A. Pascerini, of the Belgian Government, represented by P. Vlaenuninck, of the Ghent Bar, of the Spanish Government, represented by N. Diaz Abad, of the French Government, represented by F. Million, Chargé de Mission in the Legal Affairs Directorate in the Ministry of Foreign Affairs, acting as Agent, of the Portuguese Government, represented by M.L. Duarte, of the Finnish Government, represented by H. Rotkirch and T. Pynnä, of the Swedish Government, represented by A. Kruse, Departmental Adviser in the Ministry of Foreign Affairs, acting as Agent, and the Commission, represented by M. Patakia and L. Pignataro, at the hearing on 10 March 1999, after hearing the Opinion of the Advocate General at the sitting on 20 May 1999, gives the following

**Judgment**
1.  By order of 20 January 1998, received at the Court on 13 March 1998, the Consiglio di Stato (Council of State) referred to the Court of Justice for a preliminary ruling under Article 177 of the EC Treaty (now Article 234 EC) a question on the interpretation of the provisions of the EC Treaty concerning the freedom to provide services to enable it to determine the compatibility of those provisions with national legislation which, subject to exceptions, prohibits the taking of bets and reserves to certain bodies the right to organise the taking of such bets as are authorised.
2.  That question was raised in proceedings between the Questore di Verona (the police prosecuting authority of Verona) and Mr Zenatti concerning the prohibition imposed on the latter from acting as an intermediary in Italy for a company established in the United Kingdom specialising in the taking of bets on sporting events.

**Legal background**
3.  In Italy, under Article 88 of Royal Decree No 773 of 18 June 1931 approving the consolidated version of the laws on public order (GURI No 146 of 26 June 193 1, 'the Royal Decree, '[n]o licence shall be granted for the taking of bets, with the exception of bets on races, regattas, ball games and other similar contests where the taking of bets is essential for the proper conduct of the competitive event'.
4.  It is clear from the Italian Government's reply to the question put to it by the Court concerning the arrangements for applying the exception so provided for that bets may be placed on the outcome of sporting events taking place under the supervision of the Comitato Olimpico Nazionale Italiano (National Olympic Committee, 'CONI') or on the results of horse races organised though the Unione Nazionale Incremento Razze Equine (National Union for the Betterment of Horse Breeds, 'UNIRE'). The use of the funds collected in the form of bets and allocated

to those two bodies is regulated and must in particular serve to promote sporting activities through investments in sports facilities, especially in the poorest regions and in peripheral areas of large cities, and support equine sports and the breeding of horses. Under various legislative provisions adopted between 1995 and 1997, arrangements for and the taking of bets reserved to CONI and UNIRE may be entrusted, following tendering procedures and on condition of payment of the prescribed fees, to persons or bodies offering appropriate safeguards.

5.  Article 718 of the Italian Penal Code makes it a criminal offence to conduct or organise games of chance and Article 4 of Law No 401 of 13 December 1989 (GURI No 401 of 18 December 1989) prohibits the unlawful participation in the organisation of games or betting reserved to the State or to organisations holding a State concession. Moreover, unauthorised gaming and betting are covered by Article 1933 of the Civil Code, according to which no action lies for the recovery of a gaming or betting debt. Nor, except in the event of fraud, can any sum paid voluntarily be reclaimed. The main proceedings

6.  Since 29 March 1997, Mr Zenatti has acted as an intermediary in Italy for the London company SSP Overseas Betting Ltd ('sSP'), a licensed bookmaker. Mr Zenatti runs an information exchange for the Italian customers of SSP in relation to bets on foreign sports events. He sends to London by fax or Internet forms which have been filled in by customers, together with bank transfer forms, and receives faxes from SSP for transmission to the same customers.

7.  By decision of 16 April 1997 the Questore di Verona ordered Mr Zenatti to cease that activity on the ground that it was not one that could be licensed under Article 88 of the Royal Decree, since that provision allows betting to be licensed only where it is essential for the proper conduct of competitive events.

8.  Mr Zenatti initiated proceedings for judicial review of that decision before the Tribunale Amministrativo Regionale (Regional Administrative Court), Veneto and applied for an interim order suspending its enforcement. On 9 July 1997 the Tribunale Amministrativo Regionale granted an interim order to that effect.

9.  The Questore di Verona appealed to the Consiglio di Stato for that order to be set aside.

10. The Consiglio di Stato considers that the decision to be given calls for an interpretation of the Treaty provisions on the freedom to provide services. In its view, the principles expounded in the judgment of the Court of Justice in Case C-275/92 Schindler [1994] ECR 1-1039 to the effect that those provisions do not preclude legislation like the United Kingdom legislation on lotteries, in view of the concerns of social policy and the prevention of fraud which justify it, appear to be applicable by analogy to the Italian legislation on betting.

11. However, since the Community judicature has not given any judgment on legislation of that kind, the Consiglio di Stato, whose decisions are not open to appeal, considers that Article 177 of the Treaty requires it to seek a ruling from the Court of Justice. It therefore stayed proceedings pending a preliminary ruling from the Court on the following question:
'Do the Treaty provisions on the provision of services preclude rules such as the Italian betting legislation in view of the social-policy concerns and of the concern to prevent fraud that justify it?'

**The question**

12. The Italian Government and all the other Governments that have submitted observations, and also the Commission, contend that the Schindler judgment provides all that is needed for that question to be answered in the negative.

13.     Mr Zenatti, on the other hand, contends that the taking of bets on sporting events cannot be equated with the running of lotteries, with which Schindler was concerned, in particular because bets do not amount to games of pure chance but require the person laying the bet to use his skill in predicting results. He also considers that the social policy concerns and the concern to prevent fraud referred to by the national court are not sufficient to justify the legislation at issue in the main proceedings.

14.     It must be borne in mind that, in paragraph 60 of Schindler, the Court laid emphasis on the moral, religious and cultural aspects of lotteries and other types of gambling in all the Member States. The general tendency of national legislation is to restrict, or even prohibit, the practice of gambling and to prevent it from being a source of private profit. The Court also observed that lotteries involve a high risk of crime and fraud, given the size of the amounts which can be staked and of the winnings which they can hold out to players, particularly when they are operated on a large scale. They also constitute an incitement to spend which may have damaging individual and social consequences. A final consideration which, although it cannot in itself be regarded as an objective justification, the Court held to be relevant is that lotteries may make a significant contribution to the financing of benevolent or public interest activities such as social works, charitable works, sport or culture.

15.     In paragraph 61 of the judgment in Schindler the Court held that the special features of lotteries justify allowing national authorities a sufficient margin of appreciation to determine what is required to protect participants and, more generally, in the light of the specific social and cultural features of each Member State, to maintain order in society, taking into account the manner in which lotteries are operated, the size of the stakes and the allocation of the profits they yield. In such circumstances, it is for the national authorities to assess not only whether it is necessary to restrict the activities of lotteries but also whether they should be prohibited, provided that those restrictions are not discriminatory.

16.     Even though the Schindler judgment concerns the organisation of lotteries, those considerations also apply, as is clear also from the very terms of paragraph 60 of that judgment, to other comparable forms of gambling.

17.     It is true that in its judgment in Case C-368/95 Familia press v Bauer Verlag [1997] ECR I-3689, the Court declined to treat certain games in the same way as the lotteries considered in Schindler. However, that case was concerned with magazine competitions involving crosswords or other puzzles in which a number of readers who had given correct answers received a prize following a draw. As the Court held in particular, in paragraph 23 of that judgment, such draws, which are organised on a small scale and in which the stakes are small, do not constitute an economic activity in their own right but are merely one aspect of the editorial content of a magazine.

18.     In this case, on the other hand, bets on sporting events, even if they cannot be regarded as games of pure chance, offer, like games of chance, an expectation of cash winnings in return for a stake. In view of the size of the sums which they can raise and the winnings which they can offer players, they involve the same risks of crime and fraud and may have the same damaging individual and social consequences.

19.     In those circumstances, the betting at issue in the main proceedings must be regarded as gambling of a kind comparable to the lotteries at issue in Schindler.

20.     However, the present case differs from Schindler in at least two respects.

21.     First, although the laws at issue in the two cases both impose a prohibition, subject

to exceptions, upon the transactions involved, their scope is not the same. As the Advocate General observes in paragraph 24 of his Opinion, whilst the national legislation considered in Schindler involved a total prohibition on the type of gambling at issue, namely large lotteries, the legislation at issue in this case does not totally prohibit the taking of bets but reserves to certain bodies the right to organise betting in certain circumstances.

22. Second, as pointed out in some of the observations submitted to the Court, the Treaty provisions on the right of establishment may fall to be applied in a situation such as that at issue in the main proceedings in view of the nature of the relationship between Mr Zenatti and SSP, the company for which he acts.

23. On the latter point, however, since the question raised by the national court is limited to the provisions on the freedom to provide services, it is not appropriate to consider the possible applicability of other provisions of the Treaty.

24. As the Court held in Schindler, the Treaty provisions on the freedom to provide services apply, in the context of running lotteries, to an activity which enables people to participate in gambling in return for remuneration. Such an activity therefore falls within the scope of Article 59 of the EC Treaty (now, after amendment, Article 49 EC) if at least one of the providers is established in a Member State other than that in which the service is offered.

25. In this case, the services at issue are provided by the organiser of the betting and his agents by enabling those placing bets to participate in a game of chance which holds out prospects of winnings. Those services are normally provided for remuneration consisting in payment of the stake and they are cross-frontier in character.

26. It is not disputed by the parties to the main proceedings, the various Governments which have submitted observations or the Commission that the Italian legislation, inasmuch as it prohibits the taking of bets by any person or body other than those which may be licensed to do so, applies without distinction to all operators who might be interested in such an activity, whether established in Italy or in another Member State.

27. However, such legislation, preventing as it does operators in other Member States from taking bets, directly or indirectly, in Italian territory, constitutes an obstacle to the freedom to provide services.

28. It is therefore necessary to consider whether that restriction on the freedom to provide services is permissible under the exceptions expressly provided for by the Treaty or is justified, in accordance with the case-law of the Court, by overriding reasons relating to the public interest.

29. Articles 55 of the EC Treaty (now Article 45 EC) and 56 of the EC Treaty (now, after amendment, Article 46 EC), which are applicable in this area by virtue of Article 66 of the EC Treaty (now Article 55 EC), allow restrictions justified by a connection, even if occasional, with the exercise of official authority or for reasons of public policy, public security or public health. Moreover, according to the case-law of the Court (see, to that effect, Case C-288/89 Collectieve Antennevoorziening Gouda and Others [1991] ECR I-4007, paragraphs 13 to 15), restrictions on the freedom to provide services deriving from national measures which apply without distinction are acceptable only if those measures are justified by overriding reasons relating to the public interest, are suitable for securing the attainment of the objective which they pursue and do not go beyond what is necessary in order to attain it.

30. According to the information given in the order for reference and the observations of the Italian Government, the legislation at issue in the main proceedings pursues objectives similar to those pursued by the United Kingdom legislation on lotteries,

as identified by the Court in Schindler. The Italian legislation seeks to prevent such gaming from being a source of private profit, to avoid risks of crime and fraud and the damaging individual and social consequences of the incitement to spend which it represents and to allow it only to the extent to which it may be socially useful as being conducive to the proper conduct of competitive sports.

31.    As the Court acknowledged in paragraph 58 of Schindler, those objectives must be considered together. They concern the protection of the recipients of the service and, more generally, of consumers as well as the maintenance of order in society and have already been held to rank among those objectives which may be regarded as constituting overriding reasons relating to the public interest (see Joined Cases 110/78 and 111/78 Ministère Public v Van Wesemael [1979] ECR 35, paragraph 28, Case 220/83 Commission v France [1986] ECR 3663, paragraph 20, and Case 15/78 Société Générale Alsacienne de Banque v Koestler [1978] ECR 1971, paragraph 5). Moreover, as held in paragraph 29 of this judgment, measures based on such reasons must be suitable for securing attainment of the objectives pursued and not go beyond what is necessary to attain them.

32.    As noted in paragraph 21 of this judgment, the Italian betting legislation differs from the legislation at issue in Schindler, in particular in that it does not totally prohibit the transactions at issue but reserves them for certain bodies under certain circumstances.

33.    However, determination of the scope of the protection which a Member State intends providing in its territory in relation to lotteries and other forms of gambling falls within the margin of appreciation which the Court, in paragraph 61 of Schindler, recognised as being enjoyed by the national authorities. It is for those authorities to consider whether, in the context of the aim pursued, it is necessary to prohibit activities of that kind, totally or partially, or only to restrict them and to lay down more or less rigorous procedures for controlling them.

34.    In those circumstances, the mere fact that a Member State has chosen a system of protection different from that adopted by another Member State cannot affect the appraisal as to the need for and proportionality of the provisions adopted. They must be assessed solely in the light of the objectives pursued by the national authorities of the Member State concerned and of the level of protection which they seek to ensure.

35.    As the Court pointed out in paragraph 37 of its judgment of 21 September 1999 in Case C-124/97 Läärä and Others [1999] ECR I-6067 in relation to slot machines, the fact that the games in issue are not totally prohibited is not enough to show that the national legislation is not in reality intended to achieve the public-interest objectives at which it is purportedly aimed, which must be considered as a whole. Limited authorisation of gambling on the basis of special or exclusive rights granted or assigned to certain bodies, which has the advantage of confining the desire to gamble and the exploitation of gambling within controlled channels, of preventing the risk of fraud or crime in the context of such exploitation, and of using the resulting profits for public-interest purposes, likewise falls within the ambit of those objectives.

36.    However, as the Advocate General observes in paragraph 32 of his Opinion, such a limitation is acceptable only if, from the outset, it reflects a concern to bring about a genuine diminution in gambling opportunities and if the financing of social activities through a levy on the proceeds of authorised games constitutes only an incidental beneficial consequence and not the real justification for the restrictive policy adopted. As the Court observed in paragraph 60 of Schindler, even if it is not irrelevant that lotteries and other types of gambling may contribute signifi-

cantly to the financing of benevolent or public-interest activities, that motive cannot in itself be regarded as an objective justification for restrictions on the freedom to provide services.

37.   It is for the national court to verify whether, having regard to the specific rules governing its application, the national legislation is genuinely directed to realising the objectives which are capable of justifying it and whether the restrictions which it imposes do not appear disproportionate in the light of those objectives.

38.   Accordingly, the answer to the question put by the national court must be that the Treaty provisions on the freedom to provide services do not preclude national legislation, such as the Italian legislation, which reserves to certain bodies the right to take bets on sporting events if that legislation is in fact justified by social-policy objectives intended to limit the harmful effects of such activities and if the restrictions which it imposes are not disproportionate in relation to those objectives.

**Costs**

39.   The costs incurred by the Italian, Belgian, German, Spanish, French, Portuguese, Finnish, Swedish and Norwegian Governments and by the Commission, which have submitted observations to the Court, are not recoverable. Since these proceedings are, for the parties to the main proceedings, a step in the action pending before the national court, the decision on costs is a matter for that court.

**On those grounds,**
**THE COURT,**
in answer to the question referred to it by the Consiglio de Stato by order of 20 January 1998, hereby rules:
The EC Treaty provisions on the freedom to provide services do not preclude national legislation, such as the Italian legislation, which reserves to certain bodies the right to take bets on sporting events if that legislation is in fact justified by social-policy objectives intended to limit the harmful effects of such activities and if the restrictions which it imposes are not disproportionate in relation to those objectives.

———

**\* 2.12.7.   ANSWER ON BEHALF OF THE COMMISSION TO WRITTEN QUESTION E-550/00 BY ASTRID LULLING (PPE-DE), 10 APRIL 2000**[944]

Subject: Commission proceedings against restrictions imposed by the Evin law (France) on the televised broadcasting in France of sporting events held abroad

———

**2.12.8.   EUROPEAN COURT OF JUSTICE, JUDGMENT, CHRISTELLE DELIÈGE V LIGUE FRANCOPHONE DE JUDO ET DISCIPLINES ASSOCIÉES ASBL, LIGUE BELGE DE JUDO ASBL, UNION EUROPÉENNE DE JUDO AND FRANÇOIS PACQUÉE, JOINED CASES C-51/96 AND C-191/97, 11 APRIL 2000**[945]

Reference for a preliminary ruling: Tribunal de première instance de Namur – Belgium.
Freedom to provide services – Competition rules applicable to undertakings – Judokas –

---

[944] Question of 28-2-2000; OJ C 330 E, 21-11-2000, p. 185.
[945] ECR 2000, p. I-2549.

Sports rules providing for national quotas and national federations, selection procedures for participation in international tournaments.

**Keywords:**
1.   *Preliminary rulings – Admissibility – Need to provide the Court with sufficient details of the relevant factual and legal context*
     *(EC Treaty, Art. 177 (now Art. 234 EC)*
2.   *Community law – Scope – Sport as an economic activity – Included*
     *(EC Treaty, Art. 2 (now, after amendment, Art. 2 EC)*
3.   *Freedom of movement for persons – Workers – Treaty provisions Scope – Sporting activity – Limits*
     *(EC Treaty, Art. 48 (now, after amendment, Art. 39 EC)*
4.   *Freedom of movement for persons – Workers Freedom of establishment – Freedom to provide services Treaty provisions Scope – Rules aimed at regulating gainful employment in a collective manner but not emanating from a public authority – Included*
     *(EC Treaty, Arts 48, 52 and 59 (now, after amendment, Arts 39 EC, 43 EC and 49 EC)*
5.   *Freedom to provide services – Services – Definition – Sporting activity*
     *(EC Treaty, Art. 59 (now, after amendment, Art. 49 EC) and Art. 60 (now Art. 50 EC)*
6.   *Freedom to provide services – Restrictions – Sports rules making participation by professional or semi-professional sportsmen in international competitions subject to a selection procedure Permissible*
     *(EC Treaty, Art. 59 (now, after amendment, Art. 49 EC)*

**Summary**
1.   *The need to provide an interpretation of Community law which will be of use to the national court makes it necessary that the national court define the factual and legal context of the questions it is asking or, at the very least, explain the factual circumstances on which those questions are based. Those requirements are of particular importance in certain areas, such as that of competition, where the factual and legal situations are often complex. The information provided in orders for reference must not only be such as to enable the Court to reply usefully but must also give the Governments of the Member States and other interested parties an opportunity to submit observations pursuant to Article 20 of the Statute of the Court of Justice. It is the Court's duty to ensure that the opportunity to submit observations is safeguarded, bearing in mind that, by virtue of the abovementioned provision, only the orders for reference are notified to the interested parties. (see paras 30-31)*
2.   *Having regard to the objectives of the Community, sport is subject to Community law only in so far as it constitutes an economic activity within the meaning of Article 2 of the Treaty (now, after amendment, Article 2 EC). That applies to the professional or semi-professional activity of judokas, provided that they are working as employed persons or providing services for remuneration and that the activity is genuine and effective and not such as to be regarded as purely marginal and ancillary. (see paras 41, 53-54)*
3.   *The Treaty provisions concerning freedom of movement for persons do not prevent the adoption of rules or practices in the field of sport excluding foreign players from certain matches for reasons which are not of an economic nature, which relate to the particular nature and context of such matches and are thus of sporting*

    *interest only, such as, for example, matches between national teams from different countries. That restriction on the scope of the provisions in question must, however, remain limited to its proper objective and cannot be relied upon to exclude the whole of a sporting activity from the scope of the Treaty. (see para. 43)*

4.    *The Community provisions on freedom movement for persons and freedom services not only apply to the action of public authorities but extend also to rules of any other nature aimed at regulating gainful employment and the provision of services in a collective manner. The abolition as between Member States of obstacles to freedom of movement for persons and freedom to provide services would be compromised if the abolition of State barriers could be neutralised by obstacles resulting from the exercise, by associations or organisations not governed by public law, of their legal autonomy. (see para. 47)*

5.    *Sporting activities and, in particular, a high-ranking athlete's participation in an international competition are capable of involving the provision of a number of separate, but closely related, services which may fall within the scope of Article 59 of the Treaty (now, after amendment, Article 49 EC) and Article 60 of the Treaty (now Article 50 EC) even if some of those services are not paid for by those for whom they are performed. (see paras 55-56)*

6.    *Sports rules requiring professional or semi-professional athletes or persons aspiring to take part in a professional or semi-professional activity to have been authorised or selected by their federation in order to be able to participate in a high-level international sports competition, which does not involve national teams competing against each other, does not in itself, as long as it derives from a need inherent in the organisation of such a competition, constitute a restriction on the freedom to provide services prohibited by Article 59 of the Treaty (now, after amendment, Article 49 EC). (see para. 69 and operative part)*

## Parties

In Joined Cases C-51/96 and C-191/97,

REFERENCES to the Court under Article 177 of the EC Treaty (now Article 234 EC) by the Tribunal de Première Instance de Namur, Belgium, for a preliminary ruling in the proceedings pending before that court between
Christelle Deliège
and
Ligue Francophone de Judo et Disciplines Associées ASBL, Ligue Belge de Judo ASBL, Union Européenne de Judo (C-51/96)
and between
Christelle Deliège
and
Ligue Francophone de Judo et Disciplines Associées ASBL, Ligue Belge de Judo ASBL, François Pacquée (C-191/97),
on the interpretation of Articles 59 of the EC Treaty (now, after amendment, Article 49 EC), 60, 66, 85 and 86 of the EC Treaty (now Articles 50 EC, 55 EC, 81 EC and 82 EC),

## THE COURT,

composed of: G.C. Rodriguez Iglesias, President, J.C. Moitinho de Almeida, D.A.O. Edward and L. Sevón (Presidents of Chambers), P.J.G. Kapteyn, J.-P. Puissochet, G. Hirsch, P. Jann and H. Ragnemalm (Rapporteur), Judges,
Advocate General: G. Cosmas,
Registrar: H. von Holstein, Deputy Registrar, after considering the written observations submitted on behalf of:

- Ms Deliège, by L. Misson and B. Borbouse, of the Liège Bar,
- Ligue Francophone de Judo et Disciplines Associées ASBL, by C. Dabin-Serlez and B. Lietar, of the Wavre Bar,
- Ligue Belge de Judo ASBL, by G. de Smedt and L. Carle, of the Lokeren Bar, and by H. van Houtte and F. Louis, of the Brussels Bar; Ligue Belge de Judo and Mr Pacquée, by G. de Smedt (C-191/97),
- the Belgian Government, by J. Devadder, General Adviser in the Legal Service of the Ministry of Foreign Affairs, External Trade and Development Cooperation (C-51/96 and C-191/97), and by R. Foucart, Director General in the Legal Service of the same ministry (C-191/97), acting as Agents,
- the German Government, by E. Röder, Ministerialrat in the Federal Ministry of the Economy, and S. Maass, Regierungsrätin in the same ministry (C-51/96), and by E. Röder and C.-D. Quassowski, Regierungsdirektor in the same ministry (C-191/97), acting as Agents,
- the Greek Government, by G. Kanellopoulos, Member of the State Legal Service, and P. Mylonopoulos, Assistant Legal Adviser in the Special Legal Service, European Law Section, Ministry of Foreign Affairs, acting as Agents,
- the Spanish Government, by L. Pérez de Ayala Becerril, Abogado del Estado, acting as Agent (C-191/97),
- the French Government, by C. de Salins, Head of Subdirectorate in the Legal Directorate of the Ministry of Foreign Affairs, and A. de Bourgoing, Chargé de Mission in the same directorate, acting as Agents,
- the Italian Government, by Professor U. Leanza, Head of the Legal Affairs Department, Ministry of Foreign Affairs, acting as Agent, assisted by D. Del Gaizo, Avvocato dello Stato (C-51/96),
- the Netherlands Government, by A. Bos, Legal Adviser, Ministry of Foreign Affairs (C-51/96), and J.G. Lammers, Acting Legal Adviser in the same ministry (C-191/97), acting as Agents,
- the Austrian Government, by W. Okresek, Ministerialrat in the Ministry of Foreign Affairs (C-51/96), and C. Stix-Hackl, Gesandte in the same ministry (C-191/97), acting as Agents,
- the Finnish Government, by T. Pynnä, Valtionasiamies, acting as Agent,
- the Swedish Government, by E. Brattgård, Departementsråd in the Department of Foreign Trade of the Ministry of Foreign Affairs (C-51/96), and L. Nordling, Rättschef in the same department (C-191/97), acting as Agents,
- the Norwegian Government, by B.B. Ekeberg, Acting Head of Service in the Ministry of Foreign Affairs, acting as Agent,
- the Commission of the European Communities, by A. Caeiro, Legal Adviser, and W. Wils, of its Legal Service, acting as Agents, having regard to the Report for the Hearing, after hearing the oral observations of Ms Deliège, represented by L. Misson and B. Borbouse, of Ligue Francophone de Judo et Disciplines Associées ASBL, represented by B. Lietar, of Ligue Belge de Judo ASBL and Mr Pacquée, represented by L. Carle, F. Louis and T. Geurts, of the Termonde Bar, of the Belgian Government, represented by A. Snoecx, Adviser, Directorate General for Legal Affairs of the Ministry of Foreign Affairs, External Trade and Development Cooperation, acting as Agent, of the Danish Government, represented by J. Molde, Head of Division in the ministry of Foreign Affairs, acting as Agent, of the Greek Government, represented by G. Kanellopoulos, of the Spanish Government, represented by N. Diaz Abad, Abogado del Estado, acting as Agent, of the French Government, represented by A. de Bourgoing, of the Italian Government, represented by D. Del Gaizo, of the Netherlands Government, represented by M.A. Fierstra,

Assistant Legal Adviser in the Ministry of Foreign Affairs, acting as Agent, of the Finnish Government, represented by T. Pynnä, of the Swedish Government, represented by A. Kruse, Departementsråd in the Ministry of Foreign Affairs, acting as Agent, and of the Commission, represented by W. Wils, at the hearing on 23 February 1999, after hearing the opinion of the Advocate General at the sitting on 18 May 1999, gives the following

**Judgment**

**Grounds**

1.  By order of 16 February 1996 (C~51/96), received at the Court on 21 February 1996, and by judgment of 14 May 1997 (C~191/97), received at the Court on 20 May 1997, the Tribunal de Première Instance (Court of First Instance), Namur, hearing an application for interim measures in the first case and dealing with the substance in the second, referred to the Court for a preliminary ruling under Article 177 of the EC Treaty (now Article 234 EC) two questions on the interpretation of Articles 59 (now, after amendment, Article 49 EC), 60, 66, 85 and 86 of the EC Treaty (now Articles 50 EC, 55 EC, 81 EC and 82 EC).
2.  Those questions were raised in proceedings between Christelle Deliège and Ligue Francophone de Judo et Disciplines Associées ASBL (hereinafter LFJ), Ligue Belge de Judo ASBL (hereinafter LBJ) and the president of the latter, Mr Pacquée, concerning the refusal to select her to participate in the Paris International Judo Tournament in the under-52 kg category.

*Judo organisation and selection rules*
3.  Judo, a martial art, is organised at world level by the International Judo Federation (the IJF). At European level, the membership of the European Judo Union (the EJU) comprises the various national federations. The Belgian federation is the LBJ, which deals essentially with international competitions and is responsible for the selection of athletes with a view to participation in international tournaments. The LBJ is made up of two regional leagues, the Vlaamse Judofederatie (the VJF) and the LFJ. The members of the LFJ are the two regional leagues and the clubs affiliated to them. Judokas are members of a club which is itself a member of the regional league, and the latter issues licences to members enabling them to take part in courses or competitions. The holder of a licence is required to accept all the obligations imposed by the regional league under its statutes and regulations.
4.  Traditionally, these athletes are classified according to six and seven weight categories, giving a total of 14 different categories. At its Technical and Sports Meeting in Amsterdam on 5 February 1994 and its Ordinary Congress in Nicosia on 9 April 1994 the Directing Committee of the EJU adopted rules concerning participation in European Category A tournaments. Those tournaments, like the May 1996 European Championships, provided an opportunity for points to be awarded for classification on European lists as a possible basis for qualifying for the 1996 Atlanta Olympic Games. It was stipulated that only the national federations could enter their athletes and that, for each European federation, seven judokas of each sex could be entered on those lists, which meant in principle that there would be one judoka for each category. However, if no athlete was nominated in a particular category, two could be entered in another category, provided that the limit of seven men and seven women was never exceeded. As stated by the LFJ at the hearing before the Court, the judoka's nationality was irrelevant for that purpose,

the only consideration being membership of the national federation.

5.   In accordance with the selection criteria for the Atlanta Olympic Games adopted by the IJF on 19 October 1993 in Madrid, those qualifying for those games included, in each category, the first eight in the most recent world championships and a number of judokas for each continent (for Europe, nine men and five women in each category), to be selected on the basis of the results obtained by each judoka in a specified number of tournaments during the run-up to the Olympics. For that purpose, the EJU stated, at the abovementioned Amsterdam meeting and Nicosia congress, that account would be taken of the best three results achieved at Category A tournaments and senior European championships over the period extending from the 1995 World Championships to the 1996 European Championships. It also directed that it would be the federations which qualified, not judokas individually.

The main proceedings and the questions submitted.

6.   Ms Deliège has practised judo since 1983 and, since 1987, has achieved excellent results in the under-52 kg category, having been declared Belgian champion on several occasions, European champion once and under-19 world champion once, as well as winning and being highly placed in international tournaments. The parties to the main proceedings disagree as to Ms Deliège's status: she claims to practise judo professionally or semi-professionally whilst the LBJ and the LFJ contend that judo is a sport which, in Europe and in Belgium in particular, is practised by amateurs.

7.   Ms Deliège maintains that, since 1992, the officers of the LFJ and the LBJ have improperly frustrated her career development. She complains in particular that she was prevented from taking part in the 1992 Barcelona Olympics, that she was not selected for the 1993 World Championships or for the European Championships in 1994. In March 1995 Ms Deliège was informed that she had not been pre-selected for the Atlanta Olympics. In April 1995, when preparing for participation in the European Championships to be held in May, she was excluded from the Belgian team in favour of an athlete affiliated to the VJF. In December 1995 she was prevented from taking part in the Basel Category A International Tournament.

8.   The LFJ alleges that Ms Deliège has had numerous differences of opinion with the trainers, selectors and officers of the LFJ and the LBJ and that she lacks discipline, having in one instance been penalised by temporary suspension from all federation activities. Moreover, she encountered difficulties relating to the sport itself in that in Belgium there are at least four high-ranking judokas in the under-52 kg category. The LBJ states that decisions on the selection of athletes to participate in the various tournaments and championships are taken by its national sports committee, a body with joint VJF and LFJ membership.

9.   The events directly giving rise to the main proceedings concern participation in the Paris Category A International Tournament of 10 and 11 February 1996. Because the LBJ had selected two other athletes who, in Ms Deliège's view, had achieved less outstanding results than her own, on 26 January 1996 Ms Deliège made an application for interim measures to the Tribunal de Première Instance, Namur.

*Case C-51/96*

10.   Ms Deliège asked the Tribunal de Première Instance, Namur, to make an interim order directing the LFJ and the LBJ to complete all the necessary formalities for her participation in the Paris Tournament and that the Court of Justice be requested to give a preliminary ruling on the question of the possible illegality of the

rules laid down by the EJU regarding the limited number of athletes from each national federation and the authorisations issued by the federations for participation in individual Category A tournaments, having regard to Articles 59, 60, 66, 85 and 86 of the Treaty. By a writ of 9 February 1996, Ms Deliège sought to have the EJU joined as a party to the proceedings and asked the court to order all Category A tournament organisers to accept on a provisional basis any registration on her part, whether or not she had been selected by her national federation.

11. By order of 6 February 1996 the judge of the Tribunal de Première Instance, Namur, hearing applications for interim measures dismissed Ms Deliège's application as regards her participation in the Paris tournament but made an order restraining the LBJ and the LFJ from taking any decision involving non-selection of the defendant for any forthcoming competition until the parties had been given a further hearing on the other heads of claim.

12. By order of 16 February 1996 the same judge declared inadmissible the application for an order requiring the EJU to become a party to the proceedings.

13. The national court also stated that, by virtue of the case-law of the Court, sport is subject to Community law only in so far as it may constitute an economic activity within the meaning of Article 2 of the EC Treaty (now, after amendment, Article 2 EC). As a result of recent developments in the way sports operate, the distinction between amateur and professional athletes had become less clear. Leading sports personalities could receive, in addition to grants and other assistance, higher levels of income because of their celebrity status, with the result that they provided services of an economic nature.

14. According to the national court, Ms Deliège claims, on what seems, prima facie, to be an adequate legal basis, that she must be regarded as a provider of services within the meaning of Articles 59, 60 and 66 of the Treaty. The systematic requirement of a quota and selection at national level would appear to constitute a barrier to the freedom to pursue an activity of an economic nature. Moreover, it cannot reasonably be contended that the access to competitions sought by Ms Deliège would mean that anybody would be allowed to participate in any tournament, since permission to compete could be open to anyone satisfying objective requirements in terms of sporting skills, as demonstrated by experience in other comparable sports.

15. Taking account inter alia of the imminence of the Atlanta Olympics and the relative brevity of sports careers at a high level, the national court therefore considered that Ms Deliège's request that a question be referred for a preliminary ruling was ostensibly appropriate. The fact that no proceedings had been commenced on the substance did not preclude a reference being made. The question could be seen as contributing to the outcome of the proceedings for interim measures or as a measure of inquiry to expedite the proceedings on the substance, the initiation of which appeared to be being contemplated by the plaintiff.

16. Consequently, the judge of the Tribunal de Première Instance, Namur, hearing applications for interim measures sought from the Court a preliminary ruling as to:
Whether or not rules requiring professional or semi-professional sportsmen or persons aspiring to such status to have been authorised or selected by their national federation in order to be able to compete in an international competition and laying down national entry quotas for similar competitions are contrary to the Treaty of Rome, in particular Articles 59 to 66 and Articles 85 and 86.

17. Finally, as regards the adoption of a delaying measure, the national court held that the claims made by Ms Deliège against the LBJ and the LFJ could not be upheld. However, he considered that it was appropriate to afford the plaintiff protection

against serious harm by adopting a delaying measure which would not adversely affect the interests of other athletes.

18. Pending the outcome of proceedings on the substance, he therefore ordered the LBJ and the LFJ not to take any measure liable to restrict or prevent the free exercise by the plaintiff of her activity as a judoka, in particular in national or international competitions, which was not objectively justified either by reference to her physical ability or conduct or by a comparative assessment of her merits as against those of competing athletes. That measure would cease to be effective one month after the order was made unless an action on the substance was brought by Ms Deliège.

*Case C-191/97*

19. By writs of 27 February and 1 March 1996 Ms Deliège brought an action against the LFJ, the LBJ and Mr Pacquée before the Tribunal de Première Instance, Namur. She sought, first, a ruling that the system of selecting judokas for international tournaments, as established by the rules of the two abovementioned federations, was illegal in that it empowers them to act in a way which might encroach upon the right of judokas freely to provide services and upon their professional freedom, second, a reference to the Court of Justice for a preliminary ruling, third, the adoption of a delaying measure in the event of such a ruling being sought, and, lastly, an order that the LFJ and the LBJ pay her damages of BEF 30 million.

20. In its judgment, the national court considered that there was a clear risk that the Court of Justice might declare inadmissible the question submitted in Case C-51/96 on the ground that the judge hearing the application for interim measures had disposed of all outstanding matters. It therefore decided that it would be inappropriate to await the judgment of the Court of Justice in the first case and that, since the answer to the question raised in the proceedings before it was uncertain, it should seek a preliminary ruling from the Court of Justice.

21. As regards Ms Deliège's application for a delaying measure, the national court considered that it would be very difficult, or even impossible, in practice to impose such a measure whilst safeguarding the interests of all parties, and the plaintiff had not made any specific suggestion in that regard.

22. In those circumstances, the Tribunal de Première Instance, Namur, stayed proceedings pending a preliminary ruling from the Court of Justice as to:
Whether or not it is contrary to the Treaty of Rome, in particular Articles 59, 85 and 86 of the Treaty, to require professional or semi-professional athletes or persons aspiring to professional or semi-professional activity to be authorised by their federation in order to be able to compete in an international competition which does not involve national teams competing against each other. The jurisdiction of the Court to answer the questions referred to it and their admissibility

23. The LFJ, the LBJ, Mr Pacquée, the Belgian, Greek and Italian Governments and the Commission have submitted, on various grounds, that the Court has no jurisdiction to answer the question submitted in Case C-51/96 and that all or part of that question is inadmissible.

24. First, it is submitted that the national court dealt with all the heads of claim put forward by the plaintiff and thus ceased to be seised of the case. Since the main proceedings had come to an end when the matter was referred to the Court of Justice, the latter's ruling would be of no relevance for the national court. In such circumstances, it is clear from Case 338/85 Pardini v Ministero del Commercio con l'Estero [1988] ECR 2041 and Case C-159/90 Society for the Protection of Unborn Children Ireland [1991] ECR I-4685 that the Court has no jurisdiction to give a ruling.

25.    Next, the question is of a hypothetical nature and concerns a matter – amateur sport – which is not subject to Community law.

26.    Finally, the national court did not give adequate details of the factual and legislative context of the question, a requirement which is of particular importance in the field of competition, which is characterised by complex factual and legal situations (Joined Cases C-320/90 to C-322/90 Telemarsicabruzzo [1993] ECR I-393).

27.    The jurisdiction of the Court to answer all or part of the question referred in Case C-191/97 and the admissibility of that question are also contested by the LFJ, the LBJ and Mr Pacquée and by the Greek Government and the Commission. The latter submit in particular that the national court did not give sufficient details of the factual and legislative background, that the question concerns a matter unconnected with Community law, that the rights of defence of the EJU and the IJF have been infringed and that the question is hypothetical in so far as it relates to events other than those involving competition between national teams.

28.    The Court would observe, first, that the issue whether the questions submitted by the national court concern a matter unconnected with Community law, either because amateur sport falls outside the scope of the Treaty or because the events referred to by that court involve national teams, relates to the substance of the questions submitted, not to their admissibility.

29.    Second, as regards the alleged breach of the rights of defence of the IJF and the EJU, it is not for the Court to determine whether the decision whereby a matter is brought before it was taken in accordance with the rules of national law governing the organisation of the courts and their procedure (see, in particular, Case C-39/94 SFEI and Others [1996] ECR I-3547, paragraph 24, and Case C-105/94 Celestini v Saar-Sektkellerei Faber [1997] ECR I-2971, paragraph 20). It follows that it is unnecessary for the Court to address the question whether the IJF and the EJU should have been joined as parties to the main proceedings.

30.    Third, according to settled case-law, the need to provide an interpretation of Community law which will be of use to the national court makes it necessary that the national court define the factual and legal context of the questions it is asking or, at the very least, explain the factual circumstances on which those questions are based. Those requirements are of particular importance in certain areas, such as that of competition, where the factual and legal situations are often complex (see in particular Telemarsicabruzzo, cited above, paragraphs 6 and 7, Case C-67/96 Albany [1999] ECR I-5751, paragraph 39, and Joined Cases C-115/97 to C-117/97 Brentjens' [1999] ECR I-6025, paragraph 38).

31.    The information provided in orders for reference must not only be such as to enable the Court to reply usefully but must also give the Governments of the Member States and other interested parties an opportunity to submit observations pursuant to Article 20 of the EC Statute of the Court of Justice. It is the Court's duty to ensure that the opportunity to submit observations is safeguarded, bearing in mind that, by virtue of the abovementioned provision, only the orders for reference are notified to the interested parties (see, in particular, the order in Case C-458/93 Saddik [1995] ECR I- 511, paragraph 13, and the judgments cited above in Albany, paragraph 40, and Brentjens', paragraph 39).

32.    As regards Case C-191/97, which it is appropriate to consider first, it is clear from the observations of the parties to the main proceedings, the Governments of the Member States, the Norwegian Government and the Commission, submitted pursuant to the abovementioned provision of the EC Statute of the Court of Justice, that the information contained in the order for reference duly enabled them to take a position on the question referred to the Court in so far as it relates to the Treaty rules on the freedom to provide services.

33.   Furthermore, even though the Greek, Spanish and Italian Governments may have taken the view in this case that the information provided by the national court was not sufficient to enable them to take a position on the question whether the plaintiff in the main proceedings pursues an economic activity within the meaning of the Treaty, it must be emphasised that those Governments and the other interested parties were able to submit their observations on the basis of the account of the facts given by that court.

34.   Moreover, the information contained in the judgment making the reference was supplemented by that contained in the file forwarded by the national court and the written observations submitted to the Court. All that information, set out in the Report for the Hearing, was brought to the notice of the Governments of the Member States and other interested parties for the purposes of the hearing, in the course of which they were able, where appropriate, to supplement their observations (see also, to that effect, Albany, cited above, paragraph 43, and Brentjens', also cited above, paragraph 42).

35.   The information supplied by the national court, supplemented as necessary by the abovementioned details also sufficiently apprises the Court of the factual and legislative background to the main proceedings to enable it to interpret the Treaty rules on freedom to provide services in the light of the circumstances of those proceedings.

36.   On the other hand, in so far as the question submitted relates to competition rules applicable to undertakings, the Court does not consider that it has sufficient information to enable it to give any guidance as to definition of the relevant market or markets involved in the main proceedings. The judgment making the reference likewise does not clearly disclose the nature and the number of the undertakings operating in the said market or markets. Furthermore, the information supplied by the national court does not enable the Court to give an informed ruling as to the existence and extent of trade between Member States or as to the possibility of such trade being affected by the rules for the selection of judokas.

37.   It must therefore be held that the judgment making the reference does not contain sufficient information to meet the requirements referred to in paragraphs 30 and 31 of this judgment regarding the competition rules.

38.   As far as the question submitted in Case C-51/96 is concerned, the order for reference likewise does not contain sufficient details to enable the Court to give an informed ruling on the interpretation of the competition rules applicable to undertakings. On the other hand, the information set out in that order, supplemented as necessary by the details contained in the written observations submitted pursuant to Article 20 of the EC Statute of the Court of Justice and set out in the Report for the Hearing, together with the information contained in the judgment making the reference in Case C-191/97, enabled the interested parties to take a position as to the interpretation of the rules on freedom to provide services and sufficiently apprised the Court of the factual and legislative background to enable it to reply usefully on that issue.

39.   Notwithstanding their slightly different wording, the questions submitted in both cases are essentially the same and, accordingly, it is unnecessary to give further consideration to the arguments specifically challenging the admissibility of the question in Case C-51/96.

40.   It follows that the Court should answer the questions submitted to the extent to which they relate to interpretation of the Treaty rules on freedom to provide services. The questions are inadmissible, however, in so far as they concern interpretation of the competition rules applicable to undertakings.

*Interpretation of Article 59 of the Treaty*

41.   It is to be remembered at the outset that, having regard to the objectives of the Community, sport is subject to Community law only in so far as it constitutes an economic activity within the meaning of Article 2 of the Treaty (see Case 36/74 Walrave and Koch v Union Cycliste Internationale [1974] ECR 1405, paragraph 4, and Case C-415/93 Union Royale Belge des Sociétés de Football Association and Others v Bosman [1995] ECR I-4921, paragraph 73). The Court has also recognised that sporting activities are of considerable social importance in the Community (Bosman, paragraph 106).

42.   That case-law is also supported by the Declaration on Sport (Declaration 29) annexed to the final act of the Conference which adopted the text of the Amsterdam Treaty, which emphasises the social significance of sport and calls on the bodies of the European Union to give special consideration to the particular characteristics of amateur sport. In particular, that declaration is consistent with the abovementioned case-law in so far as it relates to situations in which sport constitutes an economic activity.

43.   It must be recalled that the Treaty provisions concerning freedom of movement for persons do not prevent the adoption of rules or practices excluding foreign players from certain matches for reasons which are not of an economic nature, which relate to the particular nature and context of such matches and are thus of sporting interest only, such as, for example, matches between national teams from different countries. The Court stressed, however, that that restriction on the scope of the provisions in question must remain limited to its proper objective and cannot be relied upon to exclude the whole of a sporting activity (see Case 13/76 Donà v Mantero [1976] ECR 1333, paragraphs 14 and 15, and Bosman, paragraphs 76 and 127).

44.   The selection rules at issue in the main proceedings do not relate to events between teams or selected competitors from different countries comprising only nationals of the State of which the Federation which selected them is a member, such as the Olympic Games or certain world or European championships, but reserve participation, by the national federation, in certain other international events of a high level to athletes who are affiliated to the federation in question, regardless of their nationality. The mere circumstance that the placings achieved by athletes in those competitions are taken into account in determining which countries may enter representatives for the Olympic Games cannot justify treating those competitions as events between national teams which might fall outside the scope of Community law.

45.   The LFJ submits in particular that sports associations and federations are entitled freely to determine the conditions governing access to competitions which concern only amateur sportsmen.

46.   In that regard, it is important to note that the mere fact that a sports association or federation unilaterally classifies its members as amateur athletes does not in itself mean that those members do not engage in economic activities within the meaning of Article 2 of the Treaty.

47.   As regards the nature of the rules at issue, it is clear from the judgments in Walrave and Koch (paragraphs 17 and 18) and Bosman (paragraphs 82 and 83), cited above, that the Community provisions on the free movement of persons and services not only apply to the action of public authorities but extend also to rules of any other nature aimed at regulating gainful employment and the provision of services in a collective manner. The abolition as between Member States of obstacles to freedom of movement for persons and to freedom to provide services

would be compromised if the abolition of State barriers could be neutralised by obstacles resulting from the exercise, by associations or organisations not governed by public law, of their legal autonomy.

48. It follows that the Treaty, and in particular Articles 59, 60 and 66 thereof, may apply to sporting activities and to the rules laid down by sports associations of the kind at issue in the main proceedings.

49. In view of the foregoing considerations and the conflicting views expressed before the Court, it is important to verify whether an activity of the kind engaged in by Ms Deliège is capable of constituting an economic activity within the meaning of Article 2 of the Treaty and more particularly, the provision of services within the meaning of Article 59 of that Treaty.

50. In the context of judicial cooperation between national courts and the Court of Justice, it is for national courts to establish and to evaluate the facts of the case (see in particular Case 139/85 Kempf v Staatssecretaris van Justitie [1986] ECR 1741, paragraph 12) and for the Court of Justice to provide the national court with such guidance on interpretation as may be necessary to enable it to decide the dispute (Case C-332/88 Alimenta [1990] ECR I-2077, paragraph 9).

51. In that connection, it is important to note first that the judgment making the reference in Case C-191/97 refers among other things to grants awarded on the basis of earlier sporting results and to sponsorship contracts directly linked to the results achieved by the athlete. Moreover, Ms Deliège stated to the Court – and produced supporting documents – that she had received, by reason of her sporting achievements, grants from the Belgian French-speaking Community and from the Belgian Inter-Federal and Olympic Committee and that she has been sponsored by a banking institution and a motor-car manufacturer.

52. As regards, next, the concepts of economic activities and the provision of services within the meaning of Articles 2 and 59 of the Treaty respectively, it must be pointed out that those concepts define the field of application of one of the fundamental freedoms guaranteed by the Treaty and, as such, may not be interpreted restrictively (see, to that effect, Case 53/81 Levin v Staatssecretaris van Justitie [1982] ECR 1035, paragraph 13).

53. As regards more particularly the first of those concepts, according to settled case-law (Donà, cited above, paragraph 12, and Case 196/87 Steymann v Staatssecretaris van Justitie [1988] ECR 6159, paragraph 10), the pursuit of an activity as an employed person or the provision of services for remuneration must be regarded as an economic activity within the meaning of Article 2 of the Treaty.

54. However, as the Court held in particular in Levin (paragraph 17) and Steymann (paragraph 13), the work performed must be genuine and effective and not such as to be regarded as purely marginal and ancillary.

55. As regards the provision of services, under the first paragraph of Article 60 services are considered to be services within the meaning of the Treaty where they are normally provided for remuneration, in so far as they are not governed by the provisions relating to freedom of movement for goods, capital and persons.

56. In that connection, it must be stated that sporting activities and, in particular, a high-ranking athlete's participation in an international competition are capable of involving the provision of a number of separate, but closely related, services which may fall within the scope of Article 59 of the Treaty even if some of those services are not paid for by those for whom they are performed (see Case 352/85 Bond van Adverteerders and Others v Netherlands State [1988] ECR 2085, paragraph 16).

57. For example, an organiser of such a competition may offer athletes an opportunity

of engaging in their sporting activity in competition with others and, at the same time, the athletes, by participating in the competition, enable the organiser to put on a sports event which the public may attend, which television broadcasters may retransmit and which may be of interest to advertisers and sponsors. Moreover, the athletes provide their sponsors with publicity the basis for which is the sporting activity itself.

58.    Finally, as regards the objections expressed in the observations submitted to the Court according to which, first, the main proceedings concern a purely internal situation and, second, certain international events fall outside the territorial scope of the Treaty, it must be remembered that the Treaty provisions on the freedom to provide services are not applicable to activities which are confined in all respects within a single Member State (see, most recently, Case C-108/98 RISAN. [1999] ECR I-5219, paragraph 23, and Case C-97/98 Jägerskjöld [1999] ECR I-7319, paragraph 42). However, a degree of extraneity may derive in particular from the fact that an athlete participates in a competition in a Member State other than that in which he is established.

59.    It is for the national court to determine, on the basis of those criteria of interpretation, whether Ms Deliège's sporting activities, and in particular her participation in international tournaments, constitutes an economic activity within the meaning of Article 2 of the Treaty and, more particularly, the provision of services within the meaning of Article 59 of the Treaty.

60.    If it is assumed that Ms Deliège's activity can be classified as a provision of services, it is necessary to consider whether the selection rules at issue in the main proceedings constitute a restriction on the freedom to provide services within the meaning of Article 59 of the Treaty.

61.    It must be pointed out that, in contrast to the rules applicable to the Bosman case, the selection rules at issue in the main proceedings do not determine the conditions governing access to the labour market by professional sportsmen and do not contain nationality clauses limiting the number of nationals of other Member States who may participate in a competition.

62.    Furthermore, Ms Deliège, a Belgian national, does not contend that the choice made by the LBJ, which did not select her to take part in the tournament, was based on her nationality.

63.    In addition, as indicated in paragraph 44 of this judgment, those selection rules relate not to a tournament whose purpose is to set national teams against each other but to a tournament in which, once selected, the athletes compete on their own account.

64.    In that context, it need only be observed that, although selection rules like those at issue in the main proceedings inevitably have the effect of limiting the number of participants in a tournament, such a limitation is inherent in the conduct of an international high-level sports event, which necessarily involves certain selection rules or criteria being adopted. Such rules may not therefore in themselves be regarded as constituting a restriction on the freedom to provide services prohibited by Article 59 of the Treaty.

65.    Moreover, the adoption, for the purposes of an international sports tournament, of one system for selecting participants rather than another must be based on a large number of considerations unconnected with the personal situation of any athlete, such as the nature, the organisation and the financing of the sport concerned.

66.    Although a selection system may prove more favourable to one category of athletes than another, it cannot be inferred from that fact alone that the adoption of that system constitutes a restriction on the freedom to provide services.

67.    Accordingly, it naturally falls to the bodies concerned, such as organisers of tour-naments, sports federations or professional athletes' associations, to lay down ap-propriate rules and to make their selections in accordance with them.

68.    In that connection, it must be conceded that the delegation of such a task to the national federations, which normally have the necessary knowledge and experi-ence, is the arrangement adopted in most sporting disciplines, which is based in principle on the existence of a federation in each country. Moreover, it must be pointed out that the selection rules at issue in the main proceedings apply both to competitions organised within the Community and to those taking place outside it and involve both nationals of Member States and those of non-member countries. 69 The answer to the questions submitted must therefore be that a rule requiring professional or semi-professional athletes or persons aspiring to take part in a pro-fessional or semi-professional activity to have been authorised or selected by their federation in order to be able to participate in a high-level international sports competition, which does not involve national teams competing against each other, does not in itself, as long as it derives from a need inherent in the organisation of such a competition, constitute a restriction on the freedom to provide services pro-hibited by Article 59 of the Treaty.

**Decision on costs**

*Costs*

70.    The costs incurred by the Belgian, Danish, German, Greek, Spanish, French, Ital-ian, Netherlands, Austrian, Finnish, Swedish and Norwegian Governments, and by the Commission, which have submitted observations to the Court, are not recover-able. Since these proceedings are, for the parties to the main proceedings, a step in the proceedings pending before the national court, the decision on costs is a matter for that court.

*Operative part*

On those grounds,

**THE COURT,**

in answer to the questions referred to it by the Tribunal de Première Instance de Namur by order of 16 February 1996 and by judgment of 14 May 1997, hereby rules:
A rule requiring professional or semi-professional athletes or persons aspiring to take part in a professional or semi-professional activity to have been authorised or selected by their federation in order to be able to participate in a high-level international sports competi-tion, which does not involve national teams competing against each other, does not in it-self, as long as it derives from a need inherent in the organisation of such a competition, constitute a restriction on the freedom to provide services prohibited by Article 59 of the EC Treaty (now, after amendment, Article 49 EC).

———

**\* 2.12.9.   ANSWER ON BEHALF OF THE COMMISSION TO WRITTEN QUESTION P-1323/00 BY ALEXANDRE VARAUT (UEN), 19 MAY 2000**[946]

Subject: Restrictions on televising in France of sporting events staged abroad

———

**\* 2.12.10.   EUROPEAN COURT OF JUSTICE, OPINION OF ADVOCATE GENERAL FENNELLY, QUESTORE DI VERONA V DIEGO ZENATTI, CASE C-67/98, 20 MAY 1999**[947]

———

**\* 2.12.11.   ANSWER ON BEHALF OF THE COMMISSION TO WRITTEN QUESTION E-2118/00 BY GIOVANNI PROCACCI (ELDR), 28 JULY 2000**[948]

Subject: Proceedings No 94/4855 brought by the Commission against the restrictions imposed by the Evin law on the broadcasting in France of sports events held abroad

———

**\* 2.12.12.   ANSWER ON BEHALF OF THE COMMISSION TO WRITTEN QUESTION E-2197/00 BY ASTRID LULLING (PPE-DE), 28 JULY 2000**[949]

Subject: Restrictions imposed by the Evin law (France) on the televised broadcasting in France of sporting events held abroad

———

**\* 2.12.13.   ANSWER ON BEHALF OF THE COMMISSION TO WRITTEN QUESTION P-2210/00 BY BRICE HORTEFEUX (PPE-DE) 28 JULY 2000**[950]

Subject: Commission procedure No 94/4855 to remove the restrictions imposed by the Evin Act on French televised broadcasts of sports events staged in other countries

———

**\* 2.12.14.   ANSWER ON BEHALF OF THE COMMISSION TO WRITTEN QUESTION E-3900/00 BY ASTRID LULLING (PPE-DE), 20 FEBRUARY 2001**[951]

Subject: Restrictions imposed by the Evin law on the televised broadcasting in France of sporting events from abroad

———

---

[946] Question of 17-4-2000; OJ C 374 E, 28-12-2000, p. 216.
[947] ECR 1999, p. I-7289.
[948] Question of 30-6-2000; OJ C 89 E, 20-3-2001, p. 151-152.
[949] Question of 3-7-2000; OJ C 89 E, 20-3-2001, p. 153.
[950] Question of 26-6-2000; OJ C 89 E, 20-3-2001, p. 153.
[951] Question of 13-12-2000; OJ C 174 E 19-6-2001, p. 179-180.

**\* 2.12.15. EUROPEAN COURT OF JUSTICE, OPINION OF MR ADVOCATE GENERAL TIZZANO, BACARDI-MARTINI S.A.S. AND CELLIER DES DAUPHINS V NEWCASTLE UNITED FOOTBALL COMPANY LIMITED, CASE C-318/00, 26 SEPTEMBER 2002**[952]

---

**2.12.16. EUROPEAN COURT OF JUSTICE, JUDGMENT (FIRST CHAMBER), BACARDI-MARTINI SAS, CELLIER DES DAUPHINS V NEWCASTLE UNITED FOOTBALL COMPANY LTD, CASE C-318/00, 21 JANUARY 2003**[953]

*Reference for a preliminary ruling – Freedom to provide services – Refusal to display advertisements for alcoholic drinks at a sporting event taking place in a Member State whose law allows television advertising for alcoholic drinks but being broadcast on television in another Member State whose law prohibits such advertising – Relevance of the questions for the outcome of the main proceedings*

In Case C-318/00,
Reference to the Court under Article 234 EC by the High Court of Justice of England and Wales, Queen's Bench Division, for a preliminary ruling in the proceedings pending before that court between
Bacardi-Martini SAS, Cellier des Dauphins
and
Newcastle United Football Company Ltd,

on the interpretation of Article 59 of the EC Treaty (now, after amendment, Article 49 EC),

**THE COURT,**
composed of: G.C. Rodríguez Iglesias, President, J.-P. Puissochet and M. Wathelet (Presidents of Chambers), C. Gulmann, D.A.O. Edward, P. Jann (Rapporteur), V. Skouris, F. Macken, N. Colneric, S. von Bahr and J.N. Cunha Rodrigues, Judges,
Advocate General: A. Tizzano,
Registrar: L. Hewlett, Principal Administrator,
after considering the written observations submitted on behalf of:
– Bacardi-Martini SAS and Cellier des Dauphins, by N. Green QC and M. Hoskins, Barrister, instructed by Townleys and subsequently by Hammond Suddards Edge, Solicitors,
– the United Kingdom Government, by R.V. Magrill and subsequently G. Amodeo, acting as Agents, and K. Beal, Barrister,
– the French Government, by G. de Bergues and R. Loosli-Surrans, acting as Agents,
– the Commission of the European Communities, by K. Banks, acting as Agent,

– having regard to the national court's reply to a request for clarification pursuant to Article 104(5) of the Rules of Procedure, received at the Court on 26 February 2002,
– having regard to the Report for the Hearing,
– after hearing the oral observations of Bacardi-Martini SAS and Cellier des Dauphins, represented by N. Green and M. Hoskins; the United Kingdom Govern-

---

[952] ECR 2003, p. I-905.
[953] ECR 2003, p. I-905.

ment, represented by G. Amodeo and K. Beal; the French Government,represented by R. Loosli-Surrans; and the Commission, represented by H. van Lier, acting as Agent, at the hearing on 14 May 2002,

– after hearing the Opinion of the Advocate General at the sitting on 26 September 2002,

**Gives the following judgment**

1. By order of 28 July 2000, received at the Court on 14 August 2000, the High Court of Justice of England and Wales, Queen's Bench Division, referred to the Court for a preliminary ruling under Article 234 EC two questions on the interpretation of Article 59 of the EC Treaty (now, after amendment, Article 49 EC).

2. The questions were raised in proceedings between Bacardi-Martini SAS and Cellier des Dauphins ('the claimants') and Newcastle United Football Company Ltd ('Newcastle') for compensation for the damage allegedly suffered as a result of Newcastle's interference in the performance of contracts they had concluded with Dorna Marketing (UK) Ltd ('Dorna') for the display of advertisements.

**Legal background**

3. The French Loi No 91/32 relative à la lutte contre le tabagisme et l'alcoolisme (Law No 91/32 on combating smoking and alcoholism) of 10 January 1991 (*Journal officiel de la République française* (JORF), 12 January 1991, p. 615, 'the Loi Évin') amended Article L.17 of the Code des débits de boissons (Code of licensed premises), subsequently Article L.3323-2 of the Code de la santé publique (Code of Public Health).

4. That provision authorises certain forms, listed exhaustively, of direct or indirect promotion or advertising for alcoholic drinks.

5. Under the Loi Évin, all advertising for alcoholic drinks, defined as drinks whose alcohol content exceeds 1.2 degrees, which is not expressly authorised is prohibited. Since the advertising of alcoholic drinks on television is not expressly authorised, it is prohibited.

6. That prohibition is confirmed by Article 8 of Decree No 92-280 of 27 March 1992 applying Article 27(1) of the Law of 30 September 1986 relating to freedom of communication and defining the general principles concerning the rules applicable to advertising and sponsorship (JORF, 28 March 1992, p. 4313), which provides:
'Advertising relating to products the advertising of which on television is prohibited by law and to the following products and economic sectors shall be prohibited:
- drinks having an alcohol content greater than 1.2°;
[...]'

7. The Conseil supérieur de l'audiovisuel (CSA) is an independent administrative authority responsible for guaranteeing the exercise of freedom of communication. Among other things, it monitors advertisements broadcast by audiovisual communication services. The CSA can impose administrative penalties on broadcasters who fail to comply with their obligations under the Loi Évin.

8. In 1995 the CSA adopted a code of conduct containing principles relating to the television broadcasting on French stations of sporting events taking place in France or abroad at which advertisements for alcoholic drinks appear. The principles set out in the code, which has been amended on several occasions, have no legislative force but, as stated in the preamble to the code, are accepted as an interpretation voluntarily agreed in good faith.

9. According to the CSA's code of conduct, as worded at the material time, French

producers and advertisers may not be treated differently from their foreign competitors, subject only to any limits imposed by the national law of the place of the event.

10. The code proceeds from the principle that the broadcaster must refrain from adopting an indulgent approach to advertisements for alcoholic drinks.

11. To that end, it distinguishes between 'multinational events' and 'other events' taking place abroad.

12. In the case of 'multinational events', pictures of which are transmitted in a large number of countries and thus cannot be regarded as aimed principally at a French audience, where French broadcasters broadcast pictures whose conditions of filming are not within their control, they cannot be accused of an indulgent approach to the advertisements concerned even if they appear on the screen.

13. In the case of 'other events', where the law of the host country allows the advertising of alcoholic drinks at sporting venues but the transmission is aimed specifically at a French audience, it is for all the parties negotiating contracts with the holder of the transmission rights to use all available means to prevent brand names relating to alcoholic drinks from appearing on the screen.

14. The British Code of Advertising does not prohibit the advertising of alcoholic drinks, nor does it restrict the means of advertising them. However, it limits the permitted content of the advertisements in several respects.

**The main proceedings and the questions referred for a preliminary ruling**

15. The claimants are companies incorporated under French law which *inter alia* produce and market alcoholic drinks. Newcastle is a company incorporated under English law which owns and manages a football club and stadium.

16. In the context of an agreement concluded in 1994 between a football association and several football clubs, including Newcastle, of the one part and Dorna of the other part, Dorna was appointed to sell and display advertisements around the touchline of the clubs' pitches for each home match played by the clubs' first teams.

17. Under two contracts concluded in November 1996 between the claimants and Dorna, Dorna undertook to provide the claimants with advertising time on its electronic revolving display system during a match between Newcastle and Metz, a French football club, which was to be played in Newcastle on 3 December 1996 in the third round of the UEFA Cup (Union of European Football Associations).

18. That match was to be televised in the United Kingdom and France. Newcastle had undertaken, by an agreement with CSI Ltd ('CSI'), a company incorporated under English law which *inter alia* sells television broadcasting rights for sporting events, to permit and/or procure the live broadcast of the match on French television.

19. The advertisements for alcoholic drinks which were to be shown during the match in accordance with the contracts between the claimants and Dorna complied with the requirements of English law.

20. Shortly before the start of the match, Newcastle became aware that Dorna had sold the claimants advertising space in order to display advertisements for alcoholic drinks during the match. Newcastle consequently informed Dorna that, since the match was to be broadcast by a French television station, the French legislation restricting the advertising of alcoholic drinks applied, and that Dorna should therefore remove the advertisements for the claimants from its display panels in order to comply with that legislation.

21. Since the advertisements in question could no longer be removed from the revolv-

ing displays so shortly before the start of the match, the display system was programmed in such a way that during the match they appeared for only one to two
seconds on each occasion instead of the 30 seconds provided for in the contracts.
The match was broadcast live on French television, as CSI had sold the transmission rights to the French television station Canal +.

22.   On 23 July 1998 the claimants brought proceedings against Dorna and Newcastle
in the High Court of Justice of England and Wales, Queen's Bench Division, seeking *inter alia* damages and injunctions. The proceedings against Dorna were subsequently withdrawn.

23.   In support of the claims against Newcastle, the claimants argue that breach of the
contracts concluded between themselves and Dorna is attributable to Newcastle,
that Newcastle's interference with those contracts cannot be justified by the relevant provisions of the Loi Évin because those provisions are not compatible with
Article 59 of the Treaty, and that Newcastle is therefore liable for the damage
caused to the claimants on the ground of inducing breach of contract.

24.   The claimants consider that the relevant provisions of the Loi Évin, in particular as
interpreted and applied by the CSA, infringe Article 59 of the Treaty in that they
constitute a restriction on the cross-border provision of services, since they restrict
advertising for alcoholic drinks at sporting events taking place in Member States
other than France where those events are televised in France, and/or prohibit or
restrict the televising in France of sporting events taking place in other Member
States where advertisements for alcoholic drinks are displayed at the venue of the
event.

25.   According to the claimants, the public interest which the provisions of the Loi
Évin seek to safeguard is adequately protected by the rules on the advertising of
alcoholic drinks applicable in the United Kingdom.

26.   The claimants submit, moreover, that the restrictions imposed in accordance with
the provisions of the Loi Évin are disproportionate for several reasons.

27.   In its defence, Newcastle submits *inter alia* that instructing Dorna to remove the
advertisements for the claimants on the basis of the provisions of the Loi Évin was
justified because those provisions are compatible with Article 59 of the Treaty.

28.   The High Court observes, first, that various French courts have given divergent
decisions on the applicability of the Loi Évin to cross-border broadcasts of sporting events. Second, it refers to an expert report submitted to it on the effects in
practice of the relevant provisions of the Loi Évin. It appears in particular that
matches preceding the quarter-finals of the UEFA Cup are regarded as 'other
events' within the meaning of the CSA code of conduct.

29.   Having satisfied itself that the issues raised before it did not have to be examined
from the point of view of Council Directive 89/552/EEC of 3 October 1989 on the
coordination of certain provisions laid down by law, regulation or administrative
action in Member States concerning the pursuit of television broadcasting activities (OJ 1989 L 298, p. 23), the High Court considered that the provision of Community law which applied was Article 59 of the Treaty.

30.   However, it found it inappropriate, as an English court, to make a definitive ruling
on the lawfulness of a French law with respect to Article 59 of the Treaty, particularly without the French Government having been able to submit observations on
the point.

31.   In those circumstances, the High Court decided to stay proceedings and refer the
following questions to the Court for a preliminary ruling:
'1.   Are Articles L.17 to L.21 of the Code des débits de boissons (the so-called
Loi Évin provisions), Article 8 of Decree No 92-280 of 27 March 1992 and

the provisions of the code of conduct of 28 March 1995 contrary to Article 59 of the EC Treaty (now, after amendment, Article 49 EC) in so far as they prevent or restrict

(a) the advertising of alcoholic drinks at sporting events taking place in Member States other than France when the events are to be televised in France and

(b) the broadcasting in France of sporting events taking place in other Member States at which there is advertising of alcoholic beverages?

2. If not, is the manner in which these provisions are interpreted and applied in practice by the Conseil supérieur de l'audiovisuel contrary to Article 59 of the EC Treaty (now, after amendment, Article 49 EC) in so far as they prevent or restrict

(a) the advertising of alcoholic drinks at sporting events taking place in Member States other than France when the events are to be televised in France and

(b) the broadcasting in France of sporting events taking place in other Member States at which there is advertising of alcoholic beverages?'

32. Since it considered that it was not clear on the basis of the documents submitted to the Court why an answer to the questions referred was necessary to enable the national court to give judgment in the main proceedings, the Court, pursuant to Article 104(5) of the Rules of Procedure, requested the national court to explain more fully the basis on which Newcastle could rely on the Loi Évin – assuming it to be compatible with Article 59 of the Treaty – as a defence to the claim against it.

33. In answer to that request, the High Court stated that the claims brought against Newcastle were based on 'the tort of inducing breach of contract'. It was well established in English law that a party could submit that such an interference with a contract was justified. The question of what constitutes justification in this context was a matter for the national court to decide, taking account of all the circumstances.

34. In the present case, Newcastle had submitted that it was entitled to give instructions to remove the advertisements in the stadium, *inter alia* because 'such instructions were given in the reasonable anticipation that a failure to give them would result in a breach of French law'.

35. The claimants for their part submitted that this defence was unacceptable as a matter of Community law, since the Loi Évin was in any event contrary to Article 59 of the Treaty.

36. The High Court therefore considered that it was appropriate to seek a preliminary ruling from the Court on the issue of Community law raised.

## Admissibility
*Observations submitted to the Court*

37. The French Government and the Commission submit that the questions referred are inadmissible. According to the French Government, there is no extra-territorial application of French law. It is the French television station which bought the television rights which would have had to answer for a possible breach of French law when the match which was played in England was broadcast in France. In relying on the application of French law, Newcastle's sole motive was the fear of losing the payment for the television rights.

38. The Commission adds that the High Court has not explained whether and how such financial considerations could justify inducing a breach of contract. More

generally, the High Court has given the Court no indication of how the answers to the questions referred could help it to decide the case before it.

39.    According to the claimants, on the other hand, the admissibility of the reference for a preliminary ruling derives from the fact that the national court must examine all the justifications put forward. It is not disputed that Newcastle's decision was motivated by the existence and effects of the French law. The claimants submit that this attempt at justification is invalid in that the Loi Évin is incompatible with Article 59 of the Treaty.

40.    The United Kingdom Government agrees with that argument and adds that, if it were an express or implied term of the contract between Newcastle and CSI that the broadcast of the match would comply with French law, the compatibility of the French law with Article 59 of the Treaty would indeed be of relevance for the main proceedings. In any event, the requirement imposed on the French broadcaster to negotiate compliance with the Loi Évin when matches taking place abroad are broadcast gives that law extraterritorial effect.

*Findings of the Court*

41.    It is settled case-law that it is solely for the national court before which the dispute has been brought, and which must assume responsibility for the subsequent judicial decision, to determine in the light of the particular circumstances of the case both the need for a preliminary ruling in order to enable it to deliver judgment and the relevance of the questions which it submits to the Court. Consequently, where the questions submitted concern the interpretation of Community law, the Court of Justice is, in principle, bound to give a ruling (see, *inter alia*, Case C-415/93 *Bosman* [1995] ECR I-4921, paragraph 59; Case C-379/98 *PreussenElektra* [2001] ECR I-2099, paragraph 38; and Case C-153/00 *Der Weduwe* [2002] ECR I-11319, paragraph 31).

42.    However, the Court has also held that, in exceptional circumstances, it can examine the conditions in which the case was referred to it by the national court (see, to that effect, *PreussenElektra*, paragraph 39). The spirit of cooperation which must prevail in preliminary ruling proceedings requires the national court for its part to have regard to the function entrusted to the Court of Justice, which is to contribute to the administration of justice in the Member States and not to give opinions on general or hypothetical questions (*Bosman*, paragraph 60, and *Der Weduwe*, paragraph 32).

43.    Thus the Court has held that it has no jurisdiction to give a preliminary ruling on a question submitted by a national court where it is quite obvious that the interpretation or the assessment of the validity of a provision of Community law sought by that court bears no relation to the actual facts of the main action or its purpose, or where the problem is hypothetical, or where the Court does not have before it the factual or legal material necessary to give a useful answer to the questions submitted to it (see *Bosman*, paragraph 61; Case C-437/97 *EKW and Wein & Co* [2000] ECR I-1157, paragraph 52; and Case C-36/99 *Idéal Tourisme* [2000] ECR I-6049, paragraph 20).

44.    In order that the Court may perform its task in accordance with the Treaty, it is essential for national courts to explain, when the reasons do not emerge beyond any doubt from the file, why they consider that a reply to their questions is necessary to enable them to give judgment (Case 244/80 *Foglia* [1981] ECR 3045, paragraph 17). Thus the Court has held that it is essential that the national court should give at the very least some explanation of the reasons for the choice of the Community provisions which it requires to be interpreted and of the link it establishes

between those provisions and the national legislation applicable to the dispute (order in Case C-116/00 *Laguillaumie* [2000] ECR I-4979, paragraph 16).

45. Moreover, the Court must display special vigilance when, in the course of proceedings between individuals, a question is referred to it with a view topermitting the national court to decide whether the legislation of another Member State is in accordance with Community law (*Foglia*, paragraph 30).

46. In the present case, as the questions referred are intended to enable the national court to assess the compatibility with Community law of the legislation of another Member State, the Court must be informed in some detail of that court's reasons for considering that an answer to the questions is necessary to enable it to give judgment.

47. It appears from the High Court's account of the legal context that it has to apply English law in the main proceedings. It nevertheless considers that 'the issue of the legality of the Loi Évin provisions is central to resolution of the proceedings before [it]'. It does not, however, state positively that an answer to that question is necessary to enable it to give judgment.

48. On being requested by the Court to explain more fully the basis on which Newcastle could rely on the Loi Évin, the High Court has essentially confined itself to repeating the defendant's argument that it could reasonably anticipate that a failure to give instructions to remove the advertisements in the stadium would result in a breach of French law.

49. On the other hand, the High Court has not said whether it itself considered that Newcastle could reasonably suppose that it was obliged to comply with the French legislation, and there is nothing else to that effect before the Court.

50. The United Kingdom Government has contended that the premiss for concluding that the questions referred are material could be the existence of an obligation on the part of Newcastle, in terms of its contract with CSI for the broadcast of the Newcastle-Metz match by a French television station, to comply with the French legislation. On this point, it suffices to state that the national court has not mentioned the existence of any such contractual obligation.

51. Furthermore, as the Advocate General rightly observes in point 34 of his Opinion, even if the national court were to consider that Newcastle could reasonably suppose that compliance with the French legislation required it to intervene in the contracts in question, it is not clear why that would no longer be the case if the provision with which Newcastle wished to ensure compliance turned out to be contrary to Article 59 of the Treaty.

52. The order for reference contains no information on this point either.

53. In those circumstances, the conclusion must be that the Court does not have the material before it to show that it is necessary to rule on the compatibility with the Treaty of legislation of a Member State other than that of the court making the reference.

54. The questions referred to the Court for a preliminary ruling are therefore inadmissible.

## Costs

55. The costs incurred by the United Kingdom and French Governments and by the Commission, which have submitted observations to the Court, are not recoverable. Since these proceedings are, for the parties to the main proceedings, a step in the action pending before the national court, the decision on costs is a matter for that court.

**On those grounds,**
**THE COURT,**

in answer to the questions referred to it by the High Court of Justice of England and Wales, Queen's Bench Division, by order of 28 July 2000, hereby rules:

The reference for a preliminary ruling made by the High Court of Justice of England and Wales, Queen's Bench Division, by order of 28 July 2000 is inadmissible.

———

**2.12.17.    EUROPEAN COURT OF JUSTICE, JUDGMENT, PIERGIORGIO GAMBELLI AND OTHERS, CASE C-243/01, 6 NOVEMBER 2003**[954]

*Right of establishment – Freedom to provide services – Collection of bets on sporting events in one Member State and transmission by internet to another Member State – Prohibition enforced by criminal penalties – Legislation in a Member State which reserves the right to collect bets to certain bodies*

Reference to the Court under Article 234 EC by the Tribunale di Ascoli Piceno (Italy) for a preliminary ruling in the criminal proceedings before that court against Piergiorgio Gambelli and Others on the interpretation of Articles 43 EC and 49 EC,

**The Court,**
composed of: V. Skouris, President, P. Jann, C.W.A. Timmermans and J.N. Cunha Rodrigues (Presidents of Chambers), D.A.O. Edward (Rapporteur), R. Schintgen, F. Macken, N. Colneric and S. von Bahr, Judges,
Advocate General: S. Alber,
Registrar: H.A. Rühl, Principal Administrator,
after considering the written observations submitted on behalf of:
–    Mr Gambelli and Others, by D. Agnello, avvocato,
–    Mr Garrisi, by R.A. Jacchia, A. Terranova and I. Picciano, avvocati,
–    the Italian Government, by I.M. Braguglia, acting as Agent, assisted by D. Del Gaizo, avvocato dello Stato,
–    the Belgian Government, by F. van de Craen, acting as Agent, assisted by P. Vlaemminck, avocat,
–    the Greek Government, by M. Apessos and D. Tsagkaraki, acting as Agent,
–    the Spanish Government, by L. Fraguas Gadea, acting as Agent,
–    the Luxembourg Government, by N. Mackel, acting as Agent,
–    the Portuguese Government, by L. Fernandes and A. Barros, acting as Agents,
–    the Finnish Government, by E. Bygglin, acting as Agent,
–    the Swedish Government, by B. Hernqvist, acting as Agent,
–    the Commission of the European Communities, by A. Aresu and M. Patakia, acting as Agents,
having regard to the Report for the Hearing,
after hearing the oral observations of Mr Gambelli and others, represented by D. Agnello; of Mr Garrisi, represented by R.A. Jacchia and A. Terranova; of the Italian Government, represented by A. Cingolo, avvocato dello Stato; of the Belgian Government, represented by P. Vlaemminck; of the Greek Government, represented by M. Apessos; of the Spanish Government, represented by L. Fraguas Gadea; of the French Government, represented by

---

[954] ECR 2003, not yet published.

P. Boussaroque, acting as Agent; of the Portuguese Government, represented by A. Barros; of the Finnish Government, represented by E. Bygglin; and of the Commission, represented by A. Aresu and M. Patakia, at the hearing on 22 October 2003,
after hearing the Opinion of the Advocate General at the sitting on 13 March 2003,
gives the following

**Judgment**
1.  By order of 30 March 2001, received at the Court on 22 June 2001, the Tribunale di Ascoli Peceno referred to the Court for a preliminary ruling under Article 234 EC a question on the interpretation of Articles 43 and 49 EC.
2.  The question was raised in criminal proceedings brought against Mr Gambelli and 137 other defendants (hereinafter Gambelli and others), who are accused of having unlawfully organised clandestine bets and of being the proprietors of centres carrying on the activity of collecting and transmitting betting data, which constitutes an offence of fraud against the State.

**Legal background**
*Community legislation*
3.  Article 43 EC provides as follows:-
    Within the framework of the provisions set out below, restrictions on the freedom of establishment of nationals of a Member State in the territory of another Member State shall be prohibited. Such prohibition shall also apply to restrictions on the setting-up of agencies, branches or subsidiaries by nationals of any Member State established in the territory of any Member State.
    Freedom of establishment shall include the right to take up and pursue activities as self-employed persons and to set up and manage undertakings, in particular companies or firms within the meaning of the second paragraph of Article 48, under the conditions laid down for its own nationals by the law of the country where such establishment is effected, subject to the provisions of the Chapter relating to capital.
4.  The first paragraph of Article 48 EC provides that companies or firms formed in accordance with the law of a Member State and having their registered office, central administration or principal place of business within the Community shall [...] be treated in the same way as natural persons who are nationals of Member States.
5.  Article 46(1) EC provides that the provisions of this Chapter and measures taken in pursuance thereof shall not prejudice the applicability of provisions laid down by law, regulation or administrative action providing for special treatment for foreign nationals on grounds of public policy, public security or public health.
6.  The first paragraph of Article 49 EC provides that within the framework of the provisions set out below, restrictions on freedom to provide services within the Community shall be prohibited in respect of nationals of Member States who are established in a State of the Community other than that of the person for whom the services are intended.
*National legislation*
7.  Under Article 88 of the Regio Decreto No 773, Testo Unico delle Leggi di Pubblica Sicurezza (Royal Decree No 773 approving a single text of the laws on public security), of 18 June 1931 (GURI No 146 of 26 June 1931, hereinafter the Royal Decree), no licence is to be granted for the taking of bets, with the exception of bets on races, regatta, ball games or similar contests where the taking of the bets is essential for the proper conduct of the competitive event.
8.  Under Legge Finanziaria No 388 (Finance Law No 388) of 23 December 2000

(ordinary supplement to the GURI of 29 December 2000, hereinafter Law No 388/00), authorisation to organise betting is granted exclusively to licence holders or to those entitled to do so by a ministry or other entity to which the law reserves the right to organise or carry on betting. Bets can relate to the outcome of sporting events taking place under the supervision of the Comitato olimpico nazionale italiano (Italian National Olympic Committee, hereinafter the CONI), or its subsidiary organisations, or to the results of horse races organised through the Unione nazionale per l'incremento delle razze equine (National Union for the Betterment of Horse Breeds, hereinafter the UNIRE).

9.     Articles 4, 4a and 4b of Law No 401 of 13 December 1989 on gaming, clandestine betting and ensuring the proper conduct of sporting contests (GURI No 294 of 18 December 1989 as amended by Law No 388/00, (hereinafter Law No 401/89), Article 37(5) of which inserted Articles 4a and 4b into Law No 410/89, provide as follows:

Unlawful participation in the organisation of games or bets

Article 4

1.     Any person who unlawfully participates in the organisation of lotteries, betting or pools reserved by law to the State or to entities operating under licence from the State shall be liable to a term of imprisonment of 6 months to 3 years. Any person who organises betting or pools in respect of sporting events run by CONI, by organisations under the authority of CONI or by UNIRE shall be liable to the same penalty. Any person who unlawfully participates in the public organisation of betting on other contests between people or animals, as well as on games of skill, shall be liable to a term of imprisonment of 3 months to 1 year and a minimum fine of ITL 1 000 000.

2.     Any person who advertises competitions, games or betting organised in the manner described in paragraph 1 without being an accomplice to an offence defined therein shall be liable to a term of imprisonment of up to 3 months and a fine of between ITL 100 000 and ITL 1 000 000.

3.     Any person who participates in competitions, games or betting organised in the manner described in paragraph 1 without being an accomplice to an offence defined therein shall be liable to a term of imprisonment of up to 3 months or a fine of between ITL 100 000 and ITL 1 000 000.

[...]

Article 4a

The penalties laid down in this article shall be applicable to any person who without the concession, authorisation or licence required by Article 88 of [the Royal Decree] carries out activities in Italy for the purpose of accepting or collecting, or, in any case, assisting in the acceptance or collection in any way whatsoever, including by telephone or by data transfer, of bets of any kind placed by any person in Italy or abroad.

Article 4b

[...] the penalties provided for by this article shall be applicable to any person who carries out the collection or registration of lottery tickets, pools or bets by telephone or data transfer without being authorised to use those means to effect such collection or registration.

**The main proceedings and the question referred for a preliminary ruling**

10.    The order for reference states that the Public Prosecutor and the investigating

judge at the Tribunale di Fermo (Italy) established the existence of a widespread and complex organisation of Italian agencies linked by the internet to the English bookmaker Stanley International Betting Ltd (Stanley), established in Liverpool (United Kingdom), and to which Gambelli and others, the defendants in the main proceedings, belong. They are accused of having collaborated in Italy with a book-maker abroad in the activity of collecting bets which is normally reserved by law to the State, thus infringing Law No 401/89.

11.   Such activity, which is considered to be incompatible with the monopoly on sport-ing bets enjoyed by the CONI and which constitutes an offence under Article 4 of Law No 401/89, is performed as follows: the bettor notifies the person in charge of the Italian agency of the events on which he wishes to bet and how much he in-tends to bet; the agency sends the application for acceptance to the bookmaker by internet, indicating the national football games in question and the bet; the book-maker confirms acceptance of the bet in real time by internet; the confirmation is transmitted by the Italian agency to the bettor and the bettor pays the sum due to the agency, which sum is then transferred to the bookmaker into a foreign account specially designated for this purpose.

12.   Stanley is an English capital company registered in the United Kingdom which carries on business as a bookmaker under a licence granted pursuant to the Bet-ting, Gaming and Lotteries Act by the City of Liverpool. It is authorised to carry on its activity in the United Kingdom and abroad. It organises and manages bets under a UK licence, identifying the events, setting the stakes and assuming the economic risk. Stanley pays the winnings and the various duties payable in the United Kingdom, as well as taxes on salaries and so on. It is subject to rigorous controls in relation to the legality of its activities, which are carried out by a pri-vate audit company and by the Inland Revenue and Customs and Excise.

13.   Stanley offers an extensive range of fixed sports bets on national, European and world sporting events. Individuals may participate from their own home, using various methods such as the internet, fax or telephone, in the betting organised and marketed by it.

14.   Stanley's presence as an undertaking in Italy is consolidated by commercial agree-ments with Italian operators or intermediaries relating to the creation of data trans-mission centres. Those centres make electronic means of communication available to users, collect and register the intentions to bet and forward them to Stanley.

15.   The defendants in the main proceedings are registered at the Camera di Commercio (Chamber of Commerce) as proprietors of undertakings which run data transfer centres and have received due authorisation from the Ministero delle Poste e delle Comunicazioni (Minister for Post and Communications) to transmit data.

16.   The judge in charge of the preliminary investigations at the Tribunale di Fermo made an order for provisional sequestration and the defendants were also sub-jected to personal checks and to searches of their agencies, homes and vehicles. Mr Garrisi, who is on the Board of Stanley, was taken into police custody.

17.   The defendants in the main proceedings brought an action for review before the Tribunale di Ascoli Piceno against the orders for sequestration relating to the data transmission centres of which they are the proprietors.

18.   The Tribunale di Ascoli Piceno makes reference to the case-law of the Court, in particular its judgment in Case C-67/98 *Zenatti* [1999] ECR I-7289. However, it considers that the questions raised in the case before it do not quite correspond to the facts already considered by the Court in *Zenatti*. Recent amendments to Law No 401/89 demand re-examination of the issue by the Court of Justice.

19.    The Tribunale di Ascoli Piceno refers in this context to the parliamentary working papers relating to Law No 388/00 which show that the restrictions inserted by that law into Law No 401/89 were dictated chiefly by the need to protect sports Totoricevitori, a category of private sector undertakings. The court states that it cannot find in those restrictions any public policy concern able to justify a limitation of the rights guaranteed by Community or constitutional rules.

20.    The court emphasises that the apparent legality of collecting and forwarding bets on foreign sporting events, on the initial wording of Article 4 of Law No 401/89, had led to the creation and development of a network of operators who have invested capital and created infrastructures in the gaming and betting sector. Those operators suddenly find the legitimacy of their position called in question following amendments to the rules in Law No 388/00 prohibiting on pain of criminal penalties the carrying on of activities by any person anywhere involving the collection, acceptance, registration and transmission of offers to bet, in particular on sporting events, without a licence or permit from the State.

21.    The national court questions whether the principle of proportionality is being observed, having regard first to the severity of the prohibition, breach of which attracts criminal penalties which may make it impossible in practice for lawfully constituted undertakings or Community operators to carry on economic activities in the betting and gaming sector in Italy, and secondly to the importance of the national public interest protected and for which the Community freedoms are sacrificed.

22.    The Tribunale di Ascoli Piceno also considers that it cannot ignore the extent of the apparent discrepancy between national legislation severely restricting the acceptance of bets on sporting events by foreign Community undertakings on the one hand, and the considerable expansion of betting and gaming which the Italian State is pursuing at national level for the purpose of collecting taxation revenues, on the other.

23.    The court observes that the proceedings before it raise, first, questions of national law relating to the compatibility of the statutory amendments to Article 4 of Law No 401/89 with the Italian constitution, which protects private economic initiative for activities which are not subject to taxes levied by the State, and secondly questions relating to the incompatibility of the rule laid down in that article with the freedom of establishment and the freedom to provide cross-border services. The questions of national law raised have been referred by the Tribunale di Ascoli Piceno to the Corte costituzionale (the Italian Constitutional Court).

24.    In those circumstances, the Tribunale di Ascoli Piceno has decided to stay proceedings and to refer the following question to the Court of Justice for a preliminary ruling:

Is there incompatibility (with the repercussions that that has in Italian law) between Articles 43 et seq. and Article 49 et seq. of the EC Treaty regarding freedom of establishment and freedom to provide cross-border services, on the one hand, and on the other domestic legislation such as the provisions contained in Article 4(1) et seq., Article 4a and Article 4b of Italian Law No 401/89 (as most recently amended by Article 37(5) of Law No 388/00 of 23 December 2000) which prohibits on pain of criminal penalties the pursuit by any person anywhere of the activities of collecting, taking, booking and forwarding offers of bets, in particular bets on sporting events, unless the requirements concerning concessions and authorisations prescribed by domestic law have been complied with?

## The question

*Observations submitted to the Court*

25. Gambelli and others consider that by prohibiting Italian citizens from linking up with foreign companies in order to place bets and thus to receive the services offered by those companies by internet, by prohibiting Italian intermediaries from offering the bets managed by Stanley, by preventing Stanley from establishing itself in Italy with the assistance of those intermediaries and thus offering its services in Italy from another Member State and, in sum, by creating and maintaining a monopoly in the betting and gaming sector, the legislation at issue in the main proceedings amounts to a restriction on both freedom of establishment and freedom to provide services. No justification for the restriction is to be found in the case-law of the Court of Justice stemming from Case C-275/92 *Schindler* [1994] ECR I-1039, Case C-124/97 *Läärä and Others* [1999] ECR I-6067 and *Zenatti*, cited above, because the Court has not had occasion to consider the amendments made to that legislation by Law No 388/00 and it has not examined the issue from the point of view of freedom of establishment.

26. The defendants in the main proceedings emphasise in that regard that the Italian State is not pursuing a consistent policy whose aim is to restrict, or indeed abolish, gaming activities within the meaning of the judgments in *Läärä*, paragraph 37, and *Zenatti*, paragraph 36. The concerns cited by the national authorities relating to the protection of bettors against the risk of fraud, the preservation of public order and reducing both opportunities for gaming in order to avoid the damaging consequences of betting at both individual and social level and the incitement to spend inherent therein are groundless because Italy is increasing the range of betting and gaming available, and even inciting people to engage in such activities by facilitating collection in order to increase tax revenue. The fact that the organising of bets is regulated by financial laws shows that the true motivation of the national authorities is economic.

27. The purpose of the Italian legislation is also to protect licensees under the national monopoly by making that monopoly impenetrable for operators from other Member States, since the invitations to tender contain criteria relating to ownership structures which cannot be met by a capital company quoted on the stock exchange but only by natural persons, and since they require applicants to own premises and to have been a licence holder over a substantial period.

28. The defendants in the main proceedings argue that it is difficult to accept that a company like Stanley, which operates entirely legally and is duly regulated in the United Kingdom, should be treated by the Italian legislation in the same way as an operator who organises clandestine gaming, when all the public-interest concerns are protected by the United Kingdom legislation and the Italian intermediaries in a contractual relationship with Stanley as secondary or subsidiary establishments are registered as official suppliers of services and with the Ministry of Post and Telecommunications with which they operate, and which subjects them to regular checks and inspections.

29. That situation, which falls within the scope of freedom of establishment, contravenes the principle of mutual recognition in sectors which have not yet been harmonised. It is also contrary to the principle of proportionality, *a fortiori* because criminal penalties ought to constitute a last resort for a Member State in cases where other measures and instruments are not able to provide adequate protection of the interests concerned. Under the Italian legislation, bettors in Italy are not only deprived of the possibility of using bookmakers established in another Member State, even through the intermediary of operators established in Italy, but are also subject to criminal penalties.

30.    The Italian, Belgian, Greek, Spanish, French, Luxembourg, Portuguese, Finnish and Swedish Governments, as well as the Commission, cite the case-law of the Court of Justice, in particular the judgments in *Schindler*, *Läärä* and *Zenatti*.

31.    The Italian Government relies on the judgment in *Zenatti* to show that Law No 401/89 is compatible with the Community legislation in the sphere of freedom to provide services, and even in that of freedom of establishment. Both the matter considered by the Court in that case, namely administrative authorisation to pursue the activity of collecting and managing bets in Italy, and the question raised in the main proceedings, namely the existence of a criminal penalty prohibiting that activity where it is carried on by operators who are not part of the State monopoly on betting, pursue the same aim, which is to prohibit such activities and to reduce gaming opportunities in practice, other than in situations which are expressly provided for by law.

32.    The Belgian Government observes that a single market for gaming will only incite consumers to squander more and will have significant damaging effects for society. The level of protection introduced by Law No 401/89 and the restrictive authorisation scheme serve to ensure the attainment of objectives which are in the general interest, namely limiting and strictly controlling the supply of gaming and betting, is proportionate to those objectives and involves no discrimination on grounds of nationality.

33.    The Greek Government considers that the organisation of games of chance and bets on sporting events must remain within the control of the State and be operated by means of a monopoly. If it is engaged in by private entities, that will have direct consequences such as disturbance of the social order and incitement to commit offences, as well as exploitation of bettors and consumers in general.

34.    The Spanish Government submits that both the grant of special or exclusive rights under a strict authorisation or licensing regime and the prohibition on opening foreign branches to process bets in other Member States are compatible with the policy of limiting supply, provided that those measures are adopted with a view to reducing opportunities for gaming and stimulation of supply.

35.    The French Government maintains that the fact that in the main proceedings the collection of bets is effected at a distance by electronic means and the sporting events to which the bets relate take place exclusively in Italy − which was not the case in *Zenatti* − does not affect the Court's case-law under which national laws which limit the pursuit of activities relating to gaming or lotteries and cash machines are compatible with the principle of the freedom to provide services where they pursue an objective that is in the general interest, such as the prevention of fraud or the protection of bettors against themselves. Member States are therefore justified in regulating the activities of operators in the area of betting in non-discriminatory ways, since the degree and scope of the restrictions are within the discretion enjoyed by the national authorities. It is thus for the courts of the Member States to determine whether the national authorities have acted proportionately in their choice of means, having regard to the principle of freedom to provide services.

36.    As regards freedom of establishment, the French Government considers that the restrictions on the activities of the independent Italian companies in a contractual relationship with Stanley do not undermine Stanley's right to establish itself freely in Italy.

37.    The Luxembourg Government considers that the Italian legislation constitutes an obstacle to the pursuit of the activity of organising bets in Italy because it prohibits Stanley from carrying on its activities in Italy either directly, under the freedom to

provide cross-border services, or indirectly through the intermediary of Italian agencies linked by internet. It also constitutes a restriction on the freedom of establishment. However, those obstacles are justified in so far as they pursue objectives which are in the general interest, such as the need to channel and control the desire to engage in gaming, and are appropriate and proportionate for the attainment of those objectives inasmuch as they do not discriminate on grounds of nationality, because both Italian entities and those established abroad have to obtain the same permit from the Minister for Finance to be allowed to engage in the organisation, taking and collecting of bets in Italy.

38. The Portuguese Government notes that the main proceedings have serious implications as regards the maintenance not only in Italy but in all the Member States of a system for running lotteries by public monopoly and as regards the need to preserve a significant source of revenue for the States, which replaces the compulsory levying of taxes and serves to finance social, cultural and sporting policies. In the activity of gaming, the market economy and free competition operate a redistribution of sums levied in the context of that activity which is contrary to the social order, because they are likely to move from countries where overall involvement is low to countries where it is higher and the amount of winnings more attractive. Bettors in the small Member States would therefore be financing the social, cultural and sporting budgets of the large Member States and the reduction in revenue from gaming would force governments in the smaller Member States to finance public initiatives of a social nature and other State social, sporting and cultural activities by other means, which would mean an increase in taxes in those Member States and a reduction in taxes in the big States. Furthermore, dividing up the State betting, gaming and lotteries market between three or four large operators in the European Union would produce structural changes in distribution networks for gaming lawfully carried on by those States, destroying an enormous number of jobs and distorting unemployment levels in the various Member States.

39. The Finnish Government cites in particular the judgment in *Läärä*, in which the Court acknowledged that the need for and proportionality of provisions adopted by a Member State are to be assessed solely in the light of the objectives pursued by the national authorities in that State and the level of protection they seek to provide, so that it is for the national court to determine whether, in the light of the specific detailed rules for its application, national legislation enables the aims relied on to justify it to be attained and whether the restrictions are proportionate to those aims, having regard to the fact that the legislation must be applied to all operators alike, whether they are from Italy or another Member State.

40. The Swedish Government observes that the fact that restrictions on the free movement of services are introduced for tax purposes is not sufficient to support the conclusion that those restrictions are contrary to Community law, provided that they are proportionate and do not involve discrimination as between operators, a matter for the national court to determine. The amendments to the Italian legislation made by Law No 388/00 enable an entity which has been refused authorisation to collect bets in Italy to circumvent the legislation by carrying on its activity from another Member State and prohibit foreign entities which organise bets in their own country from pursuing their activities in Italy. As the Court held at paragraph 36 of the judgment in *Läärä* and at paragraph 34 of the judgment in *Zenatti*, the mere fact that a Member State has opted for a protection scheme which is not the same as that adopted in another Member State cannot influence the assessment of the need for and proportionality of the provisions adopted in that area.

41.     The Commission of the European Communities takes the view that the legislative amendments effected by Law No 388/00 merely make explicit what was already contained in Law No 401/89 and do not introduce a genuinely new category of offences. The public-order grounds for limiting the damaging effects of betting activities relating to football matches which are relied on to justify the fact that the national legislation reserves the right to collect those bets to certain organisations are the same regardless of the Member State in which those activities take place. The fact that the sporting events to which the bets related in the case of *Zenatti* took place abroad whereas in the main proceedings here the football matches take place in Italy is irrelevant. The Commission adds that Directive No 2000/31/EC of the European Parliament and of the Council of 8 June 2000 on certain legal aspects of information society services, in particular electronic commerce, in the Internal Market (Directive on electronic commerce) (OJ 2000 L 178, p. 1) does not apply to bets, so that the outcome should be no different to that in *Zenatti*.

42.     The Commission considers that the issue is not to be examined from the point of view of freedom of establishment because the agencies run by the defendants in the main proceedings are independent and act as collection centres for bets and as intermediaries in relations between their Italian customers and Stanley, and are not in any way subordinate to the latter. However, even if the right of establishment were to apply, the restrictions in the Italian legislation are justified on the same grounds of social policy as those accepted by the Court in *Schindler*, *Läärä* and *Zenatti* with regard to the restriction on the freedom to provide services.

43.     At the hearing the Commission informed the Court that it had initiated the procedure against the Italian Republic for failure to fulfil obligations in regard to the liberalisation of the horse-race betting sector managed by the UNIRE. As regards the lottery sector, which is liberalised, the Commission referred to the judgment in Case C-272/91 *Commission* v *Italy* [1994] ECR I-1409, in which the Court held that by restricting participation in an invitation to tender for the concession of a lottery computerisation system to bodies, companies, consortia and groupings the majority of whose capital, considered individually or in aggregate, was held by the public sector, the Italian Republic had failed to fulfil its obligations inter alia under the EC Treaty.

*The Court's reply*

44.     The first point to consider is whether legislation such as that at issue in the main proceedings (Law No 401/89) constitutes a restriction on the freedom of establishment.

45.     It must be remembered that restrictions on freedom of establishment for nationals of a Member State in the territory of another Member State, including restrictions on the setting-up of agencies, branches or subsidiaries, are prohibited by Article 43 EC.

46.     Where a company established in a Member State (such as Stanley) pursues the activity of collecting bets through the intermediary of an organisation of agencies established in another Member State (such as the defendants in the main proceedings), any restrictions on the activities of those agencies constitute obstacles to the freedom of establishment.

47.     Furthermore, in reply to the questions put to it by the Court at the hearing, the Italian Government acknowledged that the Italian legislation on invitations to tender for betting activities in Italy contains restrictions. According to that Government, the fact that no entity has been licensed for such activities apart from the monopoly-holder is explained by the fact that the way in which the Italian legislation

is conceived means that the licence can only be awarded to certain persons.

48.    In so far as the lack of foreign operators among licensees in the betting sector on sporting events in Italy is attributable to the fact that the Italian rules governing invitations to tender make it impossible in practice for capital companies quoted on the regulated markets of other Member States to obtain licences, those rules constitute prima facie a restriction on the freedom of establishment, even if that restriction is applicable to all capital companies which might be interested in such licences alike, regardless of whether they are established in Italy or in another Member State.

49.    It is therefore possible that the conditions imposed by the legislation for submitting invitations to tender for the award of these licences also constitute an obstacle to the freedom of establishment.

50.    The second point to consider is whether the Italian legislation in that respect constitutes a restriction on the freedom to provide services.

51.    Article 49 EC prohibits restrictions on freedom to provide services within the Community for nationals of Member States who are established in a Member State other than that of the person for whom the services are intended. Article 50 EC defines services as services which are normally provided for remuneration, in so far as they are not governed by the provisions relating to freedom of movement of goods, capital and persons.

52.    The Court has already held that the importation of lottery advertisements and tickets into a Member State with a view to the participation by residents of that State in a lottery operated in another Member State relates to a service (*Schindler*, paragraph 37). By analogy, the activity of enabling nationals of one Member State to engage in betting activities organised in another Member State, even if they concern sporting events taking place in the first Member State, relates to a service within the meaning of Article 50 EC.

53.    The Court has also held that, on a proper construction, Article 49 EC covers services which the provider offers by telephone to potential recipients established in other Member States and provides without moving from the Member State in which he is established (Case C-384/93 *Alpine Investments* [1995] ECR I-1141, paragraph 22).

54.    Transposing that interpretation to the issue in the main proceedings, it follows that Article 49 EC relates to the services which a provider such as Stanley established in a Member State, in this case the United Kingdom, offers via the internet – and so without moving – to recipients in another Member State, in this case Italy, with the result that any restriction of those activities constitutes a restriction on the freedom of such a provider to provide services.

55.    In addition, the freedom to provide services involves not only the freedom of the provider to offer and supply services to recipients in a Member State other than that in which the supplier is located but also the freedom to receive or to benefit as recipient from the services offered by a supplier established in another Member State without being hampered by restrictions (see, to that effect, Joined Cases 286/82 and 26/83 *Luisi and Carbone* [1984] ECR 377, paragraph 16, and Case C-294/97 *Eurowings Luftverkehr* [1999] ECR I-7447, paragraphs 33 and 34).

56.    In reply to the questions put by the Court at the hearing, the Italian Government confirmed that an individual in Italy who from his home connects by internet to a bookmaker established in another Member State using his credit card to pay is committing an offence under Article 4 of Law No 401/89.

57.    Such a prohibition, enforced by criminal penalties, on participating in betting games organised in Member States other than in the country where the bettor is established constitutes a restriction on the freedom to provide services.

58.    The same applies to a prohibition, also enforced by criminal penalties, for interme-
       diaries such as the defendants in the main proceedings on facilitating the provision
       of betting services on sporting events organised by a supplier such as Stanley, es-
       tablished in a Member State other than that in which the intermediaries pursue
       their activity, since the prohibition constitutes a restriction on the right of the
       bookmaker freely to provide services, even if the intermediaries are established in
       the same Member State as the recipients of the services.

59.    It must therefore be held that national rules such as the Italian legislation on bet-
       ting, in particular Article 4 of Law No 401/89, constitute a restriction on the free-
       dom of establishment and on the freedom to provide services.

60.    In those circumstances it is necessary to consider whether such restrictions are ac-
       ceptable as exceptional measures expressly provided for in Articles 45 and 46 EC,
       or justified, in accordance with the case-law of the Court, for reasons of overriding
       general interest.

61.    With regard to the arguments raised in particular by the Greek and Portuguese
       Governments to justify restrictions on games of chance and betting, suffice it to
       note that it is settled case-law that the diminution or reduction of tax revenue is not
       one of the grounds listed in Article 46 EC and does not constitute a matter of over-
       riding general interest which may be relied on to justify a restriction on the free-
       dom of establishment or the freedom to provide services (see, to that effect, Case
       C-264/96 *ICI* [1998] ECR I-4695, paragraph 28, and Case C-136/00 *Danner*
       [2002] ECR I-8147, paragraph 56).

62.    As stated in paragraph 36 of the judgment in *Zenatti*, the restrictions must in any
       event reflect a concern to bring about a genuine diminution of gambling opportu-
       nities, and the financing of social activities through a levy on the proceeds of
       authorised games must constitute only an incidental beneficial consequence and
       not the real justification for the restrictive policy adopted.

63.    On the other hand, as the governments which submitted observations and the
       Commission pointed out, the Court stated in *Schindler*, *Läärä* and *Zenatti* that
       moral, religious and cultural factors, and the morally and financially harmful con-
       sequences for the individual and society associated with gaming and betting, could
       serve to justify the existence on the part of the national authorities of a margin of
       appreciation sufficient to enable them to determine what consumer protection and
       the preservation of public order require.

64.    In any event, in order to be justified the restrictions on freedom of establishment
       and on freedom to provide services must satisfy the conditions laid down in the
       case-law of the Court (see, inter alia, Case C-19/92 *Kraus* [1993] ECR I-1663,
       paragraph 32, and Case C-55/94 *Gebhard* [1995] ECR I-4165, paragraph 37).

65.    According to those decisions, the restrictions must be justified by imperative re-
       quirements in the general interest, be suitable for achieving the objective which
       they pursue and not go beyond what is necessary in order to attain it. They must in
       any event be applied without discrimination.

66.    It is for the national court to decide whether in the main proceedings the restriction
       on the freedom of establishment and on the freedom to provide services instituted
       by Law No 401/89 satisfy those conditions. To that end, it will be for that court to
       take account of the issues set out in the following paragraphs.

67.    First of all, whilst in *Schindler*, *Läärä* and *Zenatti* the Court accepted that restric-
       tions on gaming activities may be justified by imperative requirements in the gen-
       eral interest, such as consumer protection and the prevention of both fraud and
       incitement to squander on gaming, restrictions based on such grounds and on the
       need to preserve public order must also be suitable for achieving those objectives,

inasmuch as they must serve to limit betting activities in a consistent and systematic manner.

68.    In that regard the national court, referring to the preparatory papers on Law No 388/00, has pointed out that the Italian State is pursuing a policy of substantially expanding betting and gaming at national level with a view to obtaining funds, while also protecting CONI licensees.

69.    In so far as the authorities of a Member State incite and encourage consumers to participate in lotteries, games of chance and betting to the financial benefit of the public purse, the authorities of that State cannot invoke public order concerns relating to the need to reduce opportunities for betting in order to justify measures such as those at issue in the main proceedings.

70.    Next, the restrictions imposed by the Italian rules in the field of invitations to tender must be applicable without distinction: they must apply in the same way and under the same conditions to operators established in Italy and to those from other Member States alike.

71.    It is for the national court to consider whether the manner in which the conditions for submitting invitations to tender for licences to organise bets on sporting events are laid down enables them in practice to be met more easily by Italian operators than by foreign operators. If so, those conditions do not satisfy the requirement of non-discrimination.

72.    Finally, the restrictions imposed by the Italian legislation must not go beyond what is necessary to attain the end in view. In that context the national court must consider whether the criminal penalty imposed on any person who from his home connects by internet to a bookmaker established in another Member State is not disproportionate in the light of the Court's case-law (see Case C-193/94 *Skanavi and Chryssanthakopoulos* [1996] ECR I-929, paragraphs 34 to 39, and Case C-459/99 *MRAX* [2002] ECR I-6591, paragraphs 89 to 91), especially where involvement in betting is encouraged in the context of games organised by licensed national bodies.

73.    The national court will also need to determine whether the imposition of restrictions, accompanied by criminal penalties of up to a year's imprisonment, on intermediaries who facilitate the provision of services by a bookmaker in a Member State other than that in which those services are offered by making an internet connection to that bookmaker available to bettors at their premises is a restriction that goes beyond what is necessary to combat fraud, especially where the supplier of the service is subject in his Member State of establishment to a regulation entailing controls and penalties, where the intermediaries are lawfully constituted, and where, before the statutory amendments effected by Law No 388/00, those intermediaries considered that they were permitted to transmit bets on foreign sporting events.

74.    As to the proportionality of the Italian legislation in regard to the freedom of establishment, even if the objective of the authorities of a Member State is to avoid the risk of gaming licensees being involved in criminal or fraudulent activities, to prevent capital companies quoted on regulated markets of other Member States from obtaining licences to organise sporting bets, especially where there are other means of checking the accounts and activities of such companies, may be considered to be a measure which goes beyond what is necessary to check fraud.

75.    It is for the national court to determine whether the national legislation, taking account of the detailed rules for its application, actually serves the aims which might justify it, and whether the restrictions it imposes are disproportionate in the light of those aims.

76.     In the light of all those considerations the reply to the question referred must be
        that national legislation which prohibits on pain of criminal penalties the pursuit of
        the activities of collecting, taking, booking and forwarding offers of bets, in par-
        ticular bets on sporting events, without a licence or authorisation from the Member
        State concerned constitutes a restriction on the freedom of establishment and the
        freedom to provide services provided for in Articles 43 and 49 EC respectively. It
        is for the national court to determine whether such legislation, taking account of
        the detailed rules for its application, actually serves the aims which might justify
        it, and whether the restrictions it imposes are disproportionate in the light of those
        aims.

**Costs**

77.     The costs incurred by the Italian, Belgian, Greek, Spanish, French, Luxembourg,
        Portuguese, Finnish and Swedish Governments and the Commission, which have
        submitted observations to the Court, are not recoverable. Since these proceedings
        are, for the parties to the main proceedings, a step in the action pending before the
        national court, the decision on costs is a matter for that court.

On those grounds,
*The Court,*
in answer to the question referred to it by the Tribunale di Ascoli Piceno by an order of 30
March 2001, hereby rules:
National legislation which prohibits on pain of criminal penalties the pursuit of the activities of collecting, taking, booking and forwarding offers of bets, in particular bets on
sporting events, without a licence or authorisation from the Member State concerned constitutes a restriction on the freedom of establishment and the freedom to provide services
provided for in Articles 43 and 49 EC respectively. It is for the national court to determine
whether such legislation, taking account of the detailed rules for its application, actually
serves the aims which might justify it, and whether the restrictions it imposes are disproportionate in the light of those objectives.

Delivered in open court in Luxembourg on 6 November 2003.
R. Grass: Registrar
V. Skouris: President

———

## 2.13.   OLYMPIC GAMES*

**\* 2.13.1.   RESOLUTION OF THE EUROPEAN PARLIAMENT ON THE OLYMPIC GAMES, 13 OCTOBER 1981**[955]

———

**\* 2.13.2.   RESOLUTION OF THE EUROPEAN PARLIAMENT ON THE OLYMPIC GAMES, 24 MAY 1984**[956]

———

**\* 2.13.3.   REPORT DRAWN UP ON BEHALF OF THE COMMITTEE ON YOUTH, CULTURE, EDUCATION, INFORMATION AND SPORT ON EUROPE'S CONTRIBUTION TO OLYMPIC YEAR 1992, 9 JUNE 1988**[957]

Rapporteur: Mr K. Gerontopoulos

———

**\* 2.13.4.   RESOLUTION OF THE EUROPEAN PARLIAMENT ON EUROPE'S CONTRIBUTION TO OLYMPIC YEAR 1992, 16 SEPTEMBER 1988**[958]

———

**\* 2.13.5.   COMMUNICATION FROM THE COMMISSION TO THE COUNCIL AND THE EUROPEAN PARLIAMENT – REPORT ON THE COMMUNITY'S INVOLVEMENT IN THE 1992 OLYMPIC GAMES, 18 DECEMBER 1992**[959]

———

**\* 2.13.6.   ANSWER ON BEHALF OF THE COMMISSION TO WRITTEN QUESTION E-26/98 BY URSULA STENZEL (PPE), 13 MARCH 1998**[960]

Subject: Support for the disabled

———

**\* 2.13.7.   ANSWER ON BEHALF OF THE COMMISSION TO WRITTEN QUESTION P-353/99 BY ALEXANDROS ALAVANOS (GUE/NGL), 11 MARCH 1999**[961]

Subject: Permanent venue for the Olympic Games in Greece

———

---

\*   The full texts of documents which are marked with an asterisk (\*) are not incorporated in the book itself, but are freely accessible on the website of the ASSER International Sports Law Centre, at <www.sportslaw.nl> – documentation.

[955]   OJ C 287, 9-11-1981, p. 72.
[956]   OJ C 172, 2-7-1984, p. 117.
[957]   Doc. A2-114/88.
[958]   OJ C 262, 10-10-1988, p. 208-210.
[959]   COM(92) 575 final.
[960]   Question of 29-1-1998; OJ C 223, 17-7-1998, p. 88.
[961]   Question of 12-2-1999; OJ C 289, 11-10-1999, p. 145.

**\* 2.13.8.  ANSWER ON BEHALF OF THE COMMISSION TO WRITTEN QUESTION E-2394/00 BY LUCKAS VANDER TAELEN (VERTS/ALE), 26 SEPTEMBER 2000**[962]

Subject: Environmental impact of the 2004 Olympic Games infrastructure development in Athens

———

**\* 2.13.9.  ANSWER ON BEHALF OF THE COMMISSION TO WRITTEN QUESTION P-1335/01 BY LUCKAS VANDER TAELEN (VERTS/ALE), 13 JUNE 2001**[963]

Subject: Environmental impact of the 2004 Olympic Games infrastructure on Schinias

———

**\* 2.13.10.  ANSWER ON BEHALF OF THE COMMISSION TO WRITTEN QUESTION E-1073/01 BY STAVROS XARCHAKOS (PPE-DE) AND ANTONIOS TRAKATELLIS (PPE-DE), 22 JUNE 2001**[964]

Subject: Construction of Olympic Games facilities at Marathon – Schinias

———

**\* 2.13.11.  RESOLUTION OF THE EUROPEAN PARLIAMENT ON BEIJING'S BID TO HOST THE 2008 OLYMPIC GAMES, 5 JULY 2001**[965]

———

**\* 2.13.12.  ANSWER ON BEHALF OF THE COMMISSION TO WRITTEN QUESTION E-1809/01 BY MIHAIL PAPAYANNAKIS (GUE/NGL), 24 JULY 2001**[966]

Subject: Olympic boxing arena

———

**\* 2.13.13.  COUNCIL REGULATION (EC) NO 1295/2003, RELATING TO MEASURES ENVISAGED TO FACILITATE THE PROCEDURES FOR APPLYING FOR AND ISSUING VISAS FOR MEMBERS OF THE OLYMPIC FAMILY TAKING PART IN THE 2004 OLYMPIC OR PARALYMPIC GAMES IN ATHENS, 15 JULY 2003**[967]

———

**\* 2.13.14.  ANSWER ON BEHALF OF THE COMMISSION TO WRITTEN QUESTION P-2273/03 BY PIETRO-PAOLO MENNEA (PPE-DE), 6 AUGUST 2003**[968]

Subject: 2006 Turin Winter Olympics – ice rink – asbestos

———

[962]  Question of 13-7-2001; OJ C 136 E, 8-5-2000, p. 29.
[963]  Question of 26-4-2001; OJ C 318 E, 13-11-2001, p. 237.
[964]  Question of 5-4-2001; OJ C 340 E, 4-12-2001, p. 163.
[965]  OJ C 65 E, 14-3-2002, p. 365.
[966]  Question of 19-6-2001; OJ C 364 E, 20-12-2001, p. 211.
[967]  OJ L 183 , 22-7-2003, p. 1-5.
[968]  Question of 1-7-2003; question not yet published in the OJ.

# 2.14.   STATE AID*

## 2.14.1.   COMMISSION DECISION, 11 JUNE 1991[969]

Requiring France to suspend the implementation of the aid described below in favour of the Pari Mutuel Urbain (PMU), introduced in breach of Article 93(3) of the EEC Treaty
(Only the French text is authentic)
(92/35/EEC)

*The Commission of the European Communities,*

Having regard to the Treaty establishing the European Economic Community, and in particular Article 93(2) and (3) thereof,
Whereas:
(1)   By letter dated 27 July 1989, the Commission requested the French authorities to comment on alleged State aids granted in favour of the Pari Mutuel Urbain (PMU) and to provide all relevant information to enable the Commission to assess the measures pursuant to Articles 92 and 93 of the EEC Treaty and reminded the French authorities of their obligation pursuant to Article 93(3) of the EEC Treaty to inform the Commission in sufficient time to enable it to submit its comments, of any plans to grant or alter aid.
(2)   By letter dated 23 August 1989, the French authorities requested the Commission to extend the deadline for response by one month to which the Commission agreed by telex of 29 August 1989.
(3)   The French authorities replied by letter dated 11 October 1989 and a meeting to discuss the measures took place between the Commission and the French authorities on 6 November 1990.
(4)   By letter dated 11 January 1991, the Commission informed the French authorities that it had decided to initiate the Article 92 (3) procedure in respect of seven aid measures granted in favour of the PMU. The Commission requested the French Government to comment on the measures within a period of two months, and also requested all necessary information to enable the Commission to calculate the precise amount of these aids and the periods during which they had been provided.
(5)   The French authorities replied by letter dated 12 April 1991. The reply did not contain all the necessary information to establish the precise amount of aid and the period during which it was being granted, as well as sufficient information to enable the Commission to access the compatibility of the measures with the internal market.
(6)   On the basis of the information currently at its disposal, the Commission understands that three of the seven aid measures were only granted in the past but that the other four have an ongoing character. Of these four, the exemption from corporation tax has no financial effect at the present time because of the deficit nature of the financial position of the PMU and its members.
(7)   The Commission understands the three remaining ongoing aid measures to be as follows:

---

*   The full texts of documents which are marked with an asterisk (*) are not incorporated in the book itself, but are freely accessible on the website of the ASSER International Sports Law Centre, at <www.sportslaw.nl> – documentation.
    [969]   OJ L 14, 21-1-1992, p. 35.

### Treasury facilities

The financial resources of the PMU have been swelled to the detriment of the State by allowing it to defer on a temporary basis the payment to the State of certain charges which are levied on horserace betting. This enables the PMU to earn considerable amounts of interest during the additional period that these monies transit in the treasury resources of the PMU. The treasury facilities date from 1980 and an extension of the period of deferment was granted in 1982.

### Exemption from the one-month delay rule for VAT payment

This exemption allows the PMU to deduct immediately the VAT it has paid to suppliers compared to the normal situation under which deduction can only be made one month later. It thus enables the PMU to earn extra interest at the expense of the State.

### Exemption from the social housing levy

The PMU is an economic interest grouping composed of 10 members, all of which are racecourse undertakings. Racecourse undertakings are assimilated to professional agricultural bodies which are exempted from the payment by the employer of a charge on the employee payroll in respect of the social housing levy. As such the PMU is exempted from the payment of the social housing levy on its payroll, although it is not engaged in an agricultural activity.

(8)     The Community market for horserace betting and related services

The provision of trade statistics for service activities is generally difficult. For the service activity concerned by this case, namely horserace betting and related services, it is particularly difficult. Nevertheless the information provided below is sufficient in the Commission's opinion to demonstrate that there is trade and competition in horserace betting and related services, that the PMU and a limited number of competitors take part in this trade, that trade is increasing and that bookkeeping or tote betting cannot be considered as separate, unrelated markets whose development and functioning is independent each of the other. By these means the Commission considers that, notwithstanding the difficulty of obtaining precise trade statistics, the circumstances necessary to motivate its decision as laid down by the Court in its ruling in joined cases 296/82 and 318/82 (Leeuwarder)[970], have been satisfied.

### Market composition, competition and trade

Horserace betting is allowed and operated in all Member States except Luxembourg. Even in Luxembourg permission was granted to a bookmaking multinational to open an 'agence hippique', although the venture did not subsequently materialize.

Betting can take two forms: bookmaking, where bets are placed against the bookmaker who thus can incur a financial risk dependent upon the precise bets placed and horserace result, or under a tote or totalizator arrangement, where bets are pooled and winnings paid out as a given percentage of the betting monies received with no financial risk to the operator of the betting system. A skilled bookmaker by adjusting the 'odds he provides on bets can much reduce and even eliminate totally his inherent financial risk.

The tote is the more common form of betting and is allowed and operated in the

---

[970] [1985] ECR, p. 809.

eleven Member States mentioned. Bookmaking is additionally allowed and operated in Belgium, Germany, Ireland, Italy and the United Kingdom.

The total estimated size of horserace betting in 1989 was ECU 14 570 million. The
two largest national markets are the United Kingdom and France with totals of
ECU 8 042 million and ECU 4 456 million respectively. The third largest national
market is Germany (ECU 516 million) followed by Italy (ECU 444 million), Ireland (ECU 407 million) and Belgium (ECU 381 million). In the United Kingdom
bookmaking is the dominant form representing over 96% of all betting. In France
only the tote form is allowed, so that by definition tote betting represents 100% of
all betting.

*Ladbroke*

In the United Kingdom the major market players are Ladbroke, Brent-Walker and
Corals with market shares of approximately 25, 20 and 12% respectively. All are
organized as corporate bodies paying the normal company taxes in addition to the
special separate taxes on betting which is a common feature in the Member States.
In terms of trade, Ladbroke is the most active. It has offices in Ireland, Belgium,
Germany, Italy, Spain and the Netherlands.

In Ireland Ladbroke has 50 betting shops and in Belgium it has over 900 outlets
and is the market leader with an estimated market share of over 41%. In second
place is the PMU belge with a market share of approximately 16%, an organization separate from the PMU (France), but operating on the same principle of tote
betting. In third place is Tiercé franco-belge which is owned by Corals, with a
13% market share. It is clear that both Ladbroke and Corals trade in the Belgian
market.

In the Netherlands, Ladbroke currently operates the State monopoly on tote betting which was awarded after adjudication to Ladbroke by the Dutch authorities in
1986. At the end of 1990, Ladbroke sought to renegotiate the contract with the
competent Dutch authorities, the NDR. During the course of these negotiations a
number of Ladbroke units were visited by representatives of the NDR accompanied by representatives of the PMU. On 28 March 1991 Ladbroke gave six months
notice of its intention to terminale the contract. Subsequently both Ladbroke and
the PMU as well as certain other companies were asked to make proposals for the
provision of a computer/totalizator system. On 25 May 1991 the competent Dutch
authorities (NDR) published a press statement that they would purchase an American totalizator system. It is clear that Ladbroke is currently trading in the Dutch
market and that the PMU and Ladbroke have been in competition in that market.

*PMU*

In France, the PMU holds an effective monopoly established by law for all off-
course horserace betting. Off-course betting represents about 85% of the French
market with the remaining 15% represented by on-course betting, mainly organized by the PMU but also by individual racecourse undertakings taking bets, at
races on their own courses.

Although it is only in recent years that the PMU has actively sought to increase its
role an trade in markets for betting and related services outside France, under the
Law of 23 December 1964 the PMU was already the sole body authorized in
France for the taking of bets from abroad on French races and the placing of
French bets on foreign races.

The PMU, either directly or indirectly through commercial companies such as the
Pari Mutuel International (PMI) in which the PMU has a majority holding of

77,5% of the share capital, is actively engaged in exporting betting and related services in competitive, commercial markets in other Member States and outside the Community. Indeed, this objective is clearly stated in Article 3 of the PMI's Articles of Association.

During the 1980s, within the protected domestic market, the PMU has developed, with assistance provided by the State, a sophisticated computer system and terminals for the taking of on- and off-course bets.

At the same time it has developed the necessary skills and expertise for the television recording of French horseraces and the live transmission to betting shops and other outlets by means of satellite links and terminal equipment. Background information on horses' form and previous race results are mixed into the pictures. This is essential information in order to remain competitive for the custom of the modern punter. Ladbroke in conjunction with the other major bookmaking firms in the United Kingdom have developed similar systems for transmitting pictures and commentary of UK races.

The PMU is involved in the Belgian market in different ways.

Through its subsidiary, the PMI, the PMU established a subsidiary in Belgium on 26 May 1989 called the Pari Mutuel Belge, abbreviated to PMB. The PMB includes under its objective the organization and operation in Belgium of all forms of bets authorized by law. The PMB is constituted by a share capital which is 99,98% owned by the PMI.

It is involved in a proposal organized by a joint venture called the Groupement Hippodromes Wallons to build two new racecourses in the Wallon region of Belgium. The PMU is to provide the necessary technology and technical expertise for the taking of off-course bets, on both Belgian and French races. In connection with the provision of these services the PMU will transmit to Belgium its pictures and commentaries on French racing. According to the proposal this will involve an investment by the PMU of several hundred million Belgian francs.

As from 20 March 1991 the PMU outlets in Paris and the north-east of France can and have taken bets on Belgian races on the first and third Wednesdays of each month. An agreement introducing this arrangement was signed between the two organizations on 25 May 1990 and its implementation was made legally possible in France by Decree 91-118 of 31 January 1991.

Under the arrangements, the monies placed by punters in France are combined with the monies from Belgian punters to form a single pool of bets for the purposes of the totalizator. Winnings are paid out to punters after a retention charge by both PMU and the PMU belge. For the first three meetings the volume of the French bets exceeds those placed in Belgium, with the French bets representing an average of between 54 and 60% of the total volume of bets placed. Based on the first three meetings, the average volume of bets placed by French punters amounts to some FF 2,3 million per meeting, equivalent to approximately BF 14 million. This corresponds to an annual turnover of BF 336 million.

Whilst the figure is small compared to the total turnover for betting in Belgium of ECU 381 million, i.e. it represents around only 2%, it is based on an extrapolation of only the first three meetings. It is quite possible that as the French public become more aware of the attractions of betting on Belgian races and as the PMU extends the operation to other parts of France, these figures will increase.

More important than demonstrating the existence of interstate trade by the PMU is the fact that this is an example of the type of cooperation agreements that the PMU wishes to establish with similar organizations in Community Member States. More particularly, the PMU wishes to establish the facility to take bets in Member States outside France on horseraces held in France.

This will place the PMU in direct competition with Ladbroke. For example, 95% of Ladbroke Belgium's turnover represents the taking of bets on the results of horseraces held in France. Similarly in Germany about 40% of the bets placed relate to the results of French horseraces. The PMU wishes to capture a part of these markets and use the proceeds to support French horseracing activity.

Another example of the PMU's competition with Ladbroke can be found in the complaint that it lodged before the Belgian courts concerning the taking of bets on French races in Belgium. In that complaint, the PMU said that it was losing business to Ladbroke from punters, both in Belgium as well as in France living in the border region, who placed bets by telephone. No figures are available to the Commission to indicate the volume of telephone bets. The Commission understands that the volume of telephone bets. The Commission understands that the volume of of telephone bets, combined with the use of credit cards, which can be placed either in the same country as the caller or on a cross-border basis, is generally increasing. Certainly the trade exists, through apparently it only represents a small part of overall activity.

Another example of 'tele-betting' is the Minitel service. Under this service a punter can receive information for horserace betting through a normal television set that might be placed in his own home. A bet can be placed either through the television or by telephone. In France Minitel betting is relatively common. The Minitel service provided by the PMU in France is now being advertised and sold into Belgium. The objective must be to encourage Belgian punters to place bets on French races with the PMU rather than with other operators in the Belgian market. This brings the PMU into competition with other operators in the Belgian market and clearly, trade is again involved.

A last example of the competition between the PMU and Ladbroke in Belgium and of the exports of the PMU into Belgium is the complaint by Ladbroke on the refusal of the PMU to provide Ladbroke with television pictures and commentary on French racing for use in connection with offcourse betting. The PMU has stated its intention to supply pictures and commentary within the context of its joint venture with the Groupement Hippodromes Wallons. The Commission is investigating this complaint.

In Germany, through the PMI and its German agent, Deutscher Sportverlag, the PMU sells live television pictures and commentary on French races to German bookmakers. Based on the price list for the services charged and the number of subscribers, the Commission estimates that the PMU is realizing a turnover of approximately ECU 1 million in Germany.

There is also a complaint currently being examined by the Commission concerning the PMU's refusal to sell such coverage to the Ladbroke office in Germany. Within this complaint the Commission has become aware of the Hellmund judgment of the District Court of Saarbrücken. This case concerned the refusal of the PMU and the Deutscher Sportverlag to sell live television coverage of French races and to sell the necessary decoding equipment to receive the television pictures and sound. The German court considered that the television coverage was indispensable for the conduct of the bookmaker's business and ordered the PMU and the Deutscher Sportverlag to sell the television pictures and sound to the German bookmaker.

The Commission attaches particular importance to the judgment by the District

Court of Saarbrücken, since it not only made clear the existence of the PMU's trading activities in Germany, but also the vital importance of live TV pictures and commentary to a bookmaker's business.

In Switzerland with effect from 14 April 1991 the PMU is operating 50 outlets for the taking of bets on French horseracing. The contract to provide this service was obtained by the French PMU initially in direct competition with Ladbroke. Notwithstanding the fact that Switzerland is not a member of the Community, in the light of the Court's ruling in the Tubemeuse case (Case 142/87)[971], the Commission considers this relevant information, since the PMU's operations in Switzerland can strengthen its position in intra-Community markets and trade. It also demonstrates the general competition between the two companies for the provision of betting and related services and is another example of the export activities of the PMU.

The export activities and aims of the PMU are no secret. They have been confirmed by the French authorities, and the President of the PMU at a public press conference on 30 January 1991 made clear the policy objectives of the PMU to export its technical expertise in the area of the computerized collection and processing of off-course betting and thus to participate in international competition.

The conclusion that the Commission must draw from this lengthy list of observations is that the PMU participates either directly or indirectly in intra-Community trade, that the PMU is pursuing an active policy of export expansion and that it is one of the major market players. The information also shows that there is trade and competition in the provision of betting services in the Community, that competition in the international market is intensifying as the main market participants seek to consolidate or expand their market shares and as the barriers between national markets fall away as a result of advances in modern telecommunications and the processing power of computers.

The Commission also notes the privileged position of the PMU in this competition in that it has effectively a legally-protected monopoly in the second largest national market in the Community.

(9)     The Commission notes that the test established by the Court in the Philip Morris case (Case 730/79)[972] for establishing a distortion of competition and an effect on intra-Community trade is stated as follows

'When state financial aid strengthens the position of an undertaking compared with the other undertakings competing in intra-Community trade, the latter must be regarded as affected by that aid'.

The foregoing paragraphs have demonstrated the award of state aid and the existence of other undertakings competing in intra-Community trade. The Commission must therefore consider that the conditions for the application of Article 92(1) are fulfilled.

If this is the case then the conditions for prior notification under Article 93(3) must also certainly be applicable, because the scope of application of Article 93 (3) must be greater than that of Article 92(1). If this were not so, the Commission's capacity to assess the compatibility of aids would be much diminished and impaires. The Court has always upheld this approach.

In consequence the aids were introduced in breach of Article 93(3), in that they were not notified in advance to the Commission at the planning stage and must therefore be deemed to be unlawful.

---

[971]   [1990] ECR I, p. 959.
[972]   [1980] ECR, p. 267.

(10) In view of the above, and as the Court has acknowledge in its judgment of 14 February 1990 in Case C 301/87 *(Boussac)*[973], where an infringement of Article 93(3) has been committed, the Commission is entitled to take a provisional decision requiring France to suspend immediately the payment of aid to firms and to provide all the documents, information and particulars necessary for examining the compatibility of the aids with the common market.

Furthermore, pursuant to existing case-law, should France fail to comply with this Decision by not suspending the implementation of the scheme and the payment of the aid, the Commission could, while pursuing its examination of the substance of the case, refer the matter to the Court of justice direct in order to have such infringement established, in accordance with the second subparagraph of Article 93(2).

(11) Given the direct 'effect of Article 93(3)[974] and the clear and unconditional requirement that payment of the aid be suspended immediately, this Decision must apply in full in the French legal system. The Commission would point out in this respect that, as made clear in the case law of the Court of justice, not only national courts but also national administrative authorities, including local or regional authorities, have to apply Community law rather than national law where there is a conflict between the two[975].

(12) The Commission has also already initiated the procedure provided for in Article 93(2) in respect of the aid since it takes the view that, on the basis of the information available to it, the aid is not compatible with the common market pursuant to Article 92(1) and cannot at this stage qualify for the exemptions provided for in Article 92(2) and (3).

The Commission would point out that, should a negative final decision be taken subsequently on the aid, the Commission may require any unlawful aid that has been paid in breach of the procedural rules provided for in Article 93(3) to be repaid[976]. The abolition of the aid would involve repayment, in accordance with the procedures and provisions, of French law, in particular those relating to interest on arrears on debts due to the State, with interest starting to run on the date on which the unlawful aid was granted. This measure is necessary in order to restore the *status quo*[977] by removing the financial benefits which the firms receiving the unlawful aid have improperly enjoyed since the date on which the aid was paid.

(13) By letter dated 24 April 1991, the Commission requested France to confirm that the three ongoing aid measures had been suspended in accordance with the obligation imposed pursuant to Article 93(2) of the EEC Treaty and to confirm their position within five working days. By fax dated 30 April 1991, the French authorities informed the Commission that they had not suspended the grant of the aid,

Has adopted this decision:

---

[973] [1990] ECR I, p. 307.

[974] See judgments in Case 77/72 *Capolongo* [1973] ECR, p. 611, Case 120/73 *Lorenz* [1973] ECR 1471 and Case 78/76 *Steinicke* [1977] ECR, p. 595.

[975] See judgments in Case 166/77 *Simmenthal* [1978] ECR, p. 629 and Case 103/88 *Costanzo* [1989] ECR, p. 1839.

[976] See judgments in Case 70/72 *Kohlegesetz* [1973] ECR, p. 813 and Case 310/85 *Deufil* [1987] ECR, p. 901. See also Commission communication, OJ C 318, 24-11-1983, p. 3.

[977] See judgment in Case C-142/87 *Tubemeuse* cited above.

Article 1

France shall suspend forthwith the payment of the following aid:

–    treasury facilities enabling the PMU to defer on a temporary basis the payment of taxes levied on the horseracing bets administered by the PMU,

–    exemption from the one-month delay rule for VAT payment,

–    exemption from the payment of the social housing levy in respect of the PMU's employees,

introduced in breach of Article 93(3), and shall communicate to the Commission, within 15 days, the measures which it has taken to comply with this Decision.

Article 2

France shall, within 30 days of notification of this Decision, provide all appropriate information allowing substantive assessment of the aid referred to in Article 1.

Article 3

This Decision is addressed to the French Republic.

Done at Brussels, 11 June 1991.

For the Commission
Leon Brittan
Vice-President

———

**\* 2.14.2.  ANSWER ON BEHALF OF THE COMMISSION TO WRITTEN QUESTION E-512/96 BY GLYN FORD (PSE), 12 APRIL 1996**[978]

Subject: Football Trust grants

———

**2.14.3.  EUROPEAN COURT OF JUSTICE, JUDGMENT OF THE COURT OF FIRST INSTANCE (SECOND CHAMBER, EXTENDED COMPOSITION), KNEISSL DACHSTEIN SPORTARTIKEL AG V COMMISSION OF THE EUROPEAN COMMUNITIES, CASE T-110/97, 6 OCTOBER 1999**[979]

Decision authorising State aid for restructuring Starting point for the time-limit for bringing an action against a third party Requirements for the compatibility of the aid.

Subject matter: Competition; State Aids

**Keywords:**

1.    *Actions for annulment – Time-limits – Point from which time starts to run – Date of publication – Date on which the measure came to the applicant's knowledge – Subsidiary criterion*
     *(EC Treaty, Art. 93(2) (now Art. 88(2) EC) and Art. 173, fifth para. (now, after amendment, Art. 230, fifth para., EC)*

---

[978]  Question of 11-3-1996; OJ C 217, 26-7-1996, p. 60.
[979]  ECR 1999, p. II-2881.

2.    *State aid – Prohibited – Derogations – Aid that may be considered compatible with the common market – Discretion of the Commission Judicial review – Limits – Legality to be assessed on the basis of the elements of fact and of law existing at the time when the decision was adopted*
*(EC Treaty, Art. 92(3) (now, after amendment, Art. 87(3) EC) and Art. 173 (now, after amendment, Art. 230 EC)*

3.    *State aid – Prohibited – Derogations – Aid that may be considered compatible with the common market – Conditions – No regional aim – Irrelevant*
*(EC Treaty, Art. 92(3)(c) (now, after amendment, Art. 87(3)(c) EC)*

4.    *State aid – Prohibited – Derogations – Aid that may be considered compatible with the common market – Aid for restructuring an undertaking in difficulty – Period prescribed by the guidelines for drawing up a restructuring programma – Not binding*

5.    *State aid – Prohibited – Derogations – Aid that may be considered compatible with the common market – Aid for restructuring an undertaking in difficulty – Conditions – Prospect of viability*

6.    *State aid – Prohibited – Derogations – Aid that may be considered compatible with the common market – Aid for restructuring an undertaking in difficulty – Conditions – Aid entailing capacity reductions – Whether permissible*

7.    *Actions for annulment – Pleas in law – Pleas that can be raised when contesting a Commission decision authorising State aid – Pleas not raised during the investigation procedure – Whether admissible*
*(EC Treaty, Art. 93(2) (now Art. 88(2) EC) and Art. 173 (now, after amendment, Art. 230 EC)*

## Summary

1.    *According to the actual wording of the fifth paragraph of Article 173 of the EC Treaty (now, after amendment, Article 230 EC), the criterion of the day on which a measure came to the knowledge of an applicant, as the starting point for the period prescribed for instituting proceedings, is subsidiary to the criteria of publication or notification of the measure.*
*Since the Commission has committed itself to publishing in the Official Journal of the European Communities the complete text of decisions granting conditional authorisation for State aid adopted at the end of the procedure provided for by Article 93(2) of the Treaty (now Article 88(2) EC), time for the purposes of bringing proceedings starts to run as from the date of publication of the decision.*

2.    *The Commission enjoys a broad discretion in the application of Article 92(3) of the Treaty (now, after amendment, Article 87(3) EC). Since that discretion involves complex economic and social appraisals, the Court must, in reviewing a decision adopted in such a context, confine its review to determining whether the Commission complied with the rules governing procedure and the statement of reasons, whether the facts on which the contested finding was based are accurately stated and whether there has been any manifest error of assessment or any misuse of powers. In particular, it is not for the Court to substitute its own economic assessment for that of the Commission.*
*In the context of an action for annulment under Article 173 of the Treaty (now, after amendment, Article 230 EC), the legality of a Community measure falls to be assessed on the basis of the elements of fact and of law existing at the time when the measure was adopted. In particular, the complex assessments made by the Commission must be examined solely on the basis of the information available to it at the time when those assessments were made.*

3.      The fact that disjunctive 'or' is used in Article 92(3)(c) of the Treaty makes it clear that aid to facilitate the development either of certain activities or of certain economic areas may be regarded as compatible with the common market. It follows that the grant of authorisation for aid is not necessarily subordinate to the provision's regional aim.

4.      The fact that the period of six months – indicated in the Community Guidelines on State aid for rescuing and restructuring undertakings in difficulty as the period within which a restructuring plan must be drawn up – has been exceeded does not in itself justify a refusal to authorise aid. That time-limit is not of a binding nature; rather it is the period considered in the Guidelines to be needed, from the time when rescue aid is paid, in order to determine the measures necessary to restore the recipient undertaking to financial health.

5.      In order to satisfy the viability test required by the Community Guidelines on State aid for rescuing and restructuring undertakings in difficulty, a restructuring plan must enable the undertaking concerned to cover all its costs, including depreciation and financial charges, and to obtain a minimum return on capital such that, after completing its restructuring, the undertaking will not require further injections of State support and will be able to compete in the marketplace on its own merits alone.

6.      In the context of aid for restructuring an undertaking in difficulty, reductions in capacity provided for in a restructuring plan cannot be equated with reductions in jobs, since the relationship between the number of employees and production capacity depends on a number of factors, in particular the products manufactured and the technology used.

7.      An applicant may not rely on factual arguments which are unknown to the Commission and which it has not notified to the latter during an investigation of State aid pursuant to Article 93(2) of the Treaty (now Article 88(2) EC). On the other hand, there is nothing to prevent the interested party from raising against the final decision a plea in law not raised at the stage of the administrative procedure.
        The investigation procedure under Article 93(2) of the Treaty cannot be classed as a pre-litigation procedure against a final decision; its purpose is, on the contrary, to enable the Commission to be fully informed about all aspects of the case before it takes its decision.

## Parties

*In Case T-110/97,*
Kneissl Dachstein Sportartikel AG, a company incorporated under
Austrian law, established at Molln, Austria, represented by Georg
Diwok, of the Vienna Bar, applicant,
v
Commission of the European Communities, represented by Paul F. Nemitz and Frank Paul, of its Legal Service, acting as Agents, with an address for service in Luxembourg at the Chambers of Carlos Gómez de la Cruz, of its Legal Service, Wagner Centre, Kirchberg, defendant,
supported by
Republic of Austria, represented by Christine Stix-Hackl, acting as Agent, assisted by Michael Krassnigg, of the Vienna Bar, with an address for service in Luxembourg at the Austrian Embassy, 3 Rue des Bains,
and by
HTM Sport- und Freizeitgeräte AG, a company incorporated under Austrian law, estab-

lished at Schwechat, Austria, represented by Wolfgang Knapp, Avocat, Brussels and Rechtsanwalt, Frankfurt am Main, and by Till Müller-Ibold, Rechtsanwalt, Frankfurt am Main, with an address for service in Luxembourg at the Chambers of Arendt & Medernach, 8-10 Rue Mathias Hardt,
interveners,

APPLICATION for annulment of Commission Decision 97/81/EC of 30 July 1996 concerning aid granted by the Austrian Government to Head Tyrolia Mares in the form of capital injections (OJ 1997 L 25, p. 26),

THE COURT OF FIRST INSTANCE OF THE EUROPEAN COMMUNITIES (Second Chamber, Extended Composition), composed of: A. Potocki, President, K. Lenaerts, C.W. Bellamy, J. Azizi and A.W.H. Meij, Judges,
Registrar: J. Palacio González, Administrator,
having regard to the written procedure and further to the hearing on 24 March 1999, gives the following Judgment

**Grounds**

Legal background to the dispute
1.      Article 92(3) of the EC Treaty (now, after amendment, Article 87 EC) provides:
     'The following may be considered to be compatible with the common market:
     ...

     (c)    aid to facilitate the development of certain economic activities or of certain economic areas, where such aid does not adversely affect trading conditions to an extent contrary to the common interest.
2.      For the purposes of application of that provision, the Commission has drawn up Community Guidelines on State Aid for Rescuing and Restructuring Firms in Difficulty (94/C 368/05) (OJ 1994 C 368, p. 12, hereinafter 'the Guidelines').

**Facts**
3.      The Austrian company Head Tyrolia Mares (hereinafter 'HTM') comprises undertakings producing and marketing winter sports, tennis, diving and golf articles. In 1994, HTM had a turnover of about ATS 5 200 million, or about ECU 390 million, 45% of which was achieved in Western Europe. In June 1995, the group employed about 2 700 people. HTM's production centres are in the United States of America and in Europe (Germany, Austria, Italy, Czech Republic and Estonia). The Austrian locations are at Kennelbach (536 employees), Hörbranz (279 employees), Schwechat (395 employees) and Neusiedl (80 employees).
4.      In 1993, the public holding company Austria Tabakwerke ('AT') acquired the controlling stake in HTM for a price of USD 20 million (about ECU 16 million). AT immediately recapitalised HTM with USD 100 million (about ECU 80 million). The same year HTM obtained from AT a non-preferential shareholder loan to replace its own capital, amounting to DEM 85.25 million (about ECU 45 million)..
5.      In spite of the announced rationalisation, diversification and new investment programmes, HTM incurred heavy losses in 1993 and in 1994, mainly due to the severe decline in the world ski market since the end of the 1980s and highly negative performance in branches such as sportswear and golf equipment. High financial charges and some restructuring and extraordinary items further depressed the financial performance.

6.      After being approached by AT in January 1995 to draw up a plan to turn HTM
        round, the merchant bank SBC Warburg (hereinafter 'Warburg') was instructed, in
        March 1995, to draw up a plan for HTM's privatisation and in May 1995 Warburg
        started a procedure to select potential buyers.

7.      In order to avoid HTM's becoming insolvent, AT was forced, in April 1995, to
        inject ATS 400 million (about ECU 30 million) into the group and to convert the
        shareholder loan of about ECU 45 million granted in 1993 into new equity.

8.      In July 1995 a restructuring plan was drawn up for HTM to enable it to return to
        viability by 1997. To finance this plan and to ward off the possibility of an insol-
        vency procedure, the Austrian Ministry of Finance, in August 1995, approved
        AT's decision to inject further capital of up to ATS 1 500 million (about ECU 112
        million) into HTM, to be paid in tranches between 1995 and 1997.

9.      On 8 August 1995, the Austrian authorities informed the Commission of AT's in-
        tentions. On 1 September 1995, the Commission submitted a request for informa-
        tion to the Austrian Government, to which it responded on 21 September 1995.

10.     On 30 September 1995, HTM received payment of a tranche of ATS 373 million
        (about ECU 28 million) from AT. During September 1995, owing to the deteriora-
        tion in HTM's situation, the restructuring was abandoned in favour of immediate
        sale. On Warburg's advice, AT's board of directors decided to accept the prelimi-
        nary offer of a group of international investors led by Johan Eliasch (hereinafter
        'the Eliasch Group') and to negotiate an immediate privatisation of the entire
        HTM Group.

11.     The agreement concluded with the Eliasch Group stipulated a sales price of ATS
        10 million (about ECU 0.7 million) and a capital grant to HTM of ATS 1 190 mil-
        lion (about ECU 88 million) by AT, to be paid in several instalments. The Eliasch
        Group committed itself to injecting a further ATS 300 million (about ECU 22 mil-
        lion), of which ATS 25 million (about ECU 2 million) was to be paid as soon as
        AT's measures were approved by the Commission.

12.     AT was to receive 15% of any capital gain that the Eliasch Group might realise on
        the total or partial sale of HTM to third parties, by means of a sale of shares or a
        public offering. Finally, the Eliasch Group was obliged to maintain HTM's activi-
        ties in Austria for at least three years and to maintain employment at the
        Schwechat plant at 50% of the then current level and at 80% of the current level at
        the Hörbranz and Kennelbach plants.

13.     By letter of 10 October 1995, Kneissl Dachstein Sportartikel AG (hereinafter
        'Kneissl Dachstein'), an Austrian company producing winter sports articles (skis,
        bindings and ski boots), asked the Commission to investigate the financial aid
        granted by AT to HTM.

14.     In the last week of November 1995, the Commission was informed that the banks
        had agreed to contribute, after the change of ownership, to the restructuring of
        HTM by means of a debt write-off of ATS 630 million (about ECU 47 million)
        and by debt rescheduling.

15.     By decision of 20 December 1995, amended on 13 March 1996, the Commission
        initiated, pursuant to Article 93(2) of the EC Treaty (now Article 88(2) EC), the
        procedure for examining the compatibility with the common market, as restructur-
        ing aid for HTM, of capital injections totalling ATS 400 million (about ECU 30
        million) made in April 1995 (see paragraph 7 above) and ATS 1 190 million
        (about ECU 88 million) (see paragraph 11 above) already made or planned by AT
        in accordance with the sales agreement with the Eliasch Group.

16.     The Commission also considered that, after its conversion into a loan repayable at
        the market rate, the total amount of ATS 1 273 million (about ECU 95 million), of

which 773 million (about ECU 58 million) (see paragraphs 7 and 10 above) had already been paid to HTM, could be authorised as rescue aid.

17. For that purpose, the Commission published a communication addressed to the Member States and other interested parties, pursuant to Article 93(2) of the Treaty, concerning aid granted by the Federal Austrian Government in the form of capital injections to the company HTM (OJ 1996 C 124, p. 5).

18. At the beginning of February 1996, the Commission was informed that the conclusion of the share purchase agreement had actually taken place by the transfer of the share ownership in HTM from AT to the Eliasch Group.

19. In the examination procedure, Kneissl Dachstein submitted its observations by a document dated 30 April 1996.

20. By Decision 97/81/EC of 30 iuly 1996 concerning aid granted by the Austrian Goverment to HTM in the form of capital injections (OJ 1997 L 25, p. 26, hereinafter 'the Decision'), the Commission concluded that the capital injections of ATS 400 million (about ECU 30 million) (see paragraph 7 above) and ATS 1 190 million (about ECU 88 million) (see paragraph 11 above), or ECU 118 million, constituted State aid but, subject to certain conditions, that aid could be declared compatible with the common market as restructuring aid.

21. In the Decision the Commission observes that the alpine ski market is saturated, that it has substantial overcapacity and that a concentration of a small number of large manufacturers is to be expected. In the Commission's opinion, the same trend is underway on the market for ski-bindings and ski-boots.

22. According to the Decision, the restructuring plan envisages a return by HTM to its core activities (tennis, skis, bindings, boots and diving equipment) with the main emphasis, in the short term, on the Head brand, on marketing initiatives, on innovative and high-technology products and on the US market. Once restructuring is completed, long-term objectives include extending activities by entering new product markets (by licensing arrangements) and new geographical areas. The restructuring plan envisages operational breakeven in 1996, return to profitability by 1997 and, as an ultimate objective, HTM's flotation on the stockmarket in 1998 or 1999.

23. The restructuring plan has the following points:
  – adapting production capacity to the decline in the markets for winter-sports equipment (skis, boots and bindings) and tennis racquets. This includes use of outsourcing and the transfer of labour-intensive manufacturing processes to East European locations to bring down manufacturing costs;
  – phasing-out of unprofitable product lines and reduction of stock-keeping;
  – rationalisation and reduction of fixed costs of the sales and administrative organisation, including the merger of legal entities;
  – development and installation of a logistics system to facilitate centralised control of inventory management, inventory and shipping as well as modernisation of internal management systems and manufacturing processes.

24. The restructuring plan envisages in particular annual capacity reductions of 39% for skis, 59% for ski-bindings, 9% for ski-boots and 38% for tennis racquets. Slimming-down of staffing levels is planned in these various sectors of activity.

25. The direct cost of the restructuring measures to be carried out from 1995 to 1997 is forecast to be USD 159 million (about ECU 127 million). The main cost items are the closure of the golf business, the closure of the sportswear business, production capacity reductions and the reorganisation of the facilities at Kennelbach, Schwechat and Hörbranz. In addition, there will be severance payments for the personnel made redundant.

26.    The recapitalisation plan, which is part of the restructuring programma, provides, in addition to the capital injections by AT and debt forgiveness and interest waiver by the banks of ATS 630 million (about ECU 47 million) (see paragraph 14 above), for two capital injections from the Eliasch Group of about ECU 2 million and about ECU 20 million respectively (see paragraph 11 above) by 1998 and an international public offer which should earn USD 60 million (about ECU 48 million). Since the projected equity ratio of HTM in 1998 (7%) was regarded as being too low to compete successfully with its international competitors, the final equity contribution of the Eliasch Group and the public offer are considered vital to HTM's capital structure by further reducing the company's debts.

27.    Article 1 of the operative part of the Decision provides that the grants from Austria Tabakwerke AG to Head Tyrolia Mares in the form of capital injections amounting to ATS 1 590 million (about ECU 118 million) (see paragraph 20 above) constitute State aid within the meaning of Article 92(1) of the Treaty. That aid is considered compatible with the common market pursuant to Article 92(3)(c) as it facilitates the development of certain economic activities without adversely affecting trading conditions to an extent contrary to the common interest.

28.    Payment of that sum of ATS 1 590 million, which includes the sum of ATS 1 273 million (about ECU 95 million) already approved by the Commission as rescue aid (see paragraph 16 above), was effected in the following way: ATS 400 million (about ECU 30 million) was paid in April 1995 (see paragraph 7 above) and ATS 373 million (about ECU 28 million) on 30 September 1995 (see paragraph 10 above). Finally, provision is made for the payment of an amount of ATS 27 million (about ECU 2 million) and the staggering of payment of the balance from 31 December 1995 to 31 March 1998.

29.    In Article 2, the Decision states that, in order to ensure the compatibility of the aid with the common market, the Commission requires the Austrian Government to undertake to guarantee that the following conditions are met:

–    the restructuring plan is to be carried out as submitted to the Commission. By the end of August and the end of February each year until 1999, HTM has to deliver a report on the progress of the restructuring, showing the economic development and financial results of the company and their compliance with the restructuring plan. It must also submit the annual accounts of the companies in the group for the years 1995 to 1999 by the end of June of the following year at the latest;

–    the capacity reductions provided for in the restructuring plan are to be carried out on an irreversible basis;

–    the capital injection into HTM by the Eliasch Group of ATS 25 million (about ECU 2 million) (see paragraph 11 above) is to be effected within one month of the date of the Decision;

–    the capital injection into HTM by the Eliasch Group of ATS 275 million (about ECU 20 million) (see paragraph 11 above) is to be effected by 31 December 1998;

–    an additional contribution of fresh equity capital of at least ATS 600 million (about ECU 48 million) (see paragraph 26 above) by way of an international public offer of HTM on the capital market or by means having the same effect is to be completed by the end of 1999;

–    past losses of ATS 1 590 million (about ECU 118 million) may not be used to reduce taxable profits.

30.    Finally, Article 3 provides that the Decision is addressed to the Republic of Austria.

31.     The Decision was notified to the Austrian Government on 21 August 1996 and
        published on 28 January 1997.

**Procedure before the Court**

32.     By application lodged on 14 April 1997, Kneissl Dachstein brought an action for
        annulment of the Decision.

33.     By orders of 26 November 1997, the Republic of Austria and HTM were granted
        leave to intervene in the proceedings in support of the Commission.

34.     Upon hearing the report of the Judge-Rapporteur, the Court (Second Chamber, Ex-
        tended Composition) decided to open the oral procedure without any preparatory
        inquiry. However, it asked the parties to answer certain questions in writing.

35.     The parties present oral argument in reply to the Court's questions at the hearing
        on 24 march 1999.

**Forms of order sought by the parties**

36.     Kneissl Dachstein claims that the Court should:
        –    Declare the Decision null and void, or alternatively,
        –    Annul the Decision ex nunc;
        –    order the Commission to pay the costs;
        –    Order the interveners to bear their own costs.

37.     The Commission contends that the Court should:
        –    Dismiss the action;
        –    order the applicant to pay the costs.

38.     The Republic of Austria submits that the Court should: – Dismiss the action;
        –    order the applicant to pay the costs.

39.     HTM submits that the Court should:
        –    Declare the action inadmissible, or
        –    Dismiss the action as manifestly unfounded;
        –    order the applicant to pay HTM's costs.

**Admissibility**

40.     The Commission, supported in substance by the Republic of Austria and HTM,
        expresses doubts about the admissibility of the action, which, having been brought
        on 14 April 1997, it considers to be out of time, as the Decision was adopted on 30
        iuly 1996. Since the Decision was neither published nor formally notified to the
        applicant, the period for commencing proceedings began to run, as regards the ap-
        plicant, on the day on which it learnt of the existence of the Decision. Since it was
        reported in the press at the time of its adoption, the applicant should then have
        asked the Commission, within a reasonable period of time, to communicate the
        Decision to it. Since the applicant did not submit such a request until 18 Septem-
        ber 1996, that lapse of time cannot be regarded as reasonable.

41.     The Court merely observes that, according to the actual wording of the fifth para-
        graph of Article 173 of the EC Treaty (now, after amendment, Article 230 EC),
        the criterion of the day on which a measure came to the knowledge of an appli-
        cant, as the starting point for the period prescribed for instituting proceedings, is
        subsidiary to the criteria of publication or notification of the measure (judgment of
        the Court of Justice in Case C-122/95 Germany v Council [1998] ECR I-973,
        paragraph 35).

42.     Moreover, the Commission has committed itself to publishing in the L Series of
        the Official Journal of the European Communities the complete text of decisions
        granting conditional authorisation for State aid adopted, as in this case, at the end

of the procedure provided for by Article 93(2) of the Treaty [see Droit de la concurrence dans les Communautés Européennes, Volume II A, 'Règles applicables aux aides d'état', 1995, p. 43, paragraph 53, and p. 55, paragraph 90(d)].

43.    Since the Decision was published in official Journal L 25 of 28 January 1997, it is that latter date which started the period running as against the applicant.

44.    The argument that the action is inadmissible must therefore be dismissed.

**Substance**
*Scope of the Court's review of the compatibility of the restructuring aid in question*

45.    Acts of the Community institutions are presumed to be valid (see, to this effect, the judgment of the Court of Justice in Case 15/85 Consorzio Cooperative d'Abruzzo v Commission [1987] ECR 1005, paragraph 10). It is for parties seeking their annulment to rebut that presumption by producing convincing evidence to cast in doubt the assessments made by the defendant institution.

46.    It is also established in case-law that the Commission enjoys a broad discretion in the application of Article 92(3) of the Treaty. Since that discretion involves complex economic and social appraisals, the Court must, in reviewing a decision adopted in such a context, confine its review to determining whether the Commission complied with the rules governing procedure and the statement of reasons, whether the facts on which the contested finding was based are accurately stated and whether there has been any manifest error of assessment or any misuse of powers. In particular, it is not for the Court to substitute its own economic assessment for that of the author of the decision (judgment in Joined Cases T-371/94 and T-394/94 British Airways and Others v Commission [1988] ECR II-2405, paragraph 79).

47.    Furthermore, in the context of an action for annulment under Article 173 of the Treaty, the legality of a Community measure falls to be assessed on the basis of the elements of fact and of law existing at the time when the measure was adopted. In particular, the complex assessments made by the Commission must be examined solely on the basis of the information available to it at the time when those assessments were made (see, to this effect, British Airways and others v Commission, cited above, paragraph 81).

48.    The pleas and arguments raised by the applicant must therefore be examined in the light of the principles mentioned above.

*Objection of illegality raised against the Guidelines*

49.    Kneissl Dachstein objects that the Guidelines are unlawful in that they authorise aid not meeting the conditions laid down by Article 92(3)(c) of the Treaty. In basing its decision on the Guidelines, the Commission thus contravened that provision.

50.    The Commission and the interveners observe that the Guidelines flesh out the application of the derogations from incompatibility of aid in accordance with the aforementioned provision, and that they have never been held to be illegal by the Community judicature.

51.    The Court would reiterate here that the Guidelines indicate the course of conduct which the Commission intends to follow. They cannot therefore derogate from the provisions of Article 92 of the Treaty (see, to this effect, the judgment of the Court of Justice in Case 310/85 Deufil v Commission [1987] ECR 901, paragraph 22).

52.    Since the applicant has not shown to what extent the Commission based its decision on elements of the guidelines contrary to Article 92(3)(c) of the Treaty, its objection of illegality must be dismissed, without prejudice to the examination of its pleas of annulment in the light of the aforementioned provision.

*The first plea concerning the premiss relating to HTM's disappearance from the market*

53. Kneissl Dachstein challenges the premiss on which the Decision is based to the effect that HTM's disappearance would have harmful effects on the structure of the market by causing even tighter oligopolies to emerge. Even if the restructuring aid in question (hereinafter 'the Aid') had been prohibited, HTM would very probably have been taken over in its entirety by an investor from another sector.

54. The Commission observes that a take-over of HTM after bankruptcy would have been undertaken by a competitor and not by investors from outside the sector and would not therefore have altered the repercussions, found in the Decision, on the structure of the market.

55. According to HTM, there is no indication that, even in the event of bankruptcy and without AT's contributions, it would have been possible, or even probable, that its business would have been taken over by undertakings from outside the sector.

56. The Court finds that it follows from its very exposition that this plea is based on the unproven premiss that, if the Aid had not been authorised, HTM would not have disappeared from the market as a competitor distinct from other economic operators but would in any event have been bought by undertakings from outside the winter sports equipment sector. Quite on the contrary, the observations submitted by Kneissl Dachstein during the examination procedure show that it was keenly interested in buying HTM.

57. It is not therefore established that the Commission committed a manifest error in considering that, if the Aid had not been authorised, HTM might have disappeared from the market as an independent manufacturer.

58. In those circumstances, the plea must be dismissed.

*The second plea: infringement of the general conditions governing the authorisation of aid laid down by Article 92(3)(c) of the Treaty*

59. Kneissl Dachstein argues that the Aid does not meet the conditions laid down by Article 92(3)(c) of the Treaty. It does not promote an economic activity but only a single undertaking. The Aid does not facilitate the development of a certain area because HTM's production sites are dispersed. Finally, the Aid has no Community interest since it shifts to other undertakings and other territories the problems affecting the production and sale of winter sports articles.

60. The Court finds first of all that, since the Commission was justified in finding that HTM's survival will contribute to the maintenance of a competitive market structure, the Aid cannot be regarded as favouring a single undertaking.

61. Secondly, it is clear from the disjunctive nature of the conjunction 'or' used in Article 92(3)(c) of the Treaty that aid to facilitate development either of certain activities or of certain economic areas may be regarded as compatible with the common market. It follows that the grant of authorisation for aid is not necessarily subordinate to the provision's regional aim.

62. Finally, the complaint that the Aid presents no Community interest overlaps with the other complaints contesting the validity of its authorisation.

63. Subject to the answers to be given to those other complaints on substantive issues, this plea must therefore be dismissed.

*The third plea: absence of any link between certain capital injections and the restructuring plan*

64. Kneissl Dachstein criticises the Commission for not taking the view that the additional contribution of approximately ECU 28 million made on 30 September 1995 (see paragraph 10 above), the first tranche of approximately ECU 30 million hav-

ing already been paid in April 1995 (see paragraph 7 above), had the sole purpose of warding off the risk of HTM's insolvency and was not linked to the restructuring plan. The Aid is therefore prohibited pro tanto.

65.  According to the Commission, supported in substance by the interveners, the contributions in question could be considered to be rescue aid during the period needed to elaborate the restructuring plan and the new aid element involved in their subsequent characterisation as capital injections was authorised on the basis of the restructuring plan.

66.  The Court finds that it is clear from the exposition of the facts (see paragraphs 15 and 16 above) that the contested contributions were originally approved as rescue aid, without prejudice to the'ir subsequent authorisation as restructuring aid. It was under this new characterisation that those funds were authorised at the end of the examination procedure, on condition that the restructuring plan approved by the Decision was put into effect.

67.  It follows that the contested capital injections are to be regarded as tied into HTM's restructuring plan, irrespective of their initial approval as rescue aid, the legality of which is not the subject of this action.

68.  The plea must therefore be dismissed.

*The fourth plea: the reasonable time-limit laid down for the elaboration of the restructuring plan was exceeded*

69.  Kneissl Dachstein contends that the period of six months to which the Guidelines limit the period for drawing up a restructuring plan was clearly exceeded and that this in itself was sufficient to justify refusal to authorise the Aid.

70.  The Commission, supported in substance by the intervening parties, observes that the period of six months indicated in the Guidelines concerns the authorisation of rescue aid and not restructuring aid. moreover, whilst a restructuring plan may normally be drawn up within a period of six months, everything depends on the circumstances of the case. In the present case, complex assessments had to be carried out.

71.  The Court holds that the six-month time-limit referred to by the applicant is not of a binding nature and does not relate to the stage at which a restructuring plan as such is elaborated. That time-limit is in fact the period considered in the Guidelines to be necessary, from the time when rescue aid is paid, to determine the measures necessary to restore the recipient undertaking to financial health.

72.  Moreover, from the facts of the case set out above it does not appear that the period taken to elaborate the restructuring plan conceived by the Eliasch Group and approved by the Decision was excessive, taking into account the complexity of the case.

73.  The plea must therefore be dismissed.

*The fifth plea: the restructuring plan was inadequate*

74.  Kneissl Dachstein alleges first of all that the price paid by the Eliasch Group for HTM, which was much lower than the amount of the Aid, does not, on its own, allow the minimum return on capital required by the second paragraph of point 3.2.2 A of the Guidelines. Even in the event of sale by the Eliasch Group of its shares in HTM, the sum to be paid to AT does not represent an appropriate return.

75.  The Commission and the intervening parties state in reply that the minimum return on capital relates not to the aid granted and to the aid donors but to future economic development and to the financial results of the recipient undertaking.

76.  The Court observes that, as is explained in the second paragraph of point 3.3.2 A

of the Guidelines, the restructuring plan must, in order to satisfy the viability test, enable the undertaking to cover all its costs, including depreciation and financial charges, and to obtain a minimum return on capital such that, after completing its restructuring, the undertaking will not require further injections of State support and will be able to compete in the marketplace on its own merits alone.

77. If AT's capital injections are not to lose their characterisation as State aid, the condition of a minimum return on capital must relate not to a fair return that AT is supposed to derive from its contributions but to the restoration of the recipient undertaking's competitiveness on the basis of the approved restructuring plan.

78. The applicant's argument is based on a false premiss and must therefore be dismissed.

79. Kneissl Dachstein observes, secondly, that the Commission wrongly considered that HTM would recover its viability in the long term. The simple fact of making an operating profit, as contended by HTM, does not amount to the 'viability threshold, mentioned in the Decision. The fact alone that the recovery measures consisted only partially of internal measures already made it quite clear at the date of the Decision that, according to the market data, those measures were based on exaggeratedly optimistic assumptions about the development of the market. Although the Commission did determine in part the nature of the measures which ATM had to take, it did not estimate their specific cost. The plan did not make any differentiation between tennis articles, which the Commission in its Decision considered necessary, however, in order to enable manufacturers to maintain or increase their prices. Finally, the plan does not explain how the financing envisaged through a stockmarket flotation will operate, which the Commission described, however, as decisive.

80. The Commission and the intervening parties observe that Kneissl Dachstein has not advanced any argument to show that, after its restructuring, HTM's viability would not be guaranteed.

81. HTM states that in 1996 it was again able to make an operating profit owing to the restructuring plan put into effect.

82. The Court finds that the applicant's argument consists essentially of mere conjecture and contains nothing to show that the Commission made a manifest error in concluding that HTM would recover its long-term viability on the basis of the restructuring plan approved by the Decision.

83. In particular, the applicant has not sought to establish in what way the assumptions made by the Commission are exaggeratedly optimistic, when provision has been made for HTM to abandon unprofitable product lines, to concentrate on its core activities, to reduce administrative, manufacturing and distribution costs and to slim down its workforce.

84. It does not appear that the Commission was bound, contrary to what Kneissl Dachstein maintains, to estimate the specific cost of each of the measures to be undertaken by HTM. Besides the fact that a precise evaluation of the various items of expenditure would in any event have been uncertain owing to the prospective nature of the measures envisaged, the Commission could, in the exercise of its broad discretion, properly confine itself to an overall assessment.

85. The applicant cannot rely on the lack of measures for differentiating tennis articles allowing prices to be maintained or increased. The Decision provides generally for HTM to concentrate on innovative and high-technology products and, in particular, on the use of the latest technology for the manufacture of tennis racquets and indicates that this should, in particular, allow higher sales prices to be obtained.

86. Finally, the Commission cannot be criticised for not explaining in the Decision the

details of the financing envisaged through a stockmarket flotation planned for the end of 1999, which will occur a considerable length of time after the adoption of the Decision. It does not appear that the Commission was manifestly wrong to confine itself to laying down the principle of a fresh capital injection and stipulating that it be effected by the end of 1999 whilst leaving it to the undertaking to choose the time and means best suited to its situation as it might evolve (international issue or similar measures).

87.    It follows from the foregoing that this plea must be dismissed in its entirety.

*The sixth plea: the reduction of capacity imposed on HTM is insufficient*

88.    Kneissl Dachstein contends that the employment guarantees stipulated by the HTM sale agreement, covering a period of three years from the conclusion of that agreement, for 50% or even 80% of the staff at one of the production sites, demonstrate that the capacity reductions required by the Decision on the market in winter sports articles are insufficient, having regard in particular to the contraction in the ski and ski-boots markets which occurred between 1992 and 1997.

89.    The obligation to maintain such a level of employment prevents, for example, production capacity from being closed down for good. Furthermore, the 87% reduction in its Community ski-boot production capacity cited by HTM in its statement in intervention is in fact the result of its shifting that production to Estonia.

90.    Finally, it was clear from an article in the Salzburger Nachrichten of 2 February 1998 that HTM could have increased both sales of skis and the profit from ski sales on a world market still in decline.

91.    The Commission, supported in substance by the intervening parties, observes that the applicant has not explained to what extent it committed a manifest error in assessing the facts or a misuse of power in requiring, in the second indent of Article 2 of the Decision, the capacity reductions provided for in the restructuring plan to be carried out on an irreversible basis.

92.    The Austrian Republic explains that the employment guarantee clause concerns only three of the group's plants and considers the reduction of 20% to 50% of the numbers employed at the three Austrian plants to be objectively significant. Furthermore, the number of HTM's employees was reduced from 2 7.00 to 2 000.

93.    The Court considers that, as the Commission has rightly pointed out, the reductions in capacity cannot be equated with the reduction in jobs, since the relationship between the number of employees and production capacity depends on a number of factors, in particular the products manufactured and the technology used. The employment guarantees, limited to three of the group's sites and to three years, did not prevent the closure of the assembly plant at Neusiedl. The shifting to Estonia of ski-boot manufacture using inexpensive labour is mainly intended to reduce manufacturing costs but does not in any way exclude capacity reductions.

94.    The applicant has adduced no evidence to show that the capacity reductions required of HTM on the ski, ski-bindings and ski-boot markets, which, however, represented approximately 45% of HTM's turnover in 1994, were manifestly insufficient.

95.    In particular, the statistics on the contraction of the ski and ski-boot markets which the applicant cited at the hearing relate to a period beginning in 1992 and ending only in 1997. To that extent, they have no evidential value, since the Decision provides that the capacity reductions are essentially to be made in the very first year of the restructuring.

96.    In order to dismiss the contention concerning the increase in HTM's ski sales, it is sufficient to point out that it relates to the 1997 financial year, after the date of

adoption of the Decision, and that it shows that 425 000 pairs of skis were sold, which represented a sales volume appreciably below the 596 000 pairs sold in 1995.

97.    Finally, in the exercise of its broad discretion, the Commission could properly consider that even more severe capacity reductions would have compromised the return to viability of HTM, whose existence was considered necessary to prevent the emergence of a stronger oligopolistic structure on the markets in question. In this regard, account has to be taken of the closure of the golf business and the closure of the sportswear business as envisaged in the restructuring plan.

98.    In those circumstances, the plea must be dismissed.

*The seventh plea: the Aid was disproportionate*
99.    This plea may be broken down into five parts.

*The first part of the plea*
100.    Kneissl Dachstein complains that the Decision did not take into consideration the capital injection of approximately ECU 80 million and the shareholder loan of approximately ECU 45 million granted by AT to HTM in 1993 (see paragraph 4 above). – Admissibility

101.    The Commission, supported in substance by HTM, relies on the principle that the submissions in the administrative procedure and in the application should be strictly the same and objects that this first argument is not therefore admissible on the ground that the applicant did not raise it in the procedure in which the Aid was examined.

102.    The Court considers that it would not be admissible for the applicant to rely on factual arguments which were unknown to the Commission and which it had not notified to the latter during the examination procedure (see, to this effect, the judgment of the Court of Justice in Joined Cases C-278/92, C-279/92 and C-280/92 Spain v Commission [1994] ECR I-4103, paragraph 31, and the judgment of the Court of First Instance in Case T-37/97 Forges de Clabecq v Commission [1999] ECR II-859, paragraph 93). on the other hand, nothing prevents the interested party from raising against the final decision a legal plea not raised at the stage of the administrative procedure (see, to this effect, Forges de Clabecq v Commission, cited above, paragraph 93).

103.    The Commission's argument is based on the incorrect premiss that the examination procedure under Article 93(2) of the Treaty amounts to a prelitigation procedure against a final decision whereas its purpose is, on the contrary, to enable the Commission to be fully informed about all aspects of the case before it takes its decision (see, to this effect, British Airways and Others v Commission, cited above, paragraph 58).

104.    However, as is clear from an annex to the observations which it submitted in response to HTM's submissions in intervention, Kneissl Dachstein did in fact mention during the examination procedure that in 1993 AT had provided HTM with a capital contribution of approximately ECU 80 million (see paragraph 4 above) to reduce HTM's debt.

105.    The Commission's objection of inadmissibility to the first part of the plea must therefore be dismissed.

*Substance*
106.    Kneissl Dachstein criticises the Commission for not having addressed, in its examination of the proportionality of the Aid, the aid of approximately ECU 80 mil-

lion and approximately ECU 45 million granted by AT to HTM in 1993 (see paragraph 4 above). Although Article 92 of the Treaty was not applicable before the Republic of Austria acceded to the European Communities on 1 January 1995, the Commission took no account of the prohibition of aid laid down by Article VI of the General Agreement on Tariffs and Trade (hereinafter 'GATT) and by Article 23(1)(iii) of the Free Trade Agreement between the European Economic Communities and the Republic of Austria (OJ 1972 L 300, p. 2, hereinafter 'the Free Trade Agreement'). In those circumstances, the total amount of the aid paid to HTM is disproportionate.

107. Alternatively, the applicant submits that, if the Commission had assessed all the payments, it would have reached the conclusion that the aid granted constituted existing aid, within the meaning of Article 93 of the Treaty. The sole fact that the examination procedure provided for by that provision was not respected is in itself sufficient to warrant annulment of the Decision.

108. The Commission and the intervening parties argue in substance that neither Article 92 of the Treaty, which was not applicable at the relevant time, nor the provisions of the GATT or of the Free Trade Agreement obliged the Commission to undertake the applicable procedures in relation to the 1993 payments or to take those payments into consideration. Even supposing that the 1993 payments could be characterised as State aid, they had to be considered to be existing aid and as such were not covered by the procedure provided for in Article 93(2) of the Treaty but by the procedure laid down by paragraph (1) of that provision.

109. The Court observes that, at the time when the Commission opened the examination procedure in question (see paragraph 15 above), Article VI of the GATT and Article 23(1)(iii) of the Free Trade Agreement could no longer constitute the legal basis for assessing the compatibility with the common market of the capital grants made by AT to HTM. Moreover, Article VI of the GATT, relating to anti-dumping and compensating duties, was irrelevant and Article 23(1)(iii) of the Free Trade Agreement merely gave the contracting parties the power to intervene against public aid. The Commission could not therefore have disregarded those two provisions.

110. Furthermore, the applicant cannot validly argue that all the aid paid in 1993 and 1995 constitutes existing aid when AT's capital grants to HTM were not made on the basis of generally applicable provisions of domestic law.

111. Nor is it relevant for the applicant to claim that the amount of the Aid is disproportionate on the basis that the Commission failed to take into consideration the 1993 payments. In assessing proportionality, the Commission could only compare the capital injections made with the restructuring plan of which they constituted the necessary quid pro quo and support.

112. Moreover, the time which elapsed between the payments in 1993 and the capital injections granted from April 1995 (see paragraph 7 above) and authorised by the Decision meant that it would not have been appropriate to include them in the same single assessment of HTM's financial situation in the context of the procedure for the examination of the Aid.

113. The first part of the plea must therefore be dismissed.

*The second part of the plea*

114. Kneissl Dachstein contends that, in spite of the 1993 capital injections, HTM was able to carry over losses, the fiscal use of which gave it a supplementary advantage. However, according to point 3.2.2 C of the Guidelines, any tax credits attaching to the losses must be extinguished where aid is used to write off debt resulting from past losses.

115. The Commission replies that a carry-over of losses is unlawful only if it is attributable to aid. In the present case, it is excluded from the outset that the two injections in question constitute aid and, even if they did constitute aid, there were no grounds for taking this into account.

116. The Court may confine itself to the observation that, in reply to one of its questions, HTM stated, without being challenged on this point, that, owing to the insufficiency of its taxable profits, it was not able, in any event, to make use of the carry-over of losses from the 1993 accounting year to the years 1994 to 1997.

117. It follows that the second part of the plea must be dismissed as factually groundless.

*The third part of the plea*

118. Kneissl Dachstein maintains that unlawful aid was provided through the fact that in April 1995 AT allowed HTM to convert the shareholder loan of about ECU 45 million (see paragraphs 4 and 7 above), granted in 1993, into equity. On its view of HTM's balance sheets, that operation was a loan which, despite its non-preferential character, constituted a debt owed by the borrower. Except in the event of insolvency, which did not arise in this case, the creditor has the right to repayment of his debt. The extinction of HTM's debt occurred only at the time of the conversion of the loan into equity. The extinction of a repayment obligation, even a conditional one, led to a transfer of resources from AT to HTM.

119. The Court considers that, even if the shareholder loan had to be classified as State aid, it was from the outset, irrespective of how it was described in HTM's accounts, a non-preferential loan to replace its equity capital. Owing to HTM's serious over-indebtedness at the time when the loan was formally converted into equity, repayment of the loan was de facto excluded and the loan could not therefore be regarded as a debt of HTM vis-à-vis AT, the remission of which would have constituted an additional advantage in reality.

120. It follows that, in so far as the conversion of the loan into equity involved AT's waiver of repayment of an irrecoverable debt, it did not in itself procure HTM any economic advantage in the form of a transfer of public resources at AT's expense.

121. Consequently, the Commission did not commit any error in law in not treating that loan conversion as State aid for the purposes of assessing the proportionality of the Aid.

122. The third part of the plea must therefore be dismissed.

*The fourth part of the plea*

123. Kneissl Dachstein maintains that de facto the Aid finances the entire restructuring programma, with HTM's buyer only having to repay old debts. A private shareholder acting as vendor would have required the Eliasch Group to take on much greater risks and to make a much higher payment. In its view, the Commission has not established any relationship between the amount paid by the investors, the costs of the restructuring and, finally, the amount of the Aid.

124. The Commission, supported in substance by the intervening parties, considers that the Aid was set at the amount necessary to restore HTM's economic viability, that it was accompanied by a large reduction in HTM's capacity and that HTM had to make other considerable efforts to achieve financial health.

125. The Court observes that the direct restructuring costs evaluated by the Commission at approximately ECU 127 million in section 8.2 of the Decision represent only a part of the total amount of the costs of restructuring HTM envisaged in point 8.3 of the Decision.

126.    In response to questions from the Court, the Commission explained that, in addition to the direct restructuring costs, there are other expense items related to HTM,s financial restructuring, such as investments to achieve rationalisation, the repayment and the restructuring of debt.

127.    The Commission also explained that the total amount of the restructuring costs is financed from four different sources: Eliasch's capital injection of approximately ECU 22 million (see paragraph 11 above), the partial write-off by the banks of their debts and interest amounting to ECU 47 million (see paragraph 14 above), the Aid (approximately ECU 118 million) (see paragraph 20 above) and, finally, HTM's contribution from its own resources, amounting to 36% of the entire restructuring costs.

128.    It follows that the total amount of the restructuring costs is in fact more than ECU 290 million and that the amount of the Aid is less than half of that sum.

129.    To that extent, the fourth part of the plea must be dismissed for being based on incorrect factual premisses.

*The fifth part of the plea*

130.    Kneissl Dachstein contends that, if it had not been coupled with job guarantees, the sale of HTM would have yielded a higher sale price, which would have been the aim of any private investor. To that extent, the Decision is vitiated by a misuse of power in that it authorises aid which, for reasons of employment policy, exceeds the amount strictly necessary. The question which should have been asked was whether the closure or shutdown of the entire undertaking would not have been the least expensive option and therefore the proper step.

131.    The Court observes first of all that the behaviour of a private investor is the test for assessing the existence of State aid but that it is irrelevant in assessing its proportionality.

132.    Secondly, as is clear from the text of the Decision, the job guarantee clause concerns only three of HTM's plants, is limited in time and provides for staff reductions of 20 to 50% in those plants.

*In any case, the applicant overlooks the fact that HTM would have had to pay additional severance pay if the staff reductions had been more substantial.*

133.    Thirdly, the Court has already found that the Commission did not commit any manifest error in considering that HTM's disappearance would have been harmful as regards the maintenance of a competitive market structure. To that extent, the question whether the closure or shutdown of all of HTM's plants would have been the least costly step is irrelevant.

134.    It follows that the fifth part of the plea must be dismissed.

135.    In those circumstances, the entire plea must be dismissed.

136.    It follows from all the foregoing that the action must be dismissed in its entirety.

**Decision on costs**

*Costs*

137.    Under Article 87(2) of the Rules of Procedure, the unsuccessful party is to be ordered to pay the costs if they have been applied for in the successful party's pleadings. Since the applicant has been unsuccessful, it must be ordered to pay the costs incurred by the Commission and by the intervener HTM in accordance with their applications.

138.    Under the first paragraph of Article 87(4) of the Rules of Procedure, Member

States which intervene in the proceedings are to bear their own costs. The Republic of Austria must therefore bear its own costs.

*Operative part*
on those grounds,

*The Court of First Instance*
(Second Chamber, Extended Composition) hereby:
1.   Dismisses the application;
2.   Orders the applicant to pay the costs incurred by the Commission and by the intervener Head Tyrolia Mares;
3.   orders the Republic of Austria to bear its own costs.

————

## 2.14.4.   COMMISSION DECISION, 12 JANUARY 2001

Brüssel, den 12.01.2001
SG(2001) D/ 285046

Seiner Exzellenz
Herrn Joschka Fischer
Bundesminister des Auswärtigen
Werderscher Markt 1
D-11017 Berlin

Betrifft:   Staatliche Beihilfe Nr. N 258/00
            Deutschland Freizeitbad Dorsten

Sehr geehrter Herr Bundesminister,

### 1. Verfahren
Mit Schreiben vom 9. Mai 2000, eingegangen bei der Kommission am 10. Mai 2000, haben die deutschen Behörden gemäß Artikel 88 Absatz 3 EG-Vertrag die Finanzierung des Baus und Betriebs des Freizeitbads Dorsten notifiziert mit dem Antrag, die Kommission möge in Einklang mit Artikel 4 Absatz 2 der Verordnung (EG) Nr. 659/1999 des Rates vom 22. März 1999 über besondere Vorschriften für die Anwendung von Artikel 93 des EG-Vertrages[980] feststellen, daß die angemeldete Maßnahme keine Beihilfe darstelle. Mit Schreiben vom 29. Mai 2000, bei der Kommission eingegangen am selben Tage, haben die deutschen Behörden weitere Informationen über das Vorhaben übermittelt. Mit Schreiben vom 31. Juli 2000 erbat die Kommission weitere Informationen, die Deutschland mit Schreiben vom 6. September 2000 übermittelte; Anlagen erreichten die Kommission am 15.November 2000.

### 2. Beschreibung der Beihilfe
Die Stadt Dorsten in Nordrhein-Westfalen betreibt zwei städtische Hallenbäder und im Sommer ein Freibad. Das Hallenbad aus dem Jahr 1972 und das Freibad aus dem Jahr 1961 sind in sehr schlechtem baulichen Zustand und müßten in Kürze geschlossen werden, wenn keine Maßnahmen ergriffen würden. Für beide Bäder ist aufgrund ihres Zustandes eine Neuerrichtung wirtschaftlicher als eine Sanierung. Die Stadt hält den

---

[980] ABl. L 83 vom 27-3-1999, S. 1 ff.

Betrieb der drei Bäder für erforderlich, um den 80 000 Einwohnern der Stadt angemessene Bademöglichkeiten zur Verfügung zu stellen und so die freiwillige Aufgabe der Daseinsvorsorge zu erfüllen. Die Bäder werden von der Stadt Dorsten ferner als Schulträger zum Schulschwimmen zur Verfügung gestellt; außerdem dienen sie aufgrund öffentlich-rechtlicher Benutzungsregeln dem Vereinsschwimmen.

Aus dem Betrieb dieser Bäder erwirtschaftet die Stadt seit mehreren Jahren ein Defizit, das in den letzten Jahren bei jährlich 2,4 Millionen DEM lag. Diese Defizit stiege durch die erforderfiche Investitionen für das eine Hallenbad und das Freibad noch erheblich an, und zwar nach Berechnungen auf 3,5 Millionen DEM für die nächsten 20 Jahre. Eine Erhöhung des Haushaltsdefizits ist für die Stadt Dorsten kommunalrechtlich ausgeschlossen.

Die Stadt Dorsten hat daher 1998 beschlossen, die anstehenden Investitionen und den Betrieb der Bäder einem privaten Unternehmen zu übertragen. Dazu hat die Stadt Dorsten zwischen dem 14. Januar 1999 und dem 8. März 1999 einen europaweiten öffentlichen Teilnahmewettbewerb durchgeführt

Darin hat sie eine Konzession ausgeschrieben für den Bau und Betrieb eines Freizeitbades in Dorsten. Das Freizeitbad soll ein bestimmtes Wasserangebot umfassen, ein 25 m-Schwimmbecken innen, eine attraktive Saunalandschaft, ein Erlebnisaußenbecken mit der Möglichkeit, in Bahnen zu schwimmen, sowie ansprechende Gastronomie. Ferner muß die Eignung für das Schul- und Vereinsschwinmen gegeben sein und das Bad dafür zur Verfügung gestellt werden. Die Betreibung des städtischen Hallenbads und des Freibads sind erwünscht. Die Verknüpfung des Bades mit anderen Nutzungen aus der Freizeitwirtschaft ist vorstellbar.

Als Zuschlagskriterien waren insbesondere genannt die Attraktivität und Funktionalität des Bades bzw. der mit dem Bad kombinierten Nutzungsmöglichkeiten, städtebauliche und wirtschaftliche Gesichtspunkte für die Stadt, Risikoabsicherung, Bonität des Investors, Art und Umfang der Gewährleistung des Schul- und Vereinsschwimmens sowie die Eignung des Angebotes im Hinblick auf die Lösung der städtischen Bäderfrage.

Die Ausschreibung war im Bundesanzeiger vom 26. Januar 1999 – S. 17, Europäische Gemeinschaften – Bauaufträge – Bekanntmachung von öffentfichen Baukonzessionen und im Submissionsanzeiger vom 22. Januar 1999 veröffentlicht. Es gingen 11 Angebote ein. Die Stadt führte daraufhin Verhandlungen mit allen Bietern. Daraufhin gingen von den 11 Bietern sieben Angebote ein. Die Bewertung der Angebote führte zu dem Ergebnis, daß das Angebot der Firma Atlantis das wirtschaftlich gunstigste Angebot war.

Nach weiteren Verhandlungen wurden daraufhin zwischen der Stadt Dorsten und der Firma Atlantis Leistung und Gegenleistung in mehreren Verträgen niedergelegt. Dabei stellen sich Leistung und Gegenleistung im Wesentlichen wie folgt dar:

–   Die Firma Atlantis errichtet ein Freizeitbad auf dem für 35 Jahre nach Erbbaurecht überlassenen städtischen Grundstück. Für die Überlassung zahlt sie einen marktüblichen Erbbauzins.

–   Sie betreibt dieses bis zuin Ablauf des Erbbaurechtsvertrages zu üblichen Öffnungszeiten ganzjährig, und zwar zu sozialverträglichen Eintrittspreisen.

–   Sie reißt das alte Freibad ab und errichtet ein neues Freibad. Dieses verbleibt im Eigentum der Stadt Dorsten. Die Investitionssumme wird auf 4 Millionen DEM geschätzt. Sie betreibt das Bad gemäß dem Betreibervertrag für eine bestimmte Mindestzeit im Sommer.

–   Sie verpflichtet sich, im weiteren Hallenbad Umbaumaßnahmen durchzuführen (geschätzte Kosten: 50 000 bis 100 000 DEM), damit dort ebenfalls Schulschwimmen stattfinden kann.

–   Sie verpflichtet sich, alle drei Bäder gemäß der Belegungsvereinbarung mit der Stadt für städtisches Schulschwimmen während der gesamten Vertragslaufzeit kostenlos zur Verfügung zu stellen.

- Gleichermaßen verpflichtet sie sich, die drei Bäder gemäß dem Belegungsplan unentgeltlich für Vereinsschwimmen zur Verfügung zu stellen.
- Liegt die Besucherzahl des Freizeitbades höher als erwartet, so räumt die Firma Atlantis der Stadt Dorsten eine Gewinnbeteiligung von 10% des Nettoerlöses bei einer Jahresbesucherzahl von über 450 000 Personen ein, 15 % des Nettoerlöses, sofern mehr als 500 000 Personen jährlich das Bad besuchen.
- Sie verpflichtet sich, das städtische Personal zu übernehmen.
- Die Stadt Dorsten räumt der Firma Atlantis für die Errichtung des Freizeitbades ein Erbbaurecht für die Dauer von 35 Jahren gegen Zahlung eines angemessenen Erbbauzinses ein.
- Sie zahlt für die Dauer des Erbbaurechts einen jährlichen Zuschuß von 2 Millionen DEM ab Inbetriebnahme des Freizeitbades an die Firma Atlantis.
- Im Fall von Leistungsstörungen auf Seiten der Firma Atlantis ist im Erbbaurechtsvertrag ein entschädigungsloser Heimfallanspruch an die Stadt Dorsten vereinbart. Die Zahlung des jährlichen Zuschusses liefe in diesem Fall an die finanzierende Bank weiter, der die Firma Atlantis den Zahlungsanspruch zur Sicherung eines Investitionsdarlehens abgetreten hat.

Das Bad wird den Charakter eines modernen Freizeitbades haben und über eine Saunalandschaft sowie Gastronomie verfügen. Es wird von einem Einzugsbereich des Bades ausgegangen, der über Dorsten hinaus auch die umfiegenden Gemeinden einbezieht und ca. 50 km umfaßt, und einer jährlichen Besucherzahl von mindestens 250 000. Diese Zahlen beruhen auf einem Gutachten, das die Stadt Dorsten in Auftrag gegeben hat und das zu dem Ergebnis kommt, daß der direkte Einzugsbereich des Bades das Stadtgebiet von Dorsten sei. Aus diesem Bereich werden fast 90% der Besucher erwartet. Der indirekte Einzugsbereich werde über die Stadtgrenzen hinausreichen, aber das Gebiet der benachbarten Niederlande nicht berühren.

Ferner weist Deutschland darauf hin, daß es im erwarteten Einzugsbereich des Bades weitere vergleichbare Bäder gebe, die alle keine Gewinne erzielten und deren Verluste von den betreibenden Gebietskörperschaften getragen würden.

Deutschland ist der Auffassung, daß es sich bei der Zahlung nicht um eine Beihilfe handelt. Vielmehr stelle die Zahlung die Gegenleistung in einem Austauschvertrag dar, in dem Leistung und Gegenleistung der Vertragspartner gleichwertig seien. Durch die Zahlung würden Lasten entgolten, die der Investor im Sinne des Gemeinwohls insoweit übernehme, als er sich verpflichte, die Bäder nicht allein unter dem Gesichtspunkt der Gewinnmaximierung zu betreiben.

Nach Auffassung Deutschlands könne eine Wettbewerbsverfälschung insoweit nicht eintreten, als der Betrieb kommunaler Bäder als Aufgabe der Daseinsvorsorge wegen der dadurch verwirklichten Gemeinwohlverpflichtung nicht marktbezogen sei und regelmäßig nur defizitär betrieben werden könne. Gegenüber kommerziell betriebenen Freizeitbädern begründe der Zuschuß keinen Wettbewerbsvorteil, da er nur dazu diene, dem Investor die Nachteile auszugleichen, die durch die Übernahme der Gemeinwohlverpflichtung entstünden, und ihn so erst in die Lage versetze, ein – im Übrigen – wettbewerbsfähiges Freizeitbad zu betreiben.

Hilfsweise beruft sich Deutschland auf Artikel 86 Absatz 2 EG-Vertrag und hält die Wettbewerbsvorschriften insoweit nicht für anwendbar, da sie erforderlich seien, um im Rahmen der gewählten Aufgabenprivatisierung die Leistungen der Daseinsvorsorge sicherzustellen.

Deutschland weist abschließend darauf hin, daß die Zahlung auch nach deutschem Steuerrecht als Leistungsentgelt betrachtet werde und daher in vollem Umfang mehrwertsteuerpflichtig sei.

## 3. Würdigung

Die Kommission hat das Vorhaben gemäß Artikel 87 ff. EG-Vertrag und Artikel 61 ff. EWR-Abkommen geprüft. Sie ist bei ihrer Prüfung zu dem Ergebnis gelangt, daß die Maßnahme keine Beihilfe im Sinne von Artikel 87 Absatz 1 EG-Vertrag darstellt.

Da es sich nicht um eine staatliche Beihilfe handelt, schließt die Kommission weiterhin, daß Artikel 86 Absatz 2 EG-Vertrag keine Anwendung findet. Dieses gilt ungeachtet dessen, daß die Gegenleistung im vorliegenden Fall zum Teil für die Verpflichtung, eine Dienstleistung von allgemeinem wirtschaftlichen Interesse zu erbringen, erbracht wird, wie sie die kostenlose Überlassung der Bäder zum Schul- und Vereinsschwimmen, die Ausgestaltung der Eintrittspreise unter Beachtung sozialer Aspekte sowie einige weitere vertragliche Ausgestaltungen darstellen. Da die Voraussetzungen des Artikels 87 Absatz 1 EG-Vertrag nicht vorliegen und die Maßnahme keine staatfiche Beihilfe darstellt, findet Artikel 86 Absatz 2 EG-Vertrag keine Anwendung[981].

Eine Beihilfe im Sinne von Artikel 87 Absatz 1 EG-Vertrag liegt nämlich nur vor, wenn kumulativ alle vier Voraussetzungen dieses Tatbestandes gegeben sind, d.h. es sich um eine staatliche oder aus staatlichen Mitteln gewährte Beihilfe handelt, bestimmte Unternehmen begünstigt werden, eine Wettbewerbsverfälschung vorliegt und die Beeinträchtigung des innergemeinschaftlichen Handels gegeben ist. Die Kommission ist in ihrer Prüfung zu dem Ergebnis gelangt, daß es im vorliegenden Fall jedenfalls an einer Beeinträchtigung des innergemeinschaftlichen Handels fehlt. Daher besteht hier keine Notwendigkeit zu entscheiden, ob die anderen drei Tatbestandsmerkmale im vorliegenden Fall tatsächlich vorliegen.

Bei ihrer Entscheidung hat die Kommission folgendes berücksichtigt:

Der Handel zwischen den Mitgliedstaaten ist nur beeinträchtigt, wenn die Maßnahme hierzu zumindest potentiell in der Lage ist, wobei Handel im Sinne des Artikels 87 Absatz 1 EG-Vertrag nicht nur den Waren-, sondern auch den Dienstleistungsverkehr umfaßt. Der potentiell Begünstigte kann seine Dienstleistung – Benutzung der Schwimmbäder – hier aus offensichtlichen Gründen nicht im Ausland erbringen. Der Dienstleistungsverkehr wäre allerdings auch beeinträchtigt, wenn die Nachfrage für die Inanspruchnahme der Dienstleistung in Dorsten einen grenzüberschreitenden Charakter hätte, d.h. im Ausland entstünde.

Aus den von Deutschland übermittelten Informationen geht klar hervor, daß es sich bei dem neuen Dorstener Schwimmbad um eine moderne Einrichtung handeln wird, die für Schulschwimmen genutzt werden wird, gleichermaßen wird sie den Einheimischen zu vertretbaren Kosten als Freizeitbad dienen und dabei natürlich zugleich Besuchern der Region offenstehen. Zusätzlich zu den Kerneinrichtungen, nämlich den Bädern, wird der Komplex damit verbundene Freizeiteinrichtungen wie Sauna und Restaurantbetrieb umfassen. Aus der von Deutschland übermittelten Beschreibung deutet allerdings nichts darauf hin, daß die Einrichtung mehr als dem örtlichen Markt der Stadt Dorsten und ihren Nachbargemeinden dienen würde. Das Bad ist vielmehr in keiner Weise einzigartig in seinem Charakter in Nordrhein-Westfalen, von Deutschland ganz zu schweigen.

Die Kommission ist daher der Auffassung, daß diese Maßnahme von anderen Beihilfen durchaus unterschieden werden kann, die die Entwicklung großer Freizeitparks fördern, die auf einen nationalen, oder sogar internationalen Markt ausgerichtet sind und weit über die Region hinaus, in der sie gelegen sind, beworben werden. Kraft ihrer Natur ist es

---

[981] Vgl. die Rechtsprechung des Gerichts: Urteil des Gerichts erster Instanz vom 10. Mai 2000, SIC gegen Kommission, Rs. T-46197, Rdnr. 84; Urteil des Gerichts erster Instanz vom 27. Februar 2000, FFSA u.a. gegen Kommission, Rs. T-106/95, Rdnr. 199 und 167 ff.; vgl. auch die Mitteilung der Kommission Leistungen der Daseinsvorsorge in Europa, KOM(2000) 580 endgültig vom 20. September 2000, Nr. 27.

wahrscheinlich, daß Maßnahmen zur Förderung von Einrichtungen, die gegenüber einer internationalen Klientel beworben werden, den Handel zwischen den Mitgliedstaaten beeinträchtigen werden.
Im vorliegenden Fall wird der Einzugsbereich der Einrichtung mit ca. 50 km angegeben. Da Dorsten etwas weiter von der Grenze zu den Niederlanden entfernt liegt, kann praktisch jede Beeinträchtigung des innergemeinschaftlichen Handels ausgeschlossen werden.
Da es sich bei der Maßnahme nicht um eine staatliche Beihilfe handelt, war Deutschland nicht verpflichtet, diese bei der Kommission anzumelden[982].

**4. Entscheidung**
Daher stellt die Kommission in Einklang mit Artikel 4 Absatz 2 der Verordnung (EG) Nr. 659/1999 des Rates vom 22. März 1999 über besondere Vorschriften für die Anwendung von Artikel 93 des EG-Vertrages[983] fest, daß die Maßnahme keine Beihilfe im Sinne von Artikel 87 Absatz 1 EG-Vertrag darstellt.
Falls dieses Schreiben vertrauliche Angaben enthält, die nicht veröffentlicht werden sollen, werden Sie gebeten, die Kommission hiervon innerhalb von 15 Arbeitstagen nach dessen Eingang unter Angabe von Gründen in Kenntnis zu setzen. Erhält die Kommission keinen derart begründeten Antrag innerhalb der vorerwähnten Frist, so geht sie davon aus, daß13 Sie mit der Veröffentlichung des vollständigen Wortlauts dieses Schreibens in der verbindlichen Sprachfassung auf der Internet-Seite http://europa.eu.int/comm/sg/sgb/state-aids/ an Dritte einverstanden sind. Ihr Antrag ist per Einschreiben oder Telekopiergerät an folgende Anschrift zu richten:

Europäische Kommission
Generaldirektion Wettbewerb
Direktion G
Rue de la Loi/Wetstraat 200
B-1049 Brüssel
Telekopiergerät Nr.: 0032 2 296.98.14

Mit vorzüglicher Hochachtung
Für die Kommission
Mario Monti

—

**2.14.5.  COMMISSION DECISION, 25 APRIL 2001[984]**

Commission Européenne
Bruxelles, le 25.04.2001
SG (2001) D/ 288165

---

[982] Vgl. Artikel 88 Absatz 3 EG-Vertrag in Verbindung mit Artikel 2 Absatz 1 der Verordnung (EG) Nr. 659/1999 des Rates vom 22. März 1999 über besondere Vorschriften für die Anwendung von Artikel 93 des EG-Vertrages, a.a.O.
[983] A.a.O.
[984] OJ L 14, 21-1-1992, p. 35.
IP/01/599 – Brussels, 25-4-2001:
Commission does not object to subsidies for French professional sports clubs
*The European Commission decided on Wednesday not to object to a public subsidy scheme for professional sports clubs, notified by France, since the subsidies do not constitute state aid under the*

Son Excellence Monsieur Hubert Védrine
Ministre des Affaires étrangères
Quai d'Orsay 37
F – 75007 – Paris

Objet: Aide d'État n: N 118/00 – France
Subventions publiques aux clubs sportifs professionnels

Monsieur le Ministre,
J'ai l'honneur de vous informer par la présente de la décision de la Commission dans le
cas cité en objet.

**Aspects Procéduraux**

1.  Par leur lettre du 2 mars 2000, enregistrée au Greffe des Aides d'État le 3 mars
    2000 sous le numéro A/31889, les autorités françaises ont notifié à la Commission
    un régime de subventions publiques aux clubs sportifs professionnels français.
    Cette notification ayant été jugée incomplète, des informations complémentaires
    ont été demandées par la lettre D/52920 du 11 mai 2000. Afin d'éclaircir certaines
    éléments dans la notification, un entretien avec les autorités françaises a été
    demandé par la lettre D/54072 du 28 juillet 2000.

2.  L'entretien du 25 septembre n'ayant pas permis d'éclaircir tous les points en
    suspens, une liste de questions a été envoyée aux autorités françaises par la lettre
    D/55302 du 23 octobre 2000. À la demande des autorités françaises, une nouvelle
    réunion a eu lieu le 2 février 2001 pour préparer l'entrevue entre Mme Buffet et
    M. Monti, ayant eu lieu le 14 février 2001. Une demande de confirmation écrite
    des renseignements communiqués lors de la réunion préparatoire du 2 février a été
    envoyée par la lettre D/50598 du 9 février 2001. La réponse à celle-ci a été
    enregistrée au Greffe des Aides d'État le 13 février 2001. Un accusé de réception a
    été envoyé par le Secrétariat général le 19 février 2001 (SG D/820608).

3.  La réponse à une dernière demande d'apporter certaines précisions, transmise aux
    autorités françaises le 13 mars, a été enregistrée le 28 mars 2001.

**Description des Mesures Envisagées**

4.  Le régime en cause est notifié par les autorités françaises à la demande du Conseil
    d'État.

5.  Le régime notifié N 118/00 prévoit que les collectivités locales françaises pourront

---

*EC Treaty. It was clear from an examination of the notification that the measures are designed to
assist education and initial training and as such constitute an educational or comparable scheme.*
Under the scheme, French local authorities will be able to grant professional sports clubs with state-
approved youth training centres public subsidies of up to € 2.3 million a year per recipient club. The
sports concerned are football, basketball, rugby and volleyball. This type of education is intended by
the French authorities to provide young people with an education allowing them reach the best sporting level and to reconcile sports training with a thorough education and so enable them to find an
ordinary job (or, for those who take up sport professionally, to find a job at the end of their career).
The provision of community facilities and the prevention of violence are other targets.
The French authorities have agreed to monitor the allocation of the subsidies closely, to prevent any
overcompensation of the net cost of the training and hence any cross-subsidisation, chiefly by requiring separate accounts to be kept for training measures and for the economic activities of the professional sports clubs.

octroyer aux clubs sportifs professionnels possédant des centres de formation de jeunes agréés par les pouvoirs publics, des subventions publiques à concurrence d'un montant annuel maximal de € 2,3 millions par bénéficiaire. Les disciplines sportives concernées sont le football, le basket, le rugby et le volley. Ce régime de subventions est prévu pour une durée illimitée dans le temps.

6. Ce régime prend la suite du régime N 368/95, notifié par les autorités françaises et tacitement approuvé par la Commission en 1995 (selon les principes de l'arrêt de la Cour du 11 décembre 1973, affaire 120/73), qui est venu à extinction le 31-12-1999.

7. Les clubs sportifs professionnels possédant des centres de formation agréés se verraient proposer une convention par laquelle ils s'engageraient à organiser une filière d'enseignement scolaire, en combinaison avec la formation sportive de pointe qu'ils procurent aux jeunes sportifs. L'objectif fondamental avancé par les autorités françaises serait de fournir un système d'enseignement combiné pour faciliter aux jeunes sportifs la poursuite d'une scolarité mêlant harmonieusement l'aspect scolaire et l'aspect sportif. Le régime comporte également des mesures consistant dans l'*"animation dans les quartiers'* et la *'prévention de la violence'*.

8. Les autorités françaises justifient l'octroi des subventions par la nécessité de *'moraliser les pratiques du secteur'*, en matière de formation des jeunes sportifs, ainsi que par l'objectif d'organisation d'un enseignement combiné intégrant la formation scolaire et la formation sportive de pointe des jeunes sportifs. Elles présentent cet objectif comme étant *'d'intérêt général'*.

9. L'ensemble des coûts de fonctionnement des centres de formation des clubs sportifs professionnels relatifs à la formation, est éligible aux subventions, à l'exception des rémunérations des joueurs et des coûts des prestations de sécurité. Les autorités françaises ont indiqué que l'enseignement sportif représentait au maximum un tiers de la charge de travail quotidienne des jeunes. Sur base des dernières informations reçues des autorités françaises (chiffres pour 1999, se rapportant au régime précédent), les subventions couvriraient au moins 48 % (du budget du centre de formation).

10. Les autorités françaises se sont engagées à effectuer un contrôle adéquat de l'affectation des subventions, qui empêchera toute surcompensation du coût net de la formation et donc tout subventionnement croisé, notamment par l'obligation de tenir une comptabilité séparée entre les actions de formation et les activités économiques des clubs sportifs professionnels.

## Appréciation

11. Par le régime notifié, les autorités françaises veulent subventionner une filière d'enseignement combinant des actions de formation scolaire et des actions de formation à la citoyenneté avec des actions de formation sportive.

12. Tous les éléments disponibles indiquent que, par ce genre d'enseignement, les autorités françaises ont voulu assurer la *'(...) formation des jeunes pour leur permettre d'atteindre le meilleur niveau sportif et concilier le perfectionnement sportif avec une bonne insertion scolaire et l'acquisition d'une capacité d'insertion professionnelle (ou de réinsertion ultérieure pour ceux qui se lanceront dans une carrière de sportif professionnel), l'animation dans les quartiers, la prévention de la violence.'*[985]

13. Le soutien à la formation citoyenne, scolaire et sportive des jeunes par les clubs

---

[985] Extrait du formulaire de notification N 118/00.

professionnels peut être considéré comme une action qui relève des missions générales de l'État, dans le domaine de l'enseignement. Ceci résulte des dispositions de l'article 19-3 de la loi n° 84-610 du 16 juillet 1984 modifiée relative à l'organisation et à la promotion des activités physiques et sportives ainsi qu'aux dispositions du décret d'application notifié. Conformément aux principes développés dans l'article L.121-1 du Code français de l'Éducation, ces formations peuvent être intégrées dans un enseignement général relevant de l'Éducation nationale.

## Aspects formation scolaire et sportive

14.    L'organisation de cet enseignement s'assimile à celui relevant de l'Éducation nationale, connu sous le vocable 'sport études'. Dans la mesure où cet enseignement, externalisé, prend la relève de la filière antérieure 'sport études', tout en conservant les caractéristiques et l'organisation générales de celle-ci, le soutien financier va à des actions se situant dans le domaine de l'enseignement et donc 'hors du champ de la concurrence'. Par conséquent, le soutien à ces mesures, telles qu'elles sont prévues ne constituerait pas une aide au sens de l'article 87, §1, du traité CE. Ces mesures constituent une action d'enseignement relevant de l'Éducation nationale, qui ressort au nombre des missions générales de l'État. Cette action tombe d'ailleurs en partie dans le champ d'application de l'obligation scolaire.

15.    Il résulte de ce qui précède que le régime notifié concerne la scolarité et la formation initiale. Par conséquent, conformément aux dispositions du règlement 68/2001 de la Commission, du 12.01.2001, relatif à l'application des articles 87 et 88 du traité CE aux aides à la formation, et plus précisément à son 6è considérant, ces mesures ne tombent pas dans le champ d'application de l'article 87.

## Aspects formation à la citoyenneté

16.    Les actions de prévention de la violence, à l'attention des supporters, sont plus efficaces lorsqu'elles sont mises en œuvre par les clubs professionnels que si l'État devait s'en charger. Les actions d'animation dans les quartiers, quant à elles, concourent à la promotion du sport en général. Les autorités françaises définissent ces actions comme étant d'intérêt général. Les deux types d'action peuvent s'assimiler à des mesures d'éducation à la citoyenneté au sens large. Conformément aux principes développés dans l'article L.121-1 du Code français de l'Éducation, ces mesures peuvent s'assimiler à une action d'enseignement relevant de l'Éducation nationale, qui ressort au nombre des missions générales de l'État. Par conséquent, le soutien à ces mesures, telles qu'elles sont prévues ne constituerait pas non plus une aide au sens de l'article 87, §1, du traité CE.

17.    Les autorités françaises s'engagent à éviter toute surcompensation du coût net de la formation scolaire et sportive par un système de contrôle de l'utilisation des subventions reçues, notamment par une séparation des comptes et par l'obligation de remboursement de toutes aides utilisées à d'autres fins que celles explicitement prévues.

18.    Il faut souligner en outre que la solution dégagée au niveau communautaire dans le dossier des indemnités de transfert des joueurs de football professionnel permet de conclure qu'il n'y aura pas, en toute hypothèse, de surcompensation possible du coût de la formation des jeunes et, par conséquent, pas de 'spillover' vers l'activité

économique des clubs professionnels dans ce sport en particulier, où les transactions portent sur des sommes considérables. Pour mémoire, le nouveau régime applicable aux indemnités de transfert dans ce domaine prévoit que ces indemnités doivent servir à compenser exclusivement des coûts de formation scolaire et sportive réellement exposés par les clubs professionnels de football.

**Conclusion**

La Commission a donc décidé que:

Le régime de subventions notifié par les autorités françaises ne constitue pas une aide au sens de l'article 87, §1, du traité CE en tant qu'il concerne des actions d'enseignement qui peuvent être assimilées à la scolarité et à la formation initiale au sens du règlement 68/2001 de la Commission concernant l'application des articles 87 et 88 du traité CE aux aides à la formation.

Dans le cas où cette lettre contiendrait des éléments confidentiels qui ne doivent pas être divulgués à des tiers, vous êtes invités à en informer la Commission, dans un délai de quinze jours ouvrables à compter de la date de réception de la présente. Si la Commission ne reçoit pas une demande motivée à cet effet dans le délai prescrit, elle considérera que vous êtes d'accord avec la communication à des tiers et avec la publication du texte intégral de la lettre, dans la langue faisant foi, sur le site Internet <http://europa.eu.int/comm/secretariat_general/sgb/state_aids/>. Cette demande devra être envoyée par lettre recommandée ou par télécopie à:

Commission européenne
Direction générale de la Concurrence
Direction H – Aides d'État II
Rue de la Loi, 200
B-1049 Bruxelles
Fax: + 32 2 296.95.80

Veuillez croire, Monsieur le Ministre, à l'assurance de ma haute considération.
Par la Commission
Mario Monti
Membre de la Commission

——

**\* 2.14.6.** **ANSWER ON BEHALF OF THE COMMISSION TO WRITTEN QUESTION P-2491/02 BY PERE ESTEVE (ELDR), 26 SEPTEMBER 2002**[986]

Subject: Planning agreement involving Real Madrid football club and the free competitive market

——

**\* 2.14.7.** **ANSWER ON BEHALF OF THE COMMISSION TO WRITTEN QUESTION E-2975/02 BY PERE ESTEVE (ELDR) AND CAMILO NOGUEIRA ROMÁN (VERTS/ALE), 29 NOVEMBER 2002**[987]

Subject: Interpretation of Article 87 of the EC Treaty with regard to the planning agreement involving Real Madrid football club and the free competitive market

——

[986] Question of 28-8-2002; OJ 137E, 12-6-2003, p. 86-87.
[987] Question of 22-10-2002; OJ C 161 E, 10-7-2003, p. 57-58.

**\* 2.14.8.    ANSWER ON BEHALF OF THE COMMISSION TO WRITTEN
QUESTION E-3378/02 BY MARGRIETUS VAN DEN BERG (PSE),
8 JANUARY 2003**[988]

Subject: State aid for Dutch football clubs

---

**\* 2.14.9.    ANSWER ON BEHALF OF THE COMMISSION TO WRITTEN
QUESTION E-3413/02 BY KATHLEEN VAN BREMPT (PSE),
27 JANUARY 2003**[989]

Subject: Government aid for professional clubs

---

**\* 2.14.10.   ANSWER ON BEHALF OF THE COMMISSION TO WRITTEN
QUESTION E-537/03 BY ERIK MEIJER (GUE/NGL), 14 APRIL
2003**[990]

Subject: Local authority subsidies paid to football clubs run as businesses in order to help
them to remain competitive and to make extremely high payments to players

---

**2.14.11.    STATE AID – ITALY – AID C 70/03 (EX NN 72/03) – MEASURE IN
FAVOUR OF PROFESSIONAL SPORTS CLUBS – 'DECRETO
SALVA CALCIO' – INVITATION TO SUBMIT COMMENTS
PURSUANT TO ARTICLE 88(2) OF THE EC TREATY,
18 DECEMBER 2003**[991]

By means of the letter dated 11.11.2003 reproduced in the authentic language on the
pages following this summary, the Commission notified Spain of its decision to initiate
the procedure laid down in Article 88(2) of the EC Treaty concerning the abovementioned
aid.
Interested parties may submit their comments on the aid in respect of which the Commission is initiating the procedure within one month of the date of publication of this summary and the following letter, to: European Commission Directorate-General for
Competition
Directorate State Aid II
B – 1049 Brussels Fax (32-2) 296 95 80
These comments will be communicated to Italy. Confidential treatment of the identity of
the interested party submitting the comments may be requested in writing, stating the reasons for the request.

**Summary**
In March 2003 the Commission asked for information regarding measures adopted by
Italy concerning accounting rules for sports clubs. The Italian authorities were asked to
provide information. This information was received in June 2003.

---

[988]  Question of 27-11-2002; OJ C 242 E, 9-10-2003, p. 56.
[989]  Question of 29-11-2002; OJ C 242 E, 9-10-2003, p. 58.
[990]  Question of 14-2-2003; OJ C 280 E, 21-11-2003, p. 65-66.
[991]  OJ C 308, 18-12-2003, p. 9-13. Text with EEA relevance.

The measure is favouring sports clubs because it first of all avoids a possible re-capitalisation and secondly it may provide for a fiscal advantage. The fiscal arrangement as such may lead to an advantage to certain sports clubs depending on the financial status of the company. Football teams are undertakings which compete internationally with other football clubs in for example selling broadcasting rights and the acquisition of play-ers.

Therefore, at the present stage of procedure the Commission has come to the conclusion that the Italian authorities may grant state aid to sports clubs within the meaning of article 87(1) EC. The derogations provided for in article 87(2) and (3) EC do not seem to apply. Considering its doubts on the compatibility of the aid with the EC-Treaty, the Commission has decided to initiate the formal investigation procedure laid down in Article 88(2) of the EC Treaty.

In accordance with Article 14 of Council Regulation (EC) No 659/1999, all unlawful aid can be subject to recovery from the recipient.

**Text of letter**
'Con la presente la Commissione si pregia informare l'Italia che, dopo avere esaminato le informazioni fornite dalle autorità italiane in merito alla misura menzionata in oggetto, ha deciso di avviare il procedimento di cui all'articolo 88, paragrafo 2, del trattato CE.

IL PROCEDIMENTO

1. Sulla base delle informazioni di cui dispone la Commissione, all'atto della conversione in legge del decreto-legge 24 dicembre 2002, n. 282, il governo italiano ha adottato disposizioni in materia di bilanci delle società sportive professionistiche.

2. Con lettera D/51643 del 12 marzo 2003, la Commissione ha richiesto informazioni sulla misura in oggetto. Con lettera del 22 aprile 2003, protocollo N.5243, le autorità italiane hanno chiesto di prorogare al 14 maggio il termine per la presentazione delle informazioni. Non avendo ricevuto alcuna risposta entro la data menzionata, la Commissione ha sollecitato le informazioni in questione con lettera del 22 maggio 2003. In tale occasione, essa ha inoltre ricordato che, conformemente all'articolo 88, paragrafo 3, del trattato CE, non è consentito dare esecuzione alle misure di aiuto prima che la Commissione abbia formulato le sue osservazioni in proposito. La risposta delle autorità italiane è pervenuta il 26 giugno 2003.

DESCRIZIONE DETTAGLIATA DELLA MISURA
La misura

3. La misura introdotta con l'articolo 3, paragrafo 1 bis del decreto-legge 24 dicembre 2002, n. 282, convertito nella legge 21 febbraio 2003, n. 27, è indirizzata alle società sportive di cui alla legge 23 marzo 1981, n. 91.

4. La misura in questione permette alle società sportive di iscrivere in apposito conto – nel primo bilancio successivamente alla data di entrata in vigore della legge – l'ammontare delle svalutazioni dei diritti pluriennali delle prestazioni sportive degli sportivi professionisti, determinato sulla base di un'apposita perizia giurata. Con il consenso del collegio sindacale, tale posta sarà iscritta tra le componenti attive di bilancio quali oneri pluriennali da ammortizzare.

5. La legge precisa che le società che si avvalgono delle norme speciali introdotte dalla legge devono procedere, ai fini civilistici e fiscali, all'ammortamento della svalutazione iscritta in dieci rate annuali di pari importo.

6. Il seguente esempio illustra gli effetti della misura. Ipotizziamo che un contratto

triennale relativo alle prestazioni di un atleta professionista di costo pari a 100 abbia subito una svalutazione del 70 % nell'anno stesso dell'acquisizione. La tabella 1 riporta le norme contabili e fiscali applicate all'operazione in questione nei casi, rispettivamente, di non applicazione e di applicazione della misura in oggetto.

Tabella 1

[...]

7.    La Commissione ha invitato le autorità italiane ad illustrare il meccanismo previsto dalla misura con riferimento all'esempio summenzionato. Nella loro risposta, le autorità italiane hanno fornito i dati che figurano nella tabella 1.

8.    Le autorità italiane hanno inoltre sottolineato la peculiarità del settore del calcio, soggetto, a loro avviso, a rischi maggiori rispetto ad altre attività. Esse hanno ad esempio fatto riferimento alla vulnerabilità dei calciatori e ai danni che un infortunio può causare alle società sportive. Esse hanno altresì menzionato la falsificazione di gadget, la vendita dei biglietti al di fuori dei canali ufficiali e la pirateria sul mercato della pay-TV.

## VALUTAZIONE DELLA MISURA
Aiuto di Stato ai sensi dell'articolo 87, paragrafo 1

9.    Al fine di stabilire se la misura costituisce un aiuto di Stato ai sensi dell'articolo 87, paragrafo 1, del trattato CE, la Commissione deve stabilire se la misura in questione favorisca talune imprese o la produzione di taluni beni accordando un vantaggio di natura economica. Essa deve quindi valutare se tale vantaggio sia selettivo, e dunque tale da falsare o minacciare di falsare la concorrenza, se sia concesso mediante risorse statali e se incida sugli scambi tra Stati membri.

Talune imprese/attività economiche risultano favorite

10.    Le società sportive destinatarie della misura esercitano un'attività economica e devono pertanto essere considerate imprese ai sensi dell'articolo 87, paragrafo 1. Le società di calcio professionistiche, ad esempio, vendono i biglietti di ingresso alle partite, i diritti di trasmissione radiofonica e televisiva delle partite e le licenze su film, prodotti musicali, libri e video interattivi, concludono accordi di sponsorizzazione, percepiscono i compensi derivanti da contratti relativi a manifestazioni sportive internazionali e acquistano i diritti relativi alle prestazioni di atleti professionisti.

Vantaggio economico

11.    La misura comporta un duplice vantaggio economico per i beneficiari.

12.    Da un lato, essa consente alle società sportive di registrare la svalutazione dei contratti, riducendo quindi i costi di ammortamento, senza far apparire le perdite nello stato patrimoniale e nel conto economico. In tal modo vengono evitati i possibili effetti previsti dagli articoli 2446 e 2447 del codice civile, vale a dire la riduzione del capitale della società ed il possibile obbligo di procedere all'iniezione di nuovi capitali.

13.    Il secondo vantaggio è di natura fiscale. La misura potrebbe essere definita come un ammortamento straordinario, quale menzionato anche nella comunicazione della Commissione sulle misure di tassazione diretta delle imprese[992]. Di norma, le perdite di capitale sono deducibili ai fini fiscali quando sono 'realizzate', vale a

---

[992] Comunicazione della Commissione sull'applicazione delle norme relative agli aiuti di Stato alle misure di tassazione diretta delle imprese (GU C 384 del 10-12-1998, pag. 3).

dire, in questo caso, alla scadenza, naturale o anticipata, del contratto. Come risulta dalla tabella 1, in caso di non applicazione della disposizione in oggetto, le deduzioni non sarebbero possibili oltre la scadenza del contratto[993]. Il profilo delle deduzioni è diverso in caso di applicazione della misura: le società possono infatti beneficiare di parte degli sgravi per un periodo di dieci anni. Le società saranno pertanto autorizzate a compensare perdite registrate in passato con profitti futuri per un periodo molto più lungo. Gli effetti sulla posizione fiscale della singola società dipendono dal suo profilo di reddito e dalla durata del contratto, ma in alcuni casi, in particolare in presenza di una bassa redditività, o addirittura di perdite di esercizio, nell'anno in cui si registrano le perdite di capitale e negli anni immediatamente successivi, la possibilità di prorogare il periodo di deducibilità delle perdite rappresenta un vantaggio economico.

14. Si osserva inoltre che l'applicazione della norma è facoltativa. Essa consente pertanto alle società sportive di optare per il regime speciale solo quando consenta loro di beneficiare di un vantaggio economico.

Presenza di risorse statali

15. La misura implica l'uso di risorse statali in termini di rinuncia al gettito fiscale. Come già menzionato, la disposizione consente alle società sportive di riportare le perdite deducibili su un periodo di tempo più lungo rispetto al passato, a fronte di una riduzione delle rate d'ammortamento possibili nei primi anni. Permettendo alle società sportive di scegliere tra due metodi alternativi di imposizione, lo Stato consente a questi contribuenti di optare per il metodo per loro più conveniente e accetta quindi di rinunciare a parte del gettito fiscale.

16. Inoltre, l'attuale situazione economica delle società di calcio professionistiche, molte delle quali sono fortemente indebitate, induce a ritenere che nella maggior parte dei casi esse approfitteranno della possibilità di riportare le perdite per un periodo più lungo. Ove le società divenissero nuovamente redditizie, esse potrebbero beneficiare della modifica della legge, avvalendosi delle deduzioni fiscali alle quali non avrebbero avuto diritto altrimenti.

Carattere selettivo della misura

17. In terzo luogo, la misura è selettiva in quanto indirizzata solo alle società sportive di cui alla legge 23 marzo 1981, n. 91 e costituisce pertanto un aiuto settoriale.

18. Inoltre, possono beneficiare della misura solo le società sportive che abbiano registrato minusvalenze in relazione ai contratti con atleti professionisti e che possano iscriverle nel primo bilancio da approvare successivamente alla data di entrata in vigore della legge. La misura non ha infatti carattere permanente, ma una tantum. Essa introduce pertanto una distorsione della concorrenza non solo tra settori diversi, ma anche all'interno del settore cui si applica, in quanto favorisce le società che hanno registrato perdite rispetto a quelle che hanno i conti in ordine o che hanno già contabilizzato tali perdite in passato.

Distorsione della concorrenza e incidenza sugli scambi tra Stati membri

19. Come già menzionato al punto 10, le società sportive professionistiche esercitano svariate attività economiche. Perlomeno talune società esercitano alcune di queste

---

[993] Fatta salva la possibilità di riportare le perdite per cinque anni, qualora la società non realizzi utili sufficienti per avvalersi della totalità delle deduzioni fiscali. Questa possibilità, tuttavia, è presente anche nel quadro della nuova misura e non modifica il profilo relativo delle deduzioni fiscali.

attività su mercati internazionali. Da un lato, si tratta della vendita dei diritti di trasmissione, degli accordi pubblicitari e di sponsorizzazione e della partecipazione alle competizioni europee, come la Champions League, che danno origine a compensi relativi ai contratti stipulati dagli organizzatori. Poiché su questi mercati sono presenti anche società sportive e altri operatori economici di altri Stati membri, la misura in questione può incidere sugli scambi intracomunitari.

20. Dall'altro lato, anche quello dell'acquisizione dei diritti relativi alle prestazioni dei giocatori è un mercato internazionale. È opportuno ricordare che i giocatori professionisti presenti nei campionati europei provengono da tutto il mondo, hanno un'elevata mobilità e sono molto contesi. La disponibilità di giocatori di talento è decisiva per il successo di una società sportiva professionistica, sia in termini sportivi che commerciali. Su questo mercato operano anche società sportive di altri Stati membri e, anche per tale ragione, la misura può incidere sugli scambi tra Stati membri.

Valutazione provvisoria in merito all'esistenza di una nuova misura d'aiuto

21. Sulla base dell'analisi precedente, in questo stadio, la misura sembra soddisfare tutte le condizioni perché la si consideri un aiuto di Stato. Poiché la misura è stata introdotta per la prima volta con il decreto-legge 24 dicembre 2002, n. 282, convertito nella legge 21 febbraio 2003, n. 27 e poiché essa avvantaggia imprese operanti su mercati già aperti agli scambi intracomunitari, la Commissione ritiene, in questo stadio, che la misura in oggetto costituisca un nuovo aiuto.

Compatibilità

22. Nei casi in cui la misura costituisce un aiuto ai sensi dell'articolo 87, paragrafo 1, del trattato CE, vi sono dubbi sulla compatibilità dell'aiuto di Stato concesso in tal modo alle società sportive. Va inoltre ricordato che non possono essere autorizzati aiuti di Stato che costituiscano una violazione della legislazione comunitaria, come avviene nel caso in esame per le direttive contabili.

23. L'aiuto non sembra soddisfare le condizioni previste per una delle deroghe di cui all'articolo 87, paragrafo 2 o 3, o all'articolo 86, paragrafo 2. Quanto alla compatibilità ai sensi dell'articolo 87, paragrafo 3, lettera c), non è possibile stabilire se le condizioni per l'applicazione degli Orientamenti comunitari sugli aiuti di Stato per il salvataggio e la ristrutturazione di imprese in difficoltà siano soddisfatte. Ad ogni modo, la misura non sembra essere limitata alle imprese in difficoltà, né sembra esigere la presentazione e la realizzazione di un piano di ristrutturazione da parte del beneficiario.

24. Più in generale, la misura costituisce un aiuto al funzionamento, in quanto è destinata a permettere alle società beneficiarie di eliminare o ridurre le spese – nel caso in esame, le imposte – che avrebbero di norma dovuto sostenere in relazione alla gestione quotidiana delle loro normali attività e determina pertanto, in linea di principio, distorsioni della concorrenza (cfr. causa C-301/87, Francia/Commissione (Boussac Saint Frères), Raccolta 1990, pag. I-307; causa C-86/89, Italia/Commissione, Raccolta 1990, pag. I-3891 e causa C-156/98, Germania/Commissione, Raccolta 2000, pag. I-6857). Anche qualora si accertasse che la misura agevola lo sviluppo di talune attività economiche, la Commissione ritiene pur sempre, in questo stadio, che essa incida sulle condizioni degli scambi in misura contraria al comune interesse, considerato che i beneficiari non sono tenuti a compensare la distorsione mediante un contributo al comune interesse.

25. Le autorità italiane non hanno finora invocato nessuna delle deroghe di cui all'articolo 87, paragrafo 2 o 3, o all'articolo 86, paragrafo 2, del trattato CE.

Violazione delle direttive contabili

26. Secondo la giurisprudenza costante della Corte, il procedimento ai sensi dell'articolo 88 non deve mai pervenire a un risultato contrario a norme del trattato. Pertanto, un aiuto di Stato che, in considerazione di determinate sue modalità, contrasti con altre disposizioni del diritto comunitario non può essere dichiarato dalla Commissione compatibile con il mercato comune (cfr. a tale proposito causa 73/79, Commissione/Italia, punto 11, Raccolta 1980 pag. 1533; causa C-225/91, Matra/Commissione, punto 41, Raccolta 1993, pag. I-3203; causa C-156/98, Germania/Commissione, punto 78, Raccolta 2000, pag. I-6857).

27. Nel caso in esame, la misura stessa sembra comportare una violazione della Quarta e della Settima direttiva contabile[994]. Le società sportive di cui alla legge 23 marzo 1991, n. 91 sono costituite nella forma di società per azioni o società a responsabilità limitata e sono pertanto soggette alle disposizioni della Quarta direttiva. Esse sono soggette inoltre alle disposizioni della Settima direttiva qualora appartengano ad un gruppo e soddisfino le condizioni di cui all'articolo 1 di detta direttiva.

28. La misura nazionale di cui trattasi sembra violare i principi fondamentali di cui all'articolo 2, paragrafo 3, della Quarta direttiva e all'articolo 16 paragrafo 3, della Settima direttiva, in base ai quali i conti consolidati devono fornire un quadro fedele della situazione patrimoniale, di quella finanziaria nonché del risultato economico della società. In particolare, se i contratti con i giocatori sono considerati come immobilizzazioni immateriali, l'articolo 35, paragrafo 1, lettera b), della Quarta direttiva e l'articolo 29 della Settima direttiva dispongono che siano ammortizzati durante il periodo della loro utilizzazione. Ammortizzarli su un periodo più lungo della loro utilizzazione non è pertanto conforme alle disposizioni delle direttive contabili, considerato che l'utilizzazione di un contratto non dovrebbe di norma essere superiore alla durata del contratto. L'articolo 35, paragrafo 1, lettera c) bb), della Quarta direttiva e l'articolo 29 della Settima direttiva dispongono inoltre che, indipendentemente dal fatto che la loro utilizzazione sia o non sia limitata nel tempo, gli elementi delle immobilizzazioni devono essere oggetto di rettifiche di valore per dare a tali elementi il valore inferiore che deve essere ad essi attribuito alla data di chiusura del bilancio qualora si preveda che la svalutazione sia duratura. La misura nazionale sembra consentire alle società sportive di non effettuare le rettifiche di valore relative ai diritti sulle prestazioni di atleti professionisti anche quando si preveda che la svalutazione sia duratura. Un esame più dettagliato delle modifiche in questione può fare emergere ulteriori elementi di incompatibilità con le direttive contabili. La Commissione fa infine osservare che la misura nazionale sembra violare anche i principi contabili internazionali, (IAS) 38.

29. Di conseguenza, la modifica prevista dalla legge italiana è, ad un primo esame, contraria ai requisiti delle direttive contabili. Anche per tale ragione, la Commissione ritiene, in questo stadio, che la misura non possa essere dichiarata compatibile con il mercato comune.

CONCLUSIONE

Tenuto conto di quanto precede, la Commissione invita l'Italia a presentare, nell'ambito

---

[994] Quarta direttiva 78/660/CEE del Consiglio, del 25 luglio 1978, basata sull'articolo 54, paragrafo 3, lettera g), del Trattato e relativa ai conti annuali di taluni tipi di società (GU L 222 del 14-8-1978, pag. 11) e Settima direttiva 83/349/CEE del Consiglio del 13 giugno 1983 basata sull'articolo 54, paragrafo 3, lettera g), del Trattato e relativa ai conti consolidati (GU L 193 del 18-7-1983, pag. 1).

del procedimento di cui all'articolo 88, paragrafo 2, del trattato CE, le proprie osservazioni e a fornire tutte le informazioni utili ai fini della valutazione delle misure, entro un mese dalla data di ricezione della presente.

La Commissione invita inoltre le autorità italiane a trasmettere senza indugio copia della presente lettera ai beneficiari potenziali dell'aiuto.

La Commissione desidera richiamare all'attenzione dell'Italia che l'articolo 88, paragrafo 3, del trattato CE ha effetto sospensivo e che, in forza dell'articolo 14 del regolamento (CE) n. 659/1999 del Consiglio, essa può imporre allo Stato membro interessato di recuperare ogni aiuto illegale dal beneficiario.

Con la presente la Commissione comunica all'Italia che informerà gli interessati attraverso la pubblicazione della presente lettera e di una sintesi della stessa nella Gazzetta ufficiale dell'Unione europea. Informerà inoltre gli interessati nei paesi EFTA firmatari dell'accordo SEE attraverso la pubblicazione di un avviso nel supplemento SEE della Gazzetta ufficiale, e informerà infine l'Autorità di vigilanza EFTA inviandole copia della presente. Tutti gli interessati anzidetti saranno invitati a presentare osservazioni entro un mese dalla data di detta pubblicazione.'

———

# 2.15.   TAX*

## * 2.15.1.   ANSWER ON BEHALF OF THE COMMISSION TO WRITTEN QUESTION E-424/95 BY HUGH KERR (PSE), 4 APRIL 1995[995]

Subject: VAT on sports clubs

———

## * 2.15.2.   ANSWER ON BEHALF OF THE COMMISSION TO WRITTEN QUESTION E-1085/96 BY LAURA DE ESTEBAN MARTIN (PPE), 3 JUNE 1996[996]

Subject: VAT exemption for sports organizations

———

## * 2.15.3.   EUROPEAN COURT OF JUSTICE, OPINION OF ADVOCATE GENERAL LA PERGOLA, COMMISSION OF THE EUROPEAN COMMUNITIES V KINGDOM OF SPAIN, CASE C-124/96, 3 FEBRUARY 1998[997]

———

## * 2.15.4.   ANSWER ON BEHALF OF THE COMMISSION TO WRITTEN QUESTION E-420/98 BY GRAHAM WATSON (ELDR), 5 MAY 1998[998]

Subject: German tax regime

———

## * 2.15.5.   EUROPEAN COURT OF JUSTICE, JUDGMENT (SIXTH CHAMBER),COMMISSION OF THE EUROPEAN COMMUNITIES V KINGDOM OF SPAIN, CASE C-124/96, 7 MAY 1998[999]

———

## * 2.15.6.   ANSWER ON BEHALF OF THE COMMISSION TO WRITTEN QUESTION E-3733/98 BY BRENDAN DONNELLY (PPE), 29 JANUARY 1999[1000]

Subject: VAT on golf-club membership

———

---

*   The full texts of documents which are marked with an asterisk (*) are not incorporated in the book itself, but are freely accessible on the website of the ASSER International Sports Law Centre, at <www.sportslaw.nl> – documentation.

[995] Question of 17-2-1995; OJ C 179, 13-7-1995, p. 21.
[996] Question of 13-5-1996; OJ C 297, 8-10-1996, p. 80.
[997] ECR 1998, p. I-2501.
[998] Question of 24-2-1998; OJ C 386, 11-12-1998, p. 16.
[999] ECR 1998, p. I-2501.
[1000] Question of 11-12-1998; OJ C 207, 21-7-1999, p. 120.

**\* 2.15.7. ANSWER ON BEHALF OF THE COMMISSION TO WRITTEN QUESTION P-2751/99 BY FRANÇOISE GROSSETÊTE (PPE-DE), 20 JANUARY 2000**[1001]

Subject: Harmonisation of national legislation turnover tax

---

**\* 2.15.8. EUROPEAN COURT OF JUSTICE, OPINION OF ADVOCATE GENERAL JACOBS, SVENSKA STATEN (SWEDISH STATE) V STOCKHOLM LINDÖPARK AB AND STOCKHOLM LINDÖPARK AB V SVENSKA STATEN (SWEDISH STATE), CASE C-150/99, 26 SEPTEMBER 2000**[1002]

---

**\* 2.15.9. EUROPEAN COURT OF JUSTICE, JUDGMENT (FIFTH CHAMBER), SVENSKA STATEN (SWEDISH STATE) V STOCKHOLM LINDÖPARK AB V SVENSKA STATEN (SWEDISH STATE), CASE C-150/99, 18 JANUARY 2001**[1003]

---

**\* 2.15.10. EUROPEAN COURT OF JUSTICE, JUDGMENT (FIFTH CHAMBER), KENNEMER GOLF & COUNTRY CLUB V STAATSSECRETARIS VAN FINANCIËN, CASE C-174/00, 21 MARCH 2002**[1004]

---

**\* 2.15.11. ANSWER ON BEHALF OF THE COMMISSION TO WRITTEN QUESTION E-3327/02 BY TOINE MANDERS (ELDR), 9 JANUARY 2003**[1005]

Subject: European football finals

---

---

[1001] Question of 7-1-2000; OJ C 225 E, 8-8-2000, p. 152-153.
[1002] ECR 2001, p. I-493.
[1003] ECR 2001, p. I-493.
[1004] ECR 2002, p. I-3293.
[1005] Question of 13-11-2002; OJ C 11E, 15-1-2004, p. 48-49.

## 2.16.    TOBACCO ADVERTISING*

#### * 2.16.1.    ANSWER ON BEHALF OF THE COMMISSION TO WRITTEN QUESTION E-1584/96 BY VIVIANE REDING (PPE), 6 SEPTEMBER 1996[1006]

Subject: Sport and culture without tobacco

———

#### * 2.16.2.    ANSWER ON BEHALF OF THE COMMISSION TO WRITTEN QUESTION E-1091/98 BY GRAHAM MATHER (PPE), 30 APRIL 1998[1007]

Subject: Draft Directive on the approximation of laws, regulations and administrative provisions of the Member States relating to the advertising of tobacco products

———

#### * 2.16.3.    DIRECTIVE 98/43/EC OF THE EUROPEAN PARLIAMENT AND OF THE COUNCIL ON THE APPROXIMATION OF THE LAWS, REGULATIONS AND ADMINISTRATIVE PROVISIONS OF THE MEMBER STATES RELATING TO THE ADVERTISING AND SPONSORSHIP OF TOBACCO PRODUCTS, 6 JULY 1998[1008]

———

#### * 2.16.4. ANSWER ON BEHALF OF THE COMMISSION TO WRITTEN QUESTION E-3297/00 BY CHRIS DAVIES (ELDR), 13 DECEMBER 2000[1009]

Subject: Tobacco advertising/sponsorship

———

#### * 2.16.5.    PROPOSAL FOR A DIRECTIVE OF THE EUROPEAN PARLIAMENT AND OF THE COUNCIL ON THE APPROXIMATION OF THE LAWS, REGULATIONS AND ADMINISTRATIVE PROVISIONS OF THE MEMBER STATES RELATING TO THE ADVERTISING AND SPONSORSHIP OF TOBACCO PRODUCTS (PRESENTED BY THE COMMISSION PURSUANT TO ARTICLES 47(2), 55 AND 95 OF THE EC TREATY), 30 MAY 2001[1010]

———

---

\*   The full texts of documents which are marked with an asterisk (\*) are not incorporated in the book itself, but are freely accessible on the website of the ASSER International Sports Law Centre, at <www.sportslaw.nl> – documentation.

[1006] Question of 24-6-1996; OJ C 385, 19-12-1996, p. 18.
[1007] Question of 7-4-1998; OJ C 323, 21-10-1998, p. 112.
[1008] OJ L 213, 30-7-1998, p. 9-12. No longer in force.
[1009] Question of 25-10-2000; OJ C 151 E, 22-5-2001, p. 125-126.
[1010] OJ C 270 E, 25-9-2001, p. 97-100.

**\* 2.16.6.   OPINION OF THE ECONOMIC AND SOCIAL COMMITTEE ON THE 'PROPOSAL FOR A DIRECTIVE OF THE EUROPEAN PARLIAMENT AND OF THE COUNCIL ON THE APPROXIMATION OF THE LAWS, REGULATIONS AND ADMINISTRATIVE PROVISIONS OF THE MEMBER STATES RELATING TO THE ADVERTISING AND SPONSORSHIP OF TOBACCO PRODUCTS (PRESENTED BY THE COMMISSION PURSUANT TO ARTICLES 47(2), 55 AND 95 OF THE EC TREATY)', 17 OCTOBER 2001**[1011]

———

**\* 2.16.7.   DIRECTIVE 2003/33/EC OF THE EUROPEAN PARLIAMENT AND OF THE COUNCIL OF 26 MAY 2003 ON THE APPROXIMATION OF THE LAWS, REGULATIONS AND ADMINISTRATIVE PROVISIONS OF THE MEMBER STATES RELATING TO THE ADVERTISING AND SPONSORSHIP OF TOBACCO PRODUCTS, 26 MAY 2003**[1012]

———

---

[1011]   OJ C 36, 8-2-2002, p. 105.
[1012]   OJ L 152 , 20-6-2003, p. 16-19 (Text with EEA relevance)

# 2.17.   TRADE MARK*

## * 2.17.1.   EUROPEAN COURT OF JUSTICE, OPINION OF ADVOCATE GENERAL JACOBS, SABEL BV V PUMA AG, RUDOLF DASSLER SPORT, CASE C-251/95, 29 APRIL 1997[1013]

---

## 2.17.2.   EUROPEAN COURT OF JUSTICE, JUDGMENT, SABEL BV V PUMA AG, RUDOLF DASSLER SPORT, CASE C-251/95, 11 NOVEMBER 1997[1014]

Reference to the Court under Article 177 of the EC Treaty by the Bundesgerichtshof for a preliminary ruling in the proceedings pending before that court between
Sabel BV
and
Puma AG, Rudolf Dassler Sport
on the interpretation of Article 4(1)(b) of First Council Directive 89/104/EEC of 21 December 1988 to approximate the laws of the Member States relating to trademarks (OJ 1989 L 40, p.1),

*The Court,*

composed of: G.C. Rodríguez Iglesias, President, C. Gulmann (Rapporteur),H. Ragnemalm and M. Wathelet, (Presidents of Chambers), G.F. Mancini, J.C. Moitinho de Almeida, P.J.G. Kapteyn, J.L. Murray, D.A.O. Edward, J.-P. Puissochet, G. Hirsch, P. Jann and L. Sevón, Judges,
Advocate General: F.G. Jacobs,
Registrar: H.A. Rühl, Principal Administrator,
after considering the written observations submitted on behalf of:
–       Puma AG, Rudolf Dassler Sport, by W. Hufnagel, Patentanwalt,
–       the French Government, by C. de Salins, Deputy Director in the Legal Affairs Department of the Ministry of Foreign Affairs, and P. Martinet, Secretary for Foreign Affairs in that Ministry, acting as Agents,
–       the Netherlands Government, by A. Bos, Legal Adviser in the Ministry of Foreign Affairs, acting as Agent,
–       the United Kingdom Government, by L. Nicoll, of the Treasury Solicitor's Department, acting as Agent, assisted by M. Silverleaf, Barrister,
–       the Commission of the European Communities, by J. Grunwald, Legal Adviser, and B.J. Drijber, of its Legal Service, acting as Agents,

having regard to the Report for the Hearing,
after hearing the oral observations
–       of SABEL BV, represented by R.E.P. de Ranitz,

---

*    The full texts of documents which are marked with an asterisk (*) are not incorporated in the book itself, but are freely accessible on the website of the ASSER International Sports Law Centre, at <www.sportslaw.nl> – documentation.
   [1013] ECR 1997, p. I-6191.
   [1014] ECR 1997, p. I-6191.

–    of The Hague Bar;
–    of the Belgian Government, represented by A. Braun,
–    of the Brussels Bar;
–    of the French Government, represented by P. Martinet;
–    of the Luxembourg Government, represented by N. Decker,
–    of the Luxembourg Bar;
–    of the United Kingdom Government, represented by L. Nicoll, assisted by M. Silverleaf; and
–    of the Commission, represented by J. Grunwald, at the hearing on 28 January 1997,

after hearing the Opinion of the Advocate General at the sitting on 29 April 1997,

gives the following

**Judgment**

**Grounds**

1.    By order of 29 June 1995, received at the Court on 20 July 1995, the Bundes-gerichtshof (Federal Court of Justice) referred to the Court for a preliminary ruling under Article 177 of the EC Treaty a question on the interpretation of Article 4(1)(b) of First Council Directive 89/104/EEC of 21 December 1988 to approxi-mate the laws of the Member States relating to trademarks (OJ 1989 L 40, p. 1, hereinafter 'the Directive').

2.    That question was raised in proceedings between the Dutch company Sabel BV(hereinafter 'Sabel') and the German company Puma AG, Rudolf Dassler Sport(hereinafter 'Puma') concerning an application to register the IR mark 540 894,depicted below, [...]
      in Germany, *inter alia* for goods in classes 18 'Leather and imitation leather, prod-ucts made therefrom not included in ot her classes; bags and handbags' and 25 'Clothing, including tights, hosiery, belts, scarves, ties/cravats and braces; foot-wear; hats'.

3.    Puma lodged opposition to the registration of that mark on the ground, in particu-lar, that it was the proprietor of the pictorial mark depicted below, [...]
      which was of earlier priority and registered in Germany (under No 1 106 066), *in-ter alia* for 'leather and imitation leather, goods made therefrom (bags) and ar-ticles of clothing'.

4.    The Deutsches Patentamt (German Patent Office) considered there to be no resem-blance for the purposes of trade-mark law between the two marks and rejected the opposition. Puma therefore appealed to the Bundespatentgericht (Federal Patents Court) which partially upheld its application and held that there was a resemblance between the two marks with respect to SABEL's goods in classes 18 and 25, which it regarded as being identical or similar to the goods on the list of articles covered by the Puma mark. SABEL then appealed to the Bundesgerichtshof for annulment of the decision refusing its application.

5.    The Bundesgerichtshof provisionally considered that, applying the principles ap-plied hitherto under German law for determining whether there is a likelihood of confusion for trade-mark purposes, no such likelihood existed as regards the two marks in question.

6.    The criteria applied by the Bundesgerichtshof in order to reach that provisional conclusion are, in essence, as follows:

- In determining whether there is a likelihood of confusion, the court must focus on the overall impression made by the respective signs. It is not permissible to isolate one element out of a graphic ensemble and to restrict examination of the likelihood of confusion to that element alone. However, an individual component may be recognized as having a particularly distinctive character which characterizes the sign as a whole, and, consequently, a likelihood of confusion may be found to exist if another party's sign resembles the whole of the sign so characterized. Even in such a case, however, the two signs must be compared in their entirety and the comparison must not be confined to their individual (characterizing)elements.
- A sign may have a particularly distinctive character either *per se* or because of the reputation the mark enjoys with the public. The more distinctive its character, the greater the risk of confusion. However, since no submission had been made on that point in the present case, the starting point for examining the similarity of the two marks is that the earlier mark has normal distinguishing characteristics.
- The assessment of whether an element has such significance as to characterize the sign as a whole is, essentially, a matter for the court called upon to adjudicate on the substance of the case, subject however to its observing the rules of logic and common sense. The Bundespatentgericht cannot be criticized in law for stressing the importance of the pictorial component of the SABEL mark and considering that the textual component of the mark was of only secondary importance.
- Strict criteria must be applied with respect to the likelihood of confusion between pictorial components which are basically descriptive and have little imaginative content. The depiction of a bounding feline is a pictorial component which closely follows a natural model and reproduces the bounding motion typical of such animals. The particular features of the depiction of the bounding feline in the Puma mark, for example its depiction as a silhouette, are not reproduced in the SABEL mark. The fact that there is an analogy between the pictorial components of the two marks can therefore not be adduced as a ground for finding that there is a likelihood of confusion.

7.   None the less, the Bundesgerichtshof seeks to ascertain the importance to be accorded to the semantic content of the marks (in the present case, a 'bounding feline') in determining the likelihood of confusion. That difficulty is occasioned, in particular, by the ambiguous wording of Article 4(1)(b) of the Directive, in terms of which the likelihood of confusion 'includes the likelihood of association with the earlier trade mark'. The question therefore arises for the national court whether the mere association which the public might make between the two marks, through the idea of a 'bounding feline', justifies refusing protection to the SABEL mark in Germany for products similar to those on the list of articles covered by Puma's priority mark.

8.   The Directive, which was implemented in Germany by the Gesetz über den Schutz von Marken und sonstigen Kennzeichen (Law on the Protection of Trade Marks and Other Signs) of 25 October 1994 (BGBl I, p. 3082), contains, in Article 4(1)(b), the following provision:

'A trade mark shall not be registered or, if registered, shall be liable to be declared invalid:

(a)   ...

(b)   if because of its identity with, or similarity to, the earlier trade mark and the identity or similarity of the goods or services covered by the trade marks, there exists a likelihood of confusion on the part of the public, which includes the likelihood of association with the earlier trade mark.'

9. The tenth recital in the preamble to the Directive states:
'Whereas the protection afforded by the registered trade mark, the function of which is in particular to guarantee the trade mark as an indication of origin, is absolute in the case of identity between the mark and the sign and goods or services; whereas the protection applies also in case of similarity between the mark and the sign and the goods or services; whereas it is indispensable to give an interpretation of the concept of similarity in relation to the likelihood of confusion; whereas the likelihood of confusion, the appreciation of which depends on numerous elements and, in particular, on the recognition of the trade mark on the market, of the association which can be made with the used or registered sign, of the degree of similarity between the trade mark and the sign and between the goods or services identified, constitutes the specific condition for such protection; whereas the ways in which likelihood of confusion may be established, and in particular the onus of proof, are a matter for national procedural rules which are not prejudiced by the directive'.

10. The Bundesgerichtshof decided to stay proceedings and to refer the following question to the Court for a preliminary ruling:
'With reference to the interpretation of Article 4(1)(b) of the First Council Directive of 21 December 1988 to approximate the laws of the Member States relating to trade marks, is it sufficient for a finding that there is a likelihood of confusion between a sign composed of text and picture and a sign consisting merely of a picture, which is registered for identical and similar goods and is not especially well known to the public, that the two signs coincide as to their semantic content(in this case, a bounding feline)?
What is the significance in this connection of the wording of the Directive, in terms of which the likelihood of confusion includes the likelihood that a mark may be associated with an earlier mark?'

11. In its question the Bundesgerichtshof is essentially asking whether the criterion of the 'likelihood of confusion ... which includes the likelihood of association with the earlier trade mark' contained in Article 4(1)(b) of the Directive is to be interpreted as meaning that the mere association which the public might make between the two marks as a result of a resemblance in their semantic content, is a sufficient ground for concluding that there exists a likelihood of confusion within the meaning of that provision, taking into account that one of those marks is composed of a combination of a word and a picture, whilst the other, consisting merely of a picture, is registered for identical and similar goods, and is not especially well known to the public.

12. Article 4(1)(b) of the Directive, which sets out the additional grounds on which registration may be refused or a registered mark declared invalid in the event of conflict with earlier marks, provides that a trade mark conflicts with an earlier trade mark if, because of the identity or similarity of both the trade marks and the goods or services covered, there exists a likelihood of confusion on the part of the public, which includes the likelihood of association between the two marks.

13. Essentially identical provisions are found in Article 5(1)(a) and (b) of the Directive, which defines the situations in which the proprietor of a trade mark is entitled to prevent third parties from using signs identical with or similar to its trade mark, and in Articles 8(1)(b) and (9)(1)(b) of Council Regulation (EC) No 40/94 of 20 December 1993 on the Community trade mark (OJ 1994 L 11, p. 1).

14. The Belgian, Luxembourg and Netherlands Governments claimed that the term 'likelihood of association' was included in those provisions of the Directive at

their request, in order that they should be construed in the same manner as Article 13a of the Uniform Benelux Law on Trade Marks which adopts the concept of resemblance between marks, rather than that of likelihood of confusion, in defining the scope of the exclusive right conferred by a trade mark.

15. Those governments refer to a judgment of the Benelux Court holding that there is resemblance between a mark and a sign when, taking account of the particular circumstances of the case, in particular the distinctiveness of the mark, the mark and the sign, considered separately and together, present, aurally, visually or conceptually, a similarity such as to establish an association between the sign and the mark (judgment of 20 May 1983 in Case A 82/5 *Jullien* v *Verschuere*, Jur. 1983,vol. 4, p. 36). That decision is based on the idea that, where a sign is likely to give rise to association with a mark, the public makes a connection between the sign and the mark. Such a connection may be prejudicial to the earlier mark not only if it gives the impression that the products have the same or a related origin, but also where there is no likelihood of confusion between the sign and the mark. Since perception of the sign calls to mind, often subconsciously, the memory of the mark, associations made between a sign and a mark can result in the 'goodwill' attached to the earlier mark being transferred to the sign and dilute the image linked to that mark.

16. According to those governments, the likelihood of association may arise in three sets of circumstances: (1) where the public confuses the sign and the mark in question (likelihood of direct confusion); (2) where the public makes a connection between the proprietors of the sign and those of the mark and confuses them (likelihood of indirect confusion or association); (3) where the public considers the sign to be similar to the mark and perception of the sign calls to mind the memory of the mark, although the two are not confused (likelihood of association in the strict sense).

17. It must therefore be determined whether, as those governments claim, Article4(1)(b) can apply where there is no likelihood of direct or indirect confusion, but only a likelihood of association in the strict sense. Such an interpretation of the Directive is contested by both the United Kingdom Government and by the Commission.

18. In that connection, it is to be remembered that Article 4(1)(b) of the Directive is designed to apply only if, by reason of the identity or similarity both of the marks and of the goods or services which they designate, 'there exists a likelihood of confusion on the part of the public, which includes the likelihood of association with the earlier trade mark'. It follows from that wording that the concept of likelihood of association is not an alternative to that of likelihood of confusion, but serves to define its scope. The terms of the provision itself exclude its application where there is no likelihood of confusion on the part of the public.

19. The tenth recital in the preamble to the Directive, according to which 'the likelihood of confusion ... constitutes the specific condition for such protection', also confirms that interpretation.

20. Furthermore, the interpretation given in paragraph 18 of this judgment is not inconsistent with Article 4(3) and (4)(a) and Article 5(2) of the Directive, which permit the proprietor of a trade mark which has a reputation to prohibit the use without due cause of signs identical with or similar to his mark and do not require proof of likelihood of confusion, even where there is no similarity between the goods in question.

21. In that respect, it is sufficient to note that, unlike Article 4(1)(b), those provisions apply exclusively to marks which have a reputation and on condition that use of

the third party's mark without due cause takes unfair advantage of, or is detrimental to, the distinctive character or the repute of the trade mark.

22.     As pointed out in paragraph 18 of this judgment, Article 4(1)(b) of the Directive does not apply where there is no likelihood of confusion on the part of the public. In that respect, it is clear from the tenth recital in the preamble to the Directive that the appreciation of the likelihood of confusion 'depends on numerous elements and, in particular, on the recognition of the trade mark on the market, of the association which can be made with the used or registered sign, of the degree of similarity between the trade mark and the sign and between the goods or services identified'. The likelihood of confusion must therefore be appreciated globally, taking into account all factors relevant to the circumstances of the case.

23.     That global appreciation of the visual, aural or conceptual similarity of the marks in question, must be based on the overall impression given by the marks, bearing in mind, in particular, their distinctive and dominant components. The wording of Article 4(1)(b) of the Directive – '... there exists a likelihood of confusion on the part of the public ...' – shows that the perception of marks in the mind of the average consumer of the type of goods or services in question plays a decisive role in the global appreciation of the likelihood of confusion. The average consumer normally perceives a mark as a whole and does not proceed to analyse its various details.

24.     In that perspective, the more distinctive the earlier mark, the greater will be the likelihood of confusion. It is therefore not impossible that the conceptual similarity resulting from the fact that two marks use images with analogous semantic content may give rise to a likelihood of confusion where the earlier mark has a particularly distinctive character, either *per se* or because of the reputation it enjoys with the public.

25.     However, in circumstances such as those in point in the main proceedings, where the earlier mark is not especially well known to the public and consists of an image with little imaginative content, the mere fact that the two marks are conceptually similar is not sufficient to give rise to a likelihood of confusion.

26.     The answer to the national court's question must therefore be that the criterion of 'likelihood of confusion which includes the likelihood of association with the earlier mark' contained in Article 4(1)(b) of the Directive is to be interpreted as meaning that the mere association which the public might make between two trade marks as a result of their analogous semantic content is not in itself a sufficient ground for concluding that there is a likelihood of confusion within the meaning of that provision.

**Costs**

27.     The costs incurred by the Belgian, French, Luxembourg, Netherlands and United Kingdom Governments and by the Commission of the European Communities, which have submitted observations to the Court, are not recoverable. Since these proceedings are, for the parties to the main proceedings, a step in the proceedings pending before the national court, the decision on costs is a matter for that court.

On those grounds,
THE COURT,
in answer to the question referred to it by the Bundesgerichtshof by order of 29 June 1995, hereby rules:

The criterion of 'likelihood of confusion which includes the likelihood of association with the earlier mark' contained in Article 4(1)(b) of First Council Directive 89/104/EEC of 21 December 1988 to approximate the laws of the Member States relating to trade marks is to be interpreted as meaning that the mere association which the public might make between two trade marks as a result of their analogous semantic content is not in itself a sufficient ground for concluding that there is a likelihood of confusion within the meaning of that provision.

Delivered in open court in Luxembourg on 11 November 1997.

────

**\* 2.17.3. EUROPEAN COURT OF JUSTICE, OPINION OF ADVOCATE GENERAL RUIZ-JARABO COLOMER, ARSENAL FOOTBALL CLUB PLC V MATTHEW REED, CASE C-206/01, 13 JUNE 2002**[1015]

────

**2.17.4. EUROPEAN COURT OF JUSTICE, JUDGMENT, ARSENAL FOOTBALL CLUB PLC V. MATTHEW REED, CASE C-206/01, 12 NOVEMBER 2002**[1016]

(Approximation of laws − Trade marks − Directive 89/104/EEC − Article 5(1)(a) − Scope of the proprietor's exclusive right to the trade mark)

Reference to the Court under Article 234 EC by the High Court of Justice of England and Wales, Chancery Division, for a preliminary ruling in the proceedings pending before that court between Arsenal Football Club Plc v. Matthew Reed
on the interpretation of Article 5(1)(a) of the First Council Directive 89/104/EEC of 21 December 1988 to approximate the laws of the Member States relating to trade marks (OJ 1989 L 40, p. 1),

**THE COURT**,

Composed of: G.C. Rodríguez Iglesias, President, J.-P. Puissochet, M. Wathelet, C.W.A. Timmermans (Rapporteur) (Presidents of Chambers), C. Gulmann, D.A.O. Edward, P. Jann, V. Skouris, F. Macken, N. Colneric and S. von Bahr, Judges,
Advocate General: D. Ruiz-Jarabo Colomer,
Registrar: L. Hewlett, Principal Administrator,
after considering the written observations submitted on behalf of:
−    Arsenal Football Club plc, by S. Thorley QC and T. Mitcheson, Barrister, instructed by Lawrence Jones, Solicitors,
−    Mr Reed, by A. Roughton, Barrister, instructed by Stunt & Son, Solicitors,
−    the Commission of the European Communities, by N.B. Rasmussen, acting as Agent,
−    the EFTA Surveillance Authority, by P. Dyrberg, acting as Agent,
having regard to the Report for the Hearing,
after hearing the oral observations of Arsenal Football Club plc, represented by S. Thorley and T. Mitcheson; Mr Reed, represented by A. Roughton and S. Malynicz, Bar-

---

[1015]   ECR, p. I-10273.
[1016]   ECR, p. I-10273.

rister; and the Commission, represented by N.B. Rasmussen and M. Shotter, acting as Agent, at the hearing on 14 May 2002,
after hearing the Opinion of the Advocate General at the sitting on 13 June 2002,
gives the following

**Judgment**
1.    By order of 4 May 2001, received at the Court on 18 May 2001, the High Court of Justice of England and Wales, Chancery Division, referred to the Court for a preliminary ruling under Article 234 EC two questions on the interpretation of Article 5(1)(a) of the First Council Directive 89/104/EEC of 21 December 1988 toapproximate the laws of the Member States relating to trade marks (OJ 1989 L 40, p. 1, 'the Directive').
2.    Those questions were raised in proceedings between Arsenal Football Club plc ('Arsenal FC') and Mr Reed concerning the selling and offering for sale by Mr Reed of scarves marked in large lettering with the word 'Arsenal', a sign which is registered as a trade mark by Arsenal FC for those and other goods.

**Legal background**

*Community legislation*
3.    The Directive states, in the first recital in its preamble, that national trade mark laws contain disparities which may impede the free movement of goods and freedom to provide services and may distort competition within the common market. According to that recital, it is therefore necessary, in view of the establishment and functioning of the internal market, to approximate the laws of the Member States. The third recital in the preamble states that it is not necessary at present to undertake full-scale approximation of national laws on trade marks.
4.    According to the 10th recital in the preamble to the Directive:
'... the protection afforded by the registered trade mark, the function of which is in particular to guarantee the trade mark as an indication of origin, is absolute in the case of identity between the mark and the sign and goods or services ...'.
5.    Article 5(1) of the Directive provides:
'The registered trade mark shall confer on the proprietor exclusive rights therein. The proprietor shall be entitled to prevent all third parties not having his consent from using in the course of trade:
(a)    any sign which is identical with the trade mark in relation to goods or services which are identical with those for which the trade mark is registered;
(b)    any sign where, because of its identity with, or similarity to, the trade mark and the identity or similarity of the goods or services covered by the trade mark and the sign, there exists a likelihood of confusion on the part of the public, which includes the likelihood of association between the sign and the trade mark.'
6.    Article 5(3)(a) and (b) of the Directive provides:
'The following, *inter alia*, may be prohibited under paragraphs 1 and 2:
(a)    affixing the sign to the goods or to the packaging thereof;
(b)    offering the goods, or putting them on the market or stocking them for these purposes ...'
7.    Under Article 5(5) of the Directive:
'Paragraphs 1 to 4 shall not affect provisions in any Member State relating to the protection against the use of a sign other than for the purposes of distinguishing goods or services, where use of that sign without due cause takes unfair advantage

of, or is detrimental to, the distinctive character or the repute of the trade mark.'

8. Article 6(1) of the Directive reads as follows:
'The trade mark shall not entitle the proprietor to prohibit a third party from using, in the course of trade,

    (a)   his own name or address;

    (b)   indications concerning the kind, quality, quantity, intended purpose, value, geographical origin, the time of production of goods or of rendering of the service, or other characteristics of goods or services;

    (c)   the trade mark where it is necessary to indicate the intended purpose of a product or service, in particular as accessories or spare parts;

    provided he uses them in accordance with honest practices in industrial or commercial matters.'

*National legislation*

9. In the United Kingdom the law of trade marks is governed by the Trade Marks Act 1994, which replaced the Trade Marks Act 1938 in order to implement the Directive.

10. Section 10(1) of the Trade Marks Act 1994 provides:
'A person infringes a registered trade mark if he uses in the course of trade a sign which is identical with the trade mark in relation to goods or services which are identical with those for which it is registered.'

11. Under Section 10(2)(b) of the Trade Marks Act 1994:
'A person infringes a registered trade mark if he uses in the course of trade a sign where because –

    ...

    (b)   the sign is similar to the trade mark and is used in relation to goods or services identical with or similar to those for which the trade mark is registered,

    there exists a likelihood of confusion on the part of the public, which includes the likelihood of association with the trade mark.'

**The main proceedings and the questions referred for a preliminary ruling**

12. Arsenal FC is a well-known football club in the English Premier League. It is nicknamed 'the Gunners' and has for a long time been associated with two emblems, a cannon device and a shield device.

13. In 1989 Arsenal FC had *inter alia* the words 'Arsenal' and 'Arsenal Gunners' and the cannon and shield emblems registered as trade marks for a class of goods comprising articles of outer clothing, articles of sports clothing and footwear. Arsenal FC designs and supplies its own products or has them made and supplied by its network of approved resellers.

14. Since its commercial and promotional activities in the field of sales of souvenirs and memorabilia under those marks have expanded greatly in recent years and provide it with substantial income, Arsenal FC has sought to ensure that 'official' products – that is, products manufactured by Arsenal FC or with its authorisation – can be identified clearly, and has endeavoured to persuade its supporters to buy official products only. The club has also brought legal proceedings, both civil and criminal, against traders selling unofficial products.

15. Since 1970 Mr Reed has sold football souvenirs and memorabilia, almost all marked with signs referring to Arsenal FC, from several stalls located outside the grounds of Arsenal FC's stadium. He was able to obtain from KT Sports, licensed by Arsenal FC to sell its products to vendors around the stadium, only very small

quantities of official products. In 1991 and 1995 Arsenal FC had unofficial articles of Mr Reed's confiscated.

16. The High Court states that in the main proceedings it is not in dispute that Mr Reed sold and offered for sale from one of his stalls scarves marked in large lettering with signs referring to Arsenal FC and that these were unofficial products.

17. It also states that on that stall there was a large sign with the following text:
'The word or logo(s) on the goods offered for sale, are used solely to adorn the product and does not imply or indicate any affiliation or relationship with the manufacturers or distributors of any other product, only goods with official Arsenal merchandise tags are official Arsenal merchandise.'

18. The High Court further states that when, exceptionally, he was able to obtain official articles Mr Reed, in his dealings with his customers, clearly distinguished the official products from the unofficial ones, in particular by using a label with the word 'official'. The official products were also sold at higher prices.

19. Since it considered that by selling the unofficial scarves Mr Reed had both committed the tort of 'passing off' – which, according to the High Court, is conduct on the part of a third party which is misleading in such a way that a large number of persons believe or are led to believe that articles sold by the third party are those of the claimant or are sold with his authorisation or have a commercial association with him – and infringed its trade marks, Arsenal FC brought proceedings against him in the High Court of Justice of England and Wales, Chancery Division.

20. In view of the circumstances in the main proceedings, the High Court dismissed Arsenal FC's action in tort ('passing off'), essentially on the ground that the club had not been able to show actual confusion on the part of the relevant public and, more particularly, had not been able to show that the unofficial products sold by Mr Reed were all regarded by the public as coming from or authorised by Arsenal FC. In this respect, the High Court observed that it seemed to it that the signs referring to Arsenal FC affixed to the articles sold by Mr Reed carried no indication of origin.

21. As to Arsenal FC's claim concerning infringement of its trade marks, based on section 10(1) and (2)(b) of the Trade Marks Act 1994, the High Court rejected their argument that the use by Mr Reed of the signs registered as trade marks was perceived by those to whom they were addressed as a badge of origin, so that the use was a 'trade mark use'.

22. According to the High Court, the signs affixed to Mr Reed's goods were in fact perceived by the public as 'badges of support, loyalty or affiliation'.

23. The High Court accordingly considered that Arsenal FC's infringement claim could succeed only if the protection conferred on the trade mark proprietor by section 10 of the Trade Marks Act 1994 and the provisions of the Directive implemented by that statute prohibits use by a third party other than trade mark use, which would require a wide interpretation of those provisions.

24. On this point, the High Court considers that the argument that use other than trade mark use is prohibited to a third party gives rise to inconsistencies. However, the contrary argument, namely that only trade mark use is covered, comes up against a difficulty connected with the wording of the Directive and the Trade Marks Act 1994, which both define infringement as the use of a 'sign', not of a 'trade mark'.

25. The High Court observes that it was in view of that wording in particular that the Court of Appeal of England and Wales, Civil Division, held in *Philips Electronics Ltd v Remington Consumer Products* ([1999] RPC 809) that the use other than trade mark use of a sign registered as a trade mark could constitute an infringement of a trade mark. The High Court observes that the state of the law on this point still remains uncertain.

26. The High Court also rejected Mr Reed's argument on the alleged invalidity of the Arsenal FC trade marks.

27. In those circumstances, the High Court of Justice of England and Wales, Chancery Division, decided to stay proceedings and refer the following questions to the Court for a preliminary ruling:

'1. Where a trade mark is validly registered and

(a) a third party uses in the course of trade a sign identical with that trade mark in relation to goods which are identical with those for [which] the trade mark is registered; and

(b) the third party has no defence to infringement by virtue of Article 6(1) of [Directive 89/104/EEC];

does the third party have a defence to infringement on the ground that the use complained of does not indicate trade origin (i.e. a connection in the course of trade between the goods and the trade mark proprietor)?

2. If so, is the fact that the use in question would be perceived as a badge of support, loyalty or affiliation to the trade mark proprietor a sufficient connectiono.'

## The questions referred for a preliminary ruling

28. The High Court's two questions should be examined together.

*Observations submitted to the Court*

29. Arsenal FC submits that Article 5(1)(a) of the Directive allows the trade mark proprietor to prohibit the use of a sign identical to the mark and does not make exercise of that right conditional on the sign being used as a trade mark. The protection conferred by that provision therefore extends to the use of the sign by a third party even where that use does not suggest the existence of a connection between the goods and the trade mark proprietor. That interpretation is supported by Article 6(1) of theDirective, since the specific limitations on the exercise of trade mark rights there provided for show that such use falls in principle within the scope of Article 5(1)(a) of the Directive and is permitted only in the cases exhaustively listed in Article 6(1) of the Directive.

30. Arsenal FC submits, in the alternative, that in the present case Mr Reed's use of the sign identical to the Arsenal trade mark must in any event be classified as trade mark use, on the ground that this use indicates the origin of the goods even though that origin does not necessarily have to designate the trade mark proprietor.

31. Mr Reed contends that the commercial activities at issue in the main proceedings do not fall within Article 5(1) of the Directive, since Arsenal FC has not shown that the sign was used as a trade mark, that is, to indicate the origin of the goods, as required by the Directive, in particular Article 5. If the public do not perceive the sign as a badge of origin, the use does not constitute 'trade mark use' of the sign. As to Article 6 of the Directive, nothing in that provision shows that it contains an exhaustive list of activities which do not constitute infringements.

32. The Commission submits that the right which the trade mark proprietor derives from Article 5(1) of the Directive is independent of the fact that the third party does not use the sign as a trade mark, and in particular of the fact that the third party does not use it as a badge of origin and informs the public by other means that the goods do not come from the trade mark proprietor, or even that the use of the sign has not been authorised by that proprietor. The specific object of a trade mark is to guarantee that only its proprietor can give the product its identity of ori-

gin by affixing the mark. The Commission further submits that it follows from the 10th recital in the preamble to the Directive that the protection provided for in Article 5(1)(a) is absolute.

33.     At the hearing, the Commission added that the concept of 'trade mark use' of the mark, if found to be relevant at all, refers to use which serves to distinguish goods rather than to indicate their origin. The concept also covers use by third parties which affects the interests of the trade mark proprietor, such as the reputation of the goods. In any event, public perception of the word 'Arsenal', which is identical to a verbal trade mark, as a token of support for or loyalty or affiliation to the proprietor of the mark does not exclude the possibility that the goods concerned are in consequence also perceived as coming from the proprietor. Quite the contrary, such perception confirms the distinctive nature of the mark and increases the risk of the goods being perceived as coming from the proprietor. Even, therefore, if 'trade mark use' of the mark is a relevant criterion, the proprietor should be entitled to prohibit the commercial activity at issue in the main proceedings.

34.     The EFTA Surveillance Authority submits that, for the trade mark proprietor to be able to rely on Article 5(1) of the Directive, the third party must use the sign to distinguish – as is the primary traditional function of a trade mark – goods or services, that is, use the mark as a trade mark. If that condition is not satisfied, only the provisions of national law referred to in Article 5(5) of the Directive may be relied on by the proprietor.

35.     However, the condition of use as a trade mark within the meaning of Article 5(1) of the Directive, which must be understood as a condition of use of a sign identical to the trade mark for the purpose of distinguishing goods or services, is a concept of Community law which should be interpreted broadly, so as to include in particular use as a badge of support for or loyalty or affiliation to the proprietor of the trade mark.

36.     According to the EFTA Surveillance Authority, the fact that the third party who affixes the trade mark to goods indicates that they do not come from the trade mark proprietor does not exclude the risk of confusion for a wider circle of consumers. If the proprietor were not entitled to prevent third parties from acting in that way, that could result in a generalised use of the sign. In the end, this would deprive the mark of its distinctive character, thus jeopardising its primary traditional function.

*The Court's reply*

37.     Article 5 of the Directive defines the '[r]ights conferred by a trade mark' and Article 6 contains provisions on the '[l]imitation of the effects of a trade mark'.

38.     Under the first sentence of Article 5(1) of the Directive, the registered trade mark confers exclusive rights on its proprietor. Under Article 5(1)(a), that exclusive right entitles the proprietor to prevent all third parties, acting without his consent, from using in the course of trade any sign which is identical to the trade mark in relation to goods or services which are identical to those for which the trade mark is registered. Article 5(3) gives a non-exhaustive list of the kinds of use which the proprietor may prohibit under Article 5(1). Other provisions of the Directive, such as Article 6, define certain limitations on the effects of a trade mark.

39.     With respect to the situation in point in the main proceedings, it should be observed that, as is apparent in particular from point 19 of and Annex V to the order for reference, the word 'Arsenal' appears in large letters on the scarves offered for sale by Mr Reed, together with other much less prominent markings including the words 'The Gunners', all referring to the trade mark proprietor, namely Arsenal

FC. Those scarves are intended *inter alia* for supporters of Arsenal FC who wear them in particular at matches in which the club plays.

40.    In those circumstances, as the national court stated, the use of the sign identical to the mark is indeed use in the course of trade, since it takes place in the context of commercial activity with a view to economic advantage and not as a private matter. It also falls within Article 5(1)(a) of the Directive, as use of a sign which is identical to the trade mark for goods which are identical to those for which the mark is registered.

41.    In particular, the use at issue in the main proceedings is 'for goods' within the meaning of Article 5(1)(a) of the Directive, since it concerns the affixing to goods of a sign identical to the trade mark and the offering of goods, putting them on the market or stocking them for those purposes within the meaning of Article 5(3)(a) and (b).

42.    To answer the High Court's questions, it must be determined whether Article 5(1)(a) of the Directive entitles the trade mark proprietor to prohibit any use by a third party in the course of trade of a sign identical to the trade mark for goods identical to those for which the mark is registered, or whether that right of prohibition presupposes the existence of a specific interest of the proprietor as trade mark proprietor, in that use of the sign in question by a third party must affect or be liable to affect one of the functions of the mark.

43.    It should be recalled, first, that Article 5(1) of the Directive carries out a complete harmonisation and defines the exclusive rights of trade mark proprietors in the Community (see, to that effect, Joined Cases C-414/99 to C-416/99 *Zino Davidoff and Levi Strauss* [2001] ECR I-8691, paragraph 39 and the case-law there cited).

44.    The ninth recital of the preamble to the Directive sets out its objective of ensuring that the trade mark proprietor enjoys 'the same protection under the legal systems of all the Member States' and describes that objective as 'fundamental'.

45.    In order to prevent the protection afforded to the proprietor varying from one State to another, the Court must therefore give a uniform interpretation to Article 5(1) of the Directive, in particular the term 'use' which is the subject of the questions referred for a preliminary ruling in the present case (see, to that effect, *Zino Davidoff and Levi Strauss*, paragraphs 42 and 43).

46.    Second, the Directive is intended, as the first recital of the preamble shows, to eliminate disparities between the trade mark laws of the Member States which may impede the free movement of goods and the freedom to provide services and distort competition within the common market.

47.    Trade mark rights constitute an essential element in the system of undistorted competition which the Treaty is intended to establish and maintain. In such a system, undertakings must be able to attract and retain customers by the quality of their goods or services, which is made possible only by distinctive signs allowing them to be identified (see, *inter alia*, Case C-10/89 *HAG GF* [1990] ECR I-3711, paragraph 13, and Case C-517/99 *Merz & Krell* [2001] ECR I-6959, paragraph 21).

48.    In that context, the essential function of a trade mark is to guarantee the identity of origin of the marked goods or services to the consumer or end user by enabling him, without any possibility of confusion, to distinguish the goods or services from others which have another origin. For the trade mark to be able to fulfil its essential role in the system of undistorted competition which the Treaty seeks to establish and maintain, it must offer a guarantee that all the goods or services bearing it have beenmanufactured or supplied under the control of a single undertaking which is responsible for their quality (see, *inter alia*, Case 102/77 *Hoffman-La*

*Roche* [1978] ECR 1139, paragraph 7, and Case C-299/99 *Philips* [2002] ECR I-5475, paragraph 30).

49.   The Community legislature confirmed that essential function of trade marks by providing, in Article 2 of the Directive, that signs which are capable of being represented graphically may constitute a trade mark only if they are capable of distinguishing the goods or services of one undertaking from those of other undertakings (see, *inter alia, Merz & Krell*, paragraph 23).

50.   For that guarantee of origin, which constitutes the essential function of a trade mark, to be ensured, the proprietor must be protected against competitors wishing to take unfair advantage of the status and reputation of the trade mark by selling products illegally bearing it (see, *inter alia, Hoffmann-La Roche*, paragraph 7, and Case C-349/95 *Loendersloot* [1997] ECR I-6227, paragraph 22). In this respect, the 10th recital of the preamble to the Directive points out the absolute nature of the protection afforded by the trade mark in the case of identity between the mark and the sign and between the goods or services concerned and those for which the mark is registered. It states that the aim of that protection is in particular to guarantee the trade mark as an indication of origin.

51.   It follows that the exclusive right under Article 5(1)(a) of the Directive was conferred in order to enable the trade mark proprietor to protect his specific interests as proprietor, that is, to ensure that the trade mark can fulfil its functions. The exercise of that right must therefore be reserved to cases in which a third party's use of the sign affects or is liable to affect the functions of the trade mark, in particular its essential function of guaranteeing to consumers the origin of the goods.

52.   The exclusive nature of the right conferred by a registered trade mark on its proprietor under Article 5(1)(a) of the Directive can be justified only within the limits of the application of that article.

53.   It should be noted that Article 5(5) of the Directive provides that Article 5(1) to (4) does not affect provisions in a Member State relating to protection against the use of a sign for purposes other than that of distinguishing goods or services.

54.   The proprietor may not prohibit the use of a sign identical to the trade mark for goods identical to those for which the mark is registered if that use cannot affect his own interests as proprietor of the mark, having regard to its functions. Thus certain uses for purely descriptive purposes are excluded from the scope of Article 5(1) of the Directive because they do not affect any of the interests which that provision aims to protect, and do not therefore fall within the concept of use within the meaning of that provision (see, with respect to a use for purely descriptive purposes relating to the characteristics of the product offered, Case C-2/00 *Hölterhoff* [2002] ECR I-4187, paragraph 16).

55.   In this respect, it is clear that the situation in question in the main proceedings is fundamentally different from that in *Hölterhoff*. In the present case, the use of the sign takes place in the context of sales to consumers and is obviously not intended for purely descriptive purposes.

56.   Having regard to the presentation of the word 'Arsenal' on the goods at issue in the main proceedings and the other secondary markings on them (see paragraph 39 above), the use of that sign is such as to create the impression that there is a material link in the course of trade between the goods concerned and the trade mark proprietor.

57.   That conclusion is not affected by the presence on Mr Reed's stall of the notice stating that the goods at issue in the main proceedings are not official Arsenal FC products (see paragraph 17 above). Even on the assumption that such a notice may be relied on by a third party as a defence to an action for trade mark infringement,

there is a clear possibility in the present case that some consumers, in particular if they come across the goods after they have been sold by Mr Reed and taken away from the stall where the notice appears, may interpret the sign as designating Arsenal FC as the undertaking of origin of the goods.

58.    Moreover, in the present case, there is also no guarantee, as required by the Court's case-law cited in paragraph 48 above, that all the goods designated by the trade mark have been manufactured or supplied under the control of a single undertaking which is responsible for their quality.

59.    The goods at issue are in fact supplied outside the control of Arsenal FC as trade mark proprietor, it being common ground that they do not come from Arsenal FC or from its approved resellers.

60.    In those circumstances, the use of a sign which is identical to the trade mark at issue in the main proceedings is liable to jeopardise the guarantee of origin which constitutes the essential function of the mark, as is apparent from the Court's case-law cited in paragraph 48 above. It is consequently a use which the trade mark proprietor may prevent in accordance with Article 5(1) of the Directive.

61.    Once it has been found that, in the present case, the use of the sign in question by the third party is liable to affect the guarantee of origin of the goods and that the trade mark proprietor must be able to prevent this, it is immaterial that in the context of that use the sign is perceived as a badge of support for or loyalty or affiliation to the proprietor of the mark.

62.    In the light of the foregoing, the answer to the national court's questions must be that, in a situation which is not covered by Article 6(1) of the Directive, where a third party uses in the course of trade a sign which is identical to a validly registered trade mark on goods which are identical to those for which it is registered, the trade mark proprietor is entitled, in circumstances such as those in the present case, to rely on Article 5(1)(a) of the Directive to prevent that use. It is immaterial that, in the contextof that use, the sign is perceived as a badge of support for or loyalty or affiliation to the trade mark proprietor.

**Costs**

63.    The costs incurred by the Commission and by the EFTA Surveillance Authority, which have submitted observations to the Court, are not recoverable. Since these proceedings are, for the parties to the main proceedings, a step in the proceedings pending before the national court, the decision on costs is a matter for that court.

On those grounds,

THE COURT,
in answer to the questions referred to it by the High Court of Justice of England and Wales, Chancery Division, by order of 4 May 2001, hereby rules:
In a situation which is not covered by Article 6(1) of the First Council Directive 89/104/EEC of 21 December 1988 to approximate the laws of the Member States relating to trade marks, where a third party uses in the course of trade a sign which is identical to a validly registered trade mark on goods which are identical to those for which it is registered, the trade mark proprietor of the mark is entitled, in circumstances such as those in the present case, to rely on Article 5(1)(a) of that directive to prevent that use. It is immaterial that, in the context of that use, the sign is perceived as a badge of support for or loyalty or affiliation to the trade mark proprietor.

Rodríguez Iglesias, Puissochet, Wathelet, Timmermans, Gulmann, Edward, Jann, Skouris, Macken, Colneric, von Bahr

Delivered in open court in Luxembourg on 12 November 2002.

G.C. Rodríguez Iglesias, President
R. Grass, Registrar

———

**\* 2.17.5.   EUROPEAN COURT OF JUSTICE, OPINION OF ADVOCATE GENERAL JACOBS, ADIDAS-SALOMON AG AND ADIDAS BENELUX BV V FITNESSWORLD TRADING LTD., CASE C-408/01, 10 JULY 2003[1017]**

———

**2.17.6.   EUROPEAN COURT OF JUSTICE, JUDGMENT, ADIDAS-SALOMON AG AND ADIDAS BENELUX BV V FITNESSWORLD TRADING LTD., CASE C-408/01, 23 OCTOBER 2003[1018]**

Reference for a preliminary ruling: Hoge Raad der Nederlanden – Netherlands.
Directive 89/104/EEC – Article 5(2) – Trade marks with a reputation – Protection against use of a sign in relation to identical or similar goods or services – Degree of similarity between the mark and the sign – Effect on the public – Sign viewed as an embellishment.

Parties
In Case C-408/01,
Reference to the Court under Article 234 EC by the Hoge Raad der Nederlanden (Netherlands) for a preliminary ruling in the proceedings pending before that court between
Adidas-Salomon AG, formerly Adidas AG,
Adidas Benelux BV
and
Fitnessworld Trading Ltd,
on the interpretation of Article 5(2) of First Council Directive 89/104/EEC of 21 December 1988 approximating the laws of the Member States relating to trade marks (OJ 1989 L 40, p. 1),

*The Court*
(Sixth Chamber),
composed of: J.-P. Puissochet, President of the Chamber, C. Gulmann (Rapporteur), F. Macken, N. Colneric and J.N. Cunha Rodrigues, Judges,
Advocate General: F.G. Jacobs,
Registrar: M.-F. Contet, Principal Administrator,
after considering the written observations submitted on behalf of:
–       Adidas Salomon AG and Adidas Benelux BV, by C. Gielen, advocaat,
–       Fitnessworld Trading Ltd, by J.J. Brinkhof and D.J.G. Visser, advocaten,
–       the Netherlands Government, by H.G. Sevenster, acting as Agent,
–       the United Kingdom Government, by G.J.A. Amodeo, acting as Agent, and M. Tappin, barrister,

---

[1017]   ECR 2003, not yet published.
[1018]   ECR 2003, not yet published.

–	the Commission of the European Communities, by H.M.H. Speyart and N.B. Rasmussen, acting as Agents,

having regard to the Report for the Hearing,

after hearing the oral observations of Adidas Salomon AG and Adidas Benelux BV, represented by C. Gielen; Fitnessworld Trading Ltd, represented by D.J.G. Visser; the United Kingdom Government, represented by K. Manji, acting as Agent, and M. Tappin, and the Commission, represented by N.B. Rasmussen and F. Tuytschaever, advocaat, at the hearing on 3 April 2003,

after hearing the Opinion of the Advocate General at the sitting on 10 July 2003,

gives the following

Judgment

## Grounds of the judgment

1	By judgment of 12 October 2001, received at the Court on 15 October 2001, the Hoge Raad der Nederlanden (Supreme Court of the Netherlands) referred to the Court for a preliminary ruling under Article 234 EC two questions on the interpretation of Article 5(2) of First Council Directive 89/104/EEC of 21 December 1988 approximating the laws of the Member States relating to trade marks (OJ 1989 L 40, p. 1) ('the Directive').

2	Those questions have been raised in proceedings between Adidas-Salomon AG and Adidas Benelux BV, on the one hand, and Fitnessworld Trading Ltd ('Fitnessworld'), on the other, in connection with the marketing by Fitnessworld of sports clothing.

The legal background

3	Article 5(1) and (2) of the Directive provide:

'1.	The registered trade mark shall confer on the proprietor exclusive rights therein. The proprietor shall be entitled to prevent all third parties not having his consent from using in the course of trade:

(a)	any sign which is identical with the trade mark in relation to goods or services which are identical with those for which the trade mark is registered;

(b)	any sign where, because of its identity with, or similarity to, the trade mark and the identity or similarity of the goods or services covered by the trade mark and the sign, there exists a likelihood of confusion on the part of the public, which includes the likelihood of association between the sign and the trade mark.

2.	Any Member State may also provide that the proprietor shall be entitled to prevent all third parties not having his consent from using in the course of trade any sign which is identical with, or similar to, the trade mark in relation to goods or services which are not similar to those for which the trade mark is registered, where the latter has a reputation in the Member State and where use of that sign without due cause takes unfair advantage of, or is detrimental to, the distinctive character or the repute of the trade mark.'

4	Article 13(A)(1)(b) and (c) of the Uniform Benelux Law on Trade Marks, whose object is to transpose into Benelux law Article 5(1) and (2) of the Directive, provides:

'Without prejudice to any application of the ordinary law governing civil liability, the exclusive rights in a trade mark shall entitle the proprietor to oppose:

...

(b)   any use, in the course of trade, of the mark or a similar sign in respect of the goods for which the mark is registered or similar goods where there exists a risk of association on the part of the public between the sign and the mark;

(c)   any use, in the course of trade and without due cause, of a trade mark which has a reputation in the Benelux countries or of a similar sign for goods which are not similar to those for which the trade mark is registered, where use of that sign would take unfair advantage of, or would be detrimental to, the distinctive character or the repute of the trade mark.'

The main proceedings

5    Adidas-Salomon AG, a company established in Germany, is the proprietor of a figurative trade mark registered at the Benelux Trade Mark Office for a number of types of clothing. That mark is formed by a motif consisting of three very striking vertical stripes of equal width, running parallel, which appear on the side and down the whole length of the article of clothing. The motif may be executed in different sizes and different colour combinations, provided that it always contrasts with the basic colour of the article of clothing.

6    The mark is the subject of an exclusive licence granted in respect of the Benelux to Adidas Benelux BV, a company established in the Netherlands.

7    Fitnessworld, a company established in the United Kingdom, markets fitness clothing under the name Perfetto. A number of those articles of clothing bear a motif of two parallel stripes of equal width which contrast with the main colour and are applied to the side seams of the clothing.

8    Proceedings are pending before the Hoge Raad der Nederlanden between Adidas-Salomon AG and Adidas Benelux BV ('Adidas'), on the one hand, and Fitnessworld in connection with the marketing by Fitnessworld in the Netherlands of Perfetto clothing.

9    Adidas claims that that marketing of clothing with two stripes creates a likelihood of confusion on the part of the public, since the public might associate that clothing with Adidas' sports and leisure clothing which bears three stripes, and Fitnessworld thus takes advantage of the repute of the Adidas mark. The exclusivity of that mark could thereby be impaired.

10   The Hoge Raad takes the view that it is necessary to determine whether the reference to non-similar goods or services in Article 5(2) of the Directive and in Article 13(A)(1)(c) of the Uniform Benelux Law on Trade Marks must be interpreted as a restriction, that is to say, in the sense that the rules concerned do not apply where a sign is used in relation to similar goods or services, or whether that reference is intended merely to emphasise that those rules apply also if the goods or services are not similar, so that those rules are not restricted to cases where the sign is used for similar goods.

11   If Article 5(2) of the Directive applies to the use of a sign in relation to similar goods, the national court seeks to ascertain, first, whether the criterion to be applied is a criterion other than confusion as to origin and, second, whether the fact that the sign is viewed purely as an embellishment by the relevant section of the public is important to the assessment of the situation.

12   In that context, the Hoge Raad der Nederlanden decided to stay proceedings and to refer the following questions to the Court for a preliminary ruling:

'1.   (a)   Must Article 5(2) of the Directive be interpreted as meaning that, under a national law implementing that provision, the proprietor of a trade mark which has a reputation in the Member State concerned may also oppose the use of the trade mark or a sign similar to it, in the manner and circumstances referred to therein, in relation to goods or services which are identical with or similar to those for which the trade mark is registered?

(b)     If the answer to Question 1(a) is in the negative: where Article 5(2) of the Directive is implemented in a national law, must the concept of "likelihood of confusion" referred to in Article 5(1)(b) of the Directive be interpreted as meaning that there exists such a likelihood if a person other than the proprietor of the trade mark uses a trade mark with a reputation or a sign similar to it, in the manner and circumstances referred to in Article 5(2) of the Directive, in relation to goods or services which are identical with or similar to those for which the trade mark is registered?

2.     If the answer to Question 1(a) is in the affirmative:

(a)     Must the question concerning the similarity between the trade mark and the sign in such a case be assessed on the basis of a criterion other than that of (direct or indirect) confusion as to origin, and if so, according to what criteriono.

(b)     If the sign alleged to be an infringement in such a case is viewed purely as an embellishment by the relevant section of the public, what importance must be attached to that circumstance in connection with the question concerning the similarity between the trade mark and the signo.'

Question 1
Question 1(a)

13     Question 1(a) contains the question whether, notwithstanding the fact that Article 5(2) of the Directive refers expressly only to use of a sign by a third party in relation to goods or services which are not similar, that provision is to be interpreted as entitling the Member States to provide specific protection for a registered trade mark with a reputation in cases where the later mark or sign, which is identical with or similar to the registered mark, is intended to be used or is used in relation to goods or services identical with or similar to those covered by that mark.

14     Since the decision making the reference was registered, the Court has answered that question in the affirmative in Case C-292/00 Davidoff [2003] ECR I-389.

15     Having regard to that interpretation and for the purposes of an answer which will be helpful in resolving the dispute in the main proceedings, Question 1(a) must be understood as also seeking to ascertain whether a Member State, where it exercises the option provided by Article 5(2) of the Directive, is bound to grant the specific protection in question in cases of use by a third party of a later mark or sign which is identical with or similar to the registered mark with a reputation, both in relation to goods or services which are not similar and in relation to goods or services which are identical with or similar to those covered by that mark.

16     Adidas and the Commission contend that, on that point, an affirmative answer must be given. The Commission takes the view that such an answer is necessarily inferred from paragraph 25 of Davidoff.

17     The United Kingdom Government, by contrast, proposes a negative answer. A Member State is free to adopt provisions restricted to the express wording of Article 5(2) of the Directive, that is to say to goods or services which are not similar. It is not bound to grant the same protection also in relation to goods or services which are identical or similar. The United Kingdom Government contends, in any event, that it is for the national courts to interpret a provision transposing Article

5(2) of the Directive in relation to the question of what protection a Member State intended to confer on proprietors of marks with a reputation.

18    In that regard, it should be noted that where a Member State exercises the option provided by Article 5(2) of the Directive, it must grant to the proprietors of marks with a reputation a form of protection in accordance with that provision.

19    In Davidoff (paragraphs 24 and 25), the Court observed in support of its interpretation that, in the light of the overall scheme and objectives of the system of which Article 5(2) of the Directive is part, that article cannot be given an interpretation which would lead to marks with a reputation having less protection where a sign is used for identical or similar goods or services than where a sign is used for non-similar goods or services. It went on to hold, in other words, that where the sign is used for identical or similar goods or services, a mark with a reputation must enjoy protection which is at least as extensive as where a sign is used for non-similar goods or services (Davidoff, paragraph 26).

20    In the light of those findings, the Member State, if it transposes Article 5(2) of the Directive, must therefore grant protection which is at least as extensive for identical or similar goods or services as for non-similar goods or services. The Member State's option thus relates to the principle itself of granting greater protection to marks with a reputation, but not to the situations covered by that protection when the Member State grants it.

21    It has been consistently held that, in applying national law, in particular national legislative provisions which were specially introduced in order to transpose a directive, the national court is required to interpret its national law, so far as possible, in the light of the wording and the purpose of the directive (see, in particular, Case 14/83 Von Colson and Kamann [1984] ECR 1891, paragraph 26; Case 79/83 Harz [1984] ECR 1921, paragraph 26, and Case C-185/97 Coote [1998] ECR I-5199, paragraph 18).

22    The answer to Question 1(a) must therefore be that a Member State, where it exercises the option provided by Article 5(2) of the Directive, is bound to grant the specific protection in question in cases of use by a third party of a later mark or sign which is identical with or similar to the registered mark with a reputation, both in relation to goods or services which are not similar and in relation to goods or services which are identical with or similar to those covered by that mark.

Question 1(b)

23    Since Question 1(b) was posed only in the event of a negative answer to Question 1(a), it does not require an answer.

Question 2

Question 2(a)

24    By Question 2(a) the national court seeks essentially to ascertain whether the protection conferred by Article 5(2) of the Directive is conditional on a finding of a degree of similarity between the mark with a reputation and the sign such that there exists a likelihood of confusion between them on the part of the relevant section of the public.

25    Adidas submits that a finding of a likelihood of confusion is not necessary. It is sufficient for the national court to find a likelihood of association on the basis of a visual, aural or conceptual similarity between the mark with a reputation and the sign. The Commission also submits that a likelihood of association is sufficient.

26    Fitnessworld submits, by contrast, that the similarity between the mark and the sign must be such that it can create confusion on the part of the relevant section of the public, having regard to the visual, aural and conceptual similarities.

27      In that regard, it must be noted at the outset that, unlike Article 5(1)(b) of the Directive, which is designed to apply only if there exists a likelihood of confusion on the part of the public, Article 5(2) of the Directive establishes, for the benefit of trade marks with a reputation, a form of protection whose implementation does not require the existence of such a likelihood. Article 5(2) applies to situations in which the specific condition of the protection consists of a use of the sign in question without due cause which takes unfair advantage of, or is detrimental to, the distinctive character or the repute of the trade mark (see Case C-425/98 Marca Mode [2000] ECR I-4861, paragraphs 34 and 36).

28      The condition of similarity between the mark and the sign, referred to in Article 5(2) of the Directive, requires the existence, in particular, of elements of visual, aural or conceptual similarity (see, in respect of Article 5(1)(b) of the Directive, Case C-251/95 SABEL [1997] ECR I-6191, paragraph 23 in fine, and Case C-342/97 Lloyd Schuhfabrik Meyer [1999] ECR I-3819, paragraphs 25 and 27 in fine).

29      The infringements referred to in Article 5(2) of the Directive, where they occur, are the consequence of a certain degree of similarity between the mark and the sign, by virtue of which the relevant section of the public makes a connection between the sign and the mark, that is to say, establishes a link between them even though it does not confuse them (see, to that effect, Case C-375/97 General Motors [1999] ECR I-5421, paragraph 23).

30      The existence of such a link must, just like a likelihood of confusion in the context of Article 5(1)(b) of the Directive, be appreciated globally, taking into account all factors relevant to the circumstances of the case (see, in respect of the likelihood of confusion, SABEL, paragraph 22, and Marca Mode, paragraph 40).

31      The answer to Question 2(a) must therefore be that the protection conferred by Article 5(2) of the Directive is not conditional on a finding of a degree of similarity between the mark with a reputation and the sign such that there exists a likelihood of confusion between them on the part of the relevant section of the public. It is sufficient for the degree of similarity between the mark with a reputation and the sign to have the effect that the relevant section of the public establishes a link between the sign and the mark.

Question 2(b)

32      By Question 2(b), the national court seeks essentially to ascertain, in connection with the question concerning the similarity between the mark with a reputation and the sign, what importance must be attached to a finding of fact by the national court to the effect that the sign in question is viewed purely as an embellishment by the relevant section of the public.

Observations submitted to the Court

33      Adidas submits that the fact that a sign is used or viewed as an embellishment is of no importance to the applicability of Article 5(2) of the Directive in situations such as those described by the national court. Since that provision entitles the proprietor of a mark with a reputation to oppose the use of any sign similar to his mark, there is no requirement that the sign be distinctive. It could be any other sign, such as an embellishment.

34      Fitnessworld proposes that the question be answered to the effect that, if a sign is viewed purely as an embellishment by the relevant section of the public, there cannot in any event be an infringement to the mark.

35      The Netherlands Government considers that even the decorative use of a sign can dilute a mark with a reputation, in particular where it is a figurative mark.

36    The United Kingdom Government confines itself to contending that the fact that a sign is viewed as a mere embellishment is not relevant to the question whether that sign is similar to the mark with a reputation.

37    According to the Commission, Article 5(2) of the Directive concerns protection against the use of a sign which is similar to the mark with a reputation to such an extent that the use in question involves a likelihood of dilution of or detriment to the mark's reputation. It is in fact difficult to imagine that a sign bearing such a similarity to a mark with a reputation can be regarded as a mere embellishment. Conversely, by definition, a mere embellishment cannot be similar, within the meaning of Article 5(2) of the Directive, to a mark with a reputation.

Reply of the Court

38    The answer to Question 2(a) shows that one of the conditions of the protection conferred by Article 5(2) of the Directive is that the degree of similarity between the mark with a reputation and the sign must have the effect that the relevant section of the public establishes a link between the sign and the mark.

39    The fact that a sign is viewed as an embellishment by the relevant section of the public is not, in itself, an obstacle to the protection conferred by Article 5(2) of the Directive where the degree of similarity is none the less such that the relevant section of the public establishes a link between the sign and the mark.

40    By contrast, where, according to a finding of fact by the national court, the relevant section of the public views the sign purely as an embellishment, it does not necessarily establish any link with a registered mark. That therefore means that the degree of similarity between the sign and the mark is not sufficient for such a link to be established.

41    The answer to Question 2(b) must therefore be that the fact that a sign is viewed as an embellishment by the relevant section of the public is not, in itself, an obstacle to the protection conferred by Article 5(2) of the Directive where the degree of similarity is none the less such that the relevant section of the public establishes a link between the sign and the mark. By contrast, where, according to a finding of fact by the national court, the relevant section of the public views the sign purely as an embellishment, it does not necessarily establish any link with a registered mark, with the result that one of the conditions of the protection conferred by Article 5(2) of the Directive is then not satisfied.

**Decision on costs**

Costs

42    The costs incurred by the Netherlands and United Kingdom Governments and by the Commission, which have submitted observations to the Court, are not recoverable. Since these proceedings are, for the parties to the main proceedings, a step in the action pending before the national court, the decision on costs is a matter for that court.

**Operative part of the judgment**

On those grounds,

THE COURT

(Sixth Chamber),

in answer to the questions referred to it by the Hoge Raad der Nederlanden by judgment of 12 October 2001, hereby rules:

1.    A Member State, where it exercises the option provided by Article 5(2) of First Council Directive 89/104/EEC of 21 December 1988 to approximate the laws of

the Member States relating to trade marks, is bound to grant the specific protection in question in cases of use by a third party of a later mark or sign which is identical with or similar to the registered mark with a reputation, both in relation to goods or services which are not similar and in relation to goods or services which are identical with or similar to those covered by that mark.

2. The protection conferred by Article 5(2) of Directive 89/104 is not conditional on a finding of a degree of similarity between the mark with a reputation and the sign such that there exists a likelihood of confusion between them on the part of the relevant section of the public. It is sufficient for the degree of similarity between the mark with a reputation and the sign to have the effect that the relevant section of the public establishes a link between the sign and the mark.

3. The fact that a sign is viewed as an embellishment by the relevant section of the public is not, in itself, an obstacle to the protection conferred by Article 5(2) of Directive 89/104 where the degree of similarity is none the less such that the relevant section of the public establishes a link between the sign and the mark. By contrast, where, according to a finding of fact by the national court, the relevant section of the public views the sign purely as an embellishment, it does not necessarily establish any link with a registered mark, with the result that one of the conditions of the protection conferred by Article 5(2) of Directive 89/104 is then not satisfied.

—

## 2.18.  VANDALISM AND VIOLENCE*

* **2.18.1.  RESOLUTION OF THE EUROPEAN PARLIAMENT ON THE VIOLENCE AT THE FOOTBALL-MATCH IN BRUSSELS ON 29 MAY 1985, 13 JUNE 1985**[1019]

---

* **2.18.2.  RESOLUTION OF THE EUROPEAN PARLIAMENT ON THE TRAGEDY AT THE HEYSEL STADIUM IN BRUSSELS, 13 JUNE 1985**[1020]

---

* **2.18.3.  INTERIM REPORT DRAWN UP ON BEHALF OF THE COMMITTEE ON YOUTH, CULTURE, EDUCATION, INFORMATION AND SPORT ON VANDALISM AND VIOLENCE IN SPORT, 2 JULY 1985**[1021]

Rapporteur: Mrs. J. Larive-Groenendaal

---

* **2.18.4.  RESOLUTION OF THE EUROPEAN PARLIAMENT ON THE MEASURES NEEDED TO COMBAT VANDALISM AND VIOLENCE IN SPORT, 11 JULY 1985**[1022]

---

* **2.18.5.  FINAL REPORT DRAWN UP ON BEHALF OF THE COMMITTEE ON YOUTH, CULTURE, EDUCATION, INFORMATION AND SPORT ON VANDALISM AND VIOLENCE IN SPORT, 12 NOVEMBER 1987**[1023]

Rapporteur: Mrs J. Larive

---

* **2.18.6.  RESOLUTION OF THE EUROPEAN PARLIAMENT ON VANDALISM AND VIOLENCE IN SPORT, 22 JANUARY 1988**[1024]

---

* **2.18.7.  COUNCIL RECOMMENDATION ON GUIDELINES FOR PREVENTING AND RESTRAINING DISORDER CONNECTED WITH FOOTBALL MATCHES, 22 APRIL 1996**[1025]

---

* The full texts of documents which are marked with an asterisk (*) are not incorporated in the book itself, but are freely accessible on the website of the ASSER International Sports Law Centre, at <www.sportslaw.nl> – documentation.

[1019]  OJ C 175, 13-6-1985, p. 211.
[1020]  OJ C 175, 15-7-1985, p. 212.
[1021]  Doc. A2-70/85.
[1022]  OJ C 229, 9-9-1985, p. 99.
[1023]  Doc. A 2-215/87.
[1024]  OJ C 49, 22-2-1988, p. 168.
[1025]  OJ C 131, 3-5-1996, p. 1.

**\* 2.18.8.  AUSSCHUß FÜR GRUNDFREIHEITEN UND INNERE ANGELEGENHEITEN, BERICHT ÜBER DAS PROBLEM DES HOOLIGANISMUS UND DIE FREIZÜGIGKEIT DER FUßBALLFANS, 25 APRIL 1996**[1026]

Berichterstatterin: Frau Claudia Roth

———

**\* 2.18.9.  RESOLUTION OF THE EUROPEAN PARLIAMENT ON HOOLIGANISM AND THE FREE MOVEMENT OF FOOTBALL SUPPORTERS, 21 MAY 1996**[1027]

———

**\* 2.18.10.  REPLY ON BEHALF OF THE COUNCIL TO WRITTEN QUESTION E-682/96 BY THOMAS MEGAHY (PSE), 27 JUNE 1996**[1028]

Subject: Treatment of British football supporters in other Member States

———

**\* 2.18.11.  JOINT ACTION ADOPTED BY THE COUNCIL ON THE BASIS OF ARTICLED K.3 OF THE TREATY ON EUROPEAN UNION WITH REGARD TO COOPERATION ON LAW AND ORDER AND SECURITY, 26 MAY 1997**[1029]

———

**\* 2.18.12.  RESOLUTION OF THE COUNCIL ON PREVENTING AND RESTRAINING FOOTBALL HOOLIGANISM THROUGH THE EXCHANGE OF EXPERIENCE, EXCLUSION FROM STADIUMS AND MEDIA POLICY, 9 JUNE 1997**[1030]

———

**\* 2.18.13.  ANSWER ON BEHALF OF THE COMMISSION TO WRITTEN QUESTION E-3604/98 BY MARCO CELLAI (NI), 21 JANUARY 1999**[1031]

Subject: Fiorentina-Grasshopper football match on 3 November 1998

———

**\* 2.18.14.  RESOLUTION OF THE COUNCIL CONCERNING A HANDBOOK FOR INTERNATIONAL POLICE COOPERATION AND MEASURES TO PREVENT AND CONTROL VIOLENCE AND DISTURBANCES IN CONNECTION WITH INTERNATIONAL FOOTBALL MATCHES, 21 JUNE 1999**[1032]

———

---

[1026]  A4-0124/96.
[1027]  OJ C 166, 10-6-1996, p. 40.
[1028]  Question of 27-3-1996; OJ C 280, 25-9-1996, p. 63-64.
[1029]  OJ L 147, 5-6-1997, p. 1
[1030]  OJ C 193, 24-6-1997, p. 1.
[1031]  Question of 3-12-1998; OJ C 320, 6-11-1999, p. 58.
[1032]  OJ C 196 , 13-7-1999, p. 1-12. (No longer in force).

**\* 2.18.15.   ANSWER ON BEHALF OF THE COMMISSION TO WRITTEN QUESTION P-1661/00 BY CHRISTOPHER HEATON-HARRIS (PPE-DE), 16 JUNE 2000**[1033]

Subject: Euro 2000 football tournament

———

**\* 2.18.16.   ANSWER ON BEHALF OF THE COMMISSION TO WRITTEN QUESTION P-307/01 BY PIETRO-PAOLO MENNEA (ELDR), 10 SEPTEMBER 2001**[1034]

Subject: Violence against referees at football matches

———

**\* 2.18.17.   ANSWER ON BEHALF OF THE COMMISSION TO WRITTEN QUESTION E-2318/00 BY MARGRIETUS VAN DEN BERG (PSE), 20 SEPTEMBER 2000**[1035]

Subject: European travel ban on football hooligans travelling abroad

———

**\* 2.18.18.   ANSWER ON BEHALF OF THE COMMISSION TO WRITTEN QUESTION E-2459/00 BY CHARLES TANNOCK (PPE-DE), 22 SEPTEMBER 2000**[1036]

Subject: Seizure of passports of suspected football hooligans by the German authorities

———

**\* 2.18.19.   RESOLUTION OF THE COUNCIL CONCERNING A HANDBOOK WITH RECOMMENDATIONS FOR INTERNATIONAL POLICE COOPERATION AND MEASURES TO PREVENT AND CONTROL VIOLENCE AND DISTURBANCES IN CONNECTION WITH FOOTBALL MATCHES WITH AN INTERNATIONAL DIMENSION, IN WHICH AT LEAST ONE MEMBER STATE IS INVOLVED, 6 DECEMBER 2001**[1037]

———

**\* 2.18.20.   ANSWER ON BEHALF OF THE COMMISSION TO WRITTEN QUESTION E-3423/01 BY GLYN FORD (PSE), 19 FEBRUARY 2002**[1038]

Subject: World Cup 2002 – Commission cooperation with the Japanese and Korean authorities

———

---

[1033] Question of 18-5-2000; OJ C 72 E, 6-3-2001, p. 94-95.
[1034] Question of 2-2-2001; OJ C 81 E, 4-4-2002, p. 3.
[1035] Question of 11-7-2000; OJ C 89 E, 20-3-2001, p. 181.
[1036] Question of 24-7-2000; OJ C 89 E, 20-3-2001, p. 197.
[1037] OJ C 22, 24-1-2002, p. 1-25.
[1038] Question of 21-12-2002; OJ C 172 E, 18-7-2002, p. 56.

**\* 2.18.21. DECISION OF THE COUNCIL CONCERNING SECURITY IN CONNECTION WITH FOOTBALL MATCHES WITH AN INTERNATIONAL DIMENSION, 25 APRIL 2002** [1039]

——

**\* 2.18.22. ANSWER ON BEHALF OF THE COMMISSION TO WRITTEN QUESTION E-3103/02 BY BART STAES (VERTS/ALE), 11 DECEMBER 2002** [1040]

Subject: Identification of football supporters at European matches

——

**\* 2.18.23. ANSWER ON BEHALF OF THE COMMISSION TO WRITTEN QUESTION E-3076/02 BY GLYN FORD (PSE), 17 DECEMBER 2002** [1041]

Subject: Racism in football

——

**\* 2.18.24. ANSWER ON BEHALF OF THE COMMISSION TO WRITTEN QUESTION E-3309/02 BY STAVROS XARCHAKOS (PPE-DE), 22 JANUARY 2003** [1042]

Subject: Acts of aggression directed at Community nationals at a Turkish sports stadium

——

**\* 2.18.25. ANSWER ON BEHALF OF THE COMMISSION TO WRITTEN QUESTION E-496/03 BY CRISTIANA MUSCARDINI (UEN), 26 MARCH 2003** [1043]

Subject: Palestine: hatred spreads to football

——

**\* 2.18.26. ANSWER ON BEHALF OF THE COMMISSION TO WRITTEN QUESTION E-899/03 BY BART STAES (VERTS/ALE), 25 APRIL 2003** [1044]

Subject: Compatibility of the Belgian fan card system with Directive 95/46/EC

——

**\* 2.18.27. RESOLUTION OF THE COUNCIL ON THE USE BY MEMBER STATES OF BANS ON ACCESS TO VENUES OF FOOTBALL MATCHES WITH AN INTERNATIONAL DIMENSION, 17 NOVEMBER 2003** [1045]

——

---

[1039] OJ L 121, 8-5-2002, p. 1-3.
[1040] Question of 29-10-2002; OJ C 110 E, 8-5-2003, p. 165.
[1041] Question of 17-10-2002; OJ C 11E, 15-1-2004, p. 22-23.
[1042] Question of 21-11-2002; OJ C 192 E, 14-8-2003, p. 106.
[1043] Question of 12-2-2003; question not yet published in the OJ.
[1044] Question of 21-3-2003; OJ C 222 E, 18-9-2003, p. 241-242.
[1045] OJ C 281, 22-11-2003, p. 1-2.

Part 3

# Miscellanea

## 3.1. CHILD LABOUR

**\* 3.1.1. RESOLUTION OF THE EUROPEAN PARLIAMENT ON CHILD LABOUR IN THE PRODUCTION OF SPORTS EQUIPMENT, 13 JUNE 2002[1]**

---

## 3.2. DANGEROUS SPORTS

**\* 3.2.1. ANSWER ON BEHALF OF THE COMMISSION TO WRITTEN QUESTION E-3511/96 BY GIANNI TAMINO (V), DANIEL COHN-BENDIT (V) AND CARLO RIPA DI MEANA (V), 27 JANUARY 1997[2]**

Subject: Applicability of EU legislation on safety at the workplace to professional sport (by analogy with the 'Bosman case')

---

**\* 3.2.2. ANSWER ON BEHALF OF THE COMMISSION TO WRITTEN QUESTION P-1241/98 BY ESKO SEPPÄNEN (GUE/NGL), 8 MAY 1998[3]**

Subject: Saving the cultural heritage of Europe

---

**\* 3.2.3. ANSWER ON BEHALF OF THE COMMISSION TO WRITTEN QUESTION E-205/00 BY CAROLINE JACKSON (PPE-DE), 8 MARCH 2000[4]**

Subject: Possible EU legislation on dangerous sports

---

## 3.3. FISHING

**\* 3.3.1 ANSWER ON BEHALF OF THE COMMISSION TO WRITTEN QUESTION E-3950/96 BY JEAN-PIERRE BÉBÉAR (PPE), 29 JANUARY 1997[5]**

Subject: Deletion of the cormorant from Annex I to Directive 79/409/EEC

---

\* The full texts of documents which are marked with an asterisk (\*) are not incorporated in the book itself, but are freely accessible on the website of the ASSER International Sports Law Centre, at <www.sportslaw.nl> – documentation.
[1] OJ C 261 E, 30-10-2003, p. 587.
[2] Question of 9-12-1996; OJ C 105, 3-4-1997, p, 84.
[3] Question of 9-4-1998; OJ C 31, 5-2-1999, p. 26.
[4] Question of 4-2-2000; OJ C 280 E, 3-10-2000, p. 200.
[5] Question of 10-1-1997; OJ C 186, 18-6-1997, p. 139.

**\* 3.3.2. ANSWER ON BEHALF OF THE COMMISSION TO WRITTEN QUESTION E-1288/97 BY CAROLINE JACKSON (PPE), 7 MAY 1997[6]**

Subject: Protected status of cormorants

___

**\* 3.3.3. ANSWER ON BEHALF OF THE COMMISSION TO WRITTEN QUESTION E-1056/01 BY PAT GALLAGHER (UEN), 30 MAY 2001[7]**

Subject: Common fisheries policy – Sea angling

___

**\* 3.3.4. ANSWER ON BEHALF OF THE COMMISSION TO WRITTEN QUESTION E-805/02 BY EURIG WYN (VERTS/ALE), 19 APRIL 2002[8]**

Subject: Recreational Sea Angling (RSA) and the Common Fisheries Policy (CFP) Review

___

## 3.4.    HEALTH

**\* 3.4.1. ANSWER ON BEHALF OF THE COMMISSION TO WRITTEN QUESTION E-2449/96 BY SUSAN WADDINGTON (PSE), 25 OCTOBER 1996[9]**

Subject: Sports check-ups

___

**\* 3.4.2. EUROPEAN PARLIAMENT RESOLUTION ON FOOT-AND-MOUTH DISEASE AND THE FOOTBALL WORLD CHAMPIONSHIPS (WORLD CUP) IN SOUTH KOREA, 13 JUNE 2002[10]**

___

## 3.5.    HORSES

**\* 3.5.1. ANSWER ON BEHALF OF THE COMMISSION TO WRITTEN QUESTION E-1921/98 BY LUTZ GOEPEL (PPE), 20 JULY 1998[11]**

Subject: Use of medicinal products for horses used for sport

___

---

[6] Question of 11-4-1997; OJ C 319, 18-10-1997, p. 246.
[7] Question of 5-4-2001; OJ C 340 E, 4-12-2001, p. 158.
[8] Question of 12-3-2002; OJ C 205E, 29-8-2002, p. 220.
[9] Question of 23-9-1996; OJ C 385, 19-12-1996, p. 122.
[10] OJ C 261 E, 30-6-2003, p. 397.
[11] Question of 18-6-1998; OJ C 31, 5-2-1999, p. 43.

**\* 3.5.2. ANSWER ON BEHALF OF THE COMMISSION TO WRITTEN QUESTION E-1920/98 BY LUTZ GOEPEL (PPE), 5 AUGUST 1998**[12]

Subject: Registration of horses

___

**\* 3.5.3. REPLY ON BEHALF OF THE COUNCIL TO WRITTEN QUESTION E-2004/98 BY HARTMUT NASSAUER (PPE), 24 SEPTEMBER 1998**[13]

Subject: Council Regulation (EEC) 2377/90 of 26 June 1990 laying down a Community procedure for the establishment of maximum residue limits of veterinary medicinal products in foodstuffs of animal origin

___

**\* 3.5.4. ANSWER ON BEHALF OF THE COMMISSION TO WRITTEN QUESTION E-2428/99 BY PIIA-NOORA KAUPPI (PPE-DE), 28 JANUARY 2000**[14]

Subject: Exemption of horses used in competitions and sport from rules on veterinary medicine

___

## 3.6. HUNTING

**\* 3.6.1. ANSWER ON BEHALF OF THE COMMISSION TO WRITTEN QUESTION NO 572/84 BY MR HEMMO MUNTINGH (S – NL), 2 OCTOBER 1984**[15]

Subject: 'sport' hunting of birds

___

**\* 3.6.2. ANSWER ON BEHALF OF THE COMMISSION TO WRITTEN QUESTION E-1743/93 BY GIYN FORD (PSE), 20 JANUARY 1994**[16]

Subject: Shooting wild birds for sport on Malta

___

**\* 3.6.3. ANSWER ON BEHALF OF THE COMMISSION TO WRITTEN QUESTION E-1965/96 BY ASTRID LULLING (PPE), 11 OCTOBER 1996**[17]

Subject: Hunting insurance

___

[12] Question of 18-6-1998; OJ C 31, 5-2-1999, p. 100.
[13] Question of 29-6-1998; OJ C 13, 18-1-1999, p. 133.
[14] Question of 16-12-1999; OJ C 225 E, 8-8-2000, p. 131.
[15] Question of 20-8-1984; OJ C 308, 19-11-1984, p. 3.
[16] Question of 29-6-1993; OJ C 296, 24-10-1994, p. 18.
[17] Question of 16-7-1996; OJ C 11, 13-1-1997, p. 32.

**\* 3.6.4.  ANSWER ON BEHALF OF THE COMMISSION TO WRITTEN QUESTION E-2841/96 BY GUIDO PODESTÀ (UPE), 29 NOVEMBER 1996**[18]

Subject: Shooting of ptarmigans

———

**\* 3.6.5.  ANSWER ON BEHALF OF THE COMMISSION TO WRITTEN QUESTION E-35/00 BY ROBERT EVANS (PSE), 22 FEBRUARY 2000**[19]

Subject: Rearing of grouse and pheasants

———

**\* 3.6.6.  ANSWER ON BEHALF OF THE COMMISSION TO WRITTEN QUESTION E-3050/00 BY JEAN-CLAUDE MARTINEZ (TDI), 25 OCTOBER 2000**[20]

Subject: Elephant hunting in Africa

———

**\* 3.6.7.  REPLY ON BEHALF OF THE COUNCIL TO WRITTEN QUESTION E-3049/00 BY JEAN-CLAUDE MARTINEZ (TDI), 12 FEBRUARY 2001**[21]

Subject: Elephant hunting in Africa

———

**\* 3.6.8.  ANSWER ON BEHALF OF THE COMMISSION TO WRITTEN QUESTION E-3783/02 BY ERIK MEIJER (GUE/NGL), 4 MARCH 2003**[22]

Subject: Dangers of hunting and the need for coordination of any measures taken to prevent a further increase in fox numbers

———

**\* 3.6.9.  ANSWER ON BEHALF OF THE COMMISSION TO WRITTEN QUESTION E-377/02 BY STAVROS XARCHAKOS (PPE-DE), 21 MARCH 2002**[23]

Subject: Arbitrary killing of rare birds by licensed and unlicensed hunters

———

---

[18]  Question of 25-10-1996; OJ C 83, 14-3-1997, p. 78.
[19]  Question of 19-1-2000; OJ C 330 E, 21-11-2000, p. 72.
[20]  Question of 28-9-2000; OJ C 136 E, 8-5-2001, p. 170-171.
[21]  Question of 29-9-2000; OJ C 163 E, 6-6-2001, p. 29.
[22]  Question of 6-1-2003; OJ C 161 E, 10-7-2003, p. 144.
[23]  Question of 19-2-2002; OJ C 172 E, 18-7-2002, p. 189.

## 3.7.  JOB PROTECTION

**\* 3.7.1.  ANSWER ON BEHALF OF THE COMMISSION TO WRITTEN QUESTION E-563/99 BY ROBERTA ANGELILLI (NI), 5 MAY 1999**[24]

Subject: Reorganization of CONI (the Italian National Olympic Committee) and protecting jobs

———

## 3.8.  NOISE POLLUTION

**\* 3.8.1.  ANSWER ON BEHALF OF THE COMMISSION TO WRITTEN QUESTION E-2696/97 BY CRISTIANA MUSCARDINI (NI), 13 OCTOBER 1997**[25]

Subject: Noise pollution and sport

———

**\* 3.8.2.  ANSWER ON BEHALF OF THE COMMISSION TO WRITTEN QUESTION E-1726/03 BY MIKKO PESÄLÄ (ELDR), 23 JULY 2003**[26]

Subject: Shooting noise abatement

———

## 3.9.  SOCIAL SECURITY

**\* 3.9.1.  ANSWER ON BEHALF OF THE COMMISSION TO WRITTEN QUESTION P-100/00 BY THERESA ZABELL (PPE-DE), 7 FEBRUARY 2000**[27]

Subject: Social security arrangements for sportsmen and women

———

[24] Question of 12-3-1999; OJ C 370, 21-12-1999, p. 62.
[25] Question of 1-9-1997; OJ C 102, 3-4-1998, p. 93.
[26] Question of 14-5-2003; question not yet published in the OJ.
[27] Question of 18-1-2000; OJ C 46 E, 13-2-2001, p. 4.

# Annexes

# 1. SUBJECT INDEX*

---

\* Reference is made to section numbers instead of page numbers, as the text of documents with an asterisk are not included in this book, but are available on <www.sportslaw.nl> – documentation.

# 2. TABLES

## 2.1. TREATY ARTICLES AND OTHERS

### 2.1.1. ACT OF ACCESSION OF GREECE
Art. 3(1)    *[2.4.]* 1.
Art. 4      *[2.4.]* 1.
Art. 15(2)    *[2.4.]* 1.

### 2.1.2. ACT OF ACCESSION OF SPAIN AND PORTUGAL
Art. 3      *[2.4.]* 4.
Art. 3(1)    *[2.4.]* 2.
Art. 15     *[2.4.]* 4.
Art. 16     *[2.4.]* 4.

### 2.1.3. ASSOCIATION AGREEMENT WITH POLAND
Art. 37     *[2.7.]* 27.
Art. 37(1)    *[2.7.]* 31.
Art. 42     *[2.7.]* 27.
Art. 58(1)    *[2.7.]* 27., 31.

### 2.1.4. ASSOCIATION AGREEMENT WITH SLOVAKIA
Art. 1(2)    *[2.7.]* 31.
Art. 38     *[2.7.]* 27.
Art. 38(1)    *[2.7.]* 31.
Art. 59(1)    *[2.7.]* 27., 31.

### 5. CHARTER OF FUNDAMENTAL RIGHTS OF THE EUROPEAN UNION
Art. 21     *[2.7.]* 33.
Art. 23     *[2.7.]* 33.
Art. 24     *[3.1.]* 1.

### 2.1.6. E(E)C TREATY
Art. 2      *[1.]* 1., 20., *[2.4.]* 34., 50., 65., 101., *[2.7.]* 2., 4., *[2.10.]* 5.S7., 16., 18., 28.,
         35., *[2.12.]* 5., 8.
Art. 3      *[2.7.]* 33.
Art. 3(2)    *[2.7.]* 17.
Art. 3(b)    *[2.10.]* 5.
Art. 3(c)    *[2.6.]* 2., *[2.7.]* 2., *[2.10.]* 1., 5.
Art. 3(e)    *[2.10.]* 5.
Art. 5      *[2.4.]* 30., *[2.6.]* 2., *[2.9.]* 14., *[2.10.]* 5., *[2.13.]* 13., *[2.16.]* 6.
Art. 6      *[1.]* 38., *[2.4.]* 82., *[2.7.]* 27., *[2.10.]* 15., 16., 18., *[2.18.]* 23.
Art. 7      *[1.]* 38., *[2.6.]* 1., 2, *[2.7.]* 1., 2., 3., 4., 7., *[2.10.]* 1., 5.
Art. 7(1)    *[2.7.]* 2.
Art. 8      *[2.2.]* 2.
Art. 8(1)    *[2.4.]* 82.
Art. 10     *[2.10.]* 28.
Art. 12     *[2.7.]* 27., 35., *[2.10.]* 16., 18.
Art. 12-17    *[1.]* 9.
Art. 13     *[2.3.]* 20., *[2.7.]* 19., 20., 28., 33., *[2.9.]* 8., 11., 17.
Art. 17     *[2.7.]* 35.
Art. 28 (ex Art. 30) *[2.12.]* 5., *[3.08.]* 2.
Art. 28 (ex Art. 30) to
 Art. 30 (ex Art. 36) *[2.4.]* 43.
Art. 29     *[2.18.]* 21., 27.

**2.1.6. E(E)C TREATY** (cont.)

| | |
|---|---|
| Art. 30 | *[2.10.]* 6., 16., *[2.12.]* 5., *[2.17.]* 1., *[3.08.]* 2. |
| Art. 30(1)(a) | *[2.18.]* 21. |
| Art. 30(1)(b) | *[2.18.]* 21. |
| Art. 30-36 | *[1.]* 9. |
| Art. 34(2)(c) | *[2.18.]* 21. |
| Art. 36 | *[2.4.]* 5., *[2.17.]* 1. |
| Art. 37 | *[1.]* 9., *[2.10.]* 28. |
| Art. 39 (ex Art. 48) | *[1.]* 32., 35., *[2.7.]* 18., *[2.8.]* 21., 27., 27., 31., *[2.10.]* 16., 18., 20., 23., 27., 33., 39., *[2.12.]* 5. |
| Art. 43 (ex Art. 52) | *[2.7.]* 35., *[2.11.]* 1., *[2.12.]* 10., 17. |
| Art. 45 (ex Art. 55) | *[2.12.]* 6., 17. |
| Art. 46 (ex Art. 56) | *[2.12.]* 6., 10., 17. |
| Art. 46(1) | *[2.12.]* 17. |
| Art. 47 (ex Art. 37) | *[2.4.]* 9., *[2.10.]* 27. |
| Art. 47(2) | *[2.16.]* 4., 5. |
| Art. 48 | *[1.]* 1., 19., 1., *[2.4.]* 22., 34., *[2.6.]* 2., *[2.7.]* 1., 2., 3., 4., 8., 12., 27., 31., *[2.10.]* 1., 2., 4.S9., 11., 12., 14.S16., 18., 20., *[2.12.]* 5., 17., *[2.18.]* 3., 4. |
| Art. 48 to 51 | *[2.6.]* 1., *[2.7.]* 2., 3., 4. |
| Art. 48(1) | *[2.7.]* 27., 31. |
| Art. 48(2) | *[2.7.]* 27., 31., *[2.10.]* 6. |
| Art. 48(3) | *[2.10.]* 1. |
| Art. 48(3)(a) | *[2.10.]* 6., 18. |
| Art. 49 (ex Art. 59) | *[1.]* 33., *[2.4.]* 88., 91., 94, *[2.6.]* 2., *[2.7.]* 15., *[2.10.]* 16., *[2.12.]* 5.S8., 13., 15.S17., *[2.16.]* 6. |
| Art. 50 (ex Art. 60) | *[2.12.]* 8., 10., 17. |
| Art. 51 | *[2.6.]* 2. |
| Art. 52 | *[1.]* 19., *[2.2.]* 2., *[2.7.]* 1., 12., *[2.10.]* 5., 6., 28. |
| Art. 53 | *[2.10.]* 28. |
| Art. 55 (ex Art. 66) | *[2.12.]* 6., 8., 10., *[2.16.]* 4., 5. |
| Art. 56 | *[2.4.]* 16., *[2.12.]* 5. |
| Art. 57(1) | *[2.6.]* 2. |
| Art. 57(2) | *[2.2.]* 2., 3., *[2.4.]* 16., *[2.16.]* 3. |
| Art. 58 | *[2.10.]* 6. |
| Art. 59 | *[2.4.]* 16., 16., 22., 34., *[2.7.]* 1.S4., 15., *[2.10.]* 1., 5., 6., 15., 16., *[2.12.]* 5., 8., 15., 16. |
| Art. 59 to 66 | *[2.7.]* 2., 3., 4. |
| Art. 59(1) | *[2.7.]* 2. |
| Art. 60 | *[2.4.]* 16., *[2.7.]* 1., 4., *[2.10.]* 1., *[2.12.]* 5., 8. |
| Art. 60(3) | *[2.7.]* 2. |
| Art. 62 | *[2.7.]* 2., *[2.10.]* 1. |
| Art. 62(2) | *[2.13.]* 13. |
| Art. 63 | *[2.7.]* 1. |
| Art. 63(1) | *[2.7.]* 1. |
| Art. 63(2) | *[2.7.]* 1. |
| Art. 64 | *[2.7.]* 2., *[2.10.]* 1. |
| Art. 66 | *[2.2.]* 2., 3., *[2.4.]* 16., 16., *[2.12.]* 5, 8., *[2.16.]* 3. |
| Art. 81 (ex Art. 85) | *[1.]* 33., *[2.4.]* 42., 44., 47., 51., 54., 61., 62., 65., 67., 68., 73., 74., 75., 80., 82., 84., 88., 89., 91., 93., 94., 101., 105., *[2.10.]* 16., 18., 23., 28., 30., 39., *[2.12.]* 8. |
| Art. 81(1) (ex Art. 85(1)) | *[2.4.]* 42., 44., 49., 54., 61., 62., 65., 66., 67., 69., 70., 73., 75., 89., 92., 93., 101., 105., 107., *[2.10.]* 28., 39. |
| Art. 81(1)(c) | *[2.10.]* 28. |
| Art. 81(2) (ex Art. 85(2)) | *[2.4.]* 97. |
| Art. 81(3) (ex Art. 85(3)) | *[1.]* 33., 35., *[2.4.]* 42., 65., 75., 76., 82., 86., 88., 92., 93., 96., 97., 101., 105., 107., *[2.10.]* 28., 39. |
| Art. 81(3)(b) | *[2.4.]* 93. |
| Art. 82 (ex Art. 86) | *[2.4.]* 40., 43., 46., 47., 51., 68., 82., 88., 91., 107., *[2.10.]* 16., 18., 28., 35., 39., *[2.12.]* 8., *[2.15.]* 11. |

ANNEXES

877

**2.1.6. E(E)C TREATY** (cont.)

| | |
|---|---|
| Art. 82(b) | *[2.4.]* 40. |
| Art. 85 (now Art. 81) | *[1.]* 5., 6., 9., 19., *[2.4.]* 1., 2., 3., 4., 5., 7., 8., 9., 10., 11., 13., 15., 16., 19., 21., 22., 24., 30., 34., 35., 40., 42., 54., 62., 65., 73., 101., *[2.10.]* 1.S8., 10., 11., 13., 16., 18., 28., 39., *[2.12.]* 5., 8. |
| Art. 85 to 94 | *[2.4.]* 30. |
| Art. 85(1) | *[1.]* 20., *[2.4.]* 1., 2., 4., 5., 6., 8., 10., 13., 7., 21., 22., 15., 33., 34., 35., 37., 62., 73., *[2.10.]* 5, 7., 8., 16., 28., *[2.12.]* 5. |
| Art. 85(1)(c) | *[2.10.]* 5., 28. |
| Art. 85(3) | *[1.]* 19., *[2.4.]* 1., 2., 4., 5., 7., 10., 12., 13., 22., 34., 35., 62., 73., *[2.10.]* 4., 5., 8., 11., 16., 28., *[2.12.]* 5. |
| Art. 85(3)(a) | *[2.4.]* 62. |
| Art. 86 | *[1.]* 6., 9., *[2.4.]* 1., 2., 3, 4,, 5., 6., 7., 8., 9., 12., 13., 16., 17., 19., 21., 24., 26., 34., 35., 40., 42., 54., 60., 65., 71., 73., 101., *[2.10.]* 1., 3, 4, 5., 6., 7., 8., 13., 16., 18., *[2.12.]* 5., 8. |
| Art. 86(1) | *[2.4.]* 71 |
| Art. 86(2) (ex Art. 90(2)) | *[2.12.]* 10. |
| Art. 87 (ex Art. 92(3)) | *[2.14.]* 3., 5.S7., 10. |
| Art. 87(1) | *[2.4.]* 95., *[2.14.]* 5., 9.S 2.14.11. |
| Art. 87(2) | *[2.4.]* 62., 93., *[2.14.]* 11. |
| Art. 88 | *[2.14.]* 5.S7., 10. |
| Art. 88(2) | *[2.14.]* 11. |
| Art. 89 | *[2.4.]* 31. |
| Art. 90 | *[2.4.]* 16., 31. |
| Art. 90(1) | *[2.4.]* 60., 71 |
| Art. 90(2) | *[2.4.]* 2., 7., 13. |
| Art. 92 | *[2.14.]* 1., 3. |
| Art. 92(1) | *[2.14.]* 1., 3. |
| Art. 92(2) | *[2.14.]* 1. |
| Art. 92(3) | *[2.14.]* 1., 3. |
| Art. 92(3)(c) | *[2.14.]* 3. |
| Art. 92-94 | *[1.]* 9. |
| Art. 93 | *[2.4.]* 13., *[2.14.]* 1., 3. |
| Art. 93(2) | *[2.14.]* 1., 3. |
| Art. 93(3) | *[2.14.]* 1. |
| Art. 95 | *[2.16.]* 4., 5. |
| Art. 95(3) | *[2.16.]* 4.S6. |
| Art. 95(8) | *[2.16.]* 4., 5. |
| Art. 95-96 | *[1.]* 9. |
| Art. 100 | *[2.7.]* 3. |
| Art. 100a | *[2.16.]* 3. *[2.17.]* 1. |
| Art. 100a(3) | *[2.16.]* 3. |
| Art. 117 to 120 | *[2.10.]* 16. |
| Art. 118 | *[3.4.]* 1. |
| Art. 118b | *[2.10.]* 16. |
| Art. 126 | *[1.]* 14. |
| Art. 127 | *[1.]* 14. |
| Art. 128 | *[1.]* 13., 14., 34., *[2.10.]* 6. |
| Art. 128(1) | *[2.10.]* 6., 9. |
| Art. 128(4) | *[2.2.]* 2. |
| Art. 129 | *[2.8.]* 10., 13. |
| Art. 129(1) | *[2.8.]* 15., 16. |
| Art. 136 | *[2.7.]* 28. |
| Art. 136 to 143 | *[2.10.]* 16. |
| Art. 141 | *[2.7.]* 33. |
| Art. 149 (ex Art. 126) | *[2.6.]* 6., 7., *[2.9.]* 10., 11., 14. |
| Art. 151 (ex Art. 128) | *[1.]* 35., *[2.13.]* 10. |
| Art. 152 | *[2.8.]* 21., 26., 27., 28., 29., 30., *[2.16.]* 4. |

**2.1.11. FOURTH INTERSTATE TREATY ON BROADCASTING**
Art. 5(a)                     *[2.2.]* 6., 9.

———

## 2.2. REGULATIONS

### 2.2.1. COUNCIL REGULATIONS (EEC/EC)

| | |
|---|---|
| 17/62 | *[2.4.]* 1., 6., 7.-10., 12.-15., 33., 35.-37., 40., 42., 47., 53., 54., 62., 65., 67., 68., 73., 77., 92., 61., *[2.10.]* 4., 5., 105. |
| 99/63 | *[2.4.]* 1., 2., 4., 5., 7., 8., 10., 40., 62. |
| 19/65 | *[2.4.]* 5. |
| 67/67 | *[2.4.]* 1. |
| 1612/68 | *[2.6.]* 1., 2., *[2.7.]* 1., 2., 3., 4., 11., 18., 21., *[2.10.]* 1., 5 , 6., 15. |
| 1408/71 | *[3.9.]* 1. |
| 574/72 | *[3.9.]* 1. |
| 1430/79 | *[2.5.]* 5., 6. |
| 1697/79 | *[2.5.]* 5., 6. |
| 3626/82 | *[3.6.]* 7. |
| 1983/83 | *[2.4.]* 5., 4., 10., 15. |
| 3/84 | *[1.]* 2., 4, 5. |
| 750/87 | *[2.5.]* 3., 4. |
| 2144/87 | *[2.5.]* 5. |
| 2658/87 | *[2.5.]* 5., 6. |
| 3896/89 | *[2.5.]* 5., 6. |
| 4064/89 | *[2.4.]* 36., 49., 56., 73. |
| 610/90 | *[2.3.]* 30. |
| 2377/90 | *[3.5.]* 1., 3., 4. |
| 3831/90 | *[2.5.]* 5., 6. |
| 3832/90 | *[2.5.]* 5. |
| 3833/90 | *[2.5.]* 5. |
| 3835/90 | *[2.5.]* 5. |
| 3587/91 | *[2.5.]* 5., 6. |
| 2913/92 | *[2.5.]* 5. |
| 40/94 | *[2.17.]* 1., 2., 3., 6. |
| 118/97 | *[3.9.]* 1. |
| 338/97 | *[3.6.]* 6., 7. |
| 1310/97 | *[2.4.]* 28., 36., 73. |
| 613/98 | *[3.5.]* 1. |
| 2542/98 | *[2.4.]* 74. |
| 2842/98 | *[2.4.]* 82., 100., 107. |
| 659/99 | *[2.14.]* 11. |
| 1216/99 | *[2.4.]* 40., 42., 54. |
| 1784/99 | *[2.3.]* 27. |
| 539/01 | *[2.13.]* 13. |
| 1/03 | *[2.4.]* 101. |
| 453/03 | *[2.13.]* 13. |
| 1295/03 | *[2.13.]* 13. |

### 2.2.2. COMMISSION REGULATIONS (EEC/EC)

| | |
|---|---|
| 1074/80 | *[2.5.]* 1., 2. |
| 3040/83 | *[2.5.]* 5. |
| 2886/89 | *[2.5.]* 5., 6. |
| 2472/90 | *[2.5.]* 6. |
| 2587/91 | *[2.5.]* 6. |
| 513/92 | *[2.5.]* 5., 6. |
| 719/92 | *[2.5.]* 5., 6. |

———

## 2.3. DIRECTIVES (EEC/EC)

64/221/EEC    *[2.6.]* 1., 2., *[2.18.]* 10., 17., 18.
64/433/EEC    *[3.5.]* 1.
65/ 65/EEC    *[1.]* 20., *[2.2.]* 2., *[2.8.]* 3., 9., 10., 11.
68/360/EEC    *[2.10.]* 1.
72/462/EEC    *[3.4.]* 2.
73/148/EEC    *[2.10.]* 15.
75/319/EEC    *[1.]* 20., *[2.8.]* 3., 9., 10.
75/442/EEC    *[2.13.]* 14.
76/207/EEC    *[2.7.]* 17., 33., *[2.15.]* 8.
77/187/EEC    *[3.7.]* 1.
77/388/EEC    *[2.14.]* 3., *[2.15.]* 3., 5., 6., 7., 8., 9., 10.
79/112/EEC    *[2.8.]* 19., 25.
79/409/EEC    *[2.13.]* 9., 10., *[3.3.]* 1., 2., *[3.6.]* 1., 4., 9.
79/623/EEC    *[2.5.]* 5.
79/695/EEC    *[2.5.]* 6.
81/602/EEC    *[2.8.]* 25.
81/851/EEC    *[3.5.]* 1.
84/450/EEC    *[1.]* 20., *[2.8.]* 3., 9., 10., *[2.16.]* 6.
85/337/EEC    *[1.]* 14., *[2.13.]* 8.
88/146/EEC    *[2.8.]* 25.
88/299/EEC    *[2.8.]* 25.
88/627/EEC    *[2.4.]* 47.
89/ 48/EEC    *[1.]* 9., 3., 4., 5., 6.
89/104/EEC    *[2.17.]* 1., 2., 3., 4., 5., 6.
89/341/EEC.   *[1.]* 20., *[2.8.]* 3., 10.
89/381/EEC    *[2.8.]* 3.
89/391/EEC    *[1.]* 20., *[2.8.]* 13., 21., *[3.2.]* 1., 2.
89/552/EEC    *[1.]* 9., 13., 18., 19., 32., 41., *[2.2.]* 2., 3., 4., 5., 6., 7., 8., 9., 10., 11., *[2.4.]* 11., 16., 19.,
              34.,  63., 65., 95., 97., *[2.7.]* 33., *[2.12.]* 16., *[2.16.]* 1., 3., 4., 5., 6.,
89/622/EEC    *[2.16.]* 3.
89/686/EEC    *[2.4.]* 70.
90/239/EEC    *[2.16.]* 3.
90/388/EEC    *[2.12.]* 10.
90/426/EEC    *[3.5.]* 2., 4.
90/427/EEC    *[3.5.]* 2., 4.
91/156/EEC    *[2.13.]* 14.
91/680/EEC    *[2.15.]* 9.
92/ 27/EEC    *[2.8.]* 21., 22., 26., 29., 30.
92/ 28/EEC    *[2.2.]* 2., *[2.8.]* 11., *[2.16.]* 3.
92/ 41/EEC    *[2.16.]* 3.
92/ 43/EEC    *[2.13.]* 8., 9., 10.
92/ 49/EEC    *[3.6.]* 3.
92/ 51/EEC    *[1.]* 9., *[2.6.]* 3., 4., 5., 6., 7.
92/ 61/EEC    *[3.8.]* 1.
92/ 77/EEC    *[2.14.]* 3.
93/ 16/EEC    *[2.6.]* 3.
93/ 39/EEC    *[2.2.]* 2.
93/ 68/EEC    *[2.4.]* 70.
94/ 24/EEC    *[3.6.]* 4.
94/ 33/EC     *[1.]* 20., *[2.8.]* 21., 30., *[2.9.]* 5., 7., 9., *[3.2.]* 2.
95/ 46/EC     *[2.18.]* 22., 26.
95/ 47/EC     *[2.4.]* 42., 56.
96/ 22/EC     *[2.8.]* 19., 25., 25.
96/ 23/EC     *[3.5.]* 3.
97/ 11/EC     *[2.13.]* 8.
97/ 13/EC     *[2.12.]* 10.

----

## 2.4. RESOLUTIONS

### 2.4.1. COUNCIL RESOLUTIONS

### 2.4.2. RESOLUTIONS OF THE EUROPEAN PARLIAMENT

| 22-01-1988 | hooliganism and violence in sport | *[1.]* 10., *[2.13.]* 3., *[2.18.]* 7., 10. |
|---|---|---|
| 16-09-1988 | Europe's contribution to Olympic Year 1992 | *[1.]* 5., *[2.13.]* 4. |
| 16-09-1988 | European Community's contribution to the Olympic Year 1992 | *[1.]* 10. |
| 17-02-1989 | sport in the European Community and a people's Europe | *[1.]* 5., 10. |
| 11-04-1989 | freedom of movement of professional footballers in the Community | *[2.10.]* 2., 5. |
| 21-11-1991 | freedom of movement of professional footballers in the Community | *[2.10.]* 5. |
| 27-04-1994 | sport and doping | *[2.8.]* 8. |
| 06-05-1994 | European Community and Sport | *[1.]* 10., 14., 10., 15., 16. |
| 21-05-1996 | hooliganism and the free movement of football supporters | *[2.18.]* 10. |
| 22-05-1996 | concerning the granting of exclusive broadcasting rights to non-encrypted channels, with a view to enabling the majority of the population to participate in sporting events of general interest | *[1.]* 35. |
| 22-05-1996 | broadcasting of sports events | *[2.2.]* 1., 3. |
| 04-07-1996 | non-participation by women from certain countries at the Olympic Games | *[2.7.]* 9., 33. |
| 19-09-1996 | the role of public service, television in a multi-media society | *[1.]* 14., *[2.2.]* 3. |
| 10-10-1996 | report of the Committee of Inquiry into racism and xenophobia | *[2.18.]* 10. |
| 13-06-1997 | the role of the European Union in the field of sport | *[1.]* 14., 35., *[2.4.]* 17., *[2.7.]* 33., *[2.8.]* 15., 16., 30. |
| 13-06-1997 | to make use of the right provided for in Article 3a of the television directive in order to ensure that a substantial proportion of the public is not deprived of the possibility of following events of major social importance because the latter are broadcast on an exclusive basis | *[1.]* 35. |
| 13-06-1997 | the organisation of a European Year of Sport | *[1.]* 35. |
| 13-06-1997 | to investigate the national rules governing public subsidies for professional clubs and to seek to bring about transparency with regard to the financial situation of such clubs | *[1.]* 35. |
| 15-12-1997 | human rights in Nigeria | *[2.1.]* 3. |
| 02-02-1998 | UEFA and the Coca-Cola Cup | *[2.4.]* 17. |
| 17-12-1998 | urgent measures to be taken against doping in sport | *[1.]* 35., *[2.8.]* 15.-17., 18., 20., 21., 24., 26., 28., 29., 30., 35. |
| 13-04-1999 | criminal procedures in the European Union | *[2.8.]* 21. |
| 18-11-1999 | preparation for reform of the treaties and the next intergovernmental conference | *[1.]* 35. |
| 07-09-2000 | Commission Report to the European Council with a view to safeguarding current sports structures and maintaining the social function of sport within the Community Framework – the Helsinki Report on Sport | *[1.]* 35., *[2.7.]* 33. |
| 07-09-2000 | Commission Communication to the Council, the European Parliament, the Economic and Social Committee and the Committee of the Regions on Community Support Plan to combat doping in sport | *[2.4.]* 63., *[2.8.]* 30. |
| 05-07-2001 | Beijing's Bid to Host the 2008 Olympic Games | *[2.13.]* 11. |
| 00-03-2002 | prevention of sexual harassment and abuse of women, young people and children in sport | *[2.7.]* 33. |
| 13-06-2002 | child labour in the production of sports equipment | *[3.1.]* 1. |
| 13-06-2002 | foot-and-mouth disease and the football World Championships (World Cup) in South Korea | *[3.4.]* 2. |
| 05-06-2003 | women and sport | *[2.7.]* 33., 37. |

### 2.4.3. RESOLUTION OF THE COMMITTEE OF THE REGIONS

| 17-09-1997 | broadcasting rights of major sport events | *[2.2.]* 3. |
|---|---|---|

---

## 2.5. DECISIONS

### 2.5.1. COMMISSION DECISIONS

| 07-11-1977 | BPICA | *[2.4.]* 54. |
|---|---|---|
| 11-07-1983 | Windsurfing International | *[2.4.]* 1. |
| 17-12-1986 | Mitchell/Cotts/Sofiltra) | *[2.4.]* 73. |
| 15-09-1989 | Filmeinkauf deutscher Fernsehanstalten | *[2.4.]* 36., 49. |
| 13-07-1990 | Elopak/Metal Box - Odin | *[2.4.]* 73. |
| 19-02-1991 | Screensport/EBU Members | *[1.]* 33., *[2.4.]* 2., 3. |
| 11-06-1991 | Pari Mutuel Urbain (PMU) | *[2.14.]* 1. |

## 2.5.2. COUNCIL DECISIONS

| 03-09-1998 | Film purchased by German television stations | *[2.4.]* 42. |
| 06-02-2003 | European year of education through sport 2004 | *[2.9.]* 14. |

————

## 2.6. CASES OF THE EUROPEAN COURT OF JUSTICE*

| Case 8/55 | *Fédération Charbonnière de Belgique v High Authority* [1954 to 1956] ECR, p. 245 | *[2.4.]* 9. |
| Case 25/62 | *Plaumann v Commission* [1963] ECR, p. 95 | *[2.4.]* 13. |
| Joined Cases 56/64 and 58/64 | | |
| | *Consten and Grundig v Commission* [1966] ECR, p. 299, 347 | *[2.4.]* 73., 92. |
| Case 56/65 | *Société Technique Minière v Maschinenbau Ulm* [1966] ECR, p. 235 | *[2.4.]* 73., *[2.10.]* 5., 28. |
| Case 23/67 | *Brasserie de Haecht* [1967] ECR, p. 407, at p. 416 | *[2.10.]* 28. |
| Case 5/69 | *Völk* [1969] ECR, p. 295 | *[2.10.]* 28. |
| Case 77/70 | *Prelle v Commission* [1971] ECR, p. 561 | *[2.10.]* 6. |
| Case C-5/71 | *Zuckerfabrik Schöppenstedt v Council* [1971] ECR, p. 975 | *[2.15.]* 8. |
| Case 152/73 | *Sotgiu v Deutsche Bundespost* [1974] ECR, p. 153 | *[2.7.]* 1. |
| Case C-155/73 | *Sacchi* [1974] ECR, p. 409 | *[2.4.]* 30., *[2.10.]* 28. |
| Case 167/73 | *Commission v French Republic* [1974] ECR, p. 359, p. 371 | *[2.7.]* 1. |
| Case 2/74 | *Reyners v Belgian State* [1974] ECR, p. 631 | *[2.6.]* 1., *[2.7.]* 1. |
| Case C-33/74 | *Van Binsbergen v. Bestuur van de Bedrijfsvereniging* [1974] ECR, p. 1299 | *[2.2.]* 2., *[2.6.]* 1., *[2.7.]* 1., 2., 4. |
| **Case 36-74** | **B.N.O. Walrave and L.J.N. Koch v Association Union Cycliste Internationale Koninklijke Nederlandsche Wielren Unie and Federación Española Ciclismo [1974] ECR, p. 1405** | *[1.]* 1, 4, 9., 19., 20., 33., 38., *[2.4.]* 87., 101., *[2.6.]* 1., *[2.7.]* **1., 2.**, 4., 27., *[2.10.]* 1., 2., 5., 6., 18., 22., 28., *[2.12.]* 8. |
| Case 41/74 | *Van Duyn v Home Office* (1974) ECR, p. 1337 | *[2.7.]* 4., *[2.10.]* 1. |
| Case 71/74 | *FRUBO* [1975] ECR, p. 563 | *[2.10.]* 28. |
| Case C-36/75 | *Rutili v. Minister for the Interior* [1975] ECR, p. II-1219 | *[2.6.]* 1., *[2.10.]* 5, *[2.18.]* 18. |
| Case 118/75 | *Watson and Belmann* [1976] ECR, p. 1185 | *[2.6.]* 2. |
| **Case 13/76** | ***Gaetano Donà v Mario Mantero* [1976] ECR, p. 1343** | *[1.]* 1., 4, 9., 19., 33., *[2.4.]* 101., *[2.7.]* **3., 4.**, 31., *[2.10.]* 1., 2., 5., 6., 8., 16., 18., 28., 38., *[2.12.]* 8. |
| Case 26/76 | *Metro v Commission* [1977] ECR, p. 1875 | *[2.4.]* 13., 62., 73., 94. |
| Case 52/76 | *Benedetti v Munari* [1977] ECR, p. 163 | *[2.10.]* 5. |
| Case 71/76 | *Thieffry v Conseil de l'Ordre des Avocats á la Cour de Paris* [1977] ECR, p. 765 | *[2.6.]* 1., 2., *[2.10.]* 5. |
| Case 85/76 | *Hoffmann-La Roche v Commission* [1979] ECR, p. 461 | *[2.10.]* 5. |
| Case 11/77 | *Patrick v Ministre des Affaires Culturelles* [1977] ECR, p. 1199 | *[2.6.]* 1., 2. |
| Case 19/77 | *Miller v Commission* [1978] ECR, p. 131 | *[2.10.]* 5., 28. |
| Case 28/77 | *Tepea v Commission* [1978] ECR, p. 1391 | *[2.10.]* 5. |
| Case C-102/77 | *Hoffman-La Roche* [1978] ECR, p. 1139 | *[2.17.]* 1., 3., 4., 6. |
| Case 1/78 | *Kenny v Insurance Officer* [1978] ECR, p. 1489 | *[2.10.]* 5. |
| Case 15/78 | *Société Générale Alsacienne de Banque v Koestler* [1978] ECR, p. 1971 | *[2.12.]* 6. |
| Case 16/78 | *Choquet* [1978] ECR, p. 2293 | *[2.10.]* 5. |
| Case 22/78 | *Hugin v Commission* [1979] ECR, p. 1869 | *[2.10.]* 5. |
| Case 83/78 | *Pigs Marketing Board v Redmond* [1978] ECR, p. 2347 | *[2.10.]* 5. |
| Joined Cases 110/78 and 111/78 | | |
| | *Ministère Public v Van Wesemael* [1979] ECR, p. 35 | *[2.12.]* 6. |
| Case 120/78 | *Rewe v Bundesmonopolvewaltung für Branntwein* [1979] ECR, p. 649 | *[2.10.]* 5. |
| Case 136/78 | *Ministère public v Auer* [1979] ECR, p. 437 | *[2.6.]* 1., 2. |

* The bold printed cases relate to sport and are included full text in this volume.

Joined Cases 142/84 and 156/84

|  | BAT and Reynolds v Commission [1987] ECR, p. 4487 | *[2.10.]* 28. |
| Case 161/84 | Pronuptia [1986] ECR, p. 353 | *[2.4.]* 73. |
| Case 166/84 | Thomasdünger v Oberfinanzdirektion Frankfurt am Main [1985] ECR, p. 3001 | *[2.10.]* 5. |

Joined Cases 209 to 213/84

|  | Ministère public v Asjes [1986] ECR, p. 1425 | *[2.4.]* 30., *[2.10.]* 28. |
| Case 222/84 | Johnston v Chief Constable of the Royal Ulster Constabulary [1986] ECR, p. 1651 | *[2.6.]* 2. |
| Case 15/85 | Consorzio Cooperative d'Abruzzo v Commission [1987] ECR, p. 1005 | *[2.14.]* 3. |
| Case 53/85 | AKZO Chemie v Commission [1986] 1965 | *[2.4.]* 9. |
| Case 66/85 | Lawrie-Blum v Land Baden-Württemberg [1986] ECR, p. 2121 | *[2.10.]* 18. |

Joined Cases C-89/85, C-104/85, C-114/85, C-116/85, C-117/85 and C-125/85 to C-129/85

|  | Ahlström and Others v Commission [1993] ECR, p. 1-1307 | *[2.4.]* 15., *[2.10.]* 28. |
| Case 96/85 | Commission v French Republic [1986] ECR, p. 1475. | *[2.6.]* 2., *[2.10.]* 5. |
| Case 139/85 | Kempf v Staatssecretaris van Justitie [1986] ECR, p. 1741 | *[2.10.]* 18., *[2.12.]* 8. |
| Case 221/85 | Commission v Belgium [1987] ECR, p. 719 | *[2.10.]* 5. |
| Case 310/85 | Deufil v Commission [1987] ECR, p. 901 | *[2.14.]* 3. |
| Case 311/85 | Vlaamse Reisbureaus [1987] ECR, p. 3801 | *[2.4.]* 30. |
| Case 338/85 | Pardini v Ministero del Commercio con l'Estero [1988] ECR, p. 2041 | *[2.10.]* 18., 28., *[2.12.]* 8. |
| Case 352/85 | Bond van Adverteerders and Others v Netherlands State [1988] ECR, p. 2085 | *[2.12.]* 8. |
| Case 24/86 | Blaizot v University of Liège and Others [1988] ECR, p. 379 | *[2.10.]* 6. |
| Case 66/86 | Ahmed Saeed [1989] ECR, p. 803 | *[2.4.]* 30. |

Joined Cases 97/86, 99/86, 193/86 and 215/86

|  | Asteris v Commission [1988] ECR, p. 2181 | *[2.4.]* 62. |
| Case C-102/86 | Apple and Pear Development Council [1988] ECR, p. 1443 | *[2.15.]* 10. |
| Case 207/86 | Apesco v Commission [1988] ECR, p. 2151 | *[2.4.]* 9. |
| **Case 222/86** | **Union Nationale des Entraîneurs et Cadres Techniques Professionnels du Football (UNECTEF) v Georges Heylens and Others [1987] ECR, p. 4097** | *[1.]* 9., 19., 38., *[2.6.]* 1., 2., *[2.10.]* 6. |
| Case 247/86 | Alsatel v Novasam [1988] ECR, p. 5987 | *[2.10.]* 28. |
| Case C-267/86 | Van Eycke [1988] ECR, p. 4769 | *[2.10.]* 28. |
| Case 292/86 | Gullung v Conseils de l'Ordre des Avocats du Barreau de Colmar et de Saverne [1988] ECR, p. 111 | *[2.10.]* 5. |
| Case 81/87 | The Queen v Treasury and Commissioners of Inland Revenues, ex parte Daily Mail and General Trust [1988] ECR, p. 5483 | *[2.10.]* 5., 6. |
| Case 142/87 | Tubemeuse [1990] ECR, p. I- 959 | *[2.14.]* 1. |
| Case 143/87 | Stanton v Inasti [1988] ECR, p. 3877 | *[2.10.]* 5., 6. |

Joined Cases 154/87 and 155/87

|  | RSVZ v Wolf and Others [1988] ECR, p. 3897 | *[2.10.]* 5. |

Joined Cases 193/87 and 194/87

|  | Maurissen and European Public Service Union v Court of Auditors [1989] ECR, p. 1045 | *[2.4.]* 94. |
| Case 196/87 | Steymann v Staatssecretaris van Justitie [1988] ECR, p. 6159 | *[2.10.]* 18., *[2.12.]* 8. |
| **Case 253/87** | **Sportex GmbH & Co. v Oberfinanzdirektion Hamburg [1988] ECR, p. 3351** | *[2.5.]* 3., 4. |
| Case 301/87 | Boussac [1990] ECR, p. I- 307 | *[2.14.]* 1. |
| Case 305/87 | Commission v Greece [1989] ECR, p. 1461 | *[2.10.]* 5. |
| Case C-342/87 | Genius Holding v Staatssecretaris van Financiën [1989] ECR, p. 4227 | *[2.15.]* 8. |
| Case C-348/87 | Stichting Uitvoering Financiële Acties v Staatssecretaris van Financiën [1989] ECR, p. 1737 | *[2.15.]* 8., 9. |
| Case 374/87 | Orkem v Commission [1989] ECR, p. 3283 | *[2.4.]* 9. |
| Case 379/87 | Groener v Minister for Education and the City of Dublin Vocational Education Committee [1989] ECR, p. 3967 | *[2.10.]* 5. |
| Case C-173/88 | Skatteministeriet v Henriksen [1989] ECR, p. 2763 | *[2.15.]* 8. |
| Case C-175/88 | Biehl [1990] ECR, p. I-1779 | *[2.10.]* 5. |
| Case C-262/88 | Barber [1990] ECR, p. I-1889 | *[2.10.]* 28. |
| Case C-286/88 | Falciola. [1990] ECR, p. I-191 | *[2.10.]* 5. |

Joined Cases C-297/88 and C-197/89

|  | Dzodzi [1990] ECR, p. I-3763 | *[2.10.]* 5. |
| Case 320/88 | Shipping and Forwarding Enterprise Safe [1990] ECR, p. I-285 | *[2.10.]* 28. |

| | | |
|---|---|---|
| Case C-332/88 | *Alimenta v Doux* [1990] ECR, p. I-2077 | *[2.10.]* 18., *[2.12.]* 8. |
| Case T-7/89 | *Hercules Chemicals v Commission* [1991] ECR, p. II-1711 | *[2.4.]* 73. |
| Case T-9/89 | *Hüls v Commission* [1992] ECR, p. II-499 | *[2.4.]* 73. |
| Case C-10/89 | *HAG GF* [1990] ECR, p. I-3711 | *[2.17.]* 1., 3., 4. |
| Case T-14/89 | *Montedipe v Commission* [1992] ECR, p. II-1155 | *[2.4.]* 73. |
| Case C-49/89 | *Corsica Ferries France v Direction Générale des Douanes* [1989] ECR, p. 4441 | *[2.10.]* 5. |
| Case T-61/89 | *Dansk Pelsdyravlerforening v Commission* [1992] ECR, p. II-1931 | *[2.4.]* 73. |
| Case T-64/89 | *Automec v Commission* [1990] ECR, p. II-367 | *[2.4.]* 94. |

Joined Cases T-68/89, T-77/89 and T-78/89

| | | |
|---|---|---|
| | *SIV and Others v Commission* [1992] ECR, p. II-1403 | *[2.10.]* 5. |

Joined Cases T-79/89, T-84/89, T-85/89, T-86/89, T-89/89, T-91/89, T-92/89, T-94/89, T-96/89, T-98/89, T-102/89 and T-104/89

| | | |
|---|---|---|
| | *BASF and Others v Commission* [1992] ECR, p. II-315 | *[2.4.]* 8. |
| Case T-138/89 | *NBV and NVB v Commission* [1992] ECR, p. II-2181 | *[2.4.]* 73. |
| Case T-147/89 | *Société métallurgique de Normandie v Commission,* [1995] ECR, p. II-1057 | *[2.10.]* 5. |
| Case T-148/89 | *Tréfilunion v Commission* [1995] ECR, p. II-1063 | *[2.4.]* 73. |
| Case T-149/89 | *Sotralentz v Commission* [1995] ECR, p. II-1127 | *[2.4.]* 15. |
| Case T-150/89 | *Martinelli v Commission* [1995] ECR, p. II-1165 | *[2.4.]* 15. |
| Case T-151/89 | *Société des treillis et panneaux soudés v Commission* [1995] ECR, p. II-1191 | *[2.10.]* 5. |
| Case C-221/89 | *Queen v. Secretary of State for Transport, ex parte Factortame Ltd. and Others* [1991] | |
| ECR, p. I-3905 | *[2.2.]* 2. | |
| Case C-231/89 | *Gmurzynska-Bscher* [1990] ECR, p. I-4003 | *[2.10.]* 5. |
| Case C-234/89 | *Delimitis* [1991] ECR, p. I-935 | *[2.4.]* 73., *[2.10.]* 28. |
| Case C-288/89 | *Collectieve Antennevoorziening Gouda and Others* [1991] ECR, p. I-4007 | *[2.10.]* 5., *[2.12.]* 6. |
| Case C-292/89 | *Antonissen* [1991] ECR, p. I-745 | *[2.17.]* 1. |
| Case C-340/89 | *Vlassopoulou v Min. of Just. Bad.-Würt.* OJ C 145, 1991 | *[1.]* 9., *[2.10.]* 5. |
| Case C-363/89 | *Roux v Belgium* [1991] ECR, p. I-273 | *[2.10.]* 6. |
| Case C-368/89 | *Crispoltoni* [1991] ECR, p. I-3695 | *[2.10.]* 5. |
| Case C-10/90 | *Masgio v Bundesknappschaft* [1991] ECR, p. I-1119 | *[2.10.]* 6. |
| Case C-41/90 | *Höfner and Elser* [1991] ECR, p. I-1979 | *[2.10.]* 5., 28. |
| Case T-44/90 | *La Cinq v Commission* [1992] ECR, p. II-1 | *[2.4.]* 13. |
| Case C-76/90 | *Säger* [1991] ECR, p. I-4221 | *[2.10.]* 5. |
| Case C-159/90 | *Society for the Protection of Unborn Children Ireland v Grogan* [1991] ECR, p. I-4685 | *[2.10.]* 18., *[2.12.]* 8. |
| Case C-163/90 | *Administration des Douanes v Legros and Others* [1992] ECR, p. I-4625 | *[2.10.]* 6. |
| Case C-179/90 | *Merci Convenzionali Porto di Genova v Siderurgica Gabrielli* [1991] ECR, p. I-5889 | *[2.10.]* 18. |
| Case C-181/90 | *Consorgan v Commission* [1992] ECR, p. I-3557 | *[2.4.]* 9. |
| Case C-186/90 | *Durighello* [1991] ECR, p. I-5773 | *[2.10.]* 5. |
| Case C-204/90 | *Bachmann v Belgium* [1992] ECR, p. I-249 | *[2.10.]* 5. |
| Case C-269/90 | *Technische Universität München* [1991] ECR, p. I-5469 | *[2.4.]* 8., 13., 62. |
| Case C-300/90 | *Commission v Belgium* [1992] ECR, p. I-305 | *[2.10.]* 5. |

Joined Cases C-320/90, C-321/90 and C-322/90

| | | |
|---|---|---|
| | *Telemarsicabruzzo and Others v Circostel and Others* [1993] ECR, p. I-393-393 | *[2.10.]* 5., 15., 16., 18., 28., *[2.12.]* 8. |
| Case C-332/90 | *Steen v Deutsche Bundespost* [1992] ECR, p. I-341 | *[2.10.]* 5., 6. |
| Case C-343/90 | *Louenço Dias v Director da Alfândega do Porto* [1992] ECR, p. I-4673 | *[2.10.]* 5. |
| Case C-351/90 | *Commission v Luxembourg* [1992] ECR, p. I-3945 | *[2.10.]* 5. |
| Case C-370/90 | *The Queen v Immigration Appeal Tribunal and Surinder Singh* [1992] ECR, p. I-4265 | *[2.10.]* 5., 6. |
| Case C-2/91 | *Meng* [1993] ECR, p. I-5751 | *[2.10.]* 28. |
| **Case T-35/91** | ***Eurosport Consortium v Commission* [1991] ECR, p. II-1359** | *[2.4.]* **3.** |
| Case C-67/91 | *Asocición Espanola de Banca Privada and Others* [1992] ECR, p. I-4785 | *[2.10.]* 5. |
| Case C-83/91 | *Meilicke v ADV/ORGA* [1992] ECR, p. I-4871 | *[2.10.]* 5., 6. |
| Case C-106/91 | *Ramrath v Ministre de la Justice* [1992] ECR, p. I-3351 | *[2.10.]* 5. |
| **Case C-117/91** | ***Jean-Marc Bosman v Commission* [1991] ECR, p. I-3353** | *[2.10.]* **3., 4.**, 5. |

Joined Cases C-159/91 and C-160/91

| | | |
|---|---|---|
| | *Poucet* [1993] ECR, p. I-637 | *[2.10.]* 5. |
| Case C-168/91 | *Konstantznidis* [1993] ECR, p. I-1198 | *[2.10.]* 5. |
| Case C-198/91 | *Cook v Commission* [1993] ECR, p. I-2487 | *[2.4.]* 13. |
| Case C-225/91 | *Matra v Commission* [1993] ECR, p. I-3203 | *[2.4.]* 13. |

Joined Cases C-267/91 and C-268/91

| | | |
|---|---|---|
| | *Keck and Mithouard* [1993] ECR, p. I-6097 | *[2.10.]* 5., 6., 16. |
| Case C-271/91 | *Marshall v Southampton and South West Hampshire Area Health Authority* [1993] ECR, p. I-4367 | *[2.15.]* 8. |
| Case C-317/91 | *Deutsche Renault v Audi* [1993] ECR, p. I-6227 | *[2.17.]* 1. |
| Case C-320/91 | *Corbeau* [1993] ECR, p. I-2533 | *[2.4.]* 13. |
| Case T-7/92 | *Asia Motor France v Commission* [1993] ECR, p. II-669 | *[2.4.]* 62. |
| Case C-10/92 | *Balocchi v Ministero delle Finanze* [1993] ECR, p. I-5105 | *[2.15.]* 8., 9. |
| Case C-19/92 | *Kraus v Land Baden-Wuerttemberg* [1993] ECR, p. I-1663 | *[2.10.]* 5., 6. |
| Case T-29/92 | *SPO and Others v Commission* [1995] ECR, p. II-289 | *[2.4.]* 13. |
| **Case T-38/92** | ***All Weather Sports Benelux BV v Commission* [1994] ECR, p. II-211** | *[2.4.]* **8.** |
| Case T-43/92 | *Dunlop Slazenger v Commission* [1994] ECR, p. II-441 | *[2.4.]* 15. |

Joined Cases C-45/92 and C-46/92

| | | |
|---|---|---|
| | *Lepore and Scamuffa* [1993] ECR, p. I-6497 | *[2.10.]* 5. |
| **Case T-46/92** | ***Scottish Football Association v Commission* [1994] ECR, p. II-1039** | *[2.4.]* 9., 15, *[2.10.]* 5., 28. |
| Case C-63/92 | *Lubbock Fine v Commissioners of Customs and Excise* [1993] ECR, p. I-6665 | *[2.15.]* 8. |
| Case T-64/92 | *Chavane de Dalmassy and Others v Commission* [1994] ECR, p. II-723 | *[2.4.]* 94. |
| Case T-96/92 | *Comité Central d'Entreprise de la Société Générale des Grandes Sources and Others v Commission* [1995] ECR, p. II-1213 | *[2.4.]* 13. |
| Case C-157/92 | *Bachero* [1993] ECR, p. I-1085 | *[2.10.]* 5., 15. |
| Case C-235/92 | *P Montecatini v Commission* [1999] ECR, p. I-4539 | *[2.4.]* 73. |
| Case C-250/92 | *Gottrup-Klim v Dansk Landbrugs Grovvareselskab* [1994] ECR, p. I-5641 | *[2.4.]* 73., *[2.10.]* 5., 28. |
| Case C-272/92 | *Spotti* [1993] ECR, p. I-5185 | *[2.10.]* 5. |
| Case C-275/92 | *Schindler,* [1994] ECR, p. I-1039 | *[2.4.]* 43., *[2.10.]* 5., *[2.12.]* 6. |

Joined Cases C-278/92, C-279/92 and C-280/92

| | | |
|---|---|---|
| | *Spain v Commission* [1994] ECR, p. I-4103 | *[2.14.]* 3. |
| Case C-295/92 | *Landbouwschap v Commission* [1992] ECR, p. I-5003 | *[2.4.]* 13. |

Joined Cases C-332/92, C-333/92 and C-335/92

| | | |
|---|---|---|
| | *Eurico Italia and Others* [1994] ECR, p. I-711 | *[2.10.]* 5. |
| Case C-379/92 | *Peralta* [1994] ECR, p. I-3453 | *[2.10.]* 18. |
| Case C-386/92 | *Monin Automobiles* [1993] ECR, p. I-2049 | *[2.10.]* 5. |
| Case C-419/92 | *Scholz* [1994] ECR, p. I-505 | *[2.10.]* 5. |
| Case T-5/93 | *Tremblay v Commission* [1995] ECR, p. II-185 | *[2.4.]* 62. |
| Case C-9/93 | *IHT Internationale Heiztechnik v Ideal Standard* [1994] ECR, p. I-2789 | *[2.17.]* 1. |
| Case T-12/93 | *Comité Central d'Entreprise de la Société Anonyme Vittel and Others v Commission* [1995] ECR, p. II-1247 | *[2.4.]* 13. |
| Case C-16/93 | *Tolsma* [1994] ECR, p. I-743 | *[2.15.]* 10. |
| Case T-17/93 | *Matra Hachette v Commission* [1994] ECR, p. II-595 | *[2.4.]* 13., 73., 92., *[2.10.]* 5. |
| Case C-18/93 | *Corsica Ferries* [1991] ECR, p. I-1783 | *[2.10.]* 5., 28. |
| Case C-23/93 | *TV 10 SA v. Commissariaat voor de Media,* [1994] ECR, p. I-4795 | *[2.2.]* 2. |

Joined Cases C-46/93 and C-48/93

| | | |
|---|---|---|
| | *Brasserie du Pêcheur and Factortame and Others* [1996] ECR, p. I-1029 | *[2.15.]* 8., 9. |
| Case C-62/93 | *BP Supergas v Greek State* [1995] ECR, p. I-1883 | *[2.15.]* 8., 9. |
| Case C-316/93 | *Vaneetveld and Others* [1994] ECR, p. I-763 | *[2.10.]* 5. |
| Case C-323/93 | *Centre d'Insémination de la Crespelle v Coopérative de la Mayenne* [1994] ECR, p. I-5077 | *[2.10.]* 5. |

Joined Cases C-367/93 to C-377/93

| | | |
|---|---|---|
| | *Rodgers and Others* [1995] ECR, p. I-2229 | *[2.10.]* 28. |
| Case C-378/93 | *La Pyramide* [1994] I-3999 | *[2.10.]* 5. |
| Case C-384/93 | *Alpine Investments v Minister van Financiën* [1995] ECR, p. II-41 | *[2.10.]* 5., 6. |
| Case C-392/93 | *The Queen v H.M. Treasury, ex parte British Telecommunications* [1996] ECR, p. I-1631 | *[2.15.]* 8. |
| Case C-399/93 | *Oude Luttikhuis and Others* [1995] ECR, p. I-4515 | *[2.4.]* 73. |

| | | |
|---|---|---|
| Case C-415/93 | Union Royale Belge des Sociétés de Football Association ASBL V Jean-Marc Bosman, Royal Club Liègeois SA V Jean-Marc Bosman and Others and Union des Associations Européennes De Football (UEFA) v Jean-Marc Bosman [1995] ECR, p. I-4930. | *[1.]* 9., 11., 14., 19., 20., 26., 33., 34., 35., 36., 38., *[2.4.]* 18., 24., 47., 87., 107., *[2.7.]* 8., 14., 15., 18., 27., 31., *[2.10.]* **5., 6.,** 7., 8., 9., 11., 12., 13., 17., 18., 19., 20., 21., 28., 32., 33., 35., 39., 38., *[2.12.]* 8., *[3.2.]* 1. |

Joined Cases C-427/93, C-429/93 and C-436/93

| | | |
|---|---|---|
| | Bristol Myers Squibb v Paranova and Bayer Aktiengesellschaft, Bayer Denmark v Paranova [1996] ECR, p. I-3457 | *[2.17.]* 1., 3 |
| Case C-428/93 | Monin Automobiles [1994] ECR, p. I-1707 | *[2.10.]* 5. |

Joined Cases T-447/93, T-448/93 and T-449/93

| | | |
|---|---|---|
| | AITEC and Others v Commission [1995] ECR, p. II-1971 | *[2.4.]* 13. |
| Case C-453/93 | Bulthuis-Griffioen v Inspecteur der Omzetbelasting [1995] ECR, p. I-2341 | *[2.15.]* 8. |
| Case C-458/93 | Saddik [1995] ECR, p. I-511 | *[2.10.]* 5., 16., 18., *[2.12.]* 8. |
| Case C-470/93 | Mars [1995] ECR, p. I-1923 | *[2.10.]* 5. |
| Case C-479/93 | Francovich v Italian Republic [1995] ECR, p. I-3843 | *[2.15.]* 8. |
| **Joined cases T-528/93, T-542/93, T-543/93 and T-546/93** | **Metropole Télévision SA and Reti Televisive Italiane Spa and Gestevisión Telecinco SA and Antena 3 de Televisión v Commission [1996] ECR, p. II-649** | *[2.4.]* **13.**, 62., 73., 92., 75. |

Joined Cases T-551/93 and T-231/94 to T-234/94

| | | |
|---|---|---|
| | Industrias Pesqueras Campos and Others v Commission [1996] ECR, p. II-247 | *[2.3.]* 30. |
| Case C-5/94 | The Queen v Ministry of Agriculture, Fisheries and Food, ex parte Hedley Lomas (Ireland) [1996] ECR, p. I-2553 | *[2.15.]* 8., 9. |
| Case C-39/94 | SFEI and Others [1996] ECR, p. I-3547 | *[2.12.]* 8. |
| Case C-55/94 | Reinhard Gebhard v Consiglio dell'Ordine degli Avvocati e Procuratori di Milano [1995] p. I-4165 | *[2.10.]* 6. |
| Case C-63/94 | Belgapom, [1995] ECR, p. I-2467 | *[2.10.]* 5. |

Joined Cases C-68/94 and C-30/95

| | | |
|---|---|---|
| | France and Others v Commission [1998] ECR, p. I-1375 | *[2.4.]* 73. |

Joined Cases C-71/94, C-72/94 and C-73/94

| | | |
|---|---|---|
| | Eurim-Pharm Arzneimittel v Beiersdorf, Boehringer Ingelheim KG, Boehringer Ingelheim A/S and Farmitalita Carlo Erba [1996] ECR, p. I-3603 | *[2.17.]* 1. |
| Case T-77/94 | VGB and Others v Commission [1997] ECR, p. II-759 | *[2.4.]* 73. |
| Case T-100/94 | Michailidis and Others v Commission [1998] ECR, p. II-3115 | *[2.4.]* 75. |
| Case C-105/94 | Celestini v Saar-Sektkellerei Faber [1997] ECR, p. I-2971 | *[2.12.]* 8. |
| Case C-110/94 | Inzo v Belgian State [1996] ECR, p. I-857, | *[2.15.]* 8. |
| Case C-125/94 | Aprile v Amministrazione delle Finanze dello Stato [2000] p. I-1157 | *[2.10.]* 6. |
| Case C-143/94 | Furlanis Costruzioni Generali SpA v Azienda Nazionale Autonoma Strade (ANAS) [1995] ECR, p. I-3633 | *[2.10.]* 6. |

Joined Cases T-163/94 and T-165/94

| | | |
|---|---|---|
| | NTN Corporation and Koyo Seiko v Council [1995] ECR, p. II-1381 | *[2.4.]* 13. |
| Case C-167/94 | Grau Gomis [1995]ECR, p. I-1023 | *[2.10.]* 5. |

Joined Cases C-178/94, C-179/94, C-188/94, C-189/94, C-190/94

| | | |
|---|---|---|
| | Dillenkofer and Others v Federal Republic of Germany [1996] ECR, p. I-4845 | *[2.15.]* 8., 9. |

Joined Cases C-197/94 and C-252/94

| | | |
|---|---|---|
| | Bautiaa and Société Française Maritime [1996] ECR, p. I-505 | *[2.17.]* 1. |
| Case C-231/94 | Faaborg-Gelting Linien v Finanzamt Flensburg [19961 ECR, p. I-2395 | *[2.15.]* 9. |
| Case C-232/94 | MPA Pharma v Rhône-Poulenc Pharma [1996] ECR, p. I-3671 | *[2.17.]* 1. |

Joined Cases C-283/94, C-291/94, C-292/94

| | | |
|---|---|---|
| | Denkavit Internationaal and Others v Bundesamt für Finanzen [1996] ECR, p. I-5063 | *[2.15.]* 8., 9. |

Joined Cases T-371/94 and T-394/94

| | | |
|---|---|---|
| | British Airways and Others v Commission [1988] ECR, p. II-2405 | *[2.14.]* 3. |

| | | |
|---|---|---|
| Case C-517/99 | *Merz & Krell* [2001] ECR, p. I-6959 | *[2.17.]* 3., 4. |
| Case C-2/00 | *Michael Hölterhoff v Ulrich Freiesleben* [2002] ECR, p. I-4187 | *[2.17.]* 3., 4., 6. |
| Case C-55/00 | *Elide Gottardo v Istituto nazionale della previdenza sociale (INPS)* [2002] ECR, p. I-413 | *[2.17.]* 3. |
| Case T-80/00 | *Associação Comercial de Aveiro v Commission* [2002] ECR, p. II-2465 | *[2.3.]* 30. |
| Case C-162/00 | *Pokrzeptowicz-Meyer* [2002] ECR, p. I-1049 | *[2.7.]* 27., 31., *[2.10.]* 33. |
| **Case C-174/00** | **Kennemer Golf & Country Club v Staatssecretaris van Financiën [2002] ECR p. I-3293** | *[2.15.]* **10.** |
| **Joined Cases T-185/00, T-216/00, T-299/00 and T-300/00** | *Métropole Télévision SA (M6) (T-185/00), Antena 3 de Televisión, SA (T-216/00) Gestevisión Telecinco, SA (T-299/00) and SIC - Sociedade Independente de Comunicação, SA (T-300/00) v Commission [2002] ECR, p. II-3805* | *[2.4.]* 92. |
| Case C-267/00 | *Commissioners of Customs and Excise v Zoological Society of London* [2002] ECR p. I-3353 | *[2.15.]* 10. |
| Case C-273/00 | *Ralf Sieckmann v Deutsches Patent- und Markenamt* [2002] ECR, p. I-11737 | *[2.17.]* 3. |
| Case C-291/00 | *LTJ Diffusion SA v Sadas Vertbaudet SA* [2003] ECR, p. I-2799 | *[2.17.]* 3. |
| Case C-292/00 | *Davidoff & Cie SA and Zino Davidoff SA v Gofkid Ltd.* [2003] ECR, p. I-389 | *[2.17.]* 3., 5., 6. |
| **Case C-318/00** | **Bacardi-Martini S.A.S. and Cellier Des Dauphins v Newcastle United Football Company Limited [2003] ECR, p. I-905** | *[2.12.]* **15.** |
| **Case T-354/00** | **M6 v Commission [2001] ECR, p. II-3177** | *[2.4.]* **92.** |
| **Case T-354/00** | **Métropole Télévision (M6) v Commission [2001] ECR, p. II-3177** | *[2.4.]* **75.** |
| Case C-438/00 | *Deutscher Handballbund EV v Maros Kolpak* [2003] ECR, p. I-4135 | *[2.7.]* 27., 31. |
| | **Joined Cases C-9/01 to C-12/01** *Stéphane Monnier v Govan Sports NV, Edwin van Ankeren v Govan Sports NV Govan Sports NV v Pascal Jacobs and Govan Sports NV v Dannie d'Hondt* OJ C 254, 1-9-2001, p. 2 | *[2.4.]* 71. |
| Case C-23/01 | *Robelco NV v Robeco Groep NV.* [2002] ECR, p. I-10913 | *[2.17.]* 3., 6. |
| Case C-40/01 | *Ansul BV v Ajax Brandbeveiliging BV* [2003] ECR, p. I-2439 | *[2.17.]* 3. |
| Case C-104/01 | *Libertel Groep* | *[2.17.]* 6. |
| **Case T-121/01** | **Laurent Piau v Commission, OJ C 227, 11-8-2001, p. 31** | *[2.4.]* **67.**, 74. |
| **Case T-137/01** | **Stadtsportverband Neuss eV v Commission of the European Communities [2003] ECR, not yet published.** | *[2.3.]* **30.** |
| **Case C-206/01** | **Arsenal Football Club PLC v Matthew Reed ECR, p. I-10273** | *[2.17.]* **3.**, **4.**, 6. |
| Case C-283/01 | *Shield Mark BV v Joost Kist h.o.d.n. Memex* [2003 ECR], not yet published. | *[2.17.]* 3., 6. |
| **Case C-408/01** | **Adidas-Salomon AG and Adidas Benelux BV v Fitnessworld Trading Ltd. [2003] ECR, not yet published.** | *[2.17.]* **5.**, **6.** |
| **Case T-313/02** | **David Meca-Medina And Igor Majcen v The Commission OJ C 305, 7-12-2002 p. 62.** | *[2.4.]* **95** |

———

# DETAILED TABLE OF CONTENTS

**Previous publications by or in cooperation with the
ASSER International Sports Law Centre**
T.M.C. Asser Instituut – The Hague – The Netherlands

**Basic Documents of International Sports Organisations**, R.C.R. Siekmann and J.W. Soek, eds. (The Hague/Boston/London, Kluwer Law International 1998)

**Doping Rules of International Sports Organisations**, R.C.R. Siekmann, J.W. Soek and A. Bellani, eds. (The Hague, T.M.C.Asser press 1999)

**Arbitral and Disciplinary Rules of International Sports Organisations**, R.C.R. Siekmann and J.W. Soek, eds. (The Hague, T.M.C.Asser press 2001)

**Professional Sport in the European Union: Regulation and Re-regulation**, A. Caiger and S. Gardiner, eds. (The Hague, T.M.C.Asser press 2001)

**Mediating Sports Disputes: National and International Perspectives**, I.S. Blackshaw (The Hague, T.M.C.Asser press 2002)